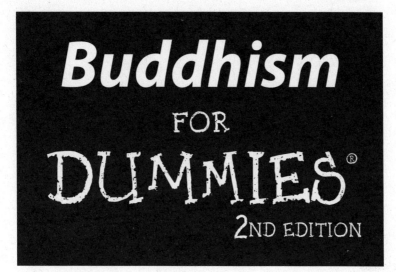

Buddhism FOR DUMMIES®

2ND EDITION

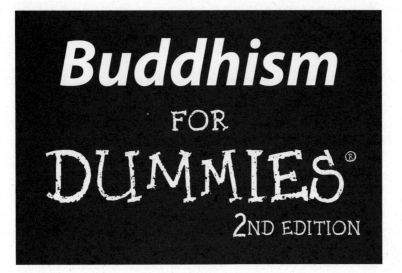

Buddhism FOR DUMMIES®

2ND EDITION

by Jonathan Landaw, Stephan Bodian,
and Gudrun Bühnemann

WILEY
Wiley Publishing, Inc.

Buddhism For Dummies®, 2nd Edition

Published by
John Wiley & Sons, Inc.
111 River St.
Hoboken, NJ 07030-5774
www.wiley.com

For general information on our other products and services, please contact our Customer Care Department within the U.S. at 877-762-2974, outside the U.S. at 317-572-3993, or fax 317-572-4002.

For technical support, please visit www.wiley.com/techsupport.

Wiley also publishes its books in a variety of electronic formats. Some content that appears in print may not be available in electronic books.

Library of Congress Control Number: 2011932088

ISBN 978-1-118-02379-2 (pbk); ISBN 978-1-118-12067-5 (ebk); ISBN 978-1-118-12068-2 (ebk);
ISBN 978-1-118-12069-9 (ebk)

Manufactured in the United States of America

15 14 13 12 11

WILEY

About the Authors

Jonathan Landaw was born in Paterson, New Jersey, in 1944 and attended Dartmouth College in New Hampshire. While there, he took a course in Asian religions taught by one of the leading authorities on Chinese thought, Professor Wing-tsit Chan (1901–1994). This course provided Jon with his first formal exposure to the teachings of the East and sparked his lifelong interest in Buddhism. This interest remained dormant while Jon attended graduate school in English literature at the University of California in Berkeley and then served in the Peace Corps, teaching the English language in Iran for three years. Not long after his stint in the Peace Corps, he was living overseas again, this time in northern India and Nepal, where he stayed throughout most of the 1970s. There he first encountered and was inspired by the living tradition of Buddhism as preserved by the refugee community that had recently fled from Chinese oppression in Tibet. By 1972, Jon was studying Buddhism full time and working as English editor of the texts being produced by the Translation Bureau of His Holiness the Dalai Lama at the Library of Tibetan Works and Archives in Dharamsala, India. Although he received training in other traditions of Buddhism during this time, the majority of his study and practice has been under the guidance of Tibetan lamas, particularly Geshe Ngawang Dhargyey (1925–1995), Lama Thubten Yeshe (1935–1984), and Lama Zopa Rinpoche (born in 1946). In 1977, Jon returned to the West, though he's managed to make periodic visits to India and Nepal since then. While living in England, the Netherlands, and now in the United States, he has continued his studies and his work editing Buddhist books for publication. He has also authored books of his own, including *Prince Siddhartha,* the story of the Buddha's life retold for children, and *Images of Enlightenment,* an introduction to the sacred art of Tibet. In addition, he's been leading meditation courses at Buddhist centers worldwide for more than 25 years. He now resides in Capitola, California, with his wife and three children.

Stephan Bodian began practicing Zen meditation in 1969 and was ordained a monk in 1974 after studying Buddhism and other Asian religions at Columbia University. He had the extraordinary good fortune to train under the guidance of several Zen masters, including Shunryu Suzuki Roshi, Kobun Chino Roshi, and Taizan Maezumi Roshi. In 1982, after a period as head monk and director of training at the Zen Center of Los Angeles, he left the monastic life to study psychology. Shortly thereafter, he married and helped raise a family.

During this period, he continued his spiritual practice by studying with several Tibetan teachers, including Sogyal Rinpoche and Namkhai Norbu Rinpoche. In 1988, he met his guru, Jean Klein, a master of Advaita Vedanta and Kashmiri yoga, with whom he spent ten years inquiring into the nature of truth. Eventually, Stephan completed his Zen training and received dharma transmission (authorization to teach) from his teacher, Adyashanti, in a lineage dating back to the historical Buddha.

In addition to authoring several books, including *Meditation For Dummies,* and numerous magazine articles, Stephan was editor-in-chief of the magazine *Yoga Journal* for ten years. Currently, he practices as a licensed psychotherapist, personal coach, writing consultant, and spiritual counselor, while offering intensives and retreats dedicated to spiritual awakening. You can reach him at `www.meditationsource.com`.

Gudrun Bühnemann is Professor and Chair of the Department of Languages and Cultures of Asia of the University of Wisconsin–Madison. She is also affiliated to the university's Religious Studies Program.

Gudrun was born in Germany. After completing studies at the universities of Bonn and Münster in Germany, she earned her Ph.D. in Buddhist and Classical Indian Studies from the University of Vienna in Austria in 1980. From 1980 to 1989, she was affiliated as a research fellow to the Bhandarkar Oriental Research Institute and Pune University, India. Her research was supported by grants from the German Academic Exchange Service, the German Research Council, and the Indian Council of Cultural Research. From 1989 to 1991 and 1991 to 1992, she was a research scholar at, respectively, Nagoya and Kyoto Universities in Japan, during which time she was supported by grants from the Japan Society for the Promotion of Science and the Bukkyo Dendo Kyokai. In 1992, she joined the University of Wisconsin–Madison, and has since been teaching the Sanskrit language and its literature, along with courses on the religions of South Asia. She has authored and edited more than 15 scholarly books and numerous articles. Her current work centers on Tantric iconography and ritual, research that takes her every summer to Nepal or India. Her website is `http://lca.wisc.edu/~gbuhnema/`.

The first edition of this book was published in 2003 under the co-authorship of Jonathan Landaw and Stephan Bodian. At the request of Wiley, Gudrun Bühnemann revised and updated this edition.

Dedication

To my mother, Ida M. Landaw, for her boundless love and support. And to the memory of my father, Louis Landaw, and of my beloved spiritual friend, Lama Thubten Yeshe.

— Jon Landaw

To my teachers, with boundless gratitude, and to the awakening of all beings everywhere.

— Stephan Bodian

Authors' Acknowledgments

Although it would be impossible for me to name everyone who had a hand in this work, several people's contributions must be acknowledged. First, I have to thank my coauthor, Stephan Bodian, for his expertise and sound judgment in giving this book a balance and breadth of view it never would have had without him.

In addition, I'd like to express my appreciation to T. Yeshe, former Buddhist nun and, for many years, a teacher associated with the Foundation for the Preservation of the Mahayana Tradition; Katherine Thanas, abbot of the Santa Cruz Zen Center; and Bob Stahl, former Theravada monk and current mindfulness-based stress reduction teacher at El Camino Hospital and the Santa Cruz Medical Clinic, for reading and offering welcome suggestions to the manuscript; and to Ven. Ajahn Amaro and Richard Kollmar for their timely contributions.

I also wish to express my gratitude to the following for their invaluable aid in providing me with a computer and the assistance to use it properly: Susan Marfield, Victoria Clark, Yorgos Hadzis, Sharon Gross, Dennis Wilson, and Elizabeth Hull.

I would also like to mention Dr. Kevin Zhu and his assistants at the Five Branches Institute in Santa Cruz and my dear friend Karuna Cayton for helping me through some particularly rough patches; and George and Betsy Cameron, whose generosity is a constant source of amazement to me. And to all those teachers who have guided me along the spiritual path, I can only offer this present work in the hope that it reflects a small portion of the insight and compassion they have always demonstrated. And lastly, to Truus Philipsen and our children, Lisa, Anna, and Kevin: thank you for being in my life.

— Jon Landaw

Any grasp of Buddhist wisdom I bring to this book can be attributed to the grace of my beloved teachers and the support of my loving friends and colleagues. In particular, I would like to thank my first Zen teacher, Kobun Chino Otogawa, who introduced me to the depths of dharma and acted as spiritual mentor and elder brother during my formative years as a practitioner; my guru, Jean Klein, who embodied the teachings of the great Zen masters and kindled the first awakening; and Adyashanti, dharma brother and heart friend, in whose presence the truth finally burst into flame.

On a day-to-day level, my dear friends have been a constant source of encouragement, especially my Thursday group; old friends Katie Darling, Barbara Green, John Welwood, and Roy Wiskar; and, above all, my wife, Lis, without whose constant love and support at every level this book would never have come into being. My heartfelt thanks to you all!

I would also like to thank Rev. David Matsumoto, Ven. Ajahn Amaro, and Dechen Bartso for taking the time to answer my detailed questions about Buddhist practice.

— Stephan Bodian

I am grateful to my colleague André Wink for initiating the process that eventually led — through his recommending my name to the publisher — to my becoming involved in preparing the second edition of *Buddhism For Dummies*. I would like to thank Tracy Boggier of Wiley Publishing and my project editor, Linda Brandon, for their help and support. My special thanks go to the technical editor, William Chu, for all the time, effort, and valuable suggestions, as well as to my copy editor, Krista Hansing.

As I revised the book for publication, numerous colleagues and friends provided information and made useful suggestions. Many thanks go to Richard J. Davidson, Susan Jensen, Amita Schmidt, Carola Roloff, the Sangha of Abhayagiri Monastery, Wendy Lewis, Shosan Victoria Austin, and Philip Pierce.

Special thanks are extended to the following individuals for providing photographs for this book and/or for granting permission to reproduce them: John C. Huntington, Susan Huntington, and Aimee Phillips of the Huntington Archive, The Ohio State University; Tatsuhiko Yokoo; Martin Stabler; Jeff Miller; Susan Jensen; Amita Schmidt; Maria Monroe; Jay Carroll; Terri Saul, Terry Barber, Richard Friday, and the Parallax Press; Liza Matthews and Shambhala Sun; Dolma Tsering, Ven. Lobsang Dechen, and the Tibetan Nuns Project; Tan Cunda, Ajahn Gunavuddho, and the Sangha of Abhayagiri Buddhist Monastery; Sudanto Bhikkhu and the Sangha of the Pacific Hermitage; Janejira Sutanonpaiboon; Mel Charbonneau and Krakora Studios; and Wendy Lewis, Tanya Takacs, Shundo David Haye, and the San Francisco Zen Center.

— Gudrun Bühnemann

Publisher's Acknowledgments

We're proud of this book; please send us your comments at http://dummies.custhelp.com. For other comments, please contact our Customer Care Department within the U.S. at 877-762-2974, outside the U.S. at 317-572-3993, or fax 317-572-4002.

Some of the people who helped bring this book to market include the following:

Acquisitions, Editorial, and Media Development

Project Editor: Linda Brandon
(Previous Edition: Allyson Grove)

Acquisitions Editor: Tracy Boggier

Copy Editor: Krista Hansing

Assistant Editor: Erin Calligan Mooney

Senior Editorial Assistant: David Lutton

Technical Editor: William Chu, PhD

Editorial Manager: Jennifer Ehrlich, Carmen Krikorian

Editorial Assistant: Rachelle Amick

Art Coordinator: Alicia B. South

Cover Photos: ©iStockphoto.com/ Bart Sadowski

Cartoons: Rich Tennant (www.the5thwave.com)

Composition Services

Project Coordinator: Sheree Montgomery

Layout and Graphics: Corrie Socolovitch, Kim Tabor

Proofreader: Bonnie Mikkelson

Indexer: Steve Rath

Publishing and Editorial for Consumer Dummies

Diane Graves Steele, Vice President and Publisher, Consumer Dummies

Kristin Ferguson-Wagstaffe, Product Development Director, Consumer Dummies

Ensley Eikenburg, Associate Publisher, Travel

Kelly Regan, Editorial Director, Travel

Publishing for Technology Dummies

Andy Cummings, Vice President and Publisher, Dummies Technology/General User

Composition Services

Debbie Stailey, Director of Composition Services

Contents at a Glance

Table of Contents

Introduction

Buddhism is much more widely known today than it was 30 years ago. Dozens of books on the subject line the shelves at your local bookstore, and hundreds of Buddhist centers throughout North America can help you find out about Buddhism directly from members of its various traditions. Buddhism even seems to be seeping into the general culture; you commonly hear casual references to it in movies and on TV.

But even with all the increased recognition, we wonder how much the general public actually knows and understands about Buddhism. Despite the number of books on the subject, we suspect that, except for folks who have pursued their interest fairly seriously, most people still have only a vague idea of what Buddhism is all about.

About This Book

So what do you do if you want to understand more about Buddhism in general, but the books you've looked at so far are too narrow — covering, for example, only one particular school, aspect, or practice? Well, the book you have in your hands may be just what you're looking for.

In this book, we cover the main themes and traditions of Buddhism without overwhelming you with too much technical jargon. (In the places where we do use technical terms, we explain them as clearly and succinctly as we can, and even provide a glossary that you can use to refresh your memory.) Because we believe that Buddhist teachings are as relevant to the human condition today as they were at the time of the historical Buddha 2,500 years ago, we avoid taking a purely theoretical approach to Buddhism, in favor of one that also shows you how you can apply its insights to your everyday life.

Conventions Used in This Book

In assigning dates, we use "BCE" (before the Common Era) and CE (in the Common Era) in place of the "BC" and "AD" that are probably more familiar to many people. These relatively new designations are coming into wider use and, being religiously neutral, seem more appropriate for a book of this nature. And don't be concerned if the dates given differ a little from dates you find in other books on Buddhism. Historians disagree on quite a few of these dates, so we simply adopted the ones that seemed most reasonable to us.

Also, throughout this book, we cite (not too often, we hope) Buddhist technical terms and personal names from the ancient Indian languages Pali and Sanskrit (in which the Buddhist scriptures were first written) and from a smattering of other Asian languages, such as Chinese, Japanese, and Tibetan. Wherever possible, we simplify the spelling of these words to reflect their approximate pronunciation, and we omit most of the marks that scholars of these languages typically employ when writing them using the Latin alphabet. If any scholars happen to be reading this book, they'll likely have no trouble identifying these terms even without their accustomed markings; for everyone else, we think that the presentation without such marks is more user friendly.

How This Book Is Organized

Buddhism is a huge subject. Not only are the teachings attributed to the Buddha himself extensive, but a succession of brilliant commentators in India and other countries have added their thoughts and interpretations to them over the years. This process has produced a large body of writings and led to the development of different Buddhist schools and traditions. In addition, as Buddhism moved from country to country, it took on different flavors. The Buddhism of Japan, for example, is different from the Buddhism of Thailand; you can even find a number of distinct forms of practice within Japan itself.

In a work like this, we can't possibly do justice to all these aspects of Buddhist thought and practice. Instead, we combine a general overview of the different traditions and schools with a more in-depth discussion of the most important themes — the themes that characterize Buddhism as a whole. Then in the list of recommended readings in Appendix B, we provide the names of books and other resources to consult to research the aspects of Buddhism that you want to explore further.

To make our presentation as clear and useful as possible, we group the topics into the following parts, each with its own unifying theme.

Part I: Embarking on a Journey: The Basics of Buddhism

We begin with an overview of Buddhism as a whole, showing how it can be regarded as a religion, a philosophy of life, and a practical approach to dealing with life's problems — all rolled into one. Then because the mind is so central to Buddhism, we take a look at how the mind creates both happiness and suffering, and how the centrally important Buddhist practices of wisdom and compassion can bring you into contact with your inner spiritual resources.

Part II: A Short History of Buddhism

History doesn't have to be a boring subject, especially when it deals with the lives and deeds of extraordinary people. In this part, we look at the history of Buddhism, beginning with the life of the historical Buddha, known as Gautama or Shakyamuni, and a summary of the most basic teachings attributed to him. We then explore how Buddhism developed in India and evolved as it spread from country to country across Asia. Finally, we show you how Theravada, Vajrayana, and Zen Buddhism grew to become the three main Buddhist traditions practiced in the West.

Part III: Behaving Like a Buddhist

In this part, we address a number of practical questions: How does someone become a Buddhist? What does being a Buddhist involve? How does Buddhism affect the way you live your life? In short, what do Buddhists actually do? To answer these questions, we look at the ways people can benefit from what Buddhism has to offer. We explore meditation and show you some of the ways you can practice it. We examine how followers of various traditions bring Buddhism into their everyday lives. And we conclude by taking you on a tour of the major Buddhist pilgrimage sites.

Part IV: Exploring the Buddhist Path

Buddhist teachings are vast and contain a wide variety of practices. In this part, we show you how all these different methods fit together. We examine the different interpretations of enlightenment and show you how you can apply the Buddhist teachings at each stage along the spiritual path. Finally, we take a look at the lives of four Buddhist masters, as inspiring examples.

Part V: The Part of Tens

If you like to receive information in bite-size, easily digestible chunks, then this is the part for you. We discuss (and dispel) ten common misconceptions about Buddhism and present ten ways that you can apply Buddhist insights to your life — all of this at no extra charge.

Part VI: Appendixes

Finally, in the appendixes, we provide some information to help round out your understanding and appreciation of Buddhism. Here you find a glossary containing many of the most commonly used Buddhist terms, as well as a list of resources to consult if you want to find out more about the different aspects of Buddhism that you encounter in this book.

Icons Used in This Book

To draw your attention to bits of information that we think are particularly important or interesting, we use the following icons throughout the text.

The information next to this icon is worth repeating. We may use this icon to highlight a thought expressed elsewhere in the book or simply to point out something that we think is especially important to keep in mind.

This text offers suggestions for ways you can get a deeper understanding of the aspect of Buddhism being discussed.

Don't be unduly alarmed by this icon. We use it to draw your attention to areas prone to misunderstandings so that you can avoid tripping up.

Next to this icon are quotations from famous Buddhist masters of the past — including those attributed to the Buddha himself — that illustrate the aspect of Buddhism being discussed.

This icon alerts you that we're retelling a traditional Buddhist story or perhaps relating an incident of a more personal nature.

Where to Go from Here

You can approach this book in several different ways. The table of contents and index are detailed enough that you can find specific topics of interest and turn directly to them, if you want. Or, because each chapter of the book is quite self-contained, you can start reading anywhere and skip around at your leisure. The cross-references we provide point out where you can find additional information on selected topics.

You can also read this book in the ordinary, straightforward manner: In other words, start at the beginning and, when you reach the end, stop. Finally, if you're like some people, you can open the book at the end and, after many detours, make your way back to the beginning. We hope that, whichever approach you follow, you find the material informative and enjoyable.

Part I

Embarking on a Journey: The Basics of Buddhism

The 5th Wave By Rich Tennant

"I'm thinking of taking a spiritual journey, but I want to make sure I look right for the trip."

In this part . . .

Want to find out what *Buddhism* actually means, and whether it's a religion, a philosophy, a psychology, or something else? Well, look no further than the pages contained in this part. We also introduce you to the Buddhist understanding of the mind and its importance, and we tell you about the treasures inside you that Buddhism wants to help you discover. That seems well worth the price of admission, doesn't it?

Chapter 1

Entering the World of Buddhism: The Basics

In This Chapter

- Realizing Buddhism's growing popularity
- Considering whether Buddhism is a religion
- Examining the role of the Buddha
- Understanding the significance of Buddhist philosophy
- Exploring Buddhist practices

Not too long ago, the West was virtually unfamiliar with the teachings of Buddhism. Back in the 1950s and '60s, for example, you could've gone about your life scarcely hearing the word *Buddhism* mentioned. Sure, you may have come across Buddhist concepts in school in the writings of American Transcendentalists like Thoreau and Emerson (who read English translations of Buddhist texts in the mid–19th century). But the fact is, if you were like most middle-class people then, you may have grown up, grown old, and died without ever meeting a practicing Buddhist — except perhaps in an Asian restaurant.

If you wanted to find out about Buddhism in those days, your resource options were few and far between. Aside from a rare course in Eastern philosophy at a large university, you'd have had to dig deep into the shelves and stacks at your local library to discover anything more than the most basic facts about Buddhism. The few books that you could get your hands on tended to treat Buddhism as if it were an exotic relic from some long-ago and faraway land, like some dusty Buddha statue in a dark corner of the Asian section of a museum. And good luck if you wanted to find a Buddhist center where you could study and practice.

Today the situation is much different. Buddhist terms seem to pop up everywhere. You can find them in ordinary conversation ("It's just your *karma*"), on television *(Dharma and Greg),* and even in the names of rock groups (Nirvana). Famous Hollywood stars, avant-garde composers, pop singers, and even one highly successful professional basketball coach practice some form of Buddhism. (We're thinking of Richard Gere, Philip Glass, Tina Turner, and Phil Jackson, but you may be able to come up with a different list of celebrities on your own.)

Bookstores and libraries everywhere boast a wide range of Buddhist titles, some of which — like the Dalai Lama's *Art of Happiness* (Riverhead Books) — regularly top *The New York Times* best-seller lists. And centers where people can study and practice Buddhism are now located in most metropolitan areas (and many smaller cities as well).

What caused such a dramatic change in just a few decades? Certainly, Buddhism has become more available as Asian Buddhist teachers and their disciples have carried the tradition to North America and Europe. (For more on the influx of Buddhism to the West, see Chapter 5.) But there's more to the story than increased availability. In this chapter, we try to account for the appeal this ancient tradition has in today's largely secular world by looking at some of the features responsible for its growing popularity.

Figuring Out Whether Buddhism Is a Religion

Wondering whether Buddhism is actually a religion may seem odd. After all, if you consult any list of the world's major religious traditions, you inevitably find Buddhism mentioned prominently alongside Christianity, Islam, Hinduism, Judaism, and the rest. No one ever questions whether these other traditions are religions. But this question comes up repeatedly in relation to Buddhism.

The answer depends on how you define *religion.* Ask most people what comes to mind when they think of religion, and they'll probably mention something about the belief in God, especially when discussing the creator of the world or universe. Our dictionary agrees. *Webster's New World College Dictionary* defines *religion* as a "belief in a divine or superhuman power or powers to be obeyed and worshiped as the creator(s) and ruler(s) of the universe."

REMEMBER

If this definition were the only definition of religion, you'd definitely have to count Buddhism out! Why? Well, we have two reasons:

- **Worship of a supernatural power isn't the central concern of Buddhism.** God (as this word is ordinarily used in the West) is absent from Buddhist teachings, although some Buddhists do worship gods and celestial Buddhas.
- **Buddhism isn't primarily a system of belief.** Although it teaches certain doctrines (as we discuss throughout Part III), many Buddhist teachers actively encourage their students to adopt an attitude that's the *opposite* of blind faith.

Many Buddhist teachers advise you to be skeptical about teachings you receive. Don't passively accept what you hear or read — and don't automatically reject it, either. Instead, use your intelligence. See for yourself whether the teachings make sense in terms of your own experience and the experience of others. Then, as the Dalai Lama of Tibet (see Chapter 15) often advises, "If you find that the teachings suit you, apply them to your life as much as you can. If they don't suit you, just leave them be."

This more practical approach agrees with both the spirit and the letter of the Buddha's own teachings. The Buddha is believed to have declared, "Do not accept anything I say as true simply because I have said it. Instead, test it as you would gold to see if it is genuine or not. If, after examining my teachings, you find that they are true, put them into practice. But do not do so simply out of respect for me."

Buddhist teachings therefore encourage you to use the entire range of your mental, emotional, and spiritual abilities and intelligence — instead of merely placing your blind faith in what past authorities have said. This attitude makes the teachings of Buddhism especially attractive to many Westerners; although it's 2,500 years old, it appeals to the postmodern spirit of skepticism and scientific investigation.

If Buddhism is *not* primarily a belief system and isn't centered upon the worship of a supreme deity, then why is it classified as a religion at all? Like all religions, Buddhism gives people who practice it a way of finding answers to the deeper questions of life, such as "Who am I?" and "Why am I here?" and "What is the meaning of life?" and "Why do we suffer?" and "How can I achieve lasting happiness?"

In addition to fundamental teachings on the nature of reality, Buddhism offers a method, a systematic approach involving techniques and practices, that enables its followers to experience a deeper level of reality directly for themselves. In Buddhist terms, this experience involves waking up to the truth of your authentic being, your innermost nature. The experience of awakening is the ultimate goal of all Buddhist teachings. (For more on awakening — or enlightenment, as it's often called — see Chapter 10.) Some schools emphasize awakening more than others (and a few even relegate it to the background in their scheme of priorities), but in every tradition, it's the final goal of human existence — whether achieved in this life or in lives to come.

By the way, you don't have to join a Buddhist organization to benefit from the teachings and practices of Buddhism. For more info on the different stages of involvement in Buddhism, see Chapter 6.

The historical Buddha

Most scholars believe that the Buddha's life largely falls within the fifth century BCE, although the exact dates of his life are unknown. According to tradition, he died at age 80, and recent research puts the year of the Buddha's death not much later than 400 BCE.

The accounts of the Buddha's life aren't historical. The earliest ones date from several centuries after his death and consist mainly of legends, some of which have striking parallels in others told about Mahavira, a religious figure of Jainism (another religion spawned on the Indian subcontinent). The legendary material on the Buddha's life is summarized briefly in this chapter and presented in more detail in Chapter 3.

Writing wasn't in use at the Buddha's time. Because the earliest Buddhist texts were orally transmitted and written down only many centuries after the Buddha's death, scholars aren't certain about what the Buddha himself taught and what was later ascribed to him.

Recognizing the Role of the Buddha

Buddhist systems are based upon the teachings given 2,500 years ago by one of the great spiritual figures of human history, Shakyamuni Buddha, who lived in the fifth century BCE. According to legendary accounts of his life (see Chapter 3), he was born into the ruling family of the Shakya clan in today's Nepal and was expected to someday succeed his father as king. Instead, Prince Siddhartha (as he was known at the time) quit the royal life at the age of 29 after he saw the reality of the extensive suffering and dissatisfaction in the world. He then set out to find a way to overcome this suffering.

After many hardships, at age 35, Prince Siddhartha achieved his goal. Seated under what became known as the *Bodhi tree* — the tree of enlightenment — he achieved the awakening of Buddhahood. Today a stone platform known as the diamond seat *(vajrasana)* near the Bodhi tree in Bodh Gaya (see Figure 1-1) marks the spot. From then on, he was known as *Shakyamuni Buddha,* the awakened (Buddha) sage *(muni)* of the Shakya clan.

Prince Siddhartha spent the remaining 45 years of his life wandering the northern part of the Indian subcontinent, teaching anyone who was interested in the path that leads to freedom from suffering. The famous Buddha statue in Sarnath (India), the place where he gave his first sermon (see Figure 1-2), shows the Buddha making the gesture of turning the wheel of his teaching. (Part III offers an overview of the entire Buddhist path.) After a lifetime of compassionate service to others, Shakyamuni died at the age of 80.

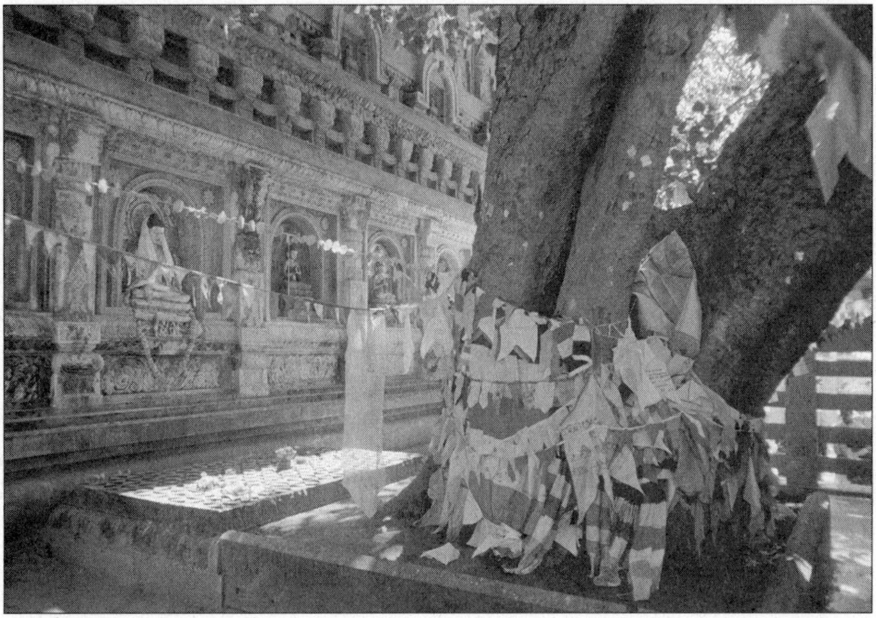

Figure 1-1: Stone platform and Bodhi tree in Bodh Gaya.

Photo courtesy of Gudrun Bühnemann.

Figure 1-2: Shakyamuni Buddha.

Photo courtesy of Gudrun Bühnemann.

The question is often asked, "What kind of being was Shakyamuni Buddha — a man, a god, or something else?" Some biographical accounts state that the Buddha was once a human being with the same hang-ups and problems as everyone else. He didn't start out as a Buddha; he wasn't enlightened from the beginning.

Only through great effort exerted over a long period of time — over many lifetimes, as the Buddhist texts tell us — did he succeed in attaining enlightenment. However, the later tradition clearly considered the Buddha an exceptional human being and elevated him to a special status. Legendary accounts of his life emphasize, for example, his miraculous birth in the Lumbini grove from his mother's side, the 32 marks of a "great man" that were found on his body, and his ability to work miracles. (See Chapter 3 for more about his birth and the 32 marks.)

The Buddhist spiritual community *(Sangha)* took great pains to preserve and transmit his teachings as purely as possible so that they could pass from one generation to the next. These extensive teachings were eventually written down, producing a vast collection (or *canon*) of the Buddha's discourses (Pali: *suttas;* Sanskrit: *sutras*).

Over the centuries, the Sangha also erected burial monuments *(stupas)* in honor of the major events in their teacher's life, which allowed later practitioners to make pilgrimage to these honored sites and receive inspiration. (Chapters 8 and 9 have more information on Buddhist devotional practices and rituals.)

Thanks to the efforts of teachers and their disciples, the Buddha's teachings (known as *Dharma*) have been handed down from generation to generation up to the present day. That's why, after 2,500 years, Buddhism is still a living tradition, capable of bestowing peace, happiness, and fulfillment upon anyone who practices it sincerely.

REMEMBER

The legends about the life of the Buddha have been a source of inspiration for Buddhists. When the Buddha is considered a mortal, he's a vital example of what each of us can achieve if we devote ourselves wholeheartedly to the study and practice of his teachings.

Understanding the Function of Philosophy in Buddhism

Socrates, one of the fathers of Western philosophy, claimed that the unexamined life isn't worth living, and most Buddhists would certainly agree with him. Because of the importance they place on logical reasoning and rational examination, many Buddhist traditions and schools have a strong philosophical flavor.

Others place more emphasis on devotion; still others focus on the direct, nonconceptual investigation and examination that take place during the practice of meditation. (For more on meditation, turn to Chapter 7.)

Like other religions, Buddhism does put forth certain philosophical tenets that sketch out a basic understanding of human existence and serve as guidelines and inspiration for practice and study. Over the centuries, a variety of schools and traditions came into existence, each with its own fairly elaborate and distinct understanding of what the Buddha taught. (For the story of these different traditions, see Chapters 4 and 5.) In addition to the discourses memorized during the founder's lifetime and recorded after his death, numerous other scriptures emerged many centuries later that were attributed to him.

Despite all its philosophical sophistication, however, Buddhism remains at heart an extremely practical religion. In the *Dhammapada (Words on Dhamma),* an ancient collection of verses on Buddhist themes, his followers have summarized the teachings as follows:

> Abstaining from all evil, undertaking what is skillful, cleansing one's mind — this is the teaching of the Buddhas. (Verse 183)
>
> Not blaming, not harming, living restrained according to the discipline, moderation in food, seclusion in dwelling, focusing on the highest thoughts — this is the teaching of the Buddhas. (Verse 185)

The Buddha has often been called the Great Physician, for good reason: He avoided abstract speculation and made his chief concern identifying the cause of human suffering and providing ways to eliminate it. (See the sidebar "The parable of the poisoned arrow" for details.) Likewise, his teachings are known as powerful medicine to cure the deeper dissatisfaction that afflicts us all. The Buddha's first and best-known teaching, the four noble truths (see Chapter 3), outlines the cause of suffering and the means for eliminating it. All subsequent teachings, such as the 12 links of dependent arising (see Chapter 13), merely expand and elaborate upon these fundamental truths.

REMEMBER

At the core of all genuine Buddhist teachings is the understanding that suffering and dissatisfaction originate in the way your mind responds and reacts to life's circumstances — not just in the raw facts of life. In particular, Buddhism teaches that your mind causes you suffering by superimposing permanence and constructing a separate self where, in fact, neither exists. (For more on the central teachings of impermanence, see Chapter 2.)

Reality is constantly changing; as the Greek philosopher Heraclitus said, you can't step into the same river twice. Success and failure, gain and loss, comfort and discomfort — they all come and go. And you have only limited control over the changes. But you can exert some control over (and ultimately clarify) your chattering, misguided mind, which distorts your perceptions, mightily resists the way things are, and causes you extraordinary stress and suffering in the process.

Happiness is actually quite simple: The secret is to want what you have and not want what you don't have. Simple though it may be, it's definitely not easy. Have you ever tried to reign in your restless and unruly mind, even for a moment? Have you ever tried to tame your anger or your jealousy, control your fear, or remain calm and undisturbed in the middle of life's inevitable ups and downs? If you have, you've no doubt discovered how difficult even the simplest self-control or self-awareness can be. To benefit from the medicine the Buddha prescribed, you have to take it — which means that you have to put it into practice for yourself. (See Chapter 17 for ten practical suggestions for putting the Buddha's teachings to use in your everyday life, and check out Chapter 14 for additional hands-on advice.)

Appreciating Buddhist Practices

Anyone interested in benefiting from the teachings of Buddhism — beyond simply discovering a few interesting facts about it — has to ask, "How do I take this spiritual medicine? How can I apply the teachings of Shakyamuni to my life in such a way to reduce, neutralize, and eventually extinguish my restlessness and dissatisfaction?" The answer is spiritual practice, which takes three forms in Buddhism:

- Ethical behavior
- Meditation (and the wisdom that follows)
- Devotion

Living an ethical life

Ethical behavior has been an essential component of the Buddhist spiritual path since the historical Buddha first cautioned his monks and nuns to refrain from certain behaviors because they distracted them from their pursuit of truth. During the Buddha's lifetime, his followers collected and codified these guidelines, which eventually became the code of discipline *(vinaya)* that has continued to shape the monastic life for more than 2,500 years. (The term *monastic* describes both monks and nuns.) From this code emerged briefer guidelines or precepts for lay practitioners, which have remained remarkably similar from tradition to tradition. (For more on ethical behavior, see Chapter 12.)

The parable of the poisoned arrow

Because intellectual activity has had such a significant place in the history of Buddhism, it may be tempting to classify Buddhism as a philosophy rather than a religion. But Shakyamuni Buddha himself warned against getting caught up in philosophical speculation. This attitude is clearly illustrated in the oft-told story of a monk named Malunkyaputta (we'll just call him the Venerable Mal, for short). Venerable Mal approached the Buddha one day complaining that he'd never addressed certain philosophical questions, such as "Is the world eternal or not?" and "Does the Buddha exist after death?" Venerable Mal declared that if the Buddha wouldn't answer these questions once and for all, he would abandon his training as a Buddhist monk.

In response, Shakyamuni described the following hypothetical situation. Suppose, he said, a man had been wounded by a poisoned arrow. His concerned relatives found a skillful surgeon who could remove the arrow, but the wounded man refused to let the doctor operate until he had received satisfactory answers to a long list of questions. "I will not have the arrow taken out," the wounded man declared, "until I know the caste to which the man who wounded me belongs, his name, his height, the village he comes from, the wood from which the arrow was made, and so forth." Clearly, such a foolish person would die long before his questions could ever be answered.

"In the same way," Shakyamuni advised Venerable Mal, "anyone who says, 'I will not follow the spiritual life until the Buddha has explained to me whether the world is eternal or not or whether the Buddha exists after death' would die long before he could ever receive satisfying answers to his questions." The truly spiritual or religious life doesn't depend at all on how these questions are answered. For, as Shakyamuni then pointed out, "Whether or not the world is eternal, you're still faced with birth, old age, death, sorrow, grief, and despair, for which I'm now prescribing the antidote."

Far from establishing an absolute standard of right and wrong, ethical guidelines in Buddhism have an entirely practical purpose: to keep practitioners focused on the goal of their practice, which is a liberating insight into the nature of reality. During his 45 years of teaching, the Buddha found that certain activities contributed to increased craving, attachment, restlessness, and dissatisfaction, and led to interpersonal conflict in the community at large. By contrast, other behaviors helped keep the mind peaceful and focused, and contributed to a more supportive atmosphere for spiritual reflection and realization. From these observations, not from any abstract moral point of view, the ethical guidelines emerged.

Examining your life through meditation

In the popular imagination, Buddhism is definitely the religion of meditation. After all, who hasn't seen statues of the Buddha sitting cross-legged, eyes half closed, deeply immersed in spiritual reflection; or picked up one of the many titles available these days devoted to teaching the basics of Buddhist meditation?

But many people misunderstand the role meditation plays in Buddhism. They falsely assume that you're meant to withdraw from the affairs of ordinary life into a peaceful, detached, and unaffected inner realm until you no longer feel any emotion or concern about the things that once mattered to you. Nothing could be farther from the truth. (We cover other misconceptions about Buddhism and Buddhist practice in Chapter 16.)

According to several Buddhist schools, the main purpose of meditation isn't to calm the mind (though this result may happen and is certainly conducive to the meditative process), nor is it to become uncaring. Instead, the purpose is to experience the profound and ultimately liberating insight into the nature of reality and yourself that we talk about in the section "Understanding the Function of Philosophy in Buddhism," earlier in this chapter — an insight that shows you who you are and what life is about and frees you from suffering once and for all. (For more on this insight, known as spiritual realization or enlightenment, see Chapter 10.)

Meditation facilitates this insight by bringing focused, ongoing attention to the workings of your mind and heart. In the early stages of meditation, you spend most of your time being aware of your experience as much as you can — an almost universal Buddhist practice known as *mindfulness.* You may also cultivate positive, beneficial heart qualities like loving-kindness and compassion or practice visualizations of beneficial figures and energies. But in the end, the goal of all Buddhist meditation is to find out who you are and thereby end your restless seeking and dissatisfaction. (For more on meditation, see Chapter 7.)

Practicing devotion

Devotion has long been a central Buddhist practice. No doubt it began with the spontaneous devotion the Buddha's own followers felt for their gentle, wise, and compassionate teacher. After his death, followers with a devotional bent directed their reverence toward the enlightened elders of the monastic community and toward the Buddha's remains, which were preserved in burial monuments known as stupas (see Chapter 4 to find out more about the stupas).

As Buddhism spread throughout the Indian subcontinent and ultimately to other lands, the primary object of devotion became the *Three Jewels* of the

Buddha, Dharma, and Sangha — the great teacher, his teachings, and the spiritual community, which preserves and upholds the teachings. To this day, all Buddhists, both lay and monastic, *take refuge* in the Three Jewels (also known as the Three Treasures or Triple Gem). (For more on taking refuge, see Chapter 6.)

Eventually, in certain traditions of Buddhism, a host of transcendent figures came to be revered. These figures include other enlightened beings (Buddhas), bodhisattvas (beings striving for enlightenment; see the next section), and celestial figures such as the goddess Tara. (See Chapter 5 for more information on Tara.) By expressing heartfelt devotion to these figures and, in some traditions, by imagining yourself merging with them and assuming their awakened qualities, you can ultimately gain complete enlightenment for the benefit of yourself and others — or so these traditions teach.

Study and reflection help clarify the Buddhist teachings, but devotion forges a heartfelt connection with the tradition, allowing you to express your love and appreciation for the teachers (and teachings) and to experience their love and compassion in return. Even traditions like Zen, which seem to deemphasize devotion in favor of insight, have a strong devotional undercurrent that gets expressed in rituals and ceremonies but isn't always visible to newcomers. For lay Buddhist practitioners who may not have the time or inclination to meditate, devotion to the Three Jewels may even become their main practice. In fact, some traditions, like Pure Land Buddhism, are primarily devotional. (For more on the different traditions of Buddhism, including Zen and Pure Land, see Chapter 5.)

Dedicating Your Life to the Benefit of All Beings

Mahayana ("The Great Vehicle" or "Great Path"), a major branch of Buddhism, encourages you to dedicate your spiritual efforts not only to yourself and your loved ones, but also to the benefit and enlightenment of *all* beings.

Many Buddhist traditions teach their followers to actively cultivate love and compassion for others — not only those they care about, but also those who disturb them or toward whom they may feel hostility (in other words, enemies). In fact, some traditions believe that this dedication to the welfare of all forms the foundation of the spiritual path upon which all other practices are based. Other traditions allow the love and compassion to arise naturally as insight deepens and wisdom ripens, while instructing practitioners to dedicate the merits of their meditations and rituals to all beings.

Engaged Buddhism

Buddhism has often been represented as a passive religion advocating introspection and withdrawal from worldly matters. For several decades, Asian proponents of what is now called (Socially) Engaged Buddhism have reinterpreted Buddhist teachings for the modern world. In this book, we talk about the work of several Buddhist reformers: B. R. Ambedkar (1891–1956), from India (Chapter 4); Buddhadasa (1906–1993) and Sulak Sivaraksa (born in 1933), from Thailand (Chapter 5); Thich Nhat Hanh (born in 1926), of Vietnam; and the 14th Dalai Lama (born in 1935), of Tibet (Chapter 15). Especially Buddhadasa and Sulak Sivaraksa have interpreted the Buddhist precepts and the teachings of Shakyamuni Buddha in new ways, making them socially and politically relevant. A good example is Sulak Sivaraksa's reformulation of the 10 Perfections of Theravada Buddhism:

1. Generosity does not mean charity (with the hope of reaping good fortune in return), but means the giving of truths and forgiveness.
2. Good conduct/morality means cultivating the normal conditions in personal and collective lives.
3. Renunciation is not simply for the ordained. For the lay, it entails the ability to quickly locate and effectively deal with the defilements circulated by capitalism, consumerism, and the mainstream mass media.
4. Wisdom means knowing the truth according to nature and the ability to resolve social problems through nonviolence.
5. Effort/endeavor implies courage or "voluntarism" in the face of obstacle(s), without neglecting the "theories and practices" of Buddhism.
6. Endurance/forbearance means flexibility, as well as fighting for good causes without being enamored by power.
7. Truthfulness means no compromise with half-truths; it means being true to oneself.
8. Resolution means fidelity or the determination to achieve the highest good for all.
9. Loving-kindness substitutes anger and hatred with love.
10. Equanimity gradually grows from the following "stages": 1) loving oneself and our equals (*metta*); 2) struggling for justice with the exploited and the excluded (*karuna*); 3) training the mind not to hate our oppressors *(mudita);* and 4) overcoming ingrained and new prejudices within us (*upekkha*), enabling us to transcend fear, hatred, anger, love, and delusion.

(*Rediscovering Spiritual Value: Alternative to Consumerism from a Siamese Buddhist Perspective,* Bangkok, 2009, pp. 66–67)

REMEMBER

Whatever the method, the teachings often emphasize that all beings are inseparable. Some traditions even counsel that, in the end, you won't be able to achieve lasting happiness and peace of mind until all beings are happy and peaceful, too. From this realization arises the vow of the *bodhisattva* (Sanskrit for "enlightenment-bound being") who dedicates his life to the enlightenment of all (see Chapter 14). Until all beings are liberated, the bodhisattva believes, his work isn't yet done. Though not every Buddhist tradition views the bodhisattva in quite the same way, all would agree that this spirit lies at the heart of Mahayana Buddhist teachings.

Chapter 2

Understanding Your Mind: The Creator of All Experience

In This Chapter

- Understanding the importance of the mind in Buddhism
- Getting to know your mind's quirks
- Recognizing your own fundamental purity
- Overcoming ignorance with wisdom
- Transforming your mind with compassion

In Chapter 1, we introduce Buddhism by contrasting what it *isn't* — a strict, rigid system of religious beliefs — with what it actually is — a practical, experience-based method for transforming your life.

At the heart of this transformation is your mind. But *mind* is a rather slippery term. Although the word pops up in conversation all the time — "She's got a sharp mind," "My mind's not very clear today," "Are you out of your mind?" and so on — its definition isn't easy to pin down.

In this chapter, we talk a little about what some traditions of Buddhism have to say about the mind, paying particular attention to the ways in which the various functions of the mind shape everything from your spiritual progress to the most ordinary, everyday life experiences. This subject is a big one, and we certainly can't cover everything relevant here. But don't worry — at this point, we're just trying to give you a general idea.

Recognizing How Your Mind Shapes Your Experience

Your mind shapes and colors all your experiences, without a single exception. The ancient collection of verses on Buddhist teachings, the *Dhammapada* (Pali: *Words of Dhamma*), verses 1–2, begins with this statement:

> Phenomena are preceded by mind, led by mind, formed by mind. If one speaks or acts with a polluted mind, suffering follows him, as a wheel follows the foot of a draught-ox.
>
> Phenomena are preceded by mind, led by mind, formed by mind. If one speaks or acts with a pure mind, happiness follows him, as an ever-present shadow.

From the Buddhist point of view, then, what goes on inside you (in your mind) is much more important in determining whether you're happy or miserable than any of the outer circumstances of your life.

Hold it right there. Does what you just read sound reasonable? Do the inner workings of your mind really have a greater effect on you than, say, your possessions or your surroundings? After all, big companies and advertising agencies spend billions of dollars every year trying to convince you that the opposite is true! In their eyes, your best shot at achieving happiness is to buy whatever they're selling. They appeal to what Jon likes to call the "if only" mentality: If only you drove a fancier car, lived in a bigger house, gargled with a stronger mouthwash, and used a softer toilet paper — then you'd be truly happy. Even if you don't believe everything advertisers tell you, don't you believe that the external conditions of your life determine how well off you are?

Get into the habit of asking yourself these types of questions when you come across new information. Investigating points brought up in a book that you're reading or teachings that you hear isn't an intellectual game or idle pastime. If done properly, such questioning becomes a vital part of your spiritual development. Merely accepting certain statements as true, while rejecting others as false without examining them closely, doesn't accomplish very much.

In this case, examination is particularly important because the questions concern the best way to live your life. Should your pursuit of happiness focus mainly on accumulating possessions and other "externals"? Or should you focus on putting your inner house in order?

To get a feel for how to start examining this issue, consider the following situation. Two friends of yours, Jennifer and Karen, take a vacation together to Tahiti. They stay in the same luxurious guesthouse, eat the same food prepared by the same master chef, lounge on the same pristine beaches, and engage in the same recreational activities. But when they get home and tell you about their trip, their stories sound like they vacationed in two completely different worlds! For Jennifer, Tahiti was heaven on earth, but for Karen, it was pure hell. For every wonderful experience Jennifer brings up, Karen tells you about two awful ones. This situation is hypothetical, of course, but doesn't it sound familiar? Hasn't something like this happened to you or your friends?

Consider one more scenario. During wartime, two friends get thrown into a prison camp. As in the previous example, both guys end up in identical situations, but this time, the outward conditions are miserable. One soldier experiences extreme mental torment due to the horrible physical conditions and ends up bitter and broken in spirit. The other manages to rise above his surroundings, even becoming a source of strength for the other prisoners. True stories like this scenario aren't rare, so how can you account for them?

These examples (and relevant ones from your own experience) demonstrate that the outer circumstances of your life aren't the only factors — or even the most important ones — in determining whether you're content. If external conditions were more important than the condition of your mind, both Jennifer and Karen would've loved Tahiti, both prisoners would have been equally miserable, and no rich and famous person would ever contemplate suicide.

REMEMBER

The more closely you look, the more clearly you'll see that your mental attitude is an important factor in determining the quality of your life. We're not saying that your outer circumstances count for nothing, nor are we implying that people have to give away all their possessions to be sincere spiritual seekers. But without developing your *inner* resources of peace and mental stability, no amount of worldly success — whether measured in terms of wealth, fame, power, or relationships — can ever bring real satisfaction. Or, as someone once said, "Money can't buy happiness; it can only allow you to select your particular form of misery."

Contrasting the Body and Mind

Even if you have a general idea of what the mind is, you may have difficulty identifying it exactly. After all, you can't point to something and say, "This is my mind." Why not? Because unlike your brain, heart, or any other bodily organ, your mind has no color, shape, weight, or other physical attribute.

But as long as you're alive, your body and mind remain intimately interconnected and have a powerful influence on one another. For example, everyone knows that drinking too much alcohol can have a potent, harmful effect on the mind. The physical properties of alcohol dull your mental capacities, lower your inhibitions, and even cause you to hallucinate.

The mind–body influence works the other way as well. For example, worrying too much can contribute to many physical ailments, including stomach ulcers, colitis (inflammation of the large intestine), and high blood pressure. This connection hasn't been lost on medical professionals. Every day, more medical professionals recognize that a patient's mental state can have an enormous effect on recovery from disease. Many hospitals now provide a variety of mind–body treatment options, including hypnotherapy, support groups, and individual counseling, to help patients heal more rapidly and completely. And a quick trip to your local bookstore presents you with even more evidence of the mind's role in the health of the body — dozens of books about the healing influence of visualizations, affirmations, and a positive state of mind line the shelves. A well-known writer even claims to have cured himself of cancer by watching one Marx Brothers movie after another! In his case, laughter really was the best medicine.

They're interconnected, but the body and mind aren't the same thing. If they were, your mental states would be nothing more than the nerve cells, electrical activity, and chemical reactions of your brain. But is this definition an adequate and satisfying explanation for what actually goes on in your mind? Can such varied and richly colored experiences as falling in love, feeling embarrassed, and getting a flash of artistic inspiration be reduced to molecular interactions?

Buddhism teaches that your mind (which is conscious of all your experiences) is formless. Hence, you can't see your mind or touch it. But being formless doesn't prevent your mind from doing what only it can do — being aware! In fact, the job of the mind is just that: to be aware (or conscious).

Approaching the Mind from Three Different Buddhist Perspectives

The various Buddhist traditions have their own particular way of talking about the mind and its role in spiritual development. To give you some idea of the richness and variety of these views, we briefly mention the approach of the three main Buddhist traditions in the West today:

- In texts of the *abhidharma,* or "higher teachings," section of the canon of the Theravada Buddhist tradition, we find a detailed analysis of the mind. These extensive teachings divide the mind's functions into different categories, such as primary and secondary, skillful and unskillful, and so on. This psychological analysis can help you precisely understand which of the many different mental functions (one abhidharma system identifies nearly 50 of them!) are arising in your mind at any given moment. The more skillful you become at identifying the complex and ever-changing nature of these mental functions as they arise, the more thoroughly you can cut through the harmful illusion of a solid, unchanging ego-identity (as we explain in Chapter 13) and achieve spiritual liberation.
- Many serious followers of the Vajrayana Buddhist tradition also study the abhidharma teachings dealing with the mind, the many different mental functions, and so forth. In addition, the Vajrayana offers techniques for contacting what it calls the *mind of clear light,* a blissful state of consciousness residing at the core of your being that's far more

powerful than any ordinary state of mind. By gaining control of this hidden treasure, skillful meditators (or *yogis* of clear light) can burn through mental obstructions rapidly and completely. This act brings them face to face with ultimate reality and, eventually, to the supreme enlightenment of Buddhahood itself.

- According to some masters in the Japanese Zen Buddhist tradition, big Mind, or Buddha nature, pervades the whole experienced universe. Everything you experience, both inside and outside yourself, is nothing other than this Mind (with a capital *m*). By contrast, the *small mind,* the analytical, conceptual mind, tends to identify itself as a limited, separate ego or self. Spiritual awakening involves a shift in identity from small mind to big Mind and to what has been called "no Mind" in Zen traditions.

REMEMBER

We talk more about the approaches of these three (and some other) Buddhist traditions throughout this book, especially in Chapter 5. But for now, we want to point out one thing: You have a choice in the way you experience your life. Your mind can be obscured or unobscured, limited or vast. The first option involves frustration and dissatisfaction. The second brings freedom and fulfillment. The so-called spiritual path enables you to shift your vision of life from the obscured to the unobscured, from the limited to the vast. And that's what Buddhist teachings are about.

Recognizing the six major types of consciousness

Because the human body comes equipped with five senses, you have five types of sensory awareness, sometimes referred to as the *five sensory consciousnesses.* In some Buddhist texts, they're given the following rather technical names, but their meaning is quite simple, so don't sweat the Latin-sounding names:

- **Auditory consciousness:** Aware of sounds
- **Gustatory consciousness:** Aware of tastes (such as bitter, sweet, and sour)
- **Olfactory consciousness:** Aware of odors
- **Tactile consciousness:** Aware of bodily sensations (such as hot and cold, rough and smooth, and so on)
- **Visual consciousness:** Aware of colors and shapes

These five types of sensory awareness, or sensory consciousness, obviously depend upon the health of your body and your sense organs. But a sixth type of awareness does *not* rely so directly on your physical senses to function. This sixth consciousness is called mental consciousness. *Mental consciousness* can be aware of *all* the previously listed items — sights, sounds, odors, tastes, and sensations — and a lot more.

Distorted appearances

Needless to say, the five types of sensory awareness depend on the conditions of their related sense organs. When you have a cold, for example, you may lose your sense of smell entirely; the olfactory consciousness continues to function well, but the nasal congestion interferes with your nose's ability to smell. Similarly, as every cook who has ever added too much salt to a soup knows, the tongue can become accustomed to certain tastes. Consider one more example: Press your finger against the side of your eye socket in a certain place and then look up into the night sky; you may see *two* moons rather than one. These examples demonstrate that you can't always trust the way things appear to your mind. If you add to the mix the various distortions created by your preconceptions and expectations, you can see that clear, undistorted perceptions aren't as common as you may think.

Seeing how certain factors affect mental consciousness

When people speak about the mind, they're generally referring to the sixth consciousness — mental consciousness. For example, if you think about your mother, even if she lives hundreds of miles away or is no longer living, you may say, "My mother has been on my mind lately." And if you think about her so strongly that her image appears to you, you're then *seeing* her — not with your *visual* consciousness, but with your *mental* consciousness. Or, as the old expression goes, you see her in your *mind's eye.*

This sixth consciousness functions in many different ways and affects everything about you, including the five sensory consciousnesses. For example, *attention* — the ability to turn your mind in a particular direction — is just one of the many different qualities associated with mental consciousness. While you're awake, all five types of sensory awareness continually receive information from your environment in the form of raw sensory data, but the amount of attention your mind pays to each piece of information in this constant stream of data can vary quite a bit.

As you read this book, for instance, you pay attention to the shape of the letters and words on the page with your visual consciousness. But how aware are you of the tactile (touch) sensations being produced as the chair (couch, bench, or patio swing) that you're sitting on makes contact with your buttocks? Pause for a moment and think about this. Until we directed your attention to these sensations just now, you were probably oblivious to them. (Of course, the situation would be different if you suddenly sat on a splinter. You wouldn't need anyone's help raising *that* kind of sensation to full awareness.)

This brief demonstration just goes to show that the quality of your sensory awareness varies greatly, depending on many factors. In some cases — such as when you look at optical illusions — you can completely mistake what you're aware of. Sense impressions are notoriously unreliable. But under certain very specific circumstances, you may experience a truly astonishing level of heightened sensory awareness. For example, professional athletes often speak about being "in the zone." When this happens, all the action (and time itself) seems to slow down, no matter how furious it may be. Athletes claim that they can see everything clearly, as if events were in super-slow motion. The entire playing field and all the other players come into sharp focus. Miraculous things can happen then.

Such dramatic changes result from an increase in your concentration, another aspect or function of your mental consciousness. *Concentration*, according to some Buddhist authorities, is the mind's ability to be steadfastly rooted in the present moment and remain fully aware of many objects. Similar to other mental abilities, concentration can be developed (for tips on developing your concentration, turn your attention to Chapter 7). Most of the time, your concentration is rather scattered — soft and fuzzy, like the light of an ordinary light bulb. By contrast, some master meditators achieve a particularly concentrated state of mind, *samadhi,* in which their mind is capable of gaining profound insights into reality. (People report that when Einstein was occupied with a particular theoretical problem, he would slip into a *samadhi*-like state of mind for long stretches of time. While in this state, he would remain motionless, oblivious to what was happening around him.)

Feeling around for your emotions

So far, in this introduction to the mind, we've emphasized certain mental activities — such as investigating and concentrating — but these activities are certainly not the only functions of the mind. Mental consciousness also includes your attitudes and emotional states, both positive and negative.

When Buddhists speak of mental development, they're not talking about becoming smarter. Mental development includes such practices as relaxing the hold that the "negative" states have on your mind and increasing the strength of your mind's "positive" qualities. (We put those words in quotation marks because "negative" and "positive" are just relative terms; don't think that one part of your mind is inherently "good" and another part inherently "bad.")

Tapping your emotional intelligence — to borrow a phrase that's become popular recently — is a large part of your mental and spiritual development.

Mind, head, and heart

In the West, the tendency is to think of the various aspects of mental consciousness as residing in one of two locations: the head or the heart. Functions such as knowing, thinking, reasoning, remembering, and analyzing — in other words, functions that most people generally think of as mental in nature — are assigned to the head. If someone has sharp academic intelligence, for example, she's often called "a real brain." When people try to figure out a difficult problem or remember something they've forgotten, they often scratch their heads, as if this activity can somehow help them jump-start their thought processes.

The emotional center of your being, on the other hand, is often assigned to the heart. When caught in the grip of strong emotions, many people grab or beat their chest. Love, bravery, and a host of other feelings are commonly said to have their home there. In fact, the heart has become the symbol of romantic feelings (think of all those Valentine's Day cards), and the English word *courage* — a brave attitude of mind — is related to the French word *coeur,* meaning "heart."

(It's interesting to note that organs other than the heart have historically been considered the seat of different emotions. In Shakespeare's day, for example, people thought of the liver as the seat of passion. This usage survives today in the insult *lily-livered,* meaning "cowardly" or "timid." Additional expressions, such as "don't vent your spleen" and "you have a lot of gall," indicate that, at one time, specific emotions were associated with other internal organs.)

Note that this sharp distinction between the emotional nature of the heart and the more intellectual qualities associated with the brain and the head doesn't exist in Buddhism. The Sanskrit word *chitta* (which we talk about again in Chapter 14) is translated as "mind," "heart," "attitude," or "consciousness," depending on its context. Similarly, the Japanese word *shin* can be translated as both "mind" and "heart."

Appreciating the Fundamental Purity of Your Mind

If you've read the previous sections of this chapter, you may have some questions at this point. For example, having recognized that the mind contains both negative and positive elements, you may be wondering whether it will always remain like this. Why should this situation ever change? Is there any reason to believe that the admirable qualities that everyone appreciates (such as benevolence) will ever replace the qualities responsible for misery (such as aversion)? In other words, can spiritual development ever really occur?

Seeing that delusions can be remedied

To answer these questions, you first need to recognize that your mind is *always* changing. A powerfully negative state of mind, such as hatred, may arise one moment, but it's certain to subside. That's the very nature of mental states: They don't last. (As the popular saying goes, "The only thing constant is change.")

Jealousy, hatred, greed, and the like lead to suffering and dissatisfaction because they're out of step with reality. They paint a misleading picture of the world. If you happen to find something attractive, the delusion of attachment exaggerates its good qualities until it appears perfect and utterly desirable. Then if you happen to discover even the slightest flaw in that very same object, your anger and disappointment may make the object appear worthless or even repulsive in your eyes. What a roller-coaster ride of emotions! A man who's totally infatuated with a woman, for example, can't find enough words to praise all her wonderful qualities. But at the divorce proceedings a short time later, he can't come up with a single good thing to say about her.

Delusions can be overcome by wisdom. (To put it another way, they can be penetrated by insight.) *Wisdom* is the positive, clarifying mental factor that aids in the process. Other positive states of mind and heart, such as compassion, aren't threatened by wisdom at all. In fact, they're strengthened by it.

Finding the sun behind the clouds

REMEMBER

From the point of view of some contemporary Tibetan Buddhist teachers, the underlying nature of the mind itself is essentially pure, uncontaminated, and unconditioned.

A powerful analogy illustrates this point. First, you need to whip up a memory of prolonged, cloudy weather. (Jon lived in northern England for a number of years, so he finds this exercise easy to do. He can remember someone once saying, "The weather wasn't so bad last week; it rained twice — once for three days, and once for four!") In these miserable conditions, it may seem as though sun has completely disappeared, that it no longer exists. But as everyone knows, the sun hasn't really disappeared, no matter what the weather is like. The clouds merely block the sun from your vision. After the winds shift and the clouds part, you can see the sun again, shining as brightly as before.

REMEMBER

In a similar manner, beneath the clouds of delusion that may be disturbing you right now (whatever confused and uncomfortable feelings of greed, anger, jealousy, and the like you may be experiencing), an essential purity still exists. This basic purity is unaffected and uncontaminated by obscuring delusions, no matter how violent they may be or how frequently they may disturb your peace of mind. This calm quality is reflected in the Zen expression, "Beneath the one who is busy is one who is not busy."

The spiritual path set forth in some Buddhist teachings, therefore, consists mainly of penetrating the inauthentic, nonessential aspects of your experience so that the sunlight of your Buddha nature — the fundamental purity of your deepest level of consciousness — can shine forth without interruption. Sometimes folks use an analogy that's more down to earth: Following the spiritual path is likened to peeling away successive layers of an onion!

An important Mahayana Buddhist text entitled *The Peerless Continuum,* attributed to Maitreya Buddha (check out Chapter 3 for more about him), contains a series of poetic analogies for this fundamental purity. The following analogy (adapted from a translation by Glenn Mullin) compares the Buddha nature that all beings share to a treasure lying hidden beneath a poor man's house.

> Under the floor of some poor man's house lies a treasure,
>
> But because he does not know of its existence
>
> He does not think he is rich.
>
> Similarly, inside one's mind lies truth itself
>
> Firm and unfading,
>
> Yet, because beings see it not, they experience
>
> A constant stream of misery.
>
> The treasure of truth lies within the house of the mind;
>
> Buddhas take pure birth into this world
>
> So that this treasure may be made known.

Tracing the Path of Wisdom and Loving Compassion

How do you go about contacting, revealing, and fulfilling the fundamental purity addressed in *The Peerless Continuum,* which we quoted in the previous section? This subject is a big one, to say the least. We discuss the process of uncovering and realizing your Buddha nature in detail throughout Part IV, but the following statements give you a quick summary:

- Cultivate the *wisdom* that unmasks ignorance, the root of all suffering.
- Generate the *loving compassion* that opens your heart to others.

In Chapter 14, we explain more about wisdom and compassion, but the following sections give you an idea of what they entail.

Wisdom: Removing the veils of misconception

REMEMBER

Buddhist teachings emphasize that every experience of suffering and dissatisfaction, *without exception,* has its root or source in ignorance.

But the term *ignorance* in this context doesn't simply mean *not* understanding or *not* knowing something, as when a person says, "I've never studied trigonometry; I'm completely ignorant of that subject." Instead, ignorance at its most troublesome — the kind of ignorance that the Buddha said was responsible for everyone's problems — is the condition of *mis*understanding or *mis*knowing the way things actually exist. Simply put, this ignorance consists of all the misconceptions that prevent you from seeing things as they really are. According to the Zen tradition, "All beings have the wisdom and virtue of the fully enlightened one. But because of their distorted views, they don't realize this fact."

When Jon's teacher and beloved spiritual friend Lama Thubten Yeshe first came to the United States in 1974, he sometimes used the example of the strained relations between blacks and whites (remember, this was before the term *African American* came into general use) to illustrate the destructive effects of ignorant misconceptions. He pointed out that when a white man and a black man encounter each other on the street, they don't actually see each other at all. All they see are their own *projections* — the distorted images from their own mind that they "project" onto the person they meet. This blanket of projections — "All black people are like this" and "All white people are like that" — prevents each man from seeing the other person *as he actually is,* in all his human complexity. The resulting atmosphere of mistrust, suspicion, and fear produces nothing but problems.

TIP

According to Buddhist teachings, you need to peel away three specific types of misconception, or ignorance, if you want to see things with the enlightened eye of wisdom and end your problems:

- Mistakenly believing that a source of suffering and dissatisfaction is actually a source of true happiness (as when an alcoholic thinks salvation can be found in a bottle)
- Mistakenly believing that something that changes from moment to moment is actually permanent, lasting, and unchanging (as when a person thinks his youthful good looks will last forever, cosmetic surgery notwithstanding)
- Mistakenly believing that people and things possess a substantial, independent, findable *self* — an individual nature of their own, separate from the whole

This last and most fundamental form of ignorance, explained in detail by proponents of Indo-Tibetan Buddhism, may not be easy to understand. Even the words used to explain it have specific meanings that aren't obvious to the casual observer. But don't worry. We explain this most subtle form of ignorance (and the preceding two) in more detail in Chapter 13.

Loving compassion: Opening your heart to others

If you find the discussion of ignorance and misconceptions heavy, this topic may be a welcome change. *Loving compassion* is a trait that everyone admires — in fact, it may be the most immediately attractive character trait of those who have advanced along a genuine spiritual path, whether they're Buddhist or not.

Witnessing examples of enlightened compassion

Consider the example of His Holiness, the Dalai Lama of Tibet (we talk more about him in Chapter 15). Many people consider the Dalai Lama to be a human embodiment of this warm and friendly attitude of loving compassion. His smiling countenance and genuine concern for others — not to mention his hearty laughter — may have done more to promote the values of true spiritual development than all the books published on Buddhism in the past several decades. And the reason this single Tibetan monk has affected so many people from all walks of life is no secret. As he himself has stated many times, "My religion is kindness."

You won't find anything complex or mysterious about this kindness, or humanity, or loving compassion, or whatever you want to call this warm feeling for others. Loving compassion can arise spontaneously in all but the most damaged of human hearts. You feel it, for example, when you sense that a small child is in danger or hear an animal howling in pain. Without regard for yourself, and without thinking about it, you immediately want to separate these helpless victims from whatever harm they're experiencing.

The only difference between such spontaneous compassion and that of a fully enlightened being — a Buddha — is its scope. Although generating genuine concern for the welfare of pets, small children, and others you feel close to probably comes easy to you, can you say the same about your attitude toward everyone? Be honest with yourself: How do you feel when you hear that someone you dislike — perhaps someone who has recently insulted you — is experiencing a problem or has just had some bad luck? If you immediately feel like rejoicing, the scope of your loving compassion is limited.

A fully enlightened being, such as Shakyamuni Buddha (one of whose epithets is the Compassionate One), no longer experiences such limitation or prejudice (see Chapter 3 for more about the historical Buddha). The compassionate concern this person extends to others isn't conditional. Whether the people experiencing difficulty have been friendly or unfriendly, supporters or sworn enemies, loving compassion arises for them all equally and spontaneously.

Overcoming selfishness and transforming your mind

Praising the beauty of unconditional love and compassion is all well and good. After all, admiring loving compassion is easy when you see it in the life and deeds of such outstanding spiritual figures as the Buddha, Jesus Christ, the Dalai Lama, and Mother Teresa.

But you may be wondering where all this leaves you. "I know I don't have unconditional love for everyone," you may be thinking. "But what should I do? Feel guilty about it? Fake it and pretend to be happy when my rival at work gets promoted above me?" Or perhaps you feel like throwing up your hands in despair, thinking, "No one like me could ever hope to live up to the example of people like the Dalai Lama or Mother Teresa. I guess I'm just no good." Or if you're feeling particularly cynical, you may even think, "I know how selfish I am, and I don't believe anyone else is really any different. All this talk about caring for others and feeling unconditional love for everyone is just a lot of pious pretense. My philosophy is, 'Look out for number one!' I'm a realist, and all this spiritual nonsense is for fools."

How can these doubts, feelings of inadequacy, and objections be answered?

TIP

Spiritual progress doesn't happen without preparation. Many Buddhists believe that it took Shakyamuni Buddha many lifetimes, from the time he first turned his mind toward the spiritual path to the time he achieved full and complete enlightenment. So expecting instant results isn't realistic. (Many traditions of Buddhism do teach that you can wake up to your enlightened nature in an instant — but it still takes years to fully actualize or embody this awakening in everyday life. For more on the different approaches to enlightenment, see Chapter 10.)

To determine whether a particular path works for you, check to see if it leads to the results it advertises. We're not talking about experiencing blinding flashes of insight or discovering that you've suddenly gained miraculous powers. Simply, are you becoming freer, more relaxed, and more open as a result of following what the Buddha — or anyone else, for that matter — has taught? Is your self-preoccupation subsiding, your wisdom growing, your joy and compassion expanding? Results like this don't happen overnight, and you needn't obsess about your progress. But when you've been practicing the teachings of Buddhism for awhile, check in to see how you're doing.

Fortunately, the Buddhist path contains the means for bringing about this desired self-transformation in the form of *meditation,* the heart of Buddhist practice. We give you a sampling of different meditative techniques and general discussions of the role of meditation in spiritual growth throughout this book. In Chapter 7, for example, you can find certain meditative techniques for dealing with the issue at hand — lessening selfishness and expanding the scope of your concern for others.

By putting meditative techniques into practice, you may discover that you do, in fact, have the power to shape the way you habitually react to others, to your surroundings, and even to yourself. With enough perseverance, you may find that you're no longer so compelled to speak, act, or even think in the limited patterns you're used to. Slowly but surely, you may find that you can liberate yourself from suffering and dissatisfaction.

And if, after some time, none of this happens — if you don't experience beneficial results at all — then simply put aside whatever you've read. After all, as the Dalai Lama often says, "You're under no obligation to follow the Buddha's teachings. Just try to be a good person. That's enough."

Part II

A Short History of Buddhism

The 5th Wave By Rich Tennant

In this part . . .

Come right in, ladies and gentlemen, and take an engaging and enlightening tour of the history of Buddhism, featuring the life of Buddha himself. Peruse this part, and you can also discover Buddha's basic teachings and see how they evolved as Buddhism spread throughout Asia and made its way through history to the present day.

Chapter 3

Surveying the Life and Teachings of the Historical Buddha

In This Chapter

- Glimpsing the early life of Prince Siddhartha
- Leaving the royal life behind
- Becoming the Buddha
- Practicing what he preached
- Waiting for the future Buddha

Gautama the Buddha, whose teachings the different schools of Buddhism developed, is thought to have lived in the fifth century BCE (before the Common Era, otherwise known as BC). We don't know when he was born, but tradition holds that he died at age 80. Scholars are still debating the year of his death. Born Prince Siddhartha, the heir of a ruling family, he gave up the royal way of life in his search for an end to all suffering. This search eventually brought him to the foot of the famous Bodhi tree — *bodhi* means "awakening" or "enlightenment" — where he reportedly reached the awakening of Buddhahood at the age of 35. This awakening earned him the title Buddha ("Awakened One"). He is also known as Shakyamuni, Sage of the Shakyas. (Shakya was the name of the clan to which he belonged.) He then spent the remaining 45 years of his life teaching those who were drawn to the path that leads from suffering and dissatisfaction toward genuine spiritual fulfillment.

On one level, Buddhism is the record of these vast and profound spiritual teachings. (On another level, of course, it's the living embodiment of these teachings in the lives of spiritual practitioners through the ages, including right now.) The accounts of the Buddha's life date many centuries after his death and include many legends. This legendary material includes inspiring teachings attributed to Shakyamuni. As in the case of Jesus, Shakyamuni's life story has been told repeatedly during the past 2,500 years, and each culture Buddhism has entered has responded to his life in its own distinctive way.

In this chapter, we give you a glimpse of the Buddha's basic teachings and some of the most significant and inspiring episodes in his life story as it has been passed down through the ages. (The complete story is too extensive to include here. If you want to read more about the Buddha's life, check out the list of books in Appendix B.)

The historical Buddha is known by different names. In this book, we have mostly referred to him as Shakyamuni (Sage of the Shakyas). Texts also refer to him as the ascetic *Gotama* (Pali) or *Gautama* (Sanskrit), Gotama/Gautama being his family name. His personal name was Siddhartha (Sanskrit; Pali: *Siddhattha,* meaning "he whose aim is accomplished"), or, according to some traditions, *Sarvarthasiddha* (Sanskrit: "all aims accomplished"). After his enlightenment, he became known by the title *Buddha* (Sanskrit: "Awakened One").

Revealing the Buddha's Early Life

Even within the traditional forms of Buddhism, you can find different ways of interpreting the events in the Buddha's life and the meaning of his enlightenment.

- An early tradition teaches that Shakyamuni was an ordinary person like you and me who happened to have uniquely favorable life circumstances (that is, plenty of spare time and energy) and an unflagging dedication to achieve full spiritual realization. This characterization suggests that, like him, you also can attain enlightenment.
- Many traditions believe that Shakyamuni began his spiritual journey a long time before his lifetime (in the fifth century BCE) and achieved significant levels of realization, but he didn't actually complete his journey until he sat under the Bodhi tree in the 35th year of his historical lifetime.
- Some traditions claim that the person who was honored as Shakyamuni actually achieved Buddhahood (that is, complete and supreme enlightenment) during a previous lifetime. He then hung out with a host of other Buddhas until the time came for him to descend to earth and demonstrate to others the spiritual path that he'd already completed.

Some traditions elevate the Buddha to mythic proportions and others view him as an exceptional human being, but they all agree that he exemplifies the ultimate fulfillment of the human condition: complete liberation from confusion and suffering.

The various Buddhist traditions broadly agree on the events of Shakyamuni's life. To begin, they say, he was born the son and heir of King Shuddhodana of the Shakya clan in the northern part of the Indian subcontinent.

Dealing with contradictions

The fact that you can interpret the Buddha's life story in different ways raises an interesting point. When you have two different and contradictory ways of explaining something, most people assume that if one explanation is right, the other must be wrong. For example, when you solve the equation $2 + x = 5$, you have only one correct answer; anything other than 3 is wrong. If you're in the habit of applying this strict "mathematical" approach to everything, the different ways of viewing the Buddha's life story may make you uneasy. "Only one of those interpretations can be correct," you may insist. "If he's a Buddha, he reached enlightenment either *during* his life as an Indian prince or *before* it. If one answer is right, the other must be wrong. So which is which?"

Buddhist teachers don't seem to feel uneasy at all about giving different explanations for the same event. We don't mean to imply that they're careless with the truth. A large part of their training involves keenly intelligent investigation of the nature of reality, so their thinking certainly isn't fuzzy. But they accept that the value of a particular explanation depends to a great extent on the intended beneficiary of that explanation. Because people have such different attitudes and inclinations from one another, the explanation that's best for one person may not be particularly helpful for another.

On one occasion many years ago, Jon had the chance to meet privately with the Dalai Lama and ask him some questions. (Chapter 15 has more on this extraordinary person.) During the interview, the Dalai Lama brought up the name of Tsongkhapa, a great Tibetan master born more than 600 years ago who had been the teacher of the very first Dalai Lama. Successive Dalai Lamas have always had the utmost respect and devotion for this particular master, and the current Dalai Lama — the 14th in this lineage — is no exception.

In general, Tibetans have great reverence for Tsongkhapa and think of him as a human manifestation of Manjushri, the bodhisattva of wisdom. But on this occasion, the Dalai Lama said (to the best of Jon's memory), "I prefer to think of Tsongkhapa as a regular human being who, through great effort, was able to complete the spiritual path in his lifetime. I find this way of thinking about him more inspiring than thinking that he was born already enlightened."

A miraculous birth

The Shakya clan lived in the part of the Indian subcontinent that lies in the southern part of present-day Nepal. The clan's leader, King Shuddhodana (shoe-*doe*-da-na), didn't have an heir to his throne. Then one night, his wife, Queen Maya (or Mahamaya), had a dream in which a beautiful white six-tusked elephant appeared to her and touched or entered her body. The wise men at court all recognized this dream as a sign that the queen was pregnant with a special child who would someday grow up to be a great leader.

Toward the end of her pregnancy, the queen left her husband's palace in the capital city of Kapilavastu and, with her entourage, headed for her parents' home to give birth — a custom that expectant mothers in many parts of India still follow today. As they passed Lumbini, the queen realized that she could give birth at any minute. So she entered the Lumbini grove and, while standing and holding on to the branch of a tree, gave birth to her son in a miraculous way: He emerged from the right side of her body without causing any pain (see Figure 3-1). The child took seven steps and proclaimed that this was going to be his last life.

Figure 3-1: Birth in the Lumbini grove.

Photographed by John C. Huntington. Photo courtesy of the Huntington Archive at The Ohio State University.

By all accounts, the child was extremely beautiful, although I'm sure you'd expect nothing less from the protagonist of this story. Numerous promising signs accompanied his birth, and in recognition of this, his proud father named him *Siddhartha* (sid-*hart*-ta), which means "he whose aim is accomplished." In some Buddhist traditions, the name appears as *Sarvarthasiddha* ("all aims accomplished").

Shortly after Siddhartha's birth, Asita (a-*see*-ta), a widely respected senior religious hermit, unexpectedly arrived in Kapilavastu. He, too, had seen the signs of an auspicious birth and had come to the royal household to check out the child for himself. King Shuddhodana greeted Asita with great courtesy and had the baby brought to him. Imagine, then, the proud parents' shock and fear when the old hermit burst into tears after taking a long look at their cherished boy.

But Asita quickly assured the royal couple that he hadn't seen anything wrong with the child, nor any signs that a disaster awaited him in the future. Quite the contrary! Asita said that the boy displayed remarkable qualities — qualities that would make him an even greater ruler than his father. And if Siddhartha were to leave the royal life and become a seeker of the truth, he would become even greater than a mere emperor: He'd become the source of spiritual guidance for the entire world!

As for his tears, Asita said, he was weeping for himself. All his life, he had wanted only to follow the spiritual path. But now that he'd met the one person who could reveal this path to him, it was too late. Asita knew that by the time Siddhartha was old enough to begin teaching, he himself would already have died.

An overprotective father

Asita's prophesy both encouraged and bothered the king. He wanted nothing more than to have his son inherit his throne and bring added glory to the royal family. Afterward, when he was an old man like Asita, Siddhartha could retire to the religious life if he wanted. But the king's priorities were clear: His son was to become a powerful and universally admired monarch.

Although he showed signs of great intelligence early on, something in the young prince's character worried his father. The child, who was brought up by his aunt, Mahaprajapati Gautami (*maha-praja-patee gau-ta-mee*), after his mother died, was extraordinarily kind and sensitive, too gentle to be a ruler of nations. He wasn't interested in the rough games of his playmates and preferred to spend his time caring for the animals that lived on the palace grounds. In one famous episode, the prince saved the life of a swan that his mean-spirited cousin, Devadatta (day-va-*dah*-ta), had shot. (Throughout Siddhartha's life, Devadatta keeps reappearing as his jealous rival.)

The king was afraid that Siddhartha's sensitive nature would lead him to abandon the royal life prematurely, so he did everything possible to hide the harsh realities of life from his son. For example, if a servant fell ill, the king removed the individual from the palace until the illness had passed. According to the stories, one of the king's gardeners was responsible for clipping and removing any flower the moment it began to wilt. In this way, the prince would be spared the pain of encountering even natural signs of decay.

The prince marries: Imprisoned in palaces of pleasure

Eventually, Siddhartha became old enough to get married and raise his own family. The king was sure that these responsibilities would keep him from abandoning the royal life, so he arranged an event where his son could meet the eligible young women in the area. (Think of the ball held in Prince Charming's honor in *Cinderella,* and you get the idea.)

At this event, Siddhartha met Yashodhara (yah-*sho*-da-ra), the daughter of a neighboring king. It was love at first sight for both of them. (Later, when fully enlightened, Shakyamuni explained this instant attraction by saying that he and Yashodhara had been married to each other in a number of previous lifetimes. They'd even mated for life as tigers at one point along the way!) But before they could marry and live happily ever after, Siddhartha had to prove that he was worthy of Yashodhara by defeating rival suitors in contests of strength and martial skill. As you may have guessed, Siddhartha was victorious, and he and Yashodhara celebrated a joyous wedding. Siddhartha was 16 years old at that time.

Soon Siddhartha and his bride were living in the three pleasure palaces (one each for the hot, cool, and rainy seasons) that his father had built for them. The palaces were all located in a vast park surrounded by a wall. In fact, the king had imprisoned Siddhartha in the palaces without the prince realizing it. Because everything and everyone inside these prisons was attractive and captivating, Siddhartha would surely never want to leave — at least, that was the king's plan. And when Yashodhara gave birth to a son, Rahula (rah-*hu*-la), the plan seemed complete.

Forbidden knowledge revealed: The four visions

But even the best-laid plans of courtiers and kings sometimes go astray. One day, a palace musician serenaded Siddhartha and his wife with a song about the beauties and wonders of the world. Intrigued by the descriptions, the prince asked his father for permission to journey beyond the palace gates to see for himself what was out there.

By this time, Siddhartha was 29 years old, and his father realized that the time had come for him to see the kingdom he would someday rule. So the king gave permission for the excursion, but not before he arranged for the removal of all unpleasant sites in the area of town that his son would visit. Finally, when everything was prepared, the prince and his charioteer, Chandaka (Sanskrit; in the Pali tradition: Channa), rode into town.

At first, the visit went very well. The people greeted Siddhartha with great joy and affection, and Siddhartha liked everything that he saw. But then Siddhartha and Chandaka ran into something that only the two of them seemed to notice — an unfortunate person who was bent over in pain and racked by cough and fever.

Siddhartha asked his charioteer to explain the meaning of this unexpected vision. "This is sickness, my lord," Chandaka replied. He then went on to explain that, sooner or later, nearly everyone experiences such disease and discomfort. The prince was startled upon realizing that, at any time, his family, friends, or companions, or he himself, could experience pain and misery. Suddenly, all his happiness and joy faded away, and he could think only about the suffering he'd just seen, a suffering that threatened everyone.

The next two times Siddhartha rode out into the city, he encountered even more disturbing sights: old age and death. The prince was devastated. He wondered how people could act so carefree and happy with the threat of sickness, old age, and inevitable death hanging over their heads.

Finally, on his fourth excursion, he discovered what he had to do. On this occasion, he saw a homeless wanderer. Despite his shabby appearance, the man possessed remarkable calm and determination. When the prince asked him who he was, the man replied, "I am one who has given up the household life to search for a way out of the suffering of the world." Siddhartha's destiny was suddenly revealed to him. He knew that he, too, would have to give up his way of life and devote himself completely to the spiritual quest.

Beginning the Quest

The four visions of sickness, old age, death, and a homeless seeker of truth (which we cover in the section "Forbidden knowledge revealed: The four visions," earlier in this chapter) mark the beginning of the prince's spiritual quest. Their importance to the history of Buddhism is undeniable, and depictions of Siddhartha's crucial encounters with them often adorn the walls of Buddhist temples.

Renouncing the royal life

When Siddhartha knew that he could no longer stay cooped up within the confines of royal life, he went to his father and asked for his permission to leave. The king reacted as many fathers would in similar situations: He blew his stack! He forbade the prince from leaving and posted a guard at all the palace exits to prevent his departure.

But the prince was determined to go. Siddhartha wanted to hold his infant son in his arms before he left, but he decided against it, fearing that he'd awaken the sleeping Yashodhara. He silently made his way past the sleeping musicians, dancing girls, and attendants and went outside, where he roused Chandaka (his charioteer) and asked him to prepare his horse, telling him that he wanted to ride out that night. Chandaka was surprised, but he obeyed the prince.

All the people in the palace, including the guards, had fallen asleep (think of the scene in *Sleeping Beauty* in which everyone is suddenly overcome by drowsiness), so Siddhartha was able to escape. He and Chandaka rode through the night, and when they stopped, the prince told Chandaka to take his horse and his royal jewelry and return to the palace without him. Chandaka began to cry and asked what he should tell the prince's family, who were sure to be devastated. "Tell them," Siddhartha replied, "that I have not left because I do not love them. It is because I *do* love them all that I must find a way to overcome the sufferings of sickness, old age, and death. If I am successful, I shall return. If I am not, then death would have eventually parted us anyway." Chandaka could do nothing but return alone.

Siddhartha was now on his own, and the first thing he did was cast off the signs of royalty. He cut his long hair, exchanged his silk clothing for the rough garb of a forest dweller, and, renouncing his former way of life completely, went in search of someone who could help him in his quest.

After his great renunciation (see the sidebar "The meaning of renunciation," later in this chapter, for more details), Siddhartha met and studied with two renowned spiritual teachers, Arada Kalama and Udraka Ramaputra. He quickly mastered the meditation techniques they taught him, but he realized that, though helpful, the techniques were insufficient to bring him the complete liberation from suffering that he desired. He'd have to go deeper.

Going to extremes and discovering the middle way

Siddhartha heard of a forest in the kingdom of Magadha where *ascetics* (people who practice austerities to attain religious insight) often gathered to practice and immediately decided to join them. On the way, he caught the attention of the ruler of Magadha, King Bimbisara (bim-bi-*sa*-ra). The king was so impressed by the young man's demeanor and dedication that he asked Siddhartha to stay and help him rule. But Siddhartha politely explained that he'd already given up one royal position and had no desire to assume another. Bimbisara then told Siddhartha that if he ever found what he was looking for, he should return and teach it to him.

Making sense of the Buddha's story

Even in this *Reader's Digest* version of Prince Siddhartha's story, you may have already encountered a number of ideas that challenge your ability to take the account at face value. For example, how could someone as bright as Siddhartha reach the age of 29 and still know nothing about sickness, old age, and death? How could the precautions of even the most overprotective father have shielded him from these grim realities?

Yet despite these objections, the story rings true on a deep level. Even in this modern world of instant, worldwide communication and the information superhighway, people manage to avoid seeing what's right in front of their eyes. The homeless fill the streets, but they remain invisible to most people. In hospitals, where death is everywhere, a dying person's true condition is often kept from him or her. And we've even heard of some communities where funeral processions can take place only at night, to avoid freaking out the general public.

Denial is the name of the game (not to mention a river in Egypt), and you can see the game being played all around you. If and when the reality of life's miseries manages to break through this wall of denial, the experience can be devastating, even life transforming. Like Siddhartha, many people turn their attention away from worldly accomplishment and toward the spiritual path as the result of some unexpected experience of suffering or loss. Of course, very few people give up everything at the first glimpse of sickness and death and search for the truth like Siddhartha did.

When Siddhartha arrived at the forest, he found five other ascetics already engaged in strict practices. The ascetics hoped to overcome suffering by winning complete control over their senses and enduring extreme pain and hardship. Siddhartha adopted these practices, and soon his extraordinary concentration and determination convinced his new companions that if any one of them was going to reach the final goal, it would be the newcomer.

Thus began what later became known as the six-year fast. Siddhartha sat exposed to the elements day and night. He ate less and less, eventually consuming nothing but the few seeds that happened to blow into his lap. His body, once so glorious and attractive, became withered and shrunken. Eventually, the practice reduced Siddhartha to little more than a living skeleton, but still he persevered (see Figure 3-2).

Finally, one day Siddhartha took stock of himself. He discovered that, in his weakened condition, he couldn't think as clearly as before; therefore, he was farther from his goal than when he'd started six years ago. Tired and dirty, he decided to refresh himself in the nearby river but nearly drowned before he could pull himself out. As Siddhartha lay on the bank recovering, he realized that if he were ever going to succeed, he'd have to follow the middle way between self-indulgence and extreme self-denial. (Later this phrase, the *middle way,* took on more meaning and became the expression that the Buddha himself often used when referring to his teachings. Even today, Buddhism is widely known as the middle way that avoids all extremes.)

Figure 3-2: Siddhartha fasting.

Photographed by John C. Huntington. Photo courtesy of the Huntington Archive at The Ohio State University.

Siddhartha sat up again, and the wife of a local herdsman soon entered the forest with an offering for the local spirits. Her name was Sujata (*sue*-ja-ta), and she had often prayed to the spirits of the forest for a baby boy. Now that she'd given birth to the child she desperately wanted, she came to the forest with a bowl of specially prepared milk rice to thank the spirits for granting her wish. When she saw Siddhartha sitting there, she mistook him for the king of the spirits who had helped her and presented the nourishing offering to him with great devotion. When his five ascetic companions saw him accept this fine meal, they were deeply disappointed. Thinking that Siddhartha had abandoned his quest, they left the forest in disgust, determined to continue their practices somewhere else.

After he'd eaten and his body regained its radiance and strength, Siddhartha thanked the woman. He told her that he wasn't the spirit she thought he was; he was just a human being searching for the path that would end all suffering. And because of her offering, he felt that he was now strong enough to succeed.

The meaning of renunciation

Long hair was one of the prominent signs of Indian royalty, and Siddhartha's decision to cut his hair symbolized his strong determination to change the entire pattern of his life and devote himself to the spiritual quest. Even today, the ceremony marking someone's formal decision to enter the Buddhist way of life often includes having a lock of hair snipped off, in imitation of the Buddha's great renunciation. Followers who choose to become ordained as a celibate monk or a nun have their entire head shaved, as a sign that they have completely renounced the life of a layperson.

But renunciation isn't really a matter of having your hair cut or changing your outward appearance in some other way. Nor does it mean that you necessarily have to give away your possessions.

The true meaning of renunciation is the decision to give up attachment. The cause of suffering and dissatisfaction is attachment, so you need to give up attachment. If you can possess something without becoming attached to it — without letting it become an obstacle to your spiritual progress or a waste of your time and energy — you don't need to give it up.

Sitting in the Shade of the Bodhi Tree: The Defeat of Mara

Siddhartha crossed the river and made his way to a large fig tree that later became known as the Bodhi tree — the Tree of Enlightenment. With some bundles of grass he'd received from a local grass cutter, he prepared a cushion and sat down with the confident determination that he wouldn't get up from that seat until he reached enlightenment.

The classical Buddhist texts describe what happened next with barely contained excitement. The accounts say that the world held its breath as the moment that would transform history approached. Siddhartha sat under the Tree of Enlightenment, and the gods rejoiced.

But not everyone was overjoyed. Mara the Tempter, the embodiment of all evil, was terrified. He knew that if Siddhartha gained enlightenment, his success would threaten the power that delusion holds over the world. Traditional texts use dramatic imagery to depict the events. As Siddhartha sat in meditation, the sons and daughters of Mara — the whole host of demonic interferences — began their attack, trying to disturb his concentration. (Take a look at Figure 3-3.)

Figure 3-3: Mara's army attacking.

Photographed by John C. Huntington. Photo courtesy of the Huntington Archive at The Ohio State University.

Violent storms of hatred arose, but beneath the Bodhi tree, all remained calm. The demonic forces unleashed a barrage of weapons, but they turned into flower petals that fell harmlessly at the feet of the determined meditator. Visions of the most enticing sensual delights then appeared to Siddhartha, along with images of his wife and son, but nothing could break his concentration.

The Bodhi tree today

You can still visit a Bodhi tree in Bodh Gaya (in northeast India) that grows on the spot where Siddhartha is believed to have attained enlightenment two and a half millennia ago. It isn't the exact same tree, but it's believed to be a direct descendant of the original.

A few hundred years after the time of the Buddha, during the reign of King Ashoka (turn to Chapter 4 for the exploits of this important monarch), Buddhism spread to the island nation now known as Sri Lanka (formerly Ceylon). At that time, a cutting from the Bodhi tree was planted on the island and became the focal point of a famous Buddhist shrine. Centuries later, after the original tree in Bodh Gaya had been destroyed, a cutting from Sri Lanka's Bodhi tree was brought back to India and planted at the original site. This tree toppled during restoration work begun in 1877, but a sapling from it was planted in its place. That's the tree you can still visit today.

Mara had just one weapon left: the seeds of doubt. Dismissing his legions, Mara appeared before Siddhartha and addressed him directly. "Show me one witness who can testify that you deserve to succeed where all others have failed," he demanded mockingly. Siddhartha responded wordlessly. He simply stretched forth his right hand and touched the earth (see Chapter 10), because the earth itself was the witness that Siddhartha had practiced the virtues (over countless lifetimes) that would now empower his attainment of Buddhahood. Mara was defeated and faded away like a bad dream.

It was the night of the full moon in the fourth Indian month (which falls in May or June of our calendar). As the moon rose higher in the sky, Siddhartha's meditative concentration deepened. He passed through different stages of deep meditative absorption. The fire of his growing wisdom burned away whatever layers of unknowing still obscured his mind. He directly and unmistakably perceived the stream of his past lives and understood exactly how past actions lead to present and future results. He saw how craving, the source of suffering, is rooted in ignorance. Gradually, he penetrated subtler levels of ignorance. Finally, as the moon was setting and the sun of the next day was rising, Siddhartha attained the ultimate goal: full and complete enlightenment. He was now an Awakened One, a Buddha.

Benefiting Others: The Buddha's Career in Full Gear

For seven weeks, Shakyamuni, Sage of the Shakyas, now known as the Buddha, remained in the vicinity of the Bodhi tree, absorbed in the limitless awareness only a fully awakened being experiences. According to traditional accounts, the Buddha thought that because no one else was likely to exert the extraordinary effort required to achieve the goal he'd attained, enjoying the fruits of enlightenment himself would be the best way to go.

As if in response to this unspoken thought, the god Brahma Sahampati appeared to Shakyamuni and, on behalf of the world, begged him to reconsider: "While it is true that beings' minds are obscured, the coverings of some are less thick than others. Certainly, there are those who can benefit from your realizations. For their sake, please teach us what you have learned." The Buddha agreed only after some hesitation. He was concerned that people would be unable to grasp the depth of his teaching.

Providing spiritual guidance: Turning the wheel of Dharma

When the Buddha thought about which individuals would be ready to receive his initial teachings, he first considered the two teachers he had studied with but realized that they already had died. So he chose his five former companions, who were continuing their strict ascetic practices without him in Sarnath, near the ancient Indian holy city of Varanasi.

The five ascetics were staying in the Deer Park at Sarnath when they saw the Buddha approach. Still believing that he'd given up the spiritual quest, they resolved not to welcome back this "quitter." But they couldn't help noticing, even from a distance, that a profound change had come over him. He radiated such peaceful assurance and benevolence that they had to greet him with great respect and offer him a seat of honor among them. Then in response to their request to reveal his experiences, he delivered his first formal teaching as an Awakened One, a Buddha.

Of all the activities of a Buddha, *turning the wheel of the Dharma* (giving spiritual instruction) is number one because an enlightened being is most helpful to others when providing instruction. As Shakyamuni himself later pointed out, a Buddha can't remove another's suffering the way you can remove a thorn from another's flesh. (If he could, everyone's problems would already be gone; the compassionate Buddha certainly would've removed them all by now.) But what a Buddha *can* do — and do with matchless skill — is reveal the path to others in ways that are best suited to each person's individual makeup.

Not every teaching that a Buddha gives is verbal. A Buddha provides spiritual inspiration and instruction by his presence and can convey great meaning even through silence. But during his lifetime, Shakyamuni Buddha did deliver many formal discourses, the first of which he gave at the Deer Park in Sarnath. The theme of this discourse was the *four noble truths,* a theme that he elaborated on and refined in the countless other teachings he gave during the remaining 45 years of his life. (The section "Understanding the Four Noble Truths," later in this chapter, delves into this subject in greater detail.)

Founding the community

As the Buddha had predicted, his five former companions were particularly ripe for spiritual instruction. Just a few words by the Buddha were enough to trigger deep insights into his teachings. They gave up all activities that the Buddha taught were harmful to the welfare of others and to their own spiritual evolution. They took ordination as monks and became the first members of the *Sangha,* the Buddhist spiritual community.

As more people became inspired by the Buddha's wisdom and compassion and benefited from his teachings, the community grew larger. This growth attracted the attention (and often aroused the jealousy) of other established teachers who, together with their own disciples, came to test and challenge the Buddha. Recognizing that the Buddha was indeed the real thing — a fully awakened master — many of the rival teachers and their followers became the Buddha's disciples. The spiritual community grew by leaps and bounds, eventually numbering in the tens of thousands.

In many respects, this community was quite revolutionary. The Buddha accepted disciples from all levels of society and treated them with equal concern and respect. His acceptance of women as disciples and his belief that they were as capable of spiritual development as men was equally unusual, given the male-dominated society of the time.

Knowing that the more conservative elements of Indian society would have great difficulty accepting a monastic community that included women, tradition has it that the Buddha hesitated for quite a while before ordaining any of his women followers. But eventually he established an order of nuns, and the aunt who raised him became its first member.

In addition to a growing community of monks and nuns, many laypeople became followers of Shakyamuni Buddha. One of these individuals was King Bimbisara of Magadha, the monarch who'd offered to share his kingdom with Prince Siddhartha before the six-year fast began. When the king became a disciple and patron of the Buddha, a large number of his subjects followed suit, and the Buddhist community suddenly grew even larger (see Chapter 4 for more on the growth of the Buddhist community on the Indian subcontinent).

Eventually, the Buddha visited Kapilavastu, where he grew up and where many members of his family and clan still lived. Many of them became his followers, including his son, Rahula, who received ordination as a monk. His father, who'd wanted Prince Siddhartha to rule his kingdom, also became one of his son's disciples, though his pride in being known as the father of the Buddha hampered his spiritual progress somewhat. Devadatta (the Buddha's cousin and lifelong rival) also joined the community, but, jealous of the Buddha's popularity, he eventually set himself up as a rival teacher, causing a split within the monastic community. (For more about some of the other significant events in the Buddha's life and teaching career, see Chapter 9, where we describe the major places of Buddhist pilgrimage.)

Who is the true brahmin?

If you'd been born in ancient India, you would've become a member of the caste — the priests, warriors, merchants, or menial workers — to which your parents belonged. Upward mobility hardly existed in this society; your birth determined everything. At the top of the heap were the priests, or *brahmins.*

The Buddha himself was not a brahmin. As Prince Siddhartha, he had been born into the ruling warrior caste, one level below that of the priesthood. The Buddha gave the word *brahmin* a new interpretation. He taught that an individual's moral character, not caste, determines his worth. So the true brahmin — the person worthy of the greatest respect — isn't the one born into a particular family. As he said, "He who is tolerant to the intolerant, peaceful to the violent, who is free from greed, who speaks words that are calm, helpful, and true and that offend no one — him I call a brahmin." These democratic sentiments, which sound so right to modern ears, were threatening to the status quo of his time. Twenty-five centuries later, they inspired many Indians (including the so-called "untouchables") who felt oppressed by the caste system to quit their traditional faith and adopt Buddhism.

Listening to the Buddha's final message: All things must pass

Finally, at the age of 80, after a lifetime of selfless, compassionate service to others, Shakyamuni fell ill. He died at the village of Kushinagara. Yet even on the last day of his life, the Buddha continued to help others, clearing away the doubts a renowned ascetic named Subhadra had about the teachings and leading him onto the path to liberation.

Finally, with many of his disciples and the people of the nearby villages gathered around him, the Buddha spoke his final words, reminding them all of the essential truths he'd been teaching throughout his life:

> Decay is inherent in conditioned things,
>
> strive with vigilance.

Entering increasingly deeper meditative states, the Buddha died. Many of his followers were overcome by grief. But some — those who understood his teachings well — remained at peace. His disciples cremated his remains (see Chapter 9 for more details) and placed his ashes within burial monuments *(stupas)* throughout the lands that he'd blessed with his presence.

Understanding the Four Noble Truths

In his first discourse at the Deer Park in Sarnath (see the section "Providing spiritual guidance: Turning the wheel of Dharma," earlier in this chapter), Shakyamuni introduced the *four noble truths,* the basis of all the rest of his teachings. The more you understand these four truths, the better you can understand what Buddhism is all about. They are the truths of

- Suffering
- The cause of suffering
- The cessation of suffering
- The path that leads to the cessation of suffering

The truth of suffering

The first of the four noble truths acknowledges the widespread experience of what is called *duhkha* in Sanskrit. (In Pali, the other ancient Indian language in which the Buddhist teachings are recorded, the term is *dukkha.*) This term is most commonly translated as "suffering," but it has a much broader range of meaning. In particular, *duhkha* conveys a sense of dissatisfaction about things not being the way you want them to be.

Certain experiences in life are so obviously painful and miserable that no one has any difficulty identifying them as suffering. For example, a headache isn't fun. When you have that familiar throbbing in your skull, sometimes all you can think about is how much you want the pain to go away. You demand relief immediately. And a headache is relatively minor compared to many physical illnesses.

Even when physical discomfort is absent, countless mental and emotional difficulties arise. In his teaching at Sarnath, the Buddha specifically mentioned that the following are unpleasant:

- Birth
- Aging
- Sickness
- Death
- Meeting with what you dislike
- Being parted from what you like
- Not getting what you want

From this list, it's clear that the term *duhkha* covers practically everything pertaining to the human existence.

But if Shakyamuni Buddha was as compassionate as he's made out to be, why did he draw attention to something as distasteful as suffering and make it the *first* of the noble truths? Partly because humans have such a large capacity for self-deception. Like the person who refuses to admit to himself that he has a life-threatening disease until it's too late to do anything about it, many people will do almost anything to avoid taking a close look at themselves and the way they truly live their lives. They just stumble along from one unsatisfactory situation to the next. Whenever they get a whiff of the flawed nature of their existence, they shrug it off and reach for another drink — or another cigarette, or TV show, or some similar distraction.

The Buddha's intention was to help people wake up from their denial and follow the path that leads to the cessation of suffering.

Taking myth and doctrine with a grain of salt

Throughout this book, but especially in this chapter, we mix the practical teachings of the Buddha, designed to help you deal with your suffering and confusion, with the mythology and Buddhist doctrines that have accrued over several thousand years. Though the elaborate stories and myths may inspire you to put the teachings into practice, you don't have to believe them to practice Buddhism. In addition, the Buddha himself didn't teach doctrine or dogma that he required his disciples to believe. Instead, he constantly encouraged them to question any concept, to make sure that it agreed with their own experience and understanding. Then he recommended that they put the ideas into practice, to make sure that they actually worked.

In one famous story about a poisoned arrow (see Chapter 1 for details), the Buddha was asked a series of theoretical questions, such as whether the world is eternal. Instead of answering in his usual way, he remained silent. When pressed, he told the following story. Suppose someone shoots you with an arrow that you know to be laced with a fast-acting poison. Do you spend time trying to find out the name and caste of the archer, where he comes from, and of what materials his bow and arrow were constructed? Of course not. Instead, you act as quickly as possible to remove the arrow and find an antidote to the poison.

In the same way, argued the Buddha, pursuing the answers to certain theoretical questions that are irrelevant to your own salvation can be a waste of precious time when you've been shot with the poison arrow of greed, hatred, and ignorance — you have only so much time to put an end to your suffering!

The truth about the four truths

Many writers and teachers have their own favorite English translations for the key terms that crop up repeatedly in the traditional Buddhist texts. For example, when talking about what's known as *dana* in both Pali and Sanskrit — the two major Indian Buddhist languages — one person may call it "generosity," another "charity," a third "giving," and a fourth "openhandedness." Plenty of other examples of the translation question abound. For instance, although *patience, tolerance,* and *forbearance* mean quite different things in English, they've all been used to translate the Sanskrit term *kshanti,* one of the main antidotes to anger. Even the Sanskrit word *duhkha* (*dukkha* in Pali), which is central to Buddha's teachings and has generally been translated as "suffering," has been rendered as "misery," "dissatisfaction," "stress," and even "oppression."

But very little variation is found from one writer to the next when it comes to the four noble truths. Almost everyone refers to them simply as the *four noble truths.* Yet something is misleading about this phrase. These words seem to imply that suffering, its cause, and so on are themselves noble, but this isn't the intended meaning at all.

The terms can be translated and interpreted in several ways, including the following:

- The truths of the noble one (the Buddha)
- The truths for the nobles
- The truths that ennoble (a person)
- The noble truths

In the Buddhist scheme of things, an arya (a noble one) is someone who has peeled away the layers of misconception blanketing the mind and who can, therefore, for the first time look upon ultimate reality directly (see Chapter 14). With this clear understanding, certain truths that previously had been hidden from view finally appear directly and unmistakably. So the four noble truths are actually the *four* things that the *noble* one (the Buddha) sees as *true.* But in this book, we stick with the more compact term *four noble truths,* the conventional translation of these terms.

The truth of suffering's cause

REMEMBER

Having pointed out how pervasive suffering is, the Buddha addresses the unspoken question, "Where does all this misery come from? What is its origin, its cause?" To answer this question, he states the second noble truth: All suffering, without exception, comes from desirous attachment or craving (Sanskrit: *trishna;* Pali: *tanha*). In other words, as long as you allow insatiable desires for this and that to lead you around by the nose, you'll be dragged from one unsatisfactory life situation to the next, never knowing true peace and satisfaction.

In essence, the Buddha is saying that if you want to find the true source of your problems, you have to look inside yourself. Suffering isn't a punishment inflicted upon you by other people, life circumstances, or some supernatural force outside yourself. Nor does suffering come to you for no reason; suffering isn't a random occurrence in a meaningless universe governed by the laws of chance (even if it has become fashionable to think so). Instead, the suffering or dissatisfaction that you experience is directly related to attitudes that arise within your own heart and mind. (See Chapter 12, where we discuss the karmic laws of cause and effect in more detail.)

You can get an idea of the relationship between attachment and dissatisfaction by thinking of some common, everyday occurrences. For example, many people head for the nearest mall when they feel restless or dissatisfied. They look for something, anything, that can fill the hollow feeling inside of them. Perhaps they spot a shirt and think how great it'll look on them. They begin to fantasize, imagining how this piece of cloth will bolster their self-esteem, make them attractive to others, and perhaps even help them catch the man or woman of their dreams and change the course of their lives!

This example may seem exaggerated, but that's exactly what desirous attachment does. It exaggerates everything. You cling to your possessions, your appearance, and other people's opinions of you in the hopes of satisfying a deep inner longing. But the more you cling, the more disappointed you become. Why? Because everything is constantly changing, and nothing can possibly live up to the unrealistic expectations you place on it. You may walk out of that mall holding the new dress or sweater you just bought, but you're really grasping an illusion. And sooner or later — usually sooner — the illusion will let you down.

REMEMBER

So the problem isn't the piece of clothing, or even the fact that you find it attractive and derive pleasure from it. The problem is your attachment to it and the unrealistic expectations this attachment can cultivate. All the grief that you experience afterward — when the dress or shirt reveals its impermanent nature by fading, fraying, or going out of style — is the direct result of your clinging.

When the Buddha spoke about desire, or clinging, as the cause of suffering, he was thinking of a lot more than the effects of mall fever. Ultimately, he was talking about the way all unenlightened beings (that is, all people who've not yet fully awakened to reality — see Chapter 10 for more on the meaning of enlightenment) cling to an unrealistic image of who and what they are. Behind the thought, "I hope I look attractive in that shirt," is a much deeper level of grasping for one's overly concrete sense of *I* itself. By clinging to this false sense of self, you not only set yourself up for disappointment and suffering as you go through this life, but you also condemn yourself to wander endlessly from one unsatisfactory life to the next. (Head over to Chapter 13 for more on this cycle of dissatisfaction and the Buddha's solution for breaking free of it.)

The truth of suffering's cessation

The third of the noble truths is the Buddha's bold declaration that there's indeed an end to suffering. (What a welcome relief after the first two rather sobering truths of suffering and its cause!) We're not talking about just a brief vacation from the cycle of dissatisfaction; we're talking about a complete cessation. The Buddha was confident in this declaration because he'd experienced this liberation and saw clearly that nothing prevents everyone else from doing the same.

Because suffering comes from desirous attachment or craving, eliminating craving leads to an end of all suffering. Craving, according to the Buddha, is eradicated by removing its cause, which is defined as ignorance (Sanskrit: *avidya*). The complete cessation of suffering is nirvana (Sanskrit). Chapter 10 explains this complex term, meaning "extinguishing," in detail. Here it means the complete eradication of greed, hatred, and delusion.

We know that giving up attachment isn't simple. You've been holding on to an unrealistic sense of self far longer than you can remember, so breaking this habit isn't going to be easy. But it can be done, and the Buddha is proof. Two and a half millennia have passed since Shakyamuni walked this earth, but his enlightened example still inspires people. And if you meet people who've trained themselves well in the methods the Buddha taught, you may be fortunate enough to see that "letting go" leads to some pretty inspiring results. (Even better, you can follow these methods and experience the same results firsthand.)

Distinguishing between attachment and desire

Many people mistakenly believe that Buddhism is down on desire. If this were true, no Buddhists would be left! The problem, according to the Buddha, lies not with your preferences and wishes, but with your relationship to them. If you don't get what you want, do you get angry or depressed? Or have you developed the inner resilience and detachment necessary to accept life the way it presents itself? After all, you have only limited control over your circumstances, so the more attached you are to having things be a certain way, the more you will inevitably suffer. The secret to a happy life is to want what you have and not want what you don't have. A simple formula, perhaps — but one that can take a lifetime of spiritual practice to master!

The truth of the path

The fourth and final noble truth contains the do-it-yourself instruction manual that leads to the cessation of suffering and the experiences of spiritual liberation and enlightenment that go along with it. (See Chapter 10 for more about the various levels of spiritual attainment.) These instructions are presented in terms of the eightfold path, symbolized by the eight spokes of the wheel of Dharma (see Figure 3-4), which we outline later in this section.

Figure 3-4: The eight-spoke wheel of Dharma.

REMEMBER

The spiritual life, whether Buddhist or otherwise, is often referred to as a path because it leads you where, in your heart of hearts, you want to go. But don't make the mistake of thinking that this path is outside you. As with the cause of suffering, the path that leads to the highest spiritual goals is within you — in what you think, say, and do.

With this in mind, consider the eight divisions of the path leading to the cessation of suffering:

- **Right view:** The path begins when you see for yourself that suffering and dissatisfaction infect the entirety of ordinary, unenlightened existence and when you understand the four noble truths.
- **Right intention:** Right intention — or right thought — involves giving up selfish attitudes that lead to further suffering and replacing them with their opposites. In place of thoughts that cause harm to yourself and others, you cultivate the intention to bring happiness to all.
- **Right speech:** Because what you say can have a powerful effect on others and can affect your own spiritual evolution as well, cultivating right speech is important. This cultivation involves speaking words that are true and not hurtful, as well as refraining from idle chatter.

- **Right action:** Just as right speech means to avoid causing harm with what you say, right action means to avoid causing harm with what you do. So in place of physically hurting others through your actions, you seek to help and protect them. In particular, you refrain from killing, stealing, and engaging in sexual misconduct.
- **Right livelihood:** You can earn your living in many different ways, but if you're intent on gaining more than just material wealth, avoid occupations that involve harm and deception. Naturally, a profession in which you can be of service to others is an excellent way of supporting yourself. But even if you don't have that kind of job, you can make sure that your dealings with others are honest and kind.
- **Right effort:** This type of effort concerns your spiritual practices. Instead of being lazy, exert continuous yet relaxed (some would say *effortless*) effort to be aware of what's arising in your mind. If it's negative, don't let it overwhelm you; if it's positive, rejoice!
- **Right mindfulness:** Mindfulness — paying close attention to what's happening right now — is essential at all levels of spiritual practice. *Mindfulness* here means constant awareness with reference to the body, the feelings, the mind, and psychic factors that lead to bondage or release.
- **Right concentration:** To develop deep insight into the nature of reality, the focus of your mind must become sharp and free of distraction and dullness. Through practicing one-pointed concentration, you will eventually be able to attain the four meditative absorptions (Pali: *jhana*).

Those elements, in brief, are the major elements of the Buddhist path. Chapters 4, 5, and 11 through 14 explain how later masters elaborated upon them and shaped them into the various Buddhist traditions that have appeared over the past 2,500 years.

The Buddha image

We don't have any idea what the Buddha looked like. In early Buddhist art, the Buddha wasn't shown in human form. Symbols, such as a wheel, a set of footprints, or the Bodhi tree, indicated his presence. The earliest Buddha images originated only several centuries after the Buddha's death, around the first century CE. They were manufactured in two places: in the region of Gandhara (in the northwestern part of the Indian subcontinent) and in Mathura (in the northern part of the subcontinent). The images from Gandhara are stylistically influenced by Greek art. Later artists depicted the Buddha with specific physical signs. These include the 32 marks of a "great man," such as elongated ear lobes, a small circle of hair between the eyebrows (Sanskrit: *urna*), and a protuberance (Sanskrit: *ushnisha*) on the top of his head. The

(continued)

(continued)

Buddha's hands frequently display meaningful gestures, such as the gesture of turning the wheel of the teaching; the meditation gesture, with both hands cupped and placed palms upward in the lap; the gesture of invoking the earth as a witness, with one hand touching the ground; or the gesture of protection, with the palm of one hand turned toward the devotee. Buddha images vary in style among Asian countries. Buddhists worship them widely, often with elaborate rituals.

Tradition has it that the Buddha recollected his past lives when he became enlightened. These lives, in which the Buddha strove as a *bodhisattva* (a being who has vowed to attain enlightenment), mostly in animal or human form, to acquire the moral perfections *(paramita)*, are the subject matter of the Jataka tales, a specific genre of Buddhist literature. These stories are extremely popular and are frequently represented in sculpture and painting.

Envisioning the Future

Shakyamuni Buddha never said he was unique.

When one of his disciples praised him extravagantly, claiming that no one anywhere was like him, the Buddha admonished him, pointing out that the disciple had no way of knowing whether the statement was true. "Instead of praising me," the Buddha suggested, "it would be far more beneficial for you simply to put my teachings into practice."

Some Buddhist traditions believe that Buddhas repeatedly appear in different times and in different places throughout the universe to help awaken those who are ready to benefit from spiritual instruction. In Theravada Buddhism, Shakyamuni is considered the 25th in the succession of Buddhas. Dipankara was the first Buddha. It is said that Shakyamuni, as the brahmin youth Sumedha in his former life, worshipped Dipankara and resolved to become a Buddha. (The past lives of Shakyamuni are described in the Jataka tales, a genre of Buddhist literature.)

Maitreya (also known as Maitri) is believed to be Shakyamuni's successor, the future Buddha in this world. We deal with this 26th Buddha in the next section.

The advent of Maitreya

REMEMBER

The name Maitreya comes from the Sanskrit word *maitri,* which means "loving-kindness." Maitreya received his name because loving-kindness — goodwill — was his main spiritual practice. (In Pali, the term for this virtue is *metta.*)

The future Buddha Maitreya (see Figure 3-5) is a source of inspiration and hope for many of Shakyamuni's followers. Realizing that they may not be able to complete the spiritual path in their present lifetime, they pray to be reborn in the first circle of Maitreya's disciples when he reappears as a Buddha, to complete their training under his guidance.

Different beliefs abound concerning when Maitreya is due to reappear on earth. Some people think that he won't be here for several thousand years, but others say the wait is just a matter of a few hundred years.

All this speculation aside, some traditional Buddhist sources say that Maitreya currently resides in Tushita Heaven. He'll remain in this cosmic way station (as Shakyamuni did before him) until the proper moment arrives for him to descend to the human realm to be born.

Figure 3-5: Maitreya, the future Buddha.

Photographed by John C. Huntington. Photo courtesy of the Huntington Archive at The Ohio State University.

Degeneration, followed by hope

According to considerably later accounts, the era of Shakyamuni's teachings is half over; in another 2,500 years, the Dharma he introduced will disappear from this planet completely. As the times grow more degenerate — in other words, as hatred, greed, and ignorance increase in strength — the world will be transformed into a battlefield. Epidemic diseases and natural calamities will become more severe and frequent, and people will begin dying of old age while they're still relatively young.

When things become as bad as they're bound to get, and people have grown stunted and deformed by their overwhelming negativities, Maitreya will show himself. Although fully enlightened, he won't appear as a Buddha at first. He'll simply show up as someone taller and more attractive than everyone else. Impressed by his beauty, people will ask him how he got to be so good-looking. He will reply, "Through the practice of morality, avoiding giving harm to any living being."

As more people are inspired to take up the practice of morality and loving-kindness, the age of degeneration will come to an end. Peacefulness will replace belligerence, and as a result, people's life span, health, and general good fortune will increase. Finally, when all the proper conditions are in place and potential disciples are sufficiently ripe for guidance, Maitreya will reappear as a glorious wheel-turning Buddha and usher in the next golden age of Dharma.

Chapter 4

The Development of Buddhism on the Indian Subcontinent

In This Chapter

- Preserving the Buddha's teachings
- Breaking down the basic Buddhist canon
- Recognizing the role of Emperor Ashoka in spreading the new religion
- Starting the engine of the Great Vehicle — new scriptures and themes
- Checking out the decline and reappearance of Buddhism in India
- Looking at Buddhism in Nepal

Buddhism began about 2,500 years ago with one person's experience of spiritual awakening. During his lifetime, Shakyamuni Buddha had contact with thousands of people. By the time of his death, the influence of his teachings extended throughout a handful of kingdoms in the northern part of the Indian subcontinent. But in the centuries that followed, Buddhist teachings spread through large parts of Asia. Today millions of people around the world practice Buddhism in some form. Interestingly enough, however, Buddhism was reintroduced into India only in the past century, about 700 years after it disappeared from the country where it was born.

The Buddha himself didn't practice "Buddhism" — he merely taught what he called the *Dharma,* the law of the cause of suffering and the path to its cessation. Because his teachings were orally transmitted for a long time and written down much later, many uncertainties surround what the historical Buddha actually taught. His disciples and their successors interpreted, clarified, and developed the Buddha's teachings, creating a variety of Buddhist schools and traditions that took the Dharma in directions the Buddha himself may not have anticipated.

In this chapter, we chronicle the growth and development of Buddhism. We concentrate on the changes the Buddha's teachings underwent as they spread throughout the Indian subcontinent (including Sri Lanka). In Chapter 5, we follow Buddhism as it transformed and adapted to the cultures of Southeast Asia, Tibet, China, Korea, Japan, and finally the West.

You may wonder what relevance the ancient history of Buddhism has today. But as you read this abbreviated account of its development, we think you'll discover issues and themes that have timeless significance — ideas that keep reappearing in Buddhist practice and thought wherever and whenever the religion takes root. Besides, it's a fascinating story.

Convening the First Buddhist Council

Before the Buddha died — or, as Buddhist scriptures put it, before he entered *parinirvana* (final liberation) — he told his disciples not to worry about being leaderless after he was gone. He said that the teachings themselves would be their guide. According to tradition, after the Buddha's death, the Venerable Mahakashyapa presided over the community of monks and gathered 500 of the Buddha's most spiritually advanced disciples to recite the precious teachings.

Gathering the council

This important communal recitation, known in Buddhist history as the First Council, was held at Rajgir, the capital of the kingdom of Magadha (see Chapter 9 for present-day Rajgir pilgrimage info). At the council, Mahakashyapa selected some of the Buddha's foremost disciples to recite from memory the teachings they'd heard. Because Ananda, the Buddha's cousin, who had been his personal attendant and constant companion for more than 30 years, had heard more of the Master's discourses than anyone else, he went first.

Ananda began each recitation with the words "Thus I have heard," to indicate that he himself had been present at the teaching he was about to relate — no second-hand information here. Then he mentioned the place where the Buddha had given that particular discourse — for example, at the Buddha's rainy-season residence near Shravasti (see Chapter 9) — and who had been in the audience on that particular occasion. After setting the scene in this way, Ananda recited from memory what he remembered. Monks who had also been present at that particular teaching were asked to confirm that Ananda's recitation was accurate. When they agreed, the recitation was accepted, and Mahakashyapa directed the assembly to commit it to memory.

Categorizing the teachings: The three baskets

The First Council formally divided the Buddha's discourses into two groups, the general discourses and the discipline (the prescriptions for monks). Later the teachings were divided into three "baskets" *(pitaka)* that make up the principal categories of the Buddhist canon, or collection of teachings. Here are the *three baskets* (*tipitaka* in Pali; *tripitaka* in Sanskrit):

- **The Basket of Discourses** (*Sutta Pitaka* in Pali; *Sutra Pitaka* in Sanskrit): Recited by Ananda, this extensive collection contains the advice the Buddha gave about the practice of meditation and related topics. The principal discourses in this basket demonstrate how you can train your mind to gain the insights that lead eventually to *nirvana* — the complete release from suffering.

  For example, within the *Sutta Pitaka,* you can find the teaching known as the *Greater Discourse on the Foundations of Mindfulness* (Pali: *Maha-satipatthana Sutta*), which contains essential instructions for gaining a clear, unmistaken realization of the four noble truths (check out Chapter 3 for more insight into these truths). Meditation practices of many Buddhist traditions were developed on the basis of this discourse.

- **The Basket of Discipline** (called the *Vinaya Pitaka* in both Pali and Sanskrit): Recited by a monk named Upali (who'd been a barber in Kapilavastu before joining the Buddha), this collection contains the more than 225 rules of conduct that guide the life of the community of monks and nuns.

  The Buddha generally formulated such rules spontaneously, in response to new situations. In other words, whenever he noticed his followers behaving in a way that was contrary to the spirit of his teachings or that could bring discredit to the community of monks and nuns (known in Sanskrit and Pali as the *Sangha*), he established the appropriate rule to govern that behavior. For example, the monk Sudinna once confessed to having sexual relations with his former wife (in order, it is said, to provide an heir who could inherit his family's property). The Buddha first rebuked him, pointing out that such behavior was unbecoming of a member of the Sangha and leads to further attachment to the world of sensual desires rather than liberation from it. Then the Buddha established the rule that forbids individuals following the monastic way of life from engaging in any sexual behavior whatsoever. (See Chapter 12 for more on the basic rules of conduct for both monastics and laypeople.)

- **The Basket of Higher Teachings** (*Abhidhamma Pitaka* in Pali; *Abhidharma Pitaka* in Sanskrit): Although the texts in this basket are of a considerably later date, one tradition has it that after Ananda and Upali finished recounting what they remembered at the First Council (by the way, some accounts state that Upali recited first), Mahakashyapa addressed the assembly. The subject of his recitation was an analysis of reality from the point of view of some early Buddhist authorities.

The Buddha often pointed out that the kind of philosophical speculation that was widespread in India at the time ("Does the world have a beginning or an end?" for example) didn't lead anywhere. But he did want his followers to know how suffering arises and how it can be eliminated. Therefore, the Buddha taught a version of the 12 links outlining the way ignorance perpetuates suffering. (We present the 12 links, according to a Tibetan tradition, in Chapter 13.) These early instructions led to the extensive teachings on philosophy and related matters that make up Buddhist "higher knowledge" studies.

Spreading the Teachings — Peacefully

When Mahakashyapa died not long after the First Council, Ananda became head of the Buddhist order. During the 40 years of his leadership, Buddhism spread throughout India as monks dispersed in all directions, following the Buddha's advice to teach "for the welfare of the many, out of compassion for the world."

Ananda himself taught thousands of disciples, setting them firmly on the path to liberation. He and the other Sangha leaders who followed — sometimes referred to as the early Buddhist patriarchs — did a lot to help Buddhism spread. The early leaders founded many monastic communities, which produced new members for the Sangha and brought a large number of lay disciples into the Buddhist fold.

REMEMBER

To the credit of the disciples involved in the rapid growth during the early years, the spread of Buddhism occurred peacefully. People became Buddhists for various reasons, but not because they were forced to.

The following scenario is typical of the way interest in Buddhism grew. A pair of simply clad monks entered a village in the early morning, having spent the previous night outdoors in the nearby forest. Carrying begging bowls, they walked from house to house seeking food, silently receiving whatever food people offered them, and then returned to the outskirts of town. Villagers who were sufficiently impressed by the calm, self-controlled demeanor of these monks often approached them after the monks had finished their one meal of the day and requested instruction. Some villagers even asked how they could join the Buddhist order.

Following the example of the Buddha, the monks responded to these requests in ways that seemed suitable — freely sharing whatever teachings they'd memorized and understood before moving on in their homeless wandering to the next village. The fact that these monks spoke respectfully with all members of society, whether they were of a high caste or low, increased their standing with the general population, and the number of Buddhists grew correspondingly.

A Fork in the Road: Managing a Developing Split in the Buddhist Community

Though peaceful, the Buddhist communities weren't free from differences — or even the occasional controversy. As Buddhist communities in India became larger and more widespread, different styles of practice emerged. For example, some monks favored a strict interpretation of the rules of discipline, while others took a somewhat more liberal approach.

Convening the Second Council

According to recent scholarship, to deal with the various concerns that were dividing the community, a second Buddhist council was held in Vaishali about 60 years after the first. The different accounts of this meeting — both accounts written by Western historians and accounts given by the various Buddhist traditions themselves — disagree about exactly what took place there.

But everyone does agree that the Second Council led to the first major *schism,* or split, within the Buddhist community. Depending on which account you follow, several thousand monks either were expelled from the council or left voluntarily because they felt that the others were interpreting the spirit of the Buddha's teachings too narrowly.

Two major Buddhist groups emerged from the Second Council. They called themselves by these names:

- **The Elders** (Sanskrit: *Sthavira;* Pali: *Thera*): Considered themselves the keepers of the Buddha's original teachings
- **The Great Community** (Sanskrit: *Mahasanghika*): Held a more liberal interpretation of the Buddha's word that they believed matched his original intentions

Over time, two major traditions of Buddhism developed. They are still followed today:

- **Theravada:** Meaning "Doctrine of the Elders," this tradition is practiced primarily in Sri Lanka and in Southeast Asian countries such as Myanmar and Thailand.
- **Mahayana:** Translated as "Great Path" or "Great Vehicle," this tradition is primarily practiced in Nepal, Tibet, Mongolia, Taiwan, Korea, and Japan.

Advancing the teachings in different ways

The way the various traditions divided and evolved, especially in the early centuries of Buddhism's development, is a complicated subject, to say the least. Because the subject is complex and views of it are shaded by the tradition each individual follows, we present only the most basic outline of the process. If you want to research this matter in more detail, we suggest that you check out different books on the subject and then attempt to unravel this complex story for yourself.

Within a couple centuries of the Buddha's death, many separate Buddhist schools were active throughout India. Each had its own version of the monastic rules. As chaotic as the situation may seem, the existence of these different schools wasn't necessarily a bad thing (especially because the different schools apparently never actually fought with one another, other than in philosophical debate).

You likely aren't too surprised to hear about divisions and subdivisions in the Buddhist community in those early years. After all, the Buddha himself didn't teach all his followers in exactly the same way. Taking into account differences in their interests and intellectual capacities, he taught in the manner that most benefited each audience. As a result, his teachings — especially those regarding the nature of the *self* (see Chapter 13) — can be interpreted in a variety of ways. It's only natural that later generations of Buddhists grouped themselves into schools identifying with the philosophical position that best suited their own understanding.

Besides purely philosophical differences, other differences emerged among Buddhists, some concerning standards of acceptable behavior and others based on language. The Buddha encouraged his followers to make the teachings they themselves had heard and understood widely available to others, and he exhorted them to do so in their native language. In this way, everyone (not just the literate and highly educated) could benefit from the teachings. India was a land of many different languages, as it is today, and these linguistic differences also helped give each school its own character or flavor.

Making Buddhism a Religion of the People: The Emperor Ashoka's Influence

In the third century BCE, a figure appeared on the Indian scene who had a dramatic effect on the entire course of Buddhist history. This figure was Emperor Ashoka, the third ruler of the powerful Mauryan dynasty established by his grandfather.

Ashoka was the individual most responsible for setting Buddhism on the road to becoming a world religion.

Transforming his approach

In the beginning of his reign (approximately 268 BCE), Ashoka followed the same warlike, expansionist policies as his father and grandfather before him. His conquests were so extensive that he eventually ruled an empire stretching over a vast portion of the Indian subcontinent.

But his bloody campaign to put down a rebellion in what is now the eastern state of Orissa involved such an enormous loss of life that Ashoka was horrified by his own actions. Deeply regretting all the suffering he'd caused, he underwent a profound spiritual transformation. Having become acquainted with the Buddhist teachings through a monk he'd met, Ashoka made the momentous decision to rule his empire according to the Buddhist principles of nonviolence and compassion.

Ashoka set out to put these lofty principles into practice on an unprecedented scale:

- He gave up military conquest and instead devoted himself to the welfare of his people.
- He established schools and hospitals, and even had wells dug along the main roads for the relief of travelers.
- In the spirit of respect and toleration, he gave royal support to many different religious institutions — not just the Buddhist ones.
- Because of his special interest in promoting the Buddhist moral code, he ordered edicts to be carved on pillars and rocks throughout his empire, exhorting his people to behave toward others with generosity, humility, and honesty.

Ashoka also promoted the practice of *pilgrimage,* visiting the various sites the Buddha had blessed with his presence (travel over to Chapter 9 for more on pilgrimages) and ordered the construction of thousands of burial monuments (known in Sanskrit as *stupas*) to the Compassionate One. With his devotion as their example, many of Ashoka's subjects developed interest in Buddhism as well, and the number of individuals professing the Buddhist faith rose dramatically, especially among ordinary laypeople.

Before Ashoka, Buddhism appealed largely to people who were well educated or highly placed in society. Afterward, it became much more a religion of the people.

Promoting Buddhism beyond India

Emperor Ashoka also sent emissaries in all directions from India to spread the word of the Buddha. Some of them supposedly reached lands as far west as Egypt, Syria, and Macedonia, although no evidence indicates that they had much of an impact in these areas.

The mission to Sri Lanka, however, turned out to be a huge success. Buddhism reached the island in the third century BCE. According to the Buddhist tradition of Sri Lanka, two of the emissaries to this island nation were the Buddhist monk Mahinda and the nun Sanghamitta, said to be Ashoka's children. They were well received by the local ruler, King Tissa, and were invited to the royal city of Anuradhapura, where a great monastery was later established. Ashoka's daughter brought with her a cutting from the original Bodhi tree under which the Buddha was believed to have achieved enlightenment, and the descendant of the tree that grew from this cutting remains a popular pilgrimage site in Sri Lanka to this day. (Check out Chapter 3 for the story of the Bodhi tree.)

How original is "original" Buddhism?

Some members of the Theravada tradition like to refer to this tradition as "original" Buddhism, implying that it's free from the later additions (and, by implication, possible distortions) that affect other (specifically, Mahayana) traditions. No one can deny that the discourses in the Pali canon of the Theravadins are the most complete written version of that section of the Buddhist canon we possess. And even Buddhists from the Mahayana traditions accept these discourses preserved in Pali as a reflection — remember that the Buddha didn't actually speak in Pali — of what the Buddha taught.

Does this mean that the discourses contained in the Pali canon reflect the original teachings of the Buddha? Keep in mind that the Buddha taught for 45 years to a wide variety of disciples and that these teachings were preserved for several hundred years in oral form only. Given these complex factors, scholars doubt whether anyone can know for certain what the Buddha taught. Similar disagreement and controversy still rage around the teachings of the historical Jesus.

But wait, there's more. The Theravada is only one of many schools that passed on their versions of the Buddha's teachings. Add up all these factors, and you can see why it's unlikely that any one Buddhist tradition, no matter how ancient, could have succeeded in recording and preserving all of Shakyamuni's original teachings. By comparison, consider the Christian tradition again: Although every Christian denomination agrees on the contents of the New Testament, each has its own favorite English translations of certain passages and its own interpretation of what the text actually means. But unless you're a true believer, you're unlikely to view a single interpretation as the one and only true gospel as Jesus himself preached it.

For 400 years or so in India, different collections of the Buddha's teachings were passed down orally, in various languages and dialects, from one generation to the next. But in the first century BCE, a version of these teachings was finally put into writing in Sri Lanka.

The particular form of the Tripitaka (the "three baskets" we mention in the section "Categorizing the teachings: The three baskets," earlier in the chapter) transcribed at that time was the one preserved in the Theravada tradition, which is believed to have arrived in Sri Lanka with Ashoka's children and primarily spread to Southeast Asia. Its language is Pali, one of India's more ancient languages.

Even now, more than 2,000 years later, many people turn to the Pali canon of the Theravada Buddhist tradition (a complete English translation was published last century by the Pali Text Society) when they want a taste of early Buddhism. (Peruse the sidebar "How original is 'original' Buddhism?" for more details.)

Two Levels of Practice in Early Buddhism

When you visit a country that subscribes to the Theravada Buddhist tradition, like Thailand, where people still practice many of the customs from the early days of Buddhism, you can get a feeling for how Buddhism must've impacted Indian society in its early years.

Members of the Buddhist order (the Sangha) relied on villagers and townspeople for their basic necessities of life, and the townspeople relied on members of the Sangha for spiritual instruction and the performance of religious rites. You can still see this interaction today, even in Thailand's overgrown capital of Bangkok. Early every morning, monks carrying begging bowls emerge from their neighborhood temples into the city's streets, where members of the local populace wait to make food offerings to them. After the monks complete their rounds, they return to their temples. Later some of the same families who gave food may gather at one of the local temples to request that the monks offer prayers or teachings on their behalf.

An important element in this interaction between monks and townspeople is known as the *collection of merit.* It's a common belief in South Asian religions that virtuous actions — such as the practice of generosity — create a store of positive energy, or merit (*punya* in Sanskrit). This meritorious energy brings about positive results in the future, in accordance with the karmic law of cause and effect (see Chapter 12 for more on karma). The person to whom you present offerings — the object, or recipient, of your virtuous actions — is known as your *field of merit,* and the more worthy your field, the more merit you create.

Because fully ordained monks (and nuns, in the few places where their lineage still exists) are among the most worthy of all fields of merit, making offerings to them is a powerful way of quickly collecting vast stores of merit. Therefore, when a woman standing in front of her house places food in the begging bowl of a monk from a nearby temple, she feels that she herself is the one who truly benefits from this act of generosity, because she receives the merit. And the merit she collects, she hopes, will bring her happiness in the future, specifically a rebirth in one of the more fortunate realms of existence (see Chapter 13, where we explain the various realms in which beings live).

This example of the interaction between monks and the townspeople neatly illustrates two levels of Buddhist practice that existed side by side in the early days of Buddhism in India — and that still exist in many places throughout the Buddhist world.

- On one level of Buddhist practice was the renounced style of the monastic community. Monks and nuns gave up family, possessions, and worldly ambition in their quest for complete liberation from suffering. They shaved their heads and donned robes, thereby eliminating (or at least minimizing) anything in their lives that would distract them from their ultimate goal, and devoted themselves primarily to the strict observance of moral precepts (check out Chapter 12 for more on these precepts) and the practice of meditation. (Chapter 7 deals with meditation in detail.)
- Many of the devoted laypeople followed the other level of Buddhist practice (traditionally regarded as inferior, from a spiritual perspective). Individuals (called householders) who chose to live an ordinary life and raise a family were generally believed to be passing up the chance to win liberation in this lifetime.

  A layperson was generally assumed to be limited to amassing enough merit — largely by supporting people who were committed to the monastic way of life — that he could achieve happiness later in this life and a favorable rebirth in the future. Then if the future rebirth was particularly fortunate, an individual might be able to devote himself to the pure practices of a fully ordained Sangha member at that time. But in the Buddha's discourses, we also read about householders who attained awakening.

Witnessing Shifting Allegiances and New Ideals

The division of the Buddhist faithful into two groups — one seeking freedom from the wheel of suffering (the pattern of recurring misery and dissatisfaction known as cyclic existence, or *samsara*) and the other hoping only for temporary comfort within it and perhaps the chance for a better rebirth in the future — was perhaps never that sharp in practice.

The system required that the townspeople continue to highly respect the ordained Sangha. Arhats, such as Ananda and some of the patriarchs who followed (see the section "Convening the First Buddhist Council," earlier in this chapter), were undoubtedly worthy of the highest esteem. But not everyone who wears the robes of a monk or a priest is a model of virtue, as is painfully evident in many religious traditions today, Buddhist and non-Buddhist alike.

Turning to the stupas

Historical evidence indicates that the growing number of *stupas* (burial monuments) located throughout India (see the section "Making Buddhism a Religion of the People: The Emperor Ashoka's Influence," earlier in the chapter) became important objects of worship for Buddhists.

The faithful regarded these monuments, originally built to house the relics of the Buddha, as indistinguishable from Shakyamuni Buddha himself. An increasing number of Buddhists, lay and monastic alike, congregated at these monuments and walked around them in the same way Shakyamuni's own disciples centuries before had walked respectfully around the Buddha before addressing him. (For more information on the location of some of these stupas, see Chapter 9.)

The stupa has been an important cult object in the Buddhist world from early times. Originally a simple burial mound, the stupa evolved over time and included elements such as gateways, a platform, a parasol-like structure on the top, and a circumambulatory passage around it. The most well-known example in India is the Great Stupa located in Sanchi (see Figure 4-1), in the modern state of Madhya Pradesh. It was built around 300 BCE but has been frequently reconstructed.

Taking a ride in the Great Vehicle: Mahayana Buddhism

Around the same time as the cult of stupas was growing, the traditions of Buddhist thought and practice subsumed under the name Mahayana began emerging in India. The word *Mahayana* means the "Great Vehicle" or "Great Path."

At the center of Mahayana doctrine is the figure of the *bodhisattva.* The Mahayanists didn't invent this term, but they did broaden its meaning. In the Theravada tradition, it is assumed that Shakyamuni Buddha had to strive for many lives as a bodhisattva, an enlightenment-bound being, before attaining awakening.

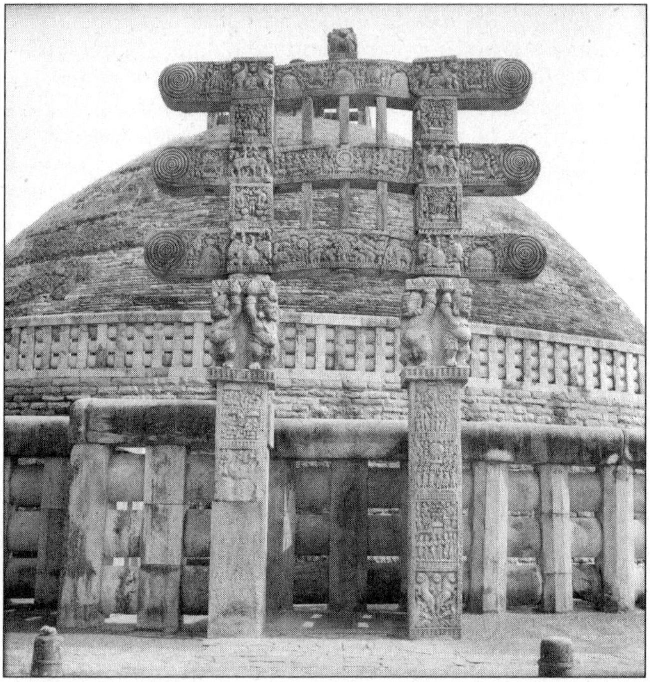

Figure 4-1: The well-known Great Stupa of Sanchi in India.

Photographed by John C. Huntington, courtesy of the Huntington Archive at The Ohio State University.

According to the Mahayana, anyone compassionate and dedicated enough to place the welfare of others before his own attainment of nirvana can achieve the same enlightenment as Shakyamuni. In other words, instead of working toward becoming an arhat and achieving liberation just for oneself, the compassionate bodhisattva's aim for Buddhahood is to bring infinite benefit to all others. This approach points to another reason for the term *Mahayana,* or "Great Vehicle": These teachings not only benefit many beings, but also lead the practitioners (the bodhisattvas) to the greatest possible achievement: supreme enlightenment.

WARNING!

For individuals who lacked this supremely altruistic intention and were intent only on their own personal liberation, the Mahayanists coined the rather negative term *Hinayana,* or "Lesser Vehicle." We've avoided using this term until now. It's used polemically, and many writers have inaccurately applied this label to entire Buddhist traditions, such as the Theravada. This categorization is grossly unfair and inappropriate.

Recognizing the Major Mahayana Themes

Certain themes characterize the Mahayana worldview and reappear in the Buddhist traditions that developed in Central Asia and the Far East:

- The compassionate bodhisattva, working for the benefit of all beings, is the ideal embodiment of spiritual fulfillment, replacing the arhat, who strives for his own liberation.
- All beings, lay as well as ordained, have the ability to achieve the highest spiritual realization, even in the midst of "ordinary" life.
- Buddhahood is an enduring principle that exists throughout the universe. Before adopting a Mahayana worldview, the faithful focused their respect on one historical person, Shakyamuni Buddha. Now they could direct their devotion toward infinite Buddhas and transcendent bodhisattvas throughout space and time.
- The nature of all existence is essentially nondualistic. That is, ultimate reality is beyond all divisions into "this" and "that" — beyond the reach of thoughts, words, and conceptions — but still capable of being directly realized through insight.

Chronicling the Rise of the Mahayana Teachings

Even though books on Buddhism often speak about the Mahayana tradition in the singular, as if only one existed, a number of different Mahayana traditions rose to prominence starting around the first century CE — and almost certainly existed in some form even before then.

To be more precise, different Mahayana sutras (or discourses) began to circulate about that time, and each one expanded the Buddhist worldview in some way. These sutras (which are mostly written in Sanskrit) claimed to be teachings of Shakyamuni Buddha that some of his disciples had preserved in secret and were now unveiling to address the needs of the historical moment. In many cases, their proponents asserted that these sutras presented the teachings in a deeper, more potent form than what had appeared before. We explain the most important of these teachings in the next few sections.

Many of these sutras never self-identify as being Mahayana and were labeled or classified as such only later. Many were originally exegetical writings that became sutras because of their followers' veneration of them or as the result of some systematizers' deliberate attempt to pass them off as the Buddha's own words.

White Lotus of the Good Dharma Sutra

Popularly known as the *Lotus Sutra,* this extensive Mahayana scripture became very influential in East Asia. (To find out more about the way the Lotus Sutra and the other Buddhist teachings and traditions mentioned in this chapter spread throughout Asia and to the West, check out Chapter 5.)

This poetic work (called *Saddharma-pundarika* in Sanskrit) presents a cosmic view of time and space and the spiritual path. As in a number of other scriptures, the events in this sutra start out at Vulture Peak near Rajgir (see Chapter 9), but they soon get a lot broader in scope. How much broader? We're talking all of existence here. Shakyamuni reveals a spectacular vision of the universe populated by countless Buddhas instructing their huge circles of disciples. He then explains that, although Buddhas like himself may teach paths that lead to lesser goals (such as individual liberation), all beings ultimately have only one final spiritual destination: the supreme enlightenment of Buddhahood.

Exposition of Vimalakirti Sutra

This work is one of the oldest and most beloved of all Mahayana scriptures. The events take place at Vaishali (site of the Second Council; see the section "Convening the Second Council," earlier in this chapter). This scripture is so popular among laypeople mainly because its central character, the layperson Vimalakirti, is described as having a more profound understanding of the teachings than even Shakyamuni's close disciple Shariputra, a monk renowned for his wisdom. This sutra (Sanskrit: *Vimalakirti-nirdesha*) also contains a famous gender-bending scene in which a goddess appears and temporarily transforms Shariputra into a woman, much to his wonder and embarrassment. This event demonstrates that all conceptual ideas, including the concepts of male and female, lack ultimate reality.

Perfection of Wisdom Sutras

This collection of discourses presents the path to supreme awakening as the union of compassionate method and insightful wisdom (see Chapters 2 and 14, which explain the connection between compassion and wisdom). Focusing on the career of the altruistically minded seeker of enlightenment, these teachings provide a philosophical foundation for many of the emerging Mahayana traditions.

In addition to outlining the bodhisattva's compassionate way of life, these sutras expand the scope and depth of Buddhist teachings on wisdom. In most earlier Buddhist texts, the insight of selflessness (see Chapters 2 and 13 for more on what it means to be without a self) is generally applied only to your ego-identity, or personality. If you want to achieve liberation, you have to penetrate this ignorant notion of self-identity to discover that there is no *I*. The *Perfection of Wisdom Sutras (Prajna-paramita)* expand — or, perhaps more accurately, transform — this insight into the truth of universal emptiness *(shunyata),* teaching that you can't find even one atom of concrete, self-existent reality anywhere in the world. (For more on emptiness, see Chapter 14.)

This view — so contrary to the ordinary notion that things exist as separately and individually as they appear — was expounded in great detail by Nagarjuna, the founder of the Madhyamika (Middle Doctrine) school of Mahayana Buddhism.

Descent into Lanka Sutra

Besides Nagarjuna's Madhyamika school, the other major philosophical school of Mahayana Buddhism is Asanga's Yogachara, which emphasizes the role of the mind in shaping and creating experience. Madhyamika points to the inherent emptiness of phenomena by demonstrating that every concept and assertion you may have about reality is untrue, but Yogachara teaches that this inherent emptiness is actually the nature of consciousness itself, which underlies all phenomena as a deeper, abiding truth. In other words, instead of saying, "There is only emptiness," Yogachara says, "There is only consciousness" — or Mind with a capital *m.* (Despite the apparent disagreement, many Buddhist masters have taught that *consciousness* and *emptiness* are merely indicators of the same indivisible, nondual (that is, inseparable) reality. For a more detailed comparison of Yogachara and Madhyamika, see Chapter 10.)

The *Lankavatara Sutra* is one of the main scriptural sources for the Yogachara school. It urges its practitioners to gain, through meditation, a direct and intuitive experience of consciousness itself, which is the deeper reality beyond the illusions generated by the conceptual mind.

World-Array Sutra

This beautiful scripture, which is really the last part of a vast collection of teachings known as the *Flower Ornament Sutra,* recounts the pilgrimage made by a young man named Sudhana — at the urging of Manjushri (see Figure 4-2), the bodhisattva of wisdom — to find the perfect teacher who can reveal to him the knowledge of enlightenment. This spiritual journey takes Sudhana to more than 50 teachers (each one instructs him in some aspect of the bodhisattva's path) until he finally meets Maitreya, the future Buddha, who has the knowledge he seeks. Maitreya shows Sudhana that all his teachers have revealed the same truth to him, but in different guises. Under Maitreya's guidance, Sudhana realizes that no difference exists between his own mind and the minds of the infinite Buddhas throughout the universe.

Sudhana's journey represents a meditator's experiences along the path to full awakening. Its vivid imagery draws the reader into an enchanted universe that stretches imagination to its limits. This sutra *(Gandavyuha)* has inspired numerous works of Buddhist art over the centuries — most notably, the reliefs that decorate the gigantic monument at Borobudur in Indonesia. (Chapter 9 has info about many pilgrimage sites, including Borobudur.) The predominant theme of this sutra, and of the various Mahayana traditions that derived from it, is the interpenetration of all universal phenomena. Everything that exists mirrors everything else, and the entire universe is like a vast hall of mirrors or net of jewels, endlessly reflecting one another.

Figure 4-2: Manjushri, the bodhisattva of wisdom.

Photographed by John C. Huntington, courtesy of the Huntington Archive at The Ohio State University.

Land of Bliss Sutras

This collection of three sutras teaches the faithful how to live and die so that they can be reborn in the *Buddha field* (or pure land) of Amitabha, who (as his name expresses) is the Buddha of Infinite Light. Described as a celestial paradise, this land is a realm or domain completely outside the wheel of samsaric suffering. The compassionate Amitabha Buddha created this land while he was still a bodhisattva, and all the conditions in this pure land are right for achieving supreme enlightenment. Even the sound of the wind passing through the trees imparts teachings.

Unlike other Buddhist approaches to enlightenment, in which you rely on your own effort to propel you toward your goal, birth in this pure land (called *Sukhavati,* the "Blissful," which is also the Sanskrit name of these sutras) largely depends on your devotion to its presiding Buddha, Amitabha. He brought this realm into existence, and you can reach it simply by maintaining faith in his saving grace. (See Chapter 5 for more on the worship of Amitabha — called Amida in Japanese — in Far Eastern Pure Land Buddhism.) The worship of Amitabha represents a general move in Mahayana Buddhism away from devotion to Shakyamuni alone and toward the worship of a vast array of Buddhas and bodhisattvas.

These brief descriptions give you a small taste of the extraordinary outburst of creative energy that produced the flowering of Mahayana over a relatively short period of time (approximately 100 BCE to 200 CE).

TIP

One important later text of Indian Mahayana Buddhism (it is not a sutra!) is the *Guide to the Bodhisattva's Way of Life,* the *Bodhicharyavatara* or *Bodhisattvacharyavatara.*The monk Shantideva, who lived in the first half of the eighth century, wrote this work, poetic as well as philosophic in nature. It details the conduct of a bodhisattva, beginning at the moment he generates the thought of enlightenment (bodhichitta) until he attains insight. (We explain bodhichitta in Chapter 14.) The Sanskrit text has been transmitted in different versions and was translated into Tibetan, Chinese, and Mongolian. This work has become something of a classic in modern times and is accessible in several good English translations.

REMEMBER

Just as the reign of Ashoka saw the Theravada Buddhism of the Pali canon spread to Sri Lanka on its way to Southeast Asia (see the section "Making Buddhism a Religion of the People: The Emperor Ashoka's Influence," earlier in this chapter), the peace and prosperity of the reign of King Kanishka in the northern part of the Indian subcontinent (first half of the second century CE) enabled the sutras of Mahayana Buddhism to begin spreading north and east on their way to China and beyond. Mahayana monks weren't the only individuals responsible for this diffusion. Merchants and other lay practitioners also established pockets of Buddhism along the trade routes of Central Asia.

Looking at the Decline and Reappearance of Buddhism in India

Buddhism eventually declined in India. But the decline didn't occur before Buddhism planted innumerable seeds that eventually flowered and took root in other lands, giving rise to the various Buddhist traditions recognized today. (Travel to Chapter 5 to find out more about the spread of Buddhism to the rest of Asia and, ultimately, the West.)

Before its decline, the Indian Sangha established numerous monasteries and several major universities that nurtured, practiced, and taught Buddhist philosophy not only to Indians, but also to visiting scholars and monks from Southeast Asia, Tibet, and China. These visitors returned home with new ideas, methods, and, above all, realizations to inspire their own and subsequent generations of spiritual seekers.

Disappearing act

You may be wondering why Buddhism declined in India, the land of its origin. Well, as is often the case, rulers of the day wanted to rule over all aspects of their domain. In the 12th century, Muslim rulers set about extending blanket control over India. Invaders destroyed major Buddhist monasteries and centers of learning, such as Nalanda and Vikramashila in present-day Bihar, in the 12th and 13th centuries. But whereas Hindu and Jain traditions survived the Muslim rule, Buddhism went into steep decline in India around the 13th century and was practiced by just a few isolated communities.

Scholars have long debated the causes for the decline of Buddhism in India. Almost everyone agrees that two factors contributed to its decline:

- **Lack of support:** Buddhism, especially in its later Vajrayana form (for the term *Vajrayana,* see Chapter 5), was largely practiced in monastic establishments and had little following among the lay population. When the major centers were destroyed, Buddhism had no firm means of survival in India.
- **Assimilation by Hindu groups:** Hindu traditions were growing in popularity. These traditions gradually assimilated a number of Buddhist ideas, and some even added the figure of the Buddha to the incarnations (avatara) of the god Vishnu.

Ambedkar: Using Buddhism as an instrument of social liberation

Ambedkar was a Hindu born into the Mahar community among the Untouchables (now called Dalits, translated as "downtrodden" or "oppressed," in many modern Indian languages). Having himself been a victim of discrimination, he attempted to use Buddhism as an instrument of social liberation. In 1956, Ambedkar formally renounced Hinduism and converted to Buddhism, along with a large number of Mahars. New converts vow to follow the eightfold Buddhist path and to renounce popular Hindu rituals and any worship of Hindu deities. Although Ambedkar propagated a form of Theravada Buddhism, some features set his Buddhism apart from other Buddhist traditions. Ambedkar's pictures or statues are common in neo-Buddhist *viharas* (meeting rooms and places of worship), revered alongside those of the Buddha. Ambedkar himself is sometimes referred to as Bodhisattva Ambedkar or Maitreya (or "the future Buddha").

Reappearing in India

But Buddhism couldn't be completely extinguished from India. A few Buddhist communities have lingered from ancient times. Other groups practicing Buddhism are Tibetans who settled in India and members of certain ethnic groups (such as Tamangs and Sherpas) living in areas bordering Nepal, Thailand, and Myanmar. But most important were the modern Buddhist movements.

Two modern movements, in particular, helped Buddhism reappear:

- **The Maha Bodhi Society:** A small group of Indians converted to Buddhism as a result of missionary activities of the Maha Bodhi Society of India. This Theravada Buddhist reform movement was founded in 1891 and has attempted to revive Buddhism in the land of its origin.
- **Ambedkar Buddhism:** The largest number of Indian Buddhists are the comparatively recent converts to the neo-Buddhist movement founded by the charismatic Bhim(rao) Ramji Ambedkar (1891–1956) in the state of Maharashtra, in the western part of India. These are the so-called Ambedkar Buddhists.

Moving Mountains: Buddhism in Nepal

As Buddhism spread over Asia, its teachings came into contact with indigenous beliefs and practices, setting in motion a complex process of assimilation and interchange of ideas. Many local Buddhist traditions developed.

When Buddhism came to the Kathmandu Valley in Nepal from India, it also developed there in specific ways. But even before this, given their position between India and Tibet, the inhabitants of the Kathmandu Valley had a long tradition of engaging with both cultures.

Buddhism continued to flourish in the Kathmandu Valley in Nepal long after its decline in India. It survived in this remote area, separated from India by formidable mountain ranges, because it suffered no major Muslim raids and thus never came under Muslim rule. When Muslims took control of India, many Buddhist teachers and monks escaped to Nepal. The Kathmandu Valley, the cultural center of Nepal, played an important role in transmitting Buddhism from India to Tibet. Tibetan scholars studied and taught in Nepal and made pilgrimages to important Buddhist sites in Nepal.

Delving into Buddhist traditions of Nepal

In addition to Hinduism, different forms of Buddhism are practiced in Nepal. Theravada, locally referred to as Shravakayana (Vehicle of the Disciples), reached the Kathmandu Valley perhaps as early as the third century BCE, and certainly no later than the first century CE. However, it was superseded by Mahayana, especially by the tantric traditions within it. Monks, mainly from Sri Lanka, reintroduced the Theravada tradition in the Kathmandu Valley in the 1930s. Theravada groups are now quite active in promoting their form of Buddhism. Vipassana meditation, which originated in the Theravada tradition, has also been popular among Newar Buddhists since the 1980s (we explain vipassana in Chapter 5). The Newars are one of several ethnic groups in Nepal and are known for their skills as artists. Newar craftsmen contributed significantly to Buddhist art and were often invited to work for patrons in Tibet. The Newars speak Newari, a Tibeto-Burman language.

In addition to the Newars of the Kathmandu Valley who practice Buddhism are Tibetans living in Nepal who follow Tibetan Buddhism. They have attracted followers among Newars and other ethnic groups in the country.

Narrowing in on Newar Buddhism

A significant portion of the Newars in Nepal practice both tantric and non-tantric forms of Mahayana Buddhism (we explain tantric forms of Buddhism in Chapter 5). These forms are therefore known collectively as Newar Buddhism. The Newar Buddhist tradition is important for several reasons. Although it developed in specific ways, it continues the Mahayana Buddhist tradition of India. It's the only Buddhist tradition that uses Sanskrit as the sacred liturgical language. Newars in Nepal have preserved and transmitted many ancient Sanskrit manuscripts that were lost in India. In particular, Buddhist texts from India that were written in Sanskrit have been faithfully transmitted, copied, and commented upon, and sometimes reworked or expanded in the Newari language. A large corpus of Buddhist ritual manuals, devotional texts, and legends is written in Newari.

An important text of Newar Buddhism is the 15th-century *Svayambhu-Purana,* which gives a mythological account of the origin of the Kathmandu Valley and the self-arisen (svayambhu) Caitya. This stupalike structure is located on a hill near Kathmandu and is an important religious monument of Newar Buddhism.

Consider these distinctive features of Newar Buddhism:

- **Caste system:** Newar Buddhism maintains a caste system. The priestly caste consists of the Shakyas and Vajracharyas.
- **Loss of living monastic communities:** With the loss of living monastic communities, Shakyas and Vajracharyas typically lead married lives as householders. These "householder-monks" undergo ordination as boys, but only for a period of three days.
- **Living tantric traditions:** Some Newars follow tantric Buddhism. They have preserved the elaborate ritual associated with the tantric tradition, which includes specific features such as dances accompanied by songs and musical instruments during which the initiated practitioners identify themselves with deities of the tantric pantheon.

Chapter 5

Watching Developments Continue to the Present Day

In This Chapter:

- Tracing the development of Buddhism in Asia
- Understanding vipassana meditation
- Exploring the spread of the Great Vehicle
- Checking out Zen and tantric Buddhism in the West

Not long after the end of the first millennium CE, Buddhism died out in India. But it reached its true peak in other lands as it evolved to meet the needs of new cultures that first tentatively and then wholeheartedly embraced it.

Chapter 4 traces the development of Buddhism in India (the homeland of its founder) as it diverged into two major currents and many minor schools. In this chapter, we follow this adaptable tradition as it spread across Asia and took various shapes by embellishing and expanding the basic teachings of the historical Buddha.

Tracing the Two Routes of Buddhism

Earlier historians suggested that Buddhism followed two routes as it spread from India to the rest of Asia:

- **Southern route:** The first, more southern, route took the tradition known as Theravada Buddhism to Sri Lanka and then into Southeast Asia to Burma (now called Myanmar), Thailand, Laos, and Cambodia (Kampuchea).
- **Northern route:** The second route carried the different forms of Mahayana Buddhism into Central Asia and across the Silk Road to China. From there, Buddhism spread to Vietnam, Korea, Japan, Tibet, and Mongolia (see Figure 5-1).

But this southern/northern classification is now considered inaccurate because it has its exceptions. Consider Indonesia, for example. Other than in its local Chinese communities, this Southeast Asian Muslim nation hasn't had its own living Buddhist tradition for many centuries. But the monumental ruins at Borobudur (see Chapter 9), which are adorned with scenes from Mahayana sutras, clearly show that so-called Northern Buddhism once thrived along the southern transmission route. Even Sri Lanka, home to Theravada Buddhism since the earliest times (around 250 BCE), hosted its own version of the Mahayana, and the Theravada tradition didn't become the official form of Buddhism for this island nation until the 12th century.

Figure 5-1: The spread of Buddhism through Asia.

Spreading the Way of the Elders Across Southeast Asia to the West

As Buddhism established itself in the various Southeast Asian countries, it faced different sets of challenges. In Sri Lanka, for instance, even after it became the official form of Buddhism, Theravada (literally, "Way of the Elders") had to confront the threat of European colonization. Beginning in the 16th century, the Portuguese and then the Dutch gained control over much of the island. The Europeans converted the people from their beliefs, and Christianity began to exercise its influence. Theravada Buddhism didn't experience a return to its former prominence until the 19th century. Nevertheless, Sri Lanka was once an ancient center of Theravada Buddhist scholarship. A famous figure in Sri Lankan Buddhism was Buddhaghosa (fifth century CE), who purportedly arrived on the island from India. We refer to his work, *Visuddhimagga (Path to Purity),* an elaborate treatise on Buddhist doctrine, in Chapters 7 and 11. Tradition has it that Shakyamuni himself visited Sri Lanka. The fifth-century chronicle *Mahavamsa (Great Chronicle)* narrates that the Buddha visited the island three times, having arrived there by air each time. On his third visit, he left his footprint on Adam's Peak, a mountain of the central part of Sri Lanka. Other important objects of religious worship in Sri Lanka include the tooth relic of the Buddha, believed to have been sent from India, which is worshipped in a temple in Kandy. In Chapter 4, we mention that a cutting from the original Bodhi tree under which the Buddha is believed to have attained enlightenment was brought to Sri Lanka and is now worshipped in the city of Anuradhapura.

Theravada and Mahayana reached Burma (now known as Myanmar) between the fifth and sixth centuries CE, but the Theravada tradition eventually prevailed. In the 11th century, the city of Pagan — adorned with thousands of Buddhist temples, of which approximately 2,000 survive today — became the capital of Burma's first unified kingdom. With the breakup of this kingdom, however, Buddhism declined and didn't return to prominence until the 19th century. Nowadays, Buddhism and other free institutions struggle to survive in the face of opposition from Myanmar's repressive regime. This nonviolent struggle is led in part by Aung San Suu Kyi (born in 1945), a Buddhist laywoman who gained international fame when she was awarded the Nobel Peace Prize in 1991. Even during this time of unrest, Myanmar's meditation tradition remains intact. The city of Yangoon has several meditation centers that welcome foreigners. Two important traditions of vipassana meditation originated in the country: the method of Mahasi Sayadaw and the one by U Ba Khin, the teacher of S. N. Goenka; both are discussed later in this chapter.

Wars and government oppression have also severely weakened the various forms of Buddhism that flourished throughout Indochina in previous centuries. Although both Laos and Cambodia (Kampuchea) were once active Theravada centers, the Buddhism that remains in the wake of the communist takeovers of the 1970s has lost much of its former vitality.

Theravada Buddhism takes root in Thailand

Thailand is a different story: It has a rich Buddhist heritage. Among the important archaeological Buddhist sites are remains of the ancient cities of Sukhothai and Ayutthaya, both declared World Heritage Sites by UNESCO.

Buddhism entered the country in about the 3rd century CE, and in the 14th century, monks from Sri Lanka revitalized the country's Theravada tradition. Today Thailand is world renowned for its opulent temples and golden statues (see Figure 5-2) and for the monks in saffron (orangey yellow) robes who walk the streets of its large cities receiving offerings from lay followers. In numerous temples and monasteries throughout Thailand, meditation is taught to laypeople. The teachers are not only monks, but also laywomen, some of whom are widely revered.

Buddhism permeates modern Thai culture. Consider the following examples of Buddhism's widespread presence:

- Buddhism is the national religion; according to the constitution, the king must be a Buddhist.
- Buddhist virtues such as gentleness and self-restraint receive widespread observance and respect.
- The connection between the lay and ordained communities is particularly close, and the laity can always be counted on to provide food, clothing, and any other support the ordained Sangha members require.
- Custom still dictates that every male spend at least several months of his life wearing the robes of a monk and living according to the rules of monastic discipline.

But as in many Buddhist countries, much of what passes for Buddhist practice today in Thailand is rather superficial and simply in need of reform. We mention here two important figures who started reform movements.

One influential authority was the monk Buddhadasa (1906–1993), an abbot at Suan Mokkh hermitage in Chaiya district, in southern Thailand. A monk *(bhikkhu)* and a scholar, he was well versed not only in Buddhist scriptures, but also in the religious and philosophical traditions of the West. His interpretations of Buddhist texts were often radically modern and his attitude toward institutionalized Buddhism was highly critical. Because of his ability to converse with people from many different cultures and walks of life, his interpretation of Buddhism has exercised considerable influence within the Buddhist world of Southeast Asia, although he never left Thailand.

A prominent figure in Thailand who was inspired by Buddhadasa is the lay Buddhist social critic, peace activist, and writer Sulak Sivaraksa (born in 1933). Criticizing traditional Buddhist religious practices, Sulak writes:

> Should we carry on spending a fortune building Buddha images of gold on high pedestals while the majority of people are starving or lack access to the most rudimentary healthcare, not to mention suffering from human rights abuses? Mindfulness should be practiced beyond the meditation hall, in places such as refugee camps or outside of military bases or even in the shopping centers so that we could bring out the seeds of peace and critical self-awareness cultivated within ourselves and engage with the world through nonviolent social action and networking.
>
> (*Rediscovering Spiritual Values,* Bangkok, 2009, p. 304)

Sulak has played a leadership role in several organizations dedicated to improving the lives of poor people in rural areas. He cofounded the International Network of Engaged Buddhist (INEB) in 1989, which has affiliated groups in more than 20 countries and focuses on environmental problems, alternative models of education, human rights, and women's issues, among other concerns. (For more information on Socially Engaged Buddhism, see the section on Thich Nhat Hanh in Chapter 15.) Like the Vietnamese monk Thich Nhat Hanh, Sulak reinterprets the traditional five Buddhist precepts in a socially relevant manner. (For his reformulation of the 10 Perfections, see the info on engaged Buddhism in Chapter 1.) Sulak was awarded the Niwano Peace Prize in May 2011 in recognition of his work.

Some members of the monastic community in Thailand have responded to the corruption within Buddhist institutions in Bangkok by retreating to the solitude of the jungle to revive the practices of the original Buddhist forest dwellers of India. Instead of adopting the familiar priestlike role of many city-dwelling monks — officiating at ceremonies on behalf of the laity and so on — these monks have adopted as simple and renounced a lifestyle as possible and have returned to the basics of their faith. Not content with treating Theravada Buddhism simply as an institutionalized religion, they devote themselves as intensely as possible to the practice of meditation. Their goal is nothing less than complete emancipation from all forms of mentally created limitations — true freedom from suffering.

The forest tradition of Thailand and neighboring Myanmar has had a major impact on the Western spiritual scene. Beginning in the 1960s, Westerners — at first just a few, but later a significant number — began making their way East in search of ancient wisdom (or, at least, an alternative to the materialistic culture in which they'd grown up). Although drugs and other distractions readily available along the hippie trail to India and beyond distracted many of these travelers, some folks actually found what they were looking for. In the United States, the forest tradition is now represented by Abhayagiri Buddhist Monastery in Redwood Valley, California, and Pacific Hermitage in White Salmon, Washington (see Chapter 8 for a detailed description). An influential teacher in the forest traditions was Ajahn Chah (1918–1992), whose life story is presented in Chapter 15.

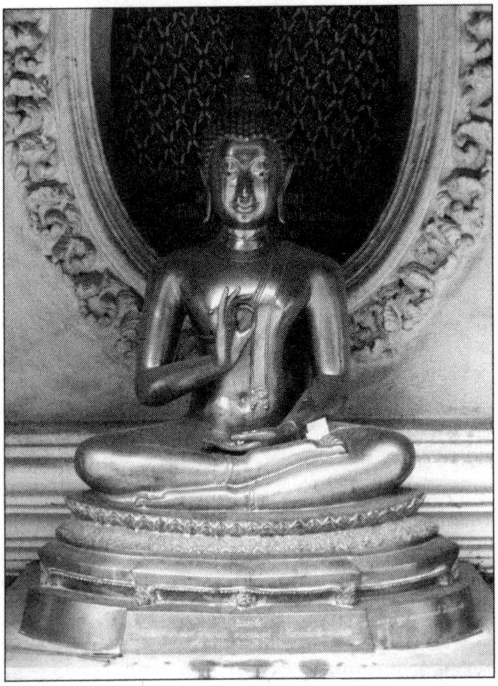

Figure 5-2: Thai Buddha statue.

Photographed by John C. Huntington, courtesy of the Huntington Archive at The Ohio State University.

Vipassana meditation gains popularity in the West

During the 1970s, a number of those pioneers who studied with Theravada masters in Southeast Asia returned to the West and began sharing what they'd learned with others, establishing centers that brought ancient Theravada practices and rituals right to America's doorstep (see Figure 5-3). Perhaps the best-known pioneer is Jack Kornfield (born in 1945), a popular author and meditation teacher who has been instrumental in introducing to the West the meditation techniques of such masters as Ajahn Chah, one of the main figures who revived the forest meditation tradition in Thailand (see Chapter 15 for more on Ajahn Chah).

Breathing it all in

The breath is a particularly good object of meditation. Unlike other objects that require considerable effort to establish and maintain — such as a visualized image of the Buddha — your breath is always available right under your nose, just waiting to be observed. In addition, you can find out a lot about your state of mind just by observing your breath. For example, rough, uneven breathing often reflects mental agitation, but as your mind grows calmer, your breathing follows suit. In fact, some meditators become so calm and focused that their breathing seems to stop altogether.

Experiencing this extraordinary calmness for the first time can be quite surprising. Your breath becomes far subtler than you're used to. When your mind has grown sufficiently calm and focused, you then direct your attention to the various sensations, feelings, and thoughts that continually appear and disappear in your body and mind (see Chapter 7 for more on this mindfulness meditation). Your task isn't to judge, compare, or engage these experiences, but merely to observe them.

Something arises and — without clinging to the pleasant or pushing away the unpleasant — you merely note the experience. This meditational technique is challenging because it's so simple. Instead of being distracted by the constant stream of chatter going on in your head, you directly confront your ever-changing experiences. When you become bored or frustrated (or when your mental chattering takes over), you note that as well. By becoming increasingly mindful of what's going on, moment by moment, you have the opportunity to gain an awareness of the way things actually exist, free of all mental projections.

Jack Kornfield (along with fellow pioneers Joseph Goldstein, Sharon Salzberg, and Christina Feldman) co-founded the Insight Meditation Society (IMS) in Barre, Massachusetts, in 1975. Since then, spiritual seekers have had access to instruction in Buddhist meditation without making the difficult journey to the East; they have to make their way only to the East Coast of the United States. (Years later, Kornfield also cofounded Spirit Rock Meditation Center in California.)

REMEMBER

The main practice taught at IMS and similar centers around the world is *vipassana* (insight) meditation. These centers have adapted their practice from the Theravada teachings of Ajahn Chah and other Thai forest masters or from those of Burmese masters such as Mahasi Sayadaw and U Ba Khin (and one of his primary disciples, S. N. Goenka), who spearheaded the revival of the Theravada practice tradition. As taught in these centers, meditation training generally begins with the preparatory practice of calming and focusing the mind by directing your attention to the rhythmic movement of the breath. When the mind is sufficiently concentrated through this or other, similar techniques, the practitioner is introduced to a technique of insight (vipassana) meditation. Its aim is direct and liberating insight into the impermanent, unsatisfactory, and selfless nature of ordinary existence (see Chapters 2 and 17 for more on these three characteristics of ordinary existence).

Theravada monasteries take root in the West

Lay meditation centers are only one Western offshoot of the Southeast Asian Theravada tradition. Followers of Ajahn Chah and other masters have established other centers in Europe, the United States, New Zealand, and elsewhere where men and women can follow the traditional lifestyle of a Theravada monk or nun without leaving their native country (see Figure 5-3).

The earliest American follower of Ajahn Chah, Ajahn Sumedho (born in 1934), founded the Amaravati Buddhist Monastery in England. Ajahn Amaro (born in 1956), who also trained with Ajahn Chah, is now abbot of the monastery. Ajahn Pasanno, another follower of Ajahn Chah, is abbot of the Abhayagiri Monastery in Redwood Valley, California (see Chapter 8 for a glimpse of life in this monastery). Although these centers may be small compared to their Asian counterparts, they maintain the monastic tradition with purity and authenticity, which bodes well for the future of Theravada in the West.

A revival of vipassana meditation got underway in the 20th century, first in Burma (now called Myanmar) and then in other Southeast Asian countries. Since then, a variety of methods have been propagated. Although they differ considerably, all claim to be based on the authority of ancient Pali texts, especially a discourse titled the *Satipatthana-Sutta* (Pali: *Sutta on the Presences of Mindfulness*). The discourse prescribes mindfulness of the body, feelings or sensations *(vedana),* the mind *(chitta),* and the psychic factors *(dharma)* that lead to bondage or release. Among the many styles of vipassana meditation, the ones promoted by Burmese master Mahasi Sayadaw (1904–1982) and by S. N. Goenka (born in 1924) have been the most influential. Mahasi's method calls for one to direct awareness to the rising and falling of the belly as one breathes, while mentally noting feelings and thoughts that arise. In the tradition of S. N. Goenka, one systematically scans the body from the head to the toes and then in the opposite direction, nonreactively monitoring the sensations felt.

Vipassana retreats last anywhere from ten days to three months or more and are conducted in complete silence, except when the leader or facilitator gives instructions or conducts personal interviews.

In addition to techniques for developing concentration and insight, centers such as IMS offer instruction in other key Buddhist practices. *Metta* (loving-kindness) meditation is particularly popular and widely taught, both on its own and as final part of the vipassana retreat schedule. Many of the Western centers also offer forms of instruction from outside the Theravada tradition and even from outside Buddhism, including courses led by Tibetan lamas, Japanese Zen masters, Christian priests, Native American shamans, and other spiritual teachers. As a result, an eclectic tradition seems to be emerging that draws its inspiration from a variety of sources and can offer spiritual services to the greater community.

Figure 5-3: Paying respects to the Triple Gem.

Photo courtesy of Abhayagiri Buddhist Monastery.

Driving the Great Vehicle to China and Beyond

In addition to Theravada, the other main division of Buddhism is the Mahayana, the self-styled Great Vehicle or Great Path that reveres the spiritual model of the *bodhisattva,* who vows to help liberate all beings in addition to himself. Theravada Buddhism made its way south to Sri Lanka and other lands, but the Mahayana Buddhism that survives today moved primarily north from the Indian subcontinent into Central Asia. From there, it trickled into China (in the first century CE) and then made its way to Korea (in the fourth century) and Japan (in the sixth century). From China, it also moved into Vietnam and Tibet (in the seventh century), although a later transmission brought Buddhism directly to Tibet from India.

The detailed story of Mahayana's movement across Asia is much more complex than that brief outline even begins to suggest, but the description provides enough detail to introduce you to the subject. While Buddhism spread from one Asian culture to another, the tradition continued to evolve back home in India, and additional teachings (the various Sanskrit sutras Chapter 4 summarizes) emerged and considerably changed the face of Mahayana Buddhism. These different scriptures eventually provided the basis for the various Mahayana traditions that sprang up across Asia.

Watching Mahayana Buddhism evolve in China

Although Mahayana Buddhism evolved in India and Central Asia, much of its later development took place in China. When it initially arrived in the first century CE, however, the Chinese didn't exactly welcome Buddhism with open arms. They were proud of their civilization (which, among other things, had produced two great philosophical traditions, Confucianism and Daoism) and looked at anything that came from foreign and "barbarian" lands with disdain. Furthermore, Buddhism's emphasis on the unsatisfactory nature of worldly life and the need to gain liberation from it didn't sit well with many Chinese. These ideas seemed to conflict with the Confucian ideal of a well-structured universe in which things worked out harmoniously if you simply carried out your proper role.

How Chinese Buddhism evolved

To get a sense of how different Buddhist schools may have evolved in China, imagine that you live in the western part of China — the area closest to India — around the third or fourth century CE. One of your friends shows you a Chinese translation of a Buddhist scripture, and you find it fascinating but difficult to understand. Because you're spiritually inclined and eager to discover the deeper meaning of what you've read, you undertake the long and difficult journey to India to find a teacher and a monastery where you can study.

As it turns out, the scriptures taught at the monastery you first encounter aren't the same as the ones you originally read. (Buddhism was undergoing rapid development, and new teachings were popping up everywhere.) The new scriptures appeal to you even more than the first scriptures you read because they present a much more understandable picture of Buddhist thought and practice. After years of intensive study as a monk, you master these new teachings, help translate them into Chinese, and return home to share them with others. As these teachings catch on, they may evolve into a distinct tradition or school of Chinese Mahayana Buddhism.

In ways like this, Chinese pilgrims to India brought back different versions of Buddhism and diversified the Buddhist landscape in China in the first half of the first millennium CE.

But in the year 220 CE, the ruling Han dynasty fell. This event swept away the sense of security and stability that the Chinese had enjoyed for centuries. In the times of uncertainty that followed, many Chinese found comfort in the new faith from India, which addressed the impermanence their society was experiencing. They also began to notice certain similarities between Buddhism and Daoism, and they equated the *Dao* (the *Way*) taught by their native philosophy with the *Dharma* explained in Buddhism. All the while, Buddhist teachings continued to arrive in China as merchants and monks made their way eastward from Central Asia. In addition, a number of Chinese made the long and difficult journey to India to learn more about Buddhism at its source (see the sidebar "How Chinese Buddhism evolved" for more details). In fact, much of the knowledge historians have of the state of Buddhism in India during the first millennium CE comes from the accounts of these early Chinese pilgrims.

Proliferation into various schools

Over the centuries, Buddhism continued to develop and evolve in China until a number of fairly distinct traditions emerged. Each tradition was associated with specific teachings, mostly of Indian origin, but with their own uniquely Chinese flavor.

During the heyday of Buddhism in China between the sixth and ninth centuries, many Buddhist traditions (so-called schools) flourished. The following are some of the most important of these, together with the *sutras* (discourses attributed to the Buddha) upon which they are based:

- **Tiantai:** Based on the *Lotus Sutra* (see Chapter 4), this tradition was named after a famous mountain in China. (For more on this tradition, check out the section "Examining Flower Ornament and Tiantai: The great unifying systems," later in this chapter.)
- **Flower Ornament:** Based on a sutra by the same name and known as Huayan in Chinese, this tradition became Kegon Buddhism in Japan (see the section "Examining Flower Ornament and Tiantai: The great unifying systems," later in this chapter).
- **Mantra:** This relatively short-lived Chinese tantric tradition survived in Japan as Shingon Buddhism (see the section "Tantra (or Vajrayana) in India, Nepal, Tibet, China, and Japan," toward the end of this chapter, for more on the Chinese and Japanese versions of this tradition).
- **Pure Land:** Based on the *Land of Bliss sutras* (see Chapter 4), this tradition inspired the development of Jodo and Jodo Shin Buddhism in Japan (see the section "The advent of two Pure Land schools in Japan," later in this chapter, for more details).
- **Meditation:** Called Chan in China and Zen in Japan, the Meditation tradition claims to be based on a direct, wordless transmission of insight (as explained in the section on Zen Buddhism later in this chapter). The *Exposition of Vimalakirti, Perfection of Wisdom,* and *Descent into Lanka* sutras strongly influenced the development of this tradition.

Don't be fazed by this rather long list of unusual names. We mention them simply to give you some idea of the richness and diversity of Chinese Buddhism in its prime.

Buddhism's appeal to the Chinese

Buddhism flourished in China because it offered something to almost everyone. Buddhism's sophistication impressed the intellectual elite, who were inspired to make their own contributions to Buddhist philosophy. And although the masses weren't interested in sophisticated philosophy, they were certainly attracted to the promise of universal salvation and to more devotional Buddhist practices, such as calling on compassionate bodhisattvas (like Guanyin) for help in this life and worshipping Buddhas (like Amitabha) for help in the next (as we explain in the section "Chronicling Pure Land and other devotional schools," later in this chapter).

Buddhism also appealed to a number of powerful local rulers, partly because they must have felt that a population trained in morality would be easier to govern. Many of these rulers also believed that Buddhist monks possessed certain magical abilities. To protect their subjects — as well as their own positions — the local rulers tried to keep these monks on their side by promoting Buddhism as much as they could.

Despite Buddhism's appeal, opposition was strong and deeply entrenched. The conflicts that often arose between the supporters of Confucianism, Daoism, and Buddhism generally had less to do with differences in belief and more to do with groups competing for the greatest share of government support and patronage. Detractors often accused Buddhists of promoting anti-Chinese values because so many of them — especially the monks — didn't seem to be fulfilling their social and family obligations. As a result of these factors and others, the influence of the different Chinese Buddhist traditions ebbed and flowed.

In fact, Buddhism as a whole went through many ups and downs in China, sometimes enjoying the strong protection of the ruling parties, and other times experiencing bitter persecution. The last major backlash took place in 845 CE when an imperial order dismantled the Buddhist monasteries and confiscated their wealth. The emperor soon withdrew the order, but not before Chinese Buddhism sank into a long, slow decline from which it never fully recovered.

After its persecution in the ninth century, Buddhism survived in China for more than 1,000 years — and even experienced some periods of brilliance — but it never again became the dynamic force it had been earlier. In the 20th century, Buddhism in China faced the additional challenges of Christianity (introduced by Western missionaries) and communism. The so-called Cultural

Revolution of the 1960s and 1970s was particularly devastating; it destroyed many traditional Buddhist institutions and further weakened an already seriously diminished Buddhist community. In addition, since the mid-1950s, the Chinese government has actively suppressed Buddhism in Tibet, dismantling monasteries and persecuting many followers. Although many different forms of Buddhist practice continue to thrive in Taiwan, the jury is still out on whether Buddhism will ever resurface on the mainland.

Examining Flower Ornament and Tiantai: The great unifying systems

Two schools of Chinese Buddhism — Pure Land and Meditation *(Chan)* — managed to survive the persecution of the ninth century relatively unscathed (see the section "Chronicling Pure Land and other devotional schools," later in this chapter). Three others — Flower Ornament, Tiantai, and Mantra — were successfully transplanted to Japan before they seriously declined at home. This section takes a closer look at the Flower Ornament and Tiantai traditions, both of which developed comprehensive philosophical systems. (For more on the Mantra tradition, see the section "Tantra (or Vajrayana) in India, Nepal, Tibet, China, and Japan," later in this chapter.)

As Mahayana Buddhism evolved in India, it gave birth to an often-bewildering array of viewpoints that caused some confusion for the early Chinese Buddhists. (For more on Mahayana in India, see Chapter 4.) The more familiar the Chinese became with the Buddhist teachings (which reached them bit by bit, not all at once), the more they wondered how the teachings fit together into a coherent whole. To make sense of this assortment of views, several Chinese schools attempted to organize these diverse Mahayana teachings according to the principles found in the particular sutra (Buddhist discourse) they cherished the most.

- **Flower Ornament:** The *Flower Ornament (Avatamsaka) Sutra* impressed the founders of this school so much that they revered it as the pinnacle of Buddhist thought. They believed that the Buddha proclaimed this sutra immediately after his enlightenment while he was still sitting under the Bodhi tree. Because the sutra presented an undiluted vision of enlightenment, they argued, no one at that time could understand it. In his wisdom and compassion, the Buddha then explained what the people *could* understand — the four noble truths (see Chapter 3) and other Theravada doctrines. The Buddha went on to deliver his advanced Mahayana sutras only after he had explained these more fundamental teachings.

No matter what else he taught, however, the massive *Flower Ornament Sutra* remained the most profound expression of the Buddha's ultimate realizations — or so the masters of the Flower Ornament tradition maintained. According to their commentaries, this sutra taught the ultimate interconnectedness of everything in the universe. Although entities seem to exist separately — this table and that chair, ordinary beings and the Buddhas — they all interpenetrate in a vast interplay of forces. Through deep and repeated contemplation of this interconnectedness, the masters believed, the spiritual practitioner could experience ultimate peace.

- **Tiantai:** The other Chinese school that attempted to arrange the diverse Buddhist teachings into a coherent whole was named after the mountain home of its founder, Zhiyi (538–597). Similar to the Flower Ornament tradition, the Tiantai claimed that the Buddha first taught the *Flower Ornament Sutra* and then, realizing it was beyond the grasp of his listeners, delivered teachings that were easier to digest. But according to Tiantai, the final and most fully expressed version of the Buddha's ultimate teaching is found in the *Lotus Sutra.*

  According to the *Lotus Sutra,* the Buddha didn't teach one doctrine to all his disciples. He revealed different paths, to suit the temperaments and abilities of his listeners. He taught some people that the path of renunciation and morality — refraining from hurting others — led to their happiness in future lives. He told others that the path of wisdom — penetrating the fiction of the self — led to complete freedom from the cycle of rebirth. And he taught others that the path of great compassion led to enlightened service for others. (To find out more about these three paths, see Chapters 12, 13, and 14, respectively.) Although these paths may seem to have different goals, Tiantai taught that the Buddha's true intention was to lead everyone, in the most effective manner, to the ultimate spiritual destination, Buddhahood.

Chronicling Pure Land and other devotional schools

Some Pure Land schools derive their inspiration and direction from the Mahayana sutras that focus on Amitabha, the Buddha of Infinite Light. Unlike the historical Buddha, Shakyamuni, who walked the earth 2,500 years ago, Amitabha is said to be a transcendental being who exists beyond the limits of ordinary time and space. (Figure 5-4 shows Amitabha.) His story transports the Buddhist faithful to a mystic realm of extraordinary wonder and beauty, but paradoxically, this realm is as close as your own heart.

According to the sutras in which Shakyamuni purportedly revealed this Buddha's existence, Amitabha dwells in the western paradise of Sukhavati, the Pure Land of Bliss. This paradise came into existence as the result of a series of heartfelt vows that Amitabha (then known as the bodhisattva Dharmakara) made before his teacher. In these vows, Amitabha stated that he would bring forth a sacred realm for the ultimate benefit of all beings upon his own attainment of Buddhahood. When a person is born into this realm, he is guaranteed to achieve full enlightenment.

The sutras dealing with Sukhavati describe its excellent qualities in exquisite detail. They even provide you with exact instructions for visualizing Amitabha (who is as red as the setting sun) and his gorgeous surroundings. But the main purpose of these sutras is simply to remind you of Amitabha's compassion.

Figure 5-4: The Buddha Amitabha.

Photo courtesy of Gudrun Bühnemann.

In India, the devoted worship of Amitabha and other transcendent Buddhas and bodhisattvas formed part of Mahayana practices in general. But in China and, later, Japan, Pure Land Buddhism became a tradition unto itself. You can get some idea of the hold Pure Land had — and continues to have — over people's hearts and minds by visiting almost any gallery of Far Eastern art. You're bound to see numerous depictions of Amitabha Buddha in both painting and sculpture. Sometimes he's seated and absorbed in meditation. Other times he's standing with his hands outstretched, welcoming everyone to join him. The fondest prayer of millions of people around the world is that this figure will appear to them at the moment of death and lead them to his western paradise.

Closely associated with Amitabha is the compassionate bodhisattva Avalokiteshvara. The *Land of Bliss sutras* describe him as standing at the right side of Amitabha, helping him welcome the deceased. The object of fervent adoration in many Asian lands, Avalokiteshvara underwent an extraordinary transformation as he made his way from India to the Far East: He became a she! (See the sidebar "Guanyin: A transgendered deity" for more information.) Buddhist devotees adore this transcendent bodhisattva, known as Guanyin in China (see Figure 5-5) and Kannon in Japan, much like Catholics adore the Virgin Mary. And like Mary, Guanyin continues to intercede on behalf of the faithful.

Figure 5-5: Guanyin, the compassionate bodhisattva.

Photo courtesy of Gudrun Bühnemann.

REMEMBER

The advent of two Pure Land schools in Japan

In Japan, Pure Land Buddhism became one of the major Buddhist traditions and diverged into two separate schools, Jodo-shu and Jodo Shinshu.

Guanyin: A transgendered deity

Many different explanations have surfaced to explain why the bodhisattva of compassion took on a female form. Some people claim that, in the Far East, compassion is understood to be a particularly feminine quality, so the sex change was somehow necessary. Others point out that even where this bodhisattva is depicted as male (in Tibet, for example, where he's known as Chenrezig; see Chapter 15), his features are soft and gentle (as befits his merciful qualities), so the gender change isn't as extreme as it may first appear. Still others maintain that Guanyin isn't actually a form of Avalokiteshvara at all: They believe that she's a blend of Tara, the Great Mother of Indian Buddhism, and local Chinese nature goddesses. (For Tara, see the sidebar "Tara, the Buddhist protectress," later in this chapter.)

However he/she is understood, millions of Buddhists around the world call upon this compassionate bodhisattva for blessings and assistance in difficult times.

- **Jodo-shu:** Literally translated from Japanese as "Pure Land School," Jodo-shu was founded by Honen (1133–1212), one of the great figures of Japanese Buddhism. Honen became a monk when he was 15 and studied with teachers from various Buddhist schools, but he became increasingly disenchanted with the Buddhism of his day.

  The 12th century was a time of social and political upheaval in Japan, and Honen felt that almost no one could successfully follow the traditional practices of Buddhism in such a degenerate age. He believed that people first needed to be reborn in the Pure Land through the vow of Amitabha, and then they could achieve enlightenment. He therefore encouraged the simple practice of mindfulness of the Buddha (Amitabha; Sanskrit: *buddhanusmriti;* Japanese: *nembutsu*), together with the cultivation of strong faith in Amitabha's saving grace. Honen interprets the *nembutsu* as chanting the homage *"Namu amida butsu,"* literally, "Homage to Amida (Sanskrit: Amitabha or Amitayus) Buddha."

- **Jodo Shinshu:** A monk named Shinran (1173–1263) was one of the many disciples who received the practice of nembutsu from Honen. In his earnest quest for spiritual fulfillment, Shinran devoted many years to serious study and practice with many Buddhist teachers. In spite of all his hard work, he remained dissatisfied and restless. Shinran felt that he hadn't achieved anything of real value. Meeting Honen was the turning point in his life. As soon as he started reciting *"Namu amida butsu,"* he experienced the peace that had eluded him for so many years. From that moment on, he gave up his monastic vows and spent the rest of his long life wandering among the common people, many of whom became devoted to him.

In 1225, Shinran began his own tradition, which he called Jodo Shinshu (True Pure Land School), to differentiate it from the tradition of his deceased master. This new tradition became increasingly popular and now has more followers than any other Buddhist denomination in Japan. Shinran's approach was radical in its simplicity. He interpreted Amitabha's vow to mean that all beings are already enlightened; they just don't realize it! According to Shinran, you don't have to do anything to reach Sukhavati — not even recite the *nembutsu.* In fact, there's nothing you *can* do; everything has been done for you already. You still pay homage to Amitabha, but not because this practice will lead you to Sukhavati. It's an expression of gratitude for having already arrived!

Under the name The Buddhist Churches of America, a subsect of Jodo Shinshu has been active in North America since Japanese immigrants first brought it with them more than 100 years ago. Still primarily popular among Japanese Americans, Jodo Shinshu has gained some non-Asian converts in recent decades and continues to be an influential force on the American Buddhist scene. (For more on the practice of Jodo Shinshu, see Chapter 8.)

The Nichiren School

A controversial figure named Nichiren (1222–1282) founded another tradition of Japanese Buddhism that deserves to be mentioned with the Pure Land schools because of some traits they have in common.

Like the Pure Land schools, Nichiren Buddhism requires little more of its followers than strong devotion and the repetition of a short phrase of homage. But unlike the Pure Land schools, the Nichiren school isn't a Japanese version of a Chinese tradition, and it doesn't direct its devotion toward Amitabha. Instead, Nichiren is a homegrown product of Japan, and the object of its devotion isn't a Buddha or a bodhisattva; it's the *Lotus Sutra.*

The *Lotus Sutra* is a Mahayana scripture that the Tiantai (Japanese: Tendai) tradition also reveres. As a follower of Tiantai (see the section "Examining Flower Ornament and Tiantai: The great unifying systems," earlier in this chapter, for more info about Tiantai), Nichiren shared in this adoration to an extraordinary degree. He believed that the *Lotus Sutra* was so powerful that you didn't have to study or even read it to benefit from it; you merely had to recite its title with faith. If you simply repeated *"Namu myoho renge kyo"* ("Homage to the *Lotus of the Good Dharma Sutra*"), your spiritual and worldly wishes would be fulfilled. And this phrase could take care of more than just your own personal wishes: Japan was going through a tumultuous period, and Nichiren felt that only faith in the *Lotus Sutra* could save it from invasion.

Offshoots of the Nichiren school

Not long after Nichiren's death, internal disputes among his followers led to the establishment of a splinter group that called itself Nichiren Shoshu (True School of Nichiren). Although it wasn't big at first, this school survived over the centuries. Then after World War II, one of its offshoots suddenly exploded into unexpected prominence. In 1937, a convert to Nichiren Shoshu founded a lay society known as Soka Gakkai (Value Creation Society). Within a few decades, fueled by the humiliation and hardship of the postwar years in Japan, this group grew into a powerful political, social, and economic force.

Members of Soka Gakkai follow the basic practice instituted by Nichiren — reciting *"Namu myoho renge kyo"* ("Homage to the *Lotus of the Good Dharma Sutra*") — and regard Nichiren as the Buddha of the present age. On their altar, practitioners keep a reproduction of a mystical diagram (mandala) called the *Gohonzon* (Object of Devotion), originally drawn by Nichiren himself, which is said to embody all the teachings of the *Lotus Sutra* and deserves the utmost adoration. Perhaps the most distinctive characteristic of Soka Gakkai, however, is their passion for promoting their religion. Evangelism isn't a trait ordinarily associated with Buddhism, but Soka Gakkai actively — some would say aggressively — encourages conversion. In terms of numbers, Soka Gakkai has been extraordinarily successful and boasts a worldwide membership of more than 12 million people, including a significant portion of the Japanese population and hundreds of thousands of followers in the West, including celebrities such as Herbie Hancock and Tina Turner.

Another offshoot of Nichiren Buddhism is the monastic order known as Nipponzan Myohoji, founded in 1917. The members of this order are strongly committed to world peace and have erected Peace Pagodas in many countries throughout the world, including Manchuria, China, Japan, England, Austria, and the United States. One of the most impressive pagodas (or stupas) is located on a hill outside Rajgir in India (see Chapter 9), where the Buddha is believed to have delivered the *Lotus Sutra* that's so central to the Nichiren tradition. Visitors to these pilgrimage sites see Nipponzan Myohoji followers walking in a regimented style around a beautiful pagoda and banging their racket-shaped drums in time to the chant *"Namu myoho renge kyo."*

Nichiren's uncompromising belief that his path was the only true path to personal and national salvation met considerable opposition. He accused the established Buddhist schools of being in cahoots with demonic forces intent on destroying Japan and made many enemies among both the Buddhist clergy and the government. He was even condemned to death, but he escaped execution — by miraculous means, according to his faithful followers. After three years in exile, he returned to Japan and lived out the rest of his life on Mount Minobu, near Mount Fuji, where he laid the foundation for the organization that would carry on his teachings after his death. (See the sidebar "Offshoots of the Nichiren school" to discover more about the present-day forms of Nichiren Buddhism.)

Zen: Taking root in the Far East — and the West

The Pure Land school (see the section "Chronicling Pure Land and other devotional schools," earlier in this chapter) became an important Mahayana tradition in China. Another form of Mahayana Buddhism that took root in China, moved to other Asian cultures, and eventually made its presence strongly felt in the West also offered a more practical approach. We're referring to Zen, arguably the most visible and widely recognized form of Buddhism in the West.

Zen has a reputation for being mysterious, so we begin this discussion with something simple: its name. The Japanese term *zen* (like the Chinese term that it comes from, *chan*) can be traced to the Sanskrit *dhyana,* meaning "meditation." Because meditation has been an important practice in Buddhism from the beginning (see Chapter 7), it has never been the exclusive property of any one tradition, and many styles of meditation exist. According to a popular legend, a monk named Bodhidharma traveled to China in the sixth century and brought with him his particular meditative approach. He is said to have started his time in China by spending nine years sitting in meditation facing a wall (see Figure 5-6). (For more on Bodhidharma, see the sidebar "Bodhidharma: A legendary Zen master.")

Figure 5-6: Bodhidharma.

Photo courtesy of Gudrun Bühnemann.

Understanding the nondual nature of Zen

For the followers of Bodhidharma's tradition, which became known as Chan (and later Zen), meditation is direct confrontation with the present moment and is capable of bringing about a penetrating insight into the true nature of reality (see Chapter 10 for more on enlightenment according to some teachers of the Zen tradition). Experiencing this moment of spiritual awakening depends not only on the meditator's own efforts, but also on the transformative influence of the master, who offers his students a special transmission outside the scriptures.

Zen traces its beginnings to just such a "special transmission" between Shakyamuni Buddha and one of his main disciples. It is believed that while seated among a group of his followers, the Buddha silently picked up a flower and showed it to the group. Sitting nearby, one of his most accomplished disciples, Mahakashyapa, smiled. Out of all the disciples, only he experienced the wordless transmission of insight that the Buddha had offered. The Buddha then said, "I have the treasury of the true Dharma eye, the ineffable mind of nirvana. Reality is formless; the subtle teaching doesn't depend on written words, but is separately transmitted apart from doctrines. This I entrust to Mahakashyapa."

What does this story try to tell us? It wants to show that ultimate reality can be clearly and directly expressed without words. In fact, although words and concepts may point to the truth (like a "finger pointing at the full moon," as the famous Buddhist saying goes), they are inadequate in expressing the truth fully because they're inherently dualistic. Words and concepts refer to a world of apparently separate, solid things and apparently separate selves that experience them. But when an awakened being looks at a flower and sees it just as it is, clearly and without conceptual overlays (that is, beyond all limited notions of "this" and "that"), no words can convey the experience. Why? Because there's no experiencer and nothing experienced. All that exists is the pure, nondual experience itself. By picking up the flower, the Buddha, according to this story, invites others to share in this nonconceptual knowing — and Mahakashyapa expresses his comprehension with a silent smile.

Awakening to this nonconceptual, nondual insight is the heart of Zen Buddhism. As Bodhidharma's tradition developed in China (influenced strongly by Daoism) and then entered Korea, Japan, and, later, Vietnam, different methods for training disciples to discover their true nature gradually evolved. Some of these different methods are found in the two schools of Zen Buddhism, Rinzai and Soto, which are active in Japan and around the world today.

Bodhidharma: A legendary Zen master

Although he may or may not have actually existed, Bodhidharma (refer to Figure 5-6) is the epitome of the tough and enigmatic Zen master whose dedication to meditation is unshakable and who teaches by direct example rather than scripture. Usually depicted with a shaved head, scruffy beard, and earring (the prototypical Gen-Xer?), the wide-eyed and concentrating Bodhidharma became a popular subject of Zen ink drawings in both China and Japan.

The instructive stories about this figure are legendary. In one, he supposedly cut off his eyelids so that he could meditate day and night without falling asleep. Clearly, this tale is meant to inspire future generations of Zen students to be diligent and focused in their practice. In another fictitious (but very popular) story, he sits impassively in the snow while a young seeker begs him for instruction. Finally, the young man cuts off his arm and hands it to Bodhidharma to show his devotion and sincerity — and Bodhidharma finally agrees to teach him. Another cautionary tale, though it's certainly not intended to encourage self-mutilation!

Profiling Rinzai and Soto: Two different Zen styles

Rinzai Zen, brought to Japan from China by the monk Eisai (1141–1215), favors the use of *koans* (loosely translated as "paradoxical stories") to confound the dualistic mind and arouse direct insight (for more on koans, see Chapter 8). Of the many hundreds of these often elusive and paradoxical questions and anecdotes, perhaps the koans best known in the West are "What is the sound of one hand [clapping]?" and "What was your original face before your parents were born?" Students focus their undivided attention on the koan they've been given and try to reveal its secret meaning, its living essence. Although no correct answers exist, constant confrontation with the koan — under the watchful eye of a skillful teacher — brings the Zen trainee to the very limit of conceptual thought — and eventually beyond.

The training offered by Soto Zen, which Dogen (1200–1253) introduced to Japan in 1227, focuses on *zazen* (sitting meditation), which is also practiced in Rinzai. Zazen is formal and demanding. It emphasizes maintaining a correct, upright posture throughout each meditation session, while remaining uninterruptedly aware of the present moment. (To help energize students who are tiring, the Zen master may strike them sharply with a stick carried specifically for that purpose. Though it may look frightening, the blow is stimulating rather than painful.) Teachers in this tradition often point out that you're not meditating to *become* a Buddha; instead, sitting in upright awareness is the way to express the Buddha nature you've always possessed.

In addition to zazen, both Rinzai and Soto Zen offer students the opportunity to have a regular personal interview with the master (known as *dokusan* in Soto and *sanzen* in Rinzai). In Rinzai, these interviews often take the form of spirited encounters in which the student attempts to present a worthy response to a koan and the master either accepts or rejects it. During retreats, participants may line up for hours to see the master and be dismissed in the first minute of the interview with instructions to return to their cushion to mull over the koan once again. In Soto, dokusan tends to occur less frequently and to be more focused on questions about posture, attitude, or everyday life practice — though certain teachers do use koans when they seem appropriate or useful.

Contemporary forms of Zen, especially those practiced in the West, are often derived from a style of Zen propagated by the Three Treasures Association (Sanbo Kyodan). This is a lay movement in the Soto Zen tradition, founded by H. R. Yasutani Roshi (1885–1973) in 1954. Given its exclusive emphasis on the experience of *kensho* (Japanese: "to see [one's true] nature"), or direct insight into the nondual nature of reality, this style of Zen actually differs from the traditional practice models found in Soto and Rinzai Zen in Japan.

Bringing Zen into your everyday life

Because Zen places great emphasis on maintaining clear awareness of the present moment, training isn't limited only to meditation sessions or koan practice. You have to bring the same clearly focused attention to the tasks of everyday life that you bring to your more formal practice. The Soto tradition, in particular, emphasizes that every activity provides an opportunity to express your true nature through wholehearted care and attention. You can find many stories of Zen masters who experienced enlightenment while doing mundane household chores like raking leaves or hanging out the laundry!

The Zen focus on the practical and immediate is reflected in its austere yet highly refined aesthetic sense, which has become an integral part of traditional Japanese culture. Practitioners lovingly apply the same clear awareness and attention to detail that they cultivate in meditation to a wide range of activities, such as preparing and serving tea, practicing archery, arranging flowers, and creating fine calligraphy. This ability to turn almost any activity into both an artistic and a spiritual experience has made Zen particularly attractive to Western artists and poets. (Did you know that Vincent van Gogh, who owned an extensive collection of Japanese prints, once painted a portrait of himself as a Zen monk?)

Recognizing Zen's appeal for the West

Of all the Buddhist traditions, Zen has perhaps the longest history of direct contact with the West — contact that its simplicity and aesthetic appeal fostered. Believe it or not, the first recorded visit of a Zen master to North America occurred in 1893, when Soen Shaku (1859–1919) attended the World Parliament of Religions in Chicago. Soen returned in 1905 to travel and teach. His disciple Nyogen Senzaki (1876–1958) accompanied him and eventually stayed in America. Though Senzaki gained few serious students, he wrote several influential books (with an American friend, Ruth McCandless) and inspired a number of Americans who went on to train in Japan and help plant the Zen seed deep in American soil. Japanese scholar D. T. Suzuki (1870–1966), another disciple of Soen Shaku, was also extremely influential. He taught at several American universities, published a series of books explaining Zen to a lay audience, and translated key Zen texts into English.

Following in Senzaki's footsteps, the next wave of Zen teachers began arriving in North America from Japan and Korea in the 1950s and 1960s. The peaceful postwar atmosphere and the growing Western interest in Zen encouraged these teachers. (The Beat poetry of Allen Ginsberg, Gary Snyder, Jack Kerouac, and others, and the interest of well-known psychologists such as Erich Fromm, demonstrated this growing Zen awareness.) By 1970, several large cities, such as New York, Los Angeles, and San Francisco, boasted burgeoning Zen centers — places where motivated students could gather to learn and practice meditation, listen to talks on Buddhist themes, and attend longer retreats (see Figure 5-7).

The San Francisco Zen Center was probably the best known of these centers. It now includes Tassajara Zen Mountain Center, the oldest Zen monastery in America (located in the wilderness near Big Sur), and Green Gulch Farm, an organic farm and practice center in nearby Marin County. The Zen Center's late founder, Shunryu Suzuki Roshi (1905–1971), gave the lectures that later became the best-selling book *Zen Mind, Beginner's Mind*

Figure 5-7: Westerners practicing zazen.

Photo courtesy of Tanya Takacs.

(Weatherhill/Shambhala). Other influential Zen masters in North America include Joshu Sasaki Roshi (born in 1907), of Mount Baldy Zen Center in southern California; Taizan Maezumi Roshi (1931–1996), of the Zen Center of Los Angeles; and the Korean master Seung Sahn (1927–2004), of the Kwan Um School of Zen (founded in 1983), based in Providence, Rhode Island, and author of several popular books, including *Dropping Ashes on the Buddha* (Grove Press).

Nowadays, most major metropolitan areas and even many smaller cities have Zen centers or sitting groups, many of them directed and led by a new generation of Zen teachers: Westerners trained by Korean or Japanese teachers and fully authorized to train others. Because of its simplicity, its practicality, and its emphasis on direct experience, Zen has enormous appeal to Westerners. They can practice it without accepting any new belief systems — or, as Zen puts it, without putting another head on top of their own.

Checking out Zen in China, Korea, and Vietnam

Most people associate Zen with Japan. But the tradition also flourished in China, Korea, and Vietnam, and masters from these countries have independently come to the West to teach. After its heyday in China, Chan (the Chinese name for Zen) gradually lost its exclusive emphasis on meditation and became more eclectic, picking up elements of Pure Land, Tiantai, and several other Buddhist schools. Although Chinese immigrants introduced the United States to Buddhism in the 1850s and 1860s, Chan didn't make much headway outside the Chinese community until Zen Master Hsuan Hua (1918–1995) founded Gold Mountain Monastery in San Francisco in 1970 and began teaching Westerners his intensive approach, including the full range of Chan practices. Since his death, Hsuan Hua's successors have continued to spread his teachings in the West.

In Korea, Zen practice had become firmly established by the sixth century CE, before it made its way to Japan, and reigned as the main form of Buddhism there for many centuries. Though suppressed during the Yi Dynasty (1392–1910), Zen (Korean: Son) managed to survive and has become a vital Buddhist school in the West, alongside Japanese Zen. In addition to Zen Master Seung Sahn, whose Kwan Um School of Zen has affiliate centers throughout the Western world, several Korean teachers have developed large followings. Although meditation has always been the primary method, Korean Zen also emphasizes the practices of chanting and bowing.

Because Vietnam, like Korea, borders China, Buddhism put down roots there in the early centuries of the first millennium CE. Over time, Zen became the predominant school. Perhaps the best-known Vietnamese Zen master to teach in the West is Thich Nhat Hanh (see Chapter 15), but Buddhist monk and scholar Dr. Thich Thien-an (1926–1980) preceded him. Thien-an arrived in Los Angeles in 1966 as a visiting professor at UCLA and stayed to teach eager Western students until his death.

From Tibet to the West: Charting the movement of the Diamond Vehicle

In the past 30 years or so, another outgrowth of Mahayana, tantric Buddhism, or Vajrayana (Diamond Vehicle), has grown to rival Zen Buddhism's popularity in the West. Vajrayana is known by a number of names (including Tantra, Path of the Mantras, and the mysterious-sounding Esoteric Vehicle). Some people equate it with Tibetan Buddhism. However, Vajrayana isn't a Tibetan invention; it developed in India and is also practiced in Nepal and Mongolia.

Like all the other forms of Buddhism, Vajrayana claims to transmit the authentic teachings of the Buddha — even though the texts (known as *tantras*) of these traditions appeared long after Shakyamuni Buddha's death. Although historians (and even other Buddhists) may have trouble accepting these late-emerging teachings as the word of the Buddha, the Vajrayana practitioners faithfully claim (like followers of some other Mahayana traditions) that the Buddha gave many teachings during his lifetime that were too advanced to be disseminated widely. Tantra was the most powerful of these advanced teachings and, therefore, was most open to abuse. Tantric practitioners purportedly kept these powerful teachings hidden from general view and passed them to only the select few who could benefit from them. Later practitioners transmitted these teachings more widely, though still with the air of secrecy, to prevent their misuse and degeneration.

Tantra

For the most part, we use the term *Vajrayana* (Sanskrit: Diamond Vehicle) in this book, but these traditions of Buddhism are often referred to as tantric Buddhism and as Mantra-naya (Path of the Words of Power, Mantras). (We do not discuss the complex issues involved in making distinctions among these three terms.) These traditions of Buddhism are based on ideas and practices stated in a category of texts called tantra.

Tantra is an esoteric tradition; to practice it, one must be initiated (empowered) by a teacher.

Some elements of tantric practice include these:

- Elaborate rituals
- Complex meditations involving the visualization of bodhisattvas and other celestial figures
- Frequent repetition of words of power (mantras)
- Mystical diagrams (mandala; see the sidebar "What is a mandala?," later in this chapter)

Tantra is often used in the West as a rather loose term referring to (unusual) sexual practices. However, rituals involving such practices appear only in a small percentage of tantric texts and only in certain traditions, where they are practiced under the supervision of a spiritual teacher.

Tantra (or Vajrayana) in India, Nepal, Tibet, China, and Japan

Vajrayana Buddhism was practiced in India in some form by the sixth century CE. It then became established in China in the eighth century as the Mantra school. This school lasted only a century in China. Kukai (774–835), also known by the title Kobo Daishi, carried it to Japan and built a temple in 816 on Mount Koya that remains the center of what became known as the Shingon (Mantra) tradition.

REMEMBER

Shingon received an early transmission of tantric teachings, which Kukai (see Figure 5-8) systematized. This school of Buddhism is still alive in Japan today.

Figure 5-8: Kukai (Kobo Daishi).

Photo courtesy of Gudrun Bühnemann.

In India, Vajrayana Buddhism continued to evolve. Maintained by scholars and master meditators, the Vajrayana tradition thrived and eventually became a major part of the training at the famous monastic universities in northern India, such as Vikramashila and Nalanda (see Chapter 9). The destruction of Nalanda by invaders in 1199 marked the demise of the Vajrayana tradition and Buddhism as a whole in India. By the beginning of the 13th century, Buddhism was no longer a viable religion in the land of its birth, even though it left a lasting imprint on the culture of the vast subcontinent (see the discussion at the end of Chapter 4 of the decline of Buddhism in India).

By the time of Buddhism's decline, the Vajrayana tradition of India was already firmly established in Nepal and Tibet. Although the tradition reached Mongolia (and even made its way back into China), Tibet remained a major center of the Vajrayana world for centuries, preserving the tantric teachings as a vital, effective tradition until the Chinese communists invaded Tibet in the 1950s. Yet Tibet's loss has been the world's gain. With the escape of the Dalai Lama in 1959 and his forced exile in India — along with the escape of a relatively small but significant number of other great teachers — Vajrayana Buddhism has become available to the West as never before.

The aim of Vajrayana practice

REMEMBER

Like other Buddhist traditions, Vajrayana practice aims at enlightenment. This tradition is distinctive, however, because of the wealth of different methods it employs to bring about enlightenment as quickly as possible. Some of these methods involve complex rituals that feature words of power *(mantras),* mystical diagrams (*mandalas;* see Figure 5-9), and stylized gestures (called *mudras*). (For more information on mandalas, see the upcoming sidebar "What is a mandala?") Other methods take place solely within the meditator's body and mind. Whether external or internal, these various methods are ultimately directed at accomplishing the radical transformation of Buddhahood.

Figure 5-9: Tibetan nuns making a sand mandala.

Photo courtesy of Tibetan Nuns Project.

What is a mandala?

Mystical diagrams (mandalas), especially from Tibet or Nepal, have received a lot of popular attention in recent years and have been displayed in many exhibitions. Because of their aesthetic appeal, art historians have taken an increased interest in them. Western psychologists have attempted to explain their symbolism from the perspective of their specialized discipline. Swiss psychologist Carl Gustav Jung's (1875–1961) observations on the mandala as a universal archetype — a primeval image — have been especially influential. But what exactly is a mandala and how should it be approached?

The Sanskrit word *mandala* refers to anything that is round or circular. But in tantric traditions, *mandala* often refers to a sacred space, which can be round, square, or any other shape. Into this space, deities are invited by uttering words of power (mantras). The center of a mandala contains an image or symbol of the main deity surrounded by minor deities. The central deity is identified with the whole mandala, while the surrounding deities are usually considered aspects of the main deity.

Mandalas are used in rituals, especially empowerment rituals (see the section "The practice of 'deity yoga'" in this chapter). Often they are created for one-time use from various materials, including colored powders. After they have fulfilled their purpose, they are dismantled. The Kalachakra Mandala, made from colored sand, has become widely known in connection with the Kalachakra (Wheel of Time) initiation the Dalai Lama gives to large groups of people. More permanent mandalas are painted on cloth. Such mandalas are now commonly used in the Tibetan and Newar Buddhist traditions as objects of general worship.

The practice of "deity yoga"

The distinctive tantric solution to the problems that arise from holding on to a limited self-identity is the practice known as *deity yoga.* Deity yoga has little to do with the "gods" and "goddesses" enjoying the celestial realms mentioned in Chapter 13. Instead, the practice enables you to dissolve your false, limiting ego-identity and replace it with something far better. By means of this profound practice, you train to see yourself as an enlightened being, a fully evolved Buddha, free from all limitations and with a radiantly pure and blissful body, speech, and mind, through which you can bring infinite benefit to others. The particular enlightened being you identify with is known in Tibetan as your *yidam,* or *meditational deity.* (See Figure 5-10 for one such meditational deity in female form.)

If done incorrectly, without the proper understanding, the practice of deity yoga can easily degenerate into a form of make-believe in which you're merely pretending to be something you're not. To avoid this pitfall, you must build your practice on a firm foundation. To start, you must be well versed in the fundamentals of the Mahayana path in general, particularly in generating the state of mind that wants to attain enlightenment for the benefit of others. Then you have to complete certain ritual practices, called *preliminaries,* which are designed to prepare you for your main practices by letting you collect a powerful reserve of positive energy and cleanse yourself of certain inner obstacles. (An example of these collecting-and-cleansing practices is offering full-length prostrations; see Chapter 8.)

The most important foundation for practice is your reliance on a fully qualified tantric master, or guru (Sanskrit). The guru, or *lama* in Tibetan, is central to Vajrayana because he introduces you to the meditational deity (such as Tara in Figure 5-10) who will act as the focal point of your practice.

Figure 5-10: Tara, the female deity of compassion.

At the *empowerment ceremony,* during which you're initiated into the practice, you need to remain undistracted by ordinary appearances — including the outward form of your guru. Instead, you visualize your guru as inseparable from the transcendent form of Shakyamuni Buddha, known as Vajradhara (see Figure 5-11). Ultimately, your practice of deity yoga is successful when you have the unshakable realization that your guru, your meditational deity, and all the Buddhas are identical with the essential nature of your own mind.

Through deity yoga, you gradually get used to the idea of being enlightened. The blessings and inspiration of your guru help empower you to view your body as the pure light body of your meditational deity (Tara in Figure 5-10, for example), radiant and blissful. In place of your ordinary speech, you recite the sound of her mantra; you practice hearing *all* sounds as indistinguishable from her mantra. At the same time, you view your environment as Tara's pure land and all your activities as Tara's wise and compassionate activities in liberating others from suffering. Ultimately, you experience your own mind and Tara's enlightened mind as one.

Figure 5-11: Vajradhara, the tantric Guru Buddha.

In the beginning stages of practice, identifying yourself and the meditational deity as one takes place largely (if not entirely) in your imagination. But at later stages, when you become adept at controlling and directing the subtle energies flowing through your body (see Chapter 11 for more about these subtle energies), you can actually experience the enlightened transformation you previously only imagined. Eventually, you can follow in the footsteps of Tibet's beloved yogi Milarepa (see Figure 5-12). Through his intense devotion to his guru Marpa and his unwavering practice, he achieved Buddhahood.

Figure 5-12: Tibet's great yogi Milarepa.

Vajrayana in the West

Vajrayana Buddhism applies many more methods than we briefly allude to here, but even this short account can give you an idea of why this form of practice has gained a growing number of Western followers in recent years. For individuals who like rituals, the many Tibetan-style Buddhist centers in the West regularly host group sessions featuring mantra recitation, chanting, and other ritualized practices (see Figure 5-13).

For folks who prefer meditation, Vajrayana presents a broad range of practices, from performing elaborate visualizations to simply resting in the mind's basic purity. The tradition also offers opportunities for academic study — as demonstrated by the rapidly increasing number of translations and commentaries rolling off the presses. But at the end of the day, the warm and compassionate lamas who teach the Vajrayana may be the most attractive feature of this tradition.

Tara, the Buddhist protectress

Tara (*tah-rah*) is an extremely popular goddess of the Mahayana pantheon. She played an important role in late Indian Buddhism (before it vanished) and later became popular among Tibetans and members of the Newar community in Nepal. She is considered the supreme mother, who nurtures and protects the faithful and can work miracles. Tara is believed to save her devotees from the eight great perils (lions, elephants, fire, serpents, thieves, water/drowning, captivity, and evil spirits). Because of her role, she has been called the Buddhist Madonna. Different religious authorities have called Tara "the mother of all the Buddhas" or a female Buddha.

Tara's name has been variously explained as "savioress," "star," and "she who leads across," for the goddess is believed to enable her devotees to cross the ocean of rebirths. More than 50 forms of Tara have been recorded. Especially well known are the Green and White Taras, along with a group of 21 forms of Tara. In art, Tara often displays the gesture of protection or charity with her right hand (refer to Figure 5-10) and holds a lotus in her left.

Every center has its own unique style and emphasis, depending on the teacher and the particular sect of Vajrayana he belongs to. (See the sidebar "Tibetan Vajrayana schools" for further details.) The Shambhala centers, established by the late Chogyam Trungpa Rinpoche (1939–1987), may be the most widespread. Trungpa was a prolific author and one of the first Tibetan teachers to adopt Western dress and familiarize himself with Western psychology and customs. But numerous other approaches are now available across North America, including a new generation of centers led by fully authorized Western teachers.

Figure 5-13: Westerners engaging in Vajrayana practice.

Photo courtesy of Shambhala Sun. Copyright Shambhala Sun.

Tibetan Vajrayana schools

As Vajrayana Buddhism spread from India to Tibet, a number of different schools (or sects) emerged. Although some cross-fertilization has always occurred between these schools, each has its own distinctive character. The schools with the greatest influence on the Tibetan Buddhism practiced in the West today are as follows:

- **Nyingma (nyeeng-mah):** This tradition is the oldest school of Tibetan Buddhism (its name means "Ancient Ones"). Padmasambhava founded this tradition and established Samye, the first monastery in Tibet, in the eighth century. Among the many lamas responsible for introducing the Nyingma lineage to the West are Dilgo Khyentse Rinpoche (1910–1991), a major teacher of lamas from all traditions; Tarthang Tulku (born in 1934), who established the Tibetan Nyingma Meditation Center and the Odiyan Buddhist Retreat Center in California; Namkhai Norbu Rinpoche (born in 1938), who lives in Italy and teaches regularly in the United States; and Sogyal Rinpoche (born in 1947), head of the worldwide Rigpa centers and author of the popular *Tibetan Book of Living and Dying* (HarperSanFrancisco).
- **Kadam (kah-dahm):** The followers of Atisha, who came to Tibet from India in 1042, started this tradition. Although this school no longer exists as a separate entity, the following three schools absorbed and transmitted its teachings.
- **Sakya (sah-kyah):** The current head of the Sakya tradition, the Sakya Trizin (born in 1945), speaks fluent English and has taught and traveled widely in the West. Among the other Sakya lamas who have been active in the United States are Deshung Rinpoche (1906–1987); Jigdal Dagchen Rinpoche (born in 1929), of the Sakya Tegchen Choling Center in Seattle; and Lama Kunga Rinpoche (born in 1935), of Kensington, California.
- **Kagyu (kah-gyew):** The previous head of the Kagyu tradition, the Sixteenth Karmapa (1923–1981), visited the United States on a number of occasions and dedicated his main center, Karma Triyana Dharmachakra, in Woodstock, New York. Other Kagyu lamas who have established centers and taught extensively in the West include Kalu Rinpoche (1905–1989), widely considered one of the greatest Vajrayana meditation masters of the 20th century; Thrangu Rinpoche (born in 1933); and Lama Lodo (born in 1939), of the Kagyu Droden Kunchab Center in San Francisco.
- **Gelug (gay-look):** Numerous lamas have represented this school in the West, including the late tutors of the Dalai Lama. Other notable lamas from this tradition who have had a great impact on the West include Geshe Wangyal (1901–1983), who founded centers in Freewood Acres and Washington, New Jersey; Geshe Lhundup Sopa (born in 1923), retired professor of the University of Wisconsin–Madison; and Lama Thubten Yeshe (1935–1984) and Thubten Zopa Rinpoche (born in 1946), of the Foundation for the Preservation of the Mahayana Tradition.
- **Rime (ree-may):** This movement combines several important lineages of Vajrayana practice. One of the leading lights of this nonsectarian movement was Jamyang Khyentse Chokyi Lodro (1896–1969). Many of Jamyang Khyentse's disciples have been influential teachers in the West, including the previously mentioned Deshung Rinpoche, Dilgo Khyentse Rinpoche, Kalu Rinpoche, Trungpa Rinpoche, Sogyal Rinpoche, and Tarthang Tulku.

Part III

Behaving Like a Buddhist

The 5th Wave By Rich Tennant

"You know how you're always saying we can learn a spiritual lesson when bad things happen to us? Well you're about to get a spiritual lesson from Herb's Towing & Collision and the Able Auto Insurance Co."

In this part . . .

Here's where it gets really interesting — practical answers to your questions about Buddhism. How do you become a Buddhist? How do you meditate? What does a typical day in the life of a Buddhist look like? What's a Buddhist pilgrimage? Where can you go? The following pages contain all this information and more, so start down the path.

Chapter 6

Turning to Buddhism

In This Chapter

- Checking out the Buddhist teachings to see if they interest you
- Making your way through the initial levels of involvement
- Committing yourself to Buddhism as a lifelong path
- Considering the wholehearted path of the monk or nun

When you know a little something about Buddhism (conceptually, at least), you may want to explore the teachings in greater detail — and perhaps even sample a Buddhist practice or two for yourself. But where do you go and what do you do to get started? "Do I need to shave my head and run off to some monastery in the forest?" you may wonder. "Or can I get a taste of Buddhism right here at home?"

Buddhism comes in many shapes, sizes, and flavors, and we're certain that a Buddhist center is located somewhere near you. (So the answer is, no, you don't have to head for a monastery just yet.) But before you get on the Internet or pick up your local phone book, you may want to read the rest of this chapter. Why? Because we think you'll enjoy it. And because this chapter offers guidelines for approaching Buddhism gradually and thoughtfully — from your initial contact, through progressive stages of involvement, and on to the (altogether optional) moment of formally becoming a Buddhist.

Proceeding at Your Own Pace

When you first start exploring Buddhism, remember that the Buddha wasn't technically a Buddhist. In fact, he didn't consider himself a member of any religion — he was a spiritual teacher who traveled around sharing some important truths about life. So you don't have to be a Buddhist, either. Buddhists and non-Buddhists alike can enjoy and put into practice the many valuable teachings that the Buddha and his disciples have provided over the centuries.

Even one of the best-known Buddhists in the West today, the Dalai Lama, advises that you don't have to change your religion to benefit from the teachings of Buddhism. (For more information on this inspiring individual — and others — check out Chapter 15.) In fact, the Dalai Lama generally discourages seekers from other faiths from becoming Buddhists — at least until they've thoroughly explored the tradition into which they were born. When asked to identify his own religion, the Dalai Lama frequently responds quite simply, "My religion is kindness."

The message of Buddhism is clear:

- Proceed at your own pace.
- Take what works for you and leave the rest.
- Most important, question what you hear, experience its truth for yourself, and make it your own.

"Ehi passiko," the Buddha was fond of declaring. "Come and see." In other words, if you feel an affinity for the teachings of Buddhism, stay for a while and explore them. If not, feel free to leave whenever you want.

Taking responsibility for your own life

Ultimately, you're responsible for deciding how you spend your life. In Buddhism, no guru or god watches over you, prepared to hand out punishment if you stray from the path.

The Buddha never insisted that his followers, even those who chose to join the monastic order by becoming monks and nuns (see Chapter 8), remain physically close to him or the rest of the spiritual community. Many of his followers wandered from place to place, meditating and sharing their understanding with others. They gathered just once each year during the rainy season to meet, receive teachings, and practice them together.

At the heart of this approach is the understanding that life itself provides you the motivation you need to turn to Buddhist practice. If and when you pay close attention to your circumstances, you may gradually discover that the Buddha had it right: Conventional life is marked by dissatisfaction. You suffer when you don't get what you want (or you get what you don't want). Often your happiness doesn't depend on external situations; it depends on your state of mind. When you realize these simple but powerful truths, you naturally look for a way out of your suffering.

Some traditions of Buddhism encourage followers to fuel their motivation — and, therefore, their devotion — to practice by remembering certain fundamental truths. The Vajrayana (the "Diamond Vehicle" described in Chapter 5) refers to these truths as the *four reminders,* which we outline in the following list. (For further information, refer to the chapters cross-referenced in parentheses.)

- **Your human rebirth is precious.** Because you now have the perfect opportunity to do something special with your life, don't waste it on trivial pursuits (see Chapter 11).
- **Death is inevitable.** Because you won't live forever, don't keep putting off your spiritual practice (see Chapter 11).
- **The laws of karma can't be altered or avoided.** Because you experience the consequences of what you think, say, and do, act in a way that brings you happiness rather than dissatisfaction (see Chapter 12).
- **Suffering (or more broadly interpreted: the feeling of dissatisfaction) permeates all limited existence.** Because you can't find lasting peace as long as ignorance veils your mind, make efforts to win true release from suffering (see Chapter 13).

These reminders can keep you from being distracted by this materialistic culture's many seductive appeals to your craving, lust, and fear. They can help you stay focused on taking responsibility for your own happiness and peace of mind. (For more on the relationship between your happiness and the state of your mind, see Chapter 2.)

Determining your level of involvement

Given their emphasis on self-motivation, Buddhist groups naturally open their doors to all seekers at every level of involvement. Traditionally, teachings on Buddhism and meditation instruction are offered freely — and, generally, free of charge — to anyone who wants to receive them. (In return, offering some form of material support, such as money, is customary.)

You can attend Sunday services at many Christian churches without becoming a member or declaring yourself a Christian, and the same goes for Buddhism. You can receive meditation instruction, listen to teachings, and even participate in meditation retreats without officially becoming a Buddhist. Some well-known teachers, like the Indian *vipassana* (insight meditation) master S. N. Goenka, even hesitate to use the term *Buddhism* because they believe that the teachings extend well beyond the confines of any one religion and apply universally to everyone, whatever their religious involvement.

The Buddha is traditionally described as a great healer whose teachings have the power to eliminate suffering at its root. Like any compassionate healer, he shared his abilities with anyone who approached him, regardless of religious affiliation. But the Buddha also made it clear that you can't benefit unless you take the medicine — in other words, unless you put the teachings into practice.

Getting Acquainted with the Teachings of Buddhism

As so often happens with any involvement, people are drawn to Buddhism for a variety of reasons. For example, consider your favorite sport. Perhaps you learned to play it as a child, and you've been involved with it ever since. Or maybe a good friend turned you on to the sport later in life. Possibly you were inspired to learn by a spectacular match you saw on TV — perhaps by the enjoyment of a family member. Or maybe you simply saw a flyer about a class at a local rec center and decided you needed the exercise.

Believe it or not, people turn to Buddhism for similar reasons. The following examples illustrate that idea.

- Some people read a book or attend a talk by a particular teacher and get so captivated by the teachings that they decide to pursue them further. Other folks tag along with a friend, without knowing anything about Buddhism, and find themselves suddenly enthralled. Still others first seek out meditation practice because they've heard that it's an effective way to reduce stress or improve their health; as meditation begins to have its desired effect, these people read more and discover that the teachings also appeal to them.
- A few folks, like the Buddha himself, have an early insight into the universal suffering of human life and feel compelled to find a solution. Even more common are the many people who experience their own deep suffering in this lifetime, try other remedies (like psychotherapy or medication, for example), and find only temporary relief. For these seekers, Buddhist teachings offer a comprehensive approach to identifying and eliminating the fundamental cause of their suffering. (For more on the cause and end of suffering, see Chapters 3 and 13.)
- And some people, for whatever reason, believe that their purpose in this lifetime is to practice the teachings and that Buddhism is the tradition they were born to study.

Whatever your particular reasons for getting acquainted with Buddhism — all are equally valid and worthwhile — this initial stage of involvement can actually last a lifetime. Some devoted, long-time meditators choose to never formally declare themselves Buddhists, even though they've studied the teachings and engaged in the practices for most of their adult lives. (Stephan's first Zen teacher cautioned him never to call himself a "Buddhist," even after he became an ordained monk.)

The following sections examine a few of the many possible ways to get acquainted with Buddhist teachings. We present them in the order in which they often occur, but you can begin getting to know Buddhism in any way you see fit, and you may keep returning to some, if not all, of these points of contact throughout your life.

Reading books on Buddhist teachings

TIP

Many excellent books on practicing Buddhist teachings are currently available, which makes this entry point a readily accessible and enjoyable place to start. You may want to stick to more popular fare at first instead of getting bogged down in the difficult language of the sutras or the riddles of the Zen masters. Check out Appendix B, where we offer a representative sample of these works.

At this stage of your involvement with Buddhism, you definitely want to keep your intellect engaged as you investigate and interpret the teachings. Does what you read make sense to you? Does it mesh with your experiences and understanding? Does it shed new light on the relationship between your thoughts, feelings, and experiences? As you read, make note of any questions you may have and make sure that they eventually get answered.

In the long run, books won't provide you with satisfying answers to all the deeper questions of life: Who am I? Why am I here? How can I realize lasting happiness? You may need to *experience* the answers directly for yourself, which is why Buddhism emphasizes putting the teachings into practice rather than merely speculating upon them intellectually.

Choosing a tradition

As you check out different books on Buddhism, you may find teachings and traditions that particularly appeal to you. Are you drawn to the practical, progressive approach of insight meditation (*vipassana*), which offers a variety of accessible practices and teachings for working with your mind? Or are you taken with the more enigmatic, formal path of Zen, with its emphasis on awakening here and now to your innate Buddha nature? Or maybe you're attracted to the elaborate visualizations and *mantras* of tantric Buddhism

(*Vajrayana*), which use the power of the spiritual teacher and other awakened beings to energize your journey to enlightenment. (For more on these different traditions, see Chapter 5.)

A few Buddhist traditions, such as the Pure Land schools, even de-emphasize meditation in favor of faith in the saving grace of Buddhist figures known as bodhisattvas (see Chapter 4). If you have a strong devotional nature, you may find one of those traditions particularly appealing.

If you came to the path through the influence of a teacher or friend, you may clearly feel that this person's tradition is the one you want to pursue. But if you're still shopping around, you may find it helpful to zero in on a particular approach before you take the next step of receiving meditation instruction. We're not saying that you can't shift directions at any point along the way, or that basic Buddhist practices and meditation techniques aren't remarkably similar across traditions. But the styles of practice, which may differ only slightly at the outset, begin to diverge rapidly as you become more actively involved in a particular tradition.

Receiving meditation instruction

If you live in a large city, you may be able to locate a class on basic Buddhist meditation at your local community college or adult education center. Nowadays, Buddhist meditation also comes in a package known as Mindfulness-Based Stress Reduction (MBSR), a program developed by researcher and longtime Buddhist meditator Jon Kabat-Zinn (born in 1944), a retired professor of the University of Massachusetts Medical School.

As a method for reducing stress, MBSR introduces basic Buddhist teachings and applies the fundamental practice of mindfulness to reduce stress. (For more on Buddhist meditation, see Chapter 7.) Research has demonstrated that MBSR is effective in alleviating a host of stress-related health problems.

If you can't locate a basic class in Buddhist meditation (or if you're already drawn to a particular tradition), check the Internet, the Yellow Pages, or a local newspaper for listings of Buddhist centers and churches. Then be sure to ask whether they provide meditation instruction to the general public. Like their Judeo-Christian counterparts, some Buddhist churches offer only weekly services, ceremonies, and community events.

TIP

If you can't find what you're looking for under the heading "Buddhism," check for listings under "Meditation" instead. Many vipassana and Zen groups that meet to sit together believe that this category more accurately describes what they do. (If you can find a copy at your local bookstore, the quarterly Buddhist magazine *Tricycle* provides an excellent listing of Buddhist groups throughout North America. Or check out *Tricycle* online at `www.tricycle.com/`.) After you make a connection, don't be afraid to ask a few questions to make sure that the organization teaches the kind of meditation you want to master. Then go ahead and take the leap!

Many centers offer an evening or one-day workshop in which you can pick up the basics of meditation in a few hours. Others offer multiweek courses, which allow you to ask questions as you experiment with the approach. In any case, make sure that you have access to ongoing support, such as phone consultations or further classes, if you need it. Although the basic techniques are generally quite simple, they can take months and even years to master, and you're almost certain to encounter a variety of obstacles and issues along the way.

Developing a meditation practice

REMEMBER

Expect to work on and develop your meditation practice for as long as you continue to meditate. Even the most accomplished meditators are constantly refining their technique. One of the joys and satisfactions of meditation is that it offers the opportunity for endless exploration and discovery. (For more on meditation practice, see Chapter 7.)

In the beginning months of your encounter with meditation, your focus will be on finding the time and a suitable location to practice and on familiarizing yourself with the basics, such as following your breath or generating loving-kindness. You'll almost certainly have questions like the following:

- What do I do with my eyes or my hands?
- My breathing seems labored and tight. Is there any way to loosen it up?
- How can I keep from losing track of my breath entirely?

Having these kinds of questions is perfectly normal, which is why follow-up guidance is crucial. More people give up meditating because they lack proper guidance than for any other reason.

In addition to technique, the teachings of Buddhism inspire and inform the practice of Buddhist meditation. Attending talks, reading books on Buddhist teachings, and meditating regularly work in combination with one another. As your meditation skills improve, the teachings make more sense to you — and as your understanding of Buddhism progresses, your meditation naturally deepens.

Finding a teacher

You may be able to meditate quite happily for months or years without feeling the need for a teacher. After all, with all the books on Buddhism available these days, the most profound teachings are just a click away at an online bookstore (or a few miles away at an offline bookstore). Sure, you may already consult a meditation instructor every now and then or attend an occasional talk by a Buddhist teacher, but choosing someone to guide you on your spiritual journey — now, that's another level of involvement entirely!

REMEMBER

In the various Buddhist traditions, the role of teacher takes different forms.

- **Theravada:** The Theravada tradition of Southeast Asia, for example, regards the teacher as a *kalyana-mitra* (Sanskrit: good friend, spiritual friend). Essentially, he's a fellow traveler on the path who advises you to "go a little to the left" or "head right a bit" when you veer off course. Other than providing this type of input, a teacher has no special spiritual authority, aside from the fact that he may be more experienced than you. The words *preceptor* and *mentor* may be the best everyday English equivalents to describe this teaching role.
- **Vajrayana:** In tantric traditions (Vajrayana), the spiritual teacher has considerable authority over his disciples. Instead of merely standing witness to vows, he initiates his disciples, of whom strict obedience is expected. The life stories of many Buddhist saints illustrate this special teacher-student relationship. Naropa (ca. 1016-1100), one of the 84 Mahasiddhas ("great accomplished ones"), had to suffer many hardships during the 12 years he served his teacher Tilopa (10th century). Likewise, the Tibetan yogi Milarepa (1040-1123) (see Chapter 5), founder of the Kagyu lineage, was made to undergo a series of ordeals by his teacher Marpa (1012-1096). Best known is the story of the four stone towers that Marpa ordered Milarepa to build and which Milarepa was then asked to tear down before they were completed.

  In the Tibetan traditions, teachers come in several shapes and sizes, including the following:

  - **Meditation instructors:** These teachers provide expert guidance in developing and deepening your practice. They may be monks or nuns or merely experienced lay practitioners.
  - **Lamas:** These teachers are often, but not always, monks. Lamas have extensive meditation training and accomplishment, and are revered by their disciples as the embodiment of wisdom and compassion.
  - **Geshes:** These teachers, who are usually monks, have extensive academic training and are experts in interpreting and expounding on the scriptures.

When you accept someone as your religious teacher, you're generally making a lifelong commitment. Although you can alter or terminate your involvement, developing hostility toward your teacher while you are in an active working relationship with him or her is believed to have serious negative karmic consequences.

- **Zen:** In Zen, practitioners regard the teacher or master (Japanese: *roshi;* Korean: *sunim*) as having considerable spiritual power and authority. Disciples deem the master to be enlightened, with the capacity to awaken similar realizations in students through words, gestures, and bearing. Close personal study with a Zen master is an essential component of Zen practice and training. Zen also has its meditation instructors and junior teachers — but behind them all stands the spiritual presence of the master.

Ordinarily, the teacher you choose depends on the tradition that appeals to you. But sometimes the process works the other way around — you're drawn to a teacher first, through his or her books or talks, and then you adopt the tradition the teacher represents. An ancient Indian saying makes the point, "When the student is ready, the teacher appears." You don't have to be in a hurry to find your teacher. As the saying suggests, finding the right teacher may depend more on the sincerity of your practice than on outer circumstances. Trust your intuition and your own sense of timing. In many traditions, establishing a relationship with a particular teacher precedes or accompanies the formal commitment to Buddhist practice.

WARNING!

One final word of caution: Be sure to check out a prospective teacher carefully before you officially become a student. Ask questions, do some research, and spend as much time with the teacher as possible. In recent years, several Buddhist teachers in the West, both Westerners and Asians, have engaged in unethical conduct that has had harmful consequences for their students and communities. As in all human interactions, don't give up your own good judgment and discernment.

Formally Becoming a Buddhist

REMEMBER

You don't need to declare yourself a Buddhist to enjoy and benefit from Buddhist practices and teachings. Some traditions even reserve formal initiation for individuals who choose the monastic life and simply ask laypeople to observe a few basic precepts. But the step of becoming a Buddhist can have profound personal significance, solidifying your commitment to a teacher or tradition and energizing your practice. For this reason, many people consider taking this significant step at some point or another in their involvement with Buddhism.

Focusing on the importance of renunciation

Many people associate renunciation with giving up material possessions and involvements and pursuing a life of detachment and withdrawal. But true renunciation is an internal (rather than external) movement or gesture — although it can certainly express itself in action. In many traditions, becoming a Buddhist involves the fundamental recognition that *samsaric* existence (see Chapter 13 for more information on *samsara*) — the world of getting and spending, striving and achieving, loving and hating and so forth — doesn't provide ultimate satisfaction or security.

In other words, when you commit yourself to Buddhism as a path, you don't renounce your family or your career; you renounce the conventional view that you can find true happiness in worldly concerns. You renounce the relentless message of the consumer society that the next car or house or vacation or accomplishment will finally relieve your dissatisfaction and bring you the contentment you so desperately seek.

Instead, you adopt the radical view that you can achieve lasting peace and happiness only by clearing your mind and heart of negative beliefs and emotions, penetrating to the truth of reality, opening yourself to your inherent wakefulness and joy, and experiencing what some Buddhists have called the "sure heart's release."

Taking refuge in the Three Jewels

The same 180-degree turnaround in consciousness that's necessary to formally become a Buddhist lies at the heart of many of the world's great religious traditions. For example, Jesus asked his disciples to renounce worldly concerns and follow him, and many Christian churches still require their members to acknowledge Jesus as their only salvation. In Buddhism, this turning (*metanoia,* literally "change in consciousness") often takes the form of taking refuge in the Three Jewels (or Three Treasures): the Buddha, Dharma, and Sangha. This is done by uttering the formula

> I take refuge in the Buddha.
>
> I take refuge in the Dharma.
>
> I take refuge in the Sangha.

This formula is repeated three times ("For the second time I take refuge...; for the third time I take refuge...").

In many traditional Asian countries, taking refuge defines you as a Buddhist, and laypeople recite the refuge vows whenever they visit a monastery or receive Buddhist teachings. For Western lay practitioners, the refuge ceremony has become a kind of initiation in many traditions, with far-reaching significance. Although it may simply involve the repetition of a prayer or chant, taking refuge implies that you turn to the Buddha, Dharma, and Sangha as your source of spiritual guidance and support. When you encounter dissatisfaction and suffering, you don't immediately assume that you can resolve it by making more money, taking the right antidepressant, or getting a better job — although these can be helpful to a limited degree.

You instead reflect on the example of the enlightened teacher (the Buddha, who discovered the path to a life free from suffering), find wise counsel in his teachings (known as the *Dharma* in Sanskrit and *Dhamma* in Pali), and seek support in others who share a similar orientation (the Sangha, or spiritual community). Many Buddhists repeat their refuge vows daily to remind themselves of their commitment to the Three Jewels.

The ancient collection of Buddhist sayings, the *Dhammapada*, emphasizes the special nature of the threefold refuge in verses 188 to 192:

> "Often do men, driven by fear, go for refuge to mountains and forest, to groves and sacred trees.
>
> But that is not a secure refuge, that is not the best refuge. Having gone to that refuge a man is not freed from all suffering;
>
> He who goes for refuge to the Buddha, the Dhamma and the Sangha, sees the four noble truths with clear understanding;
>
> The four noble truths: suffering, the origin of suffering, the cessation of suffering, and the noble eightfold path that leads to the quieting of suffering;
>
> That is indeed the secure refuge, that is the best refuge. Having gone to that refuge a man is freed from all suffering."

When you take refuge, you may appear to be relying on forces outside yourself for your peace of mind. But many great masters and teachers suggest that the Three Jewels are ultimately found inside you — in the inherent wakefulness and compassion of your own mind and heart, which are identical to the Buddha's.

Receiving the precepts

In addition to taking refuge, making a commitment to abide by certain ethical *precepts,* or guidelines, signifies an important step in the life of a Buddhist. Different traditions may emphasize either refuge or the precepts, but at their core, the traditions agree that both taking refuge and committing yourself to certain precepts mark a participant's entry into the Buddhist fold.

In the Theravada tradition laypeople take five precepts:

I undertake to observe the rule of training

to abstain from taking life;

to abstain from taking what is not given;

to abstain from sexual misconduct;

to abstain from false speech;

to abstain from taking intoxicants, which cloud the mind.

If you're a Vajrayana practitioner, for example, you generally formalize your involvement by taking refuge — and later by taking what are called the *bodhisattva vows,* in which you vow to put the welfare of others before your own. When you take refuge, you generally receive a Buddhist name to mark your new life as a Buddhist.

In the Zen tradition, you deepen your involvement by undergoing a ceremony in which you agree to abide by 16 precepts and receive a new name. (See Chapter 8 for more on this ceremony.) The 16 Zen precepts include the 3 refuges of the Buddha, Dharma, and Sangha, the 3 *pure precepts* and the 10 *grave precepts.*

The pure precepts are as follows:

Do not create evil.

Practice good.

Actualize good for others.

The 10 grave precepts are:

Refrain from destroying life.

Refrain from taking what is not freely given.

Refrain from sexual misconduct.

Refrain from untruthful speech.

Refrain from taking intoxicants.

Refrain from speaking of others' errors and faults.

Refrain from elevating yourself and blaming others.

Do not be stingy.

Do not give vent to anger.

Do not defile the Three Jewels of Refuge.

Interestingly enough, the Vajrayana refuge ceremony includes a commitment to act ethically, and the Zen precepts ceremony includes refuge vows. In the Theravada ceremony for becoming an *upasaka* (male lay practitioner) or an upasika (female lay practitioner), as conducted in certain communities in the West, participants ask to receive both the refuge vows and the precepts. Throughout Buddhism, refuge and precepts work hand in hand and reinforce each other.

Monks and nuns adhere to a lengthy code of conduct (the *vinaya*) that includes hundreds of regulations. (For more on following the precepts, see Chapter 12. For information on the connection between moral discipline [ethical conduct], concentration [meditation practice], and wisdom, see Chapter 13.)

Exploring further stages of practice

Traditionally, laypeople engage in devotional practices rather than in meditation. They chant and listen to religious sermons. They worship Buddha images with flowers, incense, and lights, and acquire religious merit (Sanskrit: *punya*) by making offerings to the community of monks and nuns. These can be offerings of food made to individual monks on an alms round or donations to the community. Rejoicing (Sanskrit: *anumodana*) in the merit earned by others is another way to acquire merit. (For the notion of accumulating merit, see Chapter 4).

Generosity (Sanskrit and Pali: *dana*) is one of the *perfections* of the practitioner in Theravada and Mahayana Buddhism (see Chapter 14 for these perfections). It is said that Shakyamuni practiced generosity and the other perfections for many lifetimes before attaining enlightenment. The Jataka tales of his past lives illustrate this virtue through stories in which he gives away everything, including his own body, to help others. The famous Vessantara Jataka tells the story of the last life of Shakyamuni before he became the Buddha. He was born as Prince Vessantara who attained perfection in generosity by giving away all his possessions and even his wife and two children.

REMEMBER

Although some traditions of Buddhism believe that becoming a monk or nun tends to accelerate your spiritual progress, they all agree that you can achieve the pinnacle of Buddhist practice — enlightenment — whether or not you become a monastic. In particular, the Mahayana tradition (see Chapter 4) offers compelling portraits of laymen and laywomen who were also great bodhisattvas, suggesting that you, too, can follow in their footsteps.

When you've become a Buddhist by taking refuge in the Three Jewels and receiving precepts, you devote the rest of your life to living according to these principles and teachings — not a small undertaking, by any standards! In most Zen centers, everyone in the meditation hall, both monks and laypeople, chants some version of this bodhisattva vow in the Mahayana tradition at the end of meditation:

Beings are numberless; I vow to save them.

Mental defilements are inexhaustible; I vow to put an end to them.

The teachings are boundless; I vow to master them.

The Buddha's way is unsurpassable; I vow to attain it.

With these kinds of promises to inspire your meditation, you definitely have your life's work cut out for you. By setting your sights on lofty goals like compassion, selflessness, equanimity, and ultimately, enlightenment, you commit yourself to a lifetime of spiritual practice and development.

Of course, you're welcome to terminate your involvement in Buddhism at any time without karmic repercussions — other than those that may reverberate through your own mind and heart. (In the Vajrayana, after you become deeply involved with a teacher, forsaking your vows gets a bit more complicated.) In fact, in Southeast Asia, especially in Thailand, it's customary and considered spiritually beneficial for laymen and laywomen (and sometimes children) to shave their heads and become monks or nuns for a few days, weeks, or months. After practicing in the monastic community briefly, they give back their robes and return to ordinary, everyday life — indelibly changed by their experience!

Entering the Monastic Way

In a number of the world's great religious traditions, the monk or nun stands as the embodiment of the spiritual ideal — the one who has given up all worldly attachments and devoted his or her life to the highest pursuits. Although Buddhism acknowledges the merit of lay practice, it, too, has traditionally placed the highest value on the acts of shaving the head, taking the full monastic vows, and entering a monastic community.

People are drawn to monastic practice for the same reasons they're attracted to Buddhism in the first place: the desire to eliminate suffering, benefit other beings, and achieve ultimate clarity and peace. Add to this mix a certain distaste for (or downright abhorrence of) conventional worldly life, and you have a good feel for the monastic impulse. Stephan's first Zen teacher used to say, "Monasteries are places for desperate people." Stephan knew exactly what he meant by this. (Of course, in some Asian countries, men and women become monks and nuns for other reasons as well, such as to escape worldly obligations, fulfill parental wishes, and so on.)

Renouncing the world

When you take monastic ordination, you leave behind the comfort and familiarity of family and friends and enter an entirely new world where the old rules no longer apply. You give external expression to your inner renunciation by cutting off your hair (a mark of personal beauty and pride), giving up your favorite clothes, and letting go of your prized possessions. (Compare these acts with Shakyamuni Buddha's own renunciation, which we describe in Chapter 3.) In essence, you strip yourself of the signs of your individuality and merge with the monastic collective, where everyone wears the same robe, sports the same haircut, sleeps on the same thin mat, and eats what is offered to sustain the body.

In the time of the Buddha (and in the traditions that continued to adhere to the full monastic code — the *vinaya*), monks and nuns were prohibited from handling or soliciting money and were allowed to own just a few simple belongings, which included items like several robes, a bowl, a razor, and an umbrella for protection from the sun. They took vows of celibacy, ate only before noon, and received their food from laypeople, either during alms rounds or through offerings brought to the monastery. The point of these regulations wasn't to cause hardship or suffering; in fact, the Buddha's approach was known as the "middle way" between asceticism (severe restrictions in the comforts of life) and materialism. Instead, the point was to free the monastics to dedicate their life to practice and teaching.

The vinaya regulations, which the Theravada tradition of Southeast Asia still follows, have been adapted somewhat in other traditions, such as Zen and Vajrayana. For example, in Japan (home to the Zen tradition), the priest, who has largely replaced the monk, trains for a period of months or years and then returns to his home temple to marry, raise a family, and serve the lay community. In Tibetan Buddhism, some lineages emphasize full monasticism (although they're not nearly as rigorous in their interpretation of the monastic code as their Theravada counterparts), but others encourage sincere seekers to combine married life and dedicated spiritual practice.

Ordaining as a monk or nun

The ceremony of ordaining as a monk or nun is a solemn and auspicious occasion marking the participant's entry into an order that dates back 2,500 years. In the West, ordination generally occurs as the culmination of years of practice as a layperson, although some people bolt from the starting gate like thoroughbred horses and head full speed for the monastery.

If you want to receive ordination, you must first ask a senior monk — often, though not always, your current spiritual teacher — for permission. Then you obtain the required robes, shave your head (in some traditions, you keep a lock to be shaved off during the ceremony itself), and set your life in order. During the ceremony, you recite the refuge vows and receive the appropriate number of precepts, depending on the level of your ordination and the tradition you follow (see Figure 6-1).

For example, there are 16 precepts (including the three refuges) in the Zen tradition (listed in the "Receiving the precepts" section, earlier in the chapter), 36 vows for the novice nun in the Vajrayana tradition, and 227 vows for the fully ordained monk in the Theravada tradition, just to name a few. After taking refuge and receiving precepts, you assume a new name (which, when translated into English, often expresses some aspect of the Buddhist path, such as "stainless love," "pure mind of patience," "holder of the teachings," and so on). At that point, you've crossed from one world into another and your life as a monastic begins.

Figure 6-1: The ordination of monks in the Theravada tradition.

Photo courtesy of Janejira Sutanonpaiboon.

Dedicating your life to Buddhist practice

If you enter a Buddhist monastery, you do so because you're eager to devote all your time and energy to the practice and realization of the teachings. To accomplish your goals, you rise early, day after day, and follow a routine consisting exclusively of meditation, chanting, ritual, study, teaching, and work. You may have limited contact with the outside world (generally, monasteries are more open to lay practitioners at certain times of the year than at others), but for the most part, you turn your attention inward, toward spiritual matters. (For a detailed description of life in a Western Theravada monastery, see Chapter 8.)

In both their structure and purpose, Buddhist monasteries resemble their Christian counterparts. Western Buddhist monks have even become interested in the Rule of Saint Benedict, the official code that has governed Catholic and Anglican monasteries for centuries. And a Carmelite (Catholic) monk and Zen practitioner Stephan knows said that he felt right at home in a Zen monastery. Whether the goal is to get closer to God or experience enlightenment, monasteries throughout the world have a remarkably similar role to play — they're places where men and women get to dedicate themselves wholeheartedly to truth.

Women in Buddhism

Like many religions, both Eastern and Western, Buddhism has traditionally failed to give women equal status with men. Buddhists over the centuries more or less mimicked the attitudes of their respective cultures, where women have traditionally been regarded as inferior and subservient. (The historical record does show that, despite the rampant sexism of the times, certain women emerged as accomplished yoginis — female practitioners of yoga — and masters. Check out the story of Dipa Ma, an Indian meditation teacher, in chapter 15.)

According to tradition, the Buddha created the female monastic order at the request of Mahaprajapati Gautami, his foster mother, and his disciple Ananda. But the full monastic ordination for women (Sanskrit: *bhikshuni;* Pali: *bhikkhuni*) died out on the Indian subcontinent. It has survived only in certain Mahayana countries (including China, Korea, and Vietnam). Instead, women in the Theravada tradition like that of Myanmar who seek to practice as nuns receive ten precepts, as well as numerous other more informal regulations.

In recent decades, however, Western women Buddhists of every persuasion have strongly criticized the institutional sexism and required their teachers and communities to recognize their full equality. The result has been the rapid emergence of women as powerful practitioners, scholars, and teachers (see the following figure of Tibetan Buddhist nuns at study). Clearly, Western Buddhists, like their Eastern ancestors, are adapting to the culture of their times. (See Appendix B for a list of books that deal with the topic of women in Buddhism.)

(continued)

(continued)

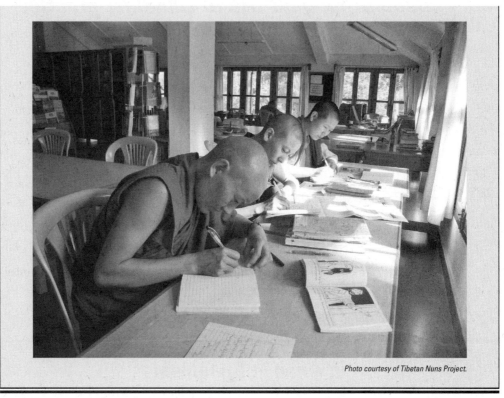

Photo courtesy of Tibetan Nuns Project.

Chapter 7

Meditation: A Central Practice of Buddhism

In This Chapter

- Tossing out misconceptions about meditation
- Finding out what meditation is really all about and how it can help you
- Concentrating on the three aspects of meditation
- Getting wise to the three kinds of wisdom

As part of their religious training, Buddhists around the world engage in a variety of different activities — from reciting prayers and studying religious texts to worshipping an image of the Buddha.

But of all the different activities you can think of, many people identify one in particular as typically Buddhist: meditation. Although not all people who call themselves Buddhists meditate — or make it part of the everyday routine that we describe in Chapter 8 — meditation is an important practice in Buddhism.

But what exactly is meditation and what can you accomplish with it? Well, we're glad you asked. In this chapter, we look into this practice more closely and try to show you why and how meditation plays such a central role in Buddhism.

Dispelling Some Meditation Myths

Because people have a lot of mistaken ideas about what it means to meditate, we want to deal with some of them right off the bat. Consider the following:

- **Meditation doesn't mean spacing out.** Many people — including quite a few Buddhists, we're afraid to say — think that meditation is some kind of vacation from reality. All you have to do is sit back, close your eyes, and let your mind drift away to never-never land. But if meditation consisted of simply letting your mind roam freely, this world would be home to a lot more highly accomplished meditators than currently occupy it. Allowing your mind to drift this way and that doesn't do anything but further ingrain whatever bad mental habits you already have.
- **The goal of meditation isn't to have your mind go completely blank, to stop thinking entirely.** Although you do eventually want to identify and eliminate certain types of distorted thinking (if you want to alleviate your suffering), as a beginner, you can't hope to simply switch off your mind like you turn off a light switch. Any attempt to do this is bound to leave you feeling frustrated.
- **Meditation isn't something you can do only while sitting down.** Although certain practices (which we describe in Chapter 8) are best done in a seated position, you can do others while standing, walking, or even lying down. (You need to be careful about using this last posture, however. What starts out as meditation can easily turn into sleep.)

Meditation objects for personality types

The fifth-century Theravada authority Buddhaghosa systematized teachings on Buddhist meditation in his classic *Visuddhimagga (Path to Purity)*. In this influential work, he classified 40 different meditation objects as suitable for different human temperaments (Chapter 2, sections 74–103 and 121–122).

The six personality types are those dominated by one of the following:

- Greed
- Aversion
- Delusion
- Faith
- Intelligence
- Speculation

The meditation teacher determines a person's temperament by the student's posture, his way of moving his body, his eating habits, other forms of behavior, and his mental states. Consider some examples of matching temperament with meditation objects:

- Meditating on the four divine abodes (see Chapter 14), for the student in whom aversion predominates.
- Meditating on repulsive things, such as the ten aspects of a decomposing corpse, for the person dominated by greed and lust.
- Meditating on the recollection of the Buddha, Dharma, and Sangha, and the recollection of good conduct, of generosity, and of the gods, for the faith-dominated person.

Defining Meditation

Meditation is a rather broad term. It denotes diverse techniques and methods developed to calm, fashion, understand, and release the mind. Thus it is usually practiced to attain specific aims, including the following:

- Mental tranquility or purification
- Insight into a religious truth
- The visualization or construction of a special perception.

Meditation techniques are found in many religious traditions, but their specifics differ with their associated belief systems. The importance of meditation in Eastern religious traditions has been overrated. (Meditation plays no significant role, for example, in Japanese Amida Buddhism.) Traditionally, Buddhist meditation is viewed as a means of attaining liberation, not as a stress-reduction technique or a form of therapy. Accordingly, it is practiced along these lines:

- Mostly by a few monks and nuns, who usually live a reclusive lifestyle
- As part of a larger system of religious beliefs and (in Vajrayana, highly ritualized) religious practices
- In intensive retreats lasting several weeks or months

Some Buddhist teachers taught that not every type of meditation is appropriate for everyone. In the Theravada Buddhist manual *Visuddhimagga (Path to Purity),* Buddhaghosa (ca. 370–450) recommended different objects of meditation for different types of individuals, depending on their predisposition (see the sidebar "Meditation objects for personality types," in this chapter). Regardless of the object, meditation is traditionally practiced in Buddhism to purify the mind, attain insight into the Buddhist truths, and ultimately, gain liberation from cyclic existence (samsara) for oneself (in Theravada) or for all beings (in Mahayana). Mental health as defined by mainstream psychology and psychoanalysis is not the purpose of meditation. This fact needs to be stressed because, in the last decades, the adaptation of Buddhist or Hindu spiritual practices in the West has generated a larger number of methods and techniques referred to as "meditation." These modern techniques have the following characteristics:

- Usually have separated from their original religious moorings
- Reportedly benefit everyone in the same way, regardless of religious beliefs
- Have been simplified to fit the modern lifestyle of the general public and thus usually ignore preparatory measures (including lifestyle changes and the observance of precepts) that were considered necessary preconditions for meditation training in Asia

Performing a balancing act

The Buddha once compared meditation to playing a stringed instrument. (You can think of a guitar, although the Buddha used an Indian lute, a vina, in his analogy.) If the strings are too loose, you can't get them to make any sound. If they're too tight, they may break when you play them.

In the same way, the mind in meditation shouldn't be too relaxed, which can lead to sleepiness, or too tight, which can make the body tense and uncomfortable and the mind itself more agitated. Instead, find a natural balance between alertness and relaxation. Then meditation will proceed easily and gracefully.

The modern techniques are usually promoted to do the following:

- Reduce anxiety and stress (that is, stabilize awareness)
- Induce relaxation (that means, enhance awareness
- Develop human potential (that is, expand awareness)

REMEMBER

The remaining parts of this chapter introduce you to some aspects of Buddhist meditation practice. In an effort to make the complex material more accessible, we present it in a somewhat simplified form, using modern terminology.

Exploring the Benefits of Meditation

In a less conventional way, we present meditation as a method for transforming your view of reality or for getting in touch with parts of yourself that you didn't previously know about. Meditation can also be considered as a method for getting to know your own mind. But why do it? "Wouldn't it be easier," you may think, "just to leave my mind alone? I've managed to muddle my way through to this point by simply letting what happens happen, so why interfere now?"

The Buddha addressed these doubts by comparing the ordinary mind — that is, the mind of ordinary, unenlightened beings — with a mad elephant. In ancient times, when wild elephants were common in India, this image made perfect sense to the Buddha's disciples; even today, many villagers have firsthand experience of the extensive destruction an enraged elephant can cause. But the mind that operates under the influence of poisons such as hatred and greed is even more destructive than a whole herd of temperamental elephants. Not only can it trample the happiness of your present life, but it also can destroy your happiness in countless future lives. The solution to this problem? You need to do something to tame the mad-elephant mind, and that something is meditation.

Examining how neuroscientists see it

For several decades, scientists have tried to study and measure the therapeutic benefits of meditation. Earlier clinical studies have mainly focused on Transcendental Meditation (TM) and Zen meditation. These studies are often flawed, in that they do not clearly define the nature of the meditation technique they examine, so they conclude that different techniques produce the same result. In addition, proponents of certain forms of meditation have conducted or sponsored certain studies themselves, so those studies, in particular, need to be treated skeptically.

Examining the benefits and possible adverse effects of meditation on individuals is a complex task. Bear in mind that different meditation techniques are likely to produce different results. Moreover, these results vary depending on an individual's predisposition and lifestyle, as well as the intensity and setting of the practice. Also keep in mind that when individuals take Buddhist or Hindu forms of meditation out of their traditional religious and philosophical context, and practice them without any preparation, they likely get different results than individuals who practice them in traditional settings. Regardless of these issues, most scientific studies of meditation have stressed the beneficial effects of the techniques, such as increased relaxation, concentration, mental alertness, and emotional control.

More recently, neuroscientists have begun to investigate Buddhist meditation. Although still in its infancy, the neuroscientific study of meditation is already showing interesting results. Richard J. Davidson, Professor of Psychology and Psychiatry at the University of Wisconsin–Madison and Director of the Laboratory for Affective Neuroscience and Waisman Laboratory for Brain Imaging and Behavior, has been examining the changes that regular meditation practice may cause in brain function. He is specifically focusing on the impact meditation has on the brain activity of practitioners of Tibetan Buddhist meditation who have completed years of intensive training (see Figure 7-1). Using brain mapping and functional Magnetic Resonance Imaging (fMRI) technology, Davidson's research demonstrates that circuits in the brain that are important in regulating attention and emotion are transformed during specific types of meditation practice. In addition, some of these circuits appear to continue to function differently in the baseline state (when one is not practicing formal meditation). The larger implications of Davidson's research are that meditation practice can alter circuits in the brain that are important for enhancing such positive qualities as equanimity and compassion. These qualities can apparently be strengthened through training that affects the brain and behavior. During practices designed to cultivate compassion, specific changes occur in brain networks that have been shown to be linked with empathy.

Researchers at other institutions are also conducting studies. Jonathan Cohen, Professor of Psychology and Codirector of the Princeton Neuroscience Institute at Princeton University, is focusing on the beneficial results of mindfulness meditation. Dr. Margaret Kemeny and Paul Ekman of the University of California at San Francisco are heading the research project "Cultivating Emotional Balance," which studies ways to reduce "destructive" emotional responses and enhance compassion and empathy through meditation.

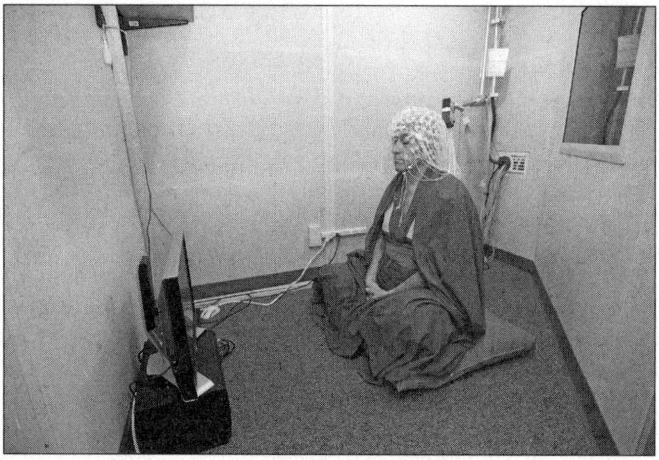

Figure 7-1: Monk undergoing brain electrical activity measurement during meditation.

Photo courtesy of Jeff Miller/University of Wisconsin-Madison.

Recognizing the condition you're in

To appreciate the value of meditation, you must check to see how your mind is operating right now. A lengthy investigation likely isn't necessary for you to realize that your mind has been subjected to some pretty heavy influences in the past. These influences have shaped your attitude, conditioning you to react to the events in your life in certain set ways. Unless you've already attained a high degree of spiritual realization, this conditioning — much of it negative — is still affecting you. (By *spiritual realization,* we mean the freedom that comes from penetrating your conditioning to the peace and clarity that lie beneath.)

For example, just think about the way your surroundings constantly bombard you with gross and subliminal messages about how you should think and behave. You walk into a store, and some super-new-and-improved-electro-thingamajig seems to jump off the shelf and demand that you buy it. Suddenly you feel that if you don't purchase that product right away, your life will be incomplete. Where did that "got to have it" impulse come from? Would you say that this kind of reaction is a spontaneous expression of your basic makeup? Is it a natural expression of your mind's fundamental purity?

Or is it a habitual response conditioned by the hours of advertising you've been exposed to?

Here's a completely different example. You see a stranger in the distance, and even though you know nothing about him and he's done nothing to you, you instantly dislike him. You may feel so uncomfortable just looking at him that your muscles begin to tense, as if you're preparing for a fight. Again, ask yourself where that aggressive impulse comes from. Is it a natural, freely arising response to some objectively real threat the stranger poses? Or does his complexion and overall appearance just happen to fit the profile of some ethnic group that you've learned to fear or identify as a potential enemy?

Some forms of conditioning, such as advertising and political propaganda, are relatively easy to identify. Other forms, such as those you were subjected to in early childhood ("You're a terrible child; you can't do anything right!"), are more difficult to recognize. Still other forms of conditioning — those that may have left their imprint on your mind in a previous lifetime — may be completely beyond your ability to recall, at least for the moment. But all these forms of conditioning shape your mind in some way. They all exert a long-lasting influence on what you do, say, and think.

REMEMBER

One of the many benefits of meditation is that it helps "deprogram" the effects of conditioning by cultivating equanimity (Pali: *upekkha*). After you recognize that you tend to react to certain situations in a way that only increases your anxiety and discomfort, you'll be motivated to neutralize as many of these damaging influences as you can. In place of the greed, hatred, ignorance, and other delusions that have shaped your responses in the past, you can choose to familiarize yourself with positive, productive states of mind, such as contentment, patience, loving-kindness, compassion, and wisdom.

WORDS OF WISDOM

Buddhist masters are fond of reminding their students that the mind can be either their worst enemy or their best friend. When you allow it to run wild, like a mad elephant, goaded by ignorant conditioning and distorted thinking, your mind is your worst enemy. But when you tame your mind and work to get past negative patterns to reach the more beneficial states of mind beneath — that is, by meditating — your mind becomes your best friend.

Cultivating equanimity

One of the first lessons you discover from meditation is how to keep yourself from responding to situations in a knee-jerk fashion — or, in Buddhist terms, how to cultivate equanimity. This accomplishment may not seem earth shattering, but it's really enormously valuable.

Maybe you have an annoying person in your life, someone you have to encounter repeatedly. (We'll call him Pat. If you find it more helpful to think of this annoying person as a woman, just switch the following pronouns from masculine to feminine.) Pat may be a family member, neighbor, co-worker, or just someone you run into on the street every day. But whoever he is, he generally rubs you the wrong way. It may be something he does or says, his tone of voice, or simply the way he looks. Or maybe he once said or did something so gross and disgusting that you can't think of him without being reminded of it. Or maybe you don't have the slightest idea why you find Pat so annoying — you just do.

The first order of business is to be clear about whether the way you react to Pat is creating a problem for you. After all, if nothing's wrong, you have nothing to fix. Simply being annoyed isn't much of a problem; after all, life is full of petty annoyances. But if you feel the uncontrollable urge to kick Pat in the shins every time you see him, you probably agree that a problem needs fixing. Simple annoyance has escalated to anger and even to hatred. Even if you manage to keep your hostility under wraps, you're still seething with anger and resentment on the inside, and you still have a problem that you definitely need to take care of before it eats you alive.

So how do you take care of hostility? Not by acting out — that only makes matters worse. If you're committed to the Buddhist approach, you've realized that the only effective way to change any situation for the better is by working first and foremost on yourself. As long as your own emotional response to a situation remains unchanged, whatever you do about the target of your negativity won't solve the underlying problem.

Turning an old phrase upside down: Don't do something — just sit there

When you're trying to work on your own mind so that you can handle difficult situations more effectively, one of the hardest decisions is figuring when to respond to these situations and when to do nothing. To return to good ol' annoying Pat, when he's pushing all your buttons, you have to decide whether you're going to confront him directly and try to resolve the conflict between the two of you, or whether you're going to refrain from responding to him at all. Each situation you face is unique, and no exact answers point to which choice is best. But to have any chance of making a wise choice, you can't simply follow your old habits blindly. When you give in to your accustomed frustration and anger, you lose the opportunity to respond with clarity and wisdom.

Meditation gives you a way to sidestep your old destructive habits. As you discover how to tame your mind through meditation, a time will come when you can deal peacefully with difficult situations *as they unfold.* In the beginning, however, this feat is virtually impossible to accomplish. You get too caught up in what's happening to act objectively or skillfully. So what's the best strategy, at least at first, to deal with difficult and stressful situations?

Do nothing. If you can avoid encountering Pat, that's great. But if meeting him is inevitable, try to put up with the annoyance as best you can, without reacting to it.

Preparing the groundwork

TIP

Although not reacting to a difficult situation may offer a short-term solution to your problem, the only truly effective long-lasting solution *begins* before you run into the problem. That's the best time to cultivate equanimity and prepare yourself for dealing skillfully with whatever you might encounter. Enter meditation.

Before you leave your room in the morning, spend a few minutes sitting quietly by yourself, allowing your mind to settle down. (See Figure 7-2 for an example of a comfortable meditation posture.) When you're ready, imagine that you're encountering the anger-provoking situation (your good buddy, annoying Pat, for example) later that day. Picture the encounter as vividly as you can in your mind's eye. Imagine him doing whatever he generally does to set you off. Then — this part requires quite a bit of practice at first — step back from the situation and simply observe what's going on. Look at the annoying person as if you were seeing him for the first time, almost as if you were watching a documentary about someone you'd never met. Notice the expressions on his face, the words and phrases he uses, his actions, and so on. Think of this process as taking an inventory, noting what you find without making any judgments.

Figure 7-2: Sitting meditation posture.

Photo courtesy of Jay Carroll/JFoto.com.

Then in a similarly objective manner, take a look at your own reactions as if observing them from the outside — as if someone else had taken your place in the encounter. Check out how you're feeling, what you're thinking, how you're responding. Be as objective as possible, like a scientist who sets up an experiment and then steps back to observe what happens.

This type of observation requires a real balancing act. You have to figure out how to alternate between two different states of mind. To begin, you have to imagine your annoying encounter vividly enough that you can react realistically within it, with feeling, as if the scene were actually happening. You're not pretending to react; you're actually re-creating your typical reactions, but on a reduced scale. Because these reactions arise in a safe, controlled environment — inside your own meditation — you're protected from creating the kind of negativity that confronting Pat in the flesh usually brings.

But as the encounter plays out in your meditation, find a corner of your mind that's not caught up in the reactions stemming from the encounter. Use this calm vantage point to observe, as dispassionately as you can, what's happening. Jon's meditation teachers compare this corner of the mind to a spy in wartime. (Some Buddhist traditions call it the *witness,* the *observer,* or simply *mindful awareness.*) The spy isn't involved in the conflict; he or she inconspicuously stays on the sidelines and simply observes what's happening on the battlefield. You may be surprised to discover that you have the capacity to observe what's happening to you without getting caught up in the action — but you do. And the more you use this capacity, the stronger it becomes — kind of like a muscle.

Changing your perspective

When you discover how to switch comfortably between the main part of your mind that re-creates the experience — in this case, the experience of an annoying encounter with the tiresome Pat — and the corner of your mind that merely observes your reactions, you can proceed in a number of different ways.

- **Experiment with different ways of viewing the situation.** Instead of seeing Pat from only your own limited perspective, try to see him through another's eyes. Someone probably thinks that Pat is a pretty good guy. Try observing *that* Pat for a while and see how your reactions to him begin to change. You may even have liked Pat in the past; if so, try to recall a time when you felt friendly toward him.

  By focusing on this kinder and friendlier version of Pat, you can start to discover positive traits in your adversary that you either forgot about or never noticed. With this discovery, your vision of Pat will start to lighten up a bit, your concrete view of him as nothing but an annoying person will begin to dissolve, and you'll notice that your own negative reactions to him will become less intense. This accomplishment opens up the possibility that your relationship with Pat may evolve over time. The two of you may even become best friends (but don't hold your breath waiting for *that* to happen). Yet even if you and Pat don't become bosom buddies overnight, at least you won't have as serious a problem with him anymore.

- **Focus less of your attention on the problem and more of your attention on your reactions to it.** Pat annoys you. That's a problem. And this annoyance probably feels quite concrete — like a lump in your chest. But as you observe this feeling more closely, you may notice that the annoyance isn't nearly as substantial as it first appeared. Like all feelings, it arises in your mind, stays there for a short time, and then subsides. There's nothing solid or concrete about it. If you don't remind yourself how much you dislike Pat, that annoying feeling will fade by itself. Experiencing the insubstantial, fleeting nature of your feelings will keep you from buying into them as strongly as you once did. This recognition alone will alleviate much of the difficulty in your relationship.

Did you notice that neither of these two approaches attempts to change Pat in any way? Instead, they change your own viewpoints and reactions. You don't have to completely forget about Pat. If he's doing something harmful and you know a skillful, effective way to help him change his behavior, go for it. But you can't count on that. The only area you definitely have power over is your own reaction, so that's what meditation seeks to work on.

Buddhist teachings offer many different methods for changing the way you look at situations so that you can reduce your discomfort, develop skillful ways to deal with difficult situations, open your heart to others, and sharpen your wisdom. We share some of these meditation techniques throughout this book, where they're appropriate. But all these techniques have certain qualities in common. They help you to

- Be more flexible and creative in how you handle potentially difficult situations
- Let go of old habit patterns that keep you trapped in dissatisfaction and frustration

Appreciating your life

Meditation has numerous other benefits. Many of these benefits involve showing up for your life with greater awareness and presence, which lets you find more enjoyment and develop a greater appreciation for other people and circumstances.

The following list details a few of these additional benefits. For more about the benefits and practice of meditation, check out *Meditation For Dummies,* 2nd Edition, by Stephan Bodian (Wiley), from which we've adapted this list.

- **Awakening to the present moment:** Meditation teaches you to slow down and take each moment as it comes.
- **Making friends with yourself:** When you meditate, you find out how to welcome every experience and facet of your being without judgment or denial.
- **Connecting more deeply with others:** As you awaken to the present moment and open your heart and mind to your own experience, you naturally extend this quality of awareness and presence to your relationships with family and friends.
- **Relaxing the body and calming the mind:** As the mind settles and relaxes during meditation, the body follows suit. And the longer you meditate (measured both in minutes logged each day and in days and weeks of regular practice), the more this peace and relaxation ripples out to every area of your life, including your health.
- **Lightening up:** Meditation enables you to find an open space in your mind in which difficulties and concerns no longer seem so threatening and constructive solutions naturally arise.
- **Enjoying more happiness:** Research has shown that daily meditation for just a few months can make people happier, as measured not only by their subjective reports, but also by brain-mapping technology. (For more on meditation research, see the section "Examining how neuroscientists see it," in this chapter).
- **Experiencing focus and flow:** Through meditation, you can discover how to give every activity the same enjoyable, focused attention that you currently give only to peak moments like playing a sport or making love.
- **Feeling more centered, grounded, and balanced:** To counter the fears and insecurities of life in rapidly changing times, meditation offers a sense of inner stability and balance that external circumstances can't destroy.
- **Enhancing performance at work and play:** Studies have shown that basic meditation practice alone can enhance perceptual clarity, creativity, self-actualization, and many other factors that contribute to superior performance.
- **Increasing appreciation, gratitude, and love:** As you begin to open to your experience without judgment or aversion, your heart gradually opens as well — to yourself and others.
- **Aligning with a deeper sense of purpose:** When you welcome your experience in meditation, you may find yourself connecting with a deeper current of meaning and belonging.
- **Awakening to a spiritual dimension of being:** As your meditation gradually opens you to the subtlety and richness of each fleeting but irreplaceable moment, you may naturally begin to see through the veil of distorted perceptions and beliefs to the deeper reality that lies beneath.

Understanding the Threefold Nature of Buddhist Meditation

The example we use earlier in this chapter of how to manage your feelings when confronted by a difficult situation emphasizes letting go of old habits and viewing the situation in a new way. The example also involves, as a starting point at least, not buying into your accustomed reactions and, instead, sitting back and "doing nothing" (that is, not reacting).

But the Buddhist teachings offer many other methods besides simply doing nothing. In Buddhism, the practice of meditation basically involves three separate but interrelated aspects or skills: mindful awareness, concentration, and insight. Though the various traditions differ somewhat in the techniques they use to develop these skills, they generally agree that mindful awareness, concentration, and insight work hand in hand and that all three are essential if you want to attain the goal of *spiritual realization* (see the section "Recognizing the condition you're in," earlier in this chapter).

Distinguishing between analytical and intuitive meditation

The great Tibetan Buddhist master Kalu Rinpoche (1905–1989) makes a useful distinction between two types of meditation — analytical and intuitive. In *analytical meditation,* you use your conceptual mind to examine and validate the teachings you receive. You can think of this approach as preparing your mind for the deeper levels of meditation by eliminating any doubts you may have and clarifying your intellectual understanding. Analytical meditation may also take the form of exploring your habitual patterns of behavior and reactivity and finding more beneficial alternatives. (Check out the section "Changing your perspective," in this chapter, for more info on this type of meditation.) But to experience the truth about reality directly, you need to advance to the second kind of meditation.

In *intuitive meditation,* you stop searching and exploring with your conceptual mind and open your awareness so that reality can reveal its nature to you. The experience is immediate, in the sense that the mind doesn't mediate your contact with reality. Instead, you have a direct insight into the way things are that can't be reduced to conceptual terms. Mindfulness meditation (see the section "Developing mindful awareness," in this chapter), sitting meditation (zazen) as practiced by students of Zen and the blend of "calm abiding" and insight practiced in the Tibetan tradition are, for the most part, forms of intuitive meditation.

Developing mindful awareness

Before you can penetrate the layers of conditioning and see clearly and deeply into the nature of existence, your mind needs to settle down enough to make such insight possible. This part of the process is where two of the three key components of Buddhist meditation come in handy: mindful awareness and concentration.

To get a better idea of how mindful awareness (often called simply mindfulness) operates, consider the popular Buddhist metaphor of the forest pool. If wind and rain constantly batter the pool, the water will tend to be agitated and cloudy with sediment and organic debris, and you won't be able to see all the way down to the bottom. But you can't calm the pool by manipulating the water. Any attempts to do so will merely cause more agitation and add to the problem. The only way to clear the water is to sit patiently, watching the pool, and wait for the sediment to settle by itself.

This patient, diligent attention is known as *mindful awareness* and is one of the cornerstones of Buddhist meditation. The Buddha taught four foundations, or applications, of mindfulness (Pali: *satipatthana*):

- Mindfulness of the body
- Mindfulness of feelings or sensations
- Mindfulness of the mind
- Mindfulness of psychic factors (dharma) that lead to bondage or release

When you're mindful, you're simply paying "bare attention" to whatever you're experiencing right now — thoughts, feelings, sensations, images, fleeting fantasies, passing moods — without judgment, interpretation, or analysis.

Most of the time, you edit and comment on your experience: "I don't like what I'm hearing." "I wish she would act differently." "I must be a horrible person to have such negative thoughts." But mindfulness meditation invites you to welcome your experience just the way it is — and if you do resist, judge, or attach meaning to your experience, you can be mindfully aware of that as well!

Beginning practitioners of mindfulness meditation generally start by paying attention to the coming and going of their breath (see the sidebar "Mindfulness of the breath: A basic Buddhist meditation," in this chapter, for more details). Over time, you gradually expand your awareness, first to your physical sensations, then to your feelings, and finally to the contents of your mind. Eventually, you may graduate to "just sitting," also known as *choiceless awareness,* in which your mind is open and expansive and you welcome whatever arises without selectively picking and choosing certain experiences to focus on.

Buddhists are generally encouraged to practice mindfulness throughout their day, in every activity (although mindfulness is especially cultivated on the meditation cushion or chair). Whether driving your car in traffic, waiting in line at the bank, picking up your kids at school, talking with a friend, or washing the dishes, you can be mindful of your feelings, sensations, and thoughts wherever you are and within whatever situation you find yourself. Mindful awareness has the added benefit of making life more enjoyable — the more you show up for your life, the more you appreciate it.

Deepening concentration

The more mindful you are, the more your concentration naturally strengthens and deepens, an additional benefit of mindfulness. If ordinary, everyday awareness resembles a 100-watt light bulb, concentration is like a floodlight or, if you finely hone and focus it, a laser beam. You may already be aware of moments in your daily life when your concentration naturally focuses and deepens — like when you're playing a sport, making love, or watching a riveting movie on TV. When you concentrate, you tend to become absorbed in what you're doing — so much so, in fact, that you may lose all self-consciousness and merge with the activity itself.

Many traditions of Buddhism encourage the development of focused concentration because it gives the mind the power to penetrate deeply into the object of meditation. Some Buddhist texts describe four levels of increasing meditative absorption, called the *jhanas* in Pali. In the Theravada tradition of South and Southeast Asia, monks and nuns are sometimes taught to advance through the jhanas until their concentration is so powerful (and their minds so calm) that they can use it to peer deeply into the waters of reality. (For more on the forest pool metaphor, see the section "Developing mindful awareness," earlier in the chapter.)

The Theravada meditation tradition as it's often practiced in the West puts less emphasis on the absorptions (jhanas), perhaps because most teachers never learned the method from their Asian teachers. The mind states encountered in the jhanas (including bliss, joy, and delight) can be so enjoyable and seductive that meditators sometimes get stuck at that level and lose interest in developing insight.

Whether or not you practice the absorptions, concentration can lend power to whatever meditative technique you're practicing. In some Vajrayana traditions, meditators learn the concentration practice known as *calm abiding,* which helps make the mind peaceful and clear (like a calm pool of water) and allows deeper penetration, or insight, to take place. Ultimately, the Vajrayana practitioners consider true meditation to be the union of this calm abiding and insight.

Developing penetrating insight

After you develop your mindfulness and deepen your concentration, you can turn your attention to reality itself. The earliest stages of meditation have definite benefits (as the section "Exploring the Benefits of Meditation," earlier in this chapter, explains), but this final stage — insight, or wisdom — lies at the heart of all Buddhist traditions.

After all, the Buddha didn't teach stress-reduction or performance-enhancement techniques. Instead, he taught a complete path leading to unsurpassable happiness and peace. To reach this noble goal, you need to experience a life-changing insight into the fundamental nature of who you are and how life functions. (Needless to say, stress reduction and performance enhancements have their own considerable relative value.) For a more detailed treatment of this life-changing insight, see Chapter 13.

Here we simply want to point out that the various Buddhist traditions differ in the methods they recommend for achieving insight and even in the contents of the insight itself.

Mindfulness of the breath: A basic Buddhist meditation

Begin by finding a quiet place where you won't be disturbed by interruptions or loud noises for 20 minutes or longer.

Set aside your preoccupations and concerns for the moment and sit down in a position that's comfortable for you. You may choose to sit cross-legged on a cushion in traditional Asian fashion or on a straight-backed or ergonomic chair. Whatever position you choose, be sure to keep your spine relatively erect (yet relaxed) so you can breathe easily and freely.

Now gently rest your attention on the coming and going of your breath. Some traditions recommend focusing on the sensation of the breath as it enters and leaves your nostrils; others prefer to focus on the rising and falling of your belly as you breathe. Whatever you choose to concentrate on, stick with it for the full meditation period. Be aware of the subtle changes and shifts in your sensations as you breathe in and out. When your mind wanders off (daydreaming or fixated thinking), gently bring your awareness back to your breath.

Don't try to stop thinking — thoughts and feelings will naturally come and go as you meditate. But remain uninvolved with them as much as possible. Enjoy the simple experience of breathing in and breathing out.

After 15 or 20 minutes, slowly move your body, stand up, and resume your everyday activities.

Resting in the nature of mind

After you become adept at mindfulness and have some insight into the way things are, you can practice the approach known as "just sitting" in Zen or as "resting in the nature of mind" in the Vajrayana tradition. Paradoxically, this technique involves the absence of all technique and mind manipulation of any kind. The Tibetans use terms like *nonmeditation* and *noncontrivance.* It's actually an advanced technique generally reserved for experienced meditators, but some teachers in the West teach it primarily, and many Westerners with some spiritual sophistication seem eager to learn it.

To rest in the nature of mind, you must have direct experience of this mind-nature, which is usually transmitted from teacher to student. In Zen, just sitting *(shikantaza)* is often described as expressing your innate Buddha nature without trying to achieve or understand anything. Because this approach requires the guidance of a teacher, we refer to it but don't attempt to teach it in this book.

- In the insight (vipassana) meditation often taught in the Theravada tradition, you discover that reality (you included) is marked by impermanence, dissatisfaction, and the absence of an abiding, substantial self.
- In the Vajrayana tradition, you recognize the vast, open, and luminous quality of the entire phenomenal world.
- In Zen, you awaken to your true nature, which is variously described as the Buddha nature, true self, no-self, suchness, and the unborn.

Despite the differences, the important point is that the insight gained from meditation practice liberates you from the suffering caused by your distorted views and habitual patterns and brings with it unprecedented levels of peace, contentment, and joy.

Developing the Three Wisdoms As the Foundation for Insight

To prepare the groundwork for gaining insight, developing the following three wisdoms (drawn from the Vajrayana tradition) can be helpful. These wisdoms involve different forms of analytical meditation. (For more on analytical meditation, see the sidebar "Distinguishing between analytical and intuitive meditation," in this chapter.)

- The wisdom gained from listening
- The wisdom gained from reflection
- The wisdom gained from meditation

The next few sections take a closer look at each of these wisdoms.

Cultivating wisdom from listening to the teachings

When you first become acquainted with the teachings of Buddhism, you rely mostly on the first of the three wisdoms: the wisdom gained from listening to (or reading about) the teachings. You can think of this wisdom as the most basic level of understanding available to you.

For example, you may want to check out what Buddhism is like or how it addresses some of the issues you're dealing with in your life. So when you find out that someone is giving a lecture on Buddhism, you decide to attend. Or maybe you go to a library or bookstore and happen to spot a book on Buddhism (like this little black-and-yellow number in your hands right now) and decide to pick it up and see what it has to say. At this point, of course, you've made no commitment to the Buddhist path; you're just browsing. But as you listen to the lecture or read the book (preferably *this* book), you begin to collect information that can form the foundation of your future understanding.

But the wisdom gained from listening isn't always wise, is it? You can hear or read something for the first time and come away from it with a completely mistaken idea of what it really means. For example, according to Mahayana Buddhist teachings, the ultimate level of truth is *shunyata,* a Sanskrit word often translated as "emptiness." (We discuss this important topic in some detail in Chapter 14.) Based on the way you ordinarily use the word *emptiness,* you could easily misinterpret this statement to mean that nothing really exists. But this notion is emphatically *not* what emptiness means here. In fact, such a misinterpretation can lead to some serious mistakes.

The more you listen or read, however, the less likely you are to make this mistake and similar mistakes. If your sources are reliable, this first wisdom becomes sharper as your collection of information grows. You begin to get a better idea of just what the Buddhist teachings are about, even though you may still not understand them in any great detail. At the very least, you're becoming somewhat familiar with certain words and phrases that appear over and over again in the teachings, and this familiarity helps point your mind in the right direction.

Cultivating wisdom from reflecting on what you heard

By itself, the wisdom gained from listening won't take you very far. If you want to progress spiritually, you have to understand the meaning of what you hear or read. You accomplish this understanding by cultivating the second wisdom: the wisdom gained from reflection.

Reflection means that you wrestle with the teachings you've heard (or read) until you extract their intended meaning. You perform this deed by engaging all your mental faculties in as close an examination and as precise an investigation as you can. These actions recall the advice ascribed to the Buddha (mentioned in Chapter 1) not to accept his teachings at face value, but to test them for yourself to see whether they're true.

To start this process, you may want to check to be sure that the teachings you've heard are logically consistent.

The Buddha taught people who differed greatly from each other in many respects — their intellectual capacities, their backgrounds, the problems they faced, and so on — so he didn't say exactly the same thing to everyone. He may have told one person to do something that he told another to avoid if it was necessary to bring each of them along the path. Even so, when you look at the Buddha's teachings as a whole, you should be able to discover an overall consistency. If you can't, either something is wrong with the teachings themselves or you haven't yet fully understood how they fit together.

So when you examine the teachings — cultivating the wisdom that comes from reflecting on what you've heard or read — ask yourself how you can put these teachings into practice in your life. Are they applicable? Do they throw light on your experience? Finally, do they work?

Cultivating wisdom from meditating on what you understand

The kind of intelligent examination we mention in the previous section is itself one form of meditation, but the third wisdom refers to something beyond that practice. Perhaps we can explain it best by using an analogy.

To flavor your favorite food, you can marinate it. The marinade you use probably consists of a special mixture of spices, oils, herbs, or wine. You may have first found out about this marinade recipe by reading it in a cookbook; this is similar to gaining the first wisdom. But reading the recipe isn't enough — you still have to figure out how to put all the ingredients together properly, which is like applying the second wisdom. If you stop here, however, all your culinary efforts will be wasted. To get the taste you want, you have to place the food into the marinade and actually let it soak up the flavor. Performing this step is like applying the third wisdom.

If you want your mind to receive the full benefit of a particular teaching, you can't simply read it and think about it intellectually. You have to apply it so thoroughly that you absorb its full flavor. In other words, you have to cultivate the wisdom of single-minded meditation, the third wisdom. In this way, you can achieve true transformation of your mind.

Two examples make this concept clear. Impermanence, or change, is a major theme in Buddhism (see Chapters 3 and 11). Things don't stay the same, not even you; whether you're prepared for it or not, each passing second brings you that much closer to the end of your life.

Reading these words is one thing, and it's another thing to examine their meaning intellectually. But for this teaching to take such deep root in your mind that it transforms your life and gives you a new perspective on your mortality, you need to go beyond the first two wisdoms. You have to reach the unshakable conclusion that you yourself will die someday and that the only thing that will count then will be how well you have taken care of your mind.

When this realization occurs, put it at the focal point of your awareness and unwaveringly place your attention on it. You're no longer simply "thinking about" your mortality, investigating to see whether the claim is true. You've done that. Now you're allowing the conclusion that you've reached — "I myself am going to die, and nothing but Dharma training can help me when I do" — to permeate your mind; you're marinating in it. Over time, you repeat this process, examining the teachings on impermanence and death and then single-pointedly meditating on the personal conclusions that you draw. Eventually, this idea will soak into your mind, transforming your attitude toward life and death from the inside out.

A second example concerns the cultivation of love, another topic of immense importance in Buddhism. Although you may have started out disliking a guy named Pat (see the section "Cultivating equanimity," earlier in this chapter, for more on Pat), after being exposed to the teachings on love, you decide to give them a try. You find out how not to buy into your limited view of this fellow and how to begin seeing him in a new light. You discover that your attitude toward him softens, and instead of wishing him ill, you want him to be happy.

At first your desire for his happiness may be rather feeble. But when you place your mind on this wish in meditation, its flavor soaks into your consciousness, transforming it. Afterward, even if Pat continues to behave annoyingly, the whole way you view him and react to him will be different. Then because something in you has changed so radically, perhaps something in Pat will open up as well. At the very least, by softening your own attitude, you give him the space to change.

Chapter 8

A Day in the Life of a Buddhist Practitioner

In This Chapter

- Examining the function of monasteries
- Exploring practice in a Theravada monastery
- Extending Zen to everyday life
- Walking in the shoes of a Vajrayana practitioner
- Spending a day with followers of the Jodo Shinshu tradition

The earlier chapters of this book explain how Buddhism evolved in Asia, grew into various different traditions, and made its way to the West. But how do you actually practice the Buddhist teachings? Sure, many Buddhists meditate, but how exactly do they meditate? What else do they do? How do they spend their time? How do their daily lives differ from yours?

In this chapter, we answer these questions by giving you a firsthand look at Buddhist practice through detailed day-in-the-life accounts of practitioners from four different traditions practiced today in the West. Buddhism comes in many different shapes and sizes, but the one thing that all these traditions have in common — and that makes them quintessentially Buddhist — is the importance they place on basic teachings. Examples of these teachings include the four noble truths and the eightfold path (see Chapter 3), the three marks of existence (impermanence, no-self, and dissatisfaction), and the cultivation of core spiritual qualities such as patience, generosity, loving-kindness, compassion, and insight.

We think that this chapter will bring the religion to life for you and make it more down to earth and immediate than any other chapter in this book.

Surveying the Role of Monasteries in Buddhism

Buddhist monks and nuns have traditionally relinquished their worldly attachments in favor of a simple life devoted to the three trainings of Buddhism (see Chapter 13 for more on the three trainings):

- **Moral discipline:** Ethical conduct
- **Concentration:** Meditation practice
- **Wisdom:** Study of the teachings and direct spiritual insight

To support these endeavors, monasteries are generally set apart from the usual commotion of ordinary life. Some monasteries are located in relatively secluded natural settings like forests and mountains; others are situated near or even in villages, towns, and large cities, where they manage to thrive by serving the needs of their inhabitants for quiet contemplation *and* the needs of lay supporters for spiritual enrichment.

REMEMBER

Wherever they're located, monasteries have traditionally maintained an interdependent relationship with the surrounding lay community. For example, in the Theravada tradition, monks and nuns rely exclusively on lay supporters for their food and financial support (for more on this, see Chapter 4). The tradition prohibits monastics (a catch-all term for monks and nuns) from growing or buying food, or earning or even carrying money. So monks and nuns often make regular alms rounds to local villages and towns (during which they receive food from their supporters) and open their doors to the laity to receive contributions of money, food, and work.

Likewise, Tibetan Buddhist monasteries are often situated near towns or villages. The monasteries draw both their members and their material support from these nearby communities. The exchange works both ways. The laity in both Tibet and Southeast Asia traditionally benefits from the teachings and wise counsel that the monks and nuns offer.

In China, the monastic rules changed to permit monks and nuns to grow their own food and manage their own financial affairs, which allowed them to become more independent of lay supporters. As a result, many monasteries in China, Japan, and Korea became worlds unto themselves, where hundreds or even thousands of monks gathered to study with prominent teachers. Here the eccentric behavior, paradoxical stories (Japanese koan; see the sidebar "Entering the gateless gate: Koan practice in Zen," in this chapter, for more information), and unique lingo of Zen flourished. (See the section "Growing a Lotus in the Mud: A Day in the Life of a Zen Practitioner," later in the chapter, for more details.)

Despite their doctrinal, architectural, and cultural differences, Buddhist monasteries are remarkably alike in the daily practice they foster. Generally, monks and nuns rise early for a day of meditation, chanting, ritual, study, teaching, and work.

Renouncing Worldly Attachments: A Day in the Life of a Western Buddhist Monk

An excellent model of Buddhist monasticism in the West is Abhayagiri Buddhist Monastery, a Theravada monastery situated in Redwood Valley, in the woods of northern California, about a three-hour drive north of San Francisco. It is one of the main monasteries of the worldwide monastic community associated with Ajahn Chah (for the life of Ajahn Chah, see Chapter 15).

Scattered around Abhayagiri's 280 forested acres are little cabins that house the monastery's roughly one dozen fully ordained monks and roughly five junior monastics in training. As in the forest tradition of tropical Buddhist countries like Thailand, where Abhayagiri's two resident teachers (who are included among the monks in residence) began their training, each practitioner has a sparsely furnished cabin for individual meditation and study.

The monastics at Abhayagiri didn't choose their strict lifestyle on a whim. The 12 fully ordained monks began as novices by adhering to first 8 and then 10 precepts before they committed to the full *vinaya* (monastic discipline), consisting of 227 rules for restraint of body, speech, and mind. (For more on precepts, check out Chapter 12.) That's no small task, as you can imagine: Just memorizing and keeping track of all those rules can be a major undertaking! The monks recite the 227 rules on the full moon and new moon days to remind them of their conduct. After confessing any transgressions of minor rules, the monks assemble in close proximity while one monk recites the 13,000 word *Patimokkha* (Pali: *Monks' Code of Discipline*) in the ancient Pali language from memory. Another monk corrects any omissions or mispronunciations. During the 50-minute recitation, the monks may not leave the area nor may anyone else enter or the recitation must begin again. The tradition of reciting the *Patimokkha* has continued for more than 2,500 years.

REMEMBER

According to the rules laid down in the *Monks' Code of Discipline*, monks must abstain from sexual activity of any kind and refrain from physical contact with the opposite sex. They can't eat solid foods after midday, sell anything, ask for or handle money, or go into debt.

Needless to say, these regulations shape monastic life in significant ways. For example, monks must rely on laypeople to deal with monastery finances, and they can't engage in any project unless the monastery has money on hand to fund it. No movies, no TV, no music, no midnight snacks. Most laypeople can't even begin to imagine a life of such utter simplicity and discipline! Yet Abhayagiri merely follows the time-honored model for Buddhist monastic life that's been passed down for thousands of years.

Although Abhayagiri is a monastery devoted to the spiritual pursuits of its monks, laypeople come and go regularly to offer food, participate in practice, renew their precepts and refuge vows, and receive teachings from the resident instructors.

Men visiting for the first time can also arrange to stay at the monastery for up to one week, as long as they agree to follow the schedule and participate in practice. For people who've stayed at the monastery before, longer visits are possible. Because the monastery isn't very old (it was founded in 1996), accommodations are quite limited.

Following a day in the life

As a monastic at Abhayagiri, you follow a schedule that's typical of Buddhist monasteries the world over. You rise at 4 a.m. — well before the sun — shower, dress, and walk the half-mile from your cabin to gather with your colleagues at the main building for chanting and meditation, which begins at 5. For the first 20 minutes, you chant various scriptures that express your devotion to practice and touch on familiar themes, such as renunciation, loving-kindness, and insight. After taking refuge in the Three Jewels (the Buddha, Dharma, and Sangha), you meditate silently with the other monastics for an hour and then participate in more chanting. (For more on meditation in the Theravada tradition, see Chapter 5.)

Following chores from 6:30 to 7:00 a.m., you meet to discuss the morning work assignments over a light breakfast of cereal and tea. After you determine your responsibilities, you work diligently and mindfully until 10:45 a.m. and then don your robes for the main meal of the day, a formal affair that laypeople offer you. After you and the other monastics help yourselves, the laity take their share and eat with you in silence. Everyone helps wash up and put things away. You then spend the afternoon meditating, studying, hiking, or resting on your own. Remember, you've seen the last of solid food until 7 a.m. tomorrow morning — and private stashes are definitely not allowed!

Tea and fruit juice are served in the main hall at 5:30 p.m., followed by a reading of a Buddhist text and discussion at 6:30, and meditation and chanting at 7:30 (see Figure 8-1). Sometime between 9 and 10 p.m. you're off to your cabin to continue your meditation or to rest in preparation for yet another long day that begins at 4 a.m.

Figure 8-1: Theravada monks chanting together.

Photo courtesy of Martin Stabler.

Though fixating on the rigors and relative strictness of such a routine is easy, we want to emphasize the joy and fulfillment that accompanies a life of such purity, awareness, and devotion to truth. Without the many distractions of postmodern lay life, the subtle insights and revelations of the spiritual life come more quickly and easily into focus. That's why the Buddha recommended the monastic life and why so many devoted practitioners have followed his example.

Punctuating the calendar with special events

In addition to the regular daily schedule we outline in the preceding section, the lunar quarters (that is, the days corresponding to the quarter, half, and full phases of the moon) and the three-month rainy-season retreat punctuate the monastic calendar.

Vipassana centers for laypeople

In addition to monasteries, the Theravada tradition in the West supports lay practice centers, much like Zen centers (see the section "Growing a Lotus in the Mud: A Day in the Life of a Zen Practitioner," later in the chapter). At these practice centers, laypeople can gather to learn how to meditate, listen to talks, attend workshops on Buddhist themes, and participate in retreats of varying lengths (from one day to three months). Frequently using the term *vipassana* (insight) rather than *Theravada,* Western teachers (some of whom have trained in Asia) staff these centers, which may be closely affiliated with nearby monasteries. (For more on vipassana meditation techniques, see Chapter 5.)

On the lunar quarters (roughly every week), you observe a kind of Sabbath: You get up when you want, set aside the usual program of meditation and work, and refrain from touching computers or phones. Instead, you go on alms rounds with the other monastics — you walk the streets of the local town in your robes, begging bowl in hand, receiving food from anyone who wishes to offer it (see Figure 8-2). Then you devote the rest of the day to personal practice.

Figure 8-2: Monks on alms round.

Photo courtesy of Martin Stabler.

Taking a bow

Stephan's first Zen teacher used to say, "Buddhism is a religion of bowing." By this he meant two things:

- Bowing expresses the surrender of self-centered preoccupation, which is one of the core teachings of Buddhism.
- Buddhists bow a great deal.

Both statements are true. In every tradition of Buddhism, bowing plays an important role. Buddhists bow to their altars, their teachers, their robes, their sitting cushions, and one another (see the following figure of a Theravada monk bowing). As a traditional expression of gratitude, respect, veneration, acknowledgement, and surrender, bowing occurs both spontaneously and in prescribed situations and contexts. In other words, sometimes you bow because you feel like it, and sometimes you bow because you're expected to.

Bowing is also a common practice in traditional Asian societies. Buddhism, bowing, and Asian culture are inextricably entwined.

Bowing in Buddhism takes different forms, depending on the culture and circumstance.

- In Southeast Asia, for example, you show respect by holding your hands in prayer position to your slightly lowered forehead. For a full bow, kneel in that position (sitting on your buttocks), lay your palms on the ground about 4 inches apart, and touch your forehead to the ground between your hands.
- In Japanese Zen, execute a half bow by holding your hands together at chest level and then bowing from the waist. For a full bow, start off with the half bow and then continue with the Southeast Asia style of bow, except with palms up rather than down.
- In Tibetan Buddhism, show respect by touching your joined hands to your forehead, throat, and heart (indicating the dedication of body, speech, and mind) and executing a full prostration by (more or less) extending the full bow of Zen until you're lying face down on the ground.

Though bowing may lapse into mere formality, the deeper intention is to express heartfelt respect and devotion. The regular practice of bowing in Buddhist monasteries and communities contributes to an atmosphere of harmony, loving-kindness, and peace. As a Westerner taught to "bow down to no one," you may find yourself resistant to the practice at first. But you may soon discover that it encourages a flexibility and openness of mind and heart that feels good inside — and it's Buddhist to the core! In any case, just remember, as Stephan's first teacher often told him: "Wherever you turn, you're simply bowing to yourself."

(continued)

(continued)

Photo courtesy of Jay Carroll/JFoto.com.

In the evening, one of the resident teachers offers a talk that's open to the lay community. Laypeople who attend and stay the night take the three refuges (the Buddha, Dharma, and Sangha) and commit to following 8 precepts for the duration of their stay — the usual 5 precepts for laypeople (with monastic celibacy in place of the customary precept governing lay sexual behavior), plus 3 precepts with a "twist" of renunciation: no eating after noon, no entertainment or self-adornment, and no lying on a high and luxurious bed (also understood as no overindulging in sleep). (For more on the five basic precepts, see Chapter 12.) Both laity and monastics practice meditation together until 3 a.m., followed by morning chanting. The rest of the day is completely unstructured, and monastics often use it to catch up on their sleep.

On Saturday nights, the monastery hosts a regular talk on a Buddhist theme that draws even more of an outside audience than the lunar gatherings.

REMEMBER

The high point of the year at Abhayagiri comes at the beginning of January, when the three-month rains retreat begins. Fashioned after the traditional monsoon assembly in India, when the wandering monks gathered to practice together, the retreat coincides with the rainiest time of the year in northern California. It gives the monks an opportunity to observe noble silence, turn their attention inward, and intensify their practice. Overnight guests and outside teaching engagements are prohibited, and the schedule becomes more rigorous, with many more group practice sessions scheduled throughout the day. In addition, monastics take turns retiring to their individual cabins during this period for solitary retreats.

Growing a Lotus in the Mud: A Day in the Life of a Zen Practitioner

Zen first gained a foothold in North America around the turn of the last century, but it didn't achieve widespread popularity until the 1960s and '70s, when Zen teachers began arriving in larger numbers and young people (discontented with the religion in which they were raised) began seeking alternatives. (Check out Chapter 5 for more details about Zen itself.)

Since that time, the uniquely Western expression of a place for Buddhist practice known as the *Zen center* has appeared in cities and towns across the North American continent. Like monasteries, Zen centers offer a daily schedule of meditation, ritual, and work combined with regular lectures and study groups. But unlike their monastic counterparts, the centers adapt their approach to the needs of busy lay practitioners who must balance the demands of family life, career, and other worldly obligations with their spiritual involvement.

Though Zen temples in Japan and Korea have lay meditation groups, nothing quite like the Zen center has ever emerged in Asia. The reason is quite simple: Lay practitioners who fervently commit themselves to Buddhist practice are far more common in the West than in Asia, where serious practitioners generally take monastic or priestly vows. Maybe this phenomenon is the result of the Western belief that we can have it all: spiritual enlightenment and worldly accomplishment. (The Judeo-Christian ethic so prominent in North America teaches that daily life is inseparable from spiritual practice.) Or perhaps Westerners simply have no choice: In a culture where the monastic style of practice isn't widely acknowledged or supported, practitioners have to make a living while studying the teachings.

REMEMBER

In any case, Buddhism has its own strong precedents for this approach: The Mahayana tradition, of which Zen considers itself a part, views lay and monastic members as equal in their capacity to achieve enlightenment. The Zen tradition, in particular, has always emphasized the importance of practicing in the midst of the most mundane activities, such as washing the dishes, driving a car, and taking care of the kids. The Mahayana tradition expresses the idea in this way:

> Just as the most beautiful flower, the lotus, grows in muddy water, so the lay practitioner can find clarity and compassion in the turmoil of daily life.

Though Zen centers form the spiritual hub of their respective communities, members continue their practice throughout the day by applying meditative awareness to every activity.

Following a day in the life

At the heart of Zen practice is *zazen* (literally, "sitting meditation"), a form of silent meditation understood by some traditions to be both a method for achieving enlightenment and an expression of your already enlightened Buddha nature. In other words, you can *be* the truth and seek it, too! How's that for a two-for-one deal?

As a Zen practitioner, you're encouraged to practice zazen on your own, but sitting with other members of the *Sangha* (spiritual community) is considered particularly effective and favorable. (Sangha is regarded as one of the Three Jewels of Buddhism, along with the Buddha and Dharma.) So, most Zen centers offer daily group meditations — usually in the early morning before work and in the evening after work. Depending on how much time you have to spare and the schedule at your local center, you can spend from one to three hours practicing Zen with others.

At *zendos* (meditation halls connected with Zen centers) across the country, meditators repeat the familiar ritual of gathering in the predawn dark to practice together. (Though Zen is best known in the West in its Japanese form, and we use Japanese terms throughout this section, remember that Zen began in China and that Korean and Vietnamese teachers introduced it to the West.)

After entering the zendo, you bow respectfully to your cushion or chair and then position yourself in preparation for zazen. Even in its Western incarnation, Zen is notorious for its careful attention to traditional formalities. Meditation begins with the sounding of a bell or gong and generally continues in silence for 30 to 40 minutes. Depending on the school of Zen to which you belong (for more on Zen schools, see Chapter 5) and the maturity of your practice, you may spend your time following your breaths, *just sitting* (a more advanced technique involving mindful attention in the present without a particular object of focus), or attempting to solve a *koan* (a paradoxical story; see the sidebar "Entering the gateless gate: Koan practice in Zen," for more details). Whatever your technique, you're encouraged to sit with an erect spine and wholehearted attention.

Between meditation periods, you may form a line with other practitioners and meditate while walking mindfully around the hall together. Following a period or two of sitting, everyone generally chants some version of the four *bodhisattva vows,* which we mention in Chapter 6:

- Beings are numberless; I vow to save them.
- Mental defilements are inexhaustible; I vow to put an end to them.
- The teachings are boundless; I vow to master them.
- The Buddha's way is unsurpassable; I vow to attain it.

During the service that follows meditation, you bow deeply three or nine times to the altar (which usually features a statue of Shakyamuni Buddha or Manjushri Bodhisattva, flowers, candles, and incense) and chant one or more important wisdom texts, which generally include the *Heart Sutra*. These texts offer concise reminders of the core teachings of Zen, and the altar represents the Three Jewels of Buddhism, the ultimate objects of reverence and refuge: the Buddha, Dharma, and Sangha.

When you finish your morning meditation, your Zen practice has just begun. Throughout the day, you have constant opportunities to be mindful — not only of what you're doing or what's happening around you, but also of the thoughts, emotions, and reactive patterns that life events trigger. Whether on the cushion or on the go, this steady, inclusive, mindful awareness lies at the heart of Buddhist practice in every tradition.

REMEMBER

In particular, the Zen tradition emphasizes taking mindful care of every aspect of your life because the deeper truth is that you're not separate from the tools you use, the car you drive, the dishes you wash, and the people you meet. The world is your very own body!

When you get behind the wheel of your car, for example, you can stop to sense the contact of your back against the seat, listen to the sound of the engine as it starts, pay attention to the condition of the road, and notice the state of your mind and heart as you head down the street. When you stop at a traffic light, you can be aware of the impatience you feel as you wait for the light to change, the sounds of the traffic around you, the warmth of the sun through the window, and so on. As you can see, every moment, from morning to night, provides an opportunity to practice.

In addition to meditation and service, most Zen centers offer weekly talks by the resident teacher and regular opportunities for private interviews with the teacher to discuss your practice. These face-to-face encounters may touch on any area of practice, including work, relationships, sitting meditation, and formal koan study. The Zen master isn't a guru endowed with special powers. Practitioners regard the master as a skilled guide and an exemplar of the enlightened way of life.

Entering the gateless gate: Koan practice in Zen

When you think of Zen, what image comes to mind? Perhaps it's the shaven-headed monks in black robes sitting silently facing the wall. Or maybe it's the Zen master making some enigmatic statement or engaging in some unusual behavior designed to rouse students from their spiritual slumber.

This last image figures prominently in the paradoxical stories known as *koans,* which teachers have used for centuries (especially in the Rinzai Zen tradition) to serve as a catalyst for awakening their students. More than an intellectual exercise, koan study is a process of spiritual reflection designed to confound the conceptual mind, bypass the intellect, and elicit a direct insight *(kensho)* into the nondual nature of reality — that is, our inherent oneness with all of life.

Some masters, especially those in the early years of Zen in China, didn't need such stories. In direct contact with their disciples during day-to-day monastic life, they had ample opportunity to transmit the teachings through their spoken words, gestures, behaviors, and, above all, their silent presence. But as monasteries grew and teachers became less accessible, the teaching encounter became increasingly confined to public dialogues and the interview room, where masters challenged and encouraged their disciples and tested their understanding.

In this context, Zen masters began using traditional questions and true stories of classic teacher–student encounters, initially to provoke kensho and then to teach different aspects of the multifaceted jewel of *prajna* (enlightened wisdom). Over the centuries, these stories and questions were collected and systematized into a kind of graduate program in living from the enlightened perspective. With Zen's emphasis on "direct transmission outside the scriptures," koans, along with the transmission stories and poems of the great masters, became the focal point of study for serious Zen practitioners, and they're still widely used today in Asia and now in the West. Among the best-known koans are "What is the sound of one hand [clapping]?" and "What was your original face before your parents were born?"

If you're a serious Zen student but can't practice at the center, because you're sick, you live too far away, or you can't arrange your calendar to include it, you can generally follow some version of this daily schedule on your own by sitting in the morning and again, if possible, in the evening. Then to energize and deepen your practice, you can make it a point to attend one or more intensive retreats each year.

Attending silent retreats

Most Zen centers in the West offer regular one- to seven-day retreats (Japanese: *sesshin*) featuring as many as a dozen periods of meditation each day, morning and evening services, daily talks on Buddhist themes, and interviews. (Korean Zen also offers retreats devoted primarily to chanting and bowing.) As a rule, these rigorous retreats are held in silence and offer an opportunity to hone your concentration, deepen your insight into the fundamental truths of Buddhism, and possibly catch a glimpse of your essential Buddha nature (an experience of awakening known in Japanese as *kensho* or *satori*). Retreats of more than one or two days are generally residential, though some centers allow you to attend part time while continuing your everyday life.

Jukai: The bodhisattva initiation or lay ordination

Jukai (Japanese: "receiving the precepts") is the ceremony of a layperson's ordination or formal entry into the practice of the bodhisattva precepts in the Zen tradition. This ceremony involves making a commitment to practice and keep the precepts for life while being a householder. In many American Zen centers, including the San Francisco Zen Center, the ceremony is a shortened version of Zaike Tokudo ("staying at home and attaining the way"). To prepare, a candidate sews a *rakusu,* a five-panel small robe patterned after the Buddha's robe, and studies the bodhisattva precepts (see Chapter 6). The ceremony then starts with an invocation to all Buddhas and bodhisattvas, to provide a framework of support for the candidates' initiation. Each candidate receives a new name and the robe he has sewn. The candidates then formally don the rakusu with a chant. Next, they avow and repent past actions stemming from greed, anger, and ignorance, and are purified with water. Thus purified, they receive the 16 precepts by reciting them after the teacher (see the following figure of a lay Buddhist ordination at the City Center in San Francisco). They receive the bloodline of the Buddhas and ancestors (Japanese: *kechimyaku*). Finally, the teachers give congratulatory statements, and the ceremony is dedicated to the welfare of all beings.

Photo courtesy of Shundo David Haye.

In keeping with the Mahayana spirit of general equality among monastic and lay practitioners, larger Zen centers often have country retreat centers that provide monastic accommodations and training for both ordained monks and nuns and lay practitioners. For example, the San Francisco Zen Center — which describes itself as one of the largest Buddhist Sanghas outside of Asia, a diverse community of priests, laypeople, teachers, and students — includes three separate facilities:

- **City Center:** This facility serves urban members.
- **Green Gulch Farm:** This location combines a suburban practice center and a working organic farm.
- **Tassajara Zen Mountain Center:** This facility is the oldest Soto Zen monastery in the United States. During the winter months, experienced Zen students from all over the world gather to participate in the fall and winter three-month practice periods. September and April are community months in which volunteers can help the monks prepare for the transitions to and from secluded monastic practice.

From late spring to early fall, Tassajara opens its gates, meditation hall, cabins, wilderness trails, and hot springs to guests, work students, and retreatants who participate in varied offerings and opportunities, ranging from relaxed day trips and vacations to extended monastic training.

All three facilities offer regular residential retreats, but the program at Tassajara is particularly intensive.

Gathering for special events

Every Zen center has its own calendar of special ceremonies and events that punctuate the year. At the San Francisco Zen Center, for example, these events include the following:

- Memorial ceremonies honoring the founder, Shunryu Suzuki Roshi
- Monthly full moon bodhisattva ceremonies
- Solstice and equinox ceremonies
- New Year's Eve and New Year's Day celebrations
- Annual Martin Luther King, Jr., ceremony
- The Buddha's birthday in April and enlightenment day in December
- Annual ceremonies honoring Bodhidharma, the founder of Chan in China, and Eihei Dogen, the founder of Zen in Japan.

Many centers also offer weekly study groups focusing on Buddhist scriptures and the teachings of the great Zen masters. Zen communities, like churches of other denominations, also sponsor social gatherings where members get to mingle and enjoy one another's company.

Devoting Yourself to the Three Jewels: A Day in the Life of a Vajrayana Practitioner

In addition to North American converts to Buddhism, the continent has many thousands of ethnic practitioners who carried their Buddhist practice with them from Asia or learned it from their Asian parents or grandparents.

Some of these Asian American Buddhists are monks and nuns (many come from Southeast Asia) who have transplanted traditional forms and practices to Western soil. But most folks are laypeople for whom Buddhism is often more a matter of devotion and ritual than meditation and study.

For these Asian Americans, being a Buddhist may involve the following actions:

- Going to the temple on the weekend to listen to a sermon
- Chanting Buddhist texts in the language of their homeland
- Participating in the special ceremonies that mark the changing of the seasons and the turning of the year
- Sharing food at temple gatherings
- Helping fellow temple members in times of need

As an ethnic lay practitioner of Tibetan Vajrayana Buddhism now living in the West, you may engage in some or all of the following daily practices (for more info on the Vajrayana Buddhism of Tibet, see Chapter 5):

- You rise early, between 5 and 6 a.m., to begin your day with meditation.
- You walk around (circumambulate) your house, which holds a sacred shrine containing statues, scrolls, and other ritual objects.
- As you walk, you finger your mala (a string of beads, a rosary) while chanting a sacred mantra such as *Om mani-padme hum* (the famous mantra of Avalokiteshvara/Chenrezig, the bodhisattva of compassion) or the longer mantra of Vajrasattva, the bodhisattva of clarity and purification.
- After cleaning your shrine, you offer 108 prostrations (see Figure 8-3 to get a glimpse of how they're done) as an expression of your devotion to and refuge in the Three Jewels (the Buddha, Dharma, and Sangha).

- You engage in a particular practice your teacher has given you, often a visualization of a particular deity accompanied by chanting, prayer, and prostrations.
- As you go about your day, you chant *Om mani-padme hum,* either aloud or silently to yourself, while cultivating the qualities of compassion and loving-kindness for all beings.
- You spend an hour or two in the evening studying certain special teachings recommended by your teacher.
- Before you go to sleep, you make offerings of incense and candles at your altar, meditate, do additional prostrations, and recite long-life prayers for your teacher(s).

As you can see, the life of a traditional Vajrayana lay practitioner is permeated by spiritual practice. Of course, some people are more devoted than others, and young people are more inclined to diverge from the traditional ways of their parents. But in general, Tibetan culture, even in exile, is filled with strong Buddhist values that often express themselves in dedicated practice.

What are mantras?

Mantras are sacred syllables, words, or sentences. Their literal meaning isn't always clearly understood, but the practice of repeating mantras isn't about an intellectual understanding of the meaning of words. Practitioners of Asian religious traditions often repeat mantras to focus the mind. Later in this chapter, we mention the mantra of Avalokiteshvara (or Chenrezig), which is popular among Tibetan Buddhists: *Om mani-padme hum.* A mantra that practitioners of the Pure Land schools in Japan chant (referred to in Chapter 5) is *Namu amida butsu* ("Homage to Amida Buddha"). More about it comes in the next section ("Trusting the Mind of Amida"). Chapter 5 also introduces an important mantra in the Japanese Nichiren School (and its offshoots): *Nam* (or *namu*) *myoho renge kyo* ("Homage to the *Lotus of the Good Dharma Sutra*").

Take a look at these characteristic features of mantras:

*Mantras are believed to be invested with divine power. It's assumed that repeating a mantra many times can access this power.

*Counting the repetitions of a mantra is done with the help of a rosary (mala), which often has 108 beads (108 is a sacred number).

*Ideally, a spiritual teacher (guru) selects a mantra and transmits it to a disciple orally. (Mantras are not meant to be picked up from books.) After receiving the transmission, the student is authorized to repeat the mantra.

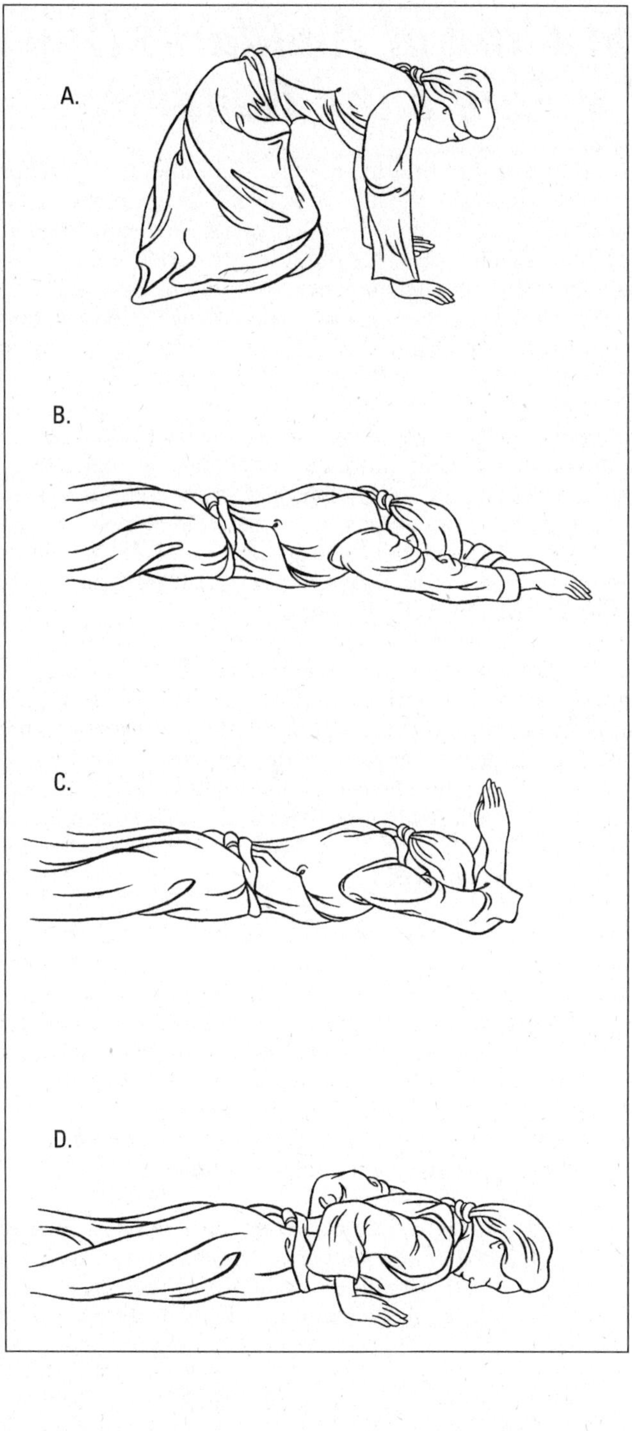

Figure 8-3: Performing full prostrations in the Tibetan style.

Trusting the Mind of Amida: A Day in the Life of a Pure Land Buddhist

Unlike most other forms of Buddhism that recommend spiritual practices (particularly meditation) as the means to attain enlightenment, Jodo Shinshu (a popular Japanese Pure Land school whose name means "The True Pure Land school") teaches its followers not to rely on their own personal practice. Instead, Jodo Shinshu instructs practitioners to rely on the "great practice" of Amida Buddha himself, who took a vow to lead all beings to enlightenment. (Check out Chapter 5 for a more in-depth discussion of Jodo Shinshu and the many facets of Pure Land Buddhism.)

As a Jodo Shinshu follower, you're taught that entry to the Pure Land (which is more a state of mind than a future realm) occurs through *other power* (that is, the power of what Amida Buddha has already accomplished) rather than through whatever you yourself may try to do. Jodo Shinshu understands Amida (or Amitabha, in Sanskrit) to be an expression of the infinite, formless, life-giving Oneness that, out of deep compassion, took form to establish the Pure Land and lead beings to Buddhahood.

Shinran (1173–1263), the Japanese founder of this tradition, did recommend certain practices, such as "hearing the Dharma" (listening to Buddhist teachings), reading scriptures and contemporary commentaries, internalizing basic Buddhist principles, and "learning to entrust yourself to the mind of Amida" rather than to your own limited effort and point of view. But the point of these practices isn't to eliminate negativity and purify your mind, as in other Buddhist traditions. You practice to realize that you're already swimming in an ocean of purity and compassion.

Shinran himself left the monastic life to marry and raise a family because he felt that making the Buddhist teachings more accessible to laypeople was extremely important. In this spirit, Jodo Shinshu emphasizes that everyday life in the context of family and friends is the perfect setting for spiritual practice. As a result, Jodo Shinshu followers lead ordinary lives that differ little from those of their non-Buddhist counterparts, except that they attempt to put into practice basic Buddhist principles, like patience, generosity, kindness, and equanimity. They get up and go to work, make dinner, and help their kids with their homework just like everyone else.

Without prescribed techniques, practice becomes a matter of attitude rather than activity. At the same time, followers of Jodo Shinshu can engage in any traditional Buddhist practice, such as meditation or the practice of mindfulness of the Buddha *(nembutsu)* by chanting the mantra *Namu amida butsu*

("Homage to Amida Buddha"), as long as they do it as an expression of their gratitude for the gift of Amida's grace (not as a means to attain enlightenment).

On Sunday mornings, followers generally gather at their local temple to listen to a talk on a Buddhist theme while their children attend the Buddhist version of Sunday school — a short sermon followed by an hour-long class about Buddhist values. If they're strongly motivated, adult members may join a discussion or study group focusing on Jodo Shinshu themes.

Seasonal holidays also bring the community together to celebrate special occasions like the Buddha's birth, enlightenment days, the vernal and autumnal equinoxes, and a summer ceremony honoring the spirits of departed ancestors. For many practitioners, the temple (like the local church or synagogue) is the focal point of social and community life. Temples often offer classes in martial arts, flower arranging, taiko drumming, and Japanese language that instill Buddhist principles and Japanese culture and values.

Chapter 9

Walking in the Buddha's Footsteps

In This Chapter

- Playing the role of a pilgrim
- Mapping out the major sites of Buddhist pilgrimage
- Exploring what happens during a pilgrimage

Two thousand five hundred years ago, Shakyamuni Buddha inspired his original disciples and their daily spiritual practice by delivering his teachings. His enlightened presence profoundly affected most of the people he met. Even when people came to the Buddha in an agitated state of mind, they often discovered that his peaceful demeanor automatically calmed them.

But what about future generations of Buddhists who don't have the opportunity of meeting Shakyamuni in person? Well, they can receive inspiration for their practice by visiting the places where he stayed during his lifetime. The custom of making a pilgrimage to the places Shakyamuni blessed by his presence has a long tradition that continues today. In this chapter, we talk about these places and some of the practices Buddhists perform while visiting them.

Visiting the Primary Places of Pilgrimage

Pilgrimage is the practice of visiting a site of religious significance to fulfill a spiritual longing or duty or to receive blessings or inspiration. Hundreds of millions of people around the world perform pilgrimage, one of the most universal of religious practices. Muslims consider it their duty to make a pilgrimage to the holy city of Mecca at least once during their lifetime. Many Jews journey to Jerusalem to pray at the Western Wall and view the great biblical battle sites. Christians may trace the footsteps of Jesus from Bethlehem to Golgotha or visit the sacred places where great saints performed miracles.

Four pilgrimage sites are of major significance for Buddhists:

- **Lumbini:** Site of the Buddha's birth
- **Bodh Gaya:** Site where he attained full enlightenment
- **Sarnath:** Site of his first discourse
- **Kushinagar:** Site where he died

According to some Buddhist traditions, visiting these and other important sites (while thinking about the events that occurred there) enables an individual of faith to accumulate merit and/or purify negative karma accumulated in past lives (see Chapter 12 for more on the concept of karma).

After the Buddha's death, his teachings flourished on the Indian subcontinent for more than a thousand years, and these pilgrimage sites grew to be important Buddhist centers (see Figure 9-1 for a map of these sites). But eventually, Buddhism began to die out in India. By the 13th century, it had virtually disappeared from the subcontinent, and many of the sites suffered from neglect and fell into ruin.

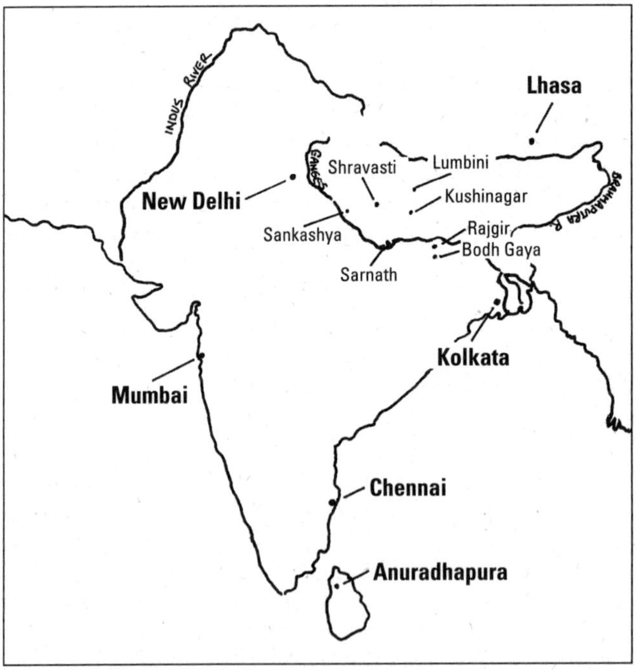

Figure 9-1: Major Buddhist pilgrimage sites in northern India and Nepal.

By the time Buddhism disappeared in the country of its birth, it had already taken root in other Asian cultures (see Chapter 5 for more on the spread of Buddhism). So when the job of reestablishing these sacred Indian sites kicked into high gear in the 19th century, many Buddhists — and Western archeologists — were up to the task. As a result of their ongoing efforts, present-day pilgrims can once again visit these sites and receive inspiration for themselves.

The next few sections take a closer look at each of the four sites.

Lumbini: A visit to the Buddha's birthplace

A good place to begin a Buddhist pilgrimage is Lumbini, which is now in Nepal near the border with India. You can get to it relatively easily by catching a train to the North Indian city of Gorakhpur and then switching to a bus that takes you across the border. (Gorakhpur is also the jumping-off point on your way to Kushinagar, site of the Buddha's death, described later in the chapter.)

The area north of modern Gorakhpur was once part of the kingdom of the Shakyas, the clan into which the Buddha was born, and Lumbini itself was his actual birthplace (see Chapter 3 for more about the Buddha's life story). Buddhist pilgrims from all over the world visit Lumbini to honor Shakyamuni, based on whose teachings Buddhism developed, and express their devotion and gratitude to him for entering this world and blazing the path leading to lasting peace, happiness, and spiritual fulfillment.

When Buddhists visit Lumbini (and the other major pilgrimage sites), they express their devotion in different ways. In the case of Lumbini, they head to the Mayadevi Temple (see Figure 9-2) purporting to encircle the exact spot where Shakyamuni was born. Adjacent to the temple is the sacred pond where Shakyamuni's mother Maya is supposed to have bathed before giving birth and where Shakyamuni is said to have been bathed after he was born. Pilgrims leave offerings at the temple as a sign of their respect. The offerings typically consist of flowers, candles, and incense. (You don't have to worry about finding the items you want to offer; Buddhist and Hindu pilgrimage sites throughout India and the surrounding area are filled with small outdoor shops selling everything you may need.)

Figure 9-2: Mayadevi Temple, Lumbini, with the sacred pond.

Photographed by John C. Huntington, courtesy of the Huntington Archive at The Ohio State University.

These pilgrimage sites are also excellent places to engage in whatever formal practices you're accustomed to performing (see Chapter 8 for some of the practices Buddhists from different traditions commonly engage in). For example, many people report that their meditations are more powerful at sites like Lumbini than they are at home, as if the place itself, blessed by the Buddha and other great practitioners of the past, gives added strength to their spiritual endeavors.

You may wonder how people know that this village is really the site of the Buddha's birth. Even though it fell into disrepair a long time ago, experts have been reasonably certain about the location of Lumbini since the end of the 19th century. At that time, archeologists uncovered an important piece of evidence — an inscribed pillar, left behind more than 2,000 years earlier by one of the most influential of all Buddhist pilgrims: the great Emperor Ashoka. (For more about Ashoka, one of the most important figures in Buddhist history, see Chapter 4.)

Bodh Gaya: Place of enlightenment

If Buddhists have a Mecca, it's Bodh Gaya, the site of the magnificent Mahabodhi Temple (see Figure 9-3). (Incidentally, *mahabodhi* means "great enlightenment" in Sanskrit.) The temple stands just east of the famous Bodhi tree (for more on the Bodhi tree, see Chapters 3 and 4). This temple (which is actually a large *stupa,* a monument housing relics of the Buddha) marks the single most important spot in the entire Buddhist world: the place where Shakyamuni is believed to have attained full enlightenment. The so-called "diamond seat," where the Buddha is supposed to have meditated, is located between the Mahabodhi Temple and the Bodhi tree (see Chapter 1).

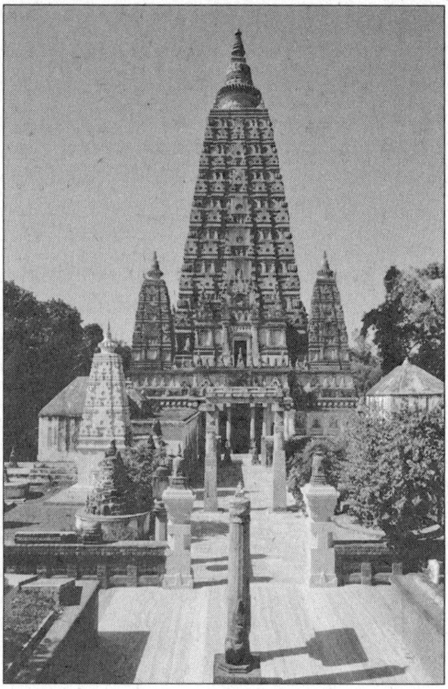

Figure 9-3: The Mahabodhi Temple in Bodh Gaya.

Photo courtesy of Gudrun Bühnemann.

Most pilgrims reach the town of Bodh Gaya by first taking a train to the city of Gaya (where you can find one of Hinduism's most holy shrines) and then continuing south 13 kilometers by taxi, auto-rickshaw, or — if you're fond of crowded conditions — bus. The road between Gaya and Bodh Gaya runs alongside a riverbed that's dry for much of the year — especially in winter. Winter is the height of the pilgrimage season here, and with good reason. Even though many Buddhists celebrate the anniversary of the Buddha's enlightenment in May or June, you may not be comfortable visiting Bodh Gaya at that time of year — unless you're a big fan of temperatures that regularly reach 120 degrees Fahrenheit and more.

Well before you enter Bodh Gaya, you can see the top of the "Great Stupa" (as the Mahabodhi Temple is often called) towering 55 meters above the surrounding plain. No one knows the age of the structure for certain, but it is likely to date from the fifth or sixth century CE.

Hindu pilgrims and Bodh Gaya

Buddhists aren't the only pilgrims who flock to Bodh Gaya. Like all Buddhist shrines, the Mahabodhi Temple attracts Hindu pilgrims as well. Many Hindus consider the Buddha to be one of the manifestations of their god Vishnu, the Preserver. They believe that whenever sufficient need arises, Vishnu descends to Earth in the appropriate form as an incarnation or "descent" (*avatara*) to provide divine assistance. The Buddha is widely regarded as the ninth major avatara of Vishnu, and some Hindus feel that his special mission was to stop the custom of animal sacrifice.

Taking a sacred walk

One of the most widely observed practices at shrines like the Mahabodhi Temple is *circumambulation,* a Latin mouthful that just means walking around.

The circumambulation of sacred objects has become a revered practice in Hindu, Jain, and certain Buddhist traditions. Pilgrims walk around a statue, shrine or another sacred object in a clockwise direction, always keeping the object of reverence on the right side. Buddhists come from all over the world to circumambulate the Mahabodhi Temple and pay their respects at the site of one of the defining moments of Buddhist history. At the height of the pilgrimage season, you can see Buddhists performing circumambulations at every hour of the day and night. And if you happen to be there on an evening of a full moon — when the power of such practices is thought to be much greater — you can easily be swept up in the swirling mass of humanity that seems to flood the area.

Feeling the Buddha's influence

The area around the Mahabodhi Temple contains many smaller stupas and shrines, some of which mark places where the Buddha is believed to have stayed during the seven weeks immediately after he attained enlightenment. Many pilgrims make circle upon circle as they walk from one of these sacred structures to the other. Throughout the extensive grounds, pilgrims take part in other religious practices as well, such as reciting prayers, making offerings, or simply sitting in quiet meditation. A favorite place for this last activity is a small room on the ground floor of the Mahabodhi Temple that's dominated by an ancient and particularly beautiful statue of the Buddha. Sitting there in front of this blessed image in the very heart of the Great Stupa gives you the feeling of being in the presence of the Buddha himself.

Buddhists from around the world have taken advantage of this special place by building temples in the area surrounding the Mahabodhi grounds. The number of temples has grown significantly in recent years. In fact, certain portions of Bodh Gaya now look like a Buddhist theme park, filled with examples of the most diverse religious architecture Asia has to offer.

"Practicing the teachings is even better"

Buddhist teachers never get tired of reminding their students that the value of their actions depends mostly on their mind and motivation. This idea is also true of the practice of *circumambulating* (walking around) holy sites, as you can see in the following story.

Dromtonpa (or, more simply, Lama Drom) was an 11th-century Tibetan master who founded the famous monastery of Radreng and is considered to be a predecessor of the line of Dalai Lamas. One day he saw an old man circumambulating the monastery and told him, "You're doing good, but practicing the teachings is even better." Thinking that he should be doing something else, the old man stopped circumambulating and began reading a Buddhist text. But soon Lama Drom came over to him again and said, "Studying texts is good, but practicing the teachings is even better." "Maybe he means meditation," the old man thought, so he stopped reading and sat down to meditate. But, when Lama Drom saw him again, he told the old man (you guessed it), "Meditating is good, but practicing the teachings is even better."

Well, at this point, the old man was pretty confused. He asked Lama Drom, "What should I do to practice the teachings?" The Lama answered, "Give up attachment to the worldly concerns of this life. Until you change your attitude, you won't be practicing the teachings."

Venturing to other notable sites

Not far from Bodh Gaya are other pilgrimage sites that, although not nearly as built up as those within Bodh Gaya itself, are still of great interest. For example, on the other side of the dry riverbed are the spots where the Buddha is believed to have spent six years fasting before his enlightenment and where he is said to have broken his fast by accepting Sujata's offering (see Chapter 3). You can also find caves used by some of the great meditators of the past in the surrounding hills.

Sarnath: The first teaching

When the Buddha decided the time was ripe to share the fruits of the enlightenment he'd achieved, he traveled to the Deer Park in Sarnath to teach his former companions. Sarnath is on the outskirts of Varanasi (or Benares, as it was formerly called in the West). Even in the time of the Buddha, Varanasi was already an ancient holy site. Varanasi is probably most famous as the place where Hindus come to cleanse themselves of impurities by bathing in the sacred waters of the Ganges River and to cremate the bodies of their loved ones.

But Buddhist pilgrims turn their attention a little to the north of Varanasi, to Sarnath, where the Buddha first turned the wheel of Dharma by teaching the four noble truths that form the basis of all his subsequent teachings (as we explain in Chapter 3). Buddhists around the world commemorate this event because the Buddha's teachings are considered his true legacy.

You can find all the sites associated with the Buddha's first teaching within a relatively new park in Sarnath. Two stupas once stood on this site. The one built by King Ashoka was destroyed in the 18th century, but the Dhamekh(a) stupa of the 6th century still remains (see Figure 9-4). During the period when Buddhism declined in India, many precious works of art were lost. Fortunately, a number of these items have since been unearthed and are currently on exhibit in Sarnath's small but excellent museum. Among the items on display is the famous Lion Capital, from the pillar Ashoka erected here. This image is now used as the national emblem of the Republic of India and appears on its currency; the wheel design also located on the capital is reproduced on India's national flag.

Figure 9-4: The Dhamekh(a) stupa in Sarnath, site of the Buddha's first teaching.

Photo courtesy of Gudrun Bühnemann.

Buddhists from various Asian countries have built temples in Sarnath as they've done in Bodh Gaya (check out the "Bodh Gaya: Place of enlightenment" section, earlier in this chapter). The tradition of learning that flourished in Sarnath during the early years of Buddhism has also been reintroduced. The Central Institute of Higher Tibetan Studies, its library, and publishing venture are all relatively new expressions of this tradition. In these and other ways, concerned individuals and groups have rekindled the Dharma flame originally lit at Sarnath.

Kushinagar: The Buddha's death

The fourth major pilgrimage site is Kushinagar, where the Buddha died.

According to tradition, sometime before he died, the Buddha announced to his closest attendant, Ananda, that the time for him to enter the state of parinirvana, or final liberation, was approaching. According to popular belief, Buddha lay down on his right side in what's known as the *lion posture,* entered progressively deeper states of meditation, and then died. Afterward, his body was cremated.

Although archeological evidence proves that numerous Buddhist monasteries once stood in Kushinagar and that King Ashoka built several stupas there, very little remains today. However, an ancient statue of the Buddha reclining in the lion posture has been restored. This statue, the Parinirvana Temple and Nirvana Stupa are among the monuments to mark the Buddha's final resting place and cremation. Many pilgrims report that Kushinagar possesses an extraordinarily calm atmosphere, making it a perfect site for peaceful meditation.

Seeing Other Important Pilgrimage Sites

Four other places of Buddhist pilgrimage in northern India deserve at least a brief mention:

- **Rajgir:** The capital city of the kingdom of Magadha, whose king, Bimbisara, was a disciple of the Buddha
- **Shravasti:** The area where the Buddha spent many rainy seasons
- **Sankashya:** The place where the Buddha is believed to have returned to Earth after teaching his mother in heaven
- **Nalanda:** The site of a world-renowned monastic university

The next few sections take a closer look at each of these sites.

Rajgir

When the Buddha left his father's palace in search of an end to all suffering (see Chapter 3 for more details), he passed through the kingdom of Magadha, where he caught the eye of King Bimbisara. The Buddha promised the king that, if his search was successful, he would return to Rajgir and teach him.

As a result of this promise, Rajgir became one of the most important places where the Buddha turned the wheel of Dharma. On a hill called Vulture's Peak, just beyond the city, the Buddha delivered some of his most important teachings (see Figure 9-5).

Figure 9-5: The Vulture's Peak at Rajgir.

Photographed by John C. Huntington, courtesy of the Huntington Archive at The Ohio State University.

Rajgir is an ancient city, and visitors can still see and use the baths where the Buddha supposedly refreshed himself. They can also view the remains of the parks given to the Buddha by his first patrons for the monastic community to use. Many important events in Buddhism's early history took place in Rajgir, including the gathering of the First Council, where 500 monks collected and compiled Shakyamuni's teachings. (To find out more about the historical development of Buddhism, including the meeting of the First Council, check out Chapter 4.)

For many of today's visitors to Rajgir, the most impressive sight is a large stupa, visible for many miles around, that Japanese Buddhists constructed on the top of the hill above Vulture's Peak. This stupa, radiantly white in the glare of the sun, is adorned on four sides with gold images illustrating the four major events in the Buddha's life mentioned throughout this chapter: his birth, enlightenment, first turning of the wheel of Dharma, and entrance into parinirvana.

Shravasti

Even today, the monsoon season in India (which lasts from about June to September in the north) makes travel difficult. During the time of the Buddha, before paved roads existed, getting around must've been close to impossible. So the Buddha remained in retreat with his disciples during this time, and he spent his first rainy season in Rajgir. But for many rainy seasons after that, he and his followers gathered at Shravasti, where a wealthy merchant had invited them to stay. The area became known as the Jetavana Grove, an often-mentioned site of the Buddha's teachings.

Many events in the life of the Buddha are associated with Shravasti, but the one that catches the imagination is the legend of the Buddha's display of miraculous powers, the "great miracle of Shravasti." Generally, Buddhists downplay the importance of the extraordinary powers that sometimes result from deep meditation. They're generally ignored or kept hidden unless an overwhelming purpose for displaying them arises. These powers aren't troublesome, but they can distract the practitioner from the true aim of meditation — spiritual realization.

According to the legend, the Buddha had good reason to display his miraculous abilities in Shravasti. During the years he traveled across India giving teachings, teachers from opposing philosophical schools often challenged him to debate points of doctrine and to engage in contests of miraculous abilities. For the first couple decades after his enlightenment, the Buddha consistently declined to take up these challenges. But eventually, he chose to accept the challenge because he realized that it would enable him to bring a large number of people into the Dharma fold. So the Buddha announced that he would meet with other spiritual teachers and engage in the contests they desired, with the understanding that whoever lost would, along with his followers, become the disciple of the winner.

You can probably guess how this contest turned out. The Buddha overwhelmed the crowds who'd gathered with a pyrotechnical display of his magical abilities — from flying through the air to producing countless manifestations of himself so that the sky was filled with Buddhas! The defeated rivals and their followers developed great faith in the Buddha, who then gave them his teachings. The whole event is still commemorated in various Buddhist lands. In Tibet, for example, Lama Tsongkhapa (whom we mention in Chapters 3 and 15 as the guru of the First Dalai Lama) instituted a 15-day prayer festival in Lhasa to mark the New Year and recall the events at Shravasti.

Sankashya

Sankashya, identified with the village of Basantpur in the Farrukhabad district of today's state of Uttar Pradesh, is the site where, according to legendary accounts, the Buddha descended after visiting his mother in heaven, where she had taken rebirth. As we explain in Chapter 3, the Buddha's mother, Queen Maya, died within a week of giving birth to him, and she was reborn in heaven. To repay her kindness, the Buddha ascended to heaven and gave her teachings on the topic of higher knowledge (abhidharma; see Chapter 4 for more on this topic). Sankashya is the spot where the Buddha, flanked by the great gods of ancient India, Indra and Brahma, is believed to have returned to Earth after this special teaching.

Nalanda

Last on the list of pilgrimage sites is Nalanda, which is located near Rajgir. At one time, Nalanda was the site of a mango grove where the Buddha often stayed. But it became famous several centuries after the time of the Buddha when an influential monastic university grew up there. This university shaped the development of Buddhist thought and practice in India and around the world. Nalanda was one of the major seats of learning in Asia, attracting Buddhists and non-Buddhists alike, and it remained influential until its destruction at the end of the 12th century.

Even though it now lies in ruins, the extensive excavations at Nalanda give visitors an idea of the huge size of this and other Buddhist monasteries of the time, as well as the enormous impact they must have had on Indian culture. The list of individuals who studied and taught at Nalanda includes many of the most revered Indian Buddhist masters, many of whose works are still studied today.

Going on Pilgrimage Today

Although Shakyamuni Buddha spent his entire life in the northern portion of the Indian subcontinent, it isn't the only part of the world where a person can go on Buddhist pilgrimage. As Buddhism spread throughout India and beyond (see Chapters 4 and 5), many different places became associated with important teachers and famous meditators, and these, too, became destinations of the devout (or merely curious) Buddhist pilgrim.

We can't possibly do justice to the large number of Buddhist holy places that pilgrims still visit to this day. Even in a relatively small area like the Kathmandu Valley of Nepal, you could spend months going from one sacred spot to another and still not see them all. The following short list, therefore, is just a sampling of the rich treasure of sites you may consider visiting some day:

- **Temple of the Sacred Tooth,** in Kandy, Sri Lanka (formerly Ceylon): A tooth said to belong to Shakyamuni Buddha is enshrined here. On the full moon of August every year, a magnificent festival is held — complete with elephants — in its honor.
- **Shwedagon Pagoda,** in Yangon (formerly known as Rangoon), Myanmar (formerly Burma): This world-famous golden monument, housing eight of the Buddha's hairs, rises over 320 feet and is the most venerated of all Burmese Buddhist shrines.
- **Mount Kailash,** in western Tibet: This remote, pyramid-shaped snow mountain is a sacred site for Hindus and Buddhist pilgrims. It is considered the home of Hindu and Buddhist deities. Pilgrims hardy enough to make the rugged journey here and complete the circuit around this sacred mountain report this pilgrimage to be a high point (literally as well as figuratively) of their lives.
- **Borobudur,** on the island of Java, Indonesia: This enormous structure of many terraces — built in the shape of a sacred diagram *(mandala)* — is located on a hill and filled with hundreds of Buddha statues and stupas.
- **The 88 Sacred Places** of Shikoku, Japan: The great Japanese Buddhist master Kukai (774–835 CE) is believed to have established a pilgrimage route around the beautiful and mountainous island of Shikoku, and people of all ages and nationalities come to complete all or part of the circuit. (For Kukai, also known as Kobo Daishi, see Chapter 5.)

- **Almost anywhere:** Inspired by Kukai's example, a number of modern-day Buddhists have established pilgrimage routes through scenic areas of their own countries. Some of the Beat poets associated with California, for example, made a practice of walking around Mount Tamalpais, a mountain north of San Francisco sacred to Native Americans. This practice continues today, and with the founding of an ever-growing number of monasteries, retreat centers, and temples in the West, trails linking them to Buddhist pilgrimage routes are bound to grow.

Part IV
Exploring the Buddhist Path

The 5th Wave By Rich Tennant

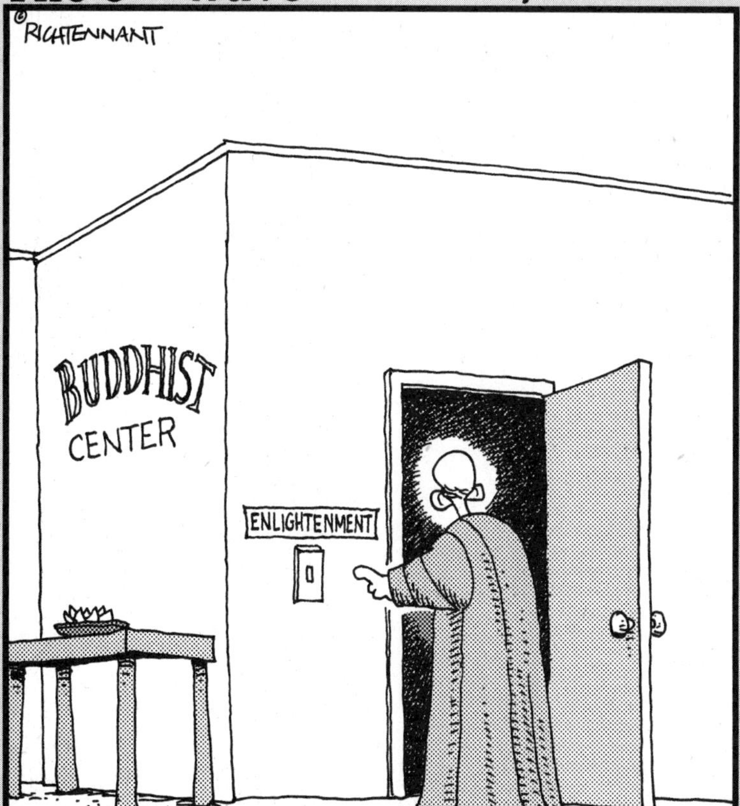

In this part . . .

You can think of this part as a handy foldout map. Here we lay out the entire Buddhist path — with the goal of enlightenment right in front of you from the beginning. Now all you have to do is get there — and with our guidance, you'll have a head start! This part lights up the important landmarks on your journey and shows you how to advance into new and inspiring terrain.

Chapter 10

What Is Enlightenment, Anyway?

In This Chapter

- Figuring out what makes enlightenment so special
- Walking along the Theravada path to nirvana
- Exploring enlightenment in the Vajrayana tradition
- Studying the path to enlightenment through the ten ox-herding pictures of Zen

A pioneering book detailing the sudden awakening experiences of ten meditators drew Stephan to the practice of Buddhism in the late 1960s. Presented in the form of letters and journal entries, these dramatic accounts chronicled years of intensive meditation practice and the powerful, life-changing breakthroughs that ultimately (though not immediately) followed. Men and women wept and laughed with joy as they finally penetrated years of conditioning and ultimately realized who they really were.

As a young college student, Stephan had experienced his share of suffering and had searched Western philosophy looking for solutions, so he was enthralled by what he read. He immediately became hooked on meditation. If those ordinary folks could wake up, he thought he could, too.

In those days, few people had even heard the word *enlightenment* used in the Buddhist context, and the available books on Buddhism for a general audience may have filled half a bookshelf, at best. Things have really changed in the past 30 years! Today books dealing with aspects of Buddhism regularly make *The New York Times* bestseller lists, and everyone seems to be seeking enlightenment in some form. You can read popular manuals for "awakening the Buddha within" or achieving "enlightenment on the run," and you can take "enlightenment intensives" at your local yoga studio. One perfume company even produces a scent they call Satori, the Japanese word for "enlightenment."

But what does enlightenment (or awakening) really mean in Buddhism? Though the current quick-fix culture has trivialized it, *enlightenment* is often considered the culmination of the spiritual path, which may take a lifetime of practice and inquiry to achieve. In this chapter, we describe (as much as words possibly can) what enlightenment is — and is not — and explain how people's understanding of it has changed as Buddhism evolved and adapted to different cultures.

REMEMBER

As you read this chapter, keep in mind that words can only point to dimensions of experience that simply can't be contained in words. To use a traditional Buddhist analogy, words are like a finger pointing at the full moon. If you get caught up in the finger, you may never get to appreciate the magnificent sight of the moon in the sky.

Considering the Many Faces of Spiritual Realization

If you read the stories of the world's great mystics and sages, you find that spiritual experiences come in a dazzling array of shapes and sizes. For example:

- Some Native American *shamans* enter altered states in which they journey to other dimensions to find allies and other healing resources for their tribe members.
- Some Hindus experience visions of deities and feelings of ecstasy through the rising of an energy known as *kundalini,* enter blissful states that last for hours, or merge in union with divinities like Shiva.
- Christian saints and mystics have encountered transformative visions of Jesus, received visitations from angels, and manifested the *stigmata* (marks resembling the crucifixion wounds of Christ) in their hands and feet.
- The Hebrew Bible is filled with tales of prophets and patriarchs who meet Jehovah in some form — as the fire in the burning bush, the voice in the whirlwind, and so on.

Though such dramatic experiences can have a transformative spiritual impact on an individual, they may or may not be enlightening, as Buddhists understand this term. In fact, most traditions of Buddhism downplay the importance of visions, voices, powers, energies, and altered states, claiming that they distract practitioners from the true purpose of the spiritual endeavor — a direct, liberating insight into the essential nature of reality.

The basic Buddhist teaching of impermanence (Pali: *anicca*) suggests that even the most powerful spiritual experiences come and go like clouds in the sky. The point of practice is to realize a truth so deep and fundamental that it doesn't change, because it's not an experience at all; it's the nature of reality itself. This undeniable, unalterable realization is known as *enlightenment.*

REMEMBER

Among the Buddha's core teachings are the *four noble truths* (see Chapter 3 for more information), which explain the nature and cause of suffering and the "eightfold path" for its elimination. This path culminates in enlightenment.

The Buddha also taught that all beings have the same potential for enlightenment that he had. Among the characteristics distinguishing ordinary beings from a Buddha are the distorted views, attachments, and aversive emotions that block the truth from their eyes.

All traditions of Buddhism would undoubtedly agree on the fundamental teachings about enlightenment that we outline in the two preceding paragraphs — after all, these teachings come from the earliest and most universally accepted of the Buddha's discourses. The traditions differ, however, over the contents of enlightenment and the precise means of achieving it. What is the actual goal of the spiritual life? What do you awaken to — and how do you get there? Believe it or not, the answers to these questions changed over the centuries as Buddhism evolved.

Most traditions believe that their version of enlightenment is exactly the same as the Buddha's. Some claim that theirs is the only true version — the deeper, secret realization that the Buddha never dared reveal during his lifetime. Other commentators insist that the realization of later Buddhist masters carried both practice and enlightenment to dimensions that the Buddha himself had never anticipated. Whatever the truth may be, the traditions clearly differ in significant ways.

In the rest of this chapter, we offer you a glimpse of enlightenment from three different points of view: Theravada, Vajrayana, and Zen. Though this brief tour certainly can't cover every conception of enlightenment within Buddhism, it does cover the basics — at least, as much as words can. Ultimately, as all traditions agree, enlightenment surpasses even the most refined intellectual understanding and simply can't be contained in our usual conceptual frameworks.

As you read the following sections, keep this old Zen adage in mind: "A painting of a rice cake cannot satisfy hunger." You can look at pictures of pastries all day long, but you won't feel fulfilled until you taste the real thing for yourself. In the same way, you can read dozens of books about enlightenment, but you won't really understand what they're talking about until you catch a glimpse of the actual experience. Does that sound like an invitation to practice Buddhism? Well, you're right — it is!

Reviewing the Theravada Tradition's Take on Nirvana

The Theravada tradition bases its teachings and practices on the Pali canon, which includes the Buddha's discourses (Pali: *suttas*) that were preserved through memorization (by monks actually in attendance), passed along orally for many generations, and ultimately written down more than four centuries after the Buddha's death. (For someone who has a hard enough time remembering a few phone numbers, such memorization skills boggle the mind.) Because these teachings are ascribed to the historical Buddha, some proponents of the Theravada tradition claim that they represent original Buddhism — that is, Buddhism as the Enlightened One actually taught it and intended it to be practiced and realized.

The Theravada tradition elaborates a detailed, progressive path of practice and realization that leads the student through four stages of enlightenment, culminating in *nirvana* (Pali: *nibbana*) — the complete liberation from suffering. The path itself consists of three aspects, or *trainings:* moral discipline (ethical conduct), concentration (meditation practice), and wisdom (study of the teachings and direct spiritual insight). (For more on the three trainings, see Chapters 8 and 13. For more on the Theravada tradition, check out Chapter 5.)

Defining nirvana

Because the Buddha considered craving and ignorance to be two of the root causes of all suffering, he often defines *nirvana* as the extinction of craving and eradication of ignorance.

REMEMBER

The term *nirvana* literally means "extinguishing," referring to the fires of craving, hatred, and ignorance that keep us unenlightened beings cycling endlessly from one rebirth to the next. Nirvana refers to a condition in which these fires are extinguished, and you're completely free of craving, hatred, and ignorance. Just because the terms used to refer to nirvana emphasize the absence of certain undesirable qualities, don't mistakenly assume that nirvana itself is negative. These seemingly negative terms point to an unconditional truth that lies beyond language and thus can't be accurately described in words. In his wisdom, the Buddha realized that positive terms, which appear to describe a limited state, may be more misleading than helpful because nirvana isn't a state and has no limitations.

REMEMBER

Nirvana is indescribable. In the Theravada tradition, it's referred to using negative terms because it's the complete opposite of samsara, the cycle of existence in which we are entangled.

However, if nirvana has a particular feeling or tone, it's generally characterized as unshakable tranquility, contentment, and bliss (see Figure 10-1). Sound appealing?

Figure 10-1: Shakyamuni Buddha, the classic embodiment of serenity and peace.

Photo courtesy of Gudrun Bühnemann.

Revealing the four stages on the path to nirvana

REMEMBER

Early Buddhism recognized four distinct levels or stages of realization, each one marked by the elimination of certain fetters (Pali: *samyojana*), or chains, that bind us.

These types of practitioners have attained the distinct stages on the path to nirvana:

- **Stream-enterer:** The practitioner has broken three of ten fetters: the erroneous view that a personality exists, doubt about the path to liberation, and attachment to rules and rituals. He has thereby entered the stream that leads to nirvana. This person purportedly will attain nirvana within seven lives.

- **Once-returner:** This person has significantly weakened two additional fetters: craving and aversion. He will be reborn as a human being no more than one time before reaching the fourth stage, that of an arhat (see the last bullet point of this list).
- **Nonreturner:** The practitioner has completely eliminated all of the five fetters previously mentioned and will not be reborn as a human being.
- **Arhat:** This person has completely broken ten fetters, including these additional five: the craving for existence in the sphere of form, the craving for existence in the formless sphere, pride, restlessness, and ignorance. He has attained full enlightenment and reached the end of suffering. The ancient collection of verses on Buddhist themes, the *Dhammapada*, describes him in verses 95 and 96 as follows:

  > "His patience is like that of the earth.
  > He is firm like a pillar and serene like a lake.
  > No rounds of rebirths are in store for him.
  > His mind is calm, speech and action are calm
  > of one who has attained freedom by true knowledge.
  > For such a person there is peace."

  At this point, the circumstances of life no longer have the slightest hold over a person; positive or negative experiences no longer stir even the slightest craving or dissatisfaction. As the Buddha said, all that needed to be done has been done. There's nothing further to realize. The path is complete.

Getting a Handle on Two Traditions of Wisdom

As Buddhism developed over the centuries, various schools emerged that differed in how they framed the path to enlightenment and how they understood the ultimate goal of this path. (For more on these developments, see Chapters 4 and 5.) Some Mahayana ("Great Vehicle" or "Great Path") schools shifted the emphasis from the experience of no-self to the experience of *emptiness.* (Chapter 14 explains the concept of emptiness.)

The two main commentarial branches of the Mahayana tradition understood emptiness (or ultimate reality) in two quite different ways. The Madhyamika (Sanskrit for "middle doctrine") school refused to assert anything about ultimate reality. Instead, these folks chose to refute and discredit any positive assertions that other schools made. The end result left practitioners without any belief or point of view to hold on to, which effectively pulled the rug out from under their conceptual minds and forced them to, in the words of the great Mahayana text, the *Diamond Sutra*, "cultivate the mind that dwells nowhere" — the spacious, expansive, unattached mind of enlightenment.

By contrast, the Yogachara (Sanskrit for "practice of yoga") school said that the world as we perceive it is only a manifestation of the mind, or *consciousness.* (This view gave rise to the other name for this school, Vijnanavada (Sanskrit for "teaching [in which] consciousness or mind [plays a special role]").

Realizing the Mind's Essential Purity in the Vajrayana Tradition

REMEMBER

The Vajrayana (or tantric) traditions of Buddhism, which began in India and flowered in Nepal, Mongolia, and Tibet, retain the basic understanding of no-self and expand on it. (Vajrayana is the name for tantric traditions within Mahayana Buddhism, which we discuss earlier in this chapter.) After you look deeply into your heart and mind (using techniques adapted from different traditions and discover the truth of no-self, you naturally open to a deeper realization of the nature of mind (or consciousness), which is pure, vast, luminous, clear, nonlocatable, ungraspable, aware, and essentially nondual.

"Nondual" simply means that subject and object, matter and spirit are "not two" — that is, they're different on an everyday level, but they're inseparable at the level of essence. For example, you and the book you see in front of you are different in obvious ways, but you're essentially expressions of an inseparable whole. Now, don't expect us to put this oneness into words the mind can understand, though mystics and poets have been trying their best for thousands of years. If you want to know more, you just may have to check it out for yourself.

Not only is the nature of mind innately pure, radiant, and aware, but it also spontaneously manifests itself in each moment as compassionate activity for the benefit of all beings. Though conceptual thought can't grasp the nature of mind, this mind-nature (like no-self) can be realized through meditation in a series of ever-deepening experiences culminating in complete realization, or Buddhahood.

In Vajrayana, the path to complete enlightenment begins with the extensive cultivation of positive qualities, like loving-kindness and compassion, and then progresses to the development of various levels of insight into the nature of mind. In some traditions, practitioners are taught to visualize themselves as the embodiment of enlightenment itself and then to meditate upon their inherent awakeness, or Buddha nature. (For more on the Vajrayana path, see Chapter 5.)

TIP

Generally, navigating the path from beginning to end requires a qualified teacher, diligent practice, wholehearted dedication, and numerous intensive retreats.

Taking the direct approach to realization

Some consider the *Dzogchen-Mahamudra* teachings the highest teaching of the Tibetan traditions. Dzogchen means "great perfection" in Tibetan, and *Mahamudra* is Sanskrit for "great seal." Both terms refer to the insight that everything is perfect just the way it is.

These two approaches are generally considered to be slightly different expressions of the same nondual realization. (For a complete explanation of nondualism, see the second paragraph earlier in this section.) Traditionally, only practitioners who completed years of preliminary practice are qualified to learn about Dzogchen-Mahamudra, but today in the West, anyone sincere and motivated enough to attend a retreat can explore this approach to enlightenment.

In Dzogchen, teachers provide their students with a direct introduction to the nature of mind, known as *pointing-out instructions.* The students then try to stabilize this realization in their meditations and ordinary lives. The goal is to embody this realization without interruption until the separation between meditation and nonmeditation drops away and the mind is continuously awake to its own inherent nature in every situation. In Mahamudra, practitioners first learn to calm the mind and then use this calmness as a foundation for inquiring deeply into its nature. When the mind recognizes its own nature, practitioners rest in this mind-nature as much as possible. (Now, don't ask us to explain what this "resting" involves — like so much else in this chapter, it eludes words.) Though the approach of Dzogchen-Mahamudra may be considered direct, mastering it is extremely difficult and may take a lifetime — at least.

Understanding the complete enlightenment of a Buddha

The Theravada tradition considers the final goal of spiritual practice, exemplified by the arhat (see the section "Reviewing the Theravada Tradition's Take on Nirvana," earlier in the chapter, for a reminder of what arhat means), to be eminently attainable in this lifetime by any sincere practitioner. In the time of the historical Buddha, numerous disciples achieved complete realization and were acknowledged as arhats, which meant that their realization of no-self was essentially the same as the Buddha's.

In the Vajrayana tradition, by contrast, the realization of Buddhahood appears to be a much more protracted path. The completely enlightened ones experience the end of all craving and other negative emotions, but these folks also exhibit numerous beneficial qualities, including boundless love and compassion, infinite, all-seeing wisdom, ceaseless enlightened activity for the welfare of all beings, and the capacity to speed others on their path to enlightenment.

Needless to say, many of the faithful (especially at the beginning levels of practice) may see such an advanced stage of realization as a distant and unattainable dream. Compounding this feeling may be the many inspiring stories of exceptional sages who meditate for years in mountain caves and achieve not only a diamondlike clarity of mind and inexhaustible compassion, but also numerous superhuman powers.

Yet dedicated Vajrayana practitioners do gradually see their efforts lead to greater compassion, clarity, tranquility, and fearlessness, along with a deeper and more abiding recognition of the nature of mind. Indeed, Vajrayana promises that everyone has the potential to achieve Buddhahood in this lifetime by using the powerful methods it provides. (For more on Vajrayana practices, see Chapter 5.)

Standing Nirvana on Its Head with Zen

The teachings about the *tathagatagarbha* (Sanskrit for "Buddha embryo" or "Buddha nature") found in some Mahayana texts have influenced the schools of Zen Buddhism. According to these teachings, all beings have the potential to become Buddhas. Instead of emphasizing a progressive path to an exalted spiritual ideal, some Zen masters teach that complete enlightenment is always available right here and now — in this very moment — and can be experienced directly in a sudden burst of insight known in Japanese as *kensho* or *satori.* Other masters teach a gradual path. Some Zen masters de-emphasize the enlightenment experience altogether, teaching that the wholehearted practice of sitting meditation (Japanese: *zazen*) — or wholehearted practice in any situation — is enlightenment itself.

Zen is filled with stories of great masters who compare their enlightenment with Shakyamuni's enlightenment and speak of him as if he were an old friend and colleague. At the same time, enlightenment (though elusive) is regarded as the most ordinary realization of what has always been so. For this reason, the monks in many Zen stories break into laughter when they finally "get it." Awakened Zen practitioners are known for their down-to-earth involvement in every activity and for not displaying any trace of some special state called "realization."

Tuning in to the direct transmission from master to disciple

A reflection of a certain attitude toward enlightenment may be found in this Chan/Zen slogan:

> A special transmission outside the scriptures,
> No dependence on words and letters.
> Directly pointing to the mind,
> See true nature, become a Buddha.

The verse makes several points, which the following list expands on:

- **Special transmission outside the scriptures:** Zen traces its lineage back to Mahakashyapa, one of the Buddha's foremost disciples who apparently received the direct transmission of his teacher's "mind essence" by accepting a flower with a wordless smile (see Chapter 5 for more info). Since then, masters have directly "transmitted" their enlightened mind to their disciples, not through written texts, but through teachings passed on from mind to mind (or, as Stephan's first Zen teacher liked to say, "from one warm hand to another"). But the truth is that enlightenment itself isn't transmitted; it has to burst into flame anew in each generation. The teacher merely acknowledges and certifies the awakening.
- **Directly pointing to the mind:** The master doesn't explain abstract truth intellectually. Instead, he points his disciples' attention directly back to their innate true nature, which is ever present but generally unrecognized. With the master's guidance, the disciple wakes up and realizes that he isn't this limited separate self, but is rather pure, vast, mysterious, ungraspable consciousness itself — also known as the Buddha nature or Big Mind.
- **See true nature, become a Buddha:** Having realized true nature, the disciple now sees with the eyes of the Buddha and walks in the Buddha's shoes. No distance in space and time separates Shakyamuni's mind and the disciple's mind. Illustrating this point, some version of the following passage appears repeatedly in the old teaching tales: "There is no Buddha but mind, and no mind but the Buddha."

REMEMBER

The great Zen masters inevitably teach that mind includes all of reality, with nothing left out. This very body is the Buddha's body, this very mind is the Buddha's mind, and this very moment is inherently complete and perfect just the way it is — a truth known as *suchness* or *thusness.* Nothing needs to be changed or added to make this body, mind, and moment more spiritual or holy than it already is — you merely need to awaken to the nondual nature of reality for yourself. (Turn your attention to the sidebar "Pure as the driven snow" for some more info.)

Pure as the driven snow

Generations of Zen teachers have told the following story, recorded in the *Platform Sutra* of the Sixth Patriarch, to illustrate the distinction between a partial, progressive view of realization and the view of the Zen masters, who understand the mind to be intrinsically pure — and, therefore, in no need of purification through various methods and practices. The Fifth Patriarch of Zen in China gathered his monks together and asked each of them to write a verse that expressed their grasp of *true nature* (also known as *Buddha nature*). If he found one among them whose wisdom was clear, he promised to pass on his lineage to him and make him the Sixth Patriarch, his successor.

That night, the head monk came forward and wrote the following verse on the monastery wall:

> The body is the Bodhi tree,
> The mind is a clear mirror.
> We must strive to polish it constantly
> And not allow any dust to collect.

When the Fifth Patriarch read the verse, he knew that it showed some relative appreciation of the value of practice, but it also clearly revealed that the person who wrote it had not entered the gate of realization — and he told this to the head monk. In public, however, he praised the verse as worthy of study. Several days later, a young, illiterate novice who worked in the kitchen threshing rice heard someone reciting the verse and asked to be taken to the wall where it was written. There he had someone inscribe the following verse:

> Bodhi [awakening] has no tree,
> The mirror has no stand.
> Buddha nature is originally clear and pure.
> Where is there room for dust to collect?

In other words, your fundamental nature needs no polishing through spiritual practice because it's never been stained — even for an instant. When the Fifth Patriarch saw this verse, he knew that he had found his successor. Even though the young novice couldn't read or write, the Fifth Patriarch acknowledged his enlightenment and made him the Sixth Patriarch of Chinese Zen.

The ten ox-herding pictures

Ever since the ten ox-herding pictures were first created in 12th-century China, Zen masters in China, Korea, and Japan have used them to instruct and inspire their students. The images illustrate the ten stages of training the mind by comparing them to the taming of an ox. They begin with an individual's search for the ox and culminate with his or her complete liberation. The images (less frequently known as the cow-herding pictures) depict, in most cases, a water buffalo. After they became popular, numerous artists drew them over the centuries, with only minor differences. There's also a series of six ox-herding pictures in which the color of the ox undergoes gradual lightening from dark to white until the ox disappears. The comparison of an ox that needs to be tamed to a practitioner's unruly mind was already being made in early Indian Buddhist texts. These texts commonly use similes that appeal to a society whose main occupation was agriculture. One example is comparing the concept of karma to a seed that is sown in the ground and eventually bears fruit.

Here we reproduce the set of ten ox-herding pictures painted by the Japanese artist Tatsuhiko Yokoo (born in 1928; see Figures 10-2 to 10-11).

The following describes each picture and explains its meaning:

- **Seeking the ox (see Figure 10-2):** The first picture shows the herder, rope in hand, wandering in search of the lost ox.

  You have the desire to practice the Buddha's teaching and are taking the first steps in Zen practice.

Figure 10-2: Seeking the ox.

Photo courtesy of Tatsuhiko Yokoo.

- **Finding the tracks (see Figure 10-3):** In the second picture, the herder finds the tracks of the ox and follows them.

  Having been introduced to the teachings of Zen, you study and practice them diligently and acquire a conceptual understanding of them.

Figure 10-3: Finding the tracks.

Photo courtesy of Tatsuhiko Yokoo.

- **Glimpsing the ox (see Figure 10-4):** In the third picture, the herder glimpses the rear of the ox.

  You've clearly seen your true nature for the first time. But this realization quickly slips into the background, and you're still a long way from making it your constant companion.

- **Catching the ox (see Figure 10-5):** In the fourth picture, the herder has caught the resistant ox and holds it by a rope.

  You're aware of your true nature in every moment and situation; you're never apart from it — even for an instant. But your mind continues to be turbulent and unruly, and you need to concentrate to keep from getting distracted.

- **Taming the ox (see Figure 10-6):** In the fifth picture, the herder leads the now-docile ox by a rope.

  Finally, as every trace of doubt disappears, the mind settles down. You're so firmly established in your experience of your true nature that even thoughts no longer distract you, for you realize that, like everything else in the universe, they're just an expression of who you fundamentally are.

Figure 10-4: Glimpsing the ox.

Photo courtesy of Tatsuhiko Yokoo.

Figure 10-5: Catching the ox.

Photo courtesy of Tatsuhiko Yokoo.

Figure 10-6: Taming the ox.

Photo courtesy of Tatsuhiko Yokoo.

- **Riding the ox home (see Figure 10-7):** In the sixth picture, the herder has mounted the ox and rides home. The ox moves of its own accord, without being led by a rope.

  Now you and your true nature are in total harmony. You no longer have to struggle to resist temptation or distraction; you're completely at peace, inextricably connected to your essential source.

- **Forgetting the ox (see Figure 10-8):** In the seventh picture, the herder is sitting outside his hut alone at sunrise.

  At last, the ox of your true nature has disappeared because you have completely and inseparably incorporated it. The ox was a convenient metaphor to lead you home. Ultimately, however, you and the ox are one! With nothing left to seek, you're thoroughly at ease, meeting life as it unfolds.

- **Forgetting both self and ox (see Figure 10-9):** The last three pictures describe the state of a Buddha after his enlightenment. In the eighth picture, we see an empty circle.

  The last traces of a separate self have dropped away, and, with them, the last vestiges of realization have vanished. Even the thought "I am enlightened" or "I am the embodiment of Buddha nature" no longer arises. You're at the same time completely ordinary and completely free of any attachment or identification.

Figure 10-7: Riding the ox home.

Photo courtesy of Tatsuhiko Yokoo.

Figure 10-8: Forgetting the ox.

Photo courtesy of Tatsuhiko Yokoo.

Figure 10-9: Forgetting both self and ox.

Photo courtesy of Tatsuhiko Yokoo.

- **Returning to the source (see Figure 10-10):** The ninth picture shows nature in full bloom, without an observer.

  After you've merged with your source, you see everything in all its diversity (painful and pleasurable, beautiful and ugly) as the perfect expression of this source. You don't need to resist or change anything; you're completely one with the *suchness* of life.

- **Entering the world with helping hands (see Figure 10-11):** In the tenth picture, an older big-bellied and bare-chested figure sits happily at rest.

  With no trace of a separate self to be enlightened or deluded, the distinction between the two dissolves in spontaneous, compassionate activity. Now you move freely through the world like water through water, without the slightest resistance, joyfully responding to situations as they arise, helping where appropriate and naturally kindling awakening in others.

Figure 10-10: Returning to the source.

Photo courtesy of Tatsuhiko Yokoo.

Figure 10-11: Entering the world with helping hands

Photo courtesy of Tatsuhiko Yokoo.

Finding the Common Threads in Buddhist Enlightenment

The experience of enlightenment, though described slightly differently and approached by somewhat different means, bears notable similarities from tradition to tradition.

- **Enlightenment signals the end of suffering and the eradication of craving and ignorance.**
- **Enlightenment also inevitably brings the birth of unshakable, indescribable peace, joy, loving-kindness, and compassion for others.**
- **Enlightenment involves being in the world but not of it.**

Chapter 11

A Matter of Life and Death

In This Chapter

- Coming to terms with your mortality
- Using death as an inspiration for practice
- Practicing the nine-point death meditation
- Coping with the death of a relative or friend
- Understanding how the different Buddhist traditions view death

Shortly before the start of the third game of the 1989 World Series between the Oakland Athletics and the San Francisco Giants, a strong earthquake hit the greater Bay Area. Jon was living just north of Santa Cruz at the time, about 10 miles from the epicenter, and witnessed firsthand the damage the quake caused. Fortunately, considering the large population of the area, relatively few lives were lost. But within 15 seconds, the event brought millions of people face to face with the fragility of their lives. The resulting emotional upheaval lingered for a long time.

The event caused many people to question some of their basic assumptions about what was really important in life. Conversations, even between strangers, quickly turned to spiritual matters. Attendance at meditation courses in the area increased dramatically and stayed high for many months after the earthquake. The event seemed to shake people up in more ways than one.

A close confrontation with death — whether through natural disaster, severe illness, or some other life-threatening event — often leads people to reevaluate and ultimately change their lives. Shakyamuni Buddha began his spiritual journey when he encountered suffering for the first time while venturing into the world outside his pleasure palaces (see Chapter 3). The path he discovered is the subject of Chapters 12, 13, and 14. In this chapter, we focus on Buddhist teachings on death, but don't be concerned if the subject matter sounds depressing. Our intention is to show how a deep appreciation of your own mortality can motivate you to become spiritually involved and how death itself can be a powerful teacher.

Taking Death Personally

You need a number of things to stay alive, such as a regular supply of food and drink, appropriate clothing and shelter, and medical care when you get sick. But as Buddhist masters like to say, dying doesn't take much at all — you merely need to breathe out and not breathe back in again.

If you stop breathing for just a few minutes, you'll soon be knocking on death's door. Death isn't remote or unusual — it's the one experience that's definitely going to happen to you (see "The story of the mustard seed" sidebar). As the old saying goes, you can rely on two absolutes in life: death and taxes.

But there's a big difference between a mere intellectual understanding that death is inevitable and a heartfelt appreciation that this reality applies to you personally. For example, if you polled a number of teenagers and asked them, "Do you think you're going to die someday?" they'd all answer "Yes." But, if you examined the way many of them live, you'd probably conclude that teenagers think that they're immortal. Think of the risks some (notice we say *some*) teenagers routinely take: binge drinking, reckless driving, extreme sports, and unprotected sex, just to name a few. Despite what they may say, some teenagers seem to believe that death happens only to other people.

We're not picking on teenagers; we're just using them as a rather obvious example. The fact is that *most* people live their lives as if they're never going to die. They confront the inevitability of their own mortality only when they're faced with the death of a loved one or a life-threatening illness of their own. And after the event passes, the window on reality that so suddenly opened quickly closes, and they forget about death — at least, for the time being.

Buddhism has always considered death to be one of the most powerful teachers, but this doesn't make it a joyless or life-denying religion. Buddhism simply acknowledges that death has an unparalleled capacity to force you to look deeply into your own heart and mind and recognize what really matters. This profound contemplation of death actually fuels your vibrant aliveness and self-awareness and motivates you to change your life in significant ways.

You may want to stop reading for a few minutes and consider your own attitude toward death. Do you ever give death much thought? Sure, you're uncomfortable with the idea of dying; most people are. You may even feel a certain anxiety as you move through life's inevitable transitions, knowing that they're bringing you closer to your ultimate demise. But do you ever consciously contemplate your own mortality and its implications for how you lead your life? Buddhism encourages you to do just that.

The story of the mustard seed

The following story is commonly told as a reminder that death awaits everyone, and you can't avoid it. Needless to say, the death of a child is one of the most poignant losses of all — and one of the most powerful reminders of impermanence.

A woman named Kisa Gotami lived in the Buddha's time. The death of her young son upset her so much that she went mad with grief. Clutching his lifeless form, she wandered from place to place looking for some medicine to cure her beloved child. Her friends felt sorry for her and said, "Gotami, why don't you approach the Buddha? Perhaps he can help you."

With infinite compassion, the Buddha told Gotami, "Go to town and bring me one tiny mustard seed. However, make certain that this seed comes from a house where no one has ever died."

The distraught mother immediately began searching house to house for the seed. Although everyone was eager to help her, they all had the same story to tell. "Last year my husband died," said one. "Three years ago, I lost my daughter," said another. "My brother died here yesterday," said a third. Everywhere she went, Gotami heard the same thing.

At the end of the day, Gotami returned to the Buddha empty handed. "What have you found, Gotami?" he asked gently. "Where is your mustard seed? And where is your son? You're not carrying him any longer."

"Oh, Buddha," she answered, "today I have discovered that I'm not the only one who has lost a loved one. Everywhere people have died; all things must pass away. I realize how mistaken I was to think that I could have my son back. I've accepted his death, and this afternoon, I had his body cremated. Now I've returned to you."

It is said that the Buddha then accepted Kisa Gotami as his disciple and ordained her as a nun in his order. Her understanding of reality deepened with her practice of Dharma and she soon achieved *nirvana* — complete liberation from suffering.

Recognizing Your Life As a Rare and Precious Opportunity

To contemplate death — or any other Buddhist theme — start right where you are at this moment. Take a close look at your present situation. We probably don't need to point out that you're a human being (unless, of course, you're reading this sentence in a bookstore on Mars).

Although your humanness may be obvious, you can take it for granted or simply dismiss it as insignificant. What's the problem with these options? From a Buddhist point of view, as a human being, you're uniquely positioned to accomplish the primary goal of spiritual training — complete liberation from suffering and dissatisfaction, resulting in a life of lasting happiness and boundless compassion for others (see Chapter 14 for a description of this compassionate way of life).

As a human being with the interest and ability to turn your mind to spiritual training, you have the capacity to achieve this goal. But here's the question: Will you choose this life direction? Your brief existence is going to come to an end all too quickly; if you don't choose wisely, you may be throwing away a rare and precious opportunity to do something valuable with the time you have left.

Why do we call your existence "a rare and precious opportunity"? With six billion people living on this planet and more being born every minute, you may not think that being human is particularly rare. But stop and consider the number of creatures in a small garden or a local pond — or a rainforest clearing. For every human being, millions of other creatures of every description inhabit the Earth. And among all these different kinds of life forms, how many species actually have the self-awareness necessary to do anything truly significant with their lives?

Even among your two-legged brothers and sisters, not too many folks have the life circumstances, interests, motivation, or innate potential to support inner growth, or spiritual awakening (see Chapter 10 for more on what it means to awaken spiritually). Many people grow up in environments so unsettled, impoverished, or violent that anything beyond mere survival is an unaffordable luxury. Others live in such remote areas or under such repressive regimes that they have no opportunity to hear valid spiritual teachings, much less practice them. And some folks simply lack the intelligence or the inclination to get the spiritual ball rolling.

By contrast, you have the time, energy, interest, and freedom to pick up this book and read about Buddhism. You probably even have life circumstances that allow you to study and practice the teachings. Compared with billions of other beings, you have a unique opportunity. You might even consider it to be "a rare and precious opportunity." Now you have to decide what to do with it.

WORDS OF WISDOM

"If you neglect the opportune moment now," wrote the great eighth-century Indian master Shantideva in his *Bodhicharyavatara* (Chapter 1, verse 4), "when can you ever hope to encounter it again?"

The turtle and the golden yoke

Drawn from traditional Buddhist sources, the following analogy graphically illustrates how unusual it is to find yourself with both the inner and outer necessities for spiritual development.

Imagine that a golden yoke is floating on the surface of the vast ocean. The winds and currents blow the yoke here and there. Deep in the ocean lives a blind turtle that, once every 100 years, swims up and briefly lifts its head above the surface. The odds are very slim that the turtle will surface at the precise point where its head will poke through the hole in the ever-wandering golden yoke.

Buddhism teaches that if you don't take advantage of the opportunities that you now enjoy, your chances of finding an optimal situation again are even less than the blind turtle's chances of being in the right place at the right time.

Facing Reality: The Nine-Part Death Meditation

According to the teachings of Buddhism, if you're going to take full advantage of this precious opportunity to do something significant with your existence, you need to keep the reality of death uppermost in your mind as a constant reminder and motivator. Otherwise, when you eventually do come to the end of your life, you may regret having wasted your time on trivial pursuits.

The following nine-part meditation on death, adapted from the Tibetan tradition (see Chapter 5), is designed to help practitioners make the most of their lives and to avoid the regret and panic that can arise if they die without properly preparing themselves for the inevitable. The meditation is written for dedicated students of Buddhism, but you may want to read it over to get a general idea of what the approach involves. Then if you want to continue, you can thoroughly examine each section, comparing it with your own experience and deeply contemplating the truths within.

As you examine the different points of the meditation, try to keep them in mind even when you're not meditating and see if they make sense in your everyday life. Then as you become more familiar with each point, you can see if your attitude and conviction begin to develop in the manner that the meditation describes.

If you decide to pursue the meditation further, you can place your new understanding and conviction at the focus of your single-pointed attention (as explained in Chapter 7) and integrate this deeper understanding into your life. Then the meditation practice won't remain a mere intellectual exercise, but will actually affect the way you both live and die.

REMEMBER

We don't intend this meditation — or the rest of the material in this chapter, for that matter — to depress or demoralize you. Its ultimate purpose is actually quite the opposite. You can use it to wake up from your illusion of immortality and set yourself firmly on the path to spiritual development. You may find it disturbing, but we really hope that you'll also find it thought provoking and even inspiring.

Understanding that your death is definite

You first have to face the cold, hard fact: Your death is a certainty. You can't get around it. You're definitely going to die. To reinforce this realization, consider the first three points in the nine-part death meditation:

- **You can't do anything to prevent the inevitable.** Nothing that you or anyone else does can keep death from occurring eventually. How well you take care of yourself, how famous you become, or where you decide to travel doesn't make any difference in the end: Death will find you. Think of the millions of people who were alive a mere 120 years ago. Not one of them is still living; death will pay you a visit, too.
- **Your lifespan is always shrinking.** With each tick of the clock and beat of your heart, the time you have left to live is growing that much shorter. When a condemned man is led to his execution, each step he takes brings him closer to his end; time is taking you steadily in the same direction.
- **You will die whether or not you've done anything worthwhile in this life.** Even if you do practice the Dharma taught by Shakyamuni Buddha, you get no assurance that you'll get very far in your practice before you punch that big time clock in the sky. Death doesn't say, "Oh, okay, I'll just wait until you're finished doing what you're doing. No, don't worry — I'll come back later." Likewise, you can't send death away from your doorstep or turn off the lights and pretend you're not home (of course, it would be nice if you could).

After you consider all the ways in which your death is certain — providing further insight from your own experience and understanding — put your foot down and decide that you *definitely* must do something to protect yourself from suffering both now and in the future. This "something" is the practice of the teachings, or following the spiritual path.

If you had a year to live . . .

The following is a meditation on life in the face of death, adapted from the work of Stephen Levine, a Buddhist teacher who has worked extensively with the dying.

1. **Sit quietly and comfortably for five minutes or so, drawing your awareness inward toward the coming and going of your breath.**
2. **Now imagine that you just got a phone call from your doctor telling you that she has discovered widespread cancer in your x-ray results and she estimates that you have about a year to live.** Take a deep breath and let it out — a year to live! Of course, you could dispute this prognosis, seek out other opinions, and battle aggressively to eliminate the cancer. But for now, just take in the news.
3. **Notice the feelings that arise — perhaps sadness, anger, fear, or regret.** Where does your mind take you: to the tragic image of leaving your loved ones behind, the frightening thought of dying alone, the many mistakes and unkindnesses for which you'd like to apologize, all the places you'd like to visit and people you'd like to see before you die?
4. **Consider what really matters most to you *right* now.** What would you need to do and say to feel complete before you die, to feel that you weren't leaving any loose ends behind and that you were dying in peace? If you really had a year to live, how would you change your life, beginning right now?

Spend at least ten minutes recording your thoughts and impressions.

Although this death meditation may seem grim, it isn't designed to depress you. Its purpose is to mobilize and motivate you to seek liberation from suffering now rather than at some random point in the future. In other words, you could say that the death meditation is intended to sober you up (without the cold shower and strong, black coffee) and open your eyes to this simple truth: Nothing lasts, everything changes, and this body also will turn to dust one day.

Realizing that the time of your death is uncertain

When you fully appreciate that your death is definite, you can turn to the next three points in the death-awareness meditation: The exact *time* of your death is most uncertain:

- **The human lifespan isn't fixed.** Although statisticians can calculate the average lifespan for a man or woman living in a particular country, you have no guarantee that you'll live to be that age (and some people may not even want to). Young people can die before their elders, and healthy people can die before people who are ill. It happens all the time. You can make a delicious meal, but you may not live to finish it; you can set out on an interesting journey, but you may not live to complete it.

- **Many factors can contribute to your death.** Open a medical textbook and read the long list of fatal diseases. Open a newspaper and read all the ways people lose their lives. Many real threats to your life exist, but you have relatively few ways to protect yourself. Even some of actions that are supposed to enhance your life can close the curtain on the final act. You need food to stay healthy, but thousands of people choke to death each year while eating. Taking a vacation is supposed to provide rest and relaxation, but thousands of people die each year in accidents while on holiday.
- **Your body is fragile.** Just because you're strong and healthy doesn't mean that it'll take a lot to kill you. Something as small as a pinprick can lead to infection, disease, and death — all in a very short time. Newspapers are full of stories about people who were apparently healthy one day and dead the next.

REMEMBER

When you fully appreciate that the time of your death is uncertain, you may naturally conclude that you can't afford to postpone your practice of the teachings any longer — you must practice *right now,* from this moment on. The point isn't to be uptight and afraid of enjoying yourself; instead, staying alert to the reality of every passing moment, being as clear and present as you can, is the key.

Using death awareness as your spiritual ally

Finally, consider these last points of the death meditation to note what you can't use at the time of your inevitable death:

- **Wealth can't help you.** Many people spend nearly all their time and energy trying to accumulate as much money and as many possessions as they can. But all the wealth in the world can't buy your way out of death. ("Um, Death, why don't you take my credit card and go buy yourself something nice?" It doesn't work. Sorry.) Rich or poor, everyone must face it. Also, no matter how many material possessions you've acquired, you can't take even the smallest particle with you. In fact, attachment to your belongings only makes letting go at the time of death more difficult.

- **Friends and relatives can't help you.** You may be the most famous or popular person in the world. An army of your supporters may surround your deathbed. But not one of them can protect you from death or accompany you on your ultimate journey. Your attachment to your friends (like your material possessions) may only make letting go and dying with a peaceful mind more difficult.
- **Even your body can't help you.** All your life, you've pampered your body by clothing it, feeding it, and taking care of it in every way possible. But as death approaches, instead of being helpful to you, your body can easily prove to be your adversary. Even if you have a spiritual practice, the pain your dying body subjects you to can make it extremely difficult for you to focus your mind on what you have to do.

REMEMBER

All these considerations lead to the inevitable conclusion that only your practice of the teachings can support you at the time of your death. (See Chapters 1 and 2 for a general understanding of Buddhism and Buddhist practice, and Chapters 12 to 14 for more specific suggestions.) Death is generally regarded as a time to practice the teachings as single-pointedly and continuously as possible, without distraction.

Reaping the Result of the Death Meditation

In the beginning, when you're first getting used to the death-awareness meditation, you may find the whole subject distasteful and rather morbid. But the farther into it you go, the more you can benefit (yep, we said *benefit*).

If you practice the meditation wholeheartedly, your life may begin to take on a direction and a purpose that it lacked before. And your spiritual practice, whatever form it happens to take, may grow in strength. If you're a practicing Buddhist and you genuinely take death awareness to heart, you may find that your attitude as you approach death is transformed as well:

- As a beginning practitioner, you may still be afraid to die, but at least you don't have any regrets, knowing that you've done everything you could and didn't waste your life.
- As an intermediate practitioner, you may not be happy about dying, but you have no fear, convinced that you can handle death and whatever comes next.
- As an experienced practitioner, you may actually welcome death because you know that it will be the gateway to awakening.

Dealing with the Death of a Loved One

Buddhism offers various practices for transcending the fear of death by realizing that there's no separate self that can die. It also acknowledges that most people don't have such a profound understanding and will naturally be afraid of death and grieve when they lose someone they love. Buddhism considers this pain completely normal and understandable, and welcomes it with compassion as a natural expression of the human condition. After all, if your heart is truly open to others and you wish the very best for them, watching them die can be extremely sad.

At the same time, even a preliminary grasp of concepts such as impermanence, selflessness, and emptiness, coupled with some appreciation of the nature of attachment and the suffering it can cause, can help ease your pain of loss. Buddhist meditation, the simple practice of being with your experience just the way it is, can be a powerful support by allowing the pain to surface and eventually release. If you don't block out your deep pain or grief or let it turn into anger or bitterness, grief can actually foster the precious spiritual quality of compassion for the suffering of others — compassion for the millions of people throughout the world who experience similar separation and pain.

Whatever your response to the death of a loved one, the most important point, from a Buddhist perspective, is to be kind and compassionate toward yourself. Instead of using Buddhist philosophy in an attempt to talk yourself out of your grief, you can tenderly allow your experience to be exactly the way it is, which can be a tremendous relief. This unconditional acceptance of the way things are lies at the very heart of Buddhism.

Surveying Attitudes toward Death in Buddhist Traditions

In this chapter, we mention that we're discussing death from a Buddhist point of view. But the truth is that not all Buddhists share a single view of death. As with so many topics, each Buddhist tradition has its own distinct way of relating to death and the process of dying.

All traditions would agree that death is a powerful motivator, that the truth of who you are doesn't die (only your body and personality), and that the moment of death can be an especially opportune time to awaken to this higher truth of who you really are. But even though different traditions share the same or similar attitudes, they often emphasize different aspects of the death experience.

The following sections offer a brief guided tour of the various ways that the major Buddhist traditions understand death. Although this quick survey can't be exhaustive, it's broad enough to give you an idea of the wealth of Buddhist approaches to this important topic.

Theravada: Getting off the wheel of existence

The theme of the Buddha's first teaching (as recorded in the Pali canon of the Theravada tradition) was how to gain release from the cycle of existence, known as samsara. (See Chapter 3 for more about the Buddha's first teachings, and Chapter 4 for more about the Theravada tradition.) *Samsara* is sometimes called a vicious circle because it consists of an endlessly repeating pattern of births, deaths, and rebirths in which no lasting satisfaction can be found. The ultimate goal of the Theravada teachings is to find a way out of this vicious circle and experience the inexpressible peace of *nirvana* — complete freedom from all suffering and dissatisfaction.

Because death is considered simply the boundary between the end of one life and the beginning of the next, your suffering doesn't end when you die. Death merely accelerates your next rebirth. The only real solution is to stop being reborn. How can you do this? Intriguingly enough, by realizing that no one dies and no one is reborn!

"That's ridiculous," you may object. "Clearly, *I'm* the one who is going to die and — assuming rebirth is true (which I'm not at all sure about) — I'm the one who's going to be reborn." But who or what is this "I" that you're talking about? By searching for an answer to this important question, you can solve the riddle of birth, death, and rebirth. So put your tray tables up and return your seats to their full, upright position; you're about to embark on an explanatory ride that may get a little bumpy.

As we discuss in more detail in Chapter 13, "I" is just a convenient way of talking or thinking about the nonstop series of events arising in your body and mind: I have a headache; I don't like the pain; I'll take an aspirin; I wonder if it'll help; I feel a little better; and so on. All these sensations, thoughts, memories, feelings, likes, dislikes, and so forth are continuously bubbling up in your experience; they last for a brief moment and then subside again — only to be replaced by others. They appear to refer back to some permanent, enduring "me," but where exactly is this "me" or "I"? In your brain? Your body? Your heart?

When you closely analyze your experiences, all you find are these ever-changing mental and physical events. Other than these momentary events, there's nothing else you can discover.

No matter how exhaustively you may search, you won't find a separate, unchanging, self-contained "I" at the core of your being who's having these experiences; you'll merely find these momentary experiences, themselves, giving rise to one another.

Death and rebirth work the same way: There's no solid, unchanging "I" that dies and then is reborn; there's only the pattern of the ever-changing momentary events perpetuating themselves. To interrupt this pattern and break free from cyclic existence (samsara), you need to give up your inborn belief in a concrete "I" (or self). This mistaken belief in a concrete "I" feeds the desires and attachments that bind you to the wheel of samsara; the insight of *no-self* — that is, the wisdom of selflessness, which helps you overcome your belief in a concrete "I" — enables you to break free from this wheel. (See Chapters 13 and 14 for more about the wheel of samsara and how to overcome false views about the "I" or "self.") The aim of Theravada practice is to develop such a degree of penetrating insight into the true nature of your existence that the causes for being reborn in samsara vanish, or dry up, and you experience the release of nirvana.

Death meditation in Theravada Buddhism

In his manual *Visuddhimagga (Path to Purity)*, the Buddhist scholar Buddhaghosa (370–450 CE) teaches the recollection or mindfulness of death as one of ten kinds of recollection. The practitioner of the recollection of death develops the thought in his mind that death will surely occur and cannot be escaped. In his manual, Buddhaghosa further distinguishes eight aspects of death (Chapter 8, sections 8–39):

- Death in the role of a murderer
- Death as the final ruin of life's accomplishments
- Death by inference — just as others have died, so will the practitioner
- Death involving one's corpse being shared with many creatures (such as worms)
- Death illustrating the fragility of life
- Death as being unpredictable
- Death as revealing the limited span of life
- Death as showing the shortness of the moment

This detailed classification in the *Visuddhimagga* shows that the meditation on death was developed and systematized to a very high degree in Theravada Buddhism.

Vajrayana: Turning death itself into the path

In the Vajrayana traditions practiced in Tibet and the surrounding regions, death is more than an unpleasant reality to be endured; it's considered an opportunity that a properly trained practitioner can use as a pathway to enlightenment itself.

To transform death into a spiritual path, you need to become well versed in the details of the dying process. You must have a good conceptual understanding of the stages you go through as you die, and you must be able to rehearse them in your daily meditation practice (and even in your dreams) as if they were actually happening to you. In fact, it is assumed that by the time *tantric yogis* (expert Vajrayana practitioners) come to the end of their lives, they've already "died" numerous times and know exactly what to expect.

According to the Vajrayana teachings, your physical form isn't the only body you possess. Underneath this physical form is a subtler "body." All the energies that support your physical and mental functions (including the way your senses operate, how your digestive system works, and even the way your mind processes thoughts and emotions) flow through this underlying body.

The main aim of Vajrayana practice is to awaken an energy far more refined than any of the other energies flowing through you. When you can do this, you have access to what's known as the *mind of clear light,* which is the priceless treasure of the tantric yogi. When this penetrating awareness is coupled with insightful wisdom, it can burn away all obstructions from your mind, allowing you to experience the purity of full enlightenment within this short life. (That's the theory, at least.)

Achieving enlightenment in this way is an extraordinary accomplishment, and even skillful Vajrayana practitioners may not be entirely successful during their lives. But every human being, whether or not she has practiced these advanced meditation techniques, naturally experiences the clear light at the time of death, at least for a moment.

The more prepared you are, the better you'll be able to remain fully conscious during this clear light of death experience and use it as your spiritual path to awakening. Even if you fail to awaken completely, you may still be able to direct your mind (through a forceful technique the Tibetans call the transference of consciousness) so that you can consciously take rebirth in a pure realm of existence (a so-called Buddha field or pure land) where everything is conducive to achieving full awakening. But if you don't reach a Buddha field, your preparation is still valuable. It provides you with a head start of sorts in your next life.

By remaining as fully conscious as possible during the dying process and controlling your rebirth, you can bring increased benefit to others in your future lives. This approach agrees with the compassionate vow to dedicate your practice to the liberation of others rather than to your own release from samsara. The Tibetans have a unique tradition in which highly skilled lamas who can direct their rebirth are discovered and then brought up in a way that enables them to continue their spiritual practices from one life to the next. For example, the 14th Dalai Lama was discovered as a child to be the reincarnation, or *tulku,* of the 13th Dalai Lama. Check out Chapter 15 for more about the way the Dalai Lama was discovered.

The Vajrayana isn't the only Buddhist tradition that uses the death experience as a pathway to enlightenment. For centuries, followers of the Chinese and Japanese schools of Pure Land Buddhism have used their devotion to Amitabha Buddha as a way of gaining access to his Buddha field at the time of their death (see Chapters 4 and 5 for more information on Pure Land Buddhism). In all these cases — whether you're practicing a highly technical yogic method or relying on your faith, devotion, and altruistic intentions — death ceases to be an obstacle to your spiritual development and becomes an opportunity to carry your development forward.

Zen: Dying the "great death" before you die

In the Zen Buddhist tradition, fearlessness in the face of death is one of the hallmarks of the truly enlightened. (For more on enlightenment, see Chapter 10; for more on Zen, see Chapter 5.) When you realize that you are the vast ocean of existence itself, life and death at the relative level become mere waves rising and falling on the surface of who you are. Your physical body may die, and this particular existence in space and time may come to an end, but you remain the unborn, the deathless, the eternal, the abiding reality — known as *Big Mind, Great Way,* or *True Self* — that underlies both life and death.

A famous (fictitious) Zen story illustrates this realization quite well. A notoriously cruel and ferocious samurai is looting and pillaging a particular village with his band of henchmen when he sees the local Zen master sitting quietly in meditation. The samurai walks up behind the master, applies the sharp blade of his sword to the master's neck, and arrogantly announces,

"You know, I am someone who could cut off your head without batting an eye." To this, the master replies calmly, "And I am someone who could have his head cut off without batting an eye." Stunned to the core by the master's response and realizing that he has met his superior, the samurai immediately bows before the master and becomes his disciple.

REMEMBER

The realization that you are the deathless, which occurs at the moment of full enlightenment (Japanese: *daikensho*), is known paradoxically as the "great death" because it signals the end of the illusion of being a separate self. For this reason, Zen urges you to "die before you die" (as the master in the previous story has already done), meaning that you put an end to separation (the idea of a separate "I") and awaken to your oneness with all of life. Only then does death lose its grip on you.

On a more everyday level, Zen emphasizes giving yourself so diligently to each activity that you completely lose yourself and leave no trace of a separate self behind. So Zen actually encourages you to die in each moment before you actually die — to let go of attachment and control with every action and every breath, just as you'll need to let go at the moment of death.

Chapter 12

Minding the Concept of Karma

In This Chapter

- Laying down the law — what goes around comes around
- Checking out ten actions you want to avoid
- Making up for your mistakes

Even if you have only a casual interest in Buddhism, you probably want to understand something about its basic principles. In this chapter, we discuss one of the most fundamental principles of Buddhist practice — being careful about your actions, words, and thoughts. Or, to put it another way, minding your karma.

Appreciating the Law of Karmic Cause and Effect

Most practitioners of South Asian religions (Buddhism, Hinduism, and Jainism) assume that your present life situation is the result of actions you committed in past lives. Your conduct in this life will have an influence on your future lives. In that sense you're ultimately responsible for your own life.

Buddhists believe that when you behave in a certain way and with a certain intention, certain results will eventually follow. If you act compassionately, in a beneficial way driven by positive motivations, the long-term results you experience will be pleasurable. But if your behavior is harmful or downright destructive, harm will come back to you in the future. This pattern is called the *karmic law of cause and effect.*

Karma is similar to other types of cause-and-effect relationships, such as the relationship between a seed and a sprout. As a song from the long-running musical *The Fantasticks* says, if you plant a carrot, you'll get a carrot, not a Brussels sprout. Buddhist teachers even talk about planting the seeds of karma and experiencing the future results (or effects) in terms of these karmic seeds ripening.

But according to Buddhist teachings, the intentions that drive the actions are more important than the actions themselves. If you accidentally squash a bug, it is believed, you bring minimal or no karmic consequences to yourself because you didn't see it and, therefore, didn't mean to hurt it. But if you crush an insect deliberately, especially out of anger or malice, you'll experience the karmic consequences of your action.

We're not talking about rewards and punishments here when we talk about karma. You're not a bad boy if you cheat on your taxes or a good girl if you help the old lady across the street. The law of karma doesn't carry that kind of judgmental baggage; it's much more practical and down to earth. The point is simple: If you act with aversion, you'll experience negative results in the future. If you act with love, you'll experience a positive outcome. Or, to continue the metaphor of the seeds: As you sow, so shall you reap.

The ancient collection of verses on Buddhist teachings, the *Dhammapada*, expresses this idea in verses 119 and 120:

"Even an evil-doer has good fortune as long as the misdeed has not matured. But when the misdeed has matured then the evil-doer experiences misfortune.

Even a good person experiences misfortune as long as the good has not matured. But when the good has matured then the good person experiences good fortune."

Experiencing Karmic Consequences

Although the basic idea of karma is simple — skillful causes lead to skillful effects; unskillful causes lead to unskillful effects — karma itself is quite complex.

According to popular notions, karma can develop (or ripen) in a number of ways. For example, consider an extremely negative action, like brutally and angrily murdering someone. According to some Buddhist traditions, if you don't cleanse yourself of this powerful negativity — in other words, if you don't purify this karma (see the "Purifying negative karma" section at the end of this chapter — you can experience its results in any or all of the following ways:

- It is believed that in this lifetime, you may experience painful, turbulent emotions such as guilt, terror, and more rage. And because of the negativity you project, you're more likely to be the victim of a violent act yourself.
- After this life, you may be reborn in a realm filled with extreme suffering. (See Chapter 13 for more about such a "hell" realm.)
- When you're born as a human again, you may have a short life filled with sickness and other difficulties.

- In your future life as a human, your surroundings won't be conducive to good health. For example, food will lack nutrition and medicines will lack the power to cure disease.
- Even as a young child in a future life, you may display a sadistic nature — taking delight in killing small animals, for example. With this kind of negative predisposition to harm others, you continue to plant the seeds for more suffering in the future. Of all the results of negative karma, this outcome is the worst because it just perpetuates misery for yourself and others.

Another reason karma can be difficult to understand is the time lag between the cause and its effect. This delay is the reason that cruel, corrupt people may thrive (at least temporarily) while compassionate, ethical people may suffer. A tremendous amount of time may pass between your action (cheating someone) and the reaction you experience (someone cheating you).

The same idea is also true for positive actions; the results may take a long time to show up. Even though some karmic effects ripen rather quickly, you don't experience most of the outcomes for one or more lifetimes! Talk about waiting (and waiting) for the other shoe to drop. As one Buddhist teacher is fond of saying, if your own back began to break just as you started to crush a bug, no one would have to warn you to stop. The connection between cause and effect would be obvious to you, and you'd naturally change your behavior. Unfortunately, the law of karma doesn't necessarily provide such immediate feedback.

Following the Buddha's Ethical Guidance

According to tradition, as Shakyamuni Buddha sat under the Bodhi tree on the night of his enlightenment (see Chapter 3), his mind achieved an extraordinary level of clarity. Among other things, he saw the pattern of cause and effect in his previous lives. He saw how his actions in earlier lifetimes led to results he experienced in later ones. Buddhists believe that he was able to perceive this pattern as clearly and directly with his mind as you can perceive colors and shapes with your eyes.

When the time came for him to provide spiritual guidance, the Buddha was able to see how the law of karmic cause and effect also shaped the lives of others. He could see the exact historical causes of their current problems and understand the reasons behind their good fortune. Because he understood their past so well, he intuitively knew the most effective way for each of them to progress spiritually. You could say that because the Buddha saw how each person tied his or her own karmic knots, he could give precise advice on the best way to untie them.

Buddhist texts give extensive guidelines that regulate the conduct of monks and nuns. Fully ordained monks and nuns must follow a large set of rules. Lay practitioners generally follow 5, 8, 10, or 16 ethical guidelines, or precepts, as listed in the next section.

Exploring the Buddhist Precepts

The five basic precepts recited by laypeople throughout the Buddhist world are probably the simplest and most universal place to start:

- I undertake to abstain from taking life.
- I undertake to abstain from taking what is not given.
- I undertake to abstain from sexual misconduct.
- I undertake to abstain from false speech.
- I undertake to abstain from taking intoxicants.

Different traditions have embellished these five precepts in their own unique ways. For example, in the Theravada tradition, novices in a monastery first take eight precepts (with the lay vow to abstain from sexual misconduct changing to abstaining from any sexual conduct); later, they take ten precepts, adding the following to the initial five:

- I undertake to abstain from eating at the wrong time (that means, after midday).
- I undertake to abstain from dancing, singing, instrumental music, and watching shows.
- I undertake to abstain from using garlands, perfumes, cosmetics and adornments.
- I undertake to abstain from using high or luxurious beds.
- I undertake to abstain from accepting gold and silver (now commonly interpreted as referring to money).

In Zen and certain other East Asian Buddhist traditions, the ten *grave precepts,* which are followed by both monks and nuns and laypeople, consist of the universal first five plus the following:

- Refrain from speaking of others' errors and faults.
- Refrain from elevating yourself and blaming others.
- Do not be stingy.
- Do not give vent to anger.
- Do not defile the Three Jewels of Refuge (the Buddha, Dharma, and Sangha).

The full precepts ceremony as part of a layperson's ordination or formal entry into the practice of the bodhisattva precepts (see Chapter 8) includes the three refuges of the Buddha, Dharma, and Sangha, the three pure precepts (do not create evil; practice good; and actualize good for others), as well as the ten grave precepts.

Arranging the precepts behind three doors

REMEMBER

In the Vajrayana tradition, the ten primary precepts, which are quite similar to Zen's precepts, are described as the ten nonvirtuous actions to avoid if you want to stop suffering. (The ten virtuous actions are simply the opposite of these nonvirtuous actions.) The Vajrayana tradition arranges these actions according to the three doors through which you make contact with your world:

- **Door number one.** The three actions of your body:
    - Killing
    - Stealing
    - Sexual misconduct
- **Door number two.** The four actions of your speech:
    - Lying
    - Divisive speech
    - Harsh speech
    - Idle gossip
- **Door number three.** The three actions of your mind:
    - Craving
    - Aversion
    - Delusion

Taking a deeper look at the ten nonvirtuous actions

The following sections look more closely at each of the ten nonvirtuous actions. The explanation we give is broadly applicable to all Buddhist traditions.

Killing

Taking another person's life bears the most karmic weight of any physical action. In the "Experiencing Karmic Consequences" section earlier in the chapter, we list some of the suffering that can result from killing — especially if it's carried out in a brutal manner while under the influence of a strong delusion like anger. Though relatively rare, such violent activity is far more common than most people would like to admit. Picking up your daily newspaper makes this point all too clear.

Although killing is listed as a physical action — something you do with your body — you can create the negative karma of taking life without lifting a finger. For example, if you order someone else to do the killing for you, you incur the full karmic consequences of the action. The amount of karma the person who actually carries out the order creates depends on several factors, including how willingly he participates in the deed.

Even when the killing is intentional, the heaviness of the karma you create — and, therefore, the heaviness of the karmic consequences you experience later — greatly depends on your state of mind. The stronger the negativity that motivates you — such as anger, jealousy, and the like — the heavier the karma you collect. Taking someone's life with great reluctance while wishing that you didn't have to is one thing, but killing someone out of hatred and rejoicing in the misery you cause is far more serious.

Who or what you kill also helps determine the strength of the karma that you create. For example, killing one of your parents is far more serious than killing an ordinary stranger. One person isn't inherently more valuable than another, but in relation to you and your particular karmic history, your parents occupy a uniquely important place because they've shown you special kindness by providing you with life. Similarly, killing a highly evolved spiritual practitioner, someone who can provide great benefit to others, is far more serious than snuffing out the life of an insect.

Don't get the idea that Buddhism condones certain types of killings because the karmic weight of killing can vary depending upon the circumstances. Not so! The Buddha taught love and compassion for all. The ethical system he voiced is based on causing others as little harm as possible.

Stealing

Although hatred often motivates killing, desire generally motivates people to steal — or take what's not given to them. To be guilty of stealing, you must take an object of value that belongs to someone else. Taking something that belongs to no one and then making use of it isn't considered stealing, because no one is harmed.

Stealing can occur in many different ways: You can sneak into a house, rob a person at gunpoint, or rip people off over the phone or on the Internet. All these types of stealing have one thing in common: They bring harm to others and yourself. The people you steal from lose their wealth or possessions, and you face the karmic consequences of your actions. For example, if you cheat someone in a business deal, you may experience great difficulty finding and accumulating the material necessities of life in the future. Just as wealth is believed to be the result of practicing generosity (see Chapter 14), poverty is assumed to be the karmic result of stealing from others in the past — even if the past happens to be a previous life.

REMEMBER

As with killing (and all the other nonvirtuous actions), stealing ultimately depends on your mind. Consider this illustration: Suppose that you visit your friends' house and accidentally take their umbrella home with you. This act isn't stealing. Your friends don't realize that their umbrella is missing, and you don't notice your mistake, so the umbrella sits in your closet for weeks. Although you have the umbrella in your home, you still haven't stolen it. One day you look in the closet and realize that you have an umbrella that isn't yours. You figure out that it belongs to your friends and decide to return it to them, but you don't get around to it. This is *still* not stealing (though it *is* procrastination). Then one day, perhaps months later, you think to yourself, "I've had this umbrella for a long time, and my friends haven't mentioned it. They obviously don't need it, so I'll just keep it." The moment you make this decision to keep what doesn't belong to you, you've taken what was not given, and that's when you accumulate the karma of stealing.

Sexual misconduct

REMEMBER

Sexual misconduct is the last of the three negative actions of body (check out the "Arranging the precepts behind three doors" section earlier in this chapter for an overview of the categories), and it refers primarily to rape and adultery. From a broader perspective, it can also refer to any irresponsible use of sexuality (like promiscuity or sexual addiction, for example). Rape and other forms of sexual abuse clearly inflict great harm on the victims — a harm that they sometimes feel for the rest of their lives. Sexual addictions are perhaps less destructive, but they often inflict emotional pain on the parties involved and rob the addict of precious time and energy that could have been spent on more constructive life pursuits.

Recent studies show that perpetrators of sexual abuse were often childhood victims of abuse. Sexual abuse is truly an evil that tends to perpetuate itself, and you don't need to have the clear understanding of a Buddha to recognize this point. But Buddhist teachings add something about this vicious circle that's not as obvious to ordinary understanding: The karmic results of committing sexual violence include having to experience it yourself in the future. In other words, although a victim of abuse may or may not grow up to be a perpetrator — and most do not — the perpetrator will definitely be a victim sometime in the future because of his transgressions (unless he or she manages to remove this karmic stain; see the "Purifying negative karma" section at the end of this chapter).

Interpreting the precepts

Though every Buddhist tradition agrees on five fundamental precepts (and the various Mahayana schools agree on five more), the traditions interpret these ethical guidelines differently. For example, Theravada tends to read them quite literally and require strict adherence to the letter of the rule; Mahayana tends to take a more situational slant, with some latitude for interpretation based on the circumstances; and the Vajrayana and Zen traditions take a more comprehensive, multidimensional approach.

As a case in point, consider the Zen tradition, which relates to the precepts on a number of levels. On the relative, mundane level, they serve as helpful guidelines for action — rules that support you in your pursuit of the enlightened way of life. On a deeper level, they refer to the contents of your mind as well as your physical actions. If you desire someone else's possessions, you're stealing; if you lust after a person's body, you're engaging in sexual misconduct. At the deepest (or ultimate) level, Zen understands the precepts as a spontaneous expression of true nature — and an accurate description of how an enlightened person naturally behaves without attempting to follow any particular rules.

For example, the enlightened person can't kill because he or she doesn't see other people as separate from himself or herself, he or she can't steal because there's nothing that doesn't belong to him or her, and he or she doesn't lie because he or she has no self to defend. At this level, the precepts provide an ideal standard against which you get to view your own tendencies and behaviors and assess the clarity of your own understanding.

Adultery also causes a great deal of grief for individuals, families, and society as a whole. Although cultural standards vary greatly from country to country (what's acceptable in some places is strictly forbidden in others), sexual behavior between two people becomes misconduct when it amounts to taking what's not given freely. If you're unfaithful to your spouse, or if you're responsible for weakening or breaking up another couple's marriage, you may experience disharmony and sexual infidelity in your own marital relationships in the future — in this life or future lives — as a karmic consequence of this illicit behavior.

Lying

REMEMBER

Lying means that you purposely mislead someone by saying something that you know isn't true. Simply making an untrue statement isn't lying; you have to intend to mislead someone into believing that you're telling the truth. Lies range from the mass deceptions often attempted by political propaganda to the small fibs and little white lies you may tell to get out of uncomfortable social situations. You don't even have to say anything to engage in this negative action; a nod of the head or a gesture can be as misleading as false words.

One of the main problems with lying is that it often forces you to cover your tracks with even more lies. You soon find that you've assembled so many lies that you can't keep your story straight anymore and must suffer the embarrassment of being found out. (You may recognize this as the plot line behind many television sitcoms.)

REMEMBER

The results of lying can be even worse than momentary embarrassment. For some people, lying becomes a habitual way of life, and they can no longer tell the difference between what's true and what's false. It's as if they're taken in by their own deceit. From a karmic perspective, Buddhists assume that, as a consequence of lying, you won't be believed even when you speak the truth.

Sometimes, however, you may find yourself in a situation where telling the unvarnished truth isn't a good idea. For example, if you know that an angry man with a gun wants to kill the person hiding behind the curtain, should you answer him truthfully when he asks you if you know where the person is? Of course not. You know that a completely truthful answer will result in murder — which is far more serious than merely veiling the truth — so you can mislead him without accruing the karmic consequences of lying. If you're devoted to the practice of compassion, you must do all you can to prevent the murder from taking place, but you need to be sure that your motive for not telling the truth is compassion for everyone involved — the would-be murderer as well as the intended victim. You not only want to save a life now, but you also want to prevent the gunman from collecting any more negative karma for the future.

Divisive speech

REMEMBER

Divisive speech refers to what you may say to break up a friendship between other people or to prevent people from getting back together after they've broken up. People can have many different motives for behaving in such a disruptive way. For example, if you're jealous of a close relationship, you may try to sabotage it for your own personal gain.

Your speech can be divisive whether the statements you make are true or false. If your intent is to split people up or prevent a reconciliation, your statements fall under the divisive category — even if they're true. According to Buddhist teachings, one result of this negative action is that you'll have a hard time finding friends and companions in the future.

TIP

One obvious case does arise in which causing disharmony between others is considered appropriate — when they're plotting to commit a crime or perform some other harmful action. If you can break up their conspiracy and prevent them from creating problems for themselves and others, you're acting with kindness. But you have to be very clear about your intentions.

Harsh speech

Harsh speech refers to the kinds of things you say when you want to hurt someone else's feelings. As with divisive speech, these insults can be true or false; your intention to belittle, embarrass, or upset someone else makes them harsh. The karmic consequences of this kind of speech — as you may guess — are believed to be that you'll be subjected to verbal abuse in the future.

In America and perhaps elsewhere, an entire tradition of humor seems to be based on insulting others. The idea of a celebrity roast, for example, is to hurl as many clever insults at the guest of honor as you can in as short a time as possible. No one is supposed to get hurt at these affairs, and the guest is expected to laugh louder than everyone else as the skewering proceeds. But occasionally, he or she does take something personally, and then things can quickly turn ugly.

Because words often carry more weight than you intend and can be more damaging than you imagine, be careful about what you say. After you develop the habit of insulting others, controlling your speech becomes more difficult. You may not be aware of the aggression inside you, but it nevertheless gives unexpected power to the words you utter "just in fun."

Idle gossip

Idle gossip is the last of the negative actions of speech. By its very nature, idle gossip is less serious than any of the other actions of body or speech mentioned in this section. The problem, however, is that it's by far the biggest waste of time.

Idle gossip includes all types of frivolous speech and can be about anything. Some people refer to it as "diarrhea of the mouth," and like harsh speech, it's a habit that's easy to fall into and difficult to break. If you spend your time and energy chattering about things that have no consequence, people eventually discount what you say as unimportant and stop taking you seriously.

Craving

Now come the three negative actions of the mind itself, beginning with craving, or desiring to possess, what you don't have. Even if you don't act on this impulse, the fact that you look at others' possessions in this greedy way creates difficulties for your mind, which begin with restlessness. Then when your desire to possess a particular item becomes strong enough, even greater problems arise. For example, if you want something badly enough, you may be tempted to steal it, which creates even worse karmic consequences.

Craving is a discontented, dissatisfied state of mind. Energizing that state of mind is the expectation (often not clearly expressed, even to yourself) that if you just possessed that one attractive item, you'd finally be happy. But as the Buddhist teachings repeatedly point out, you can't gain satisfaction by running after the various objects of the senses, no matter how attractive they may appear (see Chapter 2).

If you fail in your attempt to acquire the desired object, you're going to feel dissatisfied. But even if you're successful and get it, the object inevitably fails to live up to your exaggerated expectations. Then like saltwater, instead of satisfying your thirst, the object only makes you thirstier. In this way, you only bring yourself more discontent.

TIP

Because craving is a purely mental activity, it's harder to control than the physical and verbal actions that arise from it. To counter this disruptive mental attitude, you have to familiarize yourself with a different way of looking at things: You have to discover how to meditate (as we discuss in Chapter 7). You have to train yourself to recognize that the things you desire aren't as permanent or as inherently attractive as you imagine them to be.

Aversion

This powerful mental attitude is behind many of the things you may do or say to harm others. In this destructive state of mind, you take delight in the misfortune of others, actively wanting them to suffer. Aversion is the exact opposite of love, which is the wish for others to be happy.

As with craving, controlling this kind of harmful intention is more difficult than controlling the more obvious verbal and physical actions that arise from it. To successfully keep this attitude in check, you have to train yourself to see others as deserving of your respect, care, and love. Instead of focusing on traits that feed your aversion, familiarize yourself with others' good qualities until your heart opens toward them with compassion.

TIP

Realistically, however, sometimes your negative feelings toward someone are simply too raw and powerful for you to transform by the method we just suggested — at least for the time being. In this case, your best bet may simply be to forget about the person you're angry with and turn your attention to the feeling of aversion itself. Like a scientist examining a poisonous snake, observe this destructive emotion as carefully and objectively as you can. Don't buy into it (don't follow its demands and start shouting or fighting), but don't try to suppress it, either. Simply observe it.

As you watch your aversion dispassionately, you'll discover that, like all feelings, this negative emotion isn't as solid as it first appears. Like a wave that rises from the ocean one minute and sinks back into it the next, the aversion rises in your heart, lasts for a short while, and then disappears again. A similar wave may rise up and take its place, but it, too, will inevitably subside. If you can stand back and simply observe this process (which is similar to the breath-awareness technique that we explain in Chapter 7), your negative feelings will eventually exhaust themselves.

Delusion

Although you may have many different types of erroneous ideas, the delusion we're talking about here has a rather specific meaning. You are deluded when you actively deny the reality or existence of things that are true.

For example, according to Buddhism, the Three Jewels of the Buddha, Dharma, and Sangha are reliable guides in which you can place your faith and trust. Also, the karmic law of cause and effect that we outline earlier in this chapter is true: Your actions do have consequences not only in this life, but in future lives as well. Denying these points indicates that you've fallen under the influence of delusion. In this context, being deluded doesn't mean doubting the Buddhist teachings on karma and so forth or simply being unfamiliar with them. It means actively claiming that they're false.

For example, if you really want to commit a certain nonvirtuous action, such as adultery, you may try to convince yourself (and the other person) that nothing is wrong with what you intend to do. Besides, you may add, nobody will find out or get hurt. In this example, what you're really trying to do is excuse your misbehavior by advocating a view that flies in the face of the Buddha's teachings on cause and effect. Spreading delusion leads to serious mistakes; that's why this nonvirtuous action of mind is so dangerous.

Dealing with Transgressions

Buddhist teachings don't reveal the workings of cause and effect or identify actions to be avoided to scare practitioners. Their goal is to protect people from unwanted suffering. But what are the teachings for folks who, despite them (or without knowing about them), make mistakes anyway?

The different Buddhist traditions have different ways of addressing this question, and we consider some of these in the following sections — atoning for mistakes and purifying negative karma.

Atoning for mistakes

During the early years of the Buddha's ministry, one of his main disciples, Shariputra, asked the Buddha to formulate a code of rules for the community of monks to follow. (We mention only monks here because this particular incident occurred before women were admitted to the Sangha.) The Buddha replied that the Sangha didn't need such a code at that time because even the least-advanced monks had their feet firmly planted on the path to spiritual awakening.

But as the Sangha grew larger, conditions changed, and a code of conduct gradually emerged for these reasons:

- To help safeguard the monks from the influence of craving, aversion, and ignorance
- To ensure harmony within the Sangha itself
- To preserve good relations between the Sangha and the wider lay community

These monastic training rules didn't spring into being all at once. They developed over time as the Buddha offered guidance in individual cases (a lot like civil laws develop as a series of precedents in court cases). More than 200 rules were eventually formulated, and the custom arose of holding a meeting every two weeks (on new moon and full moon days), during which these rules were recited aloud and individual monks stepped forward to acknowledge their transgressions.

In the Theravada tradition, a monk can also make such an acknowledgment to one other monk as a daily practice of confession. As for lay followers of this tradition, when they realize that they have transgressed their precepts, they can revive them — retaking them either from a monk, by themselves in front of a Buddha image, or by simply creating the intention in their own mind to renew and retake the practices of virtuous living.

REMEMBER

The rules of conduct for monks and nuns list four grave offenses that lead to automatic expulsion from the Sangha:

- Engaging in sexual intercourse
- Stealing
- Killing a human being
- Lying about one's spiritual attainments

But most of the rules covered in the monastic code deal with far less serious offenses, and the offenders can generally atone for them by honestly admitting their transgressions. As practiced in the Theravada tradition, such a declaration of wrongdoing doesn't erase the negative karma from breaking the rule, but it does strengthen the individual's determination to avoid breaking the same rule again. Also, it lets the fellow Sangha members know that the person is still intent on following the monastic way of life as purely as he or she can.

Purifying negative karma

REMEMBER

From the perspective of certain Mahayana (or Great Vehicle) traditions, you can purify your negative karma no matter how heavy it is — though if you are a monk or nun, committing any one of the four grave offenses mentioned in the "Atoning for mistakes" section of this chapter will still get you expelled from the Sangha. (For more on the Mahayana, see Chapters 4 and 5.)

As far as purifying negative karma in the Theravada tradition is concerned, practicing virtuous living and cultivating insight are the general means for protecting yourself from experiencing the consequences of harmful actions. However, some actions — such as killing your parents — are so heavy that you may not be able to purify them completely.

In some Zen traditions, purification takes place through the following process of atonement. In addition to admitting wrongdoing and taking up a determination not to act that way again, atonement is here understood as embracing an opportunity to wipe the karmic slate clean and return to the primordial purity of your original nature.

Zen practitioners use the following verse (in some translation) in the atonement ceremony itself and also as a preamble to other important ceremonies to ensure that they're based in the purity of true nature:

> All evil karma ever committed by me since of old,
>
> On account of my beginningless greed, anger, and ignorance,
>
> Born of my body, mouth, and thought,
>
> Now I atone for it all.

In some other traditions, such as the Vajrayana, practitioners accomplish this purification by conscientiously applying the *four opponent powers* (the four R's):

- **Regret: Feeling remorse for the harm you've done; recognizing and admitting your mistakes.** Don't confuse this open and honest declaration or admission of your mistakes with guilt, which is counterproductive. Guilt traps you in the past, solidifying your identity as a "bad" person and making it more difficult to move on to more constructive behaviors.

  Regret involves acknowledging that you've made a mistake, which is the first step to undoing it. Instead of trapping you in the past, sincere regret motivates you to take care of yourself and others by changing your behaviors — both now and in the future.

- **Resolve: Determining not to repeat that destructive action.** Admitting that you've made a mistake isn't enough; you need to exert effort to keep from repeating it. The best solution is to vow never to commit that particular harmful action for the rest of your life.

  But you have to be realistic. If you think that keeping a lifelong vow would be impossible, you can try your best not to act that way again for a specific amount of time (several months, perhaps, or even the next few days). By training yourself in this way, you eventually build enough strength and confidence to stop the activity entirely.

- **Reliance: Depending upon your refuge in the Three Jewels and your dedication to others to eliminate negativity.** Whenever you commit a nonvirtuous action, you direct it against another being or against the Buddha, Dharma, and Sangha. By relying on the very same objects, you can help purify whatever negativity you engaged in.

  If your action is directed against the Three Jewels, such as by showing them disrespect (treating Buddhist texts carelessly, for example), you can begin to rectify your mistake by reminding yourself of their excellent qualities and reasserting the refuge you take in them. If you've harmed other beings, remind yourself of your compassionate intention to win enlightenment for their sake.

  These two reliances — taking refuge and developing the compassionate *bodhichitta* motivation (which we talk more about in Chapter 14) — are embodied in the following popular prayer:

  > I go for refuge, until I am enlightened,
  >
  > To the Buddha, Dharma, and Sangha.
  >
  > Through the virtue I create.
  >
  > By practicing giving and the other perfections,
  >
  > May I attain the state of a Buddha in order to benefit all sentient beings.

- **Remedy: Taking specific positive actions to counterbalance whatever negativity you created.** Specific virtuous actions directly oppose the ten nonvirtuous actions listed in the "Taking a deeper look at the ten nonvirtuous actions" section, earlier in this chapter. For example, saving and protecting the lives of others is the opposite of the first harmful action — killing. A powerful way to neutralize harm you may have committed is to do something completely contrary to the negativity you want to purify — acting out of love rather than hate, generosity rather than miserliness, compassion rather than aversion, and so on.

  Some of the generally recommended activities to counterbalance negativity include the following:

  - Serving the poor and needy
  - Visiting people in the hospital
  - Saving the lives of animals (even bait worms) about to be killed
  - Making offerings to monasteries and other religious organizations
  - Reciting passages from traditional Buddhist texts (and, better still, meditating on their meaning and putting them into practice)
  - Drawing holy images

By following the teachings, some Buddhists believe that you can save yourself from experiencing some of the most serious consequences of your negative actions — for the time being, at least. But to rid yourself of these consequences entirely, you must go deeper, as we describe in Chapter 13, which deals with breaking free of the cycle of dissatisfaction altogether.

Chapter 13

Breaking Free of the Cycle of Dissatisfaction

In This Chapter

- Digging up the three root delusions
- Spinning around the realms of cyclic existence
- Clicking on the 12 links
- Working out the three trainings

In Chapter 12 we talk about enlightenment (or awakening) and introduce the concept of nirvana. The term nirvana now even pops up in casual conversation. For example, people say things like, "Relaxing in a warm bath at the end of a hard day: Now that's my idea of nirvana!"

But what does *nirvana* actually mean? Is it a blissful feeling you can experience when you kick your meditation practice into high gear? Or is it a kind of Buddhist heaven, like a reward waiting for good Buddhists when they die?

Neither of these notions is actually correct, but at least they both convey the sense that nirvana is truly wonderful, the highest form of good, and something definitely worth reaching. Nirvana (often translated as "enlightenment" or "liberation") isn't a place for you to go. It's a state of extraordinary clarity, peace, and joy that you can attain as a result of practicing the Buddhist spiritual path.

As we explain in Chapter 10, nirvana is what you achieve when you free yourself from the underlying causes of all suffering, from craving and ignorance. Because it is the complete opposite of cyclic existence (samsara) and indescribable, Buddhists prefer to speak of nirvana in negative terms.

One way to get a handle on the rather elusive concept of nirvana is to recognize what prevents you from experiencing it. In this chapter, we present the Buddhist explanation of the mechanism (known as the 12 links) that perpetuates dissatisfaction, and the practices you need to undertake to break free from suffering and achieve lasting peace and happiness.

Feeling Like Life's a Big Rat Race

If you read the first two chapters of this book, you already have some idea of how negative states of mind — so-called delusions or defilements *(kleshas)*, such as hatred, jealousy, and so on — cause problems for you as soon as they arise. But they do more than simply cause problems. They force you to go from one unsatisfactory situation in life to another, searching for happiness and peace, but ultimately finding only disappointment and frustration.

The Sanskrit term for this pattern of recurring frustration is *samsara* (cyclic existence). This term conveys the ideas of uncontrollable wandering and restless motion that leads nowhere. If you've ever thought of your life as a rat race — your efforts to get somewhere just lead you around in circles — you've tasted the frustrating nature of samsara. Pretty bitter, huh?

Is the picture really as bleak as we've just painted it? Doesn't your life contain pleasurable aspects, moments of happiness to be enjoyed? Of course it does. But the point we want to make is that as long as your mind is under the influence of the delusions, the negative states of mind, these moments won't last. You'll inevitably experience frustration, dissatisfaction, and outright misery. That's why the Buddhist teachings say that the nature of samsara is suffering.

Remember that samsara describes not reality itself, but your distorted experience of reality based on your negative mind-states. The rat race, in other words, exists in your mind, and the way out doesn't require changing your life — it requires changing your mind. In fact, some traditions of Buddhism teach that samsara is nirvana, meaning that this life is perfect the way it is — you just have to wake up to this perfection by transforming your mind. (For more on waking up to this perfection, see Chapter 10!)

Spinning the Wheel of Life: The Meaning of Wandering in Samsara

You can easily see how patterns of frustration and dissatisfaction repeat themselves in your daily life. For example, if you're a short-tempered person who always gets angry with others, you inevitably find yourself in hostile situations where you have to confront people who dislike you. These confrontations just cause you to get even angrier. If you go to sleep in an angry state of mind, your dreams may also be disturbing. Then when you wake up the next morning, you may discover that you're already in quite a foul mood. And so it goes.

The Buddhist teachings claim that the pattern of suffering repeats itself on a much larger scale than simply waking up angry because you were upset when you went to bed. The delusions don't merely force you from one unsatisfactory experience to the next or from one unsatisfactory day to the next. They also force you to wander uncontrollably from one unsatisfactory lifetime to the next!

The teachings of Buddhism explain how deluded states of mind keep you trapped in these recurring patterns of dissatisfaction by what is called *dependent arising* or *interdependent origination.* (If you think these terms are obscure, take a look at the Sanskrit for them: *pratitya-samutpada.*) All these fancy words merely point to the same truth: Things happen to you for a reason.

From the Buddhist point of view, your life experiences, both good and bad, aren't random, meaningless events. Nor are they rewards or punishments handed out to you by some controlling force outside yourself, so blaming God or fate doesn't work. Your experiences result from a series of causes and effects that begin in your own mind. (For more about karmic cause and effect, see Chapter 12.)

Buddhists illustrate this mechanism of cause and effect in a diagram popularly known as the *Wheel of Life.* (Check out Figure 13-1 for a representation of this wheel and Figure 13-2 for a diagram of its different parts.) Perhaps the best place to begin a summary of these important teachings is at the hub of this wheel.

Figure 13-1: A Tibetan representation of the Wheel of Life.

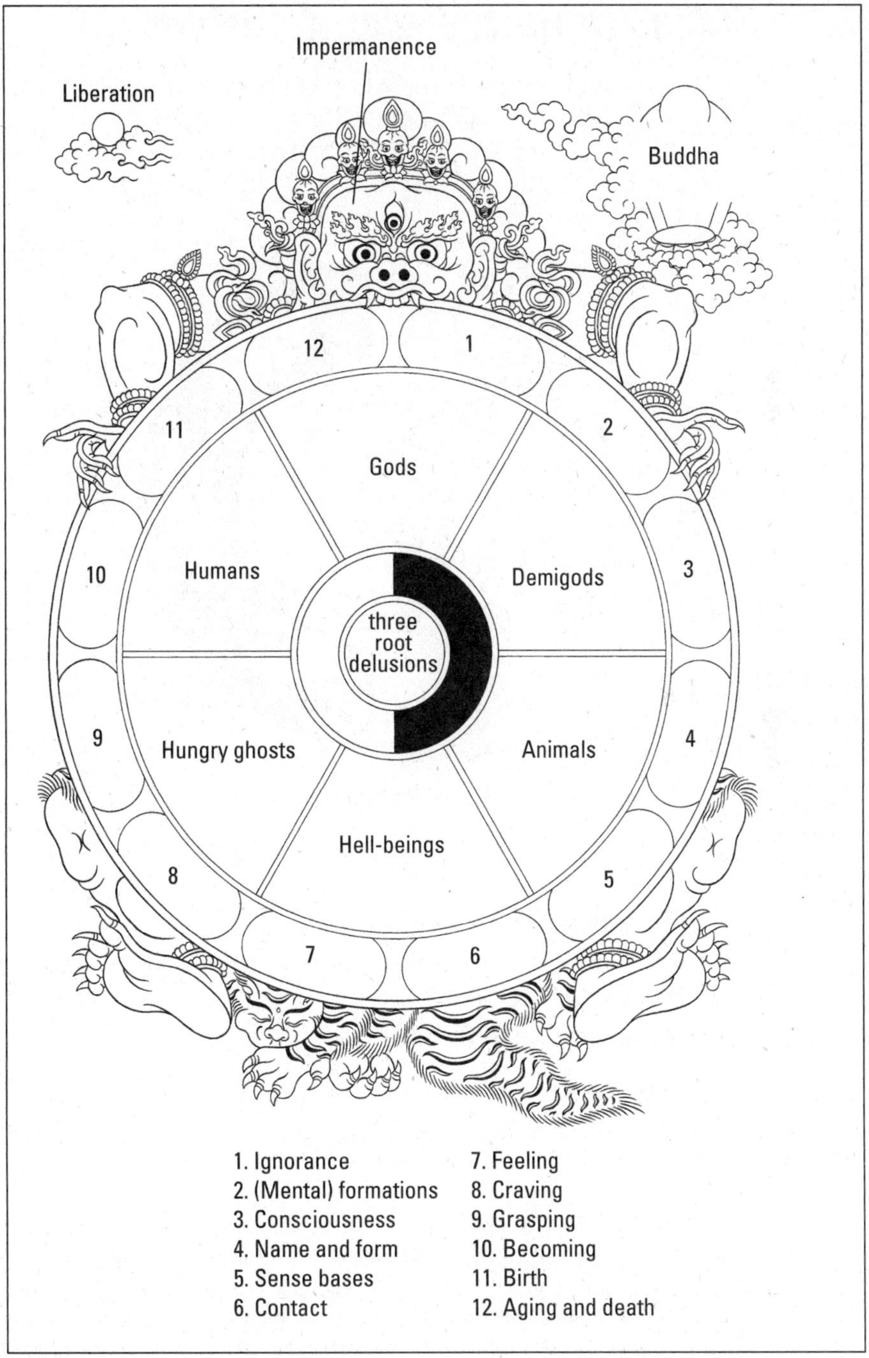

Figure 13-2: A guide to the Wheel of Life.

Identifying the root delusions

If you look at the center of the Wheel of Life (shown in Figure 13-3), you see three animals, which represent the three root delusions:

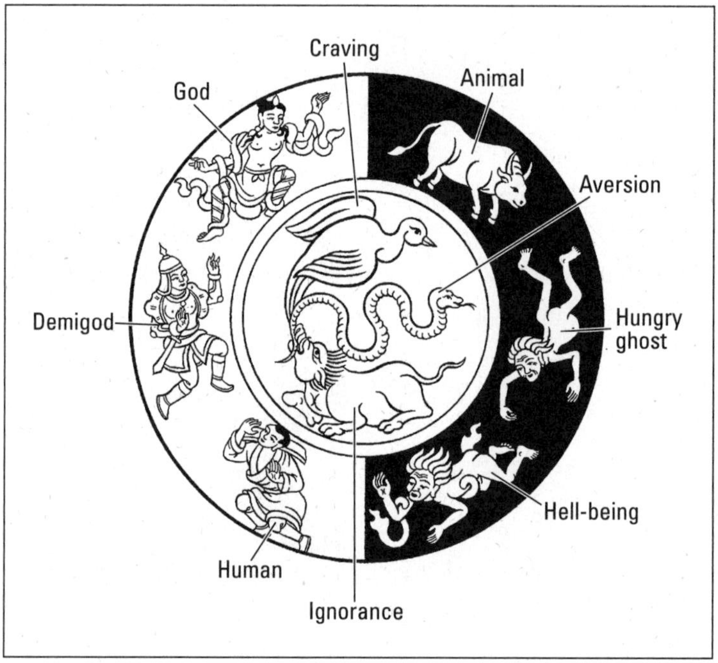

Figure 13-3: The three root delusions.

- **Pig:** Represents ignorance.
- **Rooster:** Represents craving. In some versions of the wheel, other birds take the rooster's place.
- **Snake:** Represents aversion.

If you read Chapters 1 and 2, you're already somewhat familiar with these delusions. But now we want to explore a bit more closely how they're related to one another.

Grasping at a solid self

In this representation of the Wheel of Life, the bird and snake emerge from the pig's mouth to indicate that ignorance is the source of all the other delusions. This version of ignorance doesn't simply mean to not know something. Instead, this type of ignorance holds on tightly to a mistaken idea of how things exist. You could say that it actively promotes a distorted picture of reality (see Chapter 2 for more about ignorance).

You can get an idea of how this ignorance works by performing the following exercise to discover how you ordinarily think of yourself.

1. **Use the word *I* in a sentence or two and see what you find.** For example, if you describe what you're doing right now, you may come up with something like this: "I'm sitting here reading this explanation and trying to figure out what it means."

   Notice that as soon as you talk about yourself, you automatically mention something that's going on with either your body (sitting) or your mind (trying to figure out the explanation), or both (reading). Try this little experiment several times until you clearly see that each time you use the word *I,* you're referring to some aspect of your body, your mind, or both.

2. **Take a closer look at your body and mind.** Some Buddhist philosophical texts call this body-mind combination the *basis of imputation of the I,* which is just a fancy way of stating what you've already discovered: You use the terms *I* or *me* (or your name) to refer to something going on in your mental and physical makeup. But when you slowly and carefully examine what you consist of, you discover that there is no *I* or *me*. According to Buddhist teachings, what appears to be an *I* is constituted by the five aggregates, or *skandhas*. These five aggregates are specified as material form (rupa), feeling and sensation (vedana), perceptions (samjna), mental formations (samskara), and consciousness (vijnana).

3. **Instead of coming up with an emotionally neutral statement about yourself, as you did in Step 1, bring to mind a moment of great stress or excitement.** This point is where the exercise really gets interesting. Perhaps someone insults or embarrasses you in front of a crowd, and you become uncomfortable, self-conscious, and resentful. (You can also use the example of being praised in front of others and feeling proud or getting a big head as a result, but we'll stick to just one example here.) At times like this, you probably don't think, "That person just insulted some momentary aspect of my body or mind." Instead, popping up in the center of your chest is a solid, permanent, almost tangible sense of self, and you feel like *that* is what has just been attacked: "How dare he say that about *me* in front of all these people!"

The concrete, self-existent *I* or *me* that appears to you *at that moment* has nothing whatsoever to do with your reality. You'll never find anything either inside or outside your body–mind combination that corresponds to such an apparently concrete sense of self. This apparently concrete self is solely the creation of ignorance — a bad habit of the mind. And this ignorance — sometimes called *I-grasping* or *self-clinging* because of the unrealistic way it holds on to a false image of yourself — is the root of all suffering, without exception.

The snake and the rope

The following famous analogy helps to understand how belief in the false self leads to suffering and how wisdom can eliminate that suffering. Imagine that it's nighttime and you're out walking. On the path, you see what appears to be a snake, coiled and ready to strike. Fear and panic immediately grip your heart. But when you shine a light on your would-be assailant, all you find is a piece of rope. To be on the safe side, you shine your light all around you, but no matter where you look, you can't find a snake. With the realization that a snake was never there to begin with — that it was just a figment of your imagination — you finally relax and continue on your way unafraid.

The false *I* is like the falsely imagined snake. As long as you believe that it's real — as long as you hold on to it as true — you experience fear, frustration, disappointment, and all the other forms of suffering and dissatisfaction. But when you use the light of wisdom to search long and hard enough, both inside and outside your body and mind, you discover that you can't find a solid and separate *I* anywhere. When you become convinced — not just intellectually, but in the depths of your heart — that this falsely imagined *I* never existed at all, you'll stop believing in it, and all the suffering generated by this mistaken belief will evaporate.

Watching the growth of aversion and craving

As long as you hold on tightly to a falsely imagined *I*, you continue to imprison yourself. When you think this supposedly concrete *I* is being attacked, you immediately feel defensive. You strongly dislike what's happening to you, and aversion begins to grow in your heart. You may even begin plotting revenge against your tormentor, thereby ensuring that the pattern of attacks and counterattacks continues. And so the cycle of suffering keeps on spinning.

REMEMBER

Aversion isn't the only negative state of mind that pops up. Craving and delusions arise automatically as you try to maintain or defend this ignorantly conceived *I* self. You become furious if you feel that this *I* is under attack, but you also *crave* anything that you feel would support or enhance it. This delusion is responsible for the compulsive got-to-have-it mentality. As long as you're under the influence of this I-grasping ignorance, you're feeding a desire that can never be satisfied.

You use all your energy trying to make this false *I* secure, but your efforts are doomed to fail. How can you provide security for something that never really existed in the first place? You just end up wearing yourself out and hurting others along the way.

When you're able to see that the concrete self that you've been clinging to all this time is just an illusion (generally, after extensive training in meditation), you can begin to let go of this creation of ignorance. Letting go feels like having a heavy, unnecessary burden lifted from your shoulders. No longer neurotically compelled to defend or promote this phantomlike self, you're free to experience a deep sense of contentment and peace. To put it in more mundane terms: Because you're no longer so full of yourself, you can finally chill out.

Surveying the six realms of existence

Surrounding the hub of the Wheel of Life (refer to Figure 13-1) are two semicircles (which you can also see in Figure 13-3), one light and the other dark, representing the two major types of action (or *karma*) that you can create — positive and negative. (Chapter 12 has a bunch of additional information on karma.) The three beings located in the left semicircle have accumulated positive karma that is leading them upward to the three "higher" realms of gods, demigods, and humans (refer to Figure 13-2 for a road map to all the realms), while the burden of negative karma is dragging the three beings in the right semicircle down to the "lower" realms of the animals, hungry ghosts, and hell-beings. (Don't worry, we explain these six realms in more detail later in this section.)

Don't take the terms *higher* and *lower* too literally. You won't find the gods up in the clouds or the hell-beings deep underground, even if some traditional explanations may give you that impression. Your mind creates karma and experiences its results, no matter where you may be dwelling. A particular realm, or state of existence (or, better yet, state of mind), is called "higher" or "lower" depending on the amount of obvious suffering it contains. Beings in the higher realms experience less suffering and more pleasure when compared to the beings in the three lower realms. But whether they're higher or lower, all six realms lie within the bounds of cyclic existence, and all the beings currently trapped there by ignorance carry the burden of dissatisfaction.

Here are the six realms, listed in order from highest to lowest:

- **Gods:** (See Figure 13-4, top portion.) Also called *devas* (celestial beings), gods occupy the highest position within cyclic existence and are usually depicted as living in the most sumptuous surroundings. Depending on the specific type of karma they created to be reborn here, these long-lived beings spend their lives either intoxicated by pleasure or absorbed in some form of deep concentration. Some gods mistake their realm for nirvana, but unlike true liberation, this realm (like the other five) is only temporary. When a god's powerful positive karma is exhausted — karma doesn't last forever; you use it up as you experience its results — he or she has no choice but to fall back to one of the lower, far less-enjoyable realms. So you can't even find security in the god realm. Although humans are not gods, those people who live the lifestyle of the rich and famous can be said to experience a god*like* existence, in terms of both the extraordinary pleasures available to them and the constant threat that these pleasures may be snatched from them at any moment.

- **Demigods:** (See Figure 13-4, bottom portion.) The *asuras* or demigods experience an existence similar to the one in the realm just above them (the god realm), but they can't fully enjoy the pleasures of their realm. Because their enjoyments, like their positive karma, are inferior to those of the more fortunate gods, the demigods are plagued by tremendous jealousy, the predominant delusion of this realm. This jealousy provokes them to war against their more powerful neighbors (you can see them fighting in Figure 13-4), thereby repeatedly subjecting themselves to the agony of defeat (without the corresponding thrill of victory, no less). In the human realm (which we discuss in just a second), some of the not-so-rich-and-famous experience problems of jealousy and competitiveness similar to those of the demigods.
- **Humans:** (See Figure 13-5, left.) The third realm of the three higher realms is the one you're experiencing now. As the Buddha noted at the beginning of his own spiritual journey (which we catalog in Chapter 3), this realm is filled with the suffering of sickness, old age, and death — not to mention the frustration of not getting what you want and the anguish of being separated from what you like. While living in this realm, you can experience something quite similar to the pleasures and pains of the other states of existence. In fact, that's why birth in this realm can be so fortunate: You have enough suffering to be motivated to break free from cyclic existence and enough leisure to do something about it.

Figure 13-4: The god and demigod realms.

- **Animals:** (See Figure 13-5, right.) This realm, the highest of the three lower realms, is the one with which humans have the closest connection. Although a wide range of experiences exists within this realm, the vast majority of animals lead lives of constant struggle, searching for food while trying to avoid being eaten themselves. This rough existence, driven by instincts they can't control, is a reflection of the type of behavior that's largely responsible for their birth as an animal in the first place. In addition to hunger and fear, animals suffer from heat and cold and (in the case of many domesticated animals) the pain of performing forced, heavy labor. Unfortunately, desperate circumstances or limited intelligence forces many humans to live an existence not much different from that of their animal neighbors.
- **Hungry ghosts:** (See Figure 13-6, left.) This realm is one of continual frustration, thwarted desire, and unsatisfied craving. The predominant suffering of these unfortunate beings (called *pretas* in Sanskrit and sometimes referred to as wandering spirits) is unrelieved hunger and thirst, and the main cause for being reborn here is miserliness. Often depicted as having narrow necks and cavernous stomachs, these beings have great difficulty finding and consuming food and drink. Most people haven't encountered *pretas* directly — though Jon has met a few folks who claim to have made contact with them — but you may know of Scrooges who hold on to their possessions in such a miserly fashion that, like a *preta,* they've completely banished joy from their lives.
- **Hell-beings:** (See Figure 13-6, right.) This realm is the lowest of all the realms within cyclic existence, and it's filled with the most intense suffering. The main cause for experiencing this kind of a painful rebirth is committing extremely harmful actions, such as murder, while under the influence of powerful delusions — especially hatred. Within the human realm, people who endure particularly intense forms of physical or mental agony beyond the range of ordinary experience are said to lead a hell-like existence.

Figure 13-5: The human and animal realms.

Figure 13-6: The realms of hungry ghosts and hell-beings.

REMEMBER

Although Buddhist mythology depicts these realms as having an objective existence, they're just as often used to refer to human beings who are stuck in a particular mind-state. For example, someone who never gets enough — someone who's never satisfied with the amount of material possessions he or she has — is often called a hungry ghost, and someone who's consumed with hatred is generally regarded as inhabiting the hell realm. By contrast, people may refer to someone who lives a life of wealth and ease but has little concern for spiritual matters as being stuck in the god realm.

As if the miseries depicted in this list weren't enough, a major defect of life within cyclic existence is that you can't find rest or certainty anywhere. One minute you're sipping the nectar of the gods, and the next minute you're wandering about looking for anything to quench your unbearable thirst. Even as a human, you can be buffeted up and down and around the various realms in a matter of minutes. The entire Wheel of Life is in the grip of impermanence, which is represented by the monster (sometimes identified with Yama, the lord of death, or with Mara, the tempter) in Figures 13-1 and 13-2. As your mind changes, so do your experiences.

REMEMBER

These various realms of experience, or states of existence, aren't places awaiting your visit. They're not preexisting destinations to which you're sent as a reward or punishment. You create the causes for experiencing the pleasures and pains of these realms by what you do, say, and think.

Understanding the 12 links

In teachings known as the *12 links of dependent arising,* Buddhists describe the mechanism that drives you from realm to realm within cyclic existence and keeps you trapped in suffering and dissatisfaction. There are several versions of these teachings in Buddhism and different representations of them in art. In the Tibetan depiction of the Wheel of Life introduced and explained in this book (refer to Figure 13-1), these 12 links (located around the outer rim) are presented and understood as follows:

- **Ignorance: A blind man hobbling along.** (See Figure 13-7, left.) Here, once again, ladies and gentlemen, is the root delusion ignorance, direct from the hub of the wheel (see the "Identifying the root delusions" section, earlier in this chapter). But here ignorance isn't a pig; it's a feeble blind man stumbling from one difficulty to another. He can't see where he's going because he's blinded by his own ignorance, completely mistaken about the way things (including the self) actually are. He's feeble because, even though ignorance is powerful in the sense that it's the source of all suffering, it has no firm support and, therefore, can be overcome by wisdom.
- **(Mental) formations: A potter at his wheel.** (See Figure 13-7, right.) In ignorance, you engage in actions of body, speech, and mind; these actions — or karma — shape a new life, just as the potter takes a lump of clay and shapes a new pot. (Keep in mind that as long as you continue to grasp onto a mistaken view of yourself — that's the first link: ignorance — even your positive actions will shape a new life within cyclic existence for you. Of course, this new life will be much more pleasant than one shaped by negative actions. See the explanation of the differences between the "higher" and "lower" realms of samsara in the earlier section, "Surveying the six realms of existence.")
- **Consciousness: A monkey scampering up and down a tree.** (See Figure 13-8, left.) The actions of the previous link leave impressions on your consciousness that carry over into your future lives; the monkey climbing up and down a tree symbolizes this movement from one life to the next.

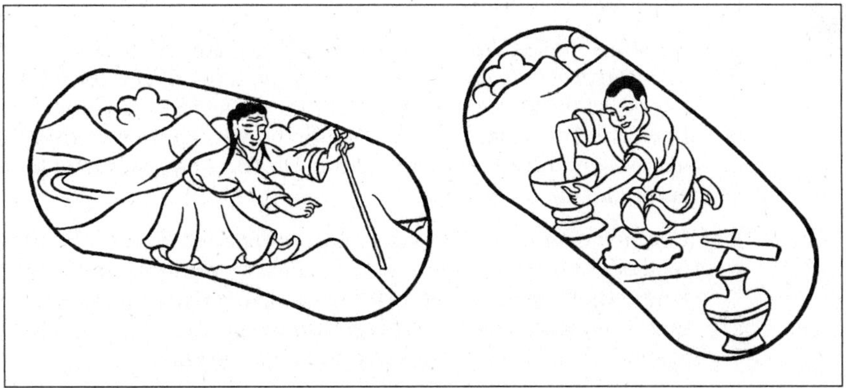

Figure 13-7: The ignorance and (mental) formations links.

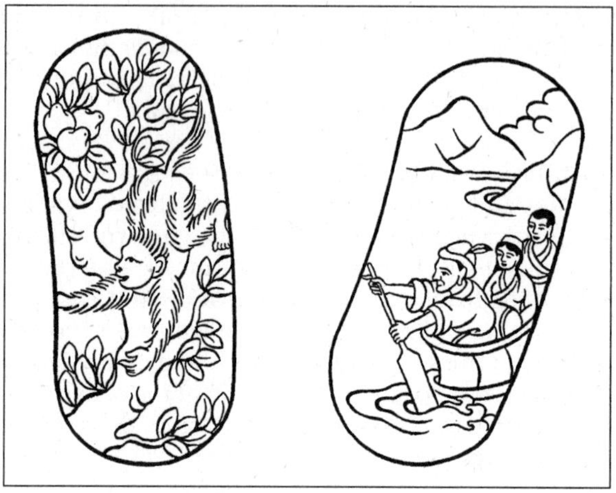

Figure 13-8: The consciousness and name-and-form links.

- **Name and form: Two people carried in a boat.** (See Figure 13-8, right.) Tibetan teachers explain this link as follows. If you're going to be reborn as a human again, your consciousness (carrying its impressions from the past) eventually enters the womb of your future mother, where it joins with the united sperm and egg of your parents. *Name,* symbolized here by one of the two travelers, refers to the mental consciousness that joins the united sperm and egg. *Form,* symbolized by the other traveler, refers to the tiny embryo that will grow into the new body for this consciousness.

  In some illustrations of the Wheel of Life, only one person is shown in the boat. In that case, the person stands for *name,* the mental consciousness coming from a previous life, and the boat symbolizes *form,* the fertilized egg into which this consciousness enters.

  REMEMBER

  Simply put, name and form refer to the newly conceived being's embryonic mind and body.

- **Six sense bases: An empty house.** (See Figure 13-9, left.) Tibetan teachers interpret this link as follows. As the fetus develops in the womb, the bases for the six senses (see Chapter 2) begin to develop. At this point, however, the senses aren't functioning yet. Therefore, their bases are symbolized by a house that, although complete on the outside, is empty inside.

- **Contact: A man and woman embracing.** (See Figure 13-9, right.) As fetal development continues, the senses eventually develop to the point where they make contact with their respective objects. This initial contact — which occurs at different times for the different sense organs — is symbolized by two people touching or kissing.

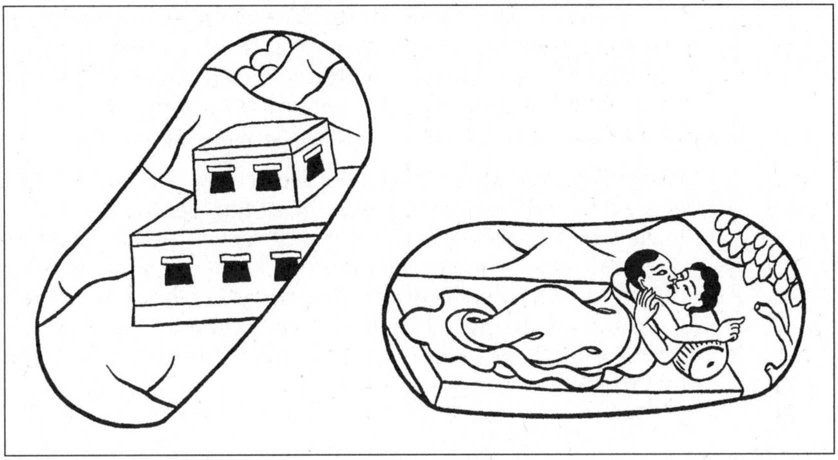

Figure 13-9: The six sense bases and contact links.

- **Feeling: A person with an arrow in his eye.** (See Figure 13-10, left.) As a result of this sensory contact, feelings of pleasure, pain, or neutrality are experienced, beginning in the womb and continuing throughout life. Through this link of feeling (sometimes called *response*), you reap the results of your past karma, experiencing pleasure as the result of virtuous actions and pain as the result of nonvirtuous or harmful actions (plus neutral feelings as the result of actions that are neither virtuous nor nonvirtuous). An arrow sticking in a person's eye graphically illustrates the immediacy and intensity of feeling.
- **Craving: A person drinking alcohol.** (See Figure 13-10, right.) The eighth link, *craving,* is the desire that arises from the feelings of the previous link. When you experience pleasure, you want it to continue; when you experience pain, you want it to stop. Your wish to repeat what feels good and to separate yourself from what feels bad is like a powerful addiction, and that's why a person drinking alcohol symbolizes this link. Like feeling, craving occurs throughout your life, but this link becomes crucial at the time of your death, when you develop an especially strong desire to continue living.
- **Grasping: A monkey snatching fruit.** (See Figure 13-11, left.) This link represents a more intense form of craving. As your desire grows, you tend to grasp at pleasurable objects the way a monkey snatches at fruit. As you approach death, you tend to grasp at a new body to replace the one you're about to lose. This action isn't a conscious, thought-out decision on your part; it's the automatic consequence of the craving and grasping that you've become accustomed to throughout your life.

Now that your old body is dying, your deeply engrained habit of I-grasping (see the "Grasping at a solid self" section, earlier in this chapter) compels you to seek a replacement. As someone once jokingly put it, "In such a state of panic, you'll probably jump into the first friendly womb that comes along."

- **Becoming: A pregnant woman.** (See Figure 13-11, right.) As the links of craving and grasping increase in strength at the time of death, they begin to ripen one of the many karmic seeds already planted on your consciousness. The potential for this seed, or *karmic impression,* to lead directly to a new life is now activated, as symbolized by the pregnant woman ready to give birth. Rebirth is assured. (This link is called *becoming,* or sometimes *existence,* because it leads to your next life coming into existence.)

Figure 13-10: The feeling and craving links.

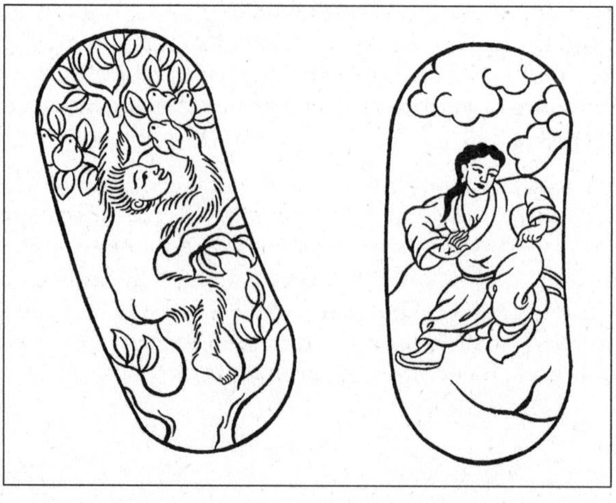

Figure 13-11: The grasping and becoming links.

- **Birth: A woman giving birth.** (See Figure 13-12, left.) The seed activated during the previous link finally ripens fully, and your dying consciousness is propelled ("blown by the winds of karma," if you want to be poetic about it) toward the circumstances of its next rebirth. A woman giving birth symbolizes this link (even though you actually first make contact with your next rebirth realm at your conception).
- **Aging and death: A person carrying a corpse.** (See Figure 13-12, right.) From the moment of your conception, the process that inevitably leads to your development, deterioration, and death begins. Along the way, you'll be forced to carry the burden of unwanted suffering, which the person carrying the corpse symbolizes.

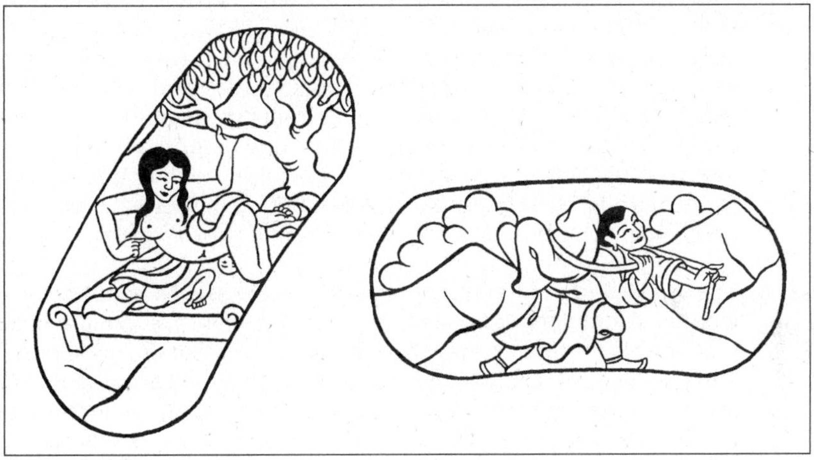

Figure 13-12: The birth and aging-and-death links.

REMEMBER

The purpose of teaching the 12 links — beginning with ignorance and ending with a corpse — isn't to bum you out or depress you. Quite the opposite! The intention is to make you acutely aware of the way your ignorantly motivated actions inevitably lead to recurring suffering, so that you'll be motivated to find a way out. The Buddha, depicted standing outside the Wheel of Life (look back at Figures 13-1 and 13-2) and pointing to the moon of liberation, or nirvana, represents this way out.

Cutting through Suffering: The Three Trainings

The question the spiritual traveler seeking liberation must ask is, "How can I cut through this 12-linked chain of dependent arising, gain release from the realms of suffering, and achieve lasting happiness and peace?"

To answer this question, you have to determine which of the 12 is the weakest link!

When, prior to his enlightenment, the Buddha spent six years engaging in austere practices of self-denial (see Chapter 3), he was essentially trying to break the sixth and seventh links — contact and feeling. He thought that if he could win sufficient control over his senses and find out how to endure even the most painful feelings, he could conquer suffering completely. But at the end of six years, he discovered that he wasn't any closer to his goal; he was just weak and exhausted. Trying to starve your senses into submission doesn't work because it addresses only the outward symptoms of suffering, not its actual causes.

Some people seem to think that they can find lasting happiness by attacking the twelfth link — aging and death. They avoid fattening foods, exercise regularly, apply special creams at the first sign of wrinkles, take their vitamins, receive hair-replacement therapy, and so on — all in the hopes that this behavior will somehow prevent them from growing old. (Some people even plan to freeze their body because they hope that doctors in the future will be able to cure them of the illnesses responsible for their deaths.) Taking care of your health is certainly worthwhile, but no matter what you do for your body, you won't be able to put off aging and death forever.

REMEMBER

The weakest of the 12 links are the ones that seem to be the strongest at first. Ignorance, craving, and grasping — the first, eighth, and ninth links — are responsible for first creating and then perpetuating the cycle of recurring suffering and dissatisfaction. Ignorance motivates the karmic actions that plant seeds of suffering in your mind; craving and grasping ripen these seeds at the time of death, sending you to a rebirth in which further suffering and dissatisfaction are inevitable.

These three links are powerful, but they're all based on a fundamental misconception — a distorted view, a lie. They all hold on to an idea about the nature of the self or *I* that conflicts with reality. In this respect, they're weak. If you can develop the wisdom that sees things the way they actually are, you can cut through these links and win complete freedom from cyclic existence (samsara). We're not talking about a detached, unfeeling withdrawal from life. Instead, we're referring to freedom from the suffering that occurs when you're caught on the Wheel of Life.

REMEMBER

The way to achieve this freedom is to engage in what is called the *three trainings,* which form a tripod on which the entire structure of Buddhist practice rests. These three trainings are as follows:

- **Moral discipline**
- **Concentration**
- **Wisdom**

The following is a traditional analogy to explain these three trainings. Imagine that you have a tree in your backyard producing poisonous fruit. Of course, you want to protect yourself and others from this dangerous situation, so you decide to get rid of the fruit. But how do you do that? You may try pruning back the branches of the tree, but this tactic helps only for a little while. Sooner or later, the branches will grow back and start producing more poison.

The poisonous fruit in this analogy stands for all deluded thoughts and actions that keep you trapped in cyclic existence, forcing you to experience suffering and disappointment over and over again. Pruning back the branches is like applying a temporary antidote to these delusions — like countering anger by practicing patience (see Chapter 14). These measures help in the short run, but as long as the source of these delusions (the tree itself) remains standing, the delusions will reappear sooner or later.

The only way to be sure that you remain completely safe from danger is to chop through the trunk of the tree so that nothing ever grows from it again. The trunk of the tree is ignorance — the mistaken view of the way you and all other things exist.

Just as you need three different things to chop down a tree (strength, a steady aim, and a sharp ax), you need the three trainings to free yourself from samsara. These three trainings work together as follows:

- **Strength (Moral discipline):** If you lack the necessary physical strength, you won't be able to swing the ax with precision and power. The same idea is true for your spiritual practices. You need the strength that comes from observing a regimen of moral discipline. You can't lead an unethical life, causing harm to yourself and others, and hope to gain the degree of concentration and insight needed to eliminate ignorance from your mind.
- **A steady aim (Concentration):** To cut through the trunk of the tree, you need a steady aim that gives you the ability to hit the same spot again and again. If you just flail around, even the sharpest ax won't help. Only a perfectly concentrated mind — which you can develop by bringing your awareness back again and again to a chosen object of meditation (see the breath-awareness technique in Chapter 7, for example) — can give you the steady aim needed to effectively wield the ax of wisdom. If your attention is lax or distracted, your aim will be untrue, and your wisdom will never penetrate.
- **A sharp ax (Wisdom):** Without a sharp ax, you won't be able to cut anything down. In this case, your ax is the wisdom you develop by hearing about, examining, and finally meditating deeply on the Buddhist teachings. Specifically, you have to develop the penetrating wisdom to directly see that the solid, concrete sense of self you've been grasping is a fiction — a false projection of your mind.

According to Buddhist teachings, if you practice the three trainings in combination with one another, you can definitely bring cyclic existence to an end and experience the inexpressible peace of liberation. You don't have to die to reach nirvana, but you do have to tame your mind. To put it another way, you need to follow the training first outlined in the eightfold path revealed in the Buddha's first discourse (which we discuss in Chapter 3). With moral self-discipline as your base and heightened concentration giving you focus, your wisdom can cut through ignorance and help you free yourself from the cycle of recurring misery in this very life.

Chapter 14

Fulfilling Your Highest Potential

In This Chapter

- Dedicating yourself to others
- Cultivating the four immeasurables (or divine abodes)
- Practicing the six perfections

Someone always seems ready to encourage you to make the most of your life. Your parents urged you to do your best. Your teachers probably nagged you to live up to your potential. Even television advertisements often harp on the same theme: Wear a particular brand of athletic shoes, and then just do it. Join the Army so you can be all that you can be!

Buddhist teachings give similar encouragement to its practitioners — though its scope and focus are quite different from those of the advertising industry and your friends, teachers, and parents. According to the teachings, you have the power to make a success not only of this life, but also of your future lives. It is assumed that you can purify your negative karma (see Chapter 12), achieve happiness and peace of mind, and eventually attain *nirvana,* which is complete liberation from the cycle of suffering and dissatisfaction (see Chapter 13). The best part is that you can do all these things regardless of your life circumstances.

Of course, such lofty goals may be the work of a lifetime, but it's good to know that you have the potential.

In this chapter, we present an overview of some Buddhist teachings about elements of the path that leads to the *actualization,* or fulfillment, of your highest potential. But first you need to be clear about exactly *why* you want to follow such a path. In other words, what's your underlying motivation? For your practice to be complete, your motivation needs to go beyond your mere personal satisfaction to include the happiness and fulfillment of others. This deep wish for the benefit of *all* beings (not just your friends — and not just other humans, either) lies at the heart of the teachings of Buddhism. In the Great Vehicle (Mahayana) tradition (of which Zen and Vajrayana, among others, consider themselves a part), this wish is expressed in the *bodhisattva vow.* In the Theravada tradition, it is implicit in the practice of the *four immeasurables* or *divine abodes* (brahmavihara).

Ordering a Round of Happiness for Everyone and Everything

Consider the following hypothetical situation. (If you think that another Buddhist analogy is coming, you're right.)

You and your entire family are at home when suddenly you smell smoke. The smoke quickly thickens, and you realize that your large two-story house is on fire. You pass a staircase leading up, but realizing that the fire will soon engulf the upper floors as well, you search for another escape route. Groping your way through the heavy smoke, you finally make it to the front door. Breaking free, you reach the yard outside. There, finally out of danger, you lie down to catch your breath.

The question is, "How do you feel now that you've reached safety? Are you content? Have you done everything you had to do?" Despite the fact that you're safe, the answer has to be no. Why? Because your family may still be trapped inside. As long as your loved ones are in danger, how can you possibly be content with just your own escape?

This analogy clearly demonstrates how incomplete you feel when you focus exclusively on your own liberation from suffering. Such self-centered preoccupation ignores the welfare of the countless other beings — human and otherwise — currently stuck in pain and dissatisfaction. Mahayana Buddhism teaches concern for all beings. With this larger picture in mind, fulfilling your highest potential must inevitably include providing for others' happiness and fulfillment as well.

REMEMBER

The determination to benefit all beings as well as (or sometimes even before) yourself is expressed in the *vow of the bodhisattva.* (For this vow, see Chapter 6.) The *bodhisattva* (Sanskrit: enlightenment-bound being) is the being who vows to remain in cyclic existence (samsara) until every living being is enlightened, too! The monk Shantideva, who lived in the first half of the eighth century, expressed this idea in his *Bodhisattvacharyavatara* ("*Guide to the Bodhisattva's Way of Life*"), also known as *Bodhicharyavatara*, (Chapter 10, verse 55) as follows:

> "As long as space abides and as long as the world abides, so long may I abide, eliminating the world's sufferings."

Dedicating Your Heart to Others

REMEMBER

In the Mahayana tradition, the bodhisattva's aspiration for awaking is known by its Sanskrit name, *bodhichitta.* Breaking the word into two parts makes it easier to understand:

- *Bodhi* means enlightenment.
- *Chitta* means mind, attitude, or heart.

Putting the two words together, you get *bodhichitta,* the aspiration for awakening or the awakening mind. Many Buddhist authors have discussed bodhichitta. Some authors understand it as the compassionate state of mind that wishes to attain enlightenment for the benefit of others. Some commentators call it simply the *awakened heart* or, as a translator we know likes to say, the *dedicated heart.* By cultivating bodhichitta, you awaken compassion in your heart for the suffering of others and dedicate your efforts to their benefit as well as your own.

Usually our compassion is conditional and limited in its scope. For example, you probably find it easy to feel compassion for a suffering family member, close friend, or small child, but your compassion for some others may not arise so spontaneously.

In many schools of Mahayana Buddhism, the goal is to develop an unconditional compassion that extends to *all* beings, regardless of whether they've helped or harmed you in the past. To aid in your cultivation of such all-encompassing "great" compassion, some teachers in the Vajrayana tradition recommend two related approaches:

- Recognizing that everyone is a member of one family
- Realizing the basic equality of yourself and others

Keeping it all in the family

If you believe in rebirth (see Chapter 13), then seeing how you're related to everyone else isn't that big of a stretch. Your past lives (as explained in certain Buddhist traditions, at least) have been infinite, so you've had more than enough time to have been born as every other being's son, daughter, sister, brother, or any other family member. For example, consider that annoying person who just cut you off on the highway or the mosquito that just left a painful bite on your arm: In a past life, each of these beings may have been your adoring mother!

Calling on Mommy Dearest — or not

One traditional method for developing great compassion and the dedicated heart begins by recognizing that, at one time, all beings have been your mother. As your mom, they've loved, protected, and cared for you in all the ways the typical Mother's Day card mentions. You can experience an immediate change in attitude (even toward an annoying person) if, for a moment, you can relate to that person as your loving mother.

These meditations for developing a compassionate, dedicated heart are part of the Buddhist mind-training tradition particularly favored by the Tibetans and must be used wisely to have the desired effect. In dealing with an annoying person, for example, the point is to shift your attitude from resentment or dislike to something positive. Therefore, when you practice visualizing a person as someone near and dear to you, make sure that you choose your role model wisely.

Traditionally, as we mention earlier, the model you first select is your own mother because she carried you in her womb, gave birth to you, and did the 1,001 things necessary to keep you alive and healthy. But when some people think about their mother, they find it difficult to remember such kindnesses. They can recall only problems — some very severe — that they've had with a rather difficult woman. In this case, don't think of others as having been your mother, because doing so may only increase your resentment toward them. Choose someone you remember as selfless and nurturing, no matter who he or she may be. Eventually, as your love, understanding, and forgiveness grow, you can open your heart to your mother as well and perhaps rediscover a bond you'd forgotten.

Getting connected to the world — through eating

Fortunately, you don't *have* to believe in rebirth to appreciate that all beings are part of one large family. As nature shows us every day, the lives of all beings on this planet are interconnected, and seeing how everyone is related to everyone else makes good sense. It has become a matter of survival.

You can use this interconnectedness to improve your meditation on great compassion. Start by thinking of anything you do on a daily basis that helps sustain or enhance your life. A good activity to begin with is eating. Imagine that you're just about to put some food into your mouth. When you can almost taste it, press your mental pause button and think about how this piece of food got to where it is now. (You can also do this meditation at the dinner table, but if you're eating with others, be prepared for some funny looks as you suddenly freeze midbite.)

Say you're about to eat a spoonful of rice. Ask yourself where the grain came from. It may have grown in a paddy field many miles away, perhaps even on another continent. Think of the many people involved in the difficult task of planting this rice. Then think about all the work it took to harvest this grain, thresh it, take it to market, and sell it. All these tasks required the strenuous effort of hundreds of people, most of whom received shockingly small pay for their backbreaking labor. But the rice hasn't yet reached your mouth: It still has to be transported, perhaps repackaged, and then sold again. Finally, it has to be prepared and served — and in many cases, you may not be involved in even these last two procedures.

You can analyze whatever you eat in pretty much the same way. In each case, you'll realize that your enjoyment of even one small bite of food is totally dependent upon a countless number of others. Even though they didn't purposely intend to benefit you, the fact remains: Without their effort, you wouldn't have the food to eat. Your enjoyment depends completely upon their endeavors.

TIP

You can apply this way of thinking to other aspects of your living situation. Ask yourself who's responsible for the house you live in, the clothes you wear, and even the language and ideas you use. In each case, the answer remains the same — other people. The more you look at things in this way, the more you can develop an appreciation of the infinite kindness you've received from others. As your heart opens to them, you'll naturally want to return this kindness in the best way possible.

Figuring out what all beings desire

A person who translated extensively for the Dalai Lama (see Chapter 15) once remarked, "I never attended a teaching by His Holiness where he didn't mention that all beings are alike in their desire to be happy and free from suffering." The translator then went on to add that you can draw one of two conclusions from this observation: Either the Dalai Lama doesn't have much to say, or this point is extremely important. You can safely opt for the second choice.

Agreeing that all beings want to be happy and to avoid unhappiness isn't difficult. In fact, thinking of any behavior *not* motivated by these twin desires is difficult. People may define happiness quite differently from one another (the music that some people like to listen to may make you cringe), but however they define it, happiness is what they want and unhappiness is what they want to avoid. Even when people harm themselves in some way — by committing suicide, for example — it's generally in a misguided attempt to get rid of pain.

Even though recognizing how universal these twin desires are isn't difficult, the implications of this apparently simple fact are profound. When a person harms you, for example, you usually take it quite personally. "He attacked me on purpose," you may think, and then you may look for ways to hurt him back. But your attitude changes significantly when you realize that your attacker is motivated by the same desire for happiness that motivates you. This fact doesn't mean that you have to sit back passively and let someone abuse you. What purpose would that serve? But it does mean that whatever action you decide to take — even if you decide to defend yourself forcefully — becomes motivated more by concern and understanding and less by the malicious desire to retaliate. Acting with this motivation in mind automatically improves the odds that your actions will be skillful and effective.

Looking at others as equal to yourself also helps reduce your selfishness, the cause of most (if not all) of your problems. Instead of constantly being involved with the tired refrain "Me, me, me," you may find yourself developing a genuine interest in the welfare of others. When you're in a group of people, for example, you may no longer feel such a terrible urge to put your wants and needs first. Instead, realizing that every person in that group also wants to be happy, you may open your heart and mind to *their* wants and needs.

The more you dedicate your heart to the welfare of others, the more you begin to realize that most people, though they claim to want happiness, engage in behaviors that only destroy their chances to find real peace and happiness. If you're honest, you'll undoubtedly find that you're making the same mistakes — and this situation doesn't change the moment you pick up a book (preferably *this* book) about Buddhism or one of the other great spiritual traditions of the world. (If it did, the publisher would definitely raise the cover price.) But at least it's a start; you're beginning to look in the right direction for true peace of mind and fulfillment.

As your understanding and sympathy for others deepen — in part as a result of dedicating your heart to their welfare — a sense of responsibility for others begins to grow in your heart as well. You begin to recognize that, in a certain sense, all beings are blind and stumbling toward the edge of a steep cliff. Who has more reason to help them than you? This train of thought may eventually result in a powerful resolve to free yourself from destructive habits and misguided points of view and to develop all the positive qualities necessary to effectively guide your family along the path to true happiness.

Nurturing the Four Divine Abodes

Just as Buddhism offers numerous meditation techniques for quieting and clearing the mind and gaining insight into the deeper truths of life, it also offers methods for cultivating the four core qualities known as the divine *abodes* or *immeasurables:*

- Loving-kindness
- Compassion
- Sympathetic joy
- Equanimity (a balanced mind)

One cautionary note: Cultivating loving-kindness and compassion doesn't involve meddling in other people's affairs or taking the morally superior attitude that declares, "I'm a bodhisattva with pure motivation who has something important to offer to you, you lowly, suffering being!" Quite the contrary: The qualities of loving-kindness, compassion, sympathetic joy, and equanimity, when practiced correctly, break down the barriers of apparent separation between yourself and others. They show you the ways in which you yourself are suffering, closed-hearted, and otherwise stuck or misguided. Whenever you find yourself pointing a finger at others, even if it's in apparent compassion, remember to turn that finger around and point it back at yourself.

Extending loving-kindness

When you practice *loving-kindness,* you value and cherish others as if they were your very own children, and you wish for them the same good fortune, health, happiness, and peace of mind that you wish for your dearest friends and family members.

By extending love to others you gradually loosen the hold that negative emotions like resentment and disappointment have over your own heart.

Meditating on the four divine abodes

In the Theravada tradition, meditations designed to cultivate loving-kindness, compassion, sympathetic joy, and equanimity have a similar structure:

1. Connect with your own innate wish for happiness and well-being.
2. Spend some time imagining a person who easily and naturally brings the quality in question to mind. In the case of loving-kindness, this person may be your mother or someone else who has loved and cared for you unconditionally. With compassion, you may think of someone you love who's experiencing great pain or suffering right now.
3. When you're in touch with the quality, direct it outward, toward yourself (quite difficult for some people), and then toward those who have benefitted from you in the past; loved ones, friends, neutral parties, and then (believe it or not) people who irritate or anger you.
4. Extend the quality to all beings everywhere.

Traditionally, certain prescribed phrases are used to generate these qualities, such as "May you be free of your pain and sorrow" (for compassion), "May your good fortune continue" (for sympathetic joy). At first, connecting with these qualities may be difficult, but don't worry (and certainly don't get upset with yourself): They're down there somewhere. When they start flowing, the practice of the divine abodes gets easier, and the qualities begin to arise more naturally and spontaneously.

Developing compassion

What exactly is compassion? Often people confuse it with the tendency to overburden themselves with the suffering of others and to harm themselves in the process of trying to help others. As some Buddhist teachers say, this habit isn't true compassion, but rather idiot compassion (or, as self-help books like to call it these days, codependency).

Genuine *compassion* (*karuna* in both Pali and Sanskrit) involves first acknowledging the suffering of others, which is common in the world, and then gradually learning to open your heart to feel it deeply without letting it overwhelm you.

If you're like most people, you understandably try to avoid feeling suffering — not only others' suffering, but also your own. After all, suffering is generally painful; besides, you may feel helpless because you can't do anything about it. And suffering often brings out other unpleasant feelings, like anger (at the cause of suffering), fear (of suffering yourself), and grief.

But genuine compassion is actually accompanied by a clear perception of the way things are. The truth is, millions of people are suffering, and you can do only so much about it. From these clear perceptions and the compassionate feelings arise the strength and skill to do whatever you can to alleviate suffering, along with the acceptance that you can do only so much.

Nurturing sympathetic joy

Strangely enough, many people find sympathizing with the suffering of others easier than rejoicing in their happiness or success. Perhaps this trait is the result of the Western "no pain, no gain" work ethic, which emphasizes struggle and hardship while being suspicious of more expansive feelings like rapture and elation. After all, how many people genuinely rejoice in even their own well-being? Or perhaps you feel jealousy rather than joy because of the tendency, especially in the West, to compete with others, to judge, compare, and demean rather than approve and appreciate. Because of these tendencies, sympathetic joy (Pali: *mudita*) can at times be difficult to develop.

Sympathetic joy cuts through the comparing, judging mind to embrace the happiness of others on their terms. Usually you view other people through the lens of your own prejudices, ideas, and expectations, and judge their efforts and accomplishments accordingly. When you cultivate sympathetic joy, however, you develop the capacity to see others clearly, just the way they are, and share in their happiness and success as if you're on the inside, feeling what they feel. By doing so you increase your own store of happiness and joy. In addition, you break down the barriers that separate you from others and establish the possibility of ongoing mutual love and support.

The practice of loving-kindness

The following steps are an exercise for connecting with the unconditional love in your heart and directing it to others. Don't hurry. Take as much time as you can; feel the love in addition to imagining it. Begin by closing your eyes, taking a few deep breaths, and relaxing your body a little each time you exhale. Then continue with the following steps:

1. When you feel relaxed, imagine the face of someone who loved you very much as a child and whose love moved you deeply.
2. Remember a time when this person showed his or her love for you and you really took it in.
3. Notice the gratitude and love that this memory stirs in your heart. Allow these feelings to well up and fill your heart.
4. Gently extend these feelings to this loved one. You may even experience a circulation of love between the two of you as you give and receive love freely.
5. Allow these loving feelings to overflow and gradually spread throughout your whole being.
6. Now consciously direct this love to yourself. You may want to use some traditional Buddhist phrases: "May I be happy. May I be peaceful. May I be free from suffering." Or you may want to choose other words and phrases that appeal to you. Just be sure to keep them general, simple, and emotionally evocative. As the recipient, be sure to take in the love as well as extend it.
7. When you feel complete with yourself for now, imagine someone for whom you feel gratitude and respect. Take some time (at least a few minutes) to direct the flow of love to this person, using similar words to express your intentions.
8. Now take some time to direct this loving-kindness to a loved one or dear friend in a similar way.
9. Direct this flow of love to someone for whom you feel neutral — perhaps someone you see from time to time but toward whom you have neither positive nor negative feelings.
10. Now for the hardest part of this exercise: Direct your loving-kindness to someone toward whom you feel mildly negative feelings, like irritation or hurt. By extending love to this person, even just a little at first, you begin to develop the capacity to keep your heart open even under challenging circumstances. Eventually, you can extend love to people toward whom you experience stronger emotions, like anger, fear, or pain.

As with any meditation, loving-kindness benefits from extended practice. Rather than a few minutes for each step, try spending five or even ten minutes. The more time and attention you give it, the more you'll begin to notice subtle (or not-so-subtle) changes in the way you feel from moment to moment. Eventually, the loving-kindness you generate in this exercise will begin to extend to every area of your life.

Establishing equanimity

Considered the culmination of the divine abodes (and the one that protects the other three), *equanimity* (Pali: *upekkha*) is balanced state of mind. This quality emerges when you meditate upon and deeply realize the essential Buddhist truth of *impermanence* (everything is constantly changing) and let go of trying to control what you simply can't control. You just let things be.

Equanimity doesn't mean passivity or indifference. You can take action to make important changes in your life with the same balance and peace of mind that you bring to sitting quietly in meditation. In equanimity, as in the other divine abodes, you're completely open to life as it presents itself. You don't shut down your heart or deny what's happening, but you have a deeper trust that life unfolds in its own meaningful and mysterious way and that you can do only so much to make a difference.

You may prefer certain life circumstances over others, but you have faith in the larger cycles, the bigger picture. Just as loving-kindness is compared to the love of a mother for her child, equanimity is compared to the love parents feel when their children become adults — providing warm support coupled with ample space and the ability to let go.

From equanimity arises fearlessness in the face of life's ups and downs — a quality that can be just as contagious as panic or rage. In the movie *Fearless,* Jeff Bridges plays a man whose equanimity during and after a plane crash radiates peace and reassurance to the other passengers. (As we describe in the "Practicing open-hearted generosity" section later in this chapter, giving the gift of fearlessness is one of the four primary forms of generosity.)

Cultivating the Six Perfections of a Bodhisattva

As you may guess, simply wanting to become enlightened so that you can help others most effectively isn't enough. You must actually follow a path that leads to this achievement.

In Buddhism, this path is outlined in numerous ways, often involving lists of some kind: the eightfold path (see Chapter 3), the three trainings (see Chapter 13), the ten stages as illustrated in the ox-herding pictures (see Chapter 10), and so on. Another helpful framework for understanding the path — one that emphasizes the cultivation of positive qualities and is used extensively for guiding students in their practice — is the set of six perfections (*paramita*).

The bodhisattva path is often said to entail a union of compassion (often called *method* because it's the means for benefiting others) and insightful wisdom into the true nature of reality. The first five perfections make up the compassionate method aspect of the path:

- Generosity
- Ethical behavior
- Patience
- Effort
- Concentration

And just as the eyes lead the body along a path, the sixth perfection gives guidance and direction to the rest:

- Wisdom

In the following sections, we largely present the interpretations of the six perfections by contemporary Tibetan teachers in the Vajrayana tradition.

Practicing open-hearted generosity

Also called giving, or even charity, *generosity* refers to the openhearted attitude that allows you to give others whatever they need without stinginess or regret.

This perfection is traditionally divided into four types:

- **Bestowing Buddhist teachings:** You don't have to be a fully qualified Buddhist master to give others spiritual guidance that leads them out of suffering, though the greater your understanding and realization of the teachings, the more effectively you can guide them. But you do have to have the proper motivation: truly wishing to benefit others and not simply looking to impress them with your knowledge.
- **Bestowing protection:** Humans and animals constantly face danger, even of losing their lives. Protecting them from danger — by scooping a bug out of a swimming pool, for example — characterizes this second form of generosity. This powerful practice not only directly benefits the beings you rescue, but it also increases your respect for the sanctity of all life. In addition, the positive karma you generate by protecting and saving the lives of others is believed to lengthen your own life span (see Chapter 12 for more on karma).

- **Bestowing material aid:** Most people think of this type of generosity when they consider the practice of giving. Because human beings need so many different things to survive and prosper, such as food, clothing, shelter, and gainful employment, you have countless opportunities to practice material giving. Sharing spare change with the homeless person on the street, donating money to your favorite charity, and buying food for a sick friend are common examples of this form of giving. Just be sure to use your discriminating wisdom when you provide material aid to someone. Giving a bottle of wine to an alcoholic, for example, may not be the wisest form of generosity.
- **Bestowing fearlessness:** Above all, you offer this precious gift to others when you display it in your own behavior — and you can't manifest fearlessness unless you cultivate it in your heart by practicing meditation and working with the distorted beliefs that cause inappropriate or excessive fear. Classical statues of the Buddha often show him in the gesture of bestowing fearlessness, with one arm raised and palm facing forward (see Figure 14-1). Because the Buddha's teachings help reduce fear and other forms of suffering, giving implicitly includes fearlessness.

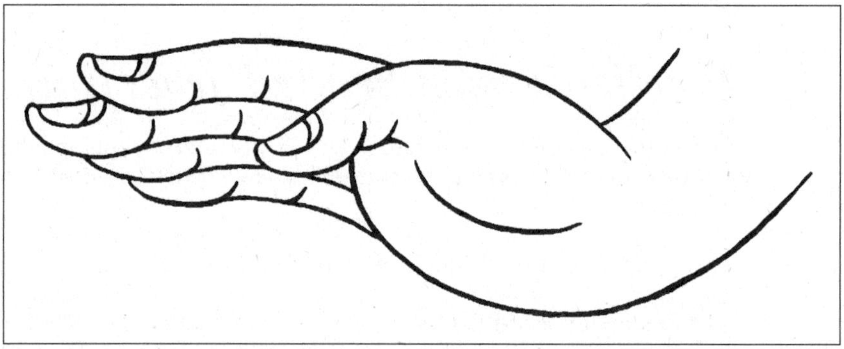

Figure 14-1: Gesture of bestowing fearlessness.

TIP

Keep in mind that the practice of generosity doesn't depend as much on *what* you give as on your *attitude* toward giving. You perfect this practice in your mind as you overcome all reluctance to help others and discover how to let go of your attachments — to material possessions, time, energy, and even points of view. In this way, generosity gradually frees you from grasping and greed.

You don't need to give anything tangible to practice generosity; even cultivating the *wish* to give counts a great deal, especially when it weakens your self-clinging. Ultimately, the deepest expression of this perfection involves the recognition that the giver, gift, and receiver are inherently one and inseparable.

Following the self-discipline of ethical behavior

This perfection is also called morality, but we're a bit cautious about using that term because it smacks too much of a puritanical attitude toward pleasure. The underlying meaning of *ethical behavior* in Buddhism is the avoidance of causing harm to others. You may want to simply call it virtue. As with generosity, the perfection of ethical behavior is traditionally divided into several types:

- **Restraint:** Your attempts to not commit negative actions while following the traditional ethical precepts fall into this category. Every effort you make to live up to the precepts or the bodhisattva vows expresses the discipline of self-restraint. The same holds true for any other vows you take as you progress along the spiritual path.
- **Accumulating virtue:** Progress along the spiritual path requires you to store up positive energy, especially when you've dedicated yourself to benefiting others. Accumulating virtue, therefore, is like charging your spiritual batteries. Throughout this book, we describe many such virtuous activities — such as making offerings to the Three Jewels, performing prostrations (see Chapter 8), praying for the welfare of others, studying Buddhist teachings, and adhering to the precepts — all of which contribute to this form of ethical discipline.
- **Benefiting others:** In daily life, you have so many opportunities to help people around you that listing them all here is simply impossible. In brief, they include everything you do with your body, speech, and mind that's directed toward the welfare of others. Even the tiny act of lighting one candle on your altar, if done with the wish of purifying the darkness of another person's mind, is an example of this form of ethical discipline.

Developing patience

REMEMBER

Patience is considered the direct opposite of anger and irritation, so it's one of the main practices of a compassionate bodhisattva. In addition to harming others, your anger and irritation have a disastrous effect on your own spiritual development. Therefore, keeping your mind as free as possible from this type of negative energy is extremely important.

Anger often arises when you feel like you're under attack, when you're not getting what you want when you want it, or when some situation or person frustrates you. But face it: The world is full of people and things that can upset you. What are you going to do, get angry at each and every one of them? Anger does unleash powerful energy, but trying to use this energy to solve your problems only creates more problems. As soon as you steamroll your way over one obstacle, two more obstacles inevitably spring up in its place.

A famous Buddhist analogy states that if you want to protect your feet from thorns, covering the entire surface of the Earth with leather is a wasteful, inefficient way of going about it. Simply cover the soles of your feet with leather, and the thorns can't harm you. In a similar fashion, you can't protect yourself from life's difficulties by trying to overwhelm them with anger. By practicing patience, however, you can keep your mind free from anger; as a result, your "problems" will no longer be able to bother you. As with wearing shoes, this approach is a much more effective way of protecting yourself.

The practice of patience is traditionally divided into three parts:

- **Remaining calm:** If you can refrain from retaliating with anger when someone or something harms or frustrates you, you're practicing this form of patience. One way to accomplish this feat is to think of how much worse you'll make the situation if you retaliate. Another way is to analyze the situation carefully and realize that the other person is ultimately attempting to find happiness, just as you are, but in an annoying and misguided way. Often the only way to improve a difficult situation is to simply refuse to engage with anger. If you do decide to confront the person, you can then do so with compassion and wisdom, which makes all the difference in the world.
- **Accepting suffering:** Even when someone or something isn't attacking or irritating you, you still continue to experience suffering in life as long as you haven't uprooted its causes within your own mind and behavior (see Chapter 13). In other words, as long as you're prey to the twin delusions of craving and aversion (wanting what you don't have and wanting to destroy what's bothering you), you're definitely going to suffer. And until you succeed in achieving full enlightenment, at which point anger disappears from your heart forever, you need to find a way to relate to this suffering that doesn't involve losing your temper.

  One way is to motivate yourself by viewing patient self-control as an opportunity to exhaust your negative karma (see Chapter 12). Another is to cultivate equanimity (one of the four immeasurables we discuss in the "Establishing equanimity" section earlier in this chapter), which allows you to accept your experience, no matter how painful. Finally, at the deepest level, anger dissolves and patience naturally arises when you view other people, including those that disturb you, as no different from yourself.
- **Developing certainty in the Buddhist teachings:** Throughout this book, we talk about the practice of the teachings — basically, training your mind — as the only reliable way of protecting yourself and fulfilling your highest potential. But old habits are hard to break, so when difficulties arise, your tendency is to react to them in the same unskillful and destructive ways you've always used. In other words, when push comes to shove, you tend to forget all the teachings you've ever heard and shove back. This third aspect of patience involves searching for the appropriate solution to each problem you face and then making the concerted effort to apply this solution directly to your present situation, no matter how hard it may be.

The empty boat

One story illustrates the foolishness of anger in light of the core Buddhist teaching of no-self, or selflessness. (In Chapter 13 we explain the concept of no-self and the five aggregates that make up what appears to be the person.) In the middle of a thick fog, a man is out fishing in his little boat when another boat slices through the mist and crashes into his. At first the man curses and yells at the person piloting the other craft, calling him names and demanding that he back off and give him space. When he looks more closely, however, he discovers that the other boat is empty — no one is manning the rudder. Suddenly, his anger disappears and he realizes the pointlessness of his rage.

In the same way, the people who seem to keep deliberately attacking you are ultimately empty of a separate, independent self. Because there's no one to blame, anger is a ridiculous waste of time.

Practicing with enthusiastic effort

In its most positive sense, *effort* (which you can think of as perseverance or commitment) is the delight you feel when doing what you know is the right thing — which, in the Buddhist context, generally means practicing the teachings. Instead of resisting, you dig in with gusto, knowing that you're on the right track. Some texts even claim that perseverance or enthusiastic effort is the most important perfection because it gives energy to the other five.

One of the main obstacles to progressing on the Buddhist path, as in any area of life, is laziness — also known as resistance. The fourth perfection is divided into three parts because each of them counters a specific form of laziness:

- **Overcoming sloth:** *Sloth* here refers to what most people mean by laziness. It includes procrastination and any of the other bad habits that may keep you from practicing the teachings right now. If you recognize what a rare and precious opportunity you have to make this life meaningful, and how easily this opportunity can be lost (see the discussion of death in Chapter 11), you'll find the energy and determination to put whatever you've mastered into practice right away.
- **Overcoming attraction to trivial pursuits:** As uncomfortable as admitting it may be, most people fill their days with unimportant distractions that aren't genuinely relaxing or fulfilling but merely occupy their time and keep them from doing what really matters in life. Watching TV, listening to talk shows, playing video games, filling out crossword puzzles — how many hours do you spend each day engaging in activities that have no deeper meaning? When you recognize how much time you waste in such trivial pursuits (and we don't mean the board game), you can deal with your addictive behavior and free up more time for Buddhist practices.

- **Overcoming defeatism:** This final form of enthusiastic effort counters whatever delusions of inadequacy or incompetence you may have. You may think that your negative mind is so strong and your practice of the teachings is so weak that you have no hope of making progress on the spiritual path.

  To weaken the hold of such defeatist ideas and eventually eliminate them from your mind altogether, you can use what are called *affirmations* (for example, "I am a loving person, and I have the power to help others") to remind yourself that you, too, despite your busy mind and unskillful behavior, possess the same inherent virtues as everyone else. Reading books on Buddhist teachings can reduce your self-doubt and fuel your perseverance. Remember that all the realized beings of the past, including Shakyamuni Buddha, were at one time as deluded as you are now. If they could generate the effort to complete their path, what's preventing you from doing the same?

Sharpening your concentration

The basic Buddhist technique for developing *concentration* is simply to choose a particular object of meditation, focus your attention on it, and then keep it there without wavering. You can choose from a wide range of objects, including your breath (see Chapter 7), a patch of color, the visualized image of Shakyamuni Buddha, or even your own mind, just to name a few.

Different traditions have their own favorite practices, and some measure of concentration is important for all of them. For example, followers of certain devotional Pure Land schools of Buddhism focus their energy on gaining rebirth in the western paradise of Amitabha Buddha. As part of their training, they may practice visualizing this Buddha and his surroundings in as much detail as possible, until the image appears with utter clarity to their mind's eye. Followers of the Rinzai Zen tradition focus much of their attention on resolving *koans* (paradoxical or enigmatic teaching stories) — such as the famous "What is the sound of one hand [clapping]?" or "What was your original face before your parents were born?" — until they break through the limitations of ordinary, conceptual thought. (See Chapter 5 for more on these two traditions.) Without strong and continuous concentration, neither the Pure Land follower nor the Zen practitioner is likely to achieve great success — and the same holds true for serious practitioners of other traditions.

Strong powers of concentration take time to develop, though occasionally a novice meditator may make surprisingly rapid advances (see the story of Dipa Ma in Chapter 15). Even though you try to focus on one specific object (your breath, for example), any number of attention grabbers can easily distract you, including:

- Sounds (of traffic, birds, and so on)
- Physical sensations (pain in your knees or itching)
- Memories (what you had for breakfast)
- Anticipations and expectations for the future (maybe what you want for lunch)
- Almost any other experience you can name

Many of these experiences are distracting because they stimulate strong desire, attachment, irritation, or frustration. For this reason, meditators trying to develop powerful, single-pointed concentration also generally practice letting go of their strong attachments and aversions by recognizing how fleeting and unsatisfactory they are (see Chapter 2). Deep concentration can grow only in a contented mind.

In the early stages of your practice, you have to be patient and persistent, firmly (but gently) placing your attention back on the meditation object every time it wanders away, which will probably happen quite a bit. But if you practice diligently enough, your attention will begin to gravitate naturally toward the meditation object (rather than the distractions) and eventually come to rest there on its own. Instead of being at the mercy of your fickle mind, you gradually become adept at controlling it.

TIP

As your concentration deepens, you naturally progress through a number of well-defined stages of meditation. Although you can read about these stages in various meditation manuals, practicing under the guidance of a competent teacher is important — at least until you're well established in the practice. Otherwise, you can get sidetracked in numerous ways. You can even practice what you think is meditation for many years, when in reality, you're only building up habits of mental dullness.

If your practice is diligent enough, you can reach a level of concentration far beyond what you normally experience. For example:

- You can develop the capacity to direct your attention to your chosen object of meditation and have it remain there with little or no effort, undisturbed by distractions or dullness.

  This level of concentration not only deepens your meditation practice, but it also has beneficial effects on your life in general. Disturbances like anger, greed, and jealousy can't easily arise in a calmly focused mind; when they do, they don't remain there for long.
- Deep concentration also brings the body and mind into balance, sometimes causing even chronic ailments to disappear.
- Deep concentration allows you to focus unwaveringly on any task, enabling you to function far more effectively at work and play.

Ultimately, however, the purpose of developing the power of deep concentration is to enable you to investigate the nature of reality. Only in this way can you develop the penetrating insight that eliminates ignorance, the root cause of all suffering and dissatisfaction. This insight, also known as wisdom, is the subject of the last of the six perfections.

Cultivating the ultimate perfection: Insightful wisdom

Buddhism encourages you to develop many different kinds of wisdom, including the ability to discriminate properly between actions that are destructive and actions that are beneficial to both yourself and others.

REMEMBER

However, the perfection of wisdom (*prajna-paramita* in Sanskrit) refers to something deeper: The perfection of *wisdom* is insight into the way things actually are, no longer misled by the false way they *appear* to exist. This wisdom reveals that the true nature of all things (you included) is marked by emptiness (*shunyata* in Sanskrit). (According to some schools of Buddhism, this wisdom reveals the *selflessness* of all things, which is another way of saying more or less the same thing.) Without this penetrating wisdom, the first five perfections are blind; without the first five, your development of the perfection of wisdom will be weak. But when they're cultivated together, in a union of compassionate method and wisdom, they give you the strength and vision to make it all the way to enlightenment.

REMEMBER

Emptiness isn't the easiest reality to comprehend. Even the different Buddhist schools have different ways of understanding it. When the Buddhist wisdom teachings state "All phenomena are empty" or "The self is empty," what exactly do they mean? Right off the bat, you have to understand that these profound teachings are *not* saying that all these things are totally nonexistent. Such things (or phenomena) as people, mountains, clouds, and so on do exist. They're just "empty," meaning they lack something. Practicing the perfection of wisdom means examining exactly what they're lacking as precisely as you can.

At this point, you may scratch your head and wonder, "What's all the fuss about understanding that things lack something they never had?" The answer is that, according to the insights of the Buddhist great masters and sages, all suffering and dissatisfaction, without exception, are rooted in your mistaken views or delusions of how things exist. Under the influence of these delusions, you superimpose qualities onto reality that reality doesn't possess. So if you want to eliminate suffering (and who doesn't?), you have to identify and eliminate all these delusions.

If you haven't directly perceived the truth, you mistakenly believe that things have a concreteness and a separateness — sometimes called an abiding, substantial self-nature — that they don't really possess. To eliminate your suffering once and for all, you need to deeply realize that phenomena are totally empty of this substantial, abiding self-nature — they're empty of all the false views you mistakenly project onto them. One translator likes to call *shunyata,* or *emptiness,* "the absence of the fantasized," meaning that phenomena are empty of your fantasies and false projections about them.

So how do you meditate on emptiness? One way is to start by identifying the habitual views you have about people and things and then recognize how limiting and badly informed these views are and how they lead inevitably to suffering and dissatisfaction (see Chapter 13). In particular, investigate your concrete views of yourself — your habit of thinking that you're this or that kind of person with particular, fixed characteristics, independent of all the moment-by-moment changes going on in your body and mind. In other words, take a long, close look at how you perpetuate a particular image of yourself — your supposed identity and what you imagine to be an abiding, substantial self.

The more you look for this solid sense of self inside you, the more elusive and ungraspable it becomes. Eventually, if you've prepared yourself well enough and your concentration is firm enough, you can experience a breakthrough to an awareness of reality "just as it is." All conceptions fall away in an experience completely beyond words or concepts. As you grow more accustomed to this penetrating wisdom — this direct experience of reality itself, free of distorted views — your realization, or enlightenment, deepens and stabilizes. Motivated by your compassionate wish to free others from their ignorantly created prisons, you can then lead them wisely and skillfully to enlightenment as well. (For more on enlightenment, see Chapter 10.)

Explaining emptiness

Contrast the way you ordinarily use the term *emptiness* with the way it's used in *Perfection of Wisdom Sutras.* For example, after a fire has destroyed a neighbor's house, you may point to the "empty" lot, indicating the absence or lack of the house that used to be there. Or you may point to a bottle that has only a little liquid left in it and say, "That bottle is almost empty."

In both these examples, you're talking about the absence of something that was once there, something that once existed. But when the wisdom teachings say that all things are empty, they don't mean that phenomena lack something that once existed. Quite the opposite! The whole point behind the Buddhist teachings on emptiness is that all phenomena, you included, are empty of something that *never* existed in the first place — a solid, permanent, substantial self or essence. (For more on emptiness, see Chapter 10.)

Chapter 15

Life Stories of Four Buddhist Masters

In This Chapter

- Discovering how a Bengali housewife becomes an honored teacher
- Understanding how a Thai monk helps revive an ancient tradition
- Following a Vietnamese Zen master who practices Engaged Buddhism
- Considering the Dalai Lama's message of peace

The other chapters in Part IV give you an idea of how a practitioner of Buddhism can develop his mind and awaken spiritually. This information is interesting and helpful (at least, we hope it is), but you may be left with a nagging question: "How can I be sure that this stuff really works?"

You may want to know for yourself whether the claims made on behalf of the Buddhist path are believable — that the path really does lead to the type of self-transformation illustrated in the stories about the Buddha and later masters (see Chapter 3). The only way to find out for sure whether the claims are true is to test the Buddhist teachings for yourself and see what happens. But not everyone feels motivated to make a serious commitment to practice without a source of inspiration who can demonstrate that the spiritual path is really worth following. Your personal teacher or spiritual mentor traditionally plays this role. (Check out Chapter 6 for more information about the different types of spiritual teachers.)

Because you probably haven't found a teacher yet, we provide you with the next best thing in this chapter: a detailed look at four modern-day Buddhist masters whom Buddhists and non-Buddhists alike admire as inspiring examples of what the spiritual life can produce. Although all four of these folks were born in Asia — and the first two died toward the end of the 20th century — their influence is still very much alive in the West.

Dipa Ma (1911–1989)

Even though Buddhist teachings are open to everyone, men — and especially monks — have dominated the history of Buddhism from its beginnings until today. This situation is regrettable but not really surprising. For several thousand years now, all the world's major cultures have been organized along patriarchal (male-dominated) lines, and Buddhist organizations simply reflect this cultural bias.

Fortunately, this unbalanced situation is beginning to change, especially in the West, where a growing number of women practitioners and teachers have achieved prominence in Buddhist circles. But whether you're a man or a woman, you can find inspiration in the life of Dipa Ma, a Bengali housewife who overcame extremely challenging life circumstances to become one of the most accomplished Buddhist masters of her day. A generation of vipassana teachers in the West reveres her.

Spending her early years as a wife and mother

Dipa Ma (see Figure 15-1), whose original name was Nani Bala Barua, was born in 1911 in a village in the Chittagong region of what's now Bangladesh, near the border with Burma (now Myanmar). Her family belonged to the Bengali Baruas, a Buddhist community. The oldest of seven children, Nani displayed an unusually strong interest in Buddhism at an early age. Instead of pretending to cook and keep house like the other little girls, she loved to spend time with Buddhist monks and make flower offerings to images of the Buddha. She also expressed keen interest in her studies, but her formal education came to an end at the age of 12, when, as custom dictated, her family gave her away in marriage to a man more than twice her age.

Fortunately, her husband, Rajani Ranjan Barua, was a kind man. He took a job as an engineer in Rangoon (now Yangon), Burma, where the couple became actively involved in the Buddhist community. Although Nani and Rajani grew to love one another, their marriage had one major flaw from the traditional point of view: It produced no children. For more than 20 years, the couple remained childless until Nani surprisingly found herself pregnant at last at age 35. But her joy didn't last long: Her long-awaited daughter died when she was 3 months old. Nani almost died from grief, but four years later, she was pregnant again. This time her daughter, whom the couple named Dipa ("light"), survived. Nani was so happy that from then on she became known as Dipa Ma — Dipa's mother. The name Dipa Ma also means "mother of light."

Figure 15-1: Dipa Ma.

Photo courtesy of Maria Monroe.

Overcoming physical ailments through meditation

During their marriage, Dipa Ma frequently asked her husband for permission to meditate, but he consistently refused, suggesting that she follow the Indian custom of waiting until she was older before pursuing a spiritual life. Throughout a life of tragedy and sorrow, Dipa Ma kept her wish to learn meditation alive. She experienced heart disease, the death of an infant son, illnesses that kept her perpetually bedridden, and finally, the heart attack and sudden death of her husband. A widow and invalid at the age of 46, Dipa Ma found herself in the depths of despair, with nothing left to do but face the prospect of death. At this point, her doctor recommended meditation as the only hope for her survival. Dipa Ma realized, more clearly than ever, that only the practice of meditation would relieve her suffering and offer her true peace. Entrusting her daughter Dipa to the care of a neighbor, she headed to the Kamayut Meditation Center in Rangoon.

Amazingly, after only one brief period of instruction, Dipa Ma managed to attain a state of deep meditative concentration. Unfortunately, she was bitten by a dog during this first retreat and had to return home to care for herself and her daughter. She continued her meditation practice at home for several years before meeting with the Bengali meditation teacher Anagarika Munindra (1914-2003) and his esteemed Burmese master, Mahasi Sayadaw (1904-1982) — both of whom were instrumental in bringing the living practice of Buddhist meditation to the West. During a retreat at Mahasi Sayadaw's meditation center Thathana Yeiktha, Dipa Ma quickly progressed through deeper meditative states until she eventually experienced the first stage of enlightenment, a moment of inexpressible stillness that changed her life forever.

At each successive stage of her inner journey, Dipa Ma broke through thicker barriers of torment and pain and let go of deeper levels of attachment. With these experiences, her health returned: Her blood pressure returned to normal, her heart palpitations all but disappeared, and she regained her physical stamina after years of illness and physical torment. Gradually, she progressed through the stages of enlightenment (see Chapter 10), relinquishing all traces of craving, aversion, and ignorance, and achieving an unflappable peace and composure until her realization was complete. Within little more than a year, the debilitated mother and housewife had been transformed into a living embodiment of the Buddhist teachings.

Sharing her story with others

Astounded and inspired by her example, the friends and neighbors who had all but given up hope for her survival just a few years before began to practice meditation themselves. Dipa Ma eventually began accepting students, teaching them how to make every moment of their lives into a meditation. For example, she taught mothers and housewives how to be steadfastly mindful whenever they washed the dishes, did the laundry, or nursed their babies. "You can't separate meditation from life," she often advised. "The whole path of mindfulness is whatever you're doing. Be aware of it." Later, when she left Myanmar and moved to a small apartment outside Calcutta (now Kolkata), she attracted a steady stream of laypeople who wanted to engage in her practical approach to mindfulness training.

Shortly after her spiritual awakening, under the guidance of Anagarika Munindra, Dipa Ma reportedly developed many of the seemingly miraculous powers that you only read about in the legends of ancient meditation masters — appearing in two places at the same time, walking through walls, and traveling in time. But she soon stopped demonstrating these *siddhis* (the name for these extraordinary powers) because, by themselves, these powers don't lead to release from suffering, which she felt was the one true goal of practice. Instead, she instructed her students to observe the precepts of pure moral behavior and dedicate themselves to the welfare of others, practices that she followed for the rest of her life.

Though she treated each person who came to her like her own son or daughter and showered everyone she met with her love and blessings, Dipa Ma could also be fierce in encouraging her students to extend themselves further, practice more diligently, and use each moment as if it were their last. In a culture that still considered women inferior, Dipa Ma told her female students that they could actually go deeper in practice than men because their minds were softer and their emotions more accessible. Among the people who came to receive instruction, encouragement, and inspiration from Dipa Ma were Westerners like Joseph Goldstein (born in 1944), Sharon Salzberg (born in 1952), and Jack Kornfield (born in 1945). These individuals went on to become some of the most influential meditation teachers in North America (see Chapter 5 for more on the spread of Buddhist meditation to the West). In the 1980s, Dipa Ma twice accepted their invitation to visit their Insight Meditation Society in Barre, Massachusetts, to help lead retreats. Her "10 Lessons to Live By" summarize her teachings. She died quietly in her small apartment in Calcutta (Kolkata) in 1989, with her daughter and a devoted student at her side, as she bowed toward the Buddha with her hands pressed together in prayer.

Ajahn Chah (1918–1992)

The Theravada ("Way of the Elders") is the oldest continually existing Buddhist tradition in the world (see Chapter 4 for more on Theravada history). Its presence in the West owes a great deal to the work of modern-day elders like the Venerable Ajahn Chah (see Figure 15-2).

Finding his way in the forest of life

Born in 1918 in a village in northeast Thailand, Ajahn Chah spent several years as a novice monk as a young man and then returned to his family to help on their farm. At the age of 20, he resumed the monastic life and took full ordination in 1939. He devoted his first years as a monk to learning Pali (the language of the Theravada scriptures) and studying the traditional Buddhist texts — the typical training in most Thai monasteries of the day.

Figure 15-2: Ajahn Chah.

Photo courtesy of Abhayagiri Buddhist Monastery.

But the death of his father led Ajahn Chah to seek more than intellectual understanding. He began a quest to discover the essential meaning of the Buddha's teachings. He had read a lot about the *three trainings* of morality, meditation, and wisdom, but he still couldn't understand how to put the teachings into practice. His burning question eventually led him to Ajahn Mun (1870–1949), the leading force in Thailand for the revival of the ancient forest-dwelling tradition of Buddhist meditation. (*Ajahn* — also spelled *Achaan* — is a term of respect given to senior monks who've begun to teach.) Ajahn Mun taught him that, although the written teachings are extensive, the central practice of mindfulness is quite simple. (For more on mindfulness, see Chapter 7.)

With the way of practice clarified, Ajahn Chah spent several years traveling around Thailand and living in cobra-infested jungles and cremation grounds — traditional places for deepening meditation practice and confronting the fear of death. After years of wandering, during which he deepened and clarified his own awakening, Ajahn Chah was invited back to his home village. Disciples began to gather around him, despite the poor shelter, scarce food, and malarial mosquitoes in the area. The purity and sincerity of his practice attracted these people in the face of such difficult conditions. Ajahn Chah founded the monastery now known as Wat Nong Pah Pong, in Ubon Ratchathani Province, in northeast Thailand, and branch monasteries gradually sprang up in the surrounding area.

Ajahn Chah became known for his great ability to tailor his explanations of Buddhist teachings to each particular group of listeners. His talks arose from the depths of his own meditative experience and were always clear, often humorous, and inevitably profound. Soon monks and laypeople from all over Thailand found their way to his monastery *(wat)* in the forest to share in his wisdom.

Blazing the monastic trail

In 1966, the newly ordained American monk Venerable Sumedho (born in 1934), who had begun training at a monastery near the Laotian border, came to stay at Wat Nong Pah Pong. The community accepted him as a disciple as long as he was willing to eat the same food and undergo the same austere practice as the other monks. By the time Venerable Sumedho had spent five rainy-season retreats at Wat Nong Pah Pong, Ajahn Chah considered him qualified to teach. Together they started the International Forest Monastery. Venerable Sumedho became the abbot of the first monastery in Thailand run by and for English-speaking monks.

Other Westerners came and went during the 1960s and 1970s, including Jack Kornfield — one of the pioneers of vipassana in the United States and a founder of the Insight Meditation Society in Barre, Massachusetts, and the Spirit Rock Center in Woodacre, California. After a stint in the Peace Corps in Thailand, Kornfield spent several years as a monk at Wat Nong Pah Pong under Ajahn Chah's guidance before he returned to the West and began to teach in 1975.

When Ajahn Chah was invited to teach in Great Britain in 1977, he brought Venerable Sumedho and several other monks with him. Seeing the Western interest in Buddhist teachings, Ajahn Chah allowed Sumedho and other monks to stay behind at the headquarters of the English Sangha Trust in London to teach. The following year, the Chithurst Buddhist Monastery was established in Sussex, England. This event marked the first time that highly trained Westerners brought the living Theravada monastic tradition to the West. (In 1984, Ajahn Sumedho moved from Chithurst to found Amaravati Buddhist Monastery in Hemel Hempstead, England. However, many monastics stayed behind, and Chithurst Monastery is still going strong under the leadership of Ajahn Sucitto.) Eventually, through Ajahn Chah's guidance and inspiration, Western disciples established additional centers in Europe, Australia, New Zealand, and elsewhere.

After several more visits to the West, Ajahn Chah's diabetes worsened and his health began to deteriorate. Like a true master, he used his worsening condition to teach his disciples about impermanence and the necessity to follow the spiritual path diligently. Even when he became bedridden and could no longer speak, his presence attracted numerous monks and laypeople to his monastery to practice. In 1992, Venerable Ajahn Chah died. He had brought untold benefit to spiritual seekers around the world.

Thich Nhat Hanh (Born 1926)

REMEMBER

The last half-century has seen the growth of a movement known as *(Socially) Engaged Buddhism,* which combines traditional Buddhist principles with non-violent social action inspired by modern teachers such as Gandhi and Martin Luther King, Jr. (You can find some books on this topic in Appendix B.)

Vietnamese Zen monk Venerable Thich Nhat Hanh (see Figure 15-3) coined the term *Engaged Buddhism.* He was one of its founders and continues to be a very influential figure in this movement. For many decades, Thich Nhat Hanh has worked tirelessly and extensively on behalf of poor and oppressed people around the world.

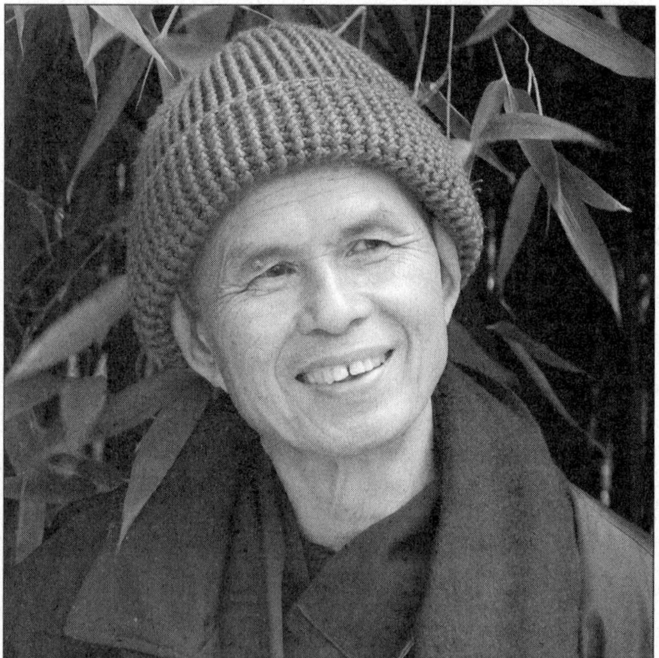

Figure 15-3: Thich Nhat Hanh.

Photo courtesy of Richard Friday with permission from Parallax Press, Berkeley, California.

Working for peace in times of war

Born in central Vietnam in 1926, Thay (Vietnamese for "teacher" or "master"), as his students call him, became a Buddhist monk in 1942. He was a founding member of a center of Buddhist studies in South Vietnam by the time he was 24. He spent two years studying and teaching comparative religion in the

United States and then returned to Vietnam. There he helped lead a resistance movement, based on Gandhi's principles of nonviolence, against the forces destroying his country during the Indochinese Wars.

Thich Nhat Hanh founded the School of Youth for Social Service, an organization that sent more than 10,000 monks, nuns, and young social workers into the countryside to establish health clinics and schools and to rebuild villages that had been bombed during the wars in Indochina. In a pattern that repeated itself many times, Thich Nhat Hanh's calls for reconciliation between the warring parties got him into trouble with both sides in the ongoing Vietnamese conflicts.

In 1966, shortly after the start of armed U.S. intervention in Vietnam, Thich Nhat Hanh traveled to the United States without any official sponsorship or sanction. His mission was to describe to the American people the suffering of their Vietnamese brothers and sisters and to appeal to both political leaders and social activists for a cease-fire and a negotiated settlement. Martin Luther King, Jr., also a proponent of Gandhi's brand of nonviolence, was so moved by Thich Nhat Hanh and his proposals that he publicly came out against the Vietnam War and, in 1967, nominated Thich Nhat Hanh for the Nobel Peace Prize. During that same visit, Thich Nhat Hanh met Thomas Merton, a well-known Catholic monk and author, who reportedly told his students, "Just the way he opens the door and enters a room demonstrates his understanding. He is a true monk."

Continuing his quest, Thich Nhat Hanh traveled to Europe, where he twice met Pope Paul VI to urge Catholic and Buddhist cooperation in helping bring peace to Vietnam. At the request of the Unified Buddhist Church of Vietnam, Thich Nhat Hanh led the Buddhist delegation to the Paris peace talks in 1969. But in 1973, when the peace settlement turned over South Vietnam to the Communists, the government refused to let him reenter his homeland. Since then, he has lived in France, where he leads meditation retreats, writes, and continues his work on behalf of peace and reconciliation. After living in exile from Vietnam for 39 years, Thich Nhat Hanh was invited to return there in 2005. He visited Vietnam for three months to teach, accompanied by a group of his monks, nuns, and lay students. He returned in 2007 and 2008 to teach.

Forging new beginnings from classic ideals

In 1982, Thich Nhat Hanh established Plum Village (`www.plumvillage.org`, a large retreat center and meditation community near Bordeaux, France, where people from around the world gather to practice mindfulness. Plum Village also serves as a refuge where activists involved in the work of peace and social justice can come for rest and spiritual nourishment, and a place where Vietnamese expatriates can find a home away from home. Since 1988, three more Plum Village practice centers in the tradition of Thich Nhat Hanh have been established. Two are located in the United States: Deer Park Monastery (in Southern California) and Blue Cliff Monastery (in upstate New York). The third is the European Institute of Applied Buddhism near Cologne, Germany.

Using Plum Village as his home base, Thich Nhat Hanh continues his frequent travels, leading retreats and giving workshops on mindfulness and social action around the world. His gentle teachings are firmly based on classical Buddhist themes, such as mindfulness, insight, and compassion. These teachings emphasize that, to achieve peace in the world, we need to be at peace ourselves. His more than 100 books of prose, poetry, and prayers have made him an internationally recognized author.

Most important, Thich Nhat Hanh established a new Buddhist lineage (or school) called the Order of Interbeing. This order is based on a reworking of the traditional Buddhist precepts (see Chapter 12 for more information on the precepts) known as the "14 Mindfulness Trainings." (An earlier version of the Mindfulness Trainings circulated under the name "14 Precepts of Engaged Buddhism.") Each mindfulness training begins with an awareness of either certain Buddhist truths or widespread inequities and injustices. Then follows a commitment to behave in a more compassionate, mindful, spiritually informed way.

WORDS OF WISDOM

For example, consider 3 of Thich Nhat Hanh's 14 Mindfulness Trainings, from his book *Interbeing* (Parallax Press):

> 1) *Aware of the suffering created by fanaticism and intolerance,* we are determined not to be idolatrous about or bound to any doctrine, theory, or ideology, even Buddhist ones. Buddhist teachings are guiding means to help us learn to look deeply and to develop our understanding and compassion. They are not doctrines to fight, kill, or die for.
>
> 5) *Aware that true happiness is rooted in peace, solidity, freedom, and compassion, and not in wealth or fame,* we are determined not to take as the aim of our life fame, profit, wealth, or sensual pleasure, nor to accumulate wealth while millions are hungry and dying. We are committed to living simply and sharing our time, energy, and material resources with those in need. We will practice mindful consuming, not using alcohol, drugs, or any other products that bring toxins into our own and the collective body and consciousness.
>
> 13) *Aware of the suffering caused by exploitation, social injustice, stealing, and oppression,* we are committed to cultivating loving kindness and learning ways to work for the well-being of people, animals, plants, and minerals. We will practice generosity by sharing our time, energy, and material resources with those who are in need. We are determined not to steal and not to possess anything that should belong to others. We will respect the property of others, but will try to prevent others from profiting from human suffering or the suffering of other beings.

Thich Nhat Hanh has made the traditional Buddhist precepts more relevant to contemporary concerns, including the growing threat to the environment, the exploitation of developing nations by multinational corporations, and the conflict and terrorism caused by religious fanaticism. Through his worldwide influence on people who work for peace, this gentle monk, who practices the slow walking and mindful awareness that he teaches, has helped further the cause of peace and justice by embodying peace and justice himself.

The Dalai Lama (Born 1935)

The world's most famous Buddhist leader is the monk Tenzin Gyatso, more popularly known as the Fourteenth Dalai Lama of Tibet (see Figure 15-4). (The title *Dalai,* Mongolian for "ocean," was bestowed upon an outstanding Tibetan lama — that is a spiritual teacher who is often a monk — more than 400 years ago by a Mongolian king. This king was so impressed by the lama's spiritual presence that he considered him to be an "ocean (of wisdom)." Each successive Dalai Lama has had *Gyatso,* which is Tibetan for "ocean," as part of his official name. By the way, the word *Tenzin* in the present Dalai Lama's name means "holder of the teachings." Because this revered spiritual teacher is so widely known in the West, we offer a somewhat more extensive account of his life and work than that of the three teachers we discuss earlier in this chapter.

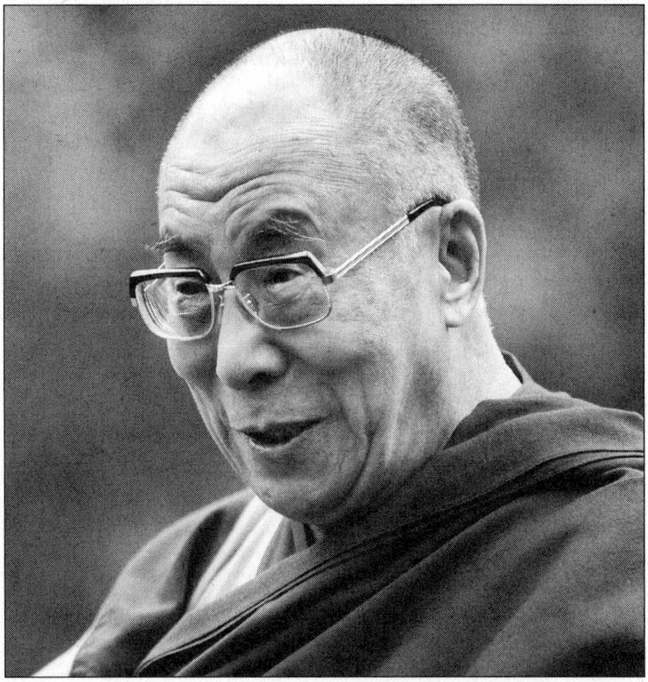

Figure 15-4: Tenzin Gyatso, the Fourteenth Dalai Lama of Tibet.

Photo courtesy of Jeff Miller/University of Wisconsin–Madison.

Understanding the legacy of reincarnation

The present Dalai Lama is the 14th in a line of Tibetan spiritual masters that stretches back more than 500 years. Included in this lineage are some of the most accomplished meditators, teachers, authors, and poets in Tibetan history. Since the time of the Fifth Dalai Lama, Lobsang Gyatso (1617–1682) — known to all Tibetans as the Great Fifth — the successors of this line have also been the spiritual and secular leaders of the Tibetan nation. (This setup is like one person holding the position of pope and king at the same time.) During the reign of the Great Fifth, the Potala Palace, the residence of the Dalai Lamas, was built in Lhasa. Aside from the Dalai Lama himself, this imposing structure remains the single most recognizable symbol of Tibet today.

One of the unique aspects of Tibetan culture is the way in which the position of spiritual and secular leader passes from one generation to the next. A person doesn't become the Dalai Lama by inheriting the throne from a deceased relative, nor does he receive this position as the result of an election. Instead, when each Dalai Lama dies, his successor is *discovered* and then installed in his place.

This system is based on the belief in rebirth (see Chapter 13 for more on this process). According to Buddhist teachings, when well-trained meditators have gained sufficient control over their mind through spiritual practice, they can remain conscious while dying and actually choose where they'll be reborn and to which parents. Selecting where they'll be reborn increases the chances that they'll be discovered at an early age (often by one or more of their former disciples). These young children (called *tulkus,* or incarnate lamas) are then educated in the same spiritual disciplines their predecessors mastered. Teachings that they gave to others are then given back to them. Because they're believed to be already familiar with these teachings from past lives, their education is said to proceed quite rapidly, allowing them to quickly resume the function for which their spiritual career has prepared them: being of maximum benefit to others.

Many incarnate lamas lived in Tibet. According to some accounts, 200 (out of approximately 1,000) managed to escape when the Chinese took Tibet in the 1950s. The most important of these *tulkus* to escape was the Dalai Lama, who is revered as the human embodiment of the bodhisattva of compassion, Avalokiteshvara in Sanskrit and Chenrezig in Tibetan. Considered the protector of the Land of Snows (Tibet), *Chenrezig* (see Figure 15-5) is the patron deity of the Tibetan people.

Reviewing the early life of the present Dalai Lama

By the time of the Great Fifth, the Dalai Lama had become the supreme secular and spiritual leader of the Tibetan people. Like the Fifth Dalai Lama, the Thirteenth was also called the *Great,* and when he died in 1933, numerous signs indicated that he would be reborn somewhere northeast of Lhasa, the capital of Tibet. The *state oracle* — a clairvoyant monk whom the government always consulted on important matters — confirmed that the search for the new Dalai Lama should concentrate on the far-northeastern province of Amdo, not far from the border with China.

Figure 15-5: Avalokiteshvara or Chenrezig, the bodhisattva of compassion.

To narrow the search, the *regent,* a lama acting as temporary ruler, decided to visit a holy site known as Oracle Lake to see if he could receive a vision of the new Dalai Lama's birthplace. At the lake, he received several visions consisting of a series of letters, an image of a three-storied monastery with a turquoise and gold roof, and a nearby house with unusual gutters surrounded by miniature juniper trees.

The committee in charge of deciphering these clues determined that the monastery must be Kumbum, a sacred site in Amdo and the birthplace of the great master Tsongkhapa, the main spiritual teacher of the First Dalai Lama. A group of high lamas, led by Keusang Rinpoche, a close friend of the Great Thirteenth, headed for Kumbum monastery to look for children in the area who showed promise of being the next Dalai Lama. When they reached the village of Taktser, which contained a house that matched the Oracle Lake image, they felt their search was coming to an end. In this house, they discovered 2½-year-old Lhamo Thondup — born on July 6, 1935. Keusang Rinpoche soon became convinced that this was the child.

When he returned to Taktser several weeks later, Keusang Rinpoche brought two canes with him. One of the canes had belonged to the Great Thirteenth. Young Lhamo grabbed that cane and declared, "This is mine! What are you doing with it?" Lhamo also took the rosary that Rinpoche was wearing around his neck — the rosary that the Thirteenth Dalai Lama had given him — and claimed it as his own. Later that evening, Keusang Rinpoche placed a number of ritual objects on a table in front of Lhamo, and the boy immediately picked up the items that had belonged to his predecessor and ignored the rest. By this time, Keusang Rinpoche knew that they had found the reincarnation of the Dalai Lama. But negotiations with the local warlord took more than a year, and the three-month journey to Lhasa didn't begin until July 1939, when Lhamo was 4 years old. The following spring, Lhamo Thondup was formally enthroned as the Fourteenth Dalai Lama and dressed in the robes of a monk. In the beginning, his tutors simply concentrated on teaching him to read. But eventually, the young boy began following the rigorous schedule of a monk. He woke up early in the morning, recited prayers, meditated, and memorized and recited texts — all before lunch! After lunch, his lessons continued with even more study of the philosophical texts that make up the most important part of a monk's education. By the time he was 12, the Dalai Lama took part in serious debate, learning how to energetically and skillfully defend and attack the different philosophical positions presented in these texts.

Dealing with the Chinese

One aspect of the Dalai Lama's training differed significantly from that of ordinary monks. In addition to his studies, he spent part of his day attending meetings with government ministers. Although he was just a child, his presence at these decision-making meetings made him aware of the enormous responsibility that he'd be expected to assume someday. And that day came sooner than anyone imagined.

In late 1949, China began amassing troops along the eastern border of Tibet. They were preparing for an invasion that would eventually engulf the whole country and bring to an end a culture and a way of life that had endured for centuries. The Chinese had wanted to incorporate Tibetan territory into China for a long time, and the Communist revolution in China (shortly after the end of World War II) gave them an opportunity to enter Tibet unopposed by the other world powers.

For the next ten years, the Dalai Lama tried to negotiate with the Chinese authorities who had assumed control of Tibet with the stated purpose of "liberating Tibet from the forces of imperialism." The only imperialist forces, however, were the invading Chinese themselves. The Dalai Lama tried to save the Tibetans from the devastation facing them, but he could do little. In 1954, China's top leaders invited the Dalai Lama to meet with them in Beijing. The officials tried to get him to see the benefits of Communism. But when he complained to Chairman Mao that Chinese soldiers were attacking and destroying Tibetan religious institutions, the core of the Tibetan cultural identity, he received a callous reply. "Religion is poison," the Chinese leader told him. At this point, the Dalai Lama realized just how terrible the situation had become.

In 1956, the Dalai Lama accepted Indian Prime Minister Nehru's invitation to travel to India to celebrate this important occasion. In India, he informed Nehru of the dangers facing Tibet and received the prime minister's assurance that if war broke out with the Chinese, the Tibetans would be welcome to seek asylum in India.

Despite the deteriorating situation, his mounting responsibilities, and the many distractions he faced, the Dalai Lama continued with his monastic studies. In early March 1959, he completed his geshe degree (roughly equivalent to a doctoral degree in philosophy and divinity). Just a few days later, the steadily worsening situation in Tibet came to a head. On March 10 (commemorated every year since then as National Uprising Day), tens of thousands of Tibetans surrounded the Dalai Lama's summer residence, the Norbu Lingka, to protect him from the Chinese forces that were about to kidnap him.

The state oracle declared that the Dalai Lama's only option was to leave for India immediately and continue the campaign to save Tibet from there. So on March 17, disguised as a soldier, the Fourteenth Dalai Lama slipped out of the Norbu Lingka and began his journey into exile. Two weeks later, after passing over some of Tibet's roughest snow-covered terrain, he reached India to begin a new life. (For a dramatic and generally accurate version of this story, check out Martin Scorsese's film *Kundun*.)

Finding freedom in exile

Nearly a million Tibetans, accounting for one-sixth of the total population, attempted to flee with the Dalai Lama in 1959 and shortly thereafter. But fewer than 100,000 actually made it safely to India and neighboring countries. In Tibet, the death toll from the brutal Chinese takeover was staggering. Many people who managed to evade the Chinese forces didn't fare much better. Disease, malnutrition, the extreme climatic differences, and the hardship of the journey killed tens of thousands.

For the young Dalai Lama, life in India was very different than life in his homeland. He soon settled into a modest residence in the North Indian town of Dharamsala, a far cry from the forbidding Potala Palace in Lhasa. In Tibet, he had lived as a virtual prisoner — both the Chinese and ancient Tibetan religious customs and institutions restricted his activities. Now he was much freer to take charge of his life and create policies more in line with his personal principles and his interest in scientific and democratic methods.

Shortly after arriving in India, the Dalai Lama set up Tibet's government-in-exile in Dharamsala and began instituting democratic reforms in the exile community, all while continuing to monitor events inside Tibet itself.

With the help of the Indian government, the Dalai Lama has opened settlement communities and reestablished monasteries. Under his guidance, children's schools, medical facilities, handicraft centers, and other cultural organizations have been established in India (and in other countries as well). In these and countless other ways, the Dalai Lama, through his promotion, support, and encouragement, has managed to preserve the Tibetan cultural identity despite the devastating destruction and genocide.

Appreciating his interest in science

The Dalai Lama has expressed a strong interest in a sustained dialogue between the sciences and Buddhism. The Mind & Life conferences that have taken place between His Holiness and leading figures in Western science since 1987 have already led to the publication of numerous books.

The Dalai Lama has received numerous awards, honorary degrees, and country citizenship from around the world. In 2007, he accepted the position of Presidential Distinguished Professor of Emory University, which has led to a fruitful exchange between modern science and the Tibetan Buddhist tradition. Faculty members of Emory University are now developing a program for educating Tibetan monks and nuns in modern science.

The Dalai Lama has shown keen interest in scientific discoveries about the workings of the brain and how they may relate to the Buddhist understanding of the mind. He has proposed that scientific research be performed on advanced Tibetan meditators so that the West can begin to document, using its own methods, the transforming effect of spiritual practices. He has helped recruit Tibetan Buddhist monks to research the effects of meditation on the brain. Chapter 7 reports on neuroscientist Richard Davidson's research on meditation. Davidson is now also studying the process of dying by carrying out experiments with advanced practitioners of Tibetan Buddhism in Dharamsala, North India. This project also has the Dalai Lama's support.

Embracing the role of Buddhist ambassador to the world

Over the years, the Dalai Lama (who is as willing to learn as he is to respond to requests for teachings) has established warm, mutually respectful relationships with leaders and followers of many other faiths. This same spirit of mutual sharing has marked his frequent contact with political leaders, social activists, psychotherapists, artists, musicians, and countless other individuals and groups from all walks of life.

The Dalai Lama has become a major participant in attempts to find common ground among the world's religions. His commentaries on the Christian gospels, for example (collected under the title *The Good Heart: A Buddhist Perspective on the Teachings of Jesus,* published by Wisdom Publications), are considered a major contribution to interfaith dialogue.

Just 50 years ago, the world of the Dalai Lama was still quite narrow. Few people had access to him, and he had limited access to the outside world. Now his smiling face and infectious laugh are known to millions of people around the globe. He spends much of his time traveling, visiting Tibetan communities abroad and giving teachings attended by thousands of participants. In March 2011, the Dalai Lama announced his decision to give up his political role as the leader of the Tibetan people in the Tibetan exile government. But even after retiring from his political responsibilities, he will remain the spiritual leader of all Tibetans.

Numerous documentaries have been made about the Dalai Lama, as well as two major movies — *Seven Years in Tibet* and *Kundun* — to which he has given extensive support.

Since receiving the Nobel Peace Prize in 1989 for his nonviolent struggle on behalf of the Tibetan people, the Dalai Lama has become the world's most widely recognized Buddhist and a revered symbol for the Buddhist virtues of wisdom, compassion, tolerance, and respect. Even people who have no interest in religion recognize and respond to his goodness, simple humanity, and humor. He has truly become a Buddhist ambassador to the world.

Part V
The Part of Tens

The 5th Wave By Rich Tennant

"I'm always endeavoring to become one with all things, however, I'm going to make an exception with this fish casserole."

In this part . . .

This part is the ultimate in one-stop shopping. You can discover (and figure out how to dispel) ten common misconceptions about Buddhism and find ten ways to apply the insights of Buddhism to your everyday life. What more could you want? Grab a cart and start loading up on knowledge.

Chapter 16

Ten Common Misconceptions about Buddhism

In This Chapter

- Getting the story on Buddhism straight
- Checking out common misconceptions
- Replacing fiction with fact

If the subject of Buddhism is relatively new to you, you may believe that your mind is like a clean slate, with no preexisting ideas about Buddhism and its teachings. But as teachers of Buddhism, we're guessing that you probably have at least a few preconceptions about Buddhists, the Buddha, or Buddhist practices. We're not saying that someone sat you down and fed these ideas to you. You could've picked them up from a comment on the nightly news, a picture in the newspaper, or a remark you overheard while watching a documentary on Asia. Though their intentions are generally good, the mainstream media are filled with distorted ideas about Buddhism.

As someone who regularly teaches (and attends) classes in Buddhist thought and meditation practice, Jon has noticed that certain misconceptions pop up repeatedly in students' comments and questions. He can even remember the misconceptions that he had while studying Buddhism for the first time. For example, after reading one or two books that emphasized the importance of eliminating desire if you want to reach Buddhahood, Jon feared that a Buddha might resemble some of the statues he'd seen in Asian art galleries — serene and balanced, to be sure, but also lifeless and cold. Jon didn't find that prospect appealing at all! But he dropped this misconception as soon as he met the Tibetan lama who eventually became his main teacher. His hearty laughter and warm, affectionate nature blew the misconception right out of the water.

In this same spirit of shining light on false impressions, we present ten common misconceptions about Buddhism in this chapter that surface more or less regularly among new (and sometimes even experienced) students of Buddhism. After explaining how these misconceptions can arise, we attempt to put them to rest. Who knows? Maybe you'll find one or two of them familiar.

Buddhism Is Only for Asians

Buddhism originated in India and then spread first to neighboring Sri Lanka and then to other Asian countries (see Chapters 4 and 5 for more on the historical development of Buddhism). Every traditional form of Buddhism (like Tibetan, Vietnamese, and Japanese Buddhism) originated in Asia. If you're like most people, the mental pictures you have of Buddhist monks and nuns are decidedly Asian. Taking that line of reasoning one step farther, some folks presume that something about Buddhism makes it appropriate for the "Eastern mentality" (whatever that means) but unsuitable for Westerners.

But Buddhism belongs to no single continent, nation, or ethnic group. As long as people suffer under the burden of negative emotions, destructive habits, and distorted thinking, the Buddhist teachings about mindfulness, wisdom, and compassion can offer effective methods for achieving lasting happiness and peace of mind.

In fact, millions of men and women in Europe and the Americas have adopted Buddhism as their spiritual path and started to adapt its rituals and forms to their needs. And a great many of the Buddhist teachers in the West these days were born and raised in the West, supplanting the Eastern teachers who carried the religion to foreign shores in previous generations.

Of course, in the United States, many Asian Americans still practice Buddhism — but now many Americans of other races and ethnic groups do, too. Buddhism is quickly becoming as American as hard work and apple pie.

To Buddhists, the Buddha Is God

Because the major Western religions are God centered, many people understandably think that Buddhists consider the Buddha to be the creator of the world and the supreme being who judges our actions, hands out rewards and punishments, plays a major role in determining our destiny, and generally has an active hand in the way our lives unfold.

But none of these concepts applies to Buddhism. As we explain in more detail in Chapter 3, the historical Buddha was a human being like everyone else. With spiritual training, he was able to penetrate the layers of attachment, anger, ignorance, and fear in his own mind and heart, and realized the origin of suffering and found the path leading to the cessation of suffering. He felt moved to lead others out of their self-created suffering and spent many years sharing his insights and methods.

There is definitely a devotional aspect in Buddhist practices. Buddha images are worshipped with offerings, and some traditions of Buddhism do revere certain Buddhas and bodhisattvas. Although Buddhists don't worship these Buddhas and bodhisattvas in exactly the same way that Jews and Christians worship God, they definitely treat these figures as objects of great devotion. Moreover, they believe that these transcendent beings can occasionally intervene in human affairs, especially by helping to empower spiritual transformation.

Buddhists Are Idol Worshippers

If you enter a Buddhist temple, you're likely to see behavior that appears to be *idolatry* (the worship of idols). Devotees stand reverentially with their palms pressed together in front of an altar decorated with flowers, incense, and other offerings and featuring a statue of the Buddha (sometimes accompanied by other strange figures). Then they suddenly bow down, in some cases stretching their body full length on the floor in the direction of the altar.

Although this scene may look like idol worship, which many belief systems warn against, when this practice — called *offering prostrations* — is explained in detail (see Chapter 8), quite a different picture emerges.

When you bow or perform prostrations conscientiously (not as an empty ritual), you humble your false pride and honor the Buddha.

Because Buddhists Think Life Is Suffering, They Look Forward to Dying

This particular misconception is one of the most popular — and most persistent — false impressions about Buddhism. And not without reason. After all, the first of the four noble truths at the heart of the Buddha's teachings is known as the truth of suffering (check out Chapter 3 for all four). Many people also have images etched into their minds of the Vietnamese monks who sat in full meditation posture, set themselves on fire in protest against war and oppression, and calmly burned to death. And a related misconception is never far behind: Buddhists consider it wrong or even sinful to have fun.

The misunderstanding can be largely dispelled if we understand that the Buddha, like a doctor, not only diagnoses suffering, but also teaches the *cessation* of suffering and the *path* that leads to this cessation. As we explain in Part IV, understanding the truth of suffering merely informs and motivates you to follow the path that leads to the *end of suffering* — the inexpressible joy and peace that dawns when you attain awakening. (For more on awakening, or enlightenment, see Chapter 10.)

In short, Buddhists aren't morbidly fixated on suffering. On the contrary, Buddhists are primarily concerned with achieving an enduring happiness and freedom that doesn't depend on the unpredictable circumstances of life. If you need proof, just look at the smiling face of the Dalai Lama, the most visible Buddhist in the West these days.

As for suicide, it's not recommended unless *excellent and compelling* reasons exist — which usually consist of saving the life of someone else. Only those Vietnamese monks can know whether they had such excellent and compelling reasons. Buddhists themselves have disagreed on this issue, but one thing is certain: The monks burned themselves not because they loved death more than life, but because they were willing to sacrifice their own lives in the hope that such a dramatic act could make a difference.

Buddhists Think That Everything Is an Illusion

The Buddhist teachings aim to remove all false, misleading views about reality because these views constitute an important source of suffering.

To express this point, certain Mahayana Buddhist texts compare the world of appearances (in which most people are completely caught up) to an insubstantial dream, mirage, or illusion. Unfortunately, some people mistakenly interpret this metaphor to mean that nothing actually exists, that things are just a figment of your imagination, and that what you do really doesn't matter because nothing makes sense anyway.

But Buddhism considers this excessively negative interpretation to be one of the biggest obstacles to spiritual development. People who fall under its spell are in danger of behaving recklessly and ignoring the workings of cause and effect ("After all, everything's just an illusion"), which just creates more suffering for themselves and others. After this misconception has taken root, it's one of the most difficult to eradicate.

You can go a long way toward avoiding this misunderstanding by inserting the little word *like* in the right spot. Things aren't illusions; things are *like* illusions: They appear to exist in one way but, in fact, exist in another way. For example, in an optical illusion, one line can look longer than another line but actually be shorter. In the same way, reality may appear to be a collection of solid, separate, material objects. In fact, however, it is a constantly changing flow, in which everything is interrelated and nothing is as separate or independent as it appears to be.

At the relative, everyday level, things do exist. Otherwise, how could we have written this chapter, and how could you be reading it? The point is that until you remove the veils of misconception obscuring your wisdom, you can't perceive reality directly, just the way it is. (To explore this concept further, check out Chapters 2, 13, and 14.)

Buddhists Don't Believe in Anything

This misconception is closely related to the one we discuss in the "Buddhists Think That Everything Is an Illusion" section. In the wisdom teachings of Buddhism, you frequently come across the term *emptiness* (Sanskrit: *shunyata*). The world of appearances that we mention in the illusion section is sometimes called *conventional* (or *relative*) truth. Buddhism gives the status of *ultimate* truth only to emptiness itself. Buddhists believe in emptiness — or, more accurately, look to experience emptiness directly for themselves — but that doesn't mean that they believe in nothing. Falling into such an extreme rejection of everything is a major pitfall on the spiritual path.

Only Buddhists Can Practice Buddhism

Some people who encounter Buddhism through a book or a teacher find that it helps them make sense of things in this world that they didn't understand before. But they hold themselves back from practicing the teachings because they think that they have to become Buddhists first — and they don't really want to go that far. Maybe they already belong to another religious tradition and don't feel comfortable with the idea of giving it up. Or maybe they're not yet ready to identify with any particular movement or "ism."

If you're one of these people, listen to Buddhist teachings and follow them if you want, but remain true to your own tradition. After all, every religion has its own outstanding qualities and values, and you may find it easier to progress spiritually in a familiar setting and community.

If you find that certain Buddhist teachings appeal to you, simply put them into practice as much as you can. The fact is, many Christians and Jews these days, including well-known ministers, rabbis, and priests, practice Buddhist forms of meditation because they find that the techniques and the teachings support and deepen their understanding and appreciation of their own tradition. Several practicing Catholics have even been recognized as Zen masters! If done correctly, Buddhist meditation can make you an even better follower of your own religion — or a better atheist, if that's what you happen to be. (For more on the stages of involvement in Buddhism, make a commitment to turn to Chapter 6.)

Buddhists Are Interested Only in Contemplating Their Navels

Undoubtedly, Buddhism places a great emphasis on silent introspection. Turn your attention inward and tame your wild and unruly mind, the teachings suggest. Many people, even experienced Buddhists, interpret this to mean that they have to turn their backs on the outside world and concentrate exclusively on getting their own act together. But this isn't the entire picture.

In certain traditions of Mahayana Buddhism, the compassionate bodhisattva is regarded as the ultimate role model. The problem is, you can't hope to help others in the most effective way possible if you're still trapped by your own negative emotions and habitual patterns such as ignorance, greed, jealousy, anger, and fear. So whether you want to help others or just help yourself, you need to start with the same step: Turn inward through meditation and other practices and work with your own mind and heart. Eventually, if your altruistic motivation is strong, you'll naturally share the wisdom and compassion you develop with the people around you.

In recent decades, some Buddhists have created social action movements of their own. These are known by the general term *(Socially) Engaged Buddhism.* If you want examples of prominent Buddhist teachers committed to social action, look no further than Thich Nhat Hanh, who was nominated for the Nobel Peace Prize in 1968 for his peace activism during the Vietnam War, and the Dalai Lama, who was awarded that prize in 1989 for his tireless work on behalf of the Tibetan people. (For more on these two important teachers, see Chapter 15; to discover more about Engaged Buddhism, check out Chapter 1 and the reading list in Appendix B.)

Buddhists Never Get Angry

The practice of meditation can be understood from several different points of view. According to some teachers in the Zen tradition, for example, the idea that you're meditating to achieve anything at all limits your practice and takes you away from the present moment. According to the point of view that the Theravada and Vajrayana traditions share, however, you engage in meditation for a variety of reasons, one of the most important of which is to overcome such inner obstacles as hatred and anger. Buddhists, therefore, have the reputation of being calm, even tempered, and unflappable when faced with adversity. Many people, even some Buddhists, think of monks and nuns as being especially incapable of anger.

But keep in mind that merely becoming a Buddhist, or putting on the robe of a monk or a nun, doesn't mean that you suddenly break all the destructive habits of a lifetime (or, as Buddhists would say, countless lifetimes). Spiritual development takes time, and expecting dramatic changes simply because you've adopted a new religion or decided to wear different clothing is unrealistic.

If you're sincere in your Buddhist practices, you may begin to notice some changes in a relatively short period of time — say, six months or a year. You may still get angry, but maybe you don't get angry as often or as violently. And when you do get angry, you don't stay angry as long as you once did. If you notice such positive signs of change, you can rejoice in them. Eventually, you may discover that situations that used to cause you to blow your stack only increase your understanding, love, and tolerance. That's when you know that you're really making progress.

Also remember that avoiding anger doesn't mean allowing others to walk all over you. People do things to one another that are harmful or just plain wrong; if you can do anything to stop or change this behavior, go right ahead. The trick is to be motivated by the positive power of love, compassion, and wisdom (if possible) when you confront the troublemaker. Try to leave the destructive power of hatred and resentment out of the picture.

Finally, we need to mention that pretending to be calm and peaceful while you're seething inside with anger is most definitely not a recommended Buddhist practice. Nor, of course, is acting out your anger toward others. The first step is to acknowledge that you're angry; the next step is to work with your anger, using one of several Buddhist practices that can help soften and ultimately defuse it. (See Chapter 7 for some ways to handle anger.) If necessary, you may need to express your anger in a clear, responsible way. But merely stuffing it down is like trying to stop a pot of water from boiling by pressing down tightly on its lid: Sooner or later, the pot will explode!

"It's Just Your Karma; There's Nothing You Can Do about It"

The term *karma* crops up often in casual conversation these days, and different people have different ideas of what it means. (If you're interested in exploring this subject in some depth, turn to Chapters 12 and 13.) For some people, karma seems to be unpredictable — kind of like luck. For others, the term means little more than *fate,* and their attitude toward life, therefore, tends to be rather fatalistic: "It's my karma to be short tempered," they may say. "That's just the way I am; what can I do?"

But Buddhism views karma (which literally means "action") as both more predictable and more dynamic than the uses of the word that we just described. You're continually engaging in actions now that will lead to karmic results in the future, and you're continually experiencing the karmic results now of actions you created in the past. In other words, your karma isn't a fixed, unchanging destiny that you must passively accept, as if it were a single, unchangeable poker hand that the universe dealt you. Instead, your karmic situation constantly shifts and changes, depending on how you act, speak, and think right now. By changing your behavior and transforming your mind and heart through Buddhist practice, you can definitely transform the quality of your life.

Buddhists Don't Know How to Count

For all we know, this statement may be true. After all, this item is the 11th in a list of 10.

Chapter 17

Ten Ways Buddhism Can Help You Deal with Life's Problems

In This Chapter

- Using Buddhist teachings to handle life's difficulties
- Laying down some general principles
- Applying specific advice to your problems

The Buddha's purpose for teaching the Dharma was entirely practical: He wanted people to be free from suffering. Simple as that. He never wanted his followers to just study, debate, and commit the teachings to memory. And he certainly didn't want people learning it just so they could claim to be expert authorities on Buddhism (unless, of course, occupying that kind of position enabled them to benefit others). The entire point of the teachings is to help people free themselves from suffering, experience peace, and realize their true nature.

Because the scope of Buddhism is so broad and profound, you can easily lose sight of the fact that the Dharma is also a practical, everyday guide. Many Buddhist traditions emphasize the importance of regular meditation practice. When you meditate each day, spending some time simply being present for your experience just the way it is, you gradually reduce your inner conflicts and make friends with yourself. In fact, meditation creates a welcoming inner space in which problems often resolve themselves. (For more on meditation, see Chapter 7.)

In this chapter, we share a few hints and suggestions, both general and specific, for using some insights from (mostly Mahayana) Buddhist teachings to help you deal with the challenges of day-to-day life. You may find that some of the pointers seem more difficult than others to put to use, and some provide nothing more than a temporary fix. But if you gradually incorporate them into your repertoire of responses, you may find that your problems gradually diminish — and your happiness and peace of mind noticeably increase.

Affirming the Basic Principles

According to later Mahayana Buddhist teachings, reality has three basic characteristics:

- It's unsatisfactory, in the sense that ordinary existence fails to give you exactly what you want out of life.
- It's impermanent, in the sense that things change.
- It lacks a concrete, abiding substance, or self-nature.

When you ignore these characteristics, you risk acting according to three corresponding misconceptions, which inevitably prevent you from living in harmony with reality. In brief, these misconceptions are as follows:

- Believing that things that are fundamentally unsatisfactory can bring lasting happiness
- Believing that things that change are permanent
- Believing that things that lack a self-nature are concrete and independent

Applying the Basic Principles

Every difficulty that you face in life is related, either directly or indirectly, to the three mistaken notions we mention in the preceding section. When you find yourself in a situation that makes you upset, frustrated, or downright miserable, try to identify which of these three misconceptions is most responsible. According to Buddhist teachings, merely identifying misconceptions and adopting a different view doesn't eradicate suffering. However, this approach can temporarily take the edge off your suffering so that you're more in tune with the way the world actually works. The following ten situations can give you a pretty good idea of how to apply some of the teachings to your problems.

Turning the page on your great expectations

You probably get upset when things go wrong in your life — no big surprise there. Being criticized, losing your job, and breaking up with your sweetheart are just a few examples of painful occurrences that can have you singing the blues (or a sad country-and-western equivalent).

But even when things go the way you want, you may be left with the nagging thought, "Is this all there is?" Although receiving praise, getting a promotion, and meeting the man or woman of your dreams sure feel good, a letdown often follows your initial euphoria. After all, you expected your good fortune to bring you some peace and satisfaction, and you're disappointed when you discover that something deep inside you remains unfulfilled.

Feeling like something is missing, even in the face of good news, points to the fundamentally unsatisfactory nature of cyclic existence, or samsara (see Chapter 13 for more about samsara and how to break out of it). As long as you permit craving and aversion to rule your mind, you'll continue to live, die, and be reborn in a state of perpetual dissatisfaction, wandering from one disappointing situation to another. That's a fact, Jack — at least, according to Buddhism.

But the situation isn't as bleak as it may appear: The Buddhist path offers an alternative to this round of unsatisfactory existence. This path doesn't require you to leave your present life and go somewhere else; it requires you to develop the self-awareness necessary to examine and change your point of view. Your disappointments provide one of the strongest motivations for making a change.

When situations don't turn out the way you hoped, don't be surprised. Instead, take a close look at your expectations; you may be suffering because you expect too much. Life hasn't signed a contract with you promising to give you everything you want. It just unfolds in its own mysterious and uncontrollable way. The more you stop resisting the way things are, the happier and more peaceful you'll be.

Accepting change gracefully

Why do people lust after other people and material objects? The answer, in part, is that those people and things appear to be so darned attractive, at least from an ordinary point of view. At first, this attractive quality seems to be a permanent, unchanging attribute of the desired objects. But a little reflection reveals that everything you see, hear, smell, taste, and touch is constantly undergoing change. You can save yourself a lot of trouble simply by accepting this reality — the reality of impermanence.

Don't just consider the impermanence of the things you desire; consider your own impermanence as well. Buddhism places great value on the awareness of death (see Chapter 11 for details). A big death waits for you at the end of your life, but you also experience a lot of mini-deaths along the way. In other words, you're constantly changing, and you're never the exact same person you were before.

As you grow older, your likes and dislikes change (think of the foods you love now but would never even think about eating as a kid), along with your looks, abilities, and interests. The objects of your passions change, too. Thinking that the object that appeals to you today will always seem that attractive to you is foolish (as we explain in the section "Watching your car rust," later in the chapter). If you can keep this little nugget of info in mind when something screams for your attention (and the contents of your wallet), you can save yourself a lot of hassles.

Remembering the reality of change not only protects you from the dangers of desire and attachment, but also serves as a safeguard against aversion and hatred. When you realize that you and the person bothering you will both be pushing up daisies before too long, what's the sense in holding a grudge?

Breaking up the concrete

Buddhism teaches that ignorance is the root cause of all suffering and dissatisfaction. Ultimately, the antidote for this ignorance is wisdom. But the question is, how can you apply what you know of this wisdom to the everyday problems you encounter? Consider this situation: A man comes up and insults you by calling you hurtful names, which makes you angry. What can you do to prevent yourself from giving in to this destructive emotional response?

In provocative situations especially, everything seems very concrete. The words directed at you appear to be a real, solid insult; the person insulting you appears to be a real, solid attacker; and an uncomfortably real and solid sense of yourself as the attackee arises in your heart in response. But by applying (Mahayana) Buddhist teachings, you can see that nothing has a concrete existence all to itself, which can save you quite a bit of emotional wear and tear.

TIP

If you immediately give in to anger after being insulted, it's too late to apply the wisdom antidote. Delusion and wisdom don't coexist very well. You'll have to be content with insightfully analyzing the situation later when you review the incident in the calm and quiet atmosphere of your meditation session. But the more you put the following advice into practice in your meditation, the better equipped you become to use your wisdom to defuse potentially dangerous situations as they happen and before they explode and engulf you.

First, take a look at the words being hurled at you. Where exactly in this combination of sounds can you find the insult itself? Can you locate it in any of the individual noises coming from the man's mouth? In a certain combination of these noises? Somewhere else? If you analyze the words in this way, taking them apart to look for the self-existent insult, you'll never find one. The insult develops its meaning in your response to the words, not in the words themselves.

In a similar way, where in the man's mental and physical makeup is the attacker himself? Can you find him in the lips and mouth that uttered the words? In some other part of his body? In its overall shape? Can you locate the concrete attacker in any of the millions of thoughts and emotions that course through the man's mind? The more closely you look, the more elusive the bad guy becomes.

Finally, where's the "you" who was insulted? Can you locate that apparently concrete entity in your ears, where the sound waves entered? In some part of your brain that processed these sound signals? In another location of your body or mind? Somewhere, anywhere, else?

REMEMBER

As you become more proficient at carefully investigating situations, you begin to realize that things aren't as substantial or as definite as they first appear. Instead of being concrete objects with hard edges, all things are actually loosely organized phenomena — feelings, thoughts, sensations, and so on — and rely to a large extent on how you perceive and interpret them. This more open view leaves no place for hatred.

Pretending to Be a Buddha

TIP

When all other ways of dealing with difficult situations fail, why not pretend that you're a Buddha? Sit quietly and let the situation, including the external circumstances and your own reactions to them, wash over you like a wave. Feel whatever you feel, but don't respond in any way.

In one scene in the movie *Little Buddha,* seductive visions of dancing girls and frightening images of attacking armies confront Keanu Reeves, but he doesn't budge. Imitate Keanu. This technique may lack spiritual sophistication, but it can get you through some difficult situations without making them worse. Besides, who knows? If you imitate a Buddha long enough, you may actually become one.

Watching your car rust

If you're like most people, you often feel disappointed by your material possessions. Cars break down, televisions go on the blink, and your good china gets chipped and cracked. All these experiences can be frustrating and lead to unexpected hassles — as well as unwanted expenses.

The fact is, you can't prevent your possessions from deteriorating. No matter how carefully you handle them or try to keep them shiny and new, they inevitably decay. But you can prevent yourself from experiencing unnecessary grief by realizing that all these material things are impermanent and, therefore, subject to change.

When you first purchase something — a new car, for example — it certainly doesn't appear impermanent. Sitting there all bright and shiny, it doesn't look like it'll ever get old and rusty or fall apart two weeks after its warranty expires. It appears to be solid and permanent, as if it'll always look the way it does right now. But this appearance is completely misleading. As the Buddha repeatedly pointed out, nothing you perceive through your five senses remains the same (as we discuss in Chapter 2 — unless that has changed, too); everything is constantly changing.

REMEMBER

The real problem isn't that things *appear* to be permanent, but that you *buy into* this false appearance and mistake it for reality. Then when things begin to fall apart, you experience unnecessary grief and anxiety. The solution is simple: Repeatedly remind yourself of the truth of impermanence, especially when you catch yourself admiring a possession as if it'll last forever.

TIP

One of Jon's friends had a grammatical trick he used to help him remain mindful of impermanence. If he owned something he thought was particularly attractive, like a watch, instead of thinking, "This is a fine-looking watch," he would purposely think, "That *was* a fine-looking watch." Referring to the object in the past tense, as if it were already broken, helped him let go of the notion that it was immune to change.

Seeing that what's yours isn't really yours

Besides becoming damaged and broken, material possessions have a habit of getting lost, which can be quite annoying, especially if the lost item is expensive or hard to replace. A particularly unhelpful attitude exaggerates your sense of loss, reinforces your annoyance, and makes the loss harder to bear. If you can reverse or overcome this attitude, you can eliminate unnecessary pain.

The attitude we're referring to is the notion of possession, which (like all unhelpful notions) is nothing more than a projection of your mind. The idea works this way: When you first see an item in a shop, you may be attracted to it, but you don't think that it belongs to you. However, as soon as you plunk down some cold, hard cash (or swipe some cold, hard plastic) and take the object home with you, your view of it begins to change. You start to think of it as yours. It begins to have something to do with you personally, as if it somehow reflects on your importance or worth as a human being. "Because I have this fancy new car or beautiful new dress or cool new pair of shoes," you think to yourself, "I'm finally the person I've always wanted to be."

Eventually, even though you know better, you begin to feel as though this item *always* belonged to you — almost as if it were part of you. Losing it is then like losing part of yourself. (The same basic pattern holds true for partners or spouses as well. Many people treat them like possessions.)

The antidote to this delusion is to recognize that the things and people you supposedly own don't really belong to you. You're just their temporary caretaker. At one point in the past, you had no connection with these items, and at a time in the future, that'll be true again. The fleeting present occupies the ground between these two points in time, and your association with these items is similarly fleeting. If you can train yourself to look at things in this way, free of all exaggerated notions of possessiveness, you can live both with them and without them, with far less anxiety.

Feeling sorry for a thief

Simply losing something is bad enough, but having it stolen from you feels far worse. If you've ever been a victim of theft, you know that this experience can be painful. In addition to losing an item of value, you feel the pain of having your personal space invaded, the pain of feeling violated.

When someone takes something from you, being angry with the thief is common. You may also wish that he gets caught or has to pay for the crime, or wish for something bad to happen to him. Your mind fills with resentment and thoughts of revenge or retribution. But these thoughts are worse than useless. They don't help you get your stuff back or help the police catch the thief; they only make you more agitated and upset.

But you can do something to make the situation better and calm yourself: You can give the stolen item to the thief. You can't physically give the object to the thief — after all, he has already taken it — but you can give it to him in your mind. Just relinquish all sense of ownership and imagine that you're presenting the object to whoever took it.

Now, this technique may seem a bit illogical — after all, you're upset precisely because you don't want to give up the item. But by offering to give it up, you're offering to give up your attachment as well. This action may seem like an empty gesture, but if you do it wholeheartedly, with the understanding that it's in the best interest of all concerned, you can replace resentment with generosity, which is definitely helpful in significant ways.

From a karmic point of view, you may have been the victim of theft because you committed a similar theft in the past (check out Chapter 12 for the lowdown on karma). Now you may be reaping the results of your past negative karma and exhausting this past karma in the process. While you're paying off your karmic debt, so to speak, the thief is accumulating his own debt and will eventually have to face the consequences.

With this understanding, you may feel some compassion for the thief, knowing that suffering awaits him in the future. You may even want to help alleviate this suffering (then again, of course, you may not). Because theft is the act of taking something that's not given, you can try to reduce the severity of the thief's future karma by voluntarily giving up the item. After all, you can't steal something that's been given to you. Even if you can't directly affect the thief's karma, generating compassion toward him feels a lot better than seething with hatred and resentment, right?

Tendering your resignation to pain

The fact that you have a physical body means that you get to experience pain and discomfort. When this pain inevitably strikes, your mental attitude largely determines how intense the pain will be.

Pain often causes people to get trapped in a "poor me" mentality. You say that life is unfair and complain about your fate. You can't think of anything except your suffering. At times like this, you're not just caught up in your pain; you're imprisoned in the negative story that you create about your condition. This claustrophobic feeling just adds to your discomfort.

REMEMBER

The solution is to turn outward and think of something or someone other than yourself. This exercise may not be easy, especially when you're experiencing a throbbing headache or some other form of intense physical pain, but it's definitely possible. The key is to recognize that many other people in the world are experiencing the same type of suffering as you are at that very minute. If you're experiencing a bad headache, for example, you can be sure that millions of others are suffering from the same affliction — and many of them are probably worse off than you.

TIP

Simply realizing that you're not alone in your suffering helps to lighten the burden of your pain and relieve your self-pity. But you can take it to another level. You can generate this compassionate thought: "May my experience of this headache be enough to exhaust the suffering of everyone else." You make the heartfelt decision to use your experience to alleviate the pain of others.

We realize that the headache of Joe from down the street may be the last thing on your mind when you're writhing in agony. And the point isn't to punish yourself. Instead, you're choosing to look at your experience from a different point of view. You still have the same headache, but you're now giving it meaning and purpose by using it to strengthen the bonds of sympathy that connect you with all other beings. Your pain is no longer a personal affliction, but an opportunity to connect with others. The main benefit of this practice is that it increases your compassion. But it sometimes brings an unexpected bonus: Your headache goes away.

Turning off the projector

Two types of annoying people exist — people you can avoid and people you can't. How can you deal with the latter?

Suppose that you live near an elderly relative whom you're expected to visit every month. For the sake of this discussion, say this person is your mother. You dread these visits because they generally end with one or both of you becoming upset. No matter how good your intentions are at the beginning, you always seem to get on each other's nerves. What can you do about this situation, short of refusing to visit her?

REMEMBER

First, keep in mind that, from a Buddhist point of view, trying to change yourself is much more effective than trying to change someone else. Second, remember that the underlying cause of most, if not all, problems can be found in the distorted views you project onto situations. Even the habit of seeing other people as annoying, for example, tends to blame them for your unhappiness, when you're the one annoying yourself.

Back to your mother. The way you behave toward her is obviously important, but the view you have of her (and ultimately of yourself) determines your behavior. So ask yourself, "Am I projecting anything onto my mother that makes it difficult for us to get along with each other?"

You may discover that you've stopped regarding her as a person in her own right. Perhaps you've fallen into the habit of thinking of her only in terms of her relationship with you. If so, you're doing her an injustice:

- As your mother, she has played a larger role in your life than you selectively remember. You may think of her as someone who's always finding fault with you, complaining about your life, putting unreasonable demands on you, and so on. But as your mother, she has related to you in many other ways as well. For example, she may have been your nurturer, your protector, and your biggest fan, among many other roles.
- Plus, she's not just your mother. She has had many different relationships with many different people. She has been someone's daughter, friend, lover, rival, wife, neighbor, and so on. In fact, she can't be defined just by her relationships. As a human being, she has had her own hopes and fears, expectations and disappointments, triumphs and challenges, and a history of experiences that you probably know little about. In short, she's a complex, multifaceted person — just like you. Thinking of her only as your mother — and a rather crabby one, at that — prevents you from finding out how interesting a person she may be.

So how do you go about improving a relationship? How do you get out of the rut into which you've fallen? You can start by sitting alone in meditation, bringing the other person to mind, and viewing him simply as a person, without your accustomed projections. All people just want to be happy and avoid suffering. Spend some time regarding someone who annoys you in this way, and allow your heart to open.

If you practice in this way for a while, you can eventually see annoying people — even your mother — in a new light. Then the next time you visit dear ol' mom, instead of relating to "your mother," try to relate to this intriguing new person you've discovered. If appropriate, ask her about some period or aspect of her life that you don't know much about. Keep the focus on her, not on her relationship to you. See where this exercise takes you.

We can't guarantee that approaching an individual as an individual and not based on his relationship with you will immediately patch up a relationship. In fact, the folks may be so taken aback by your new and unaccustomed interest in them that they become suspicious or even defensive. But if your interest is genuine — if it comes from loving concern — this new approach will eventually bear fruit. Just be patient and keep in mind that you can't hope to undo years of bad habits overnight.

Dealing with uninvited houseguests

Although some problems may arise because you take things too personally, others can occur because you don't treat things personally enough.

We've met quite a few people who can't tolerate flies, spiders, and other creepy-crawlies. If one of these insects is brave enough to enter their house, they don't hesitate to reach for the bug spray or the newspaper to annihilate it. (Before Jon lived in India, he was the same way himself, so he understands this mentality.) When these folks spot an ant, a bee, or a mosquito, all they see is a threat to their health and well-being, so they feel justified in eliminating it as swiftly as possible.

But according to the teachings of the Buddha, killing insects and other creatures has karmic consequences. Your short-term solution to one problem — swatting an unsanitary fly, for example — may set you up to experience greater problems in the future. (See Chapter 12 for more on the karmic effect of negative actions.) In addition, you get used to the act of killing, which definitely isn't a worthwhile habit to cultivate.

Clearly, if you take the teachings on karma seriously, you'll try not to harm other living beings. If you have to get rid of unwelcome intruders in your house, look for ways to do so without harming them, at least intentionally. Instead of using a chemical that kills bugs, use something that only repels them. Instead of lining your floors with poisonous ant powder, find ways to seal off the cracks that serve as ant-sized entrances. And instead of swatting mosquitoes, figure out how to catch them and take them outside.

You can find a bunch of ways to remove these critters without killing them. But most of these techniques take a lot more time and energy than simply pressing a button and letting some patented insecticide do the job for you. To convince yourself that these more humane approaches are worth the effort, change your attitude toward insects (and all creatures), recognizing that they have the same desire and right to live as you do. In other words, relate to them in a more personal manner.

If you take the time to look past the annoying buzz and painful sting of a mosquito, for instance, you can find a being that's simply struggling to survive. The little creature isn't purposely bothering you; it just views you as a source of nourishment.

When Jon lived in India, he and his housemate came up with a method that helped them see things from a critter's point of view: They gave them all names. Molly Mosquito had to be escorted out of the room at night, Betty Bee sometimes got confused and came in through a crack in the door, and Waldo Wolf-spider lived on the wall of the latrine. Although they never became pals with these little beings, they certainly never thought of harming them. We're not suggesting that you go around assigning names to all the insects in your house (after all, your friends and family may start wondering when you refer to an ant as Arnold), but you may try looking at the world from their point of view occasionally; you'll no doubt find it easier to share your living space with them.

Part VI
Appendixes

The 5th Wave By Rich Tennant

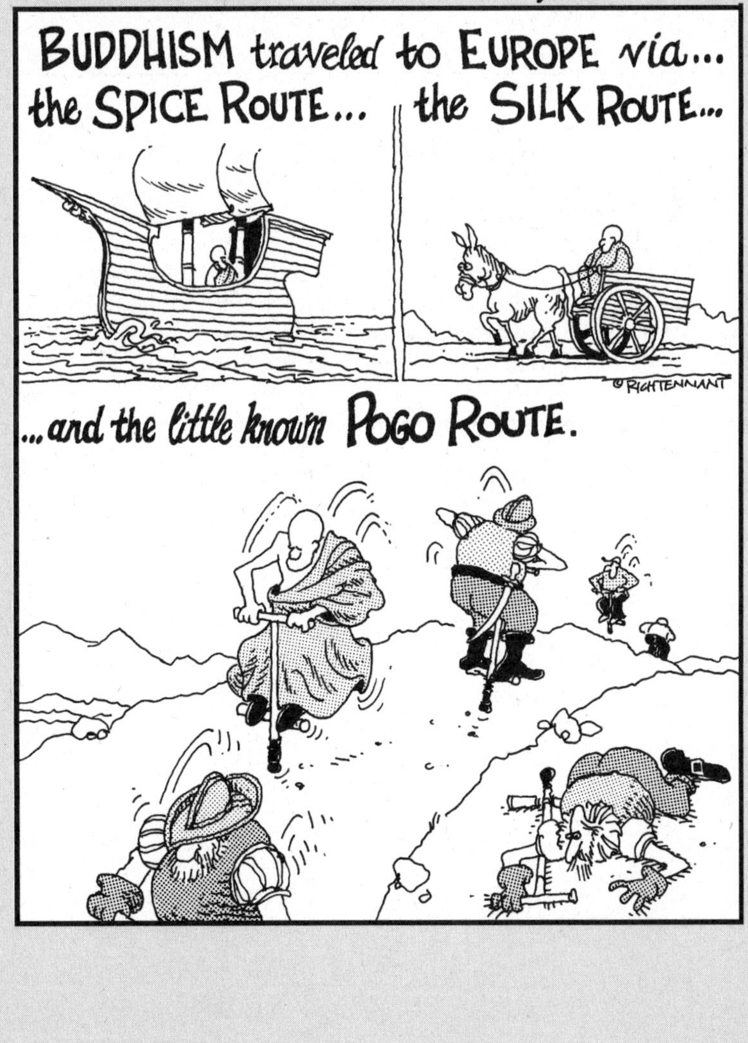

In this part . . .

This part is like a grab bag of helpful odds and ends. Can't remember what that Buddhist term means? Reach into the handy glossary and pull out a definition. Want to know more about some aspect of Buddhism that intrigues you? Glance through the list of books and other useful resources. Go ahead — pick something out.

Appendix A

Explaining Buddhist Terms

Any book on Buddhism, even an introductory work like this one, will probably contain a number of words that are unfamiliar to you. You're cruising through the text when, out of the blue, you come across words like *duhkha, avidya,* and *dhyana.* Why, you may wonder, has the author suddenly decided to switch to another language? Isn't English good enough?

The truth is, certain Buddhist terms don't have precise English equivalents — at least, not yet. As Buddhism has evolved over the centuries in Asia, a vocabulary has evolved along with it to express complex concepts and subtle experiences. But Buddhism is new to the West and, as a result, hasn't developed a terminology that all Western Buddhists can recognize and accept. For now, sticking with an Asian language for certain terms is the most accurate way to go.

But sometimes you see the same unfamiliar terms spelled differently. For example, the three terms we threw out earlier, *duhkha, avidya,* and *dhyana,* are Sanskrit, an ancient Indian language. But you may also see these terms written as *dukkha, avijja,* and *jhana.* In that case, the author is using Pali, another ancient Indian language closely related to Sanskrit. If this language lottery isn't maddening enough, sometimes these same words are adorned with strange markings above or below some of their letters. These diacritical marks (a term for slashes, dots, and squiggles) help you pronounce the words more accurately, but unless you're already a student of languages that almost no one speaks anymore, these diacritical marks can be confusing. (That's why we do without these marks in *Buddhism For Dummies.*)

As different Buddhist traditions arose in India (see Chapter 4), they transmitted their versions of the Buddha's teachings in different Indian languages. Sanskrit and Pali are the two most important of these languages, as far as Buddhism is concerned. For that reason, many Buddhist technical terms, especially the ones that are difficult to translate precisely, still appear in these ancient languages. (Similarly, certain important terms in Christian theology still appear in Greek.)

In this glossary, we provide useful — but certainly not exhaustive — definitions for the Buddhist terms you're likely to come across often in this book. To simplify matters as much as possible, most of the entries are in Sanskrit (which we signify with an S), without any diacritical marks. We list certain terms in Pali (which we mark with a P) as well, with a smattering of other Asian languages thrown in for good measure. (We use a C for Chinese, a J for

Japanese, and a T for Tibetan.) We use the Pinyin system of transliteration for words from the Chinese. Where appropriate, we also include some of the English terms we use repeatedly in this book.

One more note: When you see words in quotation marks following the glossary entry, these words are a close approximation of the literal meaning of the entry. After this info, we go on to explain the entry more fully.

abhidharma: (S) "Higher teachings." Section of the Buddhist canon dealing with psychology, philosophy, cosmology, metaphysics, and other matters (P: *abhidhamma*). See also ***tripitaka.***

Amitabha: (S) The Buddha of "infinite light," considered by some traditions to have taken a vow to lead all beings to the ***Pure Land*** over which he presides (J: *Amida*).

arhat: (S) "Worthy (of worship)." One who has attained complete liberation according to Theravada Buddhist teachings.

Avalokiteshvara: (S) A ***bodhisattva*** revered in certain Mahayana traditions as the embodiment of compassion. Known as Chenrezig in Tibet, ***Guanyin*** in China, and Kannon in Japan.

avidya: (S) "Ignorance." The root cause of all suffering (P: *avijja*).

bodhi: (S, P) "Awakening." The enlightenment of a ***Buddha.***

bodhichitta: (S) "Awakening mind." The ***bodhisattva's*** aspiration for awakening.

bodhisattva: (S) "Enlightenment(-bound) being." A previous incarnation of ***Shakyamuni*** before his ***enlightenment,*** as mentioned in the ***Jataka tales.*** Anyone who aspires to attain enlightenment (P: *bodhisatta*). One of numerous transcendent awakened beings embodying certain essential qualities of enlightenment, revered in some Mahayana traditions.

brahmavihara: (S) "Divine abode." Any one of four essential qualities (loving-kindness, compassion, sympathetic joy, and equanimity) cultivated in meditative practice.

Buddha: (S, P) "Awakened one." First of the ***Three Jewels.*** An enlightened being. See also ***Shakyamuni Buddha.***

Buddhahood: The attainment or realization of a ***Buddha*** of those following the ***Mahayana*** tradition.

Buddha nature: According to some East Asian Buddhist traditions, your true nature, indistinguishable from enlightenment; the potential to achieve enlightenment, said to exist within all beings.

cyclic existence: See ***samsara.***

deity yoga: An essential ***Vajrayana*** practice in which you identify your pure nature with a figure embodying the qualities of enlightenment.

Dharma: (S) "Law (of the universe)" taught by the historical Buddha. Second of the ***Three Jewels*** (P: *dhamma*).

dhyana: (S) "Meditation." The word means simply meditation but is also used to refer to specific states of meditative absorption (P: *jhana*; C: *Chan*, J: *Zen*).

duhkha: (S) Suffering; dissatisfaction; the unsatisfactory nature of mundane ***cyclic existence*** (P: *dukkha*).

eightfold path: Path taught by ***Shakyamuni Buddha*** leading to the cessation of suffering. Consists of right view, right intention, right speech, right action, right livelihood, right effort, right mindfulness, and right concentration.

emptiness: See ***shunyata.***

enlightenment: Awakening. See also ***bodhi.***

four noble truths: The main subject matter of the first discourse of ***Shakyamuni Buddha,*** in which he explained the reality of suffering, the cause of suffering, the cessation of suffering, and the path leading to the cessation of suffering.

Gautama: (S) Family name of the historical ***Buddha.***

Guanyin: (C) (Female) ***bodhisattva*** of mercy and compassion (J: *Kannon*). See also ***Avalokiteshvara.***

geshe: (T) "Spiritual benefactor." Degree awarded to those who've completed an intensive course of monastic study in the Tibetan tradition, roughly equivalent to a doctor of divinity.

guru: (S) "Teacher." A teacher or mentor.

Hinayana: (S) "Lesser vehicle." Term used in a disparaging way by some ***Mahayana*** Buddhists to refer to the spiritual path followed by those intent on achieving personal liberation only.

Jataka tales: (S) Stories about ***Shakyamuni Buddha's*** previous lives as a **bodhisattva,** in which he often took the form of an animal.

karma: (S) "Action." The workings of cause and effect, whereby virtuous actions eventually lead to happiness and nonvirtuous actions lead to suffering (P: *kamma*).

karuna: (S, P) "Compassion." Empathy.

kensho: (J) "Seeing true nature." A direct glimpse of your essential ***(Buddha) nature.***

klesha: (S) "Mental defilement." Mental afflictions and latent tendencies toward mental afflictions.

lama: (T) Spiritual guide and teacher; ***guru.***

liberation: See ***nirvana.***

Mahayana: (S) "Great vehicle" or "Great Path." Name of a major tradition in Buddhism.

Maitreya: (S) According to some traditions, a ***bodhisattva*** disciple of ***Shakyamuni Buddha,*** believed to be the future ***Buddha*** who will reintroduce ***Dharma*** to the world after the teachings of Shakyamuni disappear.

maitri: (S) See ***metta.***

mandala: (S) Mystical diagram.

Manjushri: (S) "Pleasing splendor." ***Bodhisattva*** revered in certain traditions as the embodiment of enlightened wisdom.

mantra: (S) Word(s) of power. Sacred syllable(s) or word(s), often in Sanskrit.

metta: (P) "Loving-kindness." Goodwill (S: *maitri*). See also ***brahmavihara.***

nembutsu: (J) "Mindfulness of the Buddha" (S: *buddhanusmriti*). For Honen (1133–1212), the nembutsu is the chanting of the homage or ***mantra:*** *Namu amida butsu* ("Homage to Amida Buddha").

Newar: Ethnic group in Nepal.

Newari: Language spoken by the ***Newars.***

nirvana: (S) "Extinguishing." Complete liberation from suffering; extinction of craving and eradication of ignorance.

paramita: (S) Perfection; a set of certain qualities that a ***bodhisattva*** cultivates.

puja: (S) Worship ritual; offering ceremony.

Pure Land: State of existence in which all conditions are favorable for attaining ***enlightenment.***

roshi: (J) "Teacher."

samadhi: (S) A developed state of mental tranquility.

samsara: (S, P) "Wandering." Cyclic existence. The cycle of death and rebirth, rooted in ignorance and full of suffering and dissatisfaction.

Sangha: (S) "(Spiritual) community." Community of three spiritual friends or more; third of the ***Three Jewels.***

satori: (J) Sudden flash of insight; a direct glimpse of your essential (Buddha) nature. See also ***kensho.***

Shakyamuni Buddha: "Sage of the Shakya clan." The historical Buddha, also known as ***Gautama*** Buddha. Buddhism is based on his teachings.

shunyata: (S) "Emptiness." The way in which things exist, devoid of all false notions of independent self-existence, and ultimately ungraspable by the conceptual mind.

Siddhartha: (S) "He whose aim is accomplished." Personal name of the historical ***Buddha*** before his awakening.

stupa: (S) Burial monument, holding relics of the Buddha or another spiritual master.

sutra: (S) Discourse, often attributed to ***Shakyamuni Buddha;*** section of the Buddhist canon (P: *sutta*).

tantras: (S) A category of texts forming the basis of the ***Vajrayana*** tradition, dealing with esoteric practices.

Tara: (S) Name of a popular goddess of the ***Mahayana*** pantheon.

Theravada: "Tradition of the elders." The tradition of Buddhism that relies on the authority of the Pali canon. The predominant tradition in Sri Lanka and Southeast Asia.

Three Jewels: ***Buddha, Dharma,*** and ***Sangha*** (S: *triratna*). Also known as the Triple Gem or Three Treasures in which Buddhists place trust: the teacher, his teachings, and the spiritual community.

tripitaka: (S) "Three baskets." The three sections into which the Buddha's teachings have been traditionally divided: ***sutra, vinaya,*** and ***abhidharma*** (P: *tipitaka*).

Vajrayana: (S) "Diamond vehicle." The ***tantric*** teachings of Buddhism; the tradition of ***Mahayana*** Buddhism that evolved in India and came to prominence mostly in Nepal, Mongolia, and Tibet.

vinaya: (S, P) "(Monastic) discipline." Section of the Buddhist canon dealing with the rules of monastic discipline and ethical behavior.

vipassana: (P) "Insight." The name of a form of meditation.

yoga: (S) Spiritual practice or discipline. Male and female practitioners of yoga are referred to as a *yogi* and *yogini,* respectively.

Zen: (J) "Meditation." A tradition of ***Mahayana*** Buddhism that first arose in China and then spread to Korea, Japan, and other Asian countries (C: *Chan*).

Appendix B

Additional Buddhist Resources to Check Out

In an introductory book like this one, we can't possibly do justice to all the many different aspects of Buddhism and its 2,500-year history. But we hope that we've sparked your interest and that you want to explore Buddhism further.

If you want to know more about Buddhism in general or any of its various traditions, you've come to the right place. This appendix offers a list of books and other resources that can help you. Within the list of magazines, we also include a few websites that contain lots of useful and interesting information about all things Buddhist, including the names of Buddhist centers near you. And as soon as you start surfing the web, you're bound to discover many more intriguing sites on your own. (An excellent place to start is `www.buddhanet.net`, the website of the Buddhist Education and Information Network.)

When we first became seriously interested in Buddhism 30 years or so ago, the *Internet* didn't exist, and the number of books on Buddhism suitable for a general reader was quite small — especially compared to the embarrassment of riches available now. Today so many Buddhist publications line bookstore shelves and fill newsstands that our biggest problem in compiling this appendix has been limiting ourselves to a manageable number of entries. From the works we left out, we could easily put together several other excellent lists. Consider this brief catalogue as your entrance into a vast world just waiting for you to explore. Enjoy!

The Story of the Buddha

The life of Shakyamuni Buddha has been told numerous times. Readers from different backgrounds have found these versions particularly inspiring.

- *The Life of the Buddha,* by Venerable H. Saddhatissa (HarperCollins). A highly respected monk-scholar from Sri Lanka drew this compelling account of the life of Shakyamuni Buddha from original Sanskrit and Pali sources.
- *The Light of Asia,* by Sir Edwin Arnold (numerous publishers). Since it first appeared in 1879, this poetic version of the Buddha's story has been an international favorite.
- *Old Path White Clouds: Walking in the Footsteps of the Buddha,* by Thich Nhat Hanh (Parallax Press). Drawing from Pali, Sanskrit, and Chinese sources, this evocative work tells the story of the Buddha's life as seen partly through the eyes of the fictional buffalo boy Svasti.
- *Prince Siddhartha,* by Jonathan Landaw (Wisdom Publications). This story of the life of the Buddha is retold especially for children — and their parents.
- *Siddhartha,* by Hermann Hesse, newly translated by Sherab Chodzin Kohn (Shambhala). Written by the Nobel Prize–winning author in 1922, this novel, set at the time of Shakyamuni Buddha, brings the reader into the world of Buddhism's founder. The translator is a longtime student of Buddhism and Eastern philosophy.

Buddhist Classics, Old and New

The following list contains some of the most influential and popular books on Buddhism.

- *Buddhist Scriptures,* by Edward Conze (Penguin Books). This compact volume contains a wide selection of useful material from Indian, Tibetan, Chinese, and Japanese sources.
- *Cutting through Spiritual Materialism,* by Chogyam Trungpa Rinpoche (Shambhala). A contemporary Tibetan lama who had a profound impact on Buddhism in the West clearly addresses the problems and pitfalls that spiritual seekers face.
- The *Dhammapada* (numerous translations by different publishers). This ancient collection (a version of it is also known as *Dharmapada*) of verses on Buddhist themes is an excellent introduction to Buddhist thought and teachings.
- The *Bodhicharyavatara* (many translations). This important Indian Mahayana text was written by the monk Shantideva in the first half of the eighth century. It details the conduct of a bodhisattva, from the moment he generates the thought of enlightenment (bodhichitta) until he attains insight.

- *The Experience of Insight: A Simple and Direct Guide to Buddhist Meditation,* by Joseph Goldstein (Shambhala). As the title implies, this book is a straightforward manual on the practice of Buddhist *vipassana* (insight) meditation. The author is one of the founders of the Insight Meditation Society in Barre, Massachusetts.
- *The Heart of Buddhist Meditation,* by Nyanaponika Thera (Red Wheel/Weiser). Originally published in 1962, this classic outlines the practice of meditation in the Theravada tradition.
- *Loving-kindness: The Revolutionary Art of Happiness,* by Sharon Salzberg (Shambhala). Filled with personal anecdotes and insights from one of the founders of the Insight Meditation Society in Barre, Massachusetts, this accessible guidebook offers meditations for cultivating not only loving-kindness, but also compassion, sympathetic joy, and equanimity.
- *Masters of Enchantment: The Lives and Legends of the Mahasiddhas,* by Keith Dowman (Inner Traditions International). Richly illustrated by Robert Beer, this work is a fascinating introduction to the ancient and magical world of Indian Vajrayana Buddhism.
- *Mother of the Buddhas: Meditation on the Prajnaparamita Sutra,* by Lex Hixon (Quest Books). More than a mere translation of a major *Perfection of Wisdom Sutra,* this is a work of rare devotional beauty that welcomes the reader to share a glorious vision of insight and compassion.
- *A Path with Heart,* by Jack Kornfield (Bantam Books). Written by the author of numerous works on Buddhist thought and practice, this bestseller provides a friendly, psychologically astute introduction to meditation. Kornfield is a founder of the Insight Meditation Society in Massachusetts and the Spirit Rock Center in California.
- *Three Pillars of Zen: Teaching, Practice, and Enlightenment,* by Philip Kapleau (Anchor Books). The first popular Zen guidebook written by an enlightened Westerner for Westerners, *Three Pillars* single-handedly introduced a generation to Zen Buddhism.
- *The Tibetan Book of Living and Dying,* by Sogyal Rinpoche (Harper SanFrancisco). Filled with teaching stories, meditations, and time-honored insights from the Tibetan Vajrayana tradition, this bestseller approaches the experience of dying — and living — with compassion and wisdom.
- *The Way of Zen,* by Alan W. Watts (Vintage Books). Written in 1957, this work by one of the most influential commentators on Eastern philosophy and religion is still one of the best introductions to the world of Zen thought and practice. Also see his *Psychotherapy East and West* (Vintage Books) for a thought-provoking discussion of the common ground between Western psychiatry and Eastern philosophy.

- *When Things Fall Apart: Heart Advice for Difficult Times,* by Pema Chodron (Shambhala). This favorite is a warm, lucid, and accessible guide to the practice of compassion, especially toward oneself, by an American Buddhist nun who is the resident teacher at a Vajrayana retreat center in Nova Scotia.
- *Zen Mind, Beginner's Mind,* by Shunryu Suzuki (Weatherhill). A classic collection of talks by the beloved Japanese-American Zen master that covers posture, attitude, and understanding from a Soto Zen perspective.

Well Worth Reading

Here are some additional titles that we think you'll like. Take a look.

- *Buddhism for Beginners,* by Thubten Chodron (Snow Lion Publications). Using a question-and-answer format, a leading American Buddhist nun addresses some of the most fundamental issues raised by those encountering Buddhism for the first time.
- *Buddhism with an Attitude: The Tibetan Seven-Point Mind-Training,* by B. Alan Wallace (Snow Lion Publications). In this work, Wallace (one of the leading Western translators and writers on Buddhism) brings the traditional techniques of thought transformation directly into the modern world.
- *The Buddhist Handbook: The Complete Guide to Buddhist Schools, Teaching, Practice, and History,* by John Snelling (Inner Traditions). This invaluable resource for anyone wanting to know more about Buddhism past and present contains appendixes that list useful addresses of Buddhist organizations in North America, major Buddhist festivals, an extensive selection of further readings, and much more.
- *Cultivating Compassion: A Buddhist Perspective,* by Jeffrey Hopkins (Broadway Books). Retired professor at the University of Virginia, interpreter for the Dalai Lama for more than ten years, and translator and editor of numerous works of Buddhism, Hopkins presents a compelling and extremely moving account of the practice of compassion in everyday life.
- *Developing Balanced Sensitivity: Practical Buddhist Exercises for Daily Life,* by Alexander Berzin (Snow Lion Publications). Author, translator, and worldwide lecturer, Berzin introduces a series of techniques adapted from traditional Buddhist sources for dealing with both insensitivity and hypersensitivity. Also check out Berzin's *Relating to a Spiritual Teacher* (Snow Lion) for a comprehensive discussion of the all-important, but often misunderstood, relationship between disciples and their spiritual guides.

- *Dharma Family Treasures: Sharing Mindfulness with Children,* edited by Sandy Eastoak (North Atlantic Books). This anthology of Buddhist writings offers a wealth of ideas for helping children bring Buddhist teachings into their daily lives.
- *The Diamond Cutter: The Buddha on Strategies for Managing Your Business and Your Life,* by Geshe Michael Roach (Doubleday). This book, by an American who completed the rigorous Tibetan geshe training, masterfully weaves together commentary on the profound *Diamond Cutter Sutra* and practical advice for running a business based on the author's experiences in the New York diamond trade. You can also check out Geshe Roach's *The Garden* (Doubleday), a beautiful parable of the Buddhist wisdom teachings.
- *The Heart of Buddha's Teaching: Transforming Suffering into Peace, Joy, and Liberation,* by Thich Nhat Hanh (Parallax Press). This clear and poetic introduction to the core teachings of Buddhism covers the four noble truths, the eightfold path, the six perfections, the 12 links, and much more.
- *The Illustrated Encyclopedia of Buddhist Wisdom: A Complete Introduction to the Principles and Practices of Buddhism,* by Gill Farrer-Halls (Quest Books). Visually attractive and easy to read, this volume provides an excellent overview of the world of Buddhism.
- *Introduction to Tantra: A Vision of Totality,* by Lama Thubten Yeshe (Wisdom Publications). This presentation of the most essential features of Vajrayana Buddhism features clarity and engaging humor.
- *Living Buddhism,* by Andrew Powell (Harmony Books). Graham Harrison's beautiful photographs richly illustrate this wide-ranging survey of Buddhist thought and practice. This book covers the development of Buddhism in India and its spread throughout Asia and to the West.
- *Lotus in a Stream: Essays in Basic Buddhism,* by Hsing Yun (Weatherhill). This work by the contemporary Chinese monk and Chan (Zen) master Hsing Yun is a well-organized and easily readable reference to the major themes of Buddhist thought and practice.
- *Mindfulness in Plain English,* by Venerable Henepola Gunaratana (Wisdom Publications). This step-by-step insight meditation manual is accessible to all readers. Of related interest is Ajahn Sumedho's slim volume *Mindfulness: The Path to the Deathless* (Amaravati Publications).
- *Moon in a Dewdrop: Writings of Zen Master Dogen,* edited by Kazuaki Tanahashi (North Point Press). These beautiful translations of writings by the Japanese Zen master Dogen (1200–1253), the founder of the Soto school, include a variety of practical instructions, as well as philosophical and poetical works.

- *Practical Insight Meditation,* by Mahasi Sayadaw (Unity Press). A revered Burmese master provides an in-depth look at mindfulness meditation: the heart of Theravada Buddhist practice.
- *Transforming Problems into Happiness,* by Lama Thubten Zopa Rinpoche (Wisdom Publications). Lama Zopa's commentary on a short thought-transformation text by a past Tibetan master is filled with practical advice that can be valuable to anyone, regardless of spiritual background.
- *Voices of Insight,* edited by Sharon Salzberg (Shambhala). This collection of articles by many of the most well-known and articulate teachers of the Theravada vipassana tradition provides an excellent introduction to the world of Buddhist meditation.
- *The Zen of Seeing: Seeing/Drawing As Meditation,* by Frederick Franck (Vintage Books). This wonderful book approaches the art of seeing/drawing as a spiritual discipline endowed with the Zen flavor of experiencing the world freshly in each moment.

By and about the Modern Masters

In Chapter 15, we introduce you to four teachers who have exerted a great influence on contemporary Buddhism. Here we present a sampling of books written by and about these illustrious teachers.

- *The Art of Happiness: A Handbook for Living,* by the Dalai Lama (Riverhead Books). This bestseller, coauthored by American psychiatrist Howard Cutler, presents many different methods for dealing with the challenges of everyday life.
- *Dipa Ma: The Life and Legacy of a Buddhist Master,* by Amy Schmidt (BlueBridge Books). This inspiring biography of Dipa Ma (1911–1989) brings to life one of the most beloved and influential Buddhist teachers of the Theravada tradition.
- *Food for the Heart: The Collected Teachings of Ajahn Chah,* introduced by Ajahn Amaro (Wisdom Publications). This compilation provides an excellent overview of Ajahn Chah's teachings, and its introduction ushers the reader into the Thai Forest Tradition that this beloved Buddhist master helped to revitalize.
- *The Good Heart: A Buddhist Perspective on the Teachings of Jesus,* by the Dalai Lama (Wisdom Publications). Invited to give his commentary on the Gospels, the Dalai Lama responds with what Huston Smith has called "arguably the best book on inter-religious dialogue published to date."

- *The Jew in the Lotus,* by Rodger Kamenetz (Harper). This engaging and often humorous account of the meeting of Jewish religious leaders and the Dalai Lama throws light on the issues facing Buddhists, Jews, and all people of faith striving to survive in the secular world.
- *Living Buddha, Living Christ,* by Thich Nhat Hanh (Riverhead Books). The Vietnamese Zen master explores the meeting ground of two of the world's major spiritual traditions. Also check out his *Going Home: Jesus and Buddha As Brothers* (Riverhead Books).
- *Meeting of Minds: A Dialogue on Tibetan and Chinese Buddhism,* by the Dalai Lama and Chan Master Sheng-yen (Dharma Drum Publications). This historical dialogue between two of the leading exponents of Tibetan and Chinese Buddhism throws much-needed light on the similarities and differences between the wisdom teachings of the Vajrayana and Zen traditions.
- *An Open Heart: Practicing Compassion in Everyday Life,* by the Dalai Lama (Little, Brown and Company). This easy-to-comprehend work provides a basic understanding of Buddhism and some of the key methods for cultivating compassion and wisdom in your daily life, no matter what your religious affiliation may be.
- *The World of the Dalai Lama: An Inside Look at His Life, His People, and His Vision,* by Gill Farrer-Halls (Thorsons). This richly illustrated and delightfully written account of the world of the Dalai Lama, both inside and outside Tibet, demonstrates the impact a life of dedication can have on others, no matter what their religious or cultural heritage.

Women and Buddhism

One of the most interesting developments in contemporary Buddhism is the increasing role that women are playing in this traditionally male-dominated sphere. The following books present a variety of points of view on this significant phenomenon.

- *Buddhist Women on the Edge: Contemporary Perspectives from the Western Frontier,* edited by Marianne Dresser (North Atlantic Books). This work contains contributions from important authors such as Pema Chodron, Jan Willis, Tsultrim Allione, Anne Klein, Thubten Chodron, and Kate Wheeler.
- *Dreaming Me: An African American Woman's Spiritual Journey,* by Jan Willis (Riverhead Books). This personal memoir takes the reader along on the author's remarkable journey from an Alabama mining camp, through undergraduate life at Cornell University, to a Tibetan Buddhist monastery, and eventually to her position as Professor of Religion at Wesleyan University.

- *The First Buddhist Women: Translations and Commentary on the Therigatha,* by Susan Murcott (Parallax Press). This look at the early history of women in Buddhism includes a translation of the earliest-known collection of women's religious poetry, the *Therigatha.*
- *Sakyadhita: Daughters of the Buddha,* edited by Karma Lekshe Tsomo (Snow Lion Publications). This collection of essays is the result of the International Conference of Buddhist Nuns held in Bodh Gaya, India, in 1987, the first such conference ever convened.
- *Turning the Wheel: American Women Creating the New Buddhism,* by Sandy Boucher (Beacon Press). This account of the challenges facing women attempting to create a vital tradition of contemporary Buddhism addresses issues of great importance to both men and women.
- *Women of Wisdom,* by Tsultrim Allione (Routledge & Kegan Paul). These biographies of six extraordinary Tibetan female mystics invite the reader to gain a deeper understanding of women's experiences of Buddhism.
- *Women Practicing Buddhism: American Experiences,* edited by Peter N. Gregory and Susanne Mrozik (Wisdom Publications). This is an interesting collection of articles by Susanne Mrozik, Thubten Chodron, and others on life stories of American Buddhist women.

Socially Engaged Buddhism

The practice of Buddhist meditation is, by its nature, a personal, private, and inner-directed activity. But the ultimate purpose of this and other Buddhist practices is to bring as much benefit to others as possible. This compassionate concern for the welfare of others has given rise to Engaged Buddhism. To find out more about this important trend in contemporary Buddhism, check out the following books.

- *Being Peace,* by Thich Nhat Hanh (Parallax Press). By one of the founders of the Engaged Buddhism movement, this book contains lectures given to activists and meditators about the importance of embodying peace in one's own life.
- *Buddhist Peace Work: Creating Cultures of Peace,* edited by David Chappell (Wisdom Publications). This compilation contains first-person accounts of the ideas and work of illustrious leaders from a wide variety of Buddhist traditions on the subject of creating and maintaining peace. Of related interest are Daisaku Ikeda's *For the Sake of Peace: Seven Paths to Global Harmony, A Buddhist Perspective* (Middleway Press) and Sulak Sivaraksa's *Seeds of Peace: A Buddhist Vision for Renewing Society* (Parallax Press).

- *Dharma Gaia: A Harvest of Essays in Buddhism and Ecology,* edited by Alan Hurt Badiner (Parallax Press). This work contains contributions by such luminaries as the Dalai Lama and Thich Nhat Hanh and authors such as Joanna Macy and Joan Halifax.
- *Engaged Buddhism in the West,* edited by Christopher Queen (Wisdom Publications). The history and teachings of Engaged Buddhism are presented here in terms of the individuals and organizations involved in Buddhist activism.
- *Socially Engaged Buddhism: Dimensions of Asian Spirituality,* by Sallie B. King (University of Hawaii Press). This important book examines how Buddhist activists have applied fundamental Buddhist teaching when engaging with social, economic, and ecological problems in the world.
- *World As Lover, World As Self,* by Joanna Macy (Parallax Press). An influential scholar of Buddhism and general systems theory shows how redefining your relationship to the world helps promote not only your own spiritual development, but also the health of the planet.

At Your Local Newsstand

If you're interested in the Buddhist perspective on current social and political affairs, you may want to look at some of the following magazines and periodicals. They're also excellent sources of up-to-date information on meditation courses and study groups organized in your local area.

- *Inquiring Mind.* Born out of the Theravada Buddhist community of insight (vipassana) meditators, this journal is highly regarded for its excellent thought-provoking interviews with Buddhist teachers, philosophers, psychologists, and artists, as well as for its poetry, stories, and humorous essays. Each issue includes an extensive international calendar of vipassana retreats and listings of events and sitting groups throughout North America (Internet: `www.inquiringmind.com`).
- *Mandala: Buddhism in Our Time.* Published by the Foundation for the Preservation of the Mahayana Tradition (FPMT), this magazine regularly features articles by and about the founder of the FPMT, Lama Thubten Yeshe (1935–1984), and its current head, Lama Thubten Zopa Rinpoche, in addition to general coverage of the Buddhist scene (Internet: `www.mandalamagazine.org`).
- *Shambhala Sun: Creating Enlightened Society.* This magazine contains articles on all facets of Buddhism and its relationship to contemporary society (Internet: `www.shambhalasun.com`). You can also take a look at *Buddhadharma: The Practitioner's Quarterly* (Internet: `www.thebuddhadharma.com`).

- *Snow Lion.* The newsletter of Snow Lion Publications is a major source of news, books, tapes, and related material on Buddhism (Internet: `www.snowlionpub.com/pages/N76.html`).
- *Tricycle: The Buddhist Review.* Reading this attractive publication, the most popular Buddhist magazine in America, is an excellent way to keep up on a wide range of issues relating to Buddhist thought and practice (Internet: `www.tricycle.com/magazine/`).
- *Turning Wheel.* Published by the Buddhist Peace Fellowship, *Turning Wheel* provides a Buddhist perspective on such current issues as ecology, peace activism, human rights, and much more (Internet: `www.bpf.org`).

Index

• A •

• B •

• C •

• D •

• E •

• F •

• G •

• H •

• I •

• J •

• K •

• L •

• M •

• N •

• O •

• P •

• R •

• S •

• T •

• U •

• V •

• W •

• Y •

• Z •

Violence and Its Alternatives

Violence and Its Alternatives
An Interdisciplinary Reader

Edited by Manfred B. Steger and Nancy S. Lind

St. Martin's Press
New York

VIOLENCE AND ITS ALTERNATIVES

ISBN 0-312-21513-4 (cloth)
ISBN 0-312-22151-7 (paper)

Library of Congress-in-Publication Data

Violence and its alternatives : an interdisciplinary reader / edited by Manfred B. Steger and Nancy S. Lind.
p. cm.
Includes bibliographical references and index.
ISBN 0-312-21513-4 (cloth : alk. paper). — ISBN 0-312-22151-7 (pbk. : alk. paper)
1. Violence. 2. Nonviolence. I. Steger, Manfred B., 1961– II. Lind, Nancy S., 1958–
HM281.V484 1999
303.6—dc21 98-48411
CIP

Design by Binghamton Valley Composition

First Edition: April, 1999
10 9 8 7 6 5 4 3 2

CREDITS AND ACKNOWLEDGEMENTS

Hannah Arendt. Excerpt from *On Violence.* New York: Harcourt Brace Jovanovich, 1970: 35–60. Copyright © 1969, 1970 by Hannah Arendt. Reprinted by permission of Harcourt Brace & Company.

Robert Paul Wolff. "On Violence," *Journal of Philosophy* LXVI, no. 19 (October 2, 1969): 601–16. Reprinted by permission of The Journal of Philosophy.

C. A. J. Coady. "The Idea of Violence," *Journal of Applied Philosophy* 3 no. 1 (1986): 3–19. Copyright © 1986: Society for Applied Philosophy.

Johan Galtung. "Cultural Violence," *Journal of Peace Research* 27 no. 3 (1990): 291–305. Copyright © 1990 by Sage Publications. Reprinted by permission from Sage Publications Ltd from Johan Galtung, Journal of Peace Research.

Walter Benjamin. "Critique of Violence" *Reflections: Essays, Aphorisms, Autobiographical Writings.* Ed. Peter Demetz. New York: Harcourt Brace Jovanovich, 1978: 277–300. Copyright © 1978 by Harcourt Brace & Company. Reprinted by permission of the publisher.

Michel Foucault. Excerpt from *Discipline and Punish: The Birth of the Prison.* Translated by Alan Sheridan (All Lane 1977, first published *as Surveiller et Punir: Naissance de la Prison* by Editions Gallimard, 1975). Copyright © 1977 by Alan Sheridan. Reproduced by permission of Penguin Books Ltd.

Jacques Derrida. Excerpt from "Force of Law: The 'Mystical Foundations of Authority' " *Cardozo Law Review* 11, no. 919 (1990): 927–945. Reprinted with permission.

Nancy Fraser. "The Force of Law: Metaphysical or Political?" *Feminist Interpretations of Jacques Derrida.* Ed. Nancy J. Holland. University Park: Penn State University Press, 1997: 157–63. This article originally appeared in Cardozo Law Review 13, no. 1325 (1991). Reprinted with permission.

Cass R. Sunstein. "Is Violent Speech a Right?" *American Prospect* 22 (Summer 1995): 34–37. Copyright © 1995 by The American Prospect, P.O. Box 383080, Cambridge, MA 02138. Reprinted with permission. All rights reserved.

Nancy C. Hartsock. "Gender and Sexuality: Masculinity, Violence, and Domination," *Humanities in Society* 7 no. 1–2 (Winter/Spring 1984): 19– 45. Reprinted with permission.

Christine Alder. "Violence, Gender, and Social Change," *International Social Science Journal* 132 (1992): 267–275. Copyright © 1992: UNESCO. Reprinted with permission.

Claire M. Renzetti. "Violence in Lesbian and Gay Relationships," *Gender Violence: Interdisciplinary Perspectives.* Ed. Laura L. O'Toole and Jessica R. Schiffman. New York: New York University Press, 1997: 285–293. Reprinted with permission from New York University Press.

Andea Dworkin. "Pornography and Grief," *Letters from a War Zone.* New York: Dutton, 1988: 19–24. Reprinted with permission.

Cindy Jenefsky. "Andrea Dworkin's Reconstruction of Pornography as a Discriminatory Social Practice." Excerpt from Cindy Jenefsky (with Ann Russo), *Without Apology: Andrea Dworkin's Art and Politics.* Boulder, CO and Oxford, England: Westview Press, 1998. Reprinted with permission of Westview Press.

Ruth Seifert. "The Second Front: The Logic of Sexual Violence in Wars," *Women's Studies International Forum* 19 no. 1–2 (1996): 35–43. Reprinted with permission from Elsevier Science.

Frantz Fanon. Excerpt from "Concerning Violence," *The Wretched of the Earth.* Trans. Constance Farrington. New York: Grove Press, 1966: 29–46. Copyright © 1963 by Presence Africaine. Used by permission of Grove/Atlantic, Inc.

Malcolm X. Excerpt from "The Ballot or the Bullet," *Malcolm X Speaks,* Ed. George Breitman. New York: Pathfinder, 1965: 31–35. Copyright © 1965, 1989 by Betty Shabazz and Pathfinder Press. Reprinted by permission.

David Nicholson. "On Violence," *Speak My Name: Black Men on Masculinity and the American Dream.* Ed. Don Belton. Boston: Beacon Press, 1995: 28– 34. Reprinted with permission by David Nicholson.

Cornel West. "Nihilism in Black America," *Race Matters.* New York: Vintage, 1994: 17–31. Copyright © 1993 by Cornel West. Reprinted by permission of Beacon Press, Boston.

Manning Marable. "Violence, Resistance, and the Struggle for Black Empowerment," *Speaking Truth to Power: Essays on Race, Resistance, and Radicalism.* Boulder: Westview Press, 1996: 124–33. Copyright © 1996 by Westview Press. Reprinted by permission of Westview Press.

Russel Barsh. "Indigenous Peoples, Racism and the Environment," *Meanjin* 49 no. 4 (1990): 723–731. Reprinted with permission of Russel Barsh.

Mary Kaldor. "The New Nationalism in Europe," *Rethinking Peace*. Ed. Robert Elias and Jennifer Turpin. Boulder: Lynne Rienner, 1994: 87–97. Copyright © 1994 by Peace Review Publications. Used with permission of Lynne Reinner Publishers, Inc.

Yael Tamir. "Pro Patria Mori! Death and the State," *The Morality of Nationalism*. Ed. Robert McKim and Jeff McMahan. New York: Oxford University Press, 1997: 227–41. Copyright © 1997 by Oxford University Press, Inc. Used by permission of Oxford University Press, Inc.

Arjun Appadurai. "Patriotism and Its Futures," *Public Culture*, 5 no. 3 (Spring 1993): 411–29. Copyright © 1993 by Duke University Press. Reprinted with permission.

Akbar S. Ahmed. "Ethnic Cleansing': A Metaphor for our Time?" *Ethnic and Racial Studies* 18 no. 1 (January 1995): 1–25. Reprinted with permission.

Georges Sorel. Excerpt from *Reflections on Violence*. Trans. T. E. Hulme and J. Roth. New York: Collier Books, 1961: 229–49. Copyright © 1950, renewed 1978 by The Times Press. Reprinted with the permission of The Free Press, a Division of Simon & Schuster.

Herbert Marcuse. "Liberation from the Affluent Society," *Critical Theory and Society: A Reader*. Ed. Stephen Eric Bronner and Douglas MacKay Kellner. New York: Routledge, 1989: 276–87. Reprinted with permission of the Literary Estate of Herbert Marcuse, Peter Marcuse, Executor. Supplementary material from previously unpublished work of Herbert Marcuse, much of it now in the Archives of the Goethe University in Frankfurt/Main, has been and will be published in a five-volume series by Routledge Publishers, England, edited by Douglas Kellner. All rights to further publication are retained by the Estate.

George Lukács. "Legality and Illegality," *History and Class Consciousness: Studies in Marxist Dialectics*. Cambridge, MA: MIT Press, 1990: 256–271. Reprinted with permission.

Manfred B. Steger. "An Autopsy of Marxist Socialism," *Peace Review* 9 no. 1 (1997): 25–31. Reprinted with permission of Manfred B. Steger and Carfax Publishing Limited, Oxfordshire, UK.

Mohandas K. Gandhi. Excerpt from *The Essential Writings of Mahatma Gandhi*. Ed. Raghavan Iyer. Delhi: Delhi Oxford University Press, 1990: 236–48; 265–68. Reprinted with permission of Navajivan Trust, which holds copyright on all the writings of Mahatma Gandhi, and Delhi Oxford University Press.

Martin Luther King Jr. Excerpt from "Love, Law, and Civil Disobedience," *A Testament of Hope: The Essential Writings and Speeches of Martin Luther King Jr.* San Francisco: HarperSanFrancisco, 1995: 263– 72. Copyright © 1961 by Martin Luther King, Jr., copyright renewed 1989 by Coretta Scott King. Reprinted by arrangement with The Heirs to the Estate of Martin Luther King, Jr., c/o Writers House, Inc. as agent for the proprietor.

bell hooks. "Beloved Community: A World Without Racism," *Killing Rage: Ending Racism*. New York: Holt, 1995: 263–72. Copyright © 1995 by Gloria Watkins. Reprinted by permission of Henry Holt and Company, Inc.

Aung San Suu Kyi. "Freedom From Fear," *Freedom From Fear and Other Writings.* Revised ed. Trans. Michael Aris. London: Penguin, 1991: 180–85. Translation copyright © 1991, 1995 by Aung San Suu Kyi and Michael Aris. Reproduced by permission of Penguin Books Ltd.

Gene Sharp. "Beyond Just War and Pacifism. Nonviolence Struggle Towards Justice, Freedom and Peace," *The Ecumenical Review* 48 no. 2 (April 1996): 233–50. Gene Sharp is Senior Scholar of the Albert Einstein Institution, Cambridge, Massachusetts; is Professor Emeritus of political science, University of Massachusetts, Dartmouth; and was formerly Associate in the Center for International Affairs, Harvard University. He has written numerous studies on the nature and potential of nonviolent struggle, including *The Politics of Nonviolent Action* (Boston: Porter Sargent, 1973). This article is a revised and expanded version of a presentation in Rome sponsored by the Justice and Peace Commission of the Unions of Superiors General of the Catholic Church. The original version was published in Italian in *Il Regno attualità (*Bologna), 14–15 July 1994. The author acknowledges the assistance of Bruce Jenkins, Fr. Donal O'Mahony, Cap., Sr. Mary Litell, Thomas E. Quigley, Elizabeth Salter, and Salpy Eskidjian.

Jennifer Turpin and Lester R Kurtz. "Untangling the Web of Violence," *The Web of Violence: From Interpersonal to Global.* Urbana: University of Illinois Press, 1997: 207–32. Copyright © 1997 by the Board of Trustees of the University of Illinois. Used with the permission of the University of Illinois Press.

CONTENTS

SECTION IV: VIOLENCE AND RACE

SECTION V: VIOLENCE AND NATIONALISM

SECTION VI: VIOLENCE AND CLASS

SECTION VII: NONVIOLENCE ALTERNATIVES

PERSONAL ACKNOWLEDGMENTS

A number of people deserve our thanks for their help in seeing this project to completion. Karen Wolny, our editor, participated in every aspect of the undertaking. James von Bockmann, Jason Hahn, and Steven Rich's assistance was invaluable. We also want to express our appreciation to our friends and colleagues: Stephen Eric Bronner, Timothy Kaufman-Osborne, Terrell Carver, Elizabeth Kelly, Jamal Nassar, Lane Crothers, Shailer Thomas, and William Tolone for providing us with many useful suggestions and insights. Finally, we would like to thank the Department of Political Science and the Graduate School at Illinois State University for their support.

INTRODUCTION

Manfred B. Steger and Nancy S. Lind

In recent years, we have heard triumphant voices proclaiming the "end of history," supposedly brought about by the "final victory" of capitalist liberal democracy over its remaining ideological competitors. Yet current affairs belie this thesis as we witness the emergence of new conflicts arising from the effects of globalization, ethnonationalism, religious fundamentalism, and international terrorism. Rather than sailing smoothly into a new century of rational concord, we continue to find ourselves enmeshed in a net of violence stitched together by crime, war, environmental degradation, and the unequal distribution of material resources. Threatened by the human capacity to unleash previously unimaginable means of violence, the very future of the world hangs in the balance. Indeed, the ominous escalation of violence on both the interpersonal and the global level represents one of the central social and political challenges for the dawning twenty-first century. In spite of the current proliferation of academic literature on the topic, however, advances in our understanding of violence and its alternatives have been hampered by a number of conceptual and institutional difficulties.

First, like most intellectuals involved in the exploration of issues that reach across different disciplines and employ various methodological approaches, students of violence find themselves confronted with the familiar problem of insufficient interdisciplinary interaction, a situation that contributes to an increasing sense of alienation, overspecialization, and isolation in the humanities and social sciences in general. Although a number of scholars have offered innovative perspectives on the causes and effects of political, social, and psychological violence, discussions of their research are often restricted to small circles of academics working in the same fields of expertise. As a result, the public learns very little about existing theories of violence. Further, the academic discourse on the topic is becoming ever more compartmentalized, thereby discouraging and marginalizing rare efforts to link related themes in projects that seek to reframe issues of violence in a more holistic manner. The magnitude of this problem is reflected in the dearth of literature on the subject, which, drawing on a broad range of methodological and cultural perspectives, would present research on violence in a language accessible to a general audience. Save for a few edited books comprised of articles by internationally known experts on violence, there exists no comprehensive collection of writings that offers a truly interdisciplinary discussion of the topic.[1]

Second, the few existing anthologies on the subject hardly ever include substantial sections on possible alternatives to violence.[2] This pervasive neglect of nonviolent alternatives in the current debates on violence becomes especially glaring when considered in light of our own violent century, which brought us nuclear and biological warfare, concentration camps, and multiple genocides. While the analysis of the mechanisms that cause and sustain structures of violence represents a crucial first step in seeking remedies, experts on violence must put more effort into developing the kind of creative imagination that enables them to formulate empowering visions of nonviolence. This constructive emphasis on alternatives to violence is particularly important for pedagogical purposes, because it could provide teachers and students with the conceptual and symbolic resources needed to affect a lasting change of violent behaviors. For this reason, it is essential that educators not only become familiar with the "classical" theories of nonviolence as presented in the writings of Mohandas K. Gandhi, Martin Luther King Jr., and other proponents of nonviolent direct action, but also initiate formal curricular proposals that support and disseminate models suitable for a comprehensive peace education.

Third, there is still little general awareness of new approaches to violence and its alternatives developed by a new generation of scholars and social activists around the world. Today, we are experiencing the quickening pace of globalization, a process that profoundly shapes our waning century. Although human lives everywhere are deeply affected by the global forces of the market, technology, and the media, neither the implications nor the opportunities presented by these changes has fully penetrated Western intellectual discourse.[3] Frequently caught within the conceptual parameters of their own cultural heritage, Western students of violence would be well advised to engage in an international exchange of ideas in order to avoid the dangers of intellectual stagnation and ethnocentric bias. To assess the significance of each methodological approach and compare the various features of different discourses on violence, scholars need to generate studies that incorporate insights developed in different cultural settings. Going beyond purely academic concerns, engaging in such a multicultural program also contributes to the development of a practical-political consciousness that might serve as a catalyst for the transformation of powerful ideologies of violence.

Striving to be sensitive to the concerns raised above, *Violence and Its Alternatives: An Interdisciplinary Reader* represents an attempt to fill the existing gap in the literature on violence by offering a comprehensive and diverse treatment of the subject that draws consciously from a variety of cultural traditions and intellectual perspectives. Methodologically eclectic and intellectually wide-ranging, this anthology of 35 contributions is divided into seven thematic sections, reflecting the importance of interdisciplinary approaches to the study of violence. Containing many of today's cutting-edge debates and controversies on the meaning, causes and effects, and ethical-political implications of violence, our collection is designed to appeal alike to students, educators, and specialists working in the field of violence studies. Overall, our reader aims to provide its audience with an exciting mix of seminal, "classical" treatments of the topic and more recent, "postmodern" contributions that analyze the ways in which popular culture has represented issues of violence. By connecting these discussions to an equally representative collection of writings by proponents of nonviolent paradigms, we hope to confront our audience with the kind of creative imaginings needed to fashion constructive alternatives to violence. Some of the central theoretical concerns raised by the contributors to the book include the following questions. What do we mean by violence? What constitutes violent behavior? What are the main forces—political, social, economic, psychological, linguistic, and cultural—that cause and sustain patterns of violence? How can we best eliminate or reduce violence in society?

As we approach the new century with its formidable social and ethical challenges, the question of violence and its alternatives will only gain in importance. As various forms of exploitation and oppression continue to raise national and global levels of conflict, indirect violence embedded in such structures of injustice will take its toll on our quality of life. Hence, we cannot afford to overlook the connection between such underlying structural forms of violence and the more obvious manifestations of direct organized violence. To meet our responsibility as citizens and scholars, we need to recognize the centrality of the global problem of violence and direct our research efforts to encourage the development and implementation of innovative nonviolent alternatives. This reader is designed to contribute to this process.

I. VIOLENCE: DEFINITIONS AND CONCEPTS

The first section of our reader introduces a variety of approaches illuminating the concept of violence. The authors represented in this section provide both the basic assumptions and the theoretical frameworks used by the other contributors in subsequent sections of the book. We begin with an excerpt from *On Violence*, **Hannah Arendt**'s controversial collection of essays on the subject, first published in 1969. In it, she asserts that power cannot be equated with violence, since violence is actually an inferior way of creating a democratic power base anchored in the organized solidarity of the people. For Arendt, "violence appears where power is in jeopardy," meaning that while violence can destroy power, it is unable to create it. The broader implications of her argument emerge in her conclusion: rather than contributing to the stability of power, the use of violence will inevitably lead to more violence. Ultimately, Arendt's innovative elucidation of the connections between violence, power, authority, strength, and force challenge conventional distinctions between "realist" and "idealist" paradigms of politics.

Published in the same year as Arendt's study *On Violence*, **Robert Paul Wolff**'s seminal essay reflects his arguments in favor of a "philosophical anarchism" that contests the legitimacy of all forms of social order based on domination and hierarchy. He proposes that the concept of violence is deliberately used by power elites to either halt change or justify the existing unequal distribution of power and privilege. For Wolff, both the concept of violence and the correlative idea of nonviolence are "inherently confused," because "these and related concepts depend for their meaning in political discussions on the fundamental notion of legitimate authority, which is also inherently incoherent." The author develops his propositions about violence in three stages, focusing on the relationship between power and authority, the unfounded distinction between "legitimate" and "illegitimate" political authority, and the ideological use of violence as a rhetorical device for domination. Wolff's steadfast refusal to divorce analytical definitions of violence from the workings of structural forces evident in "the complex class struggle for wealth and power in America" makes his essay a powerful critique of the notion that "violence" can be defined in a value-free, "objective" manner.

Johan Galtung, one of the original European founders of the burgeoning field of peace studies, clearly disagrees with Wolff on the utility of analytical definitions of violence. Indeed, his contribution centers on the idea of "cultural violence" as a follow-up to his famous introduction of the concept of "structural violence." In the former essay, published in 1969, Galtung had emphasized both the analytical and practical-political importance of distinguishing between direct and structural forms of violence. In his more recent 1990 article, included here, Galtung expands his model with the addition of the notion of "cultural violence." Defining the term as "any aspect of a culture that can be used to legitimize violence in its direct or structural form," the author goes on to cite examples of cultural violence by using a division of culture into religion and ideology, art and language, and empirical and formal science. He strongly supports the inclusion of culture as a major focus of research on peace and nonviolence—not only as deepening the quest for peace, but also as a possible contribution to the as yet nonexistent discipline of "culturology." Consistent with the thematic objectives of our reader, Galtung's contribution highlights the importance of the cultural dimension in the study of violence.

The Australian philosopher **C. A. J. Coady** concurs with Wolff in stating that there is little agreement among scholars of violence about how the concept should be understood, but he disagrees with his colleague's critique of the analytical method. Coady examines some fashionable approaches to the concept of violence and argues against "wide" definitions, particularly those of the "structuralist" variety typified by Galtung. He also offers a critique of "legitimist" definitions that incorporate some strong notions of illegitimacy into the very meaning of violence. Ultimately, the author rejects both structuralist and legitimist accounts on conceptual and practical grounds and instead presents a defense of a more restricted definition. Reflected in its thesis that understanding is sometimes best served by defining a concept such as violence in very abstract and relatively neutral terms, Coady's article represents a strong challenge to the arguments offered by Arendt, Wolff, and Galtung.

II. VIOLENCE AND LAW

The remaining six sections of our reader apply issues of violence and its alternatives to the concrete political, economic, and cultural dimensions of society. Specifically, this section deals with the subject of violence and its place in law and legal theory. Given the central role of violence as both fact and metaphor in the constitution of modern law, the contributors to this section explore the constructive, "order-making" aspects of law, while at the same time emphasizing its coercive aspects, manifested in the allegedly "legitimate" institutional violence of the state.

We start with the influential examination of the relationship between violence, law, and justice offered by the German literary critic **Walter Benjamin** in 1921. Raising the question of whether violence, in a given case, is a means to a "just" or an "unjust" end, Benjamin proceeds with an insightful discussion of "natural law" and "positive law" as two main currents in legal philosophy. Concluding that "among all the forms of violence permitted by both natural law and positive law there is not one that is free of the gravely problematic nature of all legal violence," the author emphasizes the central role of language in reaching "civil agreements," thus pointing to the possibility of creating a sphere of intersubjective "understanding" free of violence. The echoes of Benjamin's arguments can still be heard in the German philosopher Jürgen Habermas's contemporary formulation of a theory of communicative action. Benjamin's discussion closes with a highly original attempt to show how various mythical forms of violence have become bastardized as "law and order" to justify the legitimate, or law-making, violence of the state.

Next, we offer an excerpt from *Discipline and Punish*, **Michel Foucault**'s highly controversial 1975 study on penal justice and the birth of the modern prison. Guided by questions related to the discursive foundations of the "legality" of violence, the French social theorist develops his famous argument that, in modernity, violence has been transformed into a "normalizing science" resulting in the penitentiary techniques of the "carceral archipelago" and its various penal institutions. Linking the rise of the "carceral" in modernity to the emergence of other social institutions, such as the workshop, schools, hospitals, and the modern military, Foucault emphasizes the constructive role of violence in establishing far-reaching power networks that produced "systems of insertion, distribution, surveillance, and observation." In his analysis, violence does not merely destroy and injure; manifested as a modern "carceral network," it constitutes and expands various forms of knowledge, thus making a "science of law" historically possible. The academic impact of Foucault's original account of power and the formation of knowledge in modern society has been truly phenomenal. His writings have served as major catalysts for the further development of schools of social and political analysis commonly labeled "postmodernist" or "poststructuralist."

Offering such a poststructuralist "interrogation" of the relationship between law, violence, and justice that consciously engages in a critical reading of Benjamin's text, the excerpt from **Jacques Derrida**'s vanguard essay on the "Force of Law" defends the value of his "deconstructive" approach in generating profound insights into the violent origins of law. Following Foucault's line of inquiry, Derrida suggests that the concept of justice is unthinkable without enabling networks of violence, and concludes that violence is therefore deeply implicated in the legal foundation of any possible society. In her rejoinder to Derrida, the American political theorist **Nancy Fraser** criticizes the French philosopher for privileging a quasi-transcendental deconstruction of "the force of law" over a "merely" political critique of violence. In other words, Fraser accuses Derrida and other "deconstructionists" of engaging in a disempowering, metaphysical enterprise that considers any political project aimed at eliminating or reducing violence as a futile attempt to escape the very conditions that characterize the necessary relationship between violence and justice. Contra Derrida and his deconstructive approach to law and violence, Fraser outlines three aspects of a *political* critique of "the force of law" that "render visible forms of masked, structural violence that permeate and infect, legal judgment." In Fraser's view, the value of identifying various forms of violence rooted in unjust social arrangements lies in opening up the political possibility of reducing unnecessary manifestations of violence in society.

In the final contribution to this section, the American legal theorist **Cass Sunstein** focuses on the political implications of violence by exploring a particularly current aspect of violence and law in the area of freedom of speech. Using the traumatic events surrounding the 1995 bombing of a federal building in Oklahoma City, Sunstein joins the national debate about the legality of speech counseling violence or inciting hatred of public officials and the federal government. Raising the question of whether government should be allowed to control and regulate extremist forms of political dissent, she reviews a number of Supreme Court cases dealing with this issue and examines the relevance of the Court's findings in the context of modern technologies such as the Internet. While Sunstein argues against the regulation of political opinions, including the advocacy of illegal acts, she nonetheless concludes that "that principle need not, however, be interpreted to bar the government from restricting advocacy of unlawful killing on the mass media."

III. VIOLENCE AND GENDER

Our section on violence and gender reflects the increasing concerns of women who find themselves suspended in a patriarchal web of violence. Thus, our contributors analyze and challenge deep-seated structures of misogyny that lead to the legitimation and reproduction of exclusivist images of masculinity, rape mentality, hard-core pornography, sexual harassment, mechanistic thinking, domestic violence, and militarism. A familial, social, ideological, and political system in which the female is subsumed by the male, patriarchy represents a truly cross-cultural phenomenon that permeates all social institutions. As Adrienne Rich has reminded us, the violence of patriarchy is both diffuse and concrete; symbolic and literal; universal and expressed with local variations that obscure its universality. The critical work of feminists has not only opened up new avenues for the necessary reconceptualization of violence and its alternatives, but has also contributed to their political translation into concrete policy initiatives that have begun to change institutional forms of violence perpetrated against women.

We begin this section with an article by the American political theorist **Nancy Hartsock** on the connection between violence, gender, and masculine domination. Examining problematic issues such as violence and pornography, Hartsock points to the existence of an underlying "hegemony of phallocratic culture" that reflects and expresses the experience of the dominant group—white heterosexual men of a certain class in a position to make their images of masculinity hegemonic. Given that sexuality in general cannot be separated from existing power relations, Hartsock's intention is not to argue for the construction of an alternative "feminist sexuality," but rather to engage in a cultural critique of masculine power as it operates in the field defined by sexuality. As she puts it, "we need a more adequate understanding of sexuality in order to work for change. One important task is the analysis of the sexuality in the contemporary West that is tied to hostility and dominance on the one hand, and definitions of masculinity on the other." Ultimately, Hartsock's analysis reveals that even beneath the "polite" language of sexual reciprocity, one finds one-sided relations of domination and submission, and dynamics of violence, hostility, and revenge.

In her article on violence, gender, and social change, the Australian criminologist **Christine Alder** turns her analytic spotlight on those forms of violence in society that are frequently taken for granted, such as domestic violence. Arguing that in many cultures masculinity and power are linked to the ability to protect and materially support a family, Alder identifies a number of social structures of violence that close off opportunities for women. In concluding, she notes that the practice and approval of gender-based violence are more pervasive than is generally acknowledged. Hence, violence cannot be controlled through individually based strategies, for the complex nature of violence requires that the necessary social changes be diverse and wide-ranging, and that they must include macro-level alterations of the structured inequalities of race, class, and gender.

Claire Renzetti's original contribution expands the important issue of domestic violence to cases of partner abuse in same-sex relationships. The primary goal of her essay is to provide an overview of what is currently known about violence in lesbian and gay relationships as a result of empirical research. Discussing the existing similarities and differences between incidences of same-sex and heterosexual domestic violence, Renzetti finds many of the recent comparisons on the topic to be overly simplistic and falsely framed. In her view, achieving a better understanding of same-sex violence requires close attention to three main points. First, researchers must consider how people are differently located in society; second, they must examine the various meanings that specific behaviors have for the social actors involved in them; and, third, such work requires the use of diverse research methodologies that contextualize violent behavior and emotion. The author concludes by proposing the development of "findings from contextualized, collaborative studies of intimate violence among lesbian and gay couples, as well as couples from other marginalized groups and from differing cultures."

Written as a speech for a 1978 "Take Back the Night" march that was part of the first feminist conference on pornography in the United States, **Andrea Dworkin** highlights some of Nancy Hartsock's concerns, but comes to a much more radical conclusion: "Pornographers put forth one consistent proposition: erotic pleasure for men is derived from and predicated on the savage destruction of women." A pioneering theorist of the anti-pornography movement in the United States, Dworkin argues that the most insidious aspect of pornography is that it tells male truth as if it were universal truth. Incorporating in her analysis some of Foucault's insights into the "normalizing" effects of power networks, the author also uses the issue of pornography to comment on some subtle connections between physical and psychological forms of violence. Dworkin's views on the violence of pornography provoked significant academic debates that have continued to this day. Her many writings and public appearances have also contributed to heightening public awareness of the subject.

Reflecting on pornography as a violent social practice, the American social theorist **Cindy Jenefsky** offers a close reading of Dworkin's anti-pornography discourse. Focusing on the shift in Dworkin's analysis of pornography from a misogynistic cultural artifact to a discriminatory practice of sexual exploitation, Jenefsky argues that Dworkin's presentation of pornography as a violent, male-dominated social practice directly challenges current legal interpretations of pornography as a mere representation of an "idea" or a "speech." For Jenefsky, Dworkin's perspective favors an understanding of pornography in concrete, material terms as a violent *action* directed against women. Hence, the author concludes that Dworkin's writings have great *practical-political* value in that they "provide individual women with the legal mechanism for redressing class-based subordination perpetuated through the production, distribution, and consumption of pornography."

Finally, the contribution of the German sociologist **Ruth Seifert** addresses the theme of gender and violence by focusing on the gender-specific atrocities systematically committed by Serb and Croat forces in the 1992–95 Bosnian civil war. Seifert rejects the common explanation given for rapes in the context of war, which portrays such acts as "natural occurrences" to be attributed to a male anthropology or to acts of "hordes run wild." In her view, such explanations have prevented a deeper probing into the meanings and functions of collective sexual violence against women. Seifert's objective is to identify patterns of war crimes against women and to show that they have cultural functions. The author argues that such acts of violence not only destroy the physical and psychological existence of women, but also inflict harm on the culture and collective identity of the whole group, ethnicity, or nation under attack. Thus, war crimes such as the mass-rapes of women have a symbolic meaning and must be analyzed within the symbolic contexts of the nation and the gender system.

IV. VIOLENCE AND RACE

The concept of "race" represents a powerful cognitive framework that has persistently generated and sustained patterns of physical, epistemic, and symbolic violence. To be sure, prejudice against "foreigners" and alien "Others" have always existed, but "race," referring to an unchangeable human quality rooted in fixed biological categories, did not receive its "scientific" legitimation until the early nineteenth century. The conceptual violence of dividing human beings mostly along color lines into "savage" or "depraved" races and "civilized" or "higher" races became constituted as common "knowledge," endowing various racist discourses with the ideological foundations to justify colonialist and imperialist forms of domination in the name of "civilizing the lower races." Indeed, the wide acceptance of race-based ideologies in nineteenth-century Western thought proved to be the indispensable precondition for the implementation of the Holocaust and other twentieth-century manifestations of racist violence. Our reader's segment on violence and race contains the contributions of authors who survey the many forms of violence caused by the cognitive model of "race" in various cultural settings and in different historical contexts.

We begin the section with an excerpt from *The Wretched of the Earth*, **Franz Fanon**'s classical analysis of violence in colonial and post-colonial societies, first published in 1961. Arguably Africa's greatest theorist of revolution, the Caribbean-born Fanon managed to combine his extraordinary philosophical and psychological insights in a trenchant critique of racism and imperialism. Insisting on the inevitability of violence in the process of decolonization, he emphasizes its cleansing, psychological effects when employed by the colonized against their oppressor. For Fanon, no conciliation is possible in the socially constructed "Manicheistic World" of black and white, for the clashing interests of the natives and the colonizers reproduce antagonisms on the level of everyday life. Oppressor and oppressed are equally entangled in the processes of domination, exploitation, and pillage introduced by the colonizer; the postulation of objective "truths" can no longer guide a struggle in which the mediation between "good" and "evil" has become impossible. As Fanon puts it, "The naked truth of decolonization evokes for us the searing bullets and bloodstained knives that emanate from it. For if the last shall be first, this will only come to pass after a murderous and decisive struggle between the two protagonists." Thus, he celebrates the psychological release achieved through violence which enables the oppressed to free up their energies for the necessary task of building a new, liberated society. Ultimately, Fanon concludes that colonialism begins and perpetuates itself through acts of violence, and calls forth an answering violence from the colonized.

Shifting the focus to the United States in the years of the Civil Rights Movement, we turn to a short excerpt from **Malcolm X**'s famous speech on "The Ballot or the Bullet." Like Fanon, Malcolm X considers the use of violence in the civil rights struggle to be inevitable, thus emphasizing that blacks have an obligation to meet racist violence with equal force. Implicit in his argument is the rejection of King's method of nonviolence as ineffective "turn-the-other-cheek stuff," leading to a regressive strategy of "dillydallying and pussyfooting and compromising" instead of "real progress." Malcolm X instead exhorts black Americans to forge coalitions and alliances with "our African and Asian brothers," thus expanding the civil rights struggle to the level of human rights: "Let the world know how bloody his [Uncle Sam's] hands are. Let the world know the hypocrisy that's practiced over here. Let it be the ballot or the bullet."

An excerpt from **David Nicholson**'s novelistic account of his childhood experiences on the predatory streets and playgrounds of black Washington, D.C. adds a very personal and moving dimension to the intricate workings of violence in the inner city. The writer beautifully captures the daily challenges facing black youth in American urban centers: a general loss of faith in gaining satisfactory employment, the experience of space and time as fragmented and random, a feeling of dislocation and insecurity, and the existing peer pressure to join street gangs and participate in senseless acts of violence. Nicholson describes his emotional confusion after an attack on a helpless boy: "And, sickened, I learned a lesson—it felt no better to threaten violence against someone incapable of resisting than it had been to be the one threatened and equally incapable of resistance."

Next, we introduce reflections on violence and race by **Cornel West** and **Manning Marable**, two leading African American intellectuals. Both essays raise the often distorted question of black-on-black violence as well as dealing with the persistence of violent race relations in contemporary America. An excerpt from his best-selling book *Race Matters*, West's contribution follows in Nicholson's footsteps by addressing what he considers to be the most basic issue now facing black America: the nihilistic threat to its very existence. West explains that this threat is not simply a matter of economic deprivation and political powerlessness, but, first and foremost, "a profound sense of psychological depression, personal worthlessness, and social despair [that is] widespread in black America." Arguing that both liberals and conservatives tend to overlook this nihilistic threat, West proposes to counteract nihilism with an "ethic of love"—a "politics of conversion" aiming at generating a sense of dignity in a downtrodden people. He calls on black leaders to implement this politics of conversion from the bottom up through effective grass-roots organizing designed to strengthen those institutions in civil society still vital enough to promote self-worth and self-affirmation. Marable, too, calls for a new vision guided by the ideals of collective respect, shared humanity, and educational advancement. Debunking the "seductive illusion that equality between the races has been achieved in America," Marable includes in his discussion a critical assessment of the dynamics of violence within the African American community.

In the final contribution to this section, **Russel Barsh** discusses a frequently neglected dimension of racial violence. His insightful comments on "environmental racism"—the manner in which politically dominant Western countries freely impose ecological risks and hazards that they would never willingly bear themselves on relatively poor, politically isolated regions of the Third World. The victims of environmental racism are mostly indigenous peoples dependent on hunting, fishing, and agriculture who lack the power to resist these exploitative economic practices. Barsh points to the United States, Canada, and Australia as prime examples of rich Western countries that routinely impose questionable "development projects" on their indigenous populations.

V. VIOLENCE AND NATIONALISM

Whether one considers nationalism a reactionary force aiming at the restoration of an imagined traditional order, or a progressive movement of the popular interest against empire, dynasty, and privilege, one can hardly ignore nationalists' exhibited willingness to engage in violence. All types or categories of nationalism share a proclivity to endorse the use of violence against "outsiders" who are perceived as threatening the integrity of the nation. Nationalism is connected to violence in a number of ways. First, it generates conceptual and psychological dichotomies that tend to encourage political acts of violence. Second, it is involved in a struggle for political autonomy understood as the control over the instruments of coercion and the regulation of territory. The third form of nationalist violence concerns the pivotal role of warfare in the historical development of nation-states. Our section on violence and nationalism includes contributions that address these points with reference to the recent outbursts of nationalist violence around the globe.

The section starts off with **Mary Kaldor**'s 1993 investigation of the violent emergence of the "new nationalism" in Europe after the collapse of the Soviet Union in 1991. Arguing that the language of Marxism-Leninism in Eastern Europe never displaced the language of nationalism as a legitimizing principle, Kaldor offers a comprehensive explanation of the causes of the "new nationalism" and its mobilizing potential. Examining the "symbolic violence" inherent in such nationalist discourses, the author holds out hope for the revival of civil society through the efforts of transnational organizations like Amnesty International, Greenpeace, Helsinki-Watch, and Oxfam. These groups, she suggests, should cooperate with domestic trade unions, churches, and academic institutions. While stating that the new nationalism represents a limited reaction to "the oppressive nature of modernity," Kaldor never underestimates its capacity to split Eastern Europe into "small, autarchic, authoritarian, poor states" pervaded by endemic and continuous violence.

The Israeli political theorist **Yael Tamir** examines the nationalist imperative of risking one's life for the sake of the nation-state. In her view, nationalism carries a dual message of love for the nation and hostility for the Other. The ideological power of this message is especially obvious in times of war, when internal devotion and external animosity must be intensified and when the deadly cost of such attitudes is incurred. While it is commonly claimed that nations need states to secure their existence, Tamir's article suggests that the reverse is also true: "Nationalism should therefore not be seen as the pathology infecting modern liberal states but as an answer to the legitimate needs of self-defense or, to put it in even more dramatic terms, as a remedy to their malaise—namely, the atomism, neurosis, and alienation that inflict liberal states and may leave them defenseless." Her essay closes with a discussion of the strategies employed by the state to help individuals overcome their fear of death and convince them to risk their lives for the state.

The Indian anthropologist **Arjun Appadurai** offers a postcolonial perspective on the future of nationalism in the context of economic and cultural globalization. Inveighing against the view that the violence and the terror surrounding the breakdown of many existing nation-states are signs of reversion to innate, primordialist sentiments, the author considers nationalism and its institutions as socially constructed, cultural products. Appadurai cites as evidence the nationalist rhetoric of leaders who gradually construct the "nation" as a tenuous collective project. Hence, the violence employed by many recent ethnonationalist movements should not be seen as an "innate" product of our biology, but the social effect of large-scale interactions between and within nation-states. For Appadurai, nationalist violence is not so much explosive as implosive. That is, nationalism energizes local issues and implodes into various forms of violence, including the most brutal ones. In the final part of his essay, the author explores whether a postnational politics can be built in an increasingly multicultural world dominated by a single hegemon: the United States.

We close our section on violence and nationalism with a particularly salient essay by **Akbar Ahmed**, a British-Pakistani social scientist who examines the most brutal form of nationalist violence—genocide. Focusing on a number of specific cases, including the practice of "ethnic cleansing" in the recent civil war in the former Yugoslavia, the author explains nationalist violence as a consequence of the challenge to the project of modernity. Although ethnic cleansing is itself not a new phenomenon, developments in the mass media allow it to play a crucial role in influencing people in the perception of culture. Hatred of the enemy, defined simply in ethnic or religious terms, is heightened through the use of television. Ahmed suggests that cases of ethnic cleansing need to be evaluated in a global framework that encourages the development of new interdisciplinary, cross-cultural approaches to the study of nationalist violence, including its more subtle but equally tragic forms resulting from racism and exclusivist immigration policies.

VI. VIOLENCE AND CLASS

Our section on violence and class examines in detail the structural violence of capitalism as it relates to existing inequalities in private property and political power. Because of its powerful and far-reaching ability to perpetuate invidious class distinctions, to constrain the individual's social range of choices, and to limit the opportunity to develop a reflective and mindful personality, the capitalist production process assumes central importance in the analyses of the contributors. Many agree that, since they operate beyond social accountability, market forces tend to thwart reciprocity and solidarity. This is not to deny the obvious benefits of market mechanisms like the indication of demand or their ever-increasing ability to satisfy needs. Rather, as some contributors to this section argue, a *praxis*-oriented critique of the violence inherent in the market economy starts with an emphasis on the market's partiality in allocating goods and services; its tendency to ignore two-thirds of the world's population and to live off this inequality; its disregard for non-quantifiable, "useless" affinities like poetry, imagination, or cultural diversity; and its devastating effect on the planet's ecological balance and natural riches.

We start with an excerpt from *Reflections on Violence*, **George Sorel**'s famous 1906 syndicalist inquiry into the relationship between socialism and proletarian violence. Rejecting the deterministic character of Marxism as a "science," the French political thinker instead emphasizes the importance of "myths" capable of inspiring the working class to action. Sorel celebrates the mobilizing force of violence conjured up in the "myth of the general strike," which allows the revolutionary working class to challenge the rule of the bourgeoisie. Influenced by Friedrich Nietzsche's call for "transvaluation of all values," Sorel argues for the development of an ethic of proletarian grandeur that would contribute to the establishment of a "new socialism." Sorel's reflections on violence not only impacted a generation of socialist thinkers but also proved to be highly influential in the development of fascist ideology.

A key figure in the "Frankfurt School" of Social Research in Weimar Germany, **Herbert Marcuse** emerged as a prominent spokesman and theorist of the American New Left in the 1960s and 1970s. Deeply influenced by Marx and Freud, his writings reflect his attempts to enlist utopian ideals in the struggle to create a democratic-socialist society. In his speech, "Liberation from the Affluent Society," included in this section, Marcuse asserts the importance of those radical cultural currents that seemed to constitute a "great refusal" of the competitive, materialistic, and bellicose values of advanced industrial society. In his lecture, he formulates a dialectic of liberation from the structural violence of capitalism and its institutions and mechanisms of manipulation, indoctrination, and repression. While maintaining his focus on the importance of the working class for revolutionary transformation, he also suggests the integration of other marginalized groups—students, ethnic minorities, and women—in the struggle against social inequality. Marcuse ends his powerful speech with a discussion of the violent nature of revolutionary social change and the role of the intelligentsia in this process.

Born in 1885 in Budapest, Hungary, **Georg Lukács** enjoyed a long and tumultuous life as a social philosopher, literary critic, and leader in the Hungarian Communist movement. In his essay, "Legality and Illegality," written in 1920 and later incorporated into his most significant study, *History and Class Consciousness* (1923), Lukács continues on the theme of revolutionary change from a capitalist order to a socialist one, seeking to make the case for the necessary use of violence as the only realistic means by which to replace the old regime. The core of his essay is taken up with an inquiry into the problem of how best to emancipate the proletariat intellectually and emotionally from a powerful bourgeois ideology whose definitions of "law" and "legality" are rooted in its biased class perspective. Arguing that only the revolutionary process itself can bring about the reform of proletarian consciousness, he suggests that the proletariat employ a double-pronged strategy of using both "legal" and "illegal" methods in its class struggle: "Only this will bring into being the precondition for an untrammeled revolutionary attitude towards law and the state, namely the exposure of the system of law as the brutal power instrument of capitalist oppression." His innovative discussion of the violent nature of the "dictatorship of the proletariat" serves as a powerful conclusion to his essay.

Finally, the contribution of **Manfred B. Steger**, an American political theorist and coeditor of this reader, connects the 1989–91 collapse of Marxism-Leninism in Eastern Europe to two serious theoretical flaws inherent in Marxism. First, he argues that "scientific socialism" lacks insight into the connection between power and violence. The chief problem lies in Marxism's one-dimensional conception of power as an objectifiable mechanism of coercion, applied by historically determined social agents according to strict instrumental rules. As Hannah Arendt points out in the first section, Marxism exhibits a tendency to equate political power with the "organization of violence" and the "effectiveness of command." This perspective leaves out the constructive role of power and ideology understood as negotiation, compliance, and most importantly, "nonviolent" strategies of individual and collective resistance. Second, Steger observes that Marxism's deterministic teleology bypasses and downplays crucial questions of ethics, individual liberty, and political morality. While concluding that Marxism does not provide an adequate vehicle for the project of extending social equality, Steger emphasizes that the central question of socialism remains pertinent for the twenty-first century: "How can we reconcile peace, liberty, socialism, nonviolence, and democracy, while maintaining the highest possible degree of individual freedom and economic equality?"

VII. NONVIOLENT ALTERNATIVES

In a way, the contributions to this section on nonviolent alternatives can be read as responses to the question posed above. Constituting a crucial part of the reader, this segment offers imaginative alternatives to violence authored by some of the most representative proponents of nonviolence. However, we realize that both "violence" and "nonviolence" are value-laden concepts and that they can therefore hardly be disentangled from a specific normative-ethical perspective. Given our normative preference to reduce or eliminate all forms of violence, we based this section on our premise that nonviolence constitutes a regulative ideal that ought to guide social and political actors.

Naturally, we open with excerpts from **Mahatma Gandhi**'s writings outlining the scope, method, and power of nonviolence. Representing the foundation of all modern theories of nonviolence, Gandhi's work has inspired millions to consider *ahimsa* (non-harming) as both an ethical way of life and a strategy for social change. Next, we present some of **Martin Luther King**'s arguments in favor of using Gandhi's nonviolent method in the African American struggle for civil rights. King connects the core idea of nonviolence—that the means must be as pure as the end—to his celebrated discussion of "just laws" and "civil disobedience."

Influenced by King's vision of a "beloved community," the African American intellectual and social activist **bell hooks** imagines a society in which cultural and ethnic differences are maintained alongside "loving ties of care" that bind people together. Her essay develops concrete strategies for the organization of a sustained nonviolent struggle against racism, white power, and economic privilege. Most importantly, she speaks out against the "racist assumption" that there can be no meaningful bonds of intimacy between blacks and whites. Identifying existing currents of conceptual and symbolic violence, bell hooks concludes that successful efforts to create an antiracist society must be based upon a strong commitment to a democratic vision of racial justice and equality.

The Burmese human-rights activist and 1991 Nobel Peace Prize winner **Aung San Suu Kyi** explores the relationship between power, violence, and fear. The leader of Burma's League for Democracy, Suu Kyi was detained for six years by her country's ruling military junta as a "political subversive," despite an overwhelming victory by her party in 1990. Focusing on the importance of remaining uncorrupted in an environment in which fear is an integral part of everyday existence, Suu Kyi argues that nonviolence must be based on the virtue of fearlessness, cultivated through the habit of refusing to let fear of repression and suffering dictate one's political actions. Like Gandhi, she derives the energies necessary for nonviolent forms of resistance from a "revolution of the spirit," born of an "intellectual conviction of the need for change in those mental attitudes and values which shape the course of a nation's development."

Next, **Gene Sharp**, the senior scholar-in-residence at the Albert Einstein Institution in Cambridge, Massachusetts, and one of the most prominent exponents of the nonviolent method in the United States, explores the potential role of nonviolent struggle in advancing the goals of justice, freedom, and peace. After a long section outlining the nature of nonviolent struggles, Sharp surveys the official statements by several Christian churches and ecumenical bodies on the potential contributions of nonviolent action to achieve these objectives. Considering the role of churches to be crucial in a successful transformation of violence, Sharp notes that "one of the major problems in political ethics and moral theology is rooted in the use of violence for political objectives." Hence, his essay represents the attempt to convince religious and secular leaders who respect Christian thinking of the practical potential of nonviolent struggle for human liberation.

In the final contribution to this reader, **Jennifer Turpin** and **Lester Kurtz**, two American sociologists, turn their attention to the implications of nonviolent alternatives for current public policy debates. The authors emphasize that issues of personal and global violence can only be "untangled" by rethinking the pervasive use of violence in contemporary cultures. In other words, scholars need to expand their efforts to find solutions to the problems created by violence that go beyond widespread sentiments that violence can only be met with more violence. In order to learn more about violence and its alternatives, they suggest that researchers must find ways to overcome four major problems. First, funding now available for research on violence needs to be increased and diversified; second, instead of proposing quick technical fixes, researchers must address fundamental issues; third, current research must abandon its conceptual reliance on a peace-through-strength paradigm; and, fourth, we must find ways to complement a conservative approach to data collection and analysis with solid normative research designs that explore new ideas. Indeed, the editors of this reader join Turpin and Kurtz in their call to invigorate and broaden the debate on violence and its alternatives.

SECTION ONE

Violence: Definitions and Concepts

CHAPTER 1

Excerpt from On Violence

By Hannah Arendt

It is against the background of these experiences that I propose to raise the question of violence in the political realm. This is not easy; what Sorel remarked sixty years ago, "The problems of violence still remain very obscure,"[1] is as true today as it was then. I mentioned the general reluctance to deal with violence as a phenomenon in its own right, and I must now qualify this statement. If we turn to discussions of the phenomenon of power, we soon find that there exists a consensus among political theorists from Left to Right to the effect that violence is nothing more than the most flagrant manifestation of power. "All politics is a struggle for power; the ultimate kind of power is violence," said C. Wright Mills, echoing, as it were, Max Weber's definition of the state as "the rule of men over men based on the means of legitimate, that is allegedly legitimate, violence."[2] The consensus is very strange; for to equate political power with "the organization of violence" makes sense only if one follows Marx's estimate of the state as an instrument of oppression in the hands of the ruling class. Let us therefore turn to authors who do not believe that the body politic and its laws and institutions are merely coercive superstructures, secondary manifestations of some underlying forces. Let us turn, for instance, to Bertrand de Jouvenel, whose book *Power* is perhaps the most prestigious and, anyway, the most interesting recent treatise on the subject. "To him," he writes, "who contemplates the unfolding of the ages war presents itself as an activity of States *which pertains to their essence*."[3] This may prompt us to ask whether the end of warfare, then, would mean the end of states. Would the disappearance of violence in relationships between states spell the end of power?

The answer, it seems, will depend on what we understand by power. And power, it turns out, is an instrument of rule, while rule, we are told, owes its existence to "the instinct of domination."[4] We are immediately reminded of what Sartre said about violence when we read in Jouvenel that "a man feels himself more of a man when he is imposing himself and making others the instruments of his will," which gives him "incomparable pleasure."[5] "Power," said Voltaire, "consists in making others act as I choose"; it is present wherever I have the chance "to assert my own will against the resistance" of others, said Max Weber, reminding us of Clausewitz's definition of war as "an act of violence to compel the opponent to do as we wish." The word, we are told by Strausz-Hupé, signifies "the power of man over man."[6] To go back to Jouvenel: "To command and to be obeyed: without that, there is no Power—with it no other attribute is needed for it to be. . . . The thing without which it cannot be: that essence is command."[7] If the essence of power is the effectiveness of command, then there is no greater power than that which I grows out of the barrel of a gun, and it would be difficult to say in "which way the order given by a policeman is different from that given by a gunman."[8] Should everybody from Right to Left, from Bertrand de Jouvenel to Mao Tse-tung agree on so basic a point in political philosophy as the nature of power?

In terms of our traditions of political thought, these definitions have much to recommend them. Not only do they derive from the old notion of absolute power that accompanied the rise of the sovereign European nation-state, whose earliest and still greatest spokesmen were Jean Bodin, in sixteenth-century France, and Thomas Hobbes, in seventeenth-century England; they also coincide with the terms used since Greek antiquity to define the forms of government as the rule of man over man—of one or the few in monarchy and oligarchy, of the best or the many in aristocracy and democracy. Today we ought to add the latest and perhaps most formidable form of such dominion: bureaucracy or the rule of an intricate system of bureaus in which no men, neither one nor the best, neither the few nor the many, can be held responsible, and which could be properly called rule by Nobody. (If, in accord with traditional political thought, we identify tyranny as government that is not held to give account of itself, rule by Nobody is clearly the most tyrannical of all, since there is no one left who could even be asked to answer for what is being done. It is this state of affairs, making it impossible to localize responsibility and to identify the enemy, that is among the most potent causes of the current worldwide rebellious unrest, its chaotic nature, and its dangerous tendency to get out of control and to run amuck.)

Moreover, this ancient vocabulary was strangely confirmed and fortified by the addition of the Hebrew-Christian tradition and its "imperative conception of law." This concept was not invented by the "political realists" but was, rather, the result of a much earlier, almost automatic generalization of God's "Commandments," according to which "the simple relation of command and obedience" indeed sufficed to identify the essence of law.[9] Finally, more modern scientific and philosophical convictions concerning man's nature have further strengthened these legal and political traditions. The many recent discoveries of an inborn instinct of domination and an innate aggressiveness in the human animal were preceded by very similar philosophic statements. According to John Stuart Mill, "the first lesson of civilization [is] that of obedience," and he speaks of "the two states of the inclinations . . . one the desire to exercise power over others; the other . . . disinclination to have power exercised over themselves."[10] If we would trust our own experiences in these matters, we should know that the instinct of submission, an ardent desire to obey and be ruled by some strong man, is at least as prominent in human psychology as the will to power, and, politically, perhaps more relevant. The old adage "How fit he is to sway / That can so well obey," some version of which seems to have been known to all centuries and all nations,[11] may point to a psychological truth: namely, that the will to power and the will to submission are interconnected. "Ready submission to tyranny," to use Mill once more, is by no means always caused by "extreme passiveness." Conversely, a strong disinclination to obey is often accompanied by an equally strong disinclination to dominate and command. Historically speaking, the ancient institution of slave economy would be inexplicable on the grounds of Mill's psychology. Its express purpose was to liberate citizens from the burden of household affairs and to permit them to enter the public life of the community, where all were equals; if it were true that nothing is sweeter than to give commands and to rule others, the master would never have left his household.

However, there exists another tradition and another vocabulary no less old and time-honored. When the Athenian city-state called its constitution an isonomy, or the Romans spoke of the *civitas* as their form of government, they had in mind a concept of power and law whose essence did not rely on the command-obedience relationship and which did not identify power and rule or law and command. It was to these examples that the men of the eighteenth-century revolutions turned when they ransacked the archives of antiquity and constituted a form of government, a republic, where the rule of law, resting on the power of the people, would put an end to the rule of man over man, which they thought was a "government fit for slaves." They too, unhappily, still talked about obedience—obedience to laws instead of men; but what they actually meant was support of the laws to which the citizenry had given its consent.[12] Such support is never unquestioning, and as far as reliability is concerned it cannot match the indeed "unquestioning obedience" that an act of violence can exact—the obedience every criminal can count on when he snatches my pocketbook with the help of a knife or robs a bank with the help of a gun. It is the people's support that lends power to the institutions of a country, and this support is but the continuation of the consent that brought the laws into existence to begin with. Under conditions of representative government the people are supposed to rule those who govern them. All political institutions are manifestations and materializations of power; they petrify and decay as soon as the living power of the people ceases to uphold them. This is what Madison meant when he said "all governments rest on opinion," a word no less true for the various forms of monarchy than for democracies. ("To suppose that majority rule functions only in democracy is a fantastic illusion," as Jouvenel points out: "The king, who is but one solitary individual, stands far more in need of the general support of Society than any other form of government."[13] Even the tyrant, the One who rules against all, needs helpers in the business of violence, though their number may be rather restricted.) However, the strength of opinion, that is, the power of the government, depends on numbers; it is "in proportion to the number with which it is associated,"[14] and tyranny, as Montesquieu discovered, is therefore the most violent and least powerful of forms of government." Indeed one of the most obvious distinctions between power and violence is that power always stands in need of numbers, whereas violence up to a point can manage without them because it relies on implements. A legally unrestricted majority rule, that is, a democracy without a constitution, can be very formidable in the suppression of the rights of minorities and very effective in the suffocation of dissent without any use of violence. But that does not mean that violence and power are the same.

The extreme form of power is All against One, the extreme form of violence is One against All. And this latter is never possible without instruments. To claim, as is often done, that a tiny unarmed minority has successfully, by means of violence—shouting, kicking up a row, et cetera—disrupted large lecture classes whose overwhelming majority had voted for normal instruction procedures is therefore very misleading. (In a recent case at some German university there was even one lonely "dissenter" among several hundred students who could claim such a strange victory.) What actually happens in such cases is something much more serious: the majority clearly refuses to use its power and overpower the disrupters; the academic processes break down because no one is willing to raise more than a voting finger for the *status quo*. What the universities are up against is the "immense negative unity" of which Stephen Spender speaks in another context. All of which proves only that a minority can have a much greater potential power than one would expect by counting noses in public-opinion polls. The merely onlooking majority, amused by the spectacle of a shouting match between student and professor, is in fact already the latent ally of the minority. (One need only imagine what would have happened had one or a few unarmed Jews in pre-Hitler Germany tried to disrupt the lecture of an anti-Semitic professor in order to understand the absurdity of the talk about the small "minorities of militants.")

It is, I think, a rather sad reflection on the present state of political science that our terminology does not distinguish among such key words as "power," "strength," "force," "authority," and, finally, "violence"—all of which refer to distinct, different phenomena and would hardly exist unless they did. (In the words of d'Entréves, "might, power, authority: these are all words to whose exact implications no great weight is attached in current speech; even the greatest thinkers sometimes use them at random. Yet it is fair to presume that they refer to different properties, and their meaning should therefore be carefully assessed and examined. . . . The correct use of these words is a question not only of logical grammar, but of historical perspective.")[15] To use them as synonyms not only indicates a certain deafness to linguistic meanings, which would be serious enough, but it has also resulted in a kind of blindness to the realities they correspond to. In such a situation it is always tempting to introduce new definitions, but—though I shall briefly yield to temptation—what is involved is not simply a matter of careless speech. Behind the apparent confusion is a firm conviction in whose light all distinctions would be, at best, of minor importance: the conviction that the most crucial political issue is, and always has been, the question of Who rules Whom? Power, strength, force, authority, violence—these are but words to indicate the means by which man rules over man; they are held to be synonyms because they have the same function. It is only after one ceases to reduce public affairs to the business of dominion that the original data in the realm of human affairs will appear, or, rather, reappear, in their authentic diversity.

These data, in our context, may be enumerated as follows:

Power corresponds to the human ability not just to act but to act in concert. Power is never the property of an individual; it belongs to a group and remains in existence only so long as the group keeps together. When we say of somebody that he is "in power" we actually refer to his being empowered by a certain number of people to act in their name. The moment the group, from which the power originated to begin with (*potestas in populo*, without a people or group there is no power), disappears, "his power" also vanishes. In current usage, when we speak of a "powerful man" or a "powerful personality," we already use the word "power" metaphorically; what we refer to without metaphor is "strength."

Strength unequivocally designates something in the singular, an individual entity; it is the property inherent in an object or person and belongs to its character, which may prove itself in relation to other things or persons, but is essentially independent of them. The strength of even the strongest individual can always be overpowered by the many, who often will combine for no other purpose than to ruin strength precisely because of its peculiar independence. The almost instinctive hostility of the many toward the one has always, from Plato to Nietzsche, been ascribed to resentment, to the envy of the weak for the strong, but this psychological interpretation misses the point. It is in the nature of a group and its power to turn against independence, the property of individual strength.

Force, which we often use in daily speech as a synonym for violence, especially if violence serves as a means of coercion, should be reserved, in terminological language, for the "forces of nature" or the "force of circumstances" (*la force des choses*), that is, to indicate the energy released by physical or social movements.

Authority, relating to the most elusive of these phenomena and therefore, as a term, most frequently abused,[16] can be vested in persons—there is such a thing as personal authority, as, for instance, in the relation between parent and child, between teacher and pupil—or it can be vested in offices, as, for instance, in the Roman *senate* (*auctoritas in senatu*) or in the hierarchical offices of the Church (a priest can grant valid absolution even though he is drunk). Its hallmark is unquestioning recognition by those who are asked to obey; neither coercion nor persuasion is needed. (A father can lose his authority either by beating his child or by starting to argue with him, that is, either by behaving to him like a tyrant or by treating him as an equal.) To remain in authority requires respect for the person or the office. The greatest enemy of authority, therefore, is contempt, and the surest way to undermine it is laughter.[17]

Violence, finally, as I have said, is distinguished by its instrumental character. Phenomenologically, it is close to strength, since the implements of violence, like all other tools, are designed and used for the purpose of multiplying natural strength until, in the last stage of their development, they can substitute for it.

It is perhaps not superfluous to add that these distinctions, though by no means arbitrary, hardly ever correspond to watertight compartments in the real world, from which nevertheless they are drawn. Thus institutionalized power in organized communities often appears in the guise of authority, demanding instant, unquestioning recognition: no society could function without it. (A small, and still isolated, incident in New York shows what can happen if authentic authority in social relations has broken down to the point where it cannot work any longer even in its derivative, purely functional form. A minor mishap in the subway system—the doors on a train failed to operate—turned into a serious shutdown on the line lasting four hours and involving more than fifty thousand passengers, because when the transit authorities asked the passengers to leave the defective train, they simply refused.)[18] Moreover, nothing, as we shall see, is more common than the combination of violence and power, nothing less frequent than to find them in their pure and therefore extreme form. From this, it does not follow that authority, power, and violence are all the same.

Still it must be admitted that it is particularly tempting to think of power in terms of command and obedience, and hence to equate power with violence, in a discussion of what actually is only one of power's special cases—namely, the power of government. Since in foreign relations as well as domestic affairs violence appears as a last resort to keep the power structure intact against individual challengers—the foreign enemy, the native criminal—it looks indeed as though violence were the prerequisite of power and power nothing but a facade, the velvet glove which either conceals the iron hand or will turn out to belong to a paper tiger. On closer inspection, though, this notion loses much of its plausibility. For our purpose, the gap between theory and reality is perhaps best illustrated by the phenomenon of revolution.

Since the beginning of the century theoreticians of revolution have told us that the chances of revolution have significantly decreased in proportion to the increased destructive capacities of weapons at the unique disposition of governments.[19] The history of the last seventy years, with its extraordinary record of successful and unsuccessful revolutions, tells a different story. Were people mad who even tried against such overwhelming odds? And, leaving out instances of full success, how can even a temporary success be explained? The fact is that the gap between state-owned means of violence and what people can muster by themselves—from beer bottles to Molotov cocktails and guns—has always been so enormous that technical improvements make hardly any difference. Textbook instructions on "how to make a revolution" in a step-by-step progression from dissent to conspiracy, from resistance to armed uprising, are all based on the mistaken notion that revolutions are "made." In a contest of violence against violence the superiority of the government has always been absolute; but this superiority lasts only as long as the power structure of the government is intact—that is, as long as commands are obeyed and the army or police forces are prepared to use their weapons. When this is no longer the case, the situation changes abruptly. Not only is the rebellion not put down, but the arms themselves change hands—sometimes, as in the Hungarian revolution, within a few hours. (We should know about such things after all these years of futile fighting in Vietnam, where for a long time, before getting massive Russian aid, the National Liberation Front fought us with weapons that were made in the United States.) Only after this has happened, when the disintegration of the government in power has permitted the rebels to arm themselves, can one speak of an "armed uprising," which often does not take place at all or occurs when it is no longer necessary. Where commands are no longer obeyed, the means of violence are of no use; and the question of this obedience is not decided by the command-obedience relation but by opinion, and, of course, by the number of those who share it. Everything depends on the power behind the violence. The sudden dramatic breakdown of power that ushers in revolutions reveals in a flash how civil obedience—to laws, to rulers, to institutions—is but the outward manifestation of support and consent.

Where power has disintegrated, revolutions are possible but not necessary. We know of many instances when utterly impotent regimes were permitted to continue in existence for long periods of time—either because there was no one to test their strength and reveal their weakness or because they were lucky enough not to be engaged in war and suffer defeat. Disintegration often becomes manifest only in direct confrontation; and even then, when power is already in the street, some group of men prepared for such an eventuality is needed to pick it up and assume responsibility. We have recently witnessed how it did not take more than the relatively harmless, essentially nonviolent French students' rebellion to reveal the vulnerability of the whole political system, which rapidly disintegrated before the astonished eyes of the young rebels. Unknowingly they had tested it; they intended only to challenge the ossified university system, and down came the system of governmental power, together with that of the huge party bureaucracies—"*une sorte de désintégration de routes les hiérarchies*."[20] It was a textbook case of a revolutionary situation[21] that did not develop into a revolution because there was nobody, least of all the students, prepared to seize power and the responsibility that goes with it. Nobody except, of course, de Gaulle. Nothing was more characteristic of the seriousness of the situation than his appeal to the army, his journey to see Massu and the generals in Germany, a walk to Canossa, if there ever was one, in view of what had happened only a few years before. But what he sought and received was support, not obedience, and the means were not commands but concessions.[22] If commands had been enough, he would never have had to leave Paris.

No government exclusively based on the means on violence has ever existed. Even the totalitarian ruler, whose chief instrument of rule is torture, needs a power basis—the secret police and its net of informers. Only the development of robot soldiers, which, as previously mentioned, would eliminate the human factor completely and, conceivably, permit one man with a push button to destroy whomever he pleased, could change this fundamental ascendancy of power over violence. Even the most despotic domination we know of, the rule of master over slaves, who always outnumbered him, did not rest on superior means of coercion as such, but on a superior organization of power—that is, on the organized solidarity of the masters.[23] Single men without others to support them never have enough power to use violence successfully. Hence, in domestic affairs, violence functions as the last resort of power against criminals or rebels—that is, against single individuals who, as it were, refuse to be overpowered by the consensus of the majority. And as for actual warfare, we have seen in Vietnam how an enormous superiority in the means of violence can become helpless if confronted with an ill-equipped but well-organized opponent who is much more powerful. This lesson, to be sure, was there to be learned from the history of guerrilla warfare, which is at least as old as the defeat in Spain of Napoleon's still unvanquished army.

To switch for a moment to conceptual language: Power is indeed of the essence of all government, but violence is not. Violence is by nature instrumental; like all means, it always stands in need of guidance and justification through the end it pursues. And what needs justification by something else cannot be the essence of anything. The end of war—end taken in its twofold meaning—is peace or victory; but to the question And what is the end of peace? there is no answer. Peace is an absolute, even though in recorded history periods of warfare have nearly always outlasted periods of peace. Power is in the same category; it is, as they say, "an end in itself." (This, of course, is not to deny that governments pursue policies and employ their power to achieve prescribed goals. But the power structure itself precedes and outlasts all aims, so that power, far from being the means to an end, is actually the very condition enabling a group of people to think and act in terms of the means-end category.) And since government is essentially organized and institutionalized power, the current question What is the end of government? does not make much sense either. The answer will be either question-begging—to enable men to live together—or dangerously utopian—to promote happiness or to realize a classless society or some other nonpolitical ideal, which if tried out in earnest cannot but end in some kind of tyranny.

Power needs no justification, being inherent in the very existence of political communities; what it does need is legitimacy. The common treatment of these two words as synonyms is no less misleading and confusing than the current equation of obedience and support. Power springs up whenever people get together and act in concert, but it derives its legitimacy from the initial getting together rather than from any action that then may follow. Legitimacy, when challenged, bases itself on an appeal to the past, while justification relates to an end that lies in the future. Violence can be justifiable, but it never will be legitimate. Its justification loses in plausibility the farther its intended end recedes into the future. No one questions the use of violence in self-defense, because the danger is not only clear but also present, and the end justifying the means is immediate.

Power and violence, though they are distinct phenomena, usually appear together. Wherever they are combined, power, we have found, is the primary and predominant factor. The situation, however, is entirely different when we deal with them in their pure states—as, for instance, with foreign invasion and occupation. We saw that the current equation of violence with owner rests on government's being understood as domination of man over man by means of violence. If a foreign conqueror is confronted by an impotent government and by a nation unused to the exercise of political power, it is easy for him to achieve such domination. In all other cases the difficulties are great indeed, and the occupying invader will try immediately to establish Quisling governments, that is, to find a native power base to support his dominion. The head-on clash between Russian tanks and the entirely nonviolent resistance of the Czechoslovak people is a textbook case of a confrontation between violence and power in their pure states. But while domination in such an instance is difficult to achieve, it is not impossible. Violence, we must remember, does not depend on numbers or opinions, but on implements, and the implements of violence, as I mentioned before, like all other tools, increase and multiply human strength. Those who oppose violence with mere power will soon find that they are confronted not by men but by men's artifacts, whose inhumanity and destructive effectiveness increase in proportion to the distance separating the opponents. Violence can always destroy power; out of the barrel of a gun grows the most effective command, resulting in the most instant and perfect obedience. What never can grow out of it is power.

In a head-on clash between violence and power, the outcome is hardly in doubt. If Gandhi's enormously powerful and successful strategy of nonviolent resistance had met with a different enemy—Stalin's Russia, Hitler's Germany, even prewar Japan, instead of England—the outcome would not have been decolonization, but massacre and submission. However, England in India and France in Algeria had good reasons for their restraint. Rule by sheer violence comes into play where power is being lost; it is precisely the shrinking power of the Russian government, internally and externally, that became manifest in its "solution" of the Czechoslovak problem—just as it was the shrinking power of European imperialism that became manifest in the alternative between decolonization and massacre. To substitute violence for power can bring victory, but the price is very high; for it is not only paid by the vanquished, it is also paid by the victor in terms of his own power. This is especially true when the victor happens to enjoy domestically the blessings of constitutional government. Henry Steele Commager is entirely right: "If we subvert world order and destroy world peace we must inevitably subvert and destroy our own political institutions first."[24] The much-feared boomerang effect of the "government of subject races" (Lord Cromer) on the home government during the imperialist era meant that rule by violence in faraway lands would end by affecting the government of England, that the last "subject race" would be the English themselves. The recent gas attack on the campus at Berkeley, where not just tear gas but also another gas, "outlawed by the Geneva Convention and used by the Army to flush out guerrillas in Vietnam," was laid down while gas-masked Guardsmen stopped anybody and everybody "from fleeing the gassed area," is an excellent example of this "backlash" phenomenon. It has often been said that impotence breeds violence, and psychologically this is quite true, at least of persons possessing natural strength, moral or physical. Politically speaking, the point is that loss of power becomes a temptation to substitute violence for power—in 1968 during the Democratic convention in Chicago we could watch this process on television[25]—and that violence itself results in impotence. Where violence is no longer backed and restrained by power, the well-known reversal in reckoning with means and ends has taken place. The means, the means of destruction, now determine the end—with the consequence that the end will be the destruction of all power.

Nowhere is the self-defeating factor in the victory of violence over power more evident than in the use of terror to maintain domination, about whose weird successes and eventual failures we know perhaps more than any generation before us. Terror is not the same as violence; it is, rather, the form of government that comes into being when violence, having destroyed all power, does not abdicate but, on the contrary, remains in full control. It has often been noticed that the effectiveness of terror depends almost entirely on the degree of social atomization. Every kind of organized opposition must disappear before the full force of terror can be let loose. This atomization—an outrageously pale, academic word for the horror it implies—is maintained and intensified through the ubiquity of the informer, who can be literally omnipresent because he no longer is merely a professional agent in the pay of the police but potentially every person one comes into contact with. How such a fully developed police state is established and how it works—or, rather, how nothing works where it holds sway—can now be learned in Aleksandr I. Solzhenitsyn's *The First Circle*, which will probably remain one of the masterpieces of twentieth-century literature and certainly contains the best documentation on Stalin's regime in existence.[26] The decisive difference between totalitarian domination, based on terror, and tyrannies and dictatorships, established by violence, is that the former turns not only against its enemies but against its friends and supporters as well, being afraid of all power, even the power of its friends. The climax of terror is reached when the police state begins to devour its own children, when yesterday's executioner becomes today's victim. And this is also the moment when power disappears entirely. There exist now a great many plausible explanations for the de-Stalinization of Russia—none, I believe, so compelling as the realization by the Stalinist functionaries themselves that a continuation of the regime would lead, not to an insurrection, against which terror is indeed the best safeguard, but to paralysis of the whole country.

To sum up: politically speaking, it is insufficient to say that power and violence are not the same. Power and violence are opposites; where the one rules absolutely, the other is absent. Violence appears where power is in jeopardy, but left to its own course it ends in power's disappearance. This implies that it is not correct to think of the opposite of violence as nonviolence; to speak of nonviolent power is actually redundant. Violence can destroy power; it is utterly incapable of creating it.

CHAPTER 2

On Violence

By Robert Paul Wolff

Everything I shall say in this essay has been said before, and much of it seems to me to be obvious as well as unoriginal. I offer two excuses for laying used goods before you. In the first place, I think that what I have to say about violence is true. Now, there are many ways to speak falsehood and only one to speak truth. It follows, as Kierkegaard pointed out, that the truth is likely to become boring. On a subject as ancient and much discussed as ours today, we may probably assume that a novel—and, hence, interesting—view of violence is likely to be false.

But truth is not my sole excuse, for the subject before us suffers from the same difficulty that Kant discerned in the area of metaphysics. After refuting the various claims that had been made to transcendent rational knowledge of things-in-themselves, Kant remarked that the refutations had no lasting psychological effect on true believers. The human mind, he concluded, possessed a natural disposition to metaphysical speculation, which philosophy must perpetually keep in check. Somewhat analogously, men everywhere are prone to certain beliefs about the legitimacy of political authority, even though their beliefs are as groundless as metaphysical speculations. The most sophisticated of men persist in supposing that some valid distinction can be made between legitimate and illegitimate commands, on the basis of which they can draw a line, for example, between mere violence and the legitimate use of force. This lingering superstition is shared by those dissenters who call police actions or ghetto living conditions "violent"; for they are merely advancing competing legitimacy claims.

I shall set forth and defend *three* propositions about violence:

First: The concept of violence is inherently confused, as is the correlative concept of nonviolence; these and related concepts depend for their meaning in political discussions on the fundamental notion of legitimate authority, which is also inherently incoherent.

Second: It follows that a number of familiar questions are also confusions to which no coherent answers could ever be given, such as: when it is permissible to resort to violence in politics; whether the black movement and the student movement should be nonviolent; and whether anything good in politics is ever accomplished by violence.

Finally: The dispute over violence and nonviolence in contemporary American politics is ideological rhetoric designed either to halt change and justify the existing distribution of power and privilege or to slow change and justify some features of the existing distribution of power and privilege or else to hasten change and justify a total redistribution of power and privilege.

Let us begin with the first proposition, which is essential to my entire discussion.

I

The fundamental concepts of political philosophy are the concepts of power and authority.[1] Power in general is the ability to make and enforce decisions. Political power is the ability to make and enforce decisions about matters of major social importance. Thus the ability to dispose of my private income as I choose is a form of power, whereas the ability to make and enforce a decision about the disposition of some sizable portion of the tax receipts of the federal government is a form of *political power*. (So too is the ability to direct the decisions of a large private corporation; for the exercise of political power is not confined to the sphere of government.) A complete analysis of the concept of political power would involve a classification both of the means employed in the enforcing of decisions and of the scope and variety of questions about which decisions can be made.[2] It would also require an examination of the kinds of opposition against which the decision could be enforced. There is a very considerable difference between the ability a parliamentary majority has to enforce its decisions against the will of the minority and the ability of a rebel military clique to enforce its decisions against the Parliament as a whole.

Authority, by contrast with power, is not an ability but a right. It is the right to command and, correlatively, the right to be obeyed. Claims to authority are made in virtually every area of social life, and, in a remarkably high proportion of cases, the claims are accepted and acquiesced in by those over whom they are made. Parents claim the right to be obeyed by their children; husbands until quite recently claimed the right to be obeyed by their wives; popes claim the right to be obeyed by the laity and clergy; and of course, most notably, virtually all existing governments claim the right to be obeyed by their subjects.

A claim to authority must be sharply differentiated both from a threat or enticement and from a piece of advice. When the state commands, it usually threatens punishment for disobedience, and it may even on occasion offer a reward for compliance, but the command cannot be reduced to the mere threat or reward. What characteristically distinguishes a state from an occupying army or private party is its insistence, either explicit or implicit, on its *right* to be obeyed. By the same token, an authoritative command is not a mere recommendation. Authority says, "Do this!" not, "Let me suggest this for your consideration."

Claims to authority have been defended on a variety of grounds, most prominent among which are the appeal to God, to tradition, to expertise, to the laws of history, and to the consent of those commanded. We tend to forget that John Locke thought it worth while to devote the first of his *Two Treatises on Civil Government* to the claim that Europe's monarchs held their authority by right of primogenitural descent from Adam. It is common today to give lip service to the theory that authority derives from the consent of the governed, but most of us habitually accord *some* weight to any authority claim issuing from a group of men who regularly control the behavior of a population in a territory, particularly if the group tricks itself out with flags, uniforms, courts of law, and printed regulations.

Not all claims to authority are justified. Indeed, I shall suggest shortly that few if any are. Nevertheless, men regularly accept the authority claims asserted against them, and so we must distinguish a descriptive from a normative sense of the term. Let us use the term '*de facto* authority' to refer to *the ability to get one's authority claims accepted by those against whom they are asserted.* '*De jure* authority,' then, will refer to *the right to command* and to be obeyed. Obviously, the concept of *de jure* authority is primary, and the concept of *de facto* authority is derivative.

Thus understood, *de facto* authority is a form of power, for it is a means by which its possessor can enforce his decisions. Indeed, as Max Weber—from whom much of this analysis is taken—has pointed out, *de facto* authority is the principal means on which states rely to carry out their decisions. Threats and inducements play an exceedingly important role in the enforcement of political decisions, to be sure, but a state that must depend upon them entirely will very soon suffer a crippling reduction in its effectiveness, which is to say, in its political power. Modern states especially require for the successful prosecution of their programs an extremely high level of coordination of the behavior of large numbers of individuals. The myth of legitimacy is the only efficient means available to the state for achieving that coordination.

Force is the ability to work some change in the world by the expenditure of physical effort. A man may root up a tree, move a stalled car, drive a nail, or restrain another man, *by force.* Force, in and of itself, is morally neutral. Physically speaking, there may be very little difference between the physical effort of a doctor who resets a dislocated shoulder and that of the ruffian who dislocated it. Sometimes, of course, force is used to work some change in the body of another man—to punch him, shoot him, take out his appendix, hold his arms, or cut his hair. But there is in principle no significant distinction between these uses of force and those uses which involve changing some other part of the world about which he cares. A man who slips into a parking place for which I am heading inflicts an injury on me roughly as great as if he had jostled me in a crowd or stepped on my toe. If he destroys a work of art on which I have lavished my most intense creative efforts, he may harm me more than a physical assault would.

Force is a means to power, but it is not of course a guarantee of power. If I wish to elicit hard work from my employees, I can threaten them with the lash or tempt them with bonuses—both of which are employments of force—but if my workers prefer not to comply, my threats and inducements may be fruitless. It is a commonplace both of domestic and of international politics that the mere possession of a monopoly of force is no guarantee of political power. Those who fail to grasp this truth are repeatedly frustrated by the baffling inability of the strong to impose their will upon the weak.

There are, so far as I can see, *three* means or instruments by which power is exercised—three ways, that is to say, in which men enforce or carry out their social decisions. The first is force, the ability to rearrange the world in ways that other men find appealing or distasteful. In modern society, money is of course the principal measure, exchange medium, and symbol of force. The second instrument of power is *de facto* authority—the ability to elicit obedience, as opposed to mere compliance, from others. *De facto* authority frequently accrues to those with a preponderance of force, for men are fatally prone to suppose that he who can compel compliance deserves obedience. But *de facto* authority does not reduce to the possession of a preponderance of force, for men habitually obey commands they know could not effectively be enforced. The third instrument of power is social opinion, or what might be called the "symbolic" use of force. When a runner competes in a race, he may want the first-prize money or the commercial endorsements that will come to the winner, or he may even just like blue ribbons—but he may also want the acclaim of the fans. Now, that acclaim is expressed by certain uses of force—by clapping of hands and cheering, which are physical acts. But its value to the runner is symbolic; he cherishes it as an expression of approval, not merely as a pleasing sound. To say that man is a social creature is not merely to say that he hangs out in groups, nor even to say that he engages in collective and cooperative enterprises for self-interested purposes; it is most importantly to say that he values symbolic interactions with other men and is influenced by them as well as by the ordinary exercise of force and by claims of authority. This point is important for our discussion, for, as we shall see, many persons who shrink from the use of force as an instrument of political power have no compunctions about the use of social opinion or what I have called the "symbolic" use of force. Anyone who has observed a progressive classroom by a teacher with scruples of this sort will know that a day "in coventry" can be a far crueler punishment for an unruly ten-year old than a sharp rap on the knuckles with a ruler.

We come, finally, to the concept of violence. Strictly speaking, *violence is the illegitimate or unauthorized use of force to effect decisions against the will or desire of others.* Thus, murder is an act of violence, but capital punishment *by a legitimate state* is not; theft or extortion is violent, but the collection of taxes *by a legitimate state* is not. Clearly, on this interpretation the concept of violence is normative as well as descriptive, for it involves an implicit appeal to the principle of *de jure* legitimate authority. There is an associated sense of the term which is purely descriptive, relying on the descriptive notion of *de facto* authority. Violence in this latter sense is the use of force in ways that are proscribed or unauthorized by those who are generally accepted as the legitimate authorities in the territory. Descriptively speaking, the attack on Hitler's life during the second World War was an act of violence, but one might perfectly well deny that it was violent in the strict sense, on the grounds that Hitler's regime was illegitimate. On similar grounds, it is frequently said that police behavior toward workers or ghetto dwellers or demonstrators is violent even when it is clearly within the law, for the authority issuing the law is illegitimate.

It is common, but I think wrong-headed, to restrict the term 'violence' to uses of force that involve bodily interference or the direct infliction of physical injury. Carrying a dean out of his office is said to be violent, but not seizing his office when he is absent and locking him out. Physically tearing a man's wallet from his pocket is "violent," but swindling him out of the same amount of money is not. There is a natural enough basis for this distinction. Most of us value our lives and physical well-being above other goods that we enjoy, and we tend therefore to view attacks or threats on our person as different in kind from other sorts of harm we might suffer. Nevertheless, the distinction is not sufficiently sharp to be of any analytical use, and, as we shall see later, it usually serves the ideological purpose of ruling out, as immoral or politically illegitimate, the only instrument of power that is available to certain social classes.

In its strict or normative sense, then, the concept of political violence depends upon the concept of *de jure*, or legitimate authority. If there is no such thing as legitimate political authority, then it is impossible to distinguish between legitimate and illegitimate uses of force. Now, of course, under any circumstances, we can distinguish between right and wrong, justified and unjustified, uses of force. Such a distinction belongs to moral philosophy in general, and our choice of the criteria by which we draw the distinction will depend on our theory of value and obligation. But the distinctive political concept of violence can be given a coherent meaning only by appeal to a doctrine of legitimate political authority.

On the basis of a lengthy reflection upon the concept of *de jure* legitimate authority, I have come to the conclusion that philosophical anarchism is true. That is to say, I believe that there is not, and there could not be, a state that has a right to command and whose subjects have a binding obligation to obey. I have defended this view in detail elsewhere, and I can only indicate here the grounds of my conviction.[3] Briefly, I think it can be shown that every man has a fundamental duty to be autonomous, in Kant's sense of the term. Each of us must make himself the author of his actions and take responsibility for them by refusing to act save on the basis of reasons he can see for himself to be good. Autonomy, thus understood, is in direct opposition to obedience, which is submission to the will of another, irrespective of reason. Following Kant's usage, political obedience is heteronymy of the will.

Now, political theory offers us one great argument designed to make the autonomy of the individual compatible with submission to the putative authority of the state. In a democracy, it is claimed, the citizen is both law-giver and law-obeyer. Since he shares in the authorship of the laws, he submits to his own will in obeying them, and hence is autonomous, not heteronymous.

If this argument were valid, it would provide a genuine ground for a distinction between violent and nonviolent political actions. Violence would be a use of force proscribed by the laws or executive authority of a genuinely democratic state. The only possible justification of illegal or extralegal political acts would be a demonstration of the illegitimacy of the state, and this in turn would involve showing that the commands of the state were not expressions of the will of the people.

But the classic defense of democracy is *not* valid. For a variety of reasons, neither majority rule nor any other method of making decisions in the absence of unanimity can be shown to preserve the autonomy of the individual citizens. In a democracy, as in any state, obedience is heteronymy. The autonomous man is of necessity as anarchist. Consequently, there is no valid *political* criterion for the justified use of force. Legality is, by itself, no justification. Now, of course, there are all manner of utilitarian arguments for submitting to the state and its agents, even if the state's claim to legitimacy is unfounded. The laws may command actions that are in fact morally obligatory or whose effects promise to be beneficial. Widespread submission to law may bring about a high level of order, regularity, and predictability in social relationships which is valuable independently of the particular character of the acts commanded. But in and of themselves, the acts of police and the commands of legislatures have no peculiar legitimacy or sanction. Men everywhere and always impute authority to established governments, and they are always wrong to do so.

II

The foregoing remarks are quite banal, to be sure. Very few serious students of politics will maintain either the democratic theory of legitimate authority or any alternatives to it. Nevertheless, like post-theological, demythologized Protestants who persist in raising prayers to a God they no longer believe in, modern men go on exhibiting a superstitious belief in the authority of the state. Consider, for example, a question now much debated: When is it permissible to resort to violence in politics? If 'violence' is taken to mean an *unjustified* use of force, then the answer to the question is obviously *never*. If the use of force were permissible, it would not, by definition, be violence, and if it were violent, it would not, by definition, be permissible. If 'violence' is taken in the strict sense to mean "an illegitimate or unauthorized use of force," then *every* political act, whether by private parties or by agents of the state, is violent, for there is no such thing as legitimate authority. If 'violence' is construed in the restricted sense as "bodily interference or the direct infliction of physical harm," then the obvious but correct rule is to resort to violence when less harmful or costly means fail, providing always that the balance of good and evil produced is superior to that promised by any available alternative.

These answers are all trivial, but that is precisely my point. Once the concept of violence is seen to rest on the unfounded distinction between legitimate and illegitimate political authority, the question of the appropriateness of violence simply dissolves. It is mere superstition to describe a policeman's beating of a helpless suspect as "an excessive use of force" while characterizing an attack by a crowd on the policeman as "a resort to violence." The implication of such a distinction is that the policeman, as the duly appointed representative of a legitimate government, has a right to use physical force, although no right to use "excessive" force, whereas the crowd of private citizens has no right at all to use even moderate physical force. But there are no legitimate governments, hence no special rights attaching to soldiers, policemen, magistrates, or other law-enforcement agents, hence no coherent distinction between violence and the legitimate use of force.

Consider, as a particular example, the occupation of buildings and the student strike at Columbia University during April and May of 1968. The consequences of those acts have not yet played themselves out, but I think certain general conclusions can be drawn. First, the total harm done by the students and their supporters was very small in comparison with the good results that were achieved. A month of classwork was lost, along with many tempers and a good deal of sleep. Someone—it is still not clear who—burned the research notes of a history professor, an act which, I am happy to say, produced a universal revulsion shared even by the SDS. In the following year, a number of classes were momentarily disrupted by SDS activists in an unsuccessful attempt to repeat the triumph of the previous spring.

Against this, what benefits flowed from the protest? A reactionary and thoroughly unresponsive administration was forced to resign; an all-university Senate of students, professors, and administrators was created, the first such body at Columbia. A callous and antisocial policy of university expansion into the surrounding neighborhood was reversed; some at least of the university's ties with the military were loosened or severed; and an entire community of students and professors were forced to confront moral and political issues which till then they had managed to ignore.

Could these benefits have been won at less cost? Considering the small cost of the uprising, the question seems to me a bit finicky; nevertheless, the answer is clearly, No. The history of administrative intransigence and faculty apathy at Columbia makes it quite clear that nothing short of a dramatic act such as the seizure of buildings could have deposed the university administration and produced a university senate. In retrospect, the affair seems to have been a quite prudent and restrained use of force.

Assuming this assessment to be correct, it is tempting to conclude, "In the Columbia case, violence was justified." But this conclusion is *totally wrong*, for it implies that a line can be drawn between legitimate and illegitimate forms of protest, the latter being justified only under special conditions and when all else has failed. We would all agree, I think, that, under a dictatorship, men have the right to defy the state or even to attack its representatives when their interests are denied and their needs ignored—the only rule that binds them is the general caution against doing more harm than they accomplish good. My purpose here is simply to argue that a modern industrial democracy, whatever merits it may have, is in this regard no different from a dictatorship. No special authority attaches to the laws of a representative, majoritarian state; it is only superstition and the myth of legitimacy that invests the judge, the policeman, or the official with an exclusive right to the exercise of certain kinds of force.

In the light of these arguments, it should be obvious that I see no merit in the doctrine of nonviolence, nor do I believe that any special and complex justification is needed for what is usually called "civil disobedience." A commitment to nonviolence can be understood in two different senses, depending on the interpretation given to the concept of violence. If violence is understood in the strict sense as the political use of force in ways proscribed by a legitimate government, then of course the doctrine of nonviolence depends upon the assumption that there *are* or *could be* legitimate governments. Since I believe this assumption to be false, I can attribute no coherent meaning to this first conception of nonviolence.

If violence is understood, on the other hand, as the use of force to interfere with someone in a direct, bodily way or to injure him physically, then the doctrine of nonviolence is merely a subjective queasiness having no moral rationale. When you occupy the seats at a lunch counter for hours on end, thereby depriving the proprietor of the profits he would have made on ordinary sales during that time, you are taking money out of his pocket quite as effectively as if you had robbed his till or smashed his stock. If you persist in the sit-in until he goes into debt, loses his lunch counter, and takes a job as a day laborer, then you have done him a much greater injury than would be accomplished by a mere beating in a dark alley. He may deserve to be ruined, of course, but, if so, then he probably also deserves to be beaten. A penchant for such indirect coercion as a boycott or a sit-in is morally questionable, for it merely leaves the dirty work to the bank that forecloses on the mortgage or the policeman who carries out the eviction. Emotionally, the commitment to nonviolence is frequently a severely repressed expression of extreme hostility akin to the mortification and self-flagellations of religious fanatics. Enough testimony has come from Black novelists and psychiatrists to make it clear that the philosophy of nonviolence is, for the American Negro, what Nietzche called a "slave morality"—the principal difference is that, in traditional Christianity, God bears the guilt for inflicting pain on the wicked; in the social gospel, the law acts as the scourge.

The doctrine of civil disobedience is an American peculiarity growing out of the conflict between the authority claims of the state and the directly contradictory claims of individual conscience. In a futile attempt to deny and affirm the authority of the state simultaneously, a number of conscientious dissenters have claimed the right to disobey what they believe to be immoral laws, so long as they are prepared to submit to punishment by the state. A willingness to go to jail for one's beliefs is widely viewed in this country as evidence of moral sincerity, and even as a sort of argument for the position one is defending.

Now, tactically speaking, there is much to be said for legal martyrdom. As tyrannical governments are perpetually discovering, the sight of one's leader nailed to a cross has a marvelously bracing effect on the faithful members of a dissident sect. When the rulers are afflicted by the very principles they are violating, even the threat of self-sacrifice may force a government to its knees. But leaving tactics aside, no one has any moral obligation whatsoever to resist an unjust government openly rather than clandestinely. Nor has anyone a duty to invite and then to suffer unjust punishment. The choice is simple: if the law is right, follow it. If the law is wrong, evade it.

I think it is possible to understand why conscientious and morally concerned men should feel a compulsion to seek punishment for acts they genuinely believe to be right. Conscience is the echo of society's voice within us. The men of strongest and most independent conscience are in a manner of speaking, just those who have most completely internalized this social voice, so that they hear and obey its commands even when no policeman compels their compliance. Ironically, it is these same men who are most likely to set themselves against the government in the name of ideals and principles to which they feel a higher loyalty. When a society violates the very principles it claims to hold, these men of conscience experience a terrible conflict. They are deeply committed to the principles society has taught them, principles they have truly come to believe. But they can be true to their beliefs only by setting themselves against the laws of the very society that has been their teacher and with whose authority they identify themselves. Such a conflict occurs in men of weak conscience, who merely obey the law, however much it violates the moral precepts they have only imperfectly learned.

The pain of the conflict is too great to be borne; somehow, it must be alleviated. If the commitment to principle is weak, the individual submits, though he feels morally unclean for doing so. If the identification with society is weak, he rejects the society and becomes alienated, perhaps identifying with some other society. But if both conscience and identification are too strong to be broken, the only solution is to expiate the guilt by seeking social punishment for the breach of society's laws. Oddly enough, the expiation, instead of bringing them back into the fold of law-obeyers, makes it psychologically all the easier for them to continue their defiance of the state.

III

The foregoing conclusions seem to reach far beyond what the argument warrants. The classical theory of political authority may indeed be inadequate; it may even be that the concept of legitimate authority is incoherent; but surely *some* genuine distinction can be drawn between a politics of reason, rules, and compromise on the one hand, and the resort to violent conflict on the other! Are the acts of a rioting mob different only in degree from the calm and orderly processes of a duly constituted court of law? Such a view partakes more of novelty than of truth!

Unless I very much misjudge my audience, most readers will respond roughly in this manner. There may be a few still willing to break a lance for sovereignty and legitimate authority, and a few, I hope, who agree immediately with what I have said, but the distinction between violence and nonviolence in politics is too familiar to be so easily discarded. In this third section of my essay, therefore, I shall try to discover what makes the distinction so plausible, even though it is—I insist—unfounded.

The customary distinction between violent and nonviolent modes of social interaction seems to me to rest on *two* genuine distinctions: the first is the *subjective* distinction between the regular or accepted and the irregular or unexpected uses of force; the second is the *objective* distinction between those interests which are central or vital to an individual and those which are secondary or peripheral.

Consider first the subjective distinction between regular and irregular uses of force in social interactions. It seems perfectly appropriate to us that a conflict between two men who desire the same piece of land should be settled in favor of the one who can pull more money out of his pocket. We consider it regular and orderly that the full weight of the police power of the state be placed behind that settlement in order to ensure that nothing upset it. On the other hand, we consider it violent and disorderly to resolve the dispute by a fist fight or a duel. Yet what is the difference between the use of money, which is one kind of force, and the use of fists, which is another? Well, if we do not appeal to the supposed legitimacy of financial transactions or to the putative authority of the law, then the principal difference is that we are accustomed to settling disputes with dollars and we are no longer accustomed to settling them with fists.

Imagine how barbaric, how unjust, how *violent*, it must seem, to someone unfamiliar with the beauties of capitalism, that a man's ability to obtain medical care for his children should depend solely on the contingency that some other man can make a profit from his productive labor! Is the Federal Government's seizure of my resources for the purpose of killing Asian peasants less violent than a bandit's extortion of tribute at gunpoint? Yet we are accustomed to the one and unaccustomed to the other.

The objective distinction between central and peripheral interests also shapes our conception of what is violent in politics. When my peripheral or secondary interests are at stake in a conflict, I quite naturally consider only a moderate use of force to be justified. Anything more, I will probably call "violence." What I tend to forget, of course, is that other parties to the conflict may find their primary interests challenged and, hence, may have a very different view of what is and is not violent. In the universities, for example, most of the student challenges have touched only on the peripheral interests of professors. No matter what is decided about ROTC, curriculum, the disposition of the endowment, or Black studies, the typical philosophy professor's life will be largely unchanged. His tenure, salary, working conditions, status, and family life remain the same. Hence he is likely to take a tolerant view of building seizures and sit-ins. But let a classroom be disrupted, and he cries out that violence has no place on campus. What he means is that force has been used in a way that touches one of his deeper concerns.

The concept of violence serves as a rhetorical device for proscribing those political uses of force which one considers inimical to one's central interests. Since different social groups have different central interests and can draw on different kinds of force, it follows that there are conflicting definitions of violence. Broadly speaking, in the United States today, there are four conceptions of violence corresponding to four distinct socioeconomic classes.

The first view is associated with the established financial and political interests in the country. It identifies the violent with the illegal, and condemns all challenges to the authority of the state and all assaults on the rights of property as beyond the limits of permissible politics. The older segments of the business community adopt this view, along with the military establishment and the local elites of middle America. Robert Taft was once a perfect symbol of this sector of opinion.

The second view is associated with the affluent, educated, technical and professional middle class in America, together with the new, rapidly growing, future-oriented sectors of the economy, such as the communications industry, electronics, etc. They accept, even welcome, dissent, demonstration, ferment, and—within limits—attacks on property in ghetto areas. They look with favor on civil disobedience and feel at ease with extralegal tactics of social change. Their interests are identified with what is new in American society, and they are confident of coming out on top in the competition for wealth and status within an economy built on the principle of reward for profitable performance.

The "liberals," as this group is normally called, can afford to encourage modes of dissent or disruption that do not challenge the economic and social arrangements on which their success is based. They will defend rent strikes, grape boycotts, or lunch-counter sit-ins with the argument that unemployment and starvation are a form of violence also. Since they are themselves in competition with the older elite for power and prestige, they tend to view student rebels and black militants as their allies, up to the point at which their own interests are attacked. But when tactics are used that threaten their positions in universities, in corporations, or in affluent suburbs, then the liberals cry *violence* also, and call for the police. A poignant example of this class is the liberal professor who cheers the student rebels as they seize the Administration building and then recoils in horror at the demand that he share his authority to determine curriculum and decide promotions.

The third view of violence is that held by working-class and lower-middle-class Americans, those most often referred to as the "white backlash." They perceive the principal threat to their interests as coming from the bottom class of ghetto dwellers, welfare clients, and nonunionized laborers who demand more living space, admission to union jobs with union wages, and a larger share of the social product. To this hard-pressed segment of American society, 'violence' means street crime, ghetto riots, civil-rights marches into all-white neighborhoods, and antiwar attacks on the patriotic symbols of constituted authority with which backlash America identifies. Studies of the petty bourgeoisie in Weimar Germany suggest, and George Wallace's presidential campaign of 1968 confirms, that the lower middle class, when it finds itself pressed between inflationary prices and demands from the lower class, identifies its principal enemy as the lower class. So we find the classic political alliance of old established wealth with right-wing populist elements, both of which favor a repressive response to attacks on authority and a strong governmental policy toward the "violence" of demands for change.

The fourth view of violence is the revolutionary counterdefinition put forward by the outclass and its sympathizers within the liberal wing of the established order. Two complementary rhetorical devices are employed. First, the connotation of the term 'violence' is accepted, but the application of the term is reversed: police are violent, not rioters; employers, not strikers; the American army, not the enemy. In this way, an attack is mounted on the government's claim to possess the right to rule. Secondly, the denotation of the term is held constant and the connotation reverted. Violence is good, not bad; legitimate, not illegitimate. It is, in Stokely Carmichael's great rhetorical flourish, "as American as cherry pie." Since the outclass of rebels has scant access to the instruments of power used by established social classes—wealth, law, police power, legislation—it naturally seeks to legitimize the riots, harassments, and street crime which are its only weapons. Equally naturally, the rest of society labels such means "violent" and suppresses them.

In the complex class struggle for wealth and power in America, each of us must decide for himself which group he will identify with. It is not my purpose here to urge one choice rather than another. My sole aim is to argue that the concept of violence has no useful role to play in the deliberations leading to that choice.

Whatever other considerations of utility and social justice one appeals to, no weight should be given to the view that *some* uses of force are prima facie ruled out as illegitimate and hence "violent" or that other uses of force are prima facie ruled in as legitimate, or legal. Furthermore, in the advancement of dissenting positions by illegal means, no special moral merit attaches to the avoiding, as it were, of body contact. Physical harm may be among the most serious injuries that can be done to an opponent, but, if so, it differs only in degree and not in kind from the injuries inflicted by so-called "nonviolent" techniques of political action.

The myth of legitimate authority is the secular reincarnation of that religious superstition which has finally ceased to play a significant role in the affairs of men. Like Christianity, the worship of the state has its fundamentalists, its revisionists, its ecumenicists (or world-Federalists), and its theological rationale. The philosophical anarchist is the atheist of politics. I began my discussion with the observation that the belief in legitimacy, like the penchant for transcendent metaphysics, is an ineradicable irrationality of the human experience. However, the slow extinction of religious faith over the past two centuries may encourage us to hope that in time anarchism, like atheism, will become the accepted conviction of enlightened and rational men.

CHAPTER 3

The Idea of Violence

By C. A. J. Coady

Hannah Arendt once complained that the careless use in political theory of such key terms as 'power', 'strength', 'force', 'authority' and 'violence' indicated not only a deplorable deafness to linguistic meanings but a kind of blindness to significant political realities. The blame for this she traced to the obsession with reducing public affairs to "the business of dominion."[1] I share her belief that conceptual carelessness or misunderstanding about such ideas as violence has political importance and I suspect that she may be right in her diagnosis of what lies behind a good deal of such confusion. My present concern, however, is rather different from that specifically addressed by Arendt although the two are related. Nowadays, it is not so much that theorists are, as she objected, indifferent to distinctions between the key terms listed but that they offer explicit definitions of the term 'violence' which exhibit both the deafness to linguistic patterns and, more significantly, the blindness to political and moral realities of which she complained. In what follows, I shall try to support this claim by examining several fashionable definitions of violence with an eye both to their conceptual adequacy and their moral and social implications. I shall also suggest an alternative definition to the ones criticised, urge its advantages over them, and defend it against certain difficulties.

Of course, as Arendt herself was well aware, any such definitions have to cope with the untidiness, indeterminacy and variety of purpose involved in natural languages and ordinary speech contexts. Hence any definition proposed by a theorist will involve some degree of sharpening and legislation with a consequent recognition of borderline cases and the dismissal or downgrading of certain kinds of existing usage. Social and political concepts of any importance have, however, the additional interest and complexity that they may and often do embody diverse moral and political outlooks or visions and so a theorist's definitions of such terms will reflect, and often be part of, a programme for advancing certain enterprises at once both theoretical and practical. Sometimes, understanding is best served by defining a concept such as justice in very abstract and relatively neutral terms which allow competing theories and outlooks pertaining to the subject matter thus indicated to be compared and criticised. Here it has proved useful to deploy a (relatively unanalysed) contrast of concept and conception as Rawls does in his work on justice and as Dworkin recommends in the case of law.[2] Nonetheless, the literature on violence mostly proceeds in terms of definitions that aim to capture a conceptual territory believed to be at least implicit in ordinary discourse and so I shall frame my discussion in terms of definition but with the background social and political issues very much in mind. Were the concept-conception strategy applicable to the present topic it would, I believe, require only a rearrangement of what I want to say and not a revision of it.

The definition of violence provides a nice illustration of the complex interplay between concept and commitment. There are roughly three types of definition to be found in the philosophical, political and sociological literature on violence. We might label these 'wide', 'restricted' and 'legitimate'.[3] Wide definitions, of which the most influential is that of 'structural violence', tend to serve the interests of the political left by including within the extension of the term 'violence' a great range of social injustices and inequalities. This not only allows reformers to say that they are working to eliminate violence when they oppose, say, a government measure to redistribute income in favour of the already rich, but allows revolutionaries to offer, in justification of their resort to violence, even where it is terrorist, the claim that they are merely meeting violence with violence. Their own direct physical violence is presented as no more than a response to and defence against the institutional or quiet violence of their society.[4] An instance of such a wide definition is Newton Garver's: "The institutional form of quiet violence operates when people are deprived of choices in a systematic way by the very manner in which transactions normally take place."[5] But if wide definitions are naturally more congenial to the left we must not ignore the possibility of their use by the right, since it is possible for the right to see social structures as deforming in, for instance, exposing people to moral danger or leaving them too free or not economically free enough and so on.

Restricted definitions are typically those which concentrate upon positive interpersonal acts of force usually involving the infliction of physical injury. There is something to be said for this being the normal or ordinary understanding of 'violence', not only because it has the authority of dictionaries, most notably the Oxford English Dictionary, but because the proponents of the wide definitions usually take it that they are offering an extension of just such a normal or usual idea.[6] It has been argued by some that this definition has natural affinities with a reformist liberal political outlook[7] and it may be so, though I think myself that it is the most politically neutral of the definitional types (which may just show how 'liberal' it is and I am). In any case it is the type of definition in support of which I shall later argue.

The third type of definition ('legitimist') arises naturally in the context of conservative or right wing liberal political thought for it incorporates a reference to an illegal or illegitimate use of force. I think it probable that this style of definition has much more currency in the United States than elsewhere, but the usage it corresponds to does exist in other communities too. Sidney Hook is operating in this tradition when he defines violence as "the illegal employment of methods of physical coercion for personal or group ends,"[8] and Herbert Marcuse is commenting upon the usage when he says, "Thanks to a kind of political linguistics, we never use the word violence to describe the actions of the police, we never use the word violence to describe the actions of the Special Forces in Vietnam. But the word is readily applied to the actions of students who defend themselves from the police, burn cars or chop down trees."[9] One can see the advantages of this outlook for the defenders of established orders, but once more the connection, though natural, is not inevitable. Robert Paul Wolff, for one, has accepted this sort of definition in order to argue a kind of left-wing case by purporting to show that the concept of violence is incoherent.[10] I shall consider Wolff's view in detail as a representative legitimist definition, even though he gives it an untypical twist, but first I want to begin with a wide definition. The one I shall consider is that given by the Norwegian philosopher-sociologist Johan Galtung in his paper, "Violence, peace and peace research."[11]

Galtung claims in this article and elsewhere that there are various types of violence and that it is important to have a very broad concept of violence in order to accommodate them all. He distinguishes, for instance, between physical and psychological violence, giving as cases of the latter, lies, brainwashing, indoctrination and threats, but, more interestingly, he locates both of these within the category of personal violence which he then contrasts with structural violence. By so doing he generates a perspective from which one can see two types of peace. On the one hand there is negative peace which is the absence of direct or personal violence (roughly what a restricted definition determines as violence) and, on the other, positive peace which is the absence of indirect or structural violence.[12] Structural violence is also referred to as social injustice and positive peace as social justice. At this point Galtung's definition of violence should be cited, a definition which is meant to support the possibility of the two types of violence mentioned. What he says is: "Violence is present when human beings are being influenced so that their actual somatic and mental realizations are below their potential realizations."[13] Galtung confesses to some unease about this definition as soon as he formulates it, saying that it "may lead to more problems than it solves," but this avowal seems to have no more than ritual significance since no such problems are raised in the course of the article. Galtung is, however, aware that he has framed what he calls "an extended concept of violence," and feels obliged to try to justify the extension as "a logical extension." By talking of his definition as extending the concept of violence Galtung seems to be acknowledging what is, indeed, surely the case, that in its usual use the term violence covers only what he calls personal violence, whereas he wants to hold that violence also exists where social arrangements and institutions have the effect of producing substandard 'somatic and mental realisations.' Indeed, if we were to invoke the authority of the OED we might conclude that even personal violence is too extended since that authority gives a 'restricted' definition of violence in purely physical terms as follows:

> The exercise of physical force so as to inflict injury on or damage to persons or property; action or conduct characterised by this.

I shall discuss this definition later since it faces certain difficulties and requires some clarification. First we should notice, that, on this definition, there can be various metaphorical or otherwise extended uses of 'violence', 'violent', 'violently' and suchlike words which relate in more or less direct ways to episodes of the infliction of damage by physical force, e.g. "Sir John Kerr did violence to the Australian Constitution" or "Dennis waved his arms about violently" or "The violent motions of the machine surprised him." It seems plausible to treat the use of the noun 'violence' in the utterance about Sir John Kerr as an attempt to dramatise the awfulness of the governor-general's behaviour with respect to the Constitution, but the adjectival and adverbial uses are more interesting in being less metaphorical. Neither Dennis nor the machine was engaged in violence yet their movements are intelligibly described as violent because of affinities between the way their limbs and parts behaved and the way in which genuine violence manifests itself. In this respect, the employment of 'violent' and 'violently' in such contexts is like that of such expressions as 'furious' and 'furiously' since we do not suppose that the team which rows furiously is actually in a fury.

Once this is understood we should be under no temptation to think that such usages somehow license the sort of extension that Galtung is promoting. (John Harris seems to think something of the kind but we will look more closely at his view later.) Certainly it would normally be very queer to say that violence is present when (and because) a society legislates for more tax concessions for big business, or refuses to remove unjust legislation such as the denial of voting rights to certain minority groups. It seems, however, to be no less bizarre to characterise such enactments as violent in anything like the way that Dennis and the machine can be so characterised.

We should pause to eliminate some sources of possible confusion. When people speak of structural or institutional violence they often run together three things which should be kept separate. First there is what Galtung is principally concerned with, namely, the way in which people are injured and harmed by unjust social arrangements which could be otherwise even though no violence in the restricted (or 'personal') sense is being done to them. Secondly, there is the phenomenon of ordinary person-to-person violence with pronounced social or structural causes (e.g. police harassment of racial minorities, race riots, or prison brutality, to name just a few plausible candidates). Thirdly, there is the widespread readiness to resort to socially licensed violence which is implicit in much of social life. Galtung puts this into the category of 'latent violence', but appears to treat it as a type of violence,[14] which seems wrong for the perfectly general reason that tendencies and dispositions should not be confused with their displays. There are, of course, plenty of displays of the State's capacity for violence, both domestically and externally, and the role of (restricted) violence in civil life is both easy to ignore and almost equally easy to exaggerate. It is easy to ignore partly because when one has a comfortable position in society it is hardly ever personally encountered (in peacetime) and partly because second-hand knowledge of the facts tends to be clouded by euphemism. The presumed legitimacy of State violence can also create the feeling that it is a quite different activity from unauthorised violence and so lead to the legitimist idea that it is not violence at all. The point about State violence is easy to exaggerate from a different direction, especially if the distinctions made above are neglected. Some thinkers and activists speak as if nothing but violence goes on in such a State as Britain or Australia and as if political obedience rests entirely upon the fear of violent treatment by the authorities. If we are thinking of violence in some restricted sense and we do not confuse it with the capacity for violence then both of these claims are absurd. And even if we allow reference to the State's capacity for violence in discussing the roots of political obedience, then it is surely implausible to hold that most people accept political authority because they fear the State's capacity for violence against them. More plausible is Thomas Hobbes' view that the State's power to use violence ('the right of the sword') enters into most people's thinking about obedience primarily through the reassuring thought that it provides a sanction against someone else's violent behaviour. As Hobbes argued, most people in an ordered, half-decent society get such benefits from civil life as will make it clearly in their interest to accept civil authority most of the time, but this is conditional upon those who don't have such an interest (or who don't think that they have such an interest) being intimidated into conformity and upon the majority being so intimidated on those occasions (necessarily rare, so Hobbes may have believed) when conformity does not seem to be in their interests. There is some plausibility in this sort of picture of the role of violence in securing political obedience, but it is more complex than the picture often presented in popular polemics.

If Galtung is not merely concerned to draw attention to the social causes of much personal violence nor the amount of latent personal violence involved in normal social life, what good reason does he have for extending the concept of violence in the way he does?

First, let us look briefly at the formulation of his definition, which has some rather curious features. It seems to follow from it that a young child is engaged in violence if its expression of its needs and desires is such that it makes its mother and/or father very tired, even if it is not in any ordinary sense 'a violent child' or even engaged in violent actions. Furthermore, I will be engaged in violence if, at your request, I give you a sleeping pill that will reduce your actual somatic and mental realisations well below their potential, at least for some hours. Certainly some emendation is called for, and it may be possible to produce a version of the definition that will meet these difficulties (the changing of 'influenced' to 'influenced against their will' might do the job, but at the cost of making it impossible to act violently towards someone at their request, and that doesn't seem to be impossible, just unusual). I shall not delay on this, however, because I want rather to assess Galtung's reason for seeking to extend the concept of violence in the way he does. His statement of the justification of his definition is as follows:

> However, it will soon be clear why we are rejecting the narrow concept of violence—according to which violence is *somatic* incapacitation, or deprivation of health, alone (with killing as the extreme form), at the hands of an *actor* who *intends* this to be the consequence. If this were all violence is about, and peace is seen as its negation, then too little is rejected when peace is held up as an ideal. Highly unacceptable social orders would still be compatible with peace. *Hence an extended concept of violence is indispensable* but the concept should be a logical extension, not merely a list of undesirables.[15]

So, for Galtung, the significance of his definition of violence lies in the fact that if violence is undesirable and peace desirable, then if we draw a very wide bow in defining violence we will find that the ideal of peace will commit us to quite a lot. Now it seems to me that this justification of the value of his definition is either muddled or mischievous (and just possibly both). If the suggestion is that peace cannot be a *worthy* social ideal or goal of action unless it is the total ideal, then the suggestion is surely absurd. A multiplicity of compatible but non-inclusive ideals seems as worthy of man's pursuit as a single comprehensive goal and, furthermore, it seems a more honest way to characterise social realities. Galtung finds it somehow shocking that highly unacceptable social orders would still be compatible with peace, but only the total ideal assumption makes this even surprising. It is surely just an example of the twin facts that since social realities are complex, social ideals and ills do not form an undifferentiated whole (at least not in the perceptions of most men and women) and that social causation is such that some ideals are achievable in relative independence of others. Prosperity, freedom, peace and equality, for instance, are different ideals requiring different characterisations and justifications and although it could be hoped that they are compatible in the sense that there is no absurdity in supposing that a society could exhibit a high degree of realisation of all four, yet concrete circumstances may well demand a trade-off amongst them—the toleration, for instance, of a lesser degree of freedom in order to achieve peace or a less general prosperity in the interests of greater equality.

On the other hand, it may be that Galtung does not mean to say that a narrower definition of violence would provide us with a notion of peace that was not sufficiently worth pursuing, but rather that since people are against violence (narrowly construed) and for peace (narrowly construed), then their energies can be harnessed practically on a wide front against all sorts of social injustice if they come to think of peace as encompassing the whole of social justice. There are some indications in the text that this is what Galtung means and that he is not averse to achieving this goal through the promotion of what he sees himself to be confused thinking.

> The use of the term 'peace' may in itself be peace-productive, producing a common basis, a feeling of communality in purpose that may pave the ground for deeper ties later on. The use of more precise terms drawn from the vocabulary of one conflict group, and excluded from the vocabulary of the opponent group, may in itself cause dissent and lead to manifest conflict precisely because the term is so clearly understood. By projecting an image of harmony of interests the term 'peace' may also help bring about such a harmony. It provides opponents with a one-word language in which to express values of concern and togetherness because peace is on anybody's agenda.[16]

Nonetheless it is not clear how seriously this is intended. The passage occurs before the attempt at definition and it may not be charitable to take it as an indication of the true significance of Galtung's definitional strategy. If it were so taken, then it should be remarked that not only does the strategy have much the same moral status as propaganda, but it shares the disadvantages of propaganda in that it is likely in the long term to defeat the ends, good or ill, it is designed to serve. The deliberate promotion of muddle or unclarity is liable to be detected and when detected resented, because it is seen for what it is, namely, an exercise in manipulation. One is reminded of some of the Communist Party's operations with United Front (and other 'front') organisations of the 1940s and '50s, and of the subsequent damage done to numerous radical causes by the disillusionment of those who had been manipulated.

Let us suppose, however, that Galtung's strategy is not as dubious as this and let us rather interpret him as seeking to call attention to genuine similarities between personal and structural violence in the hope that once they are seen then people who are concerned to oppose the violence of, for example, war will also work to oppose the structural violence of (as it may be) inequitable tax scales, income inequities, private schools, inadequate health services and so on. (I am deliberately not using such instances of social injustice as racism which usually involve the use of 'restricted' violence, and so can lead to some confusion, as noted earlier.) To this I think there are three replies.

(a) The similarities between personal violence and structural violence seem to be far too few and too general to offset the striking differences between them. The basic similarity which Galtung's definition enshrines in a somewhat cumbersome way is that violence and social injustice both involve the production of some sort of hurt or injury broadly construed but the type of harm and the conditions of its production are terribly different.

In recent English writings on moral and political philosophy a good deal of ingenious and often impressive effort has been expended on arguments which might seem to make the similarities more convincing and the differences less striking. Most of the effort has gone into an attack upon what Jonathan Clover has called the acts/omissions doctrine and writers like Clover, Singer, Bennett, Harris and Honderich (most of them utilitarians of one sort or another) have drawn various, though related, conclusions from their critique.[17] Insofar as the discussion has served to stress the way in which various failures to act may be morally significant, it seems to me to have been of great importance. But the critique has more ambitious, if, at times, confusingly presented, intentions. So it sometimes seems that the project is to show that there is no real conceptual distinction between acts and omissions, at other times that there is a distinction but that it is never of moral significance, at other times again that there is a distinction which is sometimes morally significant but not in the special circumstances of interest to the moral theorist (e.g. euthanasia or abortion). This is not the place to explore this important issue further, but it is worth noting that while Honderich concludes that the positive acts of the violent are in the relevant respects quite unlike the omissions of the non-violent (e.g. their failure to aid third world countries) even though such omissions are seriously culpable, Harris claims that such omissions or, as he prefers, negative actions are acts of violence.[18] Some of his arguments for this conclusion are similar to Galtung's but others involve an attempt to undermine the 'restricted definition' by appeal to counter-examples. The latter I will consider when I look more carefully at attempts to provide a restricted definition, but the former can be briefly considered here.

Harris is not only interested in extending the notion of violence; more generally, he does not want to include any reference to the *manner* in which harm or injury is done, other than its being done knowingly. His definition goes as follows:

> An act of violence occurs when injury or suffering is inflicted upon a person or persons by an agent who knows (or ought reasonably to have known), that his actions would result in the harm in question.[19]

He asserts that the questions that interest about violence would be trivial if they were only concerned with injuries brought about in a certain manner. Our concern with such questions is motivated by the desire to solve 'the problem of violence', that is, 'to minimise its use or even remove it entirely from human affairs' and in the restricted sense of the term we might do this "and yet leave intact all the features of the problem of violence which make a solution desirable. Death, injury and suffering might be just as common as before, only the characteristic complex of actions by which they are inflicted would have changed."[20] And he adds that we are not so much interested in the particular methods men use to inflict injury, suffering or death, but in the fact that they cause each other such harms. As his definition indicates, Harris' primary concern, unlike Galtung's, is with personal violence, although he wants to make a dramatic extension of that category. If certain kinds of omission can count as violence then the way to structural violence is at least clearer since the damage done to people by the structures and institutions of their society can be seen as sustained by personal failures to act. Moreover a successful extension of the term 'violence' to cover omissions might make the further move to violence without individual agents more palatable.

Clearly a good deal here turns upon how we determine the question of negative actions, but even if we allow that failure to give money to Oxfam (a favoured example in the literature) with the foreseeable consequence that someone in

India dies is causing some person to die, it still does not follow that we do or must have the same interest in both kinds of deed. In fact, it is quite clear that most people are interested in and exercised about the one to a much greater degree than, and in a different way from, their concern about the other. Whether this differentiation is morally praise-worthy or defensible is another question, but the fact that they do so differentiate is indisputable. So Harris' claim that we are not really interested in the manner in which damage is caused is, as a factual claim, simply mistaken. Furthermore, such generalised differentiation is surely plausibly explained by the striking dissimilarities between what is done on the one hand in stabbing a beggar to death and, on the other hand, in ignoring his plea for assistance. These dissimilarities extend usually both to the manner of acting and to the way in which the outcome ensues. I say "usually," because although cases can be constructed in which death is immediately consequent upon our refusal of aid, the more common cases involve our negative action being, at most, merely a partial cause of death and injury and hence it is usually left open that, for instance, someone else will aid the beggar.[21] This, I suspect, is one reason why most people are more impressed by, and worried about, restricted violence than about other ways in which human beings contribute to harming one another.

A related, and important, point is that our positive actions to cause injury are standardly intentional under some relevant description (such as killing, stabbing or battering) whereas our omitting to do something which would have prevented injury or suffering may or may not be intentional with reference to that upshot even if we are fully aware that failure to act will probably have just such consequences. This will not show that the act/omission distinction *always* makes a moral difference; quite the contrary, for there will be cases where someone may omit to do something precisely because his failure to act will contribute to bringing about injury and he may even choose the negative rather than positive action in order that the victim suffer more. Imagine a malevolent nurse who stands to gain a lot from the death of a detested patient and who decides to provide a more painful death by omitting to give a vital medicine rather than simply hitting him over the head. Here, the course of intentional omission seems to be more reprehensible than the positive action. Nonetheless, the difference between the ways in which positive and negative actions are generally related to the category of the intentional does show that there is a moral significance to the distinction. Just what significance, will depend upon the role that one's moral outlook gives to intentional action. I do not claim that morality is only concerned with intentional action—the category of negligence shows that this cannot be so—but it does appear that intentional action is of distinctive importance. It is true that utilitarian moral theory either makes light of the idea or tries to stretch it so as to make all foreseen consequences of one's act intentional thus obliterating this difference between the homicidal nurse and the chap who spends all his money on his family rather than giving some of it to Oxfam whose workers will, he believes, use it to save lives. It is, I think, fairly clear that any such conceptual maneuver is a departure from ordinary thinking about intention and I am not sympathetic to the reasons usually offered for so departing but further discussion of this issue would take us into a debate about the best structure for an adequate moral theory and hence too far afield. My aim here is only to show that there is much more to the widespread interest in sharply distinguishing positive acts of violence from harmful failures to act than such theorists as Harris allow. I conclude then that the objection from dissimilarity still stands.

(b) Furthermore, even certain similarities that do exist are not all that they appear. Both the existence of social injustice (i.e. 'structural violence') and restricted violence within, or between, communities are matters for moral concern but the way in which each relates to morality seems to be different. It is hard to be confident about this if only because of the obscurity of the expression 'social justice' and the different moral understandings that are implicit in its use by different people but, on the whole, the allegation that some procedure or activity is unjust is a more decisive moral condemnation than the criticism that it is violent. It seems clear that, quite apart from the debate about just wars, some acts of domestic violence may be morally legitimate, for example, the violent restraint or hindrance of someone who is violently attacking someone else. By contrast, the idea that social injustice may be morally legitimate is more surprising. All but fairly extreme pacifists would agree that we could be morally justified in using violence to defend ourselves against violent attack but there is no ready parallel to this idea in the case of social injustice. There could indeed be a reason for restricting the liberty or wealth of a class of citizens or for otherwise injuring them but such a reason would normally preclude us from describing the restriction or injury as unjust. It is not that one social injustice has been rightly used to defeat another but rather that the good reason for using some measure which rectifies a social injustice renders that measure socially just or, at least, not unjust. This is, I think, how it would be natural to describe most justified acts of social reform, even cases of positive discrimination which are usually defended as embodiments of social justice rather than violations of it. Some may prefer to say that while this is generally so, nonetheless social injustice is sometimes morally justifiable (just as restricted violence is) because, being only one ideal amongst others, it can be overridden by some other value like maximising happiness or, more plausibly, the needs of social order. So someone might admit that slavery offends against social justice but argue that it may justifiably continue or be freshly imposed because the economy or the intellectual culture would collapse without it. Suppose such a claim were accepted as true and overriding. Would we best describe the situation by saying that slavery here is unjust but morally acceptable or by saying that slavery here is unjust and hence immoral but it is nonetheless required or necessary here to be immoral? These are difficult issues (reminiscent of some of those addressed by Machiavelli), but I think that if we allow such an overriding (as I should, in fact, be loathe to do), it is best described in the second fashion and if so, there is still no parallel with the case of restricted violence. The first form of description will, however, preserve the similarity and so suit the theorist of structural or other wide violence. The preservation is, however, purchased at a price which I suspect few such theorists would be willing to pay because it involves the admission that social injustice—usually their primary social evil—can sometimes be morally acceptable.

(c) Perhaps more important than either of these points is the fact that the wide definition of violence and peace is likely to have undesirable practical consequences. As remarked earlier, the realities of social causation are such that some ideals are achievable in relative or even total independence of others, and it is very plausible to suppose that such goals as the reduction of the level of armed conflict between or within nations or even its total elimination between them may be achievable independently of the achievement or even the significant advance of social justice within one or more such nations. Furthermore, as a corollary, it may well be that quite different techniques, strategies and remedies are required to deal with the social disorder of (restricted) violence than are needed to deal with such issues as wage injustice, educational inequalities and entrenched privilege. The use of the wide definition seems likely to encourage the cosy but ultimately stultifying belief that there is one problem, the problem of (wide) violence, and hence it must be solved as a whole with one set of techniques.

An analogy with slavery may be instructive. It would be possible to produce a Galtung-style typology of slavery which has as its sub-divisions physical slavery and structural slavery; indeed the notion of a 'wage-slave' is perhaps a contribution to this sort of enterprise. Yet not only is physical slavery, for the most part, very different from structural slavery, but it is palpably eliminable independently of eliminating structural slavery since, in much of the world, it has been eliminated whilst structural slavery remains. Furthermore, some of the methods used to eliminate physical slavery may not be appropriate to the elimination of structural slavery (e.g. the use of the British Fleet).

It is worth saying something under this heading about Harris' claim mentioned earlier that one might deal with the problem of violence narrowly conceived and indeed eliminate all such violence from the face of the earth, and yet find that "Death, injury and suffering might be just as common as before, only the characteristic complex of actions by which they are inflicted would have changed."[22] We should not here be seduced by the philosopher's typical and understandable concern for fantastic possibilities because here such a possibility will surely fail to be instructive, and the fact equally surely is that this suggested possibility is merely fantastic. Suppose, what is hard enough, that we have vastly reduced wars, revolutions, assassinations, riots, military coups, police and criminal violence, is it really conceivable that, other things being equal, the lot of mankind *could* remain unimproved with respect to death, injury and suffering?[23] One can answer "No" to this question even while believing that violence may sometimes be morally permissible and while deploring other ways in which human suffering occurs. This is because the most telling justification for violence is as a defence against other violence and because even justified violence is regrettable. In our world and any empirically similar world, a vast reduction in the level of (restricted) violence would surely mean the elimination of a great deal of what serves to bring premature death and extensive misery. Think of the parallel with slavery. No doubt many awful indignities must remain after slavery is abolished, and the act of abolition may itself create new disabilities for the former slaves but, in most imaginable circumstances, it is hard to believe that their lot is not an improved one. It seems to me that the matter is even clearer in the case of violence.

In so far then as wide definitions like Galtung's are open to the criticisms made above, their underpinnings are theoretically unsound and the practical consequences of adopting them are likely to be at the very least, disappointing.[24]

I come now to a rather different attempt at defining violence, one belonging to the 'legitimist' category and offered by Robert Wolff in his paper "On Violence."[25] We shall not here be able to engage with all of Wolff's manoeuvres in this swashbuckling piece of polemic but we should note that his strategy is to use a legitimist definition of violence in order to show that the concepts of violence and non-violence are 'inherently confused' because they rest fundamentally upon the idea of legitimate authority which is itself incoherent. He thus feels entitled to dismiss as meaningless (except for its role as 'ideological rhetoric' aimed at helping certain political interests) all debates and discussions about the morality of violence and about the respective merits of violent and non-violent political tactics.[26] Some of what I have to say bears upon these startling conclusions but I shall not comment upon his basic argument against the notion of legitimate political authority except to record my conviction that it is unsuccessful.

Wolff defines violence as meaning "the illegitimate or unauthorised use of force to effect decisions against the will or desire of others."[27] Like one interpretation of Galtung's definition, this has the consequence that one could never be violent to another if he sought to be injured but this is surely wrong, for a bank-robber's accomplice may want the robber to beat him up in order to throw the police off the scent. It also, more significantly perhaps, makes a normative political element part of the meaning of the term, violence. Wolff does allow what he calls a descriptive sense of the word too but this is not, as might be suspected, a restricted sense since it still contains a reference to political authority but this time merely *de facto* instead of legitimate. A *de facto* authority is one 'generally accepted' as legitimate in the territory. He goes on to say, "Descriptively speaking, the attack on Hitler's life during the second World War was an act of violence, but one might perfectly well deny that it was violent in the strict sense, on the grounds that Hitler's regime was illegitimate. On similar grounds, it is frequently said that police behaviour toward workers or ghetto dwellers or demonstrators is violent, even when it is clearly within the law for the authority issuing the law is illegitimate."[28]

The strange consequences of Wolff's position are here strikingly illustrated. It is tempting to think that anyone who believes that the deliberate blowing up of the conference room in the attempt to kill Hitler and thereby successfully killing and wounding others is *not* a violent act needs sympathy. Independently of any question of legitimacy, this is, on the face of it, the sort of act which should be a test of a definition of violence. If the definition doesn't determine it as an act of violence, then it is a defective definition. The question of whether the act was illegitimate or unauthorised is simply irrelevant. It may be replied that such a reaction merely shows the strength of my own commitment to a restricted understanding of the term violence but, on the contrary, it is surely rather an indication of how remote Wolff's usage is from linguistic realities, and of how difficult it is to discuss serious political issues clearly with such a definitional apparatus.

As Wolff develops his discussion this becomes even more striking. He says, for instance, *a propos* the student demonstrations at Columbia University in 1968 that it is "totally wrong" to say such things as "In the Columbia case violence was justified" even though, as he believes, the whole affair seems to have been a quite prudent and restrained use of force. Wolff believes this to be so partly because of his definition of violence since the sentence comes close to "In the Columbia case the illegitimate use of force to effect decisions against the will or desire of others was legitimate." (Actually he does not object to the sentence in quite such direct terms but argues that it implies the doctrine of legitimate government or legitimate authority, and since this is an absurdity so is the sentence itself.) Yet if there is any absurdity here it surely resides in the implications of Wolff's definition since on a more restrictive definition of violence which makes no reference to legitimate authority, etc. we can ask reasonably clear moral and political questions about the students' use of violence and hence decide the quite separate question of whether or not it was justified. Some of the issues thus raised will be similar to, if not identical with, those Wolff wants to treat in a more roundabout and, I think, contrived way by employing the much looser terminology of force.

Wolff seems at times to recognise this and in discussing what he calls "the doctrine of non-violence" he says that if violence is understood (non-strictly) as the use of force to interfere with somebody in a direct physical way or to injure him physically then the doctrine of non-violence is "merely a subjective queasiness having no moral rationale." He cites the case of a sit-in at a lunch-counter which not only deprives the proprietor of profits, but may ruin him if persisted in. Wolff says that he has been done

> a much greater injury than would be accomplished by a mere beating in a dark alley. He may deserve to be ruined, of course, but, if so, then he probably also deserves to be beaten. A penchant for such indirect coercion as a boycott or a sit-in is morally questionable, for it merely leaves the dirty work to the bank that forecloses on the mortgage or the policeman who carries out the eviction.[29]

Stirring stuff, but not, I believe, a contribution to the debate about the respective merits of violent and non-violent forms of political action or protest. This is not the place to engage in that debate but plainly it raises serious issues which are simply obscured by Wolff's treatment. Just to take the example of the sit-in: the normal defence of such an action would not be in terms of an intention to ruin the proprietor and bring him to destitution, but to bring sharply to his attention and the attention of apathetic or hostile citizens, *within* the framework of laws and conventions about the law which you all to some extent share, your beliefs that his operations have severely harmed others and are likely to bring inconvenience and financial discomfort upon him unless he mends his ways. There are numerous considerations that may be advanced to support a preference for this way of proceeding over beating him up or maiming or killing him. It may plausibly be argued that it is tactically better from the point of view of public reaction, that it has better social consequences, that violence is essentially prone to get out of hand and that the victim suffers much less. When Wolff says, "He may deserve to be ruined, of course, but, if so, then he probably also deserves to be beaten," he is engaging in no more than schoolboy bravado. Even if ruin were the object of the exercise it is far from obvious that this is worse or on a par with the effects of beating, e.g. possible permanent physical and psychological damage, if not death. One may very well have good reason for putting someone out of business without thereby being justified in mutilating or killing him.

On the assumption that no more needs to be said about Wolff's detailed argumentation, I want to conclude my consideration of legitimist definitions by raising a final objection to their procedures which is, I think, a very serious one. What will such definitions allow us to say about that pre-eminent use of violence, warfare? In the case of Wolff's definition, for instance, the absurd consequence is immediately generated that if there are two sovereign states, both of which have politically legitimate governments, then they may not be engaged in violence, even though they are bombarding each other with nuclear rockets. This will happen if both legitimate governments legally authorise the particular resort to war. This is surely not an uncommon or fantastic case. Wolff would be saved from this absurdity only by his belief that there is no such thing as political legitimacy, but others, such as Hook and Honderich, who propose legitimist definitions, have no such escape route. Honderich, it is true, explicitly excludes warfare from the scope of his discussion but purports nonetheless to be discussing political violence. The restriction of political violence to internal or domestic political contexts is, I think, astonishing and the case of warfare rightly raises difficulties for his definition which includes reference to "a use of force prohibited by law." His full definition of political violence is: "a considerable or destroying use of force against persons or things, a use of force prohibited by law and directed to a change in the politics, personnel or system of government, and hence to changes in society."[30] As we can see from this definition the problem posed by the example of warfare strikes at the roots of the legitimist outlook. For Honderich, even the *illegal* internal use of severe force by police, security organisations or even nongovernmental agencies is not political violence if it is aimed at preserving the status quo! Given Honderich's generally radical stance, this is not only a curious outcome but it exhibits starkly the tendency of legitimist theories to present the use of violence as posing a moral problem only for those who think of deploying force against the established or legitimate government. Yet surely even the legal employment of 'destroying force' raises issues about the role and nature of political violence. Comparisons between states, for instance, can rightly raise questions about the moral standing of greater or less recourse to violence, and degrees of readiness to have such recourse, in the legitimate administrations of the different polities. Such questions are not only real but they are clearly related to the questions faced by those who contemplate the use of violence against legal authority either that of their own state or of another.

Let me turn all too briefly now to a clarification and defence of a restricted definition of violence. In a sense, most of the paper has been a defence of such a definition, for it has sought to show the inadequacies of its competitors, but I think that a little more is required at least by way of clarification of possible misunderstandings.

I cited earlier the OED definition and I want to endorse something like it, but first we must distinguish violence from *force* and from *coercion*. A good deal of confusion in the literature is generated by the failure to make these distinctions. A few examples will make clear the need to distinguish. Take the examples of what Ronald Miller has called "gentle removal"[31] courteous use of force to remove unresisting but uncooperative demonstrators from a building (admittedly rare but possible) or the gentle but firm restraining of someone who wants to rush into a blazing building to rescue relatives or even, a slightly different kind of case, the use of force by a surgeon in operating to remove a piece of shrapnel from a man's leg in order to save his life. For coercion, we need only consider that threats are coercive and they need not even be threats to do violence (e.g. a threat to tell someone's wife of his disreputable behaviour). Various classical non-violent tactics of resistance and demonstration are coercive, e.g. the blocking off of a road on which officials usually proceed by having large numbers of demonstrators lie down on the roadway. Violence is, of course, one way of coercing, but only one.

Ideally at this point I should provide definitions of force and coercion, but limitations of space will have to be my excuse for dodging that difficult task here.[32] Instead I want to turn to the OED definition mentioned earlier and raise some questions about it. It defines violence as: "The exercise of physical force so as to inflict injury on or damage to persons or property; action or conduct characterised by this."

The first problem with this is that it rules out the possibility of psychological violence and there is at least a case for including it. I suspect that whether we want to allow for a non-metaphorical use of the term violence in the psychological cases will depend upon whether we can realistically view some of these cases as involving the application of force. It is useful here to think of the notion of overpowering which seems as if it must figure as an element in the analysis of force. Now if we consider a case in which someone skillfully works upon another's emotions and fears with a combination of words and deeds short of physical force, but with intentionally overpowering effects, then we may well feel that this is close enough to the physical model to be a case of violence. Newton Garver gives an interesting and profoundly sad example of the Arizona parents who decided to punish their daughter's act of adultery in an unusual way. The girl, Linda Ault, owned a dog, Beauty, of which she was very fond. According to a newspaper report,

> . . . the Aults and Linda took the dog into the desert near their home. They had the girl dig a shallow grave. Then Mrs. Ault grasped the dog between her hands, and Mr. Ault gave his daughter a .22 caliber pistol and told her to shoot the dog.
>
> Instead the girl put the pistol to her right temple and shot herself.[33]

Clearly a dreadful act, and perhaps deserving of the name of violence, but if we do so treat it this will not be because of the reasons given by Garver (which are to do with deprivation of autonomy and lead pretty quickly to a version of structural violence). There is a tendency in the literature to slide from psychological violence to structural violence, but this seems to embody a confusion since it rests on the tendency to think of psychological violence as *impalpable* and then to feel that its admission endorses the even more impalpable structural violence. However, the examples which make the category of psychological violence plausible are all very palpable indeed. In Garver's example, for instance, what strikes one is the sheer immediacy and specificity of the pressure which is brought to bear upon the unfortunate girl with such overwhelming effects. Even if she had not shot herself we would feel that she had still been the victim of severe and damaging force. The surrounding circumstances of the outrage are tinged with physical violence for not only was she ordered to kill with a gun but one imagines that force was used to get her to dig the grave and even to get her to the place of punishment (though we are given no details of this). Consequently, to describe the case as one of quiet violence and hence a half-way house to structural violence is unconvincing.

A further category concerns those cases of great damage which do not seem to involve force though they do involve physical means. Poisoning is often given as an example, and Harris gives as well the case of the Belfast children who tie a cheese-wire between two lamp-posts across a street at a height of about six feet. As one of the kids says, "There's always a soldier standing on the back of the jeep; even with the search lights he can't see the wire in the dark. It's just at the right height to catch his throat."[34] Harris concludes from such examples that we can have an *act of violence* in the absence of a *violent act*. But for most of his examples we can surely appeal to the 'accordion effect' beloved of philosophers of action. The planned and fully intended results of stretching the wire are properly describable as what the children did, as their act. Their violent act was not merely stretching gently a wire across a road but ripping a man's throat open. This resort is certainly available where the incorporated consequences are intended by the agent and Harris' cases are all of this kind. Two of his examples, however, seem to raise problems for the restricted definition, even acknowledging the accordion effect. They both focus upon the interpretation of the term 'force' in the definition rather than upon the idea of a positive act. One example is a stabbing to death with a stiletto gently slid between the ribs. (Harris somewhat painfully jokes that this is "the thin edge of the wedge.") A second example (or class of examples) concerns poisoning or gassing. I have not produced a definition of force but my instinct is to treat the stiletto case as a use of force especially when the immediate, overpoweringly forceful effects upon the victim's body are taken into account (and the killer's intention certainly encompasses them). As to poisons, if we take a case of slow poisoning (i.e. slow-acting and requiring repeated dosing) where the destructive effects are gradual and cumulative, easily mimicking a slowly acting sickness, I suspect that we should not call the poisoning a violent act—it's one that could be ordered or done by the proverbially fastidious criminal who abhors violence. By contrast, the use of poison gas in war, or the like swiftly acting poison, would be much more like dealing a blow, and fairly clearly a violent act.

The concept of force needs more attention but I shall assume that this can be successfully negotiated and that the poisoning cases can either be dealt with in the way suggested or else treated as territory which is uncomfortably borderline between violence and non-violence. It is also relevant to certain cases of poisoning that a background of violence will colour our attitudes to a particular case. Consider, for instance, a siege or a blockade which may not be violent in as much as troops or ships are just patrolling and waiting for starvation or despair to produce surrender. Nonetheless the waiting part of the siege is usually a sort of interlude in a violent campaign and the siege itself essentially involves the declared intention to use very considerable violence against anyone who attempts to leave the besieged area. Most sieges in fact produce a great deal of actual violence. Against such a background it would be natural to describe even a siege in which no shooting or killing occurred as an exercise in violence.

Finally, we might ask: what is the point in having a concept of violence of this kind? Without an answer to this question the criticism of alternative definitions is incomplete. An answer must begin by noting certain very general facts about our condition. Life is hazardous in many different ways and we may be harmed by natural disasters and accidents or by disease or the indifference and lack of consideration of our fellows or by social arrangements which are to our disadvantage. We can sometimes take steps to guard against all of these—we can avoid certain areas, move from certain communities, cultivate friends and so on. But in addition to all the hazards mentioned there is another which many people fear very greatly, namely, the forceful intrusion into their lives of those who are intent upon inflicting harm and injury upon their person. It is not surprising that this should be so and that a distinctive way of speaking should arise to mark the reality to which we react in this way.

Nor is it surprising that a particular type of concern should exist for this kind of intrusion into our lives. In the first place we know that human malevolence is liable to be effective and difficult to avoid just because it is directed by intelligence; in the second place the unjustified employment of violence damages the character and worth of the user in distinctive ways or so many people believe—hence the point of expressions such as 'bully', 'sadist', or 'thug'; thirdly, the principal way of avoiding such malevolent intrusion is to resort to violence oneself or to have agents do it for you and this in turn is dangerous both in the short or the long term as is so vividly dramatised in Hobbes' picture of a State of Nature;[35] fourthly, it is arguable that even the justified resort to violence has damaging effects upon those who employ it even where they remain physically unharmed—this argument marks one area in which pacifist contentions are commonly produced but even non-pacifists can acknowledge the appeal of some such arguments; fifthly, and relatedly, there is the fact that violence, particularly large-scale violence is hard to control and its consequences are hard to predict. The third, fourth and fifth reasons make it plausible that resort to violence even when morally justifiable should commonly be regarded as a matter for regret. More generally, all those considerations bear upon debates about the comparability of violent and non-violent tactics, about the advantages of societies with a low level of officially sanctioned violence, and the appeal as a social ideal of, what Galtung would call, negative peace.

It must of course be conceded that this ideal does not have equal weight with all who consider it. Although anyone can recognise the distinctive facts that underpin the concept of violence I have been defending, not everyone will have the same reactions to them. There will be variations in both personal and cultural terms here even amongst men and communities who are in no obvious way corrupt or wicked. There are individuals who are much more sensitive to and worried about violence than others, just as there are whole groups, such as warrior castes, for whom violence is, to some degree, an accepted and even welcome part of their lives. Such groups may be less enthusiastic than others about projects to limit the scope of violence within and between communities and an argument with them would involve exploring further the value of peace in comparison with other values as well as conducting a debate about certain empirical issues. Such a debate must await another occasion; I hope I have done something here to prepare the ground for it.[36]

CHAPTER 4

Cultural Violence

By Johan Galtung

1. DEFINITION

By 'cultural violence' we mean those aspects of culture, the symbolic sphere of our existence—exemplified by religion and ideology, language and art, empirical science and formal science (logic, mathematics)—that can be used to justify or legitimize direct or structural violence.[1] Stars, crosses and crescents; flags, anthems and military parades; the ubiquitous portrait of the Leader; inflammatory speeches and posters—all these come to mind. [However, let us postpone the examples until section 4 and start with analysis.] The features mentioned above are 'aspects of culture', not entire cultures. A person encouraging a potential killer, shouting "Killing is self-realization!" may prove that the English language is capable of expressing such thoughts, but not that the English language as such is violent. Entire cultures can hardly be classified as violent; this is one reason for preferring the expression "Aspect A of culture C is an example of cultural violence" to cultural stereotypes like "culture C is violent."

On the other hand, cultures could be imagined and even encountered with not only one but a set of aspects so violent, extensive and diverse, spanning all cultural domains, that the step from talking about cases of culture violence to violent cultures may be warranted. For that, a systematic research process is needed. This article is part of that process.

One place to start would be to clarify 'cultural violence' by searching for its negation. If the opposite of violence is peace, the subject matter of peace research/peace studies, then the opposite of cultural violence would be 'cultural peace', meaning aspects of a culture that serve to justify and legitimize direct peace and structural peace. If many and diverse aspects of that kind are found in a culture, we can refer to it as a 'peace culture'. A major task of peace research, and the peace movement in general, is that never-ending search for a peace culture—problematic, because of the temptation to institutionalize that culture, making it obligatory with the hope of internalizing it everywhere. And that would already be direct violence,[2] imposing a culture.

Cultural violence makes direct and structural violence look, even feel, right—or at least not wrong. Just as political science is about two problems—the use of

Table I. A Typology of Violence

	SURVIVAL NEEDS	WELL-BEING NEEDS	IDENTITY NEEDS	FREEDOM NEEDS
Direct Violence	Killing	Maiming Siege, Sanctions Misery	Desocialization Resocialization Secondary-Citizen	Repression Detention Expulsion
Structural Violence	Exploitation A	Exploitation B	Penetration Segmentation	Marginalization Fragmentation

power and the legitimization of the use of power—violence studies are about two problems: the use of violence and the legitimation of that use. The psychological mechanism would be internalization.[3] The study of cultural violence highlights the way in which the act of direct violence and the fact of structural violence are legitimized and thus rendered acceptable in society. One way cultural violence works is by changing the moral color of an act from red/wrong to green/right or at least to yellow/acceptable; an example being 'murder on behalf of the country as right, on behalf of oneself wrong'. Another way is by making reality opaque, so that we do not see the violent act or fact, or at least not as violent. Obviously this is more easily done with some forms of violence than with others: an example being *abortus provatus*. Hence, peace studies is in need of a violence typology, in much the same way as a pathology is among the prerequisites for health studies.

2. A TYPOLOGY OF DIRECT AND STRUCTURAL VIOLENCE

I see violence as avoidable insults to basic human needs, and more generally to *life*, towering the real level of needs satisfaction below what is potentially possible. Threats of violence are also violence. Combining the distinction between direct and structural violence with four classes of basic needs we get the typology of Table I. The four classes of basic needs—an outcome of extensive dialogs in many parts of the world[4]—are: *survival needs* (negation: death, mortality); *well-being needs* (negation: misery, morbidity); *identity, meaning needs* (negation: alienation); and *freedom needs* (negation: repression).

The result is eight types of violence with some subtypes, easily identified for direct violence but more complex for structural violence (see Table I). A first comment could be that Table I is anthropo-centric. A fifth column could be added at the beginning for the rest of Nature, the sine qua non for human existence. 'Ecological balance' is probably the most frequently found term used for environment system maintenance. If this is not satisfied, the result is ecological degradation, breakdown, imbalance. Ecobalance corresponds to survival + well-being + freedom + identity for human basic maintenance. If not satisfied, the result is human degradation. The sum of all five, for all, will define 'peace'.

But 'ecological balance' is a very broad category encompassing abiota (non-life) and biota (life) alike. Violence defined as insults to life would focus on biota, only indirectly on abiota. Moreover, there are difficult and important questions, such as 'balance for whom?' For human beings to reproduce themselves? At what level of economic activity and what numbers? Or, for the 'environment' (what an anthropocentric term!) to reproduce itself? All parts, equally, at what level, what numbers? Or for both?

Second, the mega-versions of the pale words used above for violence should also be contemplated. For 'killing' read *extermination, holocaust, genocide.* For 'misery' read *silent holocaust.* For 'alienation' read *spiritual death.* For 'repression' read *gulagl KZ.* For 'ecological degradation' read *ecocide.* For all of this together read 'omnicide'. The words might sound like someone's effort to be apocalyptic—were it not for the fact that the world has experienced all of this during the last 50 years alone, closely associated with the names of Hitler, Stalin and Reagan[5] and Japanese militarism.[6] In short violence studies, an indispensable part of peace studies, may be a horror cabinet; but like pathology they reflect a reality to be known and understood.

Then some comments on the content of the table as it stands. The first category of violence, killing, is clear enough, as is maiming. Added together they constitute 'casualties', used in assessing the magnitude of a war. But 'war' is only one particular form of orchestrated violence, usually with at least one actor, a government. How narrow it is to see peace as the opposite of war, and limit peace studies to war avoidance studies, and more particularly avoidance of big wars or super-wars (defined as wars between big powers or superpowers), and even more particularly to the limitation, abolition or control of super-weapons. Important interconnections among types of violence are left out, particularly the way in which one type of violence may be reduced or controlled at the expense of increase or maintenance of another. Like 'side-effects' in health studies, they are very important and easily overlooked. Peace research should avoid that mistake.[7]

Included under maiming is also the insult to human needs brought about by siege/blockade (classical term) and sanctions (modern term). To some, this is 'nonviolence', since direct and immediate killing is avoided. To the victims, however, it may mean slow but intentional killing through malnutrition and lack of medical attention, hitting the weakest first, the children, the elderly, the poor, the women. By making the causal chain longer the actor avoids having to face the violence directly. He even 'gives the victims a chance', usually to submit, meaning loss of freedom and identity instead of loss of life and limbs, trading the last two for the first two types of direct violence. But the mechanism is the threat to the livelihood brought about by siege/boycott/sanctions. The Gandhian type of economic boycott combined refusal to buy British textiles with the collecting of funds for the merchants, in order not to confuse the issue by threatening their livelihood.

The category of 'alienation' can be defined in terms of socialization, meaning the internalization of culture. There is a double aspect: to be desocialized away from one's own culture and to be resocialized into another culture—like the prohibition and imposition of languages. The one does not presuppose the other. But they often come together in the category of second class citizenship, where the subjected group (not necessarily a 'minority') is forced to express dominant culture and not its own, at least not in public space. The problem is, of course, that any socialization of a child—in the family, at school, by society at large—is also forced, a kind of brainwashing, giving the child no choice. Consequently, we might arrive at the conclusion (not that far-fetched) that nonviolent socialization is to give the child a choice, e.g. by offering him/her more than one cultural idiom.

The category of 'repression' has a similar double definition: the 'freedom from' and the 'freedom to' of the International Bill of Human Rights,[8] with historical and cultural limitations.[9] Two categories have been added explicitly because of their significance as concomitants of other types of violence: detention, meaning locking people in (prisons, concentration camps), anti expulsion, meaning locking people out (banishing them abroad or to distant parts of the country).

To discuss the categories of structural violence we need an image of a violent structure, and a vocabulary, a discourse, in order to identify the aspects and see how they relate to the needs categories. The archetypal violent structure, in my view, has exploitation as a center-piece. This simply means that some, the top-dogs, get much more (here measured in needs currency) out of the interaction in the structure than others, the underdogs.[10] There is 'unequal exchange', a euphemism. The underdogs may in fact be so disadvantaged that they die (starve, waste away from diseases) from it: exploitation A. Or they may be left in a permanent, unwanted state of misery, usually including malnutrition and illness: exploitation B. The way people die differs: in the Third World, from diarrhea and immunity deficiencies: in the 'developed' countries, avoidably and prematurely, from cardio-vascular diseases and malignant tumors. All of this happens within complex structures and at the end of the long, highly ramified causal chains and cycles.

A violent structure leaves marks not only on the human body but also on the mind and the spirit. The next four terms can be seen as parts of exploitation or as reinforcing components in the structure. They function by impeding consciousness formation and mobilization, two conditions for effective struggle against exploitation. *Penetration*, implanting the topdog inside the underdog so to speak, combined with *segmentation*, giving the underdog only a very partial view of what goes on, will do the first job. And *marginalization*, keeping the underdogs on the outside, combined with *fragmentation*, keeping the underdogs away from each other, will do the second job. However, these four should also be seen as structural violence in their own right, and more particularly as variation on the general theme of structurally built-in repression. They have all been operating in gender contexts even if women do not always have higher mortality rates but in fact may have higher life expectancy than men, provided they survive gender-specific abortion, infanticide and the first years of childhood. In short, exploitation and repression go hand in hand, as violence: but they are not identical.

How about violence against nature? There is the direct violence of slashing, burning, etc., as in a war. The structural form of such violence would be more insidious, not intended to destroy nature but nevertheless doing so: the pollution and depletion associated with modern industry, leading to dying forests, ozone holes, global warming, and so on. What happens is transformation of nature through *industrial activity*, leaving non-degradable residues and depleting nonrenewable resources, combined with a *world-encompassing commercialization* that makes the consequences non-visible to the perpetrators.[11] Two powerful structures at work, indeed, legitimized by economic growth. The buzzword 'sustainable economic growth' may prove to be yet another form of cultural violence.

3. RELATING THREE TYPES OF VIOLENCE

With these comments 'violence' is defined in extension by the types given in Table I, using direct and structural violence as overarching categories or 'super-types'. 'Cultural violence' can now be added as the third super-type and put in the third corner of a (vicious) violence triangle as an image. When the triangle is stood on its "direct" and 'structural violence' feet, the image invoked is cultural violence as the legitimizer of both. Standing the triangle on its 'direct violence' head yields the image of structural and cultural sources of direct violence. Of course the triangle always remains a triangle—but the image produced is different, and all six positions (three pointing downward, three upward) invoke somewhat different stories all worth telling.

Despite the symmetries there is a basic difference in the time relation of the three concepts of violence. Direct violence is an event; structural violence is a process with ups and downs; cultural violence is an *invariant*, a 'permanence',[12] remaining essentially the same for long periods, given the slow transformations of basic culture. Put in the useful terms of the French Annales school in history: 'événementielle, conjoncturelle, la longue durée.' The three forms of violence enter time differently, somewhat like the difference in earthquake theory between the earthquake as an event, the movement of the tectonic plates as a process and the fault line as a more permanent condition.

This leads to a *violence strata* image (complementing the triangle image) of the phenomenology of violence, useful as a paradigm generating a wide variety of hypotheses. At the bottom is the steady flow through time of cultural violence, a substratum from which the other two can derive their nutrients. In the next stratum the rhythms of structural violence are located. Patterns of exploitation are building up, wearing out, or torn down, with the protective accompaniment of penetration-segmentation preventing consciousness formation, and fragmentation-marginalization preventing organization against exploitation and repression. And at the top, visible to the unguided eye and to barefoot empiricism, is the stratum of direct violence with the whole record of direct cruelty perpetrated by human beings against each other and against other forms or life and nature in general.

Generally, a causal flow from cultural via structural to direct violence can be identified. The culture preaches, teaches, admonishes, eggs on, and dulls us into seeing exploitation and/or repression as normal and natural, or into not seeing them (particularly not exploitation) at all. Then come the eruptions, the efforts to use direct violence to get out of the structural iron cage,[13] and counter-violence to keep the cage intact. Ordinary, regular criminal activity is partly an effort by the underdog to 'get out', to redistribute wealth, get even, get revenge ('blue-collar crime'), or by somebody to remain or become a topdog, sucking the structure for what it is worth ('white-collar crime'). Both direct and structural violence create needs-deficits. When this happens suddenly we can talk of *trauma*. When it happens to a group, a collectivity, we have the collective trauma that can sediment into the collective subconscious and become raw material for major historical processes and events. The underlying assumption is simple: 'violence breeds violence'. Violence is needs-deprivation; needs-deprivation is serious; one reaction is direct violence. But that is not the only reaction. There could also be a feeling of hopelessness, a deprivation/frustration syndrome that shows up on the inside as self-directed aggression and on the outside as apathy and withdrawal. Given a choice between a boiling, violent and a freezing, apathetic society as reaction to massive needs-deprivation, topdogs tend to prefer the latter. They prefer 'governability' to 'trouble, anarchy'. They love 'stability'. Indeed, a major form of cultural violence indulged in by ruling elites is to blame the victim of structural violence who throws the first stone, not in a glasshouse but to get out of the iron cage, stamping him as 'aggressor'. The category of structural violence should make such cultural violence transparent.

However, the violence strata image does not define the only causal chain in the violence triangle. There are linkages and causal flows in all six directions, and cycles connecting all three may start at any point. This is a good reason why the triangle may sometimes be a better image than the three-tier stratum model.

Africans are captured, forced across the Atlantic to work as slaves: millions are killed in the process—in Africa, on board, in the Americas. This massive direct violence over centuries seeps down and sediments as massive structural violence, with whites as the master topdogs and blacks as the slave underdogs, producing and reproducing massive cultural violence with racist ideas everywhere. After some time, direct violence is forgotten, slavery is forgotten, and only two labels show up, pale enough for college textbooks: 'discrimination' for massive structural violence and 'prejudice' for massive cultural violence. Sanitation of language: itself cultural violence.

The vicious violence cycle can also start in the structural violence corner. Social differentiation slowly takes on vertical characteristics with increasingly unequal exchange, and these social facts would then be in search of social acts for their maintenance, and cultural violence for their justification—to generalize 'materialist' (meaning structural) Marxist theory. Or, the vicious cycle could start in combined direct and structural violence, with one group treating another group so badly that they feel a need for justification and eagerly accept any cultural rationale handed to them. More than one thousand years ago Nordic Vikings attacked, cheated and killed Russians. Might that not be a good enough reason for formulating the idea that Russians are dangerous, wild, primitive—meaning that one day they may come back and do the same to us as we did to them?[14] Even to the point that when Germany attacked Norway in April 1940, the official conclusion became that the Russians are dangerous because they may one day do the same. And here we see the surprise attack trauma.

Could there be still a deeper stratum, human nature, with genetically transmitted dispositions or at least predispositions for aggression (direct violence) and domination (structural violence)? The human potential for direct and structural violence is certainly there—as is the potential for direct and structural peace. In my view, however, the most important argument against a biological determinism that postulates a drive in human nature for aggression and dominance, comparable to drives for food and sex, is the high level of variability in aggressiveness and dominance. We find people seeking food and sex under (almost) all external circumstances. But aggression and dominance exhibit tremendous variation, depending on the context, including the structural and cultural conditions. Of course, the drive may still be there, only not strong enough to assert itself under all circumstances. In that case, the concern of the peace researcher would be to know those circumstances, and to explore how to remove or modify them. Here my hypothesis would be that the two terms 'structure' and 'culture' can accommodate this exploration very comfortably.

Let us reap an important harvest from this taxonomic exercise: we can use it to clarify the concept of *militarization* as a process, and militarism as the ideology accompanying that process. Obviously, one aspect is a general inclination toward direct violence in the form of real or threatened military action, whether provoked or not, whether to settle conflict or initiate it. This inclination brings in its wake the production and deployment of the appropriate hardware and software. However, it would be superficial to study militarization only in terms of past military activity records, and present production and deployment patterns:[15] this would lead to facile conclusions in terms of personnel, budget and arms control only. Good weeding presupposes getting at the roots, in this case at the structural and cultural roots, as suggested by the three-strata paradigm. Concretely, this means identifying structural and cultural aspects that would tend to reproduce the readiness for military action, production and deployment. This would include mobbing of young boys at school, primogeniture,[16] unemployment and exploitation in general. Further, the use of military production and deployment to stimulate economic growth and economic distribution; heavily nationalist, racist and sexist ideologies,[17] and so on. The combination of building military teaching and exercise components into high school and university curricula and structure,[18] and disseminating militarism as culture, should merit particular attention. Yet structure and culture are usually not included in 'arms control' studies, both being highly sensitive areas. Those taboos have to be broken.

4. EXAMPLES OF CULTURAL VIOLENCE

We turn now to the listing of six cultural domains mentioned in the introduction—religion and ideology, language and art, empirical and formal science—giving one or two examples of cultural violence from each domain. The logic of the scheme is simple: identify the cultural element and show how it can, empirically or potentially, be used to legitimize direct or structural violence.

4.1 RELIGION

In all religions there is somewhere the sacred, *das Heilige*; let us call it 'god'. A basic distinction can be made between a transcendental God outside us and an immanent god inside us, maybe also inside all life.[19] The Judaism of the Torah, founded almost 4000 years ago, envisaged God as a male deity residing outside planet Earth. A catastrophic idea; a clear case of transcendentalism as a metaphor from which many consequences follow, taken over by the other Semitic or occidental religions, Christianity and Islam. With god outside us, as God, even 'above' ('Our Father, who art in Heaven') it is not inevitable but indeed likely that some people will be seen as closer to that God than others even as 'higher'. Moreover, in the general occidental tradition of not only dualism but Manichaeism, with sharp dichotomies between good and evil, there would also have to be something like an evil Satan corresponding to the good God, for reasons of symmetry. Again transcendental and immanent representations are possible, with God and Satan possessing or at least choosing their own; or with God or Satan—not to mention God *and* Satan—being inside us. All combinations are found in all occidental religions. But the focus here is on the hard version, belief in a transcendental God and a transcendental Satan.

Whom does God choose? Would it not be reasonable to assume that he chooses those most in His image, leaving it to Satan to take the others, as indicated in Table II? This would give us a double dichotomy with God, the Chosen Ones (by God). The Unchosen Ones (by God, chosen by Satan) and Satan; the chosen heading for salvation and closeness to God in Heaven, the unchosen for damnation and closeness to Satan in Hell. However, Heaven and Hell can also be reproduced on earth, as a foretaste or indication of the afterlife. Misery/luxury can be seen as preparations for Hell/Heaven—and social class as the finger of God.

An immanent concept of god as residing inside us would make any such dichotomy an act against god. With a transcendental God, however, this all becomes meaningful. The first three choices listed in Table II are found as early as Genesis. The last one is more typical of the New Testament with its focus on right belief, not just on right deeds. The other two are found as scattered references to slaves, and to rendering unto the Lord what is of the Lord and unto Caesar what is Caesar's. The upper classes referred to as being closer to God have actually traditionally been three: Clergy, for the obvious reason that they possessed special insight in how to communicate with God; Aristocracy, particularly the *rex gratia dei*; and Capitalists, if they are successful. The lower classes and the poor were also chosen, even as the first to enter Paradise (the Sermon on the Mount), but only in the after-life. The six together constitute a hard Judaism-Christianity-Islam which can be softened by giving up some positions and turned into softer Islam, softer Christianity and softer Judaism by adopting a more immanent concept of God (sufism, Francis of Assisi, Spinoza).

The consequences in the right-hand column of Table II could also follow from premises other than a theology of chosenness; the table only postulates contributing, sufficient causes.

For a contemporary example consider the policies of Israel with regard to the Palestinians. The Chosen People even have a Promised Land, the *Eretz Yisrael*. They behave as one would expect, translating chosenness, a vicious type of cultural violence, into all eight types of direct and structural violence listed in Table I. There is killing; maiming, material deprivation by denying West Bank inhabitants what is needed for livelihood; there is desocialization within the theocratic state of Israel with second class citizenship to non-Jews; there is detention, individual expulsion and perennial threat of massive expulsion. There is exploitation, at least as exploitation B.

The four structural concomitants of exploitation are all well developed: efforts to make the Palestinians see themselves as born underdogs, at most heading for second class citizenship by 'getting used to it'; giving them small segments of economic activity; keeping them outside Jewish society both within and outside the Green Line, and dealing with Palestinians in a *divide et impera* mode (as in the Camp David process), never as one people. There is neither massive extermination nor massive exploitation A of the sort found in many Third World countries under the debt burden, which above all hits children. The violence is more evenly distributed over the whole repertory of eight types. To some, who set their sights low, defined by Hitlerite or Stalinist extermination and Reaganite exploitation A, this means that no mass violence is going on, thus proving how humane the Israelis are. Such perspectives are also examples of cultural violence, indicative of how moral standards have become in this century.[20]

4.2 IDEOLOGY

With the decline, and perhaps death, not only of the transcendental but also the immanent God through secularization, we could expect successors to religion in the form of political ideologies, and to God in the form of the modern state, to exhibit some of the same character traits. Religion and God may be dead—but not the much more basic idea of sharp and value-loaded dichotomies. The lines may no longer be drawn between God, the Chosen, the Unchosen and Satan. Modernity would reject God and Satan but might demand a distinction between Chosen and Unchosen; let us call them Self and Other. Archetype: nationalism, with State as God's successor.

A steep gradient is then constructed, inflating, even exalting, the value of Self; deflating, even debasing, the value of Other. At that point, structural violence can start operating. It will tend to become a self-fulfilling prophecy: people become debased by being exploited, and they are exploited because they are seen as debased, dehumanized. When Other is not only dehumanized but has been successfully converted into an 'it', deprived of humanhood, the stage is set for any

Table II. The Chosen and the Unchosen

GOD CHOOSES	AND LEAVES TO SATAN	WITH THE CONSEQUENCE OF
Human Species	Animals, Plants, Nature	Speciesism, Ecocide
Men	Women	Sexism, Witch-burning
His People	The Others	Nationalism, Imperialism
Whites	Colored	Racism, Colonialism
Upper Classes	Lower Classes	"Classism," Exploitation
True Believers	Heretics, Pagans	"Mentism," Inquisition

type of direct violence,[21] which is then blamed on the victim. This is then reinforced by the category of the 'dangerous it', the 'vermin', or 'bacteria' (as Hitler described the Jews); the 'class enemy' (as Stalin described the 'kulaks'); the 'mad dog' (as Reagan described Qadhafi); the 'cranky criminals' (as Washington experts describe 'terrorists'). Extermination becomes a psychologically possible duty. The SS guards become heroes to be celebrated for their devotion to duty.

Using the six dimensions of Table II, we can easily see how the chosen ones can remain chosen without any transcendental god. Thus, only human beings are seen as capable of self-reflection; men are stronger/more logical than women; certain nations are modern/carriers of civilization and the historical process more than others; whites are more intelligent/logical than non-whites; in modern 'equal opportunity' society the best are at the top and hence entitled to power and privilege. And certain tenets of belief in modernization, development, progress are seen as apodictic; not to believe in them reflects badly on the non-believer, not on the belief.

All of these ideas have been and still are strong in Western culture, although the faith in male, Western, white innate superiority has now been badly shaken by the struggles for liberation by women, non-Western peoples (such as the Japanese economic success over the West), and colored people inside Western societies. The United States, the most Christian nation on earth, has served as a major battleground, inside and outside, for these struggles. Reducing US cultural violence becomes particularly important precisely because that country sets the tone for others.

These three assumptions—all based on ascribed distinctions, gender, race and nation already given at birth—are hard to maintain in an achievement-oriented society. But if modern society is a meritocracy, then to deny power and privilege to those on the top is to deny merit itself. To deny a minimum of 'modern orientation' is to open the field to any belief, including denying power and privilege for the meritorious and a strict border between human life and other forms of life. In short, residual chosenness will stay on for a while as speciesism, 'classism' and 'meritism', regardless of the status of God and Satan.

The ideology of nationalism, rooted in the figure of Chosen People and justified through religion or ideology, should be seen in conjunction with the ideology of the stale statism. Article 9 in the postwar Japanese Peace Constitution, that short-lived effort to make some cultural peace, stipulated that "The right of belligerence of the (Japan) state will not be recognized." Evidently Japan had forfeited that right—whereas others, presumably the victors, exited from the war with the right intact, maybe even enhanced.

Where did that right of belligerence come from? There are feudal origins, a direct carry-over from the prerogative of the *rex gratia dei* to have an *ultimo ratio regis*. The state can then be seen as an organization needed by the Prince to exact enough taxes (and, after 1793, conscripts) to pay for increasingly expensive armies and navies. The state was created to maintain the military rather than vice versa, as Krippendorff maintains.[22] But the state can also be seen as one of the successors to God, inheriting the right to destroy life (execution), if not the right to create it. Many also see the state as having the right to control the creation of life, exerting authority superior to that of the pregnant woman.

Combine nationalism with steep Self-Other gradients, and statism with the right, even the duty to exercise ultimate power, and we get the ugly ideology of the nation-state, another catastrophic idea. Killing in war is now done in the name of the 'nation', comprising all citizens with some shared ethnicity. The new idea of democracy can be accommodated with transition formulas such as *vox populi, vox dei*. Execution is also done in the name of 'the people of the state X'; but like war has to be ordered by the State. Much of the pro-life sentiment against abortion is probably rooted in a feeling that abortion on the decision of the mother erodes the power monopoly of the state over life. If anti-abortion sentiment were really rooted in a sense of sacredness of the fetus (*homo res sacra hominibus*), then the pro-life people would also tend to be pacifists; they would be against the death penalty, and be outraged at the high mortality levels of blacks in the USA and others around the world. Of course, the priority for choice rather than life is another type of cultural violence, based on a denial of fetal life as human, making the fetus an 'it'.[23]

Combine the ideology of the nation-state with a theologically based Chosen People complex and the stage is set for disaster. Israel (Yahweh), Iran (Allah), Japan (Amaterasu-okami), South Africa (a Dutch 'reformed' God), the United States (the Judeo-Christian Yahweh-God) are relatively clear cases: capable of anything in a crisis. Nazi Germany (the Nazi Odin/Wotan-God) was in the same category. The Soviet Union under Gorbachev—who sees himself as the successor to Lenin after 61 years of stagnation—is probably still laboring under its calling as a Chosen People, chosen by History (capital h) as the first nation-state to enter Socialism. And France has the same superiority complex—only that any idea of being chosen by somebody would indicate that there is something above France, an intolerable idea. France chose herself, *un peuple élu, mais par lui-même*, exemplified by the archetypal act when Napoleon was to be crowned by the Pope in 1804. He took the crown from his hands and crowned himself.

4.3 LANGUAGE

Certain languages—those with a Latin base such as Italian, Spanish, French (and modern English), but not those with a Germanic base such as German and Norwegian—make women invisible by using the same word for the male gender as for the entire human species. The important movement for non-sexist writing is a good example of deliberate cultural transformation away from cultural violence.[24] The task must have looked impossible when some courageous women got started, and yet it is already bearing fruit.

Then there are more subtle aspects of language where the violence is less clear, more implicit. A comparison of basic features of Indo-European languages with Chinese and Japanese brings out certain space and time rigidities imposed by the Indo-European languages; a corresponding rigidity in the logical structure with strong emphasis on the possibility of arriving at valid inferences (hence the Western pride in being so 'logical'); a tendency to distinguish linguistically between essence and apparition, leaving room for the immortality of the essence, and by implication for the legitimacy of destroying what is only the apparition.[25] However, this is deep culture, the deeper layers of that bottom stratum in the violence triangle. The relations to direct and structural violence become much more tenuous.

4.4 ART

Let me make just one point, important for the present emergence of a European Union as the successor to the European Community of 1967.[26] How does Europe understand itself? The story tied to the "Europa" of Greek mythology is not very helpful. The understanding of Europe as the negation of the non-European environment carries us much further. And that environment at the time of the transition from the Middle Ages to the Modern Period was the gigantic Ottoman Empire to the east and the south, reaching the walls of Vienna (1683), conquering Syria and Egypt (1517), vassalizing Tripolitania, Tunisia and Algeria afterwards, leaving only the Sultanate of Fez and Morocco with the small Spanish Habsburg enclaves, two of them still there. The only non-Oriental (meaning Arab, Muslim) environment was Russia, poor, vast in space and time. Sleeping, but giant.[27]

Europe thus had to understand herself as the negation of the enemy to the south and the southeast. Thus developed the metaphor of 'oriental despotism', still very prominent in the European mind, to come to grips with the 'environment'. Typical of the 'oriental despot' was callousness and arbitrariness. Like the European Prince he killed: but he ruled by his own whim, not by law. Sexually he enjoyed an access (the harem) his European colleagues could only approximate by sneaking out at night to violate peasant girls. So did Muslims not constrained by Christian monogamy. In France a school of painting emerged in the 19th century representing oriental despotism in a setting of sex and/or violence. Henri Regnault's *Execution Without Process* and Eugene Delacroix's *The Death of Sardanapal* are good examples. Hegel, copied by Marx, also saw oriental despotism and oriental (or Asian) mode of production as negative, homogeneous, stagnant.

It belongs to this syndrome that the non-Arab part of the semicircle around Europe, Russia, also had to be seen in terms of oriental despotism. That 'despotism' could fit the tsars as a description is perhaps less objectionable—but 'oriental?' The figure has probably influenced the European image of Russia and the Soviet Union for centuries, and still does, as intended slurs on either.

4.5 EMPIRICAL SCIENCE

One example of cultural violence would be neoclassical economic doctrine, understanding itself as the science of economic activity. Strongly influenced by the Adam Smith tradition, neoclassical economics now studies empirically the system prescribed by its own doctrines, and finds its own self-fulfilling prophecies often confirmed in empirical reality. One part of neoclassical dogma or 'conventional wisdom' is trade theory based on 'comparative advantages', originally postulated by David Ricardo, developed further by Heckscher and Ohlin and by Jan Tinbergen. This is the doctrine that prescribes that each country should enter the world market with those products for which that country has a comparative advantage in terms of production factors.

In practice this means that countries well endowed with raw materials and unskilled labor are to extract raw materials, while those well endowed with capital and technology, skilled labor and scientists, are to process them. And thus it was that Portugal gave up its textile industry and became a mediocre wine producer, whereas England got the stimulus, the challenge needed to develop her industrial capacity still further. The consequences of this doctrine in the form of today's vertical division of labor in the world are visible for most people to see. Structural violence everywhere:[28] among countries and within countries.

Thus, the doctrine of comparative advantages serves as a justification for a rough division of the world in terms of the degree of processing which countries impart to their export products. Since this is roughly proportionate to the amount of challenge they receive in the production process, the principle of comparative advantages sentences countries to stay where the production-factor profile has landed them, for geographical and historical reasons. Of course, there is no law, legal or empirical, to the effect that countries cannot do something to improve their production profile—a basic point made by the Japanese economist Kaname Akamatsu.[29] But to do so is not easy when there are immediate gains to be made by not changing the status quo, for those who own the raw materials/commodities. And thus it is that the 'law' of comparative advantages legitimizes a structurally intolerable status quo. In short, this 'law' is a piece of cultural violence buried in the very core of economics.

4.6 FORMAL SCIENCE

But surely this cannot be said of mathematics? This is not so obvious. If mathematics is viewed as a formal game with one basic rule, that a theorem *T* and its negation—*T* cannot both be valid, then there may be violent consequences. Even when mathematical logic explores polyvalent logic, the tool used is bivalent logic with its strict line between valid and invalid; *tertium non datur*. And it is easily seen that it has to be that way, inference being the mortar of the mathematical edifice, with *modus ponens* and *modus tollens* being the key procedures. No inference can be made with ambiguous truth values for the antecedents or the inference.[30]

This means that mathematics disciplines us into a particular mode of thought highly compatible with black-white thinking and polarization in personal, social and world spaces. The either-or character of mathematical thought makes it an exciting game: but as a model for a highly dialectic human, social and world reality it is far from adequate. And *adequatio* is the basic requirement for culture, symbolic space, if it is to guide us in visioning a less violent potential reality.

4.7 COSMOLOGY

We return to the problem of the transition from cultural violence to violent culture. As mentioned in section I above, such global judgements could be arrived at by identifying an extensive and diverse number of cultural aspects, in religious and ideological thought, in language and art, in empirical and formal science; all of them serving to justify violence. However, there is also another approach: to explore the substratum of the culture for its 'deep culture(s)', of which there may be several.[31] We would be looking at the roots of the roots, so to speak: the cultural genetic code that generates cultural elements and reproduces itself through them. That this becomes very speculative is not so problematic; it is in the nature of science to postulate deeper layers, spelling out implications, testing the hard core of the theory around the ragged edges.

The cosmology concept is designed to harbor that substratum of deeper assumptions about reality,[32] defining what is normal and natural. Assumptions at this level of depth in the collective subconscious are not easily unearthed, not to mention uprooted. And yet, it is at this level that occidental culture shows so many violent features that the whole culture starts looking violent. There is chosenness, there are strong center-periphery gradients. There is the urgency, the *apocalypse now!* syndrome precluding the slow, patient building and enactment of structural and direct peace. There is atomistic, dichotomous thought with deductive chains counteracting the unity-of-means-and-ends. There is arrogance toward nature counteracting the unity-of-life. There is a strong tendency to individualize and rank human beings, breaking up the unity-of-man. And there is a transcendental, absolute God with awesome successors. The whole culture possesses a tremendous potential for violence that can be expressed at the more manifest cultural level and then he used to justify the unjustifiable. That there is also peace in the Occident, sometimes even emanating from the Occident, is something of a miracle, possibly due to the softer strands.

The problem is that this type of thinking easily leads to a sense of hopelessness. Changing the cultural genetic code looks at least as difficult as changing the biological genetic code. Moreover, even if it were possible, 'cultural engineering' might be a form of violence as problematic as genetic engineering is proving. Should it be left to 'chance'—meaning to those with power and privilege?[33] This is a very difficult and important field for future peace research.

5. GANDHI AND CULTURAL VIOLENCE

What did Gandhi himself have to say about these tricky problems, open as he was to exploring alternatives to both direct and structural violence? His answer was to reproduce, from his ecumenism, two axioms that in a sense summarize Gandhism: *unity-of-life* and *unity-of-means and end.* The first follows from the second if it is assumed that no life, and particularly no human life, can be used as a means to an end. If the end is livelihood, then the means has to be life-enhancing. But how do we understand "unity"? A reasonable interpretation, using the ideas developed in the preceding sections, would be in terms of closeness, against separation. In our mental universe all forms of life, particularly human life, should enjoy closeness and not be kept apart by steep Self-Other gradients that drive wedges in social space. Any justification derived from the hard core of a culture, e.g. a calling as a Chosen People, would be rejected when it conflicted with this even higher, even 'harder' axiom.

We can understand *unity-of-means-and-ends* as bringing oilier menial elements, such as acts, and facts brought about by acts, close together. They should not be kept separate by long causal chains that drive wedges in social time. To initiate long social sequences leading to take-off or revolution, investing in industry or the industrial proletariat, is not good enough. The means must be good in themselves, not in terms of distant goals, way down the road—as witnessed by the millions sacrificed on the altars of industrialism in the name of 'growth/capitalism' and 'revolution/socialism'. Justification derived from empirical confirmation, 'it works', is rejected when it conflicts with this even higher, even 'harder' axiom.

Any Self-Other gradient can be used to justify violence against those lower down on the scale of worthiness; any causal chain can be used to justify the use of violent means to obtain non-violent ends. Gandhi would be as skeptical of Marxist ideas of revolution and hard work, of sacrificing a generation or two for presumed bliss the day after tomorrow, as he would of liberal/conservative ideas of hard work and entrepreneurship, of sacrificing a social class or two for the bliss of the upper classes even today.

The conclusion drawn by Gandhi from these two axioms was respect for the sacredness of all life (hence vegetarianism) and acceptance of the precept 'take care of the means and the ends will take care of themselves'. Thus the unity-of-life doctrine is very different from a doctrine of 'ecological balance', since it means enhancing all life, not just human life; and all human life, not just the categories chosen by some (to Gandhi, distorted or misunderstood) religion or ideology. And the unity-of-means-and-ends would lead to a doctrine of synchrony, calling for work on all issues simultaneously[34] rather than the diachrony of one big stop that is assumed to trigger the *force motrice.* Archetype: the Buddhist wheel where elements of thought, speech and action tend to be at the same level of priority, not a Christian pyramid with more focus on some than others (e.g. faith vs. deeds).[35]

6. CONCLUSION

Violence can start at any corner in the direct-structural-cultural violence triangle and is easily transmitted to the other corners. With the violent structure institutionalized and the violent culture internalized, direct violence also tends to become institutionalized, repetitive, ritualistic, like a vendetta. This triangular syndrome of violence should then be contrasted in the mind with a triangular syndrome of peace in which cultural peace engenders structural peace, with symbiotic, equitable relations among diverse partners, and direct peace with acts of cooperation, friendliness and love. It could be a virtuous rather than vicious triangle, also self-reinforcing. This virtuous triangle would be obtained by working on all three corners at the same time, not assuming that basic change in one will automatically lead to changes in the other two.

But does this inclusion of culture not broaden the agenda for peace studies considerably? Of course it does. Why should peace studies be narrower than, for instance, health studies (medical science)? Is peace easier than health, less complex? And how about biology, the study of life; physics, the study of matter; chemistry, the study of the composition of matter; mathematics, the study of abstract form—all of these are fairly broad. Why should peace studies be more modest? Why draw borderlines at all in a field so terribly important in its consequences, and also so attractive to the inquisitive mind? If culture is relevant to violence and peace, and surely it is, then only the dogmatic mind will exclude it from explorations as penetrating and tenacious as the countless studies devoted to the many aspects of direct and structural violence. The only thing that is new is that the field opens for new areas of competence, such as the humanities, history of ideas, philosophy, theology. In other words, an invitation to new disciplines to join the quest for peace, and to established researchers in the field to retool—a little.

In so doing, maybe peace research could even make some contribution to rounding a major scientific enterprise still conspicuously absent from the pantheon of academic pursuits, the science of human culture, 'culturology'. Today the field is divided between 'humanities' for 'higher' civilizations and cultural anthropology for 'lower' ones; with philosophy, history of ideas and theology filling in some pieces. Concepts like 'cultural violence' span all of that, just as 'structural violence' spans the whole spectrum of social sciences. Peace research has too much to learn, so much to take, to receive. Perhaps we shall also in due time have some contributions to make: in the spirit of diversity, symbiosis and equity.

SECTION TWO

Violence and Law

CHAPTER 5

Critique of Violence

By Walter Benjamin

The task of a critique of violence can be summarized as that of expounding its relation to law and justice. For a cause, however effective, becomes violent, in the precise sense of the word, only when it bears on moral issues. The sphere of these issues is defined by the concepts of law and justice. With regard to the first of these, it is clear that the most elementary relationship within any legal system is that of ends to means, and, further, that violence can first be sought only in the realm of means, not of ends. These observations provide a critique of violence with more—and certainly different—premises than perhaps appears. For if violence is a means, a criterion for criticizing it might seem immediately available. It imposes itself in the question whether violence, in a given case, is a means to a just or an unjust end. A critique of it would then be implied in a system of just ends. This, however, is not so. For what such a system, assuming it to be secure against all doubt, would contain is not a criterion for violence itself as a principle, but, rather, the criterion for cases of its use. The question would remain open whether violence, as a principle, could be a moral means even to just ends. To resolve this question a more exact criterion is needed, which would discriminate within the sphere of means themselves, without regard for the ends they serve.

The exclusion of this more precise critical approach is perhaps the predominant feature of a main current of legal philosophy: natural law. It perceives in the use of violent means to just ends no greater problem than a man sees in his "right" to move his body in the direction of a desired goal. According to this view (for which the terrorism in the French Revolution provided an ideological foundation), violence is a product of nature, as it were a raw material, the use of which is in no way problematical, unless force is misused for unjust ends. If, according to the theory of state of natural law, people give up all their violence for the sake of the state, this is done on the assumption (which Spinoza, for example, states explicitly in his *Tractatus Theologico-Politicus*) that the individual, before the conclusion of this rational contract, has *de jure* the right to use at will the violence that is *de facto* at his disposal. Perhaps these views have been recently rekindled by Darwin's biology, which, in a thoroughly dogmatic manner, regards violence as the only original means, besides natural selection, appropriate to all the vital ends of nature. Popular Darwinistic philosophy has often shown how short a step it is from this dogma of natural history to the still cruder one of legal philosophy, which holds that the violence that is, almost alone, appropriate to natural ends is thereby also legal.

This thesis of natural law that regards violence as a natural datum is diametrically opposed to that of positive law, which sees violence as a product of history. If natural law can judge all existing law only in criticizing its ends, so positive law can judge all evolving law only in criticizing its means. If justice is the criterion of ends, legality is that of means. Notwithstanding this antithesis, however, both schools meet in their common basic dogma: just ends can be attained by justified means, justified means used for just ends. Natural law attempts, by the justness of the ends, to "justify" the means, positive law to "guarantee" the justness of the ends through the justification of the means. This antinomy would prove insoluble if the common dogmatic assumption were false, if justified means on the one hand and just ends on the other were in irreconcilable conflict. No insight into this problem could be gained, however, until the circular argument had been broken, and mutually independent criteria both of just ends and of justified means were established.

The realm of ends, and therefore also the question of a criterion of justness, is excluded for the time being from this study. Instead, the central place is given to the question of the justification of certain means that constitute violence. Principles of natural law cannot decide this question, but can only lead to bottomless casuistry. For if positive law is blind to the absoluteness of ends, natural law is equally so to the contingency of means. On the other hand, the positive theory of law is acceptable as a hypothetical basis at the outset of this study, because it undertakes a fundamental distinction between kinds of violence independently of cases of their application. This distinction is between historically acknowledged, so-called sanctioned violence, and unsanctioned violence. If the following considerations proceed from this it cannot, of course, mean that given forms of violence are classified in terms of whether they are sanctioned or not. For in a critique of violence, a criterion for the latter in positive law cannot concern its uses but only its evaluation. The question that concerns us is, what light is thrown on the nature of violence by the fact that such a criterion or distinction can be applied to it at all, or, in other words, what is the meaning of this distinction? That this distinction supplied by positive law is meaningful, based on the nature of violence, and irreplaceable by any other, will soon enough be shown, but at the same time light will be shed on the sphere in which alone such a distinction can be made. To sum up: if the criterion established by positive law to assess the legality of violence can be analyzed with regard to its meaning, then the sphere of its application must be criticized with regard to its value. For this critique a standpoint outside positive legal philosophy but also outside natural law must be found. The extent to which it can only be furnished by a historico-philosophical view of law will emerge.

The meaning of the distinction between legitimate and illegitimate violence is not immediately obvious. The misunderstanding in natural law by which a distinction is drawn between violence used for just and unjust ends must be emphatically rejected. Rather, it has already been indicated that positive law demands of all violence a proof of its historical origin, which under certain conditions is declared legal, sanctioned. Since the acknowledgment of legal violence is most tangibly evident in a deliberate submission to its ends, a hypothetical distinction between kinds of violence must be based on the presence or absence of a general historical acknowledgment of its ends. Ends that lack such acknowledgment may be called natural ends, the other legal ends. The differing function of violence, depending on whether it serves natural or legal ends, can be most clearly traced against a background of specific legal conditions. For the sake of simplicity, the following discussion will relate to contemporary European conditions.

Characteristic of these, as far as the individual as legal subject is concerned, is the tendency not to admit the natural ends of such individuals in all those cases in which such ends could, in a given situation, be usefully pursued by violence. This means: this legal system tries to erect, in all areas where individual ends could be usefully pursued by violence, legal ends that can only be realized by legal power. Indeed, it strives to limit by legal ends even those areas in which natural ends are admitted in principle within wide boundaries, like that of education, as soon as these natural ends are pursued with an excessive measure of violence, as in the laws relating to the limits of educational authority to punish. It can be formulated as a general maxim of present-day European legislation that all the natural ends of individuals must collide with legal ends if pursued with a greater or lesser degree of violence. (The contradiction between this and the right of self-defense will be resolved in what follows.) From this maxim it follows that law sees violence in the hands of individuals as a danger undermining the legal system. As a danger nullifying legal ends and the legal executive? Certainly not; for then violence as such would not be condemned, but only that directed to illegal ends. It will be argued that a system of legal ends cannot be maintained if natural ends are anywhere still pursued violently. In the first place, however, this is a mere dogma. To counter it one might perhaps consider the surprising possibility that the law's interest in a monopoly of violence vis-à-vis individuals is not explained by the intention of preserving legal ends but, rather, by that of preserving the law itself; that violence, when not in the hands of the law, threatens it not by the ends that it may pursue but by its mere existence outside the law. The same may be more drastically suggested if one reflects how often the figure of the "great" criminal, however repellent his ends may have been, has aroused the secret admiration of the public. This cannot result from his deed, but only from the violence to which it bears witness. In this case, therefore, the violence of which present-day law is seeking in all areas of activity to deprive the individual appears really threatening, and arouses even in defeat the sympathy of the mass against law. By what function violence can with reason seem so threatening to law, and be so feared by it, must be especially evident where its application, even in the present legal system, is still permissible.

This is above all the case in the class struggle, in the form of the workers' guaranteed right to strike. Organized labor is, apart from the state, probably today the only legal subject entitled to exercise violence. Against this view there is certainly the objection that an omission of actions, a nonaction, which a strike really is, cannot be described as violence. Such a consideration doubtless made it easier for a state power to conceive the right to strike, once this was no longer avoidable. But its truth is not unconditional, and therefore not unrestricted. It is true that the omission of an action, or service, where it amounts simply to a "severing of relations," can be an entirely nonviolent, pure means. And as in the view of the state, or the law, the right to strike conceded to labor is certainly not a right to exercise violence but, rather, to escape from a violence indirectly exercised by the employer, strikes conforming to this may undoubtedly occur from time to time and involve only a "withdrawal" or "estrangement" from the employer. The moment of violence, however, is necessarily introduced, in the form of extortion, into such an omission, if it takes place in the context of a conscious readiness to resume the suspended action under certain circumstances that either have nothing whatever to do with this action or only superficially modify it. Understood in this way, the right to strike constitutes in the view of labor, which is opposed to that of the state, the right to use force in attaining certain ends. The antithesis between the two conceptions merges in all its bitterness in face of a revolutionary general strike. In this, labor will always appeal to its right to strike, and the state will call this appeal an abuse, since the right to strike was not "so intended," and take emergency measures. For the state retains the right to declare that a simultaneous use of strike in all industries is illegal, since the specific reasons for strike admitted by legislation cannot be prevalent in every workshop. In this difference of interpretation is expressed the objective contradiction in the legal situation, whereby the state acknowledges a violence whose ends, as natural ends, it sometimes regards with indifference, but in a crisis (the revolutionary general strike) confronts inimically. For, however paradoxical this may appear at first sight, even conduct involving the exercise of a right can nevertheless, under certain circumstances, be described as violent. More specifically, such conduct, when active, may be called violent if it exercises a right in order to overthrow the legal system that has conferred it: when passive, it is nevertheless to be so described if it constitutes extortion in the sense explained above. It therefore reveals an objective contradiction in the legal situation, but not a logical contradiction in the law, if under certain circumstances the law meets the strikers, as perpetrators of violence, with violence. For in a strike the state fears above all else that function of violence which it is the object of this study to identify as the only secure foundation of its critique. For if violence were, as first appears, merely the means to secure directly whatever happens to be sought, it could fulfill its end as predatory violence. It would be entirely unsuitable as a basis for, or a modification to, relatively stable conditions. The strike shows, however, that it can be so, that it is able to found and modify legal conditions, however offended the sense of justice may find itself thereby. It will be objected that such a function of violence is fortuitous and isolated. This can be rebutted by a consideration of military violence.

The possibility of military law rests on exactly the same objective contradiction in the legal situation as does that of strike law, that is to say, on the fact that legal subjects sanction violence whose ends remain for the sanctioners' natural ends, and can therefore in a crisis come into conflict with their own legal or natural ends. Admittedly, military violence is in the first place used quite directly, as predatory violence, toward its ends. Yet it is very striking that even—or, rather, precisely—in primitive conditions that know hardly the beginnings of constitutional relations, and even in cases where the victor has established himself in invulnerable possession, a peace ceremony is entirely necessary. Indeed, the word "peace," in the sense in which it is the correlative to the word "war" (for there is also a quite different meaning, similarly unmetaphorical and political, the one used by Kant in talking of "Eternal Peace"), denotes this a priori, necessary sanctioning, regardless of all other legal conditions, of every victory. This sanction consists precisely in recognizing the new conditions as a new "law," quite regardless of whether they need *de facto* any guarantee of their continuation. If, therefore, conclusions can be drawn from military violence, as being primordial and paradigmatic of all violence used for natural ends, there is inherent in all such violence a lawmaking character. We shall return later to the implications of this insight. It explains the above mentioned tendency of modern law to divest the individual, at least as a legal subject, of all violence, even that directed only to natural ends. In the great criminal this violence confronts the law with the threat of declaring a new law, a threat that even today, despite its impotence, in important instances horrifies the public as it did in primeval times. The state, however, fears this violence simply for its lawmaking character, being obliged to acknowledge it as lawmaking whenever external powers force it to concede them the right to conduct warfare, and classes the right to strike.

If in the last war the critique of military violence was the starting point for a passionate critique of violence in general—which taught at least one thing, that violence is no longer exercised and tolerated naively—nevertheless, violence was not only subject to criticism for its lawmaking character, but was also judged, perhaps more annihilatingly, for another of its functions. For a duality in the function of violence is characteristic of militarism, which could only come into being through general conscription. Militarism is the compulsory, universal use of violence as a means to the ends of the state. This compulsory use of violence has recently been scrutinized as closely as, or still more closely than, the use of violence itself. In it violence shows itself in a function quite different from its simple application for natural ends. It consists in the use of violence as a means of legal ends. For the subordination of citizens to laws—in the present case, to the law of general conscription—is a legal end. If that first function of violence is called the lawmaking function, this second will be called the law-preserving function. Since conscription is a case of law-preserving violence that is not in principle distinguished from others, a really effective critique of it is far less easy than the declamations of pacifists and activists suggest. Rather, such a critique coincides with the critique of all legal violence—that is, with the critique of legal or executive force—and cannot be performed by any lesser program. Nor, of course—unless one is prepared to proclaim a quite childish anarchism—is it achieved by refusing to acknowledge any constraint toward persons and declaring "What pleases is permitted." Such a maxim merely excludes reflection on the moral and historical spheres, and thereby on any meaning in action, and beyond this on any meaning in reality itself, which cannot be constituted if "action" is removed from its sphere. More important is the fact that even the appeal, so frequently attempted, to the categorical imperative, with its doubtless incontestable minimum program—act in such a way that at all times you use humanity both in your person and in the person of all others as an end, and never merely as a means—is in itself inadequate for such a critique.[1] For positive law, if conscious of its roots, will certainly claim to acknowledge and promote the interest of mankind in the person of each individual. It sees this interest in the representation and preservation of an order imposed by fate. While this view, which claims to preserve law in its very basis, cannot escape criticism, nevertheless all attacks that are made merely in the name of a formless "freedom" without being able to specify this higher order of freedom, remain impotent against it. And most impotent of all when, instead of attacking the legal system root and branch, they impugn particular laws or legal practices that the law, of course, takes under the protection of its power, which resides in the fact that there is only one fate and that what exists, and in particular what threatens, belongs inviolably to its order. For law-preserving violence is a threatening violence. And its threat is not intended as the deterrent that uninformed liberal theorists interpret it to be. A deterrent in the exact sense would require a certainty that contradicts the nature of a threat and is not attained by any law, since there is always hope of eluding its arm. This makes it all the more threatening, like fate, on which depends whether the criminal is apprehended. The deepest purpose of the uncertainty of the legal threat will emerge from the later consideration of the sphere of fate in which it originates. There is a useful pointer to it in the sphere of punishments. Among them, since the validity of positive law has been called into question, capital punishment has provoked more criticism than all others. However superficial the arguments may in most cases have been, their motives were and are rooted in principle. The opponents of these critics felt, perhaps without knowing why and probably involuntarily, that an attack on capital punishment assails, not legal measure, not laws, but law itself in its origin. For if violence, violence crowned by fate, is the origin of law, then it may be readily supposed that where the highest violence, that over life and death, occurs in the legal system, the origins of law jut manifestly and fearsomely into existence. In agreement with this is the fact that the death penalty in primitive legal systems is imposed even for such crimes as offenses against property, to which it seems quite out of "proportion." Its purpose is not to punish the infringement of law but to establish new law. For in the exercise of violence over life and death more than in any other legal act, law reaffirms itself. But in this very violence something rotten in law is revealed, above all to a finer sensibility, because the latter knows itself to be infinitely remote from conditions in which fate might imperiously have shown itself in such a sentence. Reason must, however, attempt to approach such conditions all the more resolutely, if it is to bring to a conclusion its critique of both lawmaking and law-preserving violence.

In a far more unnatural combination than in the death penalty, in a kind of spectral mixture, these two forms of violence are present in another institution of the modern state, the police. True, this is violence for legal ends (in the right of disposition), but with the simultaneous authority to decide these ends itself within wide limits (in the right of decree). The ignominy of such an authority, which is felt by few simply because its ordinances suffice only seldom for the crudest acts, but are therefore allowed to rampage all the more blindly in the most vulnerable areas and against thinkers, from whom the state is not protected by law—this ignominy lies in the fact that in this authority the separation of lawmaking and law-preserving violence is suspended. If the first is required to prove its worth in victory, the second is subject to the restriction that it may not set itself new ends. Police violence is emancipated from both conditions. It is lawmaking, for its characteristic function is not the promulgation of laws but the assertion of legal claims for any decree, and law-preserving, because it is at the disposal of these ends. The assertion that the ends of police violence are always identical or even connected to those of general law is entirely untrue. Rather, the "law" of the police really marks the point at which the state, whether from impotence or because of the immanent connections within any legal system, can no longer guarantee through the legal system the empirical ends that it desires at any price to attain. Therefore the police intervene "for security reasons" in countless cases where no clear legal situation exists, when they are not merely, without the slightest relation to legal ends, accompanying the citizen as a brutal encumbrance through a life regulated by ordinances, or simply supervising him. Unlike law, which acknowledges in the "decision" determined by place and time a metaphysical category that gives it a claim to critical evaluation, a consideration of the police institution encounters nothing essential at all. Its power is formless, like its nowhere tangible, all-pervasive, ghostly presence in the life of civilized states. And though the police may, in particulars, everywhere appear the same, it cannot finally be denied that their spirit is less devastating where they represent, in absolute monarchy, the power of a ruler in which legislative and executive supremacy are united, than in democracies where their existence, elevated by no such relation, bears witness to the greatest conceivable degeneration of violence.

All violence as a means is either lawmaking or law-preserving. If it lays claim to neither of these predicates, it forfeits all validity. It follows, however, that all violence as a means, even in the most favorable case, is implicated in the problematic nature of law itself. And if the importance of these problems cannot be assessed with certainty at this stage of the investigation, law nevertheless appears, from what has been said, in so ambiguous a moral light that the question poses itself whether there are no other than violent means for regulating conflicting human interests. We are above all obligated to note that a totally nonviolent resolution of conflicts can never lead to a legal contract. For the latter, however peacefully it may have been entered into by the parties, leads finally to possible violence. It confers on both parties the right to take recourse to violence in some form against the other, should he break the agreement. Not only that; like the outcome, the origin of every contract also points toward violence. It need not be directly present in it as lawmaking violence, but is represented in it insofar as the power that guarantees a legal contract is in turn of violent origin even if violence is not introduced into the contract itself. When the consciousness of the latent presence of violence in a legal institution disappears, the institution falls into decay. In our time, parliaments provide an example of this. They offer the familiar, woeful spectacle because they have not remained conscious of the revolutionary forces to which they owe their existence. Accordingly, in Germany in particular, the last manifestation of such forces bore no fruit for parliaments. They lack the sense that a lawmaking violence is represented by themselves; no wonder that they cannot achieve decrees worthy of this violence, but cultivate in compromise a supposedly nonviolent manner of dealing with political affairs. This remains, however, a "product situated within the mentality of violence, no matter how it may disdain all open violence, because the effort toward compromise is motivated not internally but from outside, by the opposing effort, because no compromise, however freely accepted, is conceivable without a compulsive character. 'It would be better otherwise' is the underlying feeling in every compromise."[2] Significantly, the decay of parliaments has perhaps alienated as many minds from the ideal of a nonviolent resolution of political conflicts as were attracted to it by the war. The pacifists are confronted by the Bolsheviks and Syndicalists. These have effected an annihilating and on the whole apt critique of present-day parliaments. Nevertheless, however desirable and gratifying a flourishing parliament might be by comparison, a discussion of means of political agreement that are in principle nonviolent cannot be concerned with parliamentarianism. For what parliament achieves in vital affairs can only be those legal decrees that in their origin and outcome are attended by violence.

Is any nonviolent resolution of conflict possible? Without doubt. The relationships of private persons are full of examples of this. Nonviolent agreement is possible wherever a civilized outlook allows the use of unalloyed means of agreement. Legal and illegal means of every kind that are all the same violent may be confronted with nonviolent ones as unalloyed means. Courtesy, sympathy, peaceableness, trust, and whatever else might here be mentioned, are their subjective preconditions. Their objective manifestation, however, is determined by the law (the enormous scope of which cannot be discussed here) that unalloyed means are never those of direct, but always those of indirect solutions. They therefore never apply directly to the resolution of conflict between man and man, but only to matters concerning objects. The sphere of nonviolent means opens up in the realm of human conflicts relating to goods. For this reason technique in the broadest sense of the word is their most particular area. Its profoundest example is perhaps the conference, considered as a technique of civil agreement. For in it not only is nonviolent agreement possible, but also the exclusion of violence in principle is quite explicitly demonstrable by one significant factor: there is no sanction for lying. Probably no legislation on earth originally stipulated such a sanction. This makes clear that there is a sphere of human agreement that is nonviolent to the extent that it is wholly inaccessible to violence: the proper sphere of "understanding," language. Only late and in a peculiar process of decay has it been penetrated by legal violence in the penalty placed on fraud. For whereas the legal system at its origin, trusting to its victorious power, is content to defeat lawbreaking wherever it happens to show itself, and deception, having itself no trace of power about it, was, on the principle *ius civile vigilantibus scriprum est*, exempt from punishment in Roman and ancient Germanic law, the law of a later period, lacking confidence in its own violence, no longer felt itself a match for that of all others. Rather, fear of the latter and mistrust of itself indicate its declining vitality. It begins to set itself ends, with the intention of sparing law-preserving violence more taxing manifestations. It turns to fraud, therefore, not out of moral considerations, but for fear of the violence that it might unleash in the defrauded party. Since such fear conflicts with the violent nature of law derived from its origins, such ends are inappropriate to the justified means of law. They reflect not only the decay of its own sphere, but also a diminution of pure means. For, in prohibiting fraud, law restricts the use of wholly nonviolent means because they could produce reactive violence. This tendency of law has played a part in the concession of the right to strike, which contradicts the interests of the state. It grants this right because it forestalls violent actions the state is afraid to oppose. Did not workers previously resort at once to sabotage and set fire to factories? To induce men to reconcile their interests peacefully without involving the legal system, there is, in the end, apart from all virtues, one effective motive that often enough puts into the most reluctant hands pure instead of violent means; it is the fear of mutual disadvantages that threaten to arise from violent confrontation, whatever the outcome might be. Such motives are clearly visible in countless cases of conflict of interests between private persons. It is different when classes and nations are in conflict, since the higher orders that threaten to overwhelm equally victor and vanquished are hidden from the feelings of most, and from the intelligence of almost all. Space does not here permit me to trace such higher orders and the common interests corresponding to them, which constitute the most enduring motive for a policy of pure means.[3] We can therefore only point to pure means in politics as analogous to those which govern peaceful intercourse between private persons.

As regards class struggles, in them strike must under certain conditions be seen as a pure means. Two essentially different kinds of strike, the possibilities of which have already been considered, must now be more fully characterized. Sorel has the credit—from political, rather than purely theoretical, considerations of having first distinguished them. He contrasts them as the political and the proletarian general strike. They are also antithetical in their relation to violence. Of the partisans of the former he says: "The strengthening of state power is the basis of their conceptions; in their present organizations the politicians (viz. the moderate socialists) are already preparing the ground for a strong centralized and disciplined power that will be impervious to criticism from the opposition, capable of imposing silence, and of issuing its mendacious decrees."[4] "The political general strike demonstrates how the state will lose none of its strength, how power is transferred from the privileged to the privileged, how the mass of producers will change their masters." In contrast to this political general strike (which incidentally seems to have been summed up by the abortive German revolution), the proletarian general strike sets itself the sole task of destroying state power. It "nullifies all the ideological consequence of every possible social policy; its partisans see even the most popular reforms as bourgeois." "This general strike clearly announces its indifference toward material gain through conquest by declaring its intention to abolish the state; the state was really . . . the basis of the existence of the ruling group, who in all their enterprises benefit from the burdens borne by the public." While the first form of interruption of work is violent since it causes only an external modification of labor conditions, the second, as a pure means, is nonviolent. For it takes place not in readiness to resume work following external concessions and this or that modification to working conditions, but in the determination to resume only a wholly transformed work, no longer enforced by the state, an upheaval that this kind of strike not so much causes as consummates. For this reason, the first of these undertakings is lawmaking but the second anarchistic. Taking up occasional statements by Marx, Sorel rejects every kind of program, of utopia—in a word, of lawmaking—for the revolutionary movement: "With the general strike all these fine things disappear; the revolution appears as a clear, simple revolt, and no place is reserved either for the sociologists or for the elegant amateurs of social reforms or for the intellectuals who have made it their profession to think for the proletariat." Against this deep, moral, and genuinely revolutionary conception, no objection can stand that seeks, on grounds of its possibly catastrophic consequences, to brand such a general strike as violent. Even if it can rightly be said that the modern economy, seen as a whole, resembles much less a machine that stands idle when abandoned by its stoker than a beast that goes berserk as soon as its tamer turns his back, nevertheless the violence of an action can be assessed no more from its effects than from its ends, but only from the law of its means. State power, of course, which has eyes only for effects, opposes precisely this kind of strike for its alleged violence, as distinct from partial strikes which are for the most part actually extortionate. The extent to which such a rigorous conception of the general strike as such is capable of diminishing the incidence of actual violence in revolutions, Sorel has explained with highly ingenious arguments. By contrast, an outstanding example of violent omission, more immoral and cruder than the political general strike, akin to a blockade, is the strike by doctors, such as several German cities have seen. In this is revealed at its most repellent an unscrupulous use of violence that is positively depraved in a professional class that for years, without the slightest attempts at resistance, "secured death its prey," and then at the first opportunity abandoned life of its own free will. More clearly than in recent class struggles, the means of nonviolent agreement have developed in thousands of years of the history of states. Only occasionally does the task of diplomats in their transactions consist of modifications to legal systems. Fundamentally they have, entirely on the analogy of agreement between private persons, to resolve conflicts case by case, in the names of their states, peacefully and without contracts. A delicate task that is more robustly performed by referees, but a method of solution that in principle is above that of the referee because it is beyond all legal systems, and therefore beyond violence. Accordingly, like the intercourse of private persons, that of diplomats has engendered its own forms and virtues, which were not always mere formalities, even though they have become so.

Among all the forms of violence permitted by both natural law and positive law there is not one that is free of the gravely problematic nature, already indicated, of all legal violence. Since, however, every conceivable solution to human problems, not to speak of deliverance from the confines of all the world historical conditions of existence obtaining hitherto, remains impossible if violence is totally excluded in principle, the question necessarily arises as to other kinds of violence than all those envisaged by legal theory. It is at the same time the question of the truth of the basic dogma common to both theories: just ends can be attained by justified means, justified means used for just ends. How would it be, therefore, if all the violence imposed by fate, using justified means, were of itself in irreconcilable conflict with just ends, and if at the same time a different kind of violence came into view that certainly could be either the justified or the unjustified means to those ends, but was not related to them as means at all but in some different way? This would throw light on the curious and at first discouraging discovery of the ultimate insolubility of all legal problems (which in its hopelessness is perhaps comparable only to the possibility of conclusive pronouncements on "right" and "wrong" in evolving languages). For it is never reason that derides on the justification of means and the justness of ends, but fate-imposed violence on the former and God on the latter. And insight that is uncommon only because of the stubborn prevailing habit of conceiving those just ends as ends of a possible law, that is, not only as generally valid (which follows analytically from the nature of justice), but also as capable of generalization, which, as could be shown, contradicts the nature of justice. For ends that for one situation are just, universally acceptable, and valid, are so for no other situation, no matter how similar it may be in other respects. The nonmediate function of violence at issue here is illustrated by everyday experience. As regards man, he is impelled by anger, for example, to the most visible outbursts of a violence that is not related as a means to a preconceived end. It is not a means but a manifestation. Moreover, this violence has thoroughly objective manifestations in which it can be subjected to criticism. These are to be found, most significantly, above all in myth.

Mythical violence in its archetypal form is a mere manifestation of the gods. Not a means to their ends, scarcely a manifestation of their will, but first of all a manifestation of their existence. The legend of Niobe contains an outstanding example of this. True, it might appear that the action of Apollo and Artemis is only a punishment. But their violence establishes a law far more than it punishes for the infringement of one already existing. Niobe's arrogance calls down fate upon itself not because her arrogance offends against the law but because it challenges fate—to a fight in which fate must triumph, and can bring to light a law only in its triumph. How little such divine violence was to the ancients the law-preserving violence of punishment is shown by the heroic legends in which the hero—for example, Prometheus—challenges fate with dignified courage, fights it with varying fortunes, and is not left by the legend without hope of one day bringing a new law to men. It is really this hero and the legal violence of the myth native to him that the public tries to picture even now in admiring the miscreant. Violence therefore bursts upon Niobe from the uncertain, ambiguous sphere of fate. It is not actually destructive. Although it brings a cruel death to Niobe's children, it stops short of the life of their mother, whom it leaves behind, more guilty than before through the death of the children, both as an eternally mute bearer of guilt and as a boundary stone on the frontier between men and gods. If this immediate violence in mythical manifestations proves closely related, indeed identical to lawmaking violence, it reflects a problematic light on lawmaking violence, insofar as the latter was characterized above, in the account of military violence, as merely a mediate violence. At the same time this connection promises further to illuminate fate, which in all cases underlies legal violence, and to conclude in broad outline the critique of the latter. For the function of violence in lawmaking is twofold, in the sense that lawmaking pursues as its end, with violence as the means, what is to be established as law, but at the moment of instatement does not dismiss violence; rather, at this very moment of lawmaking, it specifically establishes as law not an end unalloyed by violence, but one necessarily and intimately bound to it, under the title of power. Lawmaking is power making, and, to that extent, an immediate manifestation of violence. Justice is the principle of all divine end making, power the principle of all mythical lawmaking.

An application of the latter that has immense consequences is to be found in constitutional law. For in this sphere the establishing of frontiers, the task of "peace" after all the wars of the mythical age, is the primal phenomenon of all lawmaking violence. Here we see most clearly that power, more than the most extravagant gain in property, is what is guaranteed by all lawmaking violence. Where frontiers are decided the adversary is not simply annihilated; indeed, he is accorded rights even when the victor's superiority in power is complete. And these are, in a demonically ambiguous way, "equal" rights: for both parties to the treaty it is the same line that may not be crossed. Here appears, in a terribly primitive form, the same mythical ambiguity of laws that may not be "infringed" to which Anatole France refers satirically when he says, "Poor and rich are equally forbidden to spend the night under the bridges." It also appears that Sorel touches not merely on a cultural-historical but also on a metaphysical truth in surmising that in the beginning all fight was the prerogative of the kings or the nobles—in short, of the mighty; and that, *mutatis mutandis*, it will remain so as long as it exists. For from the point of view of violence, which alone can guarantee law, there is no equality, but at the most equally great violence. The act of fixing frontiers, however, is also significant for an understanding of law in another respect. Laws and unmarked frontiers remain, at least in primeval times, unwritten laws. A man can unwittingly infringe upon them and thus incur retribution. For each intervention of law that is provoked by an offense against the unwritten and unknown law is called, in contradistinction to punishment, retribution. But however unluckily it may befall its unsuspecting victim, its occurrence is, in the understanding of the law, not chance, but fate showing itself once again in its deliberate ambiguity. Hermann Cohen, in a brief reflection on the ancients' conception of fate, has spoken of the "inescapable realization" that it is "fate's orders themselves that seem to cause and bring about this infringement, this offense."[5] To this spirit of law even the modern principle that ignorance of a law is not protection against punishment testifies, just as the struggle over written law in the early period of the ancient Greek communities is to be understood as a rebellion against the spirit of mythical statutes.

Far from inaugurating a purer sphere, the mythical manifestation of immediate violence shows itself fundamentally identical with all legal violence, and turns suspicion concerning the latter into certainty of the perniciousness of its historical function, the destruction of which thus becomes obligatory. This very task of destruction poses again, in the last resort, the question of a pure immediate violence that might be able to call a halt to mythical violence. Just as in all spheres God opposes myth, mythical violence is confronted by the divine. And the latter constitutes its antithesis in all respects. If mythical violence is lawmaking, divine violence is law-destroying; if the former sets boundaries, the latter boundlessly destroys them; if mythical violence brings at once guilt and retribution, divine power only expiates; if the former threatens, the latter strikes; if the former is bloody, the latter is lethal without spilling blood. The legend of Niobe may be confronted, as an example of this violence, with God's judgment on the company of Korah. It strikes privileged Levites, strikes them without warning, without threat, and does not stop short of annihilation. But in annihilating it also expiates, and a deep connection between the lack of bloodshed and the expiatory character of this violence is unmistakable. For blood is the symbol of mere life. The dissolution of legal violence stems, as cannot be shown in detail here, from the guilt of more natural life, which consigns the living, innocent and unhappy, to a retribution that "expiates" the guilt of mere life—and doubtless also purifies the guilty, not of guilt, however, but of law. For with mere life the rule of law over the living ceases. Mythical violence is bloody power over mere life for its own sake, divine violence pure power over all life for the sake of the living. The first demands sacrifice, the second accepts it.

This divine power is attested not only by religious tradition but is also found in present-day life in at least one sanctioned manifestation. The educative power, which in its perfected form stands outside the law, is one of its manifestations. These are defined, therefore, not by miracles directly performed by God, but by the expiating moment in them that strikes without bloodshed and, finally, by the absence of all lawmaking. To this extent it is justifiable to call this violence, too, annihilating; but it is so only relatively, with regard to goods, right, life, and suchlike, never absolutely, with regard to the soul of the living. The premise of such an extension of pure or divine power is sure to provoke, particularly today, the most violent reactions, and to be countered by the argument that taken to its logical conclusion it confers on men even lethal power against one another. This, however, cannot be conceded. For the question "May I kill?" meets its irreducible answer in the commandment "Thou shalt not kill." This commandment precedes the deed, just as God was "preventing" the deed. But just as it may not be fear of punishment that enforces obedience, the injunction becomes inapplicable, incommensurable once the deed is accomplished. No judgment of the deed can be derived from the commandment. And so neither the divine judgment, nor the grounds for this judgment, can be known in advance. Those who base a condemnation of all violent killing of one person by another on the commandment are therefore mistaken. It exists not as a criterion of judgment, but as a guideline for the actions of persons or communities who have to wrestle with it in solitude and, in exceptional cases, to take on themselves the responsibility of ignoring it. Thus it was understood by Judaism, which expressly rejected the condemnation of killing in self-defense. But those thinkers who take the opposed view refer to a more distant theorem, on which they possibly propose to base even the commandment itself. This is the doctrine of the sanctity of life, which they either apply to all animal or even vegetable life, or limit to human life. Their argumentation, exemplified in an extreme case by the revolutionary killing of the oppressor, runs as follows: "If I do not kill I shall never establish the world dominion of justice . . . that is the argument of the intelligent terrorist . . . We, however, profess that higher even than the happiness and justice of existence stands existence itself."[6] As certainly as this last proposition is false, indeed ignoble, it shows the necessity of seeking the reason for the commandment no longer in what the deed does to the victim, but in what it does to God and the doer. The proposition that existence stands higher than a just existence is false and ignominious, if existence is to mean nothing other than mere life—and it has this meaning in the argument referred to. It contains a mighty truth, however, if existence, or, better, life (words whose ambiguity is readily dispelled, analogously to that of freedom, when they are referred to two distinct spheres), means the irreducible, total condition that is "man"; if the proposition is intended to mean that the nonexistence of man is something more terrible than the (admittedly subordinate) not-yet-attained condition of the just man. To this ambiguity the proposition quoted above owes its plausibility. Man cannot, at any price, be said to coincide with the mere life in him, no more than with any other of his conditions and qualities, not even with the uniqueness of his bodily person. However sacred man is (or that life in him that is identically present in earthly life, death, and afterlife), there is no sacredness in his condition, in his bodily life vulnerable to injury by his fellow men. What, then, distinguishes it essentially from the life of animals and plants? And even if these were sacred, they could not be so by virtue only of being alive, of being in life. It might be well worth while to track down the origin of the dogma of the sacredness of life. Perhaps, indeed probably, it is relatively recent, the last mistaken attempt of the weakened Western tradition to seek the saint it has lost in cosmological impenetrability. (The antiquity of all religious commandments against murder is no counterargument, because these are based on other ideas than the modern theorem.) Finally, this idea of man's sacredness gives grounds for reflection that what is here pronounced sacred was according to ancient mythical thought the marked bearer of guilt: life itself.

The critique of violence is the philosophy of its history—the "philosophy" of this history, because only the idea of its development makes possible a critical, discriminating, and decisive approach to in temporal data. A gaze directed only at what is close at hand can at most perceive a dialectical rising and falling in the lawmaking and law-preserving formations of violence. The law governing their oscillation rests on the circumstance that all law-preserving violence, in its duration, indirectly weakens the lawmaking violence represented by it, through the suppression of hostile counter-violence. (Various symptoms of this have been referred to in the course of this study.) This lasts until either new forces or those earlier suppressed triumph over the hitherto lawmaking violence and thus found a new law, destined in its turn to decay. On the breaking of this cycle maintained by mythical forms of law, on the suspension of law with all the forces on which it depends as they depend on it, finally therefore on the abolition of state power, a new historical epoch is rounded. If the rule of myth is broken occasionally in the present age, the coming age is not so unimaginably remote that an attack on law is altogether futile. But if the existence of violence outside the law, as pure immediate violence, is assured, this furnishes the proof that revolutionary violence, the highest manifestation of unalloyed violence by man, is possible, and by what means. Less possible and also less urgent for humankind, however, is to decide when unalloyed violence has been realized in particular cases. For only mythical violence, not divine, will be recognizable as such with certainty, unless it be in incomparable effects, because the expiatory power of violence is not visible to men. Once again all the eternal forms are open to pure divine violence, which myth bastardized with law. It may manifest itself in a true war exactly as in the divine judgment of the multitude on a criminal. But all mythical, lawmaking violence, which we may call executive, is pernicious. Pernicious, too, is the law-preserving, administrative violence that serves it. Divine violence, which is the sign and seal but never the means of sacred execution, may be called sovereign violence.

CHAPTER 6

Excerpt from Discipline and Punish

By Michel Foucault

We have seen that, in penal justice, the prison transformed the punitive procedure into a penitentiary technique; the carceral archipelago transported this technique from the penal institution to the entire social body. With several important results.

1. This vast mechanism established a slow, continuous, imperceptible gradation that made it possible to pass naturally from disorder to offence and back from a transgression of the law to a slight departure from a rule, an average, a demand, a norm. In the classical period, despite a certain common reference to offence in general,[1] the order of the crime, the order of sin and the order of bad conduct remained separate in so far as they related to separate criteria and authorities (court, penitence, confinement). Incarceration with its mechanisms of surveillance and punishment functioned, on the contrary, according to a principle of relative continuity. The continuity of the institutions themselves, which were linked to one another (public assistance with the orphanage, the reformitory, the penitentiary, the disciplinary battalion, the prison; the school with the charitable society, the workshop, the almshouse, the penitentiary convent; the workers' estate with the hospital and the prison). A continuity of the punitive criteria and mechanisms, which on the basis of a mere deviation gradually strengthened the rules and increased the punishment. A continuous gradation of the established, specialized and competent authorities (in the order of knowledge and in the order of power) which, without resort to arbitrariness, but strictly according to the regulations, by means of observation and assessment hierarchized, differentiated, judged, punished and moved gradually from the correction of irregularities to the punishment of crime. The 'carceral' with its many diffuse or compact forms, its institutions of supervision or constraint, of discreet surveillance and insistent coercion, assured the communication of punishments according to quality and quantity; it connected in series or disposed according to subtle divisions the minor and the serious penalties, the mild and the strict forms of treatment, bad marks and light sentences. You will end up in the convict-ship, the slightest indiscipline seems to say; and the harshest of prisons says to the prisoners condemned to life: I shall note the slightest irregularity in your conduct. The generality of the punitive function that the eighteenth century sought in the 'ideological' technique of representations and signs now had as its support the extension, the material

framework, complex, dispersed, but coherent, of the various carceral mechanisms. As a result, a certain significant generality moved between the least irregularity and the greatest crime; it was no longer the offence, the attack on the common interest, it was the departure from the norm, the anomaly; it was this that haunted the school, the court, the asylum or the prison. It generalized in the sphere of meaning the function that the carceral generalized in the sphere of tactics. Replacing the adversary of the sovereign, the social enemy was transformed into a deviant, who brought with him the multiple danger of disorder, crime and madness. The carceral network linked, through innumerable relations, the two long, multiple series of the punitive and the abnormal.

2. The carceral, with its far-reaching networks, allows the recruitment of major 'delinquents'. It organizes what might be called 'disciplinary careers' in which, through various exclusions and rejections, a whole process is set in motion. In the classical period, there opened up in the confines or interstices of society the confused, tolerant and dangerous domain of the 'outlaw' or at least of that which eluded the direct hold of power: an uncertain space that was for criminality a training ground and a region of refuge; there poverty, unemployment, pursued innocence, cunning, the struggle against the powerful, the refusal of obligations and laws, and organized crime all came together as chance and fortune would dictate; it was the domain of adventure that Gil Blas, Sheppard or Mandrin, each in his own way, inhabited. Through the play of disciplinary differentiations and divisions, the nineteenth century constructed rigorous channels which, within the system, inculcated docility and produced delinquency by the same mechanisms. There was a sort of disciplinary 'training', continuous and compelling, that had something of the pedagogical curriculum and something of the professional network. Careers emerged from it, as secure, as predictable, as those of public life: assistance associations, residential apprenticeships, penal colonies, disciplinary battalions, prisons, hospitals, almshouses. These networks were already well mapped out at the beginning of the nineteenth century: "Our benevolent establishments present an admirably coordinated whole by means of which the indigent does not remain a moment without help from the cradle to the grave. Follow the course of the unfortunate man: you will see him born among foundlings; from there he passes to the nursery, then to an orphanage; at the age of six he goes off to primary school and later to adult schools. If he cannot work, he is placed on the list of the charity offices of his district, and if he falls ill he may choose between twelve hospitals. Lastly, when the poor Parisian reaches the end of his career, seven almshouses await his age and often their salubrious regime has prolonged his useless days well beyond those of the rich man."[2]

The carceral network does not cast the unassimilable into a confused hell; there is no outside. It takes back with one hand what it seems to exclude with the other. It saves everything, including what it punishes. It is unwilling to waste even what it has decided to disqualify. In this panoptic society of which incarceration is the omnipresent armature, the delinquent is not outside the law; he is, from the very outset, in the law, at the very heart of the law, or at least in the midst of those mechanisms that transfer the individual imperceptibly from discipline to the law, from deviation to offence. Although it is true that prison punishes delinquency, delinquency is for the most part produced in and by an incarceration which, ultimately, prison perpetuates in its turn. The prison is merely the natural consequence, no more than a higher degree, of that hierarchy laid down step by step. The delinquent is an institutional product. It is no use being surprised, therefore, that in a considerable proportion of cases the biography of convicts passes through all these mechanisms and establishments, whose purpose, it is widely believed, is to lead away from prison. That one should find in them what one might call the index of an irrepressibly delinquent 'character': the prisoner condemned to hard labour was meticulously produced by a childhood spent in a reformatory, according to the lines of force of the generalized carceral system. Conversely, the lyricism of marginality may find inspiration in the image of the 'outlaw', the great social nomad, who prowls on the confines of a docile, frightened order. But it is not on the fringes of society and through successive exiles that criminality is born, but by means of ever more closely placed insertions, under ever more insistent surveillance, by an accumulation of disciplinary coercion. In short, the carceral archipelago assures, in the depths of the social body, the formation of delinquency on the basis of subtle illegalities, the overlapping of the latter by the former and the establishment of a specified criminality.

3. But perhaps the most important effect of the carceral system and of its extension well beyond legal imprisonment is that it succeeds in making the power to punish natural and legitimate, in lowering at least the threshold of tolerance to penality. It tends to efface what may be exorbitant in the exercise of punishment. It does this by playing the two registers in which it is deployed—the legal register of justice and the extra-legal register of discipline—against one another. In effect, the great continuity of the carceral system throughout the law and its sentences gives a sort of legal sanction to the disciplinary mechanisms, to the decisions and judgements that they enforce. Throughout this network, which comprises so many 'regional' institutions, relatively autonomous and independent, is transmitted, with the 'prison-form', the model of justice itself. The regulations of the disciplinary establishments may reproduce the law, the punishments imitate the verdicts and penalties, the surveillance repeat the police model; and, above all these multiple establishments, the prison, which in relation to them is a pure form, unadulterated and unmitigated, gives them a sort of official sanction. The carceral, with its long gradation stretching from the convictship or imprisonment with hard labour to diffuse, slight limitations, communicates a type of power that the law validates and that justice uses as its favourite weapon. How could the disciplines and the power that functions in them appear arbitrary, when they merely operate the mechanisms of justice itself, even with a view to mitigating their intensity? When, by generalizing its effects and transmitting it to every level, it makes it possible to avoid its full rigour? Carceral continuity and the fusion of the prison-form make it possible to legalize, or in any case to legitimate disciplinary power, which thus avoids any element of excess or abuse it may entail.

But, conversely, the carceral pyramid gives to the power to inflict legal punishment a context in which it appears to be free of all excess and all violence. In the subtle gradation of the apparatuses of discipline and of the successive 'embeddings' that they involve, the prison does not at all represent the unleashing of a different kind of power, but simply an additional degree in the intensity of a mechanism that has continued to operate since the earliest forms of legal punishment. Between the latest institution of 'rehabilitation', where one is taken in order to avoid prison, and the prison where one is sent after a definable offence, the difference is (and must be) scarcely perceptible. There is a strict economy that has the effect of rendering as discreet as possible the singular power to punish. There is nothing in it now that recalls the former excess of sovereign power when it revenged its authority on the tortured body of those about to be executed. Prison continues, on those who are entrusted to it, a work begun elsewhere, which the whole of society pursues on each individual through innumerable mechanisms of discipline. By means of a carceral continuum, the authority that sentences infiltrates all those other authorities that supervise, transform, correct, improve. It might even be said that nothing really distinguishes them any more except the singularly 'dangerous' character of the delinquents, the gravity of their departures from normal behaviour and the necessary solemnity of the ritual. But, in its function, the power to punish is not essentially different from that of curing or educating. It receives from them, and from their lesser, smaller task, a sanction from below; but one that is no less important for that, since it is the sanction of technique and rationality. The carceral 'naturalizes' the legal power to punish, as it 'legalizes' the technical power to discipline. In thus homogenizing them, effacing what may be violent in one and arbitrary in the other, attenuating the effects of revolt that they may both arouse, thus depriving excess in either of any purpose, circulating the same calculated, mechanical and discreet methods from one to the other, the carceral makes it possible to carry out that great 'economy' of power whose formula the eighteenth century had sought, when the problem of the accumulation and useful administration of men first emerged.

By operating at every level of the social body and by mingling ceaselessly the art of rectifying and the right to punish, the universality of the carceral lowers the level from which it becomes natural and acceptable to be punished. The question is often posed as to how, before and after the Revolution, a new foundation was given to the fight to punish. And no doubt the answer is to be found in the theory of the contract. But it is perhaps more important to ask the reverse question: how were people made to accept the power to punish, or quite simply, when punished, tolerate being so. The theory of the contract can only answer this question by the fiction of a juridical subject giving to others the power to exercise over him the right that he himself possesses over him. It is highly probable that the great carceral continuum, which provides a communication between the power of discipline and the power of the law, and extends without interruption from the smallest coercions to the longest penal detention, constituted the technical and real, immediately material counterpart of that chimerical granting of the right to punish.

4. With this new economy of power, the carceral system, which is its basic instrument, permitted the emergence of a new form of 'law': a mixture of legality and nature, prescription and constitution, the norm. This had a whole series of effects: the internal dislocation of the judicial power or at least of its functioning; an increasing difficulty in judging, as if one were ashamed to pass sentence; a furious desire on the part of the judges to judge, assess, diagnose, recognize the normal and abnormal and claim the honour of curing or rehabilitating. In view of this, it is useless to believe in the good or bad consciences of judges, or even of their unconscious. Their immense 'appetite for medicine' which is constantly manifested from their appeal to psychiatric experts, to their attention to the chatter of criminology—expresses the major fact that the power they exercise has been 'denatured'; that it is at a certain level governed by laws; that at another, more fundamental level it functions as a normative power; it is the economy of power that they exercise, and not that of their scruples or their humanism, that makes them pass 'therapeutic' sentences and recommend 'rehabilitating' periods of imprisonment. But, conversely, if the judges accept ever more reluctantly to condemn for the sake of condemning, the activity of judging has increased precisely to the extent that the normalizing power has spread. Borne along by the omnipresence of the mechanisms of discipline, basing itself on all the carceral apparatuses, it has become one of the major functions of our society. The judge of normality are present everywhere. We are in the society of the teacher-judge, the doctor-judge, the educator-judge, the 'social worker'–judge; it is on them that

the universal reign of the normative is based; and each individual, wherever he may find himself, subjects to it his body, his gestures, his behaviour, his aptitudes, his achievements. The carceral network, in its compact or disseminated forms, with its systems of insertion, distribution, surveillance, observation, has been the greatest support, in modern society, of the normalizing power.

5. The carceral texture of society assures both the real capture of the body and its perpetual observation; it is, by its very nature, the apparatus of punishment that conforms most completely to the new economy of power and the instrument for the formation of knowledge that this very economy needs. Its panoptic functioning enables it to play this double role. By virtue of its methods of fixing, dividing, recording, it has been one of the simplest, crudest, also most concrete, but perhaps most indispensable conditions for the development of this immense activity of examination that has objectified human behaviour. If, after the age of 'inquisitorial' justice, we have entered the age of 'examinatory' justice, if, in an even more general way, the method of examination has been able to spread so widely throughout society, and to give rise in part to the sciences of man, one of the great instruments for this has been the multiplicity and close overlapping of the various mechanisms of incarceration. I am not saying that the human sciences emerged from the prison. But, if they have been able to be formed and to produce so many profound changes in the episteme, it is because they have been conveyed by a specific and new modality of power: a certain policy of the body, a certain way of rendering the group of men docile and useful. This policy required the involvement of definite relations of knowledge in relations of power; it called for a technique of overlapping subjection and objectification; it brought with it new procedures of individualization. The carceral network constituted one of the armatures of this power-knowledge that has made the human sciences historically possible. Knowable man (soul, individuality, consciousness, conduct, whatever it is called) is the object-effect of this analytical investment, of this domination-observation.

6. This no doubt explains the extreme solidity of the prison, that slight invention that was nevertheless decried from the outset. If it had been no more than an instrument of rejection or repression in the service of a state apparatus, it would have been easier to alter its more overt forms or to find a more acceptable substitute for it. But, rooted as it was in mechanisms and strategies of power, it could meet any attempt to transform it with a great force of inertia. One fact is characteristic: when it is a question of altering the system of imprisonment, opposition does not come from the judicial institutions alone; resistance is to be found not in the prison as penal sanction, but in the prison with all its determinations, links and extra-judicial results; in the prison as the relay in a general network of disciplines and surveillances; in the prison as it functions in a panoptic regime. This does not mean that it cannot be altered, nor that it is once and for all indispensable to our kind of society. One may, on the contrary, site the two processes which, in the very continuity of the processes that make the prison function, are capable of exercising considerable restraint on its use and of transforming its internal functioning. And no doubt these processes have already begun to a large degree. The first is that which reduces the utility (or increases its inconveniences) of a delinquency accommodated as a specific illegality, locked up and supervised; thus the growth of great national or international illegalities directly linked to the political and economic apparatuses (financial illegalities, information services, arms and drugs trafficking, property speculation) makes it clear that the somewhat rustic and conspicuous work force of delinquency is proving ineffective; or again, on a smaller scale, as soon as the economic levy on

sexual pleasure is carried out more efficiently by the sale of contraceptives, or obliquely through publications, films or shows, the archaic hierarchy of prostitution loses much of its former usefulness. The second process is the growth of the disciplinary networks, the multiplication of their exchanges with the penal apparatus, the ever more important powers that are given them, the ever more massive transference to them of judicial functions; now, as medicine, psychology, education, public assistance, 'social work' assume an ever greater share of the powers of supervision and assessment, the penal apparatus will be able, in turn, to become medicalized, psychologized, educationalized; and by the same token that turning-point represented by the prison becomes less useful when, through the gap between its penitentiary discourse and its effect of consolidating delinquency, it articulates the penal power and the disciplinary power. In the midst of all these mechanisms of normalization, which are becoming ever more rigorous in their application, the specificity of the prison and its role as link are losing something of their purpose.

If there is an overall political issue around the prison, it is not therefore whether it is to be corrective or not; whether the judges, the psychiatrists or the sociologists are to exercise more power in it than the administrators or supervisors; it is not even whether we should have prison or something other than prison. At present, the problem lies rather in the steep rise in the use of these mechanisms of normalization and the wide-ranging powers which, through the proliferation of new disciplines, they bring with them.

In 1836, a correspondent wrote to *La Phalange:* "Moralists, philosophers, legislators, flatterers of civilization, this is the plan of your Paris, neatly ordered and arranged, here is the improved plan in which all like things are gathered together. At the centre, and within a first enclosure: hospitals for all diseases, almshouses for all types of poverty, madhouses, prisons, convict-prisons for men, women and children. Around the first enclosure, barracks, courtrooms, police stations, houses for prison warders, scaffolds, houses for the executioner and his assistants. At the four corners, the Chamber of Deputies, the Chamber of Peers, the Institute and the Royal Palace. Outside, there are the various services that supply the central enclosure, commerce, with its swindlers and its bankruptcies; industry and its furious struggles; the press, with its sophisms; the gambling dens; prostitution; the people dying of hunger or wallowing in debauchery, always ready to lend an ear to the voice of the Genius of Revolutions; the heartless rich. Lastly the ruthless war of all against all."[3]

I shall stop with this anonymous text. We are now far away from the country of tortures, dotted with wheels, gibbets, gallows, pillories; we are far, too, from that dream of the reformers, less than fifty years before: the city of punishments in which a thousand small theatres would have provided an endless multicoloured representation of justice in which the punishments, meticulously produced on decorative scaffolds, would have constituted the permanent festival of the penal code. The carceral city, with its imaginary 'geo-politics', is governed by quite different principles. The extract from *La Phalange* reminds us of some of the more important ones: that at the centre of this city, and as if to hold it in place, there is, not the 'centre of power', not a network of forces, but a multiple network of diverse elements—walls, space, institution, rules, discourse; that the model of the carceral city is not, therefore, the body of the king, with the powers that emanate from it, nor the contractual meeting of wills from which a body that was both individual and collective was born, but a strategic distribution of elements of different natures and levels. That the prison is not the daughter of laws, codes or the judicial apparatus; that it is not subordinated to the court and the docile or clumsy instrument of the sentences that it hands out and of the results that it would like to achieve; that it is the court that is external and subordinate to the prison. That in the central position that it occupies, it is not alone, but linked to a whole series of "carceral" mechanisms which seem distinct enough—since they are intended to alleviate pain, to cure, to comfort—but which all tend, like the prison, to exercise a power of normalization. That these mechanisms are applied not to transgressions against a "central" law, but to the apparatus of production—"commerce" and "industry"—to a whole multiplicity of illegalities, in all their diversity of nature and origin, their specific role in profit and the different ways in which they are dealt with by the punitive mechanisms. And that ultimately what presides over all these mechanisms is not the unitary functioning of an apparatus or an institution, but the necessity of combat and the rules of strategy. That, consequently, the notions of institutions of repression, rejection, exclusion, marginalization, are not adequate to describe, at the very centre of the carceral city, the formation of the insidious leniencies, unavowable petty cruelties, small acts of cunning, calculated methods, techniques, "sciences" that permit the fabrication of the disciplinary individual. In this central and centralized humanity, the effect and instrument of complex power relations, bodies and forces subjected by multiple mechanisms of "incarceration," objects for discourses that are in themselves elements for strategy, we must hear the distant roar of battle.

At this point I end a book that must serve as a historical background to various studies of the power of normalization and the formation of knowledge in modern society.

CHAPTER 7

Excerpt from Force of Law: The Mystical Foundation of Authority

By Jacques Derrida

How are we to distinguish between this force of the law, this "force of law," as one says in English as well as in French, I believe, and the violence that one always deems unjust? What difference is there between, on the one hand, the force that can be just, or in any case deemed legitimate, not only an instrument in the service of law but the practice and even the realization, the essence of *droit*, and on the other hand the violence that one always deems unjust? What is a just force or a non-violent force? To stay with the question of idiom, let me turn here to a German word that will soon be occupying much of our attention: *Gewalt*. In English, as in French, it is often translated as "violence." The Benjamin text that I will be speaking to you about soon is entitled "*Zur Kritik der Gewalt*," translated in French as "Critique de la violence" and in English as "Critique of Violence." But these two translations, while not altogether *injustes* (and so not altogether violent), are very active interpretations that don't do justice to the fact that *Gewalt* also signifies, for Germans, legitimate power, authority, public force. *Gesetzgebende Gewalt* is legislative power, *geistliche Gewalt* the spiritual power of the church, *Staatsgewalt* the authority or power of the state. *Gewalt*, then, is both violence and legitimate power, justified authority. How are we to distinguish between the force of law of a legitimate power and the supposedly originary violence that must have established this authority and that could not itself have been authorized by any anterior legitimacy, so that, in this initial moment, it is neither legal nor illegal—or, others would quickly say, neither just nor unjust? I gave a lecture in Chicago a few days ago—which I'm deliberately leaving aside here, even though its theme is closely connected—devoted to a certain number of texts by Heidegger in which the words *Walten* and *Gewalt* play a decisive role, as one cannot simply translate them by either force or violence, especially not in a context where Heidegger will attempt to demonstrate his claim that originally, and for example for Heraclitus, *Dikè*—justice, *droit*, trial, penalty or punishment, vengeance, and so forth—is *Eris* (conflict, *Streit*, discord, *polemos* or *Kampf*), that is, it is *adikia*, injustice, as well. We could come back to this, if you wish, during the discussion, but I prefer to hold off on it for now.

Since this colloquium is devoted to deconstruction and the possibility of justice, my first thought is that in the many texts considered deconstructive, and particularly in certain of those that I've published myself, recourse to the word "force" is quite frequent, and in strategic places I would even say decisive, but at the same time always or almost always accompanied by an explicit reserve, a guardedness. I have often called for vigilance, I have asked myself to keep in mind the risks spread by this word, whether it be the risk of an obscure, substantialist, occulto-mystic concept or the risk of giving authorization to violent, unjust, arbitrary force. I won't cite these texts, that would be self-indulgent and would take too much time, but I ask you to trust me. A first precaution against the risks of substantialism or irrationalism that I just evoked involves the differential character of force. For me, it is always a question of differential force, of difference as difference of force, of force as *différance* (*différance* is a force *différée-différante*), of the relation between force and form, force and signification, performative force, illocutionary or perlocutionary force, of persuasive and rhetorical force, of affirmation by signature, but also and especially of all the paradoxical situations in which the greatest force and the greatest weakness strangely enough exchange places. And that is the whole history. What remains is that I've always been uncomfortable with the word force, which I've often judged to be indispensable, and I thank you for thus forcing me to try and say a little more about it today. And the same thing goes for justice. There are no doubt many reasons why the majority of texts hastily identified as "deconstructionist" for example, *mine*—seem, I do say *seem*, not to foreground the theme of justice (as theme, precisely), or the theme of ethics or politics. Naturally this is only *apparently so*, if one considers, for example, (I will only mention these) the many texts devoted to Levinas and to the relations between "violence and metaphysics," or to the philosophy of right, Hegel's, with all its posterity in *Glas*, of which it is the principal *motif*, or the texts devoted to the drive for power and to the paradoxes of power in *Spéculer—sur Freud*, to the law, in *Devant la loi* (on Kafka's *Vor dem Gesetz*) or in *Déclaration d'Indépendance*, in *Admiration de Nelson Mandela ou les lois de la réflexion*, and in many other texts. It goes without saying that discourses on double affirmation, the gift beyond exchange and distribution, the undecidable, the incommensurable or the incalculable, or on singularity, difference and heterogeneity are also, through and through, at least obliquely discourses on justice.

Besides, it was normal, foreseeable, desirable that studies of deconstructive style should culminate in the problematic of law (*droit*), of law and justice. (I have elsewhere tried to show that the essence of law is not prohibitive but affirmative.) It is even the most proper place for them, if such a thing exists. A deconstructive interrogation that starts, as was the case here, by destabilizing or complicating the opposition between *nomos* and *physis*, between *thésis* and *physis*—that is to say, the opposition between law, convention, the institution on the one hand, and nature on the other, with all the oppositions that they condition; for example, and this is only an example, that between positive law and natural law (the *différance* is the displacement of this oppositional logic), a deconstructive interrogation that starts, as this one did, by destabilizing, complicating, or bringing out the paradoxes of values like those of the proper and of property in all their registers, of the subject, and so of the responsible subject, of the subject of law (*droit*) and the subject of morality, of the juridical or moral person, of intentionality, etc., and of all that follows from these, such a deconstructive line of questioning is through and through a problematization of law and justice. A problematization of the foundations of law, morality and politics. This questioning of foundations is neither foundationalist nor anti-foundationalist. Nor does it pass up opportunities to put into question or even to exceed the possibility or the ultimate necessity of questioning, of the questioning form of thought, interrogating without assurance or prejudice the very history of the question and of its philosophical authority. For there is an authority—and so a legitimate force in the questioning form of which one might ask oneself whence it derives such great force in our tradition.

If, hypothetically, it had a proper place, which is precisely what cannot be the case, such a deconstructive "questioning" or meta-questioning would be more at home in law schools, perhaps also—this sometimes happens—in theology or architecture departments, than in philosophy departments and much more than in the literature departments where it has often been thought to belong. That is why, without knowing them well from the inside, for which I feel I am to blame, without pretending to any familiarity with them, I think that the developments in "critical legal studies" or in work by people like Stanley Fish, Barbara Herrstein Smith, Drucilla Cornell, Sam Weber and others, which situates itself in relation to the articulation between literature and philosophy, law and politico-institutional problems, are today, from the point of view of a certain deconstruction, among the most fertile and the most necessary. They respond, it seems to me, to the most radical programs of a deconstruction that would like, in order to be consistent with itself, not to remain enclosed in purely speculative, theoretical, academic discourses but rather (with all due respect to Stanley Fish) to aspire to something more consequential, to *change* things and to intervene in an efficient and responsible though always, of course, very mediated way, not only in the profession but in what one calls the *cité*, the polis and more generally the world. Not, doubtless, to change things in the rather naive sense of calculated, deliberate and strategically controlled intervention, but in the sense of maximum intensification of a transformation in progress, in the name of neither a simple symptom nor a simple cause (other categories are required here). In an industrial and hypertechnologized society, academia is less than ever the monadic or monastic ivory tower that in any case it never was. And this is particularly true of "law schools."

I hasten to add here, briefly, the following three points:

1. This configuration, this conjunction or conjuncture is no doubt necessary and inevitable between, on the one hand, a deconstruction of a style more directly philosophical or more directly motivated by literary theory and, on the other hand, juridico-literary reflection and "critical legal studies."

2. It is certainly not by chance that this conjunction has developed in such an interesting way in this country; this is another problem—urgent and compelling—that I must leave aside for lack of time. There are no doubt profound and complicated reasons of global dimensions, I mean geo-political and not merely domestic, for the fact that this development should be first and foremost North American.

3. Above all, if it has seemed urgent to give our attention to this joint or concurrent development and to participate in it, it is just as vital that we do not confound largely heterogeneous and unequal discourses, styles and discursive contexts. The word "deconstruction" could, in certain cases, induce or encourage such a confusion. The word itself gives rise to so many misunderstandings that one wouldn't want to add to them by reducing all the styles of Critical Legal Studies to one or by making them examples or extensions of Deconstruction with a capital "D." However unfamiliar they may be to me, I know that these efforts in Critical Legal Studies have their history, their context, and their proper idiom, and that in relation to such a philosophico-deconstructive questioning they are often (we shall say for the sake of brevity) uneven, timid, approximating or schematic, not to mention belated, although their specialization and the acuity of their

technical competence puts them, on the other hand, very much in advance of whatever state deconstruction finds itself in a more literary or philosophical field. Respect for contextual, academico-institutional, discursive specificities, mistrust for analogies and hasty transpositions, for confused homogenizations, seem to me to be the first imperatives the way things stand today. I am sure, or in any case I hope, that this encounter will leave us with the memory of disparities and disputes at least as much as it leaves us with agreements, with coincidences or consensus.

I said a moment ago: it only appears that deconstruction, in its manifestations most recognized as such, hasn't "addressed," as one says in English, the problem of justice. It only appears that way, but one must account for appearances, "keep up appearances" as Aristotle said, and that is how I'd like to employ myself here: to show why and how what is now called Deconstruction, while seeming not to "address" the problem of justice, has done nothing but address it, if only obliquely, unable to do so directly. Obliquely, as at this very moment, in which I'm preparing to demonstrate that one cannot speak *directly* about justice, thematize or objectivize justice, say "this is just" and even less "I am just," without immediately betraying justice, if not law (*droit*).

B. But I have not yet begun. I started by saying that I must address myself to you in your language and announced right away that I've always found at least two of your idiomatic expressions invaluable, indeed irreplaceable. One was "to enforce the law," which always reminds us that if justice is not necessarily law (*droit*) or the law, it cannot become justice legitimately or *de jure* except by withholding force or rather by appealing to force from its first moment, from its first word. At the beginning of justice there was logos, speech or language, which is not necessarily in contradiction to another *incipit*, namely, "In the beginning there will have been force."

Pascal says it in a fragment I may return to later, one of his famous "pensées," as usual more difficult than it seems. It starts like this: "*Justice, force.*—Il est juste que ce qui est juste soit suivi, il est nécessaire que ce qui est le plus fort soit suivi." ("*Justice, force* .—It is just that what is just be followed, it is necessary that what is strongest be followed.") The beginning of this fragment is already extraordinary, at least in the rigor of its rhetoric. It says that what is just must be followed (followed by consequence, followed by effect, applied, *enforced*) and that what is strongest must also be followed (by consequence, effect, and so on). In other words, the common axiom is that the just and the strongest, the most just as or as well as the strongest, must be followed. But this "must be followed," common to the just and the strongest, is "right" ("*juste*") in one case, "necessary" in the other: "It is just that what is just be followed"—in other words, the concept or idea of the just, in the sense of justice, implies analytically and *a priori* that the just be "suivi," followed up, enforced, and it is just—also in the sense of "just right"—to think this way. "It is necessary that what is strongest be enforced."

And Pascal continues: "*La justice sans la force est impuissante*" ("Justice without force is impotent")—in other words, justice isn't justice, it is not achieved if it doesn't have the force to be "enforced;" a powerless justice is not justice, in the sense of *droit*—"*la force sans la justice est tyrannique. La justice sans force est contredite, parce qu'il y a toujours des méchants; la force sans la justice est accusée. Il faut donc mettre ensemble la justice et la force; et pour cela faire que ce qui est juste soit fort, ou que ce qui est fort soit juste*" ("force without justice is tyrannical. Justice without force is contradictory, as there are always the wicked; force without justice is accused of wrong. And so it is necessary to put justice and force together; and, for this, to make sure that what is just be strong, or what is strong be just.") It is difficult to decide whether the "it is necessary" in this conclusion ("And so it is necessary to put justice and force together") is an "it is necessary" prescribed by what is just in justice or by what is necessary in force. But that is a pointless hesitation since justice demands, as justice, recourse to force. The necessity of force is implied, then, in the "*juste*" in "justice."

This *pensée*, what continues and concludes it ("And so, since it was not possible to make the just strong, the strong have been made just") deserves a longer analysis than I can offer here. The principle of my analysis (or rather of my active and anything but non-violent interpretation), of the interpretation at the heart of what I will indirectly propose in the course of this lecture, will, notably in the case of this Pascal *pensée*, run counter to tradition and to its most obvious context. This context and the conventional interpretation that it seems to dictate runs, precisely, in a conventionalist direction toward the sort of pessimistic, relativistic and empiricist skepticism that drove Arnaud to suppress these *pensées* in the Port Royal edition, alleging that Pascal wrote them under the impression of a reading of Montaigne, who thought that laws were not in themselves just but rather were just only because they were laws. It is true that Montaigne used an interesting expression, which Pascal takes up for his own purposes and which I'd also like to reinterpret and to consider apart from its most conventional reading. The expression is "*fondement mystique de l'autorité*," "mystical foundation of authority." Pascal cites Montaigne without naming him when he writes in *pensée* 293: ". . . *l'un dit que l'essence de la justice est l'autorité du législateur, l'autre la commodité du souverain, l'autre la coutume présente; et c'est le plus sûr: rien, suivant la seule raison, n'est juste de soi,' tout branle avec le temps. La coutume fait toute l'équité par cette seule raison qu'elle est reçue; c'est le fondement mystique de son autorité. Qui la ramène à son principe, l'anéantit.*" (". . . one man says that the essence of justice is the authority of the legislator, another that it is the convenience of the king, another that it is current custom; and the latter is closest to the truth: simple reason tells us that nothing is just in itself; everything crumbles with time. Custom is the sole basis for equity, for the simple reason that it is received; it is the mystical foundation of its authority. Whoever traces it to its source annihilates it.")

Montaigne was ultimately talking about a "mystical foundation" of the authority of laws: "*Or les loix*," he says, "*se maintiennent en crédit, non parce qu'elles sont justes, mais parce qu'elles sont loix: c'est le fondement mystique de leur auctorité, elles n'en ont point d'autre. . . . Quiconque leur obéit parce qu'elles sont justes, ne leur obéit pas justement par où il doibt*"[1] ("And so laws keep up their good standing, not because they are just, but because they are laws: that is the mystical foundation of their authority, they have no other. . . . Anyone who obeys them because they are just is not obeying them the way he ought to.")

Here Montaigne is clearly distinguishing laws, that is to say *droit*, from justice. The justice of law, justice as law is not justice. Laws are not just as laws. One obeys them not because they are just but because they have authority.

Little by little I shall explain what I understand by this expression "mystical foundation of authority." It is true that Montaigne also wrote the following, which must, again, be interpreted by going beyond its simply conventional and conventionalist surface: "(*notre droit même a, dit-on des fictions légitimes sur lesquelles il fonde la vérité de sa justice*)"; "(even our law, it is said, has legitimate fictions on which it founds the truth of its justice)." I used these words as an epigraph to a text on *Vor dem Gesetz*. What is a legitimate fiction? What does it mean to establish the truth of justice? These are among the questions that await us. It is true that Montaigne proposed an analogy between this supplement of a legitimate fiction, that is, the fiction necessary to establish the truth of justice, and the supplement of artifice called for by a deficiency in nature, as if the absence of natural law called for the supplement of historical or positive, that is to say, fictional, law (*droit*), just as—to use Montaigne's analogy—"*les femmes qui emploient des dents d'ivoire o-les leurs naturelies leur manquent, et, au lieu de leur vrai teint, en forgent un de quelque matière étrangère* . . ."[2]; ("women who use ivory teeth when they're missing their real ones, and who, instead of showing their true complexion, forge one with some foreign material . . .").

Perhaps the Pascal *pensée* that, as he says, "puts together" justice and force and makes force an essential predicate of justice (by which he means "*droit*" more than justice) goes beyond a conventionslist or utilitarian relativism, beyond a nihilism, old or new, that would make the law a "masked power," beyond the cynical moral of La Fontaine's "The Wolf and the Sheep," according to which "*La raison du plus fort est toujours la meilleure*" ("Might makes right").

The Pascalian critique, *in its principle*, refers us back to original sin and to the corruption of natural laws by a reason that is itself corrupt. ("*Il y a sans doute des lois naturelles; mais cette belle raison a tout corrompu,*" *Section IV, pensée 294*; "There are, no doubt, natural laws; but this fine thing called reason has corrupted everything," and elsewhere: "*Notre justice s'anéantit devant la justice divine,*" *p. 564*: "Our justice comes to nothing before divine justice." I cite these *pensées* to prepare for our reading of Benjamin.)

But if we set aside the functional mechanism of the Pascalian critique, if we dissociate it from Christian pessimism, which is not impossible, then we can find in it, as in Montaigne, the basis for a modern critical philosophy, indeed for a critique of juridical ideology, a desedimentation of the superstructures of law that both hide and reflect the economic and political interests of the dominant forces of society. This would be both possible and always useful.

But beyond its principle and its mechanism, this Pascalian *pensée* perhaps concerns a more intrinsic structure, one that a critique of juridical ideology should never overlook. The very emergence of justice and law, the rounding and justifying moment that institutes law implies a performative force, which is always an interpretative force: this time not in the sense of law in the service of force, its docile instrument, servile and thus exterior to the dominant power but rather in the sense of law that would maintain a more internal, more complex relation with what one calls force, power or violence. Justice—in the sense of *droit* (right or law) would not simply be put in the service of a social force or power, for example an economic, political, ideological power that would exist outside or before it and which it would have to accommodate or bend to when useful. Its very moment of foundation or institution (which in any case is never a moment inscribed in the homogeneous tissue of a history, since it is ripped apart with one decision), the operation that consists of founding, inaugurating, justifying law (*droit*), making law, would consist of a *coup de force*, of a performative and therefore interpretative violence that in itself is neither just nor unjust and that no justice and no previous law with its rounding anterior moment could guarantee or contradict or invalidate. No justificatory discourse could or should insure the role of metalanguage in relation to the performativity of institutive language or to its dominant interpretation.

Here the discourse comes up against its limit: in itself, in its performative power itself. It is what I here propose to call the mystical. Here a silence is walled up in the violent structure of the founding act. Walled up, walled in because silence is not exterior to language. It is in this sense that I would be tempted to interpret, beyond simple commentary, what Montaigne and Pascal call the mystical foundation of authority. I would take the use of the word "mystical" in what I'd venture to call a rather Wittgensteinian direction. These texts by Montaigne and Pascal, along with the texts from the tradition to which they belong and the rather active interpretation of them that I propose, could be brought into Stanley Fish's discussion in "Force" (*Doing What Comes Naturally*) of Hart's Concept of Law, and several others, implicitly including Rawls, himself criticized by Hart, as well as into many debates illuminated by certain texts of Sam Weber on the agonistic and not simply intra-institutional or monoinstitutional character of certain conflicts in *Institution and Interpretation*.

Since the origin of authority, the foundation or ground, the position of the law can't by definition rest on anything but themselves, they are themselves a violence without ground. Which is not to say that they are in themselves unjust, in the sense of "illegal." They are neither legal nor illegal in their rounding moment. They exceed the opposition between founded and unfounded, or between any foundationalism or anti-foundationalism. Even if the success of performatives that found law or right (for example, and this is more than an example, of a state as guarantor of a right) presupposes earlier conditions and conventions (for example in the national or intentational arena), the same "mystical" limit will reappear at the supposed origin of said conditions, rules or conventions, and at the origin of their dominant interpretation.

The structure I am describing here is a structure in which law (*droit*) is essentially deconstructible, whether because it is founded, constructed on interpretable and transformable textual strata (and that is the history of law [*droit*], its possible and necessary transformation, sometimes its amelioration), or because its ultimate foundation is by definition unfounded. The fact that law is deconstructible is not bad news. We may even see in this a stroke of luck for politics, for all historical progress. But the paradox that I'd like to submit for discussion is the following: it is this deconstructible structure of law (*droit*), or if you prefer of justice as *droit*, that also insures the possibility of deconstruction. Justice in itself, if such a thing exists, outside or beyond law, is not deconstructible. No more than deconstruction itself, if such a thing exists. Deconstruction is justice. It is perhaps because law (*droit*) (which I will consistently try to distinguish from justice) is constructible, in a sense that goes beyond the opposition between convention and nature, it is perhaps insofar as it goes beyond this opposition that it is constructible and so deconstructible and, what's more, that it makes deconstruction possible, or at least the practice of a deconstruction that, fundamentally, always leads to questions of *droit*. 1. The deconstructibility of law (*droit*), of legality, legitimacy or legitimation (for example) makes deconstruction possible. 2. The undeconstructibility of justice also makes deconstruction possible, indeed is inseparable from it. 3. The result: deconstruction takes place in the interval that separates the undeconstructibility of justice from the deconstructibility of *droit* (authority, legitimacy, and so on).

In other words, the hypothesis and propositions toward which I'm tentatively moving here call more for the subtitle: justice as the possibility of deconstruction, the structure of law (*droit*) or of the law, the foundation or the self-authorization of law (*droit*) as the possibility of the exercise of deconstruction.

CHAPTER 8

The Force of Law: Metaphysical or Political?

By Nancy Fraser

In Part One of his essay, *Force of Law: The "Mystical Foundation of Authority,"*[1] Jacques Derrida distinguishes two different ways of thinking about the relations between force and law, and justice and violence. The first approach, styled "critique," exposes the ideological, superstructural nature of law by showing that it operates in the service of social, economic, and political forces that are posited as external and prior to the law.[2] The second approach, in contrast, styled "deconstruction," addresses a relation between violence and law that is held to be more "intrinsic," "internal," and "complex," as it uncovers "the origin of authority, the foundation or ground, the position of the law" in a "violence without ground."[3] In Derrida's view, the second, deconstructive approach is the preferred one; it penetrates deeper than the critical approach to the heart of the relation between violence and law.[4]

That valuation was also presupposed in the title of the symposium that inspired this chapter. Inviting reflection "On the Necessity of Violence for Any Possibility of Justice," this title characterizes the relationship between violence and justice as one of necessity as opposed to contingency. Consequently, it suggests that violence cannot fail to be implicated in any possible legal institution in any possible society, thereby insinuating, at least to my ear, that it would be folly to aspire to eliminate it. Finally, the symposium title implies that the level at which violence is implicated in law is very deep; the suggestion is that violence constitutes the enabling ground or condition for the possibility of justice. Together, these presuppositions entail that the relationship of justice to violence needs to be approached by means of a transcendental inquiry. To be sure, this will be a *negative* or *quasi*-transcendental inquiry, since it turns out in deconstructive thought that the ground in question is precisely an *Abgrund* (abyss). Nonetheless, the fact remains that quasitranscendental reflection on violence as a necessary condition for justice will take precedence over critical forms of inquiry. Attempts to understand the relationship of violence and law through, say, critical social theory, political sociology, or cultural studies will be deprivileged as merely empirical and hence, comparatively superficial.

I have argued elsewhere that those versions of deconstruction that privilege the transcendental, even in this qualified form, incur a disability when it comes to thinking politically.[5] My argument is not the usual complaint that deconstruction leads to nihilism, immorality, or amorality. That complaint assumes that a quasi-transcendental deconstructive reflection can delegitimate practices and norms, an assumption I reject. Actually, insofar as quasi-transcendental reflection pertains to the conditions that enable *any* possible practices and norms, it cannot tell us much about *which* of those possible practices and norms are morally indefensible; nor can it tell us what moral attitude we should adopt toward actually existing practices and norms. Thus, the standard objection to deconstruction fails. However, this will provide only limited comfort to those who defend quasi-transcendentalized versions of deconstruction, as the argument cuts two ways. It tells equally against any defense of deconstruction along the following lines: Contrary to those who think deconstruction entails nihilism, precisely the reverse is true. What is really entailed by the radical ungroundedness of judgment is a paradigmatically ethical disposition: a heightened sense of responsibility, an exhortation to vigilance, and a commitment to the future that is all the more ethically intense for its lack of guarantees.[6] This response is entirely on a par with the original objection. It, too, supposes the possibility of deriving a normative conclusion from a quasi-transcendental premise. It, too, therefore, is unsound.

Thus, the argument about whether deconstruction entails nihilism or an ethics of responsibility ends in a stalemate. So long as the discussion remains on this plane, it cannot be resolved. More generally, so long as deconstruction remains committed to privileging even negative transcendental reflection, so long as it continues to concentrate its efforts on disclosing the prior, enabling *Abgrund* behind every merely critical normative judgment about every merely ontic state of affairs, it will never get to ethics or politics. For, as Aristotle understood, politics is a matter of just those contingent but warrantable normative judgments about just those historically and culturally variable practices and institutions that negative transcendental reflection seeks to get behind.[7] To assume, therefore, as Derrida does in his essay, that deconstruction must get beneath critique to a deeper mode of negative transcendental reflection, is to disable or impede the possibility of *political* thought about the relation between violence and law.

I illustrate this claim by contrasting two ways of understanding "the force of law." In Derrida's terms, these two ways are "deconstruction" and "critique." However, in my view, the crucial issue that divides them is: What is the nature of "the force of law"? Is that "force" metaphysical or political?

In Derrida's deconstructive account, "the force of law" inheres most elementally in the ungroundedness of the judge's judgment.[8] Legal judgment, in his view, is necessarily underdetermined at the moment of decision, however persuasively it may be justified ex post facto. Judging, therefore, can never be "calculation" but always involves a "leap."[9] It is here, in the "madness" or "mystique" of a radical freedom,[10] that the "violence" of legal judgment resides. "The force of law," then, is inscribed in the deep structure of judgment. It is not a matter of contingent institutions or social relations that could in principle be altered.

There are three things worth noting about this account of "the force of law." The first is the unnecessarily paradoxical character of the discussion of judgment. Derrida goes too quickly from the uncontroversial clam that judgment is not calculation to the hyperbolic and, I think, indefensible claim that it is "madness," "mystique," and "violence." There is no discussion of intermediate positions, such as those derived from the Aristotelian conception of *phronesis*, which understand judgment as neither the application of an algorithmic decision procedure nor the exercise of an irrational will. Because he fails to consider alternatives like these, which give *nonaporetic* accounts of noncalculative judgment, Derrida fails to justify his claim that judgment is shot through with aporias.[11] On substantive grounds, then, his account is flawed.

This substantive flaw in Derrida's account of judgment finds expression in a second problem at the level of his rhetoric. Why stylize as "force" or "violence" the fact that judging escapes calculation? This choice of word is troubling, regardless of whether we prefer to think of judging as *phronesis* or as "madness." It ups the rhetorical ante too quickly and risks the loss of important normative political distinctions by conflating a view about the (presumably inescapable) interplay of freedom and constraint in interpretation with (contingent, alterable) modes of individual and institutional coercion. This brings me to my third and most serious objection to Derrida's account of "the force of law." His account directs our attention to a level of so-called violence in law that is constitutive and inescapable.[12] This is a "violence" that can in no meaningful sense be called "political," as it is independent of any specific institutional or social arrangements and as it is not subject, even in principle, to change. Thus, "the force of law" in Derrida's account is essentially metaphysical.

Let me contrast that view to an alternative approach that would understand "the force of law" as political. This would be an approach that would locate law's force in contingent social relations and institutionalizations of power. It would foreswear quasi-transcendental reflection on the "violence" that must inhere in *any* possible legal institution in favor of analysis and (mere) critique of the forms of masked, structural violence that enter into social processes of judging in, for example, *our* legal system. I specify the object of critique as "forms of *masked, structural* violence" because these—as opposed to the overt, punctual violence of criminals, armies, and police—are the most difficult and most important to understand. Included here are a range of deadly systemic social processes, responsibility for which cannot easily be attributed to identifiable individual agents, but which culminate in massive harms such as malnutrition, medical neglect, and environmental toxicity.

A political critique of the "force of law" would seek to identify the various levels at which masked, structural violence enters into our institutionalized practices of legal judgment. Let me suggest three such levels that merit critical scrutiny. The first is the level of the basic constitutional principles that constrain legal interpretation. In many cases, these constitutional principles are uncontroversial and unproblematical, at least as abstractions, but in some cases, they are not. The most problematical case seems to me to be the entrenched centrality of the principle of property right in our constitution. I am not talking about the right to personal property, but rather about what we used to call in the old days "private property in the means of production." To be sure, that discourse has lost its cultural legitimacy, but the problem it names has not gone away. It is still possible in our legal system for small numbers of people to make decisions with impunity that imperil the health and livelihood of many others, while degrading the quality of life of everyone. Thus, one task for a political critique of "the force of law" would be to show how an apparatus of legal judgment can be a vehicle for the operation of masked, structural violence when it is constrained by constitutional principle to protect private property in the means of production.

A second level for critique is the deep grammar of our legal reasoning. One salient feature of this deep grammar is evident in the fact that in our legal system it is exceedingly difficult, indeed often impossible, to press claims for harms one has suffered by virtue of belonging to a social group. In contrast, it is comparatively easy to press claims in cases where the parties are identifiable individuals and the alleged harm is the result of a breach of contract or other definite assignable obligation. Thus, the deep grammar of our legal reasoning is individualistic. Problems arise, however, insofar as the legal grammar of individualism is seriously out of phase with the nature of our social system. In our social system, a great deal of harm does not take the form of individuals ripping off individuals but is rather a result of more impersonal systemic processes and of structural relations among differentially advantaged social groups. This sort of harm, however, is not usually legally admissible. In fact, the deep grammar of individualist justice presents obstacles to anyone who seeks judicial standing to claim that a systemic injustice has occurred. Thus, even before legal judging officially begins, there has already been an operation of prejudgment that has severely restricted the scope of the judge-able. This prejudgment, which embodies the individualist, deep grammar of our legal reasoning, is itself a form of masked, structural violence in the law. A political critique of "the force of law" would theorize and name it as such.[13]

Finally, there remains a third level at which a political critique could unmask the "force of law." This is the level of cultural background. When people make judgments, when they weigh the evidence and decide which principle applies and which precedent is applicable, they do so against a background of cultural assumptions. Whether we are talking about professional judges or ordinary citizens serving on juries, there are necessarily many such assumptions in play. Background assumptions—for example, about human nature, the causes of poverty, what counts as work, and proper gender roles—constitute the inescapable horizon of any judgment. Yet, in a society that is stratified by gender, color, and class, many of the most culturally authoritative and widely held assumptions about such things work to the disadvantage of subordinated social groups. They are themselves, therefore, aspects of the sociocultural structure of injustice. When they serve as elements of the tacit backdrop against which foreground legal judgments are made, they, too, become part of "the force of law."[14]

A good example of this is the congeries of androcentric assumptions that has led many judges and juries to reject self-defense as a legal defense in cases where women are accused of attacking or killing men who have battered them over a period of many years. It has been assumed that any legitimate act of "self-defense" must occur in the heat of an assault and cannot involve use of a deadly weapon against an assailant who has used "only" his fists. Yet surely those assumptions are premised on a model of male aggression that is seriously askew of many women's socialization and experience with violence.[15] To the degree that such androcentric assumptions about self-defense permeate the horizon of judgment in cases involving battered women, the "force of law" will come down with a thud on the side of patriarchy.

Let me conclude by summarizing this portion of my argument and connecting it to what went before. I have outlined three aspects of a political critique of "the force of law." In every case, the task of critique is to render visible forms of masked, structural violence that permeate, and infect, legal judgment. But the legal judgment that is the object of this critique is not any possible legal judgment whatsoever. Rather, it is a specific, institutionalized regime of justice reasoning situated in a specific, structured, sociocultural context. The point of a *political* critique of "the force of law," then, is not to identify forms of "violence" that are "necessary for any possible justice"; it is to identify forms of violence that are precisely *not* necessary.

The value of identifying unnecessary, "surplus" violence that is rooted in unjust and potentially remediable social arrangements is, I hope, obvious. This, after all, is the sort of violence we might aspire to eliminate or reduce. And that aim in the end is what dictates my own sense of priorities. To put the matter bluntly: it seems to me to have matters precisely backward to claim priority for a quasi-transcendental deconstruction of "the force of law" over a "merely" political critique.

C H A P T E R 9

Is Violent Speech a Right?

By Cass R. Sunstein

This spring, talk-show host G. Gordon Liddy, speaking on the radio to millions of people, explained how to shoot agents of the Bureau of Alcohol, Tobacco, and Firearms: "Head shots, head shots. . . . Kill the sons of bitches." Later he said, "Shoot twice to the belly and if that does not work, shoot to the groin area."

On March 23 the full text of the *Terrorist's Handbook* was posted on the Internet, including instructions on how to make a bomb (the same bomb, as it happens, that was used in Oklahoma City). By the time of the Oklahoma bombing on April 19, three more people had posted bomb-making instructions, which could also be found on the Internet in the *Anarchist's Cookbook.* On the National Rifle Association's Internet "Bullet 'N' Board," someone calling himself "Warmaster" explained how to make bombs using baby-food jars. Warmaster wrote, "These simple, powerful bombs are not very well known, even though all the materials can be easily obtained by anyone (including minors)." After the Oklahoma bombing, an anonymous notice was posted to dozens of Usenet news groups, listing all the materials in the Oklahoma City bomb, explaining why the bomb allegedly did not fully explode, and exploring how to improve future bombs.

Fifty hate groups are reported to be communicating on the Internet, sometimes about conspiracies and (by now this will come as no surprise) formulas for making bombs. On shortwave radio, people talk about bizarre United Nations plots and urge that "the American people ought to go there bodily, rip down the United Nations building and kick those bastards right off our soil." A few months ago Rush Limbaugh, who does not advocate violence, said to his audience, "The second violent American revolution is just about, I got my fingers about a fourth of a inch apart, is just about that far away. Because these people are sick and tired of a bunch of bureaucrats in Washington driving into town and telling them what they can and can't do."

In the wake of the tragedy in Oklahoma City, a national debate has erupted about speech counseling violence or inciting hatred of public officials. Of course, we do not know whether such speech had any causal role in the Oklahoma City bombing. But new technologies have put the problem of incendiary speech into sharp relief. It is likely, perhaps inevitable, that hateful and violent messages carried over the airwaves and the Internet will someday, somewhere, be responsible for acts of violence. This is simply a statement of probability; it is not an excuse for violence. Is that probability grounds for restricting such speech? Would restrictions on speech advocating violence or showing how to engage in violent acts be acceptable under the First Amendment? Aside from legal restrictions, what measures are available to the nation's leaders and private citizens to discourage incendiary hate and promote the interests of mutual respect and civility?

THE LIMITS OF PROTECTED SPEECH

Recent events should not be a pretext for allowing the government to control political dissent, including extremist speech and legitimate hyperbole. But narrow restrictions on speech that expressly advocates illegal, murderous violence in messages to mass audiences probably should not be taken to offend the First Amendment.

For most of American history, the courts held that no one has a right to advocate violations of the law. They ruled that advocacy of crime is wholly outside of the First Amendment—akin to a criminal attempt and punishable as such. Indeed, many of the judges revered as the strongest champions of free speech believed that express advocacy of crime was punishable. Judge Learned Hand, in his great 1917 opinion in *Masses* v. *United States*, established himself as a true hero of free speech by saying that even dangerous dissident speech was generally protected against government regulation. But Hand himself conceded that government could regulate any speaker who would "counsel or advise a man" to commit an unlawful act.

In the same period the Supreme Court concluded that government could punish all speech, including advocacy of illegality, that had a "tendency" to encourage illegality. Justices Holmes and Brandeis, the dissenters from this pro-censorship conclusion, took a different approach, saying that speech could be subjected to regulation only if it was likely to produce imminent harm; thus they originated the famous "clear and present danger" test. But even Holmes and Brandeis suggested that the government could punish speakers who had the explicit intention of encouraging crime.

For many years thereafter, the Supreme Court tried to distinguish between speech that was meant as a contribution to democratic deliberation and speech that was designed to encourage illegality. The former was protected; the latter was not. In 1951 the Court concluded in *Dennis* v. *United States* that a danger need not be so "clear and present" if the ultimate harm was very grave.

The great break came in the Court's 1969 decision in *Brandenburg* v. *Ohio*. There the Court said the government could not take action against a member of the Ku Klux Klan, who said, among other things, "We're not a revengent organization, but if our President, our Congress, our Supreme Court, continues to suppress the white, Caucasian race, it's possible that there might have to be some revengence taken." The speaker did not explicitly advocate illegal acts or illegal violence. But in its decision, the Court announced a broad principle, ruling that the right to free speech does "not permit a State to forbid or proscribe advocacy of the use of force or of law violation except where such advocacy is directed to inciting or producing imminent lawless action and is likely to incite or produce such action."

Offering extraordinarily broad protection to political dissent, the Court required the government to meet three different criteria to regulate speech. First, the speaker must promote not just any lawless action but "imminent" lawless action. Second, the imminent lawless action must be "likely" to occur.

Third, the speaker must intend to produce imminent lawless action ("directed to inciting or producing imminent lawless action"). The *Brandenburg* test borrows something from Hand and something from Holmes and produces a standard even more protective of speech than either of theirs.

OLD STANDARDS, NEW TECHNOLOGY

Applied straightforwardly, the *Brandenburg* test seems to protect most speech that can be heard on the airwaves or found on the Internet, and properly so. Remarks like those quoted from Rush Limbaugh unquestionably qualify for protection; such remarks are not likely to incite imminent lawless action, and in any case they are not "directed to" producing such action. They should also qualify as legitimate hyperbole, a category recognized in a 1969 decision allowing a war protester to say, "If they ever make me carry a rifle the first man I want to get in my sights is LBJ." Even Liddy's irresponsible statements might receive protection insofar as they could be viewed as unlikely to produce imminent illegality. A high degree of protection and breathing space makes a great deal of sense whenever the speech at issue is political protest, which lies at the core of the First Amendment.

But there is some ambiguity in the *Brandenburg* test, especially in the context of modern technologies. Suppose that an incendiary speech, expressly advocating illegal violence, is not likely to produce lawlessness in any particular listener or viewer. But of the millions of listeners, one or two, or ten, may well be provoked to act, and perhaps to imminent, illegal violence. Might government ban advocacy of criminal violence in mass communications when it is reasonable to think that one person, or a few, will take action? *Brandenburg* made a great deal of sense for the somewhat vague speech in question, which was made in a setting where relatively few people were in earshot. But the case offers unclear guidance on the express advocacy of criminal violence via the airwaves or the Internet.

When messages advocating murderous violence flow to large numbers of people, the calculus changes: Government probably should have the authority to stop speakers from expressly advocating the illegal use of force to kill people. There is little democratic value in protecting counsels of murder, and the ordinary *Brandenburg* requirements might be loosened where the risks are so great. Congress has made it a crime to assassinate the president, and the Court has cast no doubt on that restriction of speech. It would be a short step, not threatening legitimate public dissent, for the Federal Communications Commission to impose civil sanctions on those who expressly advocate illegal, violent acts aimed at killing people. Courts might well conclude that the government may use its power over the airwaves to ensure that this sort of advocacy does not occur.

Of course, there are serious problems in drawing the line between counsels of violence that should be subject to regulation and those that should not. I suggest that restrictions be limited to express advocacy of unlawful killing because it is the clearest case.

Authorizing the restriction of any speech, even counsels of violent crime, has risks. Government often overreacts to short-term events, and the Oklahoma City tragedy should not be the occasion for an attack on extremist political dissent. Vigorous, even hateful criticism of government is very much at the heart of the right to free speech. Indeed, advocacy of law violation can be an appropriate part of democratic debate. As the example of Martin Luther King, Jr. testifies, there is an honorable tradition of civil disobedience. We should sharply distinguish, however, King's form of nonviolent civil disobedience from counsels or acts of murder. The government should avoid regulating political opinions, including the advocacy of illegal acts. That principle need not, however, be interpreted to bar the government from restricting advocacy of unlawful killing on the mass media.

THE WIDER DEFENSE OF CIVILITY

What else might be done? First, nothing that I have said suggests that government lacks the power to limit speech containing instructions on how to build weapons of mass destruction. The *Brandenburg* test was designed to protect unpopular points of view from government controls; it does not protect the publication of bomb manuals. Instructions for building bombs are not a point of view, and if government wants to stop the mass dissemination of this material, it should be allowed to do so. A lower court so ruled in a 1979 case involving an article in the *Progressive* that described how to make a hydrogen bomb, and the court's argument is even stronger as applied to the speech on the Internet, where so many people can be reached so easily.

Second, the nation's leaders can do a good deal short of regulation. The president and other public officials should exercise their own rights of free speech to challenge hateful, incendiary speech. Although public officials could abuse these rights so as to chill legitimate protest, President Clinton's statements about hatred on the radio and the Internet were entirely on the mark. Public disapproval may ultimately have a salutary effect (as it recently did in the case of violent television shows), even without the force of law.

Third, private institutions, such as broadcasting stations, should think carefully about their own civic responsibilities. An owner of a station or a programming manager is under no constitutional obligation to air speakers who encourage illegal violence. Stations that deny airtime for such views do no harm to the First Amendment but on the contrary exercise their own rights, and in just the right way. In recent months, public and private concern about hate-mongering has encouraged some stations to cancel G. Gordon Liddy's show; this is not a threat to free speech but an exercise of civic duties. Similarly, private on-line networks, such as Prodigy and America Online, have not only a right but a moral obligation to discourage speech that expressly counsels illegal killing.

The advocacy of murder is an extreme version of a far more widespread social practice: treating political opponents, or large groups of people, as dehumanized objects of hatred and fear. Too often people who disagree are portrayed as if their political disagreement is all that they are—as if they are not real human beings who have hopes, fears, and life histories of their own. Too often the individuality of opponents is hidden behind political abstractions—"the government," "the bureaucrats," "the liberals," "the radical right," "the counterculture." The seeds of violence lie in these abstractions.

The communications media sometimes help promote violence by turning people into abstractions, but they can also help to reduce violence by telling the stories of individual people. By focusing the nation on the individuals who happened to be in a federal office building one day in April, the Oklahoma City tragedy may have helped break through the abstractions that enable government-hating extremists to commit unspeakable acts.

SECTION THREE

Violence and Gender

CHAPTER 10

Gender and Sexuality: Masculinity, Violence, and Domination

By Nancy C. M. Hartsock

Many feminists have argued that the confusion of sexuality with violence and domination must be broken. Thus, they have argued that rape is not a sexual act but rather must be recognized as an act of domination and humiliation.[1] Susan Brownmiller suggests that rape, once put "within the context of modern criminal violence and not within the purview of ancient masculine codes," will be seen to fall "midway between robbery and assault."[2] Brownmiller has highlighted the extent to which power and domination are central to rape. This has been an important theoretical and political strategy for responding to the widespread view that rape is either the act of an ordinary man strangely overcome with lust or that of a maniac continually subject to excessive lust. According to this latter view, rape is an unavoidable part of human behavior due to men's overwhelming sexual desires—desires which *must* find an outlet.[3]

Opinions such as the latter appear in more sophisticated academic garb as well. For example, Edward Shorter, in a critique of Brownmiller, suggested that while today rape may have become a political act, during the "three or four centuries before the French Revolution" rape can be charged to "sexual frustration," since there were few means of sexual release available for men in that period other than rape. It is this "huge, restless mass of sexually frustrated men" (existing, he admits, in a social system which maximized male domination) which led to rape.[4] This interpretation places the focus on sexuality, and hostility and domination drop from view.

The question of whether pornography is erotic literature or whether it involves systematic domination and degradation revolves around similar issues. Feminists have protested the violence much pornography shows directed at women: images of women in chains, being beaten, or threatened with attack carry the social message that "victimized women are sexually appealing," and that the "normal male is sexually aggressive in a brutal and demeaning way."[5] They have objected strongly to the prominence of "snuff films" (in which the pornographic action consists largely in what is claimed to be the on-camera dismemberment and death of a woman).[6] What does it mean, they ask, "when men advertise, even brag, that their movie is the 'bloodiest thing that ever happened in front of a camera' "?[7] And Gloria Steinem, distinguishing pornography from erotica, explicitly took over Brownmiller's point about rape. She argued, "Perhaps one could simply say that erotica is about sexuality but pornography is about power and sex-as-weapon—in the same way we have come to understand that rape is about violence, and not really about sexuality at all."[8]

Other feminists have argued against the dissociation of sexuality and power or domination. Given the power relations involved in everyday heterosexuality, they ask, "Can we really expect the realm of fantasy [and so pornography] to be free of the residues of that power struggle?"[9] Others go further and claim, "The desire to be sexual and the desire to be combative are complexly intertwined." They add that sexual relations are characterized by an exchange of power which should be made both explicit and consensual.[10]

Both sides in what has come to be a heated debate have important insights to offer. Yet both positions are ultimately unsatisfactory. Efforts to distinguish between erotica and degradation of or violence against women face an insoluble problem. What *is* sexually exciting in modern Western culture is hostility, violence, and domination, especially—but not necessarily—directed against women. At the same time, however, those who have taken the position that sexuality must involve exchanges of power and even combat have ignored the gender-specific nature of these connections. They have failed to recognize that sexuality as this culture constructs it is a distinctly masculine sexuality. Women's sexuality remains, as yet, unconstructed.

We need a more adequate understanding of sexuality in order to work for change—one which recognizes both the centrality of violence and domination and its connections to masculinity.

SEXUALITY AND SOCIETY

We must begin with a few words about what is meant by sexuality. Definitions of what is to be included often cover many aspects of life. For example, Freud included but did not clarify the interrelationships among such various things as libido (the basic tendency toward being alive and reproducing), the biological attributes of being male or female, sensuality, masculinity and femininity, reproductive behavior, and intense sensations in various parts of the body, especially the genitals.[11] And Jeffrey Weeks, summarizing our culture's understanding of sex, argues that in our society "sex has become the supreme secret" which is at the same time the "truth" of our being. It defines us socially and morally. Moreover, the common understanding of sexuality treats it as a "supremely private experience," which is at the same time "a thing in itself."[12]

My own reading of the literature suggests that in contrast to these definitions, we should understand sexuality not as an essence or set of properties defining an individual, or as a set of drives and needs (especially genital) of an individual. Rather, we should understand sexuality as culturally and historically defined and constructed. Anything can become eroticized, and thus there can be no "abstract and universal category of 'the erotic' or 'the sexual' applicable without change to all societies."[13] Sexuality must rather be understood as a series of cultural and social practices, meanings, and institutions which both structure and are in turn structured by social relations more generally. Thus, "sex is relational, is shaped in social interaction, and can only be understood in its historical context . . ."[14]

Because a number of theorists have argued for this position in a number of different contexts, it seems unnecessary to go into detail here, but instead to indicate that I subscribe in a general way to their arguments.[15] At the same time, because sexuality is commonly seen as rooted in human nature, it is relevant to add here a reminder about the continuing significance in my work of the essentially Marxist assumption that human activity or practice constructs a historical and constantly changing human nature, and thus, a set of historically specific and changing sexual practices and relations. It is worth reiterating this point here since in much of the literature on sexuality, possibilities for systematically changing human nature and for changing the dynamics of sexual excitement remain unaddressed, and one wonders about the extent to which many theorists hold to a view of human nature as unchanging at least in this area.[16]

HOSTILITY AND SEXUAL EXCITEMENT

If sexuality is a social and historical construction, how has contemporary Western culture shaped sexuality? There is a surprising degree of consensus that hostility and domination as opposed to intimacy and physical pleasure are central to sexual excitement. In attempting to understand these connections, the work of Robert Stoller is central.[17] Stoller contends that in our culture, "putting aside the obvious effects that result from direct stimulation of erotic bodily parts it is hostility—the desire, overt or hidden, to harm another person—that generates and enhances sexual excitement." Thus, erotic excitement must be understood as only one component of sexual excitement—others are "triumph, rage, revenge, fear, anxiety, risk."[18] Moreover, he contends, "the same dynamics, though in different mixes and degrees, are found in almost everyone, those labeled perverse and those not so labeled."[19] He suggests as well that if researchers into sexual excitement look closely they will discover that "permutations of hostility will be found far more frequently than is acknowledged today"; to underline this point, we should note that he chose the term "hostility" rather than "power" or "aggression" to indicate that "harm and suffering" are central to sexual excitement.[20] As Stoller outlines it, the mechanisms which construct sexual excitement rest most fundamentally on fetishization and on the dehumanization and objectification of the sexual object. These are associated with debasement of the object and the construction of mystery, risk, illusion, and a search for revenge. The sexual object is to be stripped of its humanity: the focus is on breasts, buttocks, legs, penises, not faces. Or an inanimate object, an animal, or a partial aspect of a human such as a breast or penis is given the personality taken from the object. These are the ways fetishization as a means for creating sexual excitement can go far beyond the clinical cases in which the fetishism is obvious. It is present in the widespread practice of treating people as though they were only organs or functions.[21]

Given our stated cultural ideals, one would not expect to find hostility at the center of sexuality. Why not intimacy, warmth, or physical pleasure? But Stoller is not alone in finding hostility in sexual excitement. A wide variety of theorists have commented on the relation of hostility and anger to sexual excitement. For example, Kinsey noted, "The closest parallel to the picture of sexual response is found in the known physiology of anger."[22] Or consider a psychologist's note that sex can be a power weapon, and that "in general it has far more intimate relationships with dominance feeling than it has with physiological drive."[23] And Kate Millett has commented that in some literary sources "the pleasure of humiliating the sexual object appears to be far more intoxicating than sex itself."[24]

Nor are references to the relation of sexual excitement and hostility limited to passing comments. These links are at the center of philosopher/pornographer George Bataille's theory and fiction. As he describes it, "sexual activity is a form of violence." The desire of the "potential killer in every man" to kill relates to the taboo on murder in the same way that the desire for sexual activity relates to the various prohibitions on it. Killing and sexual activity share both prohibitions and religious significance. Their unity is demonstrated by religious sacrifice since the latter:

> is intentional like the act of the man who *lays bare*, desires and wants to penetrate his victim. The lover *strips* the beloved of her identity no less than the bloodstained priest his human or animal victim. The woman in the hands of the assailant is *despoiled* of her being . . . loses the firm barrier that once separated her from others . . . is *brusquely* laid open to the violence of the sexual urges set loose in the organs of reproduction; she is *laid open* to the impersonal violence that overwhelms her from without.[25]

Note the use of the terms "lover" and "assailant" as synonyms and the presence of the female as victim.

Issues of sexuality and hostility appear as well in the context of analyses of racism. One writer notes that the practice of linking apes, Blacks, and Jews with the mythological satyrs "reveals that there are sensitive spots in the human soul at a level where thought becomes confused and where sexual excitement is strangely linked with violence and aggressiveness . . ."[26] Another writer, in the context of an argument about the connections between racial hostility and sexuality, makes a fairly detailed case that "the gratification in sexual conquest derives from the experience of defilement—of reducing the elevated woman to the 'dirty' sexual level, of polluting that which is seen as pure, sexualizing that which is seen as unsexual, animalizing that which is seen as 'spiritual'."[27]

In the context of these statements it is not surprising to encounter a common sense view that sex is dangerous and violent.[28] Nor should we be surprised to find hostility and violence deeply ingrained in language itself: the best known of the vulgar sexual verbs comes from the German *ficken*, meaning "to strike"; similar violent verbs are present in Latin, Celtic, Irish, Gaelic, and so forth; and consider other contemporary English terms such as "screw" or "bang."[29]

The hostility Stoller analyzes is fueled in part by danger and the construction of risk. Childhood traumas, frustrations, and dangers are turned into risks where there is a more clearly calculable outcome, where the degree of risk can be carefully controlled. This risk, then, is experienced as excitement, the childhood trauma re-created as adult sexual script. But this can only happen if the risk is simulated and the danger not too extreme.[30]

The dynamic of undoing childhood traumas and frustrations is, Stoller argues, central to the construction of sexual excitement. And while hostility is embedded in a number of social institutions and practices (e.g. humor), Stoller argues that the hostility in sexual excitement grows out of traumas and frustrations intimately connected with and threatening to the development of masculinity or femininity. He has, of course, much company in this position.[31] He concludes that sadomasochism has to be seen as a central feature of most sexual excitement, and that the desire to hurt others in revenge for having been hurt is essential for most people's sexual excitement all the time, but not all people's excitement all the time.[32]

Given the weight of evidence—both scholarly and popular—one can see how the effort to separate erotica from pornography, sexuality from violence, can gain little analytical ground. While the separation of sexuality from hostility or violence is an essential political goal, present efforts to distinguish erotica from pornography amount to blindness to a cultural reality which systematically superpositions them. Desire as domination, sexuality as hostility, then, must be recognized as the culturally hegemonic forms in which sexuality is constructed.

Some feminists have criticized Stoller's account of these dynamics. Kathleen Barry states that his argument that hostility is infused into sexuality removes responsibility from the actors, who are in most cases males. As she sums up his position, he is arguing that the fetish is created to right past wrongs, so when a woman is being raped, the rapist is not really raping her but rather is fetishizing her to right the past wrongs of being denied sexual intercourse with his mother. One can see, she adds, how this explanation plays into myth that black men rape to right the wrongs of racial injustice, or lower-class men to right past or present wrongs of poor working conditions. Moreover, Stoller's work leads to the conclusion that "sexual violence simply can't be helped—it's nature—as said Sade, as said Freud, now says Stoller . . ."[33]

There are really two issues here: the responsibility of those who commit violent acts against another, and the question of whether sexual violence is inevitable. On each point, Stoller's writing gives some support to Barry's reading, yet I think her dismissal of his insights goes too far. As I read him, Stoller is analyzing a cultural tradition of violence he neither endorses nor supports. While he puts far too much responsibility for producing "normal heterosexuals" on the mother, I do not read him as saying that rapists should not be held responsible for their acts. In addition, he explicitly raises the question of whether hostility is a real universal or is simply ubiquitous, i.e. whether gross hostility is not necessary but only usual.[34] He argues that it is probably not inevitable, even if universal, that people debase their sexual objects. He proclaims himself disappointed that sexual pleasure in most people depends on neurotic mechanisms. Finally, he suggests in a hopeful tone that perhaps there is a continuum toward less use of hostility in sexual excitement. Especially in the range of "the normative," Stoller believes there may be both hostility and affection and capacity for closeness. At the far end of the continuum, he suggests, there may be a small group of contented and secure people who are not so frightened by intimacy that they must fetishize the other person.[35] Still, Barry's view that Stoller sees the dynamic of hostility as inevitable does gain support from the fact that Stoller seems to see no way to avoid the dynamic of hostility, admits that his views put him at odds with those who see sex as a cultural and historical phenomenon (although from the text it is unclear what he means by this), and entitles his last chapter "The Necessity of Perversion."[36]

Andrea Dworkin objects to Stoller's work on other grounds. She accuses Stoller of arguing that sexual sadism is manifested in both males and females. Women too are sadists, she quotes Stoller as saying. Thus, he is justifying men's abuse of women because women are "formidable" sadists too, "despite the fact that it is not socially or historically self-evident." As she puts it, "The sexual philosophers, like the pornographers, need to believe that women are more dangerous than men or as dangerous as men so as to be justified in their social and sexual domination of them."[37] Moreover, she argues, Stoller mistakes female suffering for female triumph. The fantasies of Belle (the pseudonym of the female patient on whom Stoller bases much of his theorization of sexual excitement) are those in which she is ostensibly in the control of brutal, powerful men who try to dominate her but in Stoller's view cannot enslave her. He should have seen these sexual images as symbolic of a larger sexual reality in which she is "used, trapped, humiliated, angry, and powerless to change the values of the men who devalue her." Instead, Stoller holds that Belle chooses "sexual masochism because through it she triumphs over men whom ultimately she controls because she is the provocation to which they respond. This is an expression 'of her own oversexed nature.' She wants it, they all do."[38]

Once again, Stoller's text lends support to Dworkin's charges. He is clearly unaware of the lack of choices available to most women and far too unquestioning of the cultural institutions and cultural apparatus of male supremacy (e.g., he takes the cultural meanings of "penis" for granted and describes it as "aggressive, unfettered, unsympathetic, humiliating)."[39] There may however be a deep theoretical disagreement between Dworkin and Stoller. The latter sees not just female masochism but all masochism as, from another point of view, expressing sadism and power.[40] The correctness of Stoller's account gets support from an interesting quarter: a very similar position is taken by lesbian feminists who practice sadomasochism. As they describe the dynamics of sadomasochism among lesbian feminists, it is the masochist, or "bottom," who retains control.[41] Whatever their differences on this point, however, Stoller comes to a conclusion very similar to Dworkin's: "antagonism is established in male sexual thought as a key element in sexual excitement."[42]

Dworkin's position that Stoller attempts to assimilate male and female sexual behavior misses what I found to be one of the most intriguing and interesting aspects of his work—the existence of important but admittedly unexamined gender differences in sexual behavior and sexual excitement, differences which allow me to read Stoller as supportive of my own contention that what is culturally defined as sexuality for us is masculine sexuality, a masculine sexuality which does not grow from or express the lives of women. The area in which these differences emerge for him is in what he terms perversion.

MASCULINITY, PERVERSION, AND NORMALITY

I should note that Stoller would probably not agree with the use I have made of his arguments. In particular we part company over the meaning to be attached to, and the behaviors to be described as perversions. Despite the great prevalence of the practices he would characterize as perverse, he wants very much to keep the term as a way to characterize deviance.[43] He defines perversion as "the erotic form of hatred," a fantasy either acted out or restricted to a daydream of doing harm. It is a fantasy motivated by hostility—the wish to do harm—not by simple aggression or forcefulness.[44]

He adds:

> The more gross the hostility, the less question that one is dealing with perversion. Murder that sexually excites, mutilation for excitement, rape, sadism with precise physical punishments such as whipping or cutting, enchaining and binding games, defecating or urinating on one's object—all are on a lessening scale of conscious rage toward one's sex object, in which an essential purpose is for one to be superior to, harmful to, triumphant over another. And so it is also in the nonphysical sadisms like exhibitionism, voyeurism, dirty phone calls or letters, use of prostitutes, and most forms of promiscuity.[45]

It is interesting to note here that the psychological dynamics of perversion do not differ importantly from those Stoller has identified as typical of sexual excitement. Hostility, fetishization, and dehumanization figure centrally in both perverse and "normal" sexual excitement.[46] He attempts to distinguish variant sexual practices from perverse ones on the basis of whether or not the "aberrant" practice is or is not primarily motivated by hostility.

Stoller found two interesting puzzles in his work on perversion. First, he continually ran into the problem that by his definition, where hostility was central to perversion, a great deal, perhaps even most, of contemporary "normal" heterosexual sexual activity must be labeled perverse. Thus, he notes that we face the risk of finding that there is very little sexual behavior that might not have a touch of the perverse. He attempts to draw back from this position however: Wouldn't this ruin the meaning of the term "perverse," he asks?[47] And he complains that "the idea of normality crumbles" if one notes the ubiquity of sexual pathology in heterosexuals who are supposed to be the "normals."[48] One must deal, then, with behavior which is not in a statistical sense aberrant.

Stoller is not alone in finding this difficulty. The scholars at the Institute for Sex Research found something similar. Dworkin calls attention to a statement from *Sex Offenders: An Analysis of Types*. "If we labelled all punishable sexual behavior as a sex offense, we would find ourselves in the ridiculous situation of having all of our male histories consist almost wholly of sex offenders. . . . The man who kisses a girl [*sic*] in defiance of her expressed wishes is committing a forced sexual relationship and is liable to an assault charge, but to solemnly label him a sex offender would be to reduce our study to a ludicrous level."[49]

This last quotation points toward the second puzzle Stoller found in his work but did not analyze. Why, he asks, is perversion (that is, gross hostility or eroticized hatred) found more in males?[50] And he raises several other important and related questions: He wonders "whether in humans (especially males) powerful sexual excitement can ever exist without brutality also being present." And he asks, "Can anyone provide examples of behavior in sexual excitement in which, in human males at least, disguised hostility in fantasy is not a part of potency?"[51] And, given that psychoanalysis explains why women are as perverse as men, why has it not explained why they are not?[52]

His own analysis in *Sexual Excitement*[53] follows this pattern; as he himself notes, he has not dealt with the issue of how women are unlike men rather than like them in the construction of sexual excitement. In addition, Stoller wonders why women neither buy nor respond to pornography as intensely as men (he defines pornography by the presence of a victim, as shall be discussed further on) and begins to ask whether the question itself is wrong. Women, Stoller argues, do buy "masochistic" but "romantic" and "unsexual" stories, and thus, he suspects, the definition of pornography hinges on what is pornography for men.[54] The romantic, masochistic stories women buy raise another problem as well for Stoller: Why, he asks, given these fantasies, do so few women practice sadomasochism?[55]

Thus, Stoller's account suggests that what we treat as sexuality and sexual excitement is a gendered masculine sexuality and masculine sexual excitement.[56] This masculinity can be strikingly confirmed in a variety of areas: evidence is present in ordinary language and popular assumptions, social psychology, and literature.

The language which describes the institution our society places at the center of acceptable human sexuality, heterosexual intercourse, focuses exclusively on the experience of the man. As Janice Moulton has put it, "sexual intercourse is an activity in which male arousal is a necessary condition, and male satisfaction, if not also a necessary condition, is the primary aim . . . [whereas] female arousal and satisfaction, although they may be concomitant events occasionally, are not even constituents of sexual intercourse." While the polite language is one of symmetry, the vulgar language presents a quite different picture; for example, "if he fucked her, it does not follow that she has fucked him." The conceptual baggage of even the polite language is such that intercourse formally begins when the man's primary focus for sexual stimulation is inserted in the vagina and ends with male orgasm. Given this conceptual baggage, Moulton is led to wonder why "anyone ever thought the female orgasm had anything to do with sexual intercourse, except as an occasional and accidental co-occurrence." As she notes, "Sometimes the telephone rings, too."[57]

The assumptions embedded in common language take more explicit forms as well. Feminist writers have commented widely on the popular assumptions that what is referred to as sex drive is a male sex drive."[58] And feminists have also noted that "It was not very long ago that the notion of being sexual and being female was outrageous." Others have lamented the "total lack of images of women being motivated by sexual desire."[59] These assumptions appear as well in more professional contexts populated by sex researchers, educators, clinicians, and social workers. One feminist report from such a conference noted that "sex" was the term for heterosexual sex, and "sex" required "genital contact, male erection, and penetration."[60]

Sociological studies support both the fundamental masculinity of "sexdrive" ideas and their connections with dynamics of hostility and domination. One study of "corner boys" indicates that the "maximization of sexual pleasure clearly occurs for these boys when there is a strong component of conquest experienced in the sexual act," and suggests that without the conquest, the act is less gratifying.[61]

Kate Millett, analyzing the work of Norman Mailer, finds similar dynamics. She argues that sex for Mailer is a "thrilling test of self" (the self defined as an "athletic 'hunter-fighter-fucker' "). "Little wonder," she states, "that Mailer's sexual journalism reads like the sporting news grafted onto a series of war dispatches." On reading the work of Henry Miller, she concludes, "the pleasure of humiliating the sexual object appears to be far more intoxicating than sex itself."[62] Charles Stember underlines her point that, indeed, "for men it is a vital part of the sex act, not an added attraction."[63]

We can, then, state with some confidence that the culturally produced dynamics of hostility which structure sexual excitement correspond to a masculine sexuality which depends on defiling or debasing a fetishized sexual object.

Given this evidence, then, those who discuss sexual pleasure and desire without attending to gender differences and without recognizing that our culture has constructed sexuality in such a way that it carries a masculine gender have made an important error. We must recognize that sexuality in our culture is a power relation in which hostility, violence, and domination play central roles. This is not to say that those who argue that a nongendered sexuality must or should involve power relations are simply male-identified. This would be simplistic. Rather, it is to say that what our culture has made of sexuality expresses the experience of the ruling gender. And because of this hegemony, masculine experience sets the dynamics of the social relations in which all parties are forced to participate—women as well as men, unmasculine as well as masculine men.

Thus, an understanding of sexuality as involving power relations but not carrying a masculine gender must be seen as a kind of masculinist ideology which expresses the experience and dominance of men and, on the other hand, structures real sexual relations for women as well as men. It cannot, then, be dismissed as simply false. This should not be surprising. One should expect that in the cultural construction of sexuality, as in the development of moral judgment, the need for achievement, and so forth, it is the experience of the ruling gender which defines the terms and structures the content.[64]

Thus, we must insist that we face a gendered power relation based in what our culture has defined as sexuality. This does not change the fact that these dynamics are more typical of men than women and correspond to men's rather than women's experience.

If these are the dynamics of "normal" heterosexual excitement, we can begin to understand both the existence of rape and rape fantasies and the depiction of violence against women for purposes of arousing sexual excitement. If we cannot distinguish between sexuality and hostility, pornography and erotica, should we conclude that sexuality is inseparable from violence against women, that sex is masculine and violent, and that feminists should therefore simply stay away from sex? If hostility is so omnipresent—for men and, given our culture, women too—is there any escape?[65]

THE NATURE OF EROS

In order to move the discussion onto new and hopefully more productive ground, I propose to reformulate issues of sexuality under the heading of *eros*. Such a reformulation will allow me to put forward a broader understanding of the variety of forms taken by sexuality in our culture, and to include the sexual meanings of issues and institutions which are not explicitly genitally focused. Recasting the issue in these terms can also clarify and refine the central dynamics of sexual excitement and thus aid in tracing the association of sexuality with virility, violence, and death. In addition, such a reformulation can provide a space to develop an understanding of sexuality which need not depend on hostility for its fundamental dynamic.

Three distinct though not necessarily separate aspects of *eros* emerge from my reading of the psychological literature.[66] The first is represented by Freud's definition of *eros* as "the desire to make one out of more than one."[67] This desire may take narrowly genital form, or may appear in other, sublimated forms. Freud suggests, and Marcuse agrees, that the inhibition of the direct aims of sexual impulses and their subjugation to the control of "higher psychical agencies; which have subjected themselves to the reality principle," i.e., the repression of *eros*, is required for the development of civilization.[68] Thus, one should expect to find a number of sublimated forms of *eros*.

The second aspect of *eros* turns on the role given to sensuality and bodily concerns in social life. Historically, various societies of Western civilization have found little place for this aspect of *eros* in public life as traditionally understood. Plato was one of the first to reject it as unworthy of the citizen's concern because of the bad effects of uncontrolled appetites—likened in the *Republic* to being at the mercy of "a raging and savage beast of a master." He argued that if the soul were properly ordered, the body would be well taken care of and was therefore due no special cdncern.[69]

Creativity and generation—whether intellectual creativity in philosophy and art, physical work on the substances of nature, or the generation of children through sexual relations—emerge as the third aspect of *eros*. Some psychologists have pointed to the pleasure in the "effortful achievement of purpose" as fundamental to what makes us human. They have suggested that only when these pleasures take pathological forms can sublimation (and the civilization on which it depends) occur.[70] Freud concurs at least to some extent when he argues that

> No other technique of the conduct of life attaches the individual so firmly to reality as laying the emphasis on work; for his work at least gives him a secure place in a portion of reality, in the human community. The possibility it offers of displacing a large amount of libidinal components, whether narcissistic, aggressive, or even erotic, on to professional work and on to the human relations connected with it lends it a value by no means second to what it enjoys as something indispensable to the preservation and justification of existence in society . . . [I]f it is a freely chosen one . . . it makes possible the use of existing inclinations. . . . And yet, as a path to happiness, work is not highly prized by men.[71]

Marx's great achievement, from this perspective, was to open the possibility of a society in which the majority of people need not be driven to work only under the press of necessity. This is the society to which Marcuse refers when he suggests the possibility of "non-repressive sublimation."[72] In this case, sexuality would not be blocked or deflected from its object but rather, in attaining its object, transcend it to others. Under these conditions, Marcuse argues that sexuality could tend to grow into *eros* in a broader sense through what he terms the re-sexualizing of work. He argues that this may become a real possibility, thus eroticizing the body as a whole. These then are some important features of the third aspect of *eros*, the pleasure derived from acting in the world.[73]

These three elements—the making of one out of more than one, sensuality in a broad sense, and finally the pleasure of competent activity-represent aspects of *eros*. It is important to note that by reformulating the issues in terms of *eros* we can both clarify the underlying issues sexuality involves, and also make it possible to envision a social construction of *eros* in which hostility does not play such a central role.

But in a world of hostile and threatening others, each aspect of *eros* takes a repressive rather than liberatory form—one which points toward death rather than life. For example, the desire for fusion with another can take the form of domination of the other. Sensuality and bodily pleasures can be denied, and the third aspect of *eros*, creativity and generation, can also take forms of domination both in the world of work, where creative activity becomes alienated labor, and in reproduction, in which the creation of new life becomes either disembodied or recast as death.

These dynamics can be most fruitfully analyzed in pornography, since there we see detailed schemas for creating sexual excitement. In addition, this extensive industry illustrates how what may appear to be a series of individual actions and decisions are in fact structured and limited by society as a whole.

Because I have taken the position that it is analytically ineffective to attempt to distinguish erotica from pornography, here I propose to use as a working definition Robert Stoller's useful statement that pornography requires hostility and the presence of a victim. For Stoller: no victim, no pornography. Stoller, however, adds several important qualifications: nothing is pornographic until the observer's fantasies are added. And with the addition of these fantasies, several hostile dynamics may take place: voyeurism is the most apparent, sadism is the second, and masochism, or identification with the depicted victim, is the third.[74] Moreover, all pornography has in common a construction of risk and an evocation of danger surmounted. Thus, for Stoller there is "no nonperverse pornography, that is, sexually exciting matter in which hostility is not employed as a goal."[75] Finally, pornography will be "loathsome" to the person responding to it. Stoller here refers not only to forbidden sensuality but also to the observer's fears that hostility will be released.[76] All of these factors are part of the definition.

The fantasies of sexual excitement which appear in pornography so defined are most importantly structured by the dynamic of reversal/revenge; as a result, each aspect of *eros* takes a repressive form which points toward violence and death. The specific dynamics of reversal/revenge depend on infant and childhood experience, since the traumas of childhood are memorialized in the details of sexual excitement; the fantasies which produce sexual excitement re-create the relationships of childhood trying to undo the frustrations, traumas, and conflicts.[77] The traumas re-created in sexual excitement are, Stoller hypothesizes, memorials to childhood traumas aimed at sexual anatomy or masculinity or femininity—i.e., at gender identification. Moreover, he suggests, sexual excitement will occur at the moment when adult reality resembles the childhood trauma—the anxiety being re-experienced as excitement.[78]

Reversal/revenge (my term) is the major shift which allows anxiety to take the form of pleasure, i.e., a reversal in the positions of the actors in order to convert the trauma into revenge. In men, Stoller suggests, this dynamic of reversal/revenge leads to perversion (and, in the light of his later work, to sexual excitement more generally) constructed out of rage at giving up the early identification with the mother and concomitant ecstasies of infancy, the fear of failing to differentiate oneself from the mother, and a need for revenge on her for putting one in this situation.[79,80] This dynamic of reversal/revenge rooted in childhood trauma means that revenge fantasies can be expected to be most often directed against the mother. Stoller notes that to the degree that a child feels it has been debased, it will as an adult reverse this process in fantasy to create sexual excitement.[81] The sexual fantasies of pornography, then, can be read as patterned reversals of the traumas of childhood and as adult (male) revenge on the traumatizer. These dynamics structure each aspect of *eros* in specific ways. Some are clearest in pornography itself. Others emerge with greater clarity in the work of those Dworkin has termed the sexual philosophers, such as Mailer or Bataille.

FUSION, COMMUNITY, AND THE DEATH OF THE OTHER

In pornography, the desire for fusion with another takes the form of domination of the other. In this form, it leads to the only possible fusion with a threatening other: when the other ceases to exist as a separate, and for that reason threatening, being. Insisting that another submit to one's will is simply a milder form of the destruction of discontinuity in death since in this case one is no longer confronting a discontinuous and opposed will, despite its discontinuous embodiment. This need to destroy the other is directly connected with childhood experience. Stoller argues that sexuality and intimacy can threaten "one's sense of maleness or femaleness," and that this risk is at the same time a source of sexual excitement.[82] Pornography, then, must reduce this danger to a titillating risk if sexual excitement is to be created.

In order to reduce the danger of fusion or intimacy, pornography substitutes control. Susan Griffin in her analysis of the major themes which motivate what she terms "the pornographic mind" argues that the idea that a woman might reject a man appears at the heart of the culture of pornography.[83] The problem, she notes, is that when a woman rejects a man, he must face the reality that he does not control her. Thus, in pornography, issues of control are central to the creation of sexual excitement. One finds the importance of controlling women repeated at length: the woman is controlled, mastered, and humiliated.[84] One can remark as well the consistency of advertisements for sexual dolls in men's magazines. The makers argue that their products are better than real women because they will never say no. The dynamic of conquest and the thrill of obtaining control by overcoming a resistant will are epitomized in the figure of Don Juan, for whom excitement and gratification come not from sensual pleasure and intimacy but rather from overcoming the resistance of a woman: "Easy women do not attract him."[85] Kathleen Barry has commented on more extreme forms of this dynamic and cites passages from several stories in which women are "bound, gagged and tied into positions which render them totally vulnerable and exposed."[86]

Fetishism is a second and related move to avoid fusion and intimacy with another. Rather than concentrate on the pleasure of overcoming the will of another, fetishism avoids confronting the will by fantasizing the other as a thing rather than a human being, treating a body part as a substitute for the person, or even dispensing with the human being altogether.[87] Woman's "thingness" can also be created through her reduction to an image. The mildest of heterosexual male pornography is represented by a massive industry producing photographs of nude women which reduce the real woman to an image on the page, "imprison" her on paper, and therefore render her powerless to threaten the viewer.[88] One should view Griffin's account of Hugh Hefner's own practices in this light. Hefner, she argues, was fascinated with images as opposed to experience. He lived in a world made up of images he could control, and Griffin suggests that his control over the images allowed him both to keep a safe distance from reality and real women, and to believe that he could control this reality.[89]

The reality of women as fellow human beings can also be avoided by forbidding them to speak. Griffin notes that "a morbid fear of female speech" is central to pornography; "even the sexual action, in pornography, seems to exist less for pleasure than to overpower and silence women."[90] Her analysis of *The Story of O* takes note that the heroine is silenced: One of the first rules at Roissy is not to speak to another Woman, and later, not to speak at all.[91]

The dynamics of control and fetishization are both well illustrated by the photograph "Beaver Hunters" described by Andrea Dworkin. The naked woman in the picture, tied like a dead animal to the front of a jeep, has been hunted and subdued (the caption states that the hunters "stuffed and mounted their trophy as soon as they got her home," thus playing off and highlighting the suggestion that the woman was killed as part of their sexual use of her) and is displayed as a trophy of conquest.[92]

Third, erotic fusion and intimacy take forms structured by reversal/revenge. Here the infantile roots of the fear of intimacy are more clearly visible. Griffin points tellingly to the importance in pornography of the image of

> a woman driven to a point of madness out of the desire to put a man's penis in her mouth. So that finally, by this image, we are called back: this image reminds the mind of another scene, a scene in which the avidity to put a part of the body into the mouth is not a mystery. Here is a reversal again. For it is the infant who so overwhelmingly needs the mother's breast in his mouth, the infant who thought he might die with-

> out this, who became frantic and maddened with desire, and it was his mother who had the power to withhold.[93]

The dynamic of reversal/revenge occurs in a variety of cultural myths as well, in which the man struggles against dangerous women. One finds this struggle, for example, between Samson and Delilah, about which Griffin argues: "not only is male freedom based on female silence, but a man's life depends on the death of a woman."[94] She finds this theme in the modern novel as well—in *An American Dream* Mailer presents his protagonist as the victim who acted in self-defense when he killed his wife: "It was as if killing her, the act had been too gentle, I had not plumbed the hatred where the real injustice was stored."[95]

This is not just fiction. Lawrence Singleton, convicted of raping and cutting off the hands of a teenage girl, considered that it was he, not she, who was kidnapped and threatened. In his mind the roles were reversed and he was the victim. "Everything I did," he wrote, "was for survival."[96] Given this kind of hostility, ability to reverse roles, and deep needs for revenge, one can begin to understand why watching a woman tortured or dismembered on camera can be sexually exciting. Perhaps she should be seen as a sacrificial victim whose discontinuous existence has been succeeded in her death by "the organic continuity of life drawn into the common life of the beholders."[97]

SHAMEFUL SEXUALITY: THE DENIAL OF THE BODY

The second aspect of *eros*, too, can take a repressive form—the denial of sensuality and bodily pleasures. While this may initially strike the reader as an odd claim to make about literature and photographs intended to produce sexual and thus presumably physical excitement, the generation of this excitement relies on the experience of the body as shameful. The source of this shame can be found in childhood experience: one psychologist has commented, "The loathing and disgust that we feel for what we cannot help being interested in is our homage to the reasons we had for burying the interest."[98]

In pornography, the body—usually a woman's body—is presented as something which arouses shame, even humiliation, and the opposition of spirit or mind to the body—the latter sometimes referred to as representing something bestial or nonhuman—generates a series of dualities. Griffin captures the essence of this experience of the body when she argues that "speaking to that part of himself [the pornographer] wishes to shame, he promises, 'I'm going to treat you like something that crawled out of the sewer'."[99]

Pornography is built around, plays on, and obsessively re-creates these dualities. The dichotomy between spiritual love and "carnal knowledge" is re-created in the persistent fantasy of transforming the virgin into the whore. She begins pure, innocent, fresh, even in a sense disembodied, and is degraded and defiled in sometimes imaginative and bizarre ways.[100] Transgression is important here: forbidden practices are being engaged in. The violation of the boundaries of society breaks its taboos. Yet the act of violating a taboo, of seeing or doing something forbidden, does not do away with its forbidden status. Indeed, in the ways women's bodies are degraded and defiled in the transformation of the virgin into the whore, the boundaries between the forbidden and permitted are simultaneously upheld and broken.[101] Put another way, the obsessive transformation of virgin into whore simply crosses and recrosses the boundary between them. Without the boundary, there could be no transformation at all. And without the boundary there to violate, the thrill of transgression would disappear.

The sexual excitement striptease produces can be viewed as similar in form. It only "works" to produce sexual excitement because the exposed body is considered shameful and forbidden. The viewer is seeing something he is not entitled to see, something forbidden, and moreover, something potentially dangerous because it might have the power to change or transform him. Griffin suggests that our culture believes that the sight of a woman's flesh can turn a man into a rapist, and presumably do other things as well.[102] One finds the same view of the (female) body as loathsome, humiliating, and even dangerous in a stripper's comment that one of several styles of producing sexual excitement in striptease is "hard," that is, emphasizing the dark, hard lines of constraint provided by women's clothing, constraint of an aggressive female sexuality: "It is as if the notion of sexual woman were so overwhelming that she had to be visibly bound."[103]

Loathing for the body, in the sense that bodily needs and desires are humiliating, appears in another way in pornography in the form of the contrast between the man's self-control and the woman's frenzied abandon. It is consistently a woman who is, as Griffin puts it, "humiliated by her desire, her helplessness, and materiality."[104] These issues of control and humiliation are clear in *The Story of O.* The speech O is given her first night at Roissy is one in which the men are portrayed as fully in control of their bodies. She is told that while their costume "leaves our sex exposed, it is not for the sake of convenience . . ." and that what is done to her is "less for our pleasure than for your enlightenment." They make clear that while they make use of her, they are independent and do not need her.[105] This insistence on independence and control on one side and a victim humiliated by her own desires on the other appears frequently.[106] The presence of a victim, one who submits in fact, requires another who remains in control, who, one author suggests, establishes selfhood by controlling the other.[107] The fact that it is the woman whose body is in the control of another, and the woman who is humiliated by her desires and materality, records the reversal/revenge of infant and childhood experience.

The theme of succeeding by ignoring/overcoming the feelings of the body is related to the fear and loathing of the body. Thus Griffin can argue that Don Juan, the "femme fatale," and de Sade share the quality of being unfeeling, an unfeelingness which allows them to be "powerful and free," yet leads at the same time to feelings of numbness.[108] In pornography, feeling is conquered by projecting emotions onto the victim who is humiliated by bodily appetites, by reducing the woman to the status of a feeling body and in "snuff" films to a literal corpse.

Thus, sensuality and bodily concerns, the second aspect of *eros*, take negative forms. They become entangled with and point toward death—what Griffin has termed the death of feeling as well as the death of the body. Griffin is right to point out that the denial of the body is in part due to the fact that it is a reminder of mortality and therefore of death.[109] Indeed, as she argues in her excellent and innovative analysis of the Oedipus myth, knowledge of the body *is* knowledge of death. She holds that Oedipus's association with flesh comes from the fact that he grew up away from his father (and therefore, Griffin claims, closer to nature and the body). More importantly, though, his knowledge of the body represents knowledge of his mortality. It was this which allowed him to answer the riddle of the sphinx: "What walks on four legs in the morning, two in midday, and three in the evening?" As Griffin points out, he can answer the riddle, "Man," because he knows that he was once a vulnerable infant and will one day require a cane to aid him in the weakness of age.[110]

GENERATION, CREATIVITY, AND DEATH

The third aspect of *eros*—creativity and generation—can also take the form of domination and death. We have noted how each aspect of *eros* as constructed by pornography involves death: fusion with another requires the death (or at least submission) of the other; bodily feelings are denied because the fact of existence as embodied beings reminds us that we are mortal. In this context, it should not surprise us that issues of creativity, generation, and reproduction are reformulated in ways that link them to death.[111] These linkages appear to some extent in pornographic stories and photographs but are more clearly stated by those Dworkin has identified as sexual philosophers.

Dworkin has described an instance of these links in a genre she terms the "pornography of pregnancy." She argues that this pornography, both in pictures of pregnant women and in the accompanying text, stresses the "malevolence" of the female body, "its danger to sperm and especially its danger to the woman herself." In this vision, the "pregnancy is the triumph of the phallus over the death-dealing vagina." She notes as well that the transformation of the virgin into whore is present as well, since the pregnancy is evidence of lack of virginity.[112] Thus, reproduction comes to be linked with danger and even death. Historically, of course, reproduction did have important connections with death. It is perhaps significant that a writer such as Norman Mailer recognized these connections when he noted that sexual intercourse had lost its gravity (in part?) because pregnancy had ceased to be dangerous.[113]

French philosopher/pornographer George Bataille makes even clearer connections between *eros* and death and reformulates even reproduction itself as death. He argues that there is a "profound unity of these apparent opposites, birth and death." (Bataille is in good company: Aristotle too argued that whatever comes into being must pass away.) Yet despite their unity, Bataille gives primacy to death and argues that one must recognize a "tormenting fact: the urge towards love, pushed to its limit, is an urge toward death."[114] Moreover, reproduction is connected to continuity, but the continuity is defined by death. Indeed, "death is to be identified with continuity and both of these concepts are equally fascinating. This fascination is the dominant element in eroticism."[115] Reproduction itself seen from this perspective is better understood as death: the new entity formed from the sperm and ovum bears in itself the "fusion, fatal to both, of two separate beings."[116] One can see here traces of the roots of this view in childhood experience, and the threat to identity posed by fusion: the erotic fusion of the sexual connection not only threatens death but indeed requires it. The danger is not simply a risk to be run but is, at some level, inevitably fatal.

The separation of generation and reproduction from life takes a second, more indirect form as well: sexuality and sexual activity are portrayed in pornography as profoundly distanced from the activities of daily life. The action in pornography takes place in what Griffin has termed "pornotopia," a world outside of real time and space, where no one worries about doing dishes, or changing diapers, and women enjoy rape, bondage, and humiliation. The distance from the real world structured by daily necessities is aptly symbolized by Griffin's description of Hugh Hefner's house: "his house has no windows. Nothing unpredictable or out of his control can happen to him there. Sunrise makes no difference. . . . Food emanates from a kitchen supplied with a staff day and night. . . . [And] as if one layer of protection [or distancing] were not enough, his bedroom contains another self-sufficient and man-made world, with a desk, and food supplies, and a bed which is motorized so that it not only changes positions but also carries him about the room."[117]

This transformation of creative activity and generation into negative forms is not of course limited to sexuality but occurs in other areas of society as well. Some of the clearest examples occur in the world of work. There what could have been empowering and creative activity in conjunction with external nature becomes alienated labor in industries which pollute and destroy both their natural surroundings and the minds and bodies of those who labor, not a development of physical and mental capacities but a desruction of both.

ALTERNATIVES TO VIOLENCE AND DOMINATION

Beneath the polite language of sexual reciprocity we have uncovered not only one-sided relations of domination and submission, but also dynamics of hostility, revenge, and a fascination with death. These are the negative forms taken by *eros*, forms which in our culture define masculinity: intimacy and fusion with another pose such deep problems that they require the domination of the other or control of the actions of the other, reducing the presumably threatening person to a nonentity with no will of its (her) own. Fetishism provides a second solution to the problem of intimacy: the other who presents the possibility (or threat) of erotic fusion produces such fright that she (in most cases it is a woman) must be reduced to two-dimensional images or even a set of body parts to make it safe enough to pleasurably fantasize her victimization. And even in fantasy she must be silenced, reduced to a being without feelings or speech.

As for the second aspect of *eros*, in its negative, masculine form our existence as embodied beings does not open possibilities for sensual and physical connections with others but comes to stand as a loathsome reminder of our mortality which must be excised as much as possible from existence. Virility requires the denial of the body and its importance, whether this takes the form of control of the body of another or the portrayal of the man in heterosexual male pornography as complete master of his own body and the woman as totally at the mercy of his desires. The third aspect of *eros* too is given negative form. Creativity and generation become instead a fascination with death, and even reproduction is reformulated as concerned with death rather than life. Issues of daily life and necessity, as reminders of mortality and materiality, must be avoided.

Why are virility and domination so intimately connected? The key structuring experience can now be seen as the fear of ceasing to exist as a separate being, ceasing to exist because of the threat posed by a woman. These fears are expressed clearly in masculine sexual fantasies as these appear in pornography. Intimacy with a woman is so dangerous that she must be reduced to a nonentity or made into a thing. The body, constituting a reminder of loathsome mortality, must be denied and repressed. The whole man is reduced to the phallus; and bodily feelings are projected onto the woman who is reduced to a body without a will of her own. And in sexual fantasy and philosophy about sexual fantasy, creativity and generation take the form of a fascination with death.

The feelings of the body, because they are reminders of materiality, and worse, mortality, reminders that one will some day cease to exist, must be rejected and denied. And because to be born means that one will die, reproduction and generation either are understood in terms of death or are appropriated by men in disembodied form. Over and over, then, the fear of ceasing to exist is played out.

If women's sexuality remains unconstructed in our culture, where can we look for an alternative? I believe that women's experience does not contain an alternative sexuality, but that we can find in women's lives intimations and echoes of a different world, a world in which the erotic can be constructed as "an assertion of the life-force of women."[118] We are only at the beginning of the construction even of an alternative vision, let alone the cultural construction of an authentic female sexuality. Yet as a beginning, two disparate literatures seem particularly promising: research on maternal sexuality, and the current debate about sexuality within the feminist movement; the one concerned with sexuality as it appears in reproduction, the other concerned with sexual excitement and sexual pleasure.

Maternal sexuality is particularly interesting since it has generally been held to be nonexistent, and therefore remains culturally constructed as asexual. Perhaps one might say that this is a "feminine" sexuality, since sexuality and maternity, like sexuality and femininity, are generally held to involve a contradiction. Here the work of Niles Newton is very useful. She argues that if one looks at the three "intense interpersonal reproductive acts" available to women—coitus, parturition, and lactation—one finds marked correlations and interrelationships.[119] Yet despite her documentation of a systematic series of similarities between childbirth and sexual excitement, and between breast-feeding and coital orgasm, most women in our culture do not perceive these experiences as sexual. Some of those few women who have reported sexual feelings in nursing also reported feeling guilt about those feelings. In the case of breast-feeding, researchers who probed beyond the conventional answers did find a substantial percentage of mothers who reported that they enjoyed the experience, but described their enjoyment as not specifically sexual, but rather as feelings of tenderness and closeness.[120]

The inhibition of the sensual pleasures of breast-feeding may, Newton suggests, be similar to those which make birth orgasm rare in our culture: mother and infant are separated in the hospital, and rules about duration and timing of each sucking period are frequently enforced, Newton notes, "by persons who usually have never successfully breast fed even one baby." She concludes that "probably most people in our society would be willing to concede that we would cause coital frigidity if we prescribed the act only at scheduled times and laid down rules concerning the exact number of minutes intromission should last."[121]

The belief is that good mothers have no sexual feelings in relation to children, despite the fact that there is general agreement in the psychological literature that the early mother-child relationship should be erotic for the child.[122] What is less generally appreciated is that breast-feeding can be considered to be a reciprocal or symmetrical activity which involves not the mother alone, but also the infant. Unlike coitus, this experience can be more persuasively characterized as an "equal opportunity experience."[123] These experiences, bodily, sensual, creative in the large sense of the term, suggest that women's lives may be able to incorporate *eros* without insisting that the only fusion with another lies in the death of the other; without, for that matter, insisting that isolation or fusion are the only options.

Contemporary arguments about the nature of a "feminist sexuality" have so far produced little more than polarization.[124] Yet these arguments both raise the issue of what sexual woman might look like and also illustrate how *eros*, even in negative forms, poses different problems for women than for men. Because of masculine hegemony, one would expect that women's sexual excitement too would depend on hostility and transgression, and to some extent this is true. But even among feminists whose sexual excitement has been characterized as deeply structured by masculinist patterns, there is some evidence to support the contention that women are less perverse than men, that is, that women's sexual excitement depends less than men's on victimization and revenge. Thus one finds even in the fiction, autobiographical and political statements of lesbian proponents of sadomasochism echoes of a different experience. In terms of *eros* one finds that in terms of fusion with another, empathy with the other partner receives far more attention than separation from the other by means of domination and submission.[125] Rather than treat the body as a loathsome reminder of mortality whose needs must be projected onto the body of another, the rejection of the body takes the form of a need for permission to enjoy the pleasures of the flesh without guilt or responsibility.[126] Ironically, given the current controversy, one can compare these dynamics and issues to Anne Snitow's descriptions of the heroine's submission to greater force in Harlequin romance novels.[127]

Creativity and generation seem to play small roles in the fantasies described by Samois members. One finds little evidence of a fascination with death. The negative form of this aspect of *eros* appears only indirectly in the separation of sexuality from daily life-activity. It is perhaps significant that Snitow finds this aspect also shared by the sexual dynamics of Harlequin romances. In sum, research in these two areas suggests that women are indeed less perverse than men, that even the negative forms of *eros* take less dangerous forms for women.

Neither of these literatures provides an alternative vision. Rather, if one looks closely, one finds indications of a "muted" experience, neither fully understood nor articulated. Moreover, the construction of an alternative sexuality rooted in women's experience requires more than a vision. It would require the real power of women to define and socially construct their own sexuality. And this of course would require that women have real power.

CHAPTER 11

Violence, Gender, and Social Change

By Christine Alder

INTRODUCTION

Discussions of violence in society frequently focus on the violent crimes recorded in criminal justice statistics—assault, robbery and homicide. These crimes are most often intra-racial and intra-class: the offenders and the victims are among the economically oppressed members of our society. These offences are the cause of much human suffering and personal disaster and thus warrant careful investigation. However, there are many different forms of violence in our society, some of which are often taken for granted: in the home, parents hit their children; on the playing field, sportsmen assault each other. Other forms of violence are of increasing public interest and concern, but they may not be treated as criminal matters: at work, industrial 'accidents' occur; in our communities, dangerous chemicals are dumped; our governments turn a blind eye to the practices of some police officers; and our governments are responsible for the mass violence of war. We shall give some consideration to each of these forms of violence. The objective is to review briefly the implications of some major social changes for both the occurrence of violence and its possible reduction.

WOMEN'S LIBERATION

Women's emancipation or liberation has been one of the more popular and recurring themes in recent discussions of the implications of social change for violent crime.[1] The work of Freda Adler,[2] *Sisters in Crime*, provides a recent example of this thesis which essentially proceeds as follows: women are committing more violent crime; violent crime is masculine; women are becoming more masculine as a consequence of women's liberation.

Naffine provides a summary of now extensive literature and research that has been generated in response to Adler's argument.[3] More detailed analyses of data reveal that women have not been significantly more involved in violent crime in recent times. Female crimes remain predominantly the types of property offence consistent with traditional female role expectations (shop-lifting, fraud and petty theft). Further, female offenders are most often not the middle class women involved in the recent women's movement. In fact one study of young women found that those with more liberated views were less likely to be delinquent. Naffine concludes that, rather than the liberation of women, the social change more likely to have had an impact on increases in female property crime is the 'feminization of poverty.'

MASCULINITY

Across time and cultures, violent crime is overwhelmingly perpetrated by relatively young, economically marginalized, males.[4] Frequently, as indicated in homicide research, the violence is male to male.[5] Research in countries such as Australia and the United States indicates that somewhat more than three-quarters of all homicide offenders, and two-thirds of all homicide victims, are male.[6]

In recent years feminist research, in particular, has also drawn attention to male violence towards women. These forms of violence frequently occur in 'private', in the home, and police and other criminal justice agencies have been reluctant to define such violence as 'criminal' or to respond to such 'family' matters. Consequently, a good deal of violence against women is never recorded in official statistics.[7] Research in a number of different nations has revealed an extensive problem of domestic violence and a reluctance by formal agencies to deal with the problem.[8] Thus, despite the recent achievements of the refuge movements in many countries and their efforts to bring about social change,[9] the extent of male violence continues to be underestimated in official accounts.

While violence has been recognized as a predominantly male phenomenon, the maleness or the masculinity of the perpetrator has not been a focus of research. While a range of social characteristics of violent offenders have been analysed (their age, class, education, religion, race), their gender has been virtually ignored.[10]

Recognizing the 'maleness' of violent crime, feminist researchers have recently argued that male violence against women is an expression of male power and is used by men to reproduce and maintain their relative status and authority over women. Support for this argument is provided by an analysis of the main sources of conflict which result in male violence towards women: possessiveness and jealousy, expectations regarding women's domestic work, a sense of the right to punish 'their' women for wrongdoing, and the importance of maintaining or exercising authority.[11]

Analyses of male violence point out that the social construction of masculinity entails assumptions of power, and that both masculinity and power are linked to aggression and violence. Thus male to male confrontations are also confirmations of masculinity: a means of testing and establishing power in relation to other men.[12]

Morgan warns however against stereotyping constructions of masculinity on the basis of those presumed to be working class.[13] He points out that constructions of both masculinity and violence are in fact variable and diffuse; there are different masculinity and some violence is legitimated while some is not. For example, he notes that even within groups which encourage violence, in some circumstances a man who can control his violence may be held in higher regard than one who engages in indiscriminate violence. That is, in some male groups the control of violence is as much an expression of masculinity as engaging in violence. Further analysis of the various constructions of masculinity and their relationship to violent behaviour, Morgan argues, will facilitate the identification of ways to alter some violent processes.

Since at present there is very little research in this area it is not possible to discuss in detail changes or variations in the construction of masculinity and violence and the relationship between these across time or place. However in many cultures masculinity and power are linked to the ability to protect and materially support a family. Masculine identity is closely related to a man's work and occupational duties outside the home.[14] The relationship between economic status and violence has been the object of extensive research and it is in this arena that the consequences of social, in particular economic changes, for violent crime are most evident.

INEQUALITY AND ECONOMIC CHANGE

In his discussion of crime in America, Currie comments that "... there is an accumulated fund of sophisticated research linking serious crime with social and economic inequality."[15] While some studies have found a relationship between poverty and crime, others indicate that income inequality (the degree of relative poverty) is a better determinant of crime than absolute poverty.[16] Braithwaite and Braithwaite concluded from their study of homicide rates in 31 nations that higher homicide rates were related to the range of measures of economic inequality, including the gap between the rich and the average wage earner, the disparities in income between workers in different sectors of industry and the percentage of gross national product spent on social security.[17]

Criminal violence has been found to be strongly related to economic inequalities, particularly when those inequalities are based on race. In their research on this topic in the United States, Blau and Blau used the following independent variables: percentage black, percentage poor, income inequality and racial socioeconomic inequality.[18] In interpreting their findings, Blau and Blau argue that "aggressive acts of violence seem to result not so much from lack of advantages as from being taken advantage of, not from absolute but from relative deprivation."[19]

Such findings suggest that economic changes which entail increasing economic inequality will consequently mean increasing rates of crime, including violent crime. Braithwaite argues that there are "reasonable theoretical grounds" and "substantial empirical evidence" to suggest that a redistribution of wealth and power would diminish crime.[20]

Those who are skeptical about a link between economic status and crime argue that the relationship, observed in official crime statistics, is an artifact of race and class bias in criminal justice practice. While not denying that such bias exists, the strength of the relationship would seem to be beyond that which could be explained simply in terms of bias.[21]

Changes in unemployment rates are particularly illuminating when considering the plight of young people. Unemployment or labour force participation rates have frequently been used in studies of economic influences on crime. Studies in the US have found that unemployment rates are positively related to rates of violent crime.[22] Similarly Bechdolt concluded that the unemployment rate was a significant and strong predictor of both violent and property crime rates.[23] From a review of 63 such studies, Chiricos concluded that there was sufficient evidence of a link between unemployment and crime to remove the "consensus of doubt" in criminology about this topic.[24]

In refining the analysis of the relationship between unemployment and crime, it has been argued that, the development of social commitments requires more than simply having 'a job'. The importance and the value of work is not simply that it provides a material benefit, but that it also enables people to participate in society, to feel that they have something to contribute. Work which does not allow a person to experience a sense of worth is less likely to encourage the development of a commitment to society and thus a protection against a person's engaging in crime. Feelings of 'purposefulness' and 'alienation' can be produced by either not having a job, or by having a 'shit' job, that is, a job with no future, a job which has little social value, which does not contribute to self-worth. It can be anticipated that young people in this marginalized position will be more likely than other youth to engage in criminal behavior, including violence.

Recent changes in the structure of the labour market, such as economic specialization and technological expansion, have meant a marked decline in the jobs available to young people. For the present argument, there are two important aspects of these job losses. One, the losses are concentrated at the bottom of social class structure. It is young people who are attempting to enter the labour force without qualifications, skills or experience who are feeling the greatest pressure, since it is the unskilled and semi-skilled work that is most likely to be replaced. Two, what the resultant unemployment means for many young people is not temporary unemployment, but a closing off of entry into work. Thus, a large proportion of young unemployed people have been so for a long period, and will remain so.[25]

In many of the technologically developed countries there is a growing number of 'new marginal youth'[26] or what some have referred to as the urban 'underclass.'[27] Due to racism, in countries such as the US and the UK it is the black youths who are the hardest hit by this marginalization. In some of the Western European nations, the underclass population may be concentrated among the children of the guest-workers or other recent migrants. These are young people who are not simply out of work, they are often so far out they have ceased to look for it.[28] Such young people who cannot see the opportunity to work in either the present or the future, have little incentive to abide by the rules of a society which has abandoned them. It is suggested that the growth of this new underclass population has implications in terms of the participation of young men in street violence. This becomes apparent when we look more closely at the nature of violent crime.

Four scenarios of lethal, masculine violence have been identified in a recent study of homicide.[29] First, there was homicide in situations of sexual intimacy where the male violence was an ultimate attempt to control the behaviour of the female sexual partner. Second, homicide developed from a confrontation between males (a 'status contest'); a fight which spilled over into lethal violence. Third, homicide was observed as a consequence of another crime, such as robbery. Fourth, the homicide took place between friends, where the violence was used as a means of conflict resolution between men whose exceptional marginality meant that conventional dispute resolution procedures were unavailable. Male-to-male violence, such as found in the last three forms of homicide, account for over half of all homicides.[30] Further, these forms of violence are almost exclusively underclass or working-class male phenomena.[31]

Economic changes which increase economic marginality are likely to have as a spin-off effect an increase in the forms of masculine violence closely tied to such marginality. Evidence suggests, in fact, that while homicide rates are generally more stable than other forms of crime, upward movements in the rate are a consequence of homicides taking place between males (put another way, the rate of domestic homicides tends to be more stable over time). Further, other research indicates that it is particularly homicides of strangers that are increasing in recent years,[32] and such homicides arise almost exclusively either from masculine confrontations or out of the commission of other crimes, both of which are events most commonly involving underclass or lower class males.[33]

It was the Finnish criminologist Veli Verkko who was one of the first to observe that the variability in homicide rates is largely due to variations which occur in patterns of homicide between males.[34] To examine these findings further, Daly and Wilson[35] reviewed data from Iceland, Denmark, Australia, Canada, Brazil and the United States and concluded that "the most variable component of the homicide rate between industrial nations and between years is that perpetrated by (and, to a lesser degree upon)... disadvantaged young men... Where rates of homicide are high, the proportion of cases that involve such young men is high."[36]

These findings indicate that an understanding of the implications of economic change for violence entails consideration of the interactions between masculinity and economic status.

In societies where masculine identity is tied to work and economic independence, young men without this source of confirmation of their masculinity will do so in other ways. Violence may be used by young men in such a situation to establish a sense of power and dominance, or as a form of resistance or anger at their relative deprivation. Greenberg argues that for some young men the cultural expectations for men are contradicted by the structural constraints on male status attainment which are imposed by the larger economic and political order.[37] The resultant masculine status anxiety may result in some young men turning to whatever means are at their disposal to establish their masculinity. Thus, Greenberg argues, attempts to dominate women and other forms of interpersonal violence may produce the sense of potency not available to these young men in other spheres of life.[38]

In conclusion, then, we may say that while there may be a number of benefits which result from the movement of national economics into a post-industrial phase, one important consequence consists of the structural changes which close off opportunities for young people at the lower end of the economic spectrum to enter into viable work careers. The resultant building up of a new underclass population increases the potential for particular forms of male violence.

CORPORATE VIOLENCE

A quite different source of violence resulting from social change concerns the behaviour of large multinational corporations. Increasingly, the world is a global marketplace in which large corporations compete with each other for resources, labour, markets and profits. There are many potential benefits of multinational corporate activity as nations, especially in the underdeveloped world, come to experience new products, new sources of economic support, or expanded markets for their products. Unfortunately, these multinational organizations also have a capacity for large scale injury and death.

The search for cheaper labour, combined with the flight of capital from many developed countries, has meant a shift of various forms of productive activity into the less developed nations of the world. In these newly developing nations, the international companies may find it possible to engage in forms of production which, because of their danger, would be forbidden in the countries where the corporate headquarters are located. Huge stacks of used motor car batteries are shipped from the United States to countries in Asia where in the process of breaking them down for salvage, workers are directly exposed to concentrations of lead that would not be permitted in the United Stales. A recent report observed that a chlorine and caustic-soda corporation in Latin America, controlled by an overseas company, continued to discharge poisonous mercury into local waters, and instead of paying $650,000 for a pollution control system, declared a $3 million dollar dividend for its shareholders. This action was justified because it "would best protect the interests of shareholders in light of the unsettled political climate" of the country involved. One of the best known examples, of course, would be the tragedy of Bhopal where thousands died as a result of deadly gases released as the result of an accident in a Union Carbide plant.[39]

Consumers as well as workers have been victims of such corporate behavior. Nowhere is this better illustrated than in the pharmaceutical industry.[40] Major drug companies have distributed drugs (e.g. Depo-Provera or clioquinol) in the third world which have been banned by the more stringent drug regulations of the developed countries. The Dalkon Shield, an intra-uterine device, was sold for years in other countries after it had been banned in the United States. Pesticides which are either banned or severely restricted in Europe or North America, such as heptachlor, chlordane, endrin and others are "routinely sold" in other parts of the globe.[41] One dangerous chemical, the pesticide leptophos, was exported to such developing countries as Colombia, Egypt and Indonesia, but was never registered by the environmental protection agency of the developed country where the manufacturing was carried out. This pesticide causes delayed but lasting nervous system damage to humans, and was blamed for the deaths of several farmers and hundreds of farm animals in Egypt. Only when the workers at the production plant began to display symptoms of severe neurological damage was the manufacture of the pesticide halted.[42]

Clearly these are acts of violence which present us with the issue of whether they should also be treated as criminal acts. Both legal scholars and legal practitioners are increasingly putting the case that these are criminal actions. New criminal laws in California focus on the employers, company executives and the companies themselves, who knowingly allow life threatening faults to workers or consumers to go uncorrected. The Ford Motor Company was charged with criminal homicide in a court in Indiana for deaths which resulted when the company knowingly allowed a motor car with a serious fault to remain, uncorrected, on the road. The result, however, was an acquittal. New laws in the Netherlands have expanded the grounds whereby companies can be charged with criminal homicide when company negligence results in death.

Examples of corporate activities such as these clearly pose a significant threat to the citizens of many countries of the World. In fact, quite often the threat is much greater than that posed by the violence of more traditionally defined criminal behaviour. However, in general such violence has not been responded to with the same level of gravity of sanction that is reserved for the violent acts committed by less powerful members of our society. Our failure to confront this expanding source of violence in the world, to some extent legitimizes it.

THE LEGITIMATION OF VIOLENCE

The approval and practice of violence are more pervasive than is generally acknowledged. This becomes most apparent in studies of wife battering. In Australia, one in five adults condones the use of physical force by one spouse against another.[43] In the United States, one investigation found that one fifth of all Americans approved of slapping one's spouse on appropriate occasions. Approval of this practice increased with income and education. Public opinion polls in the United States also show widespread support for violence committed by police.[44]

These sorts of research findings indicate that in society in general some violence is accepted, normalized and even legitimized. In fact, Morgan points out, in some cases the legitimation process may be so effective that the violence is not recognized, for example corporal punishment in schools or at home.[45] The extent to which violence is legitimated in society is thought to affect the incidence of unlegitimated violence, or violent crime.

In their study of the homicide rates in 50 nations after a period of war, Archer and Gartner found support for what they referred to as the "legitimation of violence model."[46] The model suggested that the social approval of killing, or the legitimation of violence during the war period produced a lasting reduction of inhibitions against the taking of human life. Most of the combatant nations, in contrast to the noncombatant nations in the study had substantial postwar increases in their homicide rates. Further, "the increases were pervasive and occurred after both large and small wars, with several types of homicide indicators, in victorious as well as defeated nations, in nations with improved postwar economies and nations with worsened economies, among both men and women offenders, and among several age groups."[47]

Archer and Gartner conclude that when acts of violence occur, and more particularly when at least some such acts seem to be socially acceptable or even lauded, as in wartime, then general attitudes toward the use of violence shift in the direction of acceptance, and thresholds for resorting to violence fall.

This research supports the obvious, although often ignored, proposition that the extent to which we condone and allow any violence in our society will affect the rate of violent crime. If we are concerned to reduce the incidence of violent crime, then the process of social change will require that we address those norms, values and structures which legitimate and glorify other forms of violence in our society.

SOCIAL CHANGE AND VIOLENCE

While the present discussion has been concerned mainly with identifying some of the ways that developmental changes in the social, economic and political conditions of nations influence patterns of violence, it also needs to be recognized that planned social change may have important effects as well. One of the clearest examples of such effects can be found in the influence of feminists' discussions of domestic violence. In a recent book, *Women, Violence and Social Change*, for example, Dobasch and Dobasch document and evaluate the efforts of the battered-women's movement.[48] In general the goals of this movement are to provide "safety, shelter and autonomy for abused women" and to work towards the elimination of violence against women. The refuges established by this movement provide not only a haven for women and children, but they are also a visible and concrete challenge to the legacy of indifference to male violence against women.[49] This movement has also challenged both the discourse about violence against women and the criminal justice system. It thereby constitutes a vital element of efforts to bring about the social changes necessary to address the issue of male violence in society.

While the battered-women's movement has achieved a great deal, it alone cannot accomplish the breadth of social change required to respond to violence. The complexity of the nature of violence means that the necessary social changes should also be diverse and wide ranging. However it is clearly social changes that are required; violence will not be controlled through individually based strategies. It is apparent from the preceding review of the literature that the reduction of violent crimes will be more possible by a reduction in the inequalities of wealth and power in society. Overall, to change the levels of violence, we will have to change the structured inequalities of race, class and sex.

CONCLUSIONS

Social change can take many forms, and have a variety of consequences, some of which are beneficial, while some result in harm. Nowhere is this clearer than in the lessons now being learned about technological development. With the gifts of technology we have controlled famine, brought devastating diseases under control, and brought to masses of people the benefits of markedly increased standards of living. Even the most developed nations, however, have experienced the mixed blessings of technological developments.

It is in some of the most advanced cities of the world that we encounter the persistent problems of communities of underclass residents, including distinctively masculine patterns of confrontational and predatory violence. Both developed and underdeveloped countries have been threatened by ecological disasters caused by corporations, and have seen their citizens suffer the violence which results from inadequate controls over consumer products ranging from dangerous motor cars, life-threatening medical preparations, or ruinous pesticides.

What recent experiences concerned with domestic violence have demonstrated, however, is that some forms of planned social change can begin to influence not only the shape of the violence, but also how people come to view it. Human intelligence, informed debate, and collective action, in other words, can serve to bring at least some forms of violence under community control.

CHAPTER 12

Violence in Lesbian and Gay Relationships

By Claire M. Renzetti

When I first began to study partner abuse in same-sex relationships ten years ago, I was sometimes met with surprise, suspicion, and even amusement on the part of my colleagues, homosexual and straight. Many in the heterosexual academic community said that they didn't think abuse occurred in lesbian relationships, although after some reflection, they decided that it probably happened in butch-femme relationships and the batterer was the partner who "played the role of the man." Others expressed a kind of voyeuristic interest, although most did not see the topic as one worthy of serious scientific study. A number of lesbian and gay colleagues, who, unlike their straight peers, were aware of partner abuse in homosexual relationships, wondered why I, a straight woman, would study such a problem, and worried that my research would only fuel homophobic stereotypes and provide homophobes with an additional reason to denounce homosexuals.

Today, as I write this chapter, I can report that there have been important changes in professional attitudes toward partner abuse in same-sex relationships. For example, more research is being undertaken,[1] and attempts are being made to improve victim services.[2] At the same time, however, much remains the same as it was in 1985: homophobia is rampant; most battered lesbians and gay men do not receive the services they need; and the problem of same-sex partner abuse is not given the serious attention it deserves within the mainstream domestic violence movement. At a recent conference, for instance, a colleague highly regarded for his domestic violence research questioned the value of discussing lesbian battering because, as he put it, it just doesn't happen that often. Others have taken to (mis)using the data available on homosexual partner abuse to "prove" that feminist theories of domestic violence are "wrong."[3] If women do this to other women, they ask, then how can patriarchy be the cause?

My primary goal in this chapter is to provide an overview of what is currently known as a result of empirical research about violence in lesbian and gay relationships. Here I will focus on the issues of incidence and contributing factors.[4] What will become clear is that what we do know about same-sex domestic violence is far less than what we do not know. Consequently, we must be careful not to be too quick in drawing conclusions or making generalizations based on a small pool of data derived from limited samples. However, we must also commit ourselves to learning more, and so I will also suggest various topics that warrant our attention in future research.

SAME-SEX DOMESTIC VIOLENCE: WHAT IT IS, HOW AND WHEN IT OCCURS

Homosexual partner abuse may be defined as a "pattern of violent [or] coercive behaviors whereby a lesbian [or gay man] seeks to control the thoughts, beliefs, or conduct of [an] intimate partner or to punish the intimate for resisting the perpetrator's control."[5] In light of this definition it should be clear that same-sex domestic violence is quite similar to heterosexual domestic violence. Yet, there are important ways in which same-sex domestic violence is unique.

In my research with battered lesbians,[6] I found that the most common forms of physical abuse reported were being pushed and shoved; being hit with open hands or fists; being scratched or hit in the face, breasts, or genitals; and having things thrown at them. The most common forms of psychological or emotional abuse were being threatened; being demeaned in front of friends, relatives, and strangers; having sleeping and eating habits disrupted; and having property damaged and destroyed. It also was not uncommon for the partners of these respondents to abuse others in the household (e.g., children or pets).

These findings, though notable in themselves, were overshadowed by two others that I consider even more significant. First, on the questionnaire to which these women responded, there was a list of sixteen different forms of physical abuse and seventeen different forms of psychological abuse. Although some of the most severe types of abuse listed (e.g., being stabbed or shot, having guns or knives inserted into one's vagina) were relatively rare, they did occur; in fact, every type of abuse listed was experienced by at least two participants in my study. Second, the list, despite its length, was not exhaustive; respondents described numerous additional forms of abuse (e.g., being physically restrained, being forced to sever all ties and contacts with relatives and friends, partners stealing their property). Abusers would sometimes hurt or threaten to hurt themselves, as a means to control or manipulate the respondents. In addition, abusers often tailored the abuse to the specific vulnerabilities of their partners (e.g., a diabetic was forced to eat sugar as "punishment" for "misbehavior"). These findings are not unique to abusive lesbian relationships; David Island and Patrick Letellier recount numerous equally disturbing examples from their discussions with gay male victims of domestic violence.[7]

What these findings suggest is that it is not so much the form the abuse takes, but rather the motivation underlying the abuse that is important in understanding it. Research with battered heterosexual women points us in the same direction, and in listening to the stories of abused wives we hear the similarities between their abuse experiences and those of battered lesbians and gay men. In fact, one of the participants in my study told me that she was working in a battered women's shelter at the time her partner was abusing her, and it was in doing intake interviews with battered heterosexual women that she came to recognize herself as a battered woman.[8]

Nevertheless, there are important differences between heterosexual domestic violence and same-sex domestic violence. As Suzanne Pharr has pointed out, battered heterosexual women experience violence in the context of misogynism, but battered lesbians and gay men experience violence in the context of a world that is both misogynistic and *homophobic*.[9] Homophobia comes into play on several different levels, which I will consider at various points throughout the remainder of this chapter. Here, however, I wish to emphasize that homophobia may be used by an abuser as a weapon of control. More specifically, one form of abuse unique to same-sex relationships is the threat or practice of "outing," that is, threatening to reveal or actually revealing to others (e.g., relatives, employers, landlords) that an individual is lesbian or gay, when that individual wishes to conceal their sexual orientation. In our homophobic society, outing may result in abandonment by relatives and friends, the loss of a job, and a wide variety of other discriminatory behaviors, against which the victim has little or no legal recourse. In my research,[10] for instance, 21 percent of the respondents reported that their partners had threatened to out them. Several respondents stated that they quit their jobs before their partners carried through on the threat to out them at work, explaining that they felt if they left on their own and resolved their problems with their partners, they could find another job more easily than if they were outed, subsequently fired or laid off, and perhaps surreptitiously blacklisted by an employer.

AIDS also raises special issues for gay male victims of domestic violence. Although AIDS does not solely affect gay male relationships, gay men do constitute the largest percentage of people with AIDS. Island and Letellier express concern that the stress induced from the fear of contracting AIDS, from dealing with the disease if one has contracted it, or in trying to care for an infected partner is becoming an excuse for gay male domestic violence.[11] Elsewhere, Letellier outlines how AIDS may impact gay male domestic violence, particularly by increasing the difficulty abuse victims have in trying to leave their batterers.[12] For instance, an abuse victim who also has AIDS may be so dependent on his batterer for financial support and health care assistance that he decides it is better to remain in the relationship than to risk living alone. An abuse victim whose batterer has AIDS may feel tremendous guilt about leaving a dying partner with no one else to care for him. According to Letellier, abusers actively reinforce these worries in their partners.[13]

Despite the differences between same-sex and heterosexual battering, it has been argued that both occur at similar rates. It has been estimated that the incidence of domestic violence among heterosexual couples is anywhere from 12 percent to 33 percent, depending on the sample and how abuse is measured.[14] Studies of abuse in lesbian and gay male relationships have found rates ranging from almost 11 percent to more than 73 percent;[15] rates of verbal abuse have been reported as high as 95 percent.[16,17] Not surprisingly, many commentators cite these figures as evidence that violence occurs at least as frequently in lesbian and gay relationships as it does in heterosexual relationships. My own work[18] is often mistakenly cited in support of this claim,[19] when in fact my research is not a true prevalence study at all. None of the research so far on partner abuse in gay and lesbian relationships has been able to measure "true prevalence" because the studies have utilized self-selected rather than random samples. Indeed, it is doubtful that a true prevalence study of lesbian and gay partner abuse is possible as long as the stigma attached to homosexual relationships leads many lesbians and gay men to hide their sexual identities from others, including researchers. Instead, what my research and that of others does show is simply that partner abuse occurs in same-sex relationships;[20] it is not so infrequent as to be anomalous; and once it does occur, it is like to reoccur and to become increasingly severe over time.

EXPLAINING SAME-SEX PARTNER ABUSE

Little effort has been made to understand same-sex partner abuse beyond superimposing heterosexual models onto lesbian and gay relationships. For instance, research repeatedly shows that in Western societies masculinity is associated with aggression as well as dominating authority within intimate relationships. These norms of masculinity, not surprisingly, have been related to various forms of violent behavior among men, including domestic violence.[21] With increasing reports of same-sex domestic violence has come the popular stereotype that partner abuse occurs in homosexual relationships involving role-playing among the partners. Thus, it is assumed that the abuser is the masculine partner and the victim the feminine partner. However, researchers who have studied homosexual relationships report that role-playing does not characterize the majority of lesbian and gay couples. Instead, most find that role differentiation and expectations are quite diverse.[22] Moreover, research with victims of same-sex domestic violence shows that the abuser is not necessarily more "masculine" than the victim in terms of physical size, appearance, or mannerisms.[23]

The relatively few researchers who have studied domestically violent homosexual relationships have examined a number of other variables as possible contributing factors to the abuse. Again, however, most of these variables have been suggested by research with heterosexual couples, and the findings with regard to homosexual couples are equivocal at best. Consider, for example, the role of alcohol and drug abuse. In several studies of same-sex domestic violence, the use of alcohol and drugs has been found to be related to partner abuse in 33 percent to over 70 percent of the couples studied.[24] Others, however, report that although alcohol and drug use is often present in violent lesbian and gay relationships, it is neither a necessary nor a sufficient cause for partner abuse.[25] Instead, the use of alcohol and drugs often serves as an excuse for or facilitator of abuse; much abuse occurs when batterers are not under the influence of drugs or alcohol, and alcohol and drug use may follow rather than precede battering incidents.[26]

Similarly, research that has examined the role of previous exposure to domestic violence (usually in the batterer's and/or victim's family of origin) has produced inconsistent results.[27] Although Gwat-Yong Lie and coworkers[28] found that lesbians who witnessed and/or experienced domestic violence in their families of origin were more likely than those who grew up in nonviolent families to be victimized as an adult and/or to abuse their own partners, others have found no significant evidence showing the intergenerational transmission of violence in abusive lesbian and gay relationships.[29]

Feminist analyses have emphasized the importance of understanding the role of patriarchal power in the etiology of domestic violence. Unfortunately, translating power into a measurable variable for empirical research has proved difficult because of the multifaceted nature of the construct. Power operates on different levels (individual, institutional, societal) and manifests itself in numerous ways. Traditionally, power in intimate relationships has been measured in terms of which partner has greatest decision-making authority, but this approach has been extensively criticized.[30] More broadly, patriarchal power has been operationalized with measures such as the Status of Women Index, a state-by-state composite of economic, educational, political, and legal indicators of gender inequality.[31]

In studies of both heterosexual and homosexual domestic violence, however, power operationalized in one or more of these ways has not been consistently strongly correlated with abuse.

With respect to heterosexual domestic violence, for example, Kersti Yllö and

Murray Straus[32] found a curvilinear relationship between patriarchal power and abuse: High rates of abuse were found in states in which women had relatively high status as well as in those states in which women's status was relatively low. Similarly, Michael Smith reported that patriarchal beliefs and attitudes explained only 20 percent of the variance in rates of wife abuse in his Canadian study.[33] At the micro-level, most studies of heterosexual couples have shown that the risk of wife abuse increases if the male partner considers himself to be less powerful in the relationship relative to his wife or if his perceives his power relative to his wife to be waning.[34] In virtually all the empirical studies of partner abuse, power has been measured on the micro-level in terms of decision-making authority or the relative resources (i.e., money, education, status) that each partner brings to the relationship.[35] Although a few power measures in these studies were significantly correlated with the frequency and severity of partner abuse, most were not.

Nevertheless, the question of perceived power or powerlessness is not unrelated to the issue of partners' relative dependency on one another, which has been found to be strongly associated with abuse in both heterosexual and homosexual relationships. More specifically, research indicates that in heterosexual relationships, couples at greatest risk for violence were those in which husbands have high dependency (or affiliation) needs, but their wives seek relative autonomy and independence.[36] Although I know of no research that has examined empirically the role of partners' relative dependency in gay male relationships, my own research with battered lesbians produced findings consistent with those of Daniel Byrne and coworkers:[37] The greater the lesbian batterer's dependency and the greater the victim's desire to be independent, the more likely the batterer is to inflict more types of abuse with greater frequency. Batterers, both gay and straight, also have been found to have poor self-concepts and low self-esteem, which in turn are related to their dysfunctionally high dependency needs.[38]

Findings such as these have led some researchers to argue that social structural factors, such as patriarchy and gender inequality, are less important than individual personality factors in explaining partner abuse in both homosexual and heterosexual relationships.[39] More specifically, these researchers maintain that the primary causal factor of intimate violence is diagnosable psychopathology, which typically manifests as a personality disorder. The personality disorders most commonly associated with abusive behavior are borderline personality disorder, narcissism, antisocial behavior, and the aggressive-sadistic personality. The more frequent and severe the abuse, the greater the likelihood of psychopathology in the abuser.[40]

D. G. Dutton cites an impressive list of studies that show that at least among heterosexual men who are court-referred or self-referred for clinical treatment as a result of wife assault, about 80 to 90 percent have a diagnosable psychological pathology.[41] However, such data for gay and lesbian abusers are scarce, a fact that may be due in part to reluctance among some researchers in this area to begin labeling interactions in gay and lesbian relationships "sick" or "abnormal" given the negative ways homosexuality has been treated historically by most mainstream psychiatrists and psychologists. Nevertheless, V. E. Coleman[42] reports that the lesbian batterers she sees in her clinical practice often exhibit personality disorders, especially borderline and narcissistic disorders.[43]

Coleman, however, maintains that intimate violence, regardless of the sexual orientation of the couple involved, is best understood in terms of a multidimensional perspective that incorporates sociocultural variables with individual psychological factors.[44] We can perhaps best see how social structural and psychological factors may intersect by considering the issue of internalized homophobia. Internalized homophobia occurs when gay men and lesbians accept heterosexual society's negative evaluations of them and incorporate these into their self-concepts. It is analogous to internalized racism, in which people of color accept white people's prejudices against them.[45] In applying the phenomenon of internalized homophobia to same-sex domestic violence, James Shattuck asks: How might the experience of being gay or lesbian (that is, oppressed and alienated by heterosexual society, being forced to "live outside the rules") affect one's relational abilities with an intimate partner?[46] Clinicians report that internalized homophobia causes homosexuals to experience lowered self-esteem, feelings of powerlessness, obsessive closeting of sexual orientation, denial of difference between themselves and heterosexuals, and self-destructive behavior such as substance abuse.[47] It may also lead to aggression against members of one's own group, which could take the form of partner abuse.[48] Thus, societal homophobia (a social structural variable) generates internalized homophobia (a psychological variable), which, in turn, may lead to partner abuse in same-sex relationships.

Unfortunately, there is no research yet that tests the relationship between internalized homophobia and homosexual partner abuse. Such research first requires the development of a reliable and valid measure of internalized homophobia—a difficult task to say the least. In addition, researchers need to address the question of why some gay men and lesbians succumb to internalized homophobia while others do not, even though all live in a heterosexist, homophobic society. It may be the case that low self-esteem and perceived powerlessness are antecedents rather than consequences of internalized homophobia. Both, we have seen, are related to intimate violence in homosexual and heterosexual relationships. Perhaps, then, both are risk markers not only for partner abuse, but also for other dysfunctional outcomes, one of which may be internalized homophobia among gay men and lesbians.

Of course, teasing out the relationships among these and a host of other variables requires much more study utilizing more rigorous methodologies than what we have done to date. Moreover, in designing and implementing this research, there is an array of additional issues that merit serious consideration. I conclude this chapter by outlining some of them.

RESEARCH CHALLENGES

Social scientists, it seems, delight in categorization. We develop dichotomies and typologies to classify the multitude of behaviors and other phenomena we observe. Importantly, domestic violence research has shown that to ask the questions, "Is a particular individual a batterer or not?" and "Is a particular individual a victim or not?" simply establishes false dichotomies. At the same time, we now know that neither batterers nor victims constitute a homogenous group.[49] Why, then, are some of us so quick to dismiss social structural variables, such as patriarchy and gender inequality, in favor of individual psychological causes, if same-sex partner abuse at first glance does not appear to meet the criteria for our preconceived categories of "batterers" and "victims"? Knowing as we do that battering and victimization, as well as patriarchy and gender inequality, are highly complex constructs, why are we surprised when same-sex domestic violence does not always "look like" heterosexual domestic violence?

Our research on same-sex domestic violence to date has been guided by the research on heterosexual domestic violence because many of us have been trained to view scientific work according to what one of my undergraduate professors used to call the "pebble theory of knowledge." That is, each researcher, through her or his individual studies, builds on the work of other researchers, adding pebbles to the pile until eventually a "mountain of knowledge" accumulates and hopefully our questions are answered—we have discovered Truth. Thomas Kuhn referred to this process as "normal science."[50] However, as Kuhn pointed out, it sometimes becomes necessary to strike out in a new direction, to start asking different questions, to begin building a new pile of pebbles if you will. I submit that this time has come in domestic violence research.

I am not taking this opportunity to volunteer to lead this scientific revolution; I've never had much of a sense of direction, and building is hardly one of my talents. However, I can share here a number of issues that have arisen in recent discussions with feminist colleagues, and these, in turn, may serve as the basis for innovative research questions.[51]

Feminist research by women of color has taught us that we cannot assume that everyone experiences an event similarly or gives the same meaning to a particular set of interactions. Instead, in attempting to understand a phenomenon such as domestic violence, we must take *intersectionality* into account.[52] That is, we must consider how people who are differentially located in our society not only because of their sexual orientation, but also because of their race, gender, and social class, may experience a phenomenon differently and give different meanings to it. Those who are marginalized, who have been rendered "outsiders" or "the Other," often experience and define situations as problematic differently than those who are members of dominant groups.[53] Consequently, one of the major challenges for future domestic violence research is inclusivity: a careful examination of how racism, sexism, social class inequality, and homophobia may impact on both the causes and consequences of intimate violence. The goal is not to fit "others" into the dominant mold, but rather to come to a better understanding of the diversity of domestic violence experiences, the significance and meaning this violence has in the lives of different groups of people, and how this intersectionality affects outcomes, particularly institutional responses to domestic violence.

Achieving this understanding requires research that is not only inclusive, but also *contextualized*. Future domestic violence research must examine the meanings that specific behaviors have for the social actors involved in them. Research is now being done that provides analyses of heterosexual men's accounts of why they batter[54] and how heterosexual men's and women's accounts of their motivations for using violence differ.[55] To date, however, I know of no research that undertakes an analysis of whether such accounts and motives vary by race, class, or sexual orientation as well. Victoria Burbank's work also shows that the meanings and motives underlying intimate violence vary among societies, thus also alerting us to the need for more cross-cultural research.[56]

Of course, such work requires the use of diverse research methodologies. Innumerable scales and indices have been developed, with varying levels of reliability and validity, to measure an array of behaviors and affects, from the use of various types of abuse to relationship satisfaction and self-image. Nevertheless, such measures rarely if ever can place behavior and emotion in context. Nor can these measures effectively pick up on the often subtle, but no less important, differences in meanings that specific words or phrases have for members of different groups.[57] On pencil-and-paper measures and in artificial experimental settings, research participants rarely have the opportunity to ask for clarification of a term, to contextualize their responses, or even to simply to tell their stories. Our research designs, therefore, must make more use of interview, narrative, and ethnographic methods, and our research strategies must make room for genuine collaboration between researchers and participants. Fortunately, domestic violence researchers do not have to "reinvent the wheel" for this undertaking; the feminist methodologies being utilized to study a wide variety of topics are available to guide us.[58]

It should be clear at this point that I consider many of the recent comparisons between same-sex domestic violence and heterosexual domestic violence to be overly simplistic and falsely framed. In short, many of us have been asking the wrong questions and looking in the wrong places for the answers. This is not to say, however, that same-sex domestic violence and heterosexual domestic violence should be studied separately, or that findings regarding one are irrelevant to the other. Rather, what I am proposing here is simply that we stop using a specific model of heterosexual domestic violence research—one that overlooks the intersectionality of social locating variables and decontextualizes behavior and emotion—as the central organizing paradigm of our work. Indeed, what I am advocating is that we turn this paradigm on its head: That we develop, as the foundation for our mountain of knowledge, findings from contextualized, collaborative studies of intimate violence among lesbian and gay couples, as well as couples from other marginalized groups and from differing cultures.

Will we come to recognize the value of such research? If we truly seek to understand domestic violence, we must.

CHAPTER 13

Pornography and Grief

By Andrea Dworkin

I searched for something to say here today quite different from what I am going to say. I wanted to come here militant and proud and angry as hell. But more and more, I find that anger is a pale shadow next to the grief I feel. If a woman has any sense of her own intrinsic worth, seeing pornography in small bits and pieces can bring her to a useful rage. Studying pornography in quantity and depth, as I have been doing for more months than I care to remember, will turn that same woman into a mourner.

The pornography itself is vile. To characterize it any other way would be to lie. No plague of male intellectualisms and sophistries can change or hide that simple fact. Georges Bataille, a philosopher of pornography (which he calls "eroticism"), puts it clearly: "In essence, the domain of eroticism is the domain of violence, of violation."[1] Mr. Bataille, unlike so many of his peers, is good enough to make explicit that the whole idea is to violate the female. Using the language of grand euphemism so popular with male intellectuals who write on the subject of pornography, Bataille informs us that "[t]he passive, female side is essentially the one that is dissolved as a separate entity."[2] To be "dissolved"—by any means necessary—is the role of women in pornography. The great male scientists and philosophers of sexuality, including Kinsey, Havelock Ellis, Wilhelm Reich, and Freud, uphold this view of our purpose and destiny. The great male writers use language more or less beautifully to create us in self-serving fragments, half-"dissolved" as it were, and then proceed to "dissolve" us all the way, by any means necessary. The biographers of the great male artists celebrate the real life atrocities those men have committed against us, as if those atrocities are central to the making of art. And in history, as men have lived it, they have "dissolved" us—by any means necessary. The slicing of our skins and the rattling of our bones are the energizing sources of male-defined art and science, as they are the essential content of pornography. The visceral experience of a hatred of women that literally knows no bounds has put me beyond anger and beyond tears; I can only speak to you from grief.

We all expected the world to be different than it is, didn't we? No matter what material or emotional deprivation we have experienced as children or as adults, no matter what we understood from history or from the testimonies of living persons about how people suffer and why, we all believed, however privately, in human possibility. Some of us believed in art, or literature, or music, or religion, or revolution, or in children, or in the redeeming potential of eroticism or affection. No matter what we knew of cruelty, we all believed in kindness; and no matter what we knew of hatred, we all believed in friendship or love. Not one of us could have imagined or would have believed the simple facts of life as we have come to know them: the rapacity of male greed for dominance; the malignancy of male supremacy; the virulent contempt for women that is the very foundation of the culture in which we live. The Women's Movement has forced us all to face the facts, but no matter how brave and clear-sighted we are, no matter how far we are willing to go or are forced to go in viewing reality without romance or illusion, we are simply overwhelmed by the male hatred of our kind, its morbidity, its compulsiveness, its obsessiveness, its celebration of itself in every detail of life and culture. We think that we have grasped this hatred once and for all, seen it in its spectacular cruelty, learned its every secret, got used to it or risen above it or organized against it so as to be protected from its worst excesses. We think that we know all there is to know about what men do to women, even if we cannot imagine why they do what they do, when something happens that simply drives us mad, out of our minds, so that we are again imprisoned like caged animals in the numbing reality of male control, male revenge against no one knows what, male hatred of our very being.

One can know everything and still not imagine snuff films. One can know everything and still be shocked and terrified when a man who attempted to make snuff films is released, despite the testimony of the women undercover agents whom he wanted to torture, murder, and, of course, film. One can know everything and still be stunned and paralyzed when one meets a child who is being continuously raped by her father or some close male relative. One can know everything and still be reduced to sputtering like an idiot when a woman is prosecuted for attempting to abort herself with knitting needles, or when a woman is imprisoned for killing a man who has raped or tortured her, or is raping or torturing her. One can know everything and still want to kill and be dead simultaneously when one sees a celebratory picture of a woman being ground up in a meat grinder on the cover of a national magazine, no matter how putrid the magazine. One can know everything and still somewhere inside refuse to believe that the personal, social, culturally sanctioned violence against women is unlimited, unpredictable, pervasive, constant, ruthless, and happily and unselfconsciously sadistic. One can know everything and still be unable to accept the fact that sex and murder are fused in the male consciousness, so that the one without the imminent possibility of the other is unthinkable and impossible. One can know everything and still, at bottom, refuse to accept that the annihilation of women is the source of meaning and identity for men. One can know everything and still want desperately to know nothing because to face what we know is to question whether life is worth anything at all.

The pornographers, modern and ancient, visual and literary, vulgar and aristocratic, put forth one consistent proposition: erotic pleasure for men is derived from and predicated on the savage destruction of women. As the world's most honored pornographer, the Marquis de Sade (called by male scholars "The Divine Marquis"), wrote in one of his more restrained and civil moments: "There's not a woman on earth who'd ever have had cause to complain of my services if I'd been sure of being able to kill her afterward."[3] The eroticization of murder is the essence of pornography, as it is the essence of life. The torturer may be a policeman tearing the fingernails off a victim in a prison cell or a so-called normal man engaged in the project of attempting to fuck a woman to death. The fact is that the process of killing—and both rape and battery are steps in that process—is the prime sexual act for men in reality and/or in imagination. Women as a class must remain in bondage, subject to the sexual will of men, because the knowledge of an imperial right to kill, whether exercised to the fullest extent or just part way, is necessary to fuel sexual appetite and behavior. Without women as potential or actual victims, men are, in the current sanitized jargon, "sexually dysfunctional." This same motif also operates among male homosexuals, where force and/or convention designate some males as female or feminized. The plethora of leather and chains among male homosexuals, and the newly fashionable defenses of organized rings of boy prostitution by supposedly radical gay men, are testimony to the fixedness of the male compulsion to dominate and destroy that is the source of sexual pleasure for men.

The most terrible thing about pornography is that it tells male truth. The most insidious thing about pornography is that it tells male truth as if it were universal truth. Those depictions of women in chains being tortured are supposed to represent our deepest erotic aspirations. And some of us believe it, don't we? The most important thing about pornography is that the values in it are the common values of men. This is the crucial fact that both the male Right and the male Left, in their differing but mutually reinforcing ways, want to keep hidden from women. The male Right wants to hide the pornography, and the male Left wants to hide its meaning. Both want access to pornography so that men can be encouraged and energized by it. The Right wants secret access; the Left wants public access. But whether we see the pornography or not, the values expressed in it are the values expressed in the acts of rape and wife-beating, in the legal system, in religion, in art and in literature, in systematic economic discrimination against women, in the moribund academies, and by the good and wise and kind and enlightened in all of these fields and areas. Pornography is not a genre of expression separate and different from the rest of life; it is a genre of expression fully in harmony with any culture in which it flourishes. This is so whether it is legal or illegal. And, in either case, pornography functions to perpetuate male supremacy and crimes of violence against women because it conditions, trains, educates, and inspires men to despise women, to use women, to hurt women. Pornography exists because men despise women, and men despise women in part because pornography exists.

For myself, pornography has defeated me in a way that, at least so far, life has not. Whatever struggles and difficulties I have had in my life, I have always wanted to find a way to go on even if I did not know how, to live through one more day, to learn one more thing, to take one more walk, to read one more book, to write one more paragraph, to see one more friend, to love one more time. When I read or see pornography, I want everything to stop. Why, I ask, why are they so damned cruel and so damned proud of it? Sometimes, a detail drives me mad. There is a series of photographs: a woman slicing her breasts with a knife, smearing her own blood on her own body, sticking a sword up her vagina. *And she is smiling.* And it is the smile that drives me mad. There is a record album plastered all over a huge display window. The picture on the album is a profile view of a woman's thighs. Her crotch is suggested because we know it is there; it is not shown. The title of the album is "Plug Me to Death." And it is the use of the first person that drives me mad. "Plug Me to Death." The arrogance. The cold-blooded arrogance. And how can it go on like this, senseless, entirely brutal, inane, day after day and year after year, these images and ideas and values pouring out, packaged, bought and sold, promoted, enduring on and on, and no one stops it, and our darling boy intellectuals defend it, and elegant radical lawyers argue for it, and men of every sort cannot and will not live without it. And life, which means everything to me, becomes meaningless, because these celebrations of cruelty destroy my very capacity to feel and to care and to hope. I hate the pornographers most of all for depriving me of hope.

The psychic violence in pornography is unbearable in and of itself. It acts on one like a bludgeon until one's sensibility is pummeled flat and one's heart goes dead. One becomes numb. Everything stops, and one looks at the pages or pictures and knows: this is what men want, and this is what men have had, and this is what men will not give up.

As lesbian-feminist Karla Jay pointed out in an article called "Pot, Porn, and the Politics of Pleasure," men will give up grapes and lettuce and orange juice and Portuguese wine and tuna fish, but men will not give up pornography. And yes, one wants to take it from them, to burn it, to rip it up, bomb it, raze their theaters and publishing houses to the ground. One can be part of a revolutionary movement or one can mourn. Perhaps I have found the real source of my grief: we have not yet become a revolutionary movement.

Tonight we are going to walk together, all of us, to take back the night, as women have in cities all over the world, because in every sense none of us can walk alone. Every woman walking alone is a target. Every woman walking alone is hunted, harassed, time after time harmed by psychic or physical violence. Only by walking together can we walk at all with any sense of safety, dignity, or freedom. Tonight, walking together, we will proclaim to the rapists and pornographers and woman-batterers that their days are numbered and our time has come. And tomorrow, what will we do tomorrow? Because, sisters, the truth is that we have to take back the night every night, or the night will never be ours. And once we have conquered the dark, we have to reach for the light, to take the day and make it ours. This is our choice, and this is our necessity. It is a revolutionary choice, and it is a revolutionary necessity. For us, the two are indivisible, as we must be indivisible in our fight for freedom. Many of us have walked many miles already—brave, hard miles—but we have not gone far enough. Tonight, with every breath and every step, we must commit ourselves to going the distance: to transforming this earth on which we walk from prison and tomb into our rightful and joyous home. This we must do and this we will do, for our own sakes and for the sake of every woman who has ever lived.

CHAPTER 14

Andrea Dworkin's Reconstruction of Pornography as a Discriminatory Social Practice[1]

By Cindy Jenefsky

From Andrea Dworkin's first writing on pornography[2] to the early eighties when she coauthors the antipornography civil rights ordinance with Catharine MacKinnon, her analysis of pornography gradually shifts: she redefines it from a misogynistic cultural *artifact* to a discriminatory *practice* of sexual exploitation.[3] The primary, albeit *unstated*, ground for her redefinition of pornography is based on switching the argumentative premise from a concern with individual rights and liberties (pornographers' and consumers') to a concern with pornography's function on a societal level as an abrogation of the rights and freedoms of women as a class. She accomplishes this shift in her rhetorical advocacy by presenting pornography exclusively from the perspective of those harmed by it and by linguistically embedding the usually individuated pornographic image into its social and economic contexts of male domination.

According to Dworkin, pornography harms women because of its organic interaction with the material forces of white male supremacy, and every claim she makes about pornography is premised implicitly on this relationship. Within her work, pornographic products never exist in isolation from their production and consumption in this particular social context. Consequently, her analysis of pornography holistically synthesizes the product, its production, its consequences, and the hierarchical social environment in which it functions. The following examination of Dworkin's antipornography discourse illuminates the essential features of her political analysis of pornography by attending to the ways she creates a contextualized portrait of pornography that linguistically mirrors her understanding of its structural function in society.

THE PORNOGRAPHIC IMAGE: CONTENT IN CONTEXT

Dworkin traces the history of pornography to its origins in the Greek word for whore, *porné*. She explains the *porneia* as the lowest class of whores whose sole purpose in society was to be sexual servants to men. Pornography literally means "the graphic depiction of the lowest whores." She says it "does not mean 'writing about sex' or 'depiction of the erotic' or 'depictions of sexual acts' or 'depictions of nude bodies' or 'sexual representation' or any other such euphemism."[4] In *Pornography: Men Possessing Women,* Dworkin analyzes written and pictorial pornography to illustrate how the images of women consistently conform to the word's root meaning. If a woman is not already portrayed as a whore, then she is transformed into one in the course of the story while having sex or being raped—that is, suddenly she (or those around her) has an epiphany of her whorish nature and her insatiable lust for sexual servitude, including sexual abuse.[5]

Dworkin identifies the metaphysical definition of "woman as whore" as the central axis of the ideology of male domination. As a metaphysics, pornography defines what a woman is: it is "a definition of existence, not some attribute, some characteristic, some possibility. It means what women are by nature—all women, not just some women."[6] Essentializing all women as whores obscures their individual identities and defines all women according to sexual availability. Racial, ethnic, demographic, and physiological characteristics vary the ways women are used sexually in pornography, but in all cases, women are defined as naturally sexually available.

Within the governing logic of "woman as whore," anything done to women is presented *as sex* in pornography, despite the absurdity or violence of the act. Moreover, because women are defined in pornography as whores *by nature,* they are characterized as always wanting whatever "sex" they are portrayed doing. In the manner of all colonizing discourse, pornography conflates "what is done to women" with "what women want"—both are products of women's nature—thereby naturalizing and rationalizing the treatment of women pornography promotes. Forced sex is definitionally impossible within pornography's logic, for anything portrayed as sex is considered an expression of the woman's, that is the whore's, natural desire for sex. "One does not violate something by using it for what it is," writes Dworkin. Within male supremacist logic "neither rape nor prostitution is an abuse of the female because in both the female is fulfilling her natural function. . . . A whore cannot be raped, only used."[7]

In all of Dworkin's work, she insists on contextualizing pornography as *a product of* a male-dominated society. For example, in her 1981 speech, "Pornography and Male Supremacy," she asserts:

> We do not know when in history pornography as such first appeared. We do know that it is a product of culture, specifically male-supremacist culture, and that it comes after both rape and prostitution. Pornography can only develop in a society that is viciously male-supremacist, one in which rape and prostitution are not only well-established but systematically practiced and ideologically endorsed. . . . Politically, culturally, socially, sexually, and economically, rape and prostitution generated pornography; and pornography depends for its continued existence on the rape and prostitution of women.[8]

It is not merely that pornography exists *alongside* a male-supremacist society but, more importantly, it *springs from* and is inseparably intertwined with that society.

Within Dworkin's work, pornography's power, significance, and impact are derived from the existing social structure of male domination, which is both white-supremacist and economically exploitive. She argues that pornographic images obscure racism by clothing it in sexual pleasure—the same way misogyny is obscured. "The sexualization of race within a racist system," writes Dworkin, "is a prime purpose and consequence of pornography." "How," she asks, "... does one fight racism and jerk off to it at the same time? The Left cannot have its whores and its politics too."[9]

Pornography: Men Possessing Women details pornography's racist construction of the sexual nature and sexual availability of men and women.[10] She notes that the construction of male sexual domination remains constant in all pornography, as does the "valuation of the woman" as whore, as do the values the pornography promotes. What varies is the locus of the sexualization and sexual exploitation—that is, the body parts targeted. She shows how pornography's construction of Black women, for instance, uses the color of their skin as their "main sexual part"; in other words, black skin itself is fetishized as a principal sexual object. Anything done to a Black woman's skin is presented *as sex,* just as anything done to all women's vaginas is constructed as such. Black women's skin in pornography thus becomes a target of sexual abuse and exploitation.[11]

Obviously, the racism is not confined to images of women of color. Dworkin claims that in a white-supremacist society, white skin, too, is "a sexual symbol in the women of pornography: she is the boss who demands servicing." Pornography defines white women's sexuality as the so-called "civilized" standard for sexuality, while women of color, indeed all socially marginalized racial and ethnic groups, are constructed as uncivilized or savage in comparison.[12] Employing patterns of generalization commonplace in a racist society, explains Dworkin, pornography uses white women as the basis for generalizing about all women. Within pornography's white supremacist logic, all women enjoy being sexually used, humiliated, forced, insulted, and beaten because the white women say it is so; such behaviors are acceptable to do to all women because white women—the women considered "at the zenith of the hierarchy in racial terms"—desire, in fact *demand,* to be used as such.[13] The force used against the white woman "is recognized as real because she demands it"; but in demanding it, the force is simultaneously trivialized and naturalized *as sex.* "She is the initiator. She sets the terms." Dworkin writes:

> The sexuality of the woman of color is supposedly outside the constraints of civilization, that is, natural. The sexuality of the white woman is the norm of civilized sexuality. In both circumstances, the violence women experience is postulated as being the will of the women; in both circumstances, she wants it, they all do. The degree of force (perceived as such) used against the white woman establishes the norm of force acceptable in sex in white-supremacist civilization. The degree of force, then, is without limit because she wants it to be.[14]

In short, pornography uses white women to legitimize its treatment of all women *as sex.*

Dworkin's primary rhetorical strategy for ensconcing every pornographic image in its social context is to enlarge the "scene" within which she situates pornography.[15] She shifts the focus away from the discrete material artifact (the magazine, film, video, etc.) and, with a wide-angle lens, shows her audience the product in its larger context: the conditions that inspire the production of the products, the process by which these materials are produced, and the uses to which they are put. This contextualized portrait of pornography reveals its societal function as an *institution* while deemphasizing individuals' personal experiences with pornography. The three dimensions of this institution include its mass distribution as propaganda; the use of women in the production of pornography; and the consumption and use of pornography by its consumers. Comprehending Dworkin's redefinition of pornography is thus dependent upon understanding how she inextricably links pornographic representations with each process of this larger social context. Altogether, this contextualization of pornography enables her to transform what is conventionally perceived as a pornographic artifact into an entire system of sexual exploitation that functions through processes of production, consumption, and distribution.

PORNOGRAPHY AS PROPAGANDA

The essence of oppression is that one is defined from the outside by those who define themselves as superior by criteria of their own choice.[16]

Dworkin's analysis of pornography historically begins with its function as propaganda. From her first work of feminist theory to her latest writings on pornography, Dworkin incorporates an analysis of pornography's propagandistic function.[17] She considers propaganda part of the "cultural assault" that sustains any form of despotism and that functions to identify a target group and simultaneously sanction and incite systematic violence against members of this group. It is "the glove that covers the fist in any reign of terror," she states. She labels pornography "the propaganda of sexual fascism . . . of sexual terrorism" that celebrates sexual violence and sexual degradation of women.[18] "Its job in the politically coercive and cruel system of male supremacy," explains Dworkin in her speech "Pornography and Male Supremacy," "is to justify and perpetuate the rape and prostitution from which it springs."[19]

Like other forms of propaganda, pornography obscures its own violation: its use and abuse of women are disguised as sex. Dworkin states: "Pornography as a genre says that the stealing and buying and selling of women are not acts of force or abuse because women want to be raped and prostituted because that is the nature of women and the nature of female sexuality."[20] Of course, pornography could not be successful at disguising its violation were it not for the surrounding system of male supremacy that already values women as sexual objects: "Abuse means the misuse of someone. The abused person is credited with having a will, an ethic, or rights that have been violated. The female cannot be abused so long as the use made of her is sexual within the male value system, because her purpose on this earth is to be used sexually and her fundamental nature as defined by men requires rape, bondage, and pain."[21] Consequently, whatever is done to women in the name of sexuality is presented and justified *as sex,* not as abuse. In the manner of all successful propagandizing against a group of people, pornography obscures its violation by framing the forceful degradation of the targeted group in terms of the will or deservability of its members. "Force" is transformed into "the will of women" so that "what is done to women" is presented as "what women want done to them."[22] All social context is excised from the pornographic portrayals, enabling propagandists to present the images exclusively as a matter of women's free choice.

Dworkin connects society's refusal to believe women's charges of rape and battery to the male supremacist ideology that women desire, need, suggest, or demand sexual force—a belief she identifies as "the most enduring sexual truth in pornography—widely articulated by men to the utter bewilderment of women throughout the ages."[23] She shows how pornography's "fantasies" about women's so-called sexual desires are intricately related to society-wide denial of women's claims about sexual abuse. The central ideological construction of women—as insatiable whores who desire sexual dominance—functions as a lens filtering all women's claims of harassment, rape, and battery. Assaults against women thus become reframed as women's provocation or desire.[24] "Women do not believe that men believe what pornography says about women," writes Dworkin in *Pornography*. "But they do. From the worst to the best of them, they do. . . . [A victim of rape or incest] cannot comprehend what she is up against when she claims that she did not want it [to be forced into sex]. She is up against the whole world of real male belief about her real nature, expressed most purely in pornography."[25]

Dworkin considers pornography a particularly influential form of media because of its unique behavioral role in the development of sexual behaviors generally. For example, in "Why Pornography Matters to Feminists," she says that pornography "sets the standard for female sexuality, for female sexual values, for girls growing up, for boys growing up, and increasingly for advertising, films, video, visual arts, fine art and literature, music with words."[26] In an interview with Dworkin, she talks about pornography as a form of "sexual pedagogy that is exceptionally effective because, precisely because, it is not just mental; it is physiologically real to them, and they learn in their bodies about women from the pornography in a way that it doesn't matter what they think. They can think one thing, but what they do is something else." She identifies this physiological dimension of pornography as a critical factor in its effectiveness as propaganda; it is also an important feature which distinguishes it from other forms of mass media that also sexually exploit women. She considers pornography so powerfully effective because it seduces men into *experiencing* the subordination of women *as sex*—as a means to masturbate. The pornographers create a dynamic, says Dworkin, "that basically gets the man to start performing sexually."[27] Consequently, pornography is not just a belief system but includes "behavioral training"—orgasm as "a very serious reward."[28]

Pornography's success as propaganda is dependent upon its exploitation of existing racist and ethnocentric stereotypes. So, for instance, the idea within pornography that women and men of color are insatiably lustful feeds into pervasively accepted societal myths about the sexual bestiality of people of color. Similar lies are constructed about Jewish men and women in anti-Semitic pornography. The images in pornography, writes Dworkin, "do not exist in a historical vacuum. On the contrary, they exploit history—especially historical hatreds and historical suffering."[29] Pornography profits from the symmetry between its messages and the surrounding social practices and institutions: it reinforces, and is reinforced by, the existing value system.

Accordingly, Dworkin's dissection of pornography details its promotion of racial and ethnic hatreds. *Pornography: Men Possessing Women*, in particular, offers a complex analysis of how sexual exploitation functions *according to* hierarchies of race, class, and ethnicity. For example, Dworkin presents an incisive analysis of the racist sexual depictions of a series of ten photographs and accompanying text, spanning twelve pages in an issue of *Hustler*, a pornographic magazine. The photographic series is set in a jail in Mexico. There are three characters: a male jailer and a female visitor, Consuela, both of whom are Mexican, and Consuela's Anglo boyfriend who is imprisoned. The plot of the story is that Consuela wants to get into the jail to have sex with her boyfriend; to do so, she uses sex to bribe the Mexican jailer, who is portrayed as a lustful and brutish drunk. Consuela has all of the dimensions ascribed to women generally in pornography: basically, she is lustful and will do anything to have sex, especially with the Anglo boyfriend. But as Dworkin points out, Consuela's sexual allure is intensified by the color of her skin: "She is the woman sexed by the climate. The color of her skin signals the climate. . . . The heat of the climate heats the blood of 'the hot-blooded señorita,' heats her skin, heats her sex."

The racism in the photographs is not confined to the sexualization of Consuela's ethnic and racial identity. Dworkin shows how Consuela is used in the photos both to heighten and to obscure the racial antagonism between the two men. Consuela "is used by the Mexican policeman," writes Dworkin, "but she belongs to the Anglo boyfriend." In light of the fact that "Mexicans and Puerto Ricans [are] among the poorest of the poor in the United States" and that "Mexicans [are] particularly despised and exploited as aliens," the photographs embody "an imperial malice" because of the pernicious inversion of the power dynamic. The Mexican policeman is vested with power, by virtue of controlling the arms and the keys, and is constructed as the real threat both to a member of his own ethnic group and to the jailed white man. Through the symbolic manipulation of stereotypes about Mexicans, the jailer is presented as "the figure of overt force and brute sexuality" in comparison with the more delicate white male. "This, indeed, is basic to racist sexual ideology," writes Dworkin: "the white male is the civilized male, the bearer of a civilized sexuality. The darker male, the inferior male, has a brute sexual nature. . . . The white male, as the delicate male, is the sexually endangered male." Dworkin explains how the creation of such an unrealistic power dynamic between the Anglo and the Mexican male serves to bolster white supremacy and male domination, which are fused in this scene. The Mexican male

> cannot see his way clear to making an alliance with women—even the women of his peer group—based on sexual justice because he has accepted the bribe: masculinity belongs to him . . . to contaminate it through empathy with the female would mean weakening or losing it, the one thing he has, masculinity. . . . The sexuality of the racially degraded male—the only capacity allowed him—becomes both justification for taming or colonializing or castrating him and the mechanism by which he destroys himself, because he honors masculinity as authentic identity.[30]

Dworkin asserts that pornography's construction of the Mexican male's allegiance to masculinity obviates his identification with the Mexican woman and keeps him bonded to the white supremacist forces that control and dominate him. Thus she argues that pornography uses men of color, like all women, as pawns to exacerbate racial and sexual animosity, to reify racial hierarchy, and to reinforce a criminal justice system that singles out men of color as sexual predators and rapists.

Overall, Dworkin argues that pornography effectively naturalizes male sexual domination and female sexual subordination by sexualizing inequality (of many kinds). As a mass-distributed form of propaganda, then, pornography serves as ideological justification and behavioral training for sexual degradation against all culturally despised groups. Feminist theorist Patricia Hill Collins describes such naturalizing, rationalizing representations as "controlling images": hegemonic portrayals of nondominant groups used to justify relations of domination and subordination. "These controlling images," writes Hill Collins, "are designed to make racism, sexism, and poverty appear to be natural, normal, and an inevitable part of everyday life."[31] All of Dworkin's analyses of pornography articulate its function as "controlling images" without labeling the pornography as such. In the manner of "controlling images," the dissemination of pornographic propaganda ensures the maintenance of the material forces of male domination.

The notion that pornography is a form of propaganda is the most commonly understood facet of Dworkin's conception of pornography. Whether one enjoys or disdains pornography, few argue with the idea that it has an epistemic function by virtue of its mass distribution. Few, however, accord it the influence Dworkin does in the perpetuation of the ideology and the material forces of male domination, let alone its influence on actual behavior. But the fact that Dworkin attributes such power to pornography as a form of propaganda does not make her conception of pornography a radical innovation, for this does not alter the conception of the *nature* of pornography: it is still, in this context, a cultural artifact. It is just that she considers it a particularly effective artifact for reifying white male supremacy and for colonizing women.

THE PRODUCTION OF PORNOGRAPHY

Only as we turn to Dworkin's analysis of the use of women in the production of pornography is it clear why she defines pornography as an institutional *practice* of subordination instead of just an influential cultural *artifact*. The use of real women in the production of pornography changes the nature of the social phenomenon because the harm is no longer external to pornography—a result of its pervasive ideological influence—but is intrinsic to its existence. Since the harm Dworkin attributes to pornography is embodied in its production, she reconfigures its ontology from something that engenders harm to that which is *produced by* harming women.

"The First Victims"

Central to Dworkin's conception of pornography as a social practice are the concrete labor practices—specifically of the labor of women—within the pornography industry. In contrast to the perception that pornographic modeling is a matter of an individual woman's free and autonomous choice of work, Dworkin argues that the pornography industry is built upon the coercion, economic exploitation, and sexual abuse of women. In many of her works, but especially in her testimony before the Attorney General's Commission on Pornography in 1986 and in the book she coauthored with Catharine MacKinnon in 1988, *Pornography and Civil Rights,* Dworkin describes the pool of women who work within pornography as follows: almost all are poor women with little education; sixty-five to seventy-five percent of the women in pornography are incest survivors; many of these survivors entered pornography as runaways escaping abuse within their families; other women have been forced by husbands and lovers to pose for a camera, and the pictures were then put into pornographic magazines or made into commercial videos; some were forced to turn to prostitution to survive and were then forced into pornography by their pimps; others were forced into prostitution after modeling for pornography. Dworkin says that once a woman is forced into pornography—whether by parents, husband, lover, pimp, or total stranger—the pornography is then used to blackmail the woman into staying in pornography and prostitution.[32]

Based on her knowledge about the sexual and economic exploitation of women in the pornography industry, Dworkin concludes that "the first victims of pornography are the women in it."[33] Whatever is done to women in pornography is done to the women in the making of pornography. Therefore, she sees in pornography a testimony of its own abuse. In the Introduction to the 1989 edition of *Pornography: Men Possessing Women,* she calls pornographic artifacts "an archive of evidence and documentation of crimes against women." It is "a living archive," she claims, "commercially alive, carnivorous in its use of women."[34]

Linguistic Embodiment of Harm

Dworkin links together the artifacts and effects of pornography in an unusual and innovative way. Usually when one attributes harm to pornography, it is meant that it engenders harm by, for instance, creating a climate of hostility; in such a case, the pornographic artifact is still seen as a discrete object one can isolate from its effects, much as one will isolate the production of butter from its effects on the arteries. But in photographic pornography in particular, asserts Dworkin, the production of the product *is its effect;* in other words, the sexual use of the women is phenomenologically simultaneous. Therefore, she argues that pornography is harmful because its production *consists of harm to women.*

One of the complicated features of Dworkin's work on pornography is that she implicitly includes the pornography industry in every description of pornography she offers. When Dworkin describes pornographic images, she also, at the same time, describes what is being done to the women to produce the images. What pornography *is,* therefore, is always also what it *does* to women. Note, for instance, the following description of pornography from a speech titled "Pornography and Civil Rights" delivered in Madison, Wisconsin, in 1984. She is describing the content of pornography for her audience:

> The pornography being sold in this country right now features the humiliation of women as an act that gives sexual pleasure to women. . . . The pornography that is being made in this country right now includes outright torture—the kind of torture that is done to political prisoners in prison cells, the kind of torture that is recognized as torture, *not fun,* when it is done to people in prison. And the pornography in this country also includes the murder of women for sexual entertainment.
>
> Now that's the range of the entertainment. What about real life? What is the range of abuse in real life? First of all, all of the above.[35]

"The pornography [being made and sold] in this country" implies pornography as it is usually understood—as representations of women in various forms of media. If one continues to read the entire passage with such a conception of pornography in mind, it appears that Dworkin is making a causal claim about the dangerous effects of pornography's *ideas* on the treatment of women in "real life." But, in fact, the claim Dworkin is making is not only that pornography inspires the replication of what it depicts, but also that pornography "*is*" what it depicts: the sexual abuse is intrinsic to the making of pornography, not just a result of it. As she writes in *Pornography: Men Possessing Women:* "Real women are tied up, stretched, hanged, fucked, gang-banged, whipped, beaten, and begging for more. In the photographs and films, real women are used as *porneia* and real women are depicted as *porneia.*"[36]

Confining one's conception of pornography to the isolated representations of sexual activity misses the essential processes involved in the production, consumption, and distribution of pornography within a context of male domination and the harm to women involved in these processes. Consequently, with such a narrow view of pornography, it is impossible to see how it functions as a practice. Whereas pornography excises the social context to present each woman as freely choosing to be used sexually, Dworkin inverts this process and embeds the social context into every description of the pornographic image.

Dworkin abandons the notion that pornography is merely "free speech" or "propaganda"; pornography refers to the sexual exploitation of women involved in its production and is inseparable from the harm it promotes through its consumption and distribution. "Pornography happens," she writes, using the word characteristically as an active agent rather than an inert object. It is a "system of dominance and submission" and "has the weight and significance of any other historically real torture or punishment of a group of people because of a condition of birth; it has the weight and significance of any other historically real exile of human beings from human dignity, the purging of them from a shared community of care and rights and respect."[37]

REFINING THE LINKS: PORNOGRAPHY AND SEXUAL ABUSE

> *The character of pornography and its relationship to actual violence against women, if it's analogous to anything, is analogous to the way anti-Semitic literature blanketed Germany and enabled what occurred to be justified, encouraged it, incited it, promoted it.*[38]

The last addition to Dworkin's conception of pornography is its function in actively discriminating and sexually violating women. This is a notion of direct harm resulting from the consumption and use of pornographic materials. These harms are not necessarily built into the production of pornography (although they can be) but are nonetheless *intrinsic* to its contemporary existence. This dimension of harm includes the use of pornography as a "recipe book" or "how-to" manual for sexual abuse, as well as the use of pornography to directly intimidate and subordinate women. This conception of pornography's harm is different from Dworkin's earlier claim that pornography is propaganda that reflects, embodies, and bolsters the male power structure; in her works throughout the seventies, and even in *Pornography: Men Possessing Women*, she makes only very general causal claims about the ubiquity of pornography creating a climate of hostility and abuse of women. But by the time she and Catharine MacKinnon write the Minneapolis civil rights antipornography ordinance in 1983, she asserts her knowledge of direct links between pornography and the sexual abuse and subordination of women. The harm inspired by the pervasive distribution of propaganda is diffuse, even if widespread; the harm resulting from the consumption and use of pornographic materials is immediate and direct, whether it is because men use the materials in the commission of sexual abuse or because the consumption of the materials serves to directly intimidate, antagonize, and humiliate women.

The notion that pornography directly harms women is one of the central features upon which the antipornography civil rights ordinance is built. The ordinance defines pornography as a form of sex discrimination that functions to keep women subordinate to men. For if pornographic artifacts are a *direct source* of humiliation, intimidation, and violence against women, then wherever pornography is being used, a woman's right to equal treatment is threatened.

Dworkin's essay "Letter from a War Zone" contains one of her most comprehensive explanations of the direct use of pornography in sexual assault. Again, based on thousands of testimonies of women's experiences, she identifies three features that characterize pornography's direct role in sexual abuse. First, she claims that pornography is responsible for the continual *creation* of new kinds of sexual abuse: "men learned any new tricks the pornographers had to teach. We learned that anything that hurt or humiliated women could be sex for men who used pornography."[39] Examples include the use of pornography to plan and execute rape; johns' demands from prostitutes to reenact scenes from pornography; and the proliferation of cases of throat rape after the appearance of the film, *Deep Throat.* A plethora of other cases are cited throughout her work where a pornographic video, game, or photograph is used as the (often explicitly acknowledged) inspiration for a particular sexual assault.[40]

Second, Dworkin explains that men's use of pornography alters the character of their sexual behaviors: "We found that when pornography created sexual abuse . . . male sexual practice would change dramatically to accommodate violations and degradations promoted by the pornography."[41] This means that men do not merely reenact pornographic scenes that fit within their already existing repertoire of sexual fantasies and practices but, more pointedly, that men's consumption of pornography results in continuous modifications in their sexual desires and practices. As Dworkin explains in a 1993 interview, "The things that were only fantasy ideas become things that he does; and then when he sees that he can do that thing and not get hurt or caught for doing it, then there's another idea that the pornography has put there; and he goes back, and he does the next one and the next one."[42] Men who may have never hurt or humiliated or raped or tied or tortured women learn from the pornography that these activities are all part of sex (and the pornography tells them that women enjoy the activities), and then they mimic these behaviors in their own lives. In this way, pornography has a unique influence on changing the modus operandi of perpetrators, inspiring an "exceptionally dynamic" form of sadism.[43]

Essentially, Dworkin claims that the use of pornography in the commission of sexual assault changes the nature of the sexual assault. "Abuse created by pornography was different," she writes: "Once the role of pornography in *creating* sexual abuse was exposed—rape by rape, beating by beating, victim by victim—our understanding of the nature of sexual abuse itself changed." She not only argues that pornography is responsible for creating abuse, but that the pattern of abuse it creates is different from abuse outside of pornography in three fundamental ways: "the abuse [is] multifaceted, complex; the violations of each individual woman [are] many and interconnected; [and] the sadism [is] exceptionally dynamic."[44]

PORNOGRAPHY RECONFIGURED

"Pornography is *not* what pornography *says,*" assert Dworkin and MacKinnon in *Pornography and Civil Rights.* Rather, "pornography *is* what pornography *does.*"[45] Accordingly, Dworkin's discourse presents pornography strictly in terms of the harm it *does* to women. Her rhetorical reconstruction of pornography revolves around the relationship she creates within her discourse between pornography and sexual exploitation: she embeds pornography within existing systems of racial, economic, and sexual exploitation; she treats pornography as propaganda that advocates racialized sexual subordination and exploitation; and she reconfigures pornography's ontology according to its systematic racial, economic, and sexual exploitation of women used to make the pornography and of women in society as a whole.

Dworkin says that after she read Linda Marchiano's book *Ordeal,* she began to understand pornography in terms of its *civil rights violations.* In pornography, she claims, these violations are "systematic and intrinsic" because "the pornography could not exist without them."[46] Consequently, Dworkin's writing reconfigures pornography as a practice that systematically violates women's civil rights. It harms women, she writes, "inevitably by its nature because of what it is and what it does. The harm will occur as long as it is made and used. The name of the next victim is unknown, but everything else is known."[47]

This reconfiguration of pornography within Dworkin's work explicates important features of the civil rights antipornography ordinance. It is on the basis of pornography's harm to women that the ordinance classifies pornography as a practice of sex discrimination that both constitutes and causes inequality on the basis of sex. As she and MacKinnon state in the Minneapolis ordinance:

> pornography is central in creating and maintaining the civil inequality of the sexes. Pornography is a systematic practice of exploitation and subordination based on sex which differentially harms women. The bigotry and contempt it promotes, with the acts of aggression it fosters, harm women's opportunities for equality of rights in employment, education, property rights, public accommodations, and public services; create public harassment and private denigration; promote injury and degradation such as rape, battery, and prostitution and inhibit just enforcement of laws against these acts; contribute significantly to restricting women from full exercise of citizenship and participation in public life, including in neighborhoods; damage relations between the sexes; and undermine women's equal exercise of rights to speech and action guaranteed to all citizens under the Constitutions and laws of the United States and the State of Minnesota.[48]

The ordinance allows civil action against pornography on the basis of the harm it *does* to women, not on the basis of what pornography says; pornography is significant as a form of discrimination because it is a mode of action, not simply a medium of representation. Pornographic materials are defined in the ordinance according to their depictions of women *and* their relationship to the specific concrete ways women are subordinated through the production, consumption, and distribution of pornography. For someone to take action against pornography (i.e., for pornography to be deemed socially detrimental), she (or, in some cases, he) must prove that it has done something harmful to her through these practices of subordination.

This conception of pornography as social practice directly challenges current legal interpretation.[49] As Dworkin and MacKinnon explain in *Pornography and Civil Rights*, the legal system currently considers pornography "a passive reflection or one-level-removed 'representation' or symptomatic by-product or artifact of the real world. It thus becomes an idea analog to, a word or picture replay of, something else, which somehow makes what it presents, that something else, not real either."[50] In contrast, the antipornography ordinance interprets pornography in much more concrete terms: it is something injurious *done* to women, not merely morally offensive. Based on its harm, it is an *action* against women, not just speech about women.

Her reconstitution of pornography in terms of its harm is a rhetorical intervention that subverts the premises upon which pornography is currently defended—primarily as an emblem of free speech and as a crucible of sexual privacy and freedom. As Dworkin explains, "virtually all power, in cultural terms, in 'winning an argument' comes from how you define the problem. I mean, . . . a person who sets up the premises is the person who sets up the conclusion. And so I am setting up my own premises, and I think they're premises that help to undermine the general premises and, therefore, the status quo conclusion."[51]

The civil rights antipornography ordinance is constructed from the premises of Dworkin's analysis. It is designed as a material remedy to the material problem she addresses: it attempts to provide individual women with a legal mechanism for redressing class-based subordination perpetuated through the production, distribution, and consumption of pornography. It provides a legal definition and description of pornography's concrete discriminating practices from the perspective of those it subordinates. It draws upon the Fourteenth Amendment guarantee of equal protection rather than the First Amendment right to free expression. It repudiates the public/private dichotomy that protects sexual exploitation in individuals' private lives. It recognizes the injury pornography does to women (and sometimes men) and empowers those harmed by pornography to hold accountable those involved in the subordinating practices.

As Dworkin explains, the ordinance is designed to change "the power relationship between the pornographers and women."[52] Like her antipornography discourse generally, the ordinance undermines the premises of pornography by infusing the law with "the flesh-and-blood experiences of women . . . whose lives have been savaged by pornography." She writes:

> Using the Ordinance, women get to say to the pimps and the johns: we are not your colony; you do not own us as if we were territory; my will as expressed through my use of this Ordinance is, I don't want it, I don't like it, pain hurts, coercion isn't sexy, I resist being someone else's speech, I reject subordination, I speak, I speak for myself now, I am going into court to speak—to you; and you will listen.[53]

In a manner duplicating Dworkin's rhetorical confrontation with the pornography industry, the civil rights antipornography ordinance authorizes those harmed by pornography to use their concrete life experience as the basis for confronting pornography's subordination of women. The ordinance embodies the political imperative at the heart of Dworkin's feminist resistance: "to use every single thing you can remember about what was done to you—how it was done, where, by whom, when, and, if you know, why—to begin to tear male dominance to pieces, to pull it apart, to vandalize it, to destabilize it, to mess it up, to get in its way, to fuck it up."[54] The civil rights antipornography ordinance communicates faith that women can transform pain into political knowledge useful for destroying the system of male supremacy.

CHAPTER 15

The Second Front: The Logic of Sexual Violence in Wars

By Ruth Seifert

In the spring of 1993, an investigation committee of the European Community stated that the mass rapes and/or sexual torture of women in Bosnia-Herzegovina must be considered systematic, ordered acts and an important element of Serb warfare strategy. Currently, the number of raped women in the area is said to be about 60,000. The assumption that the attacks on women are deliberate military actions has for the first time become the subject of widespread discussion triggered by the events in former Yugoslavia, but it is not new. As early as 1971, an Indian novelist, referring to the mass rapes in Bangladesh, expressed his conviction that this was a premeditated crime. "The rapes were so systematic and pervasive that they had to be conscious Army policy." He suspected that the purpose was to create a new race or to dilute Bengali nationalism.[1]

Mass rapes and sexual torture of women in times of crisis and war are not new phenomena; however, only since events in the former Yugoslavia have come to international attention has widespread concern focused on the question of how to explain the rape and sexual torture of women. It seems that the reasons for this awareness are found at two different levels: First, the establishment of camps explicitly intended for sexual torture obviously marks a new stage in the escalation of violence against women; second, women now hold positions in politics, academia, science, and the media enabling them to make these incidents a political issue and to question the established, marginalising explanations that have been offered.

The explanations of sexual violence against women in civilian life as well as in war with which both the academic community and the public have been satisfied for a long time are, on closer examination, no longer tenable. They fall basically into two categories. One explanation which, even though it does not stand up to scientific scrutiny, possesses enormous ideological power, is the "sexual urge" argument. From an empirical viewpoint alone this argument is highly contestable. For rape is committed regardless of whether the urge could be satisfied in a different way. Rape in war, as one member of the U.S. Army Court of Military Review in Washington explained, "has nothing to do with the availability of willing women or prostitutes," for example, in brothels. In the "cultural vacuum" of war some men simply prefer to rape.[2] This is confirmed by rape studies which unanimously come to the conclusion that rape is not a sexual but an aggressive act (i.e., in the perpetrator's psyche it does not fulfil sexual functions). What does, however, give him satisfaction is the humiliation and abasement of his victim and the sense of power and dominance over a woman.[3] Some studies therefore describe rape as a "pseudosexual" or "anti-sexual" act: It has nothing to do with sexuality but with the exertion of sexual violence directed against women. And, finally, ethnological research reveals that rape is by no means equally common in all societies. Rather, there are rape-prone and largely rape-free societies. All modern Western societies can be considered rape-prone. Largely rape-free cultures, on the other hand, are found where, according to the prevailing Western opinion, proximity to "nature" or atavism is presumed to be closer than in our civilization, namely in smaller tribal societies. The idea that rape is an anthropological given, thus, results from a narrow ethnocentric perspective.[4] But that perspective is also ahistorical. From historical sources it can be derived that at the beginning of early modern times sexual behaviour seems to have been less violent than it is today. There is also sufficient documentary evidence that "epochs of particularly late marriage in the past were times of low rather than high bastardy."[5] Thus, whether there is an irrepressible urge or not and what consequences it has, seems more likely to depend on the social conditions and on the construction of sexuality prevailing in a particular time and culture, which, in turn, has a considerable impact on the psyche and the emotional balance of the individual.[6]

Furthermore, biochemists are highly uncertain about how to interpret scientific research concerning male aggressiveness. What has constantly been brought up in this connection is the "testosterone argument," according to which the male hormone testosterone is responsible for a higher degree of aggressiveness in men. Physiological experiments, however, do not produce smooth results that would support a biologistic view. For the crucial question is in what way hormone production and aggressiveness are really correlated. In other words: Does a high level of testosterone produce aggression, or does a certain psychological condition (namely aggressiveness) perhaps produce high levels of testosterone? Primate research has shown that this can be the case. Low-ranking males revealed an 80% decline in testosterone levels, while testosterone production increased after a male had gained a predominant status. It is also known that in situations of stress the production of testosterone decreases while anger steps it up. High levels of testosterone may, thus, be the result of aggression.[7]

But the biologistic explanation of sexual torture has to be refuted on theoretical grounds, too. For there is no conceivable mechanism that would translate the presumed biological causes (such as hormone secretion) into complex patterns of human behavior, let alone institutions. Wars, violent conflicts between people, as well as sexual attacks on women, are historical and social processes that are carried out collectively and, thus, must have a collective meaning. They are not the sum total of a couple of hundred thousand genetic predispositions for aggressiveness. Biology cannot claim to have an immediate and privileged access to reality. On the contrary: Biology, itself, is a social construct that—like all other modes of knowing—can only become a way of knowing within a certain social context. Biology is a system of classifications which helps humans make sense of their experience.[8] The argument from biology, hardly ever used any more to explain wars but nonetheless still serving as an excuse for sexual violence against women due to ideologies that continue to be effective, can be abandoned.

Another argument which tends to be brought forward chiefly by the military establishment is that acts of violence against the civilian population and, in particular, wartime atrocities against women are "regrettable side effects" of war. The Information and Press Office of the German Ministry of Defence in February 1993 stated in answer to an inquiry that psychological terrorization and the depopulation of entire areas as well as rapes were not part of military tactics. The image of man let off the leash, losing his sexual self-control in battle has also been vehemently rejected,[9] and rightly so, considering what has been said above: Biology does not prompt any man to rape. What needs to be verified is whether that other assertion is true, that is, whether attacks on the civilian population—which in times of war is for the most part made up of women—really do happen outside the boundaries of "warfare proper" and whether rapes can be regarded as excesses of singular hordes run wild.

A look at the available figures is likely to teach us otherwise. It should be borne in mind that the figures cited can only represent examples because atrocities committed against women have neither been recorded nor documented systematically. In the Chinese city of Nanking in 1937, an estimated 20,000 women were raped, sexually tortured, and murdered during the first month of the Japanese occupation. Foreign missionaries reported independently of each other at least 10 cases of gang rape a day. In response to this, the term "Rape of Nanking" soon came into general use in the press. In 1943, Moroccan mercenaries serving in the remainder of the French Army were explicitly granted the right to rape and loot in conquered Italian territory. This resulted in widespread mass rapes. After the war, the victims were awarded a small pension by the Italian government.[10] According to evidence presented at the Nuremberg war-crimes tribunal, the German command had opened a brothel in a hotel in the city of Smolensk into which women were forcibly driven. It also became known that it was the usual practice to tattoo the legend "Whore for Hitler's troops" on the bodies of captured partisan women and to use them accordingly. The French prosecutor at the Nuremberg tribunal produced evidence of mass rapes committed in retaliation for acts of the French Resistance. This proves that in some cases rape was employed as a means to achieve political-military ends. In Korea during World War II between 100,000 and 200,000 women (the "comfort women" who are now speaking out) were abducted to camps and raped or sexually tortured by the Japanese.[11] Figures on the number of women raped in the Greater Berlin area in 1945 vary. According to conservative estimates, at least 120,000 women were raped. Less conservative estimates claim that up to 900,000 women were abused. Similar things happened in other parts of Germany. In southern Baden-Württemberg, for instance, rapes were committed on a massive scale by French soldiers.[12] As already mentioned, 200,000 women were raped in Bangladesh in 1971. Many of these women were subsequently rejected by their husbands and families and ended up as a homeless, vagabond group. The government set up camps for these women but failed to furnish them with the basic facilities needed so that they soon turned into slums. Even today, more than 20 years later, there are women living in these camps. As regards the situation in Kuwait, according to official statistics at least 5,000 women are assumed to have become victims of rape during the Iraqi occupation of the country.[13]

Considering these sample figures, it seems absurd to believe that rape is a phenomenon occurring only on the periphery of war. In war zones, women apparently always find themselves on the frontline.[14] Even the Geneva Conventions, so often referred to by officials, obviously have not brought about much change. In practice they have not provided effective protection for women so far. As early as 1972, the United Nation's Economic and Social Council, in its Resolution No. 1687, expressed its "deep concern" about the persistent, almost undiminished level of brutality practised in war, especially against women, in spite of the Geneva Convention of 1949. The attendant appeal to member states to respect the humanitarian law relating to the protection of women and children went largely unheard and unheeded. In the light of their massive occurrence and the ineffectiveness of international conventions the question arises whether rapes and war brutalities against women must be regarded as integral parts of warfare.[15] What function does rape fulfil in wartime and what strategic purpose is served by sexual violence against women?

If in the following our view is narrowed to the strategic function of rape in war, it should be emphasized that this is only one aspect of sexual violence. A comprehensive analysis of the phenomenon must undoubtedly take into account many other aspects. A central issue is hatred of women in general which must be analyzed in terms of its socio-cultural as well as its psychoanalytical aspects. Without reference to the component of hostility in the construction of gender relations the specific kind of violence directed against women cannot be explained. The Croatian journalist Ines Sabalic, for example, drew attention to atrocities of a quasi-ritualistic nature centered on the femininity of the body: cases in which a woman's breasts were cut off, her stomach was slashed open or her vagina torn apart with a weapon or military tool after she had been raped. Only a hatred of femininity as such can account for that specific kind of violence.[16] But this contempt of women also exists in peacetime and manifests itself, *inter alia*, in the socially accepted pornography that displays and aestheticizes the physical violence of men against women in peacetime. Based on this hatred which is ingrained in the Western cultural unconscious, war also becomes, according to Pohl,[17] "an adventure where fantasies of destruction unconsciously directed against women are encouraged and acted out,"[18] brought to the surface in times of crisis and war when the concepts of order begin to crumble.[19]

In the following, however, attention will be focussed on the particular significance of rape in the context of war. The massive assaults on female civilians, as documented by the figures given above, have no more a place in official military theory than massive attacks on the civilian population at large. The accepted view is that unfortunately, but sometimes inevitably, it happens that civilians fall victim to acts of war. Warfare "proper" is considered to be the confrontation that takes place between soldiers. There is much to be said against this definition of war.

First, the figures on the number of civilian victims of the wars in this century give a dramatically different picture. They attest to a worldwide systematic involvement of the civilian population (mostly women and children). Far more civilians than soldiers were killed in World War I. In World War II, the former Soviet Union lost nine million soldiers, as compared to 16 million civilians. According to official statements that ratio amounted to 1:5 for the Korean War and 1:13 for the Vietnam War. UNICEF data from 1989 indicate that in the wars fought since World War II, 90% of all victims have been civilians. In an analysis conducted in 1979, the ratio for future wars was assumed to be 1:100. Faced with these figures, one can hardly speak of a regrettable and unintended involvement of the civilian population.[20]

Elaine Scarry has presented a brilliant analysis which sheds some light on the logic of the unintended involvement of the civilian population in warfare.[21] She suggests that a careful distinction must be made between the ideal concept and the reality of war. Although war in its ideal form is defined as a conflict between male armies, civilian casualties are depicted as unintentional by-products of war. Scarry poses the reasonable question: "... if injury [and death, even of civilians] is designated the 'by-product,' what is the product?" and answers it by saying that it "is the thing every exhausting piece of strategy and every single weapon is designed to bring into being: it is not something inadvertently produced on the way to producing something else but is the relentless object of all military activity."[22] Given the fact that civilian war-related deaths far outnumber military casualties, the term *by-product* is highly inappropriate both from a moral and an analytical point of view: By using words like *unforeseen or inadvertent*, civilian victims are reduced to insignificance in the context of the conflict, and their suffering is disparaged. This is also reflected in the difference that is made between civilian and military casualties. In the cultural memory, too, the loss of life among the civilian population and, in particular, the wartime experience and sufferings of women are dealt with in a completely different way than the fate of soldiers: "The victims of rape are not included in the public rite of mourning over the lost war, they are not admired as 'heroines' and do not receive any compensation."[23]

From an analytical point of view, such an approach obscures the fact that in reality the suffering of the civilian population which consists, as must be emphasised again, largely of women, constitutes a crucial element of warfare. One of the primary goals in war, as Scarry points out, is the destruction/deconstruction of culture and not necessarily the defeat of the enemy army.[24] The deconstruction of culture, however, is achieved through injuring and destroying human beings because this is the most efficient (most forceful) way in which a decision can ultimately be brought about.

The termination of a war, or its outcome, is decided not so much by the victor's clear superiority or, in other words, by his opponent's weakness and inability to influence the outcome of the war, as is illustrated by many examples. A decisive factor is rather a change of perception.[25] That is to say, a war is usually ended when one side is willing to reverse its self-image and its collective consciousness. This reversal, however, is a highly difficult process. It is, according to Scarry, nothing less than "world deconstruction" brought about by the destruction of material culture, persons and elements of consciousness.[26] It is obvious that this world deconstruction would take place on a smaller scale if wars were fought exclusively between armies and the civilian population remained uninvolved. Extending Scarry's line of argument, it can be assumed that with increasing democratization and participation of the population in politics, these processes of destruction become more significant than they were in the past (e.g., in feudal societies). For the more a people identifies with "its" government or political system and the more it is given a say in policy-making (i.e., the higher the status achieved by vast portions of the population), the more important it will be from a military-strategic point of view to affect as many inhabitants of a national territory as is possible (i.e., as many individual identities as possible) by destroying their culture and/or self-understanding.

Scarry is concerned with the function of physical violence and of the suffering and atrocities experienced in war by both men and women.[27] Women, however, have a particular place in this logic of destruction. A research project which for the first time investigated the role of women in wars arrived at surprising results. The subject of the study was the position of women in the civil warring areas of Mozambique and Sri Lanka, and it turned out that female civilians were to an extreme extent exposed to acts of war. The women living in those areas perceived war as anything but a matter concerning only men or soldiers. The analysis revealed that it was civilians rather than soldiers on whom these conflicts focussed. Sometimes they actually became the tactical targets of the operations.[28, 29]

When trying to understand the purpose of these massive assaults on women, the results of the above-mentioned study suggest the following conclusions: Sexual violence against women is likely to destroy a nation's culture. In times of war, the women are those who hold the families and the community together. Their physical and emotional destruction aims at destroying social and cultural stability. Moreover, the psychological effects mass rapes have on the community concerned may lead to the devaluation and dissolution of the entire group. The destruction of women and/or their integrity affects overall cultural cohesion. Because societies derive their specific form, their self-image and their definition of reality from cultural cohesion, its destruction is of outstanding importance.[30] This theory is corroborated by observations concerning Serb strategy in the war in former Yugoslavia. It is reported that once an area or town has been invaded, a phased course of action was followed. The first step obviously consisted in destroying objects of cultural heritage. In a second step, the intellectuals were taken captive and frequently killed because they are people who play a particularly important role in the preservation and tradition of a nation's culture. (Incidentally, a similar strategy of destruction was employed during the German invasion of Poland.)[31] The third step was the establishment of rape camps for women. Here, too, we cannot speak of a random procedure. Rather, women belonging to the intelligentsia and women of a higher status were among the first to be selected. There can be no doubt that all these strategies have the specific aim of destroying culture, that is, undermining those factors that are fundamental constituents of society and culture.[32]

Another aspect of this destruction of culture can be derived from the symbolic construction of the female body: In many cultures it embodies the nation as a whole and is so depicted in many works of art or national symbols such as the French "Marianne" personifying France, the United States' Statue of Liberty, and the Bavarian national statue "Bavaria." In many societies woman represents the symbolic system of a group, the construction of the community being produced and made visible in her person, body, and life.[33] But this also means that violence committed against women is directed against the physical and personal integrity of a group. The rape of women of a community, culture, or nation can be regarded—and is so regarded—as a symbolic rape of the body of that community.

Moreover, the social construction of the feminine implies what Wobbe calls a "vulnerability to assault," something that the construction of masculinity does not include.[34] This is shown by the well-known fact that women, even within their own society, culture, or nation, run a considerably greater risk of being bodily harmed than men. Also, communities tend to construct their rejection of strangers on the vulnerability of women. According to Wobbe, racism is frequently based on fantasies of injury inflicted on the female members of the "Us" group. But this logic also works the other way round: The "Them" group can just as well be excluded in a particular way, or "subdued," as Wobbe puts it, by exerting violence against "their" women. The consequences of these cultural attributions to women can be observed in the aggression against Croatia and Bosnia-Herzegovina, where mass rape and the sexual torture of women and girls are employed against the "Them" group as a strategy of destruction of culture and "ethnic cleansing." That strategy, however,

> is being practised on the bodies of these girls and women, in an unspeakably cruel way, in that these women—whose own social and personal existence has been destroyed—are made to generate the future of that other community by extinguishing the present of their own community.[35]

Here a further aspect of the destruction of the culture becomes obvious, that is, the idea of using rape as pollution of the enemy community. This idea was present in Bangladesh as well as in Berlin in 1945 (the idea of subverting the "pure race" Aryan project) and is an outspoken strategy of the Serbs in Bosnia who claim to imprint their identity on the Bosnian population by producing "little chef niks" or Serbs.[36] Pollution is, thus, envisaged in two ways. First, there is a racist idea of contaminating the other community's blood and genes. Second, pollution also refers to dissolving a group's spirit and identity.[37]

Finally, what needs to be pointed out is the close relationship of rape with torture which makes the term sexual torture seem more appropriate in the final analysis. The deliberate infliction of extreme pain, as in torture, has a cultural script or structure.

> This structure may be in part premeditated, seems for the most part unconscious, and is in either case based on the nature of pain, the nature of power, the interaction between the two, and the interaction between the ultimate source of each—the body, the locus of pain, and the voice, the locus of power.[38]

Torture also aims at annihilating culture, that is, a person's interior culture, by exploiting the effects of intense pain, such as the destruction of language—which is an important source of self-extension—or the obliteration of the contents of consciousness, because pain destroys the ability of elementary perception and complex thinking and feeling.[39] The same effects have been described for the rape victims in former Yugoslavia. The most frequent symptoms reported for the sexually tortured women are severe anxiety, sleeping disorders, nightmares, apathy, loss of confidence, depression, and suicidal inclinations. The rapes, which were often characterized by an extreme degree of brutality, have often resulted in a loss of identity on the part of the victims. It has been reported that in some cases the rapes have also caused an ethnic identity crisis among those Bosnians who were witnesses to the atrocities.[40]

Another important characteristic of torture is that it converts the victim's suffering into a display of power which is perfectly convincing to the torturer and the regime he represents.[41] The victim of torture experiences an extreme reduction to his or her body and to pain, an annihilating negation of the self, felt throughout the body, whereas the torturer transforms the pain into power. The victim's agony promotes his own self-extension. Part of what makes his world so huge is its juxtaposition with the small and shredded world that is left for the victim. As the victim is reduced to a bundle of pain and steadily loses ground, the tormentor senses that he is gaining territory.[42] This accounts for the frequently blatant "senselessness" of torture, when it is obvious that there is no information to be extracted from the tortured person: The translation of pain into the power of those who inflict it will in any case take place on the symbolic level.

Torture is an act of hatred and destruction of humankind. Yet, it is a highly political and, thus, "human" act. The characteristics of rape fit with this script.

For what happens in rape, that is, forcible entry into the body, is a characteristic of severe torture and constitutes the severest attack imaginable on the most intimate self and the dignity of a person. Apart from physical pain, which in many cases of rape is additionally inflicted in various ways, it means the loss of dignity, an attack on a person's identity and the loss of self-determination and control over one's own body. Because individual identity is very closely linked to sexual identity in our culture, sexual violence is also an assault on the very core of a person's self.[43]

In the last analysis, rape is committed for the same reasons as torture. According to Scarry, torture is used whenever the power in whose name it is carried out is unstable. The stronger that power becomes or the more it gains in reality, the more the incidence of torture will decrease.[44] The reality of power, therefore, no longer needs to be demonstrated by means of the incontestable reality of the sufferer's physical pain. The same motive applies in the case of rape. A comparison of low-rape and rape-prone societies reveals that the occurrence of rape is particularly high where male power has become unstable. The instability of male power and predominance as a triggering factor of rape is an aspect that is no longer put forward by feminists only. Male researchers of rape also regard it as a decisive cause of sexual violence against women.[45] In the United States, with its traditionally strong women's movement and the considerable overall achievements of women in society, rape is currently the most frequent crime of violence that has been steadily on the rise for decades.

Going back once again to what is happening in former Yugoslavia, there are two things that should be emphasized. The rape and sexual torture of women originates, on the one hand, in the political construction of the female body in a certain national context, as described above. But this alone is not a sufficient explanation for the act of rape. Although there is a national aspect to it (i.e., *Bosnian* women are raped by *Serbian* men so that, according to what was said above, the incontestable reality of tortured *Bosnian* bodies is converted into the power of the Serb regime), the fact is also that women are raped by men, which means that the incontestable reality of tortured female bodies is translated into male power. If torture is designed to consolidate power, that is, if torture is decidedly political in nature and serves a decidedly political purpose, it is to be expected that the mass rapes occurring in former Yugoslavia will also have lasting effects on the gender relationship. Therefore, they are by no means just acts of senseless brutality, but culture-destroying acts committed for strategic reasons in an ethnic conflict as well as political acts as far as the gender arrangement is concerned. The political developments that this arrangement has undergone since hostilities began have already been described.

In an analysis of the situation of women in former Yugoslavia, Vlasta Jalusić from Slovenia writes of a disciplining of the national female body taking place in practically all the constituent republics of former Yugoslavia.[46] The everyday climate is characterized by "an all-encompassing men's world; you can smell it in the air, that sense of fraternity, that heroism. It is not just uniforms, it is even the spirit that smells of the military."[47] At the same time women are disappearing from the public sphere, not only in the immediate war areas, but also in Croatia. Where women used to function as workers and had their place at least in the nonpolitical, semiofficial sectors of the socialist system, they have now become the "natural ferment" of the nation, with tasks more important and more "natural" than policy-making. The public image of women, says Jalusić, is one of "blood and soil" femininity with a pornographic connotation.[48] On the legal level, drastic limitations of free birth control and of the individual rights of women can be observed. Women's primary role is to be the biological regenerators of the nation.[49]

In Jalusić's view, the case of Yugoslavia is evidence that the nation-state principle will entail severe "public" violence against women once that principle has been adopted as a principle of government. This view is corroborated by Wobbe's[50] analysis of how communities are constituted through the national female body, and by numerous individual phenomena observed.[51, 52]

Collective antifemale violence must be interpreted within the contexts of both the formation of national identities and of gender arrangement. The latter is a factor that must also be taken into account when considering the explosive national conflicts in Eastern and Central Europe and their impact on other countries.

SECTION FOUR

Violence and Race

CHAPTER 16

Excerpt from "Concerning Violence" The Wretched of the Earth

By Frantz Fanon

National liberation, national renaissance, the restoration of nationhood to the people, commonwealth: whatever may be the headings used or the new formulas introduced, decolonisation is always a violent phenonomen. At whatever level we study it—relationships between individuals, new names for sports clubs, the human admixture at cocktail parties, in the police, on the directing boards of national or private banks—decolonisation is quite simply the replacing of a certain "species" of men by another "species" of men. Without any period of transition, there is a total, complete and absolute substitution. It is true that we could equally well stress the rise of a new nation, the setting up of a new State, its diplomatic relations, and its economic and political trends. But we have precisely chosen to speak of that kind of *tabula rasa* which characterises at the outset all decolonisation. Its unusual importance is that it constitutes, from the very first day, the minimum demands of the colonised. To tell the truth, the proof of success lies in a whole social structure being changed from the bottom up. The extraordinary importance of this change is that it is willed, called for, demanded. The need for this change exists in its crude state, impetuous and compelling, in the consciousness and in the lives of the men and women who are colonised. But the possibility of this change is equally experienced in the form of a terrifying future in the consciousness of another (species) of men and women: the colonisers.

Decolonisation, which sets out to change the order of the world, is, obviously, a programme of complete disorder. But it cannot come as a result of magical practices, nor of a natural shock, nor of a friendly understanding. Decolonisation, as we know, is a historical process: that is to say that it cannot be understood, it cannot become intelligible nor clear to itself except in the exact measure that we can discern the movements which give it historical form and content. Decolonisation is the meeting of two forces, opposed to each other by their very nature, which in fact owe their originality to that sort of substantification which results from and is nourished by the situation in the colonies. Their first encounter was marked by violence and their existence together—that is to say the exploitation of the native by the settler—was carried on by dint of a great array of bayonets and cannon. The settler and the native are old acquaintances. In fact, the settler is right when he speaks of knowing "them" well. For it is the settler who has brought the native into existence and who perpetuates his existence. The settler owes the fact of his very existence, that is to say his property, to the colonial system.

Decolonisation never takes place un-noticed, for it influences individuals and modifies them fundamentally. It transforms spectators crushed with their inessentiality into privileged actors, with the grandiose glare of history's floodlights upon them. It brings a natural rhythm into existence, introduced by new men, and with it a new language and a new humanity. Decolonisation is the veritable creation of new men. But this creation owes nothing of its legitimacy to any supernatural power; the "thing" which has been colonised becomes man during the same process by which it frees itself.

In decolonisation, there is therefore the need of a complete calling in question of the colonial situation. If we wish to describe it precisely, we might find it in the well-known words: "The last shall be first and the first last." Decolonisation is the putting into practice of this sentence. That is why, if we try to describe it, all decolonisation is successful.

The naked truth of decolonisation evokes for us the searing bullets and blood-stained knives which emanate from it. For if the last shall be first, this will only come to pass after a murderous and decisive struggle between the two protagonists. That affirmed intention to place the last at the head of things, and to make them climb at a pace (too quickly, some say) the well-known steps which characterise an organised society, can only triumph if we use all means to turn the scale, including, of course, that of violence.

You do not turn any society, however primitive it may be, upside-down with such a programme if you are not decided from the very beginning, that is to say from the actual formulation of that programme, to overcome all the obstacles that you will come across in so doing. The native who decides to put the programme into practice, and to become its moving force, is ready for violence at all times. From birth it is clear to him that this narrow world, strewn with prohibitions, can only be called in question by absolute violence.

The colonial world is a world divided into compartments. It is probably unnecessary to recall the existence of native quarters and European quarters, of schools for natives and schools for Europeans; in the same way we need not recall Apartheid in South Africa. Yet, if we examine closely this system of compartments, we will at least be able to reveal the lines of force it implies. This approach to the colonial world, its ordering and its geographical lay-out will allow us to mark out the lines on which a decolonised society will be reorganised.

The colonial world is a world cut in two. The dividing line, the frontiers are shown by barracks and police stations. In the colonies it is the policeman and the soldier who are the official, instituted go-betweens, the spokesmen of the settler and his rule of oppression. In capitalist societies the educational system, whether lay or clerical, the structure of moral reflexes handed down from father to son, the exemplary honesty of workers who are given a medal after fifty years of good and loyal service, and the affection which springs from harmonious relations and good behaviour—all these esthetic expressions of respect for the established order serve to create around the exploited person an atmosphere of submission and of inhibition which lightens the task of policing considerably. In the capitalist countries a multitude of moral teachers, counsellors and "bewilderers," separate the exploited from those in power. In the colonial countries, on the contrary, the policeman and the soldier, by their immediate presence and their frequent and direct action maintain contact with the native and advise him by means of rifle-butts and napalm not to budge. It is obvious here that the agents of government speak the language of pure force. The intermediary does not lighten the oppression, nor seek to hide the domination; he shows them up and puts them into practice with the clear conscience of an upholder of the peace; yet he is the bringer of violence into the home and into the mind of the native.

The zone where the natives live is not complementary to the zone inhabited by the settlers. The two zones are opposed, but not in the service of a higher unity. Obedient to the rules of pure Aristotelian logic, they both follow the principle of reciprocal exclusivity. No conciliation is possible, for of the two terms, one is superfluous. The settlers' town is a strongly built town, all made of stone and steel. It is a brightly-lit town; the streets are covered with asphalt, and the garbage cans swallow all the leavings, unseen, unknown and hardly thought about. The settler's feet are never visible, except perhaps in the sea; but there you're never close enough to see them. His feet are protected by strong shoes although the streets of his town are clean and even, with no holes or stones. The settler's town is a well-fed town, an easy-going town; its belly is always full of good things. The settler's town is a town of white people, of foreigners.

The town belonging to the colonised people, or at least the native town, the negro village, the medina, the reservation, is a place of ill fame, peopled by men of evil repute. They are born there, it matters little where or how; they die there, it matters not where, nor how. It is a world without spaciousness; men live there on top of each other, and their huts are built one on top of the other. The native town is a hungry town, starved of bread, of meat, of shoes, of coal, of light. The native town is a crouching village, a town on its knees, a town wallowing in the mire. It is a town of niggers and dirty arabs. The look that the native turns on the settler's town is a look of lust, a look of envy; it expresses his dreams of possession—all manner of possession: to sit at the settler's table, to sleep in the settler's bed, with his wife if possible. The colonised man is an envious man. And this the settler knows very well; when their glances meet he ascertains bitterly, always on the defensive "They want to take our place." It is true, for there is no native who does not dream at least once a day of setting himself up in the settler's place.

This world divided into compartments, this world cut in two is inhabited by two different species. The originality of the colonial context is that economic reality, inequality and the immense difference of ways of life never come to mask the human realities. When you examine at close quarters the colonial context, it is evident that what parcels out the world is to begin with the fact of belonging to or not belonging to a given race, a given species. In the colonies the economic substructure is also a superstructure. The cause is the consequence; you are rich because you are white, you are white because you are rich. This is why Marxist analysis should always be slightly stretched every time we have to do with the colonial problem.

Everything up to and including the very nature of precapitalist society, so well explained by Marx, must here be thought out again. The serf is in essence different from the knight, but a reference to divine right is necessary to legitimise this statutory difference. In the colonies, the foreigner coming from another country imposed his rule by means of guns and machines. In defiance of his successful transplantation, in spite of his appropriation, the settler still remains a foreigner. It is neither the act of owning factories, nor estates, nor a bank balance which distinguishes the governing classes. The governing race is first and foremost those who come from elsewhere, those who are unlike the original inhabitants, "the others."

The violence which has ruled over the ordering of the colonial world, which has ceaselessly drummed the rhythm for the destruction of native social forms and broken up without reserve the systems of reference of the economy, the customs of dress and external life, that same violence will be claimed and taken over by the native at the moment when, deciding to embody history in his own person, he surges into the forbidden quarters. To wreck the colonial world is henceforward a mental picture of action which is very clear, very easy to understand and which may be assumed by each one of the individuals which constitute the colonised people. To break up the colonial world does not mean that after the frontiers have been abolished lines of communication will be set up between the two zones. The destruction of the colonial world is no more and no less that the abolition of one zone, its burial in the depths of the earth or its expulsion from the country.

The natives' challenge to the colonial world is not a rational confrontation of points of view. It is not a treatise on the universal, but the untidy affirmation of an original idea propounded as an absolute. The colonial world is a Manichean world. It is not enough for the settler to delimit physically, that is to say with the help of the army and the police force, the place of the native. As if to show the totalitarian character of colonial exploitation the settler paints the native as a sort of quintessence of evil.[1] Native society is not simply described as a society lacking in values. It is not enough for the colonist to affirm that those values have disappeared from, or still better never existed in, the colonial world. The native is declared insensible to ethics; he represents not only the absence of values, but also the negation of values. He is, let us dare to admit, the enemy of values, and in this sense he is the absolute evil. He is the corrosive element, destroying all that comes near him; he is the deforming element, defiguring all that has to do with beauty or morality; he is the depository of maleficent powers, the unconscious and irretrievable instrument of blind forces. Monsieur Meyer could thus state seriously in the French National Assembly that the Republic must not be prostituted by allowing the Algerian people to become part of it. All values, in fact are irrevocably poisoned and diseased as soon as they are allowed in contact with the colonised race. The customs of the colonised people, their traditions, their myths—above all, their myths—are the very sign of that poverty of spirit and of their constitutional depravity. That is why we must put the DDT which destroys parasites, the bearers of disease, on the same level as the Christian religion which wages war on embryonic heresies and instincts, and on evil as yet unborn. The recession of yellow fever and the advance of evangelisation form part of the same balance-sheet. But the triumphant *communiqués* from the missions are in fact a source of information concerning the implantation of foreign influences in the core of the colonised people. I speak of the Christian religion, and no one need be astonished. The Church in the colonies is the white people's Church, the foreigner's Church. She does not call the native to God's ways but to the ways of the white man, of the master, of the oppressor. And as we know, in this matter many are called but few chosen.

At times this Manicheism goes to its logical conclusion and dehumanises the native, or to speak plainly it turns him into an animal. In fact, the terms the settler uses when he mentions the native are zoological terms. He speaks of the yellow man's reptilian motions, of the stink of the native quarter, of breeding swarms, of foulness, of spawn, of gesticulations. When the settler seeks to describe the native fully in exact terms he constantly refers to the bestiary. The European rarely hits on a picturesque style; but the native, who knows what is in the mind of the settler, guesses at once what he is thinking of. Those hordes of vital statistics, those hysterical masses, those faces bereft of all humanity, those distended bodies which are like nothing on earth, that mob without beginning or end, those children who seem to belong to nobody, that laziness stretched out in the sun, that vegetative rhythm of life—all this forms part of the colonial vocabulary. General de Gaulle speaks of "the yellow multitudes" and François Mauriac of the black, brown and yellow masses which soon will be unleashed. The native knows all this, and laughs to himself every time he spots an allusion to the animal world in the other's words. For he knows that he is not an animal; and it is precisely at the moment he realises his humanity that he begins to sharpen the weapons with which he will secure its victory.

As soon as the native begins to pull on his moorings, and to cause anxiety to the settler, he is handed over to well-meaning souls who in cultural congresses point out to him the specificity and wealth of Western values. But every time Western values are mentioned they produce in the native a sort of stiffening or muscular lock-jaw. During the period of decolonisation, the native's reason is appealed to. He is offered definite values, he is told frequently that decolonisation need not mean regression, and that he must put his trust in qualities which are well-tried, solid and highly esteemed. But it so happens that when the native hears a speech about Western culture he pulls out his knife—or at least he makes sure it is within reach. The violence with which the supremacy of white values is affirmed and the aggressiveness which has permeated the victory of these values over the ways of life and of thought of the native mean that, in revenge, the native laughs in mockery when Western values are mentioned in front of him. In the colonial context the settler only ends his work of breaking in the native when the latter admits loudly and intelligibly the supremacy of the white man's values. In the period of decolonisation, the colonised masses mock at these very values, insult them and vomit them up.

This phenomenon is ordinarily masked because, during the period of decolonisation, certain colonised intellectuals have begun a dialogue with the bourgeoisie of the colonialist country. During this phase, the indigenous population is discerned only as an indistinct mass. The few native personalities whom the colonialist bourgeois have come to know here and there have not sufficient influence on that immediate discernment to give rise to nuances. On the other hand, during the period of liberation, the colonialist bourgeoisie looks feverishly for contacts with the *élite*, and it is with these *élite* that the familiar dialogue concerning values is carried on. The colonialist bourgeoisie, when it realises that it is impossible for it to maintain its domination over the colonial countries, decides to carry out a rear-guard action with regard to culture, values, techniques and so on. Now what we must never forget is that the immense majority of colonised peoples is oblivious of these problems. For a colonised people the most essential value, because the most concrete, is first and foremost the land: the land which will bring them bread and, above all, dignity. But this dignity has nothing to do with the dignity of the human individual: for that human individual has never heard tell of it. All that the native has seen in his country is that they can freely arrest him, beat him, starve him: and no professor of ethics, no priest has ever come to be beaten in his place, nor to share their bread with him. As far as the native is concerned, morality is very concrete; it is to silence the settler's defiance, to break his flaunting violence—in a word, to put him out of the picture. The well-known principle that all men are equal will be illustrated in the colonies from the moment that the native claims that he is the equal of the settler. One step more, and he is ready to fight to be more than the settler. In fact, he has already decided to eject him and to take his place; as we see it, it is a whole material and moral universe which is breaking up. The intellectual who for his part has followed the colonialist with regard to the universal abstract will fight in order that the settler and the native may live together in peace in a new world. But the thing he does not see, precisely because he is permeated by colonialism and all its ways of thinking is that the settler, from the moment that the colonial context disappears, has no longer any interest in remaining or in co-existing. It is not by chance that, even before any negotiation[2] between the Algerian and French governments has taken place, the European minority which calls itself "liberal" has already made its position clear: it demands nothing more nor less than twofold citizenship. By setting themselves apart in an abstract manner, the liberals try to force the settler into taking a very concrete jump into the unknown. Let us admit it, the settler knows perfectly well that no phraseology can be a substitute for reality.

Thus the native discovers that his life, his breath, his beating heart are the same as those of the settler. He finds out that the settler's skin is not of any more value than a native's skin; and it must be said that this discovery shakes the world in a very necessary manner. All the new, revolutionary assurance of the native stems from it. For if, in fact, my life is worth as much as the settler's, his glance no longers shrivels me up nor freezes me, and his voice no longer turns me into stone. I am no longer on tenterhooks in his presence; in fact, I don't give a damn for him. Not only does his presence no longer trouble me, but I am already preparing such efficient ambushes for him that soon there will be no way out but that of flight.

We have said that the colonial context is characterised by the dichotomy which it imposes upon the whole people. Decolonisation unifies that people by the radical decision to remove from it its heterogenity, and by unifying it on a national, sometimes a racial, basis. We know the fierce words of the Senegalese patriots, referring to the manœuvres of their president, Senghor: "We have demanded that the higher posts should be given to Africans; and now Senghor is Africanising the Europeans." That is to say that the native can see clearly and immediately if decolonisation has come to pass or no, for his minimum demands are simply that the last shall be first.

But the native intellectual brings variants to this petition, and, in fact, he seems to have good reasons: higher civil servants, technicians, specialists—all seem to be needed. Now, the ordinary native interprets these unfair promotions as so many acts of sabotage, and he is often heard to declare: "It wasn't worth while, then, our becoming independent . . ."

In the colonial countries where a real struggle for freedom has taken place, where the blood of the people has flowed and where the length of the period of armed warfare has favoured the backward surge of intellectuals towards bases grounded in the people, we can observe a genuine eradication of the superstructure built by these intellectuals from the bourgeois colonialist environment. The colonialist bourgeoisie, in its narcissistic dialogue, expounded by the members of its universities, had in fact deeply implanted in the minds of the colonised intellectual that the essential qualities remain eternal in spite of all the blunders men may make: the essential qualities of the West, of course. The native intellectual accepted the cogency of these ideas, and deep down in his brain you could always find a vigilant sentinel ready to defend the Greco-Latin pedestal. Now it so happens that during the struggle for liberation, at the moment that the native intellectual comes into touch again with his people, this artificial sentinel is turned into dust. All the Mediterranean values—the triumph of the human individual, of clarity and of beauty—become lifeless, colourless knick-knacks. All those speeches seem like collections of dead words; those values which seemed to uplift the soul are revealed as worthless, simply because they have nothing to do with the concrete conflict in which the people is engaged.

Individualism is the first to disappear. The native intellectual had learnt from his masters that the individual ought to express himself fully. The colonialist bourgeoisie had hammered into the native's mind the idea of a society of individuals where each person shuts himself up in his own subjectivity, and whose only wealth is individual thought. Now the native who has the opportunity to return to the people during the struggle for freedom will discover the falseness of this theory. The very forms of organisation of the struggle will suggest to him a different vocabulary. Brother, sister, friend—these are words outlawed by the colonialist bourgeoisie, because for them my brother is my purse, my friend is part of my scheme for getting on. The native intellectual takes part, in a sort of *auto-da-fé,* in the destruction of all his idols: egoism, recrimination that springs from pride, and the childish stupidity of those who always want to have the last word. Such a colonised intellectual, dusted over by colonial culture, will in the same way discover the substance of village assemblies, the cohesion of people's committees, and the extraordinary fruitfulness of local meetings and groupments. Henceforward, the interests of one will be the interests of all, for in concrete fact *everyone* will be discovered by the troops, *everyone* will be massacred—or *everyone* will be saved. The motto (look out for yourself), the atheist's method of salvation, is in this context forbidden.

Self-criticism has been much talked about of late, but few people realise that it is an African institution. Whether in the *djemaas* [3] of Northern Africa or in the meetings of Western Africa, tradition demands that the quarrels which occur in a village should be settled in public. It is communal self-criticism, of course, and with a note of humour, because everybody is relaxed, and because in the last resort we all want the same things. But the more the intellectual imbibes the atmosphere of the people, the more completely he abandons the habits of calculation, of unwonted silence, of mental reservations, and shakes off the spirit of concealment. And it is true that already at that level we can say that the community triumphs, and that it spreads its own light and its own reason.

But it so happens sometimes that decolonisation occurs in areas which have not been sufficiently shaken by the struggle for liberation, and there may be found those same know-all, smart, wily intellectuals. We find intact in them the manners and forms of thought picked up during their association with the colonialist bourgeoisie. Spoilt children of yesterday's colonialism and of today's national governments, they organise the loot of whatever national resources exist. Without pity, they use today's national distress as a means of getting on through scheming and legal robbery, by import-export combines, limited liability companies, gambling on the stock-exchange, or unfair promotion. They are insistent in their demands for the nationalisation of commerce, that is to say the reservation of markets and advantageous bargains for nationals only. As far as doctrine is concerned, they proclaim the pressing necessity of nationalising the robbery of the nation. In this arid phase of national life, the so-called period of austerity, the success of their depredations is swift to call forth the violence and anger of the people. For this same people, poverty-stricken yet independent, comes very quickly to possess a social conscience in the African and international context of today; and this the petty individualists will quickly learn.

In order to assimilate and to experience the oppressor's culture, the native has had to leave certain of his intellectual possessions in pawn. These pledges include his adoption of the forms of thought of the colonialist bourgeoisie. This is very noticeable in the inaptitude of the native intellectual to carry on a two-sided discussion; for he cannot eliminate himself when confronted with an object or an idea. On the other hand, when once he begins to militate among the people he is struck with wonder and amazement; he is literally disarmed by their good faith and honesty. The danger that will haunt him continually is that of becoming the uncritical mouthpiece of the masses; he becomes a kind of yes-man who nods assent at every word coming from the people, which he interprets as considered judgments. Now, the *fellah,* the unemployed man, the starving native do not lay a claim to the truth; they do not *say* that they represent the truth, for they *are* the truth.

Objectively, the intellectual behaves in this phase like a common opportunist. In fact he has not stopped manœuvring. There is never any question of his being either rejected or welcomed by the people. What they ask is simply that all resources should be pooled. The inclusion of the native intellectual in the upward surge of the masses will in this case be differentiated by a curious cult of detail. That is not to say that the people are hostile to analysis; on the contrary, they like having things explained to them, they are glad to understand a line of argument and they like to see where they are going. But at the beginning of his association with the people the native intellectual over-stresses details and thereby comes to forget that the defeat of colonialism is the real object of the struggle. Carried away by the multitudinous aspects of the fight, he tends to concentrate on local tasks, performed with enthusiasm but almost always too solemnly. He fails to see the whole of the movement all the time. He introduces the idea of special disciplines, of specialised functions, of departments within the terrible stone crusher, the fierce mixing machine which a popular revolution is. He is occupied in action on a particular front, and it so happens that he loses sight of the unity of the movement. Thus, if a local defeat is inflicted, he may well be drawn into doubt, and from thence to despair. The people, on the other hand, take their stand from the start on the broad and inclusive positions of *Bread and the land:* how can we obtain the land, and bread to eat? And this obstinate point of view of the masses, which may seem shrunken and limited, is in the end the most worthwhile and the most *efficient* mode of procedure.

The problem of truth ought also to be considered. In every age, among the people, truth is the property of the national cause. No absolute verity, no discourse on the purity of the soul can shake this position. The native replies to the living lie of the colonial situation by an equal falsehood. His dealings with his fellow-nationals are open; they are strained and incomprehensible with regard to the settlers. Truth is that which hurries on the break-up of the colonialist regime; it is that which promotes the emergence of the nation; it is all that protects the natives, and ruins the foreigners. In this colonialist context there is no truthful behaviour: and the good is quite simply that which is evil for "them."

Thus we see that the primary Manicheism which governed colonial society is preserved intact during the period of decolonisation; that is to say that the settler never ceases to be the enemy, the opponent, the foe that must be overthrown. The oppressor, in his own sphere, starts the process, a process of domination, of exploitation and of pillage, and in the other sphere the coiled, plundered creature which is the native provides fodder for the process as best he can, the process which moves uninterruptedly from the banks of the colonial territory to the palaces and the docks of the mother country. In this becalmed zone the sea has a smooth surface, the palmtree stirs gently in the breeze, the waves lap against the pebbles, and raw materials are ceaselessly transported, justifying the presence of the settler: and all the while the native, bent double, more dead than alive, exists interminably in an unchanging dream. The settler makes history; his life is an epoch, an Odyssey. He is the absolute beginning: "This land was created by us;" he is the unceasing cause: "If we leave, all is lost, and the country will go back to the Middle Ages." Over against him torpid creatures, wasted by fevers, obsessed by ancestral customs, form an almost inorganic background for the innovating dynamism of colonial mercantilism.

The settler makes history and is conscious of making it. And because he constantly refers to the history of his mother country, he clearly indicates that he himself is the extension of that mother-country. Thus the history which he writes is not the history of the country which he plunders but the history of his own nation in regard to all that she skims off, all that she violates and starves.

The immobility to which the native is condemned can only be called in question if the native decides to put an end to the history of colonisation—the history of pillage—and to bring into existence the history of the nation—the history of decolonisation.

A world divided into compartments, a motionless, Manicheistic world, a world of statues: the statue of the general who carried out the conquest, the statue of the engineer who built the bridge; a world which is sure of itself, which crushes with its stones the backs flayed by whips: this is the colonial world. The native is a being hemmed in; apartheid is simply one form of the division into compartments of the colonial world. The first thing which the native learns is to stay in his place, and not to go beyond certain limits. This is why the dreams of the native are always of muscular prowess; his dreams are of action and of aggression. I dream I am jumping, swimming, running, climbing; I dream that I burst out laughing, that I span a river in one stride, or that I am followed by a flood of motor-cars which never catch up with me. During the period of colonisation, the native never stops achieving his freedom from nine in the evening until six in the morning.

The colonised man will first manifest this aggressiveness which has been deposited in his bones against his own people. This is the period when the niggers beat each other up, and the police and magistrates do not know which way to turn when faced with the astonishing waves of crime in North Africa. We shall see later how this phenomenon should be judged.[4] When the native is confronted with the colonial order of things, he finds he is in a state of permanent tension. The settler's world is a hostile world, which spurns the native, but at the same time it is a world of which he is envious. We have seen that the native never ceases to dream of putting himself in the place of the settler—not of becoming the settler but of substituting himself for the settler. This hostile world, ponderous and aggressive because it fends off the colonised masses with all the harshness it is capable of, represents not merely a hell from which the swiftest flight possible is desirable, but also a paradise close at hand which is guarded by terrible watchdogs.

The native is always on the alert, for since he can only make out with difficulty the many symbols of the colonial world, he is never sure whether or not he has crossed the frontier. Confronted with a world ruled by the settler, the native is always presumed guilty. But the native's guilt is never a guilt which he accepts; it is rather a kind of curse, a sort of sword of Damocles, for, in his innermost spirit, the native admits no accusation. He is overpowered but not tamed; he is treated as an inferior but he is not convinced of his inferiority. He is patiently waiting until the settler is off his guard to fly at him. The native's muscles are always tensed. You can't say that he is terrorized, or even apprehensive. He is in fact ready at a moment's notice to exchange the *rôle* of the quarry for that of the hunter. The native is an oppressed person whose permanent dream is to become the persecutor. The symbols of social order—the police, the bugle-cans in the barracks, military parades and the waving flags—are at one and the same time inhibitory and stimulating: for they do not convey the message "Don't dare to budge;" rather, they cry out "Get ready to attack." And, in fact, if the native had any tendency to fall asleep and to forget, the settler's hauteur and the settler's anxiety to test the strength of the colonial system would remind him at every turn that the great show-down cannot be put off indefinitely. That impulse to take the settler's place implies a tonicity of muscles the whole time; and in fact we know that in certain emotional conditions the presence of an obstacle accentuates the tendency towards motion.

The settler-native relationship is a mass relationship. The settler pits brute force against the weight of numbers. He is an exhibitionist. His preoccupation with security makes him remind the native out loud that there he alone is master. The settler keeps alive in the native an anger which he deprives of outlet; the native is trapped in the tight links of the chains of colonialism. But we have seen that inwardly the settler can only achieve a pseudo petrification. The native's muscular tension finds outlet regularly in bloodthirsty explosions—in tribal warfare, in feuds between septs, and in quarrels between individuals.

Where individuals are concerned, a positive negation of common sense is evident. While the settler or the policeman has the right the live-long day to strike the native, to insult him and to make him crawl to them, you will see the native reaching for his knife at the slightest hostile or aggressive glance cast on him by another native; for the last resort of the native is to defend his personality *vis-à-vis* his brother. Tribal feuds only serve to perpetuate old grudges deep buried in the memory. By throwing himself with all his force into the *vendetta*, the native tries to persuade himself that colonialism does not exist, that everything is going on as before, that history continues. Here on the level of communal organisations we clearly discern the well-known behaviour patterns of avoidance. It is as if plunging into a fraternal blood-bath allowed them to ignore the obstacle, and to put off till later the choice, nevertheless inevitable, which opens up the question of armed resistance to colonialism. Thus collective auto destruction in a very concrete form is one of the ways in which the native's muscular tension is set free. All these patterns of conduct are those of the death reflex when faced with danger, a suicidal behaviour which proves to the settler (whose existence and domination is by them all the more justified) that these men are not reasonable human beings. In the same way the native manages to by-pass the settler. A belief in fatality removes all blame from the oppressor; the cause of misfortunes and of poverty is attributed to God; He is Fate. In this way the individual accepts the disintegration ordained by God, bows down before the settler and his lot, and by a kind of interior restabilization acquires a stony calm.

Meanwhile, however, life goes on, and the native will strengthen the inhibitions which contain his aggressiveness by drawing on the terrifying myths which are so frequently found in underdeveloped communities. There are maleficent spirits which intervene every time a step is taken in the wrong direction, leopard-men, serpent-men, six-legged dogs, zombies—a whole series of tiny animals or giants which create around the native a world of prohibitions, of barriers and of inhibitions far more terrifying than the world of the settler. This magical superstructure which permeates native society fulfils certain well-defined functions in the dynamism of the libido. One of the characteristics of under-developed societies is in fact that the libido is first and foremost the concern of a group, or of the family. The feature of communities whereby a man who dreams that he has sexual relations with a woman other than his own must confess it in public and pay a fine in kind or in working days to the injured husband or family is fully described by ethnologists. We may note in passing that this proves that the so-called prehistoric societies attach great importance to the unconscious.

The atmosphere of myth and magic frightens me and so takes on an undoubted reality. By terrifying me, it integrates me in the traditions and the history of my district or of my tribe, and at the same time it reassures me, it gives me a status, as it were an identification paper. In underdeveloped countries the occult sphere is a sphere belonging to the community which is entirely under magical jurisdiction. By entangling myself in this inextricable network where actions are repeated with crystalline inevitability, I find the everlasting world which belongs to me, and the perenniality which is thereby affirmed of the world belonging to us. Believe me, the zombies are more terrifying than the settlers; and in consequence the problem is no longer that of keeping oneself right with the colonial world and its barbed-wire entanglements, but of considering three times before urinating, spitting or going out into the night.

The supernatural, magical powers reveal themselves as essentially personal; the settler's powers are infinitely shrunken, stamped with their alien origin. We no longer really need to fight against them since what counts is the frightening enemy created by myths. We perceive that all is settled by a permanent confrontation on the phantasmic plane.

It has always happened in the struggle for freedom that such a people, formerly lost in an imaginary maze, a prey to unspeakable terrors yet happy to lose themselves in a dreamlike torment, such a people becomes unhinged, reorganises itself, and in blood and tears gives birth to very real and immediate action. Feeding the *moudjahidines*,[5] posting sentinels, coming to the help of families which lack the bare necessities, or taking the place of a husband who has been killed or imprisoned: such are the concrete tasks to which the people is called during the struggle for freedom.

In the colonial world, the emotional sensitivity of the native is kept on the surface of his skin like an open sore which flinches from the caustic agent; and the psyche shrinks back, obliterates itself and finds outlet in muscular demonstrations which have caused certain very wise men to say that the native is a hysterical type. This sensitive emotionalism, watched by invisible keepers who are however in unbroken contact with the core of the personality, will find its fulfillment through eroticism in the driving forces behind the crisis' dissolution.

On another level we see the native's emotional sensibility exhausting itself in dances which are more or less ecstatic. This is why any study of the colonial world should take into consideration the phenomena of the dance and of possession. The native's relaxation takes precisely the form of a muscular orgy in which the most acute aggressivity and the most impelling violence are canalised, transformed and conjured away. The circle of the dance is a permissive circle: it protects and permits. At certain times on certain days, men and women come together at a given place, and there, under the solemn eye of the tribe, fling themselves into a seemingly unorganised pantomime, which is in reality extremely systematic, in which by various means—shakes of the head, bending of the spinal column, throwing of the whole body backwards—may be deciphered as in an open book the huge effort of a community to exorcise itself, to liberate itself, to explain itself. There are no limits—inside the circle. The hillock up which you have toiled as if to be nearer to the moon; the river bank down which you slip as if to show the connection between the dance and ablutions, cleansing and purification—these are sacred places. There are no limits—for in reality your purpose in coming together is to allow the accumulated libido, the hampered aggressivity to dissolve as in a volcanic eruption. Symbolical killings, fantastic rides, imaginary mass murders—all must be brought out. The evil humours are undammed, and flow away with a din as of molten lava.

One step further and you are completely possessed. In fact, these are actually organised *séances* of possession and exorcism; they include vampirism, possession by djinns, by zombies, and by Legba, the famous god of the Voodoo. This disintegrating of the personality, this splitting and dissolution, all this fulfils a primordial function in the organism of the colonial world. When they set out, the men and women were impatient, stamping their feet in a state of nervous excitement; when they return, peace has been restored to the village; it is once more calm and unmoved.

During the struggle for freedom, a marked alienation from these practices is observed. The native's back is to the wall, the knife is at his throat (or, more precisely, the electrode at his genitals): he will have no more call for his fancies. After centuries of unreality, after having wallowed in the most outlandish phantoms, at long last the native, gun in hand, stands face to face with the only forces which contend for his life—the forces of colonialism. And the youth of a colonised country, growing up in an atmosphere of shot and fire, may well make a mock of, and does not hesitate to pour scorn upon the zombies of his ancestors, the horses with two heads, the dead who rise again, and the djinns who rush into your body while you yawn. The native discovers reality and transforms it into the pattern of his customs, into the practice of violence and into his plan for freedom.

We have seen that this same violence, though kept very much on the surface all through the colonial period, yet turns in the void. We have also seen that it is canalised by the emotional outlets of dance and possession by spirits; we have seen how it is exhausted in fratricidal combats. Now the problem is to lay hold of this violence which is changing direction. When formerly it was appeased by myths and exercised its talents in finding fresh ways of committing mass suicide, now new conditions will make possible a completely new line of action.

CHAPTER 17

Excerpt from The Ballot or the Bullet

By Malcolm X

So, where do we go from here? First, we need some friends. We need some new allies. The entire civil-rights struggle needs a new interpretation, a broader interpretation. We need to look at this civil-rights thing from another angle—from the inside as well as from the outside. To those of us whose philosophy is black nationalism, the only way you can get involved in the civil-rights struggle is give it a new interpretation. That old interpretation excluded us. It kept us out. So, we're giving a new interpretation to the civil-rights struggle, an interpretation that will enable us to come into it, take part in it. And these handkerchief-heads who have been dillydallying and pussyfooting and compromising—we don't intend to let them pussyfoot and dillydally and compromise any longer.

How can you thank a man for giving you what's already yours? How then can you thank him for giving you only part of what's already yours? You haven't even made progress, if what's being given to you, you should have had already. That's not progress. And I love my Brother Lomax, the way he pointed out we're right back where we were in 1954. We're not even as far up as we were in 1954. We're behind where we were in 1954. There's more segregation now than there was in 1954. There's more racial animosity, more racial hatred, more racial violence today in 1964, than there was in 1954. Where is the progress?

And now you're facing a situation where the young Negro's coming up. They don't want to hear that "turn-the-other-cheek" stuff, no. In Jacksonville, those were teenagers, they were throwing Molotov cocktails. Negroes have never done that before. But it shows you there's a new deal coming in. There's new thinking coming in. There's new strategy coming in. It'll be Molotov cocktails this month, hand grenades next month, and something else next month. It'll be ballots, or it'll be bullets. It'll be liberty, or it will be death. The only difference about this kind of death—it'll be reciprocal. You know what is meant by "reciprocal?" That's one of Brother Lomax's words, I stole it from him. I don't usually deal with those big words because I don't usually deal with big people. I deal with small people. I find you can get a whole lot of small people and whip hell out of a whole lot of big people. They haven't got anything to lose, and they've got everything to gain. And they'll let you know in a minute: "It takes two to tango; when I go, you go."

The black nationalists, those whose philosophy is black nationalism, in bringing about this new interpretation of the entire meaning of civil rights, look upon it as meaning, as Brother Lomax has pointed out, equality of opportunity. Well, we're justified in seeking civil rights, if it means equality of opportunity, because all we're doing there is trying to collect for our investment. Our mothers and fathers invested sweat and blood. Three hundred and ten years we worked in this country without a dime in return—I mean without a dime in return. You let the white man walk around here talking about how rich this country is, but you never stop to think how it got rich so quick. It got rich because you made it rich.

You take the people who are in this audience right now. They're poor, we're all poor as individuals. Our weekly salary individually amounts to hardly anything. But if you take the salary of everyone in here collectively it'll fill up a whole lot of baskets. It's a lot of wealth. If you can collect the wages of just these people right here for a year, you'll be rich—richer than rich. When you look at it like that, think how rich Uncle Sam had to become, not with this handful, but millions of black people. Your and my mother and father, who didn't work an eight-hour shift, but worked from "can't see" in the morning until "can't see" at night, and worked for nothing, making the white man rich, making Uncle Sam rich.

This is our investment. This is our contribution—our blood. Not only did we give of our free labor, we gave of our blood. Every time he had a call to arms, we were the first ones in uniform. We died on every battlefield the white man had. We have made a greater sacrifice than anybody who's standing up in America today. We have made a greater contribution and have collected less. Civil rights, for those of us whose philosophy is black nationalism, means: "Give it to us now. Don't wait for next year. Give it to us yesterday, and that's not fast enough."

I might stop right here to point out one thing. Whenever you're going after something that belongs to you, anyone who's depriving you of the right to have it is a criminal. Understand that. Whenever you are going after something that is yours, you are within your legal rights to lay claim to it. And anyone who puts forth any effort to deprive you of that which is yours, is breaking the law, is a criminal. And this was pointed out by the Supreme Court decision. It outlawed segregation. Which means segregation is against the law. Which means a segregationist is breaking the law. A segregationist is a criminal. You can't label him as anything other than that. And when you demonstrate against segregation, the law is on your side. The Supreme Court is on your side.

Now, who is it that opposes you in carrying out the law? The police department itself. With police dogs and clubs. Whenever you demonstrate against segregation, whether it is segregated education, segregated housing, or anything else, the law is on your side, and anyone who stands in the way is not the law any longer. They are breaking the law, they are not representatives of the law. Any time you demonstrate against segregation and a man has the audacity to put a police dog on you, kill that dog, kill him, I'm telling you, kill that dog. I say it, if they put me in jail tomorrow, kill—that—dog. Then you'll put a stop to it. Now, if these white people in here don't want to see that kind of action, get down and tell the mayor to tell the police department to pull the dogs in. That's all you have to do. If you don't do it, someone else will.

If you don't take this kind of stand, your little children will grow up and look at you and think "shame." If you don't take an uncompromising stand—I don't mean go out and get violent; but at the same time you should never be nonviolent unless you run into some nonviolence. I'm nonviolent with those who are nonviolent with me. But when you drop that violence on me, then you've made me go insane, and I'm not responsible for what I do. And that's the way every Negro should get. Any time you know you're within the law, within your legal rights, within your moral rights, in accord with justice, then die for what you believe in. But don't die alone. Let your dying be reciprocal. This is what is meant by equality. What's good for the goose is good for the gander.

When we begin to get in this area, we need new friends, we need new allies. We need to expand the civil-rights struggle to a higher level—to the level of human rights. Whenever you are in a civil-rights struggle, whether you know it or not, you are confining yourself to the Jurisdiction of Uncle Sam. No one from the outside world can speak out in your behalf as long as your struggle is a civil-rights struggle. Civil rights comes within the domestic affairs of this country. All of our African brothers and our Asian brothers and our Latin-American brothers cannot open their mouths and interfere in the domestic affairs of the United States. And as long as it's civil rights, this comes under the jurisdiction of Uncle Sam.

But the United Nations has what's known as the charter of human rights, it has a committee that deals in human rights. You may wonder why all of the atrocities that have been committed in Africa and in Hungary and in Asia and in Latin America are brought before the UN, and the Negro problem is never brought before the UN. This is part of the conspiracy. This old, tricky, blue-eyed liberal who is supposed to be your and my friend, supposed to be in our corner, supposed to be subsidizing our struggle, and supposed to be acting in the capacity of an adviser, never tells you anything about human rights. They keep you wrapped up in civil rights. And you spend so much time barking up the civil-rights tree, you don't even know there's a human-rights tree on the same floor.

When you expand the civil-rights struggle to the level of human rights, you can then take the case of the black man in this country before the nations in the UN. You can take it before the General Assembly. You can take Uncle Sam before a world court. But the only level you can do it on is the level of human rights. Civil rights keeps you under his restrictions, under his jurisdiction. Civil rights keeps you in his pocket. Civil rights means you're asking Uncle Sam to treat you right. Human rights are something you were born with. Human rights are your God-given rights. Human rights are the rights that are recognized by all nations of this earth. And any time any one violates your human rights, you can take them to the world court. Uncle Sam's hands are dripping with blood, dripping with the blood of the black man in this country. He's the earth's number-one hypocrite. He has the audacity—yes, he has—imagine him posing as the leader of the free world. The free world!—and you over here singing "We Shall Overcome." Expand the civil-rights struggle to the level of human rights, take it into the United Nations, where our African brothers can throw their weight on our side, where our Asian brothers can throw their weight on our side, where our Latin-American brothers can throw their weight on our side, and where 800 million Chinamen are sitting there waiting to throw their weight on our side.

Let the world know how bloody his hands are. Let the world know the hypocrisy that's practiced over here. Let it be the ballot or the bullet. Let him know that it must be the ballot or the bullet.

CHAPTER 18

On Violence

By David Nicholson

Maybe things would have been different if instead of only being born to the culture I'd grown up in it as well. But I spent much of my childhood in Jamaica, and when my parents separated and my mother returned to America with her four children, this middle-class boy, whose dentist father and high school teacher mother had sent him to the Queen's Preparatory School in Kingston, was completely unprepared for what he found on the predatory streets and playgrounds of black Washington, D.C.

I had no sense of rhythm and I couldn't dance. I couldn't (and still can't) dribble well enough to play basketball. For years the purpose and the verbal agility of "the dozens" (which we called joneing) eluded me.

The worst, though, was the casual violence—everybody seemed to want to fight. Someone pushed someone else in line waiting to go out to the playground. Someone said something about someone else's mother. Someone said someone had said something about a third someone else's mother. Sex didn't matter (some girls terrified all but the most fearless boys) and neither did the pretext. If a serious enough offense had been committed, or even merely alleged, push soon came to shove as books were dropped and fists raised and the aggrieved parties—surrounded by a crowd gleefully chanting "Fight! Fight!"—circled each other with murder in their eyes.

Raised to believe gentlemen obeyed two essential commandments—they did not hit girls, and they did not hit anyone who wore glasses—I would have been fixed in an insoluble moral quandary if a glasses-wearing girl had dared me to fight. But somehow it was arranged that I would fight another boy in the fifth-grade class of Mrs. Omega P. Millen (so named, she'd told us, because her mother had forsworn more children after her birth). I don't remember how it happened, but someone probably offered the usual reasons—Furman had said something about my mother or I'd said something about his. The truth, though, was that Furman, fair-skinned and freckled, with curly, ginger-colored hair, was as much of an outsider because of his color as I was because of my accent. A fight would decide which of us belonged.

We met in an alley near school. When it was over, the spectators who'd gathered, jamming the mouth of the alley so that Furman and I had to be escorted in, must have been as disappointed as ticketholders who'd mortgaged their homes for ringside seats at the Tyson-Spinks title fight. Furman and I circled each other warily until he pushed me or I pushed him or someone in the crowd pushed us into each other. After a moment or two of wrestling on the dirty brick paving, rolling around on the trash and broken glass, I shoved Furman away and stood.

Memory plays tricks, of course, but I don't think I was afraid. Not as afraid as I would be later, when, coming home from the High's Dairy Store on Rhode Island Avenue with a quart of ice cream on Sunday, some bigger boy, backed by two or three of his cronies, demanded a nickel. If I said I didn't have one, they'd leave me to choose between two humiliations—having my pockets searched or fighting all three, one after the other. And I certainly wasn't as afraid as I would be when, as I walked home alone, four or five boys jumped me because I'd strayed into a neighborhood where outsiders had to be ready to fight just to walk down the street.

So what I remember feeling in the alley was not fear but puzzlement. The fight with Furman had seemed like a joke right up to the moment we'd squared off against one another. I hadn't taken it seriously, and now it felt like a piece of foolishness that had gone too far. No one else seemed to have enough sense to call a halt, so it was up to me. I found my glasses, put them on, and announced I wasn't going to fight. I'd done nothing to Furman. He'd done nothing to me. And, besides, one of us might get hurt.

There was a moment of silence and then a low grumbling of disappointment as the boys and girls who'd come expecting to see a fight realized there wasn't going to be one. I went home, one or two friends walking with me, assuring me that it was all right, I didn't have to fight if I didn't want to.

But I knew they were wrong. And I knew they knew it too.

It is a terrible thing to be condemned by others as a coward, but it is even worse to condemn yourself as one. For that reason, I brood about that time in the alley more often than is probably healthy, even given that I'm a writer and my stock in trade is memories and the past. Lately, however, I've been thinking about it as I read, or read about, the new violence-laden autobiographies by black men—Nathan McCall's *Makes Me Wanna Holler*, Kody Scott's *Monster*. I don't listen to rap music (the phrase has always struck me as an oxymoron), but I'm aware that the genre has become one of art-imitating-life-imitating-art as entertainers like Tupac Shakur are arrested and charged with crimes ranging from sexual assault to murder. And then, if all that wasn't enough, there were the T-shirts and sweatshirts featuring Mike Tyson's face and the ominous legend "I'll be back," and those bearing the legend "Shut Up Bitch, or I'll O.J. You."

More and more it's begun to seem, as we enter the middle of the 1990s, that violence and black men go together as well as the fingers of the hand make up the fist. What's most troubling is that not only has the media seized on America's enduring bogeyman, the bad nigger, as an object of fear and pity, but that black men (and women) have also gleefully embraced that image. It's as if a generation, soured by disappointment in the post–civil rights era, has given up all hope of achievement and decided that it's almost as good to be feared as it is to be respected.

And so where does that leave me, who long ago eschewed violence, whether from fear or cowardice or simply because I couldn't see the point of it? Feeling at forty-three much the same as I'd felt facing Furman in the alley—that I'd been given a choice that really wasn't a choice. If I fought, I'd become like the rest of the boys. If I didn't, I'd be a sissy. What I really wanted was just to be me.

Perhaps I'm making too much out of all this. Perhaps that afternoon in the alley was part of some perfectly normal rite of passage. Perhaps all boys test each other to find out who will fight and who will not. And perhaps by not fighting Furman or, later, any of a number of bullies and thugs, I threw away the opportunity to earn their respect. Perhaps.

All I knew then was that the rules were different from those I'd learned growing up in Jamaica, and that while almost all of the children I'd known there were also black, violence was of mystifying importance to the black boys of Washington, D.C. One reason for the difference, I see now, was poverty. My school chums in Jamaica were all middle-class, but most of us in Mrs. Millen's (and later Miss Garner's) classroom were poor enough to relish our mid-morning snack of government-issue oatmeal cookies, soft and sweet at their centers, and half-pints of warm, slightly sour milk. On winter days, windows closed and the radiators steaming, the stale air in the classroom smelled faintly of sweat and dust and urine and unwashed clothes. I remember it as the smell of poverty and of crippling apathy.

Small wonder, then, that because so many of the boys had precious little except their bodies with which to celebrate life, violence became part of that celebration. It offered them a way of feeling masculine as well as the chance to be feared, to feel important.

But I never understood the tribal nature of the violence, the randomness and the gratuitousness of it, until I saw how they'd probably been introduced to it before they were aware of what was happening, before they were old enough to understand there might be other choices. I was driving past a public housing project one gray winter afternoon when I saw two boys facing each other on the brown lawn. Each boy howled, runny-nosed in fear, as the man towering over them directed their tiny fists at each other. They couldn't have been much older than three.

Years after my abortive fight with Furman in the alley, I had a summer job downtown in the District Building, working for an agency of the city government. Five of us, all high school or college students, were summer help. We spent the day sorting building plans and building permits in a narrow, dusty back room lined with filing cabinets and ceiling-high wooden shelves. Sometimes we had to deal with citizens seeking copies of plans or permits, but most of the time we were left alone to work by ourselves, only nominally supervised.

One of the other buys (I'll call him Earl) was a freshman or sophomore at Howard. Under other circumstances—if we'd met, say, in one of the integrated church coffee houses or drama groups I'd begun to frequent because they allowed me the freedom to be black and myself in ways segregated situations did not—perhaps Earl and I might have been friends. Skinny and bespectacled, we looked enough alike to be brothers. We read books and valued them. We spoke standard English. All of that, of course, set us apart from the other boys. For that reason, instead of becoming friends with Earl, I decided to hate him.

The other boys encouraged me, aiding and abetting, but they were only accomplices, because I had made up my own mind. We goaded Earl. We taunted him. Finally, one of the other boys told me Earl had dropped some of my files and picked them up without putting them back in order. Earl hadn't, of course, and I knew it. But I also knew my choice was to fight him or become identified with him. And Earl, with his suspiciously effeminate air of striving for refinement, was not someone I wanted to be identified with.

What happened was worse than if I had beaten him, worse than if he had fought back and beaten me. Earl simply refused to fight. He crumpled, stood crying, holding his glasses, begging me to leave him alone. I didn't hit him, but

I joined with the others in making him do my work as well as his own while the rest of us sat drinking sodas or coffee, watching and making jokes.

I wish now I'd done something else. That I'd refused to fight Earl. That I'd suggested we join forces to resist the others. That I'd gone, on his behalf, to complain to our supervisor. But I didn't. And, sickened, I learned a lesson—it felt no better to threaten violence against someone incapable of resisting than it had been to be the one threatened and equally incapable of resistance.

What's missing here is the kind Ellisonian epiphany—I am who I am, and no one else—that might have long ago allowed me to let go of all this. Instead, I've had to make do with patchwork realizations and small comforts.

One evening a few years ago I was standing on the street I grew up on, talking with a man I'd known since we were both children. He is younger than I am, so I hadn't known him well. Still, I knew him well enough to know he'd been comfortable on that street in ways I had not. So I was surprised when all of a sudden he told me he had always admired me. Puzzled but curious, I asked why, and he said it was because I hadn't stayed in the neighborhood; I'd left it to live other places and see other things.

For a moment I was speechless. I knew, of course, that there were qualities—the apparent cool and the readiness to deal that we call an ability to hang—that he possessed and I lacked. I envied him those. But it was inconceivable he might also envy me.

Hard on the heels of that realization came another. Life was a series of stages and I'd passed through one, but precisely because I'd long ago left that street I hadn't known it: violence was a function of age, even for black men (like the one I was talking to) who weren't middle-class and who lacked intellectual pretensions. A wishful capacity for it might remain one of the ways we defined ourselves, and were defined; however, the truth was that after a certain point even the bad boys were forced to realize they were no longer boys and that suddenly but almost imperceptibly they'd become one step too slow to continue in the game. It's then that, for all but the most stubborn, violence becomes a matter of ritual and voyeurism: football on Sundays, heated arguments in the barbershop, the heavyweight championship on pay-per-view.

During that same sojourn in the old neighborhood, I was walking to church one winter Sunday morning. I was almost there when I heard them, and then I rounded the corner and saw a man and a woman screaming at each other beside the iron fence in front of the churchyard while a little boy watched. A few late parishioners walked past, conscientiously ignoring them.

It's been long enough now so that the details are hazy. But I remember that he pushed her, and then she pushed him, and that they were screaming at each other. And I remember their faces, his young and still beardless, adorned with that practiced air of aggrievement I remembered from my childhood after one boy had sucker-punched another and gotten caught by Mrs. Millen or Miss Garner, an insolent glare that said, "Why you lookin' at me for? I ain't did shit." The girl's face would have been pretty except that it was twisted with tears and anger. The little boy stood a little away, looking at them, and what was terrifying about it was that his face showed no expression at all.

I stepped into it, right between them, begging them to calm down, circling with them, hands out to keep them apart. He was bigger than I am, and younger. He may have pushed me once, trying to reach past to get at her. She bent to pick up a brick and lunged after him. I held her back.

Finally the police came.

An hour or so later, when I was finally home, I started to shake, thinking about what I'd done, thinking about what could have happened if he'd had a gun or a knife, or if the two of them had turned on me. Mostly, though, I thought about the little boy, looking up at me from under the hood of his parka when I stooped to ask if he was all right. He'd nodded, almost diffidently, nothing in his eyes at all that I could read. And I had thought, as I patted him on the shoulder and said, "Everything's going to be okay," that I was lying, that it wasn't going to be okay at all.

Because in that moment I could see the past—and the futures—of so many of the boys I'd first encountered on the streets and playgrounds around First Street and Rhode Island Avenue. They'd all had the same look in their eyes, the same distancing of themselves from what was happening around them. In time, I thought, this boy, too, would go on to acquire the same wariness, a quality of disguised hurt, a quality of removal and disavowal. In some important way he, like them, would cease to care. It wasn't just that these boys had come to expect to be blamed when they really had done nothing, although that was part of it. No, what was really important was that they'd made it so that it didn't matter any more. Because they'd long ago discovered that the way to survive was to hide their real selves from the world. And no matter what happened, they would never, ever, let anything touch them.

I write this now for the boy I once was who almost had his love of books and poetry beaten out of him. I write it for Earl, wherever and whoever he is, as a way of asking his forgiveness for having humiliated him in a vain attempt to avenge my own humiliations. I write it for the boy whose parents fought in front of the church that winter morning, hoping he made it whole into manhood despite the odds against him. And I write it for the boys whose names I never knew or can't remember, the ones whose eyes in elementary school were deader than any child's should ever be. Now I understand, I feel the pain they could not admit. In this way perhaps I can also one day forgive them.

C H A P T E R 1 9

Nihilism in Black America

By Cornel West

> *We black folk, our history and our present being, are a mirror of all the manifold experiences of America. What we want, what we represent, what we endure is what America is. If we black folk perish, America will perish. If America has forgotten her past, then let her look into the mirror of our consciousness and she will see the* living *past living in the present, for our memories go back, through our black folk of today, through the recollections of our black parents, and through the tales of slavery told by our black grandparents, to the time when none of us, black or white, lived in this fertile land. The differences between black folk and white folk are not blood or color, and the ties that bind us are deeper than those that separate us. The common road of hope which we all traveled has brought us into a stronger kinship than any words, laws, or legal claims.*
>
> RICHARD WRIGHT,
> *12 Million Black Voices* (1941)

Recent discussions about the plight of African Americans—especially those at the bottom of the social ladder—tend to divide into two camps. On the one hand, there are those who highlight the *structural* constraints on the life chances of black people. Their viewpoint involves a subtle historical and sociological analysis of slavery, Jim Crowism, job and residential discrimination, skewed unemployment rates, inadequate health care, and poor education. On the other hand, there are those who stress the *behavioral* impediments on black upward mobility. They focus on the waning of the Protestant ethic—hard work, deferred gratification, frugality, and responsibility—in much of black America.

Those in the first camp—the liberal structuralists—call for full employment, health, education, and childcare programs, and broad affirmative action practices.

In short, a new, more sober version of the best of the New Deal and the Great Society: more government money, better bureaucrats, and an active citizenry. Those in the second camp—the conservative behaviorists—promote self-help programs, black business expansion, and nonpreferential job practices. They support vigorous "free market" strategies that depend on fundamental changes in how black people act and live. To put it bluntly, their projects rest largely upon a cultural revival of the Protestant ethic in black America.

Unfortunately, these two camps have nearly suffocated the crucial debate that should be taking place about the prospects for black America. This debate must go far beyond the liberal and conservative positions in three fundamental ways. First, we must acknowledge that structures and behavior are inseparable, that institutions and values go hand in hand. How people act and live are shaped—though in no way dictated or determined—by the larger circumstances in which they find themselves. These circumstances can be changed, their limits attenuated, by positive actions to elevate living conditions.

Second, we should reject the idea that structures are primarily economic and political creatures—an idea that sees culture as an ephemeral set of behavioral attitudes and values. Culture is as much a structure as the economy or politics; it is rooted in institutions such as families, schools, churches, synagogues, mosques, and communication industries (television, radio, video, music). Similarly, the economy and politics are not only influenced by values but also promote particular cultural ideals of the good life and good society.

Third, and most important, we must delve into the depths where neither liberals nor conservatives dare to tread, namely, into the murky waters of despair and dread that now flood the streets of black America. To talk about the depressing statistics of unemployment, infant mortality, incarceration, teenage pregnancy, and violent crime is one thing. But to face up to the monumental eclipse of hope, the unprecedented collapse of meaning, the incredible disregard for human (especially black) life and property in much of black America is something else.

The liberal/conservative discussion conceals the most basic issue now facing black America: *the nihilistic threat to its very existence.* This threat is not simply a matter of relative economic deprivation and political powerlessness—though economic well-being and political clout are requisites for meaningful black progress. It is primarily a question of speaking to the profound sense of psychological depression, personal worthlessness, and social despair so widespread in black America.

The liberal structuralists fail to grapple with this threat for two reasons. First, their focus on structural constraints relates almost exclusively to the economy and politics. They show no understanding of the structural character of culture. Why? Because they tend to view people in egoistic and rationalist terms according to which they are motivated primarily by self-interest and self-preservation. Needless to say, this is partly true about most of us. Yet, people, especially degraded and oppressed people, are also hungry for identity, meaning, and self-worth.

The second reason liberal structuralists overlook the nihilistic threat is a sheer failure of nerve. They hesitate to talk honestly about culture, the realm of meanings and values, because doing so seems to lend itself too readily to conservative conclusions in the narrow way Americans discuss race. If there is a hidden taboo among liberals, it is to resist talking *too much* about values because such discussions remove the focus from structures and especially because they obscure the positive role of government. But this failure by liberals leaves the existential and psychological realities of black people in the lurch. In this way, liberal structuralists neglect the battered identities rampant in black America.

As for the conservative behaviorists, they not only misconstrue the nihilistic threat but inadvertently contribute to it. This is a serious charge, and it rests upon several claims. Conservative behaviorists talk about values and attitudes as if political and economic structures hardly exist. They rarely, if ever, examine the innumerable cases in which black people do act on the Protestant ethic and still remain at the bottom of the social ladder. Instead, they highlight the few instances in which blacks ascend to the top, as if such success is available to all blacks, regardless of circumstances. Such a vulgar rendition of Horatio Alger in blackface may serve as a source of inspiration to some—a kind of model for those already on the right track. But it cannot serve as a substitute for serious historical and social analysis of the predicaments of and prospects for all black people, especially the grossly disadvantaged ones.

Conservative behaviorists also discuss black culture as if acknowledging one's obvious victimization by white supremacist practices (compounded by sexism and class condition) is taboo. They tell black people to see themselves as agents, not victims. And on the surface, this is comforting advice, a nice cliche for downtrodden people. But inspirational slogans cannot substitute for substantive historical and social analysis. While black people have never been simply victims, wallowing in self-pity and begging for white giveaways, they have been—and are—*victimized*. Therefore, to call on black people to be agents makes sense only if we also examine the dynamics of this victimization against which their agency will, in part, be exercised. What is particularly naive and peculiarly vicious about the conservative behavioral outlook is that it tends to deny the lingering effect of black history—a history inseparable from though not reducible to victimization. In this way, crucial and indispensable themes of self-help and personal responsibility are wrenched out of historical context and contemporary circumstances—as if it is all a matter of personal will.

This ahistorical perspective contributes to the nihilistic threat within black America in that it can be used to justify right-wing cutbacks for poor people struggling for decent housing, child care, health care, and education. As I pointed out above, the liberal perspective is deficient in important ways, but even so liberals are right on target in their critique of conservative government cut-backs for services to the poor. These ghastly cutbacks are one cause of the nihilist threat to black America.

The proper starting point for the crucial debate about the prospects for black America is an examination of the nihilism that increasingly pervades black communities. *Nihilism is to be understood here not as a philosophic doctrine that there are no rational grounds for legitimate standards or authority; it is, far more, the lived experience of coping with a life of horrifying meaninglessness, hopelessness, and (most important) lovelessness.* The frightening result is a numbing detachment from others and a self-destructive disposition toward the world. Life without meaning, hope, and love breeds a coldhearted, mean-spirited outlook that destroys both the individual and others.

Nihilism is not new in black America. The first African encounter with the New World was an encounter with a distinctive form of the Absurd. The initial black struggle against degradation and devaluation in the enslaved circumstances of the New World was, in part, a struggle against nihilism. In fact, the major enemy of black survival in America has been and is neither oppression nor exploitation but rather the nihilistic threat—that is, loss of hope and absence of meaning. For as long as hope remains and meaning is preserved, the possibility of overcoming oppression stays alive. The self-fulfilling prophecy of the nihilistic threat is that without hope there can be no future, that without meaning there can be no struggle.

The genius of our black foremothers and forefathers was to create powerful buffers to ward off the nihilistic threat, to equip black folk with cultural armor to beat back the demons of hopelessness, meaninglessness, and lovelessness. These buffers consisted of cultural structures of meaning and feeling that created and sustained communities; this armor constituted ways of life and struggle that embodied values of service and sacrifice, love and care, discipline and excellence. In other words, traditions for black surviving and thriving under usually adverse New World conditions were major barriers against the nihilistic threat. These traditions consist primarily of black religious and civic institutions that sustained familial and communal networks of support. If cultures are, in part, what human beings create (out of antecedent fragments of other cultures) in order to convince themselves not to commit suicide, then black foremothers and forefathers are to be applauded. In fact, until the early seventies black Americans had the lowest suicide rate in the United States. But now young black people lead the nation in the rate of increase in suicides.

What has changed? What went wrong? The bitter irony of integration? The cumulative effects of a genocidal conspiracy? The virtual collapse of rising expectations after the optimistic sixties? None of us fully understands why the cultural structures that once sustained black life in America are no longer able to fend off the nihilistic threat. I believe that two significant reasons why the threat is more powerful now than ever before are the saturation of market forces and market moralities in black life and the present crisis in black leadership. The recent market-driven shattering of black civil society—black families, neighborhoods, schools, churches, mosques—leaves more and more black people vulnerable to daily lives endured with little sense of self and fragile existential moorings.

Black people have always been in America's wilderness in search of a promised land. Yet many black folk now reside in a jungle ruled by a cutthroat market morality devoid of any faith in deliverance or hope for freedom. Contrary to the superficial claims of conservative behaviorists, these jungles are not primarily the result of pathological behavior. Rather, this behavior is the tragic response of a people bereft of resources in confronting the workings of U.S. capitalist society. Saying this is not the same as asserting that individual black people are not responsible for their actions—black murderers and rapists should go to jail. But it must be recognized that the nihilistic threat contributes to criminal behavior. It is a threat that feeds on poverty and shattered cultural institutions and grows more powerful as the armors to ward against it are weakened.

But why is this shattering of black civil society occurring? What has led to the weakening of black cultural institutions in asphalt jungles? Corporate market institutions have contributed greatly to their collapse. By corporate market institutions I mean that complex set of interlocking enterprises that have a disproportionate amount of capital, power, and exercise a disproportionate influence on how our society is run and how our culture is shaped. Needless to say, the primary motivation of these institutions is to make profits, and their basic strategy is to convince the public to consume. These institutions have helped create a seductive way of life, a culture of consumption that capitalizes on every opportunity to make money. Market calculations and cost-benefit analyses hold sway in almost every sphere of U.S. society.

The common denominator of these calculations and analyses is usually the provision, expansion, and intensification of *pleasure*. Pleasure is a multivalent term; it means different things to many people. In the American way of life pleasure involves comfort, convenience, and sexual stimulation. Pleasure, so defined, has little to do with the past and views the future as no more than a repetition of a hedonistically driven present. This market morality stigmatizes others as objects for personal pleasure or bodily stimulation. Conservative behaviorists have alleged that traditional morality has been undermined by radical feminists and the cultural radicals of the sixties. But it is clear that corporate market institutions have greatly contributed to undermining traditional morality in order to stay in business and make a profit. The reduction of individuals to objects of pleasure is especially evident in the culture industries—television, radio, video, music—in which gestures of sexual foreplay and orgiastic pleasure flood the marketplace.

Like all Americans, African-Americans are influenced greatly by the images of comfort, convenience, machismo, femininity, violence, and sexual stimulation that bombard consumers. These seductive images contribute to the predominance of the market-inspired way of life over all others and thereby edge out nonmarket values—love, care, service to others—handed down by preceding generations. The predominance of this way of life among those living in poverty-ridden conditions, with a limited capacity to ward off self-contempt and self-hatred, results in the possible triumph of the nihilistic threat in black America.

A major contemporary strategy for holding the nihilistic threat at bay is a direct attack on the sense of worthlessness and self-loathing in black America. This angst resembles a kind of collective clinical depression in significant pockets of black America. The eclipse of hope and collapse of meaning in much of black America is linked to the structural dynamics of corporate market institutions that affect all Americans. Under these circumstances black existential angst derives from the lived experience of ontological wounds and emotional scars inflicted by white supremacist beliefs and images permeating U.S. society and culture. These beliefs and images attack black intelligence, black ability, black beauty, and black character daily in subtle and not-so-subtle ways. Toni Morrison's novel, *The Bluest Eye*, for example, reveals the devastating effect of pervasive European ideals of beauty on the self-image of young black women. Morrison's exposure of the harmful extent to which these white ideals affect the black self-image is a first step toward rejecting these ideals and overcoming the nihilistic self-loathing they engender in blacks.

The accumulated effect of the black wounds and scars suffered in a white-dominated society is a deep-seated anger, a boiling sense of rage, and a passionate pessimism regarding America's will to justice. Under conditions of slavery and Jim Crow segregation, this anger, rage, and pessimism remained relatively muted because of a well-justified fear of brutal white retaliation. The major breakthroughs of the sixties—more physically than politically—swept this fear away. Sadly, the combination of the market way of life, poverty-ridden conditions, black existential angst, and the lessening of fear of white authorities has directed most of the anger, rage, and despair toward fellow black citizens, especially toward black women, who are the most vulnerable in our society and in black communities. Only recently has this nihilistic threat—and its ugly inhumane outlook and actions—surfaced in the larger American society. And its appearance surely reveals one of the many instances of cultural decay in a declining empire.

What is to be done about this nihilistic threat? Is there really any hope, given our shattered civil society, market-driven corporate enterprises, and white supremacism? If one begins with the threat of concrete nihilism, then one must talk about some kind of *politics of conversion*. New models of collective black leadership must promote a version of this politics. Like alcoholism and drug addiction, nihilism is a disease of the soul. It can never be completely cured, and there is always the possibility of relapse. But there is always a chance for conversion—a chance for people to believe that there is hope for the future and a meaning to struggle. This chance rests neither on an agreement about what justice consists of nor on an analysis of how racism, sexism, or class subordination operate. Such arguments and analyses are indispensable. But a politics of conversion requires more. Nihilism is not overcome by arguments or analyses; it is tamed by love and care. Any disease of the soul must be conquered by a turning of one's soul. This turning is done through one's own affirmation of one's worth—an affirmation fueled by the concern of others. A love ethic must be at the center of a politics of conversion.

A love ethic has nothing to do with sentimental feelings or tribal connections. Rather it is a last attempt at generating a sense of agency among a downtrodden people. The best exemplar of this love ethic is depicted on a number of levels in Toni Morrison's great novel *Beloved.* Self-love and love of others are both modes toward increasing self-valuation and encouraging political resistance in one's community. These modes of valuation and resistance are rooted in a subversive memory—the best of one's past without romantic nostalgia—and guided by a universal love ethic. For my purposes here, *Beloved* can be construed as bringing together the loving yet critical affirmation of black humanity found in the best of black nationalist movements, the perennial hope against hope for transracial coalition in progressive movements, and the painful struggle for self-affirming sanity in a history in which the nihilistic threat seems insurmountable.

The politics of conversion proceeds principally on the local level—in those institutions in civil society still vital enough to promote self-worth and self-affirmation. It surfaces on the state and national levels only when grass-roots democratic organizations put forward a collective leadership that has earned the love and respect of and, most important, has proved itself *accountable* to these organizations. This collective leadership must exemplify moral integrity, character, and democratic statesmanship within itself and within its organizations.

Like liberal structuralists, the advocates of a politics of conversion never lose sight of the structural conditions that shape the sufferings and lives of people. Yet, unlike liberal structuralism, the politics of conversion meets the nihilistic threat head-on. Like conservative behaviorism, the politics of conversion openly confronts the self-destructive and inhumane actions of black people. Unlike conservative behaviorists, the politics of conversion situates these actions within inhumane circumstances (but does not thereby exonerate them). The politics of conversion shuns the limelight—a limelight that solicits status seekers and ingratiates egomaniacs. Instead, it stays on the ground among the toiling everyday people, ushering forth humble freedom fighters—both followers and leaders—who have the audacity to take the nihilistic threat by the neck and turn back its deadly assaults.

CHAPTER 20

Violence, Resistance, and the Struggle for Black Empowerment

By Manning Marable

A spectre is haunting black America—the seductive illusion that equality between the races has been achieved, and that the activism characteristic of the previous generation's freedom struggles is no longer relevant to contemporary realities. In collective chorus, the media, the leadership of both capitalist political parties, the corporate establishment, conservative social critics and public policy experts, and even marginal elements of the black middle class tell the majority of African-Americans that the factors which generated the social protest for equality in the 1950s and 1960s no longer exist.

The role of race has supposedly "declined in significance" within the economy and political order. And as we survey the current social climate, this argument seems to gain a degree of creditability. The number of black elected officials exceeds 6,600; many black entrepreneurs have achieved substantial gains within the capitalist economic system in the late 1980s; thousands of black managers and administrators appear to be moving forward within the hierarchies of the private and public sector. And the crowning "accomplishment," the November 1989 election of Douglas Wilder as Virginia's first black governor, has been promoted across the nation as the beginning of the transcendence of "racial politics."

The strategy of Jesse Jackson in both 1984 and 1988, which challenged the Democratic Party by mobilizing people of color and many whites around an advanced, progressive agenda for social justice, is dismissed as anachronistic and even "reverse racism." As in the Wilder model, racial advancement is projected as obtainable only if the Negro learns a new political and cultural discourse of the white mainstream. Protest is therefore passe. All the legislative remedies which were required to guarantee racial equality, the spectre dictates, have already been passed.

It is never an easy matter to combat an illusion. There have been sufficient gains for African-Americans, particularly within the electoral system and for sectors of the black petty bourgeoisie in the 1980s, that elements of the spectre seem true. But the true test of any social thesis is the amount of reality it explains, or obscures. And from the vantage point of the inner cities and homeless shelters, from the unemployment lines and closed factories, a different reality behind the spectre emerges. We find that racism has not declined in significance, if racism is defined correctly as the systemic exploitation of blacks' labor power and the domination and subordination of our cultural, political, educational, and social rights as human beings. Racial inequality continues, albeit within the false discourse of equality. Those who benefit materially from institutional racism now use the term "racist" to denounce black critics who call for the enforcement of affirmative action and equal opportunity legislation.

Behind the rhetoric of equality exists two crises, which present fundamental challenges to African-Americans throughout the decade of the 1990s. There is an "internal crisis"—that is, a crisis within the African-American family, neighborhood, community, cultural and social institutions, and within interpersonal relations, especially between black males. Part of this crisis was generated, ironically, by the "paradox of desegregation." With the end of Jim Crow segregation, the black middle class was able to escape the confines of the ghetto. Black attorneys who previously had only black clients could now move into more lucrative white law firms. Black educators and administrators were hired at predominantly white colleges; black physicians were hired at white hospitals; black architects, engineers, and other professionals went into white firms. This usually meant the geographical and cultural schism of elements in the black middle class from the working class and low income African-American population, which was still largely confined to the ghetto.

As black middle class professionals retreated to the suburbs, they often withdrew their skills, financial resources, and professional contacts from the bulk of the African-American community. There were of course many exceptions, black women and men who understood the cultural obligations they owed to their community. But as a rule, by the late 1980s, such examples became more infrequent, especially among younger blacks who had no personal memories or experiences in the freedom struggles of two decades past.

The internal crisis is directly related to an external, institutional crisis, a one-sided race/class warfare which is being waged against the African-American community. The external crisis is represented as the conjuncture of a variety of factors, including the deterioration of skilled and higher paying jobs within the ghetto, and the decline in the economic infrastructure; the decline in the public sector's support for public housing, health care, education, and related social services for low to moderate income people; the demise of the enforcement of affirmative action, equal opportunity laws, and related civil rights legislation; the increased racial conservatism of both major political parties and the ideological and programmatic collapse of traditional liberalism; and most importantly, the conscious decision by the corporate and public sector managerial elite to "regulate" the black population through increasingly coercive means.

The major characteristic of the internal crisis is the steady acceleration and proliferation of *violence,* in a variety of manifestations. The most disruptive and devastating type of violence is violent crime, which includes homicide, forcible rape, robbery, and aggravated assault. According to the *Sourcebook of Criminal Justice Statistics* for 1981, the total number of Americans arrested was nearly 9.5 million. Blacks comprise only 12.5 percent of the total US population, but represented 2.3 million arrests, or about *one fourth of all arrests.* Black arrests for homicide and nonnegligent manslaughter were 8,693, or about 48 percent of all murders committed in the US. For robbery, which is defined by law as the use of force or violence to obtain personal property, the number of black arrests was 74,275, representing 57 percent of all robbery arrests. For aggravated assault, the number of African-Americans arrested was 94,624, about 29 percent of all arrests in this category. For motor vehicle theft, the number of blacks arrested and charged was 38,905, about 27 percent of all auto theft crimes. Overall, for all violent and property crimes charged, blacks totaled almost 700,000 arrests in the year 1979, representing nearly one third of all such crimes.

One of the most controversial of all violent crimes is the charge of forcible rape. Rape is controversial because of the history of the criminal charge being used against black men by the white racist legal structure. Thousands of black men have been executed, lynched, and castrated for the imaginary offense of rape. Yet rape or forcible sexual violence is not imaginary when African-American women and young girls are victimized. In 1979, there were 29,068 arrests for forcible rape. Black men comprised 13,870 arrests, or 48 percent of the total. Within cities, where three fourths of all rapes are committed, blacks total 54 percent of all persons arrested for rape.

The chief victims of rape are not white women, but black women. The US Department of Justice's 1979 study of the crime of forcible rape established that overall most black women are nearly twice as likely to be rape victims than are white women. The research illustrated that in one year, about 67 out of 100,000 white women would be rape victims; but the rate for black and other nonwhite women was 115 per 100,000. In the age group 20 to 34 years, the dangers for black women increase dramatically. For white women of age 20 to 34, 139 out of 100,000 are rape victims annually. For black women the same age, the rate is 292 per 100,000. For attempted rape, white women are assaulted at a rate of 196 per 100,000; black women are attacked sexually 355 per 100,000 annually.

There is also a direct correlation between rape victimization and income. In general, poor women are generally the objects of sexual assault; middle class women are rarely raped or assaulted, and wealthy women almost never experience sexual assault. The statistics are clear on this point. White women who live in families earning under $7,500 annually have a 500 percent greater likelihood of being raped than white women who come from households with more than $15,000 income. The gap is even more extreme for African-American women. For black middle-class families, the rate of rape is 22 per 100,000. For welfare and low-income families earning below $7,500 annually, the rate for rape is 127 per 100,000. For attempted rape, low-income black women are victimized at a rate of 237 per 100,000 annually.

Rape is almost always intra-racial, not interracial. Nine out of 10 times, a white rapist's victim is a white female. Ninety percent of all black women who are raped have been assaulted by a black male. Sexual violence within the African-American community, therefore, is not something "exported" by whites. It is essentially the brutality committed by black men against our mothers, wives, sisters, and daughters. It is the worst type of violence, using the gift of sexuality in a bestial and animalistic way to create terror and fear among black women.

The type of violence which most directly affects black men is homicide. Nearly half of all murders committed in any given year are black men who murder other black men. But that's only part of the problem. We must recognize, first, that the homicide rate among African-Americans is growing. Back in 1960, the homicide rate for black men in the US was 37 per 100,000. By 1979, the black homicide rate was 65 per 100,000. In other words, a typical black male has a *six to seven times* greater likelihood of being a murder victim than a white male.

The chief victims of homicide in our community are young African-American males. Murder is the fourth leading cause of death for all black men, and the leading cause of death for black males age 20 to 29 years. Today in the US, a typical white female's statistical chances of becoming a murder victim are one in 606. For white men, the odds narrow to one chance in 186. For black women, the odds are one in 124. But for black men, the chances are one in 29. For young black men living in cities who are between age 20 to 29, the odds of becoming a murder victim are *less than one in 20*. Black young men in American cities today are the primary targets for destruction—not only from drugs and police brutality, but from each other.

The epidemic of violence in the black community raises several related questions. What is the social impact of violence within our neighborhoods? What is the effect of violence upon our children? And most importantly, how do we develop a strategy to reverse the proliferation of black-against-black crime and violence?

Violence occurs so frequently in the cities that for many people, it has become almost a "normal" factor. We have become accustomed to burglar alarms and security locks to safeguard our personal property and homes. More than one in three families keep a gun in their homes. However, we also need to keep in mind that in most of the violent crime cases, the assailant and the victim live in the same neighborhood, or are members of the same household. Half of all violent deaths are between husbands and wives. Many others include parents killing their children, or children killing parents, or neighbors killing each other. There are hundreds of murders among blacks for the most trivial reasons—everything from fighting over parking spaces to arguing over $5.

Black men are murdering each other in part because of the deterioration of jobs and economic opportunity in our communities. For black young men, the real unemployment rate exceeds 50 percent in most cities. Overall jobless rates for black men with less than a high school diploma exceed 15 percent. High unemployment, crowded housing, and poor health care all contribute to an environment of social chaos and disruption, which create destructive values and behaviors.

The most tragic victims of violence are black children. Black children between the ages of one and four have death rates from homicide which are four times higher than for white children the same age. According to the Children's Defense Fund, black children are arrested at almost seven times the rates for white children for the most serious violent crimes and are arrested at more than twice the white rates for serious property crimes. More than half of the arrests for African-American teenagers are for serious property crimes or violent crimes. For instance, the arrest rate for black youth aged 11 to 17 for forcible rape is six times higher than for whites. In terms of rates of victimization, nonwhite females are almost 40 percent more likely than white females to be raped, robbed, or victims of other violent crimes.

How do we understand the acts of violence committed by and against our children? We must begin by focusing on the cultural concept of identity. What is identity? It's an awareness of self in the context of one's environment. Identity is based on the connections between the individual and his or her immediate family and community. We don't exist in isolation of each other. We develop a sense of who we are, of who we wish to become, by interacting with parents, friends, teachers, ministers, coworkers, and others.

Our identity is collective, in that it is formed through the inputs of thousands of different people over many years. If the people relate to an individual in a negative manner, an antisocial or deviant personality will be the result. If children are told repeatedly by teachers or parents that they are stupid, the children will usually do poorly in school, regardless of their natural abilities. If children are told that they are chronic liars and untrustworthy, they will eventually begin to lie and steal. If they are physically beaten by their parents frequently or unjustly, they will learn to resort to physical violence against others. People are not born hateful or violent. There's no genetic or biological explanation for black-against-black crime. Violence is *learned* behavior.

Violence between people of color is also directly linked to the educational system. If the curriculum of our public schools does not present the heritage, culture, and history of African-Americans, if it ignores or downgrades our vital contributions to a more democratic society, our children are robbed of their heritage. They acquire a distorted perspective about themselves and their communities. If they believe that African-American people have never achieved greatness in the sciences, art, music, economics, and the law, how can they excel or achieve for themselves? Despite the many reforms accomplished to create a more culturally pluralistic environment for learning, many of our public schools are in the business of "miseducation" for people of color. Our children are frequently "cultural casualties" in the ideological warfare against black people.

The dynamics of violence within the African-American community create such chaos and destructiveness that they provide a justification for the public and private sectors' retreat from civil rights initiatives. The argument of the dominant white elites proceeds thus: "Blacks must bear the responsibility for their own poverty, crime, illiteracy, and oppression. Affirmative action is consequently harmful to blacks' interests, since it rewards incompetence and advances individuals not on the basis of merit but race alone. Blacks should stop looking to the government to resolve their problems, and take greater initiatives within the private enterprise system to assist themselves. Through private initiatives, moral guidance, and sexual abstinence, the status of the Negro will improve gradually without social dissent and disruption."

We need to recognize that, fundamentally, there would be no internal crisis among African-Americans if the political economy and social institutions were designed to create the conditions for genuine democracy and human equality. The external crisis of the capitalist political economy is responsible for the internal crisis. All of the private initiatives, and all of the meager self-help efforts mounted at the neighborhood level, and the doubling of the number of black entrepreneurs and enterprises, would not in any significant manner reverse the destructive trends which have been unleashed against our people. Institutional racism and class exploitation since 1619 have always been, and remain, the root causes of black oppression.

The epidemic of violence, in combination with the presence of drugs, has directly contributed to another type of violence—the growth of African-American suicide rates, especially among the young. From 1950 to 1974, the suicide rate of African-American males soared from 6.8 per 100,000 to 11.4 per 100,000. In the same years, the black female suicide rate rose from 1.6 per 100,000 to 3.5 per 100,000. A 1982 study by Robert Davis noted that nearly one half of all suicides among blacks now occur among people between age 20 to 34 years. Within this group, black males who kill themselves account for 36 percent of the total number of suicides. Davis also observes that within the narrow age range of 25 to 29, the suicide rate among black males is higher than that for white males in the same age group. For black men and women who live in urban areas, the suicide rate is twice that for whites of the same age group who live in cities.

These facts must be understood against the background of the social history of African-Americans. Traditionally, suicide was almost unknown within the black community during slavery and the Jim Crow period. Blacks found ways to cope with stress and the constant disappointments of life, from singing the blues to mobilizing their sisters and brothers to fight against forms of oppression. Frantz Fanon's psychiatric insight, that struggle and resistance for the oppressed are therapeutic, is confirmed by the heritage of the Black Liberation Movement. But when people lose the will to resist oppression, when they no longer can determine their friends or enemies, they lack the ability to develop the mental and spiritual determination to overcome obstacles. Suicide, once an irrational or irrelevant act, becomes both rational and logical within the context of cultural and social alienation.

The American legal system in the 1980s and 1990s also contributed to the violence within our communities in several ways. The patterns of institutional racism became far more sophisticated, as former President Reagan pursued a policy of appointing conservative, racist, elitist males to the federal district courts and the US Circuit Courts of Appeals. By 1989 Reagan had appointed over 425 federal judges, more than half of the 744 total judgeships. Increasingly, the criminal justice system was employed as a system of social control for the millions of unemployed and underemployed African-Americans. The essential element of coercion within the justice system, within a racial context, is of course the utilization of the death penalty.

According to one statistical study by David C. Baldus based on over 2,000 murder cases in Georgia during the 1970s, people accused of killing whites were about 11 times more likely to be given the death penalty than those who murdered blacks. Over half of the defendants in white-victim crimes would not have been ordered to be executed if their victims had been African-Americans. Research on the death penalty in Florida during the 1970s illustrates that Florida blacks who are accused and convicted of murdering whites are five times more likely to be given the death penalty than whites who murder other whites.

Under the conditions of race/class domination, prisons are the principal means for group social control, in order to regulate the labor position of millions of black workers. Our free market system cannot create full employment for all; and the public sector is unwilling to devote sufficient resources to launch an economic reconstruction of the central cities, which in turn would greatly reduce the drug trade. Consequently, prisons become absolutely necessary for keeping hundred of thousands of potentially rebellious, dissatisfied, and alienated African-American youth off the streets.

Between 1973 and 1986, the average real earnings for young African-American males under 25 years fell by 50 percent. In the same period, the percentage of black males aged 18 to 29 in the labor force who were able to secure full-time, year-round employment fell from only 44 percent to a meager 35 percent.

Is it accidental that these young black men, who are crassly denied meaningful employment opportunities, are also pushed into the prison system, and subsequently into permanent positions of economic marginality and social irrelevancy? Within capitalism, a job has never been defined as a human right; but for millions of young, poor black men and women, they appear to have a "right" to a prison cell or a place at the front on the unemployment line.

The struggle against violence requires a break from the strategic analysis of the desegregation period of the 1960s. Our challenge is not to become part of the system, but to transform it, not only for ourselves, but for everyone. We must struggle against an acceptance of the discourse and perceptions of the dominant white political criminal justice and economic elites in regards to black-on-black violence. If we focus solely on the need to construct more prisons and mandatory sentences for certain crimes, the crisis will continue to exist in our cities and elsewhere. People who have a sense of mastery and control in their lives do not violate their neighbors or steal their property.

An effective strategy for empowerment in the 1990s must begin with the recognition that the American electoral political system was never designed to uproot the fundamental causes of black oppression. Most of the greatest advances in black political activism did not occur at the ballot box, but in the streets, in the factories, and through collective group awareness and mobilization. Our greatest leaders in this century—W.E.B. Du Bois, Marcus Garvey, Paul Robeson, Malcolm X, Fannie Lou Hamer, Ella Baker, Martin Luther King, Jr., and many more—were not elected officials or government bureaucrats. Yet because of the electoral focus of most of the current crop of middle class black elites, we now tend to think of power as an electoral process. But there is also power when oppressed people acquire a sense of cultural integrity and an appreciation of their political heritage of resistance. There is power when we mobilize our collective resources in the media, educational institutions, housing, health care, and economic development to address issues. There is power when African-American people and other oppressed constituencies mobilize a march or street demonstration, when we use a boycott or picket line to realize our immediate objectives.

A strategy for African-American empowerment means that black politicians must be held more closely accountable to the interests of black people. Power implies the ability to reward and to punish friends and enemies alike. Can blacks continue to afford to conduct voter registration and education campaigns, and then do nothing to check the voting behavior of our elected officials? Accountability must be measured objectively according to a list of policy priorities, and not determined by political rhetoric at election time. One method to consider could be the creation of "people power" assemblies, popular, local conventions open to the general black public. Politicians of both major parties would be evaluated and ranked according to their legislative or executive records, and their responses on specific police questions. Neither the Democratic nor the Republican Party can be expected to provide this level of direct accountability.

We are losing the battle for the hearts and minds of millions of young African-Americans who have no personal memory of the struggles waged to dismantle the system of Jim Crow segregation. They have no personal experience on the picket lines, in street demonstrations, and in the development of community-based organizations which reinforce and strengthen black families, black religious, civic, and social institutions. The path forward is to create a new generation of black leaders who recognize that the effort to achieve social justice and human equality is unfinished, and that the status of black people in America could easily deteriorate to a new type of repressive environment comparable to legal segregation in the pre–Civil Rights South. We must identify and cultivate the leadership abilities of young people who display a potential and an interest in progressive social change.

We need to recognize that power in American society is exercised by hierarchies and classes, not by individuals. Part of the price for the individualism and blatant materialism within certain elements of the black upper middle class since the 1970s has been their alienation from the dilemmas confronting the black working class, the poor, and unemployed. Class elitism of any type, for a segment of the oppressed community, contributes to a disintegration of solidarity and a sense of common values, goals, and objectives. To end the dynamic of violence, we need to recognize that freedom is not rooted within individualism, in isolation from the majority. No single black woman or man in America will ever transcend the impact of racism and class exploitation unless all of us, and especially the most oppressed among us, also gain a fundamental level of cultural awareness, collective respect, material security, and educational advancement. This requires a new vision of the struggle for power, a collective commitment to the difficult, yet challenging project of remaking humanity and our social environment, rooted in a vision beyond self-hatred, chemical dependency, and fratricidal violence. This must be at the heart of our strategy for cultural resistance and empowerment for the 1990s and beyond.

CHAPTER 21

Indigenous Peoples, Racism and the Environment

By Russel Barsh

The 1990s will rewrite the history of colonialism. Environmental awareness, forced upon rich and poor countries alike by deforestation, desertification and climate change, is bringing with it a realization of the role of the environment as a medium of exploitation. European nations have not only extracted raw materials and labour from their Asian, African and American colonies, but also shifted environmental costs to their overseas territories. Some of this cost-shifting was fairly obvious. The disposal of European toxic wastes in Africa is a recent example. The decentralization of hazardous production processes and application of lower environmental standards to overseas production have also been important, and probably far more widespread.

These processes continue today, not only as an instrument of neocolonialism but also as a feature of 'internal colonialism'—that is, exploitative economic relationships *among regions* within independent states. Relatively poor, politically isolated regions are exploited as dumping grounds and high-risk production areas. Frequently these regions are the last strongholds of indigenous and tribal peoples, who are particularly marginalized and vulnerable, and powerless to defend themselves by democratic means even in relatively free societies.

ENVIRONMENTAL RACISM

Indigenous people often describe this as "environmental racism." Politically dominant groups freely impose ecological risks and health hazards on others that they would never willingly bear themselves. It is no different from arguing that other people should work harder, live more poorly and die prematurely because it is their destined lot on earth to serve superior races.

The current controversy over further development of hydroelectric power dams in northern Quebec is a convincing illustration of this phenomenon. The indigenous Cree people fought the first project in the courts and the press until they were forced to accept a settlement under which they retained control of about one-sixth of their territory and accepted compensation for the rest.[1] Now, barely fifteen years later, the nationalist provincial government of Quebec is beginning an even more ambitious engineering project that will inundate most of the rest of the Cree region. Even though the power produced by this project is destined for export to the United States, Quebec Premier Bourassa has publicly stated that, should the Crees succeed with plans to block it, Montrealers will have to read by candlelight.

Appeals to white self-interest are nothing new in Quebec, or for that matter in the rest of North America. What makes the situation in Quebec so interesting is the interaction between indigenous rights and francophone nationalism. Quebec's conservative leadership depicts the Crees and other northern indigenous peoples, who form the majority in the mineral-rich northern half of the province, as standing in the way of Québecois aspirations for independence from Canada. Indeed, there is little realistic hope for an independent Quebec unless the natural resources of the north can be exploited.

Québecois nationalists have a choice between sharing power with indigenous people—the foundation of a future bi-national state like New Zealand—or simply taking what they want because they are white. Bourassa's show of military force against the Mohawk village of Kanesatake last August provides the answer, and is a deliberate warning to all indigenous people in Quebec who might suppose that their aspirations are as important as those of Franco-Canadians. The issue at Kanesatake was not over a few acres of land slated for development as a golf course, but over making indigenous people pay, ecologically and economically, to realize other people's dreams.

The point here is that, today as in the heyday of classic colonialism, environmental racism is associated with the more virulent forms of national and racial chauvinism. It cuts across traditional class lines, because environmental matters are necessarily geographical. Resources and contaminants are related to physical rather than social space. Hence environmental contests are ideal for pitting the poor in one region against the poorer who live in another.[2]

RESOURCE FRONTIERS

Environmental racism is on the increase, reflecting the worldwide growth in consumption associated with decolonization and the diffusion of industrial technology. Since 1945 world industrial production has decentralized and newly industrializing countries have tried to secure their own sources of raw materials, leading to a decentralization and intensification of natural resource exploitation. The process has accelerated in the 1980s; over the decade, the contribution of manufacturing to the total value of exports from the 'developing' countries rose from 42 to 68 per cent.[3] The result has been a proliferation of frontiers.

This is not to suggest that the ultimate *control* of extraction or production processes has decentralized to any significant degree; the global 'debt crisis' is proof against that. Neither is it to ignore the extent to which global demand has been driven by growing per-capita consumption in the North and growing population in the South. Decentralization is an adaptation to these conditions, increasing output and transforming society faster and more completely than would have been possible within the system of centralized colonialism. It universalizes the competitive incentive to produce and consume.

The answer is not to re-centralize the world economic system but to decentralize it more completely. Rich countries are still living off the interest from the capital stock extracted from the rest of the world under colonialism. Poorer countries must still overproduce in order to repay borrowed financial capital and technology, requiring an intensified liquidation of natural resources. As a result, the

North is still eating the ecological future of the South.[4] There is a close relationship between ecological non-sustainability and the lack of a more balanced and democratic world economic system. Non-sustainability is also a characteristic of highly inequitable national economies, in which most of the population labours to support an élite.

The mechanism linking sustainability with the nature of economic relations is the ability of more powerful nations, or élites, to shift environmental costs. Shifting *financial* costs through debt, taxes or trade barriers is relatively short-term. Shifting environmental costs involves destroying the underlying productivity of nations, or regions within nations, and is a longer-term proposition.

Frontiers are the cutting edge of this process. Their existence testifies to the non-sustainability of prevailing economic structures, and their proliferation is a direct function of inequity.

The relationship between economic inequity and frontier formation has a long history, predating classic colonialism, but concentrations of capital and technology are making it more of an ecological problem. Nineteenth-century frontiers were chiefly agricultural, driven by the migration of large numbers of landless labourers, who bore most of the costs of clearing and planting themselves. This pattern can still be found along the forest edge in Amazonia and in parts of south-east Asia. More typically, however, today's frontiers depend on international financial support for technologies that make it possible to reach into very fragile habitats, such as deserts and tundra, and to accelerate the exploitation of highly productive systems, such as forests and oceans, to non-sustainable levels.

The remaining enclaves of indigenous or tribal peoples are in isolated and challenging ecosystems that until recently were far too costly for outsiders to exploit profitably. What most unites indigenous peoples, indeed, is experiencing the loss of sustainability. They are united by the experience of being on the frontier.

Indigenousness is not simply a state of mind or culture. It is a matter of one's position on the path of economic transformation from a state of self-sufficiency to interdependence and global inequalities. Britons and Germans were the indigenous peoples of the Roman Empire. Tacitus complained of them that "although their land is fertile and extensive, they fail to take full advantage of it because they do not work sufficiently hard." "One must remember," he explained, "we are dealing with barbarians."[5]

EXTRACTIVE SOCIETIES

Canada, Australia and Brazil present these processes in a special form. Each country as a whole has a European majority in political as well as economic and numerical terms, but also contains a vast expanse of territory with a distinct but thinly scattered indigenous majority. These countries have benefited historically from the ability to draw extravagantly on the natural resources of their 'bush' territories, as if these areas were uninhabited. This has led in turn to patterns of consumption and inequality that would otherwise be associated with the overseas empires of the last century. There is an interesting comparison here with the US. Until 1898, when it began colonization in the Caribbean and the Pacific, the US economy also enjoyed an internal subsidy from mining and the agricultural use of its interior territories, from which indigenous peoples were gradually removed. More recently the US has benefited far more from the key role of the dollar in international financial markets than from internal expansion.[6]

All three countries have sophisticated technological capabilities—Brazil is engaged in biotechnology and space research—but continue to earn a large part of their foreign exchange from the export of raw materials such as minerals, grain and fibre.[7] The availability of raw materials and low-cost energy also attracts a considerable amount of direct private investment from other countries, and lowers production costs for domestic producers. As a result, dominant population groups and élites enjoy standards of living much higher than the productivity of their labour would otherwise afford.

Only by this means could a country such as Australia enjoy such a high overall standard of living with an economy still so dependent on primary production. As long as they last, servant territories provide a subsidy to growth, industrialization and consumption. This subsidy, however, comes from the destruction of indigenous peoples and the ecosystems in which they live.

Such a strategy would not be possible in Europe, Asia or Andean Latin America, where population density makes the destruction of large ecosystems and the resettlement of large numbers of people a practical impossibility. Population is not the only difference. Power is also a factor in the equation. Not only are the indigenous peoples of servant territories few in numbers, they have little or no control over their lands, nor any effective voice in national decision-making. Like forests and wildlife, they have no right to complain about being sacrificed for 'development.'

This distinction between the territorial security of the European population and indigenous peoples is racist. It is also a problem for the environment, because it leaves the inhabitants of a large part of the country without the means of opposing destructive projects. This is why a society such as white Canada, which otherwise seems to have a very 'green' public conscience, can nevertheless support its lifestyle on the proceeds of megaprojects within its own national borders. This is the natural consequence of giving only Euro-Canadians the choice of what to do with the land on which they live.

ECONOMICS AND ECOLOGICAL ETHICS

Of necessity, indigenous peoples dependent on hunting, fishing and shifting cultivation evolved very sustainable forms of economic organization. Lacking the power to expand at the expense of others, they devoted themselves to achieving food security and the greatest possible social stability within their own territories. This meant reducing ecological risks and social conflict rather than increasing production. The ratio of humans to farmland and wildlife was often deliberately kept low, and surplus food was collected and preserved to guard against the vagaries of nature.[8] A small number of people living securely was preferred to the dangers inherent in expanding to the physical limits of resources.

Maintaining a dynamic balance with available resources relied, in turn, on highly co-ordinated economic activity. Rather than some form of central planning, indigenous economies employed diversification as a risk-reduction strategy. Family groups formed the basic productive units. Family harvesting and farming areas were widely dispersed, so that all available ecological niches were exploited and the blessings and curses of annual and seasonal fluctuations in resource conditions fell more or less randomly on different producers. Elaborate rituals of redistributing wealth through kinship networks then functioned to restore a rough equality. This achieved two goals. It averaged the risk of famine among all related households, and reduced the motives for social conflict.[9]

The basic productive factors in indigenous economies were labour and technology, combined non-exploitatively through kinship relations. Indigenous societies were rich repositories of observational knowledge of ecosystems, because basic productive technology was the ability to anticipate animal behaviour and interactions among species, acquired from ancestors and augmented from personal experience. The ability to organize kinsmen in labour groups for producing and processing food and materials completed the economic equation. Since kinship as such is reciprocal (every son is potentially also a father, for example), kinship-based economic structures differ from class relations.

This is not to say that the peoples we call indigenous lacked any problems related to class. Hierarchies of family groups did arise, sustained by differential access to resources. Wildlife harvesting and horticulture, however, are simply too unreliable to maintain dominance for very long. A few poor fishing seasons could raze a dynasty.

Interaction with industrialized societies has already transformed these structures almost everywhere. Some individuals gain access to outside resources in the form of wages from jobs, profit from trade or power from recruitment into colonial administration. This results in the typical, 'mixed' economy of most indigenous peoples today, which combines traditional food production with external cash income, and in which differential access to resources becomes more persistent. When the colonial system is internalized by the establishment of 'native' governments with externally financed salaries, this results in a very stable economic and political élite.

The United States is the best illustration of this process, since it devolved administrative responsibilities to its indigenous peoples more than fifty years ago. Since the 1960s Indian reservations have been torn apart by disputes over development projects, such as open-cut mining, reflecting underlying economic conflicts between primary workers and tribal technocrats.[10] All the while, Indian leaders argue for more power over their territories and people on the pretence that indigenous people are inherently better stewards of the land.

Australians have already encountered this scenario over Aboriginal land in the Northern Territory. The establishment of the Aboriginal and Tortes Strait Islanders Commission (ATSIC) has created a nationwide Aboriginal technocracy that lacks power over land, but has an advisory role with respect to the Commonwealth budget. The mere fact that Commissioners are elected will not ensure that they are genuinely accountable or free them from the construction of a distinct identity and economic self-interest. Establish an indigenous bureaucracy, and sacred land may suddenly be for sale. Indigenous people have the same right to make development choices as anyone else, of course; an inherent right, as Gandhi put it, to make their own mistakes. At the same time, it is important for indigenous peoples to acknowledge that divisions of interest exist within their own societies. Pretending to be culturally superior is dangerous. It is used by indigenous élites as an argument against the necessity of building effective, democratic institutions to deal with the new conflicts over resources and power that are evolving within their own communities.

THE PERILS OF ROMANTICISM

Moving from understanding to action in Australia or North America is fraught with danger. Neither the indigenous political movement nor the environmental movement is uniform in its social base or goals. Both, moreover, are seriously afflicted with romanticism.

The traditional sustainability of indigenous economies was not a matter of values or beliefs alone, but a product of social structures and institutions that worked against concentrations of power. Facile repetition of the idea that Indigenousness is equated with ecological sanity is a self-destructive form of racism, as unconscionable as the racist argument that would deprive indigenous peoples of the right to control their own economies and resources. Inherent superiority and inherent inferiority are two sides of the same coin.

Unfortunately, the self-delusion of indigenous leaders has often been used by environmental groups to mobilize non-indigenous support. Western romanticism is such that people will believe something said by a Brazilian Indian where they would not believe if it were said by a European. This makes Brazilian Indians very valuable, and some organizations are at great pains to recruit their own Indian chiefs and place them under contract, like movie stars. This not only creates a false issue—the preservation of supposedly pristine indigenous societies—but distorts indigenous political processes by creating a new, externally financed élite and making its survival depend on perpetuating romantic images of indigenous life.

There are natural conflicts of interest between the environmental movement in the West and indigenous peoples. Western environmentalism is dominated by recreational groups—sport fishermen and backpackers—especially in North America and Australia. They readily make tactical alliances with indigenous people against developers to save unspoiled lands, then oppose the use and control of the same land by indigenous communities. Even the more 'serious' elements of the Western movement are not entirely free from economic self-interest. Biosphere reserves in developing countries are promoted as hubs for future ecotourism by Westerners, not as homes for indigenous people.

Romanticism regarding the ecological ethics of indigenous culture gives environmental organizations an advantage in this political game, because it commits indigenous peoples to an anti-developmental stance. It accepts indigenous peoples as part of the ecosystem only as long as they do not change in any way. But traditional forms of production changed ecosystems, albeit to new, sustainable equilibria. Except in the most isolated parts of the world, moreover, indigenous territories have already been damaged by settlement and resource extraction. They are no longer as productive, and require either rehabilitation or new technologies if the inhabitants are to survive.

Designing more productive and sustainable economic structures is more difficult than removing people from the ecosystem altogether and the simplest way to remove people from the ecosystem is to limit them to activities that are no longer capable of feeding them.

SOCIAL SUSTAINABILITY

Without real democracy there can be no effective protection of the environment. This is not only a lesson from eastern Europe, where decades of authoritarianism, poorly disguised as socialism, have left a legacy of wrecked landscapes and polluted skies. It is also evident at Bhopal, and everywhere else that corporate technocrats were allowed to choose the level of acceptable risk for other people. It is clear from the desertification of Africa and in the mounting chemical loads of farmland in monsoon Asia, transformed by the development strategies of international aid agencies and financial institutions. When people get control of someone else's land, they tend to wreck it.

People are quite capable of wrecking their own land, to be sure. The destruction of the American prairies by farmers (the "Dust Bowl") is a case in point, and has parallels in Western Australia and other areas of twentieth-century agricultural expansion. There are clearly also cases of communities welcoming smelters, nuclear power stations, toxic waste dumps and large-scale logging operations for the sake of employment opportunities. In both kinds of situations the availability of information is a critical factor. Unfamiliarity with new terrain, or with new technology, can result in some spectacularly bad choices. The answer is greater public access to information and education, and more decentralized and open decision-making, not rule by well-meaning technocrats.

The key to environmental sustainability is not racial or ethnic but structural. When people have real control over their lives and feel that they enjoy a fair share of the resources around them, there is little incentive or necessity for them to over-produce or over-consume, and every reason for them to manage the land around them conservatively. Sustainable social systems are able to use ecosystems sustainably.

This is not simply a prescription for 'nasty' countries. Even in many of the most self-consciously 'free' Western countries, ecological decisions are made behind closed doors. For example, the Canadian government did not even bother to respond to a recent Royal Commission's proposal that there be a representative, public process for wildlife-management decisions.[11] What was worse, environmental groups in the country never made an issue of it, so used are they to challenging bad decisions after they are made rather than changing the nature of the decision-making process itself.

Whatever their internal difficulties, however much they are overcome with their own romantic illusions, indigenous peoples are not content with the right to complain. In their insistence on regaining real power over their lives and their lands, they can point the way to a solution for all people. To succeed, they must not only pay attention to what can be learnt from their past, but adopt realism about their present.

SECTION FIVE

Violence and Nationalism

CHAPTER 22

The New Nationalism in Europe

By Mary Kaldor

Far from ending, history seems to have accelerated since the revolutions of 1989. Germany has unified; the Soviet Union, Yugoslavia, and Czechoslovakia have fallen apart. A major war is taking place in the middle of the continent, with tens of thousands of deaths, millions of refugees, and the destruction of whole villages, towns, and historic buildings. Anti-Semitism, antigypsyism, and other forms of xenophobia are on the rise again almost everywhere in Europe.

Did those of us who devoted so much of our lives to the goal of ending the Cold War make a mistake? Was it worth being a dissident or a peace activist if this was to be the final outcome? Why did we assume that everything could be solved if the division of Europe were removed? Cold War apologists, such as John Lewis Gaddis or John Mearsheimer, told us that future generations would look back nostalgically on the period of the Cold War as a golden era of stability—the "Long Peace," they called it. Eastern European officials used to warn us that democracy was impossible because nationalist and racist feelings would be revived. Were they right after all? Was nationalism kept in check, "deep frozen" as many commentators would have it, only to reemerge when the Cold War ended?

I do not think we were wrong. People's behavior is conditioned by their immediate experience, not by memories of what happened to previous generations. Of course, those memories are rekindled and used in every nationalist conflict, but it is the current context that determines the power of memory to shape politics. I would like to argue two propositions: First, far from having been suppressed by the Cold War, the new nationalism is a direct consequence of the Cold War experience. Without the Cold War, the current wave of nationalism would not have happened, at least not in the same way and with the same virulence. Second, the new nationalism that is sweeping through Central and Eastern Europe is different from the nationalism of previous epochs, although it may share some common features. It is a contemporary phenomenon, not a throwback to the past.

Nationalism is a relatively recent phenomenon that arose in the late eighteenth century. It is extremely difficult to disentangle the concept of a nation from the concept of a nation-state. Definitions of a nation vary: a common linguistic group, inhabitants of a particular territory, an ethnic group, a group with shared cultural traditions, religion, or values. In practice, a group of human beings that define themselves as a nation usually do so because they are citizens of a particular state, because they are discriminated against by a state, or because they are interested in establishing their own state.

All nationalisms share two common features. First is the notion of citizenship—the idea that sovereignty, i.e., control of the state, is vested in the nation rather than in, say, the monarch—as in eighteenth-century Western Europe or nineteenth-century Central Europe—or foreign oppressors, as in the Third World or in the Soviet empire.

Of course, concepts of citizenship varied. Historians often distinguish between Western and Eastern nationalism—in particular, the French and the German variants of citizenship. In France, the citizens were the inhabitants of French territory. There was a notion that being French was associated with French language and culture. But this could be acquired; immigrants and minorities could assimilate. By contrast, the German notion of citizenship was ethnic. Even today, anyone of German ethnic origin can claim German citizenship.

Second, nationalism involves a sense of distinct group identity, which is defined in contrast to other groups. The rise of nationalism was linked to the rise of written vernacular languages, which in turn was linked to the expansion of the intellectual class. The discovery of print technology made the written word far more widely accessible. New publications such as novels and newspapers gave rise to new identities and communicative networks. Benedict Anderson uses the term "imagined community" to describe the way in which the people who had never met or who were not related could develop a sense of community because they read the same newspapers and novels. But it is in war that the idea of a nation is the most substantiated. The existence of an enemy, real or imagined, is an important element in forging a sense of national identity.

During the Cold War years, national sentiment seemed superseded by bloc sentiment, at least in Europe. In the East, the language of Marxism-Leninism displaced the language of nationalism as a legitimizing principle. And in the West, vague commitments to democracy and the Western way of life seemed more important than national interest. The idea of an ideological enemy seemed more convincing than a national enemy. Many commentators talked about the post-1945 European era as "postnationalist." This turned out to be wishful thinking.

Max Weber defined the state as an organization "that [successfully] claims the monopoly of the legitimate use of physical force." Pierre Bourdieu, the French sociologist, has extended that definition to cover what he calls symbolic violence, by which he means the use of language as a form of domination. It is in both the symbolic and physical senses that the state has collapsed or is collapsing in much of the postcommunist world.

The current wave of nationalism has to be understood in terms of the collapse of the communist state. First, the language of domination—the Marxist-Leninist discourse—has been totally discredited. More important, no alternative language exists that is capable of reconstructing legitimacy, i.e., mobilizing a consensus about the political rules of the game. During the communist period, there were no public political debates and no autonomous political movements or parties. There was no mechanism through which political ideas, principles, values, political groups, or even individuals could gain respect or trust in society.

To some extent, Europe, understood as a haven of peace, prosperity, and democracy and identified with the European Community, constituted a political alternative. But it soon became clear that only rich countries could join the European Community. The experience of market reform, which was associated with Western countries—especially in the former Yugoslavia, Poland, and Slovakia—quickly dispelled the mobilizing potential of the European idea. Because all politicians made use of the language of democracy, markets, and Europe and nobody really understood what it signified, it lacked the substantive content upon which to base new forms of authority.

In the aftermath of the 1989 revolutions, there were no tried and tested politicians, no established routes to power. There was a generalized distrust of politicians and parties. Given the huge expectations generated by the 1989 revolutions, every politician was bound to be disappointing.

In these circumstances, the appeal to an untainted, uncompromised ethnic, religious, or linguistic identity is one of the most effective ways to win power. In large parts of the postcommunist world, it is nationalist parties that have won elections. You vote for a politician because he (and it almost always is not she) is a Serb or a Slovak or whatever like you. The mobilization of fear, the notion that you and your people are threatened, the creation of a war psychosis in the time-honored communist tradition are all mechanisms to stay in power, to reestablish authority, to reclaim control over the means of symbolic violence. Both communist and nationalist discourse require an other—imperialism or an enemy nation. But the communist rhetoric could claim a monopoly over discourse because it was based on universalist values. The problem with the nationalist rhetoric is that it is inherently exclusionary. By nature, it is fragmentary—stimulating counterclaims to the control of symbolic violence.

Of course, there were differences among nationalist parties. Some were anti-communist and called themselves democratic. Others were simply revamped communist parties, as in Serbia or Azerbaijan. Some nationalist parties made efforts to include minorities in their nationalist project, as in the Ukraine. Others were openly exclusivist. Many commentators suggested that these differences were important. Nationalism is said to be Janus-faced. A sense of national identity is a necessary precondition for establishing democracy, for opposing totalitarianism, and for rebuilding a sense of civic responsibility. The movements in Poland, the Baltic states, and Slovenia were compared to liberation movements in the Third World. Yet sadly, the ugly face of nationalism has shown itself much more frequently than the pleasing face. In Slovenia and Croatia, and in the Baltic states, ethnically based citizenship laws have been introduced. Everywhere xenophobia and chauvinism are on the increase. In many places, paranoia about the other is whipped up and human rights are violated in the name of national security.

In addition, the Cold War machines are disintegrating. The arms buildup over the last forty years profoundly influenced economies and societies. It was naive to suppose that this process could be reversed merely by cutting defense budgets. Large parts of the postcommunist world are flooded with surplus weapons, unemployed soldiers, and arms producers. It is easy enough to form a paramilitary group by putting on a homemade uniform, buying weapons on the black market, and perhaps even employing an ex-soldier or two as mercenaries. The wars in the former Yugoslavia or the Transcaucasian region are being fought this way.

In the Croatian-occupied part of Bosnia-Herzegovina, known as the Croatian Community of Herzog-Bosne, there are, for example, several military groups. There is the official Croatian-Bosnian army, the HVO; the Muslim territorial defense force known as Armija; the extreme right-wing Hos, who wear black in memory of the Ustashe (Croatian Nazis) who ruled Croatia in 1941–1945; and a number of smaller free-lance armies such as the Croatian Falcons or the Yellow Ants. Each group has its own chain of command, sources of supply, registered license plates, and roadblocks. Similar groups can be found in the Serbian parts of Bosnia-Herzegovina and, with the breakdown of lines of command, the Yugoslav army (the JNA) has come to look more and more like a collection of paramilitary groups.

Much the same situation can be found in Transcaucasia. In Georgia, all the political parties, except the Greens, have their own militias. Shevardnadze has tried to reestablish a monopoly over the means of violence by trying to weld together these militias into a regular army. It is this ragbag of armed bands that is currently facing defeat at the hands of the Abkhazian National Guard. In Ngorno Karabakh, you see everywhere young men in various uniforms lolling around waiting to be sent to the front. They are all unpaid volunteers. The minister of defense of Ngorno Karabakh, a former Intourist guide, told me he thought it would become easier to create a regular army now that there was a "real war." In Azerbaijan, the government is employing Russian ex-Soviet army officers on yearly contracts to create a regular army. All the same, the Ministry of Defense official spokesman described the war with Armenia as a "citizens struggle. . . . We have no army and they have no army—this is a citizens struggle. All the fighting is done by irregular troops."

Private armies exist as in feudal times, but no single grouping has the legitimacy to reestablish a monopoly. None, be it an elected government or a disaffected minority, can command widespread trust in society. In these circumstances, government troops become just another paramilitary group.

In societies where the state controlled every aspect of social and economic life, the collapse of the state means anarchy. The introduction of markets actually means the absence of any kind of regulation. The kind of self-organized market institutions that are the precondition for a market economy simply do not exist. The market does not, by and large, mean new autonomous productive enterprises. It means corruption, speculation, and crime. Many of these paramilitary groups are engaged in a struggle for survival. They use the language of nationalism to legitimize a kind of primitive accumulation—a grab for land or capital. The nationalist conflicts in the former Yugoslavia and Soviet Union cannot be understood as traditional power politics; that is, not as conflicting political objectives defined by parties to the conflict, which are, in principle, amenable to some kind of compromise solution. Rather, they have to be understood as a social condition—a condition of laissez-faire violence.

Many of the characteristics of this social condition exist throughout the postcommunist world. But the situation is more extreme in the former Yugoslavia and Soviet Union, for historical and geographical reasons. Both regions are a patchwork of ethnicities; the countries of Central Europe are much more homogeneous. Both regions have histories of ethnic conflicts that politicians can easily use. This is especially true in Yugoslavia, where memories of atrocities inflicted on all communities, and especially the Serbs, during the Second World War are still vivid. And in both regions, the communist regimes—Stalin in the Soviet Union and Tito in Yugoslavia—exploited national questions in order to sustain their rule.

The new nationalism is different from the old nationalism. First, the new nationalism is antimodern, whereas earlier nationalisms were of modernization. Nationalism has, of course, always harked back to some idea of a romantic past, but the old nationalism was an essential component of modernity: It was linked to the rise of the modern state and industrialization. The early nationalists were functionalist: Nationalism, for them, was part of the march toward progress. The nation-state was a viable political unit for democracy and industry, not merely a natural institution for a historically established national community. It was a stage in human evolution, from local to national and eventually to global society. Mazzini, for example, did not support Irish independence because he thought Ireland was not viable as a nation-state. Similarly, nationalists in the Third World viewed national liberation as a precondition for modernization and development.

In contrast, the new nationalism is antimodern, not only because it is a reaction against modernity, but also because it is not a viable political project—it is out of tune with the times. This is why it is antimodern rather than postmodern. The rediscovery of cultural identity is often considered an element of postmodernism. This implies some possibility of moving beyond modernity, whatever that may involve. The new nationalism offers no such prospect. In a world of growing economic, ecological, and even social interdependence, the new nationalism wants to create ever smaller political units.

Earlier nationalisms incorporated different cultural traditions. The new nationalism is culturally separatist. It is often said that Yugoslavia was an artificial creation because it contained so many different linguistic, religious, and cultural traditions. But all modern nations were artificial. The national language was usually based on a dominant dialect, which was spread through the written word and education. At the time of Italian unification, only between 2 percent and 3 percent of Italians spoke Italian. At the first sitting of the newly created National Assembly, Massline d'Azeglio said: "We have made Italy, now we have to make Italians." The Yugoslav project was less successful than earlier national projects, perhaps because it was attempted too late or too quickly. The new nationalism is a reaction to the cultural hegemony of earlier nationalisms. It is an attempt to preserve and reconstruct preexisting cultural traditions, said to be national, at the expense of other traditions.

The new nationalism emphasizes ethnos. Cultural traditions are a birthright; they cannot be acquired. This is reflected in the citizenship laws in the Baltic countries or in Slovenia and Croatia, which exclude certain minorities and which distinguish between autochthonous, i.e., indigenous, and other minorities. There were, of course, elements of ethnicity in earlier nationalisms, especially in Germany. But now the emphasis on ethnos combined with cultural separatism contains an inherent tendency toward fragmentation. Every excluded minority discovers it is a nation. The former Yugoslavia is not only divided into Slovenia, Croatia, and Bosnia-Herzegovina, and so forth. Croatia is also divided into a Croatian and Serbian part; in Bosnia and Herzegovina, there is now a Bosnian Croatian state and a Bosnian Serbian state; and there are now distinctions between Bosnian Muslims who were once Croat and Bosnian Muslims who were once Serbs.

The antimodernism of the new nationalist movements is also reflected in their social composition. The earlier nationalist movements were more often urban and middle class, although they did become mass movements in the twentieth century. Although it is difficult to generalize, the new movements often include an important rural element. Susan Woodward has characterized the war in Bosnia-Herzegovina as a socioeconomic war, in which rural nationalists control multiethnic townspeople. In Serbia, the main support for Milosovic comes from industrial workers who live in the countryside and maintain their own smallholdings. In the nineteenth century and in Third World national liberation movements, intellectuals were extremely important. There are still, of course, nationalist intellectuals, but in today's world, where the opportunities to travel and collaborate with intellectuals in other countries have greatly increased, it is much more common to find intellectuals in Green, peace, and human rights movements that have a global consciousness. The expansion of education, and scientific and office jobs, has greatly increased the number of people who can be called intellectuals and who have international horizons. In Serbia, it is the students and the Academy of Sciences that constitute the main opposition to Milosovic. In the Transcaucasian region, it is Armenian and Azerbaijani intellectuals, supported by Russian intellectuals, who are working the hardest to overcome national conflicts.

A postmodern project would be integrating rather than unifying or fragmentative. It would emphasize cultural diversity rather than cultural homogeneity or cultural divisiveness. It would encompass the growing educated strata in society. Some people argue that the new nationalism has the potential to be integrating. Scottish nationalists talk about Scotland in Europe. Likewise, the new nation-states in Eastern Europe all say that they want to "join Europe." Indeed, the main motivation for nationalism in Slovenia and Croatia and also the Baltic states seems to have been that these people believed their chances of joining the European Community would be greater if they were unencumbered by their large backward neighbors, i.e., Russia and Serbia. Fashionable European concepts like "subsidiarity" or "Europe of the Regions" offer the possibility of combining local and regional autonomy with Europewide cooperation. But this is completely at odds with the ethnic principle of citizenship and even with the territorial sovereignty that is an essential element of all nationalisms. In practice, the new nationalism has shown itself to be closed to the outside world. New nationalist governments are reimposing control over the media, especially television; they are renationalizing rather than privatizing industry; they are introducing new barriers to travel, trade, and communication by increasing frontiers. As such, the new nationalist project is unviable; it is incapable of solving economic and environmental problems, and it is a recipe for violent unrest and frequent wars.

The second way the new nationalism differs from earlier nationalisms is the use of new technology. If the new nationalism is antimodern in philosophy, it is modern or even postmodern in technique. In place of the novels and newspapers that constructed the earlier nationalism, the new nationalism is based on new communicative networks involving television, videos, telephones, faxes, and computers. These techniques extend the possibilities for mobilizing, manipulating, and controlling public opinion. New neo-Nazis in Germany circulate anti-Semitic videos, and they use CB radios to orchestrate their demonstrations.

The use of new technology had led to the rise of transnational "imagined communities." Groups of exiles in Paris, London, and Zurich have often played an important role in national movements. But ease of communication and the expansion of expatriate communities in new countries such as the United States, Canada, or Australia have transformed the new national movements into transnational networks. In almost every significant national movement, money, arms, and ideas are provided by expatriates abroad. Irish-American support for the IRA has been well documented. Other examples include Canadian mercenaries in Croatia, American Macedonians calling for the unification of Macedonia and Bulgaria, and the Armenian diaspora supporting the claim to Ngorno Karabakh. The new nationalism has resulted, in part, from the loss of cultural identity in the anonymous melting pot nations of the New World. The dreams of the expatriates, the longing for a "homeland" that does not exist, are dangerously superimposed on the antimodern chaotic reality they have left behind. Radha Kumar has described the support that Indians living in the United States give to the Hindu nationalist movement: "Separated from their countries of origin, often living as aliens in a foreign land, simultaneously feeling stripped of their culture and guilty for having escaped the troubles 'back home', ex-patriots turn to diaspora nationalism without understanding the violence that their actions might inadvertently trigger."

Another aspect of the new technology is, of course, modern weapons. Modern military technology is immensely destructive. Even without the most up-to-date systems, villages and towns in Croatia, Bosnia, and Herzegovina have been razed. It is the combination of an antimodern philosophy with modern technology, in both military and communicative terms, that makes the new nationalism so dangerous.

The new nationalism is a dead-end phenomenon. It is a reaction to the oppressive nature of modernity, especially its statist Eastern European variant, and a rationale for a new gangsterism. It will lead at best to small, autarchic, authoritarian, poor states, and at worst to endemic, continuous violence. The conflict in Northern Ireland can be viewed as a foretaste of the new nationalism; it is a mistake to view the events in Ulster as a reversion to the past, although the various parties to the conflict—especially the various paramilitary groups—do make use of tradition. Rather, it is a contemporary antimodern phenomenon with many similarities to the new nationalisms in Eastern Europe.

The new nationalism is unviable because the nation-state as a form of organization, with extensive administrative control over clearly defined territory, is no longer an effective instrument for managing modern societies. In fact, this was already the case before World War I. The bloc system, which emerged after the Second World War as a result of the Cold War, established for a while some sort of stability, albeit oppressive, because it overcame some of the nation-state's shortcomings.

The nation-state is both too large and too small. It is too small to cope with economic interdependence, global environmental problems, and destructive military technologies. It is too large to allow for democratic accountability, cultural diversity, and the complex decisionmaking needed in the economic and environmental realms. The blocs offered a method of dealing with the problem that the nations were too small. But they greatly exacerbated the problems arising from the fact that nation-states were also too large. The new nationalism has reacted to these problems by trying to make ever smaller nation-states.

We now need a break with the idea of territorial sovereignty—the notion of more or less absolute control by a centralized administrative unit over a specific geographic area. We need greater autonomy at local and regional levels to enhance democracy, to increase people's ability to influence their own lives, to foster cultural traditions and diversity, to overcome the sense of anonymity caused by modernity, and to make sensible decisions about local economic and environmental problems. But we also need international institutions with the real power to intervene at local levels to protect human rights and democracy, to uphold environmental and social standards, and to prevent war. In other words, we need layers of political organization crisscrossing both territory and fields of activity.

Is this a utopian idea? Actually, elements of this approach already exist. The most important example is the European Community (EC). The EC is not the forerunner of a European nation-state; it is a new kind of political institution with elements of supranationality, that is, sovereignty in certain fields of activity, which allows it to interfere in member-state affairs and overrule them on some issues. The EC could become an institution capable of dealing with Europewide problems while also enhancing local and regional autonomies. The same evolution could occur in other international institutions, such as the United Nations or the CSCE (Conference on Security and Cooperation in Europe). These organizations now get their power from the nation-states, which severely limits what they can achieve. If their roles are to be extended, it will have to come from new forms of transnational political pressure.

New forms of communication have helped develop transnational networks. In certain fields, especially intellectual and managerial activity, people communicate more—through telephone, fax, and frequent travel—with others in their same field around the world than with their neighbors or their fellow nationals. If these networks have created transnational "imagined communities" based on ethnicity, they have also created more globally conscious "imagined communities." Two types of networks have a common interest, together with international institutions, in curbing the administrative sway of nation-states.

One type of network involves local layers of government: municipalities and regional governments. Since the early 1980s, local governments have become much more involved with foreign policy issues through twinning arrangements, nuclear-free or violence-free zones, and other initiatives. Organizations such as the Association of Nuclear-free Authorities, the Standing Council of Local Authorities of the Council of Europe, and the Association of European Regions potentially represent new types of transnational pressure groups.

A second type of network has emerged from the single-issue social movements of the 1970s and 1980s. These groups were much more successful at local and transnational levels than at national levels. Not able to break the grip of traditional political parties on national politics, they were much more effective than parties at creating transnational constituencies. Organizations like Greenpeace, Helsinki-Watch, Amnesty International, Oxfam, and the Helsinki Citizens Assembly can cross national boundaries and operate internationally. To these groups should be added trade unions, churches, and academic institutions, which have greatly increased their international networks in recent years. Together, they are forming what could be called transnational civil society.

Throughout Eastern Europe and especially in areas of conflict, brave groups of people, often intellectuals, are struggling to provide an alternative to violence and ethnic nationalism. They use the language of citizenship, civil society, nonviolence, and internationalism. They are supported by transnational networks such as those mentioned above. The main hope for an alternative to nationalism lies in constructing a new political culture, a new legitimate language, that might be based on an alliance between the emerging transnational civil society and international institutions.

The Balkan war provides an example of what could be done. The activities of international institutions are now greatly hampered because they are intergovernmental, which means they are seeking solutions "from above." This is because they can only make decisions based on compromise between member states, and often the compromises satisfy no one. They also assume that their negotiating partners should be the representatives of states or embryo states, yet these are the aggressive nationalists who are breaking all the norms of international behavior. Thus, international institutions are becoming parties to ethnic partition, which could mean, among other things, a loss of legitimacy for the institutions themselves.

The new nationalism is a social condition arising from the collapse of communist state structures. The new politicians may have been elected, but they do not have the legitimacy to be considered "representative" of the people because they practice exclusionary policies. There are also, in the Balkan region, municipalities, civic groups, and individuals who are trying to keep multiethnic communities together, to prevent the spread of war, to support refugees and deserters, and to provide humanitarian aid. These groups are helped by municipal and civic transnational networks, but their resources are extremely meager. If international institutions could make those groups and institutions that uphold international standards their primary partners, and could condemn all those who violate international norms, it could begin the reconstruction of legitimate political culture "from below."

The forerunners of the new groups in Eastern Europe are the dissidents of the 1970s and 1980s. Their political discourse can be traced back to the dialogue between peace groups and democracy groups across the East-West divide. In the long run, that dialogue should be remembered not for its role in ending the Cold War and ushering in a new period of turbulent nationalism, but rather for its role in establishing a new way of thinking about politics and political institutions.

CHAPTER 23

Pro Patria Mori! Death and the State

By Yael Tamir

Fortunate indeed are they who draw for their lot a death so glorious as that which has caused your mourning, and to whom life has been so exactly measured as to terminate in the happiness in which it has been passed.

—Pericles, in Thucydides,
History of the Peloponnesian War

The awareness of death, says Heidegger, confers upon human beings a sense of their individuality: "Dying is one thing no one can do for you; each of us must die alone."[1] Yet death—the commemoration and veneration of the dead, the fear of death—plays a major role in political life; it is used to strengthen communality, to build a collective identity, and to define communal obligations. The central role that the tomb of the unknown soldier plays in national ceremonies can serve to illustrate this phenomenon. By its very nature, this tomb is meant not to commemorate a particular person but to promote an *ideal* of a soldier, *our* soldier as, although his personal identity is unknown, his communal identity is certain; he is a fellow citizen. And as he has performed the ultimate act of sacrifice, he has become the perfect fellow citizen. All his flaws are forgiven, as his "good action has blotted out the bad, and his merit as a citizen more than outweighed his demerits as an individual."[2]

The glory of the fallen is closely intertwined with the glory of the state—the fact that exemplary individuals willingly give up their lives for the state is purported to prove that the state is worthy of such an offering, while the merits of the state make the sacrifice of the fallen worthwhile. The fact that citizens care about their state and are motivated to defend it is taken as a manifestation of its legitimacy, as evidence that citizens see the state as their own, cherish its existence, and support its government. This is especially true for democratic states, whose legitimacy is grounded in consent. It is therefore in the interest of such states to demonstrate that individuals are ready to risk their lives in defense of their state and that they are ready to do so for the right reasons—namely, out of identification, pride, love, and support for their country.[3]

Yet the readiness to risk one's life for one's state clashes with the most powerful individual interest—self-preservation. Why would anyone be willing to make such an offering? This is the essence of the question Einstein poses to Freud in their famous exchange of open letters.[4] In his answer Freud makes reference to the duality of the human psyche, which is motivated by erotic instincts that seek to "preserve and unite" on the one hand and by destructive instincts that seek to "kill and destroy" on the other. This duality, he argues, is reflected in the political sphere. Political life thus embodies an aspiration to promote identification and love, alongside a permission to foster hatred and aggressiveness. The subjects of these feelings are the members of two different groups: members of in-group or "us" and members of other groups or "the enemy."[5] The dual nature of political life suggests that the hope that human aggressiveness will wither away is no more than an illusion. Even those who, like the Russian communists, aspire to eliminate belligerency, Freud sarcastically observes, are "armed to day with the most scrupulous care and not the least important of the methods by which they keep their supporters together is hatred of everyone beyond their frontiers."[6]

Nationalism carries well this dual message of love and hostility. This is why it has been such an effective ally for a wide range of political ideologies. Its services are especially necessary at times of war, when internal devotion and external animosity must be intensified and when the cost of such attitudes—namely, massive, brutal, daily death—is incurred.

War is bound to sweep away the conventional treatment of death, Freud argues. At bottom "no one believes in his own death, or to put the same thing in another way, in the unconscious every one of us is convinced of his immortality." Yet at times of war death can no longer be denied; "we are forced to believe in him."[7] When death becomes "believable," it is much harder to repress the fear of death. Under such bleak circumstances one would expect that it would be much harder to convince individuals to risk their lives for the state, yet this is not necessarily the case. Quite often war incites rather than discourages the readiness of individuals to risk their lives in defending the state. Many different reasons could explain this phenomenon. War may evoke feelings of fear, revenge, humiliation; it can highlight the importance of a cause or a set of values one finds just and worthy of defense; and it can grant those who enjoy taking risks or acting recklessly and violently permission to behave in these ways. These feelings and attitudes could be harnessed by the state and used to enhance the readiness to fight. The state can also adopt a different strategy; it can attempt to confront the most painful aspect of war—death—and ameliorate the natural fear of it. This essay is an attempt to look at this latter strategy; hence it looks at the strategies states adopt in those cases in which the presence of death is evident, when the state is involved in actual fighting that demands many young lives. This—apart from my own personal background—is the reason why Israeli examples play such a major role in the argument.

At such moments of crisis, states searching for an ideology that enables them to justify their demand that their citizens risk their lives in their defense will find support in nationalism. Using a nationalist discourse, states restructure the image of both the political community and the conflict itself. Thus, creating a frame in which the difficult question of how an individual should act in relation to a certain conflict "is simplified and reinterpreted in terms of emotional ties and moral obligations to family and community . . . Cognitively, it focuses individuals' attention on a small subset of all the consequences of the choice to sacrifice for the nation or not, and thus makes the choice set simpler, while also biasing it towards the nation."[8] This restructuring of the citizen's choices is indispensable for states that foster a contractual ethos as they lack the ideological foundations necessary to incite in individuals a readiness to risk their lives for the state and is much less essential for states whose constitutive set of values provides a justification for self-sacrifice. Ironically then, an appeal to national feelings and ideology is much more necessary and effective in the case of liberal democracies.

While it is commonly claimed that nations need states to secure their existence, the argument developed here suggests that the reverse is also true. Nationalism should therefore be seen not as the pathology infecting modern liberal states but as an answer to their legitimate needs of self-defense or, to put it in even more dramatic terms, as a remedy to their malaise—namely, the atomism, neurosis, and alienation that inflict liberal states and may leave them defenseless.[9]

IN THE NAME OF THE FATHERLAND; IN THE NAME OF GOD

Before I turn to develop this argument, let me take a short interlude and explore two alternative conceptions of the state that could justify self-sacrifice without making any reference to nationalism. According to the organic view of the state, both the life and the welfare of individuals are wholly contingent on the existence and well-being of the political whole. If individuals are viewed as parts of a whole and lifeless without it, it would seem natural to say, as does Pope Pius II, that "for the benefit of the whole body a foot or a hand, which in the state are the citizens, must be amputated, since the prince himself, who is the head of the mystical body of the state, is held to sacrifice his life whenever the commonwealth would demand it."[10]

According to this description, acts performed with the welfare of the state in mind are motivated by an instinct for self-preservation. The readiness to defend the state even at the price of one's life is thus seen as no different from the readiness to raise one's arm in order to protect oneself at the risk of severe injury or even amputation. The question of why individuals would risk their lives for the state therefore receives a clear answer.

The marriage between the state and religious ideals provides an even more convincing answer to this question. If the state is endowed with a religious content, then dying in its protection could be portrayed not only as a holy obligation but also as a desirable end, as it would allow a person to enter into the *patria eterna*, into a better, heavenly world. For their self-sacrifice in the service of Christ, the fallen receive "the martyr's crown in the life hereafter."[11] The words of a Crusader's song reflect this belief:

> He that embarks to the Holy Land,
> He that dies in this campaign,
> Shall enter into heaven's bliss
> And with the saints there shall he dwell.[12]

Those who die in war thus leave this world only to become citizens of the heavenly kingdom.

According to Islam, death in a jihad (a holy war against infidels) ensures passage through the heavenly gates. During the Iran-Iraq war, both sides sent young children onto the battlefield with a key to heaven tied to a ribbon around their neck. Hizzballa warriors are promised a place in heaven for making suicide attacks, and Palestinians killed during the Intifada (Palestinian uprising) are regarded as *shahids* (martyrs). After a deadly suicide bus bombing, Hamas, the Muslim militant group that launched the attack, threatened to unleash more violence. When the late Israeli prime minister Yitzhak Rabin ordered that Hamas's top military leaders be killed on sight, the organization vowed to retaliate for Rabin's hard-line stance. Rabin must be shown, a press release stated, "that Hamas loves death more than Rabin and his soldiers love life."[13]

The religious dimension of politics turns the death in war of a brother, husband, or friend into a gain that outweighs the personal loss. "Don't come to express your condolences; come to congratulate me," said the father of the youngest victim at the Hebron massacre. "I have become the father of a *shahid*."

As these examples clearly demonstrate, when a state or a political movement is seen as a carrier of religious ideals, these ideals can endow individuals with the motivation not only to risk their lives for the state but also to die in its name.[14]

BEYOND CONTRACTARIANISM

Rational individuals could well enter a contract that reduces their risks—namely, a contract that, without granting absolute security, offers better terms than the state of nature. Yet according to Hobbes, it would be perfectly rational and legitimate for such individuals, when found in a life-threatening situation—soldiers fighting a national war, police officers trying to enforce law and order, firefighters combating a fire—to try their best to save their own skin, leaving their fellow citizens unprotected. This would be true even if individuals had willingly entered a contract committing them to some communal obligations, including the obligation to fight and die for the protection of their community. "A man who risks his life for the state accepts the insecurity which it was the only end of his political obedience to avoid."[15] This is especially true for a young man asked to serve in a wartime army. In such cases "the personal threat becomes so obvious that even a cognitively lazy follower of rules of thumb will notice that supporting the group is not in his self-interest."[16]

When facing death, Hobbes argues, individuals are justified in seeking to ensure their own self-preservation rather than abiding by the contract. True, their defection may destabilize the contract and even rescind it altogether, bringing them back to the state of nature. Nevertheless, no matter how threatening the state of nature might be, it is likely to be less threatening than the risk of immediate death. According to this analysis, the higher the risks faced by the state and the greater its defense requirements, the lower the readiness of its citizens to rally to its defense.

The threat of death seems to invalidate a contract whose main aim is the preservation of life. Death is, therefore, the "contradiction of politics."[17] In its presence, each person is left alone. But if a Hobbesian contract is necessarily abrogated in the face of external threats or internal disorder, leaving each individual to face the risks of nature alone, what might be its justification?[18]

Other contractarian approaches seem to lead to a similar deadlock. If individuals enter political agreements in order to protect their interests, life, rights, property, or well-being, agreeing to expose themselves to the dangers of death would be ridiculous, as "the means, death, would forthwith annul the end, property and enjoyment."[19] They would therefore be justified in taking any possible means in order to avoid risking their lives (though they could have good reasons to support the state's existence by a variety of "non-life-threatening actions").

Liberal morality offers no coherent guideline on such questions as "to fight or not to fight," argues Annette Baler. Liberal morality can only say "the choice is yours" and hope "that enough will choose to be self-sacrificial life providers and self-sacrificial death dealers to suit the purpose of the rest."[20] The catch, however, is that individuals reared within a liberal contractarian tradition, especially a Hobbesian one, are likely to have acquired the kind of atomistic identity that precludes the possibility of becoming self-sacrificial life providers. Liberal states thus run the risk of not having enough, or even any, individuals who will voluntarily choose to risk their lives in defense of the state. Such states must therefore stand defenseless or cultivate in their citizens an identity inconsistent with their political ethos.[21]

THE USEFULNESS OF NATIONALISM

History shows that faced with a choice between inconsistency and insecurity, liberal states have opted to foster an identity more communal in nature than their professed political ethos might have implied. They attempt to offer their citizens a stable and continuous national identity, thus imbuing the social contract with a new meaning—portraying it not only as a means to protect individual interests but also as a means to meet the need for roots, for stability, for a place in a continuum that links the past with the future.

National ceremonies, memorial days, the veneration of fallen soldiers, and the geographic and symbolic centrality of the Place de la Republique in Paris, Trafalgar Square in London, Arlington National Cemetery in Virginia, Piazza Venezia in Rome, and Mount Herzl in Jerusalem all convey the same message: the state is not merely a voluntary association but a community of fate.

But why would the insertion of nationalistic ideals and images influence the citizens' preferences and choices?[22] The answer has to do with the ability of the nationalist way of thinking to transform the self-image of individuals by portraying their personal welfare as closely tied to the existence and prosperity of their national community, as well as to its ability to contextualize human actions, making them part of a continuous creative effort whereby the national community is made and remade. By so doing, nationalism imparts special significance to even the most mundane actions and endows individual lives with meaning. It is in this sense that nationalism bestows extra merit on social, cultural, or political acts and provides individuals with additional channels for self-fulfillment that make their lives more rewarding.

Defending the continuity of their national community can thus be seen by individuals as a ground project, an endeavor on which the successful pursuit of all other significant projects is dependent. Ground projects are of the kind of projects for which it is worth fighting and risking one's life. There is no contradiction, claims Bernard Williams, in the idea of death for the sake of a ground project—"quite the reverse, since if death really is necessary for the project, then to live would be to live with it unsatisfied, something which, if it is really [a person's] ground project, he has no reason to do."[23] If a person's ground project is to live a meaningful life and if membership in a particular national-cultural community is a necessary, though by no means sufficient, condition to living such a life, a person may have a reason to risk his or her life in order to ensure the continuity and growth of his or her nation. But would not this argument lead to the paradox mentioned above? If one's purpose is to lead a worthwhile life, death would certainly thwart this goal.

One way to confront this issue is to proclaim a close link between the readiness to die for a cause and the belief that one's life is meaningful. According to Williams, the readiness to die for specific projects reaffirms the self-image of the person not as someone to whom all projects are equally external or contingent but as someone who has some constitutive commitments that make his or her life meaningful. The process is one of active equilibrium; identity generates obligations and obligations define identity. This interplay between identity and obligation is of a special importance for liberal agents whose ends and commitments are elective. By expressing readiness to risk their lives in the pursuit of some of their projects, liberal agents draw a distinction between contingent and constitutive projects, between projects that are theirs and projects that define their identity.

Ground projects need not be collective or, if they are, need not have the state, or the nation, as their object. States, however, are obviously interested in their citizens adopting collective ground projects in which the state plays a central role and will therefore devote considerable effort to cultivating a preference for such projects. As will be demonstrated in the following sections, nationalistic language and symbols are extremely useful for the purpose of endowing the state with a collective mission—that of protecting the continuity and prosperity of the nation.

The importance of endowing the state with a national task that creates a link between the present generation, its ancestors, and future generations cannot be overstated; it helps individuals conquer the fear of death by promising them an opportunity to enter the sphere of the eternal.[24] Hence even states whose main molding power is ideological adopt the genealogical and exclusivist language and symbols typical of nationalism. This is well expressed by Edmund Burke's words: "It has been the uniform policy of our constitution to claim and assert our liberties, as an ensiled inheritance derived to us from our forefathers, and to be transmitted to our posterity."[25]

Yet individuals who adopt a national project may still prefer that others defend their nation-state for them. Freeriding is especially tempting as the existence of a state is a collective good whose benefits individuals would enjoy even if they did not personally contribute to its defense. Commemoration rites and national ceremonies are meant to solve this collective action problem—namely, to convince individuals that they ought to *commit themselves* to protecting their state with their lives. In venerating and remembering the fallen, the state conveys to its citizens the following message: in committing yourself to the welfare, endurance, security, and prosperity of your state, a commitment that may force you to face danger and risk death, you will secure substantial gains; refraining from such a commitment will, on the other hand, entail social costs.

TILTING THE BALANCE: HOW TO COUNTER THE FEAR OF DEATH

The attempt to convince individuals that they should risk their lives for the state runs counter to one of the most powerful human fears—the fear of death. One might attempt to counter this fear by following Epicurus's line of argument: "Make yourself familiar with the belief that death is nothing to us, since everything good and bad lies in sensation, and death is to deprive us of sensation. So that most fearful of all bad things, death, is nothing to us, since when we are, death is not, and when death is present, then we are not."[26] Based on the Epicurean argument, Walter Glannon suggests an analysis that shows the fear of death to be irrational:

1. The state of being dead is not (good or) bad for the one who is dead.
2. If something is not bad when it is present, however, there are no rational grounds for fearing its future presence at a previous time.
3. Therefore, it is irrational for a person to fear his future state of being dead.[27]

If we accept Epicurus's argument, we ought not fear death itself, and yet we may still be anxious about the implications of that future state of affairs for our present life. Four kinds of implications suggest themselves. The first relates to our fear of the moment of death itself: What will it feel like? Will it be painful? Will I suffer? The second reflects the difficulties involved in accepting mortality, the incidental and nonessential nature of human existence, the fact that the world will go on existing without us. The third is closely related to the second and has to do with the implications of our mortality for the meaning of our life, as the fact that our existence is contingent and finite may cast doubts on the relevance and meaningfulness of our being here at all. The fourth has to do with our concern for our loved ones who might be left unsupported and unprotected.

The following sections explore some of the strategies by which states attempt to contend with these fears.[28] These strategies demand a shift in the self-image of the state and its political discourse, adding the national perspective with its promise for continuity and fraternity between generations to the liberal democratic one.

GLORIFYING DEATH

In an attempt to counter the fear of the moment of death itself, memorial rites and patriotic literature portray the deaths of patriots as peaceful and gentle, playing down any bloody or gory features. This becomes evident if we think of a following comparison of two scenes of death. The first appears in "The Silver Platter," a nationalistic poem that for many Israelis has an equal status to the Yizkor, the memorial prayer of traditional Jewish liturgy. The heart of the poem is a scene in which a young man and woman, holding hands, weary of toil and battle, quietly step forward to face the nation: "We are the silver platter / On which the Jewish state has been given you," they say, and "enveloped in shadow at the people's feet they fell."[29] The death of the young couple seems pure, sublime, even appealing. Although they have just emerged from a long and bitter national struggle, they are neither wounded nor mutilated; their appearance bears no traces of their suffering. "Silently the two approached / And stood there unmoving. / There was no saying whether they were alive or shot."[30] Death is implied but never mentioned.

This scene of death calls to mind the death of another young couple, whose story ends with these famous words:

> A glooming peace this morning with it brings;
> The sun for sorrow will not show his head:
> Go hence, to have more talk of these sad things;
> Some shall be pardoned, and some punished:
> For never was a story of more woe
> Than this of Juliet and her Romeo.

The deaths of Romeo and Juliet seem much less graceful and inviting than those of the young couple in "The Silver Platter." Romeo's and Juliet's deaths are portrayed realistically, as bloody and painful. The sight of Juliet's tormented body causes her father to moan:

> O heaven!—O wife, look how our daughter bleeds!
> This dagger hath mista'en,—for, lo his house
> is empty on the back of Montague,—
> And is mis-sheathed in my daughter's bosom![31]

While in *Romeo and Juliet* the ugliness of death is contrasted with the splendors of love, in "The Silver Platter" the glory of death is contrasted with the ugliness of War. According to George Mosse, a change in the attitude toward death in war took place during the eighteenth century: "The image of [death as] the grim reaper was replaced by the image of death as eternal sleep."[32] This shift is well expressed in Wilfred Owen's poem "Asleep," written on November 14, 1917:

> Under his helmet, up against his pack,
> After the many days of work and waking,
> Sleep took him by the brow and laid him back.
> And in the Happy no-time of his sleeping,
> Death took him by the heart.[33]

As these brief examples suggest, nationalist discourse attempts to portray the moment of death as instantaneous, gracious, and painless rather than as brutal and painful.

Moreover, nationalist literature ties death to hope and a promise for a better future, rather than to despair and destitution. Unlike Romeo and Juliet, whose deaths are motivated by despair, the youths portrayed in "The Silver Platter" are motivated by their hope that their deaths will help to achieve a nationalistic aim, the establishment of a Jewish state, which they considered worth dying for. This explains why death in *Romeo and Juliet* is the end of the story while death in "The Silver Platter" is but a beginning. "The rest," we are promised, "will be told in the annals of Israel."

PROMISING REDEMPTION FROM PERSONAL OBLIVION

The second kind of fear touches upon the human desire not to be forgotten. It is hard for people to accept that their lives will end leaving no impression, that they will wither without a trace. A man, Milan Kundera writes, "knows that he is mortal, but he takes it for granted that his nation possesses a kind of eternal life."[34] In these words Kundera captures the message that national myths convey: nations are immortal; they transcend contingency. Nationalism thus shifts finite human experience from the sphere of the mundane and contingent to the realm of the eternal.

National monuments, memorial services, funerals, and rites of commemoration constitute *les lieux de memoire*, the domains of collective memory. In performing them, the nation asserts that as long as it will endure, it will show gratitude to all who struggle and sacrifice their lives for its survival. It will turn them into heroes, perhaps even canonize them. The military cemeteries, the memorial days, are all ways of living up to this solemn oath: the fallen shall not be forgotten; they will go on living in the memory of the nation. We live because of them, and in living we save their memory and imbue their death with meaning.

On the verge of their almost certain death in battle, King Henry promises his men immortality, a chance to attain glory by entering the national pantheon:

> This story shall the good man teach his son
> And Crispin Crispian shall ne'er go by,
> From this day to the ending of the world,
> But we in it shall be remembered;
> We few, we happy few, we band of brothers.[35]

This promise is meaningful because King Henry and his men are convinced that England will go on until "the ending of the world," for if it does not, the memory of this glorious battle, and with it the promise of immortality, might wane. Members of other nations may also remember the war; for example, many of us remember the war in Marathon even though we are not Greek. But only members of the nation take a vow to remember and feel they have a moral obligation to do so.

The fallen are seen as part of the nation's chain of being, regenerating time and again with each new generation. The most striking metaphorical expression of this continuity can be found in the identification of fallen soldiers with nature. As the poet compares the rhythm of the nation to that of nature, the fallen are portrayed as "an integral part of the changing seasons, from the death of winter to the resurrection of the spring."[36] Like the drought of summer, the death of soldiers is seen as another stage of being in the life of the nation. Wilfred Owen's words, once again, provide a vivid representation of this tendency:

> Yet his thin and sodden head
> Confuses more and more with the low mould,
> His hair being one with the grey grass
> And finished fields of autumns that are old.[37]

Death in war is thus portrayed as an integral part of the national chain of being, which embodies endless regenerations. In Chaim Guri's poem, well known to all Israelis, the dead promise to return as red poppies:

> We shall raise, to break through again as then,
> and come to life again.
> We shall stride, terrible, large, as we race to the rescue,
> for it all within us still lives and floods our veins, and burns.[38]

Poppies are a symbol of renewal; in Britain they are used as a symbol of commemoration, and in Hebrew they were given an indicative name: "the blood of the Macabees." The identification of fallen soldiers with nature is represented in the heroes' grove in Germany, in the French *jardin funebre*, in the Italian Parco della Rimembranza, as well as in many forests in Israel where the names of the fallen are affixed to trees.

The notion of continuity and regeneration embodied in nationalism is of particular importance in a secular era, in which identification with the nation is "the surest way to surmount the finality of death and ensure a measure of personal immortality."[39] This is the most valuable reward for death in the service of the nation.

THE MEANING OF LIFE

Rites of commemoration attempt to break the link between the length and meaningfulness of one's life. They express a belief that one's ability to live a meaningful life depends not only on the way one lives but also on the way one finds his or her death.

This is not such an unusual claim; we can easily imagine a person who has lived a shorter but more meaningful life than another who lived longer. When comparing the misfortune entailed by the death of two individuals—Gerry, who lived to his biological limit, and Joe, who died relatively young—Jeff McMahan argues that "the explanation of why there is less reason to grieve for Gerry is simply that he has had a fair share of life. Relative to reasonable expectations, he had a rich and full life."[40] It thus seems that regrets over a person's death correspond to an estimate of the value of his or her life.

Why does Keats's death at twenty-four seem tragic while Toistoy's death at eighty-two does not? Probably because we assume that had Keats lived to be eighty-two he would have continued writing. Yet as he had defined himself as a person for whom writing was a necessary and sufficient condition for living a meaningful life, it would seem reasonable to assume that if he had to choose between being creative only until the age of twenty-four and living on to be eighty-two, or being creative only until the age of thirty-four and dying at thirty-five, he would have chosen the latter.

The relations between longevity and meaningfulness might even be inverse if the fullness and richness of one's life are closely related to the way one finds his or her death—for example, if one's life is richer and more meaningful because one has volunteered to defend one's state. Indeed, one of the strategies used to encourage soldiers to commit themselves to fight for their country is to present this commitment as an act that will make their lives more meaningful, allow them to "be all that they can be," to develop their abilities to the fullest. Military life is therefore portrayed as "exemplifying courage, strength, hardness, control over passions, and the ability to protect the moral fabric of society by living a so-called manly life."[41] The test of manliness becomes a challenge best met by war. Combat soldiers are thus seen not only as the best citizens but also as the finest people. The meaning and worthiness of their lives are defined by their readiness to face death.

MONEY, STATUS, AND SEX

Once the state has established the moral worthiness of those who are ready to risk their lives in its defense, it can offer them a series of benefits, ranging from material goods, social status, and mobility to sexual rewards, to more abstract awards such as glory, respect, and public idolization. Most of these benefits are differential; the highest go to those who join the combat units. Once individuals are convinced to join such units, the army invests great effort in building up an esprit de corps that will pressure soldiers, when the time comes, to join the actual fighting. Wartime experiences are thus depicted as embodying a moral opportunity as they allow individuals not only to develop their own character but also to express true equality and camaraderie, and experience the brotherhood of warriors.

Some rewards, however, are more concrete. For many years there was a saying in Israel: "Pilots are the best men, and the best [girls] are for the pilots." Although crude, this phrase accurately describes the terms of the sexual exchange available to those who volunteer for the most risky and prestigious units. Similar transactions are offered in other societies, too, in the shape of romantic Hollywood melodramas like *An Officer and a Gentleman*, the sexy photographs that soldiers' wives send their husbands at the front, or the license to rape the enemy's women—all varieties of sexual rewards granted to those who risk their lives for the state.

Soldiers are also rewarded with material benefits. In Israel, for instance, soldiers are entitled to financial help and to preferential treatment from university acceptance boards and job placement centers. Retired military officers are propelled to the top of the political, economic, and administrative hierarchy and enjoy wide support from "old boy" networks. In other countries where military service is voluntary, it is advocated as a major vehicle of mobilization. Army service is presented as a means to acquire education and a reliable job and even to see the world. In any case, the state tends to emphasize the economic benefits and social advantages while minimizing the dangers involved.

The reverse side of the benefits awarded for participation are the costs incurred for refusing to fight, ranging from social exclusion to the restriction of working opportunities and career development. Pericles's words again successfully capture the essence of such an exchange: "And surely, to a man of spirit, the degradation of cowardice must be immeasurably more grievous than the unfelt death which strikes him in the midst of his strength and patriotism!"[42]

When enlisting, many people probably hope that they will never need to face danger and that, if they do, the state will fulfill its promise to do its best to lessen the risks involved, come to their rescue, never leave them behind if wounded, and make an exchange for them if they are ever captured by the enemy. Committing oneself to defend the state in a distant and uncertain future in exchange for actual and immediate benefits may then seem a calculated risk.

CHAPTER 24

Patriotism and Its Futures

By Arjun Appadurai

We need to think ourselves beyond the nation.[1] This is not to suggest that thought alone will carry us beyond the nation or that the nation is largely a thought or an imagined thing. Rather, it is to suggest that the role of intellectual practices is to identify the current crisis of the nation and in identifying it to provide part of the apparatus of recognition for postnational social forms. Although the idea that we are entering a postnational world seems to have received its first airings in literary studies, it is now a recurrent (if unselfconscious) theme in studies of postcolonialism, global politics, and international welfare policy. But most writers who have asserted or implied that we need to think postnationally have not asked exactly what emergent social forms compel us to do so, or in what way. This latter task is the principal focus of this chapter.

POSTDISCURSIVE COLONIES

For those of us who grew up male in the elite sectors of the postcolonial world, nationalism was our common sense and the principal justification for our ambitions, our strategies, and our sense of moral well-being. Now, almost half a century after independence was achieved for many of the new nations, the nation form is under attack, and that, too, from many points of view. As the ideological alibi of the territorial state, it is the last refuge of ethnic totalitarianism. In important critiques of the postcolony,[2] its discourses have been shown to be deeply implicated in the discourses of colonialism itself. It has frequently been a vehicle for the staged self-doubts of the heroes of the new nations—Sukarno, Jomo Kenyatta, Jawaharlal Nehru, Gamal Abdel Nasser—who fiddled with nationalism while the public spheres of their societies were beginning to burn. So, for postcolonial intellectuals such as myself, the question is, does patriotism have a future? And to what races and genders shall that future belong?

To answer this question requires not just an engagement with the problematics of the nation form, the imagined community,[3] the production of people,[4] the narrativity of nations,[5] and the colonial logics of nationalist discourse.[6] It also requires a close examination of the discourses of the state and the discourses that are contained within the hyphen that links nation to state.[7] What follows is an exploration of one dimension of this hyphen.

There is a disturbing tendency in the Western academy today to divorce the study of discursive forms from the study of other institutional forms, and the study of literary discourses from the mundane discourses of bureaucracies, armies, private corporations, and nonstate social organizations. This chapter is in part a plea for a widening of the field of discourse studies: if the postcolony is in part a discursive formation, it is also true that discursivity has become too exclusively the sign and space of the colony and the postcolony in contemporary cultural studies. To widen the sense of what counts as discourse demands a corresponding widening of the sphere of the postcolony, to extend it beyond the geographical spaces of the former colonial world. In raising the issue of the *postnational*, I will suggest that the journey from the space of the former colony (a colorful space, a space of color) to the space of the postcolony is a journey that takes us into the heart of whiteness. It moves us, that is, to America, a postnational space marked by its whiteness but marked too by its uneasy engagement with diasporic peoples, mobile technologies, and queer nationalities.

THE TROPE OF THE TRIBE

In spite of all the evidence to the contrary, these are hard times for patriotism. Maimed bodies and barbed wire in Eastern Europe, xenophobic violence in France, flag waving in the political rituals of the election year here in the United States—all seem to suggest that the willingness to die for one's country is still a global fashion. But patriotism is an unstable sentiment, which thrives only at the level of the nation-state. Below that level it is easily supplanted by more intimate loyalties; above that level it gives way to empty slogans rarely backed by the will to sacrifice or kill. So, when thinking about the future of patriotism, it is necessary first to inquire into the health of the nation-state.

My doubts about patriotism (patria-tism?) are tied up with my father's biography, in which patriotism and nationalism were already diverging terms. As a war correspondent for Reuters in Bangkok in 1940, he met an expatriate Indian nationalist, Subhas Chandra Bose, who split with Gandhi and Nehru on the issue of violence. Bose had escaped from British surveillance in India, with the active support of the Japanese, and established a government-in-exile in Southeast Asia. The army that Bose formed from Indian officers and enlisted men whom the Japanese had taken prisoner called itself the Indian National Army, This Indian Army was roundly defeated by the British Indian Army in Assam (on Indian soil, as my father never tired of noting) in 1944, and the provisional government of Azad Hind (Free India) in which my father was minister of publicity and propaganda soon crumbled with the defeat of the Axis powers.

When my father returned to India in 1945, he and his comrades were unwelcome heroes, poor cousins in the story of the nationalist struggle for Indian independence. They were patriots, but Bose's anti-British sentiment and his links with the Axis powers made him an embarrassment both to Gandhi's nonviolence and Nehru's Fabian Anglophilia. To the end of their lives, my Father and his comrades remained pariah patriots, rogue nationalists. My sister, brothers, and I grew up in Bombay wedged between former patriotism, Bose-style, and bourgeois nationalism, Nehru-style. Our India, with its Japanese connections and anti-Western ways, carried the nameless aroma of treason, in respect to the cozy alliance of the Nehrus and Mountbattens, and the bourgeois compact between

Gandhian non-violence and Nehruvian socialism. My father's distrust of the Nehru dynasty predisposed us to imagine a strange, deterritorialized India, invented in Taiwan and Singapore, Bangkok and Kuala Lumpur, quite independent of New Delhi and the Nehrus, the Congress Party and mainstream nationalisms. So, there is a special appeal for me in the possibility that the marriage between nations and states was always a marriage of convenience and that patriotism needs to find new objects of desire.

One major fact that accounts for strains in the union of nation and state is that the nationalist genie, never perfectly contained in the bottle of the territorial state, is now itself diasporic. Carried in the repertoires of increasingly mobile populations of refugees, tourists, guest workers, transnational intellectuals, scientists, and illegal aliens, it is increasingly unrestrained by ideas of spatial boundary and territorial sovereignty. This revolution in the foundations of nationalism has crept up on us virtually unnoticed. Where soil and place were once the key to the linkage of territorial affiliation with state monopoly of the means of violence, key identities and identifications now only partially revolve around the realities and images of place. In the Sikh demand for Khalistan, in French-Canadian feelings about Quebec, in Palestinian demands for self-determination, images of a homeland are only part of the rhetoric of popular sovereignty and do not necessarily reflect a territorial bottom line. The violence and terror surrounding the breakdown of many existing nation-states are not signs of reversion to anything biological or innate, dark or primordial.[8] What then are we to make of this renewed blood lust in the name of the nation?

Modern nationalisms involve communities of citizens in the territorially defined nation-state who share the collective experience, not of face-to-face contact or common subordination to a royal person, but of reading books, pamphlets, newspapers, maps, and other modern texts together.[9] In and through these collective experiences of what Benedict Anderson[10] calls "print capitalism" and what others increasingly see as "electronic capitalism," such as television and cinema,[11] citizens *imagine* themselves to belong to a national society. The modern nation-state in this view grows less out of natural facts—such as language, blood, soil, and race—and more out of a quintessential cultural product, a product of the collective imagination. This view distances itself, but not quite enough, from the dominant theories of nationalism, from those of J. G. Herder and Guiseppe Mazzini and since then from all sorts of right-wing nationalists, who see nations as products of the natural destinies of peoples, whether rooted in language, race, soil, or religion. In many of these theories of the nation as imagined, there is always a suggestion that blood, kinship, race, and soil are somehow less imagined and more natural than the imagination of collective interest or solidarity. The trope of the tribe reactivates this hidden biologism largely because forceful alternatives to it have yet to be articulated. The historical conjunctures concerning reading and publicity, texts and their linguistic mediations, nations and their narratives are only now being juxtaposed to formulate the special and specific diacritics of the national imaginary and its public spheres.[12]

The leaders of the new nations that were formed in Asia and Africa after World War II—Nasser, Nehru, Sukarno—would have been distressed to see the frequency with which the ideas of tribalism and nationalism are conflated in recent public discourse in the West. These leaders spent a great deal of their rhetorical energies in urging their subjects to give up what they saw as primordial loyalties—to family, tribe, caste, and region-in the interests of the fragile abstractions they called "Egypt," "India," and "Indonesia." They understood that the new nations needed to subvert and annex the primary loyalties attached to more intimate collectivities. They rested their ideas of their new nations on the very edges of the paradox that modern nations were intended to be somehow open, universal, and emancipatory by virtue of their special commitment to citizenry virtue but that *their* nations were nonetheless, in some essential way, different from and even better than other nations. In many ways these leaders knew what we have tended to forget, namely, that nations, especially in multiethnic settings, are tenuous collective projects, not eternal natural facts. Yet they too helped to create a false divide between the artificiality of the nation and those facts they falsely projected as primordial—tribe, family, region.

In its preoccupation with the control, classification, and surveillance of its subjects, the nation-state has often created, revitalized, or fractured ethnic identities that were previously fluid, negotiable, or nascent. Of course, the terms used to mobilize ethnic violence today may have long histories. But the realities to which they refer—Serbo-Croatian language, Basque customs, Lithuanian cuisine—were most often crystallized in the nineteenth and early twentieth centuries. Nationalism and ethnicity thus feed each other, as nationalists construct ethnic categories that in turn drive others to construct counterethnicities, and then in times of political crisis these others demand counterstates based on newfound counternationalisms. For every nationalism that appears to be naturally destined, there is another that is a reactive byproduct.

While violence in the name of Serbs and Moluccans, Khmer and Latvians, Germans and Jews tempts us to think that all such identities run dark and deep, we need only turn to the recent riots in India occasioned by the report of a government commission that recommended reserving a large percentage of government jobs for certain castes defined by the census and the constitution as "backward." Rioting and carnage, and not a few killings and suicides, took place in North India over such labels as "other backward caste," which come out of the terminological distinctions of the Indian census and its specialized protocols and schedules. How astonishing it seems that anyone would die or kill for entitlements associated with being the member of an other backward caste. Yet this case is not an exception: in its macabre bureaucratic banality it shows how the technical needs of censuses and welfare legislation, combined with the cynical tactics of electoral politics, can draw groups into quasi-racial identifications and fears. The matter is not so different as it may appear for such apparently natural labels as Jew, Arab, German, and Hindu, each of which involves people who choose these labels, others who are forced into them, and yet others who through their philological scholarship shore up the histories of these names or find them handy ways of tidying up messy problems of language and history, race and belief. Of course, not all nation-state policies are hegemonic, nor are all subaltern forms of agency impotent to resist these pressures and seductions. But it does seem fair to say that there are few forms of popular consciousness and subaltern agency that are, in regard to ethnic mobilization, free of the thought forms and political fields produced by the actions and discourses of nation-states.

Thus, minorities in many parts of the world are as artificial as the majorities they are seen to threaten, Whites in the United States, Hindus in India, Englishmen in Great Britain—all are examples of how the political and administrative designation of some groups as minorities (blacks and Hispanics in the United States, Celts and Pakistanis in the United Kingdom, Muslims and Christians in India) helps to pull majorities (silent or vocal) together under labels with short lives but long histories. The new ethnicities are often no older than the nation-states that they have come to resist. The Muslims of Bosnia are being reluctantly ghettoized although there is fear among both Serbians and Croats of the possibility of an Islamic state in Europe. Minorities are as often made as they are born.

Recent ethnic movements often involve thousands, sometimes millions of people who are spread across vast territories and often separated by vast distances. Whether we consider the linkage of Serbs divided by large chunks of Bosnia-Herzegovina, or Kurds dispersed across Iran, Iraq, and Turkey, or Sikhs spread through London, Vancouver, and California, as well as the Indian Punjab, the new ethnonationalisms are complex, large-scale, highly coordinated acts of mobilization, reliant on news, logistical flows, and propaganda across state borders. They can hardly be considered tribal, if by this we mean that they are spontaneous uprisings of closely bonded, spatially segregated, naturally allied groupings. In the case we find most frightening today, what could be called Serbian tribalism is hardly a simple thing given that there are at least 2.8 million Yugoslav families who have produced about 1.4 million mixed marriages between Serbs and Croats.[13] To which tribe could these families be said to belong? In our horrified preoccupation with the shock troops of ethnonationalism, we have lost sight of the confused sentiments of civilians, the torn loyalties of families that have members of warring groups within the same household, and the urgings of those who hold to the view that Serbs, Muslims, and Croats in Bosnia-Herzegovina have no fundamental enmity. It is harder to explain how principles of ethnic affiliation, however dubious their provenance and fragile their pedigree, can very rapidly mobilize large groups into violent action.

What does seem clear is that the tribal model, insofar as it suggests prepackaged passions waiting to explode, flies in the face of the contingencies that spark ethnic passion. The Sikhs, until recently the bulwark of the Indian army and historically the fighting arm of Hindu India against Muslim rule, today regard themselves as threatened by Hinduism and seem willing to accept aid and succor from Pakistan. The Muslims of Bosnia-Herzegovina have been forced reluctantly to revitalize their Islamic affiliations. Far from activating long-standing tribal sentiments, Bosnian Muslims are torn between their own conception of themselves as *European Muslims* (a term recently used by Ejub Ganic, vice president of Bosnia) and the view that they are part of a transnational Islam, which is already actively involved in Bosnian warfare. Wealthy Bosnians who live abroad in countries such as Turkey are already buying weapons for the defense of Muslims in Bosnia. To free us from the trope of the tribe, as the primordial source of those nationalisms that we find less civic than our own in the United States, we need to construct a theory of large-scale ethnic mobilization that explicitly recognizes and interprets its postnational properties.

POSTNATIONAL FORMATIONS

Many recent and violent ethnonationalisms are not so much explosive as implosive. That is, rather than being rooted in some primordial substrate of affect deep within each of us that is brought up and out into wider sorts of social engagement and group action, the reverse is often the case. The effects of large-scale interactions between and within nation-states, often stimulated by news of events in even more distant locations, serve to cascade[14] through the complexities of regional, local, and neighborhood politics until they energize local issues and implode into various forms of violence, including the most brutal ones. What were previously cool ethnic identities (Sikh and Hindu, Armenian and Azerbaijani, Serb and Croat) thus turn *hot,* as localities implode under the pressure of events and processes distant in space and time from the site of the implosion. Among Bosnia's Muslims it is possible to watch the temperature of these identities change before our very eyes as they find themselves pushed away from a secular, Europeanist idea of themselves into a more fundamentalist posture. They are being pushed not only by the threats to their survival from Serbs but also by pressure from their fellow Muslims in Saudi Arabia, Egypt, and Sudan, who suggest that Bosnian Muslims are now paying the price for playing down their Islamic identity under Communist rule. Bosnian Muslim leaders have begun to explicitly state that if they do not receive help quickly from the Western powers, they might have to turn to Palestinian models of terror and extremism.

One important way to account for those cases in which cool identities turn hot and implosions from one place generate explosions in others is to remind ourselves that the nation-state is by no means the only game in town as far as translocal loyalties are concerned. The violence that surrounds identity politics around the world today reflects the anxieties attendant on the search for nonterritorial principles of solidarity. The movements we now see in Serbia and Sri Lanka, Mountain Karabakh and Namibia, Punjab and Quebec are what might be called "trojan nationalisms." Such nationalisms actually contain transnational, subnational links and, more generally, nonnational identities and aspirations. Because they are so often the product of forced as well as voluntary diasporas, of mobile intellectuals as well as manual workers, of dialogues with hostile as well as hospitable states, very few of the new nationalisms can be separated from the anguish of displacement, the nostalgia of exile, the repatriation of funds, or the brutalities of asylum seeking. Haitians in Miami, Tamils in Boston, Moroccans in France, Moluccans in Holland are the carriers of these new transnational and postnational loyalties.

Territorial nationalism is the alibi of these movements and not necessarily their basic motive or final goal. In contrast, these basic motives and goals can be far darker than anything having to do with national sovereignty, as when they seem driven by the motives of ethnic purification and genocide; thus, Serbian nationalism seems to operate on the fear and hatred of its ethnic Others far more than on the sense of a sacred territorial patrimony. Or they can be simply idioms and symbols around which many groups come to articulate their desire to escape the specific state regime that is seen as threatening their own survival. Palestinians are more worried about getting Israel off their backs than about the special geographical magic of the West Bank.

While there are many separatist movements in the world today—the Basques, the Tamils, the Quebecois, the Serbs—that seem determined to lock nationhood and statehood together under a single ethnic rubric, more impressive still are the many oppressed minorities who have suffered displacement and forced diaspora without articulating a strong wish for a nation-state of their own: Armenians in Turkey, Hutu refugees from Burundi who live in urban Tanzania, and Kashmiri Hindus in exile in Delhi are a few examples of how displacement does not always generate the fantasy of state building. Although many antistate movements revolve around images of homeland, soil, place, and return from exile, these images reflect the poverty of their (and our) political languages rather than the hegemony of territorial nationalism. Put another way, no idiom has yet emerged to capture the collective interests of many groups in translocal solidarities, cross-border mobilizations, and postnational identities. Such interests are many and vocal, but they are still entrapped in the linguistic imaginary of the territorial state. This incapacity of many deterritorialized groups to think their way out of the imaginary of the nation-state is itself the cause of much global violence because many movements of emancipation and identity are forced, in their struggles against existing nation-states, to embrace the very imaginary they seek to escape. Postnational or nonnational movements are forced by the very logic of actually existing nation-states to become antinational or antistate and thus to inspire the very state power that forces them to respond in the language of counternationalism. This vicious circle can only be escaped when a language is found to capture complex, non-territorial, postnational forms of allegiance.

Much has been said in recent years about the speed with which information travels around the world, the intensity with which the news of one city flashes on the television screens of another, of how money manipulations in one stock exchange affect finance ministries a continent away. Much has been said, too, about the need to attack global problems, such as AIDS, pollution, and terrorism, with concerted forms of international action. The democracy wave and the AIDS pandemic are to some extent caused by the same kinds of intersocietal contact and transnational human traffic.

From the perspective of the Cold War, the world may have become unipolar. But it has also become *multicentric*, to use James Rosenau's term.[15] Adapting metaphors from chaos theory, Rosenau has shown how the legitimacy of nation-states has steadily weakened, how international and transnational organizations of every type have proliferated, and how local politics and global process affect each other in chaotic but not unpredictable ways, often outside the interactions of nation-states.

To appreciate these complexities, we need to do more than what social scientists like to call comparison, putting one country or culture next to another as if they were as independent in life as in thought.[16] We need to take a fresh look at a variety of organizations, movements, ideologies, and networks of which the traditional multinational corporation is only one example. Consider such transnational philanthropic movements as Habitat for Humanity (whose volunteers seek to build new environments with fellow volunteers in far-flung locations). Take the various international terrorist organizations, which mobilize men (and sometimes women), money, equipment, training camps, and passion in a bewildering cross-hatching of ideological and ethnic combinations. Consider international fashion, which is not just a matter of global markets and cross-national-style cannibalism but is increasingly a matter of systematic transnational assemblages of production, taste transfer, pricing, and exhibition. Take the variety of Green movements that have begun to organize themselves transnationally around specific sorts of biopolitics. Consider the world of refugees. For long we have taken refugee issues and organizations to be part of the flotsam and jetsam of political life, floating between the certainties and stabilities of nation-states. What we cannot see therefore is that refugee camps, refugee bureaucracies, refugee-relief movements, refugee-oriented departments of nation-states, and refugee-oriented transnational philanthropies all constitute one part of the *permanent* framework of the emergent, postnational order. Another excellent example, closer to home perhaps, is the large number of organizations, movements, and networks of Christian philanthropy, such as World Vision, that have long blurred the boundaries between evangelical, developmental, and peace-keeping functions in many parts of the world. Perhaps the best studied of these examples is the Olympic movement, certainly the largest modern instance of a movement born in the context of European concerns with world peace in the latter part of the nineteenth century.

This movement, with its special form of dialectical play between national and transnational allegiances[17] represents only the most spectacular among a series of sites and formations on which the uncertain future of the nation-state will turn.

In all these cases, what we are looking at are not just international slogans, or interest groups, or image transfers. We are looking at the birth of a variety of complex, postnational social formations. These formations are now organized around principles of finance, recruitment, coordination, communication, and reproduction that are fundamentally postnational and not just multinational or international. The classic modern multinational corporation is a slightly misleading example of what is most important about these new forms precisely because it relies crucially on the legal, fiscal, environmental, and human organization of the nation-state, while maximizing the possibilities of operating both within and across national structures, always exploiting their legitimacy. The new organizational forms are more diverse, more fluid, more ad hoc, more provisional, less coherent, less organized, and simply less implicated in the comparative advantages of the nation-state. Many of them are explicitly constituted to monitor the activities of the nation-state: Amnesty International is an excellent example. Others, largely associated with the United Nations, work to contain the excesses of nation-states, for example, by assisting refugees, monitoring peace-keeping arrangements, organizing relief in famines, and doing the unglamorous work associated with oceans and tariffs, international health and labor.

Yet others, like Oxfam, are examples of global organizations that work outside the quasi-official United Nations network and rely on the growth of nongovernmental organizations (NGOs) in many parts of the developing world. These NGOs, which operate in a host of areas ranging from technology and the environment to health and the arts, grew from less than two hundred in 1909 to more than two thousand in the early 1970s. They often constitute major grassroots organizations for self-help that grow out of and contribute to a sense of the limited capability of national governments to deliver the basics of life in such societies as India.

Still other organizations, which we often call fundamentalist, such as the Muslim Brotherhood in the Middle East, the Unification Church, and any number of Christian, Hindu, and Muslim organizations, constitute full-service global movements that seek to alleviate suffering across national boundaries while mobilizing first-order loyalties across state boundaries. Some of these evangelical movements (such as the radical Hindu group known as the Ananda Marg, which has been held responsible for the assassination of Indian diplomats abroad) are aggressively opposed to specific nation-states and are frequently treated as seditious. Others, such as the Unification Church, simply work their way around the nation-state without directly questioning its jurisdiction. Such examples, which we still tend to see as exceptional or pariah organizational forms, are both instances and incubators of a postnational global order.

THE HEART OF WHITENESS

The term *postnational*, so far used without comment, has several implications that can now be more closely examined. The first is temporal and historical and suggests that we are in the process of moving to a global order in which the nation-state has become obsolete and other formations for allegiance and identity have taken its place. The second is the idea that what are emerging are strong alternative forms for the organization of global traffic in resources, images, and ideas—

forms that either contest the nation-state actively or constitute peaceful alternatives for large-scale political loyalties. The third implication is the possibility that, while nations might continue to exist, the steady erosion of the capabilities of the nation-state to monopolize loyalty will encourage the spread of national forms that are largely divorced from territorial states. These are relevant senses of the term postnational, but none of them implies that the nation-state in its classical territorial form is as yet out of business. It is certainly in crisis, and part of the crisis is an increasingly violent relationship between the nation-state and its postnational Others.

The United States is a particularly salient place in which to consider these propositions because, on the face of it, it has managed to retain most successfully the image of a national order that is simultaneously civil, plural, and prosperous. It appears to nurture a vibrant and complex set of public spheres, including some that have been called "alternative," "partial," or "counter" publics.[18] It remains enormously wealthy by global standards, and although its forms of public violence are many and worrisome, its state apparatus is not generally dependent on forms of torture, imprisonment, and violent repression. When this is added to the fact that multiculturalism in the United States seems to take predominantly nonviolent forms, we appear to be faced with a great, uncontested power that dominates the new world order, that draws in immigrants in the thousands, and that seems to be a triumphant example of the classic, territorial nation-state. Any argument about the emergence of a postnational global order will have to engage its greatest apparent falsification, the contemporary United States. This last section lays the groundwork for such an engagement.

Until a few years ago, I was content to live in that special space allotted to "foreigners," especially Anglophone, educated ones like myself, with faint traces of a British accent. As a black woman at a bus stop in Chicago once said to me with approval, I was an East Indian. That was in 1972. But since that happy conversation more than two decades ago, it has become steadily less easy to see myself, armed with my Indian passport and my Anglophone ways, as somehow immune from the politics of racial identity in the United States. Not only is it that after nearly three decades of being a resident alien in the United States, married to an Anglo-Saxon American woman, the father of a bicultural teenager, my Indian passport seems like a rather slight badge of identity. The net of racial politics is now cast wider than ever before on the streets of the urban United States.

My own complexion and its role in minority politics, as well as in street encounters with racial hatred, prompt me to reopen the links between America and the United States, between biculturalism and patriotism, between diasporic identities and the (in)stabilities provided by passports and green cards. Postnational loyalties are not irrelevant to the problem of diversity in the United States. If, indeed, a postnational order is in the making, and Americanness changes its meanings, the whole problem of diversity in American life will have to be rethought. It is not just the force of certain deductions that moves me to this recommendation. As I oscillate between the detachment of a postcolonial, diasporic, academic identity (taking advantage of the mood of exile and the space of displacement) and the ugly realities of being racialized, minoritized, and tribalized in my everyday encounters, theory encounters practice.

A book recently published by Random House is *Tribes: How, Race, Religion, and Identity Determine Success in the New Global Economy*.[19] Written by Joel Kotkin, "an internationally recognized authority on global, economic, political and social trends," as the dust jacket boasts, it traces the connections between ethnicity and business success. Kotkin's five tribes—the Jews, the Chinese, the Japanese, the British, and the Indians—are an odd group, but they represent primordialism with a high-tech face. They are Max Weber's pariah capitalists in late-twentieth-century transnational drag. Books like this are reminders that East Indians are still a tribe, as are the Jews and others, working the primordial lode to make their way to global dominance. So, the trope of the tribe can turn on its own premises, and we can have vast global tribes, an image that seeks to have it both ways, with primordial intimacy and high-tech strategies. However diasporic we get, like the Jews, South Asians are doomed to remain a tribe, forever fixers and dealers in a world of open markets, fair deals, and opportunity for all.

For those of us who have moved into the "national Fantasy"[20] of America from the former colonies, there is thus the seductiveness of a plural belonging, of becoming American while staying somehow diasporic, of an expansive attachment to an unbounded fantasy space. But while we can make our identities, we cannot do so exactly as we please. As many of us find ourselves racialized, biologized, minoritized, somehow reduced rather than enabled by our bodies and our histories, our special diacritics become our prisons, and the trope of the tribe sets us off from another, unspecified America, far from the clamor of the tribe, decorous, civil, and white, a land in which we are not yet welcome.

This brings us back to the pervasive idiom and image of tribalism. Applied to New York, Miami, and Los Angeles (as opposed to Sarajevo, Soweto, or Colombo), the trope of tribalism both conceals and indulges a diffuse racism about those Others (for example, Hispanics, Iranians, and African-Americans) who have insinuated themselves into the American body politic. It allows us to maintain the idea of an Americanness that precedes (and subsists in spite of) the hyphens that contribute to it and to maintain a distinction between tribal Americans (the black, the brown, and the yellow) and other Americans. This trope facilitates the fantasy that civil society in the United States has a special destiny in regard to peaceful multiculturalism—intelligent multiculturalism for us, bloody ethnicity or mindless tribalism for them.

There has developed a special set of links between democracy, diversity, and prosperity in American social thought. Built on a complex dialogue between political science (the only genuine made-in-America social science without obvious European counterparts or antecedents) and vernacular constitutionalism, a comfortable equilibrium was established between the ideas of cultural diversity and one or another version of the melting pot. Swinging between *National Geographic* and *Reader's Digest*, this anodyne polarity has proved remarkably durable and comforting. It accommodates, sometimes on the same page or in the same breath, a sense that plurality is the American genius and that there is an Americanness that somehow contains and transcends plurality. This second, post–Civil War accommodation with difference is now on its last legs, and the political correctness–multiculturalism debate is its peculiar, parochial Waterloo. Parochial because it insistently refuses to recognize that the challenge of diasporic pluralism is now global and that American solutions cannot be seen in isolation. Peculiar because there has been no systematic recognition that the politics of multiculturalism is now part and parcel of the extraterritorial nationalism of populations who love America but are not necessarily attached to the United States. More bluntly, neither popular nor academic thought in this country has come to terms with the difference between being a land of immigrants and being one node in a postnational network of diasporas.

In the postnational world that we see emerging, diaspora runs with, and not against, the grain of identity, movement, and reproduction. Everyone has relatives working abroad. Many people find themselves exiles without really having moved very far—Croats in Bosnia, Hindus in Kashmir, Muslims in India. Yet others find themselves in patterns of repeat migration. Indians who went to East Africa in the nineteenth and early twentieth centuries found themselves pushed out of Uganda, Kenya, and Tanzania in the 1980s to find fresh travails and opportunities in England and the United States, and they are now considering returning to East Africa. Similarly, Chinese from Hong Kong who are buying real estate in Vancouver, Gujarati traders from Uganda opening motels in New Jersey and newspaper kiosks in New York City, and Sikh cabdrivers in Chicago and Philadelphia are all examples of a new sort of world in which diaspora is the order of things and settled ways of life are increasingly hard to find. The United States, always in its self-perception a land of immigrants, finds itself awash in these global diasporas, no longer a closed space for the melting pot to work its magic, but yet another diasporic switching point. People come here to seek their fortunes, but they are no longer content to leave their homelands behind. Global democracy fever and the breakdown of the Soviet empire have meant that most groups that wish to renegotiate their links to their diasporic identities from their American vantage points are now free to do so: thus, American Jews of Polish origin undertake Holocaust tours in Eastern Europe, Indian doctors from Michigan set up eye clinics in New Delhi, Palestinians in Detroit participate in the politics of the West Bank.

THE FORM OF THE TRANSNATION

The formula of hyphenation (as in Italian-Americans, Asian-Americans, and African-Americans) is reaching the point of saturation, and the right-hand side of the hyphen can barely contain the unruliness of the left-hand side. Even as the legitimacy of nation-states in their own territorial contexts is increasingly under threat, the idea of the nation flourishes transnationally. Safe from the depredations of their home states, diasporic communities become doubly loyal to their nations of origin and thus ambivalent about their loyalties to America. The politics of ethnic identity in the United States is inseparably linked to the global spread of originally local national identities. For every nation-state that has exported significant numbers of its populations to the United States as refugees, tourists, or students, there is now a delocalized *transnation*, which retains a special ideological link to a putative place of origin but is otherwise a thoroughly diasporic collectivity.[21] No existing conception of Americanness can contain this large variety of transnations.

In this scenario, the hyphenated American might have to be twice hyphenated (Asian-American-Japanese or Native-American-Seneca or African-American-Jamaican or Hispanic-American-Bolivian) as diasporic identities stay mobile and grow more protean. Or perhaps the sides of the hyphen will have to be reversed, and we can become a federation of diasporas: American-Italians, American-Haitians, American-Irish, American-Africans. Dual citizenships might increase if the societies from which we came remain or become more open. We might recognize that diasporic diversity actually puts loyalty to a nonterritorial transnation first, while recognizing that there is a special American way to connect to these global diasporas. America, as a cultural space, will not need to compete with a host of global identities and diasporic loyalties. It might come to be seen as a model of how to arrange one territorial locus (among others) for a cross-hatching of diasporic communities. In this regard, the American problem resembles those of other wealthy industrial democracies (such as Sweden, Germany, Holland, and France), all of which face the challenge of squaring Enlightenment universalisms and diasporic pluralism.

The question is, can a postnational politics be built around this cultural fact? Many societies now face influxes of immigrants and refugees, wanted and unwanted. Others are pushing out groups in acts of ethnic cleansing intended to produce the very people whose preexistence the nation was supposed to ratify. But America may be alone in having organized itself around a modern political ideology in which pluralism is central to the conduct of democratic life. Out of a different strand of its experience, this society has also generated a powerful fable of itself as a land of immigrants. In today's postnational, diasporic world, America is being invited to weld these two doctrines together, to confront the needs of pluralism and of immigration, to construct a society around diasporic diversity.

But such images as the mosaic, the rainbow, the quilt, and other tropes of complexity-in-diversity cannot supply the imaginative resources for this task, especially as fears of tribalism multiply. Tribes do not make quilts, although they sometimes make confederacies. Whether in debates over immigration, bilingual education, the academic canon, or the underclass, these liberal images have sought to contain the tension between the centripetal pull of Americanness and the centrifugal pull of diasporic diversity in American life. The battles over affirmative action, quotas, welfare, and abortion in America today suggest that the metaphor of the mosaic cannot contain the contradiction between group identities, which Americans will tolerate (up to a point) in cultural life, and individual identities, which are still the nonnegotiable principle behind American ideas of achievement, mobility, and justice.

What is to be done? There could be a special place for America in the new, postnational order, and one that does not rely on either isolationism or global domination as its alternative basis. The United States is eminently suited to be a sort of cultural laboratory and a free-trade zone for the generation, circulation, importation, and testing of the materials for a world organized around diasporic diversity. In a sense, this experiment is already under way. The United States is already a huge, fascinating garage sale for the rest of the world. It provides golf vacations and real estate for the Japanese; business-management ideologies and techniques for Europe and India; soap-opera ideas for Brazil and the Middle East; prime ministers for Yugoslavia; supply-side economics for Poland, Russia, and whoever else will try; Christian fundamentalism for Korea; and postmodern architecture for Hong Kong. By also providing a set of images—Rambo in Afghanistan, "We Are the World," George Bernard Shaw in Baghdad, Coke goes to Barcelona, Perot goes to Washington—that link human rights, consumer style, antistatism, and media glitz, it might be said that the United States is partly accountable for the idiosyncrasies that attend struggles for self-determination in otherwise very different parts of the world. This is why a University of Iowa sweatshirt is not just a silly symbol in the jungles of Mozambique or on the barricades of Beirut. It captures the free-floating yearning for American style, even in the most intense contexts of opposition to the United States. The cultural politics of queer nationality is an example of this contradictory yearning in the United States.[22] The rest of this yearning is provoked by authoritarian state policies, massive arms industries, the insistently hungry eye of the electronic media, and the despair of bankrupt economies.

Of course, these products and ideas are not the immaculate conceptions of some mysterious American know-how but are precisely the result of a complex environment in which ideas and intellectuals meet in a variety of special settings (such as labs, libraries, classrooms, music studios, business seminars, and political campaigns) to generate, reformulate, and recirculate cultural forms that are fundamentally postnational and diasporic. The role of American musicians, studios, and record companies in the creation of world beat is an excellent example of this sort of down-home but offshore entrepreneurial mentality. Americans are loathe to admit the piecemeal, pragmatic, haphazard, flexible, and opportunistic ways in which these American products and reproducts circulate around the world. Americans like to think that the Chinese have simply bought the virtues of free enterprise; the Poles, the supply side; the Haitians and Filipinos, democracy; and everyone, human rights. We rarely pay attention to the complicated terms, traditions, and cultural styles into which these ideas are folded and thus transformed beyond our recognition. Thus, during the historic events of Tiananmen Square in 1989, when it seemed as if the Chinese people had become democratic overnight, there was considerable evidence that the ways in which different groups in China understood their problems were both internally varied and tied to various specificities of China's history and cultural style.

When Americans see transformations and cultural complications of their democratic vocabulary and style, if they notice them at all, they are annoyed and dismayed. In this misreading of how others handle what we still see as *our* national recipe for success, Americans perform a further act of narcissistic distortion: we imagine that these peculiarly American inventions (democracy, capitalism, free enterprise, human rights) are automatically and inherently interconnected and that our national saga holds the key to the combination. In the migration of our words, we see the victory of our myths. We are believers in terminal conversion.

The American "victory" in the Cold War need not necessarily turn pyrrhic. The fact is that the United States, from a cultural point of view, is already a vast free-trade zone, full of ideas, technologies, styles, and idioms (from McDonald's and the Harvard Business School to the Dream Team and reverse mortgages) that the rest of the world finds fascinating. This free-trade zone rests on a volatile economy; the major cities of the American borderland (Los Angeles, Miami, New York, Detroit) are now heavily militarized. But these facts are of little relevance to those who come, either briefly or for more extended stays, to this free-trade zone. Some, fleeing vastly greater urban violence, state persecution, and economic hardship, come as permanent migrants, legal or illegal. Others are short-term shoppers for clothes, entertainment, loans, armaments, or quick lessons in free-market economics or civil-society politics. The very unruliness, the rank unpredictability, the quirky inventiveness, the sheer cultural vitality of this free-trade zone are what attract all sorts of diasporas to the United States.

For the United States, to play a major role in the cultural politics of a postnational world has very complex domestic entailments. It may mean making room for the legitimacy of cultural rights, rights to the pursuit of cultural difference under public protections and guarantees. It may mean a painful break from a fundamentally Fordist, manufacture-centered conception of the American economy, as we learn to be global information brokers, service providers, style doctors. It may mean embracing as part of our livelihood what we have so far confined to the world of Broadway, Hollywood, and Disneyland: the import of experiments, the production of fantasies, the fabrication of identities, the export of styles, the hammering out of pluralities. It may mean distinguishing our attachment to America from our willingness to die for the United States. This suggestion converges with the following proposal by Lauren Berlant:

> The subject who wants to avoid the melancholy insanity of the self-abstraction that is citizenship, and to resist the lure of self-overcoming the material political context in which she lives, must develop tactics for refusing the interarticulation, now four hundred years old, between the United States and America, the nation and utopia.[23]

That is, it may be time to rethink monopatriotism, patriotism directed exclusively to the hyphen between nation and state, and to allow the material problems we face—the deficit, the environment, abortion, race, drugs, and jobs—to define those social groups and ideas for which we would be willing to live, and die. The queer nation may only be the first of a series of new patriotisms, in which others could be the retired, the unemployed, and the disabled, as well as scientists, women, and Hispanics. Some of us may still want to live—and die—for the United States. But many of these new sovereignties are inherently postnational. Surely, they represent more humane motives for affiliation than statehood or party affiliation and more interesting bases for debate and crosscutting alliances. Ross Perot's volunteers in 1992 give us a brief, intense glimpse of the powers of patriotism totally divorced from party, government, or state. America may yet construct another narrative of enduring significance, a narrative about the uses of loyalty after the end of the nation-state. In this narrative, bounded territories could give way to diasporic networks, nations to transnations, and patriotism itself could become plural, serial, contextual, and mobile. Here lies one direction for the future of patriotism in a postcolonial world. Patriotism—like history—is unlikely to end, but its objects may be susceptible to transformation, in theory and in practice.

It remains now to ask what transnations and transnationalism have to do with postnationality and its prospects. This relationship requires detailed engagement in its own right, but a few observations are in order. As populations become deterritorialized and incompletely nationalized, as nations splinter and recombine, as states face intractable difficulties in the task of producing "the people," transnations are the most important social sites in which the crises of patriotism are played out.

The results are surely contradictory. Displacement and exile, migration and terror create powerful attachments to ideas of homeland that seem more deeply territorial than ever. But it is also possible to detect in many of these transnations (some ethnic, some religious, some philanthropic, some militaristic) the elements of a postnational imaginary. These elements for those who wish to hasten the demise of the nation-state, for all their contradictions, require both nurture and critique. In this way, transnational social forms may generate not only postnational yearnings but also actually existing postnational movements, organizations, and spaces. In these postnational spaces, the incapacity of the nation-state to tolerate diversity (as it seeks the homogeneity of its citizens, the simultaneity of its presence, the consensuality of its narrative, and the stability of its citizens) may, perhaps, be overcome.

C H A P T E R 2 5

'Ethnic Cleansing': A Metaphor for Our Time?

By Akbar S. Ahmed

INTRODUCTION

Academic papers usually begin with a proposition or thesis; I wish to start with an autobiographical confession. My analysis and interest in the subject are not entirely of an academic nature. True, as an anthropologist, I am interested in ethnicity and ethnic boundaries, that is, how people define themselves and are defined by others on the basis of genealogy, language and customs. But I also approach ethnicity as someone who has had to come to terms with it in respect of my own identity, throughout my life.

From early childhood I was aware of the fact of ethnic differences which could lead to ethnic animosity and ethnic violence. Such differences accounted for my parents choosing to live in Pakistan when it was created in 1947. Large Indian provinces; as big as large European countries, were ethnically cleansed with all the attendant rape, torture and destruction. About 10 million people crossed each other as Hindus and Sikhs headed for India and Muslims for Pakistan; about one million died. Ethnic cleansing, clearly, is not a new phenomenon although it is disguised for us under a new term.

In Pakistan where I grew up and worked, although the vast majority of people belong to one religion, Islam, and Islam condemns discrimination based on ethnic background, it matters a great deal to which ethnic group you belong. In 1971 I was in what was then East Pakistan and which became Bangladesh in that year, and I saw, first-hand, the power of ethnic identity, how it could challenge successfully loyalty to a common religion.

Here, in the UK, I am given yet another identity, one based on colour and race: I am seen as black or Asian. Those who do not like Asians call them "Paki," a term which denotes racial abuse. (What they perhaps do not know is that "Paki" derives from the Urdu word pure and it is no bad thing being called pure even by swearing, snarling skinheads). Yet others learning that I am a Muslim have reservations, implying that all those with a traditional religious belief are fanatics or extremists or what the media call fundamentalists. For some Muslims, suspicious and resentful of the western establishment, I am a Fellow of a Cambridge College and therefore sullied. Multiple identities have thus been imposed on me.

Viewing the turbulence of South Asia I once envied what seemed the secure and fixed identity of being American or European. The passion generated by race and religion, I read in my American and British textbooks, was a characteristic of backward societies, those that were not modern. I now know that Northern Ireland can be as violent in its ethnic and religious hatred as the worst affected place in South Asia. In Wales and Scotland ethnic resentment against the English surfaces easily. In parts of London the colour of your skin can make you a target for abuse and assault. There are flash-points in the United States and Germany and France ready to explode into ethnic violence. To be an English-speaking male from the West in some parts of the Middle East is to know fear, to be vulnerable to the horrors of kidnapping. I no longer envied American or European identity.

Clearly I was not alone in my ethnic susceptibilities. It seemed that all of us were confronted with the same questions. What is my ethnic identity? How does the past shape it? How does it affect my life and those who are not like me? Why are the hatred and violence based on ethnic opposition so intense and so widespread? What is its relationship with the collapse of the project of modernity and the beginnings of a post–Cold War, post-Communism, postmodernity period? Is the ethnic cleansing in Bosnia a consequence of these changes and is it restricted to Bosnia alone? Has ethnic cleansing become the cognitive and affective symbol of, or metaphor for, our postmodern age?

In attempting to answer these questions my academic and personal interests in the subject coincide. I need to understand it in all its complexity to make sense of it. I therefore come to the subject with urgency and conviction and I hope with academic rigour.

BEGINNINGS AND ENDINGS

In examining the worst excesses of ethnic cleansing we are transfixed by Bosnia which has given the chilling euphemism 'ethnic cleansing' to the late twentieth century. It is the suffering of the Bosnians that challenges frontally European self-perception and self-identity, a fact not fully appreciated here in Britain.[1] Where, we may legitimately ask, are the much vaunted European liberal values humanism, civilization and the rule of law?

The ethnic killings and hatred are a consequence of the collapse of the Soviet Union, it is argued. There is even some nostalgia for the old certainties. At least there was no mass murder, no ethnic cleansing, people say, forgetting one of the champion ethnic cleansers of history, Stalin. Others argue that the excesses of Bosnia are a reflection of the ethnic violence which took place half a century ago, of an inevitable ethnic denouement. Some smugly talk of the conflict in the Balkans as typical of that area; they reflect cultural if not outright racial prejudice.

This is reductionism and simplification of complex historical events that are taking place on a global scale. There are many peoples facing persecution in our world—Muslims elsewhere in the Balkans especially in Kosovo, Palestinians, Kurds, Kashmiris, the Chittagong Hill Tribes, the East Timorese are examples.

However much Bosnia hypnotizes us, we need to broaden our frame of reference beyond Bosnia in order to draw universal principles and locate global explanations. We may then understand ethnic cleansing in our time. The explanations we provide are interlinked, some links strong, others tenuous, some fuelling the ethnic violence directly, others contributing to it more indirectly. Cumulatively they ensure that no society is immune, black or white, secular or religious, industrial or agricultural. Nevertheless, our exploration of those explanations is tentative and can only suggest further areas of research.

We note the collapse of the idea of Communism but we also need to be aware of another, more significant, collapse taking place, and that is the notion of modernity with its cluster of ideas, derived in the main from the Enlightenment, such as freedom of speech, humanism, rationality and secularism. To this was added subsequently economic and scientific progress. Sociologists like Max Weber placed these ideas firmly in Europe through explanations of a specifically European brand of Christianity. Because modernity was located in and spread from Europe over the last two centuries it allowed Europe to become the standard-bearer of civilization, indeed of the future. Cultural and racial superiority was implied. During the high noon of empire, authors like Jules Verne and H.G. Wells extolled the virtues of modern ways to and for all the world with the *naivete* of enthusiastic schoolboys but its European dimension was clearly assumed.

However, modernity had its dark side even in Europe. Bauman, citing Weber, blames it, in part at least, for the Holocaust:[2]

> The most shattering of lessons deriving from the analysis of the "twisted road to Auschwitz" is that—in the last resort—*the choice of physical extermination as the right means to the task of Entfernung was a product of routine bureaucratic procedures:* means-ends, calculus, budget balancing, universal rule application . . . The "Final Solution" did not clash at any stage with the rational pursuit of efficient, optimal goal-implementation. On the contrary, it arose out of a genuinely rational concern, and it was generated by bureaucracy true to its form and purpose.[3]

Those who believed in modernity saw other systems, Buddhist, Hindu or Islamic, for example, as anachronistic. They would be obliterated in due course in the triumphalist march of western rationalism and progress. Modernity has therefore always been viewed with ambiguity by people in Africa and Asia; it is too closely associated with European colonization and the rejection of religious and traditional ways.

We cannot say with certainty when modernity began to falter—there is no dramatic equivalent to the fall of the Berlin Wall in 1989 which symbolized the collapse of Communism. But the process of collapse had been gathering momentum. It became increasingly apparent since the middle of this century that modernity could not solve all our problems. In the last decade or two the loss of optimism combined with other developments: law and order deteriorated in the cities, unemployment grew, families fell apart and the use of illegal drugs and alcoholism spread. Bosnia, and all it stands for, was perhaps the last straw.

What follows after modernity is still uncertain. Some like Anthony Giddens note continuity in modernity and use the phrase high or late modernity.[4] Others call it postmodernity—the social condition formed by information technologies, globalism, fragmentation of lifestyles; hyper-consumerism, the fading of the nation-state and experimentation with tradition (the related concept, postmodernism, is the philosophical critique of grand narratives). Some write of a post–Cold War period or post-Communism, yet others see a time of ethnic and religious revivalism. However, in noting the revivalism we point out the yearning for premodernity, a desire to recreate a mythical past and imagined purity. In that sense the revivalism reflects anti-modernity. It is characteristic of the age that its names are not original and reflect a relationship with the past.

What is certain is that the changes after Communism, the Cold War and the failure of western modernity have universal implications. The cement binding different peoples in the large blocs and uniting them in the grand narratives has cracked. This is most notable in the former Soviet Union. But in France, in Germany, even in Britain, we can also trace the dramatic rise of racism in the last years to the dark underside of modernity. Political opinion polls reflect the growing strength of the racist. By calling the racists neo-Nazis the media acknowledge the Nazi past. We hear louder and louder the voices of racism in Europe: 'Expel the foreigners,' 'They are noisy and dirty,' 'They mean disorder and drugs,' 'They are not like us—cleanse our land of them.'

A similar process is also to be noted globally. Hindus and Muslims in South Asia, Muslims and Jews in the Middle East, Russians, and non-Russians in Russia—those ambiguous about modernity but frozen for half a century in the Cold War structures—are falling back on an imagined primordial identity, to their own traditions and culture. People define themselves in terms of the ethnic other, usually a group that has lived as neighbours.

Importantly for purposes of our argument no one group is entirely isolated from ethnic passions. If Hindus terrorize the Muslim minority in India during communal rioting, in turn, they are terrorized in Bangladesh and Pakistan by the majority Muslims. In Kashmir Muslims have been killed and tortured by the thousand. Half a million troops are deployed in Kashmir to crush the Muslim uprising. This is a great human tragedy but there is another human tragedy also taking place simultaneously in Kashmir which is not known outside India. Hindus, who have lived in Kashmir for centuries, have fled the land out of fear; Kashmir is thus ethnically cleansed of them. Most Indians only see the plight of the Hindus, most Pakistanis that of the Muslims.

Yet in order to understand ethnicity an objective approach is needed. As an anthropologist I believe my subject has much to say about the nature of ethnic conflict. Yet—somewhat to my bafflement anthropology has been conspicuous by its absence in the commentary on the major international events of the last few years like the Gulf war and the conflict in Bosnia.

Yet surely anthropologists need to explain for the general public why in some countries there is relatively little ethnic cleansing (for instance in Fiji in spite of the *coups*)? Or why it is particularly vicious in a certain period of history? Why some minorities have adjusted relatively well in an alien cultural environment (like the Sikhs in the UK), while others are less successful (consider the anti-Arab prejudice since the 1970s also in the UK)? Finally, what role does ethnicity itself play in ethnic cleansing?

REDISCOVERING ETHNICITY

The understanding of ethnicity is therefore crucial to our task. Yet despite the efforts of western social scientists the popular imagination and popular media continue to reflect traditional ignorance and prejudice when dealing with ethnicity.

Ideas and arguments about ethnicity are usually based on the assumption that ethnic identity is a characteristic of primordial and tribal societies, that only society in North America and western Europe represents modernity. Modern society has moved beyond, evolved away from, religion, belief and custom. In any case there is little nostalgia in the West for religion which is popularly associated with bigotry, superstition and intolerance. Only backward societies cling to the past. Progress, science, rationality are the key words although they are difficult to quantify; tradition, tribe and religion represent the outmoded and obsolete past. Not surprisingly western anthropologists studying African or Asian peoples once routinely classified them as 'savage,' 'primitive' or 'tribal'—you only have to glance at the titles of one of the celebrated LSE names, Malinowski, for confirmation.

Those working in or on communist societies and those of a Marxist persuasion also analysed ethnicity and religion as remains of the discredited feudal and traditional order. According to their social trajectory ethnic and religious identity, although present, would in time fade away as people became equal citizens in the modern world. Clearly this has not happened for the majority of the world population and the failure of these analysts is spectacular.

Indeed, the problem of defining key concepts such as ethnicity, race, nation and tribe that has faced social scientists is symptomatic of this malaise.[5] What, for example, is a group of Scots in the Scottish highlands? With its clans, language and customs is it a tribe, an ethnic group, a race or a nation? While the classic anthropological text on tribes, *African Political Systems,*[6] restricted the definition to groups like the Bushmen and the Zulu some anthropologists like Max Gluckman[7] included as "tribal," along with the Bushmen and the Nuba, the Scots, the Irish and the Welsh. The debate continues.

Walker Connor contributed to the discussion by combining ethnicity and nationalism and used the term "ethnonationalism."[8] He is right to underline the irrational and emotional well-springs of ethnonationalism—hence the title of his ERS/LSE lecture: *Beyond Reason*—and its capacity to influence group behaviour. But the category creates analytic problems. Surely in certain places, as in India, we need to accept the religious rather than the strictly ethnic dimension of large-scale confrontation?

Ethnicity in one place and religion in another are the central concerns of our time. Indeed, in some areas of conflict 'ethnic cleansing' is a misnomer. In most cases it is straightforward religious genocide as with the Muslims in Bosnia. So to restrict the term rigidly to ethnicity is incomplete at best and misleading at worst. When we employ the term we shall do so broadly and generally to indicate notions of exclusivity in a group, based around a cluster of symbols such as language, religion or historical memory, vehemently opposing and in turn opposed by neighbours with similar ideas of identity expressed with corresponding fervour. 'Ethnic cleansing' is the sustained suppression by all means possible of an ethnically or religiously different group with the ultimate aim to expel or eliminate it altogether.

Although we are pointing to the widespread nature and intensity of ethnic cleansing we are not suggesting it is characteristic of or exclusive to our age. Elimination, as in Bosnia, and segregation, as in the Occupied Territories of Israel, of the other (hated and weaker) group have been practised in the past: the *Reconquista* and *Inquisition* in Spain and *Glaubenskrieg* in Germany (reaching a climax with the Nazi Holocaust) are examples of the former; apartheid in South Africa and Indian Reservations in the USA for the latter.

However, the exercise of grappling with the definitions of tribe, ethnic group, race and so on may be a red herring. What we really need to analyse is why members of a group—ethnic or religious—want to oppose members of another group with such intensity that they are prepared to inflict the most horrific cruelty on them? We are thus really examining the causes for the radicalization of mass culture and the worldwide growth in and acceptance of extremism, fanaticism and violence as a solution to the ethnic problem. It is on this that we need to focus for purposes of our analysis in the otherwise amorphous and shifting global landscape.

Ethnic hatred has a mimetic quality: the opposed groups mirror the hatred, rhetoric and fears of each other. It makes everyone an outsider; and it makes everyone a target. Everywhere—in the shopping arcade, at the bus stop, in the cinema, in your living room—you are vulnerable to sudden, random violence. Anger and hatred are easily created.

The hatred is generalized, universal and maintained at a high level. For those in traditional societies it is engendered by the dangers posed to the core unit of society, the family, whether the extended or nuclear variety. In urbanized and industrialized society this threat is exacerbated as the family is under stress externally and internally: externally from migration, immigration, unemployment; internally from divorce, drugs, alcoholism. All this creates an anger at the world around and a scapegoat is easy to locate.

Members of the neighbouring ethnic group are dirty outsiders, fifth-columnists, disloyal, speak a different language and have different customs. They must be cleansed. This argument can be heard not only in the Balkans but in one form or another in other parts of the world where ethnic clashes are taking place. The mindless cruelty takes in everyone—children, the elderly, the sick—as long as they belong to the other side. It is this combination of perceived ethnic threat and personal vulnerability that forces people to fall back on community and group. There is logic here. If formal networks fail, the more informal ones may assist.

With international structures, like the UNO, not to be trusted (as in Bosnia, Palestine, Kashmir) people fall back on their own group. The belief provides a security in an age of confusion and uncertainty, protection against the imagined or real conspiracies of the enemy. It also inures us to the stories of cruelty that we know exist. By adopting an ethnic position people simplify complex ones, and by talking of national honour and glory disguise the cruelty of their compatriots.

As a parenthesis I might point out the implications of this line of argument for Edward Said's *Orientalism*,[9] Said's thesis is based on the idea of the other (for Europe it is, famously, Islam). The other is out there geographically and culturally, dark, backward and mysterious to be dominated and exploited. In contrast to this external other is the internal other which we are pointing out: it is homegrown, among us, speaking our language and reflecting our customs and sometimes it is stronger than us. Said's other is only a limited tool of analysis for our post-Orientalism argument.

Ethnic cleansing in one sense has leveled the categories that divided the global community—First World, Second World, Third World or North-South or East-West. In various degrees and in different forms ethnic cleansing is in evidence everywhere, not only in Bosnia but elsewhere from Bonn to Bombay, Cairo to Karachi. Cities like New York and Los Angeles, where entire neighbourhoods are based on colour and more or less out of bounds for those of the wrong colour, are ethnically cleansed; a similar conceptual strategy to that in Bosnia is at work. Ethnic cleansing has made us all 'primitives,' 'savages,' 'tribals'—*pace* Malinowski.

For their insensitivity during the Holocaust many governments made the puerile excuse that they were not aware of what was taking place in Germany. The gory daily news from Bosnia—or with less frequency but equal to it in the spirit of violating human rights from Israel, Iraq or India—shown on television or discussed in print has little impact on the governments of the world; they appear to have developed compassion immunity. These stories are reduced to little more than voyeurism.

As with the Holocaust many ask questions of a deep and disturbing nature: 'Why does God—if there is a God—tolerate this suffering? Why doesn't God punish the aggressor, the rapist and the murderer? What happened to the idea that good triumphs over evil?' If there is a divine parabolic lesson in Bosnia it has escaped most people.

For a Muslim events in Bosnia are truly shocking. The holy Quran clearly preaches tolerance and understanding. Indeed, there is an anthropologically illuminating verse which talks of the wonders of the world, the diversity of races, and points to this: "O Human Beings! Behold, We have created you all out of a male and a female and have made you into nations and tribes so that you might come to know one another—not that you may despise each other."[10] It is this spirit of ethnic tolerance that is under attack in our world.

Perhaps for us as academics the most distressing aspect of ethnic cleansing is the involvement of those who are educated and considered to be the pillars of modern society: the doctors, lawyers, engineers and writers. (Not surprisingly, the Jewish mass murderer who killed about fifty and wounded 200 Muslims kneeling at prayer in Hebron in February 1994 was a medical doctor.) We need to be cautious here. Although ethnic loyalty tends to be a tidal wave which sweeps all before it we can cite many courageous people precisely from this class who stand up to and expose their own community.[11]

Unfortunately these exceptions do not disprove the ethnic rule that members of the other ethnic group are considered aliens or enemies irrespective of their merits. Let us now explore some explanations for ethnic cleansing.

THE ECONOMIC ARGUMENT

Perhaps the most commonly cited man-in-the-street explanation of ethnic cleansing is the global economic crisis. It is directly related to modernity running its course, of the loss of confidence in the future for the world community. There is a general economic crisis in the world—call it recession or by some other jargon. Unemployment figures are high. Even educated people walk the streets looking for jobs. Prospects are poor. The long-term global forecast is pessimistic, keeping in view the continuing population explosion in Africa and Asia. Poverty turns men into beasts. It is in this context that minorities—the Bangladeshis in Tower Hamlets or the Muslims in Bombay—become targets of irrational emotions. Matters are made worse by pointing to those individuals who have prospered. 'They are taking all the jobs. They are being given all the housing. They must not be allowed to get away with this pampering.'

There is a strong argument to be made correlating economic deprivation and ethnic confrontation. Whether in Gaza or in Kashmir the government has made virtually no economic investment. The neglect is interpreted as ethnic prejudice. However, it is not only the minority that feels neglected. It is striking that each major section of society views its central problems in a similar light, casting itself as victim, and complains of injustice, blaming its misfortunes on the ethnic or religious enemy members of which are citizens and neighbours.

While the economic argument is valid up to a point it is also limited, for economic statistics or material progress are taken as a yardstick of life itself, an end in themselves. Yet poverty has never been an excuse for violence and intolerance; indeed, material austerity and spiritual development are central planks of most Asian religious thinking. This was made clear by the examples of the great spiritual messengers of history—Moses, the Buddha, Jesus and the Prophet of

Islam. In our century men like Mahatma Gandhi and women like Mother Teresa have advocated the message of austerity and simplicity with success. Human beings clearly cannot live by bread alone.

GLOBALIZATION AND THE MASS MEDIA

Globalization and the mass media provide us with another explanation for ethnic cleansing. Let us explore this idea with the caution that, while globalization is a characteristic of postmodernity, it is also a direct consequence and in many significant ways a continuation of modernity. Giddens in his definition of globalization draws our attention to the relationship:

> Globalisation means that, in respect of the consequences of at least some disembedding mechanisms, no one can "opt out" of the transformations brought about by modernity: this is so, for example, in respect of the global risks of nuclear war or of ecological catastrophe.[12]

Globalization draws in people all over the world who willingly or reluctantly participate in a global culture.[13]

Satellite TV, the VCR, communications technology and developments in transport have made this possible.[14] McDonald's and Mickey Mouse, "Dallas" and "Dynasty," Coca Cola and Levis, Toyota and Sony as much as ideas of mass democracy and human rights are now the universally recognized signs of this global culture whatever their country of origin. "Globalization," sighs one of the pundits studying it, "is, at least empirically, not in and of itself a 'nice thing,' in spite of certain indications of 'world progress.' "[15]

It is still early days for media studies, and the influence of the media on how people behave needs to be explored at greater length by social scientists. There is a tendency to dismiss media studies as an upstart and not take it seriously. This is a mistake because we can learn a great deal about contemporary life through media studies. Besides, it is salutary to recall the derision with which economics, sociology and anthropology—each in its turn—were greeted by fellow scientists when these subjects attempted to secure a foothold in academe.

Today TV, the VCR, satellite dishes and newspapers spread information and images more quickly and more widely than ever before in history. The consequences for our argument are enormous. For most of the population on this planet the reductive and hedonist images are a mirage, the hyper-consumerism out of reach. Envy, frustration and anger result. The need to blame someone, to find scapegoats, is great. Radicalization and violence follow.

We know that state-controlled television in Belgrade played a crucial role in manipulating and articulating Serb identity. It showed pictures of atrocities, often of Serb victims, which confirmed in people's minds the necessity to stand together against a hostile world bent on denying them dignity and statehood. Ethnic passions were aroused and ethnic cleansing appeared justified.

With its tendency to simplify complex issues the media also allow both a false and dangerous argument to circulate, one mounted by the chauvinistic and aggressive middle class, the keepers of the ethnic flame, that there is a 'global conspiracy' to keep the nation or race down and prevent it from becoming great and fulfilling its destiny, that the minorities play the role of a fifth-column in this exercise. Across the world this complaint is echoed. Let us examine the situation in India.[16]

The Hindu backlash was almost inevitable and needs to be explained. The vast majority of the population was Hindu but in the post-colonial rhetoric—secularism, national progress, socialism—Hindu identity was in danger of being submerged. Hindus felt justifiably aggrieved. Among India's founding fathers were men of great piety like Mahatma Gandhi and Sardar Patel but it was the first Prime Minister, Jawaharlal Nehru, who influenced independent India the most with his secular, tolerant and modern ideas. However, in the eyes of the traditional and orthodox, modernity appeared to demean, disempower and marginalize custom and belief. The Marxist vocabulary of the intellectuals added insult to injury.

By the 1970s with Nehru not long gone from the scene, Hindu revivalism began to gather momentum and Indira Gandhi, always a political animal, abandoned her father's position for an openly communal one. The globalization process and its aggressive cultural manifestation, especially of American origin, further alienated and threatened Indians—Hindus and Muslims—and forced them to hark back.[17]

The political and cultural atmosphere in the 1980s was charged. The mildest reservation about or the merest hint of opposition to the Hindu cause by a Muslim would risk swift, noisy and painful retribution. It would be a feeling familiar to a Muslim Bosnian in Serb-controlled Bosnia with reservations about the battle of Kosovo, a Copt about the capacity of the Egyptian state to protect Christian churches and property, a Palestinian about the fairness of the state of Israel, a Kurd about the humanity of Saddam Hussein's regime, a Jew about the Islamic revolution in Iran and a Bangladeshi Hindu about Islamic revivalism in Bangladesh.

A glance at the long list of credits of the major and popular television series depicting a mythical Hindu past, "Mahabharat," "Ramayana" and "Chanakya" (all shown in Britain) will illustrate the position of the Muslims in India today; the names are almost exclusively Hindu. It is assumed that only Hindus can make or contribute to 'religious' films. Notions of purity and exclusiveness are implied and ethnic boundaries clearly drawn. This, too, it can be argued, is a side of ethnic cleansing.[18]

This was not always so in Indian films.[19] One of the most significant contributions to the idea of a genuinely multicultural and multi-religious India was made by the Bombay cinema in the early decades of independence. It may have been an ideal but it inspired millions. One of the most famous Hindu devotional songs from the popular film "Kohinoor"[20] provides an example. It was sung on screen by Dilip Kumar (Yusuf Khan), written by Shakeel Badayuni, directed by Naushad and actually sung by Mohammad Raft, all four Muslims. This was a remarkable comment on Indian tolerance and synthesis. It reflected the spirit of the founding fathers: Mahatma Gandhi, Jawaharlal Nehru, Maulana Azad. It is this spirit which is under threat and which worries many Hindus, who wish to see it preserved. The minorities are simply terrorized by the new mass violence.

Films like "Mahabharat," "Ramayana" and "Chanakya" did not necessarily aim to have a contemporary political message but were watched by an estimated 600 million people every week and this, in itself a unique media phenomenon, created a highly religious atmosphere in the 1980s. It generated a nation-wide glow of pride and identity—a specifically Hindu pride and identity. The images projected an idealized Hindu past, a society in harmony, in flower.

Had the matter ended there—television as entertainment—that would have been admirable and innocuous. But a sub-text could be discerned: the ideal picture was shattered by invaders from outside India; Muslims were to blame. The series assisted in setting a chain of events in motion. Some media pundits in the BJP, a party floundering on the verge of extinction, at this point joined the emotions generated by the mass media and a political issue concerning the birth-place of Lord Ram at Ayodhya where a medieval mosque stood. Overnight its fortunes changed—from two seats in parliament to 119—although the results of the state election in north India indicate the support of the BJP may have peaked.

So while Hindus thrilled at the doings of the attractive warrior-hero figure of Lord Ram on television they were angered by the mosque at Ayodhya. A vigorous campaign daubed the legend "Declare with pride your Hinduism" on walls, posters and hoardings all over India. A not so subtle subliminal message was contained in this slogan: vote for those who identified with Hinduism (like the BJP). The BJP notably, but also the Congress, then recruited the stars from the television series, who were treated almost like gods in India, as their parliamentary candidates. They helped mobilize public opinion in demanding the mosque at Ayodhya be replaced by a temple. Widespread tension all over India resulted in frequent large-scale riots in the name of Lord Ram.

Hindu extremists were now offering Muslims throughout India the standard choices of ethnic cleansing: absorption into Hinduism by accepting Lord Ram and becoming "Hindu Mohammedans," or expulsion (to Pakistan or Saudi Arabia or wherever). The third choice was to prepare for the destruction of life and property. From the *Reconquista* in Spain to the Occupied Territories in Israel subjugated minorities have confronted these dilemmas.

The transformation of what its devout and thoughtful followers see as a philosophic, humane and universal religious tradition to a bazaar vehicle for ethnic hatred and political confrontation saddens many Hindus. The mosque at Ayodhya was destroyed in December 1992 and an orgy of killing followed all over India in which the paramilitary and security forces were later implicated (the world saw them on television screens idly standing by as the frenzied mob in Ayodhya went about its business). Horror stories circulated of Muslims being burnt alive or raped while video recorders filmed them. In Bombay mobs stopped men and forced them to drop their trousers; those circumcised were identified as Muslim and stabbed. The link between the media and politics, between the religious-cultural assertion of identity of one group and the persecution of another, is suggested.

There were also immediate and serious international repercussions: Hindus were attacked and their temples destroyed in Pakistan and Bangladesh while angry mobs demanded a 'holy war' against India in retaliation. In Britain tension was created between the Hindu and Muslim communities and Hindu temples were mysteriously damaged. The span of responses confirms our other argument that to understand ethnic violence we need to keep its global context before us.

Although commentators singled out the BJP as the main culprit behind the ethnic violence this is incorrect and misleading; indeed, elements in the Congress had long compromised on its secular position. Others too—influential opinion-makers like bureaucrats, media commentators and academics—had been transformed and abandoned their earlier secular neutrality on communal issues. Those who were dismayed by this trend were reduced to powerless spectators.

Let us not make the mistake of the critics of the BJP by simplification of a complex phenomenon. Beneath every case of ethnic cleansing is layer upon layer of history and culture. The movement for a separate Muslim state, the creation of Pakistan (seen by many Hindus in a religious light, as sacrilege, as the division of Mother India itself), the wars between India and Pakistan, the perception of a threatening Islamic revivalism (in neighbours like Pakistan and Bangladesh and also, of course, Iran) and the continuing problems of the Muslim minority in adjusting to the new realities of India all contributed to the ethnic suppuration.

Indeed, as early as the 1930s Gowalkar, one of the most influential Hindu ideologues, had argued that if Hitler could finish off the Jews in Germany then the Hindus ought to be able to do the same to the Muslims in India.[21] Hindu extremists even today continue to use the unsavoury language of the Nazis. The tradition of virulent propaganda against Muslims is disguised as scholarly research.[22] Muslims in these books are depicted as whoring and pillaging drunks, breaking Hindu temples and buildings. These stereotypes feed into the mass media and neatly reinforce Hindu chauvinism which is calculated to win the Hindu vote.

The argument will be made that India is, after all, Asia, Third World, backward, a society stuck in the rut of religion and tradition, that the influence on society of television is a sign of such societies. It would be incorrect. Not only in India but throughout the world what we see on our television screens helps to form our ideas. The argument that the sex and violence shown on television influence people awaits long-term statistical findings but on the surface appears plausible. They inure people to cruelty. Children grow into adulthood convinced that the simple solution is to kill or maim or hurt. Not surprisingly, American pilots, on at least one carrier, about to bomb Iraq the following day during the Gulf war, were shown sadistic, pornographic films.[23] Not surprisingly either, the young killers of little James Bulger here in the UK had grown up on a diet of "video nasties."

In December 1993 half a dozen young men raped for over an hour two young girls barely in their teens who were dragged from a McDonald's in London. About twenty other men stood round and cheered. The inspiration for this is not difficult to guess. Dozens of American films have depicted the same scene. That the gang was predominantly black gave the incident an ethnic dimension (life was also imitating art a few weeks earlier when a black—or to use the politically correct term Afro-American—gunman walked along a New York underground train shooting anyone not of his colour).

NO HEROES ANY MORE

The mass media are also responsible, because of their aggressive irreverence and unceasing probing, for the lack-lustre leadership of today. Our age has produced a distinctly mediocre set of leaders. Political scientists need to investigate this phenomenon further so that we become enlightened. Consider the list at random—Clinton in America, Major in the United Kingdom, Kohl in Germany, Yeltsin in Russia, Rao in India, Mubarak in Egypt. Many of us, I am sure, are not even aware of the names of the heads of government in China and Japan.

Charismatic leaders are not always the best leaders and those like Hitler and Stalin were ardent supporters of ethnic cleansing. So what makes some charismatic leaders extraordinary is their ability to stand up to majority opinion when it comes to matters of principle. We have the example of Mahatma Gandhi agreeing to the creation of Pakistan, however much it pained him, if that was what the Muslims wanted, and then starting a fast to death unless Hindus stopped killing Muslims in India. A Hindu fanatic killed him, accusing him of being too sympathetic to the Muslims. There was De Gaulle in France who took the unpopular decision of giving independence to Algeria. For many French it was the ultimate betrayal and De Gaulle's life was constantly under threat. And there was Churchill whose support for the Jews overruled the anti-Semitism at the Foreign Office.

In contrast, Rao in India, a year after promising to reconstruct the mosque in Ayodhya still vacillates. In France north African immigrants are the subject of the crudest form of racism and the prime minister's office talks openly of smelly and dirty aliens. Charles Pusqua and others have powerfully and mendaciously linked crime and immigration. Pusqua talks of returning immigrants to Africa "by the planeload and the boatload." He has tapped a vast reservoir of votes and added a new and dangerous dimension to both issues.

THE FAILURE OF THE NATION-STATE

The failure of the nation-state to provide justice and inspire confidence, and the frustrations that it engenders is another consequence of the collapse of modernity and of the rise of ethnic identity. Modernity was expressed by the form and idea of the nation-state. 'National identity' emerged as a by-product of the formation of the nation-state, itself impelled by 'industrialization.'[24] But in large parts of the world the nation-state itself is under challenge: in East Europe, in the lands that once constituted the USSR, in the Middle East, in South Asia and in Africa. Boundaries are being redrawn or rejected. As old states are threatened new ones are demanded or formed.

In their haste to depart, after the international climate changed following World War II, the colonialists took little time or effort when demarcating the new nations. Tribes and villages were sometimes divided between nations (in the case of the Kurds, the tribe was divided between five nations). Half a century of living together should have cemented the new states. This is not so.

One reason is the blatant discrimination that the state practises in favour of the dominant group. It is not being suggested that the state legally supports the subjugation or the elevation of a group. On the contrary, states are based on modern notions of equality and justice and in some cases appear to favour minorities (as in India where the Constitution in this regard compares favourably to the putatively advanced countries like France and Germany). Rather, that even state functionaries are now contaminated with ethnic hatred.

Most dangerously for the health of the state the majority has developed a 'minority complex'—whether in Serbia, Israel, Iraq or India. Through a process of Alice-in-Wonderland logic it has come to believe, and proclaims for all to hear, that its population is in danger of being swamped (the minority breed like rabbits); its economy is in crisis (the minority act as a brake); it is the victim of an international conspiracy (the minority are a fifth-column) and law and order have collapsed (the minority are responsible for the drugs and gun-culture). To be a member of what is seen as the pestilential minority by the majority is almost to be a *persona non grata*, irrespective of the merits of the individual (whether Muslim in India, Hindu in Bangladesh, Palestinian in Israel or Kurd in Iraq). The minority argue that the nation-state has meant suppression of their identity usually by brute force. Torture and death are common methods. Besides, the majority monopolize economic and political power, they point out. Democracy, they rightly claim, means perpetual subordination and humiliation. Ultimately, they fear, they will be wiped off the face of the earth.

A significant ethnic lesson is drawn from Bosnia. Many are now skeptical about the plausibility of plural or multicultural societies in the future. 'If the Serbs can do this to the Muslims who even married Serbs what hope is there for integration? Is the idea of integration irretrievably lost?' There were no easy answers even by optimists. The only security, it seems, was in reversion to primordial identity, a return to the idea of the tribe, of purity in an impure and menacing world.

An important idea, widely believed, is that international organizations which should have ensured justice, law and order and the rule of law have failed. The United Nations is the primary example. It has failed the Bosnians, the Palestinians and the Kashmiris. Resolution after resolution is passed regarding the destiny of these people and blatantly ignored.

For Muslims the world over Bosnia, Palestine and Kashmir signify the hostility to Islam in our times, of the persecution of Muslim minorities in particular. Muslims are convinced that fellow Muslims are being raped, killed and uprooted because of their religion. Muslim anger and anguish echo the heart-rending cry of Shakespeare's Jew: "Hath not a Jew eyes? hath not a Jew hands, organs, dimensions, senses, affections, passions?"

The historical past is evoked in each case. For instance, when discussing Bosnia Muslims believe that the West which is capable of stopping the genocide will not do so because it does not want a viable Muslim nation in Europe. The last Muslim kingdom was extinguished in 1492 in Granada, Spain, and Europeans, 500 years later, have not changed. Muslims, both globally and in Bosnia, suggest that European ideas of humanism, freedom and equality appear to be applicable only to white Europeans with a Christian background.[25] It is in this context that commentators construct the global confrontation between Islam and the West.[26]

Matters are complicated as ethnic groups across international borders are prepared to assist their oppressed kin (India accuses Pakistan of assisting the Kashmiris, Israel the Arabs of aiding the Palestinians, and so on). Once again the majority feel threatened and talk of fifth-columns. Unless free and fair channels of representation are available and unless the majority genuinely consider the needs of the minority, the democracy in these countries will be incomplete and the nation-state will continue to be challenged as the minorities demand their own state.

We also need to point to the nation-state and nuclear proliferation. In the context of our arguments, until a decade or two ago, the nuclear option did not exist outside the Cold War structure. Today it does. India and Pakistan have fought three wars. They are poised for a fourth. Tension is at a peak following the destruction of the Ayodhya mosque and the revolt in Kashmir. This time the war will be nuclear, a total war; it will also be total madness. No-one can win.

It is not difficult to conjecture what extremists on either side—Serbs or Bosnians in the Balkans, Jews or Palestinians in the Middle East, Hindus or Muslims in South Asia—would do if allowed to decide whether a bomb should be dropped on their enemy. It would solve all their problems, they will say enthusiastically. Holocaust solutions have always been popular with those who believe in eliminating supposedly inferior races.

Ethnocentric perceptions lull us into believing that nuclear weapons are more unsafe in the hands of the north Korean leaders than in American or British ones. However, any finger, whether yellow or white, on the nuclear button is dangerous although the safeguards are greater in a democracy. The fact is that nuclear proliferation poses a major danger to the world. The question of nuclear weapons needs to be addressed urgently on a global level.

RAPE AS POLICY IN ETHNIC CLEANSING

Rape is one of the most infamous acts on man's long list of infamy, one suggesting deep psychological and emotional disturbance. Because rape is so intimately tied to ideas of honour and disgrace people are reluctant to discuss it. Yet to learn about the true nature of ethnic and religious conflict social scientists need to study rape or sexual intimidation.

We know that in Bosnia rape is used deliberately as an instrument of war, a fact confirmed by innumerable international organizations and media reports. Dogs, men affected by the HIV virus and gangs taking turns are used to rape women in what have been exposed as rape camps. Small girls are raped in front of their mothers by soldiers taking turns. Rape is known as an ugly face of battle committed by soldiers in the heat of war. But in the manner it is used in the Balkans it is chillingly sinister. Civilians, administrators, students—ordinary people—are all involved as active participants or as spectators.

Bosnia is not alone in this regard. There is also considerable evidence gathered by international human rights organizations and by Indian writers that Indian troops in Kashmir are using the same tactics. There may not be official rape camps as in Bosnia but troops have regularly surrounded villages, expelled the men and raped their women all night. After the destruction of the Ayodhya mosque the police were clearly implicated in organizing riots in Bombay and Surat against Muslims which involved rape. Iraq and Israel, the former in a crude way, the latter in a more subtle manner, also use sexual tactics to intimidate minorities we learn from the book *Cruelty and Silence,* by an Iraqi expatriate writer.[27] Iraqi soldiers force Kurd women from camps taking them to be raped; Israelis lock up Arab women in security cells for the night with threatening men. An organization of brave Israeli women risked the wrath of the authorities and documented the widespread cases of sexual abuse by the Israeli police in *Women for Women Political Prisoners,* published in December 1989 in Jerusalem.

The woman is twice punished: by the brutality of the act and by the horror of her family. Notions of honour, modesty and motherhood are all violated. Rape strikes families at their most vulnerable point especially in traditional societies where, in certain tribes, illegitimate sexual acts are wiped out by death alone.[28] It is thus deliberately employed by ethnic neighbours who are fully aware of its expression as political power and cultural assertion to humiliate the internal other.

The sociological implications are clear for the purposes of our argument: rape as a final line divides one group from the other; the state, through its forces, becomes the rapist, raping its own citizens, those it is sworn to protect. Bitterness is at a peak. So is the nature of hatred in the response. Blood and revenge follow. A spiral of violence is set in motion. All the key notions of modernity—justice, rule of law, rationalism, civic society—are negated by the criminal nature of ethnic rape. For the victim and her family it is no longer an age of modernity and progress but one of barbarism and darkness.

THE USES OF THE PAST

Finally, to justify the acts of humiliation like rape and as a consequence of the general sense of disillusionment with international and national bodies, the collapse of law and order and the conviction that the only security lies in one's own people, is the increasingly creative use of historical-religious arguments which, in turn, support ethnic cleansing.

History is employed to buttress ethnic and religious polemics and, more importantly, to reclaim and re-construct ethnic identity by a whole range of commentators, academics and politicians.[29] Thus, Kosovo in the Balkans, Jerusalem in the Middle East or Ayodhya in India are not just neutral historical place names; they are also deeply emotive and affective symbols of identity. They rally the community as they provide it with a visible proof of the perfidious enemy by reviving bitter memories from a distant past. In the mass media such history translates itself into kitsch, sentimentality and commercialization; it also becomes popular and accessible. In the vacuum caused by the collapse of the grand narratives like Communism the indigenous becomes both relevant and inevitable. Honour, identity and the media, the past and the future, the rise of what is called fundamentalism or revivalism all relate to the historical reference points.

Historical-religious mythology feeds the ethnic passions of the Russians (like Zhirinovsky) and Serbs (like Arkan) who talk of a Christian crusade, Jews and Muslims in the Middle East and Hindus and Muslims in South Asia who view each other as enemies in a holy war. "God is with us," the faithful pronounce with utter conviction and sincere belief.

It is this zeal which drives men in Bosnia to burn the sign of the cross on to the bodies of innocent Muslims and impale them in crucifixion.[30] This is not the spirit of Jesus but it is a crude ethnic justification for the murder and mayhem. The first target is the village mosque. The destruction of these buildings is to be condemned on religious as well as architectural grounds, for most of them are centuries old. *The Heart Grown Bitter*, the title of an anthropological account of Greek ethnic war refugees in Cyprus by Peter Loizos, tellingly describes the plight of the ethnically dispossessed.[31]

Most academics who have dismissed such historical mythology as irrelevant to our modern lives do not fully appreciate its power and influence. We are pointing to zealous supporters of ethnic superiority who number in the millions across the world and their governments which have access to nuclear weapons.

CONCLUSION: INTO THE MILLENNIUM

Prognosis is difficult for the post-Cold War, post-Communism, postmodern age that is forming but it is likely that the next millennium will open with limited but intensely messy ethnic conflicts—with vigorous ethnic cleansing—on-going low intensity wars in which there are no real winners or losers, no major defeats or victories, no defined battlefields or boundaries. We need to pull back from this nightmare Hobbesian scenario of the future to restore a balance between tradition and modernity, local custom and culture, respect for law and the way of others. Above all, we need more imagination and tolerance in dealing with others.

It can be done. The last year or two have provided us with some dramatic examples of a silver lining to the dark ethnic cloud. Old-standing ethnic enemies shook hands, an act symbolic of the wish to remove the vast psychological and cultural barriers that divided them and their people: Rabin and Arafat in Washington, but also the British and Irish prime ministers over Northern Ireland and the black and white leaders over South Africa. In Germany, in spite of widespread and vicious ethnic violence, Dr. Ravindra Gujjula, an Indian, was elected the first Asian mayor in history. In December 1993 the Vatican reconciled with Judaism thus closing the hostility of two millennia. These significant gestures need to be more than media events and to be followed by concrete steps; the ethnic fires still rage on the ground.

Important steps need to be taken to encourage ethnic understanding. The first and most important is to underline the plurality of our world, that although people are divided by birth, language and religion they belong to the same species. To counter narrow nationalism we need to stress the extent of interdependence in today's world, growing all the time so as to encourage people to think internationally. Organizations like the United Nations, weak and ineffective in the face of ethnic crises, need urgent structural changes and larger budgets. Human rights and minority groups must be protected not only under the law but in the spirit of good neighbourliness. The idea of tolerance and understanding needs to be encouraged through the mass media. We have seen the mass media acting as a source of division, let us see its positive side.[32] For a start, it can become aware of the stereotypes it builds up of the other and avoid them.

Education is another way to discourage ethnic hatred. Ill-defined ideas and prejudices in a student's mind easily develop into prejudice for the other. Islam and Hinduism need to be taught seriously as regular subjects in Britain; Christianity in Sudan and Pakistan, and so on. We need to call for an intensification of inter-faith dialogue. There is so much common ground; spokespersons for the different faiths should point to it and act upon it. We need more Christians and non-Christians in Europe, Jews and Muslims in the Middle East and Hindus and Muslims in South Asia sitting across tables in serious discussion.

Never before in human history have the global and the local, the high and the low, the past and the present, the sacred and the profane, the serious and the frivolous been so bewilderingly juxtaposed and so instantly available to stimulate, confuse and anger the individual. Violence is almost inevitable, the ethnic victim often at hand. Globally, the disillusioned children and inheritors of modernity, live in what the academics have termed "a risk culture"[33] or "risk society."[34]

In concluding, we have pointed out the links between globalization, radicalization, sexual intimidation, the mass media, the uses of religious mythology and ethnic and religious violence in the aftermath of the collapse of modernity. There is clearly cause and effect here. We have noted that victims of ethnic intolerance in one part of the world are themselves aggressors in other parts through the acts of those who share their religion or ethnicity. Every group appears to be susceptible to the ethnic virus. Ethnic cleansing, we have suggested, ranges from the outright barbarity of death and rape camps to the more subtle but also traumatic cultural, political and economic pressures brought to bear on the minority.

In ethnic cleansing the human race faces a moral collapse leading to the most diabolical acts of cruelty. Yet our world also possesses the capacity and resources to tackle other pressing problems that we face like hunger and disease. Clearly, the global community is at some kind of dramatic crossroad, a cusp, a critical point in history.

Ethnic cleansing is the dark and ugly side of human nature. To contain it and to combat it we need first to understand it. Therefore to examine ethnic cleansing is not to look at the aberrant or the marginal or the temporary—the specialist's area of interest; it is to come face to face with our age, our nature and our aspirations; it is to confront the human condition.

SECTION SIX

Violence and Class

CHAPTER 26

Excerpt from Reflections on Violence

By Georges Sorel

Before examining what qualities the modern industrial system requires of free producers, we must analyse the component parts of morality. The philosophers always have a certain amount of difficulty in seeing clearly into these ethical problems, because they feel the impossibility of harmonising the ideas which are current at a given time in a class, and yet imagine it to be their duty to reduce everything to a unity. To conceal from themselves the fundamental heterogeneity of all this civilised morality, they have recourse to a great number of subterfuges, sometimes relegating to the rank of exceptions, importations, or survivals, everything which embarrasses them—sometimes drowning reality in an ocean of vague phrases and, most often, employing both methods the better to obscure the problem. My view, on the contrary, is that the *best way of understanding any group of ideas in the history of thought is to bring all the contradictions into sharp relief.* I shall adopt this method and take for a starting-point the celebrated opposition which Nietzsche has established between two groups of moral values, an opposition about which much has been written, but which has never been properly studied.

A. We know with what force Nietzsche praised the values constructed by the *masters*, by a superior class of warriors who, in their expeditions, enjoying to the full freedom from all social constraint, return to the simplicity of mind of a wild beast, become once more triumphant monsters who continually bring to mind "the superb blond beast, prowling in search of prey and bloodshed," in whom "a basis of hidden bestiality needs from time to time a purgative." To understand this thesis properly, we must not attach too much importance to formulas which have at times been intentionally exaggerated, but should examine the historical facts; the author tells us that he has in mind "the aristocracy of Rome, Arabia, Germany, and Japan, the *Homeric heroes*, the Scandinavian vikings."

It is chiefly the Homeric heroes that we must bear in mind in order to understand what Nietzsche wished to make clear to his contemporaries. We must remember that he had been professor of Greek at the University of Bâle, and that his reputation began with a book devoted to the glorification of the Hellenic genius (*The Origin of Tragedy*). He notices that, even at the period of their highest culture, the Greeks still preserved a memory of their former character of masters.

"Our daring," said Pericles, "has traced a path over earth and sea, raising everywhere imperishable monuments both of good and evil." It was of the heroes of Greek legend and history that he was thinking when he speaks of "that audacity of noble races, that mad, absurd, and spontaneous audacity, their influence and contempt for all security of the body, for life, for comfort." Does not "the terrible gaiety and the profound joy which the heroes tasted in destruction, in all the pleasures of victory and of cruelty," apply particularly to Achilles?[1]

It was certainly to the type of classic Greek that Nietzsche alluded when he wrote "the moral judgments of the warrior aristocracy are founded on a powerful bodily constitution, a flourishing health without forgetfulness of what was necessary to the maintenance of that overflowing vigour—war, adventure, hunting, dancing, games, and physical exercises, in short, everything implied by a robust, free, and joyful activity."[2]

That very ancient type, the Achaean type celebrated by Homer, is not simply a memory; it has several times reappeared in the world. "During the Renaissance there was a superb reawakening of the classic idea of the aristocratic valuation of all things; and after the Revolution the most prodigious and unexpected event came to pass, the antique ideal stood in person with unwonted splendour before the eyes of consciousness of humanity. . . . (Then) appeared Napoleon, isolated and belated example though he was."[3]

I believe that if the professor of philology had not been continually cropping up in Nietzsche he would have perceived that the master type still exists under our own eyes, and that it is this type which, at the present time, has created the extraordinary greatness of the United States. He would have been struck by the singing analogies which exist between the Yankee, ready for any kind of enterprise, and the ancient Greek sailor, sometimes a pirate, sometimes a colonist or merchant; above all, he would have established a parallel between the ancient heroes and the man who sets out on the conquest of the Far West.[4] P. de Rousiers has described the *master* type admirably. "To become and to remain an American, one must look upon life as *a struggle and not as a pleasure*, and seek in it, victorious effort, energetic and efficacious action, rather than pleasure, leisure embellished by the cultivation of the arts, the refinements proper to other societies. Everywhere—we have seen that what makes the American succeed, what constitutes his type—is character, personal energy, energy in action, creative energy."[5] The profound contempt which the Greek had for the Barbarian is matched by that of the Yankee for the foreign worker who makes no effort to become truly American. "Many of these people would be better if we took them in hand," an old colonel of the War of Secession said to a French traveller, but we are a proud race; a shopkeeper of Pottsville spoke of the Pennsylvania miners as "the senseless populace."[6] J. Bourdeau has drawn attention to the strange likeness which exists between the ideas of A. Carnegie and Roosevelt, and those of Nietzsche, the first deploring the waste of money involved in maintaining incapables, the second urging the Americans to becoming conquerors, a race of prey.[7]

I am not among those who consider Homer's Archaean type, the indomitable hero confident in his strength and putting himself above rules, as necessarily disappearing in the future. If it has often been believed that the type was bound to disappear, that was because the Homeric values were imagined to be irreconcilable with the other values which spring from an entirely different principle; Nietzsche committed this error, which all those who believe in the necessity of unity in thought are bound to make. It is quite evident that liberty would be seriously compromised if men came to regard the Homeric values (which are approximately the same as the Cornelian values) as suitable only to barbaric peoples. Many moral evils would for ever remain unremedied if some hero of revolt did not force the people to become aware of their own state of mind on the subject. And art, which is after all of some value, would lose the finest jewel in its crown.

The philosophers are little disposed to admit the right of art to support the cult of the "will to power;" it seems to them that they ought to give lessons to artists, instead of receiving lessons from them; they think that only those sentiments which have received the stamp of the Universities have the right to manifest themselves in poetry. Like industry, art has never adapted itself to the demands of theorists; it always upsets their plans of social harmony, and humanity has found the freedom of art far too satisfactory ever to think of allowing it to be controlled by the creators of dull systems of sociology. The Marxists are accustomed to seeing the ideologists look at things the wrong way round, and so, in contrast to their enemies, they should look upon art as a reality which begets ideas and not as an application of ideas.

B. To the values created by the *master* type, Nietzsche opposed the system constructed by sacerdotal castes—the ascetic ideal against which he has piled up so much invective. The history of these values is much more obscure and complicated than that of the preceding ones. Nietzsche tries to connect the origin of asceticism with psychological reasons which I will not examine here. He certainly makes a mistake in attributing a preponderating part to the Jews. It is not at all evident that antique Judaism had an ascetic character; doubtless, like the other Semitic religions, it attached importance to pilgrimages, fasts, and prayers recited in ragged clothes. The Hebrew poets sang the hope of revenge which existed in the heart of the persecuted, but, until the second century of our era, the Jews looked to be revenged by arms:[8] on the other hand, family life, with them, was too strong for the monkish ideal ever to become important.

Imbued with Christianity as our civilisation may be, it is none the less evident that, even in the Middle Ages, it submitted to influences foreign to the Church, with the result that the old ascetic values were gradually transformed. The values to which the contemporary world clings most closely, and which it considers the true *ethical values*, are not realised in convents, but in the family; respect for the human person, sexual fidelity and devotion to the weak, constitute the elements of morality of which all high-minded men are proud; morality, even, is very often made to consist of these alone.

When we examine in a critical spirit the numerous writings which treat, today, of marriage, we see that the reformers who are in earnest propose to improve family relations in such a way as to assure the better realisation of these ethical values; thus, they demand that the scandals of conjugal life shall not be exposed in the law courts, that unions shall not be maintained when fidelity no longer exists, and that the authority of the head of the family shall not be diverted from its moral purpose to become mere exploitation, etc.

On the other hand, it is curious to observe to what extent the modern Church misunderstands the values that classico-Christian civilisation has produced. It sees in marriage, above all, a contract directed by financial and worldly interests; it is unwilling to allow of the union being dissolved when the household is a hell, and takes no account of the duty of devotion.[9] The priests are wonderfully skillful in procuring rich dowries for impoverished nobles, so much so, indeed, that the Church has been accused of considering marriage as a mating of noblemen living as "bullies" with middle-class women reduced to the role of the women who support such men. When it is heavily recompensed, the Church finds unexpected reasons for divorce, and finds means of annulling inconvenient unions for ridiculous motives. Proudhon asks ironically: "Is it possible for a responsible man of a serious turn of mind and a true Christian to care for the love of his wife? . . . If the husband seeking divorce, or the wife seeking separation, alleges the refusal of the *conjugal right*, then, *of course*, there is a legitimate reason for a rupture, for the service for which the marriage is granted has not been carried out."[10]

Our civilisation having come to consider nearly all morality as consisting of values derived from those observed in the normally constituted family, two serious consequences have been produced: (1) it has been asked if, instead of considering the family as an application of moral theories, it would not be more exact to say that it is the base of these theories; (2) it seems that the Church, having become incompetent on matters connected with sexual union, must also be incompetent as regards morality. These are precisely the conclusions to which Proudhon came. "Sexual duality was created by Nature to be the instrument of Justice. . . . To produce Justice is the higher aim of the bisexual division; generation, and what follows from it, only figure here as accessory."[11] "Marriage, both in principle and in purpose, being the *instrument of human right*, and the living negation of the divine right, is thus in formal contradiction with theology and the Church."[12]

Love, by the enthusiasm it begets, can produce that sublimity without which there would be no effective morality. At the end of his book on Justice, Proudhon has written pages, which will never be surpassed, on the role of women.

C. Finally we have to examine the values which escape Nietzsche's classification and which treat of *civil relations*. Originally magic was much mixed up in the evaluation of these values; among the Jews, until recent times, one finds a mixture of hygienic principles, rules about sexual relationships, precepts about honesty, benevolence and national solidarity, the whole wrapped up in magical superstitions; this mixture, which seems strange to the philosopher, had the happiest influence on their morality so long as they maintained their traditional mode of living, and one notices among them even now a particular exactitude in the carrying out of contracts.

The ideas held by modern ethical writers are drawn mainly from those of Greece in its time of decadence; Aristotle, living in a period of transition, combined ancient values with values that, as time went on, were to prevail; war and production had ceased to occupy the attention of the most distinguished men of the towns, who sought, on the contrary, to secure an easy existence for themselves; the most important thing was the establishment of friendly relations between the better educated men of the community, and the fundamental maxim was that of the golden mean. The new morality was to be acquired principally by means of the habits which the young Greek would pick up in mixing with cultivated people. It may be said that here we are on the level of an ethic adapted to consumers; it is not astonishing then that Catholic theologians still find Aristotle's ethics an excellent one, for they themselves take the consumer's point of view.

In the civilisation of antiquity, the ethics of producers could hardly be any other than that of slave-owners, and it did not seem worth developing at length, at the time when philosophy made an inventory of Greek customs. Aristotle said that no far-reaching science was needed to employ slaves: "For the master *need only know how to order what the slaves must know how to execute*. So, as soon as a man can save himself this trouble, he leaves it in the charge of a steward, so as to be himself free for a political or philosophical life."[13] A little farther on he wrote: "It is manifest, then, that the master ought to be the source of excellence in the slave; but not merely because he possesses the art which trains him in his duties."[14] This clearly expresses the point of view of the urban consumer, who finds it very tiresome to be obliged to pay any attention whatever to the conditions of production.[15]

As to the slave, he needs very limited virtues. "He only needs enough to prevent him neglecting his work through intemperance or idleness." He should be treated with "more indulgence even than children," although certain people consider that slaves are deprived of reason and are only fit to receive orders.[16]

It is quite easy to see that during a considerable period the moderns also did not think that there was anything more to be said about workers than Aristotle had said; they must be given orders, corrected with gentleness, like children, and treated as passive instruments who do not need to think. Revolutionary Syndicalism would be impossible if the world of the workers were under the influence of such a *morality of the weak*. State Socialism, on the contrary, could accommodate itself to this morality perfectly well, since the latter is based on the idea of a society divided into a class of producers and a class of thinkers applying results of scientific investigation to the work of production. The only difference which would exist between this sham Socialism and Capitalism would consist in the employment of more ingenious methods of procuring discipline in the workshop.

At the present moment, officials of the Bloc are working to create a kind of ethical discipline which will replace the hazy religion which G. de Molinari thinks necessary to the successful working of capitalism. It is perfectly clear, in fact, that religion is daily losing its efficacy with the people; something else must be found, if the intellectuals are to be provided with the means of living on the margin of production.

The problem that we shall now try to solve is the most difficult of all those which a Socialist writer can touch upon. We are about to ask how it is possible to conceive the transformation of the men of to-day into the free producers of to-morrow working in manufactories where there are no masters. The question must be stated accurately; we must state it, not for a world which has already arrived at Socialism, but solely for our own time and for the preparation of the transition from one world to the other; if we do not limit the question in this way, we shall find ourselves straying into utopias.

Kautsky has given a great deal of attention to the question of the conditions immediately following a social revolution; the solution he proposes seems to me quite as feeble as that of G. de Molinari. If the syndicates of to-day are strong enough to induce the workmen of to-day to abandon their workshops and to submit to great sacrifices, during the strikes kept up against the capitalists, he thinks that they will then doubtless be strong enough to bring the workmen back to the workshops, and to obtain good and regular work from them, when once they see that this work is necessary for the general good.[17] Kautsky, however, does not seem to feel much confidence in the value of his own solution.

Evidently no comparison can be made between the kind of discipline which forces a general stoppage of work on the men and that which will induce them to handle machinery with greater skill. The error springs from the fact that Kautsky is more of a theorist than he is a disciple of Marx; he loves reasoning about abstractions and believes that he has brought a question nearer to solution when he manages to produce a phrase with a scientific appearance; the underlying reality interests him less than its academic presentment. Many others have committed the same error, led astray by the different meanings of the word *discipline,* which may be applied both to regular conduct rounded on the deepest feelings of the soul or to a merely external restraint.

The history of ancient corporations furnishes us with no really useful information on this subject; they do not seem to have had any effect whatever in promoting any kind of improvement, or invention in technical matters; it would seem rather that they served to protect routine. If we examine English Trade Unionism closely, we find that it also is strongly imbued with this industrial routine springing from the corporative spirit.

Nor can the examples of democracy throw any light on the question. Work conducted democratically would be regulated by resolutions, inspected by police, and subject to the sanction of tribunals dealing out rewards or imprisonment. The discipline would be an exterior compulsion closely analogous to that which now exists in the capitalist workshops; but it would probably be still more arbitrary because the committee would always have their eye on the next elections.[18] When one thinks of the peculiarities found in judgments in penal cases one feels convinced that repression would be exercised in a very unsatisfactory way. It seems to be generally agreed that light offences cannot be satisfactorily dealt with in law courts, when hampered by the rules of a strict legal system; the establishment of administrative councils to decide on the future of children has often been suggested; in Belgium mendicity is subject to an administrative arbitration which may be compared to the "police des moeurs;" it is well known that this police, in spite of innumerable complaints, continues to be almost supreme in France. It is very noticeable that administrative intervention in the case of important crimes is continually increasing. Since the power of mitigating or even of suppressing penalties is being more and more handed over to the heads of penal establishments, doctors and sociologists speak in favour of this system, which tends to give the police as important a function as they had under the *ancien regime.* Experience shows that the discipline of the capitalist workshops is greatly superior to that maintained by the police, so that one does not see how it would be possible to improve capitalist discipline by means of the methods which democracy would have at its disposal.[19]

I think that there is one good point, however, in Kautsky's hypothesis; he seems to have been aware that the motive force of the revolutionary movement must also be the motive force of the ethic of the producers; that is a view quite in conformity with Marxist principles, but the idea must be applied in quite a different way from that in which he applied it. It must not be thought that the action of the syndicates on work is direct, as he supposes; this influence of the syndicates on labour should result from complex and sometimes distant causes, acting on the general character of the workers rather than from a quasi-military organisation. This is what I try to show by analysing some of the qualities of the best workmen.

A satisfactory result can be arrived at, by starting from the curious analogies which exist between the most remarkable qualities of the soldiers who took part in the wars of Liberty, the qualities which engendered the propaganda in favour of the general strike, and those that will be required of a free worker in a highly progressive state of society. I believe that these analogies constitute a new (and perhaps decisive) proof, in favour of revolutionary syndicalism.

In the wars of Liberty each soldier considered himself as an *individual* having something of importance to do in the battle, instead of looking upon himself as simply one part of the military mechanism committed to the supreme direction of a leader. In the literature of those times one is struck by the frequency with which the *free men* of the republican armies are contrasted with the *automatons* of the royal armies; this was no mere figure of rhetoric employed by the French writers; I have convinced myself as a result of a thorough first-hand study of one of the wars of that time, that these terms corresponded perfectly to the actual feelings of the soldiers.

Battles under these conditions could, then, no longer be likened to games of chess in which each man is comparable to a pawn; they became collections of heroic exploits accomplished by individuals under the influence of an extraordinary enthusiasm. Revolutionary literature is not entirely false, when it reports so many grandiloquent phrases said to have been uttered by the combatants; doubtless none of these phrases were spoken by the people to whom they are attributed, their form is due to men of letters used to the composition of classical declamation; but the basis is real in this sense, that we have, thanks to these lies of revolutionary rhetoric, a perfectly exact representation of the aspect under which the combatants looked on war, a true expression of the sentiments aroused by it, and *the actual accent of the truly Homeric conflicts* which took place at that time. I am certain that none of the actors in these dramas ever protested against the words attributed to them; this was no doubt because each found beneath these fantastic phrases, a true expression of his own deepest feelings.[20]

Until the moment when Napoleon appeared the war had none of the scientific character which the later theoretists of strategy have sometimes thought it incumbent on them to attribute to it. Misled by the analogies they discovered between the triumphs of the revolutionary armies and those of the Napoleonic armies, historians imagined that generals anterior to Napoleon had made great plans of campaign; such plans never existed, or at any rate had very little influence on the course of operations. The best officers of that time were fully aware that their talent consisted in furnishing their troops with the suitable opportunities of exhibiting their ardour; and victory was assured each time that the soldiers could give free scope to all their enthusiasm, unfettered by bad commissariat, or by the stupidity of representatives of the people who looked upon themselves as strategists. On the battlefield the leaders gave an example of daring courage and were merely the first combatants, like true Homeric kings; it is this which explains the enormous prestige with the young troops, immediately gained by so many of the non-commissioned officers of the *ancien regime*, who were borne to the highest rank by the unanimous acclamations of the soldiers at the outset of the war.

If we wished to find, in these first armies, what it was that took the place of the later idea of discipline, we might say that the soldier was convinced that the slightest failure of the most insignificant private might compromise the success of the whole and the life of all his comrades, and that the soldier acted accordingly. This presupposes that no account is taken of the relative values of the different factors that go to make up a victory, so that all things are considered from a *qualitative and individualistic* point of view. One is, in fact, extremely struck by the individualistic characters which are met with in these armies, and by the fact that nothing is to be found in them which at all resembles the obedience spoken of by our contemporary authors. There is some truth then in the statement that the incredible French victories were due to intelligent bayonets.

The same spirit is found in the working-class groups who are eager for the general strike; these groups, in fact, picture the Revolution as an immense uprising which yet may be called individualistic; each working with the greatest possible zeal, each acting on his own account, and not troubling himself much to subordinate his conduct to a great and scientifically combined plan. This character of the proletarian general strike has often been pointed out, and it has the effect of frightening the greedy politicians, who understand perfectly well that a Revolution conducted in this way would do away with all their chances of seizing the Government.

Jaurès, whom nobody would dream of classing with any but the most circumspect of men, has clearly recognised the danger which threatens him; he accuses the upholders of the general strike of considering only one aspect of social life and thus going against the Revolution.[21] This rigmarole should be translated thus: the revolutionary Syndicalists desire to exalt the individuality of the life of the producer; they thus run counter to the interests of the politicians who want to direct the Revolution in such a way as to transmit power to a new minority; they thus undermine the foundations of the State. We entirely agree with all this; it is precisely this characteristic which so terrifies the Parliamentary Socialists, the financiers, and the ideologists, which gives such extraordinary moral value to the notion of the general strike.

The upholders of the general strike are accused of anarchical tendencies; and as a matter of fact, it has been observed during the last few years that anarchists have entered the syndicates in great numbers, and have done a great deal to develop tendencies favourable to the general strike.

This movement becomes understandable when we bear the preceding explanations in mind; because the general strike, just like the wars of Liberty, is a most striking manifestation of *individualistic force in the revolted masses*. It seems to me, moreover, that the official Socialists would do well not to insist too much on this point; they would thus avoid some reflections which are not altogether to their advantage. We might, in fact, be led to ask if our official Socialists, with their passion for discipline, and their infinite confidence in the genius of their leaders, are not the authentic inheritors of the traditions of the royal armies, while the anarchists and the upholders of the general strike represent at the present time the spirit of the revolutionary warriors who, against all the rules of the art of war, so thoroughly thrashed the fine armies of the coalition. I can understand why the Socialists approved, controlled, and duly patented by the administrators of *Humanite*, have not much sympathy for the heroes of Fleurus,[22] who were very badly dressed, and would have cut a sorry figure in the drawing-rooms of the great financiers; but everybody does not adapt his convictions to suit the tastes of M. Jaurès's shareholders.

I want now to point out some analogies which show how revolutionary syndicalism is the greatest educative force that contemporary society has at its disposal for the preparation of the system of production, which the workmen will adopt, in a society organised in accordance with the new conceptions.

A. The free producer in a progressive and inventive workshop must never evaluate his own efforts by any external standing; he ought to consider the models given him as inferior, and desire to surpass everything that has been done before. Constant improvement in quality and quantity will be thus assured to production; the idea of continual progress will be realised in a workshop of this kind.

Early Socialists had had an intuition of this law, when they demanded that each should produce according to his faculties; but they did not know how to explain this principle, which in their Utopias seemed made for a convent or for a family rather than for modern industrial life. Sometimes, however, they pictured their workers as possessed by an enthusiasm similar to that which we find in the lives of certain great artists; this last point of view is by no means negligible, although the early Socialists hardly understand the value of the comparison.

Whenever we consider questions relative to industrial progress, we are led to consider art as an anticipation of the highest and technically most perfect forms of production, although the artist, with his caprices, often seems to be at the antipodes of the modern worker.[23] This analogy is justified by the fact that the artist dislikes reproducing accepted types; the inexhaustibly inventive turn of his mind distinguishes him from the ordinary artisan, who is mainly successful in the unending reproduction of models which are not his own. The inventor is an artist who wears himself out in pursuing the realisation of ends which practical people generally declare absurd; and who, if he has made any important discovery is often supposed to be mad; practical people thus resemble artisans. One could cite in every industry important improvements which originated in small changes made by workmen endowed with the artist's taste for innovation.

This state of mind is, moreover, exactly that which was found in the first armies which carried on the wars of Liberty and that possessed by the propagandists of the general strike. This passionate individualism is entirely wanting in the working classes who have been educated by politicians; all they are fit for is to change their masters. These *bad shepherds*[24] sincerely hope that it will be so; and the Stock Exchange people would not provide them with money, were they not convinced that Parliamentary Socialism is quite compatible with financial robbery.

B. Modern industry is characterised by an evergrowing care for exactitude; as tools get more scientific it is expected that the product shall have fewer hidden faults, and that in use its quality shall be as good as its appearance.

If Germany has not yet taken the place in the economic world which the mineral riches of its soil, the energy of its manufacturers and the science of its technicians ought to give it, it is because its manufacturers for a long time thought it clever to flood the markets with trash; although the quality of German manufacturers has much improved during the last few years, it is not yet held in any very great esteem.

Here again it is possible to draw a comparison between industry in a high state of perfection and art. There have been periods in which the public appreciated above all the technical tricks by which the artist created an illusion of reality; but these tricks have never been accepted in the great schools, and they are universally condemned by the authors who are accepted as authorities in matters of art.[25]

This honesty which now seems to us to-day as necessary in industry as in art, was hardly suspected by the Utopists;[26] Fourier, at the beginning of the new era, believed that fraud in the quality of merchandise was characteristic of the relations between civilised people; he turned his back on progress and showed himself incapable of understanding the world which was being formed about him; like nearly all professional prophets this sham seer confused the future with the past. Marx, on the contrary, said that "deception in merchandise in the capitalist system of production is unjust," because it no longer corresponds with the modern system of business.[27]

The soldier of the wars of Liberty attached an almost superstitious importance to the carrying out of the smallest order. As a result of this he felt no pity for the generals or officers whom he saw guillotined after a defeat on the charge of dereliction of duty; he did not look at these events as the historians of to-day do; he had no means of knowing whether the condemned had really committed treason or not; in his eyes failure could only be explained by some grave error on the part of his leaders. The high sense of responsibility felt by the soldier about his own duties, and the extreme thoroughness with which he carried out the most significant order, made him approve of rigorous measures taken against men who in his eyes had brought about the defeat of the army and caused it to lose the fruit of so much heroism.

"It is not difficult to see that the same spirit is met with in strikes; the beaten workmen are convinced that their failure is due to the base conduct of a few comrades who have not done all that might have been expected of them; numerous accusations of treason are brought forward; for the beaten masses, treason alone can explain the defeat of heroic troops; the sentiment, felt by all, of the thoroughness that must be brought to the accomplishment of their duties, will therefore be accompanied by many acts of violence. I do not think that the authors who have written on the events which follow strikes, have sufficiently reflected on this analogy between strikes and the wars of Liberty, and, consequently, between these acts of violence and the executions of generals accused of treason."[28]

C. There would never have been greats of heroism in war, if each soldier, while acting like a hero, yet at the same time claimed to receive a reward proportionate to his deserts. When a column is sent to an assault, the men at the head know they are sent to their death, and that the glory of victory will be for those who passing over their dead bodies enter the enemy's position. However, they do not reflect on this injustice, but march forward.

The value of any army where the need of rewards makes itself actively felt, may be said to be on the decline. Officers who had served in the campaigns of the Revolution and of the Empire, but who had served under the direct orders of Napoleon only in the last years of their career, were amazed to see the fuss made about feats of arms which in the time of their youth would have passed unnoticed: "I have been overwhelmed with praise," said General Duhesne, "for things which would not have been noticed in the army of Sambre-et-Meuse."[29] This theatricality was carried by Murat to a grotesque degree, and historians have not taken enough notice of the responsibility of Napoleon for this degeneracy of the true warlike spirit. The extraordinary enthusiasm which had been the cause of so many prodigies of valour on the part of the men of 1794 was unknown to him; he believed that it was his function to measure all capacities, and to give to each a reward exactly proportionate to what he had accomplished; this was the Saint Simonian principle already coming into practice, and every officer was encouraged to bring himself forward. Charlatanism[30] exhausted the moral forces of the nation whilst its material forces were still very considerable. Napoleon formed very few distinguished general officers and carried on the war principally with those left him by the Revolution; this impotence is the most absolute condemnation of the system.[31]

The scarcity of the information which we possess about the great Gothic artists has often been pointed out. Among the stone-carvers who sculptured the statues in the cathedrals there were men of great talent who seem always to have remained anonymous; nevertheless they produced masterpieces. Viollet-le-Duc was surprised that the archives of Notre Dame had preserved for us no detailed information about the building of this gigantic monument and that, as a rule, the documents of the Middle Ages say very little about the architects; he adds that "genius can develop itself in obscurity, and that it is its very nature to seek silence and obscurity."[32] We might even go farther and question whether their contemporaries suspected that these artists of genius had raised edifices of unperishable glory; it seems very probable to me that the cathedrals were only admired by the artists.

This striving towards perfection which manifests itself, in spite of the absence of any personal, immediate, and proportional reward, constitutes the *secret virtue* which assures the continued progress of the world. What would become of modern industry if inventors could only be found for those things which would procure them an almost certain remuneration?

The calling of an inventor is much the most desirable of all, and yet there is no lack of inventors. How often in workshops have little modifications introduced by ingenious artisans into their work, become by accumulation fundamental improvements, without the innovators ever getting any permanent or appreciable benefit from their ingenuity! And has not even simple piece-work brought about a gradual but uninterrupted progress in the processes of production, a progress which, after having temporarily improved the position of a few workers and especially that of their employers, has proved finally of benefit chiefly to the consumer?

Renan asked what was it that moved the heroes of great wars. "The soldier of Napoleon was well aware that he would always be a poor man, but he felt that the epic in which he was taking part would be eternal, that he would live in the glory of France." The Greeks had fought for glory; the Russians and the Turks seek death because they expect a chimerical paradise. "A soldier is not made by promises of temporal rewards. He must have immortality. In default of paradise, there is glory, which is itself a kind of immortality."[33]

Economic progress goes far beyond the individual life, and profits future generations more than those who create it: but does it give glory? Is there an economic epic capable of stimulating the enthusiasm of the workers? The inspiration of immortality which Renan considered so powerful is obviously without efficacy here, because artists have never produced masterpieces under the influence of the idea that their work would procure them a place in paradise (as Turks seek death that they may enjoy the happiness promised by Mahomet). The workmen are not entirely wrong when they look on religion as a middle-class luxury, since, as a matter of fact, the emotions it calls up are not those which inspire workmen with the desire to perfect machinery, or which create methods of accelerating labour.

The question must be stated otherwise than Renan put it; do there exist among the workmen forces capable of producing enthusiasm equivalent to those of which Renan speaks, forces which could combine with the ethics of good work, so that in our days, which seem to many people to presage the darkest future, this ethic may acquire all the authority necessary to lead society along the path of economic progress.

We must be careful that the keen sentiment which we have of the necessity of such a morality, and our ardent desire to see it realised does not induce us to mistake phantoms for forces capable of moving the world. The abundant "idyllic" literature of the professors of rhetoric is evidently mere chatter. Equally vain are the attempts made by so many scholars to find institutions in the past, an imitation of which might serve as a means of disciplining their contemporaries; imitation has never produced much good and often bred much sorrow; how absurd the idea is then of borrowing from some dead and gone social structure, a suitable means of controlling a system of production, whose principal characteristic is that every day it must become more and more opposed to all preceding economic systems. Is there then nothing to hope for?

Morality is not doomed to perish because the motive forces behind it will change; it is not destined to become a mere collection of precepts as long as it can still vivify itself by an alliance with an enthusiasm capable of conquering all the obstacles, prejudices, and the need of immediate enjoyment, which oppose its progress. But it is certain that this sovereign force will not be found along the paths which contemporary philosophers, the experts of social science, and the inventors of far-reaching reforms would make us go. There is only one force which can produce to-day that enthusiasm without whose co-operation no morality is possible, and that is the force resulting from the propaganda in favour of a general strike. The preceding explanations have shown that the idea of the general strike (constantly rejuvenated by the feelings roused by proletarian violence) produces an entirely epic state of mind, and at the same time bends all the energies of the mind to that condition necessary to the realisation of a workshop carried on by free men, eagerly seeking the betterment of the industry; we have thus recognised that there are great resemblances between the sentiments aroused by the idea of the general strike and those which are necessary to bring about a continued progress in methods of production. We have then the right to maintain that the modern world possesses that prime mover which is necessary to the creation of the ethics of the producers.

I stop here, because it seems to me that I have accomplished the task which I imposed upon myself; I have, in fact, established that proletarian violence has an entirely different significance from that attributed to it by superficial scholars and by politicians. In the total ruin of institutions and of morals there remains something which is powerful, new, and intact, and it is that which constitutes, properly speaking, the soul of the revolutionary proletariat. Nor will this be swept away in the general decadence of moral values, if the workers have enough energy to bar the road to the middle-class corrupters, answering their advances with the plainest brutality.

I believe that I have brought an important contribution to discussions on Socialism; these discussions must henceforth deal exclusively with the conditions which allow the development of specifically proletarian forces, that is to say, *with violence enlightened by the idea of the general strike.* All the old abstract dissertations on the Socialist *regime* of the future become useless; we pass to the domain of real history, to the interpretation of facts—to the ethical evaluations of the revolutionary movement.

The bond which I pointed out in the beginning of this inquiry between Socialism and proletarian violence appears to us now in all its strength. It is to violence that Socialism owes those high ethical values by means of which it brings salvation to the modern world.

CHAPTER 27

Liberation from the Affluent Society

By Herbert Marcuse

I am very happy to see so many flowers here and that is why I want to remind you that flowers, by themselves, have no power whatsoever, other than the power of men and women who protect them and take care of them against aggression and destruction.

As a hopeless philosopher for whom philosophy has become inseparable from politics, I am afraid I have to give here today a rather philosophical speech, and I must ask your indulgence. We are dealing with the dialectics of liberation (actually a redundant phrase, because I believe that all dialectic is liberation) and not only liberation in an intellectual sense, but liberation involving the mind and the body, liberation involving entire human existence. Think of Plato: the liberation from the existence in the cave. Think of Hegel: liberation in the sense of progress and freedom on the historical scale. Think of Marx. Now, in what sense is all dialectic liberation? It is liberation from the repressive, from a bad, a false system—be it an organic system, be it a social system, be it a mental or intellectual system: liberation by forces developing within such a system. That is a decisive point. And liberation by virtue of the contradiction generated by the system, precisely because it is a bad, a false system.

I am intentionally using here moral, philosophical terms, values: "bad," "false." For without an objectively justifiable goal of a better, a free human existence, all liberation must remain meaningless—at best, progress in servitude. I believe that in Marx too socialism *ought* to be. This "ought" belongs to the very essence of scientific socialism. It *ought* to be; it is, we may almost say, a biological, sociological, and political necessity. It is a biological necessity inasmuch as a socialist society, according to Marx, would conform with the very *logos* of life, with the essential possibilities of a human existence, not only mentally, not only intellectually, but also organically.

Now, as to today and our own situation. I think we are faced with a novel situation in history, because today we have to be liberated from a relatively well-functioning, rich, powerful society. I am speaking here about liberation from the affluent society, that is to say, the advanced industrial societies. The problem we are facing is the need for liberation not from a poor society, not from a disintegrating society, not even in most cases from a terroristic society, but from a society which develops to a great extent the material and even cultural needs of man—a society which, to use a slogan, delivers the goods to an ever larger part of the population. And that implies, we are facing liberation from a society where liberation is apparently without a mass basis. We know very well the social mechanisms of manipulation, indoctrination, repression which are responsible for this lack of a mass basis, for the integration of the majority of the oppositional forces into the established social system. But I must emphasize again that this is not merely an ideological integration; that it is not merely a social integration; that it takes place precisely on the strong and rich basis which enables the society to develop and satisfy material and cultural needs better than before.

But knowledge of the mechanisms of manipulation or repression, which go down into the very unconscious of man, is not the whole story. I believe that we (and I will use "we" throughout my talk) have been too hesitant, that we have been too ashamed, understandably ashamed, to insist on the integral, radical features of a socialist society, its qualitative difference from all the established societies: the qualitative difference by virtue of which socialism is indeed the negation of the established systems, no matter how productive, no matter how powerful they are or they may appear. In other words—and this is one of the many points where I disagree with Paul Goodman—our fault was not that we have been too immodest, but that we have been too modest. We have, as it were, repressed a great deal of what we should have said and what we should have emphasized.

If today these integral features, these truly radical features which make a socialist society a definite negation of the existing societies, if this qualitative difference today appears as utopian, as idealistic, as metaphysical, this is precisely the form in which these radical features must appear if they are really to be a definite negation of the established society: if socialism is indeed the rupture of history, the radical break, the leap into the realm of freedom—a total rupture.

Let us give one illustration of how this awareness, or half-awareness, of the need for such a total rupture was present in some of the great social struggles of our period. Walter Benjamin quotes reports that during the Paris Commune, in all corners of the city of Paris there were people shooting at the clocks on the towers of the churches, palaces, and so on, thereby consciously or half-consciously expressing the need that somehow time has to be arrested; that at least the prevailing, the established time continuum has to be arrested, and that a new time has to begin—a very strong emphasis on the qualitative difference and on the totality of the rupture between the new society and the old.

In this sense, I should like to discuss here with you the repressed prerequisites of qualitative change. I say intentionally "of qualitative change," not "of revolution," because we know of too many revolutions through which the continuum of repression has been sustained, revolutions which have replaced one system of domination by another. We must become aware of the essentially new features which distinguish a free society as a definite negation of the established societies, and we must begin formulating these features, no matter how metaphysical, no matter how utopian, I would even say no matter how ridiculous we may appear to the normal people in all camps, on the right as well as on the left.

What is the dialectic of liberation with which we here are concerned? It is the construction of a free society, a construction which depends in the first place on the prevalence of the vital need for abolishing the established systems of servitude; and secondly, and this is decisive, it depends on the vital commitment, the striving, conscious as well as sub- and unconscious, for the qualitatively different values of a free human existence. Without the emergence of such new needs and satisfactions, the needs and satisfactions of free men, all change in the social institutions, no matter how great, would only replace one system of servitude by another system of servitude. Nor can the emergence—and I should like to emphasize this—nor can the emergence of such new needs and satisfactions be envisaged as a mere by-product, the mere result, of changed social institutions. We have seen this; it is a fact of experience. The development of the new institutions must already be carried out and carried through by men with the new needs. That, by the way, is the basic idea underlying Marx's own concept of the proletariat as the historical agent of revolution. He saw the industrial proletariat as the historical agent of revolution, not only because it was the basic class in the material process of production, not only because it was at that time the majority of the population, but also because this class was "free" from the repressive and aggressive competitive needs of capitalist society and therefore, at least potentially, the carrier of essentially new needs, goals, and satisfactions.

We can formulate this dialectic of liberation also in a more brutal way, as a vicious circle. The transition from voluntary servitude (as it exists to a great extent in the affluent society) to freedom presupposes the abolition of the institutions and mechanisms of repression. And the abolition of the institutions and mechanisms of repression already presupposes liberation from servitude, prevalence of the need for liberation. As to needs, I think we have to distinguish between the need for changing intolerable conditions of existence, and the need for changing the society as a whole. The two are by no means identical, they are by no means in harmony. *If* the need is for changing intolerable conditions of existence, with at least a reasonable chance that this can be achieved within the established society, with the growth and progress of the established society, then this is merely quantitative change. Qualitative change is a change of the very system as a whole.

I would like to point out that the distinction between quantitative and qualitative change is not identical with the distinction between reform and revolution. Quantitative change can mean and can lead to revolution. Only the conjunction, I suggest, of these two is revolution in the essential sense of the leap from prehistory into the history of man. In other words, the problem with which we are faced is the point where quantity can turn into quality, where the quantitative change in the conditions and institutions can become a qualitative change affecting all human existence.

Today the two potential factors of revolution which I have just mentioned are disjointed. The first is most prevalent in the underdeveloped countries, where quantitative change—that is to say, the creation of human living conditions—is in itself qualitative change, but is not yet freedom. The second potential factor of revolution, the prerequisites of liberation, are potentially there in the advanced industrial countries, but are contained and perverted by the capitalist organization of society.

I think we are faced with a situation in which this advanced capitalist society has reached a point where quantitative change can technically be turned into qualitative change, into authentic liberation. And it is precisely against this truly fatal possibility that the affluent society, advanced capitalism, is mobilized and organized on all fronts, at home as well as abroad.

Before I go on, let me give a brief definition of what I mean by an affluent society. A model, of course, is American society today, although even in the U.S. it is more a tendency, not yet entirely translated into reality. In the first place, it is a capitalist society. It seems to be necessary to remind ourselves of this because there are some people, even on the left, who believe that American society is no longer a class society. I can assure you that it is a class society. It is a capitalist society with a high concentration of economic and political power; with an enlarged and enlarging sector of automation and coordination of production, distribution, and communication; with private ownership in the means of production, which however depends increasingly on ever more active and wide intervention by the government. It is a society in which, as I mentioned, the material as well as cultural needs of the underlying population are satisfied on a scale larger than ever before—but they are satisfied in line with the requirements and interests of the apparatus and of the powers which control the apparatus. And it is a society growing on the condition of accelerating waste, planned obsolescence, and destruction, while the substratum of the population continues to live in poverty and misery.

I believe that these factors are internally interrelated, that they constitute the syndrome of late capitalism: namely, the apparently inseparable unity—inseparable for the system—of productivity and destruction, of satisfaction of needs and repression, of liberty within a system of servitude—that is to say, the subjugation of man to the apparatus, and the inseparable unity of rational and irrational. We can say that the rationality of the society lies in its very insanity, and that the insanity of the society is rational to the degree to which it is efficient, to the degree to which it delivers the goods.

Now the question we must raise is: Why do we need liberation from such a society if it is capable—perhaps in the distant future, but apparently capable—of conquering poverty to a greater degree than ever before, of reducing the toil of labor and the time of labor, and of raising the standard of living? If the price for all goods delivered, the price for this comfortable servitude, for all these achievements, is exacted from people far away from the metropolis and far away from its affluence? If the affluent society itself hardly notices what it is doing, how it is spreading terror and enslavement, how it is fighting liberation in all corners of the globe?

We know the traditional weakness of emotional, moral, and humanitarian arguments in the face of such technological achievement, in the face of the irrational rationality of such a power. These arguments do not seem to carry any weight against the brute facts—we might say brutal facts—of the society and its productivity. And yet, it is only the insistence on the real possibilities of a free society, which is blocked by the affluent society—it is only this insistence in practice as well as in theory, in demonstration as well as in discussion, which still stands in the way of the complete degradation of man to an object, or rather subject/object, of total administration. It is only this insistence which still stands in the way of the progressive brutalization and moronization of man. For—and I should like to emphasize this—the capitalist Welfare State is a Warfare State. It must have an Enemy, with a capital E, a total Enemy; because the perpetuation of servitude, the perpetuation of the miserable struggle for existence in the very face of the new possibilities of freedom, activates and intensifies in this society a primary aggressiveness to a degree, I think, hitherto unknown in history. And this primary aggressiveness must be mobilized in socially useful ways, lest it explode the system itself. Therefore the need for an Enemy, who must be there, and who must be created if he does not exist. Fortunately, I dare say, the Enemy does exist. But his image and his power must, in this society, be inflated beyond all proportions in order to be able to mobilize this aggressiveness of the affluent society in socially useful ways.

The result is a mutilated, crippled, and frustrated human existence: a human existence that is violently defending its own servitude.

We can sum up the fatal situation with which we are confronted. Radical social change is objectively necessary, in the dual sense that it is the only chance to save the possibilities of human freedom and, furthermore, in the sense that the technical and material resources for the realization of freedom are available. But while this objective need is demonstrably there, the subjective need for such a change does not prevail. It does not prevail precisely among those parts of the population that are traditionally considered the agents of historical change. The subjective need is repressed, again on a dual ground: firstly, by virtue of the actual satisfaction of needs, and secondly, by a massive scientific manipulation and administration of needs—that is, by a systematic social control not only of the consciousness, but also of the unconscious of man. This control has been made possible by the very achievements of the greatest liberating sciences of our time, in psychology, mainly psychoanalysis and psychiatry. That they could become and have become at the same time powerful instruments of suppression, one of the most effective engines of suppression, is again one of the terrible aspects of the dialectic of liberation.

This divergence between the objective and the subjective need changes completely, I suggest, the basis, the prospects, and the strategy of liberation. This situation presupposes the emergence of new needs, qualitatively different and even opposed to the prevailing aggressive and repressive needs: the emergence of a new type of man, with a vital, biological drive for liberation, and with a consciousness capable of breaking through the material as well as ideological veil of the affluent society. In other words, liberation seems to be predicated upon the opening and the activation of a depth dimension of human existence, this side of and underneath the traditional material base: not an idealistic dimension, over and above the material base, but a dimension even more material than the material base, a dimension underneath the material base. I will illustrate presently what I mean.

The emphasis on this new dimension does not mean replacing politics by psychology, but rather the other way around. It means finally taking account of the fact that society has invaded even the deepest roots of individual existence, even the unconscious of man. We must get at the roots of society in the individuals themselves, the individuals who, because of social engineering, constantly reproduce the continuum of repression even through the great revolution.

This change is, I suggest, not an ideological change. It is dictated by the actual development of an industrial society, which has introduced factors which our theory could formerly correctly neglect. It is dictated by the actual development of industrial society, by the tremendous growth of its material and technical productivity, which has surpassed and rendered obsolete the traditional goals and preconditions of liberation.

Here we are faced with the question: Is liberation from the affluent society identical with the transition from capitalism to socialism? The answer I suggest is: It is not identical, if socialism is defined merely as the planned development of the productive forces and the rationalization of resources (although this remains a precondition for all liberation). It is identical with the transition from capitalism to socialism, if socialism is defined in its most utopian terms: namely, among others, the abolition of labor, the termination of the struggle for existence—that is to say, life as an end in itself and no longer as a means to an end—and the liberation of human sensibility and sensitivity, not as a private factor, but as a force for transformation of human existence and of its environment. To give sensitivity and sensibility their own right is, I think, one of the basic goals of integral socialism. These are the qualitatively different features of a free society.

They presuppose, as you may already have seen, a total transvaluation of values, a new anthropology. They presuppose a type of man who rejects the performance principles governing the established societies; a type of man who has rid himself of the aggressiveness and brutality that are inherent in the organization of established society, and in their hypocritical, puritan morality; a type of man who is biologically incapable of fighting wars and creating suffering; a type of man who has a good conscience of joy and pleasure, and who works, collectively and individually, for a social and natural environment in which such an existence becomes possible.

The dialectic of liberation, as turned from quantity into quality, thus involves, I repeat, a break in the continuum of repression which reaches into the depth dimension of the organism itself. Or, we may say that today qualitative change, liberation, involves organic, instinctual, biological changes at the same time as political and social changes.

The new needs and satisfactions have a very material basis, as I have indicated. They are not thought out but are the logical derivation from the technical, material, and intellectual possibilities of advanced, industrial society. They are inherent in, and the expression of, the productivity of advanced industrial society, which has long since made obsolete all kinds of innerworldly asceticism, the entire work discipline on which Judaeo-Christian morality has been based.

Why is this society surpassing and negating this type of man, the traditional type of man, and the forms of his existence, as well as the morality to which it owes much of its origins and foundations? This new, unheard-of, and not anticipated productivity allows the concept of a technology of liberation. Here I can only briefly indicate what I have in mind: such amazing and indeed apparently utopian tendencies as the convergence of technique and art, the convergence of work and play, the convergence of the realm of necessity and the realm of freedom. How? No longer subjected to the dictates of capitalist profitability and of efficiency, no longer to the dictates of scarcity, which today are perpetuated by the capitalist organization of society; socially necessary labor, material production, would and could become (we see the tendency already) increasingly scientific. Technical experimentation, science, and technology would and could become a play with the hitherto hidden—methodically hidden and blocked—potentialities of men and things, of society and nature.

This means one of the oldest dreams of all radical theory and practice. It means that the creative imagination, and not only the rationality of the performance principle, would become a productive force applied to the transformation of the social and natural universe. It would mean the emergence of a form of reality which is the work and the medium of the developing sensibility and sensitivity of man.

And now I throw in the terrible concept: it would mean an "aesthetic" reality—society as a work of art. This is the most utopian, the most radical possibility of liberation today.

What does this mean, in concrete terms? I said, we are not concerned here with private sensitivity and sensibility, but with sensitivity and sensibility, creative imagination and play, becoming forces of transformation. As such they would guide, for example, the total reconstruction of our cities and of the countryside; the restoration of nature after the elimination of the violence and destruction of capitalist industrialization; the creation of internal and external space for privacy, individual autonomy, tranquillity; the elimination of noise, of captive audiences, of enforced togetherness, of pollution, of ugliness. These are not—and I cannot emphasize this strongly enough—snobbish and romantic demands. Biologists today have emphasized that these are organic needs for the human organism, and that their arrest, their perversion and destruction by capitalist society, actually mutilates the human organism, not only in a figurative way but in a very real and literal sense.

I believe that it is only in such a universe that man can be truly free, and truly human relationships between free beings can be established. I believe that the idea of such a universe guided also Marx's concept of socialism, and that these aesthetic needs and goals must from the beginning be present in the reconstruction of society, and not only at the end or in the far future. Otherwise, the needs and satisfactions which reproduce a repressive society would be carried over into the new society. Repressive men would carry over their repression into the new society.

Now, at this farthest point, the question is: How can we possibly envisage the emergence of such qualitatively different needs and goals as organic, biological needs and goals and not as superimposed values? How can we envisage the emergence of these needs and satisfactions within and against the established society—that is to say, prior to liberation? That was the dialectic with which I started, that in a very definite sense we have to be free from in order to create a free society.

Needless to say, the dissolution of the existing system is the precondition for such qualitative change. And the more efficiently the repressive apparatus of the affluent societies operates, the less likely is a gradual transition from servitude to freedom. The fact that today we cannot identify any specific class or any specific group as a revolutionary force—this fact is no excuse for not using any and every possibility and method to arrest the engines of repression in the individual. The diffusion of potential opposition among the entire underlying population corresponds precisely to the total character of our advanced capitalist society. The internal contradictions of the system are as grave as ever before and likely to be aggravated by the violent expansion of capitalist imperialism. Not only the most general contradictions between the tremendous social wealth on the one hand, and the destructive, aggressive, and wasteful use of this wealth on the other; but far more concrete contradictions such as the necessity for the system to automate, the continued reduction of the human base in physical labor-power in the material reproduction of society, and thereby the tendency towards the draining of the sources of surplus profit. Finally, there is the threat of technological unemployment which even the most affluent society may no longer be capable of compensating by the creation of ever more parasitic and unproductive labor: all these contradictions exist. In reaction to them suppression, manipulation and integration are likely to increase.

But fulfillment is there, the ground can and must be prepared. The mutilated consciousness and the mutilated instincts must be broken. The sensitivity and the awareness of the new transcending, antagonistic values—they are there. And they are there, they are here, precisely among the still nonintegrated social groups and among those who, by virtue of their privileged position, can pierce the ideological and material veil of mass communication and indoctrination—namely, the intelligentsia.

We all know the fatal prejudice, practically from the beginning, in the labor movement against the intelligentsia as catalyst of historical change. It is time to ask whether this prejudice against the intellectuals, and the inferiority complex of the intellectuals resulting from it, was not an essential factor in the development of the capitalist as well as the socialist societies: in the development and weakening of the opposition. The intellectuals usually went out to organize the others, to organize in the communities. They certainly did not use the potentiality they had to organize themselves, to organize among themselves not only on a regional, not only on a national, but on an international level. That is, in my view, today one of the most urgent tasks. Can we say that the intelligentsia is the agent of historical change? Can we say that the intelligentsia today is a revolutionary class? The answer I would give is: No, we cannot say that. But we can say, and I think we must say, that the intelligentsia has a decisive preparatory function, not more; and I suggest that this is plenty. By itself it is not and cannot be a revolutionary class, but it can become the catalyst, and it has a preparatory function—certainly not for the first time; that is in fact the way all revolution starts—but more, perhaps, today than ever before. Because—and for this too we have a very material and very concrete basis—it is from this group that the holders of decisive positions in the productive process will be recruited, in the future even more than hitherto. I refer to what we may call the increasingly scientific character of the material process of production, by virtue of which the role of the intelligentsia changes. It is the group from which the decisive holders of decisive positions will be recruited: scientists, researchers, technicians, engineers, even psychologists—because psychology will continue to be a socially necessary instrument, either of servitude or of liberation.

This class, this intelligentsia has been called the new working class. I believe this term is at best premature. They are—and this we should not forget—today the pet beneficiaries of the established system. But they are also at the very source of the glaring contradictions between the liberating capacity of science and its repressive and enslaving use. To activate the repressed and manipulated contradiction, to make it operate as a catalyst of change, that is one of the main tasks of the opposition today. It remains and must remain a political task.

Education is our job, but education in a new sense. Being theory as well as practice, political practice, education today is more than discussion, more than teaching and learning and writing. Unless and until it goes beyond the classroom, until and unless it goes beyond the college, the school, the university, it will remain powerless. Education today must involve the mind *and* the body, reason *and* imagination, the intellectual *and* the instinctual needs, because our entire existence has become the subject/object of politics, of social engineering. I emphasize, it is not a question of making the schools and universities, of making the educational system political. The educational system is political already. I need only remind you of the incredible degree to which (I am speaking of the U.S.) universities are involved in huge research grants (the nature of which you know in many cases) by the government and the various quasi-governmental agencies.

The educational system *is* political, so it is not we who want to politicize the educational system. What we want is a counterpolicy against the established policy. And in this sense we must meet this society on its own ground of total mobilization. We must confront indoctrination in servitude with indoctrination in freedom. We must each of us generate in ourselves, and try to generate in others, the instinctual need for a life without fear, without brutality, and without stupidity. And we must see that we can generate the instinctual and intellectual revulsion against the values of an affluence which spreads aggressiveness and suppression throughout the world.

Before I conclude I would like to say my bit about the Hippies. It seems to me a serious phenomenon. If we are talking of the emergence of an instinctual revulsion against the values of the affluent society, I think here is a place where we should look for it. It seems to me that the Hippies, like any nonconformist movement on the left, are split. That there are two parts, or parties, or tendencies. Much of it is mere masquerade and clownery on the private level, and therefore indeed, as Gerassi suggested, completely harmless, very nice and charming in many cases, but that is all there is to it. But that is not the whole story. There is in the Hippies, and especially in such tendencies in the Hippies as the Diggers and the Provos, an inherent political element—perhaps even more so in the U.S. than here. It is the appearance indeed of new instinctual needs and values. This experience is there. There is a new sensibility against efficient and insane reasonableness. There is the refusal to play by the rules of a rigged game, a game which one knows is rigged from the beginning, and the revolt against the compulsive cleanliness of puritan morality and the aggression bred by this puritan morality as we see it today in Vietnam among other things.

At least this part of the Hippies, in which sexual, moral, and political rebellion are somehow united, is indeed a nonaggressive form of life: a demonstration of an aggressive nonaggressiveness which achieves, at least potentially, the demonstration of qualitatively different values, a transvaluation of values.

All education today is therapy: therapy in the sense of liberating man by all available means from a society in which, sooner or later, he is going to be transformed into a brute, even if he doesn't notice it any more. Education in this sense is therapy, and all therapy today is political theory and practice. What kind of political practice? That depends entirely on the situation. It is hardly imaginable that we should discuss this here in detail. I will only remind you of the various possibilities of demonstrations, of finding out flexible modes of demonstration which can cope with the use of institutionalized violence, of boycott, many other things—anything goes which is such that it indeed has a reasonable chance of strengthening the forces of the opposition.

We can prepare for it as educators, as students. Again, I say, our role is limited. We are no mass movement. I do not believe that in the near future we will see such a mass movement.

I want to add one word about the so-called Third World. I have not spoken of the Third World because my topic was strictly liberation from the affluent society. I agree entirely with Paul Sweezy, that without putting the affluent society in the framework of the Third World it is not understandable. I also believe that here and now our emphasis must be on the advanced industrial societies—not forgetting to do whatever we can and in whatever way we can to support, theoretically and practically, the struggle for liberation in the neocolonial countries which, if again they are not the final force of liberation, at least contribute their share—and it is a considerable share—to the potential weakening and disintegration of the imperialist world system.

Our role as intellectuals is a limited role. On no account should we succumb to any illusions. But even worse than this is to succumb to the widespread defeatism which we witness. The preparatory role today is an indispensable role. I believe I am not being too optimistic—I have not in general the reputation of being too optimistic—when I say that we can already see the signs, not only that *They* are getting frightened and worried but that there are far more concrete, far more tangible manifestations of the essential weakness of the system. Therefore, let us continue with whatever we can—no illusions, but even more, no defeatism.

CHAPTER 28

Legality and Illegality

By Georg Lukács

The materialist doctrine that men are the product of circumstances and education, that changed men are therefore the products of other circumstances and of a different education, forgets that circumstances are in fact changed by men and that the educator must himself be educated.

Marx, *Theses on Feuerbach*

1

To gain an understanding of legality and illegality in the class struggle of the proletariat, as with any question touching on modes of action, it is more important and more illuminating to consider the motives and the tendencies they generate than merely to remain at the level of the bare facts. For the mere fact of the legality or illegality of one part of the workers' movement is so dependent on 'accidents' of history that to analyse it is not always to guarantee a clarification of theory. A party may be opportunistic even to the point of total betrayal and yet find itself on occasion forced into illegality. On the other hand, it is possible to imagine a situation in which the most revolutionary and most uncompromising Communist Party may be able to function for a time under conditions of almost complete legality.

As this criterion cannot provide an adequate basis for analysis we must go beyond it and examine the motives for choosing between legal and illegal tactics. But here it does not suffice to establish—abstractly—motives and convictions. For if it is significant that the opportunists always hold fast to legality at any price, it would be a mistake to define the revolutionary parties in terms of the reverse of this, namely illegality. There are, it is true, periods in every revolution when a romanticism of illegality is predominant or at least powerful. But for reasons which we shall discuss in what follows, this romanticism is quite definitely an infantile disorder of the communist movement. It is a reaction against legality at any price and for this reason it is vital that every mature movement should grow out of it and this is undoubtedly what actually happens.

What, then, is the meaning of the concepts of legality and illegality for Marxist thought? This question leads us inevitably to the general problem of organised power, to the problem of law and the state and ultimately to the problem of ideology. In his polemic against Duhring, Engels brilliantly disposes of the abstract theory of force. However, the proof that force (law and the state) "was originally grounded in an economic, social function"[1] must be interpreted to mean—in strict accordance with the theories of Marx and Engels—that in consequence of this connection a corresponding ideological picture is found projected into the thoughts and feelings of men who are drawn into the ambit of authority. That is to say, the organs of authority harmonise to such an extent with the (economic) laws governing men's lives, or seem so overwhelmingly superior that men experience them as natural forces, as the necessary environment for their existence. As a result they submit to them *freely*.[2]

For if it is true that an organisation based on force can only survive as long as it is able to overcome the resistance of individuals or groups by force, it is equally true that it could not survive if it were compelled to use force every time it is challenged. If this becomes necessary, then the situation will be revolutionary; the organs of authority will be in contradiction with the economic bases of society and this contradiction will be projected into the minds of people. People will then cease to regard the existing order as given in nature and they will oppose force with force. Without denying that this situation has an economic basis it is still necessary to add that a change can be brought about in an organisation based on force only when the belief of both the rulers and the ruled that the existing order is the only possible one has been shaken. Revolution in the system of production is the *essential precondition* of this. But the revolution itself can only be accomplished by people; by people who have become intellectually and emotionally emancipated from the existing system.

This emancipation does not take place mechanically parallel to and simultaneously with economic developments. It both anticipates these and is anticipated by them. It can be present and mostly is present at times when the economic base of a social system shows nothing more than a *tendency* to become problematical. In such cases the theory will think out what is merely a tendency and take it to its logical conclusion, converting it into what reality ought to be and then opposing this 'true' reality to the 'false' reality of what actually exists.[3] On the other hand, it is certainly true that even those groups and masses whose class situation gives them a direct interest, only free themselves inwardly from the old order during (and very often only *after*) a revolution. They need the evidence of their own eyes to tell them which society really conforms to their interests before they can free themselves inwardly from the old order.

If these remarks hold good for every revolutionary change from one social order to another they are much more valid for a social revolution than for one which is predominantly political. A political revolution does no more than sanction a socio-economic situation that has been able to impose itself at least in part upon the economic reality. Such a revolution forcibly replaces the old legal order, now felt to be 'unjust' by the new 'right', 'just' law. There is no radical reorganisation of the social environment. (Thus conservative historians of the Great French Revolution emphasise that 'social' conditions remained relatively unchanged during the period.)

Social revolutions, however, are concerned precisely to change this environment. Any such change violates the instincts of the average man so deeply that he regards it as a catastrophic threat to *life as such*, it appears to him to be a blind force of nature like a flood or an earthquake. Unable to grasp the essence of the process, his blind despair tries to defend itself by attacking the *immediate manifestations* of change that menace his accustomed existence. Thus in the early stages of capitalism, proletarians with a petty-bourgeois education rose up against machines and factories. Proudhon's doctrines, too, can be seen as one of the last echoes of this desperate defence of the old, accustomed social order.

It is here that the revolutionary nature of Marxism can be most easily grasped. Marxism is the doctrine of the revolution precisely because it understands the essence of the process (as opposed to its manifestations, its symptoms); and because it can demonstrate the decisive line of future development (as opposed to the events of the moment). This makes it at the same time the ideological expression of the proletariat in its efforts to liberate itself. This liberation takes the form at first of actual rebellions against the most oppressive manifestations of the capitalist economy and the capitalist state. These isolated battles which never bring final victory even when they are successful can only become truly revolutionary when the proletariat becomes *conscious* of what connects these battles to each other and to the process that leads ineluctably to the demise of capitalism. When the young Marx proposed the "reform of consciousness" he anticipated the essence of his later activity. His doctrine is not utopian, because it builds on a process which is actually taking place. It does not contemplate realising 'ideals' but merely wishes to uncover the inherent meaning of the process. At the same time it must go beyond what is merely given and must focus the consciousness of the proletariat on what is essential and not merely ephemerally the case. "The reform of consciousness," says Marx, "consists in no more than causing the world to become aware of its own consciousness, in awakening it from its dream about itself, in *explaining its own actions to it*. . . . It will then be seen that the world has long possessed a dream of things *which it only has to possess in consciousness in order to possess them in reality*."[4]

This reform of consciousness is the revolutionary process itself. For the proletariat can become conscious only gradually and after long, difficult crises. It is true that in Marx's doctrine all the theoretical and practical consequences of the class situation of the proletariat were deduced (long before they became historical 'fact'). However, even though these theories were not unhistorical utopias but insights into the historical process itself, it by no means follows that the proletariat has incorporated in its own consciousness the emancipation achieved by the Marxian theory—even if in *its individual actions* it *acts* in accordance with that theory. We have drawn attention to this process in a different context[5] and emphasised that the proletariat can become conscious of the need to combat capitalism on the economic plane at a time when politically it remains wholly within the ambience of the capitalist state. How very true this was can be seen from the fact that it was possible for Marx and Engels' whole critique of the state to fall into oblivion and that the most important theoreticions of the Second International could accept the capitalist state as *the* state without more ado and so could regard their own activity and their conflict with that state as 'opposition'.[6] For to adopt the stance of 'opposition' means that the existing order is *accepted in all essentials as an immutable* foundation and all the efforts of the 'opposition' are restricted to making as many gains as possible for the workers within the existing system.

Admittedly, only fools and innocents would have remained blind to the real power of the bouregeois state. The great distinction between revolutionary Marxists and pseudo-Marxist opportunists consists in the fact that for the former the capitalist state counts *merely as a power factor against which* the power of the organised proletariat is to be mobilised. Whilst the latter regard the state as an institution *standing above the classes* and the proletariat and the bourgeoisie conduct their war *in order* to gain control of it. But by viewing the state as the object of the struggle rather than as the enemy they have mentally gone over to bourgeois territory and thereby lost half the battle even before taking up arms. For every system of state and law, and the capitalist system above all, exists in the last analysis because its survival, and the validity of its statutes, are simply accepted as unproblematic. The *isolated* violation of those statutes does not represent any particular danger to the state as long as such infringements figure in the general consciousness merely as isolated cases. Dostoyevsky has noted in his Siberian reminiscences how every criminal feels himself to be guilty (without necessarily feeling any remorse); he understands with perfect clarity that he has broken laws that are no less valid for him than for everyone else. And these laws retain their validity even when personal motives or the force of circumstances have induced him to violate them.

The state will never have difficulty in keeping such isolated infringements under control just because it is not threatened in its foundations for a single moment. To adopt the stance of being in 'opposition' implies a similar attitude to the state: it concedes that the essence of the state is to stand outside the class struggle and that the validity of its laws is not *directly* challenged by the class struggle. This leaves the 'opposition' with two alternatives: either it will attempt to revise the laws by legal means and then, of course, the old laws remain in force until the new laws take their place. Or else it will promote the isolated infringement of the laws. Hence, when the opportunists attempt to conflate the Marxist critique of the state with that of the Anarchists, they are merely indulging their low taste for demagogy. For Marxism is concerned neither with anarchistic illusions nor with utopias. What is essential is to realise that the capitalist state *should be seen and evaluated as a historical phenomenon even while it exists.* It should be treated, therefore, purely as a power structure which has to be taken into account only to the extent to which its actual power stretches. On the other hand, it should be subjected to the most painstaking and fearless examination in order to discover the points where this power can be weakened and undermined. *This strong point, or rather weak point in the state is the way in which it is reflected in the consciousness of people.* Ideology is in this case not merely a consequence of the economic structure of society but also the precondition of its smooth functioning.

2

The clearer it becomes that the crisis of capitalism is ceasing to be a piece of knowledge gleaned by Marxist analysis and is in the process of becoming palpable reality, the more decisive will be the role played by ideology in determining the fate of the proletarian revolution. In an age when capitalism was still quite secure inwardly it was understandable that large sections of the working class should have taken up an *ideological* position wholly within capitalism. For a thoroughgoing Marxism required a posture they could not possibly sustain. Marx says: "In order to understand a particular historical age we must go beyond its outer limits."

When this dictum is applied to an understanding of the *present* this entails a quite extraordinary effort. It means that the whole economic, social and cultural environment must be subjected to critical scrutiny. And the decisive aspect of this scrutiny, its Archimedean point from which alone all these phenomena can be understood, can be no more than an aspiration with which to confront the reality of the present; that is to say it remains after all something 'unreal', a 'mere theory'. Whereas when we attempt to understand the past, the present is itself the starting-point. Of course, this aspiration is not merely petty bourgeois and utopian in character, yearning for a 'better' or 'more beautiful' world. It is a proletarian aspiration and does no more than discern and describe the direction, the tendency and the meaning of the social process in whose name it actively impinges on the present. Even so this just increases the difficulty of the task. For just as the very best astronomer disregards his knowledge of Copernicus and continues to accept the testimony of his senses which tells him that the sun 'rises', so too the most irrefutable Marxist analysis of the capitalist state can never abolish its empirical reality.

Nor is it designed to do so. Marxist theory is designed to put the proletariat into a very particular frame of mind. The capitalist state must appear to it as a link in a chain of historical development. Hence it by no means constitutes 'man's natural environment' but merely a real fact whose actual power must be reckoned with but which has no inherent right to determine our actions. The state and the laws shall be seen as having no more than an empirical validity. In the same way a yachtsman must take exact note of the direction of the wind without letting the wind determine his course; on the contrary, he defies and exploits it in order to hold fast to his original course. The *independence* which man in the course of a long historical development has gradually wrested from the hostile forces of nature, is still very largely lacking in the proletariat when it confronts the manifestations of society. And this is easily understood. For the coercive measures taken by society in individual cases are often hard and brutally materialistic, *but the strength of every society is in the last resort a spiritual strength*. And from this we can only be liberated by knowledge. This knowledge cannot be of the abstract kind that remains in one's head—many 'socialists' have possessed that sort of knowledge. It must be knowledge that has become flesh of one's flesh and blood of one's blood; to use Marx's phrase, it must be "practical critical activity."

The present acute crisis in capitalism makes such knowledge both possible and necessary. Possible because as a result of the crisis even the ordinary social environment can be seen and felt to be problematical. It becomes decisive for the revolution and hence necessary because the actual strength of capitalism has been so greatly weakened that it would no longer be able to maintain its position by force if the proletariat were to oppose it consciously and resolutely. Only ideology stands in the way of such opposition. Even in the very midst of the death throes of capitalism broad sections of the proletarian masses still feel that the state, the laws and the economy of the bourgeoisie are the only possible environment for them to exist in. In their eyes many improvements would be desirable ('organisation of production'), but nevertheless it remains the 'natural' basis of society.

This is the ideological foundation of legality. It does not always entail a conscious betrayal or even a conscious compromise. It is rather the natural and instinctive attitude towards the state, which appears to the man of action as the only fixed point in a chaotic world. It is a view of the world that has to be overcome if the Communist Party wishes to create a healthy foundation for both its legal and illegal tactics. For all revolutionary movements begin with the romanticism of illegality, but hardly any succeed in seeing their way beyond the stage of opportunist legality. That this romanticism, like every kind of Putschism, should underestimate the actual strength possessed by capitalism even at a moment of crisis is, of course, often very dangerous. But even this is no more than a symptom of the disease from which this whole tendency suffers.

The disease itself is the inability to see the state as nothing more than a power factor. And in the last resort this indicates a failure to see the connections we have just mapped out. For by surrounding illegal means and methods of struggle with a certain aura, by conferring upon them a special, revolutionary 'authenticity', one endows the existing state with a certain legal validity, with a more than just empirical existence. For to rebel against the law qua law, to prefer certain actions because they are illegal, implies for anyone who so acts that the law has retained its binding validity. Where the total, communist fearlessness with regard to the state and the law is present, the law and its calculable consequences are of no greater (if also of no smaller) importance than any other external fact of life with which it is necessary to reckon when deciding upon any definite course of action. The risk of breaking the law should not be regarded any differently than the risk of missing a train connection when on an important journey.

Where this is not the case, where it is resolved to break the law with a grand gesture, this suggests that the law has preserved its authority—admittedly in an inverted form—that it is still in a position inwardly to influence one's actions and that a genuine, inner emancipation has not yet occurred. At first sight this distinction may perhaps seem pedantic. But to realise that it is no empty and abstract invention but, on the contrary, a description of the true situation one need only recall how easy it was for typical illegal parties like the Socialist Revolutionaries in Russia to find their way back in to the bourgeois camp. One need only recall the first truly revolutionary illegal acts which had ceased to be the romantically heroic infringements of isolated laws and had become the rejection and destruction of the whole bourgeois legal system. One need only recall the way in which these acts exposed the ideological attachment of the 'heroes of illegality' to bourgeois concepts of law.[7]

The question of legality or illegality reduces itself then for the Communist Party to a *mere question of tactics*, even to a question to be resolved on the spur of the moment, one for which it is scarcely possible to lay down general rules as decisions have to be taken on the basis of *immediate expediencies*. In this wholly unprincipled solution lies the only possible practical and principled rejection of the bourgeois legal system. Such tactics are essential for Communists and not just on grounds of expediency. They are needed not just because it is only in this way that their tactics will acquire a genuine flexibility and adaptability to the exigencies of the particular moment; nor because the alternate or even the simultaneous use of legal and illegal methods is necessary if the bourgeoisie is to be fought effectively.

Such tactics are necessary in order to complete the revolutionary self-education of the proletariat. For the proletariat can only be liberated from its dependence upon the life-forms created by capitalism when it has learnt to act without these life-forms inwardly influencing its actions. As motive forces they must sink to the status of matters of complete indifference. Needless to say, this will not reduce by one iota the hatred of the proletariat for these forms, nor the burning wish to destroy them. On the contrary, only by virtue of this inner conviction will the proletariat be able to regard the capitalist social order as an abomination, dead but still a lethal obstacle to the healthy evolution of humanity; and this is an indispensable insight if the proletariat is to be able to take a conscious and enduring revolutionary stand. The self-education of the proletariat is a lengthy and difficult process by which it becomes 'ripe' for revolution, and the more highly developed capitalism and bourgeois culture are in a country, the more arduous this process becomes because the proletariat becomes infected by the life-forms of capitalism.

The need to establish just what is appropriate to revolutionary action coincides fortunately—though by no means adventitiously—with the exigencies of this educational task. To take but one example, the Second Congress of the Third International laid down in its Supplementary Theses on the question of parliamentarism that the Parliamentary Party should be completely dependent on the Central Committee of the C. P. even where this latter should be proscribed by law. Now this decision is not only absolutely indispensable for ensuring unified action. It also has the effect of visibly lowering the prestige of parliament in the eyes of broad sections of the proletariat (and it is upon this prestige that the freedom of action of that bastion of opportunism, the Parliamentary Party, is based). How necessary this is, is shown by the fact that, e.g. the English proletariat has constantly been diverted into the paths of opportunism because of its *inner subservience* to such authorities. And the sterility of the exclusive emphasis upon the 'direct action' of anti-parliamentarism no less than the barrenness of the debates about the superiority of either method constitutes proof that both are still enmeshed in bourgeois prejudices, albeit in ways that are diametrically opposed.

There is yet another reason for insisting upon the simultaneous and alternating use of both legal and illegal methods. Only this will bring into being the precondition for an untrammelled revolutionary attitude towards law and the state, namely the exposure of the system of law as the brutal power instrument of capitalist oppression. Where one or other of the two methods is used exclusively, or predominantly, even though within certain restricted areas, the bourgeoisie will be able to maintain the fiction in the minds of the masses that its system of law is the only system. One of the cardinal aims of every Communist Party must be to force the government of the country to violate its own system of law and to compel the legal party of social traitors to connive openly at this 'violation'. In certain cases, especially where nationalist prejudices obscure the vision of the proletariat, a capitalist government may be able to turn this to its own advantage. But at times, when the proletariat is gathering its forces for the decisive battle, such violations will prove all the more risky. It is here, in this caution of the oppressors which springs from considerations such as these, that we find the origin of those fatal illusions about democracy and about the peaceful transition to socialism. Such illusions are encouraged above all by the fact that the opportunists persist in acting legally at any price and thereby render possible the policy of prudence adopted by the ruling class. This work of educating the proletariat will only be directed into fruitful channels when sober, objective tactics are adopted that are prepared for every legal and every illegal method and that decide which is to be used solely on grounds of its utility.

3

However, the struggle for power will only begin this education; it will certainly be unable to complete it. Many years ago Rosa Luxemburg drew attention to the fact that a seizure of power is essentially 'premature' and this is especially true in the context of ideology. Many of the phenomena that make their appearance in the first stage of every dictatorship of *the proletariat can be ascribed to the fact that the proletariat is forced to take power at a time and in a state of mind in which it inwardly still acknowledges the bourgeois social order as the only authentic and legal one*. The basis of a soviet government is the same as that of any lawful system: it must be acknowledged by such large sections of the population that it has to resort only in exceptional cases to acts of violence.

Now it is self-evident from the very outset that under no circumstances will such recognition be forthcoming from the bourgeoisie at the beginning. A class accustomed by a tradition going back for many generations to the enjoyment of privileges and the exercise of power will never resign itself merely because of a single defeat. It will not simply endure the emergence of a new order without more ado. It must first be *broken ideologically* before it will voluntarily enter the service of the new society and before it will begin to regard the statutes of that society as legal and as existing of right instead of as the brutal facts of a temporary shift in the balance of power which can be reversed tomorrow. Whether or not the resistance of the bourgeoisie takes the form of open counter-revolution or of covert acts of sabotage, it is a naive illusion to imagine that it can be disarmed by making some sort of concession to it. On the contrary, the example of the soviet dictatorship in Hungary demonstrates that all such concessions which in this case were without exception also concessions to the Social Democrats, served only to strengthen the power consciousness of the former ruling class and to postpone and even put an end to their inner willingness to accept the rule of the proletariat.

This retreat of the power of the soviets before the bourgeoisie had even more disastrous implications for the ideology of the broad masses of the petty bourgeoisie. It is characteristic of them that they regard the state as something general and universal, as an absolute supreme institution. Apart from an adroit economic policy which is often enough to neutralise the individual groups of the petty bourgeoisie it is evident, then, that much depends on the proletariat itself. Will it succeed in giving its state such authority as to meet half-way the faith in authority of such strata of the population and to facilitate their inclinations to subordinate themselves voluntarily to 'the' state? If the proletariat hesitates, if it lacks a sustaining faith in its own mission to rule, it can drive these groups back into the arms of the bourgeoisie and even to open counter-revolution.

Under the dictatorship of the proletariat the relationship between legality and illegality undergoes a change in function, for now what was formerly legal becomes illegal and vice versa. However, this change can at most accelerate somewhat the process of emancipation begun under capitalism; it cannot complete it at one stroke. The bourgeoisie did not lose the sense of its own legality after *a single* defeat, and similarly the proletariat cannot possibly gain a consciousness of its own legality through the fact of *a single* victory. This consciousness only matured very slowly under capitalism and even now, under the dictatorship of the proletariat, it will only ripen by degrees. In the first period it will even suffer a number of setbacks. For only now will the proletariat, having once gained control, be able to appreciate the mental achievements which created and sustained capitalism. Not only will it acquire a far greater insight into bourgeois culture than ever before; but also the mental achievements essential to the conduct of the economy and the state will only become apparent to large sections of the proletariat after it has come to power.

Furthermore, it must not be forgotten that to a great extent the proletariat has been deprived of the practice and the tradition of acting independently and responsibly. Hence it may often experience the need to act thus as a burden rather than as a liberation. And finally there is the fact that petty bourgeois and even bourgeois attitudes have come to permeate the habits of life of those sections of the proletariat that will occupy leading positions. This has the effect of making precisely what is new about the new society appear alien and even hostile to them.

All these obstacles would be fairly harmless and might easily be overcome were it not for one fact. This is that the bourgeoisie for whom the problem of legality and illegality has undergone a comparable change of function, is even here much more mature and much further advanced than the proletariat.[8] With the same naive complacency with which it formerly contemplated the legality of its own system of law it now dismisses as illegal the order imposed by the proletariat. We have made it a requirement for the proletariat struggling for power that it should view the bourgeois state merely as a fact, a power factor; this requirement is now instinctively fulfilled by the bourgeoisie.

Thus, despite the victory gained by the proletariat, its struggle with the bourgeoisie is still unequal and it will remain so until the proletariat acquires the same naive confidence in the exclusive legality of its own system of law. Such a development is, however, greatly impeded by the attitude of mind imposed on the proletariat by the opportunists. Having accustomed itself to surrounding the institutions of capitalism with an aura of legality it finds it difficult to view with detachment the surviving remains which may endure for a very long time. Once the proletariat has gained power it still remains enmeshed intellectually in the trammels woven by the course of capitalist development. This finds expression, on the one hand, in its failure to lay hands on much that ought to be utterly destroyed. On the other hand, it proceeds to the labour of demolition and construction not with the sense of assurance that springs from legitimate rule, but with the mixture of vacillation and haste characteristic of the usurper. A usurper, moreover, who inwardly, in thought, feeling and resolve, anticipates the inevitable restoration of capitalism.

I have in mind here not only the more or less overt counterrevolutionary sabotage of the process of socialisation perpetrated throughout the Hungarian soviet dictatorship by the trade-union bureaucrats with the aim of restoring capitalism as painlessly as possible. I am thinking here also of the widely noted phenomenon of corruption in the soviets which has one of its chief sources here. Partly in the mentality of many soviet officials who were inwardly prepared for the return of a 'legitimate' capitalism and who were therefore intent on being able to justify their own actions when it became necessary. Partly also because many who had been involved in necessarily 'illegal' work (smuggling propaganda abroad) were intellectually and above all morally unable to grasp that from the only legitimate standpoint, the standpoint of the proletarian state, their activities were just as 'legal' as any other. In the case of people of unstable moral character this confusion was translated into open corruption. Many an honest revolutionary lapsed into a romantic hypostatisation of 'illegality', into the unprofitable search for 'illegal' openings, and these tendencies exhibit *a deficient sense of the legitimacy of the Revolution* and of the fight of the Revolution to establish its own lawful order.

In the period of the dictatorship of the proletariat this feeling and this sense of legitimacy should replace the requirement of the previous stage of the revolution, namely the stage of unfettered independence *vis-a-vis* bourgeois law. But notwithstanding this change *the evolution of the class consciousness of the proletariat advances homogeneously and in a straight line.* This can be seen most clearly in the foreign policies of proletarian states which, when confronted by the power structures of capitalist states, have to do battle with the bourgeois state just as they did when they seized power in their own state, though now the methods have partly changed.

The peace negotiations at Brest-Litovsk have already testified to the high level and the maturity of the class consciousness attained by the Russian proletariat. Although they were dealing with the German imperialists they recognised their oppressed brothers all over the world as their truly legitimate partners at the negotiating table. Even though Lenin's judgement of the actual power relationships was notable for its supreme intelligence and realistic toughness, his negotiators were instructed to address themselves to the proletariat of the world and primarily to the proletariat of the Central Powers. His foreign policy was less a negotiation between Germany and Russia than the attempt to promote proletarian revolution and revolutionary consciousness in the nations of Central Europe. Since then the home and foreign policies of the Soviet Government have undergone many changes and it has been necessary to adapt them to the exigencies of the real power situation. But notwithstanding this the fundamental principle, the principle of the legitimacy of its own power which at the same time entails the principle of the need to advance the revolutionary class consciousness of the proletariat of the world, has remained a fixed point throughout the whole period.

The whole problem of the recognition of Soviet Russia by the bourgeois states must not be regarded in isolation as involving no more than the question of the advantages accruing to Russia. It must be seen also as the question of whether the bourgeoisie will recognise the legitimacy of the proletarian revolution. The significance of this recognition changes according to the concrete circumstances in which it takes place. Its effect on the vacillating sections of the petty bourgeoisie in Russia as well as on those of the proletariat of the world remains the same in all essentials: it sanctions the legitimacy of the revolution, something of which they stand in great need if they are to accept as legal its official exponents, the Soviet Republic. All the various methods of Russian politics serve this purpose: the relentless onslaught on the counter-revolution within Russia, the bold confrontation of the powers victorious in the war to whom Russia has never spoken in tones of submission (unlike the bourgeoisie of Germany), and the open support granted to revolutionary movements, etc. These policies cause sections of the counter-revolutionary front in Russia to crumble away and to bow before the legitimacy of the Revolution. They help to fortify the revolutionary self-consciousness of the proletariat, its awareness of its own strength and dignity.

The ideological maturity of the Russian proletariat becomes clearly visible when we consider those very factors which have been taken as evidence of its backwardness by the opportunists of the West and their Central European admirers. To wit, the clear and definitive crushing of the internal counter-revolution and the uninhibited illegal and "diplomatic" battle for world revolution. The Russian proletariat did not emerge victoriously from its revolution because a fortunate constellation of circumstances played into its hands.[9] It was victorious because it had been steeled by the long illegal struggle and hence had gained a clear understanding of the nature of the capitalist state. In consequence its actions were based on a genuine reality and not on ideological delusions. The proletariat of Central and Western Europe still has an arduous road before it. If it is to become conscious of its historical mission and of the legitimacy of its rule it must first grasp the fact that the problem of legality and illegality is purely tactical in nature. It must be able to slough off both the cretinism of legality and the romanticism of illegality.

CHAPTER 29

An Autopsy of Marxist Socialism

By Manfred B. Steger

Is socialism dead? Common sense at the close of the 20th century suggests the answer is yes. The Iron Curtain in Eastern Europe has long disappeared, the Soviet Union has dissolved, Castro's Cuba is on the brink of collapse, and Chinese communism looks more and more like Singapore-style authoritarianism with a decidedly capitalist face. The admired Third Way of Scandinavian social democracy has hit a dead end, abandoning its commendable goals of full employment, rising real wages, and large welfare transfers.

Caught in a world-wide transition from nationally organized to globally integrated capitalism, the nation state-based "Keynesian socialism" of 20 years ago has found itself in a losing battle with the new internationalism of multinational corporations and expanding stock exchanges. The Western democratic Left of the 1990s has appropriated campaign slogans that barely differ from those of market liberals and conservatives.

Still, we should carefully avoid embracing Francis Fukuyama's triumphant "end of history" argument. After all, his hasty proclamation of the irreversible victory of liberal democracy over all its ideological competitors ignores the historical lessons of the last four centuries: Sometimes even the most horrendous blows to political and religious traditions cannot prevent their successful reconstitution. Modern political theorists and historians of ideas have also been known for the intellectual *hubris* of premature announcements that various socio-political systems had died. In this respect, Hegel and Marx are just as guilty as Spengler and Nietzsche.

Yet despite these words of caution, I'm nevertheless firmly convinced that Marxist socialism has lost its viability. Unlike the resilient android personified by Arnold Schwarzenegger in the film *Terminator*, no special effects will bring the body of Marxist socialism back to life again. The "intimate interconnection between Marxist political theory and practice" so effectively formulated in Marx's famous *Theses on Feuerbach* reveals serious flaws in Marxist thought that have doomed its practice, just as the political practice of authoritarian collectivism in existing socialist countries has perverted Marxist theory.

As this autopsy will show, besides numerous cuts and bruises, the mangled body of Marxist socialism has at least two chronic disorders tracing back to the earliest moments of its conception. First, it lacks insight into the role of power and coercion. Second, Marxism's deterministic teleology bypasses and downplays crucial questions of ethics, individual liberty, and political morality.

Before beginning the autopsy, let's consider two common objections to the death of socialism: First, that socialism cannot be equated with Marxism, however conceived; hence some variant of socialism might remain a viable future option. Second, that real socialism has never been tried or successfully implemented in history. In response, we can admit that it would be a mistake to confuse Marxism with socialism *per se.* There might well be a legitimate argument for the continued relevance of non-Marxist socialisms.

Yet we should remember that the equation of Marxism with "real socialism" was fiercely defended by most classical Marxist theorists. For example, in her pamphlet, *Reform or Revolution*, Rosa Luxemburg emphasized this link, building on Marx's own disdain for various forms of socialism he labelled "reactionary," "feudal," "petty-bourgeois," or "critical-utopian."

Given Luxemburg's arguments, we would be foolish to ignore the historical linkages between philosophical Marxism and the Leninist regimes of the 20th century. Even the elaborate attempts by unremitting apologists like Alex Callinicos to somehow rescue a "pure Marxism" from the claws of Leninist, Stalinist, and Maoist "aberrations" ultimately fail to prevent Marxist philosophy from being implicated in the great crimes against humanity routinely committed by state socialist regimes. If we are to take actual political practice seriously, we should recognize that the historically successful manifestations of Marxist socialism did not emerge in Luxemburg's noble dream of "democratic workers" councils, in Kurt Eisner's short-lived Bavarian *Raterepublik*, in Bela Kun's Socialist Hungary, or in Antonio Gramsci's "Red Turin," but rather in Lenin's and Mao's Third World Bolshevism.

Therefore, we should avoid intricate marxiological debates aimed at uncovering the hidden design of "real socialism." We would also gain little by engaging in dogmatic hair-splitting in order to find out "what Marx really meant." Rather, I understand "Marxist socialism" to mean two things. First, it refers to those ideological features commonly associated with the doctrine of Marx and Engels, such as the centrality of class struggle, the proletariat's emancipatory role, the materialist conception of history, the emphasis on "dialectical science," and the vision of totalizing the "communist world outlook." Second, I refer to a political program of action comprised of the "socialization of the means of production plus planned economy plus one-party rule."

Marx and Engels extended existing conceptual frameworks of power with their innovative emphasis on class, economics, and the political configuration of society as a whole. While their sociological arguments remain strong, their flawed model of political power substantially explains Marxism's recent demise. Let's examine two major defects.

In the *Communist Manifesto* as well as in other key writings, Marx and Engels introduce their concept of power as that of a "central force," and focus on the seizure of (state) power by the proletariat and the transformation of existing social and political structures by means of the "dictatorship of the proletariat." Defining political power in capitalist societies as "oppressive class rule," Marx and Engels anticipate the violent overthrow of the bourgeoisie by the proletariat organized as a politically conscious class: "The Communists disdain to conceal their views and aims. They openly declare that their ends can be attained only by the forcible overthrow of all existing conditions." They predict that after successfully implementing their ten "general measures" designed to concentrate power in the hands of the proletariat, public (proletarian) power would gradually lose its political (bourgeois) class-character, and the state as the organ of class rule would wither away.

Of course, some wondered whether the consolidation of the Communist Party and the tendency toward a centralization of power would not produce a state apparatus that had little interest in its own "withering away." Robert Michels captured this problem in his "iron law of oligarchies." While Marx and Engels did not equate the "dictatorship of the proletariat" with Lenin's "dictatorship of the Communist Party" (they even considered the possibility of a peaceful transition to socialism in some countries), both men were nevertheless committed to their vision that a violent, armed revolution would be the class struggle's logical endpoint.

Therefore, Lenin's "historical corrections" renouncing potentially peaceful transitions in England and the U.S., and his renewed emphasis on the "revolutionary conquest of political power by the armed proletariat," can be legitimately deduced from Marx's original enterprise. The fact that all real-existing socialist countries of the 20th century have actually followed Michels' oligarchical model strengthens the case against the Marxist conception of political power.

The chief problem lies in the instrumental notion that political power can be conquered as though it were an external object or commodity. Marxism does not stand alone in having such a mechanistic conceptualization of political power; it characterizes paradigms reaching as far back as Machiavelli and Hobbes. From this perspective, power is an objectifiable mechanism of coercion, applied by privileged social agents according to strict instrumental rules. As Stephen Toulmin suggests, this model closely corresponds to Newtonian physics, where power is represented as a timeless, massive force. The crucial image here is that of political power as an effective instrument, functioning both as brute force and calculated-economized violence. Unlike Machiavelli and Hobbes, whose social agents were "great men" forcing their superior will onto recurring cycles of history, Marxist theorists rely on a much more sophisticated model of social and political action based on the dialectic of class struggle. Still, as Hannah Arendt pointed out, Marxism exhibits the same remarkable tendency to equate political power with the "organization of violence" and the "effectiveness of command." This instrumental model emerges most starkly in Georges Sorel's famous *Reflections on Violence*, and in Mao's dictum that "Power grows out of the barrel of a gun."

As the political theorist Jeffrey Isaac has noted, Marxist socialism historically viewed the problem of political power as the transition to communism rather than the very constitution of communism. It lacks insights on the relationship between power, social control, and popular support of the kind we have come to associate, for example, with the tradition of nonviolence championed by thinkers such as M.K. Gandhi, Martin Luther King Jr. and Gene Sharp.

Relying on pre-established concepts, Marxist thinkers failed to develop creative ways of approaching political power. Those such as Jürgen Habermas, Claus Offe, Nicos Poulantzas, or Noberto Bobbio, who actually rethought power, state, and democracy, soon found themselves abandoning traditional Marxism in favor of liberal variants of a "radical politics." To be fair, classical Marxism did discuss power as the distortive and repressive aspects of ideology—an enterprise developed by 20th-century "critical theorists" into a more comprehensive theory of society and consciousness.

Yet these writings were not only soundly rejected by "official" Communist ideologists, but they also neglected the legitimizing dimensions of political power. What about the "constructive" role of power and ideology understood as negotiation, compliance, and most important, as strategies of individual and collective resistance? What is the relationship between nonviolence and power? What about the production of knowledge through power? How can we study mechanisms of power like sexism, racism, or homophobia, which we cannot boil down to merely economistic explanations? These are exactly the kinds of questions that inspired influential non-Marxist radicals such as Michel Foucault, Vaclav Havel and Petra Kelly.

We must also wonder why the "historicist" Marxist paradigm so readily accepts a reified Machiavellian or Hobbesian model of power that operates in seemingly fixed *loci* of human domination. Ernesto Laclau and Chantal Mouffe have called this flaw in Marxist theory "class essentialism"—the tendency to view social identities and class interests as petrified in a totalizing structure that disregards the pluralism of political struggles. In other words, Marxism not only exaggerates the part played by structurally preordained and seemingly unchanging powers in society, but also underestimates noneconomic forms of oppression, giving only scarce attention to "ordinary" networks of subjugation enmeshing women, racial, and ethnic minorities.

This omission helps explain the increasing theoretical petrification and dogmatization of Marxist socialism in our century. As soon as the living and breathing "proletariat" turned out to be yet another historical social agent that constantly changed in its composition, interests, and class character, Marxism lost much of its intellectual appeal as an "emancipatory" theory related to political reality.

The weaknesses of the Marxist model of political power also emerged when it could not explain the most significant political event of the late 20th century: the overthrow of Eastern European authoritarian communist regimes by popular nonviolent movements in the name of "solidarity" and "citizenship." The "People Power" that unleashed the 1989 Revolutions revealed that in our global age of instant information and economic interdependence, we must abandon Newtonian conceptions of political power.

Our autopsy of Marxist socialism exposes another chronic disorder: the dogmatic assumption that socialism and liberalism are inherently antagonistic. Indeed, the political program of the *Communist Manifesto* describes a conqueror who wants to incorporate territory, torn away from the enemy, as fast as possible. No common interests exist, no obligations between victor and vanquished. There are two absolute, separated classes, and their members share no common threads whatsoever. Philosophical and political expressions of pluralism are regarded as signs of false consciousness and defeatism, as are crucial liberal concepts of popular sovereignty, the rule of law, religious tolerance, individual liberty, and the rational redress of grievances. But both Marx and Engels wholeheartediy supported liberal political movements for representative and responsible government, insofar as they opposed established monarchical systems or the remains of a feudal social order. There is no reason to think that the array of democratic rights they endorsed in 1848 was merely tactical.

But the political forms of representative democracy were only accepted conditionally, as transitional goals on the way to socialism that could not constitute "socialist democracy" itself. Liberals were simply incapable of living up to the radical "democratic rights" they espoused, because their political institutions were dedicated to preserving and reproducing the private property of capitalism.

Marx also abandoned transhistorical moral standards—traditionally expressed in the natural law concepts of liberal thinkers from Locke to Kant and Mill—as passing features in the objective-teleological process of historical unfolding. Neither relying on the "beautiful dream" of socialist utopians such as Owen, Fourier, and Weitling, nor on the ethical voluntarism of moral philosophers, Marxist theorists claimed to know the coming of a fundamentally different social order as what Karl Kautsky called the "inevitable consequence of an objectively necessary process." Bourgeois notions of eternal truth and divine justice were nothing but ideological distortions hiding repressive social relations. Identifying existing contradictions at the economic base of society, Marxist socialism assumed the status of an objective social movement struggling against oppressive conditions independent of the individual's ethical ideals. But this teleological scheme of "moral historicism"—the view that whatever social structures have evolved are, *ipso facto*, morally justified—was completely undermined by the increasing tendency toward differentiation within the proletariat, coupled with the rising political importance of the middle class. Both resulted from the course of modern capitalism. The leaders of European social democracy thus grew more concerned with the growth of their labor bureaucracy and the outcomes of the next elections than with upending government. Contrary to the ominous predictions of the *Communist Manifesto*, scores of ordinary workers seemed to prefer the occasional crumbs from the capitalist table to the perils of an all-out class war. On the other hand, radical voices in Russia, China, and Cuba vigorously asserted the legitimacy of an activist interpretation of Marxism as a revolutionary doctrine for backward nations.

But Lenin and his comrades simply accentuated Marx's and Engels' fatal metaphysical blunder of constructing social developments from *a priori* formulas. Seeking to prove a thesis laid down beforehand and spinning out the logical somersaults of Hegelian philosophy, "dialectical materialists" overlooked the concrete facts of economic and political developments that could have provided the necessary empirical correction to the self-deceptions they entertained about the actual course of history. Since reality no longer corresponded to theory, communist regimes chose to lie about reality, seeking to force people, as Vaclav Havel put it, "to live the great lie." The hubristic denial of political morality by party bosses, combined with their shortsightedness about political power's decentralized workings, hastened the eventual demise of their paradigm. Rejecting the illiberalism of Marxist doctrine, Solidarity, Civic Forum, The Public Against Violence, and scores of other dissident organizations celebrated the liberal language of human rights and categorically rejected Marxist teleology. They championed a political morality that underscored the civil society as a public sphere where citizenship should be universalized.

Thus, Havel and his fellow dissidents resurrected the humanist vision of Enlightenment thinkers who argued that civil society and universal human rights protected individual liberty, institutionalized as the liberal distinction between private and public. Most of all, "People Power" liberated the political subject from the smothering objectivity of Marx's historicism, thereby encouraging individual responsibility and critical thinking.

Does the death of Marxism taint all future projects bearing the name "socialism?" Not necessarily. But the crimes of the "Marxist century" teach us that "socialism" can only refer to a transcendental, moral ideal. The "socialist goal" is only possible as a principle of cooperation; it cannot be conjured up *a priori*. The failure of Marxist socialism to acknowledge the status of socialism as a moral ideal illuminates the lingering disease that caused its death: the inability to consciously embrace the libertarian legacy of the Enlightenment.

Indeed, radical democrats ought to welcome the demise of Marxist socialism, for it allows older, ethical variants of socialism to reassert themselves. We must look at history differently, realizing that Marxism represented a long, regrettable deviation from an earlier 19th-century socialism that saw itself as the necessary social evolution of classical liberalism, guided by basic rational and humanitarian ideals.

Thus the core question of socialism remains pertinent in the 21st century: how can we reconcile peace, liberty, socialism, nonviolence, and democracy, while maintaining the highest possible degree of individual freedom and economic equality? Without indiscriminately collapsing social democracy into a new, ruthless market liberalism of the global age, the possible renewal of the socialist tradition calls for the rediscovery of non-Marxist socialist currents and their historical connections to a radical liberalism.

The language of human rights provides the most appropriate vehicle for this political program since it best articulates progressive demands: the expansion of personal rights at the expense of property rights, thus making socially consequential power accountable to the will of all citizens. In times where conservative parties assume governing responsibility, social democracy may turn into a largely defensive project, seeking to prevent the middle class from slipping, and to protect the socially disadvantaged from the worst effects of welfare rollbacks.

But even during periods of high economic growth—when progressives can pursue a more activist course—social democracy cannot shed the specific institutional form of modern liberal democracy without risking the reunification of state and society in a totalizing way, and thus the surrender of democracy as such.

While we certainly can extend political and economic democracy, the old Marxist goal of transforming the capitalist system entirely must be abandoned. Realistically appreciating the limitations of liberal democracy in our post-Soviet and post-Keynesian era forces us to acknowledge the perennial tensions between ethical principles and the political imperatives of compromise. Accepting the inevitability of some instrumental behavior under conditions of advanced capitalism, social democracy can nevertheless still fulfill important tasks. Technocrats who separate values from political activities must learn the importance of ideals guiding practice, and ethical idealists must recognize the need for pragmatic strategies in democratic politics.

As Charles W. Anderson pointed out, the justification for a more pragmatic attitude stems from the need to find the best fit between theory and practice. Those who identify with the democratic promise must keep taking stock, and balance their ideals of good practice with the intrinsic aims of the democratic enterprise itself. After the death of Marxist socialism, such a goal can no longer be viewed as the result of the inexorable workings of blind socio-economic laws but rather as an ethical protest against all forms of structural violence perpetuated by unfettered capitalism.

As long as society remains torn apart by wars, ethnic hatreds, and growing disparities in wealth and well-being, the timeless ideals of socialism will take root in those social thinkers and reformers who settle for the more modest role of mediating between different systems of thought. Even if the term "socialism" itself has been fully discredited, its ideals will survive in the name of a democratic politics that works for world peace and social justice.

SECTION SEVEN

Nonviolence Alternatives

CHAPTER 30

Excerpts from The Essential Writings of Mahatma Gandhi

By Mohandas K. Gandhi

AHIMSA—THE SCOPE AND POWER OF NON-VIOLENCE

In this age of the rule of brute force, it is almost impossible for anyone to believe that anyone else could possibly reject the law of the final supremacy of brute force. And so I receive anonymous letters advising me that I must not interfere with the progress of non-co-operation even though popular violence may break out. Others come to me and assuming that secretly I must be plotting violence, inquire when the happy moment for declaring open violence will arrive. They assure me that the English will never yield to anything but violence secret or open. Yet others, I am informed, believe that I am the most rascally person living in India because I never give out my real intention and that they have not a shadow of a doubt that I believe in violence just as much as most people do.

Such being the hold that the doctrine of the sword has on the majority of mankind, and as success of non-co-operation depends principally on absence of violence during its pendency and as my views in this matter affect the conduct of a large number of people, I am anxious to state them as clearly as possible.

I do believe that where there is only a choice between cowardice and violence I would advise violence. Thus when my eldest son asked me what he should have done, had he been present when I was almost fatally assaulted in 1908, whether he should have run away and seen me killed or whether he should have used his physical force which he could and wanted to use, and defended me, I told him that it was his duty to defend me even by using violence. Hence it was that I took part in the Boer War, the so-called Zulu rebellion and the late War. Hence also do I advocate training in arms for those who believe in the method of violence. I would rather have India resort to arms in order to defend her honour than that she should in a cowardly manner become or remain a helpless witness to her own dishonour.

But I believe that non-violence is infinitely superior to violence, forgiveness is more manly than punishment. *Kshama virasya bhushanam.* "Forgiveness adorns a soldier." But abstinence is forgiveness only when there is the power to punish; it is meaningless when it pretends to proceed from a helpless creature. A mouse hardly forgives a cat when it allows itself to be torn to pieces by her. I, therefore, appreciate the sentiment of those who cry out for the condign punishment of General Dyer and his ilk. They would tear him to pieces if they could. But I do not believe India to be helpless. I do not believe myself to be a helpless creature. Only I want to use India's and my strength for a better purpose.

Let me not be misunderstood. Strength does not come from physical capacity. It comes from an indomitable will. An average Zulu is any way more than a match for an average Englishman in bodily capacity. But he flees from an English boy, because he fears the boy's revolver or those who will use it for him. He fears death and is nerveless in spite of his burly figure. We in India may in a moment realize that one hundred thousand Englishmen need not frighten three hundred million human beings. A definite forgiveness would therefore mean a definite recognition of our strength. With enlightened forgiveness must come a mighty wave of strength in us, which would make it impossible for a Dyer and a Frank Johnson to heap affront upon India's devoted head. It matters little to me that for the moment I do not drive my point home. We feel too downtrodden not to be angry and revengeful. But I must not refrain from saying that India can gain more by waiving the right of punishment. We have better work to do, a better mission to deliver to the world.

I am not a visionary. I claim to be a practical idealist. The religion of non-violence is not meant merely for the *rishis* and saints. It is meant for the common people as well. Non-violence is the law of our species as violence is the law of the brute. The spirit lies dormant in the brute and he knows no law but that of physical might. The dignity of man requires obedience to a higher law—to the strength of the spirit.

I have therefore ventured to place before India the ancient law of self-sacrifice. For *satyagraha* and its off-shoots, non-cooperation and civil resistance, are nothing but new names for the law of suffering. The *rishis*, who discovered the law of non-violence in the midst of violence, were greater geniuses than Newton. They were themselves greater warriors than Wellington. Having themselves known the use of arms, they realized their uselessness and taught a weary world that its salvation lay not through violence but through non-violence.

Non-violence in its dynamic condition means conscious suffering. It does not mean meek submission to the will of the evil-doer, but it means the putting of one's whole soul against the will of the tyrant. Working under this law of our being, it is possible for a single individual to defy the whole might of an unjust empire to save his honour, his religion, his soul and lay the foundation for that empire's fall or its regeneration.

And so I am not pleading for India to practise non-violence because it is weak. I want her to practise non-violence being conscious of her strength and power. No training in arms is required for realization of her strength. We seem to need it because we seem to think that we are but a lump of flesh. I want India to recognize that she has a soul that cannot perish and that can rise triumphant above every physical weakness and defy the physical combination of a whole world. What is the meaning of Rama, a mere human being, with his host of monkeys, pitting himself against the insolent strength of ten-headed Ravana surrounded in supposed safety by the raging waters on all sides of Lanka? Does it not mean the conquest of physical might by spiritual strength? However, being a practical man, I do not wait till India recognizes the practicability of the spiritual life in the political world. India considers herself to be powerless and paralysed before the machine-guns, the tanks and the aeroplanes of the English. And she takes up non-co-operation out of her weakness. It must still serve the same purpose, namely, bring her delivery from the crushing weight of British injustice if a sufficient number of people practise it.

I isolate this non-co-operation from Sinn Feinism, for it is so conceived as to be incapable of being offered side by side with violence. But I invite even the school of violence to give this peaceful non-co-operation a trial. It will not fail through its inherent weakness. It may fail because of poverty of response. Then will be the time for real danger. The high-souled men, who are unable to suffer national humiliation any longer, will want to vent their wrath. They will take to violence. So far as I know, they must perish without delivering themselves or their country from the wrong. If India takes up the doctrine of the sword, she may gain momentary victory. Then India will cease to be the pride of my heart. I am wedded to India because I owe my all to her. I believe absolutely that she has a mission for the world. She is not to copy Europe blindly. India's acceptance of the doctrine of the sword will be the hour of my trial. I hope I shall not be found wanting. My religion has no geographical limits. If I have a living faith in it, it will transcend my love for India herself. My life is dedicated to service of India through the religion of non-violence which I believe to be the root of Hinduism.

Meanwhile I urge those who distrust me, not to disturb the even working of the struggle that has just commenced, by inciting to violence in the belief that I want violence. I detest secrecy as a sin. Let them give non-violent non-co-operation a trial and they will find that I had no mental reservation whatsoever.

"The Doctrine of the Sword"
Young India, 11 Aug. 1920

To
The "World Tomorrow"
396 Broadway
New York U.S.A.

My study and experience of non-violence have proved to me that it is the greatest force in the world. It is the surest method of discovering the truth and it is the quickest because there is no other. It works silently, almost imperceptibly, but none the less surely. It is the one Constructive process of Nature in the midst of incessant destruction going on about us. I hold it to be a superstition to believe that it can work only in private life. There is no department of life public or private to which that force cannot be applied. But this non-violence is impossible without complete self-effacement.

Message to "World Tomorrow"
Mahadev Desai's Diary (MSS)

Non-violence is the greatest force man has been endowed with. Truth is the only goal he has. For God is none other than Truth. But Truth cannot be, never will be, reached except through non-violence.

That which distinguishes man from all other animals is his capacity to be non-violent. And he fulfils his mission only to the extent that he is non-violent and no more. He has no doubt many other gifts. But if they do not subserve the main purpose—the development of the spirit of non-violence in him—they but drag him down lower than the brute, a status from which he has only just emerged.

The cry for peace will be a cry in the wilderness, so long as the spirit of non-violence does not dominate millions of men and women.

An armed conflict between nations horrifies us. But the economic war is no better than an armed conflict. This is like a surgical operation. An economic war is prolonged torture. And its ravages are no less terrible than those depicted in the literature on war properly so called. We think nothing of the other because we are used to its deadly effects.

Many of us in India shudder to see blood spilled. Many of us resent cow-slaughter, but we think nothing of the slow torture through which by our greed we put our people and cattle. But because we are used to this lingering death, we think no more about it.

The movement against war is sound. I pray for its success. But I cannot help the gnawing fear that the movement will fail, if it does not touch the root of all evil—man's greed.

Will America, England and the other great nations of the West continue to exploit the so-called weaker or uncivilized races and hope to attain peace that the whole world is pining for? Or will Americans continue to prey upon one another, have commercial rivalries and yet expect to dictate peace to the world?

Not till the spirit is changed can the form be altered. The form is merely an expression of the spirit within. We may succeed in seemingly altering the form but the alteration will be a mere make-believe if the spirit within remains unalterable. A whited sepulchre still conceals beneath it the rotting flesh and bone.

Far be it from me to discount or under-rate the great effort that is being made in the West to kill the war-spirit. Mine is merely a word of caution as from a fellow-seeker who has been striving in his own humble manner after the same thing, maybe in a different way, no doubt on a much smaller scale. But if the experiment demonstrably succeeds on the smaller field and, if those who are working on the larger field have not overtaken me, it will at least pave the way for a similar experiment on a large field.

I observe in the limited field in which I find myself, that unless I can reach the hearts of men and women, I am able to do nothing. I observe further that so long as the spirit of hate persists in some shape or other, it is impossible to establish peace or to gain our freedom by peaceful effort. We cannot love one another, if we hate Englishmen. We cannot love the Japanese and hate Englishmen. We must either let the Law of Love rule us through and through or not at all. Love among ourselves based on hatred of others breaks down under the slightest pressure. The fact is such love is never real love. It is an armed peace. And so it will be in this great movement in the West against war. War will only be stopped when the conscience of mankind has become sufficiently elevated to recognize the undisputed supremacy of the Law of Love in all the walks of life. Some say this will never come to pass. I shall retain the faith till the end of my earthly existence that it shall come to pass.

"Non-Violence—The Greatest Force"
The Hindu, 8 Nov. 1926

151. THE LAW OF LOVE

It takes a fairly strenuous course of training to attain to a mental state of non-violence. In daily life it has to be a course of discipline though we may not like it, like for instance the life of a soldier. But I agree that unless there is a hearty cooperation of the mind, the mere outward observance will be simply a mask, harmful both to the man himself and to others. The perfect state is reached only when mind and body and speech are in proper co-ordination. But it is always a case of intense mental struggle. It is not that I am incapable of anger, for instance, but I succeed on almost all occasions to keep my feelings under control. Whatever may be the result, there is always in me a conscious struggle to follow the law of non-violence deliberately and ceaselessly. Such a struggle leaves one stronger for it.

Non-violence is a weapon of the strong. With the weak it might easily be hypocrisy. Fear and love are contradictory terms. Love is reckless in giving away, oblivious as to what it gets in return. Love wrestles with the world as with itself and ultimately gains a mastery over all other Feelings. My daily experience, as of those who are working with me, is that every problem would lend itself to solution if we are determined to make the law of truth and non-violence the law of life. For truth and non-violence are, to me, faces of the same coin.

Whether mankind will consciously follow the law of love I do not know. But that need not perturb us. The law will work, just as the law of gravitation will work whether we accept it or not. And just as a scientist will work wonders out of various applications of the laws of nature, even so a man who applies the law of love with scientific precision can work greater wonders. For the force of non-violence is infinitely more wonderful and subtle than the force of nature, like for instance electricity. The man who discovered for us the law of love was a far greater scientist than any of our modern scientists. Only our explorations have not gone far enough and so it is not possible for everyone to see all its workings. Such, at any rate, is the hallucination, if it is one, under which I am labouring. The more I work at this law the more I feel the delight in life, the delight in the scheme of this universe. It gives me a peace and a meaning of the mysteries of nature that I have no power to describe.

"From S. S. Rajputana-III" (Letter from M. D.)[1]
Young India, 1 Oct. 1931

152. NON-VIOLENCE AS MEANS AND END

June 26, 1933

My dear Asaf Ali,

I have your long letter for which I thank you. I do not at all mind your having sent it to the Press. You had a perfect right to send me that letter and I appreciate the frankness with which you have expressed your views.

I am, as yet, unable to say anything on the present situation because I am still bed-ridden and have not been able to make an analytical study of it. I want you, however, to understand my fundamental difficulty which constitutes also my limitation. Non-violence for me is not a mere experiment. It is part of my life and the whole of the creed of *satyagraha*, non-co-operation, civil disobedience, and the like are necessary deductions from the fundamental proposition that non-violence is the law of life for human beings. For me it is both a means and an end and I am more than ever convinced that in the complex situation that faces India, there is no other way of gaining real freedom. In applying my mind to the present situation I must, therefore, test everything in terms of non-violence.

M. Asaf Ali, Esp., bar-at-law
Kucha Chelan, Delhi

Letter to M. Asaf Ali
SN 19108

Non-violence is at the root of every one of my activities and therefore also of the three public activities on which I am just now visibly concentrating all my energy. These are untouchability, *khadi,* and village regeneration in general. Hindu-Muslim unity is my fourth love. But so far as any visible manifestation is concerned, I have owned defeat on that score. Let the public, however, not assume therefrom that I am inactive. If not during my lifetime, I know that after my death both Hindus and Mussalmans will bear witness that I had never ceased to yearn after communal peace.

Non-violence to be a creed has to be all-pervasive. I cannot be non-violent about one activity of mine and violent about others. That would be a policy, not a life-force. That being so, I cannot be indifferent about the war that Italy is now waging against Abyssinia. But I have resisted a most pressing invitation to express my opinion and give a lead to the country. Self-suppression is often necessary in the interest of Truth and non-violence. If India had as a nation imbibed the creed of non-violence, corporate or national, I should have had no hesitation in giving a lead. But in spite of a certain hold I have on the millions of this country, I know the very grave and glaring limitation of that hold. India had an unbroken tradition of non-violence from times immemorial. But at no time in her ancient history, as far as I know it, has it had complete non-violence in action pervading the whole land. Nevertheless, it is my unshakeable belief that her destiny is to deliver the message of non-violence to mankind. It may take ages to come to fruition. But so far as I can judge, no other country will precede her in the fulfillment of that mission.

Be that as it may, it is seasonable to contemplate the implications of that matchless force. Three concrete questions were, the other day, incidentally asked by friends:

1. What could ill-armed Abyssinia do against well-armed Italy, if she were non-violent?
2. What could England, the greatest and the most powerful member of the League, do against determined Italy, if she (England) were non-violent in your sense of the term?
3. What could India do, if she suddenly became non-violent in your sense of the term?

Before I answer the questions let me lay down five simple axioms of non-violence as I know it:

1. Non-violence implies as complete self-purification as is humanly possible.
2. Man for man the strength of non-violence is in exact proportion to the ability, not the will, of the non-violent person to inflict violence.
3. Non-violence is without exception superior to violence, i.e., the power at the disposal of a non-violent person is always greater than he could have if he was violent.
4. There is no such thing as defeat in non-violence. The end of violence is surest defeat.
5. The ultimate end of non-violence is surest victory—if such a term may be used of non-violence. In reality where there is no sense of defeat, there is no sense of victory.

The foregoing questions may be answered in the light of these axioms.

1. If Abyssinia were non-violent, she would have no arms, would want none. She would make no appeal to the League or any other power for armed

intervention. She would never give any cause for complaint. And Italy would find nothing to conquer if Abyssinians would not offer armed resistance, nor would they give co-operation willing or forced. Italian occupation in that case would mean that of the land without its people. That, however, is not Italy's exact object. She seeks submission of the people of the beautiful land.

2. If Englishmen were as a nation to become non-violent at heart, they would shed imperialism, they would give up the use of arms. The moral force generated by such an act of renunciation would stagger Italy into willing surrender of her designs. England would then be a living embodiment of the axioms I have laid down. The effect of such conversion would mean the greatest miracle of all ages. And yet if non-violence is not an idle dream, some such thing has some day to come to pass somewhere. I live in that faith.
3. The last question may be answered thus. As I have said, India as a nation is not non-violent in the full sense of the term. Neither has she any capacity for offering violence—not because she has no arms. Physical possession of arms is the least necessity of the brave. Her non-violence is that of the weak. She betrays her weakness in many of her daily acts. She appears before the world today as a decaying nation. I mean here not in the mere political sense but essentially in the non-violent, moral sense. She lacks the ability to offer physical resistance. She has no consciousness of strength. She is conscious only of her weakness. If she were otherwise, there would be no communal problems, nor political. If she were nonviolent in the consciousness of her strength, Englishmen would lose their role of distrustful conquerors. We may talk politically as we like and often legitimately blame the English rulers. But if we, as Indians, could but for a moment visualize ourselves as a strong people disdaining to strike, we should cease to fear Englishmen whether as soldiers, traders or administrators, and they to distrust us. Therefore if we became truly non-violent we should carry Englishmen with us in all we might do. In other words, we being millions would be the greatest moral force in the world, and Italy would listen to our friendly word.

The reader has, I hope, by now perceived that my argument is but a feeble and clumsy attempt to prove my axioms which to be such must be self-proved.

Till my eyes of geometrical understanding had been opened, my brain was swimming, as I read and re-read the twelve axioms of Euclid. After the opening of my eyes geometry seemed to be the easiest science to learn. Much more so is the case with non-violence. It is a matter of faith and experience, not of argument beyond a point. So long as the world refuses to believe, she must await a miracle, i.e., an ocular demonstration of non-violence on a mass scale. They say this is against human nature—non-violence is only for the individual. If so, where is the difference in kind between man and beast?

"The Greatest Force"
Harijan, 12 Oct. 1935

A London friend has put seven questions on the working of non-violence. Though similar questions have been dealt with in *Young India* or *Harijan*, it is profitable to answer them in a single article, if perchance the answers may prove helpful.

Q. 1. Is it possible for a modern State (which is essentially based on force) to offer non-violent resistance for countering internal as well as external forces of disorder? Or is it necessary that people wanting to offer non-violent resistance should first of all divest themselves of State-authority and place themselves vis-à-vis the opponent entirely in a private capacity?

A. It is not possible for a modern State based on force, non-violently to resist forces of disorder, whether external or internal. A man cannot serve God and Mammon, nor be "temperate and furious" at the same time. It is claimed that a State can be based on non-violence, i.e., it can offer nonviolent resistance against a world combination based on armed force. Such a State was Ashoka's. The example can be repeated. But the case does not become weak even if it be shown that Ashoka's State was not based on non-violence. It has to be examined on its merits.

Q. 2. Do you think that it would be possible for a Congress government to deal with foreign aggression or internal riots in an entirely non-violent manner?

A. It is certainly possible for a Congress government to deal with "foreign aggression or internal riots" in a non-violent manner. That the Congress may not share my belief is quite possible. If the Congress changes its course, the change will prove nothing save that the non-violence hitherto offered was of the weak and that the Congress has no faith in State nonviolence.

Q. 3. Does not the knowledge that the opponent is wedded to nonviolence often encourage the bully?

A. The bully has his opportunity when he has to face non-violence of the weak. Non-violence of the strong is any day stronger than that of the bravest soldier fully armed or a whole host.

Q. 4. What policy would you advocate if a section of the Indian people tries to enforce by sword a selfish measure which is not only repugnant to others but also basically unjust? While it is possible for an unofficial organization to offer non-violent resistance in such a case, is it also possible for the government of the day to do so?

A. The question assumes a case which can never exist. A non-violent State must be broad-based on the will of an intelligent people, well able to know its mind and act up to it. In such a State the assumed section can only be negligible. It can never stand against the deliberate will of the overwhelming majority represented by the State. The government of the day is not outside the people. It is the will of the overwhelming majority. If it is expressed non-violently, it cannot be a majority of one but nearer 99 against one in a hundred.

Q. 5. Is not non-violent resistance by the militarily strong more effective than that by the militarily weak?

A. This is a contradiction in terms. There can be no nonviolence offered by the militarily strong. Thus, Russia in order to express non-violence has to discard all her power of doing violence. What is true is that if those, who were at one time strong in armed might, change their mind, they will be better able to demonstrate their non-violence to the world and, therefore, also to their opponents. Those who are strong in non-violence will not mind whether they are opposed by the militarily weak people or the strongest.

Q. 6. What should be the training and discipline for a non-violent army? Should not certain aspects of conventional military training form a part of the syllabus?

A. A very small part of the preliminary training received by the military is common to the non-violent army. These are discipline, drill, singing in chorus, flag-hoisting, signaling and the like. Even this is not absolutely necessary and the basis is different. The positively necessary training for a violent army is an immovable faith in God, willing and perfect obedience to the chief of the non-violent army and perfect inward and outward co-operation between the units of the army.

Q. 7. Is it not better under the existing circumstances that countries like India and England should maintain full military efficiency while resolving to give non-violent resistance a reasonable trial before taking any military step?

A. The foregoing answers should make it clear that under no circumstance can India and England give non-violent resistance a reasonable chance whilst they are both maintaining full military efficiency. At the same time it is perfectly true that all military powers carry on negotiations for peaceful adjustment of rival disputes. But here we are not discussing preliminary peace parleys before appealing to the arbitrament of war. We are discussing a final substitute for armed conflict called war, in naked terms, mass murder.

CHAPTER 31

Excerpt from Love, Law, and Civil Disobedience

By Martin Luther King Jr.

But there is another way, namely the way of nonviolent resistance. This method was popularized in our generation by a little man from India, whose name was Mohandas K. Gandhi. He used this method in a magnificent way to free his people from the economic exploitation and the political domination inflicted upon them by a foreign power.

This has been the method used by the student movement in the South and all over the United States. And naturally whenever I talk about the student movement I cannot be totally objective. I have to be somewhat subjective because of my great admiration for what the students have done. For in a real sense they have taken our deep groans and passionate yearnings for freedom, and filtered them in their own tender souls, and fashioned them into a creative protest which is an epic known all over our nation. As a result of their disciplined, nonviolent, yet courageous struggle, they have been able to do wonders in the South, and in our nation. But this movement does have an underlying philosophy, it has certain ideas that are attached to it, it has certain philosophical precepts. These are the things that I would like to discuss for the few moments left.

I would say that the first point or the first principle in the movement is the idea that means must be as pure as the end. This movement is based on the philosophy that ends and means must cohere. Now this has been one of the long struggles in history, the whole idea of means and ends. Great philosophers have grappled with it, and sometimes they have emerged with the idea, from Machiavelli on down, that the end justifies the means. There is a great system of thought in our world today, known as communism. And I think that with all of the weakness and tragedies of communism, we find its greatest tragedy right here, that it goes under the philosophy that the end justifies the means that are used in the process. So we can read or we can hear the Lenins say that lying, deceit, or violence, that many of these things justify the ends of the classless society.

This is where the student movement and the nonviolent movement that is taking place in our nation would break with communism and any other system that would argue that the end justifies the means. For in the long run, we must see that the end represents the means in process and the ideal in the making. In other words, we cannot believe, or we cannot go with the idea that the end justifies the means because the end is preexistent in the means. So the idea of nonviolent resistance, the philosophy of nonviolent resistance, is the philosophy which says that the means must be as pure as the end, that in the long run of history, immoral destructive means cannot bring about moral and constructive ends.

There is another thing about this philosophy, this method of nonviolence which is followed by the student movement. It says that those who adhere to or follow this philosophy must follow a consistent principle of noninjury. They must consistently refuse to inflict injury upon another. Sometimes you will read the literature of the student movement and see that, as they are getting ready for the sit-in or stand-in, they will read something like this, "If you are hit do not hit back, if you are cursed do not curse back." This is the whole idea, that the individual who is engaged in a nonviolent struggle must never inflict injury upon another. Now this has an external aspect and it has an internal one. From the external point of view it means that the individuals involved must avoid external physical violence. So they don't have guns, they don't retaliate with physical violence. If they are hit in the process, they avoid external physical violence at every point. But it also means that they avoid internal violence of spirit. This is why the love ethic stands so high in the student movement. We have a great deal of talk about love and nonviolence in this whole thrust.

Now when the students talk about love, certainly they are not talking about emotional bosh, they are not talking about merely a sentimental outpouring; they're talking something much deeper, and I always have to stop and try to define the meaning of love in this context. The Greek language comes to our aid in trying to deal with this. There are three words in the Greek language for love; one is the word *eros*. This is a beautiful type of love, it is an aesthetic love. Plato talks about it a great deal in his Dialogue, the yearning of the soul for the realm of the divine. It has come to us to be a sort of romantic love, and so in a sense we have read about it and experienced it. We've read about it in all the beauties of literature. I guess in a sense Edgar Allan Poe was talking about *eros* when he talked about his beautiful Annabelle Lee, with the love surrounded by the halo of eternity. In a sense Shakespeare was talking about *eros* when he said "Love is not love which alters when it alteration finds, or bends with the remover to remove; O'no! It is an ever fixed mark that looks on tempests and is never shaken, it is the star to every wandering bark." (You know, I remember that because I used to quote it to this little lady when we were courting; that's *eros*.) The Greek language talks about *philia* which was another level of love. It is an intimate affection between personal friends, it is a reciprocal love. On this level you love because you are loved. It is friendship.

Then the Greek language comes out with another word which is called the *agape*. *Agape* is more than romantic love, *agape* is more than friendship. *Agape* is understanding, creative, redemptive, good will to all men. It is an overflowing love which seeks nothing in return. Theologians would say that it is the love of God operating in the human heart. So that when one rises to love on this level, he loves men not because he likes them, not because their ways appeal to him, but he loves every man because God loves him. And he rises to the point of loving the person who does an evil deed while hating the deed that the person does. I think this is what Jesus meant when he said "love your enemies." I'm very happy that he didn't say like your enemies, because it is pretty difficult to like some people. Like is sentimental, and it is pretty difficult to like someone bombing your home; it is pretty difficult to like somebody threatening your children; it is difficult to like congressmen who spend all of their time trying to defeat civil rights. But Jesus says love them, and love is greater than like. Love is understanding, redemptive, creative, good will for all men. And it is this idea, it is this whole ethic of love which is the idea standing at the basis of the student movement.

There is something else: that one seeks to defeat the unjust system, rather than individuals who are caught in that system. And that one goes on believing that somehow this is the important thing, to get rid of the evil system and not the individual who happens to be misguided, who happens to be misled, who was taught wrong. The thing to do is to get rid of the system and thereby create a moral balance within society.

Another thing that stands at the center of this movement is another idea: that suffering can be a most creative and powerful social force. Suffering has certain moral attributes involved, but it can be a powerful and creative social force. Now, it is very interesting at this point to notice that both violence and nonviolence agree that suffering can be a very powerful social force. But there is this difference: violence says that suffering can be a powerful social force by inflicting the suffering on somebody else: so this is what we do in war, this is what we do in the whole violent thrust of the violent movement. It believes that you achieve some end by inflicting suffering on another. The nonviolent say that suffering becomes a powerful social force when you willingly accept that violence on yourself, so that self-suffering stands at the center of the nonviolent movement and the individuals involved are able to suffer in a creative manner, feeling that unearned suffering is redemptive, and that suffering may serve to transform the social situation.

Another thing in this movement is the idea that there is within human nature an amazing potential for goodness. There is within human nature something that can respond to goodness. I know somebody's liable to say that this is an unrealistic movement if it goes on believing that all people are good. Well, I didn't say that. I think the students are realistic enough to believe that there is a strange dichotomy of disturbing dualism within human nature. Many of the great philosophers and thinkers through the ages have seen this. It caused Ovid the Latin poet to say, "I see and approve the better things of life, but the evil things I do." It caused even Saint Augustine to say "Lord, make me pure, but not yet." So that that is in human nature. Plato, centuries ago said that the human personality is like a charioteer with two headstrong horses, each wanting to go in different directions, so that within our own individual lives we see this conflict and certainly when we come to the collective life of man, we see a strange badness. But in spite of this there is something in human nature that can respond to goodness. So that man is neither innately good nor is he innately bad; he has potentialities for both. So in this sense, Carlyle was right when he said that, "there are depths in man which go down to the lowest hell, and heights which reach the highest heaven, for are not both heaven and hell made out of him, ever-lasting miracle and mystery that he is?" Man has the capacity to be good, man has the capacity to be evil.

And so the nonviolent resister never lets this idea go, that there is something within human nature than can respond to goodness. So that a Jesus of Nazareth or a Mohandas Gandhi, can appeal to human beings and appeal to that element of goodness within them, and a Hitler can appeal to the element of evil within them. But we must never forget that there is something within human nature that can respond to goodness, that man is not totally depraved; to put it in theological terms, the image of God is never totally gone. And so the individuals who believe in this movement and who believe in nonviolence and our struggle in the South, somehow believe that even the worst segrationist can become an integrationist. Now sometimes it is hard to believe that this is what this movement says, and it believes it firmly, that there is something within human nature that can be changed, and this stands at the top of the whole philosophy of the student movement and the philosophy of nonviolence.

It says something else. It says that it is as much a moral obligation to refuse to cooperate with evil as it is to cooperate with good. Noncooperation with evil is as much a moral obligation as the cooperation with good. So that the student movement is willing to stand up courageously on the idea of civil disobedience. Now I think this is the part of the student movement that is probably misunderstood more than anything else. And it is a difficult aspect, because on the one hand the students would say, and I would say, and all the people who believe in civil rights would say, obey the Supreme Court's decision of 1954 and at the same time, we would disobey certain laws that exist on the statutes of the South today.

This brings in the whole question of how can you be logically consistent when you advocate obeying some laws and disobeying other laws. Well, I think one would have to see the whole meaning of this movement at this point by seeing that the students recognize that there are two types of laws. There are just laws and there are unjust laws. And they would be the first to say obey the just laws, they would be the first to say that men and women have a moral obligation to obey just and right laws. And they would go on to say that we must see that there are unjust laws. Now the question comes into being, what is the difference, and who determines the difference, what is the difference between a just and an unjust law?

Well, a just law is a law that squares with a moral law. It is a law that squares with that which is right, so that any law that uplifts human personality is a just law. Whereas that law which is out of harmony with the moral is a law which does not square with the moral law of the universe. It does not square with the law of God, so for that reason it is unjust and any law that degrades the human personality is an unjust law.

Well, somebody says that that does not mean anything to me; first, I don't believe in these abstract things called moral laws and I'm not too religious, so I don't believe in the law of God; you have to get a little more concrete, and more practical. What do you mean when you say that a law is unjust, and a law is just? Well, I would go on to say in more concrete terms that an unjust law is a code that the majority inflicts on the minority that is not binding on itself. So that this becomes difference made legal. Another thing that we can say is that an unjust law is a code which the majority inflicts upon the minority, which that minority had no part in enacting or creating, because that minority had no right to vote in many instances, so that the legislative bodies that made these laws were not democratically elected. Who could ever say that the legislative body of Mississippi was democratically elected, or the legislative body of Alabama was democratically elected, or the legislative body even of Georgia has been democratically elected, when there are people in Terrell County and in other counties because of the color of their skin who cannot vote? They confront reprisals and threats and all of that; so that an unjust law is a law that individuals did not have a part in creating or enacting because they were denied the right to vote.

Now the same token of just law would be just the opposite. A just law becomes saneness made legal. It is a code that the majority, who happen to believe in that code, compel the minority, who don't believe in it, to follow, because they are willing to follow it themselves, so it is saneness made legal. Therefore the individuals who stand up on the basis of civil disobedience realize that they are following something that says that there are just laws and there are unjust laws. Now, they are not anarchists. They believe that there are laws which must be followed; they do not seek to defy the law, they do not seek to evade the law. For many individuals who would call themselves segregationists and who would hold on to segregation at any cost seek to defy the law, they seek to evade the law, and their process can lead on into anarchy. They seek in the final analysis to follow a way of uncivil disobedience, not civil disobedience. And I submit that the individual who disobeys the law, whose conscience tells him it is unjust and who is willing to accept the penalty by staying in jail until that law is altered, is expressing at the moment the very highest respect for law.

This is what the students have followed in their movement. Of course there is nothing new about this; they feel that they are in good company and rightly so. We go back and read the Apology and the Crito, and you see Socrates practicing civil disobedience. And to a degree academic freedom is a reality today because Socrates practiced civil disobedience. The early Christians practiced civil disobedience in a superb manner, to a point where they were willing to be thrown to the lions. They were willing to face all kinds of suffering in order to stand up for what they knew was right even though they knew it was against the laws of the Roman Empire.

We could come up to our own day and we see it in many instances. We must never forget that everything that Hitler did in Germany was "legal." It was illegal to aid and comfort a Jew, in the days of Hitler's Germany. But I believe that if I had the same attitude then as I have now I would publicly aid and comfort my Jewish brothers in Germany if Hitler were alive today calling this an illegal process. If I lived in South Africa today in the midst of the white supremacy law in South Africa, I would join Chief Luthuli and others in saying break these unjust laws. And even let us come up to America. Our nation in a sense came into being through a massive act of civil disobedience for the Boston Tea Party was nothing but a massive act of civil disobedience. Those who stood up against the slave laws, the abolitionists, by and large practiced civil disobedience. So I think these students are in good company, and they feel that by practicing civil disobedience they are in line with men and women through the ages who have stood up for something that is morally right.

Now there are one or two other things that I want to say about this student movement, moving out of the philosophy of nonviolence, something about what it is a revolt against. On the one hand it is a revolt against the negative peace that has encompassed the South for many years. I remember when I was in Montgomery, Alabama, one of the white citizens came to me one day and said—and I think he was very sincere about this—that in Montgomery for all of these years we have been such a peaceful community, we have had so much harmony in race relations and then you people have started this movement and boycott, and it has done so much to disturb race relations, and we just don't love the Negro like we used to love them, because you have destroyed the harmony and the peace that we once had in race relations. And I said to him, in the best way I could say and I tried to say it in nonviolent terms, we have never had peace in Montgomery, Alabama, we have never had peace in the South. We have had a negative peace, which is merely the absence of tension; we've had a negative peace in which the Negro patiently accepted his situation and his plight, but we've never had true peace, we've never had positive peace, and what we're seeking now is to develop this positive peace. For we must come to see that peace is not merely the absence of some negative force, it is the presence of a positive force. True peace is not merely the absence of tension, but it is the presence of justice and brotherhood. I think this is what Jesus meant when he said, "I come not to bring peace but a sword." Now Jesus didn't mean he came to start war, to bring a physical sword, and he didn't mean, I come not to bring positive peace. But I think what Jesus was saying in substance was this, that I come not to bring an old negative peace, which makes for stagnant passivity and deadening complacency, I come to bring something different, and whenever I come, a conflict is precipitated, between the old and the new, whenever I come a struggle takes place between justice and injustice, between the forces of light and the forces of darkness. I come not to bring a negative peace, but a positive peace, which is brotherhood, which is justice, which is the Kingdom of God.

CHAPTER 32

Beloved Community: A World Without Racism

By bell hooks

Some days it is just hard to accept that racism can still be such a powerful dominating force in all our lives. When I remember all that black and white folks together have sacrificed to challenge and change white supremacy, when I remember the individuals who gave their lives to the cause of racial justice, my heart is deeply saddened that we have not fulfilled their shared dream of ending racism, of creating a new culture, a place for the *beloved community*. Early on in his work for civil fights, long before his consciousness had been deeply radicalized by resistance to militarism and global Western imperialism, Martin Luther King imagined a *beloved community* where race would be transcended, forgotten, where no one would see skin color. This dream has not been realized. From its inception it was a flawed vision. The flaw, however, was not the imagining of a *beloved community*; it was the insistence that such a community could exist only if we erased and forgot racial difference.

Many citizens of these United States still long to live in a society where *beloved community* can be formed—where loving ties of care and knowing bind us together in our differences. We cannot surrender that longing—if we do we will never see an end to racism. These days it is an untalked-about longing. Most folks in this society have become so cynical about ending racism, so convinced that solidarity across racial differences can never be a reality, that they make no effort to build community. Those of us who are not cynical, who still cherish the vision of *beloved community*, sustain our conviction that we need such bonding not because we cling to utopian fantasies but because we have struggled all our lives to create this community. In my blackness I have struggled together with white comrades in the segregated South. Sharing that struggle we came to know deeply, intimately, with all our minds and hearts that we can all divest of racism and white supremacy if we so desire. We divest through our commitment to and engagement with anti-racist struggle. Even though that commitment was first made in the mind and heart, it is realized by concrete action, by anti-racist living and being.

Over the years my love and admiration for those black and white southerners in my hometown who worked together to realize racial justice deepens, as does their love of me. We have gone off from that time of legalized segregation to create intimate lives for ourselves that include loving engagement with all races and ethnicities. The small circles of love we have managed to form in our individual lives represent a concrete realistic reminder that *beloved community* is not a dream, that it already exists for those of us who have done the work of educating ourselves for critical consciousness in ways that enabled a letting go of white supremacist assumptions and values. The process of decolonization (unlearning white supremacy by divesting of white privilege if we were white or vestiges of internalized racism if we were black) transformed our minds and our habits of being.

In the segregated South those black and white folks who struggled together for racial justice (many of whom grounded their actions not in radical politics but in religious conviction) were bound by a shared belief in the transformative power of love. Understanding that love was the antithesis of the will to dominate and subjugate, we allowed that longing to know love, to love one another, to radicalize us politically. That love was not sentimental. It did not blind us to the reality that racism was deeply systemic and that only by realizing that love in concrete political actions that might involve sacrifice, even the surrender of one's life, would white supremacy be fundamentally challenged. We knew the sweetness of *beloved community*.

What those of us who have not died now know, that generations before us did not grasp, was that *beloved community* is formed not by the eradication of difference but by its affirmation, by each of us claiming the identities and cultural legacies that shape who we are and how we live in the world. To form *beloved community* we do not surrender ties to precious origins. We deepen those bondings by connecting them with an anti-racist struggle which is at heart always a movement to disrupt that clinging to cultural legacies that demands investment in notions of racial purity, authenticity, nationalist fundamentalism. The notion that differences of skin color, class background, and cultural heritage must be erased for justice and equality to prevail is a brand of popular false consciousness that helps keep racist thinking and action intact. Most folks are threatened by the notion that they must give up allegiances to specific cultural legacies in order to have harmony. Such suspicion is healthy. Unfortunately, as long as our society holds up a vision of democracy that requires the surrender of bonds and ties to legacies folks hold dear, challenging racism and white supremacy will seem like an action that diminishes and destabilizes.

The misguided idea that one must give cultural allegiance to create harmony positively emerged from religious freedom fighters whose faith urged them to let go attachment to the things of this world (status, ethnicity, national allegiances) in order to be one with God. Negatively, it has been appropriated by the enemies of anti-racist struggle to further tensions between different racial groups, to breed fundamentalist and nationalistic feelings and support for racial separatism. Since the notion that we should all forsake attachment to race and/or cultural identity and be "just humans" within the framework of white supremacy has usually meant that subordinate groups must surrender their identities, beliefs, values and assimilate by adopting the values and beliefs of privileged class whites, rather than promoting racial harmony this thinking has created a fierce cultural protectionism. That conservative force that sees itself as refusing assimilation expresses itself in the call for cultural nationalism, for disenfranchised groups to embrace separatism. This is why black leaders who espouse black separatism are gaining political power. Many black people fear that white commodification and appropriation of blackness is a neo-colonial strategy of cultural genocide that threatens to destroy our cultural legacy. That fear is not ungrounded. Black people, however, are misguided in thinking that nationalist fundamentalism is the best or only way to either preserve our heritage or to make a meaningful political response to ending racism.

In actuality, the growth of nationalist separatist thinking among black people is an extreme expression of collective cynicism about ending white supremacy. The assumption that white folks will never cease to be racist represents a refusal to privilege the history of those whites (however few) who have been willing to give their lives to the struggle for racial justice over that of white folks who maintain racist thinking—sometimes without even knowing that they hold racist assumptions. Since white supremacist attitudes and values permeate every aspect of the culture, most white folks are unconsciously absorbing the ideology of white supremacy. Since they do not realize this socialization is taking place, many of them feel that they are not racist. When these feelings are rooted in denial, the first stage of anti-racist struggle has to be breaking that denial. This is one of the primary distinctions between the generation of white folks who were raised in the midst of white supremacist apartheid, who witnessed firsthand the brutal dehumanization of black people and who knew that "racism" permeated the culture, and this contemporary generation that either engages in historical amnesia or does not remember. Prior to desegregation, few whites would have been as arrogantly convinced that they are not racists as are most whites today, some of whom never come into contact with black people. During civil rights struggle, it was commonly understood that whites seeking to live in an anti-racist world measured their progress and their commitment by their interactions with black people. How can a white person assume he or she is not racist if that assumption has not been concretely realized in interaction? It was precisely the astute recognition on the part of freedom fighters working for racial justice that anti-racist habits of being were best cultivated in situations of interaction that was at the heart of every vision of non-racist community.

Concurrently, most white Americans who believed or believe that racism is ethically and morally wrong centered their anti-racist struggle around the desire to commune with black folks. Today many white people who see themselves as non-racist are comfortable with lives where they have no contact with black people or where fear is their first response in any encounter with blackness. This "fear" is the first sign of the internalization in the white psyche of white supremacist sentiments. It serves to mask white power and privilege. In the past the affirmation of white supremacy in everyday life was declared via assertions of hatred and/or power (i.e., public and private subordination and humiliation of black folks—the white wife who sits at her dining table eating a nice lunch while the maid eats standing in the kitchen, the white male employer paying black workers less and calling them by obscene names); in our contemporary times white belief in black inferiority is most often registered by the assertion of power. Yet that power is often obscured by white focus on fear. The fear whites direct at blacks is rooted in the racist assumption that the darker race is inherently deprived, dangerous, and willing to obtain what they desire by any means necessary. Since it is assumed that whenever fear is present one is less powerful, cultivating in whites fear of blacks is a useful neo-colonial strategy as it obscures the reality that whites do much more harm to blacks daily than vice versa. It also encourages white people to believe that they do not hold power over blacks even as their ability to project fear when there is no danger is an act of denial that indicates their complicity with white supremacist thinking. Those white people who consciously break with racist thinking know that there is no concrete reality to suggest that they should be more fearful of blacks than other people, since white folks, like blacks, are likely to be harmed by people of the same race. Let me give a useful example. When I worked as an assistant professor at an Ivy League university one of my white female students was raped by a black man. Even though she had been deeply committed to anti-racist work before the rape, during her period of recovery she found that she was fearing all black men. Her commitment to anti-racist struggle led her to interrogate that fear, and she realized that had she been raped by a white male, she would not have felt all white males were responsible and should be feared. Seeing her fear of all black males as a regressive expression of white racism, she let it go. The will to be vigilant emerged from both her commitment to ending racism and her will to be in loving community with black folks. Not abandoning that longing for community is a perspective we must all embrace if racism is to end.

More than ever before in our history, black Americans are succumbing to and internalizing the racist assumption that there can be no meaningful bonds of intimacy between blacks and whites. It is fascinating to explore why it is that black people trapped in the worst situation of racial oppression—enslavement—had the foresight to see that it would be disempowering for them to lose sight of the capacity of white people to transform themselves and divest of white supremacy, even as many black folks today who in no way suffer such extreme racist oppression and exploitation are convinced that white people will not repudiate racism. Contemporary black folks, like their white counterparts, have passively accepted the internalization of white supremacist assumptions. Organized white supremacists have always taught that there can never be trust and intimacy between the superior white race and the inferior black race. When black people internalize these sentiments, no resistance to white supremacy is taking place; rather we become complicit in spreading racist notions. It does not matter that so many black people feel white people will never repudiate racism because of being daily assaulted by white denial and refusal of accountability. We must not allow the actions of white folks who blindly endorse racism to determine the direction of our resistance. Like our white allies in struggle we must consistently keep the faith, by always sharing the truth that white people can be anti-racist, that racism is not some immutable character flaw.

Of course many white people are comfortable with a rhetoric of race that suggests racism cannot be changed, that all white people are "inherently racist" simply because they are born and raised in this society. Such misguided thinking socializes white people both to remain ignorant of the way in which white supremacist attitudes are learned and to assume a posture of learned helplessness as though they have no agency—no capacity to resist this thinking. Luckily we have many autobiographies by white folks committed to anti-racist struggle that provide documentary testimony that many of these individuals repudiated racism when they were children. Far from passively accepting it as inherent, they instinctively felt it was wrong. Many of them witnessed bizarre acts of white racist aggression towards black folks in everyday life and responded to the injustice of the situation. Sadly, in our times so many white folks are easily convinced by racist whites and black folks who have internalized racism that they can never be really free of racism.

These feelings also then obscure the reality of white privilege. As long as white folks are taught to accept racism as "natural" then they do not have to see themselves as consciously creating a racist society by their actions, by their political choices. This means as well that they do not have to face the way in which acting in a racist manner ensures the maintenance of white privilege. Indeed, denying their agency allows them to believe white privilege does not exist even as they daily exercise it. If the young white woman who had been raped had chosen to hold all black males accountable for what happened, she would have been exercising white privilege and reinforcing the structure of racist thought which teaches that all black people are alike. Unfortunately, so many white people are eager to believe racism cannot be changed because internalizing that assumption downplays the issue of accountability. No responsibility need be taken for not changing something if it is perceived as immutable. To accept racism as a system of domination that can be changed would demand that everyone who sees him- or herself as embracing a vision of racial social equality would be required to assert anti-racist habits of being. We know from histories both present and past that white people (and everyone else) who commit themselves to living in anti-racist ways need to make sacrifices, to courageously endure the uncomfortable to challenge and change.

Whites, people of color, and black folks are reluctant to commit themselves fully and deeply to an anti-racist struggle that is ongoing because there is such a pervasive feeling of hopelessness—a conviction that nothing will ever change. How any of us can continue to hold those feelings when we study the history of racism in this society and see how much has changed makes no logical sense. Clearly we have not gone far enough. In the late sixties, Martin Luther King posed the question "Where do we go from here." To live in an anti-racist society we must collectively renew our commitment to a democratic vision of racial justice and equality. Pursuing that vision we create a culture where *beloved community* flourishes and is sustained. Those of us who know the joy of being with folks from all walks of life, all races, who are fundamentally anti-racist in their habits of being, need to give public testimony. We need to share not only what we have experienced but the conditions of change that make such an experience possible. The interracial circle of love that I know can happen because each individual present in it has made his or her own commitment to living an anti-racist life and to furthering the struggle to end white supremacy will become a reality for everyone only if those of us who have created these communities share how they emerge in our lives and the strategies we use to sustain them. Our devout commitment to building diverse communities is central. These commitments to anti-racist living are just one expression of who we are and what we share with one another but they form the foundation of that sharing. Like all *beloved communities* we affirm our differences. It is this generous spirit of affirmation that gives us the courage to challenge one another, to work through misunderstandings, especially those that have to do with race and racism. In a beloved community solidarity and trust are grounded in profound commitment to a shared vision. Those of us who are always anti-racist long for a world in which everyone can form a *beloved community* where borders can be crossed and cultural hybridity celebrated. Anyone can begin to make such a community by truly seeking to live in an anti-racist world. If that longing guides our vision and our actions, the new culture will be born and anti-racist communities of resistance will emerge everywhere. That is where we must go from here.

CHAPTER 33

Freedom from Fear

By Aung San Suu Kyi

It is not power that corrupts but fear. Fear of losing power corrupts those who wield it and fear of the scourge of power corrupts those who are subject to it. Most Burmese are familiar with the four *a-gati*, the four kinds of corruption. *Chanda-gati*, corruption induced by desire, is deviation from the right path in pursuit of bribes or for the sake of those one loves. *Dosa-gati* is taking the wrong path to spite those against whom one bears ill will, and *moha-gati* is aberration due to ignorance. But perhaps the worst of the four is *bhaya-gati*, for not only does *bhaya*, fear, stifle and slowly destroy all sense of right and wrong, it so often lies at the root of the other three kinds of corruption.

Just as *chanda-gati*, when not the result of sheer avarice, can be caused by fear of want or fear of losing the goodwill of those one loves, so fear of being surpassed, humiliated or injured in some way can provide the impetus for ill will. And it would be difficult to dispel ignorance unless there is freedom to pursue the truth unfettered by fear. With so close a relationship between fear and corruption it is little wonder that in any society where fear is rife corruption in all forms becomes deeply entrenched.

Public dissatisfaction with economic hardships has been seen as the chief cause of the movement for democracy in Burma, sparked off by the student demonstrations of 1988. It is true that years of incoherent policies, inept official measures, burgeoning inflation and falling real income had turned the country into an economic shambles. But it was more than the difficulties of eking out a barely acceptable standard of living that had eroded the patience of a traditionally good-natured, quiescent people—it was also the humiliation of a way of life disfigured by corruption and fear. The students were protesting not just against the death of their comrades but against the denial of their right to life by a totalitarian regime which deprived the present of meaningfulness and held out no hope for the future. And because the students' protests articulated the frustrations of the people at large, the demonstrations quickly grew into a nationwide movement. Some of its keenest supporters were businessmen who had developed the skills and the contacts necessary not only to survive but to prosper within the system. But their affluence offered them no genuine sense of security or fulfillment, and they could not but see that if they and their fellow citizens, regardless of economic status, were to achieve a worthwhile existence, an accountable administration was at least a necessary if not a sufficient condition. The people of Burma had wearied of a precarious state of passive apprehension where they were "as water in the cupped hands" of the powers that be.

> Emerald cool we may be
> As water in cupped hands
> But oh that we might be
> As splinters of glass
> In cupped hands.

Glass splinters, the smallest with its sharp, glinting power to defend itself against hands that try to crush, could be seen as a vivid symbol of the spark of courage that is an essential attribute of those who would free themselves from the grip of oppression. Bogyoke Aung San regarded himself as a revolutionary and searched tirelessly for answers to the problems that beset Burma during her times of trial. He exhorted the people to develop courage: "Don't just depend on the courage and intrepidity of others. Each and every one of you must make sacrifices to become a hero possessed of courage and intrepidity. Then only shall we all be able to enjoy true freedom."

The effort necessary to remain uncorrupted in an environment where fear is an integral part of everyday existence is not immediately apparent to those fortunate enough to live in states governed by the rule of law. Just laws do not merely prevent corruption by meting out impartial punishment to offenders. They also help to create a society in which people can fulfil the basic requirements necessary for the preservation of human dignity without recourse to corrupt practices. Where there are no such laws, the burden of upholding the principles of justice and common decency falls on the ordinary people. It is the cumulative effect of their sustained effort and steady endurance which will change a nation where reason and conscience are warped by fear into one where legal rules exist to promote man's desire for harmony and justice while restraining the less desirable destructive traits in his nature.

In an age when immense technological advances have created lethal weapons which could be, and are, used by the powerful and the unprincipled to dominate the weak and the helpless, there is a compelling need for a closer relationship between politics and ethics at both the national and international levels. The Universal Declaration of Human Rights of the United Nations proclaims that "every individual and every organ of society" should strive to promote the basic rights and freedoms to which all human beings regardless of race, nationality or religion are entitled. But as long as there are governments whose authority is founded on coercion rather than on the mandate of the people, and interest groups which place short-term profits above long-term peace and prosperity, concerted international action to protect and promote human rights will remain at best a partially realized ideal. There will continue to be arenas of struggle where victims of oppression have to draw on their own inner resources to defend their inalienable rights as members of the human family.

The quintessential revolution is that of the spirit, born of an intellectual conviction of the need for change in those mental attitudes and values which shape the course of a nation's development. A revolution which aims merely at changing official policies and institutions with a view to an improvement in material conditions has little chance of genuine success. Without a revolution of the spirit, the forces which produced the iniquities of the old order would continue to be operative, posing a constant threat to the process of reform and regeneration. It is not enough merely to call for freedom, democracy and human rights. There has to be a united determination to persevere in the struggle, to make sacrifices in the name of enduring truths, to resist the corrupting influences of desire, ill will, ignorance and fear.

Saints, it has been said, are the sinners who go on trying. So free men are the oppressed who go on trying and who in the process make themselves fit to bear the responsibilities and to uphold the disciplines which will maintain a free society. Among the basic freedoms to which men aspire that their lives might be full and uncramped, freedom from fear stands out as both a means and an end. A people who would build a nation in which strong, democratic institutions are firmly established as a guarantee against state-induced power must first learn to liberate their own minds from apathy and fear.

Always one to practise what he preached, Aung San himself constantly demonstrated courage—not just the physical sort but the kind that enabled him to speak the truth, to stand by his word, to accept criticism, to admit his faults, to correct his mistakes, to respect the opposition, to parley with the enemy and to let people be the judge of his worthiness as a leader. It is for such moral courage that he will always be loved and respected in Burma—not merely as a warrior hero but as the inspiration and conscience of the nation. The words used by Jawaharlal Nehru to describe Mahatma Gandhi could well be applied to Aung San: "The essence of his teaching was fearlessness and truth, and action allied to these, always keeping the welfare of the masses in view."

Gandhi, that great apostle of non-violence, and Aung San, the founder of a national army, were very different personalities, but as there is an inevitable sameness about the challenges of authoritarian rule anywhere at any time, so there is a similarity in the intrinsic qualities of those who rise up to meet the challenge. Nehru, who considered the instillation of courage in the people of India one of Gandhi's greatest achievements, was a political modernist, but as he assessed the needs for a twentieth-century movement for independence, he found himself looking back to the philosophy of ancient India: 'The greatest gift for an individual or a nation . . . was *abhaya*, fearlessness, not merely bodily courage but absence of fear from the mind."

Fearlessness may be a gift but perhaps more precious is the courage acquired through endeavour, courage that comes from cultivating the habit of refusing to let fear dictate one's actions, courage that could be described as "grace under pressure"—grace which is renewed repeatedly in the face of harsh, unremitting pressure.

Within a system which denies the existence of basic human rights, fear tends to be the order of the day. Fear of imprisonment, fear of torture, fear of death, fear of losing friends, family, property or means of livelihood, fear of poverty, fear of isolation, fear of failure. A most insidious form of fear is that which masquerades as common sense or even wisdom, condemning as foolish, reckless, insignificant or futile the small, daily acts of courage which help to preserve man's self-respect and inherent human dignity. It is not easy for a people conditioned by the iron rule of the principle that might is right to free themselves from the enervating miasma of fear. Yet even under the most crushing state machinery courage rises up again and again, for fear is not the natural state of civilized man.

The wellspring of courage and endurance in the face of unbridled power is generally a firm belief in the sanctity of ethical principles combined with a historical sense that despite all setbacks the condition of man is set on an ultimate course for both spiritual and material advancement. It is his capacity for self-improvement and self-redemption which most distinguishes man from the mere brute. At the root of human responsibility is the concept of perfection, the urge to achieve it, the intelligence to find a path towards it, and the will to follow that path if not to the end at least the distance needed to rise above individual limitations and environmental impediments. It is man's vision of a world fit for rational, civilized humanity which leads him to dare and to suffer to build societies free from want and fear. Concepts such as truth, justice and compassion cannot be dismissed as trite when these are often the only bulwarks which stand against ruthless power.

CHAPTER 34

Beyond Just War and Pacifism: Nonviolent Struggle towards Justice, Freedom and Peace

By Gene Sharp

NONVIOLENT STRUGGLE AS A REALISTIC OPTION

Although major advances have been made, the world is still a long way from achievement of justice, freedom and peace. A major political and moral issue is how those goals may be achieved. This article first explores briefly the potential role of nonviolent struggle in advancing those goals, then surveys official statements by several Christian churches and ecumenical bodies on the potential contributions of nonviolent action to achieve those objectives. Together, this exploration and these statements have implications for a reconsideration of the current relevance of the traditional just war and pacifist contending positions. They also have implications for constructive action to develop the consideration and application of nonviolent struggle.

This discussion is based on the following assumptions:

- It is desirable for religious believers to deal responsibly with the issue of how to apply their principles to meet the problems of people who live in a very imperfect world and who face violations of justice, freedom and peace.
- We all share a responsibility to help people to achieve those goals themselves, to lift their oppression and to prevent and defeat violence and aggression against them.
- It is necessary and desirable to work with people with differing convictions who share a commitment to justice, freedom and peace and a willingness to act in ways which are compatible with moral principles and which respect human dignity. We are using the terms "justice," "freedom" and "peace" in the following senses:

Social justice is a condition in which all people are treated fairly and with respect, without domination, exploitation or oppression. The achievement of social justice is likely to require both means of struggle for popular empowerment and also means of constructing a more just society.

Freedom includes democratic participation in decision-making, personal and civil liberties and respect for others. It is always imperfectly achieved. New dangers to freedoms may arise from unexpected sources. Even in the best of democracies, there are often restrictions on civil liberties, manipulative controls may be applied and threats to democratic structures may arise from coups d'état and expansionist regimes. These require effective countermeasures. We also need potent programmes to prevent the rise of new dictatorships and to disintegrate existing ones.

Peace, as defined here, is the absence of or the ending of military hostilities between contending states or other fighting units (as in a civil war). A society at peace will be imperfect and usually will encompass internal conflicts and efforts to improve the society while preserving its meritorious qualities.

Peace does not always come to those who are peaceful. Peace is far from assured, despite the end of the cold war. Frequently peace is violated by military aggression, coups d'état, civil wars, bloodbaths and mass slaughters. Continuing threats to peace are posed by massive accumulations of military weaponry and the spread of nuclear, chemical and biological weapons.

Defence is needed against violations of peace. Important questions are: (1) How can defence be achieved without contributing to massive slaughters and violating religious and humane barriers against massive violence? and (2) How can attacks be prevented and defeated and peace be restored which is compatible with justice and freedom?

The goals of justice, freedom and peace are generally recognized to be good. The problems mostly concern how to achieve and preserve them. If people are not passively to submit to oppression and attacks, they must have effective means of wielding power. It is usually assumed that against great evil it is necessary to wage military struggle, perhaps with certain restrictions on the means used (*jus in bello*).

People have usually considered that alternative means of effective struggle without violence are unavailable. Violence has been perceived as the means of last resort, assumed almost axiomatically to be the most powerful means of struggle that can be used. Conflicts will clearly continue to exist in the future. In acute conflicts, if people see violence to be their most effective option, they will continue to choose violence to wage their struggle. That choice has repeatedly had its own catastrophic consequences.

However, if we see only violence as available to wage powerful struggle, we will fail to notice a major sign of hope for humanity: the growth and significance of another type of conflict, "the other ultimate sanction"—nonviolent struggle. It is sometimes also called people power, political defiance, nonviolent action, non-cooperation or civil resistance.

We should remember well the "people power" revolution in the Philippines in 1986, the ten-year nonviolent struggle in Poland which ended with the collapse of the communist system, the East German revolution and the Velvet Revolution in Czechoslovakia in 1989, the defeat of the hard-line coup in the Soviet Union in 1991. These struggles in recent years were of world significance; yet many people have already forgotten them or explained them away.

Many other cases of nonviolent struggle have occurred. Among the best known are the Gandhian struggles for India's independence in the 1920s, 1930s and 1940s and the US civil rights struggles of the 1950s and 1960s. But those are not typical of the vast range of nonviolent struggles. Other important cases include women's demonstrations in Berlin in 1943 to save their Jewish husbands, the struggle of the Norwegian teachers in 1942 against the fascist government's efforts to control the schools, the undermining of the military dictatorships of El Salvador and Guatemala in 1944, the pressure of boycotts and strikes in the 1980s in South Africa against injustices of the apartheid system. Older campaigns include the international struggles of women for the right to vote and the organization and strikes by workers in numerous countries for the right to organize and to seek fair wages and better working conditions. Nonviolent action has at times proved to be more powerful and more effective than violence.

These and other cases are relevant to finding better solutions to the moral and political problems facing us in efforts to achieve and defend justice, freedom and peace. They do not present a panacea for ongoing vast slaughters. But under certain conditions the means of nonviolent struggle applied in acute conflicts have offered a way out of cyclical predations of violence and are an option for the future.

Nonviolent struggle employs other types of power than does violence. Nonviolent action offers an alternative to violence for achieving and defending justice, freedom and peace—an approach more compatible with Christian principles and social responsibilities, an approach capable of effectiveness with fewer tragic consequences and more satisfactory long-term results.

THE NATURE OF NONVIOLENT STRUGGLE

Nonviolent action is a technique for mobilizing and applying the power potential of people and groups for pursuing objectives and interests by non-military "weapons"—psychological, political, social, economic and spiritual.

Nonviolent action includes protest, non-cooperation and intervention without physical violence. People using this technique either refuse to do things they are expected or required to do, or they insist on doing things they normally do not do or which are forbidden. The classes of specific methods or forms of action are: nonviolent protest and persuasion (consisting of symbolic acts, such as vigils, marches and display of flags); non-cooperation (including social boycotts, economic boycotts, labour strikes and many types of political non-cooperation); and nonviolent intervention (including sit-ins, hunger strikes and parallel governments).

Faced with such a challenge to their very sources of power, opponents can be expected to apply repression. This repression, however, is often ineffective in halting the nonviolent struggle and can alienate various groups, so that the repression actually weakens the opponents and strengthens the nonviolent struggle group. That process has been called "political jiu-jitsu:" the violence of the opponents may rebound to undermine their own position.

When such struggles achieve success, they do so by one or a combination of four mechanisms: *conversion* (changing the opponents' opinions or beliefs); *accommodation* (compromising to gain part of one's objectives); *nonviolent coercion* (forcing the opponents to grant the demands); or *disintegration* (causing the opponents' system or government to fall completely apart).[1]

Nonviolent struggle operates by mobilizing the power potential of people and institutions to enable them not only to wield power themselves but also to restrict or sever the sources of power of their opponents (such as authority or legitimacy, human resources, skills and knowledge, intangible factors contributing to support or obedience, material resources and sanctions).

This type of struggle enables the pillars of support to be pulled out from under the temple of oppression. Let us focus for the moment on the oppression of a dictatorship or foreign occupation (recognizing that social and economic oppression also need to be uprooted). The power of all tyrants and oppressive systems, of all dictators and aggressors, depends upon the support they receive—acceptance by the populace of the oppressors' legitimacy and the duty to obey, the operation of the economic system, the continued functioning of the civil service and the bureaucracy, the obedience of the army, the reliability of the police, the blessing of religious bodies, the cooperation of workers and managers and the like.

If you first weaken, then reduce and finally withdraw the support of all those bodies of the society, you produce something like a greatly expanded and deepened political-social strike which restricts or severs the opponents' sources of power. We understand how workers by staying off the job can paralyze a factory. Think of a political society applying the same principle of non-cooperation against oppression: religious and moral leaders denounce the regime as meriting no obedience whatever and preach the duty of disobedience and nonviolent revolution against it; civil servants stay home or operate as they please, ignoring the orders of the regime; soldiers disobey and mutiny, or even join the demonstrators; police refuse to arrest patriotic resisters; capitalists and business managers shut down their economic activities; workers stay home on strike; transportation is shut down. Everything is paralyzed. Imagine a dictator under those conditions issuing orders for the revolution to be put down tomorrow—and being ignored by everyone.

To maximize the power of this nonviolent struggle, developing and applying wise strategy is highly important. Yet only rarely do those seeking to use this type of struggle fully recognize the critical importance of preparing a comprehensive strategic plan before they act. For various reasons resisters have often not even attempted to think and plan strategically how to accomplish their objective. As a result, the chances of success are drastically reduced, even eliminated. There is no plan to guide the use of one's own resources most effectively in order actually to gain the goals of the conflict. One's strength is dissipated. One's actions are ineffective. Sacrifices are wasted and one's cause is not well served.

By contrast, the formulation and adoption of sound strategies increase the chances of success.[2] One's strength and actions are focused to serve the main strategic objectives. Casualties may be reduced and the sacrifices may serve the main goal more effectively. Directed action in accordance with a strategic plan enables concentrating strengths to move towards the desired goal.

It is profoundly significant that this technique has been and can be used by people who reject a belief in the positive good of "nonviolence," who do not accept a moral prohibition on the use of violence and who support the possibility of "justified war" under established criteria. In specific conflicts on behalf of issues such as liberation, justice and defence it is possible for masses of people who do not believe in "nonviolence" nevertheless to use this nonviolent technique instead of violence.

Contrary to the usual assumption, only rarely in the multitude of past cases of nonviolent struggle has principled nonviolence been a significant factor in adopting and implementing the technique. Pragmatic factors were very important even in the leadership of both Gandhi and Martin Luther King (both of whom are atypical in the history of leaders of nonviolent struggles). In various discussions with those involved in serious nonviolent conflicts—in the occupied West Bank, in Panama, in Beijing, in Lithuania, Latvia and Estonia and in many other cases—

pragmatic considerations have always been cited in response to questions about the motives for choosing the means of nonviolent action.

Nonviolent struggle can be practised by imperfect people in an imperfect world, who are nevertheless able to act without use of violence. Such means are available to all people who share a desire for justice, freedom and peace. While few individuals are able to "turn the other cheek" in the spirit of love and forgiveness, many more are able to understand that for their particular objectives nonviolent action offers the best chances of success. Human stubbornness coupled with the assertion of human dignity and the use of nonviolent means has its virtues.

When this type of action is understood as a non-doctrinal technique, operating by understandable processes, capable of producing humane results more effectively and efficiently than violence, it has the potential to be widely adopted in situations in which people and institutions might otherwise resort to violence.

THE HISTORICAL GROWTH OF NONVIOLENT ACTION

Nonviolent struggle has a history that goes back many centuries. One example from the pre-Christian era occurred in Rome in 494 BCE, when the plebeians, rather than murder the consuls in an attempt to correct grievances, withdrew from the city to a hill (later called "the Sacred Mount"). There they remained for some days, refusing to make their usual contributions to the life of the city. An agreement was then reached pledging significant improvements in their life and status.[3]

Assessing historical trends in the use of nonviolent action is difficult, since there is nothing approximating a complete historical survey of its practice. But some well-informed scholars have suggested that this technique is being practised to a much greater extent in the late 20th century than previously. There clearly appears to be an acceleration in the incidence, scale and importance of the use of nonviolent struggle throughout much of the world.

As recently as 1980, few people would have thought that nonviolent struggle would within a decade be a major force in shaping the course of politics around the world. Since then we have experienced, in addition to the examples of "people power" mentioned above, the people's defiance campaign for civilian government in Thailand in 1992, the nonviolent independence struggles of Lithuania, Latvia and Estonia, the brave uprising in Burma in 1988 and the courageous demonstrations in China in 1989—the last two with many lives lost and without immediate success, though both now continue under new circumstances.

Looking back a little further, since 1970 politically significant nonviolent action has also occurred in at least the following countries: Australia, Japan, South Korea, India, Pakistan, Sudan, South Africa, Morocco, Israeli-occupied Palestinian territories, Iran, Mexico, New Caledonia, Argentina, Chile, Brazil, the United States, West Germany, Norway, France, Algeria, Nigeria, Madagascar, Armenia, Moldova, the Ukraine, Georgia, the Philippines, Panama, Yugoslavia, Bolivia, Haiti, Ireland and Nicaragua. Clearly, some of the recent and current cases have not yet succeeded while others have produced dramatic changes, even toppling powerful established governments, such as those of the Shah of Iran and Marcos of the Philippines. It should be cautioned, however, that without careful attention to the transition to a democratic or more just system, a new dictatorship can arise from the ruins of the old one.

The lifeblood of dictatorships—submission—can be cut off by the power derived from the ability of people and their independent institutions to organize despite governmental prohibitions to meet their human, social, economic and political needs and, when necessary, to resist and fight aggressors, dictators and oppressors. Nonviolent struggle is not weak, but strong. It is not the way of the timid, but of the brave. Nonviolent action is "armed struggle" in which people wield nonviolent weapons which, when refined and prepared, can be more powerful than violence for the causes of justice, freedom and peace.

LONG-TERM CONSEQUENCES OF NONVIOLENT STRUGGLE

In place of passive submission to oppression, therefore, or reliance on social reformers and revolutionaries to gain control of the state apparatus to change oppressive social systems, another course is possible. Through the dual skills of wielding power by nonviolent struggle and a constructive programme of building more just and democratically controlled institutions, people will be able to bring a more just social order into being incrementally. People will become increasingly empowered to confront the forces of domination and to dissolve them, as they conduct constructive efforts to build on a less centralized basis a more free and just society.[4]

The recent and widespread use of nonviolent struggle is certain to have profound and continuing consequences in all political systems. The depth of those long-term results will vary with the degree to which this technique is used strategically wisely. Whole populations have learned that even in the face of tyrannical governments, terroristic regimes and oppressive social systems they are not helpless. People can see they have an immense power potential which, with difficulties and costs, they can mobilize actively to shape their own futures and remove or block the forces of domination. Such knowledge once gained cannot be easily erased.

Whether nonviolent struggle can truly be a major factor in resolving those political and ethical problems depends in large degree on its actual capacities and future potential in refined and developed forms. If the effectiveness of nonviolent struggle against ruthless regimes can be clearly established, then our future may not only be one of immense difficulties, but also of unprecedented grounds for realistic hope for humanity. That possibility brings very great responsibilities to all people who would seek a better society and a peaceful world, one in which the goals of justice, freedom and peace are coupled with realistic strategies to achieve and maintain them.

NONVIOLENT STRUGGLE FOR DEFENCE?

While constantly pursuing a variety of measures to make political freedom fuller and more vibrant in the face of the forces of centralized manipulation, control and repression, new programmes are required. The aims of these are both to block the rise of dictatorships, as through defence against coups d'état, and also to disintegrate existing dictatorships. For both objectives the widespread application of political noncooperation and popular defiance will be essential.[5]

Nonviolent struggle can also be applied for national defence against both coups d'état and foreign aggression. On the basis of research, feasibility studies, contingency planning, preparations and training of the population and leadership groups, a policy of "civilian-based defence" would seek to deter and defend by reliance on massive public defiance and widespread non-cooperation. The aim would be both to deny the attackers their objectives and also to make impossible the consolidation of their rule. This non-cooperation and defiance may be combined with other forms of action intended to subvert the loyalty and reliability of the attackers' troops and functionaries.

Writings on civilian-based defence were used by defence planners during the 1991 crises in Lithuania, Latvia and Estonia to protect themselves against Soviet attacks. These countries are now in the process of incorporating some type of modest civilian-based resistance components alongside their limited military capacities. Sweden also has a non-military resistance component within its total defence policy. Several other European countries have conducted some type of investigation or feasibility studies on the potential of this policy.[6] Interest also exists in Thailand in the potential of a specifically anti-coup defence capacity.

Official adoption of a civilian-based defence policy would usually be a phased incremental introduction and gradual expansion of the civilian-based capacity, with many countries probably maintaining both military and civilian means for the foreseeable future. As with the adoption of nonviolent action in struggles for social justice and freedom, the refinement and adoption of civilian-based defence would contribute to the progressive replacement of reliance on violence with application of prepared nonviolent forms of struggle.

CHRISTIAN RESPONSES TO THIS OPTION

The development of practical and effective nonviolent means of waging conflicts against injustice, dictatorship and aggression produces a new situation for those concerned to apply religious principles in the real and imperfect world in which we live. One of the major problems in political ethics and moral theology is rooted in the use of violence for political objectives.

The recognition, refinement and increasing effectiveness of nonviolent struggle could also potentially contribute to a more satisfactory resolution of the key problem of how to wield power effectively in the real world, so as to be able to influence the actual course of events, while not becoming enmeshed in the constant cycle of violence, thus violating important ethical, moral or religious principles and ideals. The contention here is that effective means of struggle can be both nonviolent and effective, both moral and practical.

One of the criteria for a "justified war" (*jus ad bellum*) is that it is the means of last resort, that all other "peaceful" options have been tried and have failed to produce the needed result. Such reliance on violence as the ultimate sanction is based on an assessment or assumption that it is the strongest and most effective means available to counter an attack, that the use of only weaker means or submission without any resistance would ensure that the opponents' violence would be successful in achieving its objectives. Such weakness and submission have been deemed to have their own problems, including moral ones.

However, the view that counter-violence is the strongest and most effective means available is not a judgment based on ethics, morality, norms, precepts or scriptures. It is an assumption about social and political reality. Therefore, it needs to be asked whether it is in fact true that counter-violence is the strongest and most effective means available to resist injustice, destroy an oppressive system, or counteract a violent attack.

Which are in fact the most powerful "means of last resort" is now an empirical question. To answer it requires data, analysis and evaluation of the relative effectiveness of violent versus nonviolent means of conducting conflicts. It requires examination of the two main means of waging struggles (as distinct from such milder measures as conciliation, negotiation and the like). The data required would come primarily from social, political and historical sources.

It is not true that violence is without question the most effective and powerful means of conducting open acute conflicts, especially for the goals of justice, freedom and peace. On the contrary, nonviolent struggle has often proved more effective than violent struggle. Furthermore, nonviolent struggle has been improvised on many occasions in struggles for justice, freedom and even for national defence purposes instead of war.

Where nonviolent struggle is for pragmatic reasons accepted for use in situations in which otherwise violence would have been applied, the moral situation is changed fundamentally. A variety of secondary moral or ethical problems would predictably arise or continue in the application of the nonviolent option. For example, under what conditions are extreme psychological pressures justified? When should international economic sanctions be applied? However, the most serious moral or ethical problems in the past have been aggravated because they have been associated with the use of violence in acute conflicts. It was at least in part to deal with these problems that the theories of justified war were developed—both *jus ad bellum* (under what conditions is resort to war justified?) and *jus in bello* (if it is justified, within what limits should it be conducted?).

However, the increase in the effectiveness of nonviolent struggle and its deliberate adoption in policies to deal with acute conflicts produces a new situation, in which one of the major conditions for a "justified war" (*jus ad bellum*)—that there is no available effective alternative to violence—no longer exists.

The development of pragmatic nonviolent struggle as a third practical but at the same time more moral option is a possibility which was not contemplated in the centuries-old arguments between exponents of pacifism and of "justified war." This option means that what is religiously and morally required and what is practically required become essentially the same. The distinction between the ideal and the real can be removed. The development of this option would follow the lines of another insight, that the development of nonviolent struggle as a pragmatic option makes it possible for a society of people who do not believe in principled nonviolence nevertheless to accept nonviolent policies and courses of action.

Therefore, the old arguments between pacifists and exponents of justified wars can now be bypassed. Instead, attention, resources and thought can now be concentrated on development, critical examination and implementation of a type of struggle which appears to be a higher synthesis of the better components of each of those past positions. This higher synthesis then becomes one which may make possible a new integration between ethics and politics, by providing a way to face crises with behaviour which is simultaneously in harmony with religious injunctions not to kill and politically responsible because of its capacity successfully to resist hostile forces attempting to impose or maintain injustice, dictatorship or war.

CHRISTIAN NON-PACIFIST VOICES

Recognizing that nonviolent struggle raises important policy and theological issues quite separate from the arguments for and against pacifism, several prominent

Christian calls have been made for exploring the potential of nonviolent struggle in acute internal and international conflicts. These have come from both Catholics and Protestants, and date back to at least the 1930s.

Protestant theologian Reinhold Niebuhr, in his famous book *Moral Man and Immoral Society*, recognized the inevitability of conflict in society and therefore the need for coercion. If that coercion is not to be by violence, he argued, one must "choose those types of coercion which are most compatible with, and least dangerous to, the rational and moral forces of society."[7] "Nonviolent coercion and resistance . . . is the type of coercion which offers the largest opportunities for a harmonious relationship with the moral and rational factors in social life."[8] The advantages of nonviolent methods are great, he argued, but they "must be pragmatically considered in the light of circumstances." He understood that this technique was not yet adequately developed and concluded that "there is no problem of political life to which religious imagination can make a larger contribution than this problem of developing nonviolent resistance."[9]

A brief but very important Catholic statement came in 1986 from the Congregation for the Doctrine of the Faith, in its "Instruction on Christian Freedom and Liberation." In the context of a discussion of the need for "a very rigorous analysis of the situation" where "armed struggle" is considered "as a last resort to put an end to an obvious and prolonged tyranny," it declared:

> Indeed, because of the continual development of the technology of violence and the increasingly serious dangers implied in its recourse, that which today is termed "passive resistance" shows a way more conformable to moral principles and having no less prospects for success.[10]

In the foundation document attached to their 1986 pastoral letter "In Defense of Creation: The Nuclear Crisis and a Just Peace," the Council of Bishops of the United Methodist Church encouraged "special study of nonviolent defence and peacemaking forces," citing "a vast—but neglected—history" of nonviolent defiance against "foreign conquerors, domestic tyrants, oppressive systems, internal usurpers and economic masters."

> Among notable modem examples are Gandhi's satyagraha (soul force) in India, Norway's resistance during Nazi occupation to keep schools free of fascist control, Martin Luther King Jr's civil rights movement and Solidarity in Poland . . . Every prospect that either military establishments or revolutionary movements might effectively replace armed force with nonviolent methods deserves Christian support.[11]

The 1987 report of the Episcopal diocese of Washington on nuclear weapons also noted the topic of nonviolent resistance for defence, but treated the topic with considerable skepticism:

> We also recognize as legitimate the perspective of nonviolent resistance, and accept it as a personal option and as a possible collective approach to conflict resolution . . . We are honestly troubled, however, by the claim that nonviolent resistance can be effective in settling conflicts between nations. Most of us have difficulty seeing how it meets the responsibility to protect the innocent from oppression's spread, or to prevent suffering, although we understand it as a valid means of resisting internal oppression and injustice. Nonviolent resistance was indeed successfully used

as a means to achieve human and civil rights in the United States during the 1960s.[12]

The general assembly of the Presbyterian Church (USA) also addressed the policy of civilian-based defence as an alternative to nuclear deterrence in its 1988 policy statement about Christian responsibilities in the nuclear age:

> A strategy of civilian-based defence, grounded in nonviolent resistance, is now a matter of serious study at several major universities. Civilian-based defence involves work stoppages, strikes, slow-downs, boycotts, demonstrations, disabling key components of the infrastructures and other nonviolent means as ways of refusing to consent to be governed by an invading power. There is risk of failure in such an alternative, as there has always been in conventional military defence. For civilian-based defence to have a chance of success would require a degree of national consensus, discipline and devotion which we do not believe exists in this country at the present time. We do believe, however, that the church needs to give careful study to the growing literature in this field.[13]

ASSESSMENTS BY THE WORLD COUNCIL OF CHURCHES

In the years since its founding after the second world war, various bodies of the World Council of Churches have discussed the potential relevance of nonviolent action in facing both international conflicts and struggles for social justice. These statements have varied in their terminology and the clarity of their references to nonviolent action as a technique used by diverse groups, to moral or religious nonviolence, or to various peaceful means of conflict resolution.[14] Nevertheless, some of those statements have unmistakably discussed nonviolent action as a technique of action sometimes applied by groups which do not share a religious conviction regarding nonviolence, which is the focus of central interest here.

The "Martin Luther King Jr Resolution" adopted by the WCC's fourth assembly (Uppsala 1968) directed the central committee "to explore means by which the World Council could promote studies on nonviolent methods of achieving social change."[15] In 1971 the central committee, meeting in Addis Ababa, asked the sub-unit on Church and Society "to conduct a two-year study on the problems and potentialities of violence and nonviolence in the struggle for social justice." The committee had received a report from an ad hoc staff group which had spoken of an "increasing reluctance to pose the issue as 'violence' versus 'non-violence,' " preferring "a search for more pertinent Christian criteria for evaluating alternative coercive strategies."[16]

In 1972 Church and Society organized a consultation on "Violence and Nonviolence in Social Change" in Cardiff, Wales; and its report was commended to the churches by the central committee in August 1973 for study, comment and action.[17] The report dealt extensively with how Christians could effectively oppose the forces of an oppressive society, and contained significant passages on the relevance of nonviolent action. These included the following:

> The world and the churches have been both inspired and challenged in recent years by examples of new and sophisticated nonviolent move-

> ments for justice and freedom. Some of these—for example the Gandhian movement—have been non-Christian. Others—such as that of Martin Luther King—have been Christian. Together their witness has brought the churches of the world to examine anew the style of their involvement in the struggle for world justice and peace.[18]

Later, it continued:

> We are convinced that far too little attention has been given by the church and by resistance movements to the methods and techniques of nonviolence in the struggle for a just society. There are vast possibilities for preventing violence and bloodshed and for mitigating violent conflicts already in progress, by the systematic use of forms of struggle which aim at the conversion and not the destruction of the opponent and which use means which do not foreclose the possibility of a positive relationship with him. Nonviolent action represents relatively unexplored territory: initiatives being taken by various groups and individuals to help the exploration happen deserve the strongest possible support from the WCC and the churches.

The report then pointed to some complexities in the application of nonviolent forms of struggle:

> We reject, however, some facile assumptions about nonviolence which have been current in the recent debate. Nonviolent action is highly political. It may be extremely controversial. It is not free of the compromise and ambiguity which accompany any attempt to embody a love-based ethic in a world of power and counter-power, and it is not necessarily bloodless. Moreover, most struggles for freedom—and most government actions—have been, as a matter of fact, mixtures of violent and nonviolent action . . . In all of these Christians will have hard choices to make. The more these choices are informed by a responsible spirit and knowledge of constructive nonviolent options, the more creative they will be.

The report also sought to dispel some oversimplifications concerning both violent and nonviolent means: "Violence should not be equated with radicalism and revolution, nor nonviolence with gradualism and reform, nor vice versa." It concluded with a series of questions which exponents of the differing convictions about the use of violent and nonviolent means should ask themselves.[19]

In acting on the Cardiff statement, the central committee called attention to specific topics:

> We welcome the statement's clarification of the nature of nonviolent action . . . Nonviolence must not be equated with mere passivity or disengagement in the face of injustice. On the contrary, understood in the tradition of Gandhi, King and Luthuli, it is an active, highly political, often controversial and sometimes very dangerous form of engagement in social conflict.

It went on to recommend

> that WCC units and sub-units be encouraged to develop fresh initiatives appropriate to their respective programmes, to stimulate and assist churches and Christians throughout the world to more careful study of, and more courageous engagement in, nonviolent action in support of the oppressed.[20]

The WCC's fifth assembly (Nairobi 1975) adopted a policy guideline on "the need . . . to explore further the significance of nonviolent action for social change and the struggle against militarism."[21]

In 1979 the central committee encouraged "further exploration and continuing implementation of the report on 'Violence, Nonviolence and the Struggle for Social Justice,' paying serious attention to the rights of conscientious objectors and the need to promote peaceful resolution of conflicts." The same year the Commission of the Churches on International Affairs (CCIA) convened a small consultation in Chambesy, Switzerland, on peaceful resolution of conflict with representatives of the Historic Peace Churches, scholars and activists seeking viable alternatives to military-dominated systems of national defence.

In 1980 the executive and central committees called on WCC member churches "to initiate and encourage innovative measures for peaceful resolutions of conflicts." Ecumenical thinking was reported to have "moved more and more in the direction of the need for justice as a means of avoiding and resolving conflicts, to eliminate the root causes of war to be found in economic injustice, oppression and exploitation and . . . restrictions on human rights," as the central committee stated at its meeting in Dresden in 1981.

In preparation for the sixth assembly (Vancouver 1983) an informal international consultation on "Violence, Nonviolence and Civil Conflict" was held in Northern Ireland, co-sponsored by the Corrymeela Community and the WCC, in March 1983. Its report submitted to the WCC general secretary, commented that "the level of the current debate about violence and nonviolence in civil conflicts does not match the complexity of the international situation today and the actual experience of people regarding the use of violence for political ends . . . This complexity makes it even more difficult today to draw up general guidelines for a Christian response in particular situations of violence."

The "traditional questions must be reopened," the report continued, including the criteria for the legitimacy of governmental power and the individual right of resistance (including by violence) against "unjust structures." "This applies also to the role of violence and nonviolence in social change." The question was raised whether the criteria of Christian just war theories could simply be applied to civil conflicts:

> The report of 1973 employed both pacifism and just war theory. Since then, both traditional positions have felt their inadequacies in the debate on militarism, modern sophisticated means of mass destruction and revolutionary conflicts. The time seems ripe for a new attempt at bridge-building between them.[22]

The report urged strengthening of international institutions to assist resolution of both local and international conflicts, but contained no specific recommendations for the examination of the potential of nonviolent action in social and international conflicts.

The WCC's seventh assembly (Canberra 1991) had in mind especially the conflicts which had followed the collapse of the communist systems in Eastern and Central Europe when it referred to the "complex intertwined set of issues" arising "at once virtually all around the globe."

> It is not surprising, therefore, that no clear definitions of either the problems or of possible solutions are at hand, or that our own grasp of applicable moral, ethical and theological categories is inadequate.

The central committee, meeting in August 1992, agreed "that active nonviolent action be affirmed as a clear emphasis in the programmes and projects related to conflict resolution. . . ."[23] WCC general secretary Emilio Castro pointed out that

> the two issues at stake belong together: an overall estimation of the potentialities of active nonviolence in the world today; and the actual handling of conflict situations, which still has to be discussed more fully. We are not saying—and the Council has never been able to say—that war is not permitted in any circumstances. We are saying that lessons learned in nonviolent approaches can help us in such a situation.[24]

At its 1994 meeting in Johannesburg, South Africa, the WCC central committee recommended the establishment of a Programme to Overcome Violence, whose purpose was to challenge and transform the global culture of violence in the direction of a culture of just peace.[25] In this connection a consultation was held in Corrymeela in June 1994 on "Building a Culture of Peace: The Churches' Contribution." WCC general secretary Konrad Raiser said in his opening address that "if one considers the resources and the energies invested in the education and preparation of young men for the task of fighting in wars, then it becomes obvious that the social competence in the nonviolent resolution of conflicts is gravely underdeveloped."[26]

The Corrymeela consultation made no specific call for the consideration, development and promotion of nonviolent action and nonviolent means of struggle in social conflicts and for defence. Later that month, the board of CCIA, meeting in Kitwe, Zambia, focused on "building and rebuilding communities of justice, peace and ecological sustainability." It accepted conflict as a "normal aspect of life in human community" and pointed out that conflict "does not necessarily lead to violence and war." Its programme sought among various other objectives "to contribute to the delegitimization of war and violence and to the promotion of peace with justice." Mediation work was among specific recommendations. Nothing more specific related to developing nonviolent action or its use as a substitute for violence was recommended.[27]

CATHOLIC BISHOPS' STATEMENTS

The Roman Catholic bishops of the United States in their 1983 pastoral letter *The Challenge of Peace: God's Promise and Our Response* stressed the importance of attention to nonviolent struggle, especially that applied for purposes of national defence. They indicated the potential of this approach for gaining the support both of adherents to just war theory and of pacifists. "We believe work to develop nonviolent means of fending off aggression and resolving conflict best reflects the call of Jesus both to love and to justice."[28] The bishops continued: "Nonviolent means of resistance to evil deserve much more study and consideration than they have thus far received. There have been significant instances in which people have successfully resisted oppression without recourse to arms."[29] In this connection they cited examples of nonviolent resistance by Danes and Norwegians during the second world war, and noted that nonviolent struggle can take many forms, depending on the situation, including for national defence:

> There is, for instance, organized popular defence instituted by government as part of its contingency planning. Citizens would be trained in the techniques of peaceable noncompliance and non-cooperation as a means of hindering an invading force or nondemocratic government from imposing its will.

Citing the requirements of effective nonviolent action, they concluded that, although it may not always succeed, "before the possibility is dismissed as impractical or unrealistic, we urge that it be measured against the almost certain effects of a major war." Then, in a significant departure from the standard theological positions regarding justified war and pacifism, they noted:

> Nonviolent resistance offers a common ground of agreement for those individuals who choose the option of Christian pacifism . . . and those who choose the option of lethal force allowed by the theology of just war. Nonviolent resistance makes clear that both are able to be committed to the same objective—defence of their country.[30]

In conclusion, compared with the threats of existing military policies, "practical reason as well as spiritual faith" demand that nonviolent popular defence be given "serious consideration as an alternative course of action."[31]

The Catholic bishops' reflection, *The Harvest of Justice is Sown in Peace*, on the occasion of the tenth anniversary of the 1983 pastoral letter, was published in November 1993. In the intervening years significant new applications of nonviolent struggle had occurred, conducted almost entirely by people who did not believe in pacifism.

The Catholic bishops in 1993 raised again the two traditions of "nonviolence and just war" and also referred to both "the success of nonviolent methods in recent history" and the post-cold war pressures for limited military engagement and for humanitarian intervention. The statement referred to the diverse views within the Catholic Church on the validity of the use of "force" (meaning violence), stating that:

> 1) In situations of conflict our constant commitment ought to be, as far as possible, to strive for justice through nonviolent means.
>
> 2) But when sustained attempts at nonviolent action fail to protect the innocent against fundamental injustice, then legitimate political authorities are permitted as a last resort to employ limited force to rescue the innocent and establish justice.[32]

The bishops' new statement cited the "new importance" of "nonviolence" which should not be "confused with popular notions of non-resisting pacifism." This "nonviolence" was not "simply a personal option or vocation, [and] recent history suggests that in some circumstances it can be an effective public undertaking as well."[33]

The bishops then quoted what Pope John Paul II had written about the Eastern European revolutions in his encyclical *Centesimus Annus* (1993), on the 100th anniversary of *Rerum Novarum:*

> It seemed that the European order resulting from the second world war . . . could only be overturned by another war. Instead, it has been overcome by the nonviolent commitment of people who, while always refusing to yield to the force of power, succeeded time after time in finding effective ways of bearing witness to the truth.[34]

The bishops went on to say:

> These nonviolent revolutions challenge us to find ways to take into full account the power of organized, active nonviolence. What is the real potential power of serious nonviolent strategies and tactics—and their limits? What are the ethical requirements when organized nonviolence fails to overcome evil and when totalitarian powers inflict massive injustice on an entire people? What are the responsibilities of and limits on the international community?
>
> One must ask, in light of recent history, whether nonviolence should be restricted to personal commitments or whether it also should have a place in the public order with the tradition of justified and limited war. National leaders bear a moral obligation to see that nonviolent alternatives are seriously considered for dealing with conflicts. New styles of preventative diplomacy and conflict resolution ought to be explored, tried, improved and supported. Nations should promote research, education and training in nonviolent means of resisting evil. Nonviolent strategies need greater attention in international affairs.
>
> Such obligations do not detract from a state's fight and duty to defend against aggression as a last resort. They do, however, raise the threshold for the recourse to force [violence] by establishing institutions which promote nonviolent solutions of disputes and nurturing political commitment to such efforts. In some future conflicts, strikes and people power could be more effective than guns and bullets.[35]

The statement reviewed the just war criterion of "last resort:" that violence "may be used only after all peaceful alternatives have been seriously tried and exhausted." The section on the just war tradition ended with the recommendation that "important work needs to be done in refining, clarifying and applying the just-war tradition to the choices facing our decision-makers in this still violent and dangerous world."[36]

The bishops also encouraged integration of "Catholic teaching on justice, nonviolence and peace into the curriculum and broader life of our educational endeavours," observing that "we will not fashion new policies until we repudiate old thinking." They concluded:

> Changes we could barely imagine ten years ago have taken place before our eyes. Without violence, the hope, courage and power of ordinary people have brought down walls, restored freedoms, toppled governments and changed the world.[37]

In April 1994 the Mexican Catholic bishops addressed essentially this same issue in the context of domestic conditions in their country, including violence, poverty, injustices, mistreatment of ethnic groups and distrust of institutions. Despite the temptation to resort to violence against such grievances, the bishops rejected "violence as a way to resolve problems, for violence begets more violence." "We must absolutely reject all violence, whether verbal or physical." Rather, said the bishops, quoting the 1986 statement from the Congregation for the Doctrine of the Faith cited earlier, "that which today is termed passive resistance shows a way more conformable to moral principles and having no less prospects for success."[38]

THE ECUMENICAL ASSEMBLIES OF BASEL AND SEOUL

At the end of the 1980s two major international ecumenical gatherings on the themes of justice, peace and the environment were held, one in Europe in Basel, one at a global level in Seoul, Korea. The documents produced by these assemblies made clear references to nonviolent action, and the document from Seoul mentioned its application to national defence.[39]

The European Ecumenical Assembly on Peace and Justice was convoked in Basel in May 1989 by the Roman Catholic bishops of Europe and the Conference of European Churches, and jointly presided over by Russian Orthodox Metropolitan Alexy of Leningrad (now patriarch of Moscow) and the Catholic archbishop of Milan, Cardinal C. M. Martini.

The final document, discussed and approved by the great majority of more than 500 delegates, includes several passages relevant to our theme, among them a commitment to "a nonviolent solution of conflicts from one end of the earth to the other."[40] In Section VI, "Fundamental Affirmations, Commitments, Recommendations and Perspectives for the Future," it states:

> At all levels in the church and in the society, there ought to be developed a peace education oriented to peaceful resolution of conflicts. In every situation, the nonviolent alternative ought to have priority in the resolution of conflicts. Nonviolence ought to be seen as an active dynamic and a constructive force based on the absolute respect for the human person.[41]

Less than a year later, in March 1990, the WCC organized a world "convocation" on Justice, Peace and the Integrity of Creation (JPIC) in Seoul. Although the involvement of the Catholic Church was almost nil compared to Basel, and Orthodox participation very reserved, the meeting of 400 delegates and almost as many observers and guests was a very significant step in the involvement of the churches at a global level with these themes.[42]

One of the affirmations voted at Seoul states: "We are called to seek every possible means of establishing justice, achieving peace and solving conflicts by active nonviolence."[43] The security of nations and of peoples was the focus of one of the covenants, which developed that commitment with repeated references to the promotion of "forms of nonviolent defence" and to the "cultures of active nonviolence." One of these passages recommended "developing and coordinating justice and peace ministries including a global nonviolent service which can advance the struggle for human rights and liberation and serve in situations of conflict, crises and violence."[44] A later section on "the demilitarization of international relations and the promotion of nonviolent forms of defence" recommended that those purposes could be advanced "through a defensive, non-threatening and non-offensive posture or security measures and the development of civilian-based defence."[45] Yet another section of the document was headed: "For a culture of active nonviolence which is life-promoting and is not a withdrawal from situations of violence and oppression but is a way to work for justice and liberation."[46]

THE NEED FOR FRESH POLITICAL AND THEOLOGICAL CONSIDERATION

It is evident that a diverse range of prominent Christian leaders, denominations, churches, ecumenical assemblies and other authoritative bodies have, in varying degrees of precision, pointed to nonviolent struggle and even specifically civilian-based defence as meriting serious exploration and practice in acute conflicts in which violence otherwise would likely be used. These thinkers and groups have done so after considering both morality and efficacy.

These statements add significant weight to the call made earlier in this article for both careful consideration of the practical potential of nonviolent struggle for liberation and defence, and also for fresh theological examination of the possibilities of moving beyond the old pacifist and justified war positions and arguments. Sound new political and theological positions may now be possible.

It now remains to be seen to what extent and how Christians—and also religious and secular leaders who respect Christian thinking—will act upon the important counsels offered in these important challenges.

CHAPTER 35

Untangling the Web of Violence

By Jennifer Turpin and Lester R. Kurtz

The argument underlying this volume is that our current perspectives on violence are too narrowly conceived; research approaches, theories of violence, and policy debates must be broadened. We now turn our attention to the implications of these insights for current public policy debates. Recent public attention to problems of violence is heartening, but we are convinced that the debates are narrowly conceived, misguided, and will not solve the problems they are intended to alleviate.

In this conclusion, we argue that the tendency to see violence as the consequence of aberrant behavior committed by deviant individuals at the margins of society obscures the central role violence plays in the very foundations of the social order and the fundamental dilemmas that humans face as they move into the twenty-first century. The problems created by violence will not be solved by acting on the margins but by rethinking the pervasive use of violence in contemporary cultures.

LINKING PERSONAL AND GLOBAL VIOLENCE

Current approaches to violence precipitate two conceptual difficulties. First, most people feel forced to choose between a micro-and macrolevel approach to theory, research, and policy. This forced choice leads to two false alternatives, one of which ignores the effect of microlevel processes and individual choices on broad historical trends; the other screens out the impact of broad sociocultural, macrolevel situations on individuals choosing to engage or not engage in violent behavior. Our argument is that violence is caused not simply by individual psychological factors, biological impulses, or social-structural factors alone but by a web of causal connections between personal-level and global-level structures, processes, and behaviors.

Second, current perspectives on violence promote efforts to find a "technical fix" to the problems that violence creates, especially in the pragmatic technical cultures that now dominate much social organization. Technical solutions often provide temporary relief, but they also deflect our attention from the underlying nontechnical problems that are not easily remedied.

A sociology of knowledge-oriented analysis of these approaches suggests that they are unduly shaped by cultural biases and attempts by ruling elites to maintain the status quo. The lack of attention to micro/macro linkages, which has been a primary focus of this volume, is a major difficulty facing the general public, scholars, and policy makers around the world. Although broad generalizations are difficult to make on such matters, our impression is that the collapse of socialist experiments at the end of the twentieth century has narrowed our field of vision even further. Individualistic solutions that ignore larger structural causes of violence now dominate the policy scene, as played out in two related models.

The criminal model of violence distinguishes between legitimate and illegitimate violence and requires the identification of criminals, whether in neighborhoods or geopolitical regions, who transgress national or international law. According to this paradigm, problems of violence are created by outlaws and thugs who deviate from civil norms and make life miserable for decent, law-abiding citizens and nations. According to this theory, we must punish individual criminals: we put them in prison, drive them from power, execute them by the state (or rebel forces), or somehow expunge them from the civil society in which they are wreaking havoc.

A more liberal alternative to the criminal model of deviance is the medical or psychotherapeutic model: miscreants (from petty thieves to dictators) are maladjusted and require treatment. We should rehabilitate or treat (sometimes medicate) gang members and prison inmates for aggressive personality disorders.

A more recent trend is to teach miscreants conflict resolution techniques that can facilitate their dealing with personal struggles in a less violent manner. The conflict resolution movement, which has had dramatic success in a number of spheres, while promising in many respects, is still only a Band Aid applied to a deep wound. It usually represents yet another technical fix, so popular in modern cultures that excel in technology. Conflict resolution is similar to the search for the ultimate weapon that will end all war or the frantic effort to build more prisons or improve the treatment that often accompanies individualistic approaches to solving the problems of violence.

These individualistic and technically oriented solutions are rooted in the broader process of cultural framing in which the policy debates are conducted, and it is to that process that we now turn our attention. From our perspective, the analysis of violence, and any proposed solutions to the problems it creates, must encompass a broad frame that includes many voices heretofore excluded from the debate. At the core of our approach is the conclusion that individual propensities to violence are not ordinarily enacted except in what Elias calls a "culture of violent solutions." That is, any psychobiological vulnerabilities to engaging in violent behavior are discouraged and are rarely acted on unless the broader culture allows or encourages such behavior. On the other hand, even in a culture that promotes violent solutions, not all individuals will be violent. Moreover, even the most violent individuals are not so all of the time. Violence, from our perspective, is thus a result of the dialectical interaction of micro-and macro-level processes. Solutions to the problem of violence must address all levels—as well as the interactions among them. Most of our current struggles with the issue are framed in such a way as to blind us to significant elements of the problem.

In the discussion that follows, we will explore the ways in which people define policy issues and narrow their alternatives. After exploring two mainstream approaches to violence that frame current policy debates, we will outline a third perspective that we believe addresses significant problems with conventional approaches and provides some promising alternatives.

PUBLIC DISCOURSE ABOUT VIOLENCE

Public policy positions on the problem of violence tend to fit within two major frames, although elements of a third, alternative frame occasionally enter the debate. The first frame is a "peace through strength" or "law and order" frame that emphasizes the use of tough measures, usually involving violence against deviant individuals or nations, to solve problems of violence (the traditional so-called conservative position in U.S. culture). A second frame is the traditionally liberal "legal control" frame that emphasizes rational legal procedures that place boundaries around the use of violence (e.g., such measures as arms and gun control). A final, alternative frame that has seldom been part of the mainstream debate is the "common security and nonviolent conflict" approach that combines elements of the first two positions but emphasizes the interdependence of individuals and nations and promotes the use of nonviolent techniques for solving conflicts. A narrative expresses each frame, linking macrolevel cultural orientations with microlevel motivations and actions, as Smith observes.[1] Individuals thus fit events into "moralizing narrative frames" to assess the ethical status and efficacy of particular acts of violence. This process is a political one, although not exclusively within the realm of the state. Collective and individual rituals thus reaffirm the narratives of the frame and express the boundaries of a culture's repertory of acceptable behavior.

People are socialized into a culture; its norms are internalized through a variety of cultural processes, from the mundane storytelling of village folktales or corporal punishment of children by conservative Christian parents[2] to the high drama of political spectacles and denunciation of counterrevolutionaries by Chinese communists.[3] Often the cultural boundaries are so pronounced and the institutions that enforce them so powerful that evidence contradicting the culturally accepted frames becomes almost invisible. Thus, the Chinese official Yuan Mu insists that photographs of violence taken in Tiananmen Square on June 4, 1989, are falsifications.[4] Others contend that the Holocaust is a hoax or that its scope has been vastly embellished.

In the discussion that follows, we will explore the narratives, characteristics, and methods of each approach, as well as its fundamental assumptions and policy implications. We will also evaluate the problems with each perspective and what must happen in order to stop the cycles of violence within that framework.

PEACE THROUGH STRENGTH AND LAW AND ORDER

Whether violence is occurring within a community or among nations, the peace through strength position advocates the use of whatever means are required—often violent ones—to stop "illegitimate" violence in its tracks. This approach gives birth to the criminal model of violence discussed above and relies on deterrence through intimidation to mitigate violent behavior, thus strengthening military and police forces and pursuing technological developments such as weapons arsenals, surveillance techniques, and so on that will punish offenders. Advocates call for more prisons, tougher sentences, and the death penalty, or military action against aggressors. For the most part, such actions are carried out by the state—the police or military and the criminal justice system, but at the extreme, if the state is perceived as ineffective, vigilante groups may intervene.

A number of assumptions lie behind this perspective. First, the only way to stop violence is with superior force, usually one that relies on violence. A second assumption is that the world is inhabited by many evil people who must be deterred from violence through intimidation and punished should deterrence fail. Advocates of the law and order position contend that we cannot appease or coddle aggressors and criminals: the only language such people understand is force, and it will do no good to reason with them. In fact, efforts to deal rationally with "deviants" may allow them to perceive authorities as weak and vulnerable, thus resulting in efforts to exploit the weakness, like Hitler did with the British before World War II.

Finally, peace through strength advocates contend that such measures as arms and gun control do nothing to mitigate violence. On the contrary, they simply hamper legitimate efforts of law enforcement officials and the military, leaving them at a disadvantage. Criminals and aggressors will always obtain the weapons they need, whether legal or not, so that demilitarization will simply disarm legitimate authorities and honest citizens, while criminals and international aggressors will proceed illegally, cheat on treaties, and ignore the law.

Several implications follow from this perspective—most importantly, that military and police systems must have the most advanced weapons available, thus requiring continual force modernization. Second, tough laws must be enacted to enhance deterrence and punish aggressors. The central issue here, as with all frames, is whether the perspective is an accurate depiction of human nature. We contend that the peace through strength approach misreads the dynamics of conflict and inadvertently compels opposing forces to escalate their fights and to proliferate their weapons.

The major problem with the peace through strength frame is that it often perpetuates an upward spiral of violence and thus results in widespread devastation, a police state, war, or—at its extreme—a nuclear holocaust. Moreover, it does not address many of the individual or structural causes of violence, such as fear, greed, and inequality, or foster nonviolent means to engage in conflict or pursue one's desired goals. On the contrary, the peace through strength approaches serve primarily to suppress violent behavior through brute force, regardless of the precipitating factors. Ironically, it is the most effective approach in preventing the weak and powerless from becoming violent, while provoking those with more resources to escalate their aggression. As the military or police become more sophisticated in their ability to destroy, so do their opponents, so that the conflict takes on a life of its own—as it often does—and escalates beyond the control of all involved parties. The most obvious example of this problem is the superpower arms race of the cold war, which escalated to such extremes that the entire planet was placed at risk by a complex system of nuclear weapons and redundant weapons delivery systems. Although the danger appears to have subsided somewhat because of the collapse of the Soviet Union, the weapons system itself is still very much in place, and the perceived increase in security may be as much a consequence of social amnesia as the result of a substantial change in the situation.[5]

Although less threatening in its scope, the arms race between police and illegal forces in various urban areas and regions of ethnic conflict in the United States,

Russia, the Middle East, and elsewhere mirrors the larger global process, as does the conflict between various parties making overlapping territorial claims from the so-called warlords of Somalia to the street gangs of Los Angeles.

In such situations, ruling civil authorities feel compelled to "up the ante" by "damping down," "getting tough," escalating the level of armaments, and reducing the civil rights of the populations involved. When the peace is kept by a "balance of terror" within the family, community, or worldwide, everyone feels the pressure to escalate violence and armaments. Terrified citizens who feel vulnerable and unprotected by the state often turn to private systems of security, buying guns for their own homes and—especially among the economic elite—hiring armed bodyguards to protect them.[6]

A major consequence of this situation is the set of high social and economic costs of living in a militarized zone. As C. Wright Mills noted, we all now live in a "war neighborhood."[7] Although he was referring to what now seems a rather crude set of long-range weapons delivery systems, the proliferation of weapons at the local level—even among schoolchildren—makes his remarks even more salient.

The high cost of the ongoing escalation of violence globally and in many local contexts around the world involves not only the physical consequences of widespread violence, and the psychological toll of the balance of terror, but also what Victor Sidel calls "destruction without detonation."[8] That is, the militarized context in which we live has its costs even when the weapons are not fired, in terms of the way economic resources are spent, the effect of the threat of violence on children, and the social construction of evil that poisons interpersonal, interethnic, and international relations. A wide range of political costs of this approach includes the growth of the national security state at the national level, police states at the community level, and a vast system of propaganda, deliberate secrecy, and deception that undermines public trust.[9]

The cycles of escalating violence sustained by these dynamics can only be halted by a technological breakthrough that enables the "good guys" to gain control over the criminals and aggressors who threaten the social order. This search for an ultimate technical fix to the problem runs the gamut from the Strategic Defense Initiative (SDI, or Star Wars) and first-strike nuclear weapons of the Reagan era to sophisticated arms and management techniques for police forces. Some thought that the invention of the machine gun would put an end to combat, because it was so ghastly that no one would dare to use it. But, the weapon to end all weapons, like the war to end all wars, appears as a mirage on the distant desert of an increasingly armed planet.

THE LEGAL CONTROL FRAME

A second major frame in the violence debate is the traditional liberal position that calls for a rule of law that imposes reason on chaotic forces and aims to stop violence with legal progress and procedures designed to impose rational order. This frame emphasizes arms control negotiations and treaties in the international sphere, effective law enforcement and gun control legislation combined with social programs to treat offenders at the domestic level, and a legal framework to protect human rights. Efficient military and criminal justice systems are necessary but should be combined with such efforts as job training, rehabilitation of offenders, and more recently, programs to teach conflict resolution techniques to "at risk" populations.

Several assumptions lie behind this approach, which follows the Western Enlightenment tradition that places a premium on rational thought and efforts to control both natural and social environments. The core assumption, for our purposes, is that the only way to stop violence is to maintain the rule of law. Disputes among civilized people should be fought in the courtroom, not on the battlefield. Human beings, according to this approach, are basically rational and can be taught to act in a rational fashion when shown the costs and benefits of the alternatives.

Unlike the peace through strength frame, this perspective usually maintains that we already have enough weapons and guns, prisons, and tough laws and that an escalation of arms will not alleviate the problem. Moreover, new opportunities exist in the post-cold war era for the establishment of a reasoned global social order governed by rational discourse, international trade and cultural exchanges, and international law. New techniques of arms verification to enforce treaties at the international level and sophisticated techniques of conflict resolution and behavioral therapy at community and individual levels will enable people to make slow, steady progress toward a less violent world.

The legal control framework has a number of implications for public policy, notably (1) an international legal framework is necessary to sustain a stable global social order, (2) violence would be reduced by improving law enforcement and military techniques, while maintaining civil liberties, protecting human rights, and placing strict limits on military and police authorities, and (3) criminal justice and international peacekeeping efforts need significant reforms and increased resources in order to maintain the peace from local to global levels.

The international legal framework involves the elaboration of an arms control regime that expands the efforts of the last few decades, with interstate negotiations and treaties and mechanisms for monitoring agreements and imposing sanctions on violators. Legal control advocates maintain a wide range of positions regarding the nature of the international order that would best serve the process of legal control. They usually claim that successful international trade agreements and the development of new forms of arms verification provide the foundation on which such an order can be built. Moreover, the structure for negotiating, concluding, and monitoring such agreements has been established through decades of arduous work that could bear fruit in the post-cold war period.

At the community level, the legal control framework would systematically upgrade the criminal justice and law enforcement systems in order to rationalize the entire process of peacekeeping. The effort to make criminal justice a science reflects these kinds of concerns, as does the ongoing professionalization of the police, who in more "enlightened" cities are now armed with conflict resolution techniques and computer databases as well as guns and assault rifles. Hence, journals such as the Police Chief attend to such issues as those addressed in Gary Buchanan's article,[10] "Handcuffing All Arrested Persons: Is the Practice Objectively Reasonable?"[11]

Finally, such reform of the social control system will require a major effort, with the expenditure of substantial resources to upgrade and rationalize police and military forces, establish rehabilitation programs and treatment centers, train police and military officers, and upgrade technological services available to them. From this perspective, crime control is essentially a management problem, in which individuals who fail to cooperate with the larger system are brought back into line.

Similarly, a legal control system at an international level requires the elaboration of international organizations such as the United Nations. Nationally based militaries would give way to a sophisticated arrangement of collective security arrangements. Effective multinational peacekeeping and police forces would be deployed by the international community, and violators of international law—individuals or collectivities, public or private—would be brought before the World Court. Convicted offenders would be subjected to rational sanctions to deter them and others from future violations.

The legal control framework is appealing to many who find the peace through strength approach too aggressive, but its major stumbling blocks are formidable: it is individualistic in its proposed solutions, despite its so-called social programs, and it is ultimately hampered by the "bureaucratic shuffle." That is, the legal control approach must be implemented by large, inefficient bureaucratic systems in which no one takes responsibility. These systems also result in a bureaucratic distancing between officials and the "clients" whom they serve, which ironically results in the hidden bureaucratized violence common in the modern world.

The assumption of this approach—that humans can act rationally—has some serious problems. Although certainly capable of rational calculation, humans often engage in violence precisely because of nonrational motivations, or because of a complex combination of rational and nonrational, individual and social forces, as Lifton suggests occurred among the Nazi doctors. Perhaps the only way to break the cycles of burgeoning bureaucratic administration of violence is the mass mobilization of social movements across national and social boundaries—a mobilization that demands a humanization of large-scale social organizations in much the same way that movements within the civil societies of Eastern Europe challenged their states in the late 1980s and early 1990s. Such movements push us toward the third frame, that of common security and nonviolent conflict.

COMMON SECURITY AND NONVIOLENT CONFLICT

> *All problems could be peacefully resolved if adversaries talked to each other on the basis of love and truth. All through history, the way of truth and love has always won. This was the belief and vision of Mahatma Gandhi and this vision remains good and true today.*
>
> Ronald Reagan, speech to the United Nations,
> September 25, 1984

The final frame has not been central to the mainstream debates in most societies because of its radical departure from accepted assumptions about security. Four recent developments, however, make it a more imaginable alternative: (1) increased doubts, raised by the specter of a nuclear holocaust, about the conventional wisdom regarding security, (2) Mikhail Gorbachev's advocacy of a common security perspective while serving as president of the Soviet Union in the 1980s, (3) the global diffusion of nonviolent struggle from Gandhi's anticolonial movement to the prodemocracy movements of the late twentieth century, and (4) increasing public discontent with the threat of violence that saturates daily life.

The common security approach emphasizes the interdependence of all humans. Although differing in substantial ways from the two previous frames, it also draws upon elements of both of them: it recognizes both the importance of strength and confidence as an element of security and the need for a rational order based on law. In the place of deterrence through intimidation advocated by both peace through strength and legal control perspectives, however, the common security approach emphasizes cooperation when possible and creative nonviolent conflict when necessary.

The common security perspective advocates the construction of institutions that mitigate the causes of violence, rather than emphasizing the organization of social control agents like the military and police. Common security relies on the provision of basic economic security and human rights for all, systematic training of the civil population in the techniques of nonviolent struggle and conflict resolution, and the cultivation of cultural prohibitions against the use of violence to solve even problems of violence. In short, the common security approach would replace a "culture of violent solutions," as Elias calls it, with a culture of nonviolent solutions. New cultural narratives would be woven that delegitimate violence.[12]

The fundamental assumption of the common security approach is that no one is secure until everyone is, because we all live in the same "global village." A second assumption is that strength is necessary in order to maintain the peace, an assumption similar to the peace through strength position. Weakness will be exploited by others, so some form of deterrence must be adopted. Strength is not measured in terms of military might or weapons technology, however, but by means of a variety of other criteria. Thus, the ability to deter is also redefined in this perspective: people are deterred from undesirable behavior by a variety of factors, only one of which is the threat of violence. In everyday life, for example, people are deterred from harming those whom they love, respect, or with whom they wish to maintain civil relations for fear of the consequences that aggressive actions will have for others and themselves. Deterrence results from a complex combination of rewards and sanctions that lie along a continuum between the most violent and the most nonviolent.[13]

That violent solutions may provide temporary relief of a problem, but do not work in the long run, is a third assumption of the common security approach to violence. Behind this notion is the cycle of violence thesis: "Violence begets violence." Those whose aggression is stopped by today's violence may retaliate tomorrow.

This assumption clearly demonstrates the importance of cognitive framing: we readily observe evidence confirming our general frame in order to sustain our preferred argument, while conveniently ignoring any counterevidence that might negate it. Anecdotal evidence can easily be provided to "verify" the cycle of violence thesis, but counterevidence can be provided just as easily by peace through strength advocates who claim that unchecked aggressors are genuine threats. The common security frame addresses this dilemma by offering an alternative to simply ignoring a genuine threat or "wishing it away." Nonviolent struggle with opposing forces, which may seem foreign to some peace through strength advocates, requires standing up to opponents but fighting in such a way as to attack their aggressive or unwanted behavior, rather than the people themselves.[14]

A fourth assumption of the common security approach is that structural violence can be as destructive as other kinds of violence. This aspect of the approach is significant, because it shifts the focus of definitions of security and deterrence from attention to strictly military or overt forms of violence toward other ways in which people are made insecure or are physically harmed. Emanating from efforts in the field of peace studies to distinguish between positive and negative peace,[15] this argument implies that solutions to the problem of violence must include more than increased use of force to defend against deviants at the local or global level, exploring such matters as economic security, at least as long as malnutrition and poverty remain major killers.

Fifth, conflict does not have to be a "zero sum game," as it is sometimes perceived.[16] According to some conventional wisdom, a conflict must end in victory by one party only at the expense of the other; the goal of nonviolent conflict is to conduct a dispute as creatively as possible, so that all parties benefit from its resolution. Whereas violent conflict inherently accentuates differences between partisans, nonviolent struggle seeks to minimize boundaries between people.

Gandhi, for example, argues for separating the "doer from the deed;"[17] when engaged in struggle, the nonviolent activist seeks to destroy unjust systems but not the people who are involved in them. While this approach may seem idealistic to many, it was both a moral and pragmatic stance for Gandhi, who always treated the British individuals with tremendous respect, and often affection, while standing squarely against the British colonial system.

This principle has become a central element of conflict resolution approaches that emphasize "fair fighting" and respect for opponents as a significant way of changing the nature of any conflict and moving it toward a positive resolution. It also served as a hallmark of the nonviolent political revolutions of recent decades; in the Philippines' "People Power" revolution, for example, efforts to oust dictator Ferdinand Marcos were dramatically assisted by the fact that large sections of the military were persuaded to defect, in part because of the way in which they were treated by the demonstrators, who gave them flowers, food, and cigarettes.[18] It may well be that the massacre at Tiananmen Square in Beijing in 1989 was precipitated in part by a breakdown in the nonviolent discipline of the demonstrators, who had held the square peacefully for seven weeks and, until hours before the military stormed the square, had generally treated the soldiers with respect and dignity.[19]

The differentiation between behavior and people goes to the heart of the link between micro- and macrolevel processes that lead toward or away from violence. Violence may be perpetuated by systems, but it is carried out against individuals. Although we do not have sufficient data to prove it, the highest probability for violence occurs, we would argue, when certain structural conditions and individual motivations converge. When individuals feel threatened or wish to obtain something they do not have (fundamental emotions that are not as different as they might appear superficially) and their sociocultural context proffers only violent solutions to their dilemma, they are more likely to engage in violence to achieve their wishes.

The dynamics of human conflict are such that individuals engaged in it often find themselves swept along by the escalating events in which significant aspects of their personal identities are invested in its outcome. As conflicts escalate, issues become abstracted, opponents are often vilified as part of the rhetoric of the struggle, and the outcome becomes a matter of moral and personal consequence.

Several studies[20] suggest that violence is more likely to be perpetrated when the distance between the perpetrator and the victim increases. The "social construction of evil," by which opponents are dehumanized and perceived as the personification of evil, enhances the probability that a conflict will become violent.

Violent responses to complex situations have been a fundamental part of human life for thousands of years; twentieth-century technologies have so transformed the consequences of violent response, however, that conventional approaches are now called into question. Moreover, the long range of contemporary weapons means that no personal contact occurs between perpetrators and victims.

A final assumption of the common security approach is that nonviolence is morally and strategically superior to violence. One central dilemma in the issue of violence is the gap between what is often considered moral and that which is defined as effective. In *The Fate of the Earth*, Jonathan Schell remarks that the advent of nuclear weapons forces us to be either a strategic or a moral idiot.[21] On the one hand, that which is usually defined as strategically superior (i.e., the effective use of superior force to deter or sanction one's opponent) becomes morally offensive if it threatens widespread destruction. On the other hand, if one eschews the use of weapons of mass destruction on moral grounds, one opens oneself up to attack and appears strategically naive.

This tension between the moral and the strategic emerged with particular poignancy in the nuclear debates in the United States during the early 1980s. Alarmed by the threat of a nuclear holocaust, the National Conference of Catholic Bishops undertook an extensive study of the ethical implications of nuclear weapons and concluded that nuclear war is morally indefensible because it violates two fundamental principles of the church's traditional "just war" teachings. The principle of proportionality requires that the good caused by a war must outweigh its harmful consequences; the principle of discrimination prohibits the intentional use of violence that kills noncombatants.

Defense Secretary Caspar Weinberger's report to Congress grappled surprisingly, for the first time in history, with the ethical virtues of particular strategic and weapons policies.[22] Ironically, in responding to the bishops' critique of the indiscriminate nature of nuclear weapons, the Pentagon developed an argument that justified the escalation of the superpower nuclear arms race. The new, sophisticated weapons under development—so-called counterforce weapons—were declared moral because they were targeted on military installations, weapons systems, and so on. In contrast, earlier and existing systems were less accurate and were used for targeting cities and other "soft" (i.e., civilian) targets. Thus, a whole set of new weapons delivery systems from the MX missile and the Trident D5 (submarine-launched) missiles to the stealth bomber were justified by the Pentagon on moral as well as strategic grounds.

The nuclear holocaust debates of the 1980s called into question the strategic relevance of such weapons programs. Ostensibly created for deterrence purposes, nuclear weapons were seen by some as having a limited strategic value, especially in light of the nuclear winter studies that suggested that the explosion of even a relatively small percentage of the world's nuclear weapons could result in the possible annihilation of all human, and most other, life on earth.

In an effort to expand the technical fix approach to the problem of international violence, and to "regain the moral high ground," peace through strength advocates proposed the Strategic Defense Initiative (SDI, or Star Wars) designed to protect against nuclear attack. Questions about its feasibility were raised in many quarters; ultimately, advocates admitted that its purpose was to "enhance deterrence," rather than protect against an actual attack. It merely provides a numerical advantage by destroying some unknown portion of the aggressors' weapons before they reach their targets. Advocates promoting the program, however, questioned the deterrence effectiveness of all advanced weapons systems. The ultimate spokesman for the "peace through strength" approach, President Ronald Reagan, argued that if deterrence were to work, "it must work perfectly, because if it doesn't work perfectly, it fails utterly."[23] By promoting a "final solution" that became widely ridiculed, advocates of this frame undermined their position in the public debate. Reagan ended his term by promoting peace through friendship, because of his negotiations and personal relationship with common security advocate Mikhail Gorbachev. One of the great ironies of the 1980s is that Reagan, who was elected on a peace through strength platform and dramatically increased the U.S. military budget in the first years of his presidency, concluded his tenure in office by promoting friendly relations with the nation he had earlier designated the "focus of evil in the modern world."

The moral superiority of nonviolence is seldom questioned; it is the practical side that is problematic, even among many who would prefer nonviolence to violence. Even Gandhi admitted that the effectiveness of nonviolence could not be asserted, only demonstrated. Nonviolent direct action, so foreign to most ways of perceiving solutions to the problem of violence, carries little validity with those who have not experienced its potential power. On the other hand, participants in the Indian Freedom Movement, the U.S. civil rights movement, or recent nonviolent revolutions in Eastern Europe and elsewhere confirm its power. Even in those cultural contexts, however, the efficacy of violence remains strong.

REFRAMING THE PROBLEM OF VIOLENCE

The common security approach requires a reframing of public policies at all levels, from local to global. This framebreaking implied by the common security perspective requires nothing less than rethinking basic approaches to human relations from the family to the world system.

It is not possible to address the entire range of implications for that reframing process, but we will suggest three significant areas in which the common security approach to violence differs substantially from most conventional frames: (1) it defines deterrence as a broad social process, rather than as a strategy of military and criminal justice systems, (2) it expands the repertory of nonviolent means of struggle (when deterrence fails), and (3) it transforms cultural values and socialization processes, such as the link between masculinity and violence that encourages the socialization of young men in such a way as to require violent behavior on their part in order to prove their "manhood."

Efforts to deter violence would focus not on more effective means of confronting violence with violence but on a broad range of issues that addresses the assumptions just outlined. Deterrence policies would emphasize the cultivation of friendly relations across boundaries that are the site of violent confrontation, from class and race divisions within the community to international, alliance-driven, and ideological boundaries within the world system. Common security approaches contend that aggression is deterred through a variety of means that address the concern that parties will have about protecting their own interests, relationship, or alliance. It does not necessarily rely on altruism, although it does not deny the possibility that people may engage in altruistic behavior, especially when relating with people for whom they care.

At the interpersonal level, people are frequently deterred from engaging in aggressive behavior because they are afraid that they might harm someone who might then retaliate or sever a relationship. Sometimes the motivating factor may even be genuine concern about the well-being and safety of the other. At more abstract levels of social organization, this more humane element may be obscured by the distancing mechanisms of bureaucratic institutions, vilification of certain groups or nationalities, or the politics of international relations. Even at the most abstract levels, individuals act on behalf of structures, which may help to explain why some puzzling events occur, such as the thawing of the cold war. Although many economic and geopolitical factors converged to bring about the development of friendly relations between the United States and the former Soviet Union, even sociologists must take into account the dramatic impact of the personal relationship forged between the two unlikely partners of Gorbachev and

Reagan. A relationship of mutual respect and affection seemed to develop between the two when they began meeting face-to-face at the initiative of the charismatic Gorbachev.[24] These personal interactions between two leaders who had both a sense of their role in history and reputations for affability apparently broke through the formal structures that defined them as bitter enemies. The valence of the relationship changed from negative to positive, but its intensity did not diminish.

A related element of the reframing of conflict required by the common security approach is the need to expand the repertory of nonviolent solutions to conflict. It is nothing less than a call to transform the "culture of violent solutions," as Elias puts it, so that the dominant alternatives to social organization and social conflict are not deeply rooted in violence.[25]

We are quite adept at violence because the peace through strength approach has been so important historically, especially in macrolevel human relations. We have the technical know-how, institutional infrastructure, and a wide range of options in our cultural repertory for carrying out violent conflict in a sophisticated manner on a wide variety of fronts. In fact, the world spends about U.S. $2 billion each day (almost half of that by the United States) on its militaries, and another very large sum on paramilitary and police forces and private arsenals. Compared to that remarkable mobilization of resources, very little is spent on nonviolent means of conflict and on research to address the causes of war and violence.

"If you want to get tough on crime, rock a crack baby," a Catholic bishop remarked recently. Each baby born in poverty and raised in a violent neighborhood without opportunities for meeting his or her basic needs is a candidate for violence. It is not simply a matter of addressing the individual orientation of such a person and providing techniques for dealing with conflict nonviolently—although such a program might help in a number of ways. The fundamental structures that produce a world in which half of the population lives on the verge of starvation, while a small percentage lives in unprecedented wealth, cannot simply be supported indefinitely by force.

Thus, a final implication of the call for reframing in this perspective is the need for a broad transformation of contemporary cultures, so that violence is devalued and nonviolence promoted. Since the vast majority of violence is committed by men,[26] we must break the link between cultural definitions of masculinity and violence that can be found in most of the world's cultures. It involves the creation of what Eisler[27] calls a partnership, rather than dominator, social organization, making alternative models of leadership part of the cultural repertory. As long as we require that manliness be proven through the adept use of violence and that boys be taught from a very early age that they must demonstrate their strength through violence and the use of weapons, it is difficult to imagine a significant move toward a nonviolent global order.[28]

The dialectic between micro- and macrolevels again becomes important. On the one hand, the socialization of young men is shaped profoundly by the culture of violence that is imposed from the top. On the other hand, the ongoing process of teaching boys to use violence for solving problems reproduces the culture of violence across generations. It is difficult to tell one's young son not to destroy his enemies on the playground when the country's president uses such methods to solve international problems. By the time our sons become heads of state, they have been taught repeatedly the efficacy of violence in solving problems: by their parents and peers, through popular culture, the media, video games, the political leaders of their respective countries, and sometimes by their religious leaders. These cycles of violence cannot be solved either by transforming individuals on a case-by-case basis or by imposing nonviolent dictums from above but through a complex process of cultural and individual transformation. Although individuals may be taught to "use words" or enlarge their repertory of conflict techniques, such actions will not be sufficiently widespread without a broader cultural shift. Historic cultural changes, however, do not take place without the courageous action of individuals who contradict existing cultural frames. The kind of cultural transformation required by the common security approach is possible only with massive transnational social movements that mobilize public opinion in opposition to existing frames and that cultivate cooperation between civil society and state agencies, from community to global levels.

The common security and peace through strength approaches have some important common threads that may not be immediately apparent. Both share a suspicion toward the state, which is inconsistent in both approaches; each has some ambivalence about the state that results in internal contradictions. Peace through strength advocates tend to oppose excessive state intervention in other spheres but often place a heavy burden on the state to provide the kind of military and police forces necessary to check violence with violence. Common security advocates tend to be oriented toward forging a democratic civil society as a force opposing the state, which is so often hierarchical and violent. Even in the most democratic of political systems, there is no other entity for undertaking the kind of social transformation demanded by social movements, which are usually better at resisting than ruling (witness the difficulties faced by post-Soviet societies in Eastern Europe).

The common security approach also emphasizes the creation of social institutions that promote nonviolence, mitigate violence, and address the sources of potential violence. If the world community could spend $2 billion a day on that process rather than on military training and arms, the world would be much less violent.

Erich Fromm notes that if people behave the way nations do, we institutionalize them, by putting them in a jail or a mental hospital.[29] Large-scale human social organization is so oriented toward violent conflict, and the amount of resources spent on the conduct of violence is so enormous, that it should not surprise us that we resort so frequently to violence.

One model for this sort of institution building is the concept of nonviolent peacekeeping systems—what Gandhi called *Shanti Sena* (peace brigades)—organized at all levels, from the neighborhood to the world. As Gandhi conceptualized them, local citizen peace brigades would work in a community to address the potential sources of violence. When no overt conflict is raging, the *Shanti Sena* would engage in "constructive work," meeting the needs of the local community: if there is a housing shortage, they should help local residents build homes; if the community needs a water supply, they should help residents dig wells. When an overt conflict breaks out, members of the brigade intervene nonviolently, acting as mediators or placing themselves directly between the conflicting parties, attempting to manage the conflict in a nonviolent fashion.[30]

Such an approach—advocated only at the margins a few decades ago—has entered into the mainstream, not so much as an idealistic dream but as a concrete form of action, beginning with the Indian Freedom Movement, which culminated in India's independence in 1947, and then elaborated in the U.S. civil rights movement and other nonviolent social movements around the world, such as the Filipino "People Power" movement, and finally, the successful prodemocracy movements of the former Soviet bloc.[31]

Although we should not expect the peace brigade concept to be adopted by the Pentagon or Kremlin any time in the near future, it has matured over time, and a number of serious efforts to develop a plan for a system of nonviolent "civilian-based defense" have emerged in recent decades, notably in the work of Gene Sharp.[32] Peace brigade proposals have actually been considered practical policy in a few cases: Costa Rica exists without an army but in relative peace with its violent neighbors; a movement to abolish the army was widely popular in Slovenia before the civil war shattered the peace; the newly independent Lithuania is considering a nonviolent defense system as part of its national security.

Less dramatic, but quite remarkable, measures that emphasize nonviolent conflict and common security include the increasing sophistication and systematic use of conflict resolution techniques in international and ethnic conflicts, such as that between the Palestine Liberation Organization (PLO) and Israel.[33]

Finally, many creative ideas about the cultivation of a nonviolent civic culture that promotes free expression, equal opportunity, and mutual support have emerged from resistance movements in various parts of the world.[34] From the essays and plays of Vaclav Havel[35] to the actions of nonviolent prodemocracy movements in Thailand[36] and Latin America,[37] it may be that the groundwork for a less violent culture is being laid toward the end of humanity's most violent century. At the community level, experiments in nonviolent conflict and its resolution thrive: in Gandhian "constructive workers" in India, Christian-based communities in Latin America, the Quaker "Alternatives to Violence" training in U.S. prisons, and elsewhere around the world.

We are not blind, of course, to the tremendous obstacles to the transition from a violent to a nonviolent culture. We will briefly discuss three major problems with an implementation of the common security approach: (1) cultural resistance and the complexity of such a transformation, (2) our collective ignorance about alternatives to violence and a lack of structures for facilitating nonviolent conflict, and (3) the virtually inevitable resistance by powerful interests who profit from the status quo and will fight to maintain it.

In a global culture saturated with violence, the idea of a nonviolent world sounds like the idealistic ramblings of marginal sociologists and peace activists. Two factors make it possible to imagine. First, the power of nonviolent struggle has been demonstrated for the first time on a large scale in the twentieth century, from the Indian Freedom Movement to various social movements especially in the United States, Philippines, Argentina, Palestine, and the former Soviet bloc. The fact that nonviolent approaches have now been demonstrated changes the nature of the argument in their favor from a primarily moral to a more strategic one.

Second, despite the flaws of a nonviolent approach, conventional approaches look increasingly defective in the nuclear age. As Gwynne Dyer puts it, violence has been a part of human life for five thousand years; in the twentieth century, it has simply been too costly.[38] Is it really more idealistic to imagine the transformation of human social organization toward nonviolence than to expect humans to survive if we continue down the path of violent solutions? Do increasingly sophisticated weapons of mass destruction, the proliferation of armaments around the world, and the widespread distribution of guns in schools and homes provide more security? Perhaps the shock of the nuclear threat in the 1980s and the violence of daily life for so many (including even the wealthy and powerful) around the world in the 1990s provide the kind of awareness of our addiction to violence that will lead us to seek some therapeutic measures.[39]

A second obstacle to the common security approach is our collective ignorance of nonviolent alternatives. For centuries—perhaps millennia—we have cultivated warfare techniques, invented new means of destruction, and rationalized our strategies for violent conflict. In the twentieth century, preparation for the use of violence and its actual practice consume an enormous proportion of human resources. We are very adept at it and getting better all the time.

Nonviolent struggle, on the other hand, while also as old as human life, is less well developed. It is only in the last millisecond of the long day of human history that we have discovered large-scale nonviolent action, systematized plans of action, and laid the groundwork for future development. There is no Strategic Integrated Operation Plan (SIOP) for a nonviolent defense system, and no large-scale system that develops necessary technologies and battle strategies, recruits and trains combatants, and carries out conflicts in a nonviolent manner. We have only the scattered fragments of Gandhi's writings and stories about his work, the teachings of Martin Luther King Jr., Sharp's Politics of Nonviolent Action, a few documentary films and scholarly works on nonviolence and conflict resolution, a handful of research institutes studying, and religious organizations promoting, nonviolent change, and the recently developed tradition of nonviolent social movements, with their stories, pamphlets, and collective wisdom. Perhaps we do not need or want a Pentagon for nonviolent struggle, which should be democratically forged and wherever possible homegrown, but we should not be surprised that, when the forces of violence meet those of nonviolence, the latter look shabbily prepared and sloppy compared to the twentieth-century culmination of centuries of discipline and training in violence.

Finally, the interests organized against such a transformation are formidable: the largest block of capital resources available for capital formation exists in the U.S. military budget, and those who control it will not relinquish it lightly. Certainly, it appears to be in the vested interests of those who control the missiles and the guns, as well as those who make them, to resist the sort of dramatic social transformation required by the common security perspective, and perhaps to resist it violently.

Developments since the fall of the Soviet bloc demonstrate the nature of the obstacles to taking the nonviolent path. In the former Soviet Union, just days after Boris Yeltsin led crowds of unarmed demonstrators in the street to challenge the Soviet military troops and tanks with flowers and words, the new Russian president himself was dispersing his new troops around the country and making compromises with his military establishment. Gandhi-reading Lech Walesa requested NATO to admit his new Poland into their military alliance. Self-proclaimed change-oriented presidential candidate Bill Clinton, now in charge of the world's most powerful military machine, called for dramatic reductions in government but asked for only a 4 percent reduction in the U.S. military budget, swollen to nearly twice its pre-Reagan size.

The only way to break this kind of impasse, it would seem, is what we call the "Eisenhower solution:" that is, a popular mass movement that mobilizes a social and cultural transformation sufficient to pressure the state into making changes. We call it the Eisenhower solution because Dwight Eisenhower, commander of Allied Forces in Europe during World War II and subsequently president of the United States, claimed that "people of the world want peace so badly that some day governments had better get out of their way and let them have it."[40]

THE POLITICS OF VIOLENCE RESEARCH

Critics who contend that the problems created by violence are widespread but can only be met with violence are, in the final analysis, correct about the vagueness of the alternatives. We simply do not know enough about how to solve these problems beyond escalating the violence.

Part of our problem is our lack of knowledge, and the current processes for learning about violence and its alternatives are too meager and misguided. We contend that the current myopia in research must be overcome because of four major problems. First, the foundations and government funding now available for research on violence tend to support status quo systems and are locked into disciplinary frameworks. Second, most current research and policy recommendations tend to frame violence in individualistic terms and propose solutions that involve technical fixes at the margins of society, rather than address the fundamental issues. Third, current research is dominated by a peace through strength frame that screens out many of the insights from the legal control frame and most of the common security approach. Finally, even the style of research that is funded narrows our vision by taking a conservative approach to data collection and analysis, a tactic that further reinforces existing paradigms.[41]

Foundations and other institutions interested in advancing our understanding of violence need to "break frame." The most dramatic example of how the current funding process works is the fact that the largest amount of funding for social science research in all fields (not just violence) is controlled by the U.S. Army Research Institute for the Behavioral and Social Sciences, which had an annual research budget of $59.9 million in 1988. Although a small portion of the overall Pentagon budget, that amount exceeds the total combined social science research budget of all other sources of federal finding in the United States, including the National Science Foundation, the National Institute of Mental Health, and the Department of Education.[42]

The individualistic focus of research is underscored by the fact that the Army Research Institute employs 197 psychologists out of its 213 scientists, and only five sociologists.[43] Although their research agenda includes a number of topics, a primary objective is how to make members of the armed forces fight more efficiently, manage more effectively, and stay in the military longer. Thus, the military spends vast amounts of money to study itself and to analyze alternative military strategies.[44]

The end of the cold war offers an opportunity to engage in new thinking about violence; indeed, some new government officials seem to be willing to consider alternative approaches. In Eastern Europe, considerable conceptual and practical progress has been made in this area, growing out of the movements resisting communist domination of that region.[45]

Some new possibilities are also emerging in the West, especially in the field of nonviolent conflict resolution,[46] which is rapidly becoming an established field. Similarly, the number of university peace studies programs has escalated dramatically in recent years, especially in Europe and the United States, but elsewhere as well. A handful of peace institutes were founded after World War I and more following World War II, but only in the 1970s and 1980s did the academic study of peace and conflict become widespread. In 1970, there were two peace studies programs at U.S. universities; in 1990, there were about 250.[47]

Following years of lobbying for an alternative to the military academies, the U.S. Congress established the U.S. Peace Institute in 1984. This official agency faced considerable political turmoil from the outset, with its Reagan-appointed governing board sometimes opposing the procedures favored by those influential in the institute's creation. Nonetheless, it has managed to fund a number of important projects, primarily in the area of conflict resolution techniques.

More surprisingly, U.S. Attorney General Janet Reno recently made the following statement, which represents a sharp departure from previous frames emanating from that office:

> One of our greatest challenges in the 1990s is to make the prevention and treatment of violence a top priority.
>
> If we can make peace education and nonviolent conflict resolution a part of everyone's life; if we take it to the housing projects and make it a part of every resident's life; if we can take it to domestic violence programs and prevention programs throughout the United States; if we can say that before anyone gets married they should go through a conflict resolution course, we will make great strides in the 1990s.
>
> If we can bring this program to bear at every level of our society, we will be able to look back 10 years from now and be proud of what we did through education, prevention and showing people how to be peaceful.[48]

It is no accident that this new cognitive frame at the Justice Department comes from the America's first female attorney general. Similar shifts will occur if we expand our frames of reference in other ways, by including perspectives from various cultures and subcultures around the world other than those that have traditionally dominated research. Papers from "Studying Violence," a seminar held by the Indian Council of Peace Research in 1973, repeatedly identified social, rather than individualistic, causes of and remedies for violence. According to Sugata Dasgupta, for example, "the seedbed of violence" lies "in the disfunctionality of the societal process."[49]

American scholarship tends to dominate social science approaches around the world and, to the extent to which it shapes U.S. policy, has a global impact. Research on violence in the United States tends, however, to reflect the individualistic culture of the country as well as—even though often unintended—the hegemonic structures of international capital. As long as we remain within the frames provided by conventional scholarship, we will fail to untangle the web of violence we have woven. We hope that this volume will be an initial step toward broadening debate and opening new alternatives.

NOTES

Introduction

1. One notable exception is Jennifer Turpin and Lester R. Kurtz, eds., *The Web of Violence. From Interpersonal to Global* (Urbana, IL: University of Illinois Press, 1997). Unfortunately, however, their collection includes only eight contributions.
2. See, for example, Hannah Brady, ed., *Defining Violence* (Aldershot: Avebury, 1996); and Pamela Taylor, ed., *Violence in Society* (London: Royal College of Physicians of London, 1993).
3. For the development of such global models of intellectual exchange, see Fred Dallmayr, "Introduction: Toward a Comparative Political Theory," *Review of Politics* 59.3 (Summer 1997), pp. 421–427.

Chapter 1

1. Georges Sorel, *Reflections on Violence,* "Introduction to the First Publication" (1906), (New York 1961): 60.
2. *The Power Elite* (New York 1956): 171; Max Weber in the first paragraphs of *Politics as a Vocation* (1921). Weber seems to have been aware of his agreement with the Left. He quotes in the context Trotsky's remark in Brest-Litovsk, "Every state is based on violence," and adds, "This is indeed true."
3. *Power: The Natural History of Its Growth* (1945), (London 1952): 122.
4. Ibid., p. 93.
5. Ibid., p. 110.
6. See Karl von Clausewitz, *On War* (1832), (New York 1943): ch. I; Robert Strausz-Hupé, Power and Community (New York 1956): 4; the quotation from Max Weber: "*Macht bedeutet jede Chance, innerhalb einer sozialen Beziehung den eigenen Willen auch gegen Widerstand durchzusetzen;*" is drawn from Strausz-Hupé.
7. I chose my examples at random, since it hardly matters to which author one turns. It is only occasionally that one hears a dissenting voice. Thus R. M. McIver states. "Coercive power is a criterion of the state, but not in essence. . . . It is true that there is no state, where there is no overwhelming force. . . . But the exercise of force does not make a state." (In *The Modern State* [London 1926]: 222–225.) How strong the force of this tradition is can be seen in Rousseau's attempt to escape it. Looking for a government of no-rule, he finds nothing better than "*une forme d'association . . . par laquelle chacun s'unissant à tous n'obéisse pourtant qu'à lui-même.*" The emphasis on obedience, and hence on command, is unchanged.
8. I am quoting from the important book *The Notion of the State,* by Alexander Passerin d'Entréves, the only author I know who is aware of the importance of distinguishing between violence and power. "We have to decide whether and in what sense 'power' can be distin-

guished from 'force', to ascertain how the fact of using force according to law changes the quality of force itself and presents us with an entirely different picture of human relations," since "force, by the very fact of being qualified, ceases to be force." But even this distinction, by far the most sophisticated and thoughtful one in the literature, does not go to the root of the matter. Power in Passerin d'Entréves's understanding is "qualified" or "institutionalized force." In other words, while the authors quoted above define violence as the most flagrant manifestation of power, Passerin d'Entréves defines power as a kind of mitigated violence. In the final analysis, it comes to the same. (*The Notion of the State, An Introduction to Political Theory* was first published in Italian in 1962. The English version is no mere translation; written by the author himself, it is the definitive edition and appeared in Oxford in 1967. For the quotations, see pp. 64, 70, and 105.)

9. Ibid., p. 129.
10. *Considerations on Representative Government* (1861), Liberal Arts Library, pp. 59 and 65.
11. John M. Wallace, *Destiny His Choice: The Loyalism of Andrew Marvell* (Cambridge 1968): 88–89. I owe this reference to the kind attention of Gregory DesJardins.
12. The sanctions of the laws, which, however, are not their essence, are directed against those citizens who—without withholding their support—wish to make an exception for themselves; the thief still expects the government to protect his newly acquired property. It has been noted that in the earliest legal systems there were no sanctions whatsoever. (See Jouvenel, *op. cit.*, p. 276) The lawbreaker's punishment was banishment or outlawry; by breaking the law, the criminal had put himself outside the community constituted by it.

    Passerin d'Entréves (*op. cit.*, pp. 128 ff.), taking into account "the complexity of law, even of State law," has pointed out that "there are indeed laws which are 'directives' rather than 'imperatives', which are 'accepted' rather than 'imposed', and whose 'sanctions' do not necessarily consist in the possible use of force on the part of a 'sovereign'." Such laws, he has likened to "the rules of a games, or those of my club, or to those of the Church." I conform "because for me, unlike others of my fellow citizens, these rules are 'valid' rules."

    I think Passerin d'Entréves's comparison of the law with the "valid rules of the game" can be driven further. For the point of these rules is not that I submit to them voluntarily or recognize theoretically their validity, but that in practice I cannot enter the game unless I conform; my motive for acceptance is my wish to play, and since men exist only in the plural, my wish to play is identical with my wish to live. Every man is born into a community with preexisting laws which he "obeys" first of all because there is no other way for him to enter the great game of the world. I may wish to change the rules of the game, as the revolutionary does, or to make an exception for myself, as the criminal does; but to deny them on principle means no mere "disobedience," but the refusal to enter the human community. The common dilemma—either the law is absolutely valid and therefore needs for its legitimacy an immortal, divine legislator, or the law is simply a command with nothing behind it but the state's monopoly of violence—is a delusion. All laws are " 'directives' rather than 'imperatives'." They direct human intercourse as the rules direct the game. And the ultimate guarantee of their validity is contained in the old Roman maxim *Pacta sunt servanda.*
13. *Op. cit.*, p. 98
14. *The Federalist.* No. 49.
15. *Op. cit.*, p. 7. Cf. also p. 171, where, discussing the exact meaning of the words "nation" and "nationality," he rightly insists that "the only competent guides in the jungle of so many different meanings are the linguists and the historians. It is to them that we must turn for help." And in distinguishing authority and power, he turns to Cicero's *potestas in populo, auctoritas in senatu.*
16. There is such a thing as authoritarian government, but it certainly has nothing in common with tyranny, dictatorship, or totalitarian rule. For a discussion of the historical background and political significance of the term, see my "What is Authority?" in *Between Past and Future: Exercises in Political Thought* (New York 1968), and Part I of Karl-Heinz Lübke's valuable study, "*Auctoritas bei Augustin*" (Stuttgart, 1968), with extensive bibliography.
17. Wolin and Schaar, in *op. cit.*, are entirely right: "The rules are being broken because University authorities, administrators and faculty alike, have lost the respect of many of the students." They then conclude, "When authority leaves, power enters." This too is true, but, I am afraid, not quite in the sense they meant it. What entered first at Berkeley was student power, obviously the strongest power on every campus simply because of the students' superior numbers. It was in order to break this power that authorities resorted to violence, and it is precisely because the university is essentially an institution based on authority, and therefore in need of respect, that it finds it so difficult to deal with power in

nonviolent terms. The university today calls upon the police for protection exactly as the Catholic church used to do before the separation of state and church forced it to rely on authority alone. It is perhaps more than an oddity that the severest crisis of the church as an institution should coincide with the severest crisis in the history of the university, the only secular institution still based on authority. Both may indeed be ascribed to "the progressing explosion of the atom 'obedience' whose stability was allegedly eternal," as Heinrich Böll remarked of the crisis in the churches. See "Es wird immer spläter," in *Antwort an Sacharow* (Zurich, 1969).

18. See the *New York Times*, January 4, 1969, pp. 1 and 29.
19. Thus, Franz Borkenau, reflecting on the defeat of the Spanish revolution, states: "In this tremendous contrast with previous revolutions one fact is reflected. Before these latter years, counter-revolution usually depended upon the support of reactionary powers, which were technically and intellectually inferior to the forces of revolution. This has changed with the advent of fascism. Now, every revolution is likely to meet the attack of the most modern, most efficient, most ruthless machinery yet in existence. It means that the age of revolutions free to evolve according to their own laws is over." This was written more than thirty years ago (*The Spanish Cockpit* [London, 1957; Ann Arbor 1963]: 288–289) and is now quoted with approval by Chomsky (*op. cit.*, p. 310). He believes that American and French intervention in the civil war in Vietnam proves Borkenau's prediction accurate, "with substitution of 'liberal imperialism' for 'fascism'." I think that this example is rather apt to prove the opposite.
20. Raymond Aron, *La Révolution Introuvable*, 1968, p. 41.
21. Stephen Spender, *op. cit.*, p. 56, disagrees: "What was so much more apparent than the revolutionary situation [was] the nonrevolutionary one." It may be "difficult to think of a revolution taking place when . . . everyone looks particularly good humoured," but this is what usually happens in the beginning of revolutions—during the early great ecstasy of fraternity.
22. There is some controversy on the purpose of de Gaulle's visit. The evidence of the events themselves seems to suggest that the price he had to pay for the army's support was public rehabilitation of his enemies—amnesty for General Salan, return of Bidault, return also of Colonel Lacheroy, sometimes called the "torturer in Algeria." Not much seems to be known about the negotiations. One is tempted to think that the recent rehabilitation of Pétain, again glorified as the "victor of Verdun," and, more importantly, de Gaulle's incredible, blatantly lying statement immediately after his return, blaming the Communist party for what the French now call *les événements*, were part of the bargain. God knows, the only reproach the government could have addressed to the Communist party and the trade unions was that they lacked the power to prevent *les événements*.
23. In ancient Greece, such an organization of power was the polis, whose chief merit, according to Xenophon, was that it permitted the "citizens to act as bodyguards to one another against slaves and criminals so that none of the citizens may die a violent death." (*Hiero*, IV, 3.)
24. "Can We Limit Presidential Power?" *The New Republic*, 6 (April 1968).
25. It would be interesting to know if, and to what extent, the alarming rate of unsolved crimes is matched not only by the well-known spectacular rise in criminal offenses but also by a definite increase in police brutality. The recently published Uniform Crime Report for the United States, by J. Edgar Hoover (Federal Bureau of Investigation, United States Department of Justice, 1967), gives no indication how many crimes are actually solved—as distinguished from "cleared by arrest"—but does mention in the Summary that police solutions of serious crimes declined in 1967 by 8%. Only 21.7 (or 21.9)% of all crimes are "cleared by arrest," and of these only 75% could be turned over to the courts, where only about 60% of the indicted were found guilty! Hence, the odds in favor of the criminal are so high that the constant rise in criminal offenses seems only natural. Whatever the causes for the spectacular decline of police efficiency, the decline of police power is evident, and with it the likelihood of brutality increases. Students and other demonstrators are like sitting ducks for police who have become used to hardly ever catching a criminal.

    A comparison of the situation with that of other countries is difficult because of the different statistical methods employed. Still, it appears that, though the rise of undetected crime seems to be a fairly general problem, it has nowhere reached such alarming proportions as in America. In Paris, for instance, the rate of solved crimes declined from 62% in 1967 to 56% in 1968, in Germany from 73.4% in 1954 to 52.2% in 1967, and in Sweden 41% of crimes were solved in 1967. (See "Deutsche Polizei," in *Der Spiegel*, April 7, 1967.)
26. Solzhenitsyn shows in concrete detail how attempts at a rational economic development were

wrecked by Stalin's methods, and one hopes this book will put to rest the myth that terror and the enormous losses in human lives were the price that had to be paid for rapid industrialization of the country. Rapid progress was made after Stalin's death, and what is striking in Russia today is that the country is still backward in comparison not only with the West but also with most of the satellite countries. In Russia there seems not much illusion left on this point, if there ever was any. The younger generation, especially the veterans of the Second World War, knows very well that only a miracle saved Russia from defeat in 1941, and that this miracle was the brutal fact that the enemy turned out to be even worse than the native ruler. What then turned the scales was that police terror abated under the pressure of the national emergency; the people, left to themselves, could again gather together and generate enough power to defeat the foreign invader. When they returned from prisoner-of-war camps or from occupation duty they were promptly sent for longer years to labor and concentration camps in order to break them of the habits of freedom. It is precisely this generation, which tasted freedom during the war and terror afterward, that is challenging the tyranny of the present regime.

Chapter 2

1. What follows is a summary of analyses I have published elsewhere. The concept of political power is treated in Chapter III of *The Poverty of Liberalism* (Boston: Beacon Press, 1968). The concepts of legitimacy and authority are analyzed in my essay on "Political Philosophy" in Arthur Danto, ed., *The Harper Guide to Philosophy* (New York: Harper & Row, 1970).
2. See Robert A. Dahl, "The Concept of Power," *Behavioral Science* (July 1957), for just such a classification.
3. See "Political Philosophy," in Danto, *op. cit.*

Chapter 3

1. Hannah Arendt, *On Violence*, (London 1970): 43–44.
2. John Rawls, *A Theory of Justice*, (Oxford 1972): 5–6. Ronald Dworkin, *Taking Rights Seriously*, (Duckworth [new impression] 1978): 134–6, 266 and also in lectures in Oxford in 1982. I have some reservations about Dworkin's use of the concept/conception distinction but this is not the place to discuss them nor even to argue a case for believing (as I do) that the distinction is likely to have less fruitful application in the case of violence than in that of justice or law.
3. There is a discussion of those types under the labels "expansive," "observational" and "narrow" in K. W. Grundy and M. A. Weinstein, *The Ideologies of Violence*, (Columbus, Ohio 1974): 8–13. Their discussion is useful, but not entirely convincing.
4. It is not just that they can accuse their critics of like behaviour and, crying "tu quoque," expose their inconsistency. This is the interpretation Ted Honderich places upon this sort of use of the notion of structural violence (see Ted Honderich, *Violence For Equality—inquiries in political philosophy*, Penguin 1980: 96–100) but Honderich fails to observe that revolutionaries can try to justify their own violence as a form of defence against structural violence.
5. Newton Garver, "What violence is," *The Nation*, 24 June 1968, p. 822. This is reprinted in James Rachels and Frank A. Tillman (Ed.), *Philosophical Issues—a contemporary introduction*, (New York 1972): 223– 228. The quoted passage is on p. 228 and future references in the text to Garret will be cited from Rachels and Tillman.
6. Cf. N. Garver, op. cit., p. 224 and J. Galtung, "Violence, peace and peace research" *The Journal of Peace Research*, vol. 6, 1969, p. 168 and 173.
7. Cf. K. W. Grundy and M. A. Weinstein, *op. cit.*, pp. 10–11, where they also see it as involved in revolutionary attitudes to totalitarian regimes.
8. Quoted in Grundy and Weinstein, *op. cit.*, p. 12.
9. *New York Times Magazine*, 27 October 1968, p. 90.
10. Robert Paul Wolff, "On Violence," *Journal of Philosophy*, vol. 66, 1969.
11. Galtung, *op. cit.*
12. Ibid., p. 183.
13. Ibid., p. 168.
14. Ibid., p. 172.
15. Ibid., p. 168.
16. Ibid., p. 167.

17. See Jonathon Glover, *Causing Deaths and Saving Lives*, (Harmondsworth 1977); Peter Singer, *Practical Ethics*, (Cambridge 1979); John Harris, *Violence and Responsibility*, (London 1980); Ted Honderich, *Violence for Equality*, (Harmondsworth 1980).
18. Honderich, *op. cit.*, pp. 96–99 and 152–154; Harris, *op. cit.*, Chapter 2.
19. Harris, *op. cit.*, p. 19.
20. Actually Harris has some special views about poisoning and other "non-forceful" positive acts of killing which are germane to his position here but which I shall consider later.
21. The dissimilarities with respect to the ways in which outcomes are tied to positive acts and to failures to act do not obtain universally since there may be circumstances in which a positive act takes a long time to realise its outcome and allows for some high prospect of failure, but I do not think that this sort of case can yield a model for the normal case of action and hence it does not vitiate a contrast drawn in terms of that case.
22. Harris, *op. cit.*, p. 18.
23. Harris, *op. cit.*
24. I do not mean to deny the value of metaphorical or extended employments of the term violence in appropriate contexts. Heinrich Böll's novel, *The Lost Honour of Katherina Blunt*, for instance, is subtitled, "How violence develops and where it can be lead" and it makes impressive play with the devastating effects of media smears and distortions upon the personality of an innocent woman caught up in a police investigation. Katherina's actual violence (she eventually murders the journalist principally responsible for the destruction of her reputation) is made to seem an almost natural, healthy reaction against the unscrupulous power of the popular press which has shattered her private world in ways analogous to a series of blows. There may well be a case for treating some of the episodes in the narrative as psychological violence, a category about which I shall have more to say later, but much of the novel's success lies in its symbolic and metaphorical deployment of the idea of violence and the ironic parallels between the effects of violence and the impact of journalistic irresponsibility and sensation-seeking.
25. Robert Paul Wolff, "On Violence" *Journal of Philosophy*, LXVI, 1969.
26. Ibid., p. 602.
27. Ibid., p. 606.
28. Ibid.
29. Ibid., p. 610.
30. Honderich, *op. cit.*, p. 154. Honderich's general definition of violence makes reference neither to law nor political change but only to a use of force etc. "that offends against a norm" (p. 153). He could thus admit a category of illegal State violence and presumably even such legal State violence as could be construed as offending against a norm (whatever that might mean). Yet the facts remain that, (i) he shows no interest in working with the broader notion of violence, (ii) gives no idea of what sort of norms he has in mind, and (iii) is, in any case, committed to seeing these exercises of violence as nonpolitical whatever their rationale.
31. R. Miller, "Violence," Ed. J. A. Shaffer, (New York 1971): 27.
32. Cf. Miller *op. cit.*
33. Garver, *op. cit.*, pp. 225–26.
34. Harris, *op. cit.*, p. 16.
35. The mention of Hobbes should remind us that one traditional way of viewing the legitimacy of the State is to see it as the safest form of the agency defence against the dangers of violence. Here too we may locate some of the point behind legitimist definitions of violence because the authorized violence of the State is seen as so contrasting with the violence against which it offers protection as not to deserve the name violence at all. Nonetheless, violence it is and even where authorized there remain moral questions about its employment.
36. Versions of this paper were read at philosophy colloquia in Oxford and London in 1983, when I was a Visiting Fellow at Corpus Christi College, Oxford, and particularly benefited from comments by Alan Ryan, G. A. Cohen and C. C. W. Taylor. It originally appeared in *Philosophical Papers*, vol XIV (1), May 1985.

Chapter 4

1. Thus, "cultural violence" follows in the footsteps of the concept of "structural violence," introduced in this journal over 20 years ago in "Violence, peace and research." For a recent very constructive critique and effort to develop the idea further see Roth (1988). A similar concept is introduced in Saner (1982).
2. There have been many efforts to create the "new man" (and woman?). In the West each new

branch of Christianity is an effort, so is humanism, so is socialism. But any inculcation in others of any single culture is in itself an act of direct violence (meaning intended by the actor), usually implying desocialization from one culture and resocialization into another—including the very first socialization of the young (defenseless) child. However, if culture is a *conditio sine qua non* for a human being, we are born with none (only predispositions), and inculcation is an act of violence, then we are faced with the basic problem of education: is "educate" a transitive or intransitive verb? Of course it is both related hermeneutically. Peaceful education, including socialization would probably imply exposure to multiple cultures and then a dialogue, as argued below. Neither Christianity nor humanism is good at this: in fact, we still do not know how to do it. It should be noted that to impose a culture on somebody, whether done directly or structurally, is not what is meant here by cultural violence. Cultural aspects legitimizing that imposition, however, for instance because the culture is "higher" (monotheistic, modern, scientific, etc.), would be violence built into that culture, in other words, cultural violence. "Empirical or potential legitimation of violence" is the key to cultural violence.

3. We then schematically divide control mechanisms into internal and external, positive and negative: identifying "internal, both positive and negative" as good and bad conscience respectively; external positive as reward and external negative as punishment. "Internalization" is conscience deeply rooted in the person system, "institutionalization" is punishment/reward deeply tooled in the social system. Both serve to make the act come from "naturally, normally, voluntarily." This piece of elementary social science may serve to locate cultural and structural violence centrally in general social science theory construction.
4. Johan Galtung, "The Basic Needs Approach," in Katrin Lederer; David Antal and Johan Galtung, Eds. *Human Needs: A Contribution to the Current Debate*. Cambridge, MA: Oelgeschlager Gunn and Hain; Königstein: Anton Hain (1980): 55–125.
5. For an attempt to compare the three systems (not just Hitlerism and Stalinism, as is now very common under *glasnost* revisionism), see Galtung (1984).
6. There are strong similarities built around *shinto* themes of chosenness. For an analysis see Ienaga (1978), particularly p. 154 for the concept of *hakko ichiu* (the eight corners of the world under one roof).
7. The easy approach is to dump all "side-effects" at the doorsteps of some other disciplines demanding that they shall clean it up conceptually, theoretically, and in practice—as economists are wont to do.
8. A document consisting of the Universal Declaration of 1948, the two Covenants of 1966 and an Optional Protocol. The Bill has not yet attained the standing it deserves, among other reasons because of US failure to ratify the Covenants.
9. Johan Galtung, "How Universal Are the Human Rights? Some Less Applaudable Consequences of the Human Rights Tradition." Paper prepared for the Nobel Symposium on Human Rights, Oslo, June (1988).
10. Johan Galtung, *Peace and Social Structure Essays in Peace Research*, vol. III. (Copenhagen: Ejlers) 1978.
11. Hence, it is at this level environmental degradation has to be counteracted, through de-industrializing and de-commercializing processes, not by converting one type of pollution or depletion to another through patchwork approaches to this major global problem.
12. Johan Galtung, *Methodology, and Ideology Essays in Methodology*, vol. I. (Copenhagen: Ejlers, 1977).
13. Hans Ruedi Weber, "The Promise of the Land, Biblical Interpretation and the Present Situation in the Middle East," *Study Encounter*, vol. 7, no. 4 (1971): 1–16.
14. Rather, it is almost incredible how peaceful that border high up in the North has been between such a small and such a big country, supposed by some to be eager to fill any "power vacuum."
15. This, of course, is the general approach taken by the Stockholm International Peace Research Institute, in the SIPRI Yearbook and other publications: very useful as documentation at the surface level, but it does not deepen the understanding sufficiently for any real countermeasures to be imagined and enacted.
16. These factors are very often held to be important in explaining Japanese aggressiveness, [e.g. Benedict (1972), Ienaga (1978) also quotes these factors.]
17. When the tram passed the Imperial Castle in Tokyo, passengers used to stand up and bow toward the Emperor. And the *shinto* Yasukuni shrine is still a major center of the national and nationalist constructions in Japan. After his party's defeat in the 23 July 1989 elections, the new LDP Prime Minister, Kaifu, did not visit the shrine on the anniversary of the capitulation 15 August 1945, well knowing that the winds were blowing more from the left.

18. Nowhere have I seen a clearer example of such deep integration of the military into the university as with the Reserve Officers Training Corps (ROTC) in the USA, which even permits the military to buy students with scholarships and to give classes filled with militarist propaganda.
19. Another theological distinction of equal importance is whether we are born with original sin (as some Christians would claim), original blessing (as others would claim), both (a Hindu-Buddhist karmaist position?) or neither (an atheist position). The combination transcendental God/original sin has tremendous implications for controlling people, as Luther understood well.
20. For more details, see Galtung (1989a. ch. 3; 1989b). For an excellent study of the theme of chosenness, see Weber (1971).
21. This is a major theme of a fascinating and scary dystopian novel (Atwood, 1997). I am indebted to Carolyn DiPalma for this reference.
22. Ekkehart Krippendorff, Staat und Krieg. *Die historische Logik politischer Unvernunft* (Frankfurt: Suhrkamp, 1985).
23. My own position, not very original, is this: the fetus is life, hence sacred. Everything possible should be done to avoid a situation where life is destroyed, willfully or not. After all alternatives have been exhausted, the decision belongs to those who created that life, generally a woman and a man, with veto power to the woman and right of consultation to the man.
24. Casey Miller and Kate Smith, *The Handbook of Nonsexist Writing* (New York: Harper & Row [2nd ed.] 1988).
25. Johan Galtung and Fumiko Nishimura, "Structure, Culture and Languages: An Essay Comparing the Indo-European, Chinese and Japanese Languages," *Social Science Information*, vol. 22, no. 6, (December 1983): 895–925.
26. Johan Galtung, *Europe in the Making* (New York and London: Taylor and Francis, 1989).
27. Mogens Trolle Larsen, "Europas Lys," in Hans Boll-Johansen and Michael Harbsmeier, eds, *Europas Opdagelse*. (Copenhagen; Ejlers 1988): 9–37.
28. Johan Galtung, "A Structural Theory of Imperialism," *Journal of Peace Research*, vol. 8., no. 2, (1971): 81–117.
29. His basic point is simply this: use all surplus value accumulated to improve the factors of production, not for luxury consumption by the owners of the factors of production, to get out of the trap. Simple and wise, this is what Japan did, but hardly what Japan today would like to see too many others do.
30. Johan Galtung, *Methodology and Development Essays in Methodology*, vol. III. (Copenhagen: Ejlers, 1988).
31. An important poststructuralist position: digging deep, below the surface, is not a transition from multiplicity to simplicity. "Deep occidental culture," for instance, is not unambiguous. I would, for instance, argue that Christianity can be understood only in terms of at least two readings, a hard reading (more transcendental, original-sin oriented) and a soft reading (immanent, original-blessing oriented). Others see a more complex variety of deep cultures. The step from one to two is a necessary condition.
32. Cosmology is defined, roughly, as "the deep cultural assumptions of a civilization, including the general assumptions underlying the deep structures; defining the normal and natural."
33. When does the culture, particularly the deep culture, have sufficient plasticity (Scholem) for the culture to be moulded, reshaped? In times of crises? After a deep trauma has been inflicted, including the trauma of inflicting deep traumas on others? We know little except that these are crucial questions.
34. Look at Gandhi's life: The political agenda he took on was staggering—*swaraj*: the exploration of *satyagraha* and *sarvodaya*; the uplift of the Indians in South Africa, the *harijans* in India, the women; and the communal struggle between Hindus and Muslims. At no point did Gandhi say: I will concentrate on one of these, and the rest will follow.
35. Johan Galtung, "How Universal Are the Human Rights? Some Less Applaudable Consequences of the Human Rights Tradition." Paper prepared for the Nobel Symposium on Human Rights, Oslo, June 1988.

Chapter 5

1. One might, rather, doubt whether this famous demand does not contain too little, that is, whether it is permissible to use, or allow to be used, oneself or another in any respect as a means. Very good grounds for such doubt could be adduced.
2. Unger, *Politik und Metaphysik*, Berlin, 1921, p. 8.

3. But see Unger, pp. 18ff.
4. Sorel, *Réflexions sur la violence*, 5th ed., Paris, 1919, p. 250.
5. Hermann Cohen, *Ethik des reinen Willens*, 2nd ed., Berlin, 1907, p. 362.
6. Kurt Hiller in a yearbook of *Das Ziel.*

Chapter 6

1. Crime was explicitly defined by certain jurists such as Muyart de Vouglans, 1767: 108 and 1780: 3, or Rousseaud de la Combe, 1–2.
2. Moreau de Jonnés, quoted in Touquet.
3. *La Phalange,* 10 August 1836.

Chapter 7

1. *Essais III, XIII, De l'expérience, ed.* Pléiade, p. 1203
2. *Livre II, ch. XII,* p. 601 Pléiade

Chapter 8

1. Jacques Derrida, "Force of Law: The 'Mystical Foundation of Authority,' " *Cardozo Law Review* 11 (1990): 919.
2. Ibid., pp. 940–1.
3. Ibid., p. 943.
4. Ibid., pp. 942–5.
5. Nancy Fraser, *The French Derrideans: Politicizing Deconstruction or Deconstructing the Political? in her Unruly Practices: Power, Discourse, and Gender in Contemporary Social Theory* (Minneapolis: University of Minnesota Press, 1989): 69.
6. Derrida's essay contains one version of this defense. See Derrida, "Force of Law," 960–69. For another version, see Drucilla Cornell, "Time, Deconstuction, and the Challenge to Legal Positivism: The Call to Judicial Responsibility," *Yale Journal of Law and Humanities* 2 (1990): 267.
7. Aristotle, "Politics: Book I," in *The Politics of Aristotle*, trans. Ernest Barker (London: Oxford University Press. 1946).
8. See Derrida, *supra* note 1, pp. 960–9.
9. Ibid., pp. 960–3.
10. Ibid., p. 967. ("The instant of decision is a madness, says Kierkegaard.")
11. Ibid., pp. 960–9.
12. Ibid., pp. 942–3.
13. For a book that I consider a model of this sort of critique, see generally Patricia J. Williams, *The Alchemy of Race and Rights* (Cambridge: Harvard University Press, 1991). Interestingly, Williams uses deconstructive techniques in the service of critical, as opposed to quasi-transcendental, reflection.
14. Again, the outstanding exemplar is Patricia J. Williams, *supra* note 13.
15. See Elizabeth Schneider, "The Dialectic of Rights and Politics: Perspectives from the Women's Movement," *New York University Law Review* 16 (1986): 589, 642–8 (argument that issues of sexual harassment and legal protection for batted women emerged from feminist thinking of the 1970s).

Chapter 10

1. Susan Griffin, *Rape: The Power of Consciousness.* New York: Harper & Row, 1979; Andrea Medea and Kathleen Thompson, *Against Rape.* New York: Farrar, Straus & Giroux, 1974; and Heidi Hartmann and Ellen Ross, "Comments on 'On Writing the History of Rape'," *Signs* 3:4 (Summer 1978).
2. Susan Brownmiller, *Against Our Will.* New York: Simon and Schuster, 1975: 423–4. My own view is that it is more an assault than a robbery, the latter term being too bound up with an exchange mentality.

3. See for example, Medea and Thompson, *Against Rape*, 32. See also Brownmiller's conversations with reporters in Vietnam (*Against Our Will*, 87–118).
4. Edward Shorter, "On Writing the History of Rape," *Signs* 3:2 (Winter 1977): 471–82, esp. 474.
5. Women Against Violence Against Women Newsletter, June 1976: 1.
6. Not only do "snuff" films claim to depict a woman's death and dismemberment, but one of the selling points of the advertising is that the actress is really killed on camera. See Beverly La Bell, "Snuff—the Ultimate in Woman-Hating," in *Take Back the Night*, ed. Laura Lederer. New York: Morrow, 1980.
7. *Aegis*, November/December 1978: 3.
8. Gloria Steinem, "Erotica and Pornography: A Clear and Present Difference," in *Take Back the Night*, p. 38.
9. Paula Webster, "Pornography & Pleasure," *Heresies* 12 (1980): 49–50.
10. For the quotation, see Virginia Barker, "Dangerous Shoes, or What's a Nice Dyke like Me Doing in a Get-up Like This," *Coming to Power*, ed. Samois. Palo Alto: Palo Alto University Press, 1981.
11. Robert Stoller's restatement on Freud, *Perversion*. New York: Pantheon, 1975: 6, 12–14, 23.
12. Jeffrey Weeks, *Sex, Politics, and Society*. Essex, U.K.: Longman, 1981: 12.
13. This argument is made in greater depth by Robert Padgug, "Sexual Matters," *Radical History Review*, No. 20 (Spring/Summer 1979), quoted material from p. 11. I should note that while his case is similar to mine, he does not focus as much as I do here on the effects of structured social relations. Nor am I using his definition of *praxis* as "language, consciousness, symbolism and labor" since that strikes me as too compartmentalized.
14. See Weeks, p. 12. Weeks gives a series of factors which should be taken as guidelines in studying sexuality: he includes the kinship and family system, economic and social changes, changing forms of social regulation, the political moment, and the existence of cultures of resistance.
15. See especially Weeks's discussion of the different strategies of investigating sexuality in *Sex, Politics, and Society*, 1–18; *Radical History Review*, special issue on Sexuality, No. 20 (Spring/Summer 1979); Sherry B. Ortner and Harriet Whitehead, "Accounting for Sexual Meanings," in Ortner and Whitehead, eds., *Sexual Meanings: The Cultural Construction of Gender and Sexuality*. New York: Cambridge University Press, 1981: 1–27; Adrienne Rich, "Compulsory Heterosexuality and Lesbian Existence," *Signs* 5:4 (Summer 1980); Ann Ferguson, Jacquelyn Zita, and Kathryn Pyne Addelson, "On Compulsory Heterosexuality and Lesbian Existence: Defining the Issues," *Signs* 7:1 (Autumn 1981).
16. One can find these assumptions for example in Amber Hollibaugh and Cherrie Moraga, "What We're Rollin' Around in Bed With," *Heresies* 12 (1980); Paula Webster, "Pornography and Pleasure," *Heresies* 12 (1980). Webster does state that masculinity and femininity are social constructions but at the same time argues that the images one gets in pornography are at least demystifying, and that our fantasies can be used to map the zones of arousal, thus accepting unquestioningly the erotic conventions of our culture. See also Barbara Lipschutz, "Cathexis," in *What Color is Your Handkerchief?* Berkeley: Samois, 1979: 9. One of the basic problems in much of this feminist literature is that while authors state that they see sexuality as a cultural creation, they often go on to argue in ways that suggest that changing one's sexuality is an impossibility: one must simply accept it. But if sexuality is a social relation and is culturally and historically specific, then those of us who are committed to changing other social relations must include sexuality as one of the dimensions of our existence open to change.
17. I should note at the outset that I have many difficulties with the positions he takes and I note them here in part to indicate that the points I take from him for use are just that, not an endorsement of the position he puts forward. In particular, I oppose his unquestioning acceptance of the existence of the vaginal orgasm. See *Sexual Excitement: The Dynamics of Erotic Life*. New York: Pantheon, 1979: 88 and *Perversion*, p. 23; his stress on the centrality of maternal responsibility in producing "normal" heterosexuals (See *Perversion*, pp. 138, 154, 161); and his account of how people become homosexuals (for example, *Perversion*, p. 153). Nor do I share his concerns: I do not believe homosexuality should be considered either a perversion or a diagnosis, nor am I interested in the psychological origins of gender identity (see *Perversion*, pp. xvi, 199f). At times as well, Stoller's discussion is marred by a masculine understanding of the world, for example his statement that "It is hard to imagine a little girl, confronted with this task, who would not envy boys and their aggressive, penetrating, hedonistic, arrogant, unfettered, God-granted, antisocial, unsympathetic, humiliating penis"

(see *Sexual Excitement*, p. 74). Thus, he seems to accept without question the social and cultural meanings associated with the penis.

18. See *Sexual Excitement*, p. 26.
19. Ibid., p. 6.
20. Ibid., pp. 23, 6.
21. See *Perversion*, p. 8, 59; *Sexual Excitement*, p. 8.
22. Andrea Dworkin, *Pornography: Men Possessing Women* (New York: W. B. Putnam's Sons, 1979): 182, quoting Alfred C. Kinsey, Wardell B. Pomeroy, Clyde E. Martin, and Paul H. Gebhard, *Sexual Behavior in the Human Female* (Philadelphia: W. B. Sounders and Co, 1953): 705. She adds that the reference indicates that this physiology is true of both males and females. Her own style of presentation suggests that she does not believe this to be true.
23. A.H. Maslow, "Self-Esteem (Dominance-Feeling) and Sexuality in Women," *Journal of Social Psychology* 16 (1942): 291, quoted in Charles Herbert Stember, *Sexual Racism*. New York: Harper & Row, 1976: 145.
24. *Sexual Politics*. New York: Doubleday, 1970: 304, quoted by Stember, p. 150.
25. George Bataille, *Death and Sensuality*. New York: Arno Press, 1977: 90
26. O. Mannoni, *Prospero and Caliban*. New York: Praeger, 1964: 111, quoted by Stember, p. 164.
27. Stember, p. 149. The gender dimensions of this statement are not accidental, nor is the notion of pollution.
28. See immediately following discussion in Deirdre English, Amber Hollibaugh, and Gayle Rubin, "Talking Sex: a Conversation on Sexuality and Feminism," *Socialist Review*, No. 58 (July-August 1981): 52.
29. Barbara Lawrence, "Four-Letter Words Can Hurt You," *Philosophy and Sex*, ed. Robert Baker and Frederick Elliston. Buffalo, New York: Prometheus Books, 1975: 32.
30. See *Perversion*, pp. 7, 105–9; *Sexual Excitement*, pp. 18–21
31. *Perversion*, p. xii. This is a common psychoanalytic position, but see also Ann Snitow, "Mass Market Romance: Pornography for Women is Different," *Radical History Review*, No. 20 (Spring/Summer 1979): 153.
32. See *Sexual Excitement*, p. 113.
33. Kathleen Barry, *Female Sexual Slavery*. New York: Avon Books, 1979: 230, 233.
34. See *Sexual Excitement*, pp. 23, 33.
35. Ibid., pp. 13, 31, 35.
36. See *Perversion*, p. 208.
37. Dworkin, *Pornography: Men Possessing Women*, pp. 135–6.
38. Ibid., p. 151.
39. See *Sexual Excitement*, p. 74.
40. See *Sexual Excitement*, p. 124. See also *Perversion*, p. 58, where Stoller argues that the masochist is never really a victim because she or he never really relinquishes control.
41. See Pat Califia's statement that the bottom is the superior in "A Secret Side of Lesbian Sexuality," *The Advocate*, December 27, 1979, or in "Feminism and Sadomasochism," *Heresies* 12 (1980): 31; she notes that the "stubbornness and aggressiveness of the masochist is a byword in the S/M community."
42. See *Pornography*, p. 158.
43. See *Perversion*, p. 97.
44. Ibid., p. 44.
45. Ibid., p. 56.
46. One can compare Barry's definition of perversion as "not just that which is wrong, bad, or evil, but that which distorts, devalues, depersonalizes, warps, and destroys the person as she or he exists in time and space. It involves destruction of the human being in fact. Accordingly . . . sexuality that is fostered through the arrested male sex drive which objectifies, forces, and violates, whether it is heterosexual or homosexual, is perversion." Objectification itself, she argues, is perversion (p. 266).
47. Ibid., p. 97.
48. Ibid., p. xvii.
49. Paul Gebhard, John H. Gagnon, Wardell B. Pomeroy, and Cornelia V. Christenson, *Sex Offenders: An Analysis of Types*. New York: Harper & Row, 1965: 6, cited in Dworkin, p. 52.
50. Ibid., p. 9.
51. Ibid., p. 88.
52. Ibid., p. 98, 135ff.
53. See *Sexual Excitement*, pp. 220–1.

54. See *Perversion*, pp. 89–91.
55. On this point, Stoller seems to subscribe to the idea/argument that sexuality is a social construction when he notes that female masochism should be expected to be related to women's power in a particular culture, and states that masochism should not at all be considered a biological drive. See *Sexual Excitement*, pp. 119, 122 (respectively).
56. This in and of itself should not be surprising. McClellan's work on need for achievement, since re-done by Matins Horner, or Lawrence Kohlberg's work on the stages of moral development, since re-done by Carol Gilligan and Susan Freeman, provide two important examples of other areas in which this has been true.
57. Janice Moulton, "Sex and Reference," *Philosophy and Sex*, ed. Baker and Elliston.
58. Barry, p. 255ff., cites a number of authors in support of her point.
59. Amber Hollibaugh, "Talking Sex," p. 46. Deirdre English laments the "total lack of images of women being motivated by sexual desire," p. 53.
60. Carole Vance, "Gender Systems, Ideology, and Sex Research: An Anthropological Analysis," *Feminist Studies* 6:1 (Spring 1980): 133. See also Weeks, who notes that among those who see sex as a driving force, it is held to be basically male, and to have a firmly heterosexual orientation, p. 3.
61. William F. Whyte, "A Slum Sex Code," *American Journal of Sociology* 49 (July 1943): 27, quoted by Stember, p. 146. "Corner boys" refers to the street corner culture of lives lived both marginally employed and outdoors in the collectively inhabited spaces of street corners.
62. Kate Millett, *Sexual Politics*. New York: Doubleday, 1970: 327, quoted by Stember, p. 146.
63. See Stember, p. 150.
64. My point here is identical in form to Marx's point that the ideology of the ruling class expresses the dominant material relations in the form of ideas, and that this ideology, and the institutions which support it, structure the existence of the dominated classes as well.
65. Note that the patient with/on whom Stoller worked out his theory of sexual excitement was a woman.
66. I should note that my definition here differs from that of others who have used the term. Stoller uses the term as a narrower reference than "sexuality," arguing that most of what we label "sexual excitement" has many different parts, only one of which can be characterized as erotic excitement. The others include triumph, rage, revenge, fear, anxiety, and risk. See *Sexual Excitement*, p. 26. In contrast, I take *eros* to be the more inclusive term. Nor is my definition the same as that put forward by Susan Griffin, who states, "The very force of *eros*, the very brilliance of vitality, the irrepudiability of feeling, that *eros* cannot be reasoned out of existence . . ." See *Pornography and Silence*. New York: Harper & Row, 1981: 77.
67. Sigmund Freud, *Civilization and Its Discontents*, trans. Joan Riviera. Garden City, NY: Doubleday, 1958: 57. Freud, however, does not recognize the possibility of making one out of more than two.
68. Ibid., pp. 42–3.
69. *Republic* I: p. 329c and III: p. 403d, respectively, in Paul Shorey, trans., *The Collected Dialogues of Plato*. Princeton: Princeton University Press, 1978. All references to dialogues are from this collection unless otherwise noted. In this context, the uniqueness of Marx's contribution to political thought is marked by the centrality of the place given to human sensuous experience, one indicating a respect for rather than devaluation of the body—with all its needs and failings. What could be more explicit than his critique of Feuerbach's materialism for not conceiving of reality itself as "human sensuous activity"? See "Thesis I," in Robert Tucker, ed., *The Marx-Engels Reader*, 1st ed. New York: Norton, 1975: 143.
70. See Dorothy Dinnerstein, *The Mermaid and the Minotaur*. New York: Harper & Row, 1976: 140. Note her discussion of Norman Brown's *Life Against Death*, pp. 135–51. See also Herbert Marcuse, *Eros and Civilization*. Boston: Beacon Press, 1955.
71. Ibid., p. 21.
72. Ibid., p. 211.
73. See Marcuse, pp. 220, 222. I differ with him on the possibilities for a "re-sexualized work" since it seems that the pleasure of acting on the world is in itself an "erotic" one.
74. See *Perversion*, pp. 64–5.
75. Ibid., p. 86.
76. Ibid., p. 91.
77. Ibid., pp. 4, 80; *Sexual Excitement*, p. 77.
78. *Perversion*, p. 105.
79. Ibid., p. 99.
80. Stoller makes this point in the context of an argument that perversion "may be a gender

disorder in the development of masculinity." On this point, see my argument in Chapter 10 of *Money, Sex, and Power: Toward a Feminist Historical Materialism*. New York: Longman, 1983.

81. Ibid., p. 119; *Sexual Excitement*, p. 13.
82. Stoller regards this as a tentative hypothesis, See *Sexual Excitement*, p. 21. He notes that the perversion is a fantasy which is a defensive structure raised to preserve pleasure, and that perversion arises as a way of coping with one's gender identification. See *Perversion*, pp. xiv, xii, respectively.
83. See *Pornography and Silence*, p. 144. I have relied heavily on her description of the major themes found in contemporary pornography. But I have many fundamental and important disagreements with her. I do not believe that the problems we face can be traced to the pornographic *mind*. Nor do I believe that pornography endangers our lives because action begins in the mind and then moves to reality. Rather, I hold that what endangers our lives is the same social structure which produces pornography as well as other attacks on humanity. Griffin misses the importance of institutions, in part because she focuses on the mind. Thus, she can hold that the pornographer cuts off the heads of nature, and others grow, and for this reason the violence must accelerate. In addition, I am not concerned, as Griffin is, about addressing questions of whether the pornographer is a revolutionary of the imagination or whether pornography is catharsis—worthy subjects, but not my own. Nor do I think pornography is fundamentally rooted in religion (as she claims, p. 16). Nor do I share the mysticism which invades her work—e.g. her references to "sacred image of the goddess, the sacred image of the cow, the emblematic touch of divinity in the ecstasy of the sexual act . . ." (see p. 71). I find her evaluation of the "heart" as an organ between mind and appetite difficult to accept (see p. 81). Why not the liver?, I found myself asking. The "heart" as a model for feeling is a cultural, not universal construction. I list this variety of disagreements to indicate my various difficulties with her analysis, and to indicate that, as with Stoller's work, points are being taken over and used in my own framework of analysis. I should note in addition that I found it extremely difficult to translate Griffin's account into my own terms. Thus, my references to *Pornography and Silence* should be seen as references to the place in her work where I found the material I make use of, to places where her work highlighted issues for me, not as references to arguments she has made, unless clearly indicated as such.
84. Ibid., p. 34.
85. See *Perversion*, p. 57.
86. Ibid., pp. 208–9.
87. See Griffin, pp. 41, 49; *Perversion*, p. 133.
88. See Griffin, p. 133.
89. Ibid., pp. 122–3.
90. Ibid., pp. 89–90.
91. See Griffin's chapter on silence, pp. 201–50.
92. See Dworkin, pp. 25–6.
93. Ibid., p. 61.
94. Griffin's point here is echoed by Stoller, who underlines that the major way for looking to be sexually exciting is for the man to believe he is acting sadistically and revengefully on an unwilling woman. See *Perversion*, pp. 108–9.
95. Quoted in *Pornography and Silence*, p. 91.
96. Amanda Spake, "The End of the Ride," *Mother Jones*, April 1980: 40.
97. See George Bataille, *Death and Sensuality*, p. 91. For a more complete account of the commonalties of sexual activity and ritual sacrifice, see p. 91ft.
98. See Dinnerstein, p. 135.
99. See Griffin, pp. 24–8, 59.
100. For an analysis of how this works, see Angela Carter, *The Sadeian Woman*. New York: Pantheon, 1978: 38–77; for a very different analysis, more like that put forward here, see Griffin, pp. 21–5. See also Dworkin's synopsis, pp. 167–75, of Bataille's *Story of the Eye* with the (to me) odd centrality of egg fetishism—a proof, if one is needed, that anything can be eroticized.
101. See Jessica Benjamin, "The Bonds of Love: Rational Violence and Erotic Domination," *Feminist Studies* 6:1 (Spring 1980): 154.
102. See Griffin, p. 30. See also the discussion of the power dynamics of striptease from the stripper's point of view, where when the show is going well the stripper is in complete control; Seph Weene, "Venus," *Heresies* 12 (1980): 36–8.
103. See Weene, 37. The other types she mentions are "soft and powerless," "not-a-woman,"

and "rich." It is interesting to note that each of these ways of producing sexual excitement relies on a move away from dailiness.

104. See Griffin, page 64.
105. See Benjamin, p. 157. She is quoting from *The Story of O*, by Pauline Reage, trans. S. d'Estree. New York: Grove Press, 1965: 15–7.
106. Griffin gives a number of examples, see *Pornography and Silence*, pp. 64–6, 68.
107. See Benjamin, p. 155.
108. Griffin, 56–8. Griffin analyzes *The Story of O* as an account of how O "unlearns all the knowledge of her body" (219 ff). But it should, I believe, rather be read as a series of ever-increasing attacks on the body and, more precisely, the will of another.
109. Ibid., p. 29.
110. See Griffin, pp. 132–8. See also the Apollo story in *Oresteia*, which is an attempt to deny this.
111. Griffin makes a similar seeming but different point. She argues, in p. 32, that pornography contains three levels of death—the links of death with sex, the fear of the body, and the death of self-image.
112. See Dworkin, pp. 217–23.
113. See Mailer, *Prisoner of Sex*. Boston: Little, Brown, 1971: 126, quoted in Dworkin, p. 54.
114. See Bataille, p. 42. While Adrienne Rich acknowledges the sometimes violent feelings between mothers and children, she quite clearly does not put these at the heart of the relation.
115. Ibid., p. 13.
116. See Bataille, p. 14; see also p. 101.
117. See Griffin, p. 123. She uses this description to make the point of the obsessive need for control.
118. Audre Lorde, "The Master's Tools Will Never Dismantle The Master's House," *This Bridge Called My Back*, ed. Cherrie Moraga and Gloria Anzaldua. Watertown, Mass.: Persephone Press, 1981: 99.
119. Niles Newton, "Interrelationship Between Sexual Responsiveness, Birth, and Breast-Feeding," *Contemporary Sexual Behavior*, ed. Joseph Zubin and John Money. Baltimore: Johns Hopkins University Press, 1971: 95.
120. Ibid., pp. 80–3.
121. Ibid., p. 84.
122. Susan Weisskopf, "Maternal Sexuality and Asexual Motherhood," *Signs* 5:4 (Summer 1980): 770.
123. The quoted phrase is Janice Moulton's, from "Sex and Reference." In addition I am indebted to Sarah Begus for pointing this out to me. See "Sexual Relations of Domination" (mimeo), p. 20.
124. See for example Gayle Rubin, "The Leather Menace: Comments on Politics and S/M," *Coming to Power*, ed. Samois, and, for another view, *Off Our Backs* 12:6 (June 1982).
125. See Pat Califia, "Feminism and Sadomasochism," p. 32; Amber Hollibaugh and Cherrie Moraga, "What We're Rollin' Around in Bed With," *Heresies* 12 (1980): 60; Pat Califia, *Sapphistry* (N.p.: Naiad Press, 1980): 124, 125, 128.
126. For example, Pat Califia's statement that "most of us feel some guilt or shame about being sexual," in *Sapphistry*, p. 131. See also Sarah Zoftig, "Coming Out," pp. 88, 93; Califia, "Jessie," p. 167; Gayle Rubin, "The Leather Menace," p. 215; and Sophie Schmuckler, "How I Learned to Stop Worrying and Love My Dildo," 98–9, all in *Coming to Power*.
127. Snitow, "Mass Market Romance," p. 151.

Chapter 11

1. C. Smart, *Women, Crime and Criminology*, (London: Routledge & Kegan Paul, 1976): 70–76.
2. F. Adler, *Sisters in Crime*, (New York: McGraw-Hill, 1975).
3. N. Naffine, *Female Crime: The Construction of Women in Criminology*, (Sydney: Allen & Unwin, 1987).
4. M. Wolfgang and F. Ferracuti, *The Subculture of Violence: Towards an Integrated Theory in Criminology*, (London: Tavistock Publications, 1967); See also M. Daly and M. Wilson, *Homicide* (New York: Aldine De Gruyter, 1988).
5. K. Polk and D. Ranson, "Patterns of Homicide in Victoria," in D. Chappel, P. Grabosky and H. Strang (eds.), *Australian Violence: Contemporary Perspectives*, (Canberra: Australian Institute

of Criminology, 1991); See also Daly and Wilson, *Homicide;* and A. Wallace, *Homicide: The Social Reality,* (Sydney: New South Wales Bureau of Crime Statistics and Research, 1986).

6. A. Wallace, *Homicide: The Social Reality*, and M. Wolfgang and F. Ferracuti, *The Subculture of Violence: Towards an Integrated Theory in Criminology.*
7. J. Hanmer, J. Radford, and E.A. Stanko, *Women, Policing and Male Violence: International Perspectives,* (London: Routledge, 1989).
8. R.E. Dobasch and R.P. Dobasch, *Women, Violence and Social Change* (London: Routledge, 1992): Ch. 1.
9. Ibid.
10. J. Allen, "The 'Masculinity' of Criminality and Criminology: Integrating Some Impasses," in *Understanding Crime and Criminal Justice,* (Sydney: Law Book Company, 1988): 16.
11. Dobasch and Dobasch, *Women, Violence and Social Change,* p. 4.
12. J. Messerschmidt, *Capitalism, Patriarchy and Crime: Toward a Socialist Feminist Criminology* (Totowa, N.J.: Rowmand & Littlefield, 1986); see also Daly and Wilson, *Homicide.*
13. D.H.J. Morgan, "Masculinity and Violence," in J. Hanmer and M. Maynard (eds.) *Women, Violence and Social Control,* (London: Macmillan, 1987).
14. Messerschmidt, *Capitalism, Patriarchy and Crime: Toward a Socialist Feminist Criminology.*
15. E. Currie, *Confronting Crime: an American Challenge* (New York: Pantheon Books, 1985).
16. J. Belknap, "The Economies-Crime Link," *Criminal Justice Abstracts* (March 1989) for a review of these studies.
17. J. Braithwaite and V. Braithwaite, "The Effects of Income Inequality and Social Democracy on Homicide," *British Journal of Criminology* 20 (1980).
18. J. Blau and P. Blau, "The Cost of Inequality: Metropolitan Structure and Violent Crime," *American Sociological Review* 47 (1982).
19. Ibid., p. 126.
20. J. Braithwaite, *Inequality, Crime and Public Policy,* (London: Routledge & Kegan Paul, 1979): 230.
21. Ibid., pp. 32–46; and Currie, *Confronting Crime: an American Challenge.*
22. J. B. Kau and R. Rubin, "New Estimates of the Determinants of Urban Crime," *Annals of Regional Science* 9 (1975).
23. B.V. Bechdolt, "Cross-sectional Analysis of Socioeconomic Determinants of Urban Crime," *Review of Social Economy* 33 (1975).
24. T. Chiricos, "Rates of Crime and Unemployment: An Analysis of Aggregate Research Evidence," *Social Problems* 34 (1987).
25. K. Polk, "The New Marginal Youth," *Crime and Delinquency* 30 (1984); T. Duster, "Crime, Youth Unemployment and the Black Urban Underclass," *Crime and Delinquency* 30 (1987).
26. Polk, "The New Marginal Youth."
27. Duster, "Crime, Youth Unemployment and the Black Urban Underclass."
28. Currie, *Confronting Crime: an American Challenge.*
29. Polk and Ranson, "Patterns of Homicide in Victoria."
30. Wallace, *Homicide: The Social Reality.*
31. Polk and Ranson, "Patterns of Homicide in Victoria."
32. Daly and Wilson, *Homicide.*
33. Polk and Ranson, "Patterns of Homicide in Victoria."
34. V. Verkko, *Homicides and Suicides in Finland and Their Dependence on National Character,* (Copenhagen: G.E.C. Gads Forlag, 1951).
35. Daly and Wilson, *Homicide.*
36. Ibid., p. 285.
37. D. Greenberg, "Delinquency and the Age Structure of Society," in A. Pearl, D. Grant and E. Wenk (eds.) *The Value of Youth* (Davis, Cal.: Responsible Action, 1978).
38. Ibid., p. 65.
39. R. Mokhiber, *Corporate Crime and Violence: Big Business Power and the Abuse of the Public Trust,* (San Francisco: Sierra Club Books, 1989).
40. J. Braithwaite, *Corporate Crime in the Pharmaceutical Industry,* (London: Routledge & Kegan Paul, 1984).
41. Mokhiber, *Corporate Crime and Violence: Big Business Power and the Abuse of the Public Trust.*
42. Ibid., p. 187.
43. Public Policy Research Centre, 1988. Domestic Violence Attitude Survey, conducted for the Office of the Status of Women, Department of the Prime Minister and Cabinet, Canberra.
44. D. Archer and R. Gartner, *Violence and Crime in Cross-National Perspective,* (New Haven, Conn.: Yale University Press, 1984): 63.

45. Morgan, "Masculinity and Violence."
46. Archer and Gartner, *Violence and Crime in Cross-National Perspective.*
47. Ibid., p. 96.
48. Dobasch and Dobasch, *Women, Violence and Social Change.*
49. Ibid.

Chapter 12

1. See Hamberger and Renzetti 1996; and Renzetti and Miley 1996.
2. See Margolies and Leeder 1995; Renzetti 1995; and Renzetti and Miley 1996.
3. e.g. Dutton 1994.
4. Space limitations preclude a discussion of services and treatment issues. For a discussion of these topics, see Margolies and Leeder 1995; Renzetti 1992; and Renzetti and Miley 1996.
5. See Hart 1986: 173.
6. See Renzetti 1992.
7. See Island and Letellier 1991.
8. Renzetti 1992.
9. See Pharr 1986.
10. Renzetti 1992.
11. Island and Letellier 1991.
12. Letellier 1996.
13. Ibid.
14. See Koss 1990; Straus 1993; and Straus and Gelles 1990.
15. See Island and Letellier 1991; Lie, Schilit, Bush, Montagne, and Reyes 1991.
16. Kelly and Warshafsky 1987.
17. For other incidence estimates, see Bologna, Waterman, and Dawson 1987; Brand and Kidd 1986; Coleman 1990; Lie and Gentlewarrior 1991; and Gardner-Loulan 1987.
18. Renzetti 1992.
19. See e.g. Harris and Cook 1994.
20. e.g. Island and Letellier 1991.
21. Messerschmidt 1993.
22. Blumstein and Schwartz 1983; and Tanner 1978.
23. Renzetti 1992.
24. See Coleman 1990; Kelly and Warshafsky 1987; and Schilit, Lie, and Montagne 1990.
25. e.g. Island and Letellier 1991; and Renzetti 1992.
26. See also Gelles 1993.
27. This should not be surprising, given that research with heterosexual couples has also generated confounding findings. Compare, for example, DeMaris 1990; Forsstrom-Cohn and Rosenbaum 1985; Kalmuss 1984; O'Leary 1993; and Straus, Gelles, and Steinmetz 1980.
28. Gwat-Yong Lie et al. 1991.
29. See Coleman 1990; Kelly and Warshafsky 1987; and Renzetti 1992.
30. See Renzetti and Curran 1995.
31. Yllö and Straus 1990.
32. Ibid.
33. See Michael Smith 1990.
34. Gondolf 1988; and Finkelhor, Gelles, Hotaling, and Straus 1983.
35. Bologna, Waterman, and Dawson 1987; Coleman 1990; Kelly and Warshafsky 1987; and Renzetti 1992.
36. Byrne, Arias, and O'Leary 1992.
37. See David Byrne et al. 1992.
38. Byrne 1996; Coleman 1990; and Walker 1989.
39. Dutton 1994; Letellier 1994; and O'Leary 1993.
40. Dutton 1994.
41. Ibid.
42. See V.E. Coleman 1994.
43. See also Island and Letellier 1991.
44. See V.E. Coleman 1994.
45. Allport 1958; and Margolies, Becker, and Jackson-Brewer 1987.
46. James Shattuck 1992.
47. Margolies et al. 1987; Nicoloft and Stiglitz 1987; Riddle and Sang 1978; and Vargo 1987.

48. James Shattuck 1992.
49. See Gelles 1995.
50. See Thomas Kuhn 1970.
51. I am indebted to my colleagues—Angela Browne, Walter DeKeseredy, Rebecca and Russell Dobash, Ann Goetting, Ed Gondolf, Demie Kurz, Beth Ritchie, Kersti Yllö, and many others—who attended the Wheaton College Conference on Feminism and Domestic Violence, June 22–25, 1995, for raising these issues and, through their provocative discussions, leading me to think carefully about how the issues relate to research on same-sex domestic violence, an area that I feel is well suited for exploring these issues empirically. Special thanks to Kersti Yllö for organizing the conference and providing me the opportunity to take part in it.
52. See Crenshaw 1994.
53. See Patricia Hill Collins 1986; and James Crenshaw 1994.
54. e.g. Adam and Cayouette 1995; Barnett, Lee, and Thelen 1995; and Eiskovits and Buchbinder 1995.
55. e.g. Barnett, Lee, and Thelen 1995.
56. See Victoria Burbank 1994a, 1994b.
57. For example, I am reminded of a verbal exchange I had several years ago with a member of the battered lesbians support group with whom I was working to develop a questionnaire. While trying to understand the woman's objection to my use of a particular word on the questionnaire I said, "Now, let's get this straight . . ." at which point she interrupted me and said, "That's what I mean: No matter how hard you try, we'll never get it straight." We shared a good laugh, but her point was well taken.
58. See e.g. Reinharz 1992; and Patricia Maguire 1987.

Chapter 13

1. Georges Bataille, *Death and Sensuality* (New York: Ballantine Books, 1969): 1.
2. Ibid., p. 11.
3. Donatien-Alphonse-Francois de Sade, *Juliette*, trans. Austryn Wainhouse (New York: Grove Press, 1976): 404.

Chapter 14

1. This essay is excerpted from Cindy Jenefsky (with Ann Russo), *Without Apology: Andrea Dworkin's Art and Politics* (Boulder, CO and Oxford, England: Westview Press, 1998).
2. Andrea Dworkin, *Woman Hating* (New York: Dutton, 1974).
3. Ibid. The antipornography civil rights ordinance was first introduced in Minneapolis in 1983 and Indianapolis in 1984. This ordinance was the first initiative in the United States to legislate against pornography on the basis of its violation of women's civil rights. It is a civil law, *not* criminal, and is amended to existing antidiscrimination law. Accordingly, it defines pornography in terms of its subordinating practices, not its representational content, and these subordinating practices are derived directly from women's experiences of discrimination through the production, trafficking, and use of pornography. In general, the ordinance seeks to provide litigants legal redress—in the manner of all antidiscrimination law—against those who discriminate against them. Ordinance of the City of Minneapolis Amending Title 7, Chapters 139 and 141 of the Mpls. Code of Ordinances relating to Civil Rights, 30 December 1983; the last revision of the Minneapolis ordinance was 13 July 1984. See also Indianapolis, Indiana City-County General Ordinance No. 35 of the Code of Indianapolis and Marion County, 11 June 1984. For a complete copy of this ordinance, along with one drafted for the City of Indianapolis, one that appeared on the ballot in Cambridge, Massachusetts, in 1985, and a model ordinance sent to antipornography activists, see Andrea Dworkin and Catharine A. MacKinnon, *Pornography and Civil Rights: A New Day for Women's Equality* (Minneapolis: Organizing Against Pornography, 1988): Appendices A-D. (*Pornography and Civil Rights* is currently out of print, but the full text is available on the Andrea Dworkin web site: http://www.igc.apc.org/womensnet/dworkin.) For a brief sketch of some of the places where the ordinance was introduced, see Dworkin's Introduction to the 1989 edition of *Pornography: Men Possessing Women* (New York: Dutton, 1989): xxviii-xxxii; and Gail

Dines and Rhea Becker, "A Conversation with Andrea Dworkin," *Sojourner: The Women's Forum* (June 1990): 20.

4. Andrea Dworkin, *Pornography: Men Possessing Women* (New York: Perigee, 1981): 200.
5. Dworkin, *Pornography,* esp. chs. 5, 6 & 7; see also "Feminism: An Agenda" (1983), in *Letters from a War Zone* (London: Secker & Warburg, 1988): 148.
6. Andrea Dworkin, "Pornography and Civil Rights," unpublished speech delivered at the University of Wisconsin—Madison, 13 October 1984; see also *Pornography,* 203–204.
7. Dworkin, *Pornography,* 203–204.
8. Dworkin, "Pornography and Male Supremacy" (1981), in *Letters,* 229–230.
9. Dworkin, *Pornography,* 217.
10. See also "Pornography Is a Civil Rights Issue" (1986), in *Letters,* 277.
11. Dworkin, *Pornography,* 215–216.
12. Dworkin, *Pornography,* 164–165.
13. Andrea Dworkin, "Pornography Happens" (1993), in *Life and Death: Unapologetic Writings on the Continuing War Against Women* (New York: Free Press, 1997): 129.
14. Dworkin, *Pornography,* 164–165.
15. This notion of the term "scene" is derived from Kenneth Burke's rhetorical theory. Burke explains symbolic action (language) in terms of five basic elements which comprise his dramatistic pentad: act, scene, agent, agency, and purpose. The relationship between these elements within any symbolic action reveals clues about a rhetor's motives or attitudes toward the subject matter of the discourse. Burke describes scene as the "container" of the act, the background or context in which an act is performed by a particular agent. The scene—like the other elements in the pentad—is not necessarily fixed; it can be widened or narrowed in scope. Dworkin's emphasis of scene over agent reveals a sociological (institutional) rather than a psychological (individual) perspective on a situation. This approach yields a materialist analysis which makes the context itself the key to understanding the motive for action. *A Grammar of Motives* (Berkeley: University of California Press, 1969), esp. 3–20.
16. Dworkin, *Pornography,* 149.
17. *Woman Hating* (1974) is her first work of feminist theory. For her latest publications on the topic, see *Life and Death,* esp. "Free Expression in Serbian Rape/Death Camps" (1993): 73–76.
18. Dworkin, "Pornography: The New Terrorism" (1977), in *Letters,* 199, 201. Similarly, in *Pornography* she discusses this propaganda in terms of the male "power of naming" which, as with any other dominant form of propaganda in a system of oppression, "is upheld by force, pure and simple," Dworkin, *Pornography,* 17–18.
19. Dworkin, "Pornography and Male Supremacy," in *Letters,* 231.
20. Dworkin, "Pornography and Male Supremacy," in *Letters,* 231. This concept is also integral to her analysis in *Pornography.*
21. Dworkin, "Women Lawyers and Pornography" (1980), in *Letters,* 239–240.
22. See the chapter titled "Force" in *Pornography* for an intricate discussion of pornography's obfuscation of its use of force, 129–198.
23. Dworkin, *Pornography,* 166.
24. There is abundant, readily available evidence of men not believing women when they say "no." Of particular note is the 1992 legal case of *State* v. *Crawford,* cited in Catharine MacKinnon's "Defamation and Discrimination." A jury in South Carolina acquitted Crawford of marital rape, even after viewing a videotape of the event where the defendant is shown having intercourse with his wife and penetrating her with objects while her hands and legs are bound with rope, her mouth is gagged, her eyes are covered with duct tape, and she is screaming in resistance. MacKinnon writes: "Crawford testified he did not think his wife was serious when she said 'no.' " As the videotape was being shown to the jury, Crawford's lawyer asked, " 'Was that a cry of pain and torture? Or was that a cry of pleasure?' " Even with pictures of the rape, the jury was unable to distinguish if the sex acts were forced on Trish Crawford; that is, the jury was unable to distinguish between a woman's pain and her pleasure, between force and desire. Catharine A. MacKinnon, "Defamation and Discrimination," *Only Words* (Cambridge: Harvard University Press, 1993): 114, notes 3 & 4, respectively.
25. Dworkin, *Pornography,* 167 and 179, respectively.
26. Dworkin, "Why Pornography Matters to Feminists" (1981), in *Letters,* 204.
27. Andrea Dworkin, interview with author, Brooklyn, N.Y., 22–23 June 1989.
28. Dworkin, "Feminism: An Agenda," in *Letters,* 148.

29. Dworkin, *Pornography,* 143.
30. All quotations about this series of photographs are taken from *Pornography,* 153–160.
31. Patricia Hill Collins, *Black Feminist Thought: Knowledge, Consciousness, and the Politics of Empowerment* (New York: Routledge, 1991), 68. For a later discussion of the two major types of controlling images, see Patricia Hill Collins, "Toward a New Vision: Race, Class, and Gender as Categories of Analysis and Connection," *Race, Sex & Class: An Interdisciplinary Journal* 1 (Fall 1993): 32–34.
32. Dworkin, "Pornography Is a Civil Rights Issue," in *Letters,* 276–307; and Dworkin and MacKinnon, *Pornography and Civil Rights,* 42–43 and 70–72. See also the BBC documentary on Dworkin's work "Against Pornography: The Feminism of Andrea Dworkin," *Omnibus* (London: BBC, 1991).
33. Dworkin, "Pornography and Civil Rights."
34. Dworkin, Introduction to 1989 edition of *Pornography,* xxxvii.
35. Dworkin, "Pornography and Civil Rights."
36. Dworkin, *Pornography,* 201. See states similarly in her speech "Pornography and Civil Rights": "In many of the films that are being sold in this country right now, the rapes are real, the force is real, the hitting is real, the tying up is real. The women are really being raped, and the women are really being hurt." See also: "Pornography and Male Supremacy," in *Letters,* 232.
37. Dworkin, Introduction to 1989 ed. of *Pornography,* xxxviii.
38. Elizabeth Wilson, "Interview with Andrea Dworkin," *Feminist Review* 1 (June 1982): 26.
39. Dworkin, "Letter from a War Zone" (1979), in *Letters,* 315.
40. See for example "Letter from a War Zone," in *Letters,* 315–319; "Pornography Is a Civil Rights Issue," in *Letters,* 278–279; Introduction to 1989 ed. of *Pornography,* xvi–xxiv.
41. Dworkin, "Letter from a War Zone," in *Letters,* 315.
42. Andrea Dworkin, interview with author, Brooklyn, N.Y., 25–26 May 1993.
43. Dworkin, "Letter from a War Zone," in *Letters,* 315.
44. Dworkin, "Letter from a War Zone," in *Letters,* 315 (Dworkin's italics). See also "Violence Against Women: It Breaks the Heart, Also the Bones" (1984), in *Letters,* 178–179.
45. Dworkin and MacKinnon, *Pornography and Civil Rights,* 37–38 (authors' italics).
46. Dworkin, "Letter from a War Zone," in *Letters,* 313.
47. Dworkin, "Against the Male Flood" (1985), in *Letters,* 262.
48. Dworkin and MacKinnon, *Pornography and Civil Rights,* Appendix A, 99–100.
49. The Dworkin-MacKinnon civil rights antipornography ordinance has sparked much comment and controversy among legal (and political) theorists on the legal intricacies and implications of the ordinance. This body of material is too voluminous to cite in its entirety; for a sampling of this controversy, consult the following works and their bibliographic references: Margaret Baldwin, "The Sexuality of Inequality: The Minneapolis Pornography Ordinance," *Law and Inequality: A Journal of Theory and Practice,* 2 (August 1984): 629–653; Michael A. Gershel, "Evaluating a Proposed Civil Rights Approach to Pornography: Legal Analysis as If Women Mattered," *William Mitchell Law Review,* 11 (1985): 41–80; June Callwood, "Feminist Debates and Civil Liberties" and Lisa Duggan, Nan Hunter, and Carole S. Vance, "False Promises: Feminist Antipornography Legislation in the U.S.," both in *Women Against Censorship,* ed. Varda Burstyn (Vancouver: Douglas & McIntyre, 1985), 121–129 and 130–151, respectively; Penelope Seator, "Judicial Indifference to Pornography's Harm: *American Booksellers v. Hudnut,*" *Golden Gate University Law Review,* 17 (Fall 1987): 297–358; Donald Downs, *The New Politics of Pornography* (Chicago: University of Chicago Press, 1989); Catharine A. MacKinnon, "Pornography as Defamation and Discrimination," *Boston University Law Review,* 71 (1991): 793–815; Kathleen A. Lahey, "Pornography and Harm: Learning to Listen to Women," *International Journal of Law and Psychiatry,* 14 (1991): 117–131; Richard Delgado and Jean Stefancic, "Pornography and Harm to Women: 'No Empirical Evidence?' " *Ohio State Law Journal,* 53 (1992): 1037–1055; Nadine Strossen, "A Feminist Critique of 'the' Feminist Critique of Pornography," *Virginia Law Review,* 79 (August 1993): 1099–1190; Susan M. Easton, *The Problem of Pornography: Regulation and the Right to Free Speech* (London: Routledge, 1994).
50. Dworkin and MacKinnon, *Pornography and Civil Rights,* 26.
51. Dworkin, interview with author, 1993.
52. Dworkin, "Against the Male Flood," in *Letters,* 273.
53. Dworkin, "Pornography Happens," in *Life and Death,* 135–136.
54. Dworkin, "Remember, Resist, Do Not Comply" (1995), in *Life and Death,* 175.

Chapter 15

1. Susan Brownmiller, *Against our Will: Men, Women and Rape* (New York: Simon & Schuster, 1975): 85.
2. Ibid., p. 76.
3. Harry Feldmann, *Vergewaltigung und ihre psychischen Folgen: Ein Beltrag zur post-traumatischen Belastungsreaktion*. (Stuttgart: Enke 1992).
4. Peggy Reeves Sanday, "Rape and the Silencing of the Feminine," in Sylvana Tomaselli and Roy Porter (Eds.), *Rape*. (London: Basil Blackwell 1986): 84–101.
5. Roy Porter, "Rape—Does it have a Historical Meaning?" in Tomaselli and Porter, *Rape*, p. 216–36.
6. Ibid. p. 220; Jeffrey Weeks, *Sexuality and its Discontents: Meanings, Myths and Modern Sexualities*. (London: Routledge & Kegan, 1985).
7. John Archer and Barbara Lloyd, *Sex and Gender*. (New York: Cambridge University Press, 1989).
8. Bob Connell, *Gender and Power: Society, the Person and Sexual Politics*. (Cambridge, UK: Polity Press, 1987). See also Gisela Bock, "Geschichte, frauengeschichte, geschlechtergeschichte." *Geschichte und Gesellschaft*, 14, (1988): 364–512.
9. Tageszeitung daily newspaper, February 17, 1993.
10. Michael Walzer, *Just and Unjust Wars: A Moral Argument with Historical Illustrations*. (New York: Basic Books, 1977): 133f; See also Susan Brownmiller (1975).
11. See Susan Brownmiller (1975).
12. Helke Sander, and Barbara Johr, *BeFreier und Befreite. Krieg, Vergewaltigung, Kinder* (Munich: Kunstmann Verlag, 1992).
13. Jean R. Sasson, *The Rape of Kuweit. The True Story of Iraqi Atrocities Against A Civilian Population*. (New York: Knightsbridge, 1991).
14. This seems to be true even for the "home front." Pohl reports a marked increase in the number of rapes committed in Israel during the Gulf War in 1991. A similar observation is reported from those parts of the former Yugoslavia not or no longer immediately involved in the war. According to information from the emergency hotlines in Belgrade, the incidence of sexual violence against women has increased 100%. From Zagreb it was reported that death threats against women and rape even within the family increased by at least 30% after the outbreaks of violence. Especially after TV broadcasts with a nationalistic bias, an immediate surge in anti-female violence could be observed. See Rolf Pohl, "Männlichkeit, Destruktivität und Kriegsbereitschaft." In *Logik der Destruktion. Der zweite Golfkrieg als erster elektronischer Krieg und die Möglichkeiten seiner Verarbeitung im Bewußtsein* (1992): 157. Series published by the Political Science Institute of the University of Hanover; Elisabeth Raiser, "Vergewaltigungen als Kriegsslrategie." *Junge Kirche. Zeitschrifi europäischer Christinnen und Christen* (1993) p. 6; Maja Korać, "Understanding ethnic-national identity and its meaning: Questions from women's experience," *Women's Studies International Forum*, 18 (5/6): 133–43.
15. Alexandra Stiglmayer, (Ed.) *Mass rape. The War Against Women in Bosnia-Herzegovina*. (Lincoln, NE: Nebraska University Press, 1993).
16. Ines Sabalic and Ruth Seifert, *Nirgends erweihnt—doch überail geschehen*. (Munich: Gleichstellungsstelle [Equal Rights Office for Women] of the City of Munich, 1993).
17. See Pohl (1992).
18. *Ibid*., p. 161.
19. Ruth Seifert, "War and Rape: A Preliminary Analysis," in Alexandra Stiglmayer (Ed.), *Mass rape. The War Against Women in Bosnia-Herzegovina* (Lincoln, NE: Nebraska University Press, 1993): 54–72.
20. Carolyn Nordstrom, "Women and War: Observations from the field" MINERVA. Quarterly Report on Women and the Military (IX/l 1991): 1; Richard Gabriel, *The Culture of War: Invention and Early Development* (New York: Greenwood, 1991): 14.
21. Elaine Scarry, *The Body in Pain: The Making and Unmaking of the World* (New York: Oxford University Press, 1985).
22. Ibid., p. 72f.
23. Ingrid Schmidt-Harzbach, "Eine woche im April," in Helke Sander & Barbara Johr (Eds.), *Befreier und BeFreite, Krieg, Vergewaltigung, Kinder* (Munich: Kunstmann, 1992): 43.
24. See Scarry (1985).
25. Scarry (1985) mentions the Vietnam War as an example: "The defeat of the United States by North Vietnam did not entail the loser's inability to continue or to renew military hostilities; its military prowess was in the period beginning with its defeat many times that of

North Vietnam. Instead, the war was ended because there was no longer any support for it in the United States. The American Public considered changing the national self-definition a lesser evil than continuing the war" (p. 98).

26. Ibid., p. 92.
27. Ibid.
28. See Nordstrom (1991).
29. In this context an important question is how atrocities against women are dealt with by political and military leaders. A young German historian has concerned herself with that question in her MA thesis. She found that during World War II, contrary to army regulations that provided capital punishment for rapists, sexual violence against women was, in most cases, handled with great indulgence by the military leadership in the German Wehrmächt as well as in other armies. Her preliminary result is that lack of prosecution and thus toleration in a military context can be tantamount to an order (Beck, 1994).
30. See Nordstrom (1991).
31. The Polish *intelligentsia*, as bearers of Polish nationalism and culture, were considered particularly dangerous by Nazi strategists. The orders for the ethnic annihilation of the Jewish population of Poland were extended to include non-Jewish Polish intellectuals (Nuremberg Documents NO-3732; Broszat, 1963).
32. See Ines Sabalic, *Personal Communication*, 1993.
33. Theresa Wobbe, *Die Grenzen des Geschlechts. Konstruktionen von Gemeinschaft und Rassismus* (Mitteilungen des Instituts für Sozialforschung Frankfurt, 2, 1993): 106.
34. Ibid.
35. Ibid., p. 106, author's translation.
36. See Stiglmayer (1993).
37. Adrien K. Wing and Sylke Merchán, *Rape, Ethnicity and Culture: Spirit Injury from Bosnia to Black America* (1994). Unpublished manuscript.
38. See Scarry (1985), p. 51.
39. Ibid.
40. Vera Folnegović-Smalc, "Psychiatric Aspects of Rapes in the War Against the Republics of Croatia and Bosnia-Herzegovina," in Alexandra Stiglmayer (Ed.), *Mass Rapes: War against Women* (Lincoln, NE: Nebraska University Press, 1993): 219ff.
41. See Scarry (1985): 27.
42. Ibid., p. 36.
43. Harry Feldmann, *Vergewaltigung und ihre psychischen Folgen: Ein Beltrag zur post-traumatischen Belastungsreaktion* (Stuttgart: Enke, 1992): 6.
44. See Scarry (1985).
45. Nicholas Groth and William F. Hobson, "Die Dynamik sexueller Gewalt," in Jürgen Heinrichs (Ed.), *Vergewaltigung. Die Opfer und die Täiter* (Braunschweig: Holtzmeyer, 1986): 87–98; see also Feldmann (1992).
46. Vlasta Jalusić, "Zurück in den 'Naturzustand'? Desintegration JugosfaWiens and ihre Folgen für die Frauen." (*Feministische Studien*, 2, 1992): 9–21.
47. Ibid., p. 18.
48. Ibid.
49. For an elaboration on the social and legal consequences, see Andejelka Millic, "Women and Nationalism in the Former Yugoslavia," in Nanette Funk & Magda Mueller (Eds.), *Gender Politics and Post-Communist Reflections from Eastern Europe and the former Soviet Union* (New York: Routledge, 1993): 109–122.
50. See Wobbe (1993).
51. See, for example, Endnote 1; Elizabeth Raiser, "Vergewaltigungen als Kriegsslrategie," *Junge Kirche. Zeitschrifi europäischer Christinnen und Christen* (1993): 4–10.
52. More research on the meaning of violence against women in a nationalistic context is necessary. Let it suffice here to suggest that it may serve to establish certain gender relations in a nationalistic context and a specific relationship between men and the state.

Chapter 16

1. We have demonstrated the mechanism of this Manichean world in *Peau Notre, Masques Blancs*, (Éditions du Seuil).
2. Fanon is writing in 1961. (Transl.)
3. Village assemblies. (Transl.)

4. See chap. V, "Colonial War and Mental Disorders," in *The Wretched of the Earth* (New York: Grove Press, 1966).
5. Highly trained soldiers who are completely dedicated to the Moslem cause. (Transl.)

Chapter 21

1. This is the James Bay–Northern Quebec Agreement (1975). For a detailed account of the negotiations, see Harvey Felt, "Political articulations of hunters to the States," *Études Inuit Studies*, 3, 2, 1979: 37–52.
2. To its credit, the Canadian Labour Congress has given consistent support to indigenous people, working against the efforts of Tory and nationalist politicians, particularly in Quebec, to make land rights and claims a race issue.
3. *World Economic Survey* 1990 (United Nations, New York, 1990): Figure III. 2.
4. See the remarks on modern capitalism made by Rabindranath Tagore in his *Nationalism* (Macmillan, London, 1917): "It is carnivorous and cannibalistic in its tendencies, it feeds upon the resources of other peoples and tries to swallow their whole future."
5. Tacitus, *Germania*, c. 26, and *Agricola*. c. 11.
6. Russel Barsh, "Indian Resources and the National Economy," *Policy Studies Journal* 16, 4, 1988: 799–825.
7. In 1988 75 percent of the value of all exports from all countries consisted of manufactured goods (see *World Economic Survey* 1990, Figure III. 2). In 1987 manufactures comprised only 61 percent of Canada's exports, 50 percent of Brazil's, and a mere 19 percent of Australia's (Conference on Trade and Development, *Handbook of International Trade and Development Statistics* 1989 (United Nations, New York, 1990, Table 4.1).
8. Population control was widely practised. See Henry de Laszlo and Paul S. Henshaw, "Plant materials used by primitive peoples to affect fertility," *Science* 119, 1954: 626–31; and Charles Hudson, "Cherokee concepts of natural balance," *Indian Historian*, 3, 4, 1970: 51–4.
9. See, for example, Hugh Brody, *Maps and Dreams: Indians and the British Columbia Frontier* (Norman & Hobhouse, London, 1981); and Wayne Suttles, *Coast Salish Essays* (University of Washington Press, Seattle, 1989).
10. By "primary workers" I refer to Indian hunters, fishermen, farmers and ranchers. Reservation farmers and ranchers are structurally more like peasants, as their land is largely managed and controlled by Federal and Tribal officials. See Joseph G. Jorgenson (ed.), *Native Americans and Energy Development* II (Anthropology Resource Center, Cambridge, Mass., 1984); Russel Barsh, "Plains Indian agrarianism and class conflict," *Great Plains Quarterly*, 7, 2, 1987: 83–102; and Norman Chance, "Subsistence research in Alaska: premises, practices and prospects," *Human Organization*, 46, 1, 1987: 85–9.
11. Report of the Royal Commission on Seals and the Sealing Industry in Canada (Minister of Supply and Services, Ottawa, 1986), Volume 1, recommendations 37 and 38. The author was a member of the Commission.

Chapter 23

1. Martin Heidegger, in R. Olson, "Death," *The Encyclopedia of Philosophy*, ed. P. Edwards (New York: McMillan, 1967): 309.
2. Pericles, in Thucydides, *The History of the Peloponnesian War* (Encyclopedia Britannica, 1952): 398.
3. Hence individuals who fight for the state but are motivated by a desire to ensure certain rewards for themselves, such as members of the Foreign Legion and other mercenaries, are not considered patriots, and their action cannot serve to support the legitimacy of the state.
4. The interchange was arranged by the International Institute of Intellectual Cooperation under the auspices of the League of Nations and was first published simultaneously in German, French, and English in Paris in 1933.
5. Thucydides, *History of the Peloponnesian War*, p. 398.
6. S. Freud, "Reflection upon War and Death," *Character and Culture* (Collier, 1963): 114.
7. Ibid., pp. 122, 124.
8. P. C. Stern, "Why Do People Scarify for Their Nations," *Political Psychology* 16, no. 2 (1995): 232.

9. I explain this point in greater detail in my book *Liberal Nationalism* (Princeton: Princeton University Press, 1993), chap. 6.
10. E. H. Kantorowicz, "Pro Patria Mori in Medieval Political Thought," *American Historical Review* 56 (1950): 490.
11. Ibid.
12. Ibid., p. 481.
13. Jerusalem, Associated Press, October 24, 1994.
14. In some cases, not only the state but also the nation will be endowed with religious ends, and therefore the distinction between religious and nationalistic arguments will be obscured.
15. M. Walzer, *Obligations: Essays on Disobedience, War, and Citizenship* (Cambridge, Mass.: Harvard University Press, 1970): 82.
16. Stern, "Why Do People Scarify for Their Nations?" p. 234.
17. Walzer, *Obligations*, p. 82.
18. Ibid., p. 86. Moreover, a contract that forces individuals to surrender all their authority in return for only partial security might not be attractive. If all that the contract can offer is a new spread of risks, exchanging permanent fears and threats for periods of extensive protection alternating with periods of substantial risk, then the price of subscribing to absolute authority might be considered far too high.
19. Georg Wilhelm Friedrich Hegel, quoted in *Ibid.*, p. 89.
20. Annette Baler, cited in R. Rorty, "Why Can't a Man Be More like a Woman, and Other Problems in Moral Philosophy," *London Review of Books*, 24 February 1994.
21. Contractual states that are defenseless are unable to fulfill the role that justifies their creation. Losing their main source of justification implies not only that these states cannot call upon their members to protect them with their lives but also that they do not deserve such protection.
22. I have provided a much more detailed answer to this question in *Liberal Nationalism*, chap. 2.
23. B. Williams, *Moral Luck* (Cambridge: Cambridge University Press, 1981): 13.
24. See my discussion of these issues in "The Enigma of Nationalism," *World Politics* 47, no. 3 (1995), and in "Reconstructing the Landscape of Imagination," *National Rights and International Obligations*, ed. S. Cancy, D. George, and P. Jones (Boulder, Colo.: Westview, 1996): 85–102.
25. Edmund Burke, in J. Waldron, *Nonsense on Stilts* (London: Methuen, 1987): 118.
26. Epicurus, in *The Extant Remains*, ed. C. Bailey (Oxford: Oxford University Press, 1926): 85.
27. W. Glannon, "Epicureanism and Death," *Monist* 76 (1993): 224.
28. One may rightly comment that if Epicurus's argument is rejected—namely, if people fear the state of being dead rather than being concerned about the implication of future death for their present lives—the task of the state becomes much more difficult. Presumably the reason states embark upon a project that fits Epicurus's argument is neither because they have considered the validity of his argument nor because they have been convinced by it but because its consequences are easier to confront.
29. "The Silver Platter," Natan Altermann:

And the land was silent. The incarnate sun
Flickered languidly
Above the smoldering borders.
And a nation stood—cloven hearted but breathing . . .
To receive the Miracle.
The one miracle and only . . .
The nation made ready for the pomp. It rose to the crescent moon.
And stood there, at pre-dawn garbed in festive and fear—then out they came
A boy and a girl
Pacing slowly towards the nation.
In workaday garb and bandoleer, and heavy-shod,
Up the path they came
Silently forward.
They did not change their dress, and had not yet washed away
The marks of the arduous day and night of fire-line.
Tired, oh so tired, forsworn of rest,
And oozing sap of young Hebrewness—
Silently the two approached

And stood there unmoving.
There was no saying whether they were alive or shot.
Then the nation, tear-rinsed and spellbound, asked,
Saying: Who are you? And the two soughed
Their reply: We are the silver platter
On which the Jewish state has been given you.
They spoke. Then enveloped in shadow at the people's feet they fell.
The rest will be told in the annals of Israel.

30. Ibid.
31. W. Shakespeare, "Romeo and Juliet," *The Complete Works* (New York: Oxford University Press, 1959): 164.
32. George L. Mosse, *Fallen Soldiers: Reshaping the Memory of the World Wars* (Oxford: Oxford University Press, 1950): 39. This change in the perception of death transformed the Christian cemetery into a peaceful wooded landscape of groves and meadows.
33. Wilfred Owen, "Asleep," *The Collected Works of Wilfred Owen*, p. 57.
34. M. Kundera, *The Book of Laughter and Forgetting* (Middlesex, Eng.: Penguin, 1980): 229.
35. W. Shakespeare, "Henry V," *The Complete Works*, p. 491. Although this text was written in a prenational era, it has repeatedly been used in later periods to evoke national feelings and commitments.
36. Mosse, *Fallen Soldiers*, p. 44.
37. Owen, "Asleep."
38. H. Guri, "Here Our Bodies Are Casted."
39. A. D. Smith, *National Identity* (Reno: University of Nevada Press, 1991): 160.
40. J. McMahan, "Death and the Value of Life," *Ethics* 99 (1988): 51.
41. Mosse, Fallen Soldiers, p. 27. This discussion can explain some of the major sources for the marginalization of women in modern politics.
42. Pericles, in Thucydides, *History of the Peloponnesian War*, p. 398.

Chapter 24

1. Earlier versions of this essay were presented at the Center for the Critical Analysis of Contemporary Culture at Rutgers University, at the Center for Transcultural Studies (Chicago), and at the University of Illinois.
2. A. Mbembe, "The Banality of Power and the Aesthetics of Vulgarity in the Post-colony," *Public Culture* 4.2 (1992).
3. B. Anderson, "Census, Map, Museum," *Imagined Communities* (rev. edition). (New York and London: Verso, 1991).
4. E. Balibar, "The Nation Form: History and Ideology," in E. Balibar and I. Wallerstein (eds.) *Race, Nation, Class: Ambiguous Identities* (London and New York: Verso, 1991).
5. H.K. Bhabha, *Nation and Narration* (London and New York: Routledge, 1990).
6. P. Chatterjee, *Nationalist Thought and the Colonial World: A Derivative Discourse?* (London: Zed Books, 1986).
7. A. Mbembe, "Belly-up: More on the Postcolony," *Public Culture* 5.1 (1992).
8. J. Comaroff and J.L. Comaroff, "Of Totemism and Ethnicity," *Ethnography and the Historical Imagination* (Boulder, CO: Westview Press, 1992).
9. J. Habermas, *The Structural Transformation of the Public Sphere* (Cambridge, MA: MIT Press, 1983); C. Calhoun, *Habermas and the Pubic Sphere* (Cambridge, MA: MIT Press, 1992).
10. Anderson 1991, see endnote three.
11. M. Warner, *The Letters of the Republic: Publication and the Public Sphere in Eighteenth Century America* (Cambridge, MA: Harvard University Press, 1990); B. Lee, "Going Public," *Public Culture* 5.2 (1993).
12. Lee 1993, see endnote eleven.
13. E. Hobsbawm, "Ethnicity and Nationalism in Europe Today," *Anthropology Today* 8.1 (1992).
14. J. Rosenau, *Turbulence in World Politics: A Theory of Change and Continuity* (Princeton, NJ: Princeton University Press, 1990).
15. Ibid.
16. See the convergence between this proposal and the argument from the Chicago Cultural Studies Group (1992): 537.
17. J. MacAloon, *This Great Symbol: Pierre de Coubertin and the Origins of the Modern Olympic Games*

(Chicago: University of Chicago Press, 1981); S.Y. Kang, J. MacAloon, and R. DaMatta, *The Olympics and Cultural Exchange* (Seoul: Hanyang University, Institute for Ethnological Studies, 1988).

18. L. Berlant and E. Freeman, "Queer Nationality," *Boundary* 19.1 (1992); N. Fraser, "Rethinking the Public Sphere: A Contribution to the Critique of Actually Existing Democracy," in C. Calhoun, *Habermas and the Public Sphere* (Cambridge, MA: MIT Press, 1992); M. Hansen, "Unstable Mixtures, Dilated Spheres: Negt and Kluge's The Public Sphere and Experience: Twenty Years Later," *Public Culture* 5.2 (1993); B. Robbins, *The Phantom Public Sphere* (Minneapolis: University of Minnesota Press, 1993); Black Public Sphere Collective, *The Black Public Sphere: A Public Culture Book* (Chicago: University of Chicago Press, 1995).
19. J. Kotkin, *Tribes: How Race, Religion, and Identity Determine Success in the New Global Economy* (New York: Random House, 1993).
20. L. Berlant, *The Anatomy of National Fantasy: Hawthorne, Utopia, and Everyday Life* (Chicago and London: University of Chicago Press, 1991).
21. I am grateful to Philip Scher, who introduced me to the term *transnation*.
22. Berlant and Freeman 1992, see endnote eighteen.
23. Berlant 1991, see endnote 20.

Chapter 25

1. See Bell-Fialkoff 1993; Meron 1993; Mestrovic 1994; Schopflin 1993; and Vulliamy 1994.
2. Bauman 1991, p. 14.
3. Ibid., p. 17.
4. See Anthony Giddens 1991.
5. See Barth 1969; Helm 1971; Ahmed 1976, 1980; Godelier 1977; and Ahmed and Hart 1984.
6. See Fortes and Evans-Pritchard 1940.
7. See Max Gluckman 1971.
8. See Walker Connor 1993.
9. Edward Said 1978; see also Said 1993.
10. Surah, *Al-Hujurat,* Verse 13.
11. For example, Mestrovic in the Balkans in 1994; the Jewish women in Israel in 1993: Makiya in Iraq in 1993 and Padgaonkar—with too many others to name—in India in 1993. Padgaonkar, chief editor of *The Times of India,* was dubbed the chief editor of *The Times of Pakistan* in Bombay by Hindu communalists when he attempted balanced reporting of the riots after Ayodhya and published the book *When Bombay Burned;* this is the equivalent of the white liberal who earns himself the contemptuous title "nigger lover" from his people for supporting black issues.
12. Giddens 1991, p. 22.
13. See Nash 1989; Giddens 1990, 1991; Robertson 1991; Beck 1992; Fukuyama 1992; Ahmed 1993e; Huntington 1993; Moynihan 1993; Ahmed and Donnan 1994; Turner 1994; and Ahmed and Shore, in press.
14. For an illuminating discussion on ideology and mass communication see Thompson 1990; for the role of the media in disasters and relief see Benthall 1993.
15. Robertson 1992, p. 6.
16. For the recent high-quality literature on religion and the rise of extremism in India, mainly written by Indians, see Engineer 1984; Akbar 1988; McLeod 1989; Phadnis 1989; Graham 1990; Gopal 1991; Tully 1991; Das 1992; Madan 1992; Ahmed 1993b, 1993d; Basu *et al.*, 1993; Padgaonkar 1993.
17. A point perceptively raised by Iyer 1992; also see Amin 1994.
18. The process works both ways in South Asia: the popular Pakistani series "Dhoop Kinarey"—also shown in Britain—has almost all Muslim names in the credit list.
19. See Ahmed 1992b.
20. Kohinoor 1960.
21. See Gowalkar 1938.
22. See Oak 1990; Elst 1992.
23. "Dying to Please Nobody" by Marilyn French in *The Sunday Times*, 10 October 1993.
24. See Gellner 1983; Giddens 1991.
25. See Ahmed 1992c, 1993c; Mestrovic 1994; also *Impact International* and "Q" News published in London.

26. See Ahmed 1988, 1992a, 1993a, 1993e; Huntington 1993.
27. See Makiya 1993.
28. See Ahmed 1980.
29. See Ahmed 1993b, 1993d.
30. See Goytisolo 1993; Yusuf 1993.
31. See Peter Loizos 1981.
32. For example, see Benthall 1993 for its impact on disasters and relief.
33. Giddens 1991, p. 3.
34. Title of Beck 1992; also see Giddens 1990; Ahmed 1992a; Ahmed and Donnan 1994; Turner 1994; Ahmed and Shore, in press.

Chapter 26

1. Nietzsche, *Généalogie de la moral*, trad. franç, pp. 57–9.
2. Nietzsche, *op. cit.* p. 43.
3. Nietzsche, *op. cit.* pp. 78–80.
4. P. de Rousiers observes that everywhere in America approximately the same social environment is found, and the same type of men at the head of big businesses; but "it is in the West that the qualities and defects of this extraordinary people manifest themselves with the greatest energy; . . . *it is there that they key to the whole social system is to be found*": (La Vie Américaine: ranches, fermes, et usines, pp. 8–9; cf. p. 261).
5. De Rousiers, *La Vie américaine: l'education et la société*, p. 325.
6. De Rousiers, *La Vie américaine: ranches, fermes, et usines*, pp. 303–5.
7. J. Burdeau, *Les Maîtres de la pensée contemporaine*, p. 145. The author informs us on the other hand that "Jaurès greatly astonished the people of Geneva by revealing to them that the hero of Nietzsche, the *superman*, was nothing else but the proletariat" (p. 139). I have not been able to get any information about this lecture of Jaurès; let us hope that he will some day publish it, for our amusement.
8. It is always necessary to remember that the resigned Jew of the Middle Ages was more like the Christians than his ancestors.
9. Epistle to the Ephesians, v. 25–31.
10. Proudhon is alluding sarcastically to the frequently very comic nullifications of marriage, pronounced by the Roman courts, for physiological reasons. Proudhon, *op. cit.* vol. vi. p. 39. We know that the theologians do not like legitimate method of fulfilling it.
11. Proudhon, loc. cit. p. 212.
12. Proudhon, (Euvres, vol. xx. p. 169). This is extracted from the memoir he wrote in his own defence, after he had been condemned to three years in prison for his book on Justice. It is worth while noting that Proudhon was accused of attacking marriage! This affair is one of the shameful acts which dishonoured the Church in the reign of Napoleon III.
13. Aristotle, *Politics*, book I, chap. vii. 4–5.
14. Aristotle, *op. cit.* book I, chap v. 13, 14.
15. Xenophon, who represents in everything a conception of Greek life very much earlier than the time in which he lived, discusses the proper method of training an overseer for a farm (*Economics*, pp. 12–14). Marx remarks that Xenophon speaks of the division of labour in the workshop, and that appears to him to show a *middle-class instinct* (*Capital* vol. i, p. 159, col. 1); I myself think that it *characterises* an observer who understood the importance of production, an importance of which Plato had no comprehension. In the *Memorabilia* (book ii, p. 7) Socrates advises a citizen who had to look after a large family, to set up a workshop with the family; J. Flach supposes that this was something new (*Laçon du 19 avril 1907*): it seems to me to be rather a return to more ancient customs. The historians of philosophy appear to me to have been very hostile to Xenophon because he is too much of an *old Greek*. Plato suits them much better since he is more of an *aristocrat*, and consequently more detached from production.
16. Aristotle, *op. cit.* book i, chap v. 9 and 11.
17. Karl Kautsky, *La Révolution sociale*, French translation, p. 153.
18. The managers of manufactories would constantly be busying themselves with how to ensure the success of the government party at the next election. They would be very indulgent to workmen who were influential speakers, and very hard on men suspected of lack of electoral zeal.

19. We might ask if the ideal of the relatively honest and enlightened democrats is not at the present moment the discipline of the capitalist workshop. The increase of the power given to the mayors and State governors in America seems to me to be a sign of this tendency.
20. This history has also been burdened by a great number of adventures, which have been fabricated by imitating real ones, and which are very like those which later on *The Three Musketeers* rendered popular.
21. Jaurès, *Études socialistes*, pp. 117–8.
22. The battle of Fleurus, won in 1794 by General Jourdain, was one of the first decisive triumphs of the revolutionary army. *The Chant du Départ* was written by J.M. Chénler shortly before this battle.
23. When we speak of the educative value of art, we often forget that the habits of life of the modern artist, founded on an imitation of those of a jovial aristocracy, are in no way necessary, and are derived from a tradition which has been fatal to many fine talents. Lafargue appears to believe that the Parisian jeweller might find it necessary to dress elegantly, to eat oysters, and run after women in order to be able to keep up the artistic quality of this work (i.e. in order to keep his mind active; the artistic quality of his work, destroyed by the wear of daily life in the workshop, will be reconstituted by the gay life he leads outside) (*Journal des économistes*, September 1884, p. 386). He gives no reasons to support this paradox; we might moreover point out that the mentality of Marx's son-in-law is always obsessed by artistocratic prejudices.
24. This is an allusion to play by Octave Mirbeau with that title.—*Trans.*
25. See the chapter in Ruskin's *Seven Lamps of Architecture* entitled "Lamp of Truth."
26. It must not be forgotten that there are two ways of discussing art; Nietzsche attacks Kant for having "like all the philosophers meditated on art and the beautiful as a *spectator* instead of looking at the esthetic problem from the point of view of the artist, the *creator*" (*op. cit.* p. 178). In the time of the Utopists, esthetics was merely the babbling of amateurs, who were delighted with the cleverness with which the artist had been able to deceive the public.
27. Marx, Capital, French translation, vol. iii, first part, p. 375.
28. P. Bureau has devoted a chapter of his book on the *Contrat de Travail* to an explanation of the reason which justify boycotting of workmen who do not join their comrades in strikes; he thinks that these people merit their fate because they are notoriously inferior both in courage and as workmen. This seems to me very inadequate as an account of the reasons which, in the eyes of the working classes themselves, explain these acts of violence. The author takes up a much too intellectualist point of view.
29. Lafaille, *Mémoires sur les campagnes de Catalogue de 1808 à 1814*, p. 336.
30. The chariatanism of the followers of Saint Simon was as disgusting as that of Murat; moreover, the history of this school is unintelligible if we do not compare it with its Napoleonic models.
31. General Donop strongly insists on the incapacity of Napoleon's lieutenants who passively obeyed instructions that they never tried to understand, and the fulfillment of which was minutely overlooked by their mater (*op. cit.* pp. 22–29 and 32–34). Napoleon's armies were valued in proportion to the exactitude with which they carried out the orders of their master; initiative being little valued, it was possible to estimate the conduct of the generals like the ability of a good pupil who has learnt his lessons well; the Emperor gave pecuniary rewards to his lieutenants, proportionate to the measure of merit he recognized in them.
32. Viollet-le-Duc, *Dictionnaire raisonné de l'architecture française*, vol. iv, pp. 42–3. This does not contradict what we read in the article "Architect." From that we learn that the builders often inscribed their names in the cathedrals (vol. i, pp. 109–11); from that it has been concluded that these works were not anonymous (Bréhier, *Les Eglises gothiques*, p. 17), but what meaning had these inscriptions for the people of the town? They could only be of interest to artists who come later on to work in the same edifice and who were familiar with the traditions of the *schools*.
33. Renan, *Histoire du peuple d'Israël*, vol. iv, p. 191. Renan seems to me to have identified too readily glory and immortality; he has fallen a victim to a figure of speech.

Chapter 28

1. *Anti-Duhring*, p. 205.
2. Which is not to say that they *approve* of them.
3. A case in point is the role played by natural law as a prelude to the bourgeois revolutions.
4. Nachlass I, pp. 382–3. [Correspondence between Marx and Ruge, 1843.] The italics are mine.

5. Cf. The essay "Class Consciousness."
6. This can be seen at its clearest in the polemic between Pannekoek and Kautsky in 1912.
7. Today Boris Savinkov is fighting in the White Polish camp against proletarian Russia. In the past he was not only the celebrated organiser of almost all the great assassinations under Czarism but also one of the first theoreticians of romantic illegality.
8. This remains true as long as it is fighting against a proletarian state that has not yet properly established itself.
9. This constellation existed equally for the German proletariat in November 1918 and for the Hungarian proletariat at the same time and also in March 1919.

Chapter 30

1. Mahadev Desai published the above extract from a discourse given by Gandhi at the evening prayer, during his voyage to London.

Chapter 34

1. For a fuller study of the nature of nonviolent struggle, see Gene Sharp, *The Politics of Nonviolent Action.*
2. See Peter Ackerman and Christopher Kruegler, *Strategic Nonviolent Conflict: The Dynamics of People Power in the Twentieth Century*, Westport, CT, and London, Praeger, 1994.
3. Frank R. Cowell, *The Revolutions of Ancient Rome*, tr. W.P. Dickson, London, Thames and Hudson, rev. ed. 1962, pp. 42–3. Cowell's account is based on Livy.
4. See Gene Sharp, "Popular Empowerment" and "The Problem of Political Technique in Radical Politics," *Social Power and Political Freedom*, Boston, Porter Sargent, 1980, pp. 309–48 and pp. 181–94.
5. See Gene Sharp and Bruce Jenkins, "Against the Coup: A Guide to Effective Action to Prevent and Defeat Coups d'Etat," Occasional Paper No. 2, New York, International League for Human Rights, 1994; and "From Dictatorship to Democracy: A Conceptual Framework for Liberation," Cambridge, Albert Einstein Institution, 1994, and (in English and Burmese) Bangkok, Committee for the Restoration of Democracy in Burma, 1994.
6. See Gene Sharp with Bruce Jenkins, *Civilian-Based Defense: A Post-Military Weapons System*, Princeton, NJ, and London, Princeton UP, 1990.
7. Reinhold Niebuhr, *Moral Man and Immoral Society*, London, SCM Press, 1937, p. 238.
8. Ibid., p. 250f.
9. Ibid., p. 254.
10. "Instruction on Christian Freedom and Liberation," section 79, published in *Origins*: NC Documentary Service. Vol. 15, no. 44, 17 April 1986, Washington, D.C., Catholic News Service, 1986. The Congregation's earlier "Instruction on Certain Aspects of the 'Theology of Liberation' " (1984) had condemned violence ("To put one's trust in violent means in the hope of restoring more justice is to become the victim of a fatal illusion: Violence begets violence and degrades man . . . The overthrow by means of revolutionary violence of structures which generate violence is not ipso facto the beginning of a just regime"—adding that "we are not talking here about abandoning an effective means of struggle on behalf of the poor for an ideal which has no practical effects"). However, it did not explicitly point to nonviolent struggle as an alternative to violence in struggles for greater justice. In *Origins*, Vol. 14, no. 13, 13 Sept. 1984, sections 7, 10, 11. I am grateful to Thomas Quigley for these two references.
11. Council of Bishops, *In Defense Of Creation—The Nuclear Crisis and a Just Peace: Foundation Document*, Nashville, Graded Press, 1986, p. 80. I am grateful to John McCartney for information on the United Methodist Church.
12. *The Nuclear Dilemma: A Christian Search for Understanding. A Report of the Committee of Inquiry on the Nuclear Issue*, Cincinnati, Forward Movement Publications, 1987, p. 109.
13. Christian Obedience in a Nuclear Age: A Policy Statement Adopted by the 200th General Assembly, Louisville, Office of the General Assembly, PC (USA), 1988, p. 7.
14. The difficulties here have been compounded by a general lack of terminological clarity; in fact, the central committee of the WCC in 1971 spoke of "the semantic confusion which surrounds words like 'violence', 'revolution', 'power' and 'liberation' " and pointed to the need for terminological clarification to facilitate future discussions (Minutes, Geneva, WCC, 1971, Appendix VIII, p. 246). The central committee in August 1973 also pointed to the

conceptual problem of an enlarged concept of violence in its statement "Violent, Nonviolence and the Struggle for Social Justice," reprinted in *Violence, Nonviolence and Civil Conflict*, Geneva, WCC, 1983, p. 18 n. 2.

15. Norman Goodall, ed., *The Uppsala Report 1968*, Geneva, WCC, 1968, p. 270.
16. *Violence, Nonviolence and Civil Conflict*, p. 16; Minutes of the Addis Ababa central committee meeting, Appendix VIII, p. 246.
17. Published in *The Ecumenical Review*, Vol. 25, no. 4, Oct. 1973; cited here from *Violence, Nonviolence and Civil Confli*ct.
18. Ibid., p. 21.
19. Ibid., pp. 28–32.
20. lbid., p. 19.
21. A survey of these developments is found in a report prepared by the WCC's Commission of the Churches on International Affairs (CCIA), submitted to the Committee on Programme Unit III (Justice, Peace and Creation) at the meeting of the WCC central committee in Johannesburg, South Africa, January 1994 (Document C. 11, dupl.).
22. "Violence, Nonviolence and Civil Conflict: The Report of the Corrymeela Consultation," *Violence, Nonviolence and Civil Conflict*, pp. 9–15.
23. Cf. "Overcoming the Spirit, Logic and Practice of War," *Programme to Overcome Violence: An Introduction*, Geneva, WCC, Programme Unit III, 1995, p. 7.
24. Minutes of the 1992 central committee meeting, Geneva, WCC, 1992, p. 95.
25. *Programme to Overcome Violence*, p. 17.
26. Ibid., p. 29.
27. Ibid., pp. 94–8.
28. The Challenge of Peace: God's Promise and Our Response: A Pastoral Letter on War and Peace, Washington, D.C., US Catholic Conference, 1983, p. 25.
29. Ibid., p. 70.
30. Ibid.
31. Ibid., p. 71.
32. US Catholic Bishops, "The Harvest of Justice Is Sown in Peace," *Origins*, Vol. 23, no. 26, 9 Dec.1993, p. 453.
33. Ibid.
34. Ibid., p. 453f.
35. Ibid., p. 454.
36. Ibid., p. 454f.
37. Ibid., p. 463f.
38. Conferencia del Episcopado Mexicano. *Por la Justicia, La Reconciliación y la Paz en Mexico*, Cuautitln Iacalli, Mexico, Mexican Bishops Conference, 1994, paras 28, 35; English translation by Thomas Quigley in *Origins*, 1994, Vol. 24, No. 3.
39. I am grateful to Guido Mocellin of *Il Regno attualita* for recommending inclusion of passages from these important ecumenicai assemblies, and to Sr Mary Litell OSF and Stephen Coady for help in connection with their documentation.
40. Peace With Justice: The Official Documentation of the European Ecumenical Assembly, Geneva, Conference of European Churches, 1989, p. 54.
41. Ibid., p. 60: see also pp. 31, 42, 46, 50, 95, 97, 127, 129.
42. The final document of the Seoul convocation consists of three parts: a preamble, ten affirmations about justice, peace and integrity of creation, and a covenant in four areas related to economics, militarism, climate change and racism. Only the affirmations were fully discussed and voted on by the participants.
43. *Now is the Time: The Final Document and Other Texts from the World Convocation on JPIC*, Geneva, WCC, 1990, p. 17. This was in Affirmation VI: "We affirm the peace of Jesus Christ."
44. Ibid., p. 27.
45. Ibid., p. 28.
46. Ibid., pp. 28–9.

Chapter 35

1. See Philip Smith, "Civil Society and Violence: Narrative Forms and the Regulation of Social Conflict," *The Web of Violence: From Interpersonal to Global*. Ed. Jennifer Turpin and Lester R. Kurtz. Urbana, IL: University of Illinois Press, 1997.

2. See Christopher Ellison and John Bartkowski, "Religion and the Legitimation of Violence: Conservative Protestantism and Corporal Punishment," *The Web of Violence: From Interpersonal to Global.* Ed. Jennifer Turpin and Lester R. Kurtz. Urbana, IL: University of Illinois Press, 1997.
3. See Yuan-Horng Chu, "The Counterrevolution—A Family of Crimes: Chinese Communist Revolutionary Rhetoric, 1929–89," *The Web of Violence: From Interpersonal to Global.* Urbana, IL: University of Illinois Press, 1997: 69–90.
4. Ibid.
5. Jennifer Turpin, "Nuclear Amnesia." Paper presented at the annual meetings of the American Sociological Association, August, Miami, FL. (1993).
6. In residential areas of New Delhi, for example, many homes look like fortresses, complete with high walls and guard towers staffed by well-armed guards.
7. C. Wright Mills, *The Causes of World War Three*, (New York: Simon and Schuster, 1958).
8. Victor Sidel, "Buying Death with Taxes," *The Final Epidemic*, Ed. Ruth Adams and Susan Cullen. Chicago: Educational Foundation for Nuclear Science, 1981: 36.
9. Edward S. Herman and Noam Chomsky, *Manufacturing Consent: The Political Economy of the Mass Media*, (New York: Pantheon, 1988); Sam Marullo, *Ending the Cold War at Home: From Militarism to a More Peaceful World Order*, (Lexington, MA: Lexington Books, 1993); Lester R. Kurtz, *The Nuclear Cage: A Sociology of the Arms Race*, (Englewood Cliffs, NJ: Prentice-Hall, 1988).
10. Gary W. Buchanan, "Handcuffing All Arrested Persons: Is the Practice Objectively Reasonable?" *Police Chief* 60 (1993): 26–34.
11. cf. Arthur Hudson, "Special Needs Unit: Probation Program Offers Officer His Toughest Challenge," *Corrections Today* 56 (July 1993): 20–23.
12. See Philip Smith, endnote one.
13. Lester R. Kurtz, "The Geometry of Deterrence," *Peace Review* 6:2 (1994): 187–94. Lester R. Kurtz and Sarah Beth Asher, Eds. Forthcoming. *The Geography of Nonviolence*, Oxford: Blackwell.
14. Mohandas K. Gandhi, *Non-Violent Resistance*, (New York: Schocken, [1951] 1961); Lester R. Kurtz, "Nonviolent War: An Idea Whose Time Has Come?" *Gandhi Marg* 14 (October 1992): 450–62.
15. See Birgit Brock-Utne, "Linking the Micro and Macro in Peace and Development Studies," *The Web of Violence: From Interpersonal to Global.* Urbana, IL: University of Illinois Press, 1997.
16. Nancy Bell and Lester R. Kurtz, "Social Theory and Nonviolent Revolution: Rethinking Definitions of Power." Paper presented at the Peace Studies Association, Boulder, CO. (1991).
17. Mohandas K. Gandhi, *Non-Violent Resistance*, (New York: Schocken, [1951] 1961): 203.
18. Stephen Lee. Forthcoming. "The Philippines and Nonviolence," *Experiments in Peace: Student Studies in Nonviolence*, Ed. Margaret Zimmerman and Lester R. Kurtz. New Delhi: Gandhi-in-Action; Jose Blanco. Forthcoming. "Filipino People Power: An Interpretation in Faith," *Geography of Nonviolence*, Ed. Lester R. Kurtz and Sarah Beth Asher.
19. Some have speculated that agents provocateurs planted by the government may have incited the crowds to turn against the soldiers. See Gene Sharp and Bruce Jenkins, "Nonviolent Struggle in China: An Eye-witness Account," *Nonviolent Sanctions* 1 (Fall 1989): 5.
20. For example, Stanley Milgram, *Obedience to Authority: An Experimental View*, (New York: Harper and Row, 1975).
21. Jonathan Schell, *The Fate of the Earth*, (New York: Alfred A. Knopf, 1982). Seminar on Studying Violence, 1972. *Studying Violence.* New Delhi: Indian Council of Peace Research.
22. Caspar W. Weinberger, Department of Defense Annual Report to the Congress, Fiscal Year 1984, (Washington, D.C.: Government Printing Office, 1983).
23. Quoted by Alan Myer, "The Political and Strategic Context of the Strategic Defense Initiative." Address at "Star Wars: The Strategic Defense Initiative," a symposium sponsored by the Southwestern Regional Program in National Security Affairs and the Military Studies Institute, Texas A&M University, 16–17 November, College Station, TX. (1984).
24. Jennifer Turpin, "Gorbachev, the Peace Movement, and the Death of Lenin," *Why the Cold War Ended: A Range of Interpretations*, Ed. Ralph Summy and Michael Salla. (Westport, Conn.: Greenwood Press, 1995): 69–80.
25. See Riane Eisler, *The Web of Violence: From Interpersonal to Global*, (Urbana, IL: University of Illinois Press, 1997).
26. John Archer, Ed. *Male Violence*, (London: Routledge, 1994).

27. See Eisler, endnote twenty-five.
28. See Brock-Utne, endnote fifteen.
29. Erich Fromm, *May Man Prevail? An Inquiry into the Facts and Fictions of Foreign Policy*, (Garden City, NY: Anchor, 1961).
30. Mohandas K. Gandhi, *Non-Violent Resistance.* (New York: Schocken, [1951] 1961): 86.
31. Lester R. Kurtz and Sarah Beth Asher, Eds. Forthcoming. *The Geography of Nonviolence*, (Oxford: Blackwell).
32. Gene Sharp, *The Politics of Nonviolent Action*, 3 vols. (Boston: Porter Sargent, 1973); see also Gene Sharp, *Civilian-Based Defense*, (Princeton: Princeton University Press, 1991).
33. Sourad Dajani, Forthcoming. "Nonviolent Civilian Resistance in the Occupied Palestinian Territories: A Critical Reevaluation," *Geography of Nonviolence*, Ed. Lester R. Kurtz and Sarah Beth Asher. (Oxford: Blackwell).
34. Peter Ackermann and Christopher Kruegler, *Strategic Nonviolent Conflict: The Dynamics of People Power in the Twentieth Century*, (New York: Praeger, 1994).
35. Vaclav Havel, "The Power of the Powerless," *Without Force or Lies, Voices from the Revolutions of Central Europe in 1989–90*, Ed. William Brinton and Alan Rinzler, (San Francisco: Mercury House, 1990).
36. Chaiwat Satha-Anand. Forthcoming. "Nonviolent Practices, Professional Class and Democracy: The Bangkok Case, May 1992," *Geography of Nonviolence,* Ed. Lester R. Kurtz and Sarah Beth Asher. (Oxford: Blackwell).
37. Ronald Pagnucco and John D. McCarthy, "Advocating Nonviolent Direct Action in Latin America: The Antecedents and Emergence of SERPAJ," *Religion and Politics in Comparative Perspective*, Ed. Bronislaw Misztal and Anson Shupe. (Westport, Conn.: Praeger, 1992); see also Crueza Maciel. Forthcoming. "Nonviolence in Latin America," *Geography of Nonviolence*, Ed. Lester R. Kurtz and Sarah Beth Asher. (Oxford: Blackwell).
38. Gwynne Dyer, *War.* (New York: Crown, 1985).
39. See Johan Galtung, "Is There a Therapy for Pathological Cosmologies?" *The Web of Violence: From Interpersonal to Global.* Ed. Jennifer Turpin and Lester R. Kurtz. Urbana, IL: University of Illinois Press, 1997.
40. Dwight D. Eisenhower. "Peace in the World: Acts, Not Rhetoric Needed," Vital Speeches of the Day 19 (May 1953).
41. Enlightenment rationality certainly represents a culmination of this sort of thinking, but similar approaches can be found in many other cultures. Confucian thought in Chinese civilization, so influential throughout Asia, for example, emphasizes a hierarchical order and a formal rationality that produces many results similar to the utilitarian rationality of the West, although it did not develop in the same way.
42. Lester R. Kurtz, "War and Peace on the Sociological Agenda," *Sociology and Its Publics*, Ed. Terence C. Hallida and Morris Janowitz. (Chicago: University of Chicago Press, 1992).
43. James Bynam, telephone interview, 24 September 1988.
44. Morris Janowitz and R. W. Little, *Sociology and the Military Establishment*, (Beverly Hills, CA: Sage, 1974).
45. Vaclav Havel, "The Power of the Powerless," *Without Force or Lies*, ed. (Brinton and Rinzler, 1990).
46. Louis Kriesberg, *The Sociology of Social Conflicts.* (Englewood Cliffs, N.J.: Prentice-Hall, 1982); see also Kriesberg, "Consequences of Efforts at Deescalating the American-Soviet Conflict," *Journal of Political and Military Sociology* 14 (Fall 1986).
47. Robert Elias and Jennifer Turpin, "Thinking about Peace," *Rethinking Peace.* Ed. Robert Elias and Jennifer Turpin. (Boulder, Colo.: Lynne Rienner Publishers, 1994).
48. See Lester R. Kurtz, "War and Peace on the Sociological Agenda."
49. Sugata Dasgupta, "Violence, Development, and Tensions," *Studying Violence.* (New Delhi: Indian Council of Peace Research, 1972).

SELECTED BIBLIOGRAPHY

Ackermann, Peter and Christopher Kruegler. *Strategic Nonviolent Conflict: The Dynamics of People Power in the Twentieth Century.* New York: Praeger, 1994.

Adam, David and S. Cayouette. "Treatment Models of Men Who Batter," *Feminist Perspectives on Wife Abuse.* Ed. Kersti Yllö and Michele Bograd. Newbury Park, CA: Sage, 1988.

Adler, Freda. *Sisters in Crime.* New York: McGraw-Hill, 1975.

Aegis, November/December 1978: 3. Document of the Illinois Department on Aging.

"Against Pornography: The Feminism of Andrea Dworkin," *Omnibus.* London: BBC, 1991.

Ahmed, Akbar S. *Millennium and Charisma among Pathans: A Critical Essay in Social Anthropology.* London: Routledge, 1976.

——— 1980. *Pukhtun Economy and Society: Traditional Structure and Economic Development in a Tribal Society.* London: Routledge.

——— 1988. *Discovering Islam: Making Sense of Muslim History and Society.* London: Routledge.

——— 1991. "Anthropology 'Comes Out'?" *Anthropology Today* 7, no. 3 (June).

——— 1992a. *Postmodernism and Islam: Predicament and Promise.* London: Routledge.

——— 1992b. "Bombay Films: The Cinema as Metaphor for Indian Society and Politics," *Modern Asian Studies* 26, no. 2, Cambridge University Press: 289–320.

——— 1992c. "Palestine Revisited," *Newstatesman and Society,* 20 November.

——— 1993a. *Living Islam: From Samarkand to Stornoway.* London: BBC Books.

——— 1993b. "The History-Thieves: Stealing the Muslim Past?" *History Today* 43 (January).

——— 1993c. "New Metaphor in the 'New World Order,' " *Impact International,* 12 March-8 April: 24–7.

——— 1993d. "Points of Entry: The Taj Mahal," *History Today* 43 (May).

——— 1993e. "Media Mongols at the Gates of Baghdad," *New Perspective Quarterly* 10 (Summer).

Ahmed Akbar S. and Hasting Donnan. *Islam, Globalisation and Postmodernity.* London: Routledge, 1994.

Ahmed, Akbar S. and David Hart. *Islam in Tribal Societies: From the Atlas to the Indus.* London: Routledge, 1984.

Ahmed, Akbar S. and Cris Shore. *The Future of Anthropology: Its Relevance to the Contemporary World.* London: Athlone, (eds) in press.

Akbar M. J. *Riot after Riot.* India: Penguin, 1988.

Allen, J. "The 'Masculinity' of Criminality and Criminology: Integrating some Impasses," *Understanding Crime and Criminal Justice.* Sydney: Law Book Company, 1988.

Allport, Gordon. *The Nature of Prejudice.* New York: Doubleday, 1958.

Amin, Samir. "India Faces Enormous Danger from Globalization," *Mainstream* XXXII, no. 9 (15 January 1994) New Delhi.

Anderson, Benedict. "Census, Map, Museum," *Imagined Communities* (rev. edition). New York and London: Verso, 1991.

Anderson, Charles. *Pragmatic Liberalism*. Chicago: University of Chicago Press, 1990.
Antal, David and Johan Galtung. *Human Needs: A Contribution to the Current Debate*. Cambridge, MA: Oelgeschlager Gunn & Hain; Königstein: Anton Hain, 1980.
Archer, Dane and Rosemary Gartner. *Violence and Crime in Cross-National Perspective*. New Haven, CT.: Yale University Press, 1984.
Archer, John. *Male Violence*. London: Routledge, 1994.
Archer, John and Barbara Lloyd. *Sex and Gender*. New York: Cambridge University Press, 1989.
Arendt, Hannah. "What is Authority?" *Between Past and Future: Exercises in Political Thought*. New York 1968.
——— 1969. *On Violence*. New York: Harcourt Brace Jovanovich.
Aristotle. "Politics: Book I," *The Politics of Aristotle*. Trans. Ernest Barker. London: Oxford University Press. 1946: chap. vii. 4–5, 13–4.
Atwood, Margaret. *The Handmaid's Tale*. New York: Ballantine, 1987.
Baldwin, Margaret, "The Sexuality of Inequality: The Minneapolis Pornography Ordinance," *Law and Inequality: A Journal of Theory and Practice* 2 (August 1984): 629–53.
Balibar, Etienne. "The Nation Form: History and Ideology," *Race, Nation, Class: Ambiguous Identities*. Ed. Etienne Balibar and Immanuel Wallerstein. London and New York: Verso, 1991.
Barber, Benjamin. "An Epitaph for Marxism," *Social Science and Modern Society* (December 1995): 22–6.
Barker, Virginia. "Dangerous Shoes, or What's a Nice Dyke like Me Doing in a Get-up Like This," *Coming to Power*. Ed. Samois. Palo Alto: Palo Alto University Press, 1981.
Barnett, Ola W., C. Y. Lee, and R. E. Thelen. "Gender Differences in Forms, Outcomes and Attributions for Interpartner Aggression." Paper presented at the Fourth International Family Violence Research Conference, Durham, NH, July 1995.
Barry, Kathleen. *Female Sexual Slavery*. New York: Avon Books, 1979: 225, 230, 233.
Barsh, Russel 1987. "Plains Indian Agrarianism and Class Conflict," *Great Plains Quarterly* 7, no. 2 (1987): 83–102.
——— 1988. "Indian Resources and the National Economy," *Policy Studies Journal* 16, no. 4: 799–825.
Barth, Frederick. "Introduction and Pathan Identity and its Maintenance," *Ethnic Groups and Boundaries: The Social Organization of Culture Difference*. London: Allen and Unwin, 1969.
Basu, Tapan. *Khaki Shorts and Saffron Flags: A Critique of the Hindu Right*. London: Sangam Books, 1993.
Bataille, Georges. *Death and Sensuality*. New York: Ballantine Books, 1969.
Bauman, Zygmunt. *Modernity and the Holocaust*. Oxford: Polity Press, Cambridge with Blackwell Publishers, 1991.
Bechdolt, Burley V. "Cross-sectional Analysis of Socioeconomic Determinants of Urban Crime," *Review of Social Economy*, no. 33 (1975): 132–40.
Beck, Birgit. *Krieg und Frauen: Vergewaltigung als Waffe*. Paper presented at the Annual Conference of the Arbeitskreis Historische Friedensforschung, Bad Urach, October 7–10, 1994.
Beck, Ulrich. *Risk Society: Towards a Net Modernity*, Trans. Mark Ritter. London: Sage Publications, 1992.
Belknap, Joane. "The Economics-Crime Link," *Criminal Justice Abstracts* (March 1989).
Bell, Nancy and Lester R. Kurtz. "Social Theory and Nonviolent Revolution: Rethinking Definitions of Power." Paper presented at the Peace Studies Association, Boulder, CO, March 1991.
Bell-Fialkoff, Andrew. "A Brief History of Ethnic Cleansing," *Foreign Affairs* (Summer 1993).
Benedict, Ruth. *The Chrysanthemum and the Sword*. London: Routledge, 1972.
Benjamin, Jessica. "The Bonds of Love: Rational Violence and Erotic Domination," *Feminist Studies* 6, no. 1 (Spring 1980): 29, 154–5, 157.
Benthall, Jonathan. *Disasters, Relief and the Media*. London: I. B. Tauris and Company, 1993.
Berlant, Lauren G. *The Anatomy of National Fantasy: Hawthorne, Utopia, and Everyday Life*. Chicago and London: University of Chicago Press, 1991.
Berlant, Lauren G. and E. Freeman. "Queer Nationality," *Boundary* 19, vol. 1 (1992).
Betz, Jospeh. "Violence: Garver's Definition and a Deweyan Correction," *Ethics* 87, no. 4 (July 1977): 339–51.
Bhabha, Homi K. *Nation and Narration*. London and New York: Routledge, 1990.
Black Public Sphere Collective. *The Black Public Sphere: A Public Culture Book*. Chicago: University of Chicago Press, 1995.
Blanco, Jose. "Filipino People Power: An Interpretation in Faith," *Geography of Nonviolence*. Ed. Lester R. Kurtz and Sarah Beth Asher (forthcoming).

Blau, Judith and Peter Blau. "The Cost of Inequality: Metropolitan Structure and Violent Crime," *American Sociological Review*, no. 47 (1982): 126.

Blumstein, Philip and Pepper Schwartz. *American Couples*. New York: William Morrow, 1983.

Bologna, M. J., C. K. Waterman, and L. J. Dawson. "Violence in Gay Male and Lesbian Relationships: Implications for Practitioners and Policy Makers." Paper presented at the Third National Conference for Family Violence Researchers, Durham, NH, July 1987.

Borkenau, Frank. *The Spanish Cockpit: An Eye Witness Account of the Political and Social Conflict of the Spanish*. Ann Arbor: University of Michigan Press, 1963.

Brady, Hannah. *Defining Violence*. Aldershot: Avebury, 1996.

Braithwaite, John 1979. *Inequality, Crime and Public Policy*. London: Routledge & Kegan Paul.

——— 1984. *Corporate Crime in the Pharmaceutical Industry*. London: Routledge & Kegan Paul.

Braithwaite, John and Valerie Braithwaite. "The Effects of Income Inequality and Social Democracy on Homicide," *British Journal of Criminology*, no. 20 (1980): 45–53.

Brand, Pamila A. and Aline H. Kidd. "Frequency of Physical Aggression in Heterosexual and Female Homosexual Dyads," *Psychological Reports* 59 (1986): 1307–13.

Brinton, William M. and Alan Rinzler. *Without Force or Lies: Voices from the Revolutions of Central Europe in 1989–90*. San Francisco: Mercury House, 1990.

Brock-Utne, Birgit. "Linking the Micro and Macro in Peace and Development Studies," *The Web of Violence: From Interpersonal to Global*. Urbana, IL: University of Illinois Press, 1997: 149–160.

Brody, Hugh. *Maps and Dreams; Indians and the British Columbia Frontier*. London: Norman & Hobhouse, 1981.

Broszat, Martin. *Zweihundert Jahre deutsche Polenpolitik*. Munich: Ehrenwirth, 1963.

Brownmiller, Susan. *Against our Will: Men, Women and Rape*. New York: Simon & Schuster, 1975.

Buchanan, Gary W. "Handcuffing All Arrested Persons: Is the Practice Objectively Reasonable?" *Police Chief* 60 (1993): 26–34.

Burbank, Victoria K. 1994a. *Fighting Women: Anger and Aggression in Aboriginal Australia*. Berkeley: University of California Press.

——— 1994b. "Cross-Cultural Perspectives on Aggression in Women and Girls: An Introduction." *Sex Roles* 30: 167–76.

Burke, Kenneth. *A Grammar of Motives*. Berkeley: University of California Press, 1969: 3–20.

Burke, Edmond. *Nonsense on Stilts*. By J. Waldron. London: Methuen, 1987: 118.

Byrne, C., I. Arias, and K. K. O'Leary. "Autonomy as a Predictor of Marital Violence." Poster presented at the Annual Meeting of the Advancement of Behavior Therapy, Boston, November 1992.

Byrne, Daniel. "Clinical Models for the Treatment of Gay Male Perpetrators of Domestic Violence," *Violence in Gay and Lesbian Domestic Partnerships*. Ed. Claire Renzetti and Charles H. Miley. New York: Harrington Park, 1996.

Bynam, James. Telephone Interview with Lester R. Kurtz. 24 September 1988.

Calhoun, Craig. *Habermas and the Pubic Sphere*. Cambridge, MA: MIT Press, 1992.

Califia, Pat 1979. "A Secret Side of Lesbian Sexuality," *The Advocate*, December 27.

——— 1980a. "Feminism and Sadomasochism," *Heresies* 12: 31–2.

——— 1980b. *Sapphistry*. N.p.: Naiad Press: 124, 125, 128, 131.

——— 1981. "Jessie," *Coming to Power*. Ed. Samois. Palo Alto: Palo Alto University Press: 167.

Callinicos, Alex. *The Revenge of History: Marxism and the East European Revolutions*. University Park, PA: Penn State University Press, 1991.

Callwood, June. "Feminist Debates and Civil Liberties," *Women Against Censorship*. Ed. Varda Burstyn. Vancouver: Douglas & McIntyre, 1985: 121– 151.

Carter, Angela. *The Sadeian Woman*. New York: Pantheon, 1978: 38–77.

Chance, Norman. "Subsistence Research in Alaska: Premises, Practices and Prospects," *Human Organization* 46, no. 1 (1987): 85–9.

Challenge of Peace: God's Promise and Our Response: A Pastoral Letter on War and Peace, Washington, D.C., US Catholic Conference, 1983: 25, 70–1.

Chatterjee, Partha. *Nationalist Thought and the Colonial World: A Derivative Discourse?* London: Zed Books, 1986.

Chiricos, Theodore. "Rates of Crime and Unemployment: An Analysis of Aggregate Research Evidence," *Social Problems*, no. 34 (1987): 187–212.

Chu, Yuan-Horng. "The Counterrevolution—A Family of Crimes: Chinese Communist Revolutionary Rhetoric, 1929–89," *The Web of Violence: From Interpersonal to Global*. Urbana, IL: University of Illinois Press, 1997: 69–90.

Clausewitz, Karl von. *On War.* Trans. J.J. Graham. 8th Impression. New York: Barnes & Noble, 1968.
Coleman, V.E 1990. "Violence between Lesbian Couples: A Between Groups Comparison." Ph.D. diss. Ann Arbor, MI: University Microfilms International.
——— 1994. "Lesbian Battering: The Relationship between Personality and the Perpetration of Violence," *Violence and Victims* 9: 139–52.
Collins, Patricia Hill. "Learning from the Outsider Within: The Sociological Significance of Black Feminist Thought," *Social Problems* 33, no. 6 (1986): S14–S32.
——— 1991. *Black Feminist Thought: Knowledge, Consciousness, and the Politics of Empowerment.* New York: Routledge: 68.
——— 1993. "Toward a New Vision: Race, Class, and Gender as Categories of Analysis and Connection," *Race, Sex & Class: An Interdisciplinary Journal* 1 (Fall): 32–4.
Comaroff, Jean. and John L. Comaroff. "Of Totemism and Ethnicity," *Ethnography and the Historical Imagination.* Boulder, CO: Westview Press, 1992.
Commager, Henry Steele. "Can We Limit Presidential Power?" *The New Republic* 6 (April 1968).
Conferencia del Episcópado Mexicano. *Por la Justicia, La Reconciliación y la Paz en Mexico,* Cuautitln Iacalli, Mexico, Mexican Bishops Conference, 1994, paras 28, 35; English translation by Thomas Quigley in *Origins* 24, no. 3 (1994).
Connell, Bob. *Gender and Power. Society, the Person and Sexual Politics.* Cambridge, UK: Polity Press, 1987.
Connor, Walker. "Beyond Reason: The Nature of the Ethnonational Bond," Annual ERS/LSE Lecture, *Ethnic and Racial Studies* 16, no. 3 (July 1993).
Cornell, Drucilla. "Time, Deconstuction, and the Challenge to Legal Positivism: The Call to Judicial Responsibility," *Yale Journal of Law and Humanities* 2 (1990): 267.
Cowell, Frank Richard. *The Revolutions of Ancient Rome.* Rev. ed. Trans. W.P. Dickson. London: Thames and Hudson, 1962: 42–3.
Currie, Elliott. *Confronting Crime: An American Challenge.* New York: Pantheon Books, 1985.
Dajani, Souad. "Nonviolent Civilian Resistance in the Occupied Palestinian Territories: A Critical Reevaluation," *Geography of Nonviolence.* Ed. Lester R. Kurtz and Sarah Beth Asher (forthcoming).
Dallmayr, Fred. "Introduction: Toward a Comparative Political Theory," *Review of Politics* 59 no. 3 (Summer 1997): 421–27.
Daly, M. and M. Wilson. *Homicide.* New York: Aldine De Gruyter, 1988.
Das, Veena. *Mirrors of Violence: Communities, Riots and Survivors in South Asia.* Delhi: Oxford University Press, 1992.
Dasgupta, Sugata. "Violence, Development, and Tensions," *Studying Violence.* New Delhi: Indian Council of Peace Research, 1972: 2–11.
Delgado, Richard and Jean Stefancic, "Pornography and Harm to Women: 'No Empirical Evidence?' " *Ohio State Law Journal* 53 (1992): 1037–55.
DeMaris, A. "The Dynamics of Generational Transfer of Courtship Violence: A Biracial Exploration," *Journal of Marriage and the Family* 52 (1990): 219–73.
Derrida, Jacques 1990. "Force of Law: The 'Mystical Foundation of Authority,' " *Cardozo Law Review* 11: 927–45.
——— 1994. *Spectres of Marx.* New York: Routledge.
Dines, Gail and Rhea Becker, "A Conversation with Andrea Dworkin," *Sojourner: The Women's Forum* (June 1990): 20.
Dinnerstein, Dorothy. *The Mermaid and the Minotaur.* New York: Harper & Row, 1976: 135–51, 71, 211.
Dobasch, R. Emerson and Russell P. Dobasch. *Women, Violence and Social Change.* London: Routledge, 1992.
Donatien-Alphonse-François de Sade. *Juliette.* Trans. Austryn Wainhouse. New York: Grove Press, 1976.
Dutouquet, Hippolyte-Ernest. *De la condition des Classes Pauvres à la Campage.* Paris: Librairie de Guillaumin, 1846.
Downs, Donald. *The New Politics of Pornography.* Chicago: University of Chicago Press, 1989.
Duggan, Lisa, Nan Hunter, and Carole S. Vance. "False Promises: Feminist Antipornography Legislation in the U.S.," *Women Against Censorship.* Ed. Varda Burstyn. Vancouver: Douglas & McIntyre, 1985: 121–51.
Duster, Troy. "Crime, Youth Unemployment and the Black Urban Underclass," *Crime and Delinquency,* no. 33 (1987): 300–16.
Dutton, Donald G. "Patriarchy and Wife Assault: The Ecological Fallacy," *Violence and Victims* 9 (1988): 167–82.

Dworkin, Andrea 1979. *Pornography: Men Possessing Women.* New York: W. B. Putnam's Sons: 25–6, 52, 54, 61, 135–36, 151, 158, 167–75, 182.

——— 1974. *Woman Hating.* New York: Dutton.

——— 1981. *Pornography: Men Possessing Women.* New York: Putnam: 200.

——— 1984. "Pornography and Civil Rights." Unpublished speech delivered at the University of Wisconsin—Madison, 13 October.

——— 1988a. "Feminism: An Agenda" (1983), *Letters from a War Zone.* London: Secker & Warburg: 148.

——— 1988b. "Pornography: The New Terrorism" (1977), *Letters from a War Zone.* London: Secker & Warburg: 199, 201.

——— 1989a. *Pornography: Men Possessing Women.* New York: Dutton, 1989: xxviii-xxxii.

——— 1989b. Interview with Cindy Jenefsky, Brooklyn, N.Y., 22–23 June.

——— 1997. *Life and Death: Unapologetic Writings on the Continuing War Against Women.* New York: Free Press: 73–76, 148, 129, 175, 178–179, 204, 231, 239–240, 262, 276–307.

Dworkin, Andrea and Catharine A. MacKinnon, *Pornography and Civil Rights: A New Day for Women's Equality.* Minneapolis: Organizing Against Pornography, 1988: Appendices A-D.

Dworkin, Ronald. *Taking Rights Seriously.* Cambridge: Harvard University Press, 1977.

Easton, Susan M. *The Problem of Pornography: Regulation and the Right to Free Speech.* London: Routledge, 1994.

Eisenhower, Dwight D. "Peace in the World: Acts, Not Rhetoric Needed," *Vital Speeches of the Day* 19 (May): 418–21.

Eisler, Riane. "Human Rights and Violence: Integrating the Private and Public Spheres," *The Web of Violence: From Interpersonal to Global.* Ed. Jennifer Turpin and Lester R. Kurtz. Urbana, IL: University of Illinois Press, 1997: 161–186.

Eiskovits, Zvi and E. Buchbinder. "Talking Violence: A Phenomenological Study of Metaphors Violence Men Use." Paper presented at the Fourth International Family Violence Research Conference, Durham, NH., July 1995.

Elias, Robert, and Jennifer Turpin. "Thinking about Peace," *Rethinking Peace.* Ed. Robert Elias and Jennifer Turpin. Boulder, CO: Lynne Rienner Publishers, 1994: 1–12.

Ellison, Christopher G. and John P. Bartkowski. "Religion and the Legitimation of Violence: Conservative Protestantism and Corporal Punishment," *The Web of Violence: From Interpersonal to Global.* Ed. Jennifer Turpin and Lester R. Kurtz. Urbana, IL: University of Illinois Press, 1997: 45–68.

Elst, Koenraad. *Negationism in India: Concealing the Record of Islam.* New Delhi: Voice of India, 1992.

Engels, Frederick. *Anti-Dühring.* Moscow: Foreign Languages Publishing House, 1962.

Engineer, Asghar Ali. *Communal Riots in Post-Independence India.* London: Sangam Books, 1984.

English, Deirdre, Amber Hollibaugh, and Gayle Rubin. "Talking Sex: A Conversation on Sexuality and Feminism," *Socialist Review,* no. 58 (July-August 1981): 46, 52–3.

Epicurus. *The Extant Remains.* Ed. C. Bailey. Oxford: Oxford University Press, 1926: 85.

Epistle to the Ephesians, v. 25–31. Biblical passage.

Federalist, no. 49.

Feldmann, Harry. *Vergewaltigung und ihre psychischen Folgen: Ein Beltrag zur post-traumatischen Belastungsreaktion.* Stuttgart: Enke, 1992.

Felt, Harvey. "Political Articulations of Hunters to the States," *Études Inuit Studies* 3, no. 2, (1979): 37–52.

Ferguson, Ann, Jacquelyn Zita, and Kathryn Pyne Addelson. "On Compulsory Heterosexuality and Lesbian Existence: Defining the Issues," *Signs* 7, no. 1 (Autumn 1981).

Fernandez, C. and Naresh Fernandes. "A City at War with Itself," *Padgaonkar* (1993).

Finkelhor, David, Richard J. Gelles, Gerald T. Hotaling, and Murray A. Straus. *The Dark Side of Families: Current Family Violence Research.* Beverly Hills, CA: Sage, 1983.

Folnegovič-Smalc, Vera. "Psychiatric Aspects of Rapes in the War Against the Republics of Croatia and Bosnia-Herzegovina," *Mass Rapes: War against Women.* Ed. Alexandra Stiglmayer. Lincoln, NE: Nebraska University Press, 1993.

Forman, James D. *Communism: From Marx's Manifesto to 20th-Century Reality.* Rev. ed. New York: Watts, 1979.

Forsstrom-Cohn, B. and A. Rosenbaum. "The Effects of Parental Marital Violence on Young Adults: An Exploratory Investigation," *Journal of Marriage and the Family* 47 (1985): 467–72.

Fortes, Meyer and Edward Evans-Pritchard. *African Political Systems.* Oxford: University Press, 1940.

Fraser, Nancy 1989. *The French Derrideans: Politicizing Deconstruction or Deconstructing the Political?*

in her Unruly Practices: Power, Discourse, and Gender in Contemporary Social Theory. Minneapolis: University of Minnesota Press.
——— 1992. "Rethinking the Public Sphere: A Contribution to the Critique of Actually Existing Democracy," *Habermas and the Public Sphere.* Ed. Craig Calhoun. Cambridge, MA: MIT Press.
Freud, Sigmund 1958. *Civilization and Its Discontents.* Trans. Joan Riviera. Garden City, NY: Doubleday.
——— 1963. "Reflection upon War and Death," *Character and Culture.* Collier.
Fromm, Erich. *May Man Prevail? An Inquiry into the Facts and Fictions of Foreign Policy.* Garden City, N.Y.: Anchor, 1961.
Fukuyama, Francis 1989. "The End of History?" *The National Interest* 3, no. 18 (Summer).
——— 1992. *The End of History and the Last Man.* London: Hamish Hamilton.
Gabriel, Richard. *The Culture of War: Invention and Early Development.* New York: Greenwood, 1991.
Galtung, Johan 1969. "Violence, peace and peace research," *The Journal of Peace Research* 6, no. 3: 167–91.
——— 1971. "A Structural Theory of Imperialism," *Journal of Peace Research* 8., no. 2: 81–117.
——— 1977. *Methodology, and Ideology Essays in Methodology,* vol. I. Copenhagen: Ejlers.
——— 1978. *Peace and Social Structure Essays in Peace Research,* vol. III. Copenhagen: Ejlers.
——— 1980a. "The Basic Needs Approach," *Human Needs: A Contribution to the Current Debate.* Ed. Katrin Lederer, David Antal and Johan Galtung. Cambridge, MA: Oelgeschlager Gunn & Hain; Königstein: Anton Hain: 55–125.
——— 1980b. *Peace and World Structure Essays in Peace Research,* vol. IV. Copenhagen: Ejlers.
——— 1984. *Hitlerisme, stalinisme, reaganisme. Tre variasjoner over et temaav Orwell* [Hitlerism, Stalinism, Reaganism. Three Variations on a Theme by Orwell: in Norwegian]. Oslo: Gyldendal.
——— 1988a. "How Universal Are the Human Rights? Some Less Applaudable. Consequences of the Human Rights Tradition." Paper prepared for the Nobel Symposium on Human Rights, Oslo, June.
——— 1988b. " 'A Structural Theory of Imperialism,' Ten Years Later," *Transarmament and the Cold War: Peace Research and the Peace Movement. Essays in Peace Research,* vol. VI Copenhagen: Eljers: 298–310.
——— 1988c. *Methodology and Development Essays in Methodology,* vol. III. Copenhagen: Ejlers.
——— 1989a. "The "Middle East" Conflict," *Solving Conflicts: A Peace Research Perspective.* Honolulu, HI: University of Hawaii Press: 37–57.
——— 1989b. *Nonviolence and Isreal/Palestine.* Honolulu, HI: University of Hawaii Press.
——— 1989c. *Europe in the Making.* New York and London: Taylor & Francis.
——— 1997. "Is There a Therapy for Pathological Cosmologies?" *The Web of Violence: From Interpersonal to Global.* Ed. Jennifer Turpin and Lester R. Kurtz. Urbana, IL: University of Illinois Press: 187–206.
Galtung, Johan and Fumiko Nishimura, 1983. "Structure, Culture and Languages: An Essay Comparing the Indo-European, Chinese and Japanese Languages," *Social Science Information* 22, no. 6 (December): 895–925.
Gandhi, Mohandas K. *Non-Violent Resistance.* New York: Schocken, 1961.
Gardner-Loulan, JoAnn. *Lesbian Passion: Loving Ourselves and Each Other.* San Francisco: Spinsters/ Aunt Lute, 1987.
Garver, Newton. "What Violence Is," *Philosophical Issues—A Contemporary Introduction.* Ed. James Rachels and Frank A. Tillman. New York: Harper & Row, 1972.
Gebhard, Paul, John H. Gagnon, Wardell B. Pomeroy, and Cornelia V. Christenson. *Sex Offenders: An Analysis of Types.* New York: Harper & Row, 1965: 6, 9, 88, 98, 135.
Gelles, Richard 1993. "Alcohol and Other Drugs Are Associated with Violence—They are Not Its Cause," *Current Controversies in Family Violence.* Ed. Richard J. Gelles and Donileen R. Loseke. Newbury Park, CA: Sage.
——— 1995. "Violence, Abuse, and Homicide: A Continuum of Violence or Distinctive Behaviors." Paper presented at the Fourth International Family Violence Research Conference, July, Durham, NH.
Gellner, Ernest. *Nations and Nationalism.* Oxford: Blackwell, 1983.
Gershel, Michael A. "Evaluating a Proposed Civil Rights Approach to Pornography: Legal Analysis as If Women Mattered," *William Mitchell Law Review* 11 (1985): 41–80.
Giddens, Anthony. *Consequences of Modernity.* Cambridge: Polity Press, 1990.
——— 1991. *Modernity and Self-identity: Self and Society in the Late Modern Age.* Cambridge: Polity Press.

Glannon, Walter. "Epicureanism and Death," *Monist* 76 (1993): 224–34.
Gluckman, Max. *Politics, Law and Ritual in Tribal Society*. Oxford: Basil Blackwell, 1971.
Godelier, Maurice. *Perspectives in Marxist Anthropology*. Cambridge: Cambridge University Press, 1977.
Gondolf, Edward W. *Research on Men Who Batter: An Overview, Bibliography and Resource Guide*. Bradenton, FL: Human Services Institutes, 1988.
Goodall, Norman. *The Uppsala Report 1968*. Geneva: WCC, 1968: 270.
Christian Obedience in a Nuclear Age: A Policy Statement Adopted by the 200th General Assembly, Louisville, Office of the General Assembly, PC (USA), 1988: 7.
Gopal, Sarvepalli. *Anatomy of a Confrontation: Ayodhya and the Rise of Communal Politics in India*. India: Penguin, 1991.
Gowalker, Madhav Sadashiv. *We or Our Nationhood Defined*. India: Nagput, 1938.
Goytisolo, Juan. "Terror Town," *Newstatesman and Society*, 17–31 December 1993.
Graham, Bruce. *Hindu Nationalism and Indian Politics: The Origins and Development of Bharatiya Jana Sangh*. Cambridge: Cambridge University Press, 1990.
Greenberg, D. "Delinquency and the Age Structure of Society," *The Value of Youth*. Ed. A. Pearl, D. Grant and E. Wenk. Davis, CA: Responsible Action, 1978.
Griffin, Susan 1979. *Rape: The Power of Consciousness*. New York: Harper & Row.
——— 1981. *Pornography and Silence*. New York: Harper & Row.
Groth, Nicholas with William F. Hobson. "Die Dynamik Sexueller Gewalt," *Vergewaltigung. Die Opfer und die Täter*. Ed. Jürgen Heinrichs. Braunschweig: Holtzmeyer, 1986.
Grundy, Kenneth W. and Michael A. Weinstein. *The Ideologies of Violence*. Columbus, OH: Merrill, 1974.
Habermas, Jürgen 1968. *Technik und Wissenschaft als 'Ideologie'*. Frankfurt.
——— 1983. *The Structural Transformation of the Public Sphere*. Cambridge, MA: MIT Press.
Hamberger, L. Kevin and Claire M. Renzetti. *Domestic Partner Abuse: Expanding Paradigms for Understanding and Intervention*. New York: Springer, 1996.
Handbook of International Trade and Development Statistics 1989. United Nations, New York, 1990.
Hanmer, Julia, Jill Radford, and Elizabeth Ann Stanko. *Women, Policing and Male Violence: International Perspectives*. London: Routledge, 1989.
Hansen, M. "Unstable Mixtures, Dilated Spheres: Negt and Kluge's The Public Sphere and Experience: Twenty Years Later," *Public Culture* 5, no. 2 (1993).
Harris, John. *Violence and Responsibility*. London: Routledge & K. Paul, 1980.
Harris, Richard Jackson and Cynthia A. Cook. "Attributions about Spouse Abuse: It Matters Who the Batterers and Victims Are," *Sex Roles* 30 (1994): 553–65.
Hart, Barbara. "Lesbian Battering: An Examination," *Naming the Violence*. Ed. Kerry Lobel. Seattle: Seal Press, 1986.
Hartmann, Heidi and Ellen Ross. "Comments on 'On Writing the History of Rape'," *Signs* 3, no. 4 (Summer 1978).
Hartsock, Nancy C.M. *Money, Sex, and Power: Toward a Feminist Historical Materialism*. New York: Longman, 1983: 119.
Haug, Frigga. "The End of Socialism in Europe: A New Challenge for Socialist Feminism?" *Feminist Review* (Winter 1991): 37–48.
Havel, Vaclav 1989. *Living in Truth*. London: Faber & Faber.
——— 1990. "The Power of the Powerless," *Without Force or Lies*. Ed. Brinton and Rinzler: 43–127.
Heidegger, Martin in R. Olson, "Death," *The Encyclopedia of Philosophy*. Ed. P. Edwards. New York: McMillan, 1967: 309.
Helm, J. *Essays on the Problem of Tribe*. American Ethnological Society (USA): University of Washington Press, 1971.
Herman, Edward S. and Noam Chomsky. *Manufacturing Consent: The Political Economy of the Mass Media*. New York: Pantheon, 1988.
Hobsbawm, Eric J. "Ethnicity and Nationalism in Europe Today," *Anthropology Today* 8, no. 1 (1992).
Hollibaugh, Amber and Cherrie Moraga, "What We're Rollin' Around in Bed With," *Heresies* 12 (1980): 60.
Honderich, Ted. *Violence For Equality—Inquiries in Political Philosophy*. Harmondsworth, Middlesex: Penguin, 1980.
Hoover, J. Edgar. Uniform Crime Report for the United States. Federal Bureau of Investigation, United States Department of Justice, 1967.
Hudson, Arthur. "Special Needs Unit: Probation Program Offers Officer His Toughest Challenge," *Corrections Today* 56 (July 1993): 20–3.

Hudson, Charles. "Cherokee Concepts of Natural Balance," *Indian Historian* 3 no. 4 (1970): 51–4.
Huntington, Samuel P. "The Clash of Civilizations," *Foreign Affairs* (Summer 1993).
Ienaga, Saburo. *The Pacific War: 1931–1945.* New York: Random House, 1978.
Isaac, Jeffrey 1987. *Power and Marxist Theory.* Ithaca: Cornell University Press.
——— 1995. "The Strange Silence of Political Theory," *Political Theory* (November): 636–52.
Island, David and Patrick Letellier. *Men Who Beat the Men Who Love Them.* New York: Harrington Park, 1991.
Iyer, Krishna. 1992 review of Ahmed 1992a, *Economic and Political Weekly* (Bombay) 7 (November).
Iyer, Raghavan. *The Essential Writings of Mahatma Gandhi.* Delhi: Oxford University Press, 1993, c1991.
Jalusić, Vlasta. "Zurück in den 'Naturzustand'? Desintegration Jugosfawiens and ihre Folgen für die Frauen." *Feministische Studien* 2 (1992).
Janowitz, Morris and Roger W. Little. *Sociology and the Military Establishment.* Beverly Hills, CA: Sage, 1974.
Jenefsky, Cindy (with Ann Russo). *Without Apology: Andrea Dworkin's Art and Politics.* Boulder, CO and Oxford, England: Westview Press, 1998.
Jorgenson, Joseph G. *Native Americans and Energy Development II.* Cambridge, MA: Anthropology Resource Center, 1984.
Jouvenel, Bertrand de. *Power: The Natural History of Its Growth.* London: Batchworth Press, 1952.
Kalmuss, Debra S. "The Intergenerational Transmission of Marital Aggression," *Journal of Marriage and the Family* 46 (1984): 11–9.
Kang, Sin-p'yo, John MacAloon, and Roberta DaMatta. *The Olympics and Cultural Exchange.* Soule: Hanyang University, Institute for Ethnological Studies, 1988.
Kantorowicz, Ernest Hartwig. "Pro Patria Mori in Medieval Political Thought," *American Historical Review* 56 (1950): 490.
Kau, James B. and Paul Rubin. "New Estimates of the Determinants of Urban Crime," *Annals of Regional Science,* no. 9 (1975): 68–76.
Kelly, E. E. and L. Warshafsky. "Partner Abuse in Gay Male and Lesbian Couples." Paper presented at the Third National Conference for Family Violence Researchers, Durham, NH, 1987.
Kinsey, Alfred C., Wardell B. Pomeroy, Clyde E. Martin, and Paul H. Gebhard. *Sexual Behavior in the Human Female.* Philadelphia: W. B. Sounders and Co, 1953: 705.
Korać, Maja. "Understanding Ethnic-National Identity and its Meaning: Questions from Women's Experience," *Women's Studies International Forum* 18 (May/June 1995).
Koss, M. P. "Changed Lives: The Psychological Impact of Sexual Harassment," *Ivory Power: Sexual Harassment on Campus.* Ed. Michele A. Paludi. Albany: State University of New York Press, 1990.
Kotkin, Joel. *Tribes: How Race, Religion, and Identity Determine Success in the New Global Economy.* New York: Random House, 1993.
Kriesberg, Louis. *The Sociology of Social Conflicts.* Englewood Cliffs, NJ: Prentice-Hall, 1982.
——— 1986. "Consequences of Efforts at Deescalating the American-Soviet Conflict," *Journal of Political and Military Sociology* 14 (Fall): 215–34.
Krippendorff, Ekkehart. *Staat und Krieg. Die historische Logik politischer Unvernunft.* Frankfurt: Suhrkamp, 1985.
Kuhn, Thomas S. *The Structure of Scientific Revolutions.* Chicago: University of Chicago Press, 1970.
Kundera, Milan. *The Book of Laughter and Forgetting.* Middlesex, Eng.: Penguin, 1980: 229.
Kurtz, Lester R 1988. *The Nuclear Cage: A Sociology of the Arms Race.* Englewood Cliffs, NJ: Prentice-Hall.
——— 1992a. "Nonviolent War: An Idea Whose Time Has Come?" *Gandhi Marg* 14 (October): 450–62.
——— 1992b. "War and Peace on the Sociological Agenda," *Sociology and Its Publics.* Ed. Terence C. Hallida and Morris Janowitz. Chicago: University of Chicago Press: 61–98.
——— 1994. "The Geometry of Deterrence," *Peace Review* 6, no. 2: 187– 94.
Kurtz, Lester R. and Sarah Beth Asher. *The Geography of Nonviolence.* Oxford: Blackwell (forthcoming).
La Bell, Beverly. "Snuff—the Ultimate in Woman-Hating," *Take Back the Night.* Ed. Laura Lederer. New York: Morrow, 1980.
Laclau, Ernesto and Chantal Mouffe. *Hegemony and Socialist Strategy.* London: New Left Books, 1985.

Lahey, Kathleen A. "Pornography and Harm: Learning to Listen to Women," *International Journal of Law and Psychiatry* 14 (1991): 117–31.

Larsen, Mogens Trolle. "Europas Lys," *Europas Opdagelse.* Ed. Hans Boll-Johansen and Michael Harbsmeier. Copenhagen: 1988: 9–37.

Laszlo, Henry de and Paul S. Henshaw. "Plant Materials Used by Primitive Peoples to Affect Fertility," *Science* 119 (1954): 626–31.

Lawrence, Barbara. "Four-Letter Words Can Hurt You," *Philosophy and Sex.* Ed. Robert Baker and Frederick Elliston. Buffalo, NY: Prometheus Books, 1975: 32.

Lee, Benjamin. "Going Public," *Public Culture* 5, no. 2 (1993).

Lee, Stephen. "The Philippines and Nonviolence," *Experiments in Peace: Student Studies in Nonviolence.* Ed. Margaret Zimmerman and Lester R. Kurtz. New Delhi: Gandhi-in-Action (forthcoming).

Lenin, Vladimir Il'ich. *Collected Works.* Vol. 23. Moscow: Progress Publishers, 1964.

Letellier, Patrick 1994. "Gay and Bisexual Domestic Violence Victimization: Challenges to Feminist Theory and Responses to Violence," *Violence and Victims* 9: 95–106.

——— 1996. "Twin Epidemics: Domestic Violence and HIV Infection among Gay and Bisexual Men," *Violence in Gay and Lesbian Domestic Partnerships.* Ed. Claire M. Renzetti and Charles H. Miley. New York: Harrington Park.

Lie, Gwat-Yong and Sabrina Gentlewarrior. "Intimate Violence in Lesbian Relationships: Discussion of Survey Findings and Practice Implications," *Journal of Social Service Research* 15 (1991): 41–59.

Lie, Gwat-Yong, Rebecca Schilit, Judy Bush, M. Montagne, and L. Reyes. "Lesbians in Currently Aggressive Relationsips: How Frequently Do They Report Aggressive Past Relationships?" *Violence and Victims* 6 (1991): 121–35.

Lipschutz, Barbara. "Cathexis," *What Color is Your Handkerchief?* Berkeley: Samois, 1979: 9.

Locke, John. *Two Treatises on Civil Government.* 1690.

Loizos, Peter. *The Heart Grown Bitter: A Chronicle of Cypriot War Refugees.* Cambridge: Cambridge University Press, 1981.

Lorde, Audre. "The Master's Tools Will Never Dismantle The Master's House," *This Bridge Called My Back.* Ed. Cherrie Moraga and Gloria Anzaldua. Watertown, MA.: Persephone Press, 1981.

Lübke, Karl-Heinrich. *"Auctoritas" bei Augustin, mit einer Einleitung zur römischen Vorgeschichte des Begriffs.* Stuttgart: W. Kohlhammer, 1968.

MacAloon, John. *This Great Symbol: Pierre de Coubertin and the Origins of the Modern Olympic Games.* Chicago: University of Chicago Press, 1981.

Maciel, Crueza. "Nonviolence in Latin America," *Geography of Nonviolence.* Lester R. Kurtz and Sarah Beth Asher (forthcoming).

MacKinnon, Catharine A. 1991. "Pornography as Defamation and Discrimination," *Boston University Law Review* 71: 793–815.

——— 1993. "Defamation and Discrimination," *Only Words.* Cambridge: Harvard University Press: 114.

Madan, T. N. *Religion in India.* Oxford and Delhi: Oxford University Press, 1992.

Maguire, Patricia. *Doing Participatory Research: A Feminist Approach.* Amherst: Center for International Education, School of Education, University of Massachusetts, 1987.

Mailer, Norman. *Prisoner of Sex.* Boston: Little, Brown, 1971: 126.

Millett, Kate. *Sexual Politics.* New York: Doubleday, 1970: 304, 327.

Makiya, Kanan. *Cruelty and Silence: War, Tyranny, Uprising, and the Arab World.* London: Jonathan Cape, 1993.

Mannoni, Octave. *Prospero and Caliban.* New York: Praeger, 1964: 111.

Marcuse, Herbert. *Eros and Civilization.* Boston: Beacon Press, 1955: 220, 222.

Margolies, Liz, and E. Leeder. "Violence at the Door: Treatment of Lesbian Batterers," *Violence against Women* 1 (1995): 139–57.

Margolies, Liz, Martha Becker, and Karla Jackson-Brewer. "Internalized Homophobia: Identifying and Treating the Oppressor Within," *Lesbian Psychologies.* Ed. Boston Lesbian Psychologies Collective. Urbana: University of Illinois Press, 1987.

Marquand, David. "After Socialism," *Political Studies* (1993): 43–56.

Marullo, Sam. *Ending the Cold War at Home: From Militarism to a More Peaceful World Order.* Lexington, MA.: Lexington Books, 1993.

Marx, Karl. "Thesis I," *The Marx-Engels Reader.* 1st ed. Ed. Robert Tucker. New York: Norton, 1975: 143.

——— *Capital.* Vol i. French translation; p. 159, col. 1.

Maslow, Abraham H. "Self-Esteem (Dominance-Feeling) and Sexuality in Women," *Journal of Social Psychology* 16 (1942): 291.

Mbembe, Achille. "The Banality of Power and the Aesthetics of Vulgarity in the Post-Colony," *Public Culture* 4 no. 2 (1992).

Mbembe, Achille. "Belly-up: More on the Postcolony," *Public Culture* 5 no. 1 (1992).

McFadden, Robert. "Minor Mishap Shuts Down IRT as Riders Balk at Leaving Train," *New York Times*, 4 January, 1969: 1, 29.

McLeod, W. H. *Who is a Sikh? The Problem of Sikh Identity*. Oxford: Clarendon Press, 1989.

McMahan, Jeff. "Death and the Value of Life," *Ethics* 99 (1988): 51.

Medea, Andrea and Kathleen Thompson. *Against Rape*. New York: Farrar, Straus & Giroux, 1974: 32.

Meron, Theodor. "The Case for War Crimes Trials in Yugoslavia," *Foreign Affairs* (Summer 1993).

Messerschmidt, James 1986. *Capitalism, Patriarchy and Crime: Toward a Socialist Feminist Criminology*. Totowa, NJ: Rowmand & Littlefield.

——— 1993. *Masculinities and Crime: Critique and Reconceptualization of Theory*. Lanham, MD: Rowman and Littlefield.

Mestrovic, Stjepan G. *The Balkanization of the West: The Confluence of Postmodernism with Postcommtmism*. London: Routledge, 1994.

Milgram, Stanley. *Obedience to Authority: An Experimental View*. New York: Harper and Row, 1975.

Millič, Andjelka. "Women and Nationalism in the Former Yugoslavia," *Gender Politics and Post-Communism. Reflections from Eastern Europe and the former Soviet Union*. Ed. Nanette Funk and Magda Mueller. New York: Routledge, 1993.

Mill, John Stuart. *Considerations on Representative Government*. London, 1861.

Miller, Casey and Kate Smith. *The Handbook of Nonsexist Writing*. New York: Harper & Row, 1988.

Miller, William Robert. *Nonviolence: A Christian Interpretation*. New York: Association Press, 1964.

Mills, C. Wright 1956. *The Power Elite*. New York: Oxford University Press.

——— 1958. *The Causes of World War Three*. New York: Simon and Schuster.

Minutes of the Addis Ababa Central Meeting in Geneva, WCC, 1971, Appendix VIII: 246.

Mokhiber, Russell. *Corporate Crime and Violence: Big Business Power and the Abuse of the Public Trust*. San Francisco: Sierra Club Books, 1989.

Morgan, David H.J. "Masculinity and Violence," *Women, Violence and Social Control*. Ed. Jalna Hanmer and Mary Maynard. London: Macmillan, 1987.

Mosse, George L. *Fallen Soldiers: Reshaping the Memory of the World Wars*. Oxford: Oxford University Press, 1950: 39.

Moynihan, Daniel Patrick. *Pandaemonium: Ethnicity in International Politics*. Oxford: Oxford University Press, 1993.

Myer, Alan. "The Political and Strategic Context of the Strategic Defense Initiative." Address at "Star Wars: The Strategic Defense Initiative," a symposium sponsored by the Southwestern Regional Program in National Security Affairs and the Military Studies Institute, Texas A&M University, College Station, TX, 16–17 November 1984.

Nachlass. "Nachlass I," *Aus dem literarischen Nachlass von Karl Marx, Friedrich Engels and Ferdinand Lassalle*. Herausgegeben von Franz Mehring, Stuttgart: 1902: 382–3.

Naffine, Ngaire. *Female Crime: The Construction of Women in Criminology*. Sydney: Allen & Unwin, 1987.

Nash, Manning. *The Cauldron of Ethnicity in the Modern World*. Chicago: University of Chicago Press, 1989.

New York Times Magazine, 27 October 1968: 90.

Newton, Niles. "Interrelationship Between Sexual Responsiveness, Birth, and Breast-Feeding," *Contemporary Sexual Behavior*. Ed. Joseph Zubin and John Money. Baltimore: Johns Hopkins University Press, 1971: 80–4, 95.

Nicoloft, Lee K. and Eloise A. Stiglitz. "Lesbian Alcoholism Etiology, Treatment and Recovery," *Lesbian Psychologies*. Ed. Boston Lesbian Psychologies Collective. Urbana: University of Illinois Press, 1987.

Niebuhr, Reinhold. *Moral Man and Immoral Society*. London: SCM Press, 1937: 238, 250, 254.

Nietzsche, Friedrich Wilhelm. *Généalogie de la Moral*. Trad. franç: 43, 57–59, 78–80, 117–8.

Now is the Time: The Final Document and Other Texts from the World Convocation on JPIC. Geneva: WCC, 1990: 17, 27–9.

Nordstrom, Carolyn. "Women and War. Observations from the Field. MINERVA," *Quarterly Report on Women and the Military* IX/I (1991).

Nuclear Dilemma: A Christian Search for Understanding. A Report of the Committee of Inquiry on the Nuclear Issue. Cincinnati: Forward Movement Publications, 1987: 109.

Oak, Purushottam Nagesh. *Some Blunders of Indian Historical Research.* New Delhi: Bharati Sahitya Sadan, 1990.

O'Leary, K. Daniel. "Through a Psychological Lens: Personality Traits, Personality Disorders, and Levels of Violence," *Current Controversies on Family Violence.* Ed. Richard J. Gelles and Donileen R. Loseke. Newbury Park, CA: Sage, 1993.

Ortner, Sherry B. and Harriet Whitehead. "Accounting for Sexual Meanings," *Sexual Meanings: The Cultural Construction of Gender and Sexuality.* Ed. Sherry Ortner and Harriet Whitehead. New York: Cambridge University Press, 1981: 1–27.

"Overcoming the Spirit, Logic and Practice of War," *Programme to Overcome Violence: An Introduction.* Geneva: WCC, Programme Unit 111, 1995: 7.

Padgaokar, Dileep. *When Bombay Burned.* New Delhi: UBS Publishers and Distributors, 1993.

Padgug, Robert. "Sexual Matters," *Radical History Review,* no. 20 (Spring/Summer 1979): 11.

Pagnucco, Ronald and John D. McCarthy. "Advocating Nonviolent Direct Action in Latin America: The Antecedents and Emergence of SERPAJ," *Religion and Politics in Comparative Perspective.* Ed. Bronislaw Misztal and Anson Shupe. Westport, CT.: Praeger, 1992: 125–47.

Passerin d'Entréves, Alessandro. *The Notion of the State.* Oxford: Clarendon Press, 1967.

Peace With Justice: The Official Documentation of the European Ecumenical Assembly, Geneva, Conference of European Churches, 1989: 31, 42, 50, 54, 60, 95, 97, 127, 129.

Pericles, Cicero in Thucydides, *The History of the Peloponnesian War.* Encyclopedia Britannica, 1952: 398.

Phadnis, Urmila. *Ethnicity and Nation-Building in South Asia.* New Delhi: Sage Publications, 1989.

Pharr, Suzanne. "Two Workshops on Homophobia," *Naming the Violence.* Ed. Kerry Lobel. Seattle: Seal Press, 1986.

Plato 1978a. "Republic I," *The Collected Dialogues of Plato.* Trans. Paul Shorey. Princeton: Princeton University Press: 329c.

——— 1978b. "Republic III," *The Collected Dialogues of Plato.* Trans. Paul Shorey. Princeton: Princeton University Press: 403d.

Pohl, Rolf. Männlichkeit. "Destruktivität und Kriegsbereitschaft," *Logik der Destruktion. Der zweite Golfkrieg als erster elektronischer Krieg und die Möglichkeiten seiner Verarbeitung im Bewußtsein.* Series published by the Political Science Institute of the University of Hanover, 1992: 157–77.

Polk, Ken. "The New Marginal Youth," *Crime and Delinquency,* no. 30 (1984): 462–79.

Polk, Ken and David Ranson. "Patterns of Homicide in Victoria," *Australian Violence: Contemporary Perspectives.* Ed. Duncan Chappell, Peter Grabosky, and Heather Strang. Canberra: Australian Institutes of Criminology, 1991.

Porter, Roy. "Rape—Does it have a Historical Meaning?" *Rape.* Ed. Sylvana Tomaselli and Roy Porter. London: Basil Blackwell, 1986: 216–36.

Public Policy Research Centre. Domestic Violence Attitude Survey, conducted for the Office of the Status of Women, Department of the Prime Minister and Cabinet, Canberra, 1988.

Rachels, James and Frank A. Tillman. *Philosophical Issues—A Contemporary Introduction.* New York: Harper & Row, 1972: 223–8.

Radical History Review, special issue on Sexuality, no. 20 (Spring/Summer 1979).

Raiser, Elisabeth. "Vergewaltigungen als Kriegsstrategie," *Junge Kirche. Zeitschrifi europäischer Christinnen und Christen* 1 (1993).

Randie, Michael. *People Power: The Building of a New European Home.* Stroud, U.K.: Hawthorne Press, 1991.

Rawls, John. *A Theory of Justice.* Cambridge, MA: Belknap Press of Harvard University Press, 1971.

Réage, Pauline. *The Story of O.* Trans. Sabine d'Estree. New York: Grove Press, 1965: 15–7.

Reinharz, Shulamit. *Feminist Methods in Social Research.* New York: Oxford University Press, 1992.

Renan, Ernest. *Histoire Du Peuple D'Israél.* Vol. IV. Paris: Calmann-Levy, 1893.

Renzetti, Claire M. 1992. *Violent Betrayal: Partner Abuse in Lesbian Relationships.* Newbury Park, CA: Sage.

——— 1995. *Information Packet on Lesbian Battering.* Harrisburg, PA: National Resource Center on Domestic Violence.

Renzetti, Claire M. and Daniel J. Curran. *Women, Men and Society: The Sociology of Gender.* Boston: Allyn and Bacon, 1995.

Renzetti, Claire M. and Charles H. Miley. *Violence in Gay and Lesbian Domestic Partnerships.* New York: Harrington Park, 1996.

Report of the Royal Commission on Seals and the Sealing Industry in Canada. Volume 1, recommendations 37 and 38. (Ottawa: Minister of Supply and Services, 1986).

Rich, Adrienne. "Compulsory Heterosexuality and Lesbian Existence," *Signs* 5, no. 4 (Summer 1980).

Riddle, Dorothy I. and Barbara Sang. "Psychotherapy with Lesbians," *Journal of Social Issues* 34 (1978): 84–100.

Robbins, Bruce. *The Phantom Public Sphere.* Minneapolis: University of Minnesota Press, 1993.

Robertson, Roland 1991. "The Globalization Paradigm: Thinking Globally," *Religion and Social Order.* Ed. David G. Bromley. Greenwich, CT: JAI Press, 1991.

——— 1992. *Globalization: Social Theory and Global Culture.* London: Sage Publications.

Rorty, R. "Why Can't a Man Be More like a Woman, and Other Problems in Moral Philosophy," *London Review of Books,* 24 February 1994.

Rosenau, James. *Turbulence in World Politics: A Theory of Change and Continuity.* Princeton, NJ: Princeton University Press, 1990.

Roth, Michael 1988. "Strukturelle und personale Gewalt: Probleme der Operationalisierung des Gewaltbegriffs von Johan Galtung," *HSFK Forschungsbericht,* no. 1 (April 1988).

Rousseaud de la Combe, G. *Traité des maiti(res Criminelles.* 1741.

Rubin, Gayle. "The Leather Menace: Comments on Politics and S/M," *Coming to Power.* Ed. Samois. Palo Alto, CA: Palo Alto University Press, 1981: 215.

Ruskin, John. "Lamp of Truth," *Seven Lamps of Architecture.* New York: John Wiley & Sons, 1885.

Sabalic, Ines and Ruth Seifert. *Nirgends erwähnt-doch überall geschehen.* Munich: Gleichstellungsstelle (Equal Rights Office for Women) of the City of Munich, 1993.

Said, Edward 1978. *Orientalism.* London: Routledge.

——— 1993. *Culture and Imperialism.* London: Chatto and Windus.

Sanday, Peggy Reeves. "Rape and the Silencing of the Feminine," *Rape.* Ed. Sylvana Tomaselli and Roy Porter. London: Basil Blackwell, 1986: 84–101.

Sander, Helke and Barbara Johr. *BeFreier und Befreite. Krieg, Vergewaltigung, Kinder.* Munich: Kunstmann Verlag, 1992.

Saner, Hans. "Personale, strukturelle und symbolische Gewalt," *Hoffnung und Gewalt. Zur Ferne des Friedens.* Basel: Lenos & Z Verlag, 1982: 73–95.

Sasson, Jean R. *The Rape of Kuweit. The True Story of Iraqi Atrocities Against a Civilian Population.* New York: Knightsbridge, 1991.

Satha-Anand, Chaiwat. "Nonviolent Practices, Professional Class and Democracy: The Bangkok Case, May 1992," *Geography of Nonviolence.* Ed. Lester R. Kurtz and Sarah Beth Asher (forthcoming).

Scarry, Elaine. *The Body in Pain: The Making and Unmaking of the World.* New York: Oxford University Press, 1985.

Schell, Jonathan. *The Fate of the Earth.* New York: Alfred A. Knopf, 1982.

Schilit, Rebecca, Gwat-Yong Lie, and Marilyn Montagne. "Substance Use as a Correlate of Violence in Intimate Lesbian Relationships," *Journal of Homosexuality* 19 (1990): 51–65.

Schmidt-Harzbach, Ingrid. "Eine Woche im April," *Befreier und BeFreite. Krieg, Vergewaltigung, Kinger.* Ed. Helke Sander and Barbara Johr. Munich: Kunstmann, 1992: 21–45.

Schmuckler, Sophie. "How I Learned to Stop Worrying and Love My Dildo," *Coming to Power.* Ed. Samois. Palo Alto, CA: Palo Alto University Press, 1981: 98–9.

Schneider, Elizabeth. "The Dialectic of Rights and Politics: Perspectives from the Women's Movement," *New York University Law Review* 61 (1986): 589, 642–48.

Schopflin, George. "The Rise and Fall of Yugoslavia," *The Politics of Ethnic Conflict Regulation.* Ed. John McGarty and Brendan O'Leary. London: Routledge, 1993.

Seator, Penelope, "Judicial Indifference to Pornography's Harm: American Booksellers v. Hudnut," *Golden Gate University Law Review* 17 (Fall 1987): 297–358.

Seifert, Ruth. "War and Rape: A Preliminary Analysis," *Mass Rape: The War Against Women in Bosnia-Herzegovina.* Ed. Alexandra Stiglmayer. Lincoln, NE: Nebraska University Press, 1993: 54–72.

Seminar on Studying Violence. *Studying Violence.* New Delhi: Indian Council of Peace Research, 1972.

Shakespeare, William. "Romeo and Juliet," *The Complete Works.* New York: Oxford University Press, 1959: 164.

Sharp, Gene 1973. *The Politics of Nonviolent Action.* 3 vols. Boston: Porter Sargent.

——— 1980. *Social Power and Political Freedom.* Boston: Porter Sargent.

——— 1991. *Civilian-Based Defense.* Princeton: Princeton University Press.
Sharp, Gene, and Bruce Jenkins 1989. "Nonviolent Struggle in China: An Eye-witness Account," *Nonviolent Sanctions* 1 (Fall): 1, 3–7.
——— 1990. *Civilian-Based Defense: A Post-Military Weapons System.* Princeton, NJ, and London: Princeton UP.
——— 1994a. "Against the Coup: A Guide to Effective Action to Prevent and Defeat Coups d'Etat." Occasional Paper No. 2. New York: International League for Human Rights.
——— 1994b. "From Dictatorship to Democracy: A Conceptual Framework for Liberation." Cambridge: Albert Einstein Institution, 1994; and (in English and Burmese) Bangkok: Committee for the Restoration of Democracy in Burma.
Shattuck, James. "Organizing Domestic Violence Offender Services: Building Coalitions." Paper presented at the fourteenth National Lesbian and Gay Health Conference, Los Angeles, CA, July 1992.
Shorter, Edward. "On Writing the History of Rape," *Signs* 3, no. 2 (Winter 1977): 471–82.
Sidel, Victor. "Buying Death with Taxes," *The Final Epidemic.* Ed. Ruth Adams and Susan Cullen. Chicago: Educational Foundation for Nuclear Science, 1981: 35–47.
Singer, Peter. *Practical Ethics.* Cambridge, New York: Cambridge University Press, 1979.
Smart, Carol. *Women, Crime and Criminology.* London: Routledge & Kegan Paul, 1976.
Smith, Anthony D. *National Identity.* Reno: University of Nevada Press, 1991: 160.
Smith, Michael. "Sociodemographic Risk Factors in Wife Abuse: Results from a Survey of Toronto Women," *Canadian Journal of Sociology* 15, no. 1 (1990): 39–58.
Smith, Philip. "Civil Society and Violence: Narrative Forms and the Regulation of Social Conflict," *The Web of Violence: From Interpersonal to Global.* Ed. Jennifer Turpin and Lester R. Kurtz. Urbana, IL: University of Illinois Press, 1997: 91–116.
Snitow, Ann. "Mass Market Romance: Pornography for Women is Different," *Radical History Review,* no. 20 (Spring/Summer 1979): 151, 153.
Sorel, Georges. *Reflections on Violence,* "Introduction to the First Publication" (1906). New York, 1961.
Spake, Amanda. "The End of the Ride," *Mother Jones* (April 1980): 40.
Steinem, Gloria. "Erotica and Pornography: A Clear and Present difference," *Take Back the Night.* Ed. Laura Lederer. New York: Morrow, 1980: 38.
Stember, Charles Herbert. *Sexual Racism.* New York: Harper & Row, 1976: 145–6, 149, 150, 164.
Stern, Paul C. "Why Do People Scarify for Their Nations," *Political Psychology* 16, no. 2 (1995): 232.
Stiglmayer, Alexandra. *Mass Rape. The War Against Women in Bosnia-Herzegovina.* Lincoln, NE: Nebraska University Press, 1993.
Stoller, Robert 1975. *Perversion.* New York: Pantheon.
——— 1979. *Sexual Excitement: The Dynamics of Erotic Life.* New York: Pantheon.
Straus, Murray A. "Physical Assaults by Wives: A Major Social Problem," *Current Controversies on Family Violence.* Ed. Richard Gelles and Donileen Loseke. Newbury Park, CA: Sage, 1993.
Straus, Murray, and Richard J. Gelles. "How Violent Are American Families: Estimates for the National Family Violence Resurvey and Other Studies," *Physical Violence in American Families.* Ed. Murray Straus and Richard Gelles. New Brunswick, NJ: Transaction Press, 1990.
Straus, Murray A., Richard J. Gelles, and Suzanne Steinmetz. *Behind Closed Doors.* New York: Doubleday, Anchor, 1980.
Strausz-Hupé, Robert. *Power and Community.* New York, 1956.
Strossen, Nadine. "A Feminist Critique of 'the' Feminist Critique of Pornography," *Virginia Law Review* 79 (August 1993): 1099–1190.
Suttles, Wayne. *Coast Salish Essays.* Seattle: University of Washington Press, 1989.
Tagore, Rabindranath. *Nationalism.* London: Macmillan, 1917.
Tamir, Yael 1993. *Liberal Nationalism.* Princeton: Princeton University Press.
——— 1995. "The Enigma of Nationalism," *World Politics* 47, no. 3.
——— 1996. "Reconstructing the Landscape of Imagination," *National Rights and International Obligations.* Ed. S. Cancy, D. George, and P. Jones. Boulder, CO.: Westview: 85–102.
Tanner, Donna M. *The Lesbian Couple.* Lexington, MA: Lexington Books, 1978.
Taylor, Pamela. *Violence in Society.* London: Royal College of Physicians of London, 1993.
Thompson, John B. *Ideology and Modern Culture.* Cambridge: Polity Press, 1990.
Toulmin, Stephen. *Cosmopolis: The Hidden Agenda of Modernity.* Chicago: University of Chicago Press, 1990.
Tucker, Robert. *The Marx-Engels Reader.* New York: W.W. Norton, 1978.

Tully, Mark. *No Full Stops in India*. London: Viking, Penguin Books Ltd, 1991.

Turner, Bryan S. *Orientalism, Postmodernism and Globalism: Intellectuals in the Modern World*. London: Routledge, 1994.

Turpin, Jennifer. "Nuclear Amnesia." Paper presented at the annual meetings of the American Sociological Association, August 1993, Miami, FL.

——— 1995. "Gorbachev, the Peace Movement, and the Death of Lenin," *Why the Cold War Ended: A Range of Interpretations*. Ed. Ralph Summy and Michael Salla. Westport, CT.: Greenwood Press: 69–80.

Turpin, Jennifer and Lester R. Kurtz. *The Web of Violence. From Interpersonal to Global*. Urbana, IL: University of Illinois Press, 1997.

US Catholic Bishops, "The Harvest of Justice Is Sown in Peace," *Origins* 23, no. 26 (9 Dec. 1993): 453–4.

Vance, Carole. "Gender Systems, Ideology, and Sex Research: An Anthropological Analysis," *Feminist Studies* 6, no. 1 (Spring 1980): 133.

Vargo, Sue. "The Effects of Women's Socialization on Lesbian Couples," *Lesbian Psychologies*. Ed. Lesbian Psychologies Collective. Urbana: University of Illinois Press, 1987.

Verkko, Veli. *Homicides and Suicides in Finland and Their Dependence on National Character*. Copenhagen: G.E.C. Gads Forlag, 1951.

Violence, Nonviolence and Civil Conflict. Geneva: WCC, 1983, vol. 2: 16–18.

Viollet-le-Duc, Eugène-Emmanuel. *Dictionnaire Raisonné de l'architecture Française du Xie au SVIe siècle*, IV. Paris: Morel, 1867: 42–43, 109–11.

Vulliamy, Ed. *Seasons in Hell: Understanding Bosnia's War*. New York: Simon and Schuster, 1994.

Wade, Francis C. "On Violence," *Journal of Philosophy* 68 (June 1971): 369–77.

Wallace, Alice 1986. *Homicide: The Social Reality*. Sydney: New South Wales Bureau of Crime Statistics and Research.

——— 1989. "Trying to See My Sister," *Living by the Word*. New York: Harcourt Brace Jovanovich.

Wallace, John M. *Destiny His Choice: The Loyalism of Andrew Marvell*. London: Cambridge University Press, 1968.

Walzer, Michael 1970. *Obligations: Essays on Disobedience, War, and Citizenship*. Cambridge, MA.: Harvard University Press.

——— 1977. *Just and Unjust Wars. A Moral Argument with Historical Illustrations*. New York: Basic Books.

Warner, Michael. *The Letters of the Republic: Publication and the Public Sphere in Eighteenth Century America*. Cambridge, MA: Harvard University Press, 1990.

Weber, Hans Ruedi. "The Promise of the Land, Biblical Interpretation and the Present Situation in the Middle East," *Study Encounter* 7, no. 4 (1971): 1–16.

Webster, Paula. "Pornography & Pleasure," *Heresies* 12 (1980): 49–50.

Weeks, Jeffrey 1981. *Sex, Politics, and Society*. Essex, U.K.: Longman: 1–18.

——— 1985. *Sexuality and its Discontents. Meanings, Myths and Modern Sexualities*. London: Routledge & Kegan.

Weene, Seph. "Venus," *Heresies* 12 (1980): 36–8, 64.

Weinberger, Caspar W. *Department of Defense Annual Report to the Congress, Fiscal Year 1984*. Washington, D.C.: Government Printing Office, 1983.

Weisskopf, Susan. "Maternal Sexuality and Asexual Motherhood," *Signs* 5, no. 4 (Summer 1980): 770.

Whyte, William F. "A Slum Sex Code," *American Journal of Sociology* 49 (July 1943): 27.

Williams, Bernard. *Moral Luck*. Cambridge: Cambridge University Press, 1981.

Williams, Patricia J. *The Alchemy of Race and Rights*. Cambridge: Harvard University Press, 1991.

Wilson, Elizabeth, "Interview with Andrea Dworkin," *Feminist Review* 1 (June 1982): 26.

Wing, Adrien K. and Sylke Merchàn. *Rape, Ethnicity and Culture: Spirit Injury from Bosnia to Black America*. Unpublished manuscript, 1994.

Wolff, Robert Paul 1968. *The Poverty of Liberalism*. Boston: Beacon Press.

——— 1969. "On Violence," *Journal of Philosophy* 66 (October): 601–16.

——— 1970. "Political Philosophy," *The Harper Guide to Philosophy*. Ed. Arthur Danto. New York: Harper & Row.

——— 1971. "Violence and the Law" *The Rule of Law*. New York: Simon and Schuster.

Wolfgang, Marvin and Franco Ferracuti. *The Subculture of Violence: Towards an Integrated Theory in Criminology*. London: Tavistock Publications, 1967.

Women Against Violence Against Women Newsletter, June 1976: 1.

United Nations World Economic Survey. New York: United Nations, 1990.

Wright, Richard. *12 Million Black Voices.* New York: Viking Press: 1941.

Yllö, Kersti and Michele Straus. "Patriarchy and Violence against Wives: The Impact of Structural and Normative Factors," *Physical Violence in American Families.* Ed. Murray S. Strauss and Richard Gelles. New Brunswick, NJ: Transaction Publishers, 1990.

Yusuf, Feyyaz. "Christian Radicalism Stirs the Serbs," *'Q' News,* 10–17 December 1993.

Zoftig, Sarah. "Coming Out," *Coming to Power.* Ed. Samois. Palo Alto, CA: Palo Alto University Press, 1981: 88, 93.

INDEX